U0632237

纪念雷海宗先生诞辰一百一十周年 蔡美彪题

中国第四届世界古代史国际学术研讨会论文集

南开大学历史学院
中国世界古代中世纪史研究会 编

中华书局

图书在版编目(CIP)数据

纪念雷海宗先生诞辰110周年 中国第四届世界古代史国际学术研讨会论文集/南开大学历史学院,中国世界古代中世纪史研究会编. —北京:中华书局,2016.3
ISBN 978-7-101-11338-9

Ⅰ.纪… Ⅱ.①南…②中… Ⅲ.①雷海宗(1902~1962)-纪念文集②世界史-古代史-研究-国际学术会议-文集 Ⅳ.①K825.81-53②K12-53

中国版本图书馆CIP数据核字(2015)第264374号

书 名	纪念雷海宗先生诞辰110周年 中国第四届世界古代史国际学术研讨会论文集
编 者	南开大学历史学院 中国世界古代中世纪史研究会
责任编辑	张继海
出版发行	中华书局 (北京市丰台区太平桥西里38号 100073) http://www.zhbc.com.cn E-mail:zhbc@zhbc.com.cn
印 刷	北京市白帆印务有限公司
版 次	2016年3月北京第1版 2016年3月北京第1次印刷
规 格	开本/880×1230毫米 1/16 印张49¾ 插页8 字数1200千字
印 数	1-600册
国际书号	ISBN 978-7-101-11338-9
定 价	198.00元

本书出版得到范曾先生捐赠设立的"雷海宗基金"的资助

编委会 (以姓氏笔划为序)

王以欣　王敦书　叶　民　江　沛　杨巨平　杨栋梁
陈志强　范　曾　侯建新　晏绍祥　郭小凌　魏宏运

常　务：杨巨平
主　编：王敦书

历史学家雷海宗

历史学家雷海宗

1927年在美国芝加哥大学获博士学位

1929年在南京玄武湖（合影者张景茀）

1943年西南联大历史系1943级毕业纪念（前排左一孙毓棠，左二郑天挺，左三噶邦福，左四雷海宗，左五吴晗，左六王信忠，左七邵循正。照片提供者二排左一何兆武）

1946年全家合影

1949年春，在北平郑天挺寓所，北大、清华历史系部分教授合影。前排左起：谢国桢、雷海宗、邓广铭、向达、余逊、杨人楩、孔繁霱、赵万里；后排左起：郑天挺、孙毓棠、周一良、张政烺、邵循正

1956年在卢沟桥（左三为郑天挺）

1957年全家合影

雷海宗墓
（在北京万安公墓，旁立者王敦书）

Department of History
Nankai University
Tientsin, China
September 15, 1962

炳棣:

首先我须致歉: I owe you a thousand apologies, 因为我早就应该与你回信。你寄给我的贺年片信，伯在1959年年底寄给我的你那一本精心之作 Studies on the Population of China 和我的论文，我都已收到；你以开封寄的我的论文，我也都已送交南开大学图书馆。读你那本书和论文之後，感到极为欣幸。最近人收到，本年八月十一日的信和所附的各种学术刊物書你的巨的是口同声的赞美评论摘要，我更是无法形容时所感到的欣悦和赞叹。你仍在盛年，我深信你以後在学术上所要作出的成绩，一定还要超过你已有的极不平凡的成绩。我希望，我最少还有機会看到你今後一部分的成绩；我眼前正在急切盼望早读到你那本关于 social mobility 的新书。

我近三四年，一直在病中，大部分的時间不能从事工作因为弱的神衰，朋友间的信息往来也都断绝。我过去曾经屡次提笔，想要给你写信，每次都连提起我。搁置，没有能力写下去，以致劳你在万里之外长期惦念一惦及，内疚至深。最近一年，虽未完全康復，我已开始任课，因仍在病中，领导方面对我特别周注，叫我只担任一门课，以免劳累。课为新兴即洲国史学，主要是讲西方近三四三千年的史学学展情况。我极力希病能早日好轉，以後可以多担任些工作。

我知道你将要担任芝加哥大学历史学系的中国史教授，非常欣慰，你今后必能更顺利地从事教学工作和学术研究工作。芝加哥市听说并于有一个专门收藏中国善本资料的善本馆，对你从事经常性的研究，可能有帮助；当然，有特别专门的研究，恐怕你需借助于东部的几个大善本馆。

我的病不好不坏，请勿多念。每月都有我照顾进药，再次到医院就诊，都有青年同事陪伴，扶我上车下车。内子虽已年逾花甲，大致尚属健康；她叫我向你、心学俗多多致意，并告诉你们的两个孩子，祝万里之外有一对老人有常常想到他们。小女现于北京大学西语系任讲师；她已自有家庭，也已有一儿一女；她工作较忙，不能多来天津，所以经常只是我与内子两人相依度日。

你写信给我，谈你在国外的工作和情况，用英文比较方便，今后尽管仍用英文。我给你写信项项碎碎也谈我的情况，用中文较为便利。
　　此祝

阖府安好。　　　　　　海宁 1962. 9. 15

2012年6月15日"雷海宗先生诞辰110周年纪念会"合影

目 录

【下编】 世界古代史研究

【古希腊史】

【罗马史】

【中世纪、拜占廷帝国史】

【附录】

【上编】

伟大的预言者

在雷海宗先生诞辰 110 周年纪念会上的讲话

龚 克 南开大学校长

各位专家，老师们、同学们：

今天是南开校园倍感荣耀的日子。海内外百余位历史学人在此汇聚一堂，纪念一位中国近代学术史上声誉卓著的历史学家、世界史学科的奠基人之一、已故的南开大学教授雷海宗先生，为此，我代表南开大学向各位来宾表示热烈的欢迎和诚挚的感谢！

今年是雷海宗先生诞辰一百一十周年。十年前，也就是雷先生百年诞辰之际，南开大学也曾举办同样隆重的纪念会和学术研讨会。对于一位曾为南开史学，也为中国的世界史学科做出杰出贡献的伟大学者，南开是不会忘记的。如今，他所开拓的学术事业正在南开乃至整个中国发扬光大，结出硕果。

南开史学的成绩源于老一辈史学家的艰苦创业、悉心培植和多年的学术积累与传承，雷海宗先生在其中功不可没。雷先生年轻时曾留学美国芝加哥大学，获哲学博士学位。1927 年回国后，先后在南京中央大学、金陵女子大学、武汉大学、清华大学、西南联大任教，讲授外国史和中国史课程，是一位学贯古今中西的学术泰斗和著名的爱国民主人士。1952 年全国高等院校院系调整，雷先生从清华调任南开，担任南开历史系的世界史教研组主任，成为南开世界史学科的奠基人。南开世界史学科能有今日之规模，与雷先生的重大贡献密不可分。1957 年，雷先生遭受无端政治打击，人生陷入低谷，但他在受到极不公正的对待且身患重疾的情况下依然坚守讲坛，为学生授课，直至生命的最后时刻。当年的学生曾撰文回忆雷先生在南开的"最后一课"，我读后深为感动。那是多么伟大的人格！一代学术巨擘的早逝，是南开之痛，也是中国学术界的巨大损失。所幸，经雷先生的高足，我校王敦书教授的悉心整理编辑，雷先生的著述和遗稿陆续出版，如《伯伦史学集》、《西洋文化史纲要》、《世界上古史讲义》等，为我们留下了丰富的学术遗产。

雷海宗先生是享誉国内外的学术大师。他的渊博学识、治学理念与实践和有幸存世的遗稿，都是我辈世代享用的精神遗产。今天的学术环境当然仍有改进余地，但与雷先生当年景况已不可同日而语。南开正在努力创造一个宽松自由的学术环境，让学者们的才华得到充分施展；南开也比往昔任何时候都更加珍惜人才，爱护人才，善待人才。今天，国内外史学家们再次聚首南开，让我们共同努力，将雷先生的学术思想和理念发扬光大，用更丰富的学术成果告慰这位史学大师。相信在大家的共同努力下，雷海宗学术思想和治学理念的研究将获得进一步的深化。希望各位继续支持、关心南开史学的发展，使雷先生开创的南开史学事业得以发扬光大，也希望南开学人继续努力，使雷先生的治学精神得以发扬光大！

（2012 年 6 月 15 日）

雷海宗先生和中国古代哲学
（主题报告）

范　曾　南开大学

今天在座的，我曾经听过课的老教授辜燮高先生也来了。我是应向辜燮高先生永执弟子礼的。今天我作为南开大学的校友，在雷海宗先生纪念会上交一份关于历史哲学的答卷。

我们知道，1957 年，对中国的知识分子无疑是个寒冷的季节。那时候我 18 岁，在南开大学历史系上学。最初看到，在《人民日报》上刊登的雷海宗的讲话下面有一个编者按。其实我在看雷海宗的文章时，我觉得没有问题呀。他认为马克思主义的辩证法和唯物论到 1895 年恩格斯逝世以后，基本上没得到很好的发展。这里，确切地说，是指从第二国际到第三国际的这个过程。我想，对西方历史了如指掌的人对这段历史是非常清楚的。可是，当时掌握着文化生杀大权的康生，他对这段历史并不了解。不仅他不了解，就是以后也领导我们的某些理论干部，自认为对第二国际有了解，可是也不能够不出些笑话。有一次，胡乔木领导大家学习"无产阶级专政和叛徒考茨基"，结果他在会上朗读很长的一段，就像刚才龚校长念的这个文章似的，念完以后说："这个写得多么好啊，讲得多么透彻啊！"就在当时，胡耀邦同志的秘书孙长江在旁边讲："哎，胡老嗳，你不要弄错了，这是考茨基的话呀！"不要以为他身居高位，一定他的"学"和"识"就超过当时像雷海宗先生这样的人。我想雷海宗，从那以后，他的晚境肯定比较凄凉。这个反右运动是席卷了全国大学的一个大运动。当时雷海宗的处境可谓是"交游莫救视，左右亲近，不为一言"。可是这时候呢，历史系站出了一个很瘦小的教授，杨志玖先生。他在反右学术讨论会上讲，雷先生是学术问题呀，不是政治问题。差点为这个问题，杨志玖先生也被打成"右派"。所幸当时魏宏运先生调查清楚了，杨志玖先生出身中农，出身中农的教授还不是很多，后来就成了右倾。所以，怀念雷海宗和杨志玖，我同样有一种感怀。我曾经在杨志玖先生执教 60 周年的一个大会上送给了他一首诗，里面有句：大名有雷，先生不右。先生根本就不右，他讲的是一个真理。雷先生是个什么样的人，他是个卓越的、高屋建瓴式的学者，是个预言家式的学者，要言不繁。比如讲，1895 年这句话成为近代研究共产主义史的史学界必须重视的一句话。再比如，他曾经讲，下个世纪 50 年代，就是我们现在的本世纪 50 年代将出现一个西欧大帝国。你们看欧共体如何？欧共体现在货币统一了，他们还准备搞共同的宪法。雷先生他有天才的预感，这不是一般历史学家所能有的。再比如讲，对中国一些史学上的问题，对史学分期问题，对中国历史上少数民族和汉族大交融，淝水之战的地位问题，他都有很精辟的看法。今天我讲的是"雷海宗先生和中国古代哲学"。

各位看，这是孔子像和老子像。孔子 73 岁，眉毛画得够长。这是我画的。对于孔子，我们可以在《史记·孔子世家》里看到，这是个很怪的人。身体高大，高丈余。丈余呢，就是今天一尺算七寸的话，也接近姚明的高度，而且头顶凸起。头顶凸起，孔丘之名即源于此。头顶鼓起一个包，这不是我造谣啊，孔子是这样的。至于老子呢，《史记·老子韩非列传》记载了三位老子。一个是生于河南苦县的老聃，李耳。一个姓老，叫老莱子。一个就是我经常画的骑着青牛出函关到秦国去的老子。这说明什么问题，说明老子史实的记载不像孔子这么确切。就是从春秋晚期到西汉汉武帝这几百年，他已经很模糊了。孔子的门下弟子非常多，他本身就是中国第一部编年史的作者，所以

孔子的年龄我们记得很清楚：公元前551年到公元前479年。老子没有这样的机会。

　　在雷海宗先生的论述中，我们对中国古典哲学深受启发的是，他将其源流大分为二：其一、老子的哲学，这在雷海宗先生认为是纯粹的哲学。其二是孔子的哲学，这是解决现实人生的哲学。但他们有着不可分割的联系。老子的哲学可以上溯为夏、商之世已然存在的古老的筮，亦即纯粹的卦。而卦在远古蒙昧时期，是人们对天地鬼神由敬畏而产生的占卜之术。当然这不是哲学。那么孔子的哲学呢，上溯到史。这个是雷海宗先生非常精辟的见解，而且是符合历史事实的见解。那么这个筮呢，它是用一种蓍草来占卜。而这种蓍草占卜，筮卜术本身不是哲学。一直到战国时代的屈原还请女巫师来占卜。"索藑茅以筳篿兮，命灵氛为余占之"，他还是拿着这种草请灵氛为其占卜。这个习惯从公元前21世纪绵延到公元前11世纪，以至到公元后。所以，雷海宗先生认为最原始的筮不是哲学。可是，它到后来与前哲学有相当的关系。由不是哲学的筮到前哲学，标志是什么呢？就是司马迁在《报任安书》里讲，"古者富贵而名摩灭，不可胜记，惟倜傥非常之人称焉。盖文王拘而演《周易》"。文王拘演《周易》，这个演《周易》使原始的筮法渐渐走上了哲学之路。我想，当初在文王演易时，已经开始有了易相、易数和易理的萌芽。所以孔子所读的《易经》，我想是周初传下来的版本，语焉简略，非常精炼的语言，没有一定的学养和阅历是无法卒读的。孔子所谓："加我数年，五十以学《易》，可以无大过矣"。可见《易》在孔子心目中的崇高地位，而其"韦编三绝"，足见其学易之勤奋。那么孔子学易以后，他不会学而不言，他有门下弟子这么多，他会有很多对于学易的感悟、体会。比如，《易传》讲"作《易》者其有忧患乎？"他说作《易》的人是不是有他的忧愁，有他的人间忧患呢。这说明不同的人看《易经》会有不同的立场。那么，从雷海宗先生的文章里，我们可以看到，就是从原始的筮法，这纯粹的卦，到前哲学，到老子说的纯哲学，这中间又增加了些什么呢？在《易经》的变化上，我想，在孔子之后，严格地讲，在西汉之世，渐渐地有了上下象、上下象、上下系辞、文言、序卦、说卦、杂卦。这个《十翼》，就是我的名字，我取的字叫十翼，人家以为是长了十个翅膀，不是。这是伪托孔子的十篇文章的名字。自战国至西汉，大体是伪托孔子《十翼》产生的时期。虽为伪托，我想孔子的门人们当会将孔子的关于《易》的言说载录，所谓伪托，只是假孔子之名，便于流传之意。因此《十翼》：上下象、上下象、上下系辞、文言、说卦、序卦、杂卦，孔子本人是见不到的。可是雷海宗先生考量上下象、上下象和文言里面的一些章句。到了老子《道德经》的时候，这里就说得非常通达。他认为这些应该是断定老子出生年月的一个很好的标

志。雷海宗先生据老子《道德经》的语言的渊源（譬如万物负阴而抱阳，祸福相仍，物极必反等等），考订老子应在孔子之后，最晚在庄子之前（这在庄子《天下篇》中可明显看到），我想是切合实际的妙语。他就是从上下象、上下象和文言这五篇里面看到了消息。我想，上下系辞、序卦、说卦和杂卦应该晚于这个上下象和上下象。因为这个《十翼》不是出于一人之手。《十翼》虽然是伪托孔子的书，可是你知道，古代有些学者重学不重名，他希望让自己的学术流传，不一定要自己挂上名字，孔子的名望大。而且这种说法，从孔子的门人，孔子的门人的门人传递下来，总结出来就是《十翼》。对中国的《易经》，意义非同一般。我想周初也有易相，就是以大自然的事物，当时就选了天、地、风、雷、水、火、山、泽八个图像。这八个图像就是所谓八卦。我们不太相信刘歆和孔安国所流传下来的伏羲八卦，就是所谓的坤震离兑乾巽坎艮这样的图，这个伏羲时不可能有。我想，我们对刘歆的学问还是非常佩服的。可是刘歆有改古书的前科，所以对他和孔安国所提供出来的非常确切的卦象，我们质疑可能就是刘歆和孔安国辈的作品。可是不要因人废言。因为虽然刘歆对《古文尚书》是有些篡改，可是八卦图像和当时王莽篡夺政权可能关系不大。我想，为什么司马迁称周文王是倜傥非常之人，倜傥非常之人一定有卓而不群的贡献。我想，这些东西在周初应该已开始形成。所以，孔子所读的《易经》，我想是周初传下来的版本。语言简略，缺乏一定学问和阅历的人是无法卒读的。孔子说："加我数年，五十以学《易》，可以无大过矣"，可见《易》在孔子心目中的崇高地位，其"韦编三绝"也足见学《易》之勤奋。战国至西汉大致是伪托孔子《十翼》产生的时间。虽为伪托，我想孔子的门人，再加门人的门人，当会将孔子关于《易》的言说载入。所谓伪托就是加孔子之名，便于流传之意。因此《十翼》，孔子本人是见不到的。我们知道，在《庄子》的"天下篇"里，庄子对儒家当然驳斥得体无完肤。对墨家驳斥，对名家驳斥，唯有听到老聃，"闻其风而悦之"。这"天下篇"当然也不是庄子的作品，可却是《庄子》书里一篇很重要的文章，我想当时就收入了，因为这篇文章很能反映庄子的全部思想。庄子"闻其风而悦之"，说明庄子一定在老子之后。孔子讲："凤鸟不至，河不出图，洛不出书，吾已矣夫。"那么，河图、洛书，孔子没有看到，孔子所看到的是周初版本的《易》，那么，到西汉末年，刘歆、孔安国这个八卦图，我们讲，刚才已谈到，它和政治没有关系，不要因人而废言。

孔子对宇宙本体论的兴趣不如老子，他关注的是现实的政治，因此他与弟子们所修订之《尚书》、《礼记》、《春秋》、《春秋外传》（《国语》）则大体重视"史"。由于孔子在重史的同时，并未忘情于《易经》，《易传》云"作易者其有忧患乎"，孔子重《易》，所注重的也是人间忧患。因此孔子同样敬天，而且以天与人之间的桥梁自勉。当时孔子有个学生叫陈子禽，对子贡讲："夫子之不可及也，犹天之不可阶而升也"（《论语·子张》）。孔夫子的学问之高啊，宛如登天不可以一阶一阶地通上去。而且有个地方小吏也讲，"天将以夫子为木铎"，就是希望夫子发出振聋发聩的声音。孔子自己也说："人能弘道，非道弘人"，所以在孔子的《论语》里，我们会看到尧、舜，看到商代的圣人：微子、箕子、比干，会看到周公。尤其对周公，"甚矣，吾衰也；久矣吾不复梦见周公"。我很衰弱，我很久没在梦里见到周公了。他认为这些人能弘道，这些人弘扬了天所展示的道。因此，如果说《十翼》的确孔子思想的渗透，那么《系辞》所讲的"天垂象"、"圣人则之"的思想，完全可以认为是孔子思想对《易经》的渗透。而老子说的，则是老子对《易经》的使用。雷海宗先生对孔子源于史，而老子源于筮的结论，真所谓妙悟者不在多言，简赅精炼如此，令人惊叹。

所谓上古的史，其实不光是史。《报任安书》讲："文史星历近乎卜祝之间，固主上所戏弄，倡优所畜，而流俗之所轻也。"他讲"文史星历，近乎卜祝之间"，就是文、史、星历和卜祝有着同样的地位。同样的地位，正好是讲一个源于史，一个源于筮。那么司马迁这段话当然是他受宫刑后的一种发愤之言。可是，司马迁讲"文、史、星历"，不仅仅是讲它的地位，是"主上所戏弄，倡优所畜"，而是讲它和卜祝有相同的地位。

在读懂雷海宗先生高论之后，我曾用两句话来概括《老子》和《论语》：《老子》是自然的人格化，包括《道经》三十七篇和《德经》四十四篇。而《论语》呢，是人格的自然化。正如《系辞》所谓："天生神物，圣人则之；天地变化，圣人效之；天垂象，见吉凶，圣人象之；河出图，洛出书，圣人则之。"虽然孔子未见《十翼》，然而心向往之。

下面我画了一个图，诸位可以看看这个图。这个图一边是史，一边是筮。这个史当然可以上溯到《尚书》。《尚书》当然有《洪范》、《虞书》、《尧典》、《舜典》、《大禹谟》、《皋陶谟》、《益稷》这些篇章。这里面有个《大禹谟》，我们要注意，是从伪《古文尚书》里出来的。《古文尚书》有两个，一个就是汉武帝时候在孔宅墙壁里发现的，这是用虫鸟篆写的，所以称《古文尚书》。到了东晋的时候，有个梅赜献出一本他伪造的《古文尚书》。伪造的《古文尚书》里有《大禹谟》。那《大

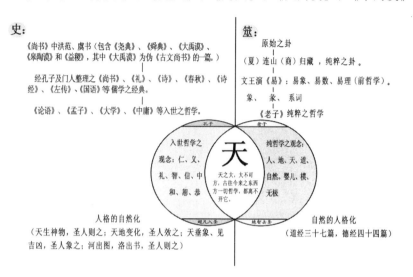

史：
《尚书》中洪范、虞书（包含《尧典》、《舜典》、《大禹谟》、《皋陶谟》和《益稷》，其中《大禹谟》为伪《古文尚书》的一篇。）

经孔子及门人整理之《尚书》、《礼》、《诗》、《春秋》、《诗经》、《左传》、《国语》等儒学之经典。

《论语》、《孟子》、《大学》、《中庸》等入世之哲学。

入世哲学之观念：仁、义、礼、智、信、中和、恕、恭

天

天之大，大不可方，古往今来之东西万一切哲学，都离不开它。

纯哲学之观念：人、地、天、道、自然、婴儿、朴、无极

筮：
原始之卦

（夏）连山（商）归藏，纯粹之卦。

文王演《易》：易象、易数、易理（前哲学）。
象、彖、系词

《老子》纯粹之哲学

人格的自然化
（天生神物，圣人则之；天地变化，圣人效之；天垂象，见吉凶，圣人象之；河出图，洛出书，圣人则之）

自然的人格化
（道经三十七篇，德经四十四篇）

禹谟》为什么现在还聊备一格留存着，说明它虽然伪，可是有一定的价值。孔子和他的弟子们整理《尚书》、《礼记》、《春秋》、《诗经》。然后到了南宋朱熹的时候，《大学》、《中庸》从《礼记》里拿出来，和《论语》、《孟子》并称为"四书"。那么，大体上，儒家的入世哲学的理念渐渐化为现实的很重要的一些东西，比如仁、义、礼、智、信、中和、恕、恭，等等。人格的自然化就是人对自然的一种趋近。人能弘道。那么筮的这边，当然，根据中国古代传说，谁也没见到，夏代有《连山》，商代有《归藏》，到了周，周文王演《易》，雷海宗先生认为这是个前哲学。那么到了老子，雷海宗先生讲，这是一个纯粹的哲学。纯粹哲学的关键词是人、地、天、道、自然，然后回归于朴、婴儿、无极。大体上，在我读雷海宗先生对中国古代哲学大分为二的时候，我的体会大体就是这样。雷海宗先生在他的文章里，对16世纪王阳明给予极崇高的评价。他认为这是中国500年来最伟大的思想者。前天晚上我和王敦书先生见面。王敦书先生讲，这句话可以讲是一个终极性结论。老实说，中国从12世纪的理学到16世纪王阳明的心学，这个里程碑式人物就是朱熹和王阳明。王阳明在他的《传习录》里全面展开他对心学问题的看法。当然他最终是为了解决"知"和"行"的问题。在王阳明的心目里，"知"和"行"，不是先"知"而后"行"，或者先"行"而后"知"。"知"的开始就是"行"的开始。比如讲，我内心知道我应当爱母亲，你爱母亲的"行"已经开始了。这是王阳明《传习录》里面很重要的一个观念。《传习录》特别强调心灵，心外无物。心外无物甚至心外无天，那么心外无天，那天理在哪呢？心明就是天理。这和朱熹就不一样。朱熹讲，在没有天地之前，总还有一个"理"，王阳明不会同意这个看法。王阳明的哲学思想当然是受南宋陆九渊这些人的影响。我们知道"鹅湖之会"有陆九渊和朱熹的辩论。朱熹就讲，陆九渊过于简单，陆九渊讲，朱熹过分琐碎。当时参加这个会的当然还有很多大学者。我想，古代学人之所以伟大，那就是治学的精神。朱熹到了晚年给陆九渊写信，讲我们当时在鹅湖时的辩论，今天我认为你说的对，我想改我的文章，可是我年已迟暮，无能为力了。因为他作的很多古籍的诠注，那时是作为一个范

本的。我们从古代学人的身上能够学到这种精神，从朱熹对陆九渊的态度就可以看出来。王阳明同样非常尊重人对至善的追求。我前年写了一篇文章，就是《一词圣典：至善》，我写王阳明和笛卡尔。王阳明是 16 世纪中国的大思想家，雷海宗先生称之为 500 年来最伟大的思想家，这一点不为过。笛卡尔被认为是西方理性主义之父。他们用的方法是完全不一样的。我们知道笛卡尔本身是生理学家、数学家，他一定要通过自己的实践，一辈子做去伪存真的工作，还要回到一个纯粹信念，他认为纯粹信念是人类与生俱来的。王阳明也认为，至善也是本然的存在，所以每个人都可以成为圣人。王阳明讲，我看到满街的人都是圣人，满街人看到我也是圣人。这说明什么，王阳明对人的与生俱来的本根，根本善，有充分的自信，他自信不仅对自身，而且他把他的这个大爱普及到满街的人，都可能是如此。

下边是我的结论：

雷海宗先生已远离我们而去，然而他博大的学识和史学家的睿智，将和英国的汤因比、德国的斯宾格勒一样永驻人类的文化史，像长青不败之树，永葆其美妙青春。

忆雷海宗先生在南开的岁月

魏宏运 南开大学

雷海宗（1902年6月17日——1962年12月25日）是学界公认的史学大师。2002年12月15日，南开大学历史学院为纪念先生诞辰百年，举行了学术讨论会。此时，他的高足王敦书整理出版了雷师的著作《伯伦史学集》，并由中华书局出版。据此书，认识的或不认识的，写出不少缅怀和评论文章，汇集于《雷海宗与二十世纪中国史学》一书，2005年也由中华书局出版。今年是雷师诞辰110周年，历史学院再次于6月15日，举行纪念会，中外人士百余人参加，发言者从不同的角度，称赞这位博学的大家。

雷师的一生，其治学有诸多独特之处，诸如学贯古今，跨越东西；译注斯宾格勒的《西方的没落》，以其文化史观，观照中外历史，是介绍文化史观到中国的第一人；打破王朝体系治中国历史的模式，主张不该一律按朝代划分段落；在抗日战争时期，和林同济、陈铨等形成战国策派，师从尼采思想，在昆明出版《战国策》杂志；研究欧洲史，必须了解基督教的历史和地位；晚年，主张以生产工具的发展论述中国社会的分期。在教学方面，讲课艺术高超，思想严密，论述深刻；没有讲稿，人名、地名、时间、历史事件脱口而出，又擅长历史对比，等等。

雷师以知识渊博、平易近人，颇受师生爱戴。这里，我讲几个故事，以表示我的深切怀念。

雷先生早年就读芝加哥大学，回国后，先后任教武大、西南联大、清华大学，并担任清华大学历史系主任。1952年全国院系调整，他和北大历史系主任郑天挺先生一起调到南开。规定郑任系主任兼中国史教研室主任，雷任世界史教研室主任。

为安排郑、雷二师的生活，学校派我到北京大学和清华大学了解情况，我带回雷师在思想改造中的自我反省材料，这是和旧思想决裂，树立新的人生观的榜样，在京津高校广为传诵。

雷师的书籍很多，我派了几位同学装书，以汽车运到天津。南开教师住宅一直很紧张，郑师是单身，由杨石先校长腾出一间14多平方米来住。雷师有家属，住在校东门内东平房约50—60平方米，每间都很小。

郑、雷来后，南开历史系声望大震。记得《往事并不如烟》的作者章诒和讲，她父亲说，学历史专业应到南开去，可见南开历史系被视为历史学术重镇。

解放初，根据市委文教部要求，南开大学和天津大学共同办起马列主义夜校，每周请苏联专家和人民大学教师讲马克思主义哲学，雷、郑和我都去听课。郑、雷非常认真，从未旷课。雷说，这是他第一次接触马克思学说。

郑师认为我和其他两位助教基础知识差，请雷师在他的家中给我们讲先秦史，郑师和杨志玖、王玉哲两位教授也来听讲。

五十年代前，是雷师最忙的时期。他除了自己讲课，还组织教研室诸同仁学习苏联教学经验，预讲，听讲，组织课堂讨论，有的教师就是根据他的讲述来讲的。教育部又委托他编写《世界上古中古史讲义》。教育部制定的教学大纲中要开设物质文明史，各校都开设不出来，只有雷担当这一课程，仅讲蒙古人民骑马所穿的裤子就讲了几个小时。

不幸的厄运降临，雷师在《人民日报》记者组织的一次座谈会上，讲到1895年恩格斯逝世后，马克思主义有很大发展，而马克思主义的社会科学则处于停滞状态。《人民日报》对讲话作了按语，说"1895年以来马克思主义就没有发展"。康生认为这是"右派"言论，中宣部长陆定一也讲，天津市委再不批雷海宗就要犯"右派"机会主义的错误。就在这时，北京大学物理系学生谭天荣到南开煽风点火，否定中国共产党的领导，校方陷于混乱。历史系学生会主席刘健清请雷师在校大礼堂批判谭天荣。雷质问谭："你读过黑格尔哲学吗？"谭说："读过一部分。"雷说："你能读外文书吗？"谭说："不能。"雷说："你请教过北大对黑格尔哲学颇有研究的贺麟先生吗？"谭说："没有。"雷先生最后指着主席台挂着的语录标语说："领导我们事业的核心力量是中国共产党，指导我们思想的理论基础是马克思主义。"这一问一答，谭非常尴尬，学校立即平静下来。这表明雷师是坚决拥护共产党的。

但是《人民日报》的编者按语扭曲了雷讲话的原意，雷写信请其更正，也置之不理。天津市委认为雷讲的是学术问题，可以争鸣，但事情的发展越来越严重。在中央的敦促下，天津也顶不住了。文教部长梁寒冰找我说："不批不行了。"我说："雷的声望很高，批不起来。"梁说："那就先从校外批。"在北京，毛主席的秘书田家英、历史所所长尹达、中央党校和马列学院教授孙定国等在北京民族饭店还组织了一次批判会，南开派郑天挺、吴廷璆和我参加，主要批判两个问题，一是马列主义停滞论，一是中国没有奴隶社会发展阶段。

经过这一番折腾，雷师受的压力很大，身体日益衰弱，并患了尿毒症。雷师母张景弗讲："从此无人敢进我们家门，当时我能向谁求援，又有谁敢来帮助？我们二人终日默默相对，食不甘味，寝不安眠。"这是实情，其痛苦是难以忍受的。"左"的思潮不知伤了多少知识分子的身心，伤害了多少人的家庭。

由于群众希望听到雷师的讲课，我和系主任郑天挺、办公室主任于可商议，请雷师再登讲台，讲授"外国史学名著选读"和"外国史学史"，他欣然答应。系里先后派曹忠屏和王敦书照顾他的生活。由其家中坐三轮车到主楼一楼东边阶梯大教室讲授，这是雷师执教鞭的最后一课，真是鞠躬尽瘁，死而后已！

先生逝世，风范长存，经市委统战部批准，在主楼一小教室举行了追悼会，由我致悼词，赞扬雷师为中国文化作出了巨大贡献。如今学界普遍认为曾经批判雷海宗两个观点的文章，都是站不住脚的。雷海宗的学术观点没有错，历史终于作出了公正的结论，雷师可含笑于九泉矣！

雷海宗先生南开教学轶事

辜燮高　南开大学

1952 年院系调整，雷先生到南开大学历史系，任世界史教研室主任。从 52 年到 55 年的三个学年间，教研室经常教课的只有雷先生和我二人。当时杨生茂先生先是去党校学习，后调去编世界史方面的中学教科书，直至 55 年下半年才回系；而梁卓生先生也是在 55 年才由高教部下放到南开历史系的；其间还有个别学中国史的先生曾短期教世界史作为去中国史教研室的过渡。

这三学年（52-55 年）雷先生经常教的基础课是世界古代史和世界现代史，再搭一门选修课。我经常教的基础课是世界中古史和世界近代史，再加选修课英国史。此外，雷先生还给全系助教讲过《古文观止》。有一年中文系有世界通史课，由我们二人共同讲授。这里谈谈怀念雷先生的几件事。

1. 关于 52-53 学年的世界中古史。当时我是年轻教师，上课前先在雷先生处试讲，听讲的还有教研室的两位助教。52-53 年还没有苏联的教学大纲，因此怎样讲完全由自己决定。雷先生提出两点：一是摆脱西洋史影响，讲成真正的世界史；一是反对西欧中心论，由东向西讲。因此我讲的时候，便从朝鲜、日本、越南讲起，然后是蒙古人扩张、印度，再向西讲。我也是学西洋史的底子，东方国家过去也还大致接触过，成问题的是撒哈拉以南的非洲（黑非洲）。南开图书馆没有这方面的材料，于是由雷先生先讲我记，再由我整理后向学生讲，记得当时如加纳已讲到了。其次是拉丁美洲，我知道也不多。于是由雷先生补充材料。雷先生对年轻教师的确起到传帮带的作用，我受益良多。

2. 当时学生真想学历史的并不多，因此进入历史系大都有专业思想问题。雷先生高质量的讲课内容和高超的讲课技术（笔记便是一篇文章），对于稳定学生专业思想起到极好作用。还有一点，雷先生的世界古代史已经给了学生应有的世界史知识（如西方历法），使我接手讲中古史方便不少。记得 50-51 年我在另一所大学讲世界中古史时，古代史也是一位老先生讲的，我接手发现许多世界史基本知识还得给学生讲，使我增加不少困难，这一点也得特别感谢雷先生。

3. 雷先生是学贯中西的名教授，但非常谦虚。他曾对我讲，思想改造后，别人对这方面提的意见还能接受，但在业务方面就不一样了，其实这是固步自封，不利于业务进步的。

怀念雷先生，提出以上几点，是我感到最突出的。

雷海宗先生的"三为"之道堪为后生楷模

朱 寰 东北师范大学

今年是国内外著名历史学家雷海宗先生诞辰 110 周年，我们纪念雷先生，希望把他为人、为学、为师的"三为"之道的基本精神继承下来，发扬光大、利国益民、泽被后世。

雷海宗先生，字伯伦，河北省永清县人。他主要生活在 20 世纪前半期，即 20 世纪前 60 年。他生活的这个年代，如果从 1840 年鸦片战争算起，到 1945 年第二次世界大战结束，这一百多年间是中国人民有史以来最为艰难险恶的历史时期。这一百多年的前半段，中国开始遭受西方帝国主义列强的侵略和压迫，特别是后半段，即 1894 年中日甲午战争之后，直到 1945 年二战结束，这半个多世纪，中华民族一直遭受日本军国主义的疯狂侵略和大举进攻的严重威胁，国难当头，失土丧民，家破人亡，险象环生。这一个世纪国破家亡的历史使中国人民真正懂得了一个道理："落后就要挨打"。要想让中国不挨打，就必须迎头赶上，学习和实践西方的现代科学技术，改变旧中国社会经济、政治、文化和科学技术的落后状态。这正是我们父祖辈以来中国人的共识。雷海宗先生正是生活和奋斗在这个时代。他 1917 年入北京崇德中学，1919 年转入北京清华高等学堂学习，这是一所留学美国的预备学校。雷先生出国之前，正处在"五四运动"时期，又是身处北京的知识青年，自然深受爱国思想和新文化思潮的洗礼。1922 年清华毕业后，雷先生怀着满腔热情，为国家为民族赴美留学，进入芝加哥大学，主修历史学，兼修哲学。一位热血的知识青年在国难当头的时候出国留学，自然怀抱着爱国、救国和建国的满腔热情和雄心壮志。

首先，我认为雷先生的"为人"之道，堪为我们晚辈的楷模。雷先生作为一位正派中国人，爱国家、爱人民的崇高思想，一切为国家、为人民的伟大精神，是非常值得我们学习和发扬的。这种思想和精神在雷先生的言行和文章中可以看得清清楚楚。

雷先生在抗日战争初期写的文章《时代的悲哀》中指出："今日的世界正处在一个大的动乱时代，到处都是问题，每一个问题又好似都没有妥善的解决方策，以致人心普遍的不安，被一种莫可名状的忧郁心理所笼罩，一若非常的大祸随时就要临头的模样"。雷先生忧国忧民的心态，跃然纸上。他特别称赞中国士兵在抗日战场上的英勇杀敌行为，谴责那些官宦绅士贪生怕死、疯狂逃生的怯懦行径。雷先生在 1938 年（民国 27 年）10 月写成的《抗战建国中的中国》一文中指出："生，固然可贵；但是不惜任何代价以求苟生，还不如死！士兵的英勇，真可谓非常而可钦；后方有责者的狂逃，实在是反常而可耻。"雷先生在《此次抗战在历史上的地位》一文中，对中国的抗战给予极高的评价，他说："此次抗战不只在中国历史上是空前的大事，甚至在整个人类历史上也是绝无仅有的奇迹"。雷先生在抗战时期的一切言行，以国家民族的大义为重，在为人方面充分表现了爱国、救国和建国的高贵品格，实为后生学习的楷模。

其次，雷先生的"为学"之道也是值得我们晚辈学习的。雷先生的治学品格，概括起来，有三个明显特点：这就是勤奋、广博、创新。人们在学术的广阔天地里，不管哪一门学问，自然科学也好，社会科学也好，或者哲学文学也好，所有的学人都知道这样一个道理："书山有路勤为径，学海无涯苦作舟。"要取得任何一点学术上的成就，都离不开勤奋刻苦。不坐冷板凳是办不到的。常言道："宁坐板凳十年冷，不写文章一句空。"雷先生的学术成就是极其广博、深邃的，可以说是淹古通今、中外交融。就中国古代历史学而言，雷先生是考证周武王伐殷的准确年代是公元前 1027 年的第一人；就世界历史学而言，雷先生又是把德国历史哲学家施本格勒的"文化形态史观"介绍到中国来的第一人。雷先生前后给学生开过的课程不下十几门，既有中国历史，又有世界历史；既有史学理论，又有史料学和史学史，可以说，历史学的课程，门类俱全。这是从另一个侧面反映出先生学识的广博精深。雷先生治学方面，我认为最重要特点是善于独立思考，勇于发表个人的独立见解，在学术上不断推陈出新，体现了一种开创精神，也是值得我们后辈认真学习和发扬的。例如，雷先生接受了西方的"文化形态史观"，他就按照这种理论认真研究中国全部历史，根据中国历史上文化形态的演变，他提出了自己的独立见解，认为中国历史形态的变化实现了两周的理论，并在抗战以后有望实现第三周的开端。不管其他学者是否同意雷先生这个观点，但这是先生根据自己的理论，结合中国历史实际，经过深思熟虑，认真研究而提出来的独立见解。我认为这是雷先生反对中国古史学中的繁琐考据和材料堆砌，推陈出新，而提出的新观点、新见解。学术创新必须在正确的理论指导下，不断地研究探索中外各国的历史实际，才有可能实现历史学的创新。雷先生在学术上从不抱残守缺，而是与时俱进。"1948 年后期，全国解放的形势日益明朗。尽管有关当局给雷海宗提供机票动员他'南飞'，但他认为国民党大势已去，不得人心。……毅然决定留在北平清华园，迎接解放，与人民同呼吸，共命运。新中国成立后，在党的关怀教育下，他积极参加土改、抗美援朝和思想改造等运动，转变政治立场和世界观。他开始系统学习马克思主义，感到发现了一个新的世界，似乎恢复了青年时期的热情，进一步加强了建设社会主义新中国的决心。"雷先生在 1951–1952 年间发表的学术性成果多是对罗马教廷和美帝国主义进行口诛笔伐的批判性文章。后来雷先生在南开大学编写的《世界上古史讲义》，彻底摆脱了从前的文化形态史观，完全按照马克思主义观点，运用丰富的材料，对世界上古史进行系统的阐述。既有自己的体系，又不受苏联历史学大国沙文主义的影响。因此教育部决定将此书作为全国高等学校交流讲义，正式出版发行。由此可见雷先生的学术观点随着时代的发展而不断进步的。

最后，雷先生于 1927 年在美国芝加哥大学获得博士学位之后，立即回国任教，决心把毕生的精力全部贡献给祖国的高等教育事业，为国家培养高级建设人才。雷先生自回国任教以来，非常关心学生，爱护学生，千方百计教好课，解决学生学习上的困难，关心学生的日常生活。1931 年雷先生在武汉大学任教时，给学生讲授"欧洲通史"课，因为当时没有教材和中文参考书，雷先生给学生印发了详细的讲授提纲。迄今武汉大学图书馆善本室内还藏有雷先生撰写的讲授提纲《欧洲通史》（二）铅印本。该提纲共 300 页（600 面），分四十九章，每章末开列外文参考书目，合计约三百余种。"全部提纲体系完整，层次鲜明，子目详尽细致，覆盖面极广而条理一目了然。"这部教学提纲的印发，对于学生的学习极为方便有利。

1932 年雷先生回到母校清华大学任教，"他面向全校学生，开设'中国通史'课程，并编选大量史料，以《中国通史选读》为名，作为铅印讲义发给学生，共 7 册 43 章 769 节 930 页（1860 面）。全书内容从史前石器时代一直编到清末溥仪退位。材料选自各方面文献，系统完整，极其丰富"。

为了使学生学得好，雷先生尽心竭力，鞠躬尽瘁，创造一切条件，促进学生提高学习质量。不仅如此，雷先生待人极为宽厚，律己极严，无微不至地关心学生生活上的具体困难。1941 年初冬在昆明西南联大时，何炳棣教授第一次留美应试失败，后来又得知身处沦陷区的老父在天津逝世，雷先生怕何炳棣生活发生困难，亲切温情地问他，是否需要到其它大学教书，做讲师或副教授？当何回答说，为了潜心治学，不在乎名义待遇，坚决留在西南联大。雷先生特别称赞何的决定。三个月后，何炳棣为家务回金华，在浙赣路上碰到了九级历史系学长王文杰回福建奔妻丧，王告诉何说，他路费的极大部分是雷先生私人供给他的。

首都师大荣誉校长齐世荣教授在纪念雷先生的文章中也提到："雷先生对学生十分关心，不仅关心他们的学习，而且关心他们的生活。我读大四时，生活比较困难。一天课后，雷先生对我说，美国波摩那大学来了一个研究生，学中国近代史，想写关于梁启超的论文，他的中文程度还需要提高。你可去给他补习中文，借机会练练英文，并增加点收入。我听了以后十分感动，不知道老师如何知道我最近生活困难。"大量事实说明雷先生不仅关心学生们的学习成绩，而且还关心学生们的生活状况。雷先生的为师之道的基本精神是非常值得我们晚辈学习和发扬的。

雷先生在做人方面，严于律己，宽以待人；对国家和人民，充满了热爱，具有高度责任感；毕生热衷于科学教育事业，成为一代史学大师；热爱劳动人民，关心青年的成长。雷先生的"三为"之道，值得我们晚辈好好学习继承，并发扬光大，为国家的发展、中华民族的复兴做出自己的贡献。

（2012 年 4 月 15 日于长春）

在雷海宗先生诞辰110周年纪念会上的发言

张文朴　中国前驻加拿大大使

感谢南开大学历史学院和王敦书先生的盛情邀请，能有机会参加今天的纪念会，使我受益良多。

我于1947—51年间就读于清华大学历史系，毕业后被统一分配到中央国家机关，当了一名普通干部，从事一般的行政工作，从此与历史科学渐行渐远。在校时只上过雷先生的一门课——美国史，对雷先生在历史科学上的巨大贡献知之甚少，只了解先生精通西洋史，不知道他也是中国古代史的一位大家，对于他博古通今、学贯中西、擅长于对中外历史进行比较研究，且在史学理论体系方面有独创性的建树，更是一无所知。回想起来，自己真是经泰山而不知其高，涉江海而不知其深，在知识宝库面前徘徊而未能窥其门庭！所以今天对雷先生博大精深的学术成就无从置喙，只是带着某种抱撼的心情对雷先生表达我的敬意和思念。特别是雷先生在上个世纪40年代末拒绝南行，毅然留在北平迎接解放。以后又以极大热情从事新中国的学术建设，但在1957年却横遭摧残。回顾这段经历，使我为老师感到心痛，为国家感到心痛。他在得到部分昭雪以后，又以抱病之躯，重上讲堂，这种精神真值得我们敬佩。

如前所述，由于我离开学校以后就再无缘于历史科学的研究和深造，本科四年所学有限的基础知识，对我后来多年从事的"文秘"工作虽说有用，但只是提供一种"通才教育"所能提供的文化铺垫。当然，有这个铺垫和没有还是不同的。那时我对人自称是"万金油"，但内心认为还是比较高级的"万金油"。

由于某种机缘巧合，到了上个世纪七十年代，我有幸应召参加了国家的外事工作。那时我已过了不惑之年，又没有经过什么专业培训（现在叫"充电"），深感自己的知识准备不足，尤其在国际经济和法律知识方面，要逊于我们的外国（主要是西方）同行。然而幸好有几十年前打下的历史知识的基础，加上它的综合性质能起触类旁通的作用，使我在同西方外交官和政界人士进行交流甚或交锋时，不仅不感到气馁，反而觉得底气十足。这是因为，除了在外交上道理常在我们方面以外，即使在知识水准、视野广度和思辨能力方面我们也不落下风，因此在许多场合能做到不仅"理直"，而且"气壮"。

我的外交生涯中的一段重要经历是在上个世纪80年代初，以一名中级外交官的身份，参与了有关中美关系的工作，包括参加了中美间第三个联合公报（俗称《八·一七公报》）的谈判和拟订工作。这个公报的主旨是要解决和限制美国向台湾出售武器的问题。在这一过程中，我深感当年从雷先生那里学到的一些美国历史知识对我有极大的帮助。虽说学业已荒疏多年，但毕竟使我对要打交道的国家的历史有一个梗概的了解。有时还能将一些史实材料直接用到工作中去。例如，在为领导人起草的谈话材料中，以南北战争为例，证明一个主权国家不惜一切代价维护国家统一的正当性。

又如，引用当年美国联邦政府为阻止英国向南方提供武器，甚至一度不惜诉诸武力这一事例，证明美国坚持向台湾出售武器在法理上的荒谬。

回顾这段经历，我想说的是：即使对我这个在历史科学方面未能成材的弟子，雷先生和其他各位先师们当年的栽培和心血也没有白费，是起了作用的。如果说若干年来我在不同岗位上还能做些事情，那在很大程度上是拜他们所赐。谨以此告慰雷先生和各位老师们的在天之灵，并表达我对他们的无限感激。

对于雷海宗先生史学的三点初步体会

刘家和　北京师范大学

一　雷先生史学的渊博性

请先谈"渊博"。渊之意为深，不待多说。至于博，则或有误解。《荀子·修身》曰"多闻曰博"，又曰"多而乱曰耗"。所以"多闻"只是博的必要条件，不多闻不能成其为博；可是"多闻"不是博的充分条件，即多闻未必真博。《说文》："博，大、通也。"《玉篇》："博，广也，通也。"所以这里说雷先生之渊博，是说他的学问既深且广而又通。据个人体会，他的渊博主要表现在两个方面：

（一）博通中外历史

雷先生在美国留学的博士论文是关于法国近代史方面的。可是他回国后并非专门教西洋史。他也教中国通史，写关于中国史的论文。这已经说明他的多闻，但又不仅于此。他也讲世界通史，而且他还设计了自己的贯通中外的世界史提纲。他的世界通史不同于实为西洋史的"世界通史"。这就是他的既广又通的严格意义上的博。

（二）博通古今历史

雷先生既然讲中外通史，当然通知古今史事。不过，这还只是事情的第一个层面。在雷先生那里，更重要的是要有贯通古今的史识。这就要求有进一步之思维深度，方能称其为渊博。他讲文明周期，指出中国与外国之历史皆有大体一致的周期，是其同；但又言中国文明有第二期，在抗战期间更倡言第三期，是其异。且不论其具体是非得失，可以确定的是，一则是他秉持一种深厚的爱国热情，二则是他具有古今之变的通识。古与今之间有变化，但其间又有内在的相通性或一贯性。把古今之变看成为一种变与常的统一，这就是通识。

二　雷先生史学的前沿性

雷先生史学之前沿性表现于史学方法论和反西方中心论两个方面。

（一）在史学方法论方面

雷先生不仅有个人史学研究与教学之实践，还有一种对于史学实践的方法论上的反思。这主要表现在他本人讲述、其门人谷霁光先生记录、王敦书先生整理的 1932 年史学方法课程笔记中。此笔记前半部分基本讲史学考证（或史料批判）的方法，所参考的外国教本基本是朗格诺瓦与瑟诺博的《史学原论》。不过，他在讲"外评"、"内评"（今通译为外、内考证）时，并非照本宣科，而是结合中国固有的历史文献学的传统加以比较与联通，分别以校勘之学、训诂之学与之相对应。这是否是牵强附会呢？不是。如所周知，这一史学方法在中国可谓古已有之，而大盛于清代乾嘉时期（1736–1811）。所以，他所用阐释性之举例，也由外国实例改易为中国实例。这样就不止于外国史学之简单的引进，而是以中外史学之传统相互参照而求其精神上之内在的沟通。

在西方，此一历史文献批判传统，滥觞于尼布尔（1776–1831），而大盛于兰克（1795–1886）。兰克的史学成了西方 19 世纪史学的主流。1824 年，他出版了成名之作《拉丁与条顿民族史》。在此书序言中，他写下了以下名言："历史指定给本书的任务是：评判过去，教导现在，以利于未来。可是本书并不敢期望完成这样崇高的任务。它的目的不过是说明事情的真实情况而已（Er will bloss zeigen wie es eigentilich gewesen.）。"[1]在兰克看来，只要把史料收集完全并做好严密的考证，历史本身就会自然地呈现出来，不需史家任何主观之见的介入。（其实，中国的崔述（1740–1816）也曾于《考信录提要》中明确反对"以己度人，以今度古"[2]）兰克的这部名著的丰富而严密的考证性的注释，也标志出他的史学特色。兰克以讲习班的方式教授弟子，在欧美影响很大。德国伯恩海姆之《史学方法教本》[3]与法国朗格诺瓦与瑟诺博之《史学原论》可以说是兰克历史文献考证方法之综合与详论。这种史学的考证或批判方法确有其重要性。雷先生在讲史学方法时援引朗格诺瓦与瑟诺博之《史学原论》，可说是对于兰克史学积极方面的继承，其实也是对于清代乾嘉时期史学文献考证传统之继承。当然，兰克纯客观主义的史学观念是有其片面性与局限性的。

或谓兰克史学为纯客观主义的史学，其实并不准确。难道兰克的史料批判不正是其主观理性的运用吗？其实，在乾嘉时期史家崔述那里也有同样的问题。再者，史学家的主观能动性难道仅仅能够表现在史料的考证上吗？到了 19 世纪晚期至 20 世纪初期，针对这个问题，德国学者狄尔泰（1833–1911）以及文德尔班（1848–1915）、李凯尔特（1863–1936）纷纷提出新说。他们都认为，史料本身不能自我呈现为历史，要理解历史人物，必须经过史家的体验或直观；而且，史学有异于自然科学，即其是非（真）与价值（善）是难以分割的。意大利学者克罗齐（1866–1952）在这一趋势之下又有了自己的拓展。1916 年，他出版了《历史学的理论与实践》（1920 有英译本）。此书在 20 世纪早期无疑处于西方非马克思主义的史学理论的前沿。

雷先生于 1930 年译出克罗齐《史学的理论与实践》之第一章《历史与记事》（傅任敢先生译为《历史与编年史》似更准确，但亦未敢必）。此章既为此书之首篇，实亦此书立论之基础。此章之核心内容为"一切历史皆为当代史"，事虽古远，而今人（史家）思想、精神能与之相通者，即为当代史；即使一小时前之事，而今人（史家）思想、精神不能与之相通者，即为"记事"（于此亦可见 ANNALS 在此译为编年史，难通），而决不能称之为当代史。在他看来，治记事者为学者，写历史者为史家。二者相异亦相须为用。雷先生的《课程笔记》所说的"学者"（外评家）与"史家"（内评家）之分看来源自克罗齐之说。当然，乾嘉学者章学诚（1738–1802）也曾将史学研究成果分为"记撰"与"著述"两类，大体相当。雷先生的《课程笔记》里具体论说克罗齐的内容不多，其中涉及"想

---

① 转引自古奇：《十九世纪历史学与历史学家》中译本，商务印书馆，页 178。
② 《崔东壁遗书》，顾颉刚编，上海古籍出版社，页 4。
③ Ed. Bornheim, *Lehrbuch der historischen Methode*, 1889. 按有中译本，一时不记原中译书名。

象"，但笔记明显不全。无论如何，当时才 30 岁的雷先生的学术眼光是非常趋向学术前沿的。

（二）在反对西方中心论方面

雷先生在这一方面显然是受到了斯宾格勒的《西方的没落》的影响的。不过，他不是在简单地照搬，而是在文化周期说中独特地提出了中国文化的第二周期说。我们可以对这种文化周期说的理论从理论上作种种分析与批判，因为它不过是一种缺乏事实根据的思辨的主观构建。不过，汉帝国与罗马帝国在人类历史上的地位有鲜明的相似之处，这是不争的事实；而在其后魏晋南北朝与罗马之分为东西以及日耳曼世界同拜占廷帝国的对立却不可同日而语，这同样是不争的事实。中西之间的巨大历史差别是值得史学家们认真、严肃深思的。雷先生敏锐地注意到这一点，这就既来源于又超越于斯宾格勒，走到了斯宾格勒的更前沿。限于篇幅，此处恕不烦赘。

三　雷先生史学的启发性

在这方面，我想以提出并试答问题的形式简单地谈两点体会。

（1）雷先生以海外名校的博士归国的身份在名大学里讲授世界史，那是无人可以质疑的。可是他又讲授中国通史。那时候，比他年长而又饱读经史的学者尚大有人在。在当时自由竞争的学术气氛中，他不仅能在讲台上自有特色地站起来，而且赢得学者们的尊重。难道他真是对于中国历史文化在微观的积累方面果然胜过当时的博学鸿儒们吗？看来未必。那么他是怎么能够成功的呢？唯一的关键似乎就在于，他以自己的世界史知识为背景看出并说了中国历史上前人没有看出并说出的问题与道理。反之，他在外国留学，学的都是外国人已经看出并说明了的道理，按照常规，他只能亦步亦趋地跟在人家后面做传播工作。可是，他对于外国的学问又有着自己的新理解，这又何以成为可能？因为他是一位中国学者，具有自己的文化历史底蕴。因此，他才能突破外国人"不识庐山真面目"的中心盲点，看出并说出自己的新见地来。愚意以为，这正是雷先生值得我能深思并学习的地方之一。

（2）雷先生以历史学为自己的专业，学于斯、教于斯以终生。可是，当我们一看他的文章、撰史大纲以及《课程笔记》等等，总难免因为他的眼界之开阔与夫见解之新颖而有豁然之感。这又是为什么？在《课程笔记》里，他对于史学主张从哲学、科学与艺术三个层面进行考察、理解。当然。这本身并非他自己的发明。西方有人这样看，中国唐代史学家刘知几不是也曾说过史学三长才、学、识吗？所以，在这个问题上不是知道与不知道的问题，而是是否真能身体力行的问题。历史从来就是多方面、多层次的，史学因此也从来就是多方面、多层次的。要做到这一点，就不仅需要中外通、古今通（雷先生这方面的特色上文已经说到），而且需要多方面学术知识的贯通。雷先生在这方面也十分出色。宋代史学家郑樵强调的"会通"、清代史学家章学诚所说的"横通"，都是这个意思。这一点，在我们今天来说已经远非易事。不过，我们今天正面临中华文明伟大复兴时期，史学界需要形成新一代的史学大家，难道不需要作这样的努力吗？雷先生早年生活在那个"风雨如晦"时代的中国尚且给我们作了示范，这实在是一种弥足珍贵的启示。

洛克菲勒基金会档案中有关雷海宗先生的史料三则
——纪念先生 110 周年诞辰

刘桂生　清华大学

今年是雷海宗先生诞辰 110 周年。我本来准备写一篇回忆先生 1950——1951 年在清华历史系"世界史"课上及课间谈 19 世纪学术"高峰"问题的文章，还没有写完，收到周启博先生（周一良师的二公子）从美国寄来他发表在网上的《美国救济中国人文学者的往事》一文，谈的是抗日战争时期美国洛克菲勒基金会资助几所大学邀请中国学者赴美讲学的事。我稍稍翻阅，发现其中有几则与雷先生有关的史料，过去还没有见过。当然，我知道，资中筠教授前些年在《关于雷海宗先生二三事》一文中谈及此事，也谈到雷先生被邀请，又"谢绝"赴美等等。不过，资中筠教授却没有介绍档案的细节。[①] 这次周启博先生的文章介绍得比较详细，我喜出望外，决定改变主意，不写那篇回忆先生谈学术"高峰"问题的文章，改为写这篇介绍史料的文章，赶上先生诞辰 110 周年纪念大会，向国内学人介绍。我想，这几则史料（主要是出自友人笔下的评语），先生生前不一定见过，但很可以作为一种"祭品"，献于先生灵前。

＊　　　　＊　　　　＊

抗日战争时期美国邀请中国学人赴美讲学，美方在重庆主持其事的是费正清教授和夫人费慰梅

[①] 资中筠教授的文章发表在《博览群书》2003 年第 8 期，后收入南开大学历史学院编《雷海宗与二十世纪中国史学——雷海宗先生百年诞辰纪念文集》（中华书局，2005 年版）中，相关段落文字如下：

"1992 年，我在美国做访问学者时因研究洛克菲勒基金会与中国的关系，曾到洛氏基金会档案馆查档案。忽然发现几份饶有兴趣的文件：1943 年至 1944 年间，中国抗战最艰苦的岁月，时任美国驻华使馆文化官员的著名中国通费正清与清华大学美国教授温德联名给洛克菲勒基金会写信，大意谓，中国最著名的一些人文社会科学教授现在生活陷于极端困境，连温饱和健康都难以保证（其中提到闻一多罹肺病等等），为抢救这批对中国的复兴极为宝贵的知识精英，建议洛氏基金会有选择地分批资助一些教授赴美讲学，既可以对他们改善生活不无小补，又可以加强美国的中国学。由于中国知识分子自尊心极强，直接由基金会出面，他们可能不肯接受，因此建议由美国国务院出面与中国政府谈，作为两国文化交流项目，中美双方共同协商决定名单，再由洛氏基金会拨款给美国有兴趣的大学，由他们出面聘请对等学科的教授。这一方案果然付诸实施，名单分 A、B 两批，A 是被认为不但著名而且最有创造力的学者，雷海宗在这一名单上。其他有闻一多、费孝通、冯友兰、梁思成、罗常培等十几位教授。多数都应邀成行，利用这一机会，在学术上成绩斐然。例如费孝通的《乡土中国》（英文原著）就是在此期间完成的，冯友兰也是在这一年开始与卜德教授合作翻译他的《中国哲学史》。雷先生却婉拒不就，理由是现在正是学校最困难时期，西南联大需要他，他不能在这个时候离开。梅贻琦校长曾亲自动员他接受邀请，但是他留意已决，终于没有去。这一情节见于基金会在华工作人员向总会汇报工作的信中，完全事务性一笔带过，未加任何评论。而这几句话给我留下很深的印象，引起我很大的心灵震撼。"

女士。在昆明，则有多年在清华外文系、当时在西南联大外文系的温德（Robert Winter）①教授。从档案中得知，他原来也是洛克菲勒基金会的工作人员。在解放战争时期，众所周知，他是第二条战线上学生爱国运动的著名的同情者。

这次被邀请的中国学者共 22 人。这 22 人分为 A、B 两类：A 类 8 人；B 类 14 人。雷先生的名字在 A 类中，简历是：

> 雷海宗，年 42，芝加哥大学博士，
> 清华大学历史系教授，1933 年——现在。
> 专长：中国古代史。

名字后面有一段批语，出自温德之手，如下：

> A 类中最杰出的候选人。大概 A、B 两类加在一起，他也是最优秀的。聪慧，勇敢，善于表达。如可能，毫无疑问他应该有机会去美国一年。他和太太②，太太的兄嫂③、太太嫂子的嫂子，都可以住在一处。这一大家人都令人喜欢，受人尊重。

这是史料第一则。据周文，档案号是：Folder 412，Box 49，Series 601，RG 1.1，RAC（Rockefeller Archive Center）。

*　　　　*　　　　*

邀请名单确定后，费正清等于 1943 年 12 月 22 日把它送交洛克菲勒基金会。随后，在美国发生一场奥伯林学院（Oberlin College）④ 和帕莫纳学院（Pomona College）⑤ 两校"争聘"雷海宗先生的"争夺战"。两校都是素以历史、政治等学科著称的名校。结果，奥伯林学院获胜。我们在另一

---

① 现将温德（Robert Winter or Bob Winter）教授的简历介绍如下：
1887 年：生于印地安纳（Indiana）州之克劳福特斯维尔（Crawfordsvielle）的一个德国移民家庭。显示了语言和文学天赋。
1913 年：在瓦巴什学院获得文学硕士学位，留校任教。
1914 年：往法国、意大利留学，并在中学主持外语教学，授法语、西班牙语。
1920 年：在芝加哥大学罗马语系（含法、意、西、葡、罗马尼亚、卡塔兰（Catalan）等语言）任助理教授，有机会与中国留学生闻一多、张景钺等相识。
1923 年：到南京，任教于东南大学，与吴宓、楼光来等中国学者相识。吴宓为他取"温德"这一中文名字。开始了解中国国情、民情和文化。
1925 年：经闻一多、张景钺二人之介绍，由清华学校校长曹云祥聘至清华外语系任教。
1928 年：任国立清华大学外语系教授，抗日战争爆发后亦兼任国立西南联合大学外语系教授。
1953 年：转任北京大学外语系教授。
1987 年：以百岁高龄逝世于北大校园。
他一生，除 1943 年 7 月到 1945 年 3 月返美 1 年零 8 个月之外，在中国整整度过了 62 个年头。
② 雷太太名张景茀。
③ 雷太太的哥哥是北京大学生物系教授张景钺，他太太是清华大学生物系教授崔芝兰。
④ 奥伯林学院（Oberlin College）：地址在俄亥俄州的罗兰（Lorain）郡，成立于 1833 年，由长老会创办，设文理学院和音乐学院，是美国历史上第一所男女合校并重视有色人种青年教育的高等学府，素以历史、政治等学科著称。中国孔祥熙、宋子文等人留学该校。1835 年到该校任教，1851——1866 年间担任校长的神学家芬尼（Charles Grandison Finney），改造、发展了基督教的加尔文主义，使之形成一新教派（New School Calvinism），在美国被称为"奥伯林神学"。该校近年在美国大学排名中，位于前 20 名。
⑤ 帕莫纳学院（Pamona College）：地址在加州克雷蒙特（Claremont）市，成立于 1887 年。校园环境优美，有"园中大学"（College in a Garden）之称。制度多模仿英国牛津、剑桥等大学，而与美国一般大学有所不同。该校 2008 年在美国大学文理学院排名中，高居第 8 位。

张聘定后的名单中，看见一条批语，也是温德写的，内容如下：

> 聪慧，勇敢，善于表达。编写历史教科书时不向执政党的沙文主义妥协。他和他的家庭在中国知识阶层生活中占重要地位。可能有点过分推崇斯本格勒（Osward Spengler）的学术。戈培尔推崇斯本格勒，但斯本格勒并没有借此攀附纳粹。

这是第二则史料。它的出处，周文说是在费正清 1944 年 2 月 22 日给基金会人文主管斯蒂文斯的信中。档案号和上条一样。

＊　　　　＊　　　　＊

雷先生由奥伯林学院聘定后，消息传到中国。1944 年底，消息从中国传回，雷先生的答复是：

> "他的国家和学校现在比美国更需要他"。因此，不能来美国。

基金会第 44343 号拨款文件中，有这样一段话：

> 在已拨出的 5 笔款项中，有给奥伯林学院的 8,000 美元。因该院邀请的中国学者不克来美，故将此款收回。

这件材料是雷先生"谢绝"赴美讲学的"旁证"。上两者合称第三则史料，档案号亦与上则同。

＊　　　　＊　　　　＊

这三则史料有助于我们加深对雷先生的认识：

第一、温德认为雷先生"可能有点过分推崇斯本格勒"。但是，笔锋一转，他马上把斯本格勒与纳粹的区别说个清楚明白。这样运笔，显然是为防雷先生因此而无端受到牵连。

第二、温德看出，雷先生在"编写历史教科书"问题上，"不向执政党的沙文主义妥协"。这几句话表明，在这位美国学者心目中，雷先生是个人格和思想独立的学者，是个道德主体，有判断是非的道德世界在心中。这样的分析有助于加深对雷先生的认识。

第三、雷先生在民族存亡的生死关头，不肯离开故土，毅然、决然地"谢绝"赴美讲学的邀请。这种爱国思想、牺牲精神，正是从他那蕴蓄已久的"道德世界"中绽放出来的光华。这种精神，前引资中筠教授的文章，已阐发得十分清楚，大家可以参阅，这里就不需多费笔墨了。

2012 年 6 月 6 日于北京清华园

（本文引用史料均摘自周启博先生《美国救济中国人文学科的往事》一文，谨此申明，并致谢忱。）

师恩重于山——雷海宗的最后十年

王敦书　南开大学（笔述）、王坚　天津师范大学（整理）

　　雷海宗诞生于1902年，今年6月18日，将迎来他的110周年诞辰。出生于牧师家庭的他，自幼即打下良好的旧学与新学功底。1922年，他从清华学堂毕业，公费留美，入芝加哥大学主修历史学，副修哲学。5年后，他获哲学博士学位并回国。其后，历聘于南京中央大学、金陵女子大学和武汉大学；1932年，他回母校清华服务，后长期担任清华历史学系主任（1935-1949，中间因抗战间断），并统领大家云集的西南联合大学（抗战时期，由北京大学、清华、南开合并而成）史学系（1938-1946）；1952年，他因院系调整离开清华，来到天津南开大学，在那里，他一直工作到1962年病逝。作为一个成名很早的大学者，雷海宗早年就享有盛誉；后来，虽然他因为被错划为"右派"等原因，影响和名气曾一度衰落，但是，今天，"其声如雷，其学似海，史学之宗"，这三句巧妙地将他的名字嵌入的评语，又一次得到众口传诵。

　　南开大学教授王敦书先生，是雷海宗先生的关门弟子。他1955年毕业于北京大学历史系，1957年考入南开大学，师从雷海宗，攻读世界上古中古史专业的副博士研究生（当时向苏联学来的一种学位制度，大致与硕士相当，但实行四年制，有博士候选人之意）。1961年王先生回系工作，又成为雷海宗的同事。从师从雷先生，受其亲炙，并先后被打成"右派"，到在其指点之下一起做翻译，做研究，再到为雷先生送终，最后又在雷先生身后为其整理文稿，编纪念文集，推动并亲自做雷先生生平与思想的研究，这位高足，已经成为雷海宗先生的世界里不可或缺的一部分。

　　讲述雷海宗到南开后的晚年岁月，相信没有比王先生更合适的人选。

父亲之交　师生之恩

　　我与雷师的关系，用几句话来概括，很不容易。考虑再三，是否可用："父亲之交，师生之恩。受教恨短，勉承师学。凄凉送终，情同父子。"

　　雷师1922年毕业于清华学堂，我的父亲1923年清华毕业，他们是差一年的同学，彼此认识，但不很熟。以后美国留学和返国工作，都不在一个城市，可能未再见面。1947和1948年清华迁回北平后接连两年举行盛大校庆，父亲都带我（当时我上初中二和初中三年级）从天津去北平参加清华校庆，见到了潘光旦、刘崇乐等长辈，但没遇见雷先生。1950年，我决定明年高中毕业后第一志愿报考清华历史系。父亲特告我，雷先生是著名的大史学家，嘱我考上清华后应好好向雷师请教学习。

　　1951年10月，我考入清华历史系，在系开学典礼大会上见到了雷先生。当时，人很多，没有时间做自我介绍。从父亲的关系说，按过去的礼节，我应称雷师为"雷年伯"。但这时，我只能随大流，称他雷先生，此后也一直如此。

　　解放后，雷师积极参加了各种政治运动。他解放前有过反苏反共的言行，作为战国策派的主要成员，曾遭到左派的批判，而且过去还是国民党员，在党内担任过一定职务，所以解放后，他曾受到管制（后撤销），并且不再担任清华历史系主任之职。1952年初思想改造运动时，他在全系范围内做了思想检查，对过去的反动言行、战国策派理论与斯宾格勒的历史哲学进行了自我批判，并接受大家的批评帮助。作为学生，我参加了大会，听到了雷师和其它教师的检查。我是新生，刚17岁，对这一切毫无所知，所以没有发言，听了检查和批判，只知道这些东西是洪水猛兽，反动透顶。据说，雷师的检查是检查得比较好的。我还有一个印象，1951年前后，雷师曾在北京的某一报纸上发表一篇谈自己思想改造的短文，说开始懂得了"为人民服务"的丰富内容与真正意义。第二学期，雷师给高年级同学讲授世界中古史，并不给一年级开课。我曾旁听过世界中古史课，很受教益，但没有坚持下去，以为以后还有的是机会上雷师的课。而且，我也没有去雷师家拜访他。所以，在清华一年级期间，我始终没有与雷师单独专门谈过话。1952年全国高校院系调整，当我知道北大、清华、燕京三校历史系合并和雷师将调往南开的消息后，确实为今后不能再听雷师的课感到遗憾，并后悔前一时期未能坚持听完雷师的课。

　　对于1952年调南开一事，雷师后来没有跟我谈过他的想法和心情，这里只能谈谈我个人的看法和感觉。当时三校三个历史系合并为一个北京大学历史系，人满为患，势必要调走一些人。问题是：调走谁和调往何处？我觉得，从业务水平来说，雷师学贯古今中外，自应留在北大历史系。但从政治状况来说，他调离北大是很自然乃至必然的。南开是全国著名的大学，抗战时期与清华、北大合组成西南联大；天津离北京很近，是全国第三大的直辖市，所以，能调往南开就算是不错的了。雷师有自知之明，对于离开清华、北大前往南开，我想他应有心理准备，并能够接受。

　　对于南开，雷师是有感情的，觉得自己与南开似乎有缘分。他知道自己将调南开的消息后，曾对清华的邻居张岱年教授说，二十五年前留学回国时，南开曾向他发过聘书，当时未能成行，而现在终于要去了，看来晚年将在南开度过。我觉得，雷师说的是一个事实。当时他的心情，与其说是自嘲，不如说是感慨，或者说是"四分感慨，三分无奈，三分自嘲"。

　　到南开后，校里领导对雷师是尊重和重用的，生活上也尽可能给以照顾。从居住条件来说，当时南开没有较优良富裕的教授住宅。听雷师母说起，雷师仅夫妇二人来南开，对居住条件要求不高，只希望厕所有能坐的抽水马桶，因雷师解大手的时间较长，甚至有时候坐在那里看书报。南开就把校门口新盖的二居室的平房拨给他们，有单独的厨房厕所和能坐的抽水马桶卫生设备，虽比清华时的条件差些，但也就可以了。

　　当时和雷师一起来南开的，还有郑天挺先生。南开历史系突然增加两个大师级的著名史学家，实力和声望大增。该系原来的教师队伍的力量并不算弱，但缺乏大师级的名教授，而且世界史方面稍差一些，尤其杨生茂先生有一段时期被借调到北京去编历史教科书，世界史人手就感不足。雷师来后，大大充实提高了南开世界史的力量。从1952至1957年，雷师在南开主要讲授世界古代史，他声音如雷，学问如海，口才好，讲课极有条理，深受学生欢迎，课讲得好是全国闻名的。由于杨生茂先生暂离南开，他讲授的世界近代史课就由新从燕京大学调来的林树惠先生任教。但林先生口才欠佳，原来也不是研究世界史的，因而不受学生欢迎，课讲不下去了，只好由作为世界史教研组主任的雷先生代教，林先生则随班听课。按一般情况说，林先生此时的心情肯定是不高兴的，甚至会发生误会，牵怒于雷师。然而，实际情况是，林先生不但没有埋怨雷先生，反而深深敬佩雷师的教学学问和道德为人。1957年我到南开后，一次与林先生聊天时，他特别谈到此事，并赞叹说："雷先生的课讲得太好了，他讲歌德的《浮士德》，讲得都玄了。"雷师母在怀念雷师的文章中说，批判雷先生时，有一位教师为雷师不平，称"雷海宗是我最好的老师"，这位教师就是林树惠先生。此外，雷师还开过物质文明史一课。他不但给学生正式讲课，而且还单独给青年教师讲专业英语和中国古代史。雷师不但世界史好，对中国史更有研究，在清华历史系二十年间一直讲中国通史和殷周史与秦汉史。据雷师母说，雷师在家中给青年教师讲中国上古史时，甚至老先生也来旁听。雷师非常关心南开在哲学社会科学领域的外文藏书情况，与南开大学图书馆馆长冯文潜教授及其它专家合作，努力进行这方面的图书资料建设，大有成效。南开大学图书馆的教师阅览室的社会科学方面的外文工具书当时是全国一流的。在此期间，雷师写了多篇文章，主要都在他任编委的《历史教学》杂志发表。总之，雷师来南开后，对南开历史系的发展做出了巨大的贡献。

人们说，郑天挺和雷海宗调到南开是南开历史系的幸事，这确实如此。

以上是我所知道的雷师到南开来之后的一些情况。这一时期我不在南开，与雷师也没有接触，对他的情况了解不多，而且多为间接听来的。

我自己与雷师的直接接触，始于1952年10月初。那一日我在天津火车站排队买火车票回清华，突然有人从后面拍我肩膀，回头一看没想到竟是雷先生。他说来南开办些手续，现返清华，于是我们同车赴京。在火车上两个多小时中，雷师先仔细了解我的学习情况和中外文基础知识，然后耐心细致而又高屋建瓴地给我讲应如何读书治学，并如数家珍地具体告我从世界古代史直到世界近现代史，乃至国别史应读哪些名家的代表作。这是我第一次单独聆听雷师的教诲，尤其是雷师主动对我耳提面命、言传身教。如果说父亲为我打下了学习世界近现代史和国际关系史的基础，雷师则在两三个小时内把我领进了整个世界史从古至今的殿堂，并画龙点睛地授我以打开这神圣殿堂大门的锁钥。真是听师一席谈，胜读十年书，师恩重于山。

之后三年，我在北大历史系学习，没有再见过雷师。

1955年夏，我大学毕业，由历史系领导统一分配工作。当时，南开历史系需要进人，我是有心去南开做雷师的研究生或助教的，但一切应服从组织分配，而且之前也不知有去南开的名额，所以只能心向往之。后来，几经周折，我被分配到武昌建筑工程学校任教。据说南开方面曾想过要我，但我已去武汉，来不及了。

1956年春，周恩来总理做了关于知识分子问题的报告，全国学术空气大为活跃、浓厚起来，雷师开始招收世界上古中古史专业副博士研究生。在雷师的关怀下，我回到天津报考。11月中旬考完后，我告别雷师回武昌。令我终生难忘的是，12月初，我意外地收到雷师寄来的亲笔长信，他首先告诉我以特优成绩被南开大学录取，随后语重心长，嘱我今后当在他的指导下刻苦读书，在哲学社会科学、古今中外历史和古文外语各方面打下深厚的基础，几年后方能登堂入室，以便更上一层楼。由此，我深刻地体会到雷师对我关怀之深、期望之切、要求之严和做学问之不易，并把自己的学习志趣定位到世界上古中古史领域。

1957年2月，我向南开大学历史系报到，正式成为雷师1957年唯一招收的也是最后的一个副博士研究生。

受教恨短　勉承师学（一）

入学后，雷师让我查录下图书馆内世界上古史方面的全部外文书目，然后逐一给我说明该书的主要内容和价值，指导我看最重要的书。并告诉我写文章最好深入浅出，即内容要深刻，但表达要浅显易懂。有时因问题太深奥不得不得深入深出，但要尽可能讲清楚，让人看明白。最要不得的是浅入深出，即言而无物，没有价值，却咬文嚼字，故弄玄虚。雷师让我继续随堂听他给本科一年级同学讲的世界上古史课程以及给世界史青年教师讲的专业英语，并没有另外单独给我讲课。

1957年春，全国开展帮助党内整风运动，号召大家大鸣大放，夏季时即转为反"右派"斗争运动。雷师始终没有跟我谈过他对此运动和自己的表现与受到批判的看法与心情。当时，我只是系里的一个刚入学不久的非党团员的研究生，对此时校、系领导与雷师之间的关系与谈话皆不清楚。我只能谈一下自己对此的认识和感受。

一开始，雷师是和全国绝大多数的高级知识分子一样，心情振奋、知无不言地参加助党整风的。4月间，他先后两次参加关于"百家争鸣"的座谈会，主要谈发展社会科学的问题。有一次他这样说：

> 对马克思和恩格斯树立的新的社会科学的看法，大家在理论上是一致的，承认马列主义应该发展，可是实际上是停止了发展，还停留在恩格斯死时1895年的地方。1895年以后，列宁、斯大林在个别问题上有新的提法，但他们主要谈当前革命问题。从了解整理几千年来人类历史经验，建立新的社会科学来说，基本上停留在1895年，教条主义者就是这样。马克思、恩格斯生平也是经常修改他们的学说，他们注意到当时每一个社会科学部门的发展情况，掌握社会科学研究的材料和成果。可是以后人们就以为他们已解决了一切问题，社会科学不能再发展了。事实上并不如此，1895年以后社会科学上新材料很多，对旧材料有很多新的认识。我们今天的任务，就是要把1895年到今天62年的课补上。

雷师这段话，后来被批判为污蔑"马克思主义停滞在1895年"。《人民日报》不久刊载了他的发言，并加编者按和编者注，中间有这样的话："雷先生认为列宁对于马克思主义只是'在个别问题上有新的提法'，马克思主义'基本上停留在1895年'，这却是违反了事实。"

我觉得，雷师看到《人民日报》对他发言的编者按和注后，应该有被敲响警钟之感，会隐约觉察到自己也有可能遭到批评或批判。但他认为当时仍在整风和鸣放，并没有"收"，而且将学术问题与政治问题分开，所以才根据"百花齐放、百家争鸣"的方针，一面去信向《人民日报》做解释与澄清，一面继续于6月在天津社会科学学会学术讲座上做《世界史分期与上古中古史中的一些问题》的报告，并在《历史教学》1957年第7期予以发表，认为奴隶社会并不是人类历史上原始社会后普遍、必经的一个社会形态与历史阶段。而"否定奴隶社会"和"马克思主义停滞在1895年"却成为他受到批判和划为"右派"的两个主要"罪状"。

5、6月间，北大学生谭天荣到南开"煽风点火"，曾分别访问过雷师等三名教授。随后，在南开大礼堂召开了由三教授谈与谭天荣谈话情况的大会。雷师在发言中指出，自己曾询及谭学习哲学及读黑格尔著作情况，奉劝他谈黑格尔思想时，应该多读一点黑氏的著作，并说中国是个大国，人口众多，贫困落后，要治理好必定会遇到许多困难，出现不少问题。他指着主席台两侧的标语牌说：我相信这两句话，那就是——领导我们事业的核心力量是中国共产党，指导我们思想的理论基础是马克思主义。话音一落，掌声满堂。

雷师在大礼堂的讲话，固然是真话和心里话，但已有所警惕，并在心里绷上了"被敲响警钟"这根弦。过了些日子，他在天津市九三学社（他是其市委委员之一）做了关于民主问题的长篇报告（后刊载于该学社的刊物），结合自己在美国留学时的感受和参加土改的亲身体会完全正面地批判美国的资产阶级民主，歌颂我国的社会主义民主。我想，这时他应该不仅有所警惕，而是已经预感到反右斗争风暴的气息了。

6月底，雷师给本科生讲的世界上古史课程结束。最末一堂课上，他最后说，宇宙无穷大，有无数的恒星，有的恒星有行星，可能有的行星的环境条件接近于地球，这种行星也可能出现像人类这样的高等生物，他们也可能组成为社会，这种社会也一定经过五种生产方式和奴隶社会吗？讲完后宣布下课，大阶梯教室近二百个听课者全体起立，热烈鼓掌不绝。上这门课的南开历史系1956年级学生共九十人，其中很多是调干转业生，是新中国成立前后即参军或参加工作至1956年转考大学者。他们有头脑，有思想，有工作经验，读书用功，出"右派"也多，大概十好几个。

1957年6月后，全国整风运动转入反"右派"斗争，南开大学反右斗争至7月底初步告一段落，放暑假。历史系教师和研究生中只划了两个"右派"，教师和研究生各一人，雷师和我当时都没有受到批判。我想，雷师之所以未受批判，可能是由于他的学术和政治地位都比较高，批判他要慎重一些；他的一些发言有学术性，与政治问题交织在一起，一时不易分清；而关于谭天荣的讲话和关于民主问题的报告却比较正确，站在党和人民的一边，所以一时没有动他。我以为，天津市和南开大学学校及历史系的党的领导方面肯定对批不批判雷海宗的问题是有所考虑和研究的。8月中下旬暑假尚未结束，忽接到系里召开全体教师批判雷海宗大会的通知。据说，是康生在北京召开的一次会上公开点的名。他问天津来参加会议的市委负责人，天津为什么不批判雷海宗？因此，天津市和南开大学立刻多次召开了揭发批判雷师的大大小小的不同会议，整理和发表这方面的材料与文章。我参加了历史系两次由雷师做检查和大家进行批判的大会，另外还有雷师不出席的背靠背的多次会议。作为雷师所欣赏的弟子，我感到压力很大。但由于师生之情和有某种共鸣，并觉得别人已把言都发了，没什么可加的，我始终一言不发，没有讲过揭发批判雷师的话和写这方面的材料与文章。这大概也是我后来被划为"右派"的原因之一。

受到批判后，雷师停止了教学工作，他的心情肯定是痛苦的，健康急剧恶化。此外，他过去最喜欢的学生丁则良教授在反右斗争时，服安眠药自沉于北大未名湖，后来听雷师母说，雷师听此噩耗后曾痛哭不已。由于他受到批判，而自己也处于很不利的地位，此后我没有再到他家去过，除了批判会与某些公开场合，也没有见过他和与他交谈。

1957年12月初的一个傍晚，我在南开大学中央的道路上散步，在苍茫的暮色中看到远方蹒跚地走来了一个扶杖的老人。走近一看，发现竟是雷师。看四周无人，我就走向前去难过地叫了一声雷先生。雷师见是我，就关心地问我最近的学习情况如何？听什么课？在看什么书？有什么问题？我简单汇报了自己的学习情况，说在听世界中古史的课，看这方面的外文参考书，顺便向他请教问题。雷师说，天气冷，在道旁寒风中不便久谈。明后天将把问题的答复写下来，插在系里各人的信件袋中。然后，我们匆匆告别。两天后，我果然在我的信件袋中发现了雷师的亲笔答复。雷师在受到批判、健康恶化、心情沉痛之际，还如此关心我的学习，并迅速写出答复亲手放在我的信袋里，真使我感激涕零，永志不忘。现在想来，仍痛感师恩深重，恩重如山。

1958年2月，南开进行反"右派"斗争补课和处理"右派"运动。我在历史系受到了批判，被补划为"右派"，接受的处分是：取消研究生资格，另行分配工作。雷师受到的是降职降薪处分，由二级教授降为五级，工资由280元降至170多元。3月下旬，我即随队参加下放劳动，未敢向雷师告别。1960年10月底，才在南开大学农场被摘掉"右派"分子的帽子。

总起来看，我真正正式作为雷师的副博士研究生或者说关门弟子，不过几个月，不到半年。所以，我用"受教恨短"四个字来形容。雷师是大学问家，"勉承师学"是说我想勉力继承雷师的衣钵，但只能勉强做到一点点。

受教恨短　勉承师学（二）

虽然名义上不再做雷师的副博士研究生，但我后来仍有不少机会，受教于雷师，可惜时间仍不长，不过一两年。

1961年3月底我从农场回南开历史系，系领导让我做资料员。我是"摘帽右派"，而雷师是尚未摘帽的全国史学界最大的"右派"，因此，我不敢去看他。在农村农场劳动期间，我与他没有接触，对他的情况一无所知。回系后，听说他身体不好，在家养病，不担任教学科研工作。在过去的三年中，南开历史系甚至天津市可能开过批判雷师的大会，至少在全国性刊物上发表了多篇批判他的文章，南开历史系也铅印辑录了雷师以前写的部分文章供批判之用。由于当时我不在系里，详情不知。

该年5月初，郑天挺先生从北京参加全国文科教材会议回来，对我说：外国史学方面决定编译《外国史学名著选》，南开历史系承担了两件选译的任务，经商量决定，将具体的工作交给你完成，有问题可以向雷先生请教。于是，怀着兴奋的心情，相隔近四年，我再登雷师之门。

先生和师母见到我很高兴，但明显地显得憔悴衰老了，雷师近几年来身患严重的慢性肾脏炎和贫血症，双腿浮肿，血色素甚低。我简单地汇报了自己三年多的情况，着重地说明选译外国史学名著的任务，雷师欣然接受对我的指导和校改译稿的工作。

首先，选译李维的《罗马史》。雷师指导我选译该书最著名和精彩的关于高卢人攻入罗马的段落，并约好每周星期一至星期五我翻译一段，星期六晨将英译本与我的汉译稿送往雷师家中，由他在周末校改。几周后，选译工作完毕。雷师抱病在身，但仍紧张而认真地对我全部的译稿、注释与李维简介做了精心指点和仔细修改，使我在六周的时间内在英语理解、汉译文字、工具书使用和罗马史研究等方面大大提高一步，终生受用不尽。

1961年4月，苏联发射载人宇宙飞船上天成功，加加林成为人类第一个宇航员。五、六月间，一次我到雷师家送《罗马史》译稿时，雷师正在如厕。等候中我无意地发现书桌上放着几页雷师亲笔写的英文长诗，拿起一看，原来是歌颂加加林上天的。未及细阅，雷师就出来了。我就放下诗稿，与先生谈有关选译之事。此后，我再没有见过这一诗稿，也没有与雷师谈过此事，因为"偷看"老师手写的东西，即使无意也是有些不礼貌和不好意思的。雷师英语极佳，写的英文长诗，当为文学精品。尤可注意者，雷师有浪漫的"天人合一"的思想，也曾写过关于人类进入"航空时代"的文章。在《人生的境界（一）——释大我》一文末，他展望：或进步不已的今日人类，或高于人类的新的灵物，终有一天能彻底明了宇宙，与宇宙化一，小我真正成了大我，大我就是小我。因此，当他知道加加林登上太空，人类开始由"航空时代"进入"航天时代"的消息后，受到极大鼓舞，心潮澎湃，情不自禁地用英文写此长诗，歌颂人类对宇宙的征服与前进。可惜，诗佚人亡，渺不可知。不然，由此诗中，我们可以进一步明了先生当时的内心情境和精神面貌。

至1961年底，全国又有一大批"右派"分子被摘掉"右派"帽子，雷师也在其中。既摘掉了"右派"帽子，就有资格讲课，而雷师又健康日差，系里就提出要"抢救遗产"，希望雷师早日开课。这样，先生就在1962年春重登讲台，给历史系高年级本科生开设外国史学名著选读一课，由曹中屏同志任助教。我随班听课，在需要时为雷师选的名著有关段落从英文译成中文，由先生修改后油印发给同学参考。

教室在主楼一楼西侧大阶梯教室，可容纳二百多人。雷师家在校门口，离主楼甚远，先生身体衰弱，双腿浮肿，步履艰难，就扶着拐杖来回坐三轮车前往教室，由曹中屏接送。此课是一学期课，每周一次连上两节课。先生虽抱病讲课，依然"声音如雷，学问如海"，精神抖擞，旁征博引，内容丰富。听课的人包括南开历史系高年级本科生，还有大批外系乃至校外的旁听者，整个阶梯教室坐得满满的，盛况仍与1956年时相同。上课时，大家用心听，认真记笔记，只是由于雷师是受到批判的人，就不再给他鼓掌了。

1962年9月，雷师为南开历史系高年级本科生讲外国史学史一课。不久，曹中屏同志赴朝鲜留学，系里让我接替他原来担任的协助雷师教课与陪伴他去医院看病的工作。雷师记忆力极好，几乎过目不忘，讲课备有大纲，从不写讲稿。但讲外国史学史课时，我在他家曾发现他亲笔写的此课的讲稿，可见他在一生最后时刻认真的献身精神与负责的教学态度。先生曾让我抽调检阅部分同学的听课笔记本，以了解他们听课的情况。到11月时，雷师病重，行走困难，此课中断，殊为可惜。

雷师平常每星期去看病，最后几次已上不去楼，是由我背他上二楼的。还有一次，曾陪他去一个老中医私人家中看病。由于经常陪他看病，最后几个月我们接触较多，等候看病时通过交谈聆听教诲，获益匪浅，也使我对先生有更多的认识和了解。谈话内容主要为学术问题，有时也涉及其它方面。

一次，偶然谈到国民党和蒋介石，先生说自己原来与蒋介石没有直接的接触，对其认识不深，抗日战争后期蒋介石曾见过雷师，直接谈过话，由此获得的对蒋的印象不佳，觉得他不够当国家领袖的资格与气魄。先生还说过，闻一多是自己的好友与老同学，对闻一多被暗杀感到非常悲痛，他保留着暗杀闻一多的子弹头，以表示对好友的怀念和对国民党杀人凶手的痛恨。

雷师知识面极广，几乎无所不知，还都有自己的看法。试举一例。一次聊天，我说，小时候觉得时间过得非常慢，等周末来到好出去玩，感到彷佛要等好久，而盼过年更觉得太漫长了。可长大后，就觉得日子过得快多了，而老年人感到时间过得更快，好像一转眼就过了一年，又老了一岁。这是否是个心理问题？雷师说：是这样，好像大家都有过如此的心理和感觉，不过也许背后还有更深一层的道理。时间是物质存在和运动过程的形式，是客观的，不以人的意志为转移的，彷佛是绝对的。但不同的物质或称物体的存在与运动过程的时间不同，时间可能有相对性。我们所称的时间与计时单位年月日，是分别指地球围绕太阳一周、月亮绕地球一周与地球自转一周的时间，这可以说是自然的时间，其快慢长短是固定不变的。而生物的时间可能有所不同，有所谓 biological time（生物学的时间）的说法。生命的生长与运动实质是新陈代谢的活动，新陈代谢过程的时间就是生物学的时间，是有快慢的。小时候生命在成长，生命力旺盛，新陈代谢活动得快，相对于固定不变的自然时间，就觉得日子过得慢和长。长大了，尤其是衰老了，新陈代谢活动就愈来愈慢，相对于不变的自然时间，就觉得日子过得愈来愈快和短了。这也许有点道理。我不禁深深佩服先生学问的广博。

凄凉送终　情同父子

1962 年 12 月初，雷师病情恶化，经诊断为由肾脏炎导致的尿毒症与并发的心力衰竭，于是住进总医院，这是天津市最好的医院。系里让我全天候陪伴，还派一些世界史方面的青年教师轮流照顾。系领导郑天挺主任和魏宏运党总支书记都来医院看过雷师。先生在天津家中只有雷师母一人，女儿女婿均在外地，他们在 12 月中旬都赶来天津伺候雷师。先生病况愈来愈重，最后三天，已昏迷不醒。

12 月 25 日亦即基督教圣诞节凌晨零点 30 分，先生的心脏停止了跳动。一代"史学之宗"，过早地与世长辞，年六十岁，身边只有雷师母、女儿、女婿和我四人。

两天后，系里让我告诉雷师母，总医院方面听说雷师是大学者，脑子特别好，希望能按惯例将先生的大脑留作标本，师母表示同意。所以，雷师的大脑当时是留在天津市总医院的。大约三天后，我一人代替系里和雷师母一家（他们因悲痛与需要相伴都留在家中）去总医院太平间，送先生遗体去天津市北仓火葬场火化。看遗体送入火化炉后，在场只有一个工作人员，我怀着崇敬而悲痛的心情向先生行了三鞠躬礼，然后让工作人员关炉门点火，送雷师在严寒的隆冬岁末驾鹤西行灵归道山。三天后，我一人前往北仓殡仪馆取回雷师的骨灰，骨灰盛放在雷师母特为此准备的一个景泰蓝的坛子中，师母等人由于伤心没有前去，并让我取回后暂存放在系里。系里开了追悼会，让我去校门口雷家接师母全家。师母给我系上已准备好的黑膀纱，到会场后发现别人没有戴黑纱，我就显得突出了。后来，文化大革命时有人为此事给我贴大字报，说我是屎克螂戴花圈。追悼会在南开大学主楼二楼历史系的一个教室中举行，系领导致了悼词，历史系教师约出席几十人，气氛是沉默和悲痛的。

因女儿在北大工作，雷师母准备迁往北京定居。一次，我去雷家，师母告诉我，有人跟她说，王敦书这么好地为雷师做一切的事，可惜你只有一个女儿而且早已结婚，那你就认他做干儿子吧。

我想，雷师母这样说，就是有这个意思，于是就答应了，称她为干妈，以后在信中都如此称呼，而且在雷师母及其家人面前提到雷师时也称他作干爹。这样，我就成为雷师自己不可能知道的去世后的义子，所以我用"凄凉送终，情同父子"来概括我与雷师最后的关系。

尾　声

雷师骨灰安葬于北京万安公墓。我曾两次去北京看望雷师母，并去雷师墓前行礼。文革期间，联系中断。

文化大革命爆发后不久，1966年8月，南开历史系有人写出《雷海宗阴魂不散》的大字报，说系里有人仍保留着雷师的著作和书。我看到后，吓得回家只好忍痛将雷师的著作和译文的手稿焚毁，但保留雷师赠我的书，只将有雷师印章与签名手迹的扉页撕去。

文化大革命结束后，1979年我和雷师的"右派"分子问题得到改正，与雷师母恢复联系。她过去曾来信说整理出雷师的遗稿。我问她，现在遗稿还有没有？她说，文化大革命爆发，全家吓得不得了，抄家时雷师的遗稿、日记乃至照片都焚毁了，荡然无存。

1982年，《中国历史学年鉴》约我写雷海宗简介并加以刊登，这大概是自1957年批判雷师以来第一篇比较正面地介绍他生平的文章，也可以说有些开始为他恢复名誉吧。之后十年中，我先后发表多篇介绍与纪念雷师的文章。《史学理论》1988年第4期刊载我的《雷海宗关于文化形态、社会形态和历史分期的看法》一文后，一位澳大利亚学者阅后在文章中说此文意味着中国开始为雷海宗恢复名誉。1992年，南开大学历史系举行了雷师诞辰九十周年纪念会；2002年12月，又召开了雷师诞辰一百周年的大型纪念会。进入21世纪以后，雷师的旧著也纷纷出版或再版。

为纪念雷师诞辰110周年，南开大学历史学院将于2012年6月16日召开大型纪念会。

我有过写一本雷海宗传的想法，别人早就多次劝我这样做，但我觉得自己对雷师尤其是早年与抗日战争时期的情况了解不足，掌握的材料不够多，不敢当此重任。雷师有写日记的习惯，这是写他的传记的极宝贵的史料与根据，可惜被销毁，荡然无存。我没有见过他的日记本，只看到过他病危时在病床上潦草地写的几行字：南开某某人来看我。

总起来说，雷师一生的浮沉与中国国家的命运紧密相连。新中国成立后，因为左的路线，雷师受到批判是自然和必然的。但南开历史系领导对雷师还是比较温和宽容的。系主任郑天挺先生是雷师的老友与同仁，对雷师关心照顾自不待言。历史系党的领导干部魏宏运先生，按历史系刘泽华教授的提法，执行"中左"路线，即不"极左"过分激烈。他对雷师执行党的统战政策和高级知识分子政策，虽不得不批判雷师，但对雷师的人格与学问是尊重和佩服的。他说雷师学问渊博，记忆力强，课讲得好，能用英语思维，1952年初思想改造运动时思想检查得比较好，并提出让雷师讲课以"抢救遗产"。文化大革命时，被批为雷师的保护伞与黑后台。在雷师的两次纪念会上都发了言，并写了纪念文章。

（本文正文部分基本上是根据王敦书先生笔述直接整理而成；整理成文后，又经王敦书先生审定。特此说明，并致谢。同时感谢天津人民出版社任洁、伍绍东为联系采访所提供的帮助。）

Lei Hai Zong–A view from outside

Fritz-Heiner Mutschler（穆启乐）　德国德累斯顿大学 / 北京大学

Ladies and Gentlemen,

Let me first of all say that I feel very honoured to be given the opportunity of speaking at this function in memory of Lei Hai Zong, the famous scholar and revered teacher of world history.

Obviously, there are aspects of Lei Hai Zong's work about which a Western Classicist like myself cannot say anything substantial. On the other hand, it is a characteristic of this work that it transcends national and cultural boundaries to such an extent that even a Western Classicist finds there many ideas worth pondering.

I will concentrate my short remarks on two subjects which seem to me both central to Lei Hai Zong's work and still relevant for scholarship nowadays, the first one being Lei Hai Zong's theory of historical cognition, the second one his view of the course of universal history.[1]

If one looks at Lei Hai Zong's theory of historical cognition two points are of particular importance. On the one hand his idea that the process of historical research comprises three main steps: (1) the ascertainment of the historical facts, (2) the interpretation of these facts, and (3) the presentation of the results of these procedures in literary form.[2] On the other hand there is his distinction between what he calls absolute and relative past, that is the past as it happened independently from us and the past as we reconstruct it in our scholarly endeavour.[3] Both points are worth pondering and in combination lend to Lei Hai Zong's theory an amazing actuality.

We can see this if we compare Lei Hai Zong's theory with that of the current leading German theoretician of history, Jörn Rüsen.[4] The degree of concurrence is striking. In Rüsen, too, we have the distinction between three components of historical research. First by sober and strictly scientific examination of all primary and

---

[1]　The basis of my brief appraisal is the collection of essays 雷海宗《伯伦史学集》中华书局 2002 with the illuminating introductory preface on Lei Hai Zong's life and work by the editor Wang Dunshu. For help with understanding the Chinese articles I thank my student Zhu Yingchao.

[2]　Cf. 《伯伦史学集》(s. footnote 1), p. 6f.

[3]　Cf. in particular 《历史过去释义》in 《伯伦史学集》(s. footnote 1), pp. 259–263.

[4]　For Rüsen's theory of historical research cf. the "trilogy": *Historische Vernunft. Grundzüge einer Historik I: Die Grundlagen der Geschichtswissenschaft*. Göttingen 1983; *Rekonstruktion der Vergangenheit. Grundzüge einer Historik II: Die Prinzipien der historischen Forschung*. Göttingen 1986; *Lebendige Geschichte. Grundzüge einer Historik III: Formen und Funktionen des historischen Wissens*. Göttingen 1989; and the collection of essays: *History. Narration – Interpretation – Orientation*, New York / Oxford 2005.

secondary sources one has to ascertain as many historical facts as possible. Second these facts have to be interpreted, that is they have to be connected with each other especially in terms of cause and effect, which is not possible without certain theoretical assumptions concerning e.g. the workings of human psyche, the relationship between economic, social, and political developments etc. Third the results of these procedures have to be presented in literary form, as R ü sen would say, in a narrative which will have to observe artistic and aesthetic rules.

The most important point of agreement between the two theoreticians, however, consists in the significance which both of them, in relation to the investigation of the past, attribute to the present. Just as for Lei for Rüsen, too, the whole process of historical research is embedded in the present of the historian and is shaped by this present's needs, concerns, hopes, beliefs, prejudices and emotions. It is these needs, concerns, hopes etc. which stimulate the historian's activity and to which he tries to respond by the presentation of the results of his work to his contemporaries.

The only point of divergence between the two theoreticians I can see lies in the fact that Lei Hai Zong, in view of this situation, feels forced to term historical research as subjective whereas Rüsen claims that even if historical research does not lead to objective knowledge in a radical sense of the word, it nevertheless provides results which are verifiable or falsifiable and therefore have the potential of being inter−subjectively valid.

How should we explain this astonishing extent of agreement between Rüsen and Lei Hai Zong? Two things are important. On the one hand, because of Lei Hai Zong's admirable familiarity with Western thought both authors build in part on the same, i.e. the Western, tradition of historical thinking. But I think that something else is more important. In my opinion the far−reaching agreement between Lei Hai Zong's and R ü sen's theories has its main reason in the simple fact that the analysis of the historian's activity the two theoreticians give is valid, i.e. that they describe correctly what was, is, and always will be happening when historians set out to scientifically investigate the past. To have developed this kind of valid analysis is to the credit of both of them, but it fills us with particular admiration that Lei Hai Zong did it already in the middle decades of the last century.

I come to my second topic, Lei Hai Zong's view of the course of universal history.[1] As is well known Lei Hai Zong was greatly influenced by Arnold Spengler's work on "The decline of the West". Lei shared Spengler's view of a number of great world cultures as decisive units of universal history and also the belief in a cyclical movement of these cultures in the course of which each of them was bound to pass through a fixed sequence of particular stages of its political, social, economic, military, religious and cultural development. But there was another idea, particularly close to Lei's heart, and that was the idea that in one respect Chinese culture was different from the others, because it alone had proven itself able to pass, after the completion of the first cycle, through a second one, and could even be considered to be about to enter a third one.

What are we to think of this view of the course of universal history? I start with two points which I consider problematic; the first one is general, the second one more specific. My more general reservation: I don't doubt that looking at the historical development of cultures we can discover parallels. But I think we can observe the absolute and through−going parallelism which Lei has in mind only by force, i.e. by adapting our observations to our preconceived ideas and by neglecting the richness and diversity of history. The second, more concrete

---

① Cf: in particular 《历史的形态与例证》 and "Historical Sketch" in 《伯伦史学集》 (s. footnote 1), pp. 243−258 and 493−567.

point: Being a Westerner, and in addition a classicist, for whom the connection between the Greco-Roman and the modern Western worlds is a given, it is peculiar to read that only Chinese culture knows the phenomenon of revitalization, of taking off for a second cycle. As soon as we take the Greco-Roman and the Western cultures not as two different cultures, but as one, it becomes clear that we can observe here the same ability to revitalize itself which Lei Hai Zong wants to reserve for Chinese culture alone.

But it would not be right to limit one's comments on Lei's view of the course of universal history to these critical remarks; for there are aspects of this view which are still of interest nowadays. The first one is the concentration on cultures as the decisive units of historical development. This approach implies an assumption which has gained ground in the course of the last decades and which has lead to what people call "the cultural turn" in historical studies.[1] The assumption purports that the different spheres of human life like politics, economy, religion, art etc. are so closely connected with each other that we have to take into account all of them in their interrelatedness if we want to come to a full understanding of what has happened. The integrated and holistic approach which follows as a consequence from this assumption was certainly something which Lei Hai Zong himself aspired to and for which he was qualified like few because of his interdisciplinary interests which pertained to philology, philosophy, archaeology, history of the arts just as well as to political and social history in the narrow sense of the word.

Another point. Lei Hai Zong's approach to universal history was not only culture-oriented but it is decidedly intercultural in the sense that it was decidedly directed towards the comparative study of the great cultures. In this way, however, Lei Hai Zong's approach is of immediate significance for today's scholarship. For in view of the fact that the different parts of the world have now really grown together and that the different cultures of the world are now in daily contact, intercultural comparison will become or rather is already becoming an important part of historical studies, and as it seems to me, offers one of the rare possibilities to break new ground and to do truly original work.

In this work, however, and this is my third point, Lei Hai Zong's ideas can be of help. For in doing intercultural comparison it is one of the most difficult things to decide what to compare, to find categories of description which bear fruit because they let us see similarities and differences which are important. Lei Hai Zong's work on the development of world cultures uses many and manifold categories and it is up to us to try them out and to make good use of them even if this use is different from that of Lei Hai Zong.

Thus, it seems that Lei Hai Zong's view of the course of universal history, even if it will meet nowadays more with scepticism than with acclamation, has nevertheless the potential to inspire and stimulate present and future research.

I would like to end, however, not with Lei Hai Zong's significance as a scholar but with a reflection concerning him and us as human beings.

As we heard before Lei Hai Zong was convinced that our perception of the past is shaped by the concerns of our present. This is certainly true for Lei Hai Zong himself. Especially the years of the Kangri were of uttermost importance for the development of his thinking and we are probably justified to say that his theory of a possible third cycle of Chinese culture was as much the expression of a heartfelt desire as it was a scientific hypothesis.

---

[1] A useful presentation of this "turn" is provided by V.E. Bonnell / L. Hunt (eds.), *Beyond the Cultural Turn*, Berkley 1999.

Against this background I think we are justified to ask ourselves how Lei Hai Zong would possibly reshape his vision of the course of universal history under the circumstances of our here and now. I could imagine the following—and I am not denying that I am bringing in now my own concerns and hopes. I think that Lei Hai Zong first of all would feel vindicated with respect to his theory of a third cycle of Chinese culture. I could also imagine that he would concede the possibility that not only Chinese but also Western culture started a second or—in my reckoning—a third cycle and that other cultures, too, have the chance of rejuvenating themselves. But above all I would like to assume that he would complement his idea of a cyclical development of the great cultures by that of a linear one, which is to say by the idea of a directional movement at the end of which the cultures of the world have started to merge into one common culture of humankind.

Now, it is difficult to say whether Lei Hai Zong would really be willing to modify his scientific ideas in the described way. But as far as I got to know him through his work and the testimony of others I am relatively sure that in this new und unparalleled situation in world history, which is ours, he would call upon us as human beings to work with full commitment towards a state of affairs where in this globalized world the different nations, peoples and cultures both peacefully compete and amicably cooperate with each other, being aware of a fundamental set of shared characteristics but also acknowledging remaining differences and accepting each other's particularities.

附：译文（叶民译）

女士们，先生们：

首先，感谢你们给我这个机会，在纪念著名学者和令人尊敬的世界史教授雷海宗先生的会议上发言。我感到非常荣幸。

毫无疑问，作为一个西方古典学者，我不可能对雷海宗的著作给予实质性的全面评价，但是，雷先生著作的一个特点是它已经完全超越了民族和文化的界限，以至于我这个西方古典学者也感到他的诸多思想值得探讨。

我的简短发言主要集中在两点，我觉得，这两点可能是雷海宗著作的中心，并且同当今的学术有所关联：一是雷海宗的历史认识论；二是他的世界历史进程观[1]。

在雷海宗的历史认识论中有两点最重要：一方面，他认为历史研究的进程包括三个主要步骤：（1）甄别史实；（2）解释史实；（3）以书面文字形式表达这些程序的结果[2]。另一方面，在他称之为"绝对的过去"和"相对的过去"之间有明显的区别，"绝对的过去"是指独立于我们之外而发生的过去，而"相对的过去"是指我们通过学术上的努力而重构的过去[3]。这两种观点都值得仔细思考，并且合起来使雷海宗的理论具有令人惊叹的现实性。

如果我们把雷海宗的理论同当今德国著名史学理论家约尔恩·于森[4]（Jörn Rüsen）的观点做个

① 拙作的资料基于中华书局 2002 年版《伯伦史学集》（雷海宗著），编者王敦书在前言中对雷海宗的生平和著作给以详尽的介绍。在中文论文的理解方面我得到了我的学生诸颖超的帮助，在此致谢。

② 参见《伯伦史学集》（页下注 1），第 6 页。

③ 参见《历史过去释义》，载于《伯伦史学集》（页下注 1），第 259—263 页。

④ 关于于森历史研究"三步骤"方法参见该作者著述：《历史的理性—史学原理 I：史学基础》，哥廷根 1983 年版；《重构过去—史学原理 II：历史研究的原则》，哥廷根 1986 年版；《生动的历史—史学基础 III：史学的体用》，哥廷根 1989；同时参见论文集《历史，叙述－解释－取向》，纽约／牛津，2005 年版。

对比，会发现两者竟然不谋而合，令人惊叹。于森认为，我们在历史研究过程中有三个不同的组成部分：第一，必须通过对全部第一和第二手史料的严肃认真的科学考察，确定尽可能多的历史事实。第二，必须解释这些事实，即它们之间应该相互联系，尤其是因果联系。要解释这种联系，必须运用某些理论假设，它们涉及，例如，人类心理的作用，经济、社会和政治发展之间的关系，等等。第三，以上程序所形成的结果，应当用书面文字的形式呈现出来，于森认为，应当在叙述中遵循艺术和美学的规则。

然而，这两位理论家之间最重要的契合点在于，他们在考察过去时都赋予现在以重要的意义。两者都认为，历史研究的整个过程是嵌入于历史研究者的当今时代中，是由当今时代的需求、关怀、希望、信仰、偏见和情绪等因素所形成的。正是这些需求、关怀、希望等等刺激历史学者的活动，而历史学者试图通过自己著作的成果向同时代人展示其对这些因素的回应。

我认为，两个学者的唯一分歧在于：雷海宗面对这种状况，感到不得不将历史研究视为主观的，而于森却主张，即使历史研究并不导致根本意义上的客观知识，然而它却提供了可被证实的或可被证伪的结果，因而这些结果具有成为跨主观而有效的可能性。

我们应如何解释存在于森和雷海宗之间的令人惊叹的相同之处？重要的有两点。一方面，由于雷海宗对西方思想令人称羡地了如指掌，因此两者理论都部分地建立在相同的西方传统历史思想基础上。但我认为另外一点更为重要，两者理论的广泛的一致性主要基于这样一个简单的事实，即这两个理论家对历史学者的活动所做的分析是妥当有效的，也就是说，他们正确地描述了历史学家开始科学地探究过去时以前、现在、直到未来所做的一切活动。信赖于他们二人之赐，这种妥善的分析得以发扬光大。但让我们尤其感到敬佩的是，雷海宗早在上世纪中期就已经取得这种成就。

现在谈谈我的第二个主题：雷海宗的世界历史进程观[①]。众所周知，雷海宗深受斯宾格勒《西方的没落》一书的影响，他赞同斯宾格勒的思想，认为一些伟大的世界文化是世界历史的决定性单位，并相信这些文化进行周期性的运动，每种文化在此运动过程中必然固定地经过一系列在其政治、社会、经济、军事、宗教和文化发展上的独特阶段。但在雷海宗的内心深处还特别有另外一种思想，即中国文化不同于其它文化，因为只有它证明自己能在完成第一个周期之后，经过第二个周期，并且甚至考虑可能进入第三个周期。

我们应如何看待这种世界史进程观？我先提出两个商榷性意见，一个是总体性的，另一个是更专门的。我的比较总体性的保留意见是：在考察这些文化的历史发展中，毫无疑问，我们可以找到平行和相似性。但我想我们只能够"勉强"观察到雷海宗思想中的这种绝对和彻底的平行相似性，所谓"勉强"就是把我们的考察去适应我们预设的观念，并且忽视历史的丰富多样性。第二个是我比较具体的保留意见。作为一个西方人，尤其是一个古典学者，对我来说，古代希腊罗马和现代的西方世界之间的相互联系是既定的，当我阅读到只有中国文化具有复兴的现象，并向第二个周期起飞时，我不能不感到奇怪。只要我们不把希腊罗马文化和西方文化看作是两个不同的、而是同一个文化时，我们显然可以从它身上看到同样的复兴能力，而这种能力雷海宗只希望保留在中国文化身上。

然而，如果把对雷海宗的世界历史进程观的评价局限于这些批评性的意见，那是不对的。因为这种观点至今仍然在很多方面具有影响力。第一是它集中于将诸文化作为历史进程的决定性单位。这种方法包含一个设想，它在最近几十年中普及开来，导致历史研究中的所谓"文化转变"[②]。这种设想认为人类生活的不同领域如政治、经济、宗教、艺术等等彼此非常紧密相联，因此，如果我们

---

① 参见《历史的形态与例证》和《中国历史概略（英文论文 Historical Sketch）》，载于《伯伦史学集》（参见页下注 1）第 243-258 页和第 493-567 页。

② 关于"转变"问题的有益的解释参见邦纳尔和亨特（V.E. Bonnell / L. Hunt）所著《超越"文化转变"》伯克莱 1999 年版。

想要充分理解过去所发生的一切，就必须在它们相互关联中考察所有方面。这种综合的、整体的方法就是随着这种假设而形成的，并且肯定是雷海宗本人所致力的；也只有少数象雷海宗这样的学者才有资格驾驭这种方法，因为他具有跨学科的兴趣，涉及语言学、哲学、考古学、广义的人文科学历史和狭义的政治社会史各个方面。

第二点，雷海宗对于世界历史的研究方法不仅是文化取向性的，而且断然是跨文化性的，因为它明确地指向对诸重要文化的比较研究。然而，在这方面它对于当今的学界会有直接的意义。因为事实上当今世界的不同地域真正形成一体，而且当今世界的不同文化联系频繁，跨文化比较将成为或者已经形成历史研究的一个重要部分，在我看来，这种比较方法为开垦新的学术领域、为从事真正的原创性的研究工作提供了宝贵的可能性。

第三点，我认为，在这种研究工作中，雷海宗的思想是有益的。因为从事跨文化比较研究的一个最困难之处是决定比较的内容、寻找有效的描述类型，然后我们才会看到关键的相似性和区别。雷海宗的关于世界文化进程的论著中使用了多种多样的类型，我们可以进一步提炼并充分利用它们，即使我们的运用方法同雷海宗的方法有所不同。

因此，尽管雷海宗关于世界历史进程的观点似乎在今天受到的怀疑多于赞赏，然而它仍然有可能对当前和将来的研究有启发和激励作用。

但是，在我发言的结尾，我并不想把雷海宗作为一个重要的学者来评价，我宁愿把他看作同我们一样的人类的一员来反思。

如前所述，雷海宗深信，我们对于过去的理解是由我们现在的关怀所决定的。这一点真实地体现在雷海宗身上。抗日战争的年代对他的思想发展产生重要的影响，大概我们可以这样认为：他的关于中国文化可有第三周期的理论，既是一种科学的假设，也是是一种心愿的表现。

在此背景下，我觉得我们可以自问，如果雷海宗身处我们此地此刻的现实，他会如何重新改造自己的世界历史进程观呢？我会做如下想象，并不否认其中带有我自己的关怀与希望。我想雷海宗首先会感到他的中国文化第三周期的理论被证明是正确的。我还会想象，他会对这样一种可能性做出让步：不仅中国文化，而且西方文化开始了第二——或者我认为——第三周期，而且其它文化也有机会重新焕发生机。但最重要的是，我愿以为，他会用一种线形理论来完善自己关于伟大文化的周期发展的理论，这种线形理论就是通过一种方向性运动，最终世界诸文化开始融合成一种人类的共同文化。

现在，雷海宗是否真正愿意用上述方式修正他的观点，我们不得而知，但就我通过他的著作以及他人的陈述而对他的了解，我相对地确信，如果他处于我们当今世界历史中崭新的、前所未有的时代，他会号召作为人类的我们怀着充分的承诺，为实现这样的国际事务状态而努力，在此状态中，全球化世界上的不同国家、民族和文化彼此和平竞争、友好合作，既认识到大家在根本形态上共同的特征，同时也承认互相存在的差异，接受彼此的特殊个性。

我的发言到此结束，谢谢大家！

雷海宗的史学：中国与世界

Leif Littrup（李来福）丹麦哥本哈根大学

1927 年，二十五岁的雷海宗（Barnabas Hai-Tsung Lei）在美国芝加哥大学获得历史学博士学位。他的博士导师是著名的美国历史学家詹姆斯·汤普逊（James Westfall Thompson, 1869–1941），研究欧洲中古和近代早期的专家。雷海宗的博士论文名为《杜尔阁的政治思想》（*The Political Ideas of Turgot*）。杜尔阁是十八世纪法国启蒙时代的一位自由经济学家和政治家。雷氏的论文共有 136 页，芝加哥大学图书馆还保存着这篇论文。他的书目是令人印象深刻的，大部分是法文论著。

回国后，他在南京中央大学和金陵女子大学教授历史，以后在武汉大学任教一至两年。1932 年，蒋廷黻邀请他回清华大学教授历史，很快就任系主任之职。抗日战争时期，他在昆明的西南联大任教。从 1952 年起，他赴南开大学教授世界史。然而，1957 年被错划为史学界五大"右派"分子之一后，他的健康状况很快就恶化了，教学也停止了。

他回国后撰写的第一篇学术论文是 1928 年发表的"评汉译韦尔斯的《世界史纲》"。他认为韦尔斯（Wells）写这本书所用资料大部分来自欧洲，基本上持西方人的史观，虽然也利用其他民族的资料，但只是利用这些资料来支持自己的历史观，而不是采用历史学者的史料批判做法。雷海宗还就韦尔斯的书究竟是小说还是世界通史展开讨论。他批评《史纲》是韦尔斯"鼓吹世界大同的一本小说杰作"，而作为世界通史是没有价值的，用这本书向中国人介绍世界史是比较容易误导他们的。我们如今注意到，韦尔斯的书对中国世界历史学科的发展还是发挥了作用的。譬如吴于廑先生，武汉大学著名的世界史学家，在 19 世纪 80 年代还记得，韦尔斯的书是他年轻时阅读的第一部通史（universal history）著作，影响他把世界史作为其毕生的工作。

雷海宗到南开前，既教授中国史，也教授世界史，还编撰了一些教科书与史料集，两者兼而有之。中国历史学家在国外无论学中国史还是外国史，回国后有不少人专攻中国史。这常常同获取资料的问题有关，外语问题也不可忽视。雷海宗使用外文资料很多，在外语方面游刃有余。他自己重视中国史，尤其是中国上古史的原因，可能同当时的形势有关。那个时代的中国人、中国的领袖、中国的知识分子都想在世界上赋予中国一个应有的位置。作为一位爱国的历史学家，雷海宗自然重视中国史及其在人类历史上的地位。他研究中国史时既关注中国的情况，也介绍外国史，尤其是欧洲史，以及地中海的历史。譬如，他在《中国的兵》中也介绍古希腊雅典的历史学家和军事家色诺芬（Xenophon）。

1935 年，他写了英文的《中国历史概略》，发布在英文的《中国年鉴》（*The Chinese Yearbook 1936–1937*）上，从古代一直讲到当代的中国历史。该文显然受到德国史家施本格勒（O. Spengler）提出的"文化形态史观"的影响，认为不同的文化在不同的时间和地域有独自产生和自由发展的历史。

每个文化虽然有其特点，但经过固定的生命周期必然趋于毁灭。每个文化都要经历从开始到最后毁灭的一个周期。按雷海宗的看法，中国历史是世界上唯一经历了两个周期的文化（以后可能还有第三周）：第一周从中国历史开端至公元383年的淝水之战，是古代文化的时代。中国文化是比较独立的，跟其它地区交流较少。第二周是胡人的佛教文化。在这个时期，中国受周边民族和国家的影响比较强烈，有些民族甚至侵入中国，成为中国的皇帝。七十多年后读这篇文章，有的地方我觉得不易苟同。雷海宗把中国历史当然看作人类历史的一部分，但其独立性可能过多了。如果只看亚欧大陆的东部和西部，这是有道理的，两个地方相互隔离，因而都是比较独立的。然而，周边民族和国家却离中国很近，应该同他们相互交往，而不只是外域民族的来华和汉化。他对中国历史的这种看法对我们的世界史学科是有影响的。可以说，他一方面强调中国根本上是独立的，好像被置于一般的世界史之外，另一方面也强调，要学中国史，必须注重它与外国史的相似之处。

雷先生到达南开大学后，他的工作集中于世界历史的教学和写作上。如果他的职业生涯没有这么短，他对中国世界史学科的发展一定会有重要影响，也会对外国的世界历史学的发展构成影响。世界史学科就是在他那个时代开始步入一个新阶段。联合国教科文组织就是在50年代开始出版其期刊《世界史》，也想发表一部真正的世界史著作，可惜雷海宗没有参加这项工作。

他在文化多元论方面做出了贡献。譬如，他既认为古代中国文化是比较独立发展的，也认为，甚至在生产力不发达的上古各地区，其文化发展在很大程度上依然是脉络相通的。作为人类和文化之间交流的媒体，游牧人可能是最重要的，其他旅行者应该也发挥了作用。

他清楚地指出，学习世界历史应以中国在世界上的地位为出发点："中国是世界上最早的文明古国之一，在古代世界历史上，中国占有重要地位。因此我们在学习世界史的过程中要注意两个问题：第一要注意中国与世界其他地区的联系和彼此间的互相影响；第二要注意中国对世界人类文明发展的贡献。同时，我们中国人学习世界历史，则必须要从中国的角度来看世界，这样就能够在很大程度上纠正过去把'世界史'看成是'西洋史'的错误看法。"我完全同意这种看法。我们研究世界史，最有收获的常常是从自己的位置出发，可以说是以自己为世界的中心。然而，雷海宗的建议可能有缺陷。他自己是学历史的，他所学的大部分是中国历史和欧洲－地中海的历史。这样，他不是从中国出发，慢慢地学习周边国家的历史，了解他们的历史文化，跟中国历史有什么关系，跟他们周边的民族与国家有什么关系，以后扩展至亚欧大陆的西部，这个他好像没有强调。

1949年后，他也显示出，他并不排斥新的研究思路和工作环境。他开始学习马克思主义，用其来解释历史。作为严肃的学者，他希望为人类，特别是中国的进步建立一个新的理论基础，但不应过于教条。不幸的是，正是这种态度使他陷入严重的麻烦。我们对此都感到遗憾，这是中国史学史和国际史学史不应忽视的一个问题。

雷海宗先生无疑是20世纪的一位伟大历史学家，不仅在中国伟大，在国际上也很了不起。他既研读中国历史，也研读外国史，那时是很少有人研读外国史的。他学识渊博，兼通中外史学和其他学科的知识。将他的几篇有代表性的文章尽快译成英文是非常好的，有助于丰富外国人对世界历史的了解，帮助我们解决世界历史上的一些问题，也有助于了解中国历史学家在其生活的关键时期的工作环境，当然也有助于我们了解雷海宗先生本人。

独立思考精神、批判思维与学术创新

刘北成 清华大学历史系主任

尊敬的主席先生、各位师长、各位同仁、各位同学：

因职务之故，我非常有幸代表清华大学历史系出席南开大学历史学院主办的"雷海宗先生诞辰110周年纪念会"。在此，我非常感谢南开大学历史学院，特别是王敦书先生的盛情邀请。

雷海宗先生与清华大学有着深厚的渊源。他在 1919 — 1922 年就读清华学堂高等科。1932 — 1952 年在清华大学（包括西南联大）任教 20 年，曾任历史系主任和文学院代理院长。总算下来，雷先生有 23 年在清华大学学习和工作。雷先生后来在南开工作十年，再加上西南联大的 8 年，雷先生与南开也有 18 年的渊源。雷先生在 60 岁辞世，他的大部分岁月、最富有创造力的岁月是在清华和南开度过的，而清华和南开，尤其这两个学校的历史学科也以有雷先生这样的杰出学者、杰出教授倍感骄傲。

当然，雷海宗先生不仅属于清华大学和南开大学，他更是中国现代学术史上一位彪炳史册的学者。提到雷先生的名字，我们会立即想到与雷先生相关的两件事，一是他的学术贡献，二是他的政治遭遇。

说到学术贡献，无论在学术研究方面，还是在现代历史学科的建设方面，雷先生都是重要的开拓者。此外，雷先生独立儒雅的人格体现了中国士林的优秀品格，也给我们留下一份精神财富。

雷先生的政治遭遇也给我们留下宝贵的启示，在今天尤为重要。雷先生在1957年发表一个讲话，其内容被归纳为"马克思主义的社会科学自1895年恩格斯死后发展停滞"。任何观点都是可以争议的，这个讲话的具体表述也可以争议。但是，总的来看，其实质是提倡学术创新，体现了雷先生的独立思考精神和批判思维。这段讲话因遭到严酷的政治打压反而凸显其弥足珍贵的价值。雷先生本人因此而遭受政治迫害，从反面证明了学术自由以及公民自由乃是学术创新的基本条件。

改革开放 30 多年来，情况已经发生很大变化。现在，创新已经成为学界和社会的时髦词汇，但是创新的意涵仍值得探讨，创新的条件仍有待改善。

什么是创新？创新应该以独立思考和批判为前提，不墨守成规，不唯上，不唯书，只唯实。只看是否遵循科学方法，是否符合实际。

什么是创新的条件？当下，以规定课题、工程为导向的科研支持体制和评价体制是否有利于人文社会科学创新？如何保障学术自由，促进思想解放？我们需要反思。

今天，我们纪念雷海宗先生，不仅要缅怀先哲的道德文章，而且也要思考如何改进我们的现状，做出不负先哲期望、无愧时代的努力。谢谢大家！

文科创新型人才的培养与学术研究的环境

刘新成　首都师范大学校长

非常高兴有机会参加南开大学举办的纪念雷海宗先生诞辰110周年的纪念活动。事实上10年前纪念雷先生百年诞辰的时候，我就曾陪同齐世荣先生来过这个会场。当时聆听了许多老先生的发言，受益匪浅，所以这次接到王敦书先生的邀请电话，我非常高兴。但王先生要求我发言，这给我很大压力，因为与上次纪念活动的发言者相比，我实在是没有发言的资格。余生也晚，未能登堂入室，亲承謦欬，甚至未曾有幸得瞻先生风采，只是读过先生的著作，勉强可算私淑弟子吧，所以真不知该说些什么。但是既然王先生布置了任务，我也只好勉力为之。我做了一点功课，即重读了《雷海宗先生百年诞辰纪念文集》和《伯伦史学集》、《贻书堂史集》中的部分文章。我看书的时候，由于这些年从事学校管理工作，便产生了一些与史学相关，但又不属史学研究范畴的体会，今天就从这些体会中拣出两点来向大家汇报。

首先谈谈关于史学或曰文科人才培养的体会。现在我们常说要培养创新型人才，但什么样的人才算创新型人才？具备什么素质才能创新？在这方面，雷先生提供了一个"个案"：作为历史学一代宗师，雷先生显然属于创新型人才，因此总结雷先生的学养特点，大概有助于我们弄明白史学乃至文科创新型人才所应具备的基本素质。那么雷先生的学养特点是什么呢？几乎所有回忆雷先生的文章都谈到了先生的两大突出特点：学贯中西和跨学科素养。所谓学贯中西，并非以中学或西学为主，而对另一种兼有涉及，而是将中学西学全都真正吃透和领会，并且融会贯通。所谓跨学科素养，是说除史学外，雷先生于人类学、社会学、政治学、语言学等等都有相当程度的造诣。目前我们培养的本科生或研究生当然做不到中西贯通和具备多学科素养，因为现在高校的文科人才培养方案就没有将这两点作为培养的目标和取向。这是我们作为高校教师和管理者应该惕悟的。

造成高校文科培养方案这种缺陷的原因，一是对专业的理解比较肤浅，将专业知识范围限定在一级学科甚至二级学科之内，认为此外的知识都是非专业性的，不必硬性要求。然而从当今学术发展的跨学科趋势来看，不管学什么学科，都至少应该把各科基础知识纳入学习范围之内，这种兼收并蓄的知识学习并不等同于目前高校实行的通识教育。我们需要重新对文科的跨学科教育制定专门标准，认真落实，否则我们的文科毕业生真是很难进行知识创新。在传统的历史学科一分为三，成为三个一级学科的今天，我们这些历史学科的教师尤其应该注意这一点。

二是学业负担太轻，学术训练不足。要在限定的学制内打好国学和西学基础，并掌握多学科知识殊非易事，按道理说，学业负担应该是相当沉重的。然而目前我国高校文科生的学业负担却远远不够。我曾在一次采访中就中美两国文科大学生的课业量进行对比，指出我国文科生的课业量（主要是作业量）普遍偏少，我认为这是影响文科人才培养质量的重要原因之一。我的这个看法得到周围教师、学生，特别是学生的广泛认同，这说明学生并不缺少学习热情，问题可能出在教育者身上。

文科培养方案上述缺陷的直接后果是学生读书少，阅读量小，读写训练不足。回顾雷先生的教书生涯，他对学生的阅读质量和数量是相当重视的。他上"史学方法"课，列出一张外文理论名著大单，让学生任选一本精读（这对本科生来讲，不是件容易事！），他作指导，学生互相交流。20世纪30-40年代雷先生在清华讲中国通史，其讲义就是史料汇编，共计7册，1860页。从某种意义上讲，文科学习——特别是人文学科的学习——就等于阅读，只要会读书（包括会选书），多读书，读懂书，知识和方法的掌握就尽在其中了。而在这当中，达到一定阅读量是最基本的，可当前我们的文科学生恰恰是读书数量严重不足。

是不是改进专业培养方案就一定能出人才？也不一定，还有一个学者个人的学术抱负或曰"风骨"问题。王敦书先生曾经说过，雷先生在美国以并非中国人擅长的"杜尔阁的政治思想"为题做博士论文，而回国后不以国人生疏的外国史博取学术声望，却大讲中国史，这说明雷先生始终以做一流学问为取向，而毫无投机取巧之心，这与时下以找个好工作、获批好项目、或是提职报奖为取向的"学术"追求，真有云泥之别。所以培养创新型人才还是要讲人格塑造的。资中筠先生在回忆雷先生的文章中提到了学识与风骨，说明两者之间是有联系的。完美的专业培养方案最多只能解决学识问题，而真正成才还要有风骨，二者缺一不可。在这里，风骨大致可以视为一种自我期许，一种学术抱负和人格追求。当然资先生在"学识和风骨"之后还谈到了"遭遇"。雷先生的悲惨遭遇其实与其学识与风骨相关联，倘若雷先生不具备如此的学识与风骨，倒是很可能在那场荒谬的政治运动中平安无事。因此如何创造一种环境，使那些真正具有学识与风骨的人能够为国家富强民族振兴发挥全部能力，至少不让他们的能力受到抑制，精神受到痛苦，身心受到迫害，这是值得各级管理者认真思考的。

其次谈谈有关史学研究的一点体会。重读雷先生的著作，我意外发现，当今国内乃至国际的所谓"学术前沿"，其实雷先生在半个多世纪以前就几乎已经触及了。比如环境史，堪称当今史学热点，而雷先生早在上世纪50年代就指出要重视气候变化对人类历史的影响（南开大学历史学院编：《雷海宗与二十世纪中国史学》，中华书局2005年版，第94-95页）。如今颇受关注的"全球史观"以其"整体"视野见长，而雷先生早年在介绍文化形态学的时候就意识到"迄今没有全人类的历史，只有各个文化的历史"。他在《上古中晚期亚欧大草原的游牧世界与土著世界》一文中曾说：即使在生产力不发达的上古时期，"世界（各地）的发展在很高的程度上仍然是脉络相通的"（《伯伦史学集》，中华书局2002年版，第342页）。他在论述"上古时的中国"时提醒研究者，要注意中国与世界其他地区的联系和彼此间的相互影响（南开大学历史学院编：《雷海宗与二十世纪中国史学》，中华书局2005年版，第180页），这些意见与当代全球史学者倡扬的"文化互动研究"颇为相通。据王永兴先生回忆，当年雷先生指点他，教授中国古代史的人要好好研究欧洲中世纪史，以便在对比当中深入解读中国古代史。这说明雷先生已经注意运用比较史学的方法。正如刘家和先生所说，雷先生的中国史文章（如《断代问题与中国史的分期》等）均以世界为背景，具有中外比较的性质（同上书，第131页）。在对待西学问题上，雷先生坚决反对简单化倾向，他批评将西方文艺复兴时代提出的古代、中世纪、近现代三段式分期法套用于我国，并针对"欲追求现代化必彻底抛弃传统"的说法，指出西文中现代（Modern）一词出现时，其含义非但不是"非古"，而且恰恰是"复古"。（同上书，第72页）在这里雷先生已经触及了不同语境中的"话语"解读问题。今天，当我们的人文社会科学研究很大程度上仍然不得不沿用西方的概念、范式、理论、规则的时候，我们事实上仍然面临同样的问题。早在1954年，雷先生就从时序对比的角度对西方史学界将奥斯曼帝国兴起、堵塞东西陆路交通视为葡萄牙海外探险动因的观点提出过质疑，并以此为例说明"西方中心主义"如何妨碍了学术研究的客观性。雷先生的这一看法和研究方法，在今天仍有借鉴意义（同上书，第74页）。凡此种种，均说明雷先生确有"先见之明"，尽管他的观点、看法未必成熟和准确，但如果循此路径深入下去，或许我们的世界史教学和研究水平早就能够达到更高的水平，在某些领域甚或可以引领国际学术也未可知。但正如马克尧先生所言，雷先生的许多真知灼见并没有得到进一步发挥（同上书，第141页）。这是非常遗憾的。究其原因，当然与当时的政治环境有关，但能说与学术环境毫无关系吗？可悲的是，当前的政治环境已经比雷先生当年好了许多，但学术环境仍有不利于学术进步之处。没有严格和自觉的学术规范，没有平和公允的学术批评，没有自由宽松的研究条件，对于学术的敬畏之情和探究兴趣不足，而急功近利之心迫切。这些大家已经说得很多了，而且发现问题牵涉广泛，盘根错节，恐非短时能有改变，这里不说也罢。

以上就是我重读雷先生著作的两点体会。总之我以为，只有好好治学才是对雷先生的最好纪念。

继承和发扬雷先生的精神和学术遗产

庞卓恒　天津师范大学

各位老前辈和中青年朋友们，我今天有机会在这里讲几句我对雷海宗先生的精神遗产和学术遗产的一点体会。我要感谢王敦书先生和南开大学举办这样一个会议，给我这样一个机会。我就简单讲这两个问题：雷先生留下的精神遗产主要是什么遗产。我觉得主要是两个精神：一个是爱国精神，一个是科学精神。

爱国精神，我觉得突出地体现在他的《中国的兵》、《中国文化和中国的兵》、《无兵的文化》这些文章。我们看出来，这是一个什么精神呢，跟鲁迅的那个精神是一致的，哀其不幸，怒其不争，是本着这么一种精神写出来的。刚才，我看到刘桂生教授公布了一段当年洛克菲勒基金会已经批准邀请他作为 A 类学者到美国讲学一年，那后面一段是，他的回答是，我的国家和我的学校现在更需要我留在中国。这样我就更加感到他的爱国精神。这样的遗产是我们应当继承的。

科学精神是什么精神，我就特别突出地感到他对马克思主义的一种科学的态度，对待马克思主义的这样一个坚持，这样一种科学精神。最突出的一点，我过去也讲过一些，那就是否认奴隶制是一个独立的社会形态。他实际上认为古希腊罗马的那种社会形态实际上是封建制的一种变态，变种。这个精神很了不起啊！雷海宗先生是解放后才学习马克思主义的，他一学进去，那真是以一种很严谨的深厚的科学精神来对待它。当时，可以说吧，就我所了解的马克思主义的学术史，恐怕他是第一个提出来的。古希腊罗马不能够用一个奴隶制的社会形态来概括它，它就是一个封建制的变种。这个观点真是石破惊天。到现在，我还想不到，我读过一些西方的马克思主义学者的一些书，我没有看到他们提出过这样的看法。在中国学者中，他是提出这种看法的第一人。第二个人就是我的老师胡钟达先生。我到现在还不大知道，胡钟达先生是不是跟雷海宗先生交换过这方面的看法（王敦书插话：没有）。但他们两位可以说是从不同的学术研究角度认识了同一个问题，提出了同样的论断。而这个论断是个什么论断呢？恰恰就是我后来读到的马克思的三大形态，三大阶段的学说，是和马克思吻合的。马克思确实就是把奴隶制、封建制、行会制和家长制统统看作是同一个人类社会的第一大阶段。但是马克思的这个学说，这个思想，雷海宗先生在那个时候一定是不知道的，没有读到过的，因为这是马克思在 1857–1858 年的经济学手稿里头写出来的，论述了这三大形态，三大阶段。而这是马克思《资本论》的第一个手稿，这个手稿一直到上个世纪 40 年代才由苏联出版了它的德文版。而且德文版是印数很少的，我记不清印了多少册，印数很少的。后来所谓的五大形态，五种生产方式，我的老师胡钟达先生考证过，那是列宁最先模糊地提出来的。后来斯大林把它规范化地提出来了。他们两位都没有读到过马克思三大形态三大阶段的论述。40 年代苏联才出版了德文版，那时列宁已经去世了，斯大林那时是非常忙的，他也不懂德文，他们都没有读到过。但是五种生产方式，五大形态就从那时以后成为法定的论断，具有法定的权威性。可是我们不知道，马克思一百多年前就说过，是三大形态三大阶段，雷海宗先生当时也肯定不会知道，但是他居然从他自己的马克思主义理论的学习当中得出了马克思早就说过的，我们后来大家都不知道的那么一个结论。这实在是很了不起的。所以我非常佩服。雷海宗先生学马克思主义绝对不是就是为了一种政治上的需要，就是为了装一个门面，表一个态，来谋得一个什么职位。他完全是科学的精神。这种科学的精神居然达到了他所不知道的但马克思本人早就论述出来的这么一个结论，这么一个论断。所以我是非常佩服的。后来我的老师胡钟达先生到了文革以后把他的观点说出来，他也是主张大封建论，古希腊罗马，资本主义以前整个社会都可以说成是封建社会，泛封建论，大封建论，这是雷海宗先生头一个提出来的。我在这里说明一下，我个人并不认为五种生产方式是完全错误的，它有它的道理，把世界史分为上古史和中古史这两段，我觉得也有道理，但是三大形态，我们需要更好地去理解。

　　归纳起来，就是科学精神、爱国精神，这是我们应该继承和弘扬的雷先生的精神遗产。他的学术遗产也是跟这两大精神有关的，中国和西方的比较，这是他的一种学术遗产，他画了一个大的轮廓，三大形态、大封建论，都是他的科学精神的表现，也是他的学术遗产，都值得我们好好研究。

从世界史到环球史

汪荣祖　台湾中央大学

所谓"世界史"（world history）早已行之有年，但长期以来其观点与内容无异是"西方的历史"（the history of the West），如韦尔斯（H. G. Wells）著名的《世界史纲》（Outline of History）虽声称是"一部单纯的人类生活史"（being a plain history of life and mankind），但对早期中国只见轻描淡写，自认"中国史对欧洲人而言所知甚少"[1]。就以西洋史而论，雷海宗教授生前对这本书也有严厉的批评："书虽名为世界史，实只头绪错乱参杂质的西洋史"[2]。然而威氏世界史纲的汉文译本（初版于1928年）在二战之前的中国，一直颇为风行[3]。

二十五卷本的《史家世界史》（Historians' History of the World）虽拥有大量的材料，但无非是许多国别史的综合[4]。喀拉地（John Garraty）与盖彼得（Peter Gay）合撰的三卷本《世界史》（History of the World），第一卷是各区域史的合编，其余两卷则是编年史，中国史部分不断被切割[5]。曾享盛名的汤恩比（Anord Toynbee）完成十卷本《历史之研究》，几乎包揽人类所有的文明，但其论点颇多争议，于中华文明尤多误解[6]。其余在西方制作的所谓世界通史，皆不足以言通。

在中国，已故周谷城教授曾出版《世界通史》，试图聚焦于各地区的国家与文化的相互关系，特别是欧亚之间的关系。周氏有意突破世界史的欧洲中心史观，不认为世界史是西方文明向世界各地传播的历史。但周氏并未完成其预定的计划，写到工业革命就戛然而止[7]。

全世界进入二十一世纪以来，"环球史"（global history）概念日益当红，有取代世界史之势，实由于近世之变局，不得不以全球的视野观照人类的历史。人类发生环球性的接触，或可追溯久远，但直到近世，各国、各洲、各文化之间始有广泛的互动，而后才有全球化时代的到来。环球化时代确实会感受到天涯若比邻，而全球性的接触愈来愈密切。不过，新时代最后是否会真正消除国界，进入世界大同，犹不可知。国家观念以及民族主义仍然甚为强固，世界各国人民之间在思维与心理

---

① Herbert G. Wells, *The Outline of History: Being a Plain History of Life and Mankind*, vol. 1 (Garden City: Doubleday & Company, 1971), p. 150.

② 见雷海宗，《评汉译韦尔斯著世界史纲》，《伯伦史学集》，南开史学家论丛雷海宗卷，北京：中华书局，2002，页616。

③ 梁思成等译，《世界史纲》，上海：商务印书馆，1935。

④ Henry S. Williams (ed.), *The Historians' History of the World: A Comprehensive Narrative of the Rise and Development of Nations as Recorded by the Great Writers of All Ages* (London: The Times, 1907–1908).

⑤ John A. Garraty and Peter Gay, *A History of the World*, 3 vols. (New York: Harper & Row Publishers, 1972).

⑥ 参阅汪荣祖，《史学九章》，北京：三联书店，2006，页39–61。

⑦ 参阅周谷城，《世界通史》，2册，石家庄：河北教育出版社，2000。

层面的鸿沟犹深，难以超越，真正的环球整合依旧是可望而不可及的目标。

在比较各自孤立的"前近代"（pre-modern），天涯海角之相遇全靠机缘。在人类历史上不知有多少次失之交臂的交往。就东西相遇而言，公元前326年亚历山大大帝（Alexander, the great）曾跨越大山，进入印度。虽然曾因兵变迫使他撤退到巴比伦（Babylon），但并未稍减其继续东进的意志。只因33岁英年早逝，使他壮志未酬。若天假岁月，他很可能会接触到战国时代（403–221 BCE）的中国人民与诸子百家。若然，则希腊哲人与先秦诸子共创"中希文化"（Sino-Hellenic culture），恐非凭空无据的想象。后汉的班超知道西方有大秦帝国，遂派甘英于公元97年往访。甘英抵达里海边的巴西雅（Parthia），只因误听当地人横渡地中海到罗马帝国需时三个月之久而折返。若甘英毅然前往，洛阳与罗马的交往早就可以建立。另一失之交臂的事例是阿罗本主教（Bishop Alopen of Antioch）于公元635年率队到唐朝京师长安，成立以拜火教（Nestorian abbey）为名的基督教。许多中国的官绅对此甚感兴趣，于781年有上千的中国人在长安参与此教活动[1]。只因唐廷困于内部问题，无暇让基督教成为沟通大唐中国与拜占廷（Byzantine）帝国之间的桥梁，错失良机。佛教与海商有助于六到七世纪中国与其他地区的联系，但主要在亚洲。几世纪之后，蒙元在十三世纪建立了欧亚帝国，打开了东西交通，马可波罗（Marco Polo）东来，将中国的生活与文化传播到欧洲，但蒙古帝国的衰亡瞬即终止了欧亚之间的往来。直到十六世纪，由于地理的大发现，欧亚之间的连接才到达前所未有的程度。耶稣会教士利玛窦（Mateo Ricci）来华传教，成功地使儒者如徐光启、李之藻辈受洗入教。但最后由于礼仪之争，导致利玛窦想要建立的中国基督教梦想之破灭[2]。中国也失去跟上欧洲科技的良机，最后于十九世纪被列强打开门户，屡遭侵略，国势日衰，无法与世界其他各国有任何有意义的交往与合作可言，有的是相互之间的摩擦与仇视。在当时中国既不了解世界，世界也无兴趣了解中国。

在近代才出现的全球性的自由贸易与商业来往，并没有能够整合全球经济。列强之间的竞夺反而使环球化变得政治化，产生压迫、仇恨与民族主义。第一次世界大战终结了欧洲世纪，民族自觉、集体安全、自由贸易，似乎促进了环球化，但情况并不如预期，1929年的经济大恐慌激化保护主义，萎缩了世界上的商业来往。法西斯主义的高涨引发二战，德、日等法西斯帝国主义的惨败为美利坚世纪铺了路，战后美国借其庞大的经济与军事实力将全球许多地方推向环球化，但美国想要的新世界秩序并未如愿，随之而来的是美苏对抗的冷战时代。苏联帝国于1990年代初崩溃之后，才结束两极世界。然而由美国主导的世界秩序既不明确，环球议题诸如人权、环境、通商也更趋复杂。不过由于洲际通航的频繁、讯息网络的密集、数据处理的迅速、电子媒体的普及，无不造就全球的一体性[3]。虽然如此，正在冒升的新型环球性格是否会成为历史的主轴，以及普世经验，都值得关注。

当今世界由于科技的进步，使地理空间大幅缩小，国际旅行既省时又省钱。国际合作兴隆，世界经济有前所未有的整合。但快速的环球化同时也加速了世界上的分裂、不平等与冲突。国际合作往往伴随国际竞争，一直没有出现一个环球性的社会结构，国家体制也无消失的迹象。毫无疑问，在全球化时代仍然存在无从否定的差异性。

如何才能达成环球文化的融合？有鉴于环球交往与物质文明的流通，在衣食住行育乐等方面日

---

[1] 引自徐子明所写"What the World's History Might Have Been"一文，载《宜兴徐子明先生遗稿》，台北：华冈出版社，1975，页3。

[2] 详阅 Donald W. Treadgold, *The West in Russia and China* (Cambridge: Cambridge University Press, 1975), vol. 2, pp. 8–12.

[3] 简明环球史可参阅 Jürgen Osterhammel and Niels P. Peterson, *Globalization: A Short History* (Princeton: Princeton University Press, 2003), esp. chaps. v and vi.

趋一致，已无多大差异。学者包定（Kenneth Boulding）认为人类的生活形态与风格会愈来愈相像①。包定虽难言在可预见的将来会有一种人类共同的语言，但英文似乎已可在各地通用。总之，包定肯定环球文化之融合是可以达到的。史家汤恩比同样乐观预期未来的人将同是孔子、老子、苏格拉底（Socrates）、柏拉图（Plato）的后代②。不过，近年环球文化专家羽石（Mike Featherstone），并不如此乐观，如谓："若无世界政府，文化整合是不可能的，而环球一国更极不可能出现"（It would be impossible to identify an integrated global culture without the formation of a world state—a highly unlikely prospect）③。笔者以为全球化既不应也无必要导致单一的文化。人文世界不必要像自然界那样一致而有规律，十九世纪德国历史哲学家赫德（Johann Gottfried Herder）有言：人类有语言、习俗、性格之异，不必强同④。赫德虽不及见前所未有的全球化进程，他所说的语言、习俗、性格之异渐趋淡化，但这些差异不可能完全消失，也无消失的必要。更值得注意的是，每一个国家的历史与文化经验具有特殊性。清末民初的章太炎无意中呼应了赫德所说，历史乃是维系一个国家或文化特色最关键的要素之一。在此一意义上，一国之史乃国之精髓，国家赖以生存与持续⑤。特殊的历史经验使语言与心灵表达绝然异趣⑥。诚如章太炎所说，"社会之学与言质学者殊科，几何之方面，重力之形式，声光之激射，物质之化分，验于彼土者然，即验于此土者亦无不然。若夫心能流衍，人事万端，则不能据一方以为权概，断可知矣"⑦。章氏之言一如意大利哲人维柯（Giambattista Vico）之区分"心界"（World of Minds）与"天界"（World of Nature），或所谓的"外知识"（outer knowledge）与"内知识"（inner knowledge）。维柯的"内知识"就是他的"新科学"（Scienza nuova；New Science），他提升了心智之学，并将之与物质之学并肩⑧。即使有朝一日，全球化打破国界种姓，特殊的历史也不会消失。然则，各国的特殊历史必然能在全球化的进程中留存，而不致于影响全球化的和谐，反而能有助于相互了解。特殊而悠久的中国历史自也不能例外。

各自异趣的历史与文化若能在全球化之下，欣欣向荣，犹如思想史大师柏林（Isaiah Berlin）所说的"文化多元论"（cultural pluralism）。大一统的文化很可能造成"文化霸权"，单调无趣的一元文化，以及武断的共同真理。时至今日，已少有人仍然认为全球化就是西化，"全球主义"（globalism）并非要全然"普世"，只能留下无关紧要的"特殊"。

仅仅靠科技与交通显然不能使世界融为一体，还需要经由理念上的一致与共同准则，才能顺应环球化。转向环球化至今主要由西方推动，特别是美国，但环球化不能等同西化或美国化。环球共同认可的准则必须经由相互了解、容让，才能适用各国家、各文化。欲达此目的，必须要在互动日益频繁的世界里，洞察各民族与文化的异趣。货真价实而有效的"寰宇性"（globosity）的建立，不能仅靠政治上的合作与经济上的整合，而且要认真对待东西文化之异与南北地域的差距。总之，要相互了解，而历史是最好的管道。

接下来的问题是如何超越昔日世界史的格局，撰写一部包容全球、统合多元历史文化，确具世界观点的环球史。此一工程少不得时间绵长、内容丰富的中国史之参与。换言之，中国史如何对环

① Kenneth E. Boulding, *The Meaning of the Twentieth Century* (New York: Harper & Row Publishers, 1964), p. 18.

② Arnold Toynbee, *Civilization on Trail and the World and the West* (Oxford: Oxford University Press, 1948), p. 85.

③ Mike Featherstone, "Global Culture: An Introduction," in Mike Featherstone (ed.), *Global Culture: Nationalism, Globalization and Modernity* (London: Sage Publications, 1990), p. 1.

④ Isaiah Berlin, *Vico and Herder: Two Studies in the History of Ideas* (New York: Vintage Books, 1976), p. 159; 参阅汪荣祖，《康章合论》，台北：联经出版事业有限公司，1988，页55-56。

⑤ 引自徐复，《訄书详注》，上海：上海古籍出版社，2000，页831-832。

⑥ 章炳麟，《齐物论释》，收入章炳麟，《章太炎全集》，第6册，上海：上海人民出版社，1985，页28-29。

⑦ 章炳麟，《社会通诠商兑》，收入《章太炎全集》，第4册，页323。

⑧ 参阅汪荣祖，《史传通说》，台北：联经出版事业有限公司，1988，页198。

球史的写作有所贡献，以便建立如当代史家麦克尼尔（John R. McNeill）所谓的"既多元而又可行的全人类的网络"（a pluralistic and plausible "human web"）[1]。中国的特殊历史经验无疑能为全球相互了解提供极具价值的知识，网络的互通已拥有人类历史的中心地位[2]。时至二十世纪，对许多西方的政治人物或知识分子而言，中国依然是一个"神秘"的国度。中国史虽于二战后在欧美主要的大学讲授，但被视为地区研究的一部分，并未融入人类历史之中。

当中国在全球化时代崛起，中国与世界上其他民族与国家的联系、互动、理解，以及建立共同准则，益见重要。互联网大大增进了信息的传播，而历史知识是最好的信息。世人可从历史的镜子里洞察中国的面貌。在此意义上，中国史的参与有助于环球和谐，减低疑惧而能在全球化的过程中追求共同目标，增进共同价值，庶几建立属于世界性的人网，以友谊与合作而非敌对与对抗联系各国人民。然则，历史知识足以为认识与和谐当前世界之用。

中国史对环球史的贡献不应是穿插的、片段的，而必须是融为一体的。将中国史天衣无缝写入环球史并不简单，今日之专业史家大都是专家，专治一端，鲜能掌握全球性的历史知识，从大量史料中选取并作判断，而近年流行解构历史知识，将历史知识零碎化，皆与全球视野背道而驰。此外，民族主义声势未减也难以追求公平正义的全球观点。然而全球化时代毕竟需要环球史，或可从环球联系较多的近代史开始。随着"全球主义"（globalism）的成长，使不同的人民与多元文化同居于地球村里，而中国史不仅写入环球史，且成为人类知识不可分隔的一部分。至少有二方面的议题亟待写入环球史。

其一是人民苦难史。中国历史像他国历史一样，充斥叛乱、战争，瘟疫，以及自然灾害，但人民受灾、受害、受难的苦难史少见入史。例如长达十五年的太平天国战争，也许是人类史上最惨烈的内战，受难者不下二千万人，而史册所载大都是战役、制度、理念，很少提到战争暴力下的人民创伤[3]。当太平天国结束时，东南富庶之地满目沧夷，昔日繁华的城镇几无人烟。一如翼王石达开的诗句所说，"我志未酬人亦苦，东南到处有啼痕"[4]此一人间悲剧始自洪秀全 1850 年 6 月的金田起兵，一开始双方伤亡皆众，所用兵器不仅仅是弓矛，且发洋枪洋炮。1852 年 4 月的永安一役，四名清将阵亡；桂林之围乌兰泰伤重而死；1853 年正月武昌城陷，巡抚以下官员不是战死就是被杀；当攻下南京时，总督陆建瀛与两万旗兵几乎尽被杀戮。苏州陷落时，巡抚及其十余下属自尽，百分之二十到三十之居民被杀害，另外百分之二十到三十之人跳井或悬梁自尽。富裕的苏州在战前的 1830 年约有三百四十余万纳税人，到战后的 1865 年只剩下一百二十余万，几乎损失了三分之二的人口[5]。太平军方面，伤亡亦重，西王萧朝贵、南王冯云山均于早期战殁；1855 年自南京北征，全军覆没，而西征初胜后败，在武昌拉锯战多年，至 1854 年 10 月 14 日武昌易手，死伤数字难以估算[6]。1856 年太平天国内部的自相残杀，惨烈不下于恶战，当北王韦昌辉与燕王秦日纲奉天王洪秀全之命突袭

[1] 阅 John R. McNeill and William H. McNeill, *The Human Web: A Bird's-Eye View of World History* (New York: W. W. Norton & Company, 2003).

[2] 上引书，页 3。

[3] 参阅 Franz H. Michael in collaboration with Chung-li Chang, *The Taiping Rebellion: History and documents* (Seattle: University of Washington Press, 1976).

[4] 诗句见石达开，《石达开全集》，台中：普天出版社，1971，页 30。

[5] 据苏州府志，该府 1830 年的人口数字是 3,412,694 人，1865 年则降到 1,288,145 人，见高纪言等编辑，《中国地方志集成：江苏府县志》第 13 册，南京：江苏古籍出版社，1991，页 343-344。

[6] 阅 Franz H. Michael, *The Taiping Rebellion*, pp. 69, 97, 103-104, 123, 153; 参阅汪荣祖，《走向世界的挫折：郭嵩焘与道咸同光时代》，北京：中华书局，2006，页 15-24，45。

东王杨秀清,东王本人之外,相关者包括妇孺在内均遭杀害。杨秀清的首级高悬竹竿示众[1]。当时充当佣兵的爱尔兰人亲眼目击"极其恐怖的杀戮"(horrendous slaughter):"有些地方尸体堆集五、六尺高,有的是自己吊死,有的被炮弹严重灼伤致死",一周之后,又见到成群之人,或五、或十、或百、或千被绑赴刑场斩首[2]。洪秀全又诱杀东王的六千卫士。此后三月,凡与东王有关者,包括五百女兵在内,赶尽杀绝。1856年10月初,石达开从武昌到南京,对惨酷杀戮表示愤怒,寻即遭到威胁而逃离天京,然其家眷仍不能幸免于难。此一天京血案,据估计至少有两万人丧身[3]。天王虽杀北王与燕王,仍不能平愤,内斗与自相残杀不断,犹如德国哲学家尼采(Frederich Nietzsche)所说的"无端之苦难"(pointlessness of suffering)。曾国藩、曾国荃兄弟最后于1864年7月15日攻破天京,三日恐怖的巷战,十万太平男女除自杀外,包括忠王李秀成在内均遭处决。研究太平天国的汉学家梅谷(Franz Michael)指出杀俘由于太平军之狂热与曾氏兄弟之策略[4],但无可忽视的是残忍之结局。长期战争不仅伤亡无数,繁华之东南残破不堪。一个外国商人发现战后苏州几乎是空城,到处见有腐尸与白骨[5]。在十八世纪富裕一时的扬州也被太平天国战争所摧毁,战后的瘟疫更增添了死亡率。一位于1853年二月至七月住在扬州的无名氏目击城陷,记下战后瘟疫使"尸体堆集如山,阻塞巷道"[6]。当清军于1861年9月5日克复安庆, 16,000名太平军无一生还。翌年英王陈玉成被俘后,于6月4日处死。石达开孤军奋战六年后,穷途末路,在四川投降,希望能放过剩下的2,000名部下。然而他以33岁英年被凌迟处死后,属下无一幸免,惨酷的杀俘事件引起在华外国人的抗议。事实上,政府军不仅杀俘,而且杀害涉嫌通敌或附敌的平民百姓。

太平天国之役造成的悲惨世界,只是中国历史上的一页,有关战争、暴力、杀戮、谋害、饥荒、疾病、灾难、破坏等史实不胜枚举,但作史者很少致力于把这些惨绝人寰的人民苦难入史,更少能分析暴行的心态。读史者应知古人的苦难,以及他们如何面对恐惧,应付创伤。如将历代中国人民的苦难写入环球史,才是一部比较完整的全球苦难史,增益对人类命运的了解。

其二是环境史。自然环境对人文的影响无疑是全球性的,人与环境的互动也有世界性的含意。自然对历史中国所扮演的角色自将有助于全球环境史之理解,特别是从明到清经历了影响深远的"小冰期"(Little Ice Age),波及整个十七世纪世界,覆盖之下,无远弗届,中国大地自不例外。中国人对自然环境变迁的看法与反应必可丰富全球环境史的内容,交换中外的生态信息更能完整显示自然在历史上对环境留下的痕迹,使读史者更能理解气候变化、植被与动物的分布,以及在历史空间里土地形态的转化。

历史上的生态变迁足以对生灵与文化留下难以磨灭的后果,诸如疾病与瘟疫、森林的消失,以及旱涝成灾。中国历史上的生态无疑有助于理解自然环境自古至今全球性的变迁过程[7],如森林覆盖在近五百年来的中国,快速锐减。明代开国之初,华北森林仍然茂密[8],经人口激增与城市发展需要

---

[1] 太平天国内斗可参阅简又文, *The Taiping Revolutionary Movement* (New Haven: Yale University Press, 1973), pp. 294–295; Jonathan D. Spence, *God's Chinese Son: The Taiping Heavenly Kingdom of Hong Xiuquan* (New York: W. W. Norton & Company, 1996), p. 242; Michael, *The Taiping Rebellion*, pp. 109–115.

[2] Spence, *God's Chinese Son*, p. 243.

[3] 阅徐彻,《天京事件中韦昌辉杀人问题新探》,载社会科学战线编辑部编《中国近代史研究论丛》,长春:吉林人民出版社,1981,页60–71. 作者认为北王不可能杀掉两万人,此数应是整个事件死亡总数。

[4] Michael, *The Taiping Rebellion*, p. 174.

[5] 目击者见闻可见之于1865年1月13日的上海的报章。

[6] 无名氏,《广陵史稿》,见《四库未收书辑刊》,第2辑,北京:北京出版社,1997,第4册,卷16,页13。

[7] 参阅 Mark Elvin, *The Retreat of the Elephants: An Environmental History of China* (New Haven: Yale University Press, 2004).

[8] Walter C. Lowdermilk and Dean R. Wickes, *History of Sail Use in the Wu T'ai Shan Area* (Shanghai: North China Branch of Royal Asiatic Society), pp. 4–5.

大量燃料和建材之后，林木逐渐耗损，久之长城沿边的森林面积大幅减少，森林砍伐到明末已深入四川、贵州、云南等偏远地区[1]。持久的砍伐导致中国林木覆盖面积的锐减，改变了土地形态，造成近代中国严重的沙漠化以及旱涝等灾害[2]。

为了耕种，清除林地，势必缩减各类动物的生存空间，许多物种包括熊猫在内在十七世纪面临灭绝的危机[3]，老虎为了觅食，出而伤人。明清时代的黄河以南地区，广阔的森林显著缩减，迫使成群的华南虎到乡镇觅食，有记载老虎曾进入杭州的住宅区内[4]。晚明时期江南虎患甚炽，一直延续到清朝。当乾隆皇帝执政的十八世纪，乡民仍需设置捕虎的陷阱，以策安全[5]。至清中叶，由于不断的猎虎，虎踪渐稀，最后凶猛的老虎几成面临灭绝的动物[6]，成为另类的生态问题。

中国史的生态观，包括生态危机、人与自然的关系、环境意识、生态政策、以及疾病对社会文化造成的严重后果，无疑会对环球空间里的环境议题有所贡献，得到更平衡而完备的知识。环球生态学仍然是正在发展中的课题，需要跨文化的挹注。若无充分的中国生态史知识，全球的环境史必然是不完整的，只能具备地区性的意义，欲理解自然对人生的诸多影响，必须要迈向跨地区、跨文化的大道。

全球化至今仍限于洲际联系、政治合作，经济整合；国家与文化之间的哲学与心理上的诸多鸿沟，依旧未能跨越。真正全球化时代的来临，需要清除国家间的歧异，协调文化上的不一致，以便形成各方皆能认同的准则。欲达此目的，具有全球视野的环球史，允有必要。

反映全球化时代的环球史宜超越以西方为中心的世界史格局，必须包容中国的历史经验在内。中国史的书写也应该具有环球观点，超越旧时代的朝代史与新时代的国别史。不过，中国史的全球化并不是要将特殊的历史经验普世化，而是要将中国的特殊写入"多元的人网"（a pluralistic human web），诸如特殊的中国苦难故事以及生态危机，都将会丰富这两方面的全球知识。历史上中国人受到灾难的伤痛，以及如何面对大自然所赐与的生存空间，都会对环球史有莫大的贡献。历史学者为了环球史，必须克服民族情绪、避免专攻一端，以及消除后现代之虚无，使中国史真正成为全世界人类历史的一部分，提供丰富的历史经验，有助于世人之间的相互了解，不再是独门独户的汉学。

2012 年 4 月 22 日初稿

2012 年 11 月 10 日二稿

---

[1]　参阅蓝勇，《明清时期皇木采办研究》，《历史研究》，第 6 期 (1994)，页 86–98。

[2]　参阅丁建民，徐廷弼，《我国的森林》，北京：商务印书馆，1985。

[3]　参阅何业恒，《大熊猫的兴衰》，《中国历史地理论丛》，第 4 册 (1998)，页 10–11。有关帝国晚期华南生态后果可参阅 Robert B. Marks, *Tigers, Rice, Silk, and Silt: Environment and Economy in late Imperial South China* (Cambridge: Cambridge University Press, 1998), pp. 309–332。

[4]　见陈继儒，《虎荟》，在王云五等编，《丛书集成》，第 1364 册，北京：中华书局，1983。

[5]　许秋垞，《闻见异辞》，第 2 册，在《丛书集成三编》，第 67 册，台北：新文丰出版社，1996。

[6]　参阅蓝勇，《清初四川虎患与环境复原问题》，在《中国历史地理论丛》，第 3 册 (1999)，页 203，210。

百家争鸣中的我与雷海宗——兼谈"唯心"、"唯物"及"批判"

吕万和　天津社会科学院

1957 年 8 月 14 日，天津市召开"科技（学术）界反右斗争大会"，闪电式地突然批斗南开大学历史系教授雷海宗，定为大"右派"。我和冯承柏同志当时同在天津市委文教部科学处工作，随之受牵连。冯被定为"阶级异己分子"，开除党籍。我成为天津市委机关五名处分最重（监督劳动）的"极右分子"之一。科学处随之撤销。

此案经过，冯先生已写《雷海宗先生 1957 年蒙难始末》。我则三次参加纪念雷先生的研讨会，欲言又止，总觉得自己的思想梳理不清。今已垂老，理应如实交代，对我本人（或可称 "我辈"）当年的 "思维模式"、"行为模式"作一些反思，并补充冯文未曾写及的一些内情。

"大地回春"（1956 年 6 月—1957 年 3 月）

我与雷先生素不相识。大学时代听高班同学谈及雷海宗，印象是：（1）学识丰厚，"一把黑纸扇"，纵论古今中外。（2）反苏反共，有点赞扬法西斯。这种印象似乎形成一种"思维模式"。"批胡风"、"批胡适"，更加强了对 "唯心论"的警惕。

党中央召开的"知识分子问题会议"（1956 年 1 月）震动了上述"思维模式"。毛泽东多次倡导"百家争鸣、百花齐放"，知识分子顿感 "大地回春"。

我听到的内部传达报告中，有两次感受最深。

其一是：天津市委副书记兼宣传部长王亢之传达陆定一同志关于百家争鸣的报告，其中说道：以往两大阵营斗争，西方资产阶级场总是挥舞四面旗帜：自由、和平、民主、民族自决。而今，我们已经把"和平""民主""民族独立"这三面旗帜从资产阶级手中夺了过来。只有"自由"这个旗帜，仍在西方资产阶级手中。"百家争鸣、百花齐放"，就是要把"自由"这面旗帜从资产阶级手中夺过来！

其二是：1957 年 3 月 17 日毛泽东在天津党员干部会议上的讲话（我听的是录音）。

轻松活泼，谈笑风生。一开始说：讲什么呀？就讲"百家争鸣、百花齐放"吧！明确指出：过去几十年，我们是"叫化子打狗"，搞阶级斗争，推翻帝国主义、封建主义、官僚资本主义的统治。如果从鸦片战争算起，到打败蒋介石，抗美援朝，镇压反革命，土地改革，城市的民主改革，一直到 1956 年的社会主义改造高潮，则经历了 116 年。现在，大规模的阶级斗争基本结束。敌我矛盾还有、但是不多了。"万晓塘（天津市公安局长），你的工作还有，但是不多了。"今后，主要是人民内部矛盾，解决的办法是说服，不是压服。是"百家争鸣，百花齐放"。今后的任务，是"向自然界开战""向科学进军"。"在座的有没有大学教授呀？大学教授请举手！"（据说台下只有两人举手），"你的势力不大呀、少得可怜呀！"号召党员干部学科学、学技术，当好教授、工程师、医生，管好工厂、学校、医院，搞好建设。

1956 年 6 月，天津市委文教部建立科学处，初期只有三人。我们走访专家，组建各种学会及科联、科普、科委；编制 "天津市 12 年科学发展远景规划"。九个多月期间，工作异常顺利，体现当年上下同心，到处振奋。这九个月期间，中宣部召开了 "科学处工作座谈会"、"学术刊物和大学学报编辑部座谈会"、"全国哲学社会科学规划会议" 等重要会议，传达指示、听取汇报，通报学术思想动态。北京、上海等地学术界出现活泼生机。如：生物学界对李森科学说，哲学界对形式逻辑、唯心论，经济学界对商品和价值规律、政治经济学（社会主义部分），以及民族学、社会学、人口学等都有所质疑或建议。

与北京、上海等地相比，天津学术界相当沉寂。我和冯承柏都很关注雷海宗先生。冯勤奋好学，对雷先生多有了解。我的亡妻崔树菊是雷先生的学生，我得以浏览雷先生的讲稿。加以冯文潜先生（冯承柏父）热心支持，我们得以比较深入地了解雷先生的学术思想。1956 年初冬，我与雷先生晚间长谈后，深夜借宿南开，次晨一早就向文教部副部长王金鼎作了汇报（他原任南开党委书记，仍住南开）。他连连说："情况了解得好"，指示我们写简报，向上反映。简报发出，有关领导和中宣部科学处等都认为：应当鼓励雷先生讲演、写文章。于是，决定举办 "学术讲座"，请雷先生讲世界上古史分期和奴隶制问题。

风云幻变（1957 年 4 月—6 月）

恰当此时，《人民日报》理论组来津组织座谈百家争鸣（1957 年 4 月 14 日），是为 "天津十教授座谈"。雷先生发言主旨是：马克思主义在革命理论方面有很大发展。但在社会科学、历史学方面，许多论点仍然停留在恩格斯逝世的 1895 年。《人民日报》在报道中却把雷的发言归结为 "马克思主义基本上停留在 1895 年"，并且使用通栏标题，加了长长的按语，表示 "我们不能同意"（4 月 21、22 日）。各界对此议论纷纷，南开园更是一片哗然。

雷先生这些话，二十多天前在天津市委召开的座谈会上就说过，冯承柏写了简报，中宣部领导肯定看到，并无惊异。两、三天前，市委书记王亢之与王金鼎通电话说：《人民日报》对雷的发言要加编者按，征求天津市委意见。金鼎连连说："不合适""不合适"。我恰在电话机旁，也说了 "不合适"。

现在，事出意外，我请示金鼎怎么办？金鼎对《人民日报》的作法不满，说："我是不同意加按语的"，并且说 "亢之同志也是不同意的。"

我急赴北京。面见中宣部科学处处长于光远同志。我请示：天津应否表态支持《人民日报》？原定雷海宗的学术讲演是否仍然举行？光远同志答称："他们（指《人民日报》）按他们的，你们照常让雷讲演，届时作好记录，通知《人民日报》参加。"我又问：是否仍属 "百家争鸣"？林涧青同志插话：还是 "百家争鸣吧！"。光远同意。

雷先生随即致函《人民日报》，申述发言本意。杨志玖先生仗义执言，直说："贵报对雷先生的批评和雷先生的原意并不相同。"《人民日报》均 "来函照登"（4 月 28 日及 5 月 7 日）。杨先生在天津继续批评《人民日报》并为雷鸣不平，《天津日报》也照登（5 月 10 日）。

事态如此，似乎体现 "百家争鸣"。我却忐忑不安，总觉得不支持《人民日报》不妥。部领导有此同感，指示我和冯承柏写一短文，用河北大学孙延龄的名义投送《天津日报》，意在 "留此存照"。此文颇费心机，既不能硬说雷先生宣称 "马克思主义停滞"，又不能不持《人民日报》。想了一下，搬出列宁在《卡尔·马克思》一文中的那段经典论断，认为：真正的社会科学和历史学是在马克思主义理论指导下建立、发展起来的，如是则"革命理论和社会科学密不可分"，结语发问："《人民日报》的按语与雷先生的论点是否完全无关？"杨先生随即"敬复"：不应当把列宁的个别论点当成不能更动的经典。（《天津日报》5月16日、30日）。

6月2日，按照原定计划，雷先生作了题为《世界史分期与世界上古中古史中一些问题》的讲演。听众热烈鼓掌。6月5日，《人民日报》详加报道，并在同版刊出批评尚钺压制学术上不同意见的文章，似乎是在表态：雷的言论属于"学术问题"。7月初，天津《历史教学》全文刊出雷先生的讲演。

该不该"批判"雷海宗？（1957年7月-8月）

此时，"整风"已转入"反右"，文教部全力投入"反右"。我在文教系统"反右"办公室负责秘书组。天津市领导和南开大学党委对雷先生的态度并未动摇。南开并且安排雷先生登台讲演，批判美国资产阶级民主和北大学生中的"右派"言行。他手指会场标语，高声朗读："领导我们事业的核心力量是中国共产党"，"指导我们思想的理论基础是马克思主义"。《人民日报》详加报道（1957年6月29日）。仿佛认同雷先生与"右派"有别。

然而，北京已大张旗鼓，批判学术界的大"右派""妄图复辟资产阶级社会科学"。《人民日报》字里行间透露：翦伯赞批评了"我的同行雷海宗"。天津科联、科普的陈哲同志奉派住北京饭店参与活动。我坐不住了，经批准，抽身前往北京，与陈哲一同参加"全国科技学术界反右斗争大会"，听到翦伯赞、郭沫若在大会上点名批判雷海宗。陈哲告我：康生在内部有一个报告，我请他一定拿到记录。

我异常紧张地来到中宣部。中宣部已开展反右，科学处那位曾经综合介绍哲学社会科学界思想动态的同志已被审查。我见到于光远同志，郑重请示：应当如何对待雷海宗？他回答说：雷的那些学术性言论，仍属"百家争鸣"。至于他是不是"右派"，应由天津市委决定。

我回到北京饭店，拿到康生报告记录一看，认定：不能不批雷海宗！

回到天津，交上康生报告纪录，我向领导表示：天津也应召开科技（学术）界反右大会，并提请考虑：应否批判雷海宗。领导未及表态。七月中旬，天津高等学校学生中的"反右"告一段落，准备放暑假。我抓紧与冯承柏研究、拟定"天津市科技界反右斗争大会"草案，要求冯整理雷海宗的材料。他有些抵触，说："我不明白，我们是组织争鸣，还是组织批判。"我说：听领导决定。

大会草案不难拟定，问题在于是否点名批判雷海宗？不点，怕犯错误。点了，怎么批判？这时，部长梁寒冰传达陆定一同志的报告说："在学术问题上，不要当盖子。在政治问题上不要当瞎子。"我们据此研究，如何对待雷海宗？我说：世界上古史分期、奴隶制之类，完全是学术问题，自应"百家争鸣"，不能当"盖子"。雷先生如果有反动言行，当然要进行"政治斗争"，不能当"瞎子"。但尚无材料。

是否点名批判雷海宗？我认为：雷先生的"文化形态史观"是"唯心论"。陆定一报告强调："百家争鸣"中也要批判唯心论。一般地说，"唯心论"是世界观问题。但是，公然对抗党的理论基础——马克思主义唯物论，就很难说不带有"政治斗争"性质。何况当时的权威说法是：反对教条主义，但不允许攻击马克思主义的基本原理。雷先生的讲演涉及"五种生产方式"，当时，这是公认的"基本原理"（尽管我本人不是这种看法），又使用了"马克思主义停滞"的提法，这都很不好说。

于是，我在大会草案点名批判名单的最后，加上了雷先生的名字、括注问号，请部领导决定。我的解释是："政治斗争"和"百家争鸣"两者之间，还可以有一个层次：批判"唯心论"。其性质是"思想批判"。要冯承柏按这一思路整理材料。我幻想：主动进行"思想批判"，也许能避免"政治斗争"。

这个草案先呈送主管科学处工作的副部长王金鼎。他仍然说："雷海宗不点。"我征询南开大学藤维藻同志的意见，他回答说："雷海宗是在市里（市级座谈会）放的火，要批市里批。"我把草案送呈部长梁寒冰，附纸写明金鼎和藤维藻的意见，请部长审定。梁寒冰批示："雷的问题，中央、北京已经点名，天津不提，是否合适？我即去中宣部开会（"全国宣传部、文教部部长会议"），回来后研究决定。"

8月初，梁寒冰回到天津，立刻传达中宣部部长陆定一在大会上的严厉批评：说："天津市委右倾，不批雷海宗！"又传达康生的严厉指责："为什么不批雷海宗？天津高等学校的反右要重搞！"文教部随即向市委呈送检讨（我受命起草）：承认错误严重，保证彻查。

梁寒冰还说：在陆定一严厉批评之前，康生在小组会上就当面指责梁寒冰："雷海宗还没批，你们天津的反右就结束了？"梁当场解释说："不是这样，我们已经作了计划，回去就召开大会，批判雷海宗。"

批斗雷海宗的大会迅速召开。各大学随即通知学生返校。我受命为大会起草领导发言，冯承柏整理的材料成为大会批斗雷海宗的基本资料。市委文教部随之责令我和冯承柏检查交待，进而揭发批判，终至不得不说我是"组织右派向党进攻、掩护右派退却"，冯承柏是"资产阶级在党内的传声筒"。

如何反思？

历史学（History）的本意，应该是"探索、讲述真实的重要故事（往日之事）"，以促进"反思"，提高自觉。"雷案"今已澄清，该当如何反思？

南开大学已三次隆重召开纪念雷先生的研讨会，出版了纪念文集。近又刊出雷先生的短评时论集：《历史·时势·人心》。雷先生热爱祖国，坚决抗日，对美国的侵略扩张企图也相当警惕。他坚信抗日战争必将胜利、中华优秀文化必将浴火重兴。他反对蒋介石集团的腐败独裁，对新中国充满希望。

我等受牵连者均获改正。对我的改正结论是："吕万和在1956年为贯彻党的双百方针，搜集有关情况，组织座谈访问，并经领导审阅起草印发有关简报，反映一些教授的情况、意见、和学术见解，均属职责范围的正常工作活动，且有些学术观点吕也并不同意。"（市文教组党委，1979年1月15日）。

康生的高压直接导致这场灾难。已确知：1956年春，康生插手中宣部工作后即来天津，3月间已掌握雷海宗的上述发言。《人民日报》派记者来津与康生有无关联令人难测。雷海宗登台讲演批判"右派"，康生得知后大发雷霆，拍桌子说："难道雷海宗成了左派？"南开学生放假，康生更加震怒，说："雷海宗还没批，你们就放假了？"陆定一对天津的严厉指责来自康生的震怒。

康生为何有如此威力？我辈为何不能"坚持原则"？这类大问题，恕我无力反思。我只能对我本人当年的困惑，谈一些粗浅认识。

关于"唯心""唯物"及"批判"

当年我认为："雷海宗的文化史观是唯心论，必须批判"。而今我不免质疑：文化史观是否"唯心论"？所谓"唯心论"是否必须批判？何谓"批判"？甚至，"唯心论"、"唯物论"这两个译名是否准确？

这两个译名源自日本的早期社会主义者。一个"唯"字，容易简单认定：似乎哲学家非此即彼，完全对立，无法相容。这种看法是否符合实际？试问：稍有常识者谁能否认物质的存在先于精神？贺麟先生是公认的唯心论哲学家，有同学曾在课堂上向他质问："到底先有物质，还是先有精神？精神是不是物质活动的产物？"贺麟先生唯有苦笑，说：这类科学常识，谁不承认？

另一方面，"精神变物质""思想领先、政治挂帅""能动的反映"，这些精辟论点出自辩证唯物论哲学，难道不是对精神的极其高度的重视？

哲学家在不同研究领域，或重视研究"物"（物质），或重视研究"心"（理想、精神），既相互驳难，也相互促思，这才是哲学史所揭示的人类思维发展规律。去掉一个"唯"字，具体评介各派学者在宇宙观、历史观、人生观、伦理观、认识论、方法论等哲学各领域的贡献和局限，既关注两者的对立，也关注两者的相互促思，是否有助于防止僵化武断，促进思维的发展？加上一个"唯"字，只讲两者的对立，甚至闻"心"色变，动辄斗争，是否会助长僵化武断，阻碍思维创新？

雷先生的"文化形态史观"应否归入"唯心论"？根据王敦书先生的精要阐述，我粗浅理解、试作概括如下：

历史活动是人类（指新石器时代以后的人类）各群体（种族、部族、民族），在特定环境下（地理、自然、历史条件），谋求生存、发展的活动。"文化形态"则是人类各群体发展到高级阶段（足以创造文化）的历史活动。"文化"既有共性，又因环境、群体不同而各具特色，形成各种"文化形态"。"文化"是物质和精神的统一。物质文化中，最重要的是生产工具，它决定"文化形态"的整体面貌，是历史分期（石器时代、铜器时代、铁器时代、机器时代）的基准。精神文化包括经济、政治、法律等各项制度以及礼仪、习俗、思想、艺术、宗教等等。各种文化无不凝聚群体精神。政治（或统治）状态的演变和由此导致的群体精神状态，警示各种"文化形态"的兴衰。

迄今已知"文化形态"有七：埃及、巴比伦、印度、中国、希腊罗马、回教和欧西。欧西和中国两种之外，其他五种皆经历"形成、发展、兴盛、衰败"，"一个周期"而消亡。其过程又大致经历五个阶段：封建时代、贵族国家时代、帝国主义时代、大一统时代（至此盛极转衰）、以至政治破裂、甚至文化灭绝。

欧西文化形态方兴未久，但已出现两次世界大战等足资警示的兆端。

中国文化形态则比较特殊。古典的中国文化是"华夏文化"，起自殷商西周封建，历经春秋贵族统治、战国王帝统治，至秦汉大一统盛极，魏晋转衰，是为"第一周期"。但"华夏文化"并未"灭绝"，反因"五胡乱华"、印度佛教输入，以及南方地区的开发和融入，形成"胡汉混合、梵华同化"的"中国文化"，是为"第二周期"。两周期分界线是"淝水之战的胜利"（公元383年）。第二周期的中国文化，政治上虽然大致墨守秦汉，思想文艺上则代有生机。历经隋唐盛世，宋元开拓，明清转衰。

欧西文化入侵，中国文化面临严重挑战。日本全面侵华，中国文化更是濒临生死存亡。雷先生坚信：伟大的抗日战争必将胜利。中国文化定能浴火重生，"更旧创新"，进入第三个周期。他大声疾呼："二千年来养成的元气，今日全部拿出，作为民族文化保卫战的力量。此次抗战的英勇，大半在此。"（《伯伦史学集》，第197～202页。）并写专文：《建国——在望的第三周文化》，说："生逢二千年来所未有的乱世，身经四千年来所仅见的外患，担起拨乱反正、抗敌复国、更旧创新的重任——那是何等难得的机会！何等伟大的权利！何等光荣的使命！"（《中国文化与中国的兵》，商务，2001年，第168～185页。）

雷先生从世界史看中国史，力求融会中西、贯通古今，促进反思、提高民族发展的自觉性。他评述兴亡陈迹，指点兴亡征兆，痛砭中国历代腐朽统治者的奢靡腐败及由此导致的积弱衰颓，高呼重振元气，弃弱图强，奋起抗敌，"更旧创新"。其学术贡献弥足珍惜，其爱国热忱更是感人。

史观不等于史学。雷先生的学术贡献学界公认。这里只是讨论上述史观应否归入"唯心论"，绝非妄评雷先生的史学。

诚然，上述"史观"不是马克思主义史观。其涵盖范围基本上限于古代、中世纪史。所列"一周期而消亡"的五种"文化形态"，也可以说是古代中世纪时期欧亚非各地王朝、帝国的兴替史。

古代中世纪时期（原始社会时期更不用说），各地群体交融不易，解决冲突、争夺和扩张的手段主要是军事掠夺和征讨杀戮，确实有"一周期而亡"的"文化形态"。至于所列七种文化形态能否涵盖全球各地、所列五种文化形态是否"完全绝灭"、政治分裂是否必然"文化绝灭"（根种基因毫无留存）、"中华文化"是否唯一延续至今的"文化形态"等等，也并非不可讨论。

近现代社会与古代中世纪的传统社会迥然不同。由于新航线的开辟、机器时代和工业化、资本主义和社会主义，信息化、全球化以及军事文化等各方面的发展，人类各地群体，交往日益密切，相互依存、相互交融日益成为主流。这种巨大变化，显然不是"欧西文化形态"一词数语所能概括，也不是"文化形态史观"及其"周期论"所能涵盖。马克思主义史观吸收既往成果，考察了原始社会以来、特别是资本主义诞生后的人类历史，其基本概念和理论结构的科学性（周全、严密、明确）显然不是"文化形态史观"所能比及的。当然，马克思主义史观也在发展，不存在所谓"终极真理"。

雷先生的"文化形态史观"确实重视精神文化和民族精神，但毫未否认自然环境、物质文化的存在及其对精神活动的制约。它十分重视生产工具、十分关注社会集团之间的利益冲突与斗争，怎能说是"唯心论"？文化是物质与精神的统一，精神文化（文化环境）体现在物质文化（物质环境）之中，这是谁也不能否认的"客观存在"或"客观现实"。人类的发展程度越高，精神活动、国民素质所起的作用越大。智力劳动者日益成为主要劳动力。创造性的智力劳动日益成为先进的生产力。"共产主义"的伟大理想更是鼓舞人类前进的精神动力。

社会科学和史学等人文学科的研究对象是人的社会活动，怎能不重视精神活动的研究？马克思主义史学难道不重视研究人类的精神活动？"人文环境"、"景由心造"、"贵在创意"、"人口素质"、"文化传统"、"商品的文化内涵"、"两军相逢勇者胜""软实力""规划领先"以及法学、经济学有关"人性""行为"的种种论点，难道都要归入"唯心论"？持这类论点者有谁会弱智到否认物质的存在及其对精神活动的制约？

哲学和人文学科（历史学等）应当建立在科学的基础上，但不等于科学，更不能代替科学。世界是多元、多层次的。各种学科、各个方面，各个专题、各种角度的学术研究，反映了世界的多元多层。各种论点各有其适用范围。某些论点有所偏颇也完全正常。各种论点，展开争鸣，相互驳难，恰可取长补短，交融增益。哲学家则纠偏持正，综合论衡，这才是"批判"的真正含义。

当年我曾幻想：对"文化形态史观"主动进行"思想批判"，或可避免政治斗争。结果则所谓"批判"，就是"不容置辩""一棍子打死"的"无情斗争"。

"批判"这个译语，大概也是源自当年日本的早期社会主义者或马克思主义者。不知为什么要把它变成"一棍子打死"的"无情斗争"。

当年，冯承柏说：他不明白"何为争鸣，何为批判？"。王金鼎同志更说："批判"，是一个高水平的学术用语。马克思的《政治经济学批判》、《黑格尔法哲学批判》，康德的《三大批判》是什么水平？我们动辄进行的"批判"又是什么水平？这些话我至今怀念。我想起，贺麟先生在"西洋哲学史"课堂上讲到康德的《三大批判》时，在黑板上郑重写了三行字：《纯理论衡》《行理论衡》《品鉴论衡》。今日深感：贺先生这个提示具有重大的意义。

批判（critique）是反对盲从武断，审视既往和现存，认真检验论证，承前启后，更旧创新。决非强词夺理、不容置辩的中世纪对异端的裁判。"批判精神"就是用理性衡量一切的"启蒙精神"，就是"高水平的争鸣"，其目的是为了达到纠偏持正的"论衡"。

教育学重视培育"批判性思维"，"辩证法"的实质是"辩答求真"。"我思故我在"，"怀疑是思考之始"。恢复"批判"这个用词的深刻含义，提倡高水平的百家争鸣，无疑是发展创新思维的必由之路。

至于"斗争"一词又当如何界定使用，这又是大问题，恕不多言。联想到这类译名颇多源自日本。有的水平很高。比如"哲学"，就比梁启超译作"智学"更准确。Communism一词，我国最初曾译作"安民真谛"（音义兼顾）。"共产主义"的译名大概出自日本的基督教社会主义者。近闻有主张译作"大同主义"者。既已通行，不必深究，准确理解就好。

雷海宗先生是我国开拓世界史学科的一代宗师

徐德源、刘明翰 中国青年政治学院

今年（2012年）是雷先生诞辰110周年，也是他逝世的忌辰50周年。雷先生是我国《大百科全书》（外国史卷）中列为中国八位杰出的历史学家之一。他的生命之火黯然熄灭，含冤被"打成右派"时，年仅55岁，正是应为祖国高教事业大展才华的中年。我们不仅应纪念他的诞辰，更应追忆他的忌辰，缅怀和探索他对历史科学，特别是对世界史学科的卓越贡献。

通过对《伯伦史学集》①、雷著《西洋文化史纲要》②和《世界上古史讲义》③等许多著述的阅读，我们了解到雷海宗先生学贯中西，博古通今，治学严谨，满腹经纶。他是我国也是世界上开拓史学、锐意创新的前辈。他对世界史学科的突出贡献，概括说来主要表现在下述四个方面：

（一）他以马克思主义基本原理，辩证的唯物史观为指导，对世界历史的分期、西洋文化史和世界上古史等发表了自成体系的创新灼见。

雷先生在《伯伦史学集》中，辑录了他涉及世界史领域的众多论析，以及他发表过的包括天主教专题等六篇论文和四篇书评。他精辟地指出："真正的史学不是繁琐的考证或事实的堆砌"，而应当"于事实之外须求道理，要有哲学的眼光，对历史作深刻透彻的理解。有价值的史学著作应为科学、哲学和艺术的统一"。④雷先生在许多论文和所写的书评中，表述了他的鲜明观点。例如，指出了"地理大发现"一词，"乃纯欧洲立场的名词"，"含有浓厚侵略及轻蔑的气味，把欧洲以外的地方看为发现、开发、剥削的对象"。⑤

他主张：不可忽略并详细论析"游牧部落在世界史中的地位"，⑥他还反复强调"由于各地生产力的不同，因而各个地区的发展极不平衡。"⑦

雷先生早在而立之年时期（1928—1935年）所发表的几篇述评，都简而精，颇有见地。他对当时西方名家韦尔斯著的《世界史纲》，指出"书虽名为世界史，实仅为'西洋史'。"此书中文译本的错误共约二百条之多，乃出版书局粗疏之故，影响了书的史学价值。

雷先生在评道森著《人类行径》一书时，结合史实，指出"此书题目与内容太不相符"，"不

---

① 雷海宗：《伯伦史学集》，中华书局，2002年9月版。
② 雷海宗：《西洋文化史纲要》，上海古籍出版社，2001年7月版。
③ 雷海宗：《世界上古史讲义》，中华书局，2012年4月版。
④ 《西洋文化史纲要》，上海古籍出版社，2001年，第6页。
⑤ 《伯伦史学集》，中华书局，2002年，第329页。
⑥ 雷海宗：《上古中晚期亚欧大草原的游牧世界与土著世界（公元前1000–公元570）》，《伯伦史学集》，第345–373页。
⑦ 雷海宗：《世界上古史讲义》，第14章"世界上古史总结"，中华书局，2012年，第391页。

妥当与错误处不少"，一些措辞颇不当，不应遗漏处不少……。[①]此外，对某些外国人的著作在评论时也给与肯定。如评拉托来特著的《中华民族之历史与文化》，肯定了"书中地位的分配大致是为得体。"书中所选的"古今大事与重要潮流"令人满意。"他的著作是外国人一本合用的中国指南，也值得中国人一读。"[②]雷先生在评论古德里奇著《乾隆文字狱》一书中，见解深邃。指出乾隆时代"由外表看来虽然极威，实际这是衰落时期的开始；……所以对汉族愈发畏忌，因而更加紧的压迫"，还提出："这书最有价值的一部分恐怕还是后面附录的《禁书现存目录》。"[③]通过雷先生的几篇述评，看出他的学识甚为广博和精湛

（二）提倡多元史观，反对欧洲中心论，反对传统的帝王将相体系，强调社会生产方式决定社会历史的发展。

雷先生一再指出过，历史是多元的，是各个不同的文化在不同的时间、地域，产生和自由发展的历史。他认为历史学研究的对象普遍称为"过去"，而过去有二，一为绝对的，一为相对的。把过去的事实看成某时某地发生过的独特事实，这个"过去"，是绝对的和固定不变的。但是，史学的"过去"则是相对的。历史学必须研究清楚一件史实的前因和后果，以及当时的地位和今天的意义，便之成为活的历史事实。对历史的了解虽凭借传统的事实记载，但了解程序的本来是一种人心内在的活动，是一种时代精神的表现，是一种宇宙人生观用于过去事实的思想反应。[④]

雷先生在教学和科学研究中，长期以来一贯是力图破除欧洲中心论的惯例和王朝体系对历史学束缚的。他一向强调要"纠正过去把'世界史'看成'西洋史'"的错误看法。[⑤]他也一再论述过"决定社会历史发展的绝不是自然环境，自然环境仅只是一定限度之内影响这社会历史的发展，加速或延缓发展的过程。但这种影响又随着社会生产的提高和人对自然控制、利用的增强而逐渐减弱。推动社会历史向前发展的唯一决定力量是社会生产方式。"[⑥]

（三）雷先生主张世界史并非外国史，必须包括中国史，而且应大力弘扬中华文明对世界的贡献。

他在世界史的教学和研究工作中，不仅逐渐摆脱了原来他曾经发挥过的斯宾格勒的形态史观的框架以及影响，而且也反对照搬苏联结构。多年来，雷先生强调的是：

1. 世界史必须包括中国史，应纠正中国史与世界史完全脱节的现象。通过经济、政治、文化，以及人民性和民族性等各个方面，说明中国在世界史的地位和作用。

2. 在世界史的内容中，重视各地区、各个部族、种族之间的相互关系和影响整体和世界全局来研究和阐述世界历史。

3. 必须积极评价和弘扬中华文明。"中国的特殊发展，产生了中国特征，就是人民性和民族性的突出表现。在封建范畴内，中国发展最高，经济最富裕，政治最统一。在这种较高的基础上，人民也有较高的组织力和斗争性。……世界各地在封建范畴内均发展较低，所以没有民族出现，它们成为民族一般为进入资本主义社会过程中的事。所谓'中国封建社会长期停滞'，实际并非停滞，而是在封建范围内长期发展及高度发展。"[⑦]

4. 他还指出，面对百年来在帝国主义侵略下祖国的积弱和科技落后的现实，应充分肯定中国传统文化的积极方面，坚信中华民族具有坚强的生命力，必须担负起"更旧创新"的光荣使命。

---

① 《伯伦史学集》，中华书局，2002 年，第 628–630 页。
② 《伯伦史学集》，中华书局，2002 年，第 621–624 页。
③ 《伯伦史学集》，中华书局，2002 年，第 625–627 页。
④ 雷海宗撰，王敦书整理：《西洋文化史纲要》，上海古籍出版社，2001 年，第 7 页。
⑤ 雷海宗：《世界上古史讲义》，中华书局，2012 年，第 9 页。
⑥ 雷海宗：《世界上古史讲义》，中华书局，2012 年，第 8 页。
⑦ 雷海宗：《世界上古史讲义》，第一章"总论——中国与世界"，中华书局，2012 年版，第 30–31 页。

（四）在历史学的研究方法上，雷先生倡导多学科应互融的综合研究方法，要重视历史学的纵横比较，他曾将历史学研究形象地比喻为类似"房屋的建筑工程"。

雷先生曾指出过，有价值的史学著作，应为科学、哲学和艺术的统一：要做审查、鉴别与整理材料的分析工作；以一贯的概念与理论来贯穿说明史实的综合工作；用艺术的手段以叙述历史的表现工作。[①]他对三者的关系有深刻的论析，指出分析是必要的历史基础，有如建筑房屋时，选择合适的地点，准备充分而必不可缺的建筑材料；综合乃史学的主体，属于修建房屋中最重要的工程。是否具有综合的能力和水平，房屋建筑工程负责人的理论水平是关键。艺术是对所建房屋的美容和装饰。全部工程中，应一定的哲学观点消化史料，解释历史、对历史作透彻的了解非常重要。

（五）世界史教学和研究过程中应注意的问题。

他指出："在科学不断进步、教学不断改善的今日，是不会有十全十美的课本的。课本的缺点恐怕主要须靠教师同志在教学实践中去发现，发现后提出与编者商榷。"[②]雷先生根据当时高级中学课本《世界近代现代史》上册中存在的问题提出了两点：一个是"没有考虑亚洲各国所当占有的恰如其分的地位，这对于培养学生世界范围地看世界问题很重要，而不能养成以欧美为中心地看世界问题的习惯。"再一个是课本中只讲英美法俄四国，将17、18世纪后欧洲各国基本删除，以致对19世纪各国革命的历史来历全然不清，这种体例是不可取的，不能把历史简单化。教学中所用的课本"如能编得视线概括、认识全面，对于整个问题的解决是可以发生一定的推动作用的。[③]

再者，尽人皆知，世界史涉及的国别众多，难度很大。我们从事世界史教学和科研的人员，所掌握的资料比其他部门的材料更少，而且还必须掌握一门、两门以上的外语，才能阅读国外书刊中的研究成果和资料。因此，从事世界史工作的人员对自己应提出更高的要求，加倍努力，认真学习并以马克思、恩格斯的理论为指导。需知"马克思、恩格斯是在资产阶级社会科学的基础上用新方法和新观点为无产阶级建立了新的社会科学。我们要体会马克思、恩格斯研究问题的方法，而不是光揣摩他们的结论。"[④]雷海宗先生远在55年前，曾语重心长地写过："在科学文化事业的大环节中，社会科学恐怕是我们最弱的一环，而这个最弱的一环又极少引人注意，好似它是可有可无，无关重要。他对三者的关系有深刻的论析，指出分析目前社会科学工作很薄弱，同国家建设特别不相称……。"[⑤]

总的来看，雷先生主张对马克思主义应坚持和发展的观点是正确的。他对社会科学、特别是世界史学科如何贯彻"双百方针"所表述的意见，是有启发意义的。早在十年前纪念雷海宗先生诞辰100周年时，我们曾根据雷先生著的《西洋文化史纲要》一书的内容，写出过《欧洲文艺复兴史的理性启迪——雷海宗论欧洲文艺复兴》的论文，[⑥]概述并评价了雷先生对文艺复兴史研究的贡献，故不再赘述。雷海宗先生当之无愧地是我国开拓世界史学科卓有贡献的一代宗师，我们历史学界应当永远纪念和缅怀他！

---

① 雷海宗：《西洋文化史纲要》，上海古籍出版社，2001年，第6—7页。
② 雷海宗：《读高级中学课本〈世界近代史〉上册》，《伯伦史学集》，中华书局，2002年，第637页。
③ 同上，第637，638页。
④ 雷海宗：《在天津教授们关于"百家争鸣"的座谈会上发言》，原在于《人民日报》，1957年4月21、22日，辑入《伯伦史学集》，第639,641页。
⑤ 雷海宗：《给〈人民日报〉的信》，原载于《人民日报》1957年4月28日，辑入《伯伦史学集》，第643页。
⑥ 南开大学史学院编：《雷海宗与二十世纪中国史学》，《雷海宗先生百年诞辰纪念文集》，中华书局，2005年，第147–155页。

记雷海宗先生在教学和学术上的业绩
——纪念先生诞辰 110 周年

李长林 湖南师范大学

关于雷海宗先生在高等学校从事教学和学术活动方面的业绩，学人多有论述，已辑入中华书局 2005 年出版的《雷海宗先生百年诞辰纪念文集》中，下面就我知悉的一些有关情况，加以补记，进一步展现大师的风采。

雷先生在从事大学历史教学方面确为名师，这表现在他能开出多门课，并且教学效果极佳。

据 1995 年清华大学出版社出版的《清华校史丛书·清华人物志》第三册介绍他在 1932 年至 1938 年执教清华大学期间，讲授过中国通史、中国上古史、秦汉史、欧洲中古史、史学方法、史学名著选读等课程，其中中国通史为一年级不分专业的必选课，其内容是讲述史前至最近民族政治社会经济变迁之大势，兼及宗教与思想之发展。

他讲课从不带讲稿，连提纲也不要，深入浅出，条理清晰，生动诱人，使众学子在欢快、渴求下获得了知识和启示。一位学生在《教授印象记》一文中写道："他走进教室，于是他摘下那顶旧呢帽放在台子角上，一枚校徽老是倒插在上面，他真没功夫管这些。你看，喘着气，脸上的红潮还来不及退，他就在黑板上写了一个《战国之社会经济》，信口讲了下去，讲来又是那么的轻快、流利、生动，使历史上一个个人物都活了起来，一件件事都在墙壁上来回的撞，任你是笔记专家也有时会怪你的手欠灵。看过他的《殷周年代考》，又该知道他说话与作文，是一样的严密新颖，使你宁可张嘴听不愿提笔写。他不是讲到吕不韦书成后，悬千金求增减一字的故事吗？这士大夫高傲得太使人发笑了。"

据何炳棣回忆，二十世纪二三十年代，清华大学历史系以陈寅恪先生为首的学者重考证，当时任历史系主任的蒋廷黻为了加强史学结合研究，聘请雷海宗先生来清华大学历史系工作。(详见忻平:《何炳棣教授访问记》，《史学理论研究》，1997 年第 1 期)。雷先生来清华大学以后，引进斯本格勒的文化形态史观，开展史学的综合研究。蒋廷黻在清华大学历史系三年工作总结中，特别提到雷先生的综合史观，较易引起学生共鸣。

雷先生在清华大学开设中国通史课时，编著有讲义《中国通史选读》共 7 册 43 章 769 节，近 90 万字。1934 年由清华大学铅印出版。2006 年由北京大学出版社重印出版，在重印出版说明中，评价了这部讲义。指出："每节起始，为雷海宗先生所撰简明评述，勾勒历史变迁之大势，其下则为史学元典的选录，编者有意引导读者从元典入手，于基本文献中领悟中国史学的内在解释系统。而全书之章节架构，又显出编者以世界史眼光治中国史的新意。或可说，本书是依据中国史学基本文献编辑而成的一部很有特色的通史。"

《中国通史选读》反映了雷先生对中国史研究的成果，这引起陈寅恪先生的重视，曾推荐雷先生主编三卷本英文版《中国通史》，表明他并不否认综合，至少希望之让欧美汉学界了解中国由自己的综合（参见桑兵著：《国学与汉学——近代中外学界交往录》第18页注③，浙江人民出版社，1999年版）。

雷先生1938–1946年在西南联大执教期间，还是担任多门课程的教学，据西南联合大学校友会编的《西南联合大学校史》（北京大学出版社2006年版）第120–121页记载，雷先生开设有秦汉史、罗马帝国制度史、西洋文化史、西洋史学史、西洋中古史、西洋近古史（16–18世纪），外系中国通史，共七门，是十名教授中开课最多者，其次为刘崇鋐教授，共开五门。雷先生教学效果很好，学生多有赞誉。

雷先生在西南联大期间，既教书，又育人，据校友马识途回忆，1944年5月3日由西南联大历史学会主办了"五四"纪念会（实为中共地下党策划），出席晚会的教授有张奚若、闻一多、周炳林、吴晗和雷海宗，在会上他们的发言阐述了五四运动伟大的历史意义，会开的很成功。（详见西南联大校友会编的《云南文史资料选辑》，第三十四辑《西南联合大学建校五十周年专辑》），云南人民出版社，1988年版，第254页）

西南联大附近的文林街上有个文林教堂，教堂牧师是位名叫吉尔伯·贝克（Gibert Baker）的英国人，他颇为风雅，西南联大迁来不久就结识了多名教授，其中雷海宗先生常来此讲演。（见鲲西：《清华园感旧录》，上海古籍出版社2002年版第80页），可见雷先生还热衷于公益活动.

雷先生在西南联大工作期间的1940年4月国民政府教育部成立了史地教育委员会，雷先生同吴稚晖、张其昀、蒋廷黻、顾颉刚、钱穆、陈寅恪、傅斯年等聘为委员，此举反映了雷先生在文教界的威望。

1946年西南联大结束，雷先生在这年10月回到北平清华大学的清华园，讲授的主要课程有西洋近古史、西洋文化史、史学方法、西洋史学名著选读、商周史、秦汉史和中国通史，其中西洋文化史和西洋近古史的讲授给学生留下深刻的印象。他讲起课来，总是围绕中心题目加以发挥，深入浅出，从不"跑野马"，西洋近古史这门课第一章照例是宗教改革，第一堂从中世纪基督教在欧洲的重大作用讲起，以"七礼"（或称"七圣事"）为例，说明当时一个人从出生到死都离不了教会，婴儿一出生，要受洗礼。长大成人结婚，要由教士主持婚礼；临终前，要行敷油礼。这么一讲，立刻引起了学生的极大兴趣。然后，他再讲教会的腐败，很自然的引起了路德的宗教改革，使学生深为受益。他讲课几乎每堂课都有一些令人难忘的名言警句，在讲《堂吉诃德》这部名著的划时代意义时，他说："它使全欧洲在一阵大笑声中结束了骑士文学。"同学们也在一阵大笑声中受到了教益。

在讲课的同时，他先后发表了《历史过去的释义》、《欧美民族主义的前途》、《理想与现实》、《两次世界大战后的世界人心》、《如此世界，如此中国》、《论中国社会的特质》等专论文章。既不乏创见，也反映出其时他对共产党和人民解放战争还不了解，甚而有所误解。尽管如此，在清华解放前夕，有人动员他"南飞"，并愿为他提供机票，他拒绝了，乃决定留了下来。

令人难忘的是雷先生同学生迎接解放军的一桩故事。1948年12月15日，中国人民解放军进驻海淀，清华园解放了，全校师生为之欢呼。18日这一天，雷海宗先生和历史系的几位同学一起去玉泉山，同解放军官兵进行了欢快的交谈。据他的学生万邦儒说：那天雷先生和我们一起去玉泉山看望解放军，回学校时在西校门，看到校门口墙上贴着一张布告，上面写着：

中国人民解放军第十三兵团政治部布告

为布告事，查清华大学为中国北方高级学府之一，凡我军政民机关一切人员，均应本我党我军既定爱护与重视文化教育之方针，严加保护，不准滋扰。尚望学校当局及全体同学，照常进行教育，安心求学，维持学校秩序。特此布告，俾众周知！

此布

政治部主任 刘道生

中华民国卅七年十二月十八日

大家围着观看，有同学情不自禁地朗读着。雷海宗先生出于历史学家对历史文物和史料的敏感，向大家说："这是一件重要历史文物，应妥善保存。"可见，随着人们解放战争的节节胜利，雷海宗先生的思想认识也在发展变化着，此时他已看到了人民解放战争必将彻底胜利。万邦儒等人把这张布告小心翼翼地揭了下来，送到历史系保存。如今这份重要历史文物，仍存放在清华大学档案馆内。雷海宗和全校师生一起欢快地迎接了北平的解放。

解放后，雷海宗为新中国的诞生而欢庆，他积极参加思想改造、土地改革等运动，从思想感情上体会到"为人民服务"的真正意义。他开始系统学习马克思主义，感到发现了一个新世界，似乎恢复了青年时代的热情。他在《读毛主席〈论反对日本帝国主义的策略〉》一文中充满激情地写道："每读到毛主席分析实际问题与指示具体策略的文章，都有一个最强烈的感觉，就是问题分析的透彻与策略指示的正确，也就是说，这些分析与指示都是有预见性的。例如《论反对日本帝国主义的策略》。"

以上雷先生回到清华园的事迹，均见《清华人物志》第三册。

上世纪50年代，雷先生在南开大学工作期间，他积极从事学术研究时，既搞阳春白雪，也重下里巴人，他注意科普工作，他先后在《历史教学》上发表有关世界史领域若干混乱概念的辩误。雷先生还对世界地理的若干概念进行了订误。

据雷海宗先生在《翻译中的小问题一束（二）》（载于1950年12月出版的《翻译通报》第一卷第六期）中指出："英伦三岛"这个错误译名由来已久，在满清末年已经流行，当初也并不是译自British Isles，乃是由误解而来。当时的联合王国，主要有三部分，就是英格兰、苏格兰、爱尔兰，当时人又模模糊糊的知道'联合王国'是一个岛国，所以就望文生义的认为三个'兰'就是三个岛，塑造出这个奇特的名词。"后来人们对联合王国的了解增多，知道它并非三岛。

多年以后，商务印书馆资深译著编辑周颖如在她写的《译稿编辑生涯三十年》一书中，特别提到了雷先生这则订误，鉴于时下仍有人沿用"英伦三岛"这个误译，周颖如呼吁不要因约定俗成而继续误用。（详见周颖如《译稿编辑生活三十年》，世界图书出版公司，2011年版第97—98页）

我们在回顾雷先生学术研究的丰硕成果时，应注意到中国港台学者对雷先生及战国策派的学术成就的评论，有关评论见之于岳麓书社2003年出版的许冠三的《新史学三十年》一书的第十二章。另广西师范大学出版社2007年出版的王尔敏著的《20世纪非主流史学与史家》一书，在前言中列有"战国策学派"专目，对战国策派有言简意赅的评论，指出："战国策派的学人发表的史学、文学、哲学各样论著，表达知识分子对于国家当前处境、世界前途以及文化信持，抗敌决心，一一暴表其种种解析估断，在艰辛中，鼓舞国人团结精神，奋斗意志。战国策学派之一群学者，所取定名为战国策颇具深意。一在表面看清世界大局，一在表明所当时代。这些学者在世界眼光上，在文化使命上，在学问造诣上，俱远远超过浅薄夸张、眼高手低的科学主义史学派。战国策学派之学者群，除沈从文一人外，俱是游学国外而对西方有深入了解。他们在这样艰危的国难时代，表现出对国家有信心，对西方文化有批评，对西方历史参考透熟，有全面、全程评估，对西方文学哲学也有批评，所站是中国知识分子立场。鄙人多年治史所见，战国策学派成员是20世纪的百年中人才精英，为最杰出学界领袖，抱负中国文化使命，以中国为主体。然而却在抗战之后面对国际主义潮流，——被人诬为法西斯主义，而备遭难堪对待，下场可悲。"

　　另王尔敏在《20世纪非主流史学与史家》有专章评论属战国策派的学者沙学浚关于历史地理学的研究成果，并指出大陆学者研究战国策派时对沙氏的研究成果有所疏漏。王氏有关沙氏研究成果的论述，对研究雷海宗的史学思想也有帮助，因为过去学术界曾认为雷先生宣扬过地缘政治学。

批评欧洲中心论第一人——雷海宗先生评韦尔斯

陈志强　南开大学

"著者是西洋著作界一个富有普通常识而缺乏任何高深专门知识的人，所以在他的脑海中'历史'一个名词就代表'西洋史'，而他的历史观也就是他以西洋史为根据所推演出来的一个历史观。"[1]这段话出自雷海宗先生于1928年3月4日发表于《时事新报》的一篇书评，后为1930年中央大学历史系所编《史学》第1期转载，而被评介的书籍即是韦尔斯所著，由梁思成等翻译并有梁启超等参与校订的中文版《世界史纲》。如果我没有说错的话，这篇书评完全可以证明雷海宗先生是我国第一位明确批评欧洲（西洋）中心论的学者。

"欧洲中心论"是从19世纪开始在欧洲流行起来的一种思想理论，"欧洲中心论者是以欧洲为世界历史发展中心的。他们用欧洲的价值观念衡量世界一切。"[2]最初，这种思想观念是伴随着欧洲工业文明的兴起而兴起，而欧洲人对亚洲特别是中国文明的崇拜也是从这个时期发生逆转的，诚如弗兰克所说："欧洲对亚洲的这种仰望直到19世纪欧洲开始工业化和推行殖民主义之后才发生变化。欧洲的工业化和殖民主义活动深刻地改变了欧洲人的观念和态度，包括他们的历史学和社会科学。"[3]以某个地区或民族为中心的历史观自古有之，从亚洲到欧洲自有文字以来撰写历史的古代历史作家都不能摆脱以各自地区和本民族为中心的历史观念。近代以来，世界发生了从农业文明向工业文明发展的重大社会转型，为了认识和解释这一复杂的变化，多种理论观点纷纷出台。其中，"欧洲中心论"随同欧洲经济、政治、军事、文化等诸多方面形成的优势和扩张活动而占据了国际思想文化理论领域的制高点，成为欧洲话语"霸权主义"的重要组成部分。

近200年来，一大批社会思想家、历史家、文化理论家等在各自的学科领域中，自觉或不自觉地成为"欧洲中心论"的编造者、鼓吹者和传播者。弗兰克批评说"这种欧洲中心观念包含着若干支脉。有些支脉特别受惠于卡尔·马克思和沃纳·桑巴特这样的政治经济学家，另外有些支脉则受惠于埃米尔·涂尔干、乔治·齐美尔和马克斯·韦伯这样的社会学家。"包括孟德斯鸠、卢梭、斯宾格勒、汤因比、魏特夫、桑巴特、布罗代尔，直到当代的沃勒斯坦，等等都不能免除欧洲中心论的影响。[4]吴于廑则指出，赫尔德、黑格尔"看来好像是颇能从全世界着眼了，但实际上列出东方是为了否定东方，中国和印度等等根本就不让在世界史上插足。""朗克在晚年编世界通史，不但无视欧洲以外，而且无视东欧，分给欧洲以外的一点篇幅，不过是点缀而已。本世纪之初，威廉士……

---

[1] 雷海宗：《评汉译韦尔斯著《世界史纲》》，《伯伦史学集》，王敦书编，中华书局2002年，第614页。

[2] 吴于廑：《时代和世界历史》（写于1964年），《吴于廑学术论著自选集》，第10页。

[3] 弗兰克：《白银资本——重视经济全球化中的东方》，刘北成译，中央编译出版社2000年，第36页。

[4] 弗兰克：《白银资本——重视经济全球化中的东方》，刘北成译，中央编译出版社2000年，第38—40页。

剑桥三史以及法国《人类的进化》等书……在以欧洲为中心这一基本观点上，和威廉士书如出一辙。……所以不论地理知识如何扩大，历史文献如何积累和传播，都不能保证近代西方对于世界史的研究具有全面的世界观点。"[1]"汤因比的历史思想，实际是别具一格的西方文明中心论。他给这个思想披上了一件眩目的博学的外衣，让人相信世界的历史就是许多文明生生灭灭而最后是西方文明胜利和独存的历史。""看来要反对欧洲中心论还须探索一下如何在世界史中正确体现世界的观点。"[2]"欧洲中心论"史学家们的关键弱点在于习惯于以欧洲为主体，而更多地是囿于种族和阶级成见，不能以世界为一全局，因而也就不能如实地考察世界的历史。就此而言，雷海宗先生敏锐地注意到韦尔斯《世界史纲》的重大理论缺陷，并尖锐指出"我们若详细审查一下，就知道他的书实在不是'史'——至少不是世界史，最好也不过成为前有四不像之长序中间被无关之事所参杂的一本西洋史。"[3]30年后，吴于廑先生在评价同一问题时也说，"晚出的西欧文明则是汇合过去一切文化成就的顶点。这种乐观的自信的一线论弥漫于19世纪后叶及20世纪初期的西方史学界。英国费边主义者威尔斯（H. G. Wells）在1920年发表的《世界史纲》就是这一思想最典型而通俗的代表。"[4]雷海宗先生明确指出此书的理论弱点首先表现在其谋篇布局方面，"所以26章内西洋史就占了16章——61.5%——的地位；其余10章的一小块余地，韦尔斯先生慷然慨然的让亚述人、巴比伦人、埃及人、印度人、中国人、犹太人、回人、蒙古人、日本人去拥拥挤挤的凑热闹。"[5]细查韦尔斯《世界史纲》全书共38章，除了从宇宙到形成人类的12章外，涉及"最初文明"到"近代帝国主义的浩劫"的26章中，详细描述了希腊人、希腊的思想、文学和艺术、亚历山大大帝的一生、亚历山大城的科学和宗教、罗马帝国的兴亡、两个西方的共和国、从提比利乌斯、格拉古到罗马的神皇、海洋和大平原间的罗马诸帝、基督教的兴起和西罗马帝国的衰亡、西罗马帝国和拜占廷帝国衰落期间、基督教世界和十字军东征、西方文明的复兴、列强时代、欧洲君主、议会和列强、美国和法国的新的民主共和国、拿破仑的生平事业、欧洲19世纪的现实和想像、近代帝国主义的浩劫等，而把其他文明作为点缀简略穿插其中，难怪遭到雷海宗先生的嘲讽。[6]

学术界广泛反对欧洲中心论大约始于欧洲爆发第二次世界大战前后，因为残酷的现实沉重打击了弥漫在思想文化界的那种对欧洲文明极端乐观的信念，同时学术界对于世界其它文明研究的新发现和新成果也越来越有力地否定了欧洲中心论的思想根据。被吴于廑先生赞誉为"在这个问题上一再阐发疑义的最有代表性的人物"[7]的巴拉克拉（劳）夫在其1978年出版的《当代史学主要趋势》中详细分析了反思欧洲中心论的思潮，认为甚至像斯塔夫里亚诺斯这样声称"站在月球上观察世界的立场……依然是以西方为中心"，是"经过掩饰的西方中心论。"[8]如果说巴拉克拉夫把包括苏俄学者在内的欧洲中心论者称作"西方种族中心论"显得更为尖刻的话，那么他比雷海宗先生首先提出否定欧洲中心论的意见晚了半个世纪。作为我国世界史学科的开创性人物，雷海宗先生先于国际学术界反思欧洲中心论思潮，深刻洞察到欧洲中心论的理论缺陷，从评论韦尔斯这部"名作"入手，在我国最先提出了对欧洲中心论的批判，并富有先见之明地告诫我国读者必须防止欧洲中心论的不

① 吴于廑：《时代和世界历史》（写于1964年），《吴于廑学术论著自选集》，第10-11页。
② 吴于廑：《时代和世界历史》（写于1964年），《吴于廑学术论著自选集》，第13-14页。
③ 雷海宗：《评汉译韦尔斯著〈世界史纲〉》，《伯伦史学集》，王敦书编，中华书局2002年，第614页。
④ 吴于廑：《巴拉克劳夫的史学观点与欧洲历史末世感》（写于1959年），《吴于廑学术论著自选集》，第234页。
⑤ 雷海宗：《评汉译韦尔斯著〈世界史纲〉》，《伯伦史学集》，王敦书编，中华书局2002年，第614页。
⑥ 韦尔斯：《世界史纲：生物和人类的简明史》（上下卷），吴文藻、谢冰心、费孝通等译，广西师范大学出版社2001年版。
⑦ 吴于廑：《巴拉克劳夫的史学观点与欧洲历史末世感》（写于1959年），《吴于廑学术论著自选集》，第232页。
⑧ 巴拉克拉（劳）夫：《当代史学主要趋势》，杨豫译，上海译文出版社1987年，第248页。

良影响,可惜没有受到国人的关注。①为此,他特别注意到韦尔斯小说家的背景。韦尔斯全称赫伯特·乔治·韦尔斯(Herbert George Wells),1866 年出生于英国肯特郡,在英国皇家学院接受高等教育,曾任教于伦敦大学,后从事新闻工作,撰写过多部科幻小说,如《时间机器》、《隐身人》、《当睡着的人醒来时》和《不灭的火焰》等。诚如雷海宗先生所说,他算不上历史学家,因此"韦尔斯既是善于运用笔墨的小说家,他当然能写出一本前后一致的世界史来。"②毫无疑问,韦尔斯的生平背景特别是其教育背景和工作经历都决定了其思想必定受到"欧洲中心论"的强烈影响。但正是因为韦尔斯的非专业历史家的身份,决定了他并不是刻意宣传欧洲中心论。雷海宗先生就此特别指出,"评者不敢相信著者是看其他一切民族为无足轻重,只有西洋人为上帝的骄子的。其真正的原因,据评者揣想是一种不知不觉中的混乱是非。"③

欧洲中心论的实质是以欧洲作为世界的中心,并以欧洲的价值标准看待世界,因此就引申出欧洲特殊论、欧洲至上论、欧洲模式普世论、欧洲主导论等多种观念。对此,当代学者多有反思与批判。弗兰克尖锐地指出,"工业革命的来临以及欧洲开始在亚洲推行殖民主义的活动,促成了欧洲思想的转变,结果,即使没有'虚构'全部历史,也至少发明了一种以欧洲为首和在欧洲保护下的虚假的普遍主义。到 19 世纪后半期,不仅世界历史被全盘改写,而且'普遍性的'社会'科学'也诞生了。这种社会'科学'不仅成为一种欧式学问,而且成为一种欧洲中心论的虚构。"④为此他全盘否定了以前所有持有欧洲中心论的作家,声称"我们所引述的公认的社会科学理论几乎都渗透着欧洲中心论的偏见和自负。……但是所有公认的说法都需要我们认真地反思和质疑。"⑤这样的质疑声早在弗兰克的这一呼吁之前 70 年就已经由雷海宗先生提出了,并点明韦尔斯断章取义为己所用的手段,"不过处于现在的世界,任人都知道'历史'与'西洋史'不是可以互相混用的名词,所以韦尔斯作《史纲》的时候不得不把西洋以外的诸民族勉强拉进来,但他的历史观是早已固定了,并且是以西洋历史为根据的;所以他参考其他民族史籍的时候,不知不觉中,一定是只将可以证明他的历史观的——至少不同他历史观相背的——事迹引用。"⑥类似的批评也出现在弗兰克的评论中,"在对马克思产生过影响的古典政治经济学家中,斯密([1776]1937:348)曾表示感谢'有关中国以及(古代)埃及和……印度斯坦的财富和发展的精彩报道'。但是,在这方面,马克思却偏爱诸如孟德斯鸠、卢梭这样的哲学家以及詹姆斯·穆勒等人。"⑦

在剖析韦尔斯《世界史纲》持有的欧洲中心论时,雷海宗先生还注意到作者采取的扭曲史实牵强附会的手法,举出第 22 章"希腊思想与人类社会之关系"为例。他对这一章中只谈雅典及其价值与影响,而无视其他重要文明,提出质问:"但世界上同时的两个思想非常发达的区域——春秋战国诸子的中国与释迦牟尼前后诸家的印度——为什么却半句不题?……对于印度韦先生尚把佛教提了一提,对于中国他不但除了孔子外只字未提,并且将秦始皇焚书的事故放在希腊之先。这显然证明韦尔斯看中国古史为一种讨厌的障碍,故随便先把它略叙几句,以了结一场该发生的公案,然后再不慌不忙的归入正文——西洋史。除此之外,我再也想不出第二个缘故来解释这种牵强事实掩抹事实的痕迹。"⑧对于这种按照作者主观意图随意编排历史事实的现象,比弗兰克更早明确怀疑欧

① 韦尔斯的这部书至今仍在国内热销,受到史学界的热捧,一再重印,2001 年广西师范大学出版社再版旧译本后,2006 年上海人民出版社再版梁思成译本,2008 年上海三联出版社则出版了颜世俊、刘仲达翻译的新中文版等。
② 雷海宗:《评汉译韦尔斯著〈世界史纲〉》,《伯伦史学集》,王敦书编,中华书局 2002 年,第 614 页。
③ 雷海宗:《评汉译韦尔斯著〈世界史纲〉》,《伯伦史学集》,王敦书编,中华书局 2002 年,第 614 页。
④ 弗兰克:《白银资本——重视经济全球化中的东方》,刘北成译,中央编译出版社 2000 年,第 39 页。
⑤ 弗兰克:《白银资本——重视经济全球化中的东方》,刘北成译,中央编译出版社 2000 年,第 46 页。
⑥ 雷海宗:《评汉译韦尔斯著〈世界史纲〉》,《伯伦史学集》,王敦书编,中华书局 2002 年,第 614 页。
⑦ 弗兰克:《白银资本——重视经济全球化中的东方》,刘北成译,中央编译出版社 2000 年,第 39 页。
⑧ 雷海宗:《评汉译韦尔斯著〈世界史纲〉》,《伯伦史学集》,王敦书编,中华书局 2002 年,第 615 页。

洲中心论的巴拉克拉夫也指出，"E.M.茹可夫提出的那种关于世界史的分期方法，即把17世纪的'英国资产阶级革命'、1789年的法国革命以及1917年的俄国革命指定为'符合逻辑的人类进步道路上'的关键步骤'。①如果说茹可夫的观点具有代表性，这似乎说明苏联的世界历史概念甚至比西方非马克思主义历史学家更带有西方中心论的性质。"②在这里，巴拉克拉夫与其前辈学者雷海宗先生得出了同样的结论，前者说"由于当代世界基本上是由西方形成的，由此而产生的结果，如果说是下意识的话，就是西方种族中心论。"后者则指出韦尔斯种种欧洲中心论表现，"……十有八九他那是受下意识的指导而作的。"③中、英两国世界史资深学者对欧洲中心论的批评意见如出一口，在世界范围学术批判案例中实属罕见，惟有区别的是，雷海宗先生的观点早出了半个世纪。可见，最早批判欧洲中心论的雷海宗先生不仅指出了韦尔斯这部世界史在篇幅比例方面轻视欧洲以外地区的表现，而且具体分析了该书是如何贬低其他文明突显欧洲文明的。其手段有三，其一曰随意选材，其二曰牵强附会，其三曰掩抹史实。早在上世纪20、30年代就能对欧洲中心论提出如此条理分明的深刻批评意见，实在难得，也为后辈人作出了榜样。

　　近半个世纪以来，否定欧洲中心论或者反思欧洲中心论史观几乎成为学术界的共识，如今没有任何严肃的学者再公开鼓吹欧洲中心论了，因为无论是人类历史发展的现实还是学术研究特别是考古研究的成果都证明，这种源于欧洲列强世界范围殖民扩张的思想理论之错谬。但是，在如何认定欧洲中心论的动机上，学界还存在诸多不同的看法。如前引文中，雷海宗先生明确指责韦尔斯认为"只有西洋人为上帝的骄子"这种欧洲特殊论，除此之外，他进一步提出这部书具有的"帝国主义意识形态"，"《史纲》中的许多章，如果独立，都是很好的通俗历史小册。但只因为韦尔斯硬要把它们拉拢起来，编成一本有系统有先后的所谓世界史，所以倒把事情弄糟了。书名虽为世界史，实只头绪错乱参杂质的西洋史。西洋历史家每将埃及巴比伦亚述等国拉入'西洋'的圈中，强迫他们作'西洋史'的开幕人，已是不通！几乎可说是一种对已死民族的帝国侵略主义；现在韦尔斯把一部比此还不若的一本西洋史硬叫作世界史，是越发没有道理了。"据此，雷海宗先生认为，"欧美现在正在大同主义日渐风行国家主义极盛转衰的时代；《史纲》就是鼓吹大同主义的一本名著。韦尔斯不过是国家主义反动时代的一个产儿，他的《史纲》是受欧洲大战激感而写出的。"④我们不甚了解雷海宗先生所处时代人们对各种思潮的称谓是否准确，对书评中提及的各种理论也还需要认真的对号入座，但是，雷海宗先生将韦尔斯及其《世界史纲》置于历史发展的大背景中去分析，将其纳入时代巨变的环境中去看待，分析鞭辟入里，看法入木三分，这就远远超出了一般书评就书论书就作者论作者的高度，使我们对韦尔斯及其作品又多了一层认识，也使后人对欧洲中心论的多种表现又加深了时代性的解读。相比而言，后来的一些认识似乎欠缺了一些。例如有大学者认为"欧洲资产阶级的史学家讲世界史，以欧洲为中心，如果不坚持侵略，不以欧洲为侵略中心，原没有什么不可。但我们自己讲世界史，如果也以欧洲为中心，则大不可。"⑤前引巴拉克拉夫的著作中，明确将欧洲中心论归为民族主义的历史学，认为"是因为受到爱国主义的压力以及在19世纪非常强大的那种信念的复兴所造成的，这种信念认为历史学的主要目的是铸造民族意识。"正是从这个动机出发，近代欧洲学者形成了欧洲中心论，因此巴拉克拉夫把欧洲中心论称为"西方种族中心论"。⑥尽管巴拉

---

① "世界历史分期方法"，载《第11届国际历史科学大会报告》，第1卷（1960年），第79-83页。

② 巴拉克拉（劳）夫：《当代史学主要趋势》，杨豫译，上海译文出版社1987年，第248页。

③ 巴拉克拉（劳）夫：《当代史学主要趋势》，杨豫译，上海译文出版社1987年，第256页。雷海宗：《评汉译韦尔斯著《世界史纲》》，《伯伦史学集》，王敦书编，中华书局2002年，第615页。

④ 雷海宗：《评汉译韦尔斯著《世界史纲》》，《伯伦史学集》，王敦书编，中华书局2002年，第、第616-617、619页。

⑤ 周谷城：《评没有世界性的世界史》，《文汇报》1961年2月7日，见《周谷城学术论著自选集》，北京师范大学出版社1992年版，第124页。

⑥ 巴拉克拉（劳）夫：《当代史学主要趋势》，杨豫译，上海译文出版社1987年，第237、256页。

克拉夫属于欧洲传统史学的叛逆者，但是，吴于廑先生在 1959 年专论其史学思想的文章中仍然认为他难以摆脱欧洲中心论的巢臼，只是"他的学说比传统西方史学更多一层宿命论的色彩，在本质上是一丘之貉。"而欧洲中心论就是"19 世纪后叶资本主义在欧洲历史上的新的发展以及伴随这些发展而产生的西方资产阶级充满自大狂的思想意识，不可避免地要在历史学领域里得到反映。"①"实质上是为帝国主义的'世界国家'说教。"惟有不同的是，"巴拉克拉夫怎样貌为超脱和明智，也掩饰不了西方史学界的那种末世的哀愁。"②这种看法大体上达到了雷海宗先生书评的水准，而晚出的弗兰克也许说到了问题的实质，"历史家之所以撰写'民族的'历史，是因为受到这么强大的影响，从而反过来丛意识形态上支持欧洲和美洲的'民族主义'，为统治阶级的意识形态、政治和经济利益服务。"③

行文至此，笔者深为雷海宗先生的先见之明所折服。尽管他在 80 多年前就尖锐地批判了欧洲中心论，并告诫世人"研究历史时，最好读别的书，对韦尔斯的书愈少过问愈好。"④但是，我们今天仍然面临清除欧洲中心论的重要任务，特别是许多读者不能分辨《世界史纲》存在的严重理论缺陷和错谬，误将玻璃球当成明珠。一些误导之词借助现代电子技术，大肆吹捧和广泛传播早为我国世界史学大师批评的欧洲中心论及其通俗代表作品《世界史纲》，说"《世界史纲》的叙述笔法，威尔斯的书，深入浅出，文笔畅达，无'高头讲章'之深奥，无诘屈聱耳之艰涩，读来令人赏心悦目，爱不释手。加之最早读到的梁译本的译文。梁思成等先贤，均是精通英语擅长国文的人，由他们译出的书，自然如历史学家雷海宗所说的'又精致又正确'，这不仅便于我们从专业上放心使用，而且便于读者的阅读。"⑤公开曲解雷海宗先生原意竟然到了如此程度，更觉得有必要重申雷海宗先生对欧洲中心论的严厉批判。

① 吴于廑：《巴拉克劳夫的史学观点与欧洲历史末世感》（写于 1959 年），《吴于廑学术论著自选集》，第 244、246 页。
② 吴于廑：《巴拉克劳夫的史学观点与欧洲历史末世感》（写于 1959 年），《吴于廑学术论著自选集》，第 250、251 页。
③ 弗兰克：《白银资本——重视经济全球化中的东方》，刘北成译，中央编译出版社 2000 年，第 24 页。
④ 雷海宗：《评汉译韦尔斯著《世界史纲》》，《伯伦史学集》，王敦书编，中华书局 2002 年，第 620 页。
⑤ http://book.douban.com/review/1319585/ 2012-4-30/12:00；http://baike.baidu.com/view/351270.htm ；http://www.cReader.com 2001-10-25/13:56:20；http://dict.youdao.com/wiki/%E4%B8%96%E7%95%8C%E5%8F%B2%E7%BA%B2/#，2012-4-30/12：00.

雷海宗对中国古代历史特点的揭示
——读雷海宗《断代问题与中国历史的分期》

邹兆辰　首都师范大学

摘要：雷海宗先生于1936年发表了《断代问题与中国历史的分期》一文，后又改名为《中国文化的两周》。此文以文化形态史观，对中外历史的断代问题，对中国历史的具体分期提出了自己独具匠心的见解；并且通过中外历史的比较，揭示出中国历史的重要特点。本文从学术史的角度，研究其内容及思想蕴含，并力图阐释其具有的学术价值。

1932年，正值而立之年的雷海宗回到清华大学任教，重点从事中国通史的教学，同时讲授"殷周史"和"秦汉史"两门选修课。同时，开设"史学方法"一课，向学生介绍西方史学理论和方法。从1934年起便在《清华学报》上发表有关中国史的文章。1935年，清华大学又创办《社会科学》杂志，雷海宗即在其创刊号上发表长文《中国的兵》；1936年，雷海宗又在《社会科学》杂志上发表《无兵的文化》和《断代问题与中国历史的分期》两篇论文。1940年，他将《断代问题与中国历史的分期》一文改名为《中国文化的两周》，与其他几篇文章合成《中国文化与中国的兵》一书出版。1942年，他又写了《历史的形态与例证》，1946年，他将此文与相关的几篇文章汇集成《文化形态史观》一书出版。由此看来，《断代问题与中国历史的分期》一文，是雷海宗以文化形态史观探讨中国历史的滥觞，影响比较大，值得我们认真研读。

一　在断代问题上的独特见解

1. 阐明历史分期工作的意义

雷海宗在文章中开宗明义地指出："历史就是变化，研究历史就为的是明了变化的情形。若不分期，就无从说明变化的真相。"[①]他认为，以往的分期方法是不负责任的，只粗枝大叶地把历史分为上古、中古、近代，就算了事。"比较诚恳一点"的，则分为上古、中古、近古、近世、近代、现代等，这种笼统的分期方法"比不分期也强不了许多。"因为这种分期，"对于变化的认清并没有多大的帮助"，所以要进行分期，就"必须多费一点思索的工夫"。按照雷海宗先生的意思，历史分期是为了阐明历史的变化，为了了解历史的真相，就必须认真思考，提出具有意义的历史分

[①]《历史·时势·人心》，第64页，天津人民出版社2012年版。

期方法。

2. 西方正统分期法的思想来源

雷海宗从世界史学思想史的角度，重点对西洋史上有关上古、中古、近代的正统分期法的来源进行了探究。他认为这是文艺复兴时代的产物。因为当时的文人，对过去几百年以至近千年的历史产生了反感，认为那是野蛮人的时代或黑暗的时代，或者称为中间的时代。他们有一种崇拜古代的思想，认为他们时代的精神与罗马人以至希腊人较为接近。他们认为希腊、罗马的时代是经典的时代，或称为古代或上古，那是"理想时代"或"黄金时代"。而自己所处的时代，就是摩登时代（Modern Age）或新时代。这种来自文艺复兴时代的崇拜古代的心理逐渐延续下来，为人们所公认，历史的三段分法也就延续了下来。

3. 西方正统分期法的弊端

雷海宗认为，这种分期方法对埃及、巴比伦和波斯，除了与希腊、罗马发生关系以外，对这些民族"一概置诸不理"，而且由于地下的发掘的成果把古代越拉越长。但"地下发现的史实太生硬，除了用生吞活剥的方法之外，万难与传统的历史系统融合为一。"近年来，"更把民族、血统完全间断，文化系统线索不明的新石器时代与旧石器时代也加上去"，甚至有人从开天辟地或天地未形成之前讲起。这样使人怀疑史学到底有没有范围，是否一种"大而无外的万宝囊"。

4. 中国史分期上的问题

雷海宗认为，对于中国史的分期断代的问题并没有解决。有人参考西洋史的三段划分法，把中国史分为三段或五段。同时，在中国史学上也有西洋史同样的问题，把地下发现的石器时代，也加在中国历史的前边，"于是中国史戴上一顶石头帽子"。北京猿人发现之后，国人甚至认为"中国历史可以向上拉长几十万年"。他认为，这是一种"盗谱高攀的举动"，因为"北京猿人早已断子绝孙，我们决不会是他的后代。"他强调，"地方与民族打成一片，在一定的时间范围以内才有历史。民族已变，文化的线索已断，虽是同一个地方，也不是同一的历史。"[①]同一地方也有历史，但那是属于地质学或自然地理学的范围以内，不属于史学范围。

5. 必须认清文化上的独立性才可谈分期

雷海宗认为，"西洋"一词在欧美人用来意义已经非常含混，到中国就更加空泛。实际上"西洋"有三种不同的意义，可称为泛义的、广义的、狭义的。狭义的西洋专指中古以下的西欧，就是波兰以西的地方，近四百年来又包括新大陆，这是以日耳曼民族为主创造的文化。广义的西洋，除中古与近代的欧西外，又加上希腊罗马的所谓经典文化，也就是文艺复兴时代的所谓上古文化。泛义的西洋，除希腊罗马与欧西外，又添上回教与地下发掘出来的埃及、巴比伦以及新石器时代，甚至再加上欧洲的旧石器时代。他认为，狭义的用法，最为妥当；广义的用法，还可将就；泛义的用法，绝要不得。因为文化是个别的，断代应当以每个独立的文化为对象，不能把几个不同的个体混为一谈而牵强分期。"我们必须把每个文化时间与空间的范围认清，然后断代的问题以及一切的史学研究才能通行无阻。"[②]

---

① 《历史·时势·人心》，第67页，天津人民出版社2012年版。
② 《历史·时势·人心》，第69页，天津人民出版社2012年版。

二 对中国历史各阶段特点的揭示

雷海宗此文的重点在于说明中国历史的分期，这是一个十分独特的见解。

他把四千年来的中国史分为两大周：第一周。由最初到公元383年的淝水之战，大致是华夏民族创造文化的时期，外来的血统与文化没有重要的地位，这一周的中国可以称为"古典的中国"。第二周从公元383年到写文章的当时（1936年），是北方各种胡族屡次入侵，印度的佛教深刻地影响中国文化的时期。这时的中国已经不是纯华夏族的古典中国，而是胡汉混合、梵华同化的新中国，是一个综合的中国。

雷海宗把第一大周的中国史分为五个时代：（一）封建时代（公元前1200—前771年）；（二）春秋时代（公元前770—前473年）；（三）战国时代（公元前473—前221年）；（四）帝国时代（公元前221年—公元88年）；（五）帝国衰亡与古典文化没落时代（公元88年—383年）。

第二大周也可分为五期：（一）南北朝、隋、唐、五代（公元383—960年）；（二）宋代（公元960—1279年）；（三）元明（公元1279—1528年）；（四）晚明盛清（公元1528—1839年）；（五）清末中华民国（公元1839年以下）。

雷海宗的这种分期方法，不仅是对中国历史的时代进行了断限，划分出了历史的阶段，更重要的是他揭示了各个时期的历史特点：

1. 盘庚迁殷以后的商周是封建时代。

他根据《竹书纪年》记载，在公元前1300年，即盘庚迁殷的时候，可认为是封建时代的开始。但是，他并没有认为在此以前中国就没有历史。比如，公元前3000年以后，黄河流域进入新石器文化阶段。这时期的遗物可以证明，这时期的人已经是日后华夏民族的祖先。到公元前1700年左右，已经出现两个强大的部落——夏和商。可以断定，这时必有较可靠的历法并发明了文字。周灭商以后，周王把东方领土征服，封子弟功臣为诸侯，周建立起封建的制度，天子只直接统辖王畿，诸侯是世袭的。到约公元前900年左右，封建帝国渐呈裂痕，周平王东迁后进入春秋时代。这一时期的精神生活为宗教所包办，人与神的界限并不严明。

2. 春秋时代是大国争霸的时代。

平王东迁以后，实际独立的列国并争，齐、晋、秦、楚四大国特别强盛，中原的小国成为争夺的对象。列国内部已经统一，在国君的统治下，贵族包揽政治，所以也是封建残余的时代。吴与越的争霸，是最后的春秋战争。春秋大部分时间是在宗教的笼罩之下，但由于大局的剧变，出现独立的思潮。有为旧制度辩护的人，如孔子；有反对旧制度的人，如邓析；也有逃避现实的人，如一些隐士。

3. 战国时代是战争最烈的时代，但也是百家争鸣的时代。

这一时代，各国内部都起了社会变化，残余贵族被推翻，诸侯成了专制独裁的君主。人民都要去当兵，战争以尽量屠杀为手段，以夺取土地为目的。各家争鸣，都提出适当的方案去解决当前的严重问题。儒、墨、法、阴阳都希望人君实行他们的理想以平天下。

4. 秦、西汉及东汉中兴的三百年是中国的帝国时代。

秦始皇创立了自古未有的新局面，此后的二千年统一是常态，分裂是变局。秦、西汉、东汉中兴的三百年，统一最长、最稳固、最光荣，二千年来中国的基础都立于这三个世纪。秦始皇设立的制度，成为此后历朝谨守的遗产，中国的疆土也在汉武帝时立下大致规模。社会制度也凝结于此时，传统的宗法社会受到打击，重农抑商政策使大地主势力日盛。儒教成为国教，孔子虽然没有成神，素王也演化为一个很神秘的人物。道家渐渐变成道教，各种迷信成了其教义。汉的精神界是儒、道、阴阳合同统治的天下。

5. 汉末三国魏晋时期是帝国衰退时代。

汉和帝以下，帝国衰退日益显著。内政日坏，外族势力日大，北部边疆成了胡人的天下。在内外交迫的形势下，大小的变乱不断发生，把帝国命运断送。三国鼎立之后，晋虽临时统一，但内部不能整顿，外力不能消灭。三国魏晋百年挣扎，胡人终于占据中原，汉人大批南迁。淝水之战是一个决定历史命运的战争。当时胡人如果胜利，后果不堪设想。精神方面也呈衰颓状态，儒教渐渐被人厌弃，颓废的老庄学说兴盛，清谈流行，平民社会迷信程度加深，佛教暗中侵入，胡人血统也在开始内侵。

在中国历史的第二大周里，中国历史也呈现一些特点。第二周也分为五期或五个时代，由于在政治社会方面一千五百年里没有什么本质的变化，大体上是保守流传秦汉帝国所创设的制度。

1. 南北朝、隋、唐、五代是一个大的过渡、综合与创造的时代。

南北朝二百年间，北方胡族与汉人同化，江南蛮人也被汉人同化。到隋统一宇内，这个新的汉族才能创造一个能与秦汉媲美的大帝国。南北朝佛教大盛，以儒、道为代表的旧文化感到外力的威胁，新旧文化竞争的空气紧张。当种族混一时，佛教已与旧有文化打成一片。伟大的隋唐帝国与灿烂的隋唐文化都是南北朝二百年酝酿的结果。隋唐帝国是一个原由胡汉混成，现在仍由胡汉合作的二元大帝国。佛教的各派别在此时达到最高的程度。安史之乱后，政治上的强盛时期已成过去，文化发展也渐衰弱，帝国的统一名存实亡，佛教的极盛时期也已经过去。因此，南北朝、隋、唐、五代代表一个整个的兴起、极盛与转衰的文化运动。

2. 宋代的三百年是一个整理清算的时代。

北宋统一后，各种难题仍不能解决，府兵制破裂，军队成了流民集团，财政紊乱，人民负担繁重，科举制度僵化，人才难以出现，国家的难题无人应付。外族侵占的土地没有能力收复，每年还需要向辽、夏入贡，才得苟安。整个中国极需彻底地整顿。王安石变法代表一个面面俱到的整理计划，处处针对各种积弊，以图挽回中国的颓运。但守旧势力太强，变法完全失败。中原又丧于外人，宋朝只得渡江偏安。最后连江南也不能保，中国第一次亡于异族。宋代的理学是一种调换招牌的运动。宋代诸子调和了中国式的佛教、原有的道教与正统的儒教，产生一个混合物，可称为新儒教。

3. 元明两代是一个失败与结束的时代。

元代使整个中国受制于外族，这是过度保守、过度松散的政治社会的当然命运。蒙古人不肯汉化，但不久却也腐化，不到百年就被推翻。明是唐以后唯一的整个中国自治统一的时代，东北、西北等塞外土地被并入帝国的范围，这比宋代大有可观，但内里的腐败也不能掩盖。科举制度僵化为八股文技术，民族的心灵被封闭，难以找到经世的通才。政治的发展达到腐败的尽头，如廷杖制度，如宦官专权。政治未上轨道，整个局面感到是人类史上的一大污点，整个民族与文化发展到绝望状态。黑暗中的一线光明就是汉族闽粤系的向外发展，证明这个民族尚未走上绝境，内在的潜力仍能打开新的生路。元、明两代的思想界也同样缺乏生气。程朱理学在宋末已成正统派别，思想方面很难再有新的进展。但王阳明是人类史上的少见的全才，他是最后的有贡献的理学家，是明代唯一的伟人。

4. 晚明盛清是政治文化完全凝结的时代。

明以下的三百年间，没有产生一个惊人的天才，也没有创造一件值得纪念的特殊事业，三个世纪的功夫都在混混沌沌的睡梦中过去。明末，西洋人、鞑靼、日本、满洲四种势力都有破灭明朝的可能，而成功的是满洲，整个中国二次亡于异族。但满人不想摧毁中国传统文化，一概追随明的规模，一切都平平庸庸。在沉寂的三百年中，清朝对西南边省的汉化运动，是唯一影响远大的事件。清代理学没有新的进展，盛清时的智力都集中于训诂考据，没有新的创造。

5. 鸦片战争以下的近百年，是传统政治文化总崩溃的时代。

中国民族与文化的衰征已非常明显，满人经二百年统治后已经开始腐化，政治社会不见有复兴的希望，精神方面也没有一点新的冲动。西洋的政治机构、经济组织、文化势力，猛烈冲击中国，中国最后一败涂地，最近才开始对西洋的真相有所认识。代表传统文化的帝制和科举都已废除，都市已大致西洋化。中国文化的第二周已经快到结束的时候。

三　在中外历史比较中揭示中国历史的特点

在分析了中国历史各个阶段的历史特点以后，雷海宗又把中国历史与世界历史进行了比较，探讨其中的共同点和特殊性。

他认为："从人类史的立场看，中国历史的第一周并没有什么特别，因为其他民族的历史都有类似的发展。任何文化区，大概起初总是分为许多部落或小国家，多少具有封建的意味。后来这些小国渐渐合并为少数的大国，演变成活泼生动的国际局面。最后大国间互相兼并，一国独盛，整个的文化区并为一个大帝国。这种发展，在以往的时候可以说是没有例外的。在比较研究各民族的历史时，整个文化区的统一是一个不能误会的起发点。"① 他根据埃及、希腊、罗马和中国的例子来说明这一历史情况。他断定，一个文化区由成立到统一，大致不能少于一千年，不能多于一千五百年。其他民族由于材料的缺乏，不是那么清楚，但是可以以此来推论，也可以大体断定，如印度，如巴比伦。

同时他还认为，用这个方法也可以对将来的大概趋势能够比较认清。比如，西洋文化，最初限于欧西，后来普及到整个欧美并泛滥于全球，这个有关人类命运的文化的前途怎样呢？他说："如果西洋文化不是例外，它大概也终久要演化到统一帝国的阶段。"不过这件事何时实现，比较难说。根据中国和希腊的情况来推算，西洋封建与列国并立的两时代，一般以公元 1500 年左右为枢纽；以此推算西洋大帝国的成立当在公元 2050 年左右。现在西洋正发展到中国战国中期的阶段，少数列强激烈竞争与称雄世界，多数弱小国家完全失去自主的情况，就相当于扩大的中国的战国，未来的大局似乎除统一外，别无出路。

以上他所说的是中国文化与世界文化的共同性。但这种共同性只是体现在中国文化的第一周上，而中国文化的第二周"在人类史上的确是一个特殊的例外"。没有其他的文化，我们能确切的说它曾有过第二周返老还童的生命。埃及帝国被波斯征服，因而渐渐消灭，有一千一百年；巴比伦帝国也被波斯征服与消亡不过一千五百年。罗马帝国由成立到灭亡不过一千五百五十年。但是，中国由秦并六国到今日已经过二千一百五十年，在年代方面不是任何其他文化可能及的。其他任何比较持久的文化在帝国成立以后也没有能与中国第二周相比的伟大事业。在中国历史的第二周，"二千年间大体能维持一个一统帝国的局面，保持文化的特性，并在文化方面能有新的进展与新的建设，这是人类史上绝无仅有的奇事。其他民族，不只在政治上维持如此之长，并且在文化方面也绝没有这种二度的生命。"他说："能创造第二周的文化才是真正值得我们自夸于天地间的大事。……这在人类史上是只有我们曾能作出的事，可以自负而无愧。"②

由此看来，按雷海宗先生的观点，在人类史上仅仅中国有这种第二周文化，其他国家都没有，这就是中国历史的最突出的特点。

四　对文章的总体评价

雷海宗这篇文章是在 1936 年发表的。这时距离他 1927 年从美国芝加哥大学获博士学位回国不

---

① 《历史·时势·人心》，第 79 页，天津人民出版社 2012 年版。
② 《历史·时势·人心》，第 81 页，天津人民出版社 2012 年版。

到十年。1927年他在南京中央大学主要讲授世界史，1931年到武汉大学也是讲授世界史，但是他已经开始了对中国史的研究。1932年来到清华大学讲授中国史也不到四年。这时候，他还是一位年仅34岁的青年教师。但是，他已经具有很好的中国史和世界史的教学与研究的功底，能够做到学贯中西。同时，他在美国除主修历史外，还副攻哲学，获得的是哲学博士。因此，他具有很强的理论思维能力。对于西方的新的学术思想、学术理念有很敏锐的感觉，并且能够用之来对中外历史问题进行深入的审视。《断代问题与中国历史的分期》一文就是他运用文化形态史观来认识断代问题，认识中国历史的分期和中国历史特点的尝试。

1. 以时代特征为标准的分期方法

雷海宗把中国的历史分为两大周，每周五个时期。这是他个人的独具特色的一种历史分期方法，体现了以文化形态史观来观照中国的历史的一种努力。确实，他对每一个时代的把握，不是单纯地考虑朝代的更替，也不是时间的长短，而是以其时代特征为标志的。在文化形态史观的学者看来，历史是多元的，每一个民族的历史都是一种独立的文化发展，包括政治的组织形式，民族关系的状况，宗教、哲学的发展，这些情况的综合就形成它特殊的时代特征。比如，西周的时代是封建的时代，春秋的时代是大国争霸的时代，战国的时代是百家争鸣的时代，秦和两汉是帝国时代，汉末魏晋是帝国衰退的时代等等。第二周的历史也各有其时代特征，虽然他没有给它们定出名称，而只是以朝代名来划分。例如，南北朝、隋、唐、五代是一个大的过渡、综合与创造的时代，宋代便是一个整理的时代，元明是失败与结束的时代，晚明盛清则是完全凝结的时代，清鸦片战争以后则是总崩溃的时代。而标志这些变化的核心内容就是政治和文化。

这种分期方法，从一定程度上说确实反映了中国历史发展变化的外在表现，体现了这一时代的历史特征。用这种方法去研讨中国历史的分期，并进而探讨各个阶段的历史活动内容，就能够找到具有代表性的历史事件、历史关系、历史制度、历史人物。用这种历史观，的确能看到世界上不同时期、不同民族、不同国家的历史的共同性，也能发现其显著的特殊性。

2. 分期方法的局限性

雷海宗此文，以政治文化为中心来划分历史的时代，也是有明显的局限性的。这种分期方法，不考虑生产力发展水平，不考虑生产方式的状况，只以政治文化为中心来划分历史阶段，就难免看不到历史发展的真正进步。历史的真正进步，应该是以生产力的发展为中心，通过生产方式的变化从而产生相应的社会经济组织、政治状态、文化状态、社会状态的变化发展。没有经济发展这根主线，就会把社会历史发展的不同历史阶段混淆起来，甚至根据一些表面现象来判断历史的发展水平。例如，他在文中说今日的西洋文明，还处于列国称雄的时代，还没有形成统一的帝国，认为这个发展阶段相当于中国战国中期的局面，将来会发展到统一帝国的局面，就像中国的秦帝国的统一一样。他预计到2050年前后会实现这种统一。从分散的列国争雄到实现统一，建立大帝国，这也许是历史的一种趋势。但是，西洋文明发展到今天，绝对不能说只相当于中国的战国中期，因为对这期间的生产力的发展，文明的进步，现代化的进展都不考虑在内，把不同历史阶段的国家发展进行这样表面的类比是不妥当的。因为它不符合历史的基本事实，也不符合历史发展的辩证规律。

3. 雷海宗在历史分期方法上的与时俱进

1936年，雷海宗发表《断代问题与中国历史的分期》一文时，他还没有掌握唯物史观，他只能以他当时所接受的文化形态史观来探讨中国史的分期问题。但是在新中国成立以后，他开始掌握唯物史观，体现在历史分期问题上，就改变了30年代对历史分期问题的主张。

我们看到2012年中华书局出版的王敦书先生整理的雷海宗先生《世界上古史讲义》，在其总论中开宗明义地就讲到历史分期问题。他说："人类社会的发展过程，按其生产方式的不同，亦即社会性质的不同来划分其各个历史阶段，则有不同历史阶段，即氏族社会、奴隶社会、封建社会、资本主义社会与共产主义社会。"但他也强调，世界史的分期不能完全按照社会发展史的五个阶段来划分，因为学习历史除了这种社会阶段的观念以外，还需要具有严格的时代与年代的观念。因此，"就某一个个别的地区和民族的历史分期来说，则应在其历史的发展过程中，依其标志着生产方式发生根本变革的重大历史事件所发生的年代来分期。"①这说明，雷海宗先生在1952-1953年讲授世界上古史时，已经接受了唯物史观，把人类社会历史发展的一般规律与关系历史发展的重大事件的年代结合起来进行分期。他把世界历史的分期划分为氏族社会（公元前三千年以前）、上古（公元前三千年至公元五、六世纪间，以奴隶社会为主）、中古（公元五、六世纪间至十七世纪，以封建社会为主）、近代（公元1640年至1918年，以资本主义为主）与现代（自1917年十月革命至现在，社会主义与资本主义之间的斗争时期）五个时期。

在讲到上古中国历史的概述时，他也有了新的历史阶段的划分方法。他说："上古中国历史的发展大致可以分为三大阶段：第一阶段是氏族社会转入阶级时期，约当'虞'夏两代；第二阶段是统一形式下封建分裂时期——商殷至战国；第三阶段是大一统时期——秦至南北朝。在概述上古中国历史内容时，他更是着重讲了不同历史阶段社会经济的发展，阶级斗争的情况，同时也讲思想文化的发展。

新中国成立以后，雷先生已经不再强调他的中国史的两周说，也不同意用两周说来套用五种生产方式。据30年代曾经听过雷先生讲课的卞僧慧先生回忆：1950年他重访清华，曾问过先生，以先生往日的两周分期法来看今天中国社会分期各说，如以原始共产社会和奴隶社会相当于第一周，以封建社会和半殖民地半封建社会相当于第二周，魏晋封建说是否更可取？先生答：这是两回事，不能比附。②这说明他已经在以唯物史观重新认识中国古代历史的分期，不同意把自己过去的两周说来勉强比附五种生产方式说。

雷海宗先生关于中国史的两周说的分期方法，是在他在上世纪三、四十年代尚未接受唯物史观时对中国历史分期问题的一种尝试性的分期方法，并且他将这种理论作为他的文化形态史观的重要内容。这种观点，在那个时代有其学术价值和现实的意义，并渗透着爱国主义的精神。它的出现，代表那一代学人对于中国历史发展特点的一种理性的思考，一种中外比较的宏观的探索，也体现出对于中华民族前途与命运的积极关切。

---

① 《世界上古史讲义》，第1页，中华书局2012年版。
② 南开大学历史学院编：《雷海宗与二十世纪中国史学》，第40-41页，中华书局2005年版。

雷海宗对国际汉学研究的关注——以 1930 年代的书评为例

朱政惠 华东师范大学

雷海宗（1902-1962）是我国现代史上著名历史学家，他不仅精通中国历史，对西方历史也很娴熟，史学理论研究上犹有特别建树。他还十分关注国际汉学，注意其研究动态，用批判眼光看待分析其研究成果。1930 年代，他曾在《清华学报》发表数篇对国际汉学著作的评论文章，虽然这类文章在其一生所撰论文中比例不是很高，但却是其学术研究中一个值得关注的亮点。

雷先生书评的一个重要特点，就是从大局上关心当时有重要影响的汉学著作，关心那些能体现学术前沿、有突出特点的成果，包括学术活跃度相当高的学者的作品。他所写的《赖德烈：〈中国人的历史与文化〉》①就是这样的一篇书评。作者赖德烈（Kenneth Scott Latourette）当时已是耶鲁大学教授，刚成立不久的美国中国学研究促进会（The Committee on the Promotion of Chinese Studies）会长，对推动美国汉学发展有很多想法和举措。他写这本书就是希望很好宣传中国历史，接得上卫三畏的《中国总论》。他说卫三畏 1883 年对该书修订后，没出现过新的有这样份量的专著，希望自己的作品能成功。②当时国际汉学界颇为肯定赖的这本新书，称赞是书为卫三畏后又一部重要的专论中国研究的总括性著作。著名远东专家宓亨利（Harley Farnsworth MacNair）称，这无疑是一本"新的里程碑性质的中国历史研究专著"，对欧美国家了解中国有普及意义。③荷兰汉学家戴闻达（J. J. L.Duyvendak）认为，赖书成功促进了美国中国学，"拉近了美国汉学与当代学术的距离"，有利于了解"越来越重要的中国"。④雷海宗抓住对这本书的评论，显然注意到国际汉学研究的这一热点，为此而用心去撰写评论感想。他当时还撰写了《费子智：〈中国文化简史〉》⑤的书评。这是英国人费子智（C.P.Fitzgerald）的作品，此书看似简略，影响却很大，以后也多次再版。雷海宗当然也注意到了这本书的价值，希望看个究竟，掂掂份量，评个子丑寅卯。这就是他这方面书评的一个重要特点。在他看来，那些或可代表国际汉学界学术旨趣与前沿走向的著作，是中国学术界应该了解和

① Kenneth Scott Latourette, *The Chinese ,Their History and Culture*（《清华学报》1935 年第 2 期）

② Kenneth Scott Latourette, *The Chinese, their history and culture*, New York, The Macmillan Company, 1934. Preface.

③ Harley Farnsworth MacNair, Untiled, *The American Political Science Review*, Vol. 28, No. 3 (Jun., 1934).

④ J. J. L. Duyvendak, Untiled, *Pacific Affairs*, Vol. 7, No. 2 (Jun., 1934)。一些评论还说，这本书"一定会引起历史学和社会科学研究师生的极大兴趣"，"对那些专职于中国文化和生活方向的研究者的影响也是无可估量的"。其它书评还有如：Sister Justina, Untiled,The Americas,Vol.3,No.2(Oct.,1946).pp.270–271, Cyrus H. Peake, Untiled,*Journal of the American Oriental Society*, Vol. 56, No. 4 (Dec., 1936), C.W.Bishop,Untitled,*Geographical Review*,Vol.24,No.4(Oct.,1934),pp.686–687 等。

⑤ C.P.Fitzgerald, *China:A Short Cultural History*（《清华学报》1936 年第 4 期）.

把握的，这方面的工作要及时做。

他对国际汉学著作的评价，很关心其原创程度的分析，即在西方相关研究中的原创程度，与中国同类成果相比较的原创程度。他对这一问题看得很重，认为是学术发展之本，所评论的几书都有这样的意图。他称有的著作不一定完善，但只要有这一份特质，应该得到相应重视。他所写的《傅路德：〈乾隆朝的文字狱〉》[1]就体现这一点。他说这方面的研究在美国实在罕见，著者傅路德（Luther Carrington Goodrich）是在做一次"勇敢的尝试"，包括有其"动人见解"。他说举国上下人心惶惶之后，官方史书很难寻找相应资料，私人日记、野史笔记也仅发现一二，作者作此探索不易，是"深得史家恢复往绩的本行"。他还肯定书中的一些学术观点，包括对乾隆大开文字狱原因的分析。[2]当时，欧美学者对此著作的重视，也都是注意其选题的大胆，称是西方语言的作者"所完全忽视的"，"甚至中国学者也没有给予过恰当的重视"。[3]费正清也评论称其尝试勇气十足。[4]雷先生这种对创新理念的强调，还包括对著作中文献资料引用突破程度的考察。他认为《乾隆朝的文字狱》有价值，还在于其后面所附的禁书目录，虽然后人会发现其中或有遗漏，但已属很重要的参考书目了。包括赖德烈的《中国人的历史与文化》，他也认为其每章后面所开列书目的价值高，"因为西方中国学者近年来研究的结果，至今尚无人统计整理"，称读者对赖教授的这类努力"应欢迎感激"。

雷海宗的评论还很看重这些著作的编纂框架、谋篇布局、详略安排，认为能反映出学者的编纂意图，是学术主旨的体现，得失分析的窗口。他说赖德烈《中国人的历史与文化》分上、下两部分处理的方式是合适的。他很肯定该书上册上起石器时代、下迄 1933 年通史的写法，说以往西人所著中国通史不出两类：一类专讲秦汉以上的中国，以后二千年的史实"反倒三言两语了事"；一类只注意鸦片战争以下的外交史，"把以往四千年的一大段公案缩为一篇短序"——赖氏力避两类"易犯的错误"，就另有蹊径了。他认为赖书上册以四分之一的篇幅论述上古秦汉时代的做法也很巧妙，为明了整个中国历史，有关中国文化创造期的历史应该有"相当的认识"；而六朝至满清中期占二分之一篇幅，以后一百年历史又有四分之一地位，比例也很合适，"作为一种简单的中国通史，这个篇幅的分配可算恰当"。关于费子智的《中国文化简史》，他认为编纂处理也不错——当时西方人比较偏重 19 世纪以下中国历史研究，而费书能叙述从古代到太平天国这一段中国文化史，就足以让西方人了解到这三千年的文化史。他认为作者把这三千年历史分成七个时期的做法也比较妥适，"大致可称恰当"。当然他对这些著作的评价，还很重视其学术理念的考察。他批评一些中国学者的通史著作把宝贵篇幅让位于历代官制及其干燥事实描述的做法，认为只能对那些"想象力枯竭的学究"发生兴趣——这样写便只有名称的改变，"无本质的变化"，"往往是纸上的宪法，不是实际的制度"。他指出，赖德烈的书（《中国人的历史与文化》）就很注意"古今的大事与重要潮流"，虽有制度描述，但也只是秦汉创制，以后相袭，省了无限笔墨。他还十分赞同其下编的写法，涉及政治、经济、宗教、社会、语言、文学各方面的探讨，称这种对中国文化的鸟瞰是"很周到的社会写照"，不只对欧美人大有帮助，就是中国读者"也能从其中得些新的

---

① Luther Carrington Goodrich , *The Literary Inquisition of Chien-Lung*（《清华学报》1935 年第 4 期）
② 傅路德认为乾隆打开文字狱的原因是因为社会已见衰相，皇帝的心理问题是起始的一个重要原因。
③ Carroll B.Malone,The Literary Inquisition of Chien-lung by Carrington Goodrich ,Journal of the American Oriental Society ,Vol.55,No.4(Dec.,1935),pp.477-479.
④ 费正清所说的，是指这本书以后，傅路德成为哥伦比亚大学中国学研究的主要领军人物，也一度是美国东方学会的主席。有关傅路德的评论，还可以参见：Thomas D.Goodrich, Luther Carrington Goodrich (1894-1986): Bibliography, *Journal of the American Oriental Society* ,Vol.113,No.4(Oct.-Dec.,1993),pp.585-582.

知识"。①他认为这种充实的、有关社会横切面的描述，足以帮助我们"明白自己团体以外的社会"。笔者发现，这是他与当时西方书评颇不一样的观点。②

诚然，雷的评论也很用心观察这些著作的史料运用、作者的中国历史认识及其相关理解的准确程度。他认为这是学者基本功的反映，也有个对子孙后代负责的问题。这方面的探讨，批评多于肯定。大致有这样几类：其一，揭露对中国历史认识的谬误。他说赖德烈称汉代有儒家、墨家、法家，却把很重要的阴阳家忘记了。他还批评刘向受过佛教影响的观点，说那时刘向可能连浮屠的名字也不曾听到。关于唐代北方人自称汉人、南方人自称唐人的说法，他也表示不同意见，称著者研究中国多年，"决不至以为长江以南的人都自名为唐人"。费子智在书中称明太祖建都金陵正确、明成祖北迁失策，他也表示不同看法，认为明成祖如不北迁，"将来不知要演出多少次靖难"，北迁"绝对的必需"。其二，批评对中国历史理解的无据。他说赖德烈在著作中说孔子不幽默，但这种说孔子不幽默的观点本身"就非常幽默"。他说费子智称中国最早的法家是商鞅的说法也没有证据，称秦始皇坑儒是因为他们私下藏书的说法也不知出于何典。其三，批评这些著作中汉名、译音的混乱。他说傅路德的翻译还是不敢恭维，"中文程度似乎还不能胜任"，"时常遇到上下不连贯、意义不清楚，或情节可疑的词句"，其他学者也有此类问题。他对这些错误的揭露不遗余力，用辞尖刻。雷先生说，涉及广泛的研究错误似乎难免，但被批评者应该知错，反省更正，不能固执己见，谬种流传。

很显然的，这些评论即使在今天看来也很有道理，到位的。雷先生能对当时国际汉学家的著作有如此深入尖锐的批评，是其学识才干的不凡体现。没有坚实的中国学术根底，没有融贯东西的渊博学识，没有介入国际学术前沿的深切关怀，写出这样的文章是不可能的。

介于两次世界大战间的 1930 年代上半期，在西方尤其是美国，出于远东战略的考虑，加强了对中国问题的探讨，美国中国学研究促进会就是这时候诞生的。一批美国本土汉学家如恒慕义、赖德烈、傅路德、卜德、韦慕庭等相继走上舞台，形成新的汉学家队伍。这支队伍与欧洲汉学家汇合，汇成影响颇巨的欧美汉学团队。由此，国内学术界也出现了对国际汉学发展的关注，与国际汉学界频繁互动。报章杂志注意对国际汉学动态介绍，出版社组织对汉学名著翻译，研究机构派遣学者海外访学。③当时的学术界已有一种学术自觉，希望了解国际汉学研究最新情况，把握这些异域中国研究成果前沿。诚然，一个多世纪的积贫积弱，多少使国学大家们感受到中国研究主流地位受挑战的困惑，有所谓汉学正统"西京还是东京"的慨叹。④雷海宗对国际汉学的关注及其评论，与当时这样的历史背景及其学术关怀有关。作为清华历史系主任的他，也许不能抽暇写更多这样的批评文章，但就这几篇，已足够显示其境界与水平，体现了中国学术界的一种大气反馈，是其历史意识和时代意识的可贵履践。

雷海宗的这类书评尽管不多，但却是其学术生涯的可贵足迹，是他学术遗产中值得关注的方面。今天适当回顾，仍有其借鉴意义。究竟怎样看待国际汉学界出现的此类成果？究竟怎样评价研究者

---

① 他认为研究者应该有这样的问题意识：现在的城市市民或乡村人士，都不能做到对城乡两方面的同时了解；即使是城市市民，也往往对自己团体以外的情况十分隔膜。

② 美国学术界有书评就批评下卷的写法，例如普拉特（J.H.Pratt）的一篇书评说，他不认为该书下卷的八个方面的分析及其总结是必要的，读者并不认为这是需要的，他们宁可多花时间自己去研究。（J.H.Pratt, Untitled,*Journal of the Royal Asiastic Society of Great Britain and Ireland,* No.1（Jan.,1936），pp.104–106）

③ 如王钟麟《最近日本各帝大研究中国学术之概况》（南京：金陵大学 1932 年）、于式玉编《日本期刊三十八种中东方学论篇目》（北平：哈佛燕京学社引得编纂处，1933 年）、燕京大学历史学系史学消息社编《国外汉学论文提要分类目录》（北平：禹贡学会发行部，1937 年）、于式玉与刘选民编《一百七十五种日本期刊中东方学论文篇目》（北平：哈佛燕京学社引得编纂处，1940 年）、中法汉学研究所编《18 世纪、19 世纪之法国汉学》（1943 年）等。

④ 郑天挺《五十自述》，《天津文史资料选辑》第 28 辑第 8 页。

的思想观点、研究方法与存在问题？而作为批评者言，自身的才识、抱负和理念又如何良性铸就？这都需要好的历史经验。在海外中国学日趋发展和我们对它们日益关注的今天，雷先生的这些经验是值得注意的，可以从中找到影子和启迪。

自由主义与民族主义的纠缠
——以 1930-40 年代"战国策派"思潮为例

江　沛　南开大学

摘要：在近代中国社会发展中，拯救民族危机与向现代转型是发展的两条主线，由此形成了既要反对西方侵略、维护民族尊严，就要倡导中国文化独立性，反对西方文化传入，既要开放中国，学习西方以融入世界，就必须反对民族主义思潮，批判传统文化的相互矛盾的双线走向。在九一八事变后民族危机上升为中国社会主要矛盾，"战国策派"主要人物与追求自由主义信仰的众多知识界人士一样，在思想理念上发生了迎合民族主义思潮的转变，倡导"国家至上、民族至上"，呼吁个人自由暂时让位于民族自由，为时势所迫主张集权政治，并将民主政治与民主主义硬性割裂。救亡与启蒙的两难，观念与现实的冲突，自由主义内核与民族主义外衣的交织，在战国策学人论述中表现十分突出，也是那个动荡时代知识群体中思潮繁杂现象的典型反映。

关键词：战国策派思潮；自由主义；民族主义

19 世纪中叶至 20 世纪的中国，社会形态从传统向现代转型的趋势日益明显，这一趋势所独有的复杂性及矛盾性，不仅推动着现代经济的快速变动，深刻影响着社会结构的多重整合，也使思想潮流呈现出了新旧杂陈、变与不变的特征。在这一背景下，近代中国诸多思潮都难以纯粹追求学术旨趣，都必须面对"救亡图存"时代需求的诘问。以文化形态史观为学术理念、以西学改造中国文化为根本取向的"战国策"派思潮，同样努力为现实政治献"策"，并呈现出时代挤压下的学术性与政治性思考交织、自由主义与民族主义理念纠缠的复杂形态。

一　近代中国的双线走向与自由主义、民族主义思潮的矛盾

19 世纪中叶始，近代中国在欧美列强的压迫下被迫开放，并开始接受由欧美列强主导的现代经济体系，中国丧失了诸多主权，深陷"亡国灭种"的危机。现代工商业的进入对于传统农业、手工业的有力冲击，导致大批失业者出现及传统经济的衰败，使得排外情绪有了广泛的民众基础。在两千年来形成的"天朝大国"心态和近代民族国家思潮的基础上，中国思想界及民众日渐积累出恢复民族独立的强烈意愿，在形成巨大凝聚力的同时产生了以盲目排外为特征的义和团运动，也孕育了以救国为根本指归的一批思想家，形成了影响近代中国走向的激进民族主义思潮。

在这一过程中，现代思想体系的重要理念如自由、民主、博爱、平等、人权等价值判断，开始传入以儒家文化为核心的中国，与旧有的专制、人治、绝对平均等理念产生了尖锐冲突。思想界日渐理解，中国落伍于世界并非只是曾被蔑视为"奇技淫巧"的科技及工商业之不足，更深层的原因在于中国文化是传统农业社会的产物，从中难以找到适应现代化进程的要素。因此，中国社会的根本转变，不仅在于现代经济的引入，更在于思想观念与制度体系的更新，于是清末民初便有蔚为大观的新思潮纷涌景象。

由此，中国社会与文化开始陷入如李泽厚先生所言的"救亡压倒启蒙"的深刻悖论[①]。一是在外来侵略的背景下必须追求民族独立，强调中国文化的独立性，因此要高扬民族主义大旗。这种思潮与"天朝大国"及文化至上的心态揉合为一，造就了近代中国激进民族主义思潮的甚嚣尘上，进而反对侵略中国的西方所象征着的现代资本主义及其意识形态；而在现代经济及思想体系的猛烈冲击下，中国社会、文化及制度又不可避免地开始从传统形态向现代转型，必须要以"列国酵素"培养新文化因子，因此要倡导现代经济、制度与自由主义理念，同时当然要反对传统的农业文明及意识形态。

于是悖论出现了。中国社会及思想界一方面要倡导民族主义以"救亡"，强调"中体西用"观，要反对以西方为代表的外来侵略，指斥现代经济体系是中国社会沦落的根本原因，民主共和体制是北洋时代兵灾难息、政局混乱的元凶，这一思潮矛头所指自然也包括现代化的经济体系及其理念（以自由主义为代表），另一方面，为摆脱"东亚病夫"的地位以圆强国之梦，又必须融入以西方为代表的现代世界经济体系，学习现代性的生产方式及制度文明进而批判中国传统文化，当然要做到这一点，就不能任由激进民族主义横行。在毛泽东归纳的近代中国社会根本任务的"反帝国主义、反封建主义"演变轨迹中，自由主义与民族主义思潮的碰撞，构成近代中国社会及文化发展中本质性的矛盾与困境。

如胡适、鲁迅、陈独秀等人倡导与中国传统文化彻底决裂，以自由主义理念对中国社会及文化进行根本改造的激进改革，对于具有"学成文武艺，货与帝王家"的群体性格特征、强调"天下兴亡、匹夫有责"的入世文化观的中国知识人而言，显然是难以接受的。而强调民族主义的"救亡"以保存中国文化的生命力，更能获得广泛支持，也极易被政治势力所依赖。民族主义思潮与政治力量的结合，使得民族主义在不同时期的意识形态中始终强势，多数知识分子也同样遵从之[②]，由此也决定了近代以来自由主义思潮及以自由主义知识群体的弱势命运。

"战国策"派学人均生于20世纪初，成长于清末民初中国社会及文化的转型期，思想接受了"五四"时期新文化的熏陶，又有留学欧美的教育背景，西学及世界发展对其的影响远大于中国文化，但中国文化的烙印及民族主义思潮的喧嚣也同样刻骨铭心。1930年初他们学成归国之时，国民党"党国"体制下的中国，社会动荡不安，内战不已，九一八事变更进一步加深了中国社会的危机。"一二·九"运动中青年学生提出的"偌大华北，已安不下一张平静的书桌"的口号，正是此时学术界、文化界主流心态的真实写照。

二 民族主义的诉求与自由主义的妥协

民族主义的兴盛，是近代中国百年危机压力下的重要现象，其核心理念在于维护传统文化、强化民族自尊、自信的凝聚力，伸张中华民族的自决权，同时也为政治统治奠定合法性基础。然而，

① 《启蒙与救亡的双重变奏》，李泽厚：《中国现代思想史论》，东方出版社1987年6月版，第41页。
② 许纪霖：《紧张而丰富的心灵：林同济思想研究》，《历史研究》2003年第4期。

民族主义本质上是一种非理性思潮，过于强盛就会引发诸多冲突。民族主义者认为，人类最重要的生存单位是民族或种族，个人是微不足道的，甚至要求牺牲个人利益以获得民族利益的实现，主张权力及资源的独占，鼓吹反普世的价值相对主义，理念庞杂又常被随意曲解，时常妨碍自由主义的伸张与民主政治的推行①。

1931年的九一八事变及此后中日战争的全面爆发，刺激了民族主义思潮席卷全国，"抗战文化"、"抗战歌曲"、"抗战文学"、"抗战诗歌"、"抗战电影"等风起云涌。在文化政治化或意识形态化的过程中，民族主义主题的表述极为醒目，知识分子群体的入世传统，又为其推波助澜。

在此背景下，蒋廷黻、丁文江、钱端升、胡适等自由主义者先后发生了转向②，"战国策"派学人同样极力表达支持民族主义思潮及其现实政治象征、服务抗战的主张，也唯如此，方能在文化界获得一席之地。"战国策"派学人声言："本社同人，鉴于国势危殆，非提倡及研讨战国时代之大政治 (High Politics) 无以自存自强。而大政治例循'唯实政治'(Real Politics) 及'尚力政治'(Power Politics)、大政治而发生作用，端赖实际政治之阐发，与乎'力'之组织，'力'之驯服，'力'之运用，本刊有如一'交响曲'(Symphony)，以大政治为'力母题'(Leitmotif)，抱定非红非白，非左非右，民族至上，国家至上的主旨，向吾国在世界政治角逐中取得胜利之途迈进。"③此后，"战国策"派学人经常使用"民族至上"、"国家至上"、"民族主义"、"民族意识"等几个含义不尽相同的名词，阐释其改造国民性及中国文化特质的主张，但本质相去不远。"非白非红，非左非右"，表明了"战国策"派思潮鲜明的文化自由主义的中立宗旨；"民族至上、国家至上"，则是其认识近代世界和中国文化总体规律的逻辑结果，也是其对民族主义诉求的积极响应④。

与纯粹受民族主义思潮影响而起者不同，"战国策"派对于民族主义的认识，基于文化形态史观的理论逻辑。在他们看来，世界上各个独立发展的文化区域间自古以来就存在民族与国家间的竞争⑤，而15世纪地理大发现后特别是19世纪以来，世界进入了文化整合时代，"西洋文化，都是世界的主流。"⑥在整体发展中，民族或国家就成为各个文化生存与发展的基本单位或称"时代的界线"，以民族间、国家间的关系、矛盾、斗争为要素的民族竞争，是世界历史的"时代的大前提"和重要特征之一⑦。因此，在民族主义至上的"大战国时代"，每个民族都面临着竞争生存的大问题。就中国而言，"远自鸦片战争以来，就始终是一个彻头彻尾的民族生存问题。说到底，一切是手段，民族生存才是目标。在民族生存的大前提下，一切都可谈，都可做。在民族生存的大前提外做工夫，无往而不凶。这是百余年来大战国局面排下的铁算"⑧。这一时期，"'国家至上，民族至上'，原来并不只是一种抗战期内的口号，乃是一种世界时代精神的回音"⑨陈铨明确提出，所谓"战国时代"实际上就是民族主义高扬的时代，"民族主义，至少是一这个时代环境的玉律金科，'国家至上，民族至上'的口号，确是一针见血"⑩。何永佶认为：随时代的发展，"中国已不是'大一统'的'世界'，而是在紧张严肃的角逐中的一员。这世界尚无'大一统'的象征，春秋战国时代的一切，

① 江沛：《战国策派思潮研究》，天津人民出版社2001年版，第220-221页。参见翁贺凯：《民族主义、民族建国与中国近代史研究——"西方学理"与"中国问题"》，郑大华、邹小站主编：《中国近代史上的民族主义》，社会科学文献出版社2007年版，第39页。
② 张太原：《〈独立评论〉与20世纪30年代的政治思潮》，社会科学文献出版社2006年版，181-194页。
③ 《本刊启事（代发刊词）》，昆明《战国策》第2期（1940年4月15日）。
④ 江沛：《战国策派思潮研究》，第220页。
⑤ 雷海宗：《历史的形态——文化历程的讨论》，重庆《大公报·战国副刊》1942年2月4日。
⑥ 林同济：《民族主义与二十世纪——列国阶段的形态论》，重庆《大公报·战国副刊》1942年6月17日。
⑦ 林同济：《柯伯尼宇宙观——欧洲人的精神》，重庆《大公报·战国副刊》1942年2月14日。
⑧ 林同济：《廿年来思想转变与综合》，昆明《战国策》第17期（1941年7月20日）。
⑨ 林同济：《第三期的中国学术思潮——新阶段的展望》，昆明《战国策》第14期（1940年11月1日）。
⑩ 陈铨：《政治理想与理想政治》，重庆《大公报·战国副刊》1942年1月28日。

可于现在世界见之"①。贺麟也称："中国的民族主义运动的外观上是反抗帝国主义势力在经济上、政治上和军事上的压迫；其内在意义是反抗保守的军阀和封建主义；文化理智方面，它是对过去的传统和习俗的反抗。"②"战国策"派学人对于民族主义思潮的倡导，显然具有一定的学理依据，是从中国文化在"战国时代"如何在竞争中求生存出发的。他们与不少知识界人士倡导"民族至上"、"国家至上"，提倡以"民族文学"培养"民族意识"，目的在于重建中国文化，使千年灿烂文明"摆脱了一切'颓萎'色彩而卷土重来再创出一个壮盛的、活泼的、更丰富的体系"③。

自清末至1930年代，在世界化进程的洗礼中，中国的新学思潮渐次形成，它们意识到以西方为代表的世界化进程是中国社会发展的唯一取向，但却无视这一取向是以生活方式及思维方式的彻底更新为前提的。因此，多数新思潮都有从技术层面上学习西方的特征，诸如"科学救国"、"教育救国"、"军事救国"、"实业救国"、"体育救国"等不一而足，唯独极少提倡"民主救国"和"自由救国"！这些思潮表露的急功近利心态是清晰可见的，本质仍是"中体西用"，仍然抱定中国文化具有适应世界现代化进程的天然合理性，只要利用西学补足科技及工商业上的不足，中国文化仍可独步天下。因此，在面临救亡图存的现实需求面前，诸多思潮都有与民族主义思潮合作的思想基础，常常会"不问国家构成的情形，便以一种对象不确定的国家忠诚感'报效祖国'，这对国家的现代转轨毫无助益不说，反而发挥了助纣为虐的反作用，成为国家主义的牺牲品"④。

有所不同的是，"战国策"派学人虽然在现实主张上迎合民族主义思潮，但他们并没有在价值层次上彻底放弃自由主义，也决不同意回归传统。林同济、雷海宗等人认为，中国文化自救决不能复古，"救大一统文化之穷，需要'列国酵素'"，决不能死抱"大一统型"的"骄态与执见。"⑤在他们主张里，没有民族主义式的盲目排外与文化保守⑥，强调以开放的胸襟不断吸收西方现代文化精神，谋求通过民族主义的胜利获得国家独立，进而实施自由主义的理念完成宪政并走上自由主义的坦途。

三　"个人自由"让位于"民族自由"

考察某一个学派或思潮时，如以中国近代组织严密的革命型政党或秘密社团的形态切入，则差之毫厘，失之千里。具有自由主义、民族主义多重复杂性的学派或思潮，内部不同的声音和丰富的形象，正是其学术个性及信仰自由的价值体现。

"战国策"派的学人构成，本身即存在着教育及知识背景的不同，民族主义的压力对于学人群体也产生的不同影响，导致其在对一些重大理念的表述不一，对现实政治的主张存在分歧。

民国之后，社会与经济的现代化进程因中国与世界一体化而迅速发展，但民族危机压力、政治权力更替、地方势力难以遏制，都使得思想文化的多元化，并未能在政治制度与思想价值上呈现出自由主义的形态，要求集权及专制的呼声，反使不少自由主义知识分子发生了暂时转向，这一转变只是无力应付救亡图存危机的反映之一，他们寄希望于依赖政治强人实现自己的理想，但从对中国政治与文化发展的思路上看，他们并未真正放弃对民主自由的追求，不应简单看作是对中国近代民主潮流的反动。

---

① 何永佶：《政治观：钱向与内向》，昆明《战国策》第1期（1940年4月1日）。

② 《基督教与中国的民族主义运动》（1929年），贺麟：《文化与人生》，商务印书馆1988年版，第149页。

③ 林同济：《形态历史观》，重庆《大公报·战国副刊》1941年12月3日。

④ 任剑涛：《建国之惑：留学精英与现代政治的误解》，中国政法大学出版社2012年版，第21页。

⑤ 《卷头语》，林同济、雷海宗：《文化形态史观》，上海：大东书局1946年版，第3-4页。

⑥ 暨爱民认为：战国策派学人是一群文化民族主义者，旨在复兴民族文化，是一种非常有启发性的提法。参见暨爱民：《文化民族主义："战国策派"与文化重建》，郑大华、邹小站主编：《中国近代史上的民族主义》，第235-249页。

战国策派学人是从文化形态史观来认识当时世界的，他们倾心于近代西方以自由、平等、民主为核心观念的文化精神，但当他们认为世界进入"大战国时代"的同时，又极力地强调民族主义、国家主义，强调全能国家与集权；面对抗日战争的残酷现实，林同济、陈铨的一些言论更将服从国家、民族需要以获取民族独立放在第一位，他们错误地将民族生存与民主自由二者对立起来并义无反顾地选择了前者。如陈铨声言："二十世纪的政治潮流，无疑的是集体主义。大家第一的要求是民族自由，不是个人自由，是全体解放，不是个人解放。在必要的时候，个人必须要牺牲小我，顾全大我，不然就同归于尽。"①林良桐认为："战国时代所需求的，是国家的安全与强盛；民主政治所企图的，是个人的自由与繁荣。前者重团体，后者重个人；前者利于强有力的政府，后者利于无为的政府。"虽然他们想"努力寻求二者调和的方案，可是直到现在仍滞留于原则与理想的时期"。"我并不是主张独裁，但我只指出民主的弱点；假设我们能寻求一种方案，使政府不至于太强而压抑自由，复不至太弱不能抵御外侮，有最高的效率，有最大的安全，我固馨香而祝之。如其不能，则我们似亦不必过分迷信民主政治。御侮重于个人，安全重于自由"②。何永佶说：一个国家，"谁来做大官都行，只要他确能增进国家的总力量，以备'大政治'不时之需。只要他的设施，系向着时代的方向走"③。

陈铨从哲学和文学的角度考察近代中国的社会与文化危机。陈铨认为："二十世纪的政治潮流，无疑的是集体主义。大家第一的要求是民族自由，不是个人自由，是全体解放，不是个人解放。"④他认为五四运动倡导的民主和科学精神，"在西洋自然有历史的背景，有清楚的界限，在中国却成了个人自由无限伸张的工具。对于一切的传统都重打倒，对于任何的英雄，都不佩服"，是知识群体在近代中国民族危机面前"一盘散沙"的重要原因。因此，怎样改变教育方针，发扬中华民族的潜在精神、培养英雄崇拜的风气，"是中国目前最切急的问题"⑤。他试图引进尼采思想、提倡"力"与"英雄崇拜"，以文学培养"民族意识"来改造国民劣根性、凝聚民族向心力，以使中国能在世界民族竞争中生存和发展。在这里，陈铨混淆了中国传统个人主义与近代西方自由主义间的本质差别，将抗战期间战场上及大后方出现的一些消极抗战问题，完全归因于"五四运动的流弊"，甚至声称"平民教育要太发达，中国民族，一定更不能崇拜英雄，更是一盘散沙，这次抗战，更没有人去拼命了"⑥，则走到了否定近代中国现代性走向的极端。在介绍尼采政治思想时，陈铨提出："假如战争是人类进化不可少的工具，那么民主政治和社会主义，自然不适宜于战争"⑦，其指向还是可以揣测到的。

在这里，战国策派学人出现了割裂挽救民族危机与以现代理念重建中国文化间关系的重大理论失误，似乎民主政治不适宜抗战，只有政治集权方可御侮，民族危机过后，再倡行政治民主与自由主义理念。作为书生的他们，没有意识到在缺乏民主传统与有效程序的中国，政治集团为利益驱使而集权，具有丰厚的生存土壤，集权体制能否顺利向民主体制过渡，是一个十分复杂的问题。从雷海宗将中国古代士大夫阶层集权牵强比喻为"一党专政"可知，"牺牲小我、顾全大我"并非"战国策"派学人的初衷与理想，客观上却迎合了国民党政治权威主义的理论与实践。正是在"民族至上"的前提下，战国策派学人踏着救亡压倒启蒙的动人节拍，不自觉地跳起以全能政治节制民主政治的

① 陈铨：《五四运动与狂飙运动》，重庆《民族文学》第1卷第3期（1943年9月7日）。
② 林良桐：《民主政治与战国时代》，昆明《战国策》第15-16期（1941年1月）。
③ 何永佶：《政治观：外向与内向》，昆明《战国策》第1期（1940年4月1日）。
④ 陈铨：《五四运动与狂飙运动》，重庆《民族文学》第1卷第3期（1943年9月7日）。
⑤ 陈铨：《论英雄崇拜》，昆明《战国策》第4期（1940年5月15日）。
⑥ 陈铨：《论英雄崇拜》，昆明《战国策》第4期（1940年5月15日）。
⑦ 陈铨：《尼采的政治思想》，昆明《战国策》第9期（1940年8月5日）。

镖铐之舞，自然会招致不少左翼文化人的严厉批判①。当然，一些文章出于政治宣传需要，将"战国策"派学人与陈立夫等所谈"民族至上"、"国家至上"合二为一，似乎两者在里应外合，并称"战国策"派学人要替国民党统治"提供学理依据"的说法，也有失过激。

综上所述，"战国策"派学人倡导的"民族至上"、"国家至上"观念，导源于其所尊奉的文化形态史观及近代中国文化危机的现实需要，它既要追求民族独立、融合近代西方文化精神以重建中国文化的价值，又要为民族救亡而鼓吹放弃个人自由的原则，甚至与政治保守主义纠缠不清。这种两难的尴尬，正是近代中国文化思潮的重要特征之一。

四 自由主义内核与民族主义外衣的交织

尽管本人认为对"战国策"派学人不应以革命型政党或社团的惯性思维去理解，但学人们在自由主义基本理念上还是有相当多共性的，在民族主义的表述上同样如此。如果将之放在20世纪中国历史与社会变动的大格局下去考察，或许能较为真切地理解"战国策"派学人思想的杂芜。所以称自由主义为其思想的内核，源于其来自共同的西式教育背景及文化形态史观的逻辑，他们并不仅从中国文化的传统出发而是以未来为出发点的；所以称民族主义为其思想的外衣，则是由于其已认识到，思想服务于现实需求毕竟只是权宜之计。

雷海宗声称："今日的世界，在西洋文化的笼罩下，呈现一个人类开化后的空前现象，就是世袭君主制的大致消灭。多数国家都是共和国，少数的国家只维持一个傀儡的世袭君主，实权却操在另外一个选举的或用其他法产生的执政者手中。真有实权的君主在今日已是凤毛麟角，"并称："政治上任何实权者的世袭制度，在今日的世界绝无地位。"②雷海宗显然看出了世界政治体制向民主化方向发展的大趋势。

以世界民主化政治潮流参照中国，何永佶尖锐批判了"军队私人化"、"割据自私"的地方主义势力，主张"军队国家化"。他认为："惟其军队国家化，始有宪政可谈，始有法治可讲，军队而不国家化，则朝立宪法，而暮即可毁坏，所谓人权保障——宪法的精髓——在军队私人化下，不过是一种空谈。国人羡于英、美等国的法治宪政，而不知他们的宪政，正是建筑于军队国家化的大前提下"③。何永佶准确归纳了近代独裁国家的政治文化特征："'这国家是本党造的，所以这国家应为本党某某主义的甚么国'，这是道地的独裁者的口吻"，明确主张中国采用西方民主政体。他指出：民主与独裁的区别"不限于政制，而根本在于一种精神、心理、思想之分。在独裁的国家内，人们习惯于视一切'反对'为'反叛'，故凡口出半个不字批评政府的，都认为是'反动'，该枪毙。在民主的国家内，人们习惯于'反对'与'反叛'之截然不同，目的一致而意见尽可不一致，意见一致而办法尽可不一致"，也即"意志统一而不是意见的统一。"④他认为这个"近代政治的窍妙"，"不但我们中国人不懂，即德意人亦不懂"⑤。将国民党政权与德意法西斯政权相提并论，充分表达了何永佶对于当时中国政治的极度不满。

关于政治的权能问题，何永佶一针见血地指出："'权'从甚么地方来，'责'就向那个地方负。"以往帝王认为权力得之于天，只向天而不向人民负责，皇帝以下的官吏认为权力来自于帝王，

① 胡绳：《论反理性主义的逆流》，重庆《读书月报》第2卷第10期（1941年1月1日）。收入《胡绳文集（1935–1948）》，重庆出版社1990年版。汉夫："战国"派的法西斯主义实质》，重庆《群众》第7卷第1期（1942年1月25日）。
② 《世袭以外的大位承继法》，雷海宗：《中国文化与中国的兵》，重庆：商务印书馆1940年版，第223–224页。
③ 何永佶：《政治观：外向与内向》，昆明《战国策》第1期（1940年4月1日）。
④ 何永佶：《反对与反叛》，昆明《战国策》第3期（1940年5月1日）。
⑤ 何永佶：《意志统一与意见统一》，昆明《云南日报》1940年5月5日。

就只向帝王负责而不向人民负责；而在民主国家里，官吏民选机制决定着他要向人民负责。这是民主与独裁国家在权力的源与责关系上的根本区别。在民主机制下，以国会等各种方式对政府实行"限权"；而独裁国家则要把一切权力集中起来，不允许其他权力的干涉[1]。

针对当时一些人视美国式的选举制度为浪费、奢侈的认识，何永佶指出：民主国家的领袖必须要由选举产生。尽管三四十年代的美国总统竞选费用昂贵，每次合计要花费 1500 万美元，五千万选民平均每人要摊上三毛钱。他认为，这笔费用与独裁国家领袖靠内战流血换取的代价相比要小得多。他认为，民主选举最好有两个大党，党派过多则容易产生过多的矛盾，导致政权更替过于频繁，不利于政治稳定。在他眼中，美国的民主制度是中国政体改造最理想的参照物[2]。

贺麟对于民主政体也有一些非常有趣的观点。他认为，"没有法律的政治，就是乱政，无治，即无有组织，不能团结，未上轨道的政治"。他认真剖析了法律与自由间不可或缺的关系后，区别了申韩式的法治、诸葛式的法治和近代民主式的法治三种政体，申韩式的法治特点是"厉行铁的纪律，坚强组织，夺取政权，扩充领土，急近功，贪速利，以人民为实现功利政策的工具；以法律为贯彻武力征服或强权统治的手段；以奖赏为引诱人图功的甘饵；以刑罚为压迫人就范的利器"；诸葛式的法治特点是"信赏罚，严纪律，兼有申韩之长，一方面要去偏私，以求达到公平开明的政治。其有为国为民的忠忧，而无急功好利的野心"；近代民主式的法治特征为"以'人民自由立法，自由遵守'为原则。政府非教育人民的导师，而是执行人民意志的公仆。人民既是政府训练出来的健全公民，故政府亦自愿限制其权限，归还政权给人民。政府既是人民公共选出来的代理者，人民相信政府，亦自愿赋予政府充分权力，俾内政外交许多兴革事业，可以有效率的进行无阻"[3]。随后，贺麟提出：在训政时期，应当采取诸葛式的法治，而到宪政时期则应该采取近代民主式的法治。

雷海宗虽然在文化理念上明确意识到"西洋文化中国不妨尽量吸收，实际也不得不吸收"[4]，但他同时认为，民主政治在中国的确立还有漫长的道路要走。特别是处于"战国时代"的中国，倡行完全西方式的民主政体缺乏社会与经济的支撑，似乎并无能力在短期内纠正散漫无力的国民性以凝聚国力。正是在这一前提下，他也声称，在现时世界上不少国家里，"共和制度与民主主义是两回事，两者可合可分，并无绝对必要的联系。反之，凡不终日闭眼在理想世界度生活的人，都可看出今日的大势是趋向于外表民主而实际独裁的专制政治"。他特别举出德国、苏联、意大利三国为例来说明其观点，这一认识在当时欧洲及国内颇具代表性。在这里，雷海宗的自由主义理念因环境而退让，政治保守主义意识开始占据上风；一方面他清醒地意识到了实现民主政治的世界趋势和必备条件，另一方面为时势所迫不得不主张集权政治，并将民主政治与民主主义硬性割裂。救亡与启蒙的两难，观念与现实的冲突，在雷海宗思想上体现得非常明显，也是"战国策"派学人思想意识的典型反映。

其实，林良桐的有关说法，道出了战国策派学人思想上的极端矛盾："战国时代需要一个大权在握的政府，'要政府有大权，即不容多党存在；如容多党存在，则政府必不能有大权'（钱端升先生语）。然而'政党仍是民主政治所必需的条件。在全能国家中，一党专政，一党治国，严格言之，就不成其为政党'（吴文藻先生语）"[5]。林良桐虽然看到了这一矛盾，并称在"努力寻求二者调和的方案，可是直到现在仍滞留于原则与理想的时期"。他明确声称："我并不是主张独裁，但我只指出民主的弱点；假设我们能寻求一种方案，使政府不至于太强而压抑自由，复不至太弱不能抵御

---

[1] 何永佶：《权责论》，重庆《东方杂志》第 41 卷第 23 期（1945 年 12 月 25 日）。

[2] 何永佶：《从美国大选说到政党政治的"窍"》，重庆《大公报》1944 年 11 月 14 日。

[3] 《法治的类型》（1938 年 8 月），贺麟：《文化与人生》，第 46—48 页。

[4] 《无兵的文化》，雷海宗：《中国文化与中国的兵》，第 156 页。

[5] 林良桐：《民主政治与战国时代》，昆明《战国策》第 15—16 期（1941 年 1 月）。

外侮,有最高的效率,有最大的安全,我固馨香而祝之。如其不能,则我们似亦不必过分迷信民主政治。御侮重于个人,安全重于自由。"[1]这一段话,清楚地展现了战国策派学人救亡高于一切的基本思路,也显露出他们对民主体制的认识不足。他们没有意识到,在拯救民族危机的同时,民主体制虽会对个人自由做出一定限制,但并非以个人丧失自由、国家废除法治为前提。特别是在中国这样有几千年集权政治文化传统的国家里,以危机为理由倡导集权政治,实际上会使自身滑向政治现代化的对立面。

结　语

综上所述,战国策派学人基本的政治理念中,具有意识认同与现实选择间的重大矛盾。留学欧美多年的林、雷、陈、何、贺等人,无论是在检讨中国的政治传统抑或是考察近代西方的政治文化,都是以西方现代性价值标准进行的,他们几乎一致认为,在西方"坚强生动的政治机构"冲击下,以集权独裁为特征的传统中国政治机制难以招架,要求全面引入"列国酵素"以重建中国文化,自然不会将导致中国两千年来"没有政治社会上真正的变化,只有易姓王天下的角色更换"[2]的王权主义与专制体制当成抗战的法宝。整体考察战国策派思潮,尽管其主张较为庞杂甚至有前后矛盾之处,但并不能得出战国策派学人反对民主政体甚至不具有自由主义思想内核的结论。

不可否认,战国策派学人对民主政治认识的明显转变,是在欧洲战事中各国体制发生变化及中日战争需要的前提下进行的。战国策派学人看到了德、意、日等国集权体制在战争中的高效能,看到了欧美各国在应付战争时建立"危机政府"的相对集权,也看到了两者间独裁与民主的本质差别。面对近代中国危机和抗日战争的艰苦局面,他们忽略了欧美诸国与中国支撑战时体制的基本社会形态间的不同,似乎战时欧美的转变就是潮流,从而割裂了救亡图存与倡行民主政治间的关系。他们不反对民主政治,却错误地以为民主体制必然附带不利于抗战的诸如个人主义散漫等问题,要救亡图存只能缓行民主政治。如任剑涛所言,类似战国策派学人这样的留学精英群体,在当时普遍支持缓行民主政治的国家建构理念,纯属对现代国家建构的严重误解,"既掩盖了国家建构的特质,又扰乱了公众对国家现代转轨的视线,还成为人们顶礼膜拜的学术权威见解。因此,对其进行严肃的学术批判,有关毋庸置疑的必要性与重要性"[3]。

此外,战国策派学人是在忽视了集权与民主体制间相互转化的条件与难度后发生认识偏差的。与战国策派某些观点相近的王赣愚,有一个堪称代表性的表述:"近几年来,中国政治可说是朝着两个方向走,一面为求事权统一,指挥灵活,以期增进行政效率,适合抗战需要;一面又积极团结全国力量,使人民之自由,与更多之参政机会。前的倾向,姑称之'集权',而后的倾向,则称之为'民主',为抗战要实行'集权',为建国要促进'民主',这中间存着绝对的联系性,丝毫没有冲突。"[4]贺麟也称,在训政阶段,"人民不可因政府之权力集中,而误会政府为法西斯化,而妄加反抗。政府亦应自觉其促进人民自由,实现宪政,达到近代民主式的法治的神圣使命,不可滥用职权,不必模仿法西斯的独裁"[5]。然而,一旦政治保守主义思潮转化为政治实践后,如何保证战时集权体制增进效能、稳定秩序而不是相反?如何有效地限制权力并防止其滥用?如何保证战时集权体制会为和平建国所必须的民主政治体制的实现创造必要前提?如何促成两者间顺利而和平的转换?对于这些

---

① 林良桐:《民主政治与战国时代》,昆明《战国策》第15—16期(1941年1月)。
② 《无兵的文化》,雷海宗:《中国文化与中国的兵》,第142页。
③ 任剑涛:《建国之惑:留学精英与现代政治的误解》,第24页。
④ 王赣愚:《集权与民主——一年来国内政治的动向》,昆明《今日评论》第3卷第1期(1940年1月7日)。
⑤ 《法治的类型》(1938年8月),贺麟:《文化与人生》,第50页。

重大问题，战国策派学人几乎都没有明确答案，自然会受到来自左翼文化人和自由主义者的批判。国民党战时集权体制在稳定社会秩序、增加效能、向民主体制转化方面的恶劣表现，令战国策派学人始料未及。正是在抗战结束前后，战国策派学人先后回归到对自由主义的认同上，再一次发出政治自由主义的呐喊。1945 年 8 月，何永佶在系列文章里集中讨论了对战后中国民主政治建设的设想，希望国共团结；要求中国从此成为与世界潮流合拍的"地缘国家"而不再是自以为是的"天下国"；要求中国人要培养"程序化"的头脑；重视言论自由，力求做到"多数决定"；希望行政机构能够增加效率，做到"快得利"（英文 quickly 的谐音）[1]。他认为，"只有民主才能使中国人民现在尚在沉闷起来的聪明才智发挥出来，使之创造新文化，蔚为奇花异卉"[2]。

其三，战国策派学人的政治主张在由民主向集权的转变中，除了对民主或集权体制在效率、能力等技术层面的选择之外，还有一个价值层面的意义。他们清楚地指出："西方的个人主义，尽管讴歌个性的独尊，却始终忘不了社会。它是承认社会的……'法律为治'从来是他们一切自由谈的根基。"[3]民主政治的价值基础是承认个体的自由与权利，其制度的着眼点即在保障个人的自由与权利；专制体制的价值基础是否认个人的自由与权利，其制度的着眼点是在权力的集中上。林同济所称的"国命潮流"，是"注重统一与集权，是一种向心运动，目的要在层级结构打翻后，再把那些日形'原子化'Atomized，'散沙化'的个人收拾起来而重建一个新集体。具体形态的表现，多半是政权集中，军队统一，经济干涉，国教创立等项。最适当的象征可说是百家争鸣后所多少都要产生出来的思想统治的主张"[4]。陈铨也认为："二十世纪的政治潮流，无疑的是集体主义。大家第一的要求是民族自由，不是个人自由，是全体解放，不是个人解放。"[5]显然，"战国策"派学人在价值层面上对自由主义精神发生了疑虑。所以如此，是由于"战国策"派学人首先是民主主义者，其次才是自由主义者，一旦二者发生冲突，他们往往会以牺牲后者为代价。他们似乎没有意识到，民主实现与自由获得，二者是不可偏废的。

如何才能实现真正意义上的民主政治，保证其本质不被变异，是一个至今仍在探讨的难题。在价值层面上，战国策派学人群体对民主自由的崇尚是显然的，但在战时特定环境下，他们在实践层面上却发生了政治意识的转变，这种转变不应视为对民主政体的非难，将之看作他们对西方现代性在意识认同与现实选择间的矛盾所致更为恰当。战国策派学人群体中所发生的忽视自由意识及对民主政治的认识流变，在 20 世纪上半叶知识群体中具有相当的典型性。

考察"战国策"学人对于民族主义的倡导必须要注意到特定的时代背景，否则极易对一些足以引发歧义的词句进行离题万里的解释，从而误解"战国策派"的核心价值。雷海宗曾说过：我们反对传统文化中的"文德"，但也"绝不是提倡偏重武德的文化"[6]。何永佶在批判中国人缺乏严格意义下的宗教意识时，在感叹西方人的"天召"与"使命"感时，曾举希特勒为例说："他的种种行为，我们不赞成。"[7]林同济也明确指出："希特勒的办法是以武力征服一切，把国家、个性与贵士遗风一概蹂躏起来而建立一个机械性的'车同轨，书同文，以法为教，以吏为师'的秦始皇式的世界帝国"，这种极权体制"终使文化走上颓萎的孽程。希特勒绝对要不得！"[8]谷春帆坚定地认为："中国固需

---

① 何永佶：《想一想明天》，重庆《世界日报》1945 年 8 月 14 日。

② 何永佶：《论我国民主政治》，重庆《世界日报》1945 年 10 月 9 日。

③ 岱西：《中国人之所以为中国人》，昆明《战国策》第 1 期（1940 年 4 月 1 日）。

④ 林同济：《形态历史观》，重庆《大公报·战国副刊》1941 年 12 月 3 日。

⑤ 陈铨：《五四运动与狂飙运动》，重庆《民族文学》第 1 卷第 3 期（1943 年 9 月 7 日）。

⑥ 《建国——在望的第三周文化》，雷海宗：《中国文化与中国的兵》，第 217 页。

⑦ 何永佶：《中西人风格一较》，林同济编：《时代之波》，重庆：在创出版社 1944 年版，第 34 页。

⑧ 林同济：《文化的尽头与出路——战后世界的讨论》，林同济、雷海宗：《文化形态史观》，第 177 页。

要民族主义，但只是中国式理性的民族主义，而不是军国式疯狂的民族主义"①。他特别指出："中国人之民族怨毒，已积百年，难以一泄而尽，"因此，克服激进民族主义情绪至关重要，"如何使新兴的民族主义与向来和平主义，谋一妥帖调和处置之方，而成为中国式的民族主义，合理的民族主义，尤为以后百年来中国史上之大问题"。②读着这些旗帜鲜明的文字，并将"战国策"派思潮放在时代背景下细加思考后，相信应该有所感悟。

附英文摘要：

Entanglement of Liberalism and Nationalism:
the 1930–40′s Ideological Trend of Zhanguoce Clique
Jiang Pei
(School of History, Nankai University)

Abstract: As far as modern Chinese society was concerned, to save the national crisis and to achieve modern transformation were the two major developing lines during the course. Thus for one thing, advocating the Chinese cultural independence and resisting the coming of Western culture was crucial for the resistance of the Western aggression and the defending of national dignity, and for another, we must oppose nationalist thought, criticize our traditional culture and learn from the West in order to open the door and integrate China into the world, which composed two conflicting routes. Since the 9·18 Incident, national crisis had risen up to become the major social contradiction in China. Like most intellectuals pursuing liberal beliefs, representatives of the *Zhanguoce* Clique converted their thought and began catering to nationalist ideas, advocating "state supremacy and national supremacy", and calling for the temporary replacement of individual freedom with national freedom. Confronted with pressing moments, they proposed a totalitarian state, and rigidly fragmented democratic politics and democracy. *Zhanguoce* Clique's discourse evidently displayed the dilemma between salvation and enlightenment, the conflict of concept and reality, and the entanglement of liberalism core and nationalism imagery, which also reflected the ideological complexity of the whole intellectual group during that turbulent era.

Keywords: the Ideological Trend of *Zhanguoce* Clique, liberalism, nationalism

---

① 谷春帆：《中国会成为近代民族主义国家么？》，昆明《今日评论》第2卷第5期（1939年7月23日）。
② 谷春帆：《中国应采的民族主义》，昆明《今日评论》第2卷第7期（1939年8月6日）。

雷海宗对《古史辨》第二册的书评：翻译和解读

竹元规人 日本福冈教育大学

摘要：雷海宗先生早年发表过对《古史辨》第二册的书评。这书评是雷先生通过对《古史辨》第二册的评论表明自己研究中国上古史的方法的，可以说相当于他《孔子以前之哲学》的序论，不失为学术史上的重要资料。因为这书评从来没被注目，所以本文除了讨论这书评的内容和意义之外，还附载英文原文和中文翻译，提供参考。

　　雷海宗 1927 年获得美国芝加哥大学博士学位，同年返国，在中央大学文学院史学系任教。当时留美学生在中国学界里的势力越来越大，他也属于那一群体。但当时"海龟"们不一定一帆风顺，回国刚任教时，就难免遇到一些困难。现代中国留学生年轻任教授的代表学者，可以胡适为首。他1917 年回国在北京大学上课时，学生们议论："他是一个美国新回来的留学生，如何能到北京大学里来讲中国的东西？"①胡适"在北大，于初到后数日，即于某晚大礼堂讲墨学，到者百余人，反应不甚良好。我（引者注：毛以亨）与傅斯年曾去听讲，回来觉得类于外国汉学家之讲中国学问。曾有许多观点，为我们所未想到，但究未见其大，且未合中国人之人生日用标准。胡先生后来在北大研究所，与马叙伦同任中国哲学讲师。马氏担任老庄，而胡氏则指导墨学，马氏首言，欲讲名法，不可不先讲老庄，口若悬河，滔滔不绝。而当时之胡先生，口才亦不甚好，遂使研究员十六人中，十五人皆随马氏研老庄。当时哲学系，班长是赵健，觉得不好意思，乃声称愿随胡先生研墨经，借以解围。"②当时公费留学生相当于往年的进士秀才，就是大家羡慕的对象。未曾出过国门的学者、学生们，对西方现代学问的了解当然比不上留学生，但对于中国的学问，却大有可言。雷海宗刚回国时也遇到一些流言蜚语："在中央大学时，只是一个刚从国外回来的青年，讲授的又是外国史，有些冬烘先生妒火中烧，竟胡说他中国史学问不够，中文水平不高。"他的反应是："这当然不是雷先生所能容忍的。所以随即大写中国史文章，并讲授中国史，无不大得好评，誉满全国，远非冬烘之流所能望其项。"③

　　可见雷海宗当年受到的压力之大，而他不肯充耳不闻，要正面克服压力。他早年写的"中国史文章"是《殷周年代考》（1931 年发表）和《孔子以前之哲学》（1932 年发表），还有对《古史辨》第二册的书评（1931 年发表）。我们不仅要关注这些文章的内容本身，更要关注雷氏选这些题材的

---

① 顾颉刚：《古史辨》第一册自序，朴社，1926 年版，第 36 页。
② 毛以亨：《初到北大的胡适》，王汎森先生提供，谨致谢忱。
③ 蒋孟引：《雷海宗先生给我的教益》，收入南开大学历史学院编：《雷海宗与二十世纪中国史学：雷海宗先生百年诞辰纪念文集》，北京：中华书局，2005 年版，第 113—114 页。

含义和意图。这些论文不像是因为发现了什么问题而写的文章，却似乎是经过精心考虑后刻意选择的题目，意在对付另一种对他而言更大的压力——就是在当时学界里怎样才能成一家之言的问题。

先就当时史学界的大概情况做个说明。自从梁启超1902年发表《新史学》以来，中国学人不断进行创立新史学的各种尝试和努力。与新史学的开展同步进行的是研究机构的设立。1921年北京大学研究所国学门成立，大致包括章太炎派和胡适派，1920年代后期，章派的朱希祖担任北大历史系主任，追求与"社会科学"结合的史学。1926年胡适的高足顾颉刚编写的《古史辨》出版，他同时南下到厦门大学国学研究院，随即转到广州中山大学，与刚从留学回来的傅斯年一起创办语言历史学研究所，推进语言学、民俗学和历史学的研究。傅氏1928年以后主持中央研究院历史语言研究所，重视考古发掘，要重建中国上古史。清华则1925年成立国学研究院，聘请梁启超、王国维、陈寅恪、李济等学者，虽然持续的时间很短，却培养了一批下一代的学人中坚。另外还有南京的柳诒征、缪凤林等所谓"南高派"，与胡适和所谓北大派对立。当时马克思主义史学还没有充分开展，郭沫若的名著《中国古代社会研究》是1928年出版的。还有一些重要的史学家，就不一一赘述了。

也就是说，雷海宗回国任教的1927年，恰恰是中国现代史学上的顶级学者们逐渐形成自己的阵地，大张旗鼓地开展研究的时候。梁启超、王国维和胡适早已成名，顾颉刚的疑古风靡一时，傅斯年得到国民政府的大力支持，有了制度上的依靠。雷氏的早期著作就是针对这种情况而发的。

我在这篇文章里要翻译介绍雷氏1931年发表的对《古史辨》第二册的书评。原篇名为：H. T. Lei, "Book Review: Ku, *Discussions in Ancient History*"，刊载于 *The Chinese Social and Political Science Review*(《中国社会与政治科学评论》)，vol.15, No.2, 1931年7月，第300–307页。这杂志是从1916年至40年代在北京出版的英文期刊，持续的时间较长，一些著名学者投稿，可算是当时重要的社科类期刊之一。然而，可能因为是英文期刊的缘故，所以至今没得到充分重视，至今出版的雷先生文集也还没收入过这篇书评。

这篇文章实际上是借书评的形式表明雷氏研究古代史的态度和方法，因此十分重要。他对《古史辨》显然持有否定态度，语调比较激烈。他认为："顾先生正在陷入固执己见的巨大危险之中。……在摧毁模范帝王和不可能的圣人们的时候，顾氏把战国和汉代的学者们、思想家们塑造为典型的造伪者和不可能的创造者。""在破除古代儒家塑造的圣主明君的偶像同时，他险些同样错误地造出一个新偶像，那就是无所不在的战国造伪者偶像。"[1]雷氏提出研究古代史时的两个前提。第一："从印刷术以前的时代流传至今的文献作品非常稀少。"第二：随着时代的变化，人们的兴趣也转移，所以战国时代的人不注意保存西周时代和春秋时代的书，导致文献遗失。只有《诗经》、《书经》和《易经》比较完整地传下来了。[2]所以："当我们因某种信仰或理念，据我们所知，第一次出现在后世的著作中，就将它们归在那个时代时就要特别谨慎，因为，据我们所知，我们知道的真是很有限。"[3]具体来说，不能把尧舜传说归于战国时代的伪造，那么，在战国时代的政治潮流里面探讨造伪的原因，当然无意义了。[4]

雷海宗建议参考西欧封建时代，那么会发现："就制度和观念这两大文明的基础而言，封建时代一般构成后来各个时代的基础。"[5]又建议参考欧洲中世纪和古代希腊的神话传说，就会知道：神和半神半人变成人的"过程很早就开始了，实际上发生于封建时代早期。其次，他会发现，很少

---

[1] H. T. Lei, "Book Review: Ku, Discussions in Ancient History," *The Chinese Social and Political Science Review*, vol.15, No.2, 1931.7, pp.301，307.

[2] Ibid., pp.301–302.

[3] Ibid., p.303.

[4] Ibid., p.304.

[5] Ibid., p.304.

能够找出使某个特定的神或神话人物变成历史英雄的确凿无疑的原因。"①提出这些观点时，他引用傅斯年对顾氏《秦汉统一的由来和战国人对于世界的想象》的批评，虽然没有讨论傅氏提到的"传说之越国远行"的问题。这些建议是要求在与西方历史的比较下研究中国古代史的，前提是各个地域的上古史共有某种普遍性的原理。因为留存的文献稀少，所以更要重视世界史上的原理，弥补史料的缺乏。

文献稀少时不能仅依据那些文献进行推测，这一批评与张荫麟提出的对"默证法"的批评②相同。张氏的批评主要是根据史学方法论的（他引用 Ch. V. Langlois and Ch. Seignobos, *Introduction to the Study of History*, 1898），虽然成为对疑古的具有代表性的批评，但并不等于古史的重建。而雷氏的建议表明研究上古史的另一方法，更有积极意义。总之，他面对当时颇有影响的疑古思潮，提出自己的另一条道路。这篇书评可算是他为了在当时的史学情况里面确立自己立场的重要作品，也不失为讨论《古史辨》的学术史上的一篇重要论文。

另外，雷氏还提出一个问题："顾先生……似乎过分相信《诗经》是历史记录。……诗人们从来不重视历史事实，甚至是自己的时代的事实。难以置信的是，率而疑古的顾先生，竟然坚信在所述历史事件数百年之后才写成的颂诗。"③到底中国古代的哪种文献能相信，这也是一个重要问题，这个问题与雷氏的中国古代哲学史观密切相关。雷氏在 1932 年发表的另一篇早年重要论文《孔子以前之哲学》里面，提出作为上古哲学史料重视《尚书》和《易经》的想法：

> 普通研究中国哲学的，都看孔、老为最早的哲学家，前此毫无哲学思想可言。然而凡稍明哲学进化的人都可看出孔、老的思想是哲学已到成熟时代的思想，在他们背后一定还有悠久的历史，并且决不止是宗教信仰史，乃是真正的思想发展史。……孔、老以前哲学史料的缺乏是无可讳言的事实。但侥幸还有《尚书》与《周易》两部书能帮助我们寻出西周与春秋时代思想进化的线索。因材料过少，进化的步骤虽不十分清楚，然而大致的前后关系还可看出。所以本文的取材几乎完全是出于《书》、《易》两经的。④

原来，胡适在当时"开风气"的《中国哲学史大纲》卷上里面，撇开《尚书》和《易经》，认为《诗经》是最古的史料⑤。顾氏重视《诗经》的想法也可能受到胡氏的直接影响。雷海宗的想法是与胡适截然相反的。

雷氏认为《尚书·周书》和《易经·象传、象传》是西周末年的哲学史料，其根据是："《周书》中大多篇都富于哲学思想，不似周初政治方定时所宜有。且大多篇体裁一致，文体一致，思想一致，极似是出于一人或一组人之手。吾人皆知西周末叶宣王（公元前 827 至 782 年）幽王（781 至 771 年）时诗歌曾大放光辉，《小雅》中所存名篇甚多。这是中国历史上文艺初次大盛。恐怕此时或此时前

① Ibid., p.306.

② 张荫麟：《评近人对于中国古史之讨论》，《古史辨》第二册，第 271-273 页。

③ H. T. Lei, "Book Review: Ku, *Discussions in Ancient History*", pp.306-307. 关于顾颉刚对《诗经》的重视，笔者去年作过一个学术报告，论文待发表。我们同时要注意的是，虽然雷氏在对《古史辨》第二册的书评比较激烈地批评顾氏的方法，但雷氏并不是全盘否定顾氏的学术思想和学术成果。雷氏在对顾氏《古史辨》第一册自序英译本的书评（载于《中国社会政治科学评论》，第 17 卷第 4 期，1934 年 1 月）和《汉代学术史略》的书评（载于《清华学报》第 11 卷第 2 期，1936 年）里，并不持有否定态度，而在《孔子以前之哲学》里面，还征引顾氏《周易卦爻辞中的故事》。他当然采取就事论事的态度，不为门户之见所囿。

④ 雷海宗：《孔子以前之哲学》，王敦书编：《伯伦史学集》，北京：中华书局，2002 年版，第 13 页。

⑤ 胡适：《中国古代哲学史》（原《中国哲学史大纲》卷上），季羡林主编：《胡适全集》，第 5 卷，合肥：安徽教育出版社，2003 年版，第 212-213 页。

后散文文学也发达起来，真正的哲学思想也在此时萌芽起来。一般史官就把他们历代所保存的史料加以系统化与哲学化而作成今日《周书》中多篇"①，"西周末叶是中国古代文化的一个大过渡时代：一方面伟大的封建帝国渐趋破裂，列国日见盛强；一方面文学界又有新的发展。在这种时期思想方面也不会完全寂寞，《彖》、《象》二传大概就是这种新思潮之下的产品。"②

同样，他认为《周易·系辞传》和《尚书·虞书》是春秋时代的哲学史料："今人总喜欢说《系辞》是战国末或秦、汉间的产品（注：见《古史辨》卷三）。……但我们若看《系辞》，就可见出它的思想只能说是与老、庄同系，而绝对不能说它有阴阳家的口吻。所以它不会是战国末期或秦、汉间的产品。……至於秦汉时代的人，可说完全不知哲学为何物，只知把古代哲学著作来附会或误解，伟大的创作更谈不到了。从积极方面看，我们可断定《系辞》是《彖》、《象》与《老子》之间的作品。"③因为"一个制度极盛时代，并不用人替它辩护，到它将衰或已衰时都需要辩护。……到东周初年列国并起天子无权而仍欲恢复旧权的时代，辩护宣传家的时机就到了。《虞书》中所描写的显然是一个理想的'协和万邦'的大封建帝国，《尧典》一篇把这种理想尤其形容得淋漓尽致。……所以《虞书》为春秋时代作品，可无疑义。"④

雷氏对史料的这些看法与其说是根据文献的精细考据，不如说是依据古代史的原理。像他在对《古史辨》第二册的书评提出的那样，上古的史料留存的很少，在这种情况下指出某书的伪造或晚出是容易而危险的，且没有意义：

> 疑古过度而定《老子》为战国晚期作品的，由崔东壁《洙泗考信录》及梁启超《评胡适之中国哲学史大纲》。此外同一论调的文字甚多，无需列举。近来一般的风气是把一本古书在可能的范围内定到最晚的时期，以示批评力之精锐。这在崔东壁时代是革命的举动，到现在已成了天经地义。这在古籍湮没的今日本是非常容易的事。古籍湮没，参考比较的标准缺乏；我们若不顾一本书整个的系统与地位而专事于枝节的吹求，恐怕把先秦遗籍都断为汉人所伪托，也非难事。⑤

为了了解"整个的系统与地位"，就要看清各种思想的悠久的渊源，尤其是从宗教而哲学的演进过程："一个哲学家的思想除时代背景外，都有它的渊源；这渊源不外两种——前代的哲学家，与当时或前代传下的宗教。最早的哲学，无论东西，都是由宗教信仰宗教术语演化出来的。"⑥思想的系统存在于一个时代前、后的整个过程中，所以不能只看思想或思想家出现的某个特殊的时代背景："当然每个思想家都有他的特殊的时代背景；但一个大思想家的哲学决不能完全以时代背景来解释。"⑦这也是对胡适的批评，因为胡适原来主张从时势来说明学说的发生："我们现在要讲哲学史，不可不先研究哲学发生时代的时势，和那时势所发生的种种思潮。"⑧

可见，《孔子以前之哲学》是根据世界古代哲学史的原理，对现代中国学术史上占重要地位的胡适的《中国哲学史大纲》进行批评，进而提出一种新的哲学史观。此外，我们还看到，雷海宗在"《古史辨》第二册书评"里对疑古提出的批评，在《孔子以前之哲学》一文中已发展为具体的古史研究。

---

① 雷海宗：《孔子以前之哲学》，第 15 页。
② 同上，第 15–17 页。
③ 同上，第 24–25 页。
④ 同上，第 27 页。
⑤ 同上，第 26 页。
⑥ 同上，第 26 页。
⑦ 同上，第 37 页。
⑧ 胡适：《中国古代哲学史》，第 221 页。

〈原文〉

Ever since the first volume of the *Discussions in Ancient Chinese History* appeared in 1926, students of ancient China have been waiting for the succeeding volumes with impatience, often wondering whether they would ever be published. So the appearance of the second volume gives most of us a feeling of relief. Readers of this Review perhaps can still recollect Mr. Ku's thesis as put forth in the first volume–that ancient Chinese history was a putch–work, pieced together, polished up, and perfected in the course of centuries; that ancient history, as a complex in the racial consciousness, receded back earlier and earlier as the centuries passed; and that, to give the most glaring examples, tha Saint–Emperors Yao（尧）, Shun（舜）, and Yu（禹）were fabrications of the Ch'un–Ch'iu（春秋）and Ch'an（战国）periods.

In the new volume the viewpoint and method are the same as in the first; no progress has been made in the "discussions." It is divided into three parts. Part one is the most similar to the earlier one; it contains a few essays by Mr. Ku and others, pointing out the holes of ancient tradition. The starting point of the discussions is furnished by a lecture of Mr. Ku's on the "The Origins of Chinese Unification by the Ch'ins（秦）and the Hans（汉）and the world–views of the Ch'an Kuo Period." Two series of essays on the last king of the Yin Dynasty and on the lore of Chiang–Yüan（姜嫄）complete the First Part. Part two is devoted to Confucius and Confucianism. Mr. Ku's essay on "The Confucius of the Ch'un Ch'iu Period and the Confucius of the Han Dyansty" furnishes the starting point. Part three is a collection of criticisms and reviews of the whole or parts of Mr. Ku's first volume. Taken as a whole, that which strikes the reader most at the first glance is the paucity of contribution made by Mr. Ku in this new volume. The work of others comprises at least eight–tenths of the total, and the few essays that Mr. Ku does contribute do not show that he has learned very much from others' views–a fact which surprises at least one of his readers a great deal.

The first volume introduced new blood, as it were, into the study of ancient china; but the new volume, showing no progress whatever, makes us feel that Mr. Ku is in very great danger of becoming a man obsessed with one idea. His obsession, not to be broken by the strongest factual evidence is that whatever there is of ancient Chinese civilization–philosophy, literature, general ideas, institutions, history as a cognition of the past–is largely, if not *in toto*, a fabrication of the Ch'an–Kuo and Han periods. The people of these two much belaboured ages, if they could return to earth, might be greatly astonished to find that, after so many centuries of peaceful rest, they are being overwhelmed with so much undeserved credit. In destroying model emperors and impossible saints, Mr. Ku is making the Ch'an–Kuo and Han scholars and thinkers into model fabricators and impossible creators. Before discussing a few points in detail, let us make one or two general remarks that no student of ancient China can afford to ignore.

First of all, very few literary works have come down to us from the ages before the printing press, and the burning of the books by the first Chinese emperor and the destruction of his palace after the downfall of his dynasty make us feel fortunate indeed that so many reliable works of the Ch'an–Kuo period still remain. The official histories of the various states, of which there was probably only one copy, were all burned by imperial decree. Most of the works of individual authors were also destroyed; at most one copy of each work was deposited in the palace, which was burned a few years later by the famous Hsiang Yu 项羽. And the destructive wars after the downfall of the Ch'in dynasty perhaps worked further havoc by destroying a large part of the few books that scholars ventured to conceal within walls. The loss of one copy of a book at that age meant much more than that of a thousand now, for that copy might often mean the only copy remaining of that particular work. Now, as long as a book has some intrinsic value, it is almost impossible for it to be lost; but, then, nothing but luck made for the survival of the most valuable literary, philosophical, or scholarly product.

Secondly, a point related to the first is that interests change with the ages. The people of the Ch'an-Kuo period were no longer interested in much of what the Ch'un-Ch'iu period had thought, believed, or done; and still less, in that of the Western Chou period. What we war no longer interested in, of course, we take little interest to preserve. So the books of the Western Chou period. What we are no longer interested in, of course, we take little interest to preserve. So the books of the Western Chou and Ch'un Ch'iu periods, which, if we could only know, would have given us a far different picture of ancient China, have almost all been lost, perhaps more through neglect than through destruction by fire and sword. Only two works by compilers, probably for tutorial purposes（the Shih-King and the Shu-King）and one work for divination purposes（the Yi-King）have come down to us more or less intact. This point has never been brought up with sufficient emphasis; so we may say a few more words on it. We all know that the inscriptions on the tortoise shells and animal bones discovered in Honan give us a fairly clear picture of the institutional history and religious beliefs of the later Yin dynasty. But the later age of the Western Chou is a long night of darkness, relieved only by the Shih-King and Shu-king which after all tell us very little and with little certainty. The Ch'un-Ch'iu period is no less dark, as far as philosophy and letters are concerned. The earliest philosophers we know of were all born at the end of the period. But the thought of Confucius is that of a late age, representing a humanistic reaction to a long age of mysticism and metaphysics. Lao-tse, the work if not the man, represented the final expression of pure metaphysics, while Chuang-tze after him already belonged to a later age of mysticism and metaphysics, a new reaction to the prevailing humanistic thought of the followers of Confucius and Mo-tse. Though we don't know the name of even one of the philosophers and religious leaders before Confucius, yet we feel certain that they must have existed. Otherwise, Confucius and Lao-tze would be totally inexplicable freaks. Who can tell what these thinkers, each with his own particular（but for us unknown）ends in view, might have done with the gods and demi-gods and heroes of the primitive age!

With these two considerations in mind, we should be very careful in assigning a belief or idea to a late age just because it first appeared, as *far as we know*, in a book of that age, because, as far *as we know, we really know very little.*

To give a few examples, Mr. Ku seems to be convinced that the Yao and Shun stories were largely creations of the late Ch'an-Kuo period, and therefore unwarrantably questions the few passages in the Confucian Analects about these two Saint Emperors. He also assigns the first part of Shu-King, the Yu-Shu（虞书）to the Ch'an-Kuo period; though, from the astronomical phenomena mentioned in it, it seems to be fairly certain that it was a product of the early Ch'un Ch'u period. Now, the Yao and Shun were originally demi-gods in primitive Chinese mythology seems to be quite certain. But it is very dangerous to say that they must have been humanized by the Ch'an-Kuo philosophers just because the strongest political current of that day is toward unification. Philosophers have a way of expounding ideas that have little or no apparent connection with the actual political or social movements of their age. Then, it seems a rather prejudiced view to regard the Yao-Tien（尧典）as political-philosophical propaganda for unification, of which the reviewer can see very little. If anything, it will be straining our credulity less to say that it is an idealization of the nominal overlordship of a feudal king at a time(the Ch'un-Ch'iu period) when the feudal forms still remained more or less intact, though real feudalism had ended with the callapse of the Western Chou Dynasty.

Another point on which Mr. Ku is never tired of insisting is that the institutions described in the Yü-kung（禹贡）and the division of China into nine administrative districts were all ideas of the Ch'an-Kuo period. Here again is simply another expression of Mr. Ku's incurable obsession. One of his critics points out to him that the nine districts as an administrative fact antedated the Ch'an-Kuo period, as shown by the Shih-King and bronze inscriptions （p.15）. If Mr. Ku would spend some time studying the feudal age of Western Europe, he would have a higher regard for the Western Chou and Ch'un Ch'iu periods; he would find that in the fundamentals of civilization, both institutions and ideas, feudal ages are as a rule the basis of all the succeeding ages. In this particular instance, he would see that it is the rule for a feudal king or emperor to divide his country into administrative districts, though he has effective control only over the royal domain. As has been pointed out above, Chinese students of history are very unfortunate in having lost almost all the records of the ages of cultural creation; so none but the most rash would draw far-reaching conclusions on the basis of the scanty material that remains. The earliest ages that we know more or less fully, the later Ch'un Ch'iu and the Ch'an-Kuo periods, are late ages in the history of Chinese civilization; they are the inheritors, not the creators, of Chinese culture. The intricate political organizations and complex international system and the mature, even decadent character of the philosophical systems of the Confucian and post-Confucian times leave us no doubt whatever that the real ages of creation lay far behind. Though it is dangerous to put too much reliance on analogy, yet, with the history of the West as well as of other cultures as a basis of comparison, we may with confidence believe that the beginning of glorious cultural creation in China must have been far back in the late Yin Dynasty, around the fourteenth and thirteenth centuries B. C. —a belief well borne out by the tortoise shell inscriptions. It is a great mistake characteristic of pedants to give too much credit to the Ch'an-Kuo period just because more of the books of that age have been preserved.

Another peculiarity of Mr. Ku's method is that while he seems to be well-endowed with wild fancy (which enables him to draw preposterous conclusions, such as identifying the Chinese King of the Underworld with the God of the River Nile, a point which he made in his first volume), he has very little trained imagination. One of his ablest critics, Mr. Fu Ssu-Nien（傅斯年）sums up this point very well: --

> "I think ……one of your mistakes is to try to find a concrete cause for everything, ignoring the migration of traditions and legends. For instance, in explaining the Flood, you feel obliged to prove that K'uai-Chi（会稽）must have had a flood in the early age; or, in explaining the Wei-Shu（纬书）you must find out why the people of that age created them. As a matter of fact, parables and cosmologies often travel thousands of miles without regard to concrete situations. The story of the Flood as recorded in the Book of Genesis was copied from the Babylonians, who, for all we can tell, might have learned it from another people that we don't know. So, in studying the fanciful stories in the Wei-Shu and the stories of the Chinese Flood and the nine districts, we must not forget this phenomenon of migration… If you must find rational and concrete causes for everything, it would amount to making a mark on a moving boat in order to locate a lost sword, forgetting that the boat is moving all the time while the sword remains motionless beneath the running current." (p.14)

This really disqualifies Mr. Ku as a student of ancient history, in which myth and fact are inseparably mixed. It would be a very good idea for Mr. Ku to study the myths and legends of the European Middle Ages and of the Ancient Greeks and to find how gods and demi-gods become human heroes; he would find out, first, that the process of transformation begins very early, in fact, early in the feudal age, and secondly, that the cases are rare where hard and fast concrete causes can be found for the transformation of a particular deity or mythical figure into a historical hero.

One more fundamental point in Mr. Ku's methodology may be questioned. He seems to have undue faith on the Shih-King as a record of history. While discussing the traditional history of the Yin and Western Chou dynasties, he makes the highly questionable attempt to reconstruct their history from the Odes. Poets never have very high regard for historical facts, even facts of their own age. It is incredible how Mr. Ku, so rash in his doubts, can put so much faith on the Odes written hundreds of years after the events described.

Mr. Ku's book has been called epoch-making; we can still recognize the justice of this opinion. But it is epoch-making only in the negative sense; he has succeeded in pointing out the untrustworthiness of ancient Chinese history as recorded in the books. But the method of Mr. Ku is extremely questionable; that he can ever get a true picture of ancient China unless he discards his deep obsessions is quite impossible. Every student of ancient China should be grateful for Mr. Ku's destructive work. But in destroying the old Confucianist Idol of Model Emperors and Philosopher-Kings he is in danger of setting up a new idol no less false, the idol of the ubiquitous Ch'an-Kuo fabricators. Mr. Ku may still be broadminded enough to discard this idol of his own making if he can be made to see its vanity; but a new dogmatic school of ancient history, the Ku-ist school, is rising among the younger students who, in the course of time, may distort Chinese history just as much as ancient philosophers. So let us beware!

H. T. Lei

雷海宗

Ginling College,

Nanking.

〈翻译〉

　　1926 年《古史辨》第一册出版之后，研究中国古代的学者们对后续诸卷翘首以待，时常惦记，不知是否又有几卷已经出版了。第二册的出现终于让大家松了口气。读这篇书评的读者也许还记得顾先生在第一册里提出的观点——就是说，中国上古史是缀补、拼贴而成的，经过几个世纪的润色加工而得以完善；作为种族意识之复合体的上古史，时代越后，追溯越前；最明显的例子是，圣王尧、舜、禹是春秋战国时代的伪造。

　　在新的卷册里面，观点和方法与第一册一样。在"辨"中没有任何进步。分为三个部分。第一部分与第一册最相近，包括顾先生和别人的几篇论文，指出古代传统的缺陷。以顾先生的一篇演讲《秦汉统一的由来和战国人对于世界的想象》为首展开"考辨"，辅之以关于殷商末代君王和姜嫄传说的两种系列论文构成第一部分。第二部分关注孔子和儒教。以顾先生的论文《春秋时的孔子和汉代的孔子》开篇。第三部分集合了各种对于顾先生《古史辨》第一册整体或局部的批评和评论。总体来讲，大部分读者第一眼得到的印象是，在这一新的卷册里面顾先生贡献不足。其他人的作品至少占全部的百分之八十，而且顾先生的少数几篇论文也没显示出他认真吸取了别人提出的许多意见——这一事实至少让我这个读者深感惊讶。

　　第一册确实给中国古史研究注入了新鲜血液。但最新的卷册完全没有显示出任何进步，让我们感到顾先生正在陷入固执己见的巨大危险之中。他的偏执不为强有力的事实证据所动摇，他认为古代中国文明——哲学、文学、一般观念、制度以及历史作为关于过去的认知——全部或者大部分都是战国和汉代的伪造。如果这两个备受争议的时代的人们能够起死回生的话，他们一定会惊讶地发现，在安息千百年之后，他们正被大量名不符实的信任所淹没。在摧毁模范帝王和不可能的圣人们的时候，顾氏把战国和汉代的学者们、思想家们塑造为典型的造伪者和不可能的创造者。在对几个具体问题进行详细讨论之前，先总论研究中国古代的学者们不可忽视的一、两个问题。

首先，从印刷术以前的时代流传至今的文献作品非常稀少，幸运的是，经过秦始皇的焚书，秦王朝覆灭之后，秦国宫殿被毁，仍有为数众多可信的战国时代的作品被保留下来。各国的官方史记可能只有一份副本，根据皇帝的饬令全部被烧毁了。大多数个人著述也同样被毁。顶多每部著作有一套复本收藏于皇宫，几年后被著名的项羽烧毁了。而且秦亡后的破坏性战争造成了更大的浩劫，使士人们冒险藏于夹壁中的珍稀书籍大部分毁于一旦。当时一本著作的一个复本的遗失要比现在遗失一千个复本的损失大得多。因为那可能是某部著作仅存于世的孤本。现在，一部著作书只要稍有价值，几乎不可能丧失。可是，那时大部分有价值的文学、哲学或学术性作品只有靠运气才能流传下来。

其次，跟第一点有关的是，随着时代的变化，兴趣也转移了。战国时代的人们，对春秋时代的思考、信仰和事迹的大部分已经不感兴趣了，西周时代就更不用说了。对已经不感兴趣的东西，我们不怎么注意保存。所以西周时代和春秋时代的书几乎全部遗失了，与其说是由于战火不如说由于忽视，如果我们能够读到的话，一定会极大改变我们对古代中国的印象。只有两部可能为教育目的而编辑的作品（《诗经》和《书经》），一部为占卜而编的作品（《易经》）或多或少完整地流传下来。这一点从来没得到充分强调。因此我们要多说一点。众所周知，在河南发现的龟甲和兽骨上的铭文使商代晚期的制度史和宗教信仰相当清晰地呈现在我们面前。但是西周晚期如同漫漫长夜，漆黑一片，只是通过《诗经》和《书经》情况才有所改观，不过它们的内容太少，而且很不确定。春秋时代完全不在黑暗中，至少就哲学和文学而言。我们所知道的最早的哲学家都生在那时代的末期。但是孔子的思想属于后世的思想，代表人文主义对漫长的神秘主义和形而上学时代的反应。老子，其作品而非其人，代表纯粹形而上学的总结。在他之后的庄子已经属于后来的神秘主义和形而上学，其思想是针对占主流地位的孔孟门徒的人文思想的新的反应。虽然孔子之前的哲学家和宗教领袖的名字我们连一个都不知道，但我们确信他们是存在的。否则孔子和老子就成了完全无法解释的怪人。谁知道这些思想家们出于个人的特殊目的（我们对此一无所知）会对原始时代的神、半神半人和英雄们做些什么！

心中有了这两点考虑，当我们因某种信仰或理念，据我们所知，第一次出现在后世的著作中，就将它们归在那个时代时就要特别谨慎，因为，据我们所知，我们知道的真是很有限。

举例来说。顾先生好像确信尧舜故事大部分是战国后期的创造，所以无端地怀疑《论语》里关于这两个圣王的段落。他也把《书经》的最初部分《虞书》归在战国时代。尽管，根据《虞书》里谈到的天文现象，似乎可以肯定这是春秋时代早期的作品。现在似乎可以确信，尧舜起源于中国原始神话中的半神半人。可是如果认为战国时代的哲学家们使他们化身为人，只因当时巨大的政治潮流倾向统一，那就太危险了。哲学家们有办法解释与他们那个时代的实际政治、社会运动没有明显关系的观念。所以，把《尧典》视为对大一统的政治－哲学的宣传毋宁说是一种偏见，作为评论者，我就完全看不出来。如果有什么的话，不用说，那就是使我们更加轻信，它把（春秋时代）封建君主名义上的统治理想化了，尽管封建制度已随西周王朝的瓦解而荡然无存，封建方式却貌似原封未动地保存下来。

顾先生始终坚持的另一观点是，《禹贡》所描述的制度和把中国分为九个行政区的区划全是战国时代的观念。这只是顾先生无药可治的偏执狂的另一种表现。一个批评者向他指出，九州作为行政区划的事实早于战国时代，《诗经》和青铜器铭文证实了这一点 (p.15)。如果顾先生肯花点时间研究一下西欧封建时代的话，他准会对西周和春秋时代另眼相看；他会发现，就制度和观念这两大文明的基础而言，封建时代一般构成后来各个时代的基础。在这个特定的情形下，他会看到封建君王或皇帝总是把邦国划分为行政区，虽然他只能在王室属地范围内进行有效统治。如上面指出的那样，中国的历史学者非常不幸，因为文化创立时代的几乎所有记录已荡然无存。所以只有最轻率的人才会依据稀少的传世史料得出广泛的结论。春秋晚期和战国时代是我们多少有些了解的最早时代，在中华文明史上属于晚生时期，它们是中华文化的继承者，不是创造者。繁琐的政治组织、复杂的邦际体系，儒家和后儒家时代的哲学体系所具有的成熟乃至颓废的特征，使我们确信真正的创造发明时代在很久很久以前。虽然过度依赖类比是危险，但以西方和其它文化的历史为基础进行比较，使我们确信，灿烂辉煌的中华文化的创立始于殷代后期，约公元前 14 世纪、13 世纪，——这种信念恰因甲骨文而产生。学究们的特点是太相信战国时代，因为那个时代有更多的书籍被保存下来，这是大错特错的。

顾先生的方法另有一古怪之处，他看似沉醉于疯狂的想象之中（以致于得出中国的冥王等同于尼罗河的神这类荒谬的结论，这是他在第一卷提出的一个观点），但他缺乏训练有素的想象力。在一些才华横溢的批评者当中，傅斯年先生对此做了很好的总结：

> 我总觉得你这篇文里，……颇犯一种毛病，即是凡事好为之找一实地的根据，而不大管传说之越国远行。如谈到洪水必找会稽可以有洪水之证，如谈到纬书便想到当时人何以造此等等。其实世界上一些寓言(Parables)，一些宇宙论(Cosmologics)，每每远到数万里。洪水之说，今见之于 Genesis 者，实由巴比伦来。其在巴比伦者由何来，今不可得而考。纬书上一些想象，及洪水九州等观念，我们不可忘传说走路之事也。……如必为一事找他的理性的、事实的根据，每如刻舟求剑，舟已行矣，而剑不行，凿矣。（p.14）

这就否定了顾先生作为古史学者的资格。在古史中，神话和事实不可分离地混杂在一起。顾先生最好去研究一下欧洲中世纪和古代希腊的神话传说，看看神和半神半人是怎么变成人类英雄的。首先，他会发现，转变的过程很早就开始了，实际上发生于封建时代早期。其次，他会发现，很少能够找出使某个特定的神或神话人物变成历史英雄的确凿无疑的原因。

顾先生的方法论中的另一个基本观点也值得商榷。他似乎过分相信《诗经》是历史记录。在考证殷代和周代的传统历史时，他试图通过颂诗重建那段历史，这种做法很值得商榷。诗人们从来不重视历史事实，甚至是自己的时代的事实。难以置信的是，率而疑古的顾先生，竟然坚信在所述历史事件数百年之后才写成的颂诗。

顾先生的书被称为划时代的。我们还是认可这种看法有其合理性，但这种划时代只具有消极意义。他成功指出了文献记载的中国古史的不可信性。但顾先生的方法很有问题。除非放弃他根深蒂固的偏执妄想，否则他不可能了解古代中国的真正面貌，但这是不可能的。每个研究中国古代的学者都应该感谢顾先生的破坏工作。但在破除古代儒家塑造的圣主明君的偶像同时，他险些同样错误地造出一个新偶像，那就是无所不在的战国造伪者偶像。假使顾先生能够看出这偶像是空虚的话，那么他也许还有足够胸襟抛弃自己造出的偶像。但是，一个新教条主义的古史学派——顾氏学派已在年轻学者当中兴起，总有一天他们会跟古代哲学家们一样歪曲中国历史。所以我们要提高警惕！

H. T. Lei

雷海宗

金陵大学

南京

雷海宗西方古典奴隶制学术思想的发展及启示

甄修钰、李艳辉　内蒙古大学

摘要：20世纪50年代，雷海宗先生在西方古典奴隶制问题上曾提出：雅典不等于希腊、雅典奴隶制社会"孤岛论"、罗马奴隶制社会"特例论"、希腊和罗马基本上是铁器时代早期的封建社会形态等一系列学术思想。雷先生的这些观点在当时学术争论政治化的特殊时代遭到不公正批判，并为此付出了沉痛的代价。然而，雷先生的学术思想并没有因其作古而销声匿迹，考察改革开放以来国内外马克思主义学术界有关西方古典奴隶制的研究成果，不难发现，雷先生的那些学术思想不仅在国内外马克思主义学术界仍后继有人，而且与马克思主义创始人的理论也并不矛盾。

关键词：雷海宗；古希腊罗马；奴隶制；启示

雷海宗先生是我国著名的学贯中西的史学大师，他虽然没有给我们留下正式出版的必读性经典著作，但却为我们留下了求真求实的优良学风。20世纪50年代，雷海宗先生在西方古典奴隶制问题上曾提出：雅典不等于希腊、雅典奴隶制社会"孤岛论"、罗马奴隶制社会"特例论"、希腊和罗马基本上是铁器时代早期的封建社会形态等一系列学术思想。但在那个特殊时代，雷先生的观点受到了责难。现在，学术争论已进入正态时代，雷先生这些观点尽管本意上是为了"使自己的认识能够少犯片面的错误，能够逐渐比较接近真实"[①]，但实际上仍然是学术界需要共同关注的重大理论问题。

一　雷海宗先生的古典奴隶制学术思想

1957年，雷海宗先生在《历史教学》七月号上发表学术论文《世界史分期与上古中古史中的一些问题》，文中就"亚细亚生产方式"、生产工具发展史、生产工具与"生产力"的关系、铜器铁器与社会性质等问题阐述了自己的观点。其中，最引人注目的是雷先生有关希腊罗马的奴隶制及其社会性质问题。归纳他的观点，大体有三个方面：

第一，奴隶制不等于奴隶社会。

雷先生认为："西欧在资本主义萌芽和资本主义初期的这三个世纪中，由于控制了全世界的重要海上航线(注意：又是一个控制海上交通的例子)，大量把落后的非洲人运到新大陆为奴。我们说

[①] 雷海宗：《世界史分期与上古中古史中的一些问题》，《历史教学》1957年第7期。

这是奴隶社会的残余。它比罗马的规模不晓得大多少倍,哪有这样大的残余?"①雷先生进一步指出:"由原始社会末期到资本主义社会,一直有奴隶制,只在特殊条件下可以得到特殊的发展,世界历史上并没有一个奴隶社会阶段。既然如此,历史上也就没有一个所谓奴隶社会向封建社会过渡或转化的问题。这个问题虽然谈了很久,实际它有如希腊神话中的雅典娜女神,是从天父丢斯的头脑中忽然跳出来的。上古、中古之间并无重大的变化,真正重大的变化发生在公元前1100年以下几个世纪间铜器转入铁器的一段。"②雷先生在这里告诉我们一个常识:奴隶制在原始社会末期就已产生,直到美国南北战争时期还存在,而后者的规模远远超过罗马,但它终归是奴隶制,而不是奴隶社会或"残余"。

第二,雅典不等于希腊。

就奴隶制而言,雷先生反对把雅典等同于希腊。"称古希腊为奴隶社会或类似的说法,并不是什么新的看法,这是文艺复兴以后几百年来欧洲学者的传统看法。这种看法出于错觉,出于在'雅典'和'希腊'两个概念间画等号的错觉。几百年来欧洲学者推崇古希腊传下的作品为经典或古典,而这些作品绝大部分都出自雅典,所以在崇古的文人的心目中,完全不自觉地就把雅典扩大为希腊,雅典代表希腊,雅典就是希腊。对于雅典以外的希腊,他们不是不知道,而是视而不见,听而不闻,不能进入他们的意识深处。十九世纪欧洲学术发展到非常高的程度,但仍很少有人体察得到,雅典和另外几个类似的城邦,只不过是希腊世界中的几个孤岛,雅典并不能代表希腊世界。我们学希腊史,是由欧洲人的地方学来的,自然地也就承受了欧洲人的错觉,并且青出于蓝,把这个错觉进一步发挥:雅典扩大为希腊,希腊扩大为全世界,全世界必须要有雅典式的、最少是近似的奴隶制度。象这样的凿空之作,在学术发展史上恐怕是很难找到第二个例的。"③

雷先生之所以称雅典是奴隶制的"孤岛",是因为从特萨利亚一直到伯罗奔尼撒半岛的广大内陆地区,再到整个克里特岛,如此大的范围并不是奴隶制占主导地位的社会。"至于以农业为主的内陆国家,则更没有一般所想象的奴隶景象。它们根本没有条件大量奴役外人或落后部族,就近奴役当地语言文化相同相近的人,只能为农奴,不能为奴隶。例如克里特岛上有几十个希腊城邦,社会组织大同小异。统治阶级为公民和战士,被统治阶级在一般希腊文字中也称为'奴隶',实际他们在当地另有专名。他们有国奴和私奴之分,国奴经营国家的公地,私奴属于个人或家族。私奴为主人经营土地,按定额交租;得有私产,得有家室,由法律承认;主人死而无子,他们并得继承主人的财产。只有两种权利他们不能享受:不能当兵,不能在公共体育场参加体育活动。希腊半岛北中部广大农业区的提撒利亚的情况,也与克里特几乎完全一样。另外,斯巴达称为希洛人的农民,地位实际也与此相同,只是所受的待遇较为严酷,并且没有对主人土地的继承权。这主要地是作风不同,不是根本制度的不同。"④雷先生进一步认为,"但即或在雅典,奴隶与农业的关系也很浅。土地上仍有很多小自耕农。大地主虽用少量奴隶,但土地往往出租或雇工经营。土地关系,主要是封建性的"⑤。

第三,古希腊罗马不等于奴隶社会。

在雷先生笔下,特萨利亚、斯巴达、克里特已无奴隶景象,雅典虽然有奴隶景象,但实质是封建社会的"变种"。因为,"奴隶的大量使用,限于工商业,只有在象雅典这一类的特殊工商业城邦,工商业奴隶有高度发展的可能。但即或是关于雅典,许多情况也不象一般想象得那样清楚的……奴

① 雷海宗:《世界史分期与上古中古史中的一些问题》,《历史教学》1957年第7期。
② 雷海宗:《世界史分期与上古中古史中的一些问题》,《历史教学》1957年第7期。
③ 雷海宗:《世界史分期与上古中古史中的一些问题》,《历史教学》1957年第7期。
④ 雷海宗:《世界史分期与上古中古史中的一些问题》,《历史教学》1957年第7期。
⑤ 雷海宗:《世界史分期与上古中古史中的一些问题》,《历史教学》1957年第7期。

隶使用于各种生产事业上，但也大量使用于家庭服役，富贵之家尤其如此。劳动生产，奴工与自由工并肩工作，工头有时为奴隶，监督自由工人。关于城内生产劳动中奴工与自由工的比例，我们也无法知道，我们只知道一个具体例证。公元前408年雅典修建一座神庙，雇工71人，其中外侨35人，公民20人，奴隶16人。此例有否代表性，我们不能判断。一般所谓典型奴隶社会的雅典，在奴隶制度最盛的公元前五四世纪间，并未见到奴隶对奴隶主的起义斗争，一切重大的政治斗争均为自由人内部不同阶级或阶层之间的斗争，有似封建社会自由身分或半自由身分人民对统治阶级的斗争"[1]。

至于罗马，当它成为地中海霸主时，"罗马得以随心所欲地经由方便的海路向非罗马、非拉丁、非意大利的异族地区侵略征服，大量奴役人口，送到意大利和西西利去作土地奴隶。这种奴隶几乎每年都有补充，地中海上许多地方真正呈显了千里无人烟的惨象。他们贱于牛马；牛马或需重价收买，或需抚养成长。这些奴隶都是自己长大成人的，价格极低，所以主人对他们完全不知爱惜，鞭挞逼工，死了无关，市场上的贱价奴隶好似是无穷无尽的。罗马土地奴隶的生死周转率极快。在全部上古史上，我们只知道这一个例证。假如全世界都如此，人类早已灭绝了。也就在这个时期，罗马史上接连不断地出现奴隶起义。这种情形，显然不能持久。公元前30年罗马统一了整个地中海，无新地可再征服，奴隶制立刻发生危机，贱于牛马的奴隶来源一断，土地奴隶制马上就难再维持下去，很快地就有奴隶被释放为封建性的隶农。罗马式的土地奴隶制度，不只在亚非大陆没有，在希腊也向来没有见到。没有罗马的特殊条件，是不可能出现罗马的土地奴隶制的"[2]。

基于雅典是孤岛式的工商业奴隶制，罗马是短命的土地奴隶制，因此，就古希腊和古罗马整个历史而言，"古典社会的多数地方，包括雅典的农业部分，包括公元前三世纪以上的罗马，实际是封建社会。雅典、罗马的短期特殊发展，只能看为封建社会的变种发展。这种变种，并不限于封建社会，到资本主义社会，只要条件适合，它也可出现。历史上第一次大量用土地奴隶的是罗马，第二次就是十六、十七、十八世纪的西欧"[3]。

雷先生的这些观点在当时学术争论政治化的特殊时代遭到不公正批判，并为此付出了沉痛的代价。然而，雷先生的学术思想并没有因其作古而销声匿迹，考察改革开放以来国内外马克思主义学术界有关西方古典奴隶制的研究成果，不难发现，雷先生的那些学术思想不仅在国内外马克思主义学术界仍后继有人，而且与马克思主义创始人的理论也并不矛盾。

二 马克思主义经典作家有关古典奴隶制的理论及国内外学者的理解

雷先生的上述观点在当时那种特殊的情况下被轻易带上了"反马克思主义"的帽子，但在今天看来，雷先生的那些观点与马克思主义经典作家有关古典奴隶制的论述不仅不矛盾，而且后继有人。

第一，马克思主义经典作家有关古典奴隶制的主要观点：

首先，特萨利亚和斯巴达是农奴制。

1882年，恩格斯致信马克思时明确提到，"我很高兴，关于农奴制的历史，照实业界人士的说法，我们'达成协议'了。毫无疑问，农奴制和依附关系并不是某种特有的中世纪封建形式，在征服者迫使当地居民为其耕种土地的地方，我们到处，或者说几乎到处都可以看得到，——例如在特萨利亚很早就有了"[4]。

关于斯巴达，恩格斯在1859年9—10月给《美国新百科全书》写词条时认为，黑劳士是奴隶。"最

① 雷海宗：《世界史分期与上古中古史中的一些问题》，《历史教学》1957年第7期。
② 雷海宗：《世界史分期与上古中古史中的一些问题》，《历史教学》1957年第7期。
③ 雷海宗：《世界史分期与上古中古史中的一些问题》，《历史教学》1957年第7期。
④ 《马克思恩格斯全集》第35卷，北京：人民出版社，1971年，第131页。

初，组成多立斯社会的各个阶级——不仅构成贵族阶级的全权公民，而且无全权的珀里俄科，甚至奴隶——都必须服兵役。"①但恩格斯在1884年写《家庭、私有制和国家的起源》时则改变了他在1859年的看法。"斯巴达至少在其全盛时代，还不知有家务奴隶，而处于农奴地位的黑劳士则另外居住在庄园里，因此，斯巴达人占有他们妻子的机会比较少。"②这足以表明，恩格斯这时对斯巴达的社会性质有了新的看法，或者说纠正了他在1859年时有关黑劳士是"奴隶"的观点，而这种纠正我们应特别重视。

其次，古典奴隶制占主导地位的时间比较短。

马克思在《资本论》第1卷（1872年）中明确指出："小农经济和独立的手工业生产，一部分构成封建生产方式的基础，一部分在封建生产方式瓦解以后又和资本主义生产并存。同时，它们在原始的东方公有制解体以后，奴隶制真正支配生产以前，还构成古典共同体在其全盛时期的经济基础。"③马克思和恩格斯在《资本论》第3卷（1894年）中又同样指出："自耕农的这种自由小块土地所有制形式，作为占统治地位的正常形式，一方面，在古典古代的极盛时期，形成社会的经济基础，另一方面，在现代各民族中，我们又发现它是封建土地所有制解体所产生的各种形式之一。"④

林志纯先生对马克思这两段话做过专门的分析。他认为，"'古典古代'或'古典公社'（社会）的全盛时代，具体正是指公元前5至4世纪希腊城邦和公元前3至2世纪罗马共和国"⑤。这就意味着：古希腊从提修斯至公元前4世纪，古罗马从塞尔维乌斯·图里乌斯至公元前2世纪，其经济基础还不是奴隶制经济，而是小农经济。这样，古希腊占有"半边天"的特萨利亚和斯巴达（还不包括克里特）是农奴制，而剩下的另一半直到古典古代极盛时期还不是奴隶制经济占主导地位；在古罗马，直到古典古代极盛时期同样也不是奴隶制经济占主导地位，古典古代极盛时期之后，即公元前2世纪之后，奴隶制经济虽然开始占主导地位。但众所周知，古罗马在公元1世纪时便出现隶农制和佃农制了。到帝国繁荣时代结束后，即从塞维鲁王朝开始，"帝国繁荣时代的庞大的生产已收缩为小农业和小手工业，这种小农业和小手工业都不能容纳大量奴隶了。只有富人的家庭和供他们显示豪华的奴隶，在社会上还有存在余地"⑥。这样，"以奴隶劳动为基础的大庄园经济，已经不再有利可图；而在当时它却是大规模农业的唯一可能形式。现在小规模经营又成了唯一有利的形式"⑦。

看来，就奴隶制而言，在马克思主义经典作家笔下确实存在着雅典不等于希腊的情况，以及古罗马奴隶制短暂的情况，或者说，雷先生的看法与马克思主义经典作家的相关论述并非对立。

第二，国内外马克思主义古典史学术界有关古典奴隶制的主要观点：

首先是现代西方古典史研究中马克思主义学派有关古典奴隶制的观点。

早在1961—1962年间，英国《今日马克思主义》开展社会发展阶段问题的讨论时，J·西蒙在其带有总结性的《社会发展中的阶段》一文中，提出"社会经济形态的基本序列"是"原始共产主义——封建主义——资本主义"⑧。

晏绍祥先生对这一学派有过专门的介绍。"芬利曾经指出，在古代希腊，除了斯巴达等极少数的例外，一般来说，人们并不担心奴隶起义的威胁。而在古典时代的前期和后期，奴隶制都不是主要的剥削形式，即使在古典时代，在那些奴隶制比较发达的地区，奴隶制也只能在大生产中取得支

① 《马克思恩格斯全集》第14卷，北京：人民出版社，1964年，第354页。
② 《马克思恩格斯选集》第4卷，北京：人民出版社，1994年，第61页。
③ 《马克思恩格斯文集》第5卷，北京：人民出版社，2009年，第388页。
④ 《马克思恩格斯文集》第7卷，北京：人民出版社，2009年，第911页。
⑤ 林志纯主编：《世界上古史纲》（上册），天津：天津教育出版社，2007年，第17页。
⑥ 《马克思恩格斯选集》第4卷，北京：人民出版社，1994年，第150页。
⑦ 《马克思恩格斯选集》第4卷，北京：人民出版社，1994年，第149页。
⑧ 胡钟达《胡钟达史学论文集》，呼和浩特：内蒙古大学出版社，1997年，第183–184页。

配地位，社会的绝大多数，乃是和奴隶制没有关系的小农。另一古史学者德圣克罗阿把阶级斗争定义为剥削及其对剥削的抵抗，认为只要存在剥削及其对剥削的反抗，便有阶级斗争存在。在古代希腊，由于统治阶级主要依靠剥削奴隶及依附劳动者而使自己免除劳动，因此，奴隶和奴隶主之间始终存在着尖锐的斗争。可是，在叙述古代希腊的阶级斗争时，他仍把自由民内部的冲突作为主要内容，而对奴隶和奴隶主之间的矛盾语焉不详，难以提出几条有力的证据。此外，德圣克罗阿也不能不承认，在古代希腊世界，奴隶制只是有产阶级取得剩余价值的主要途径，社会的主要生产者仍然是那既不剥削别人，也不受他人剥削的小所有者。法国学者韦尔南援引马克思的阶级定义，宣称真正的阶级只存在于近代世界。在希腊，由于独特的城邦结构的作用，阶级斗争主要发生在公民内部，表现为富有公民和贫穷公民之间的冲突。而在罗马，正象马克思指出的那样，阶级斗争主要发生于大、小土地所有者之间。奴隶仅是阶级斗争中的看客，最多追随主人，成为主人的帮凶和打手，并没有自己独立的政治和经济要求，不构成一个独立的阶级。所以，奴隶和奴隶主之间的矛盾虽然是古代社会的基本矛盾，却不是主要矛盾，在阶级斗争中仅具有次要的意义。"①

看来，要论证古典社会是奴隶制社会，必须同时证明古典社会的主要矛盾是奴隶主和奴隶之间的矛盾。但以上学者从社会主要矛盾这个角度的论述却表明：雷先生在20世纪50年代就提出的有关古典奴隶制社会的局部性、特例性及暂时性的观点不仅没有过时，而且确实抓住了古典社会的复杂性和特殊性。正如郭小凌先生正确评价的那样，"他认为奴隶制在雅典和罗马的发展只是特殊的、局部的、暂时的现象，只能看作是整个封建社会大背景下的变种。这一看法较剑桥大学教授芬利提出的类似看法早了23年，至今仍没有失去重要的参考价值"②。

其次是俄罗斯古典史研究中马克思主义学派有关古典奴隶制的观点。

早在1966年，苏联学者Ю·М·柯比夏诺夫在其《封建社会、奴隶制和亚细亚生产方式》一文中就提到，"以兴盛时期的罗马帝国为例，它被认为是奴隶占有制社会的典型例子。奴隶（就其经济方面的含义而言）是农业、手工业和大型建筑业中劳动者的少数。很大一部分奴隶，即几乎所有的生产者都是在城市和乡村交纳代役租的。大部分劳动者属于小生产者的范畴。罗马历史的各个时期都是如此。因此不能把罗马国家（无论是王政、共和国，还是帝国）看作是奴隶占有制国家"。他进一步认为，"至于所谓的奴隶占有制生产方式，它在任何时候、任何地方，都不曾有过"。因此，"封建社会和资本主义是历史上已知的仅有的两种阶级社会形态"③。

俄罗斯著名古典史学者库济辛是一位马克思主义学者，他于1996年主编的《古希腊史》一书体现了苏联解体后的俄罗斯古希腊史的研究成果。对于古希腊奴隶制问题，该书的观点与雷先生的观点有相同之处。在古风时代，希腊"城邦居民的主体是自由的小生产者，首先是农民（在雅典，他们被称作第三等级和第四等级），以及自食其力的工商业者。公元前6世纪，奴隶的数量并不多，只有在大的地产和手工作坊中使用奴隶劳动，因而奴隶在城邦中的作用还不大"④。到古典时代，古希腊城邦的"中等阶层的居民在城邦居民总数中占有相当高的比重，而城邦又采取措施来保持公民集体的稳定，因此不会有太剧烈的财产分化"⑤。所以，"在希腊任何一个城邦，自由小土地所有者都是最重要的社会集团之一。城邦制度的稳定性，民主制度的作用，社会政治冲突的性质，都取决

① 晏绍祥：《古代希腊历史与学术史初学集》，武汉：湖北人民出版社，2003年，第368–369页。
② 郭小凌《生不逢时的雷海宗——雷海宗先生〈西洋文化史纲要〉一书读后》，引自南开大学历史学院：《雷海宗与二十世纪中国史学》北京：中华书局，2005年，第188页。
③ 〔俄〕Ю·М·柯比夏诺夫：《封建社会、奴隶制和亚细亚生产方式》甄修钰译，丁士超校，载《史学理论》，1988年第3期。
④ В.И. Кузищина/Под ред История древней Греции. М.: Высш.шк, 1996.с129.
⑤ В.И. Кузищина/Под ред История древней Греции. М.: Высш.шк, 1996.с163.

于这个集团的经济状况、政治积极性及其成熟程度。小土地所有者一般被称为农民，这个术语也适用于希腊各城邦的农民。应当指出的是，古典农民的许多特点既有别于古代东方的公社成员，又有别于封建社会的农民"①。此外，"还有一些其他类型的依附性劳动者。如在斯巴达、彼奥提亚的城市、特萨利亚、阿卡地亚以及其他一些城邦中，农业中的主要生产者不是奴隶（奴隶不是很多），而是一些处于另一种社会和法律地位的劳动者。他们在斯巴达被称为希洛人，在一些特萨利亚城市被称为珀涅斯泰人（пенесты），在克里特岛被称为沃伊克（войкеи）或克拉罗泰人（кларот），在赫拉克利亚（Гераклей）被称为马里安金人（мариандин）"②。这就是说，古典时代的希腊，无论是雅典，还是斯巴达、特萨利亚及克里特等地区，都不是奴隶制占主导地位。但"从公元前4世纪开始，可以说奴隶的数量大幅度增加，农业、手工业作坊和各类商业部门开始广泛使用奴隶劳动。在雅典经济中，奴隶的广泛使用扩大了生产的规模，20—25公顷的以及配有15—20个奴隶的庄园开始普及，20—30个或更多奴隶的作坊遍布各地。这种状况不论在雅典还是在希腊的其他城邦都比较普遍"③。

至于古罗马地区，库济辛在2002年主编的《古罗马史》中也有专门分析。"在公元前3—2世纪时……家长奴隶制发展为所谓的古典奴隶制，即奴隶制生产方式达到了相当成熟的程度，罗马社会总体来说具备了奴隶制社会性质。"④此时，"奴隶的数量不断增长，成为罗马—意大利社会人数众多的阶层，奴隶占有制在决定性的经济领域——农业、采矿业、金属加工、建筑业——开始普及。但是，自由人和半自由人的劳动在各个部门仍继续使用，并成为公元前2至1世纪罗马国民经济中另一个重要的部门"⑤。同时，"在公元前2至1世纪，奴隶的数量特别多，但是，古代居民的数量，包括奴隶的数量知道的并不准确。学者们对古典时代奴隶和自由民的数量特别关注。19世纪末20世纪初的德国历史学家贝洛赫（Ю. Белох）把奴隶和自由民的比例定为3：5（奴隶占37.5%，自由民占62.5%）。美国历史学家韦斯特曼（У. Уестерман）认为其比例是1：2（奴隶占33%，自由民占67%）"⑥。这样，古罗马即使在古典奴隶制时期，奴隶的劳动并没有完全代替自由民。尤其值得注意的是，在1—2世纪时，古罗马的奴隶制度开始发生变化。"如果说公元前2—1世纪时，罗马政府不过问奴隶和主人之间的相互关系，并支持和保护家长的权利，那么，到2世纪时，奴隶不仅被视为主人的个人财产，而且在一定程度上被视为国家的臣民。统治奴隶的不仅有主人，还有罗马政府。帝国的元首干预奴隶与主人的相互关系，力求制止特别残暴对待奴隶事件的发生。"⑦奴隶制度向缓和方面演化的情况还表现在1世纪时有关奴隶地位的法律文献中，如克劳狄的有关被遗弃的病奴如恢复健康可获自由、哈德良的有关主人杀奴要判罪、安敦尼·皮乌斯的有关杀奴等于杀普通人等法令⑧。看来，古罗马的奴隶制社会确实是比较短暂的一个特例。

最后是国内古典史学者有关古典奴隶制的观点。

国内与雷先生古典奴隶制观点大致相同的后继者主要是胡钟达先生。他"以今日之我与昨日之我论战"，发表了这方面的系列论文。他认为，"在古希腊、罗马的整个历史中，仍然是'希洛特'型和'科洛尼'型以及其他类似的生产关系占优势"，因此，"只要把'封建主义'的含义和使用范围加以扩大，则不仅中世纪的欧洲社会是封建社会，整个古代东方社会、古代希腊罗马社会也都

---

① В.И. Кузищина / Под ред　*История древней Греции*. М.: Высш .шк, 1996. c165.
② В.И. Кузищина / Под ред　*История древней Греции*. М.: Высш .шк, 1996. c161.
③ В.И. Кузищина / Под ред　*История древней Греции*. М.: Высш .шк, 1996. c207.
④ В.И. Кузищина / Под ред　*История Древнего Рима*[M]. М.: Высш .шк, 1996. c97.
⑤ В.И. Кузищина / Под ред　*История Древнего Рима*[M]. М.: Высш .шк, 1996. c99.
⑥ В.И. Кузищина / Под ред　*История Древнего Рима*[M]. М.: Высш .шк, 1996. c100—101.
⑦ В.И. Кузищина / Под ред　*История Древнего Рима*[M]. М.: Высш .шк, 1996. c251.
⑧ С.И. Ковалева / Под ред　*История Рима*[M]. Санкт-Петербург, 2002. c688—689.

可以认为是封建社会。亚细亚的、古代的、封建的生产方式可以认为是同一封建社会经济形态的不同类型或模式"①。胡先生为了论证他的古典奴隶制"特例论"和"插曲论"，在方法论上也有说明：一是，重新强调恩格斯《家庭、私有制和国家的起源》一书中所引有关雅典奴隶数字不准确或夸大了②。二是，列宁的《论国家》是不可靠的速记稿③。同时，马克思、恩格斯、列宁时期的古典史研究还很薄弱，尤其是马克思时期，苏美尔文明、爱琴文明、哈拉巴文明还不为人们所知。列宁也承认，有关古代史知识还很薄弱④。三是，高尔亭法典肯定类似黑劳士型劳动者的沃伊克有财产权，俄罗斯学者"卡扎玛诺娃以厄福鲁斯那一段话为据来证明沃伊克实际上并无财产权，完全是牵强附会，是对原文意义的误解或曲解"⑤。如果克里特不是奴隶社会，与克里特类似的斯巴达和特萨利亚也不是奴隶社会，这样，希腊的农奴制就不是"半边天"问题了，而是大部分地区了，支撑奴隶社会的基石于是被抽掉了，"整个大厦就要倾塌了"⑥。四是，不论从马克思的《资本主义生产以前的各种形式》和《资本论》中有关论述来看，还是从西欧的历史实际来看，"奴隶制和农奴制一样，都是在原始社会解体时期就已出现，而不是在奴隶社会末期作为封建主义的'萌芽'才出现的"⑦。因此，"那种认为封建社会必须脱胎于奴隶社会，原始社会假如没有受到先进生产力的影响只能发展为奴隶社会而不能发展为封建社会，并且把创立这种理论的'荣誉'归之于马克思和恩格斯，事实上是毫无根据的"⑧。

当然，用胡先生的上述观点来论证雷先生古典奴隶制观点的学术价值还不足以令人信服。因此，我们有必要简述一下"五种生产方式说"学者对古典奴隶制的看法。

林志纯先生是著名的"五种生产方式说"学者，也是古典史大师级学者，他在其主编的《世界上古史纲》一书中，特别重视马克思有关"小农经济……还构成古典社会全盛时期的经济基础"的论述，并专门做了分析。林先生认为，"'古典古代'或'古典公社'（社会）的全盛时代，具体正是指公元前5至4世纪希腊城邦和公元前3至2世纪罗马共和国。这时，尽管各地奴隶制在末后已有相当大发展，但只要自耕农民阶级尚未彻底破产，尚未完全被奴隶制排挤，经济基础总还不是奴隶制经济，而仍然是小农经济"⑨。对于典型的古罗马奴隶社会而言，"公元前111年的托利乌斯土地法宣告公有地制度的灭亡，私有制的胜利；它同时也表示了城邦共和国小农经济基础的彻底破坏，奴隶制经济和大地产的胜利"。但"到公元1世纪，情况就有变化，隶农或佃农（colonus）制出现了。这是后来中世纪庇护制（patrocinium）的开端"⑩。看来，从公元前111年的托利乌斯土地法宣告公有地制度的灭亡，到公元1世纪隶农或佃农（colonus）制的出现，古罗马的奴隶制社会确实比较短暂。

李雅书和杨共乐两位先生是研究古罗马史的专家，他们对"古代所有制"的含义与奴隶制的本质差别做了专门分析，并根据二者的关系对古罗马的历史分期进行了新的划分⑪。他们认为，"马克思所指的古代所有制形式决不是奴隶所有制形式，而完全是一种与奴隶制绝然不同的独立的所有制

---

① 胡钟达《胡钟达史学论文集》，呼和浩特：内蒙古大学出版社，1997年，第187页。
② 胡钟达《胡钟达史学论文集》，呼和浩特：内蒙古大学出版社，1997年，第230–231页。
③ 胡钟达《胡钟达史学论文集》，呼和浩特：内蒙古大学出版社，1997年，第227页。
④ 胡钟达《胡钟达史学论文集》，呼和浩特：内蒙古大学出版社，1997年，第224–226页。
⑤ 胡钟达《胡钟达史学论文集》，呼和浩特：内蒙古大学出版社，1997年，第283页。
⑥ 胡钟达《胡钟达史学论文集》，呼和浩特：内蒙古大学出版社，1997年，第285页。
⑦ 胡钟达《胡钟达史学论文集》，呼和浩特：内蒙古大学出版社，1997年，第175页。
⑧ 胡钟达《胡钟达史学论文集》，呼和浩特：内蒙古大学出版社，1997年，第181页。
⑨ 林志纯主编：《世界上古史纲》（上册），天津：天津教育出版社，2007年，第17页。
⑩ 林志纯主编：《世界上古史纲》（下册），天津：天津教育出版社，2007年，第216–217页。
⑪ 李雅书，杨共乐：《对古代罗马史若干理论问题的重新考察》，《世界历史》，1993年第4期。

形式。它从氏族社会中发展而来，最后又被奴隶制等因素的发展所否定。正因为如此，所以，建立在古代所有制基础上的社会也决不是奴隶社会，它只能是与其基础相适应的古代社会和公民共同体。公元前6世纪塞尔维乌斯改革以来的罗马社会就是这种古代社会的典型。在罗马，这种古代社会一直存在了3个多世纪，只是到公元前2世纪中叶以后，由于奴隶制的发展才破坏了这种社会所赖以存在的基础，导致了古代社会的灭亡"①。因此，公元前2世纪中后期到公元1世纪中叶，是古代社会的衰落和奴隶制社会的建立时期。1世纪中叶到2世纪末叶，是罗马奴隶社会的完善和发展期。3世纪初叶到5世纪中叶，是罗马奴隶制社会的衰落和瓦解时期②。看来，在李先生和杨先生笔下，古罗马的奴隶制社会也大体限于1世纪中叶到2世纪末叶，或者说古罗马奴隶制占主导地位的时间也比较短。

总之，国内外学者有关古典奴隶制的观点也有力证明了：雷先生对古典奴隶制的分析完全符合古希腊罗马的历史实际。

三　雷海宗先生古典奴隶制学术思想的启示

雷先生的古典奴隶制学术思想在特殊的环境下虽然被认为是离经叛道，但当学术环境进入正态时期，雷先生求真求实的精神就会得到一大批响应者，并使我们后人不得不考虑这种现象的启示意义：

第一，学术争论不能政治化。

据陈吉生先生考察，与雷先生发表古典奴隶制学术观点的同时还有另两位学者，即黄现璠和李鸿哲。黄先生于1957年6月出版的壮族历史上第一本简略通史《广西僮族简史》中说："唐以前和唐末宋初，僮族的社会是奴隶社会或封建社会，抑是氏族部落社会，值得提出研究。依汉族社会发展史，由氏族部落社会，经奴隶社会，进到封建社会。但社会性质的决定，应该根据社会生产力、经济、政治等发展的实际情况而定，不能公式化机械的硬套。唐以前和唐末宋初，认为僮族社会是奴隶社会或封建社会，文献上都没有记载，惟有氏族部落社会尚可由各方面材料加以推断。"③同年7月，雷先生在《历史教学》上发表了众所周知的《世界史分期与上古中古史中的一些问题》一文。同年10月，李鸿哲接着发表了《"奴隶社会"是否社会发展必经阶段？》一文，公开置疑主流史学定为一尊的"有奴论"，最后得出结论："奴隶社会说在理论上站不住脚，不符合历史事实，违背历史唯物主义，多年来为人所信从，实在是一种教条主义的偏向。但这一种教条却不是从马克思的经典著作中得来的，它是由郭沫若先生、斯特鲁威院士等提倡起来的。由于这一种教条的存在，苏联和我国史学家们曾花费很多力气在古代各国历史上找寻奴隶。假若奴隶社会说本身根本不能成立，那么这些工作和争论岂非徒劳无功！"④

因此，后人把黄现璠、雷海宗、李鸿哲称为中国"无奴"学派的"三剑客"，也可称为"英雄所见略同"现象，因为黄先生与雷先生的"亮剑"仅仅相差1个月，加之他们所从事的专业不同，所以他们的"共识"未必是相互沟通的结果，而是对教条主义或公式化难以接受的勇敢挑战。但遗憾的是在那个特殊时代，我们不能很好地把握"政治上求同存异，学术上求异存同"的原则，结果使本来可以通过讨论来丰富完善的学术问题政治化、教条化和公式化了。

---

① 李雅书，杨共乐：《对古代罗马史若干理论问题的重新考察》，《世界历史》，1993年第4期。
② 李雅书，杨共乐：《对古代罗马史若干理论问题的重新考察》，《世界历史》，1993年第4期。
③ 参见黄现璠《广西僮族简史》，广西人民出版社，1957年。转引自陈吉生《试论中国历史学的无奴学派》，中国世界古代史研究网，http://www.cawhi.com/show.aspx?id=7112&cid=16，2010-07-01。
④ 李鸿哲：《"奴隶社会"是否社会发展必经阶段？》，《文史哲》1957年第10期。

第二，应重视社会发展规律的多样性统一。

历史无疑有规律性，但也有丰富多彩性和复杂性。夸大规律性，会导致教条主义和公式化；夸大多样性，会导致历史无规律可循。

众所周知，在雷先生时期，即使"有奴"学派的观点也不完全一致，尤其是在中国古代史分期的讨论上，奴隶社会和封建社会的断限竟然相差了1500年。学者们把它归纳为"三论五说"。"三论"是指以吕振羽、范文澜、翦伯赞、邓拓、嵇文甫、杨向奎、徐中舒、王亚南、赵光贤、王玉哲、李埏为代表的西周封建论；以郭沫若、杨宽、吴大琨、白寿彝、田昌五、林甘泉为代表的战国封建论（解放初期郭沫若的古史分期主张多次变动，至1952年他的《奴隶制时代》一书出版时，改为主张战国封建说）；以尚钺、王仲荦、日知（林志纯）、何兹全、王思治、赵俪生为代表的魏晋封建论。以上三论，一般认为是在中国古史分期讨论中所形成的"有奴论"的三大学派。所谓"五说"，即以李亚农、唐兰、祝瑞开、吴慧为代表的春秋封建说；以黄子通、夏甄陶、金景芳为代表的秦统一封建说；以侯外庐、赵锡元为代表的西汉封建说；以周谷城、郑昌淦为代表的东汉封建说；以梁作干为代表的东晋封建说①。

"三论五说"的现象足以表明中国古史分期和中国古史本身的复杂性，当然也不排除大讨论之所以进入死胡同有教条主义和公式化的原因，最后只好把郭沫若战国封建论等同于马克思主义的官方史学理论。

更为重要的现象是，"无奴"学派的"三剑客"虽然在当时的环境下失去了话语权，但在今天仍后继有人。据陈吉生统计，"无奴"学派现已发展到50多人，其中较有代表性的是张广志、胡钟达、沈长云、晁福林等学者②。陈吉生不仅列举了"无奴"学派的姓名和正式发表的论文，而且还就"无奴"学派的发展壮大情况、主要观点及特点等加以考察。他的研究表明，"无奴"学派的"三剑客"之所以后继有人，其阵容之所以不断发展壮大，是因为"有奴"学派的观点确实存在不少问题。因此，我们今天的讨论必须重视社会发展规律的多样性统一，或者说在讨论社会形态问题时，应充分重视"无奴"学派的观点。

第三，应重视理论与实际相统一。

仅以古希腊罗马史而言，既然马克思明确提到："小农经济"是"构成古典社会全盛时期的经济基础"，而历史事实也表明古希腊的奴隶制是在公元前4世纪开始占主导地位，古罗马的奴隶制是公元前2世纪开始占主导地位，那么，我们的教材直到现在仍然把公元前4世纪希腊城邦的危机纳入古典时代，把公元前337年的科林斯会议作为古典时代终结的标志，这显然是与理论和实际相矛盾的。事实上，伯罗奔尼撒战争结束后，即公元前4世纪的希腊城邦危机显然是一个新的时期。至于古罗马史，李雅书和杨共乐两位先生已有新的分期，这个分期是否有采用和完善的必要，我们的教材目前仍无反映，仍是王政、共和、前期帝国、后期帝国的陈旧划分。

总之，前资本主义社会各个阶段确实还存在着不少困扰学术界的理论问题，需要学者们深入讨论，而这种深入讨论尤其需要有雷先生的求真求实的精神。

① 参见黄现璠《广西僮族简史》，广西人民出版社，1957年。转引自陈吉生《试论中国历史学的无奴学派》，中国世界古代史研究网，http://www.cawhi.com/show.aspx?id=7112&cid=16，2010-07-01。
② 转引自陈吉生《试论中国历史学的无奴学派》，中国世界古代史研究网，http://www.cawhi.com/show.aspx?id=7112&cid=16，2010-07-01。

20世纪初中国历史学者为提升中国史研究的
国际地位所做出的努力
——以陈寅恪、傅斯年、雷海宗为例

马亮宽、李慎令 聊城大学

摘 要： 20世纪初期，科学教育思潮、救国思潮在中国兴起，有些留学欧美的青年学者利用西方历史学的理论和方法研究中国史，试图提高中国人民的民族自信心和爱国心，"为中国而豪外国"，其中傅斯年、陈寅恪、雷海宗等堪称代表。他们的努力取得了西方学术界的关注和重视，提高了中国历史学研究的国际地位。

关键词： 中国史研究；陈寅恪；傅斯年；雷海宗

20世纪初，中国哲学社会科学的研究和传承出现了一些明显的特点，在历史学领域表现得尤为突出。许多青年历史学者在对中国传统学术进行批判的同时，以高度的社会责任感对中国历史学术进行改造或重建，其目的是提高民族的历史自信力，实现科学教育救国的目标。

一

清末民初，中国有一批有志青年，怀着医国救民的理想留学欧美各国，学习先进的科学技术。正如有人所评论："这段期间在欧陆负笈求学的，民初中国知识分子，亲眼目睹了欧洲在一次大战过后的满目疮痍，以及战后各国的整建与复原所做的努力，再想起远在万里以外的苦难祖国，正遭逢国内外变局的摧残！因此而激起了一股豪气干云的情操。要'究天人之际'、要'通古今之变'、要'成一家之言'的呐喊响彻云霄。当时，在欧陆时常往来的一批浮云游子，包括了傅斯年、陈寅恪、俞大维、罗家伦、毛子水、赵元任……等，这些人日后学成归来，大多数都成了中国现代史里具有举足轻重力量的'优异分子'。"①这批青年学子回国后除部分人从政外，大部分终生从事学术研究和教育，其中部分学者借鉴西方的历史研究理论和方法，致力于对传统史学的改造，身体力行，奠定了中国历史学发展和创新的基础。

陈寅恪、傅斯年、雷海宗堪称这批学人的典型代表。他们认为，中国历史悠久，有着优秀的历史研究传统，但是，历史研究方法和理论已经落后于时代，必须借鉴西方科学的理论和方法，结合

---

① 《傅孟真传记资料》（一），（台）天一出版社1979年版，第50页。

中国历史研究的传统优势，确立中国史研究的优势地位。对此，傅斯年等留学归国后，在阐述学术研究中如何处理中国与外国的关系时强调："现在中国希望制造一个新将来，取用材料自然最重要的是欧美的物质文明，即物质以外的东西也应该取精神于未衰败的外国。"①至于如何认识当时中国历史学的研究现状和国际上地位，傅斯年、陈寅恪等人都有正确的评断。傅斯年在《历史语言研究所工作之旨趣》中对历史学、语言学、考古学研究的发展方向进行了系统的阐述："在中国境内语言学和历史学的材料是最多的，欧洲人求之尚难得，我们却坐看他毁坏和亡失，我们着实不满这个状态，着实不服气，就是物质的原料以外，既便学问的原料，也被欧洲人搬了去乃至偷了去。我们很想借几个不陈的工具，处理些新获见的材料，所以才有这历史语言研究所的设置。"②很显然，傅斯年争取建立历史语言研究所，就是改变中国历史研究现状，实现其在中国历史学、语言学研究方面"为中国而豪外国"③的理想。

陈寅恪对于 20 世纪初中国历史学研究落后状况有更深刻的认识，他曾论述说："当时史学地位之卑下若此，由今思之，诚可哀矣，此清代经学发展过甚，所以转致史学之不振也。近二十年来，国人内感民族文化之衰颓，外受世界思潮之激荡。其论史之作，渐能脱除清代经师之旧染，有以合于今日史学之真谛，……。"④陈寅恪 1931 年发表《吾国学术之现状及清华之职责》中对中国的学术现状进行了评估，对社会科学诸学科评价甚低。他说："西洋文学哲学艺术历史等，苟输入传达，不失其真，即为难能可贵，惶问其有所创获。……至于本国史学文学思想艺术史等，疑若可以几于独立者，察其实际，亦复不然。近年中国古代及近代史料发见虽多，而具有统系与不涉傅会之整理，犹待今后之努力。今日全国大学未必有人焉，能授本国通史，或一代专史，而胜任愉快者。东洲邻国以三十年来学术锐进之故，其关于吾国历史之著作，非复国人所能追步。……今日国虽幸存，而国史已失其正统，若起先民于地下，其感慨如何？"⑤结合陈寅恪 1929 年《北大学院已巳级史学毕业生赠言》："群趋东邻受国史，神州士夫羞欲死。田巴鲁仲两无成，要待诸君洗斯耻。添赋迁儒自圣狂，读书不肯为人忙。平生所学宁堪赠，独此区区是秘方。"⑥这些都说明陈寅恪对中国史研究的不满和担忧，在同时代的另一篇文章中对中国古代史研究状况再次进行评论说："寅恪不敢观三代两汉之书，而喜谈中古之降民族文化之史，故承命不辞。……今日吾国治学之士，竞言古史，察其持论，间有类乎清季夸诞经学家之所为者。"⑦陈寅恪对 20 世纪 20—30 年代研究中国古代史者不满意，主要因为传统学者的研究夸诞不实，无法使中国历史研究在国际上取得优势地位。

相对陈寅恪、傅斯年诸人在欧美留学兼收并蓄不同，雷海宗在美国留学 5 年，主修历史学，对西方史学理论和方法有了系统全面的了解，回国后先后任教于中央大学、清华大学，抗战期间长期担任西南联合大学历史系主任。雷海宗回国不论教课还是学术研究，以兼通中外，改造旧史学为己任，研究方向则转向中国古代史，如 1931 年发表在《文哲季刊》的《殷周年代考》，1932 年发表在《金陵学报》的《孔子以前之哲学》，皆为先秦历史与哲学，1932 年调入清华大学主要讲授中国通史，研究和著述也以中国古代史为主，他的代表作《中国的兵》、《皇帝制度之成立》，也都是 20 世纪 30 年代前期的成果。雷海宗在史学理论观念方面深受德国历史哲学家斯宾格勒文化形态史观影响，回国后结合中国历史发展历程及特点，以世界文化演进周期理论论证中国历史文化周期的演进，他

① 《傅斯年全集》第三卷，湖南教育出版社 2003 年版，第 13 页（以下引用该书只注卷数与页数）。
② 《傅斯年全集》第三卷，第 9 页。
③ 王汎森、潘光哲、吴政上主编《傅斯年遗札》第一卷，（台）中研院历史语言研究所 2011 年版，第 113 页。
④ 《陈寅恪集·金明馆丛稿二编》，三联书店 2009 年版，第 270 页。
⑤ 《陈寅恪集·金明馆丛稿二编》，三联书店 2009 年版，第 361—362 页。
⑥ 《陈寅恪集·诗集》，三联书店 2009 年版，第 19 页。
⑦ 《陈寅恪集·金明馆丛稿二编》，三联书店 2009 年版，第 270 页。

认为："世界几个文明区的发展进程虽各有特点，但发展的节奏、时限和周期大致相同，都经过封建时代、贵族国家时代、帝国主义时代、大一统时代和政治破裂与文化灭绝的末世，这五个阶段，最后趋于毁灭。"雷海宗通过对中国历史发展进程进行研究，认为中国历史发展已经经历了两个周期，正由第二生命周期进入第三生命期，就像木本花一样，"今年开放，明年可再重开，若善自培植，可以无限的延长生命"。①很显然，雷海宗的结论告诉人们，中国历史文化不断更新发展，不会走其他文化一个周期结束就必然灭亡的老路，雷海宗的文化周期理论论证了中国历史文化的不断更新演进，在当时无疑可以提高中国人民的民族自信心。从某种意义上说，雷海宗对中外历史文化的比较从另一个层面提高了中国历史研究的历史地位。

二

陈寅恪、傅斯年、雷海宗等深知，要实现科学教育救国这一伟大目标，必须团结起来，建立学术组织，实现集众式研究，推动科学研究不断进步，同时要加强与欧美的联系，学习和吸收他们的研究成果，才能赶上和超越他们。为此，这些学者在回国之初，积极组建学术研究组织，如北京大学国学门、中央研究院历史语言研究所等，其中傅斯年、陈寅恪是历史语言研究所的领袖，在史语所建立后，聘请了欧美汉学研究的领导人士米勒、伯希和、珂罗倔伦三人为通信研究员。实际上是借此加强与欧美汉学研究中心建立学术联系。傅斯年、陈寅恪等人在建立学术机构，组织有关学者进行集众式研究的同时，还筹办了学术刊物，不断地将其研究成果、研究动态向世界公布，传达学术研究的信息，其中以《历史语言研究所集刊》最具代表性。

陈寅恪、傅斯年、雷海宗等一代学人争取中国历史学术国际地位的努力从某种意义上说获得了成功，他们的学术研究在 20 世纪 30—40 年代引起西方汉学界的关注和推重，这里仅举几个例子加以证明：

陈寅恪是最受西方学术界推重的中国学者之一。陈寅恪出身于官宦士大夫家庭，自少年时期开始留学日本，以后又留学美国、欧洲，前后近 20 年，在留学期间，刻苦学习和研究各国语言和历史等学科。回国后任职于清华大学和历史语言研究所，毕生致力于语言、历史方面的研究，其学术成就受到西方学术界的重视。1938 年，英国牛津大学聘陈寅恪为汉学教授，并授予英国皇家学会研究员职称，这是欧洲汉学界对陈寅恪学术地位的肯定。"伟大的汉学家伯希和认为陈先生能以批判性的方法并利用各种不同文字的史料从事他的研究，是一位最优秀的中国学者。""是西方汉学家难以超越的。"②当时一位了解陈寅恪的中国学者也评论说："欧美任何汉学家，除伯希和、斯文赫定、沙畹等极少数人外，鲜有能听得懂寅恪先生之讲者。不过寅公接受牛津特别讲座之荣誉聘请，至少可以使今日欧美认识汉学有多么个深度，亦大有益于世界学术界也。"③

陈寅恪接受了聘请，曾两次计划经香港乘船赴英国牛津大学就职，皆因第二次世界大战激烈进行，航路中断而未能成行，但欧洲汉学界与陈寅恪的联系没有中断。1943 年，牛津大学担任中国宗教和哲学课程的高级讲师修中诚到中国访问，专程到桂林拜访陈寅恪，两人就陈寅恪赴英就职进行合作研究等事项进行了商讨，陈寅恪委托修中诚向牛津大学校方转达他学术研究合作的计划，计划中有两项内容值得特别注意：一是将新、旧《唐书》以比较研究的形式译成英文，时间计划 5—6 年完成；二是委任雷海宗、邵循正、孙毓棠三人用英文撰写三卷本的中国历史。陈寅恪提交的计划书说明他答应就任牛津大学中文教授不是贪图虚名和改善生活环境，而是代表中国与西方学术界合

① 许冠三：《新史学九十年》，岳麓书社 2003 年 9 月版，第 294 页。
② 程美宝：《陈寅恪与牛津大学》，《历史研究》2000 年第 3 期，第 155 页。
③ 蒋天枢：《陈寅恪先生编年事辑》，上海古籍出版社 1997 年版，第 118 页。

作，推广中国学术。特别应强调的一点，合作撰写英文的中国历史书，陈寅恪推荐的第一个人是雷海宗，说明他对雷海宗的认可和推重。陈寅恪虽然因国际形势的变化没能到牛津大学就职，但欧洲汉学界一直与他保持联系，对其学术地位继续给予褒奖和推崇。1944 年，经陶育礼（Dodds）、汤恩比（Toynbee）、库克（Cook）三名院士联名推荐，经英国学术院院士大会通过陈寅恪为通讯院士的提案，从此，陈寅恪作为英国学术院通讯院士的记录一直保留在《英国学术院院刊》，直到 1975 年，英方确认陈寅恪去世。①

自 20 世纪 30 年代开始，西方汉学界对中国历史文化领域的研究认识和评价不断提高，来中国访问考察、寻求合作的学者不断增多，多数来访者都是以平等甚至求学问道的心理来考察和交流。其中包括伯希和、李约瑟等知名的汉学家。伯希和是世界著名的法国汉学家，其晚年对中国历史研究的成就相当推崇，对陈寅恪、傅斯年等学者也相当敬重。正如当时学者所评论："且伯君认识及称述中国学人之贡献，尤为其他汉学者所不及，此可于伯君著作及言论见之。"②1943 年 3 月，英国学者李约瑟、陶育礼（E.R.Dodds）等，率领英国文化科学使团到中国考察访问，先后到重庆、宜宾李庄考察交流，在访问期间会见了王世杰、朱家骅、梅贻琦、蒋梦麟、叶企荪、傅斯年等科技文化界上层人士。李约瑟等人在李庄等地考察时对史语所科研人员在艰苦、简陋的环境下认真从事学术研究的精神所感动，同时对他从事中国科学技术史研究给予了全力合作和支持。尤其是傅斯年，被李约瑟认为是"大学者"，他在致夫人的信中评论傅斯年等人说："那里的学者是我迄今会见的人们中最杰出的，因这个学科一直是中国学者特别擅长的，这也是意料中的事。"③李约瑟这次对中国考察访问前后近四年，当 1946 年，李约瑟回国时，傅斯年所致的欢送词中对李约瑟在中国的作为给予了高度评价："当他居留在中国期间，他曾有一次回到英国去了几个月，在那里他作了多次关于中国科学工作的演讲，因此在英国学术圈内激起对中国的新评价。"④

总之，陈寅恪、傅斯年、雷海宗等人都是 20 世纪的学术大师，他们学贯中西、知识渊博，由于他们的积极努力，完成了中国历史学研究从传统向现代的科学转型。他们在中国历史研究方面取得的成就获得了西方学术界的认可和较高评价。

①　《陈寅恪研究》，九州出版社 2013 年版，第 62 页。
②　《傅斯年全集》，第五卷，第 469 页。
③　陈怀宇：《在西方发现陈寅恪》，北京师范大学出版社 2013 年 3 月版，第 142 页。
④　《傅斯年全集》，第五卷，第 496 页。

雷海宗：十年一觉南开梦——访南开大学教授王敦书

王　坚　天津师范大学

陈乐民先生在《欧洲文明十五讲》中，曾对雷海宗（1902–1962，字伯伦，河北永清人）的一生作了这样的鸟瞰：

> 雷海宗先生何许人也？你们可能都没有人知道了。他是过去的清华大学教授，早年留学美国，回来以后在武汉大学教书，再后来又到清华大学历史系教书。我在清华大学的时候，人们说他讲课"其声如雷，其学如海，史学之宗"，他就是这么一位大学问家。雷先生在1952年院系调整的时候，本来应该调到北大历史系。不知道是何缘故，所有的清华大学文科的名牌教授都调到北大来了，少数的调到社科院去了，独独雷海宗先生调到南开大学。南开大学得人啊，因此，南开大学历史系最有它的特色。得一位老师，兴一个学科。当然后来雷海宗先生也免不了和其他的教授一样戴上了"右派"帽子。

这段概述虽然精辟，但过于简短，非但不能交待细节，反而会引起人们更多的好奇和疑问：雷先生1952年"独独"调到南开大学，究竟是为什么？后来他为什么会被错划为"右派"？这位"大学问家"到南开后，工作并逝世于斯，总共时间不过十年，其中，尚有近半时间因政治运动而受厄，那么，他又如何能在这充满艰辛的寥寥数年间，再造人生的高峰？再往上溯，在强手如云的民国学界，雷先生究竟又有何过人之处，以至于被称为"其声如雷，其学如海，史学之宗"？……

正是带着这些好奇与疑问，笔者找到了南开大学教授，也是雷海宗关门弟子的王敦书先生。

王敦书，1955年毕业于北京大学历史系，1957年考入南开大学，师从雷海宗，攻读世界上古中古史专业的副博士研究生（当时向苏联学来的一种学位制度，大致与硕士相当，但实行四年制，有博士候选人之意），1961年，回历史系工作，又成为雷海宗的同事。从师从雷先生，受其亲炙，并先后被打成"右派"，到在其指点之下一起做翻译，做研究，再到为雷先生送终，最后又在雷先生身后为其整理文稿，编纪念文集，推动并亲自做雷先生生平与思想的研究，这位高足，已经成为雷海宗先生的世界里不可或缺的一部分。

要了解雷海宗一生的光荣与梦想，尤其是他到南开后的遭际和变迁，相信没有比王敦书先生更合适的访问人选。

"其声如雷" 今看摇落

回忆是从 1952 年雷海宗先生的调动开始的。

1952 年,全国高校院系调整,雷海宗由清华大学历史系调到天津南开大学。虽然这并不尽如人意,但是在雷海宗心中,并无太多遗憾。他知道自己将调南开的消息后,曾对清华的邻居张岱年教授说,二十五年前留学回国时,南开就向他发过聘书,当时未能成行,而现在终于要去了,看来晚年也将在南开度过。对于南开,他是有感情的,觉得自己与南开似乎有缘分。

王敦书先生回忆说:"关于 1952 年秋调到南开一事,雷师没有跟我谈过他的想法和心情,所以我只能谈谈个人的看法和感觉。当时北大、清华、燕京三校历史系合并为一个北京大学历史系,人满为患,势必要调走一些人。问题是:调走谁和调往何处?我觉得,从业务水平来说,雷师学贯古今中外,自应留在北大历史系;但从政治状况来说,调离北大却是很自然乃至必然的。南开是全国著名的大学,抗战时期与清华、北大合组成西南联大;天津离北京很近,是全国第三大的直辖市,所以,能调往南开就算是不错的了。清华另外两位教我的师长丁则良和何基,还分别被调往长春的东北人民大学和东北师范大学。雷师有自知之明,对于离开清华、北大,前往南开,我想他应有心理准备和能够接受的。他对张岱年先生讲的话,是 1992-1993 年间清华同仁召开纪念雷师诞辰九十周年会议时,我听张先生发言说的。我觉得,他说的是一个事实,当时雷师的心情与其说是自嘲,不如说是感慨,或者说是'四分感慨,三分无奈,三分自嘲'。"

与雷海宗一起到南开的,还有郑天挺先生。南开历史系本来不弱,但缺乏大师级的名教授,世界史方面也稍差一些,雷郑两人联袂而来,大大充实了它的力量。对于他们,南开大学的领导是相当重视的。

王先生回忆说:"对雷师,南开的领导是尊重和重用的,生活上也尽可能给以照顾。从居住条件来说,当时南开没有较优良富裕的教授住宅。听雷师母说起,雷师仅夫妇二人来南开,对居住条件要求不高,只希望厕所有能坐的抽水马桶,因雷师解大手的时间较长,甚至有时候坐在那里看书报。南开就把校门口新盖的二居室的平房拨给他们,有单独的厨房厕所和能坐的抽水马桶卫生设备,虽比清华时的条件差些,但也就可以了。雷师来南开后,一边担任讲课的重任,一边写文章,工作是比较顺利的。"

然而,1957 年那个难忘的夏天来临之后,一切都改变了。

那是 8 月 14 日,一次紧急会议,打破了假期中南开大学校园的宁静。

这一日,天津科协举行反"右派"斗争大会,按当时天津市委的决定,雷海宗定为"右派"。他在这一年前后的发言、讲话、文章,都成为罪证。

据说,雷海宗此次被定为"右派",是康生在北京召开的一次会上公开点的名。他问天津来参加会议的市委负责人,天津为什么不批判雷海宗?此后,天津市和南开大学立刻召开大大小小多次会议,揭发批判雷海宗,整理和发表这方面的材料与文章。

厄运,似乎突如其来;不过,之前早已是山雨欲来风满楼。

1949 年以前,雷海宗不但曾加入国民党,担任过党内职务,还是"战国策"派代表人物。抗战时期,他提出和国民党"民族第一"、"国家第一",各党派平息内争、全力抗战等口号相一致的主张,当时就曾受到中共南方局属下一些知识分子的批判。1949 年以后,他虽然之前拒绝过国民党当局的"南飞"动员,毅然留在清华园,之后又积极参加共产党的各种政治运动,还写文章批判美国的"门户开放"政策及罗马教廷,但是,因为"历史问题",他在清华时,就已经是不得不作检讨,并被批判为"反动的'战国策'派代表人物"了。

王先生说:"解放后,因为担任过国民党党内的职务,雷师曾受到管制(后撤销),并且不再担任清华历史系主任之职。1952年初思想改造运动时，他在全系范围内做了思想检查，对过去的反动言行、战国策派理论与斯宾格勒的历史哲学进行了自我批判，并接受大家的批评帮助。不过，据说，雷师的检查是检查得比较好的。我还有一个印象，1951年前后，雷师曾在北京的某一报纸上发表一篇谈自己思想改造的短文，说开始懂得了'为人民服务'的丰富内容与真正意义。"

调南开后，很快到了1957年春。

那时，全国开展帮助党内整风运动，号召大家大鸣大放，雷海宗响应号召，4月间，他先后两次参加关于"百家争鸣"的座谈会，主要谈发展社会科学的问题。作为一代史学宗师，雷海宗此时虽然接受并按照马克思主义来研究历史，不过，他对马克思主义的理解与态度，毕竟和那些教条主义者及政治实用家是不一样的。他说出了自己的独立思考，其中，最著名的，是这样一段话：

> 对马克思和恩格斯树立的新的社会科学的看法，大家在理论上是一致的，承认马列主义应该发展，可是实际上是停止了发展，还停留在恩格斯死时1895年的地方。1895年以后，列宁、斯大林在个别问题上有新的提法，但他们主要谈当前革命问题。从了解整理几千年来人类历史经验，建立新的社会科学来说，基本上停留在1895年，教条主义者就是这样。马克思、恩格斯生平也是经常修改他们的学说，他们注意到当时每一个社会科学部门的发展情况，掌握社会科学研究的材料和成果。可是以后人们就以为他们已解决了一切问题，社会科学不能再发展了。事实上并不如此，1895年以后社会科学上新材料很多，对旧材料有很多新的认识。我们今天的任务，就是要把1895年到今天62年的课补上。

这段话，后来被批判为污蔑"马克思主义停滞在1895年"。《人民日报》不久刊载了他的发言，并加编者按和编者注，中间有这样的话："雷先生认为列宁对于马克思主义只是'在个别问题上有新的提法'，马克思主义'基本上停留在1895年'，这却是违反了事实。"

王先生回忆说："鸣放一开始，雷师是和全国绝大多数的高级知识分子一样，心情振奋、知无不言地参加助党整风的。他看到《人民日报》对他发言的编者按和注后，我觉得应该有被敲响警钟之感，会隐约觉察到自己有可能遭到批评或批判。但他认为当时仍在整风和鸣放，并没有'收'，而且将学术问题与政治问题分开，所以才根据'百花齐放、百家争鸣'的方针，一面给《人民日报》去信做解释与澄清，一面继续于6月在天津社会科学学会学术讲座上做《世界史分期与上古中古史中的一些问题》的报告，并在《历史教学》1957年第7期予以发表，认为奴隶社会并不是人类历史上原始社会后普遍、必经的一个社会形态与历史阶段。而'否定奴隶社会'和'马克思主义停滞在1895年'却成为他受到批判和划为"右派"的两个主要'罪状'。"

是年5、6月间，北大学生谭天荣到南开"煽风点火"，曾分别访问过雷海宗等三名教授。随后，三教授在南开大礼堂参加大会，谈谭天荣访问时的谈话情况。雷海宗发言，指出自己曾询及谭学习哲学及读黑格尔著作情况，奉劝他谈黑格尔思想时，应该多读一点黑氏著作，并说中国是个大国，人口众多，贫困落后，要治理好必定会遇到许多困难，出现不少问题。发言时，他还指着主席台两侧的标语牌说：我相信这两句话，那就是——领导我们事业的核心力量是中国共产党，指导我们思想的理论基础是马克思主义。话音一落，掌声满堂。

王先生说："雷师在大礼堂的讲话，固然是真话与心里话，但已有所警惕，并在心里绷上了'被敲响警钟'这根弦。过了些日子，他在天津市九三学社（他是其市委委员之一）做了关于民主问题的长篇报告（后刊载于该学社的刊物），结合自己在美国留学时的感受和参加土改的亲身体会，完全正面地批判美国的资产阶级民主，歌颂我国的社会主义民主。我想，这时他应该不仅有所警惕，而是已经预感到"反右"斗争风暴的气息了。6月底，雷师给本科生讲的世界上古史课程结束。最末一堂课上，他最后说，宇宙无穷大，有无数的恒星，有的恒星有行星，可能有的行星的环境条件接近于地球，这种行星也可能出现像人类这样的高等生物，他们也可能组成为社会，这种社会也一定经过五种生产方式和奴隶社会吗？讲完后宣布下课，大阶梯教室近二百个听课者全体起立，热烈鼓掌不绝。"

讵料6月伊始，"鸣放"已经悄然转换为"反右"。不过，7月底，暑假已经开始，南开大学"反右"斗争初步告一段落。当时历史系教师和研究生中只划了两个"右派"，雷海宗并未受到批判。

王先生说："我想，雷师之所以那时尚未受批判，可能是由于他的学术和政治地位都比较高，批判他要慎重一些；他的一些发言有学术性，与政治问题交织在一起，一时不易分清；而关于谭天荣的讲话和关于民主问题的报告却比较正确，站在党和人民的一边，所以一时没有动他。我以为，天津市和南开大学学校及历史系的党的领导方面肯定对批不批判雷海宗的问题是有所考虑和研究的。"

然而，到了8月，经康生公开点名后，雷海宗就再也无法逃脱厄运了。

虽然与后来"文革"中的知识分子惨状相比，早逝的雷海宗遭遇的政治磨难并不算太重。但是，随着政治上被打入冷宫，重则饱受口诛笔伐的围攻，轻则遭遇降职降薪的处分，中间又看饱人间冷暖、世态炎凉，却是不免的了。

大批判后，雷海宗由原来的二级教授降为五级，工资也由280元调为170多元。被迫停止教学工作的他，心情十分痛苦，健康也急剧恶化。

王先生回忆说："雷师受批判后，我也处于不利的地位，后来被补划为"右派"，1960年才摘帽。虽然听说雷师身体不好，但我不敢去看他并交谈，只有一次偶然的例外。那是1957年12月初的一个傍晚，我在南开大学中央的道路上散步，在苍茫的暮色中看到远方蹒跚地走来了一个扶杖的老人。走近一看，发现竟是雷师。看四周无人，我就走向前去难过地叫了一声雷先生。雷师当时正受批判、健康恶化、心情沉痛之际，却非常关心我的学业。1961年5月初，郑天挺先生交待我承担《外国史学名著选》中的一项选译任务（选译李维《罗马史》），并嘱我有问题可以向雷先生请教。於是我再登雷师之门，先生和师母见到我很高兴，但他们明显地显得憔悴衰老了。雷师那几年更是身患严重的慢性肾脏炎和贫血症，双腿浮肿，血色素甚低。"

横祸飞来，一代宗师，不但老病孤独，而且正常的教学与研究，也受到严重影响。

"其声如雷"，人们以之形容雷海宗讲课的风采；其实，以此语形容他过去的学术声望，同样恰当。然而，错划为"右派"后，他长期停课（后短期复课），个人的学术声望，随着人生逐渐步入寒冬而慢慢跌进谷底。昔日的身外光芒，也都一一黯淡下来，渐行渐远渐无穷，终于，随着他的过早谢世，几乎完全退出了大众的视野。

人们暂时地遗忘了这位宗师。所以，本文开头所引述陈乐民先生的话，第一句就是："雷海宗先生何许人也？你们可能都没有人知道了。"

"其学似海"　昔时称盛

由于政治原因和"反右"斗争，雷海宗的著作长期不能出版或重版；至"文化大革命"时，甚至他所留下的文稿、日记、相片等遗物，也都被家属在惊吓与无奈当中付之一炬……到后来，王敦书先生欲为其作一小传，资料竟也一度不可得——仿佛这只飞鸿，根本就不曾飞过天空。

然而，雷海宗过去的学术辉煌，却是令人瞩目的。

在强手如云的民国学界，能长期担任清华历史学系主任（1935-1949，中间因抗战间断），并统领大家云集的西南联合大学（抗战时期，由北京大学、清华、南开合并而成）史学系（1938-1946），这自非一般人所能。雷海宗以其别具特色的研究风格、自成体系的史学理论、兼通中西的渊博学识、挥洒自如的讲课艺术，不但做到了这一点，还得到三句将他的名字巧妙嵌入的评语——"其声如雷，其学似海，史学之宗"，可谓不易。

雷海宗出生于牧师家庭，自幼就打下旧学和新学的良好功底。1922 年，深受"五四"新思潮影响的他毕业于清华学堂，并公费留美，入芝加哥大学主修历史学，副修哲学。据同窗回忆，当时血气方刚的中国留学生们，一到美国花花世界，不免要受其影响，但雷海宗却不受干扰，专心读书，心无旁骛。5 年后，他拿出一篇研究法国近代重要政治家與思想家杜尔阁政治思想的论文，获得哲学博士学位，并受到导师器重。正如王敦书先生所说："与外国学生相比，中国学生自然以中国学问见长，雷海宗以纯外国历史为研究对象而获得优秀成绩，这是难能可贵的。"然而，这只是雷海宗学术辉煌的起步之作。

王先生说："雷师归国后，先在南京中央大学和金陵女子大学任职；4 年后，转任武汉大学史学系与哲学系合聘教授；再到次年，也就是 1932 年，他回到阔别 10 年的母校——清华大学；如果把抗战南迁后清华合并到西南联大的那几年也算入，他一直为清华服务 20 年，直到 1952 年调整到南开。回国伊始，雷师授课与治学便有自己的独特之处。第一是他的强调中外贯通、东西并重，并不以他负笈芝加哥大学时专修的世界史为限；第二则是注重改造中国传统史学，纠正其偏于'记事'等弊病，主张不搞烦琐的考证或史实的堆砌，而是于事实之外求道理，以哲学的目光观察历史，以写出熔科学、哲学和艺术于一体的有价值的史学著作。他自己身体力行，1935 年接替蒋廷黻出掌清华史学系后，继续推行'历史学和社会科学并重，历史之中西方史与中国史并重，中国史内综合与考据并重'的办系方针，力争使清华跻身当世一流。"

已故著名史学家蒋孟引回忆，刚回国、年纪轻轻的雷海宗在中央大学讲授西洋史，竟然惹来嫉妒，有人说他中国史学问不够，中文水平不高，"这当然不是雷先生所能容忍的"，于是他"随即大写中国史文章，并讲授中国史，无不大得好评，誉满全国，这远非冬烘之流所能望其项背"。

雷海宗回国后，不几年就在教学与著述中，均取得不俗的成绩。他批评韦尔斯的《世界史纲》是"鼓吹世界大同的一本小说杰作"，介绍引进克罗齐的史学理论，考订孔子以前的哲学，推断殷周的年代（其中，他推定周室元年为公元前 1027 年，今日渐成学界共识，被他的另外一位高足、著名史学家何炳棣称为"雷海宗的年代"），这些早期的成绩，就已体现出他打通中西、不拘流俗的格局。

他在武汉大学讲授欧洲通史的提纲，后经王敦书先生整理，命名《西洋文化史纲要》出版。这虽然只是一个提纲，不是完整的书稿，却紧抓重大历史事件与社会变革，讲述了整个欧洲、尤其是西欧的历史，举凡西方宗教、哲学、文学、科学、史学等的嬗变、发展及其流派，均有所阐发。它原名虽是《欧洲通史》（二），实际上却是一部西洋文化史，陈乐民先生就认为它是"研究西方文化必备的工具书"。他推荐这本书时还说："我看了（它）之后，实在是佩服。纲要中都是些大题目，小题目，但是你看那些大题目、小题目的安排，你可以感到他思想的开放和钻研的深度。"

王先生说："雷师到清华后，重点从事中国史的教学与研究。他在课堂上的魅力先不说，这段时期，正是他攀上个人学术生涯顶峰的阶段。他将古今中西兼熔于一炉，以哲学消化史料，解释历史，努力打破欧洲中心论和中国传统的王朝更替体系，建立起自己独树一帜，既博大精深又针砭时弊的史学体系。正是这些，使雷师的学术声望达到了常人难以企及的高峰。"

雷海宗留下的文字，并不算多；他创立的有关于中国历史文化的体系，主要见之于《中国文化与中国的兵》及《文化形态史观》两本集子，尤其是前者。他从三个方面来讨论中国传统文化：

首先，是皇帝制度。他认为，皇帝把天下视为他的私产，人民等同于他的奴婢臣妾，在他以下，丞相与小民同样卑微，人人但听天命，毫无主人意识，因而顾不上关心国家团体命运。在皇帝制度这种全民平等的独裁统治下，民众只知消极拥护，处于一盘散沙的状态，这时只有皇帝是维系天下的惟一势力。而辛亥革命摧毁了皇帝制度，所以当前的关键，应是在中国建立一个新的元首制度。

其次，是家庭制度。他认为"东汉以下二千年间，大家族是社会国家的基础"，它一方面强化了汉民族的凝聚力，但也正因为"宗法的家族太盛"，民众以家族而不是民族、国家为核心，孝道张而国家、民族意识弱，"国家因而非常散漫"，近代以来随着西洋文化的冲击，大家族制度遭到破坏，小家庭逐渐兴盛，这是一个趋势，但两种家庭制度各有利弊，所以得调和出一种平衡的家族制度。

最后，是兵。他认为中国经历了贵族当兵到流民当兵，兵匪不分，军民相互仇视的蜕变，在汉代时军人便受到鄙视，所谓"好铁不打钉，好汉不当兵"也。中国军队的孱弱，使之根本无力承担保卫国家的责任，历史上只好借助羌胡兵，现今也"不足以抵抗西洋或彻底西洋化的国家"。东汉以降，兵的问题"永未解决"，是中国长期积弱的主要原因。"兵可说是民族文化基本精神的问题"，中国这种"无兵的文化"，导致汉代以后中国社会没有"本质的变化"，"旧中国传统的污浊、因循、苟且、侥幸、欺诈、阴险、小器、不彻底，以及一切类似特征，都是纯粹文德的劣根性。一个民族或一个人，既是软弱无能以至无力自卫，当然不会有直爽痛快的性格"。他主张抛弃文德的虚伪与卑鄙，但也不要学日本式"纯粹武德的暴躁与残忍"，而是要"恢复战国以上文武并重的文化"，创造光明磊落的人格、风气和文化。

王先生说："雷师对中国文化有贬有褒，更有所寄托。他对旧文化提出批评，是因为他认为'若要创造新生，对于旧文化的长处与短处，尤其是短处，我们必须先行了解'。他深受德国历史哲学家斯宾格勒文化形态史观的影响，但又不为西欧中心论所束缚，他以渊博的学识，论述了中国文化发展的独特性，并在此基础上建立了自己的体系。他认为其它文化，除欧西因历史起步晚尚未结束外，皆按照封建时代、贵族国家时代、帝国主义时代、大一统时代和政治破裂与文化灭绝的末世这五个阶段的进展，经形成、发展、兴盛、衰败一周期而亡。惟独中国文化四千年来却以公元 383 年淝水之战为分界线，经历了两个周期。第一周'古典的中国'结束以后，由于胡人血统的渗透，以及印度佛教的传入，而且中国文化由黄河流域扩展到长江和珠江流域，中国文化获得了新的生机，返老还童，进入了第二周——'胡汉混合、梵华同化'的综合中国时期。雷师不但打破了欧洲中心论，也不同于中国的传统王朝体系，他的学说，不但独树一帜，而且提出了中国文化革新的重大问题。他认为中国传统文化无法进行自身革新，必须有外来文化的作用才能带来动力。他以为一种文化的新生与其是否具有开放的意识是紧密相关的。"

据何兆武先生回忆，雷海宗曾在给一位同学的题词中这样写道："前不见古人，历史可以复活古人；后不见来者，历史可以预示来者。"他研究历史，最大的抱负正是要"复活古人"，并"预示来者"。

雷海宗并不否认他的学术有为现实服务的强烈意识，他抨击检讨中国文化的劣根性，主张中国要勇于向正在强势扩张的西方文化开放，却是希望国人要有文化的自信，"不致再似过去的崇拜盲从，而是自动自主的选择学习"。他的理想，是要借欧风美雨带来的机遇，使中国文化在第二周之后，进入第三周的生长期。他这样说道："若勉强作一个比喻，我们可说文化如花，其他的文化都是草本花，一度开放，即告凋死；中国似为木本花，今年开放，明年可再重开，若善自培植，可以无限的延长生命。第二周的文化虽在人类史上已为例外，但既有第二周，也就可有第三周。"

王先生说："从一二·九运动到卢沟桥事变，这是雷海宗一生中的一个重大转折点。他从一个基本上不参与政治的学者，变为开始积极议政，将学术与政治连结起来。他检讨自己前此的注意力集中于传统文化的弱点，对中华民族的坚强生命力，只略为提及，但抗战开始后，这种缄默已不能继续维持了。他强调中国之有两周文化是其他民族历史上所绝无的现象，是我们大可自豪于天地间的。他在抗战这场'两千年来所未有的乱世'、'四千年来所仅见的外患'当中，看到了中国文化

第三周开幕的契机。"

雷海宗认为，为了实现抗战的胜利，不仅要养成文武兼备的文化，破除传统中国"无兵的文化"，而且要保持一个平衡的家庭制度，讲究忠孝，鼓励生育，还要有战时领袖来稳定局面。这三个方面，恰好触及传统文化的根本。而此时陷入大战与强权政治中的欧西文化，则正相当于我国古代的"战国时代"，其发展趋势，将是走向大一统帝国的建立。面临这样的局面与机遇，中国要有应对之策，要"担起拨乱反正、抗敌复国、更旧创新的重任"，以实现第三周文化的伟业。1940 年，雷海宗与林同济等人创办《战国策》半月刊，次年，又在重庆《大公报》上开辟副刊《战国》，被时人称为"战国策派"，他们主要基于的便是以上的考虑。也正因此，他們才有与国民党"民族第一"、"国家第一"的鼓吹撞车，并遭南方局批判之事。

对雷海宗这一套自成格局的史学体系，誉之者固然不少，毁之者亦有人在。

据何兆武先生回忆，1941 年春，雷海宗在云南大学的一次讲演中系统地阐发了他的史学观点。他一一比较世界各大文明的兴衰周期，从中总结出一套文化形态演变的普遍规律。演讲结束，主持人林同济先生作结论，赞美他这一理论是一曲"历史学家的浪漫"。对这种"浪漫"，誉之者欣赏其视野之开阔，批判之有力，体系之博大，立论之宏伟，关怀之深切，称其为近代以来史学家著述中所少见。雷海宗，亦被誉为"贯中外、通古今、兼宏微、融史哲"的大师。

而毁之者，老前辈中有陈寅恪，后生新秀中有吴晗，据何炳棣所记，他们大抵是讥刺雷海宗史实、制度的处理工夫不够。雷在清华和西南联大开中国通史课，分在为非历史系本科生开设的乙组。在考辨分析史料的细致周到上，这一组整体上确实不如陈寅恪等人。对此，雷海宗自己也直认不讳。

然而，雷海宗却有自己独到的考虑。比如，有人说他在《中国的兵》中对三国以下讲得未免太简单，他说：这种批评著者个人也认为恰当，但两千年来兵的本质的确没有变化，如考证起来，"作一篇洋洋大文并非难事。但这样勉强叙述一个空洞的格架去凑篇幅，殊觉无聊。反之，若从侧面研究，推敲两千年来的历史有什么特征，却是一个意味深长的探求"。他是主张以哲学的目光来洞察历史的，更为注重的是要把握历史的本质和全局；对于中国传统史学的偏于记事，他颇多批评；他并不轻视"考据"，但是更注重"义理"。

王先生说："雷师也写极好的考据文章，如《殷周年代考》、《汉武帝建元始于何时》与指出章学诚不足的关于蓝鼎元《饿乡记》的文章，但他更重视历史的意义与道理，如见《史学方法课程笔记》、《历史警觉性的时限》等。传统的治学方法与态度，有'考据'、'义理'及'经世致用'三者，雷师显然是重义理与致用的。晚年时，他一次还和我谈起中国古代古文学派和今文学派的争论问题，他一针见血地说，说到底其实是一个争饭碗的问题。我觉得，他的眼光很敏锐。此外，雷师对哲学也很有研究，常从哲学的高度来看问题，看历史。他在美国芝加哥大学留学时副科学习哲学；回国后发表的第一篇论文是《孔子以前的哲学》；在武汉大学时，也是历史学系与哲学系的合聘教授。一次，他与我谈起历史学时，用英文说，History is philosophy, teaching by examples.（历史是以实例教人的哲学。）我觉得，这是对历史与哲学的关系乃至历史学本身的一个相当经典性的定位。"

对陈寅恪、吴晗与雷海宗的学术分歧，王先生还专门谈了他的看法："关于陈寅恪先生对雷师的讥刺，我从来没有听他谈过，他是很尊敬陈先生的。我对陈先生没有研究，也没有见过他，不知他是否写过这方面的话。我想大家有此印象恐怕主要来自于何炳棣先生所写的《雷海宗专忆》一文。不过，请注意，我在《雷海宗与二十世纪中国史学——雷海宗先生百年诞辰纪念文集》一书中转载何先生此文时，在叙及此事处加了一个注说：据程美宝对陈寅恪赴牛津大学讲学档案的研究（见《陈寅恪与牛津大学》，载《历史研究》2000 年第 3 期），陈寅恪在牛津的研究计划包括由雷海宗、邵循正、孙毓棠三人用英文写一部 3 卷本约 1500 页并附所需地图及详细索引的《中国通史》，这说明至少此时陈寅恪对雷海宗的中国史研究是有所肯定与认同的，不然他不会将由雷海宗领衔写这部书列入自己的研究计划了。何先生看到此注后，在电话中对我说，这个注加得好，表示感谢。当然，陈寅恪与雷海宗的学术思路可能不完全相同，陈先生也许更重考据。他们之间的关系大概是孔子所说的'君子和而不同'的情况。作为后辈，我们不应斤斤计较于何先生所听说的陈先生对雷师的讥刺这一面，更应看到陈先生将请雷师带头写中国史作为自己研究计划的另一面。况且，何先生讲此事的本意在于敬仰雷师的大过于人的容忍与学术道义方面的自信。至于吴晗先生，他与雷师之不同，更包括政见之不同。吴先生治学也重视现实与政治。不过，雷师是战国策派；吴先生是左派，他的《朱元璋传》是影射国民党蒋介石的。我到清华历史系上学时，吴先生已不在清华教课了，但系里盛传着毛主席曾与他交谈历史的佳话。"

"史学之宗" 爝火不息

雷海宗的史学体系，主要完成于1949年之前；1949年后，由于时代的特殊关系，他没有写出能和之前的最高成就相媲美的著作。但是，在这有限而且近半时间无法正常从事研究的十余年中，他仍然留下了不少可圈可点的文字。

王先生说："解放初，雷师仍旧留在清华任教，他除了写作学术性的批判文章之外，还发表《古今华北气候与农事》等文章。他到南开之后，编写了《世界上古史讲义》，并被教育部定为全国高等学校交流讲义，准备铅印出版。这部讲义既摆脱了他原来发挥的斯宾格勒文化形态史观的框架，也不完全沿用苏联教科书的一般结构，它打通中国史与世界史的界限，强调中国人学习世界史，要从中国的角度来看世界；还重视各地区、各种族之间的相互关系和影响，从总体上来把握世界史；尤其还对上古史中不同地区奴隶社会转入封建社会的总问题，提出了自己的创见。这些贡献之外，雷师还精心译注斯宾格勒《西方的没落》一书有关章节，多有独创精到之见。我翻译《李维〈罗马史〉选》，也由他亲自指导，认真校改；雷师的关怀备至，使我学到许多东西，终生受用不尽。"

学术研究，是雷海宗事业的一部分；传道授业解惑，也是他的职业和终生使命。他晚年的不少研究，如《世界上古史讲义》，本身就是为构建高校世界史教学体系而做的努力。1957年那一场厄运之后，雷海宗因为政治环境及自身健康的原因，不可能再花很大精力用于著述，但是对课堂讲学，他仍是一有机会，就全力以赴、当仁不让的。

王先生说："雷师晚年在著述之外，大部分精力献身于教育事业。他回国以后一直在高等学校工作、教书，作为一位名教授和教育家，他的教书育人是极具特色和众口叫绝的。雷师声音洪亮，讲课极有条理，深入浅出，鞭辟入里，内容丰富，生动活泼。他讲解历史事件既材料翔实，又说明前因后果，更揭示性质意义娓娓动听，使人听了感到余兴未尽。每节课他计时精确，下课时恰好讲完一个题目，告一个段落，下节课再讲新的，前后衔接自如。他的记忆力极强，走上课堂，只拿几支粉笔，但讲得井井有条，滔滔不绝，人名、地名、年代、史实准确无误。他学问渊博，研究精深，口才好，思路清楚，懂多门外语，教学认真负责，又讲究教学方法，使讲课成为一门艺术，挥洒自如，引人入胜。早年他在清华和西南联大为非历史系本科生开设的中国通史课，选课人数极多，课堂总是挤得满满的，其中还有不少慕名而来的旁听者，已故著名世界史学家吴于廑先生就是这样的旁听者，当时他已是南开大学经济研究所的研究生了。雷师对学生十分爱护，不仅指导他们的学习，而且关心他们的生活。所以，在来南开以前，雷师在杏坛便已留下诸多的故事、佳话。"

对雷海宗的讲课，虽然也有人颇有微词，但显然都淹没在学生们对他的叹服声中。王先生对雷氏讲课风格的描述，可以互见于雷氏门生的诸多回忆文字。他对学生学习与生活的关怀，不仅溢于言表，而且总是很实际深入。

著名世界史家、首都师范大学前校长齐世荣先生曾回忆："我读大四时，生活比较困难。一天下课后，雷先生对我说，美国波摩那大学来了一个研究生，学中国近代史，想写关于梁启超的论文。他的中文程度还需提高，你去给他补习中文，注意借机会练练英文，并增加点收入。我听了后十分感动，不知道老师如何知道我最近生活困难……通过这件事，可以说明雷先生是多么地爱护学生，他既注意学生的学习成绩，也关心他们的生活状况。"

丁则良和何炳棣是雷海宗很喜欢的学生，丁学贯亚欧，攻宋史、苏联史、亚洲史等，很有成绩；何中西兼通，致力于中国历史上人口土地、社会流动、先秦诸子等问题的研究，成为驰名国际的中国史学家。雷海宗与他们之间师生感情之深厚，同样一言难尽。丁则良留英回国，1957年被错划为"右派"，访苏归来即自沉于北大未名湖，噩耗传到雷海宗那里，他痛哭不已，以泪洗面。何炳棣留在美国，但他每有新著，辄必寄恩师；雷海宗逝世不久，他在给雷师母的信中，说1962年圣诞雷师去世那日，自己虽在美国，但似有感应；其后，他与恩师家人通信不辍，慰问甚勤，甚至还在他们困难的时候予以经济支援。在他眼中，雷海宗"是真正兼具基督教和儒家品德的学人"。

王先生说："雷师的课讲得好是全国闻名的。他来南开后，由于讲授世界近代史课的杨生茂先生暂离南开，该课就由新从燕京大学调来的林树惠先生任教。但林先生口才欠佳，原来也不是研究世界史的，因而不受学生欢迎，课讲不下去了，只好由作为世界史教研组主任的雷师代教，林先生则随班听课。按一般情况说，林先生此时的心情肯定是不高兴的，甚至会发生误会，牵怒于雷师。然而，实际情况是，林先生不但没有埋怨雷先生，反而深深敬佩雷师的教学学问和道德为人。1957年我到南开后，一次与林先生聊天时，他特别谈到此事，并赞叹说："雷先生的课讲得太好了，他讲歌德的《浮士德》，讲得都玄了。"雷师母在怀念雷师的文章中说，批判雷先生时，有一位教师为雷师不平，称'雷海宗是我最好的老师'，这位教师就是林树惠先生。此外，雷师还开过物质文明史一课。他不但给学生正式讲课，而且还单独给青年教师讲专业英语和中国古代史。雷师不但世界史好，对中国史更有研究，在清华历史系二十年间一直讲中国通史和殷周史与秦汉史。据雷师母说，雷师在家中给青年教师讲中国上古史时，甚至老先生也来旁听。雷师非常关心南开在哲学社会科学领域的外文藏书情况，与南开大学图书馆馆长冯文潜教授及其它专家合作，努力进行这方面的图书资料建设，大有成效。南开大学图书馆的教师阅览室的社会科学方面的外文工具书当时是全国一流的。在此期间，雷师写了多篇文章，主要都在他任编委的《历史教学》杂志发表。总之，雷师来南开后，对南开历史系的发展做出了巨大的贡献。"

雷海宗晚年对南开历史学科的这些贡献，被陈乐民先生引以为南开之幸，概括为"得一位老师，兴一个学科"。

1961年底，摘掉"右派"帽子的雷海宗又有了讲课的资格，然而，他的健康状况却不容乐观。当时，南开历史系提出要"抢救遗产"，希望他能早日开课。于是1962年春，雷海宗就重新登上讲台，给历史系高年级本科生开设了外国史学名著选读一课。

王先生说："雷师这门课，我也随班听课，在需要时为雷师选的名著有关段落从英文译成中文，由先生修改后油印发给同学参考，记得曾译过色诺芬的《居鲁士教育记》中关于居鲁士品格的部分、普鲁塔克的《凯撒传》中关于凯撒被刺杀的部分和吉本的《罗马帝国衰亡史》中关于公元410年罗马城为西哥特人攻陷的部分。这门课上课的教室，是在主楼一楼西侧大阶梯教室，可容纳二百多人。雷师家在校门口，离主楼甚远，先生身体衰弱，双腿浮肿，步履艰难，就扶着拐杖来回坐三轮车前往教室，由助教曹中屏接送。此课是一学期课，每周一次连上两节课。吴于廑先生列出了从古至今大约十位外国的著名史家及其著作，雷师还增加了几个，如布莱斯的《神圣罗马帝国》和福尼埃尔的《拿破仑传》等，对每个史家及其名著讲一至二周。先生虽抱病讲课，依然'声音如雷，学问如海'，精神抖擞，旁征博引，内容丰富。听课的人包括南开历史系高年级本科生，还有大批外系乃至校外的旁听者，整个阶梯教室坐得满满的，盛况仍与1956年时相同。上课时，大家用心听，认真记笔记，只是由于雷师是受到批判的人，不再给他鼓掌了。"

1962 年 9 月，雷海宗又为南开历史系高年级本科生讲外国史学史一课。他的记忆力本来极好，几乎过目不忘，所以以往讲课，都是有大纲而无讲稿。但开这门课时，却认真地准备了讲稿。然而，到 11 月时，他就因为病重，行走困难，而不得不将此课中断了。

后来，另一位学生肖黎，生动地记述了最后的那些日子里，雷海宗在讲堂上的形象：

> 上课铃响后，只见一位小老头拄着拐杖，一步一步地挪动着双腿，吃力地坐在讲台后的一把椅子上。看着他那痛苦的样子，我不觉生出几分恻隐之心。在那一瞬间，阶级斗争的观念就像是断了线的风筝，无影无踪。此刻，教室里异常安静。突然，洪钟般地声音响起，只见他腰板直了，精神也振作起来了，与他刚进教室时简直判若两人。37 年过去了，讲课的具体内容早已忘记。只依稀记得他讲的是印度的寡妇殉葬。他上课什么也不带，却对历史事件、人物、地名、年代都十分熟悉，脱口而出。他的外文极好，一会儿是希腊文，一会儿又讲一个词语如何从希腊文演变为拉丁文、英文的，斯拉夫语系有什么特点，侃侃而谈。

在"与人斗，其乐无穷"的年代里，对病入膏肓的雷先生也是不会放过的。每次先生讲完课后，都要组织一场"消毒"课。一些"左派"挖空心思地找出种种"毒素"，以显示他们洞察一切的本领。我想，雷先生如果知道，他为了"将自己的学识献给人民"而抱病上讲台，却被一些人视为"贩毒"者，他岂不要挥舞拐杖，质问苍天："公理安在？"

最难忘的是雷先生的最后一课。他大概也知道自己将不久于人世，这是他人生中的最后一课。犹如回光返照，他一直处于亢奋之中，情绪十分激昂，声音更加洪亮。课间休息时，同学们还是窃窃私语，不敢和他接近。他仍然一个人孤独地坐在那里。我鬼使神差地走过去，就是想和他说几句话。不知从哪里来的勇气，我压低声音说："雷先生，您多保重！"先生用异样的眼光注视着我，他点点头，什么也没说。最后一堂课结束了，依然没有例行的致意和掌声。雷先生孤独地拄着拐杖走了。在这难以言表的时刻，同学们都走到窗前，目送着他登上回医院的车渐渐地远去。

上完最后几课，雷海宗已是油灯行将熬尽。

王先生说："雷师开外国史学史课后不久，系里安排我为他做些教学辅助工作，并陪伴他去医院看病。雷师平常每星期去天津市总医院或第一中心医院看慢性肾脏炎病和 259 医院血液研究所看贫血症，最后几次已上不去楼，是由我背他上二楼的。"

1962 年 12 月 25 日，雷海宗的心脏停止了跳动。一代"史学之宗"，甫及六十岁，便过早地与世长辞。

多年前，雷海宗曾经撰文，称赞战国以前的贵族当兵，"男子都以当兵为职务，为荣誉，为乐趣。不能当兵是莫大的羞耻"。他说：在整部《左传》里，"我们找不到一个因胆怯而临阵脱逃的人"。这样一种"直爽痛快"和"光明磊落"的人格，正是他所心仪的。（见《中国的兵》）

而雷海宗自己，虽然晚年多难，但是，他又岂肯临阵逃脱呢！"日月出矣，爝火不息"，身外光芒日渐黯淡的他，仍旧以亲身证明：这种"兵"的精神，在他自己身上永远燃烧，从来没有一丝熄灭过。

尾　声

"文化大革命"结束后，1979 年，雷海宗的"右派"问题得到改正。

折戟沉沙铁未销，自将磨洗认前朝。从那时起，蒙尘数十年的雷海宗，终于又一次渐渐地开始为世人所知。

王敦书先生说：“总起来说，雷师一生的浮沉与中国国家的命运紧密相连。从三十年代直至1957年，雷师是名闻遐迩的史学大家。后来因为左的路线，雷师受到批判是自然和必然的。但南开历史系领导对雷师还是比较温和宽容的。“文革”结束后，雷师不但个人名誉得到恢复，他在学术研究、教育教学上的巨大贡献，亦渐渐得到越来越多人的关注和承认。1982年，《中国历史学年鉴》约我写雷海宗简介并加以刊登，这大概是自1957年批判雷师以来第一篇比较正面地介绍他生平的文章，也可以说有些开始为他恢复名誉吧。之后十年中，我先后发表多篇介绍与纪念雷师的文章。《史学理论》1988年第4期刊载我的《雷海宗关于文化形态、社会形态和历史分期的看法》一文后，一位澳大利亚学者阅后在文章中说此文意味着中国开始为雷海宗恢复名誉。1992年，南开大学历史系举行了雷师诞辰九十周年纪念会；2002年12月，又召开了雷师诞辰一百周年的大型纪念会。进入21世纪以后，雷师的旧著也纷纷出版或再版。2012年6月18日，是雷师110年诞辰，6月16日，南开大学历史学院将召开大型纪念会。”

一代“史学之宗”，“其学如海”，“其声如雷”，虽经摇落，但终必复振。

（以上是笔者对王先生的采访所得，打引号的是他的原话，无引号的是笔者的认识与发挥，有的地方也融入了王先生以前所写有关文章中的一些话。全文完稿后经王先生审校改正，特此致谢！）

【综论】

The Western Futures of Ancient History[①]

Oswyn Murray，Oxford University

Abstract：The secular study of 'ancient history' in western Europe has always been connected with the classical tradition and the influence of Greece and Rome on the formation of European culture. The critical study of other ancient civilizations (Israel, Egypt, the Near East, India, China, Japan) arrived late and has remained peripheral to the study of the origins of western culture.

The outlook of Ancient History is therefore limited, and has centred around two separate concepts, imperialism and liberty. The first interest explains the fundamental importance of Roman history with its exemplification of the fate of empires to rise, decline and fall. The second interest includes the history of political liberty and democratic forms of government, together with personal liberty and the rise of the individual: this is seen in terms of a continuing process of development from antiquity to the present, and as exemplified in the history of ancient Greece. These two ideas explain both the weaknesses and the strengths of western attitudes to the past.

The role of Jewish history in this conception of 'ancient history' is of course problematic, and points to a number of weaknesses in the western tradition. I shall explore this question through the tradition of Josephus translations in Britain, the first attempt to adapt Jewish history to the western tradition in H.H. Milman's highly controversial *History of the Jews* (1830), and the first serious Jewish attempt

---

[①] These reflections were first formulated as a keynote speech for the 2012 International Symposium on Ancient World History in China, June 16–18, Nankai University, Tianjin. They were subsequently developed for a meeting of the European Network for the Study of Ancient Greek History at Tel Aviv University in October 2012, and delivered to seminars at Duke and Northwestern Universities during a visit to the USA. In 2013 they were presented to the Hong Kong Academy of Sciences, to Tokyo University, at a conference at Thessalonica University on 'Knowing Future Time', and at seminars on the Josephus tradition in Oxford and on 19th century nationalism in Durham. I am very grateful to all the participants for their comments, often in opposition.

to characterise what is unique about Jewish History in the work of Heinrich Graetz.

Time present and time past

Are both perhaps present in time future,

And time future contained in time past.

If all time is eternally present

All time is unredeemable.

T.S. Eliot, *Four Quartets: Burnt Norton* (1944)

The study of historiography is not part of the 'classical tradition': the purpose of the study of the past of ancient history is to influence its future, and to clarify the methods and principles that may determine the activity of writing history. All history is and has always been written in and for the present, and is valid only as a myth for the present or as a step towards the future. Unless we are aware of the constraints of tradition on this picture, future histories will continue to be determined by the past: in order to liberate ourselves from tradition and prevent the preoccupations of the present and its past from distorting the future of history, we must investigate the roots of our current concerns.

The study of 'ancient history' in western Europe has always been connected with the influence of Greece and Rome on the formation of European culture. The critical and comparative study of this tradition with other ancient civilizations such as Israel, Egypt, the Near East, India, China, and Japan to create an 'ancient world history', arrived late and has remained peripheral to the study of the origins of western culture. My purpose in this brief paper is to explore the consequences of this fact.

The western outlook on 'Ancient History' is therefore limited, and has since the eighteenth century centred around two distinct concepts; these are imperialism and liberty. The first interest, imperialism, explains the fundamental importance of Roman history with its exemplification of the fate of empires, to rise, decline and fall. It began with the discussion provoked by the famous French author Montesquieu in his work *Considérations sur la grandeur et décadence des Romains*, published in Holland in 1734. In this short essay Montesquieu traced the growth of the Roman empire in the second century BC and attributed it to the vertu of the Romans, their moral and political character. He showed how moral and political corruption followed, until the traditional liberty of the Romans was extinguished in a monarchic form of government, and their moral character was corrupted by the luxury consequent on empire. This analysis was part of a general movement in the early 18th century to contrast the declining power of the French monarchy under its greatest ruler, Louis XIV, in the face of the rise of the English version of constitutional monarchy, in a country essentially governed by the merchant classes after the Glorious Revolution of 1688. The success in war of the English armies under the Duke of Marlborough and the creation of an English naval empire around the world were making it clear that absolute monarchy and territorial conquest were incompatible with the modern expansion of overseas trade based on government by the landed aristocracy and the merchants of the city of London. The message of Montesquieu was accepted by all the thinkers of the Enlightenment, and became the basis of the new critical historiography which reached its zenith in the famous work of Edward Gibbon, in which the whole history of Europe from antiquity to the Renaissance was incorporated into a *History of the Decline and Fall of the Roman Empire* (1776–88).

This perception has dictated the shape of Roman history ever since. The fundamental questions remain the same today as they were formulated in the 18th century: how did Rome become an imperial power, on the basis of what political structures was her success achieved, how was her political, social and economic development affected by the consequent advent of luxury and wealth, and why did the system end by only finding stability under a form of absolute monarchy that was incompatible with political liberty? It was only the advent of a new religion, Christianity, and the impact of nomadic barbarian invasions that introduced a new dynamic to history; but that required a break with the past that was only partially resolved in the Renaissance. From this perspective of ancient history as Roman history, it is empire, its rise and fall, that provides the questions to which we still seek answers. And much of the justification of western imperialism in the modern age has been based on the model of the Roman example, from Edmund Burke's eighteenth century analysis of the faults and virtues of English imperialism in Ireland, north America and India, to the systematic education of administrators for the British Indian Empire on principles that were directly derived from Roman provincial administration. The French and German empires were no different: throughout Europe the virtues and vices and indeed the methods of imperialism have always been conceived in terms of the ancient Roman example.

The second interest, the history of liberty, includes the history of political liberty and democratic forms of government, together with personal liberty and the rise of the concept of the individual: this is seen in terms of a continuing process of development from antiquity to the present, and as especially exemplified in the history of ancient Greece. It explains the obsession of historians of ancient Greece with Athens and the principles of democratic government. We still idealise Athenian democracy as the best form of government, and discuss modern governmental systems in relation to this ancient example. We are still obsessed with the idea of liberty, both political and personal; and as a consequence we judge all forms of government, whatever their historical traditions, in relation to standards that are seen as absolute. This strand in the history of the ancient world is often seen as consequent on the Hegelian view of history as the history of liberty, and on the concern of the Romantic period with the idea of the creativity of the original artistic genius, standing outside tradition. And it is believed that the nineteenth century philosophical movement known as Utilitarianism established the apotheosis of democracy and liberty in the *History of Greece* (1846–56) composed by the Utilitarian radical politician George Grote.

But in fact this concern with liberty and democracy is too a product of the eighteenth century, and of much the same impulse that inspired Montesquieu. The catalyst was the presentation by the Frenchman Nicolas Boileau in 1674 of an obscure ancient work of literary criticism known as *Longinus On the Sublime*. In the last chapter of this work the author mentions an ancient theory that relates artistic creativity to political liberty. This work with its emphasis on the importance of the sublime was fundamental to literary theory in the 18th century, and its conclusion was interpreted as an explanation and a vindication for the renewed literary activity in contemporary Britain after the Glorious Revolution. The literature of ancient Greece and especially Athens was interpreted as being a consequence not of aristocratic patronage but of political liberty and Athenian democracy. This view of the benefits of democracy became widespread in the 18th century, and lies behind the change from an almost universal dismissal of democratic forms of government as dangerous, unjust and anarchic to an increasing idealisation of democratic institutions. This in turn led to a close identification of ancient Athens with modern Britain and subsequently modern America. The difference between ancient and modern democracy was rightly seen as a difference between direct and representative democracy: the most important innovation in 18th century political theory, due largely to Montesquieu again, was the realisation that representation could be harnessed to the idea of democracy. Despite this obvious difference it was believed that ancient and modern democracy shared common characteristics. The consequent rise of the principle of democratic representative government justified the historical movement from aristocratic forms of government to a new 'democratic', capitalist, oligarchic control of government by the bourgeoisie.

These two strands, imperialism and democracy, have in our generation come together in the new democratic imperialism of the United States of America, which seeks to promote the principles of democracy and capitalism under an American imperial hegemony held to be self-evidently the teaching of human history, for in Hegelian terms the triumph of the individual and of liberty is the lesson of history.

Yet each of these theoretical approaches is problematical in a number of respects, and concentration on them to the exclusion of all others represents an impoverishment of the varieties of human experience. Let us consider each concept in turn.

Imperialism is not synonymous with exploitation and expropriation; it requires an ideology to persuade the master race to conquer and even more to maintain control over other societies: you must believe in your mission or the rulers will lose the will to rule. The Romans came to believe that their version of Greco-Roman civilization was a gift that would benefit all who came under their domination; in this they were helped by a conception of citizenship that (with certain conditions) was perhaps the most inclusive that the world has experienced. The result was that in the end all subjects of the empire became Roman citizens, and were eligible for the benefits of empire; these benefits of course changed over time, but always remained real enough, and could and did include the possibility of even becoming the emperor himself. The later western model built on this conception of the benefits of civilization, and added to it the principle of conversion to Christianity as the true faith. But it was always recognised that in principle, if in the distant future the subject peoples should embrace these western principles of government and western religion, such empires would dissolve themselves into some unspecified relationship, whether of universal citizenship or of independence. Moreover whereas the Roman conception of empire had been of an eternal empire *(Roma aeterna)*, there was built into its successor, the 18th century conception of empire, the notion of decline and fall; there was therefore always a 'dying fall', a sense of a future ending embodied in western imperialism: the end of empire is envisaged in its beginning. Of course history falsified or usurped these dreams in a variety of ways. But the pure conception of imperialism as exploitation never existed in the west (with the possible exception of the Belgian Congo); and while the analysis of imperialism in terms of its economic benefit to the ruler may help, it is not sufficient to explain all human motivation involved.

The ideas of democracy and freedom are equally problematic. Direct and representative democracy have been recognised to be wholly different forms of government since the 18th century. Direct democracy is only suitable for small scale institutions in which the members of the group can meet and make decisions in a form of assembly which contains only those who will execute those decisions. It is today seldom practised even in groups small enough to qualify, and the right to decide or even influence decisions has become simply a residual right confined to occasional almost ritual events. No-one believes in direct ancient democracy as practised by the ancient Athenians, and few people would wish to see its return as a viable form of government. In the 19th century it was agreed to be dependent on a form of political education which was essentially unattainable, and the 20th century added the even less democratic idea of the need for expertise. These criticisms of democracy go back at least to Plato's Protagoras.

They have been incorporated into the theory of representative government, which allows an elite to rule with the consent of the majority. The problem that results is that of all forms of government in all periods, the creation of a divide between the rulers and the ruled. In ancient Greek terms all modern forms of government are not democracies, but either tyrannies or oligarchies, depending on whether they obey the rule of law or not.

At least since the time of Benjamin Constant's famous essay 'On the liberty of the ancients compared to the liberty of the moderns' (1819) it has been recognised that this difference between ancient and modern democracy is the determining factor behind the difference between ancient and modern conceptions of liberty:

[Ancient] liberty consisted in exercising collectively but directly most aspects of ancient sovereignty, deliberating in the public square about war and peace, concluding with foreigners treaties of alliance, voting on laws, pronouncing legal judgments, examining the accounts and the decrees and the decisions of magistrates, making them appear before the assembled people, putting them on trial, condemning or acquitting them. But at the same time that this was what the ancients called liberty, they admitted as compatible with their collective liberty the total subjection of the individual to the authority of the community.

Modern ideas of liberty in contrast privilege the freedom of the individual from interference by a system controlled by the ruling classes. Far from deriving from ancient world conceptions of liberty it is a consequence of centuries of conflict between the various sects of the Christian religion, which resulted in the assertion of the freedom of the individual conscience in religious matters. In the modern age this has become extended beyond the sphere of religion to all aspects of the private life of the individual.

Modern writers have wrestled with these differences between ancient and modern democracy and ancient and modern liberty; Isaiah Berlin for instance tried to distinguish between a positive *'freedom to'* (act), which was more akin to ancient political freedom, and a negative *'freedom from'* (interference) which seemed to him to be exemplified in the modern concept of the freedom of the individual. The most recent attempts to relate ancient and modern ideas of freedom and democracy tend to emphasise the importance of duties or responsibilities in the ancient ideas of community life leading to a constraining of the freedom of the individual, in contrast to the absolute selfishness and the anarchic consequences of modern liberty. In that sense the modern western conceptions of democracy and liberty might well indeed learn the limitations of these ideas from studying the ancient world view.

My reflection is however intended to contrast these two conceptions of history derived from ancient western ideas, with the traditions of history that are found elsewhere. It is clearly not true that these two sets of problems exhaust all the historical possibilities that the long history of human society exemplifies. If we reflect on other historical traditions, we can see that this western conception has many faults. It does not consider the necessity of order or decorum in the construction of civilizations, or the significance of continuity and tradition, as exemplified for instance in the Chinese tradition.

Even within western culture this dual tradition also almost completely ignores one of the most powerful forces in historical formation, the importance of religion and the way that beliefs about the divine world structure and permeate almost all social systems: after the collapse of the grand nineteenth century theories of universal religion, it was not until J-P Vernant offered a social and psychological interpretation of ancient religion that it escaped from the sterile grip of myth and ritual antiquarianism. Ancient western history has indeed been inclined until very recently to regard ancient religion as unimportant and irrelevant, no doubt partly due to the bias against all forms of polytheism as primitive and faulty representations of a divine world that was only revealed by God through the true religion of Christianity: so, while apparently ignoring religion, ancient western history has also been profoundly conditioned by a negative reaction to the advent of Christianity.

But it is not of course only Christianity that appears to be marginalised by the dominant western conception of ancient history. Another religion has claims to be far older than Christianity, and possesses a complex historical tradition at least as old as the Chinese—Judaism. The question of how Jewish history might be incorporated into ancient history also began as early as the eighteenth century, as a part of the enlightenment revival of the study of history. This built in turn upon a much neglected aspect of the work of the sole surviving Jewish historian in the ancient classical tradition, Josephus. For it was really Josephus who, in his *Jewish Antiquities*, even more than in his account of the Jewish War, set out to normalise the Jewish historical tradition in terms of classical historiography: he was indeed himself an ancient historian, and shared with them many of the political and rational attitudes that made his account compatible with the canons of ancient history. Independently of the holy texts of Judaism and Christianity it was he who made it possible for later generations to compare and contrast the Jewish historical tradition with that of Greece and Rome. In terms of later generations he therefore bridged the gap between sacred and secular history, and may be regarded as perhaps the most important of all ancient historians for the future of historical writing.

Already in antiquity Josephus was performing this function for the early Christian Church. This explains their interest in copying his works, and even in improving them at a very early date, by interpolating the notorious references to Jesus Christ, his brother James and John the Baptist; by this means Josephus could be made to offer historical support not just to the Old Testament, but also to the Gospel narrative. Josephus has indeed always been more highly regarded in the Christian tradition than in Judaism itself, which tends to regard him as a renegade and a traitor.

Translations of Josephus into the modern European languages were very popular, and especially in Protestant England. At first they were simple translations. The earliest was by Thomas Lodge, the contemporary of Shakespeare in 1602, 'faithfully translated out of the Latin and French'.[1] This was arranged as a continuous historical narrative, from the Antiquities to the Life, the Jewish Wars, Against Apion, and the martyrdom of the Maccabees. Exactly a century later in 1702 Sir Roger L'Estrange offered a new translation, following almost the same order, but with the Life coming after the Jewish Wars and Philo's Legation added to extend the historical account. He added two 'discourses' and several 'remarks', on the veracity and chronology of Josephus.[2] This edition was reprinted in Dundee in 1766.[3] But in the meantime the most popular of all the translations of Josephus, that by William Whiston had been published in 1737. This became the most widely read and most widely owned book after the Bible in the English speaking world for the next two centuries.[4]

Whiston had been the successor of Isaac Newton as Professor of Mathematics at Cambridge, and like Newton he combined an interest in ancient chronology with scriptural scholarship[5] To him Josephus appeared to present a narrative of Jewish history exactly comparable to that found in classical ancient historians, and

---

[1] The Famous and Memorable Workes of Josephus, A Man of much Honour and Learning Among the Jews. Faithfully translated out of the Latin, and French, by Tho. Lodge, Doctor in Physicke. Humfrey Lownes 1609. First edition 1602 acc to catalogue.

[2] The Works of Flavius Josephus: translated into English By Sir Roger L'Estrange, Knight. London Richard Sare 1702.

[3] Published by Henry Galbraith, Dundee.

[4] The Genuine Works of Flavius Josephus the Jewish Historian. London 1737. The standard bibliography of Josephus by L.H. Feldman claims, but does not list some 217 editions of this translation.

[5] James E. Force Furze, *William Whiston Honest Newtonian* 2002 ; *Memoirs of the Life and Works of William Whiston* (1753).

like his predecessors he arranged his translation of the various works to provide a chronological narrative. But in many later editions of his translation an interesting transformation occurred: the narrative of Josephus was combined with a section usually entitled something like 'Sequel to the history of the Jews; continued to the present time.'

The first person to realise the possibility of recording a continuous history of Judaism in this manner was the Huguenot antiquary and friend of Pierre Bayle, Jacques Basnage, Sieur de Beauval (1653–1723), who published in 1706–7 in the Netherlands a work that was immediately translated into English with the author's approval.[①] The English title-page reads:

The History of the Jews from Jesus Christ to the Present Time: Containing their Antiquities, their Religion, their Rites. The Dispersion of the Ten Tribes in the East, and the Persecutions this Nation has suffered in the West. Being a Supplement and Continuation of the History of Josephus. Written in French by Mr Basnage. Translated into English by Tho. Taylor, A.M. London 1708.[②]

Despite its claim to be a supplement to Josephus, Basnage's work did not include the text of Josephus itself. The earliest edition of Josephus to have combined the two elements in a single volume appears to have been the lavishly illustrated folio of George Henry Maynard, which claims to be a new translation prepared under the royal licence of George III and contains, after the usual works of Josephus and Philo and an appendix defending the authenticity of his references to Christianity, 'a Continuation of the History of the Jews from Josephus down to the present Time Including a Period of more than One thousand seven hundred Years.'[③] The 'Translator's Address to the Reader' ends with the statement:

To compleat the work, we have annexed a Supplement, collected from authentic Manuscripts, bringing down the Jewish History to the present times, which, being an attempt entirely new, we flatter ourselves, will stamp an additional value upon our undertaking, and make it in every respect worthy the patronage of a judicious and candid public.

I say that it appears to be the earliest because there is also a second similarly undated but contemporary illustrated edition by 'Thomas Bradshaw D.D. Late of Emmanuel College Cambridge, Lecturer of Painswick, near Gloucester; Master of the Grammar School of Painswick; Chaplain of Pentonville-Chapel and Afternoon-Preacher of Allhallows-Barking, published by Royal Authority and Act of Parliament.' This similarly claims 'The whole Newly Translated from the Original in the Greek and Hebrew Languages, and Diligently Revised, Corrected, and Compared with other Translations .. to which is added a Continuation of the History of the Jews from the Death of Josephus to the Present Time, including a period of more than 1700 Years.'[④] I have not yet investigated the relationship between these two competing editions, but they cannot be independent of each other.

① *L'histoire et la religion des Juifs depuis Jesus-Christ jusqu'à present. Pour servir de suplément et de continuation à l'Histoire de Josèphe* (5 volumes) Rotterdam 1706–7, 1711, 1716.

② There is a copy of this relatively rare work in Balliol College Library. For Basnage see A. Sutcliffe, *Judaism and Enlightenment* (Cambridge 2003) 79–89.

③ *The Whole Genuine and Complete Works of Flavius Josephus, the learned and authentic Jewish Historian and celebrated Warrior.* Translated from the Original in the Greek Language To which is added Various Useful Indexes also a Continuation of the History of the Jews from Josephus down to the present Time Including a Period of more than One thousand seven hundred Years, by George Henry Maynard, Ll.D. The date of this work is 1785 according to the Harvard University catalogue.

④ The date of this work is given as [1792?] in the Harvard catalogue.

The tradition of updating Josephus to provide a complete history of Judaism continued. In the (again undated) nineteenth century family edition of Whiston's Josephus that I inherited from my grandfather I find that this long sequel of 222 pages terminates with a full account of the debate inside and outside the British Parliament on the Jewish Emancipation Bill of 1847, which was provoked by the election of Lionel de Rothschild as MP for the City of London, and his inability to take up his seat because he would not swear the normal religious oath required of Members of Parliament. The debate was indeed the highpoint for the articulation of English philosemitism; speakers included Lord John Russell the Prime Minister, Gladstone, Disraeli, Sir Robert Peel and Lord Ashley the evangelical Zionist (who surprisingly spoke against the Bill). The Bill passed in the Commons by a majority of 73 (277 votes to 204) but was rejected by the House of Lords, and Rothschild did not take up his post until another election success in 1858.[1] It was however the debate in 1847–8 that saw the most memorable and thoughtful speeches. Since it does not mention the final triumph of Rothschild I deduce (perhaps wrongly) that my family edition was published between 1848 and 1858. It would indeed be an interesting study to follow the successive stages of this conception of the continuity of Jewish history under the protection of Josephus.

The first modern Jewish history was not therefore as revolutionary as it might have seemed, for it built on this tradition. H.H. Milman's three volume work *The History of the Jews* of 1830 begins, like Josephus, with Moses, and in its earlier stages is essentially a rationalistic account of his narrative and the Old Testament.[2] For the later period, Milman disparages Basnage and prefers the German Jewish historian Isaac Jost.[3] Milman's work was published contemporaneously with the earliest English translations of the new German scientific histories of the ancient classical world by August Boeckh (1828), B.G. Niebuhr (1828–32) and C.O. Müller (1830).[4] Milman was a close friend of many of the translators who were responsible for these works, and his book is (as his first reviewers saw) an early product of the new interest in German critical history and theology that came to be known as the Higher Criticism. Although his History was generally welcomed in orthodox Jewish circles, it caused an immense scandal in the English Protestant community because it applied rational historical principles to the narrative of a sacred text: the ideas that Abraham was a simple Arab sheikh and that the Jews were a Palestinian tribe fighting for their existence among hostile neighbours were simply too much to accept. The publisher was forced to abandon the series that Milman's book was intended to inaugurate, and Milman himself remained theologically suspect for the rest of his distinguished career: a liberal churchman, who compounded doubts about his orthodoxy when he edited the standard nineteenth century edition of Gibbon, he never rose beyond the status of Dean of Canterbury. Ultimately of course Milman's History, revised to take account of later German scholarship, became the standard narrative history of the Jews in English, and

---

[1] There is an excellent account of the Jewish Question from 1833 to 1858 in Gertrud Himmelfarb, *The People of the Book: Philosemitism in England from Cromwell to Churchill* (New York 2011) ch. III.

[2] I have used primarily the second edition, also of 1830, which seems to differ in only minor details from the first. Milman revised his text for the 1863 edition, shortly before his death in 1868; this is most easily available in the Everyman's Library.

[3] *Geschichte der Isräeliten seit der Zeit der Maccabäer*. For the verdict see Milman vol III p. 158f: 'We differ from Jost, who is a pupil of Eichhorn, on many points, particularly the composition of the older Scriptures, but we gladly bear testimony to the high value of his work, which, both in depth of research and arrangement, is far superior to the desultory, and by no means trustworthy, volumes of Basnage.'

[4] On these see my account in the *History of Oxford University*.

remained in print for most of the twentieth century.[①]

Milman defends his approach in the introduction to the third volume of the first edition, and again towards the end of his life in the preface to the edition of 1863:

What should be the treatment by a Christian writer, a writer to whom truth is the one paramount object, of the only documents on which rests the earlier history of the Jews, the Scriptures of the Old Testament? Are they, like other historical documents, to be submitted to calm but searching criticism as to their age, their authenticity, their authorship; above all, their historical sense and historical interpretation? … (Everyman edn. p. 4)

Lawgivers, prophets, apostles, were in all other respects men of like passions (take the word in its vulgar sense) with their fellow-men; they were men of their age and country, who, as they spoke the language, so they thought the thoughts of their nation and their time, clothed those thoughts in the imagery, and illustrated them from the circumstances of their daily life. They had no special knowledge on any subject but moral and religious truth to distinguish them from other men; were as fallible as others on all questions of science, and even of history, extraneous to their religious teaching….

This seems throughout to have been the course of providential government: lawgivers, prophets, apostles, were advanced in religious knowledge alone. In all other respects society, civilisation, developed itself according to its usual laws, The Hebrew in the wilderness, excepting as far as the Law modified his manners and habits, was an Arab of the Desert. Abraham, excepting in his worship and intercourse with the One True God, was a nomad Sheik. The simple and natural tenor of these lives is one of the most impressive guarantees of the truth of the record. (ibid p.7-8)

But problems always remained. While allowing for the insertion of Jewish history into the prevailing conceptions of the progress of civilisation, and for the possibility of comparisons such as Moses with Solon, it was not entirely possible to reconcile the principles of Jewish history with those adopted in the new scientific history of ancient Greece and Rome. Even discarding miracles and the direct intervention of God in history in favour of a rational approach, there remained two fundamental problems. Throughout the long tradition of Sacred History the Jews had been regarded as the Chosen People, and their history was the history of the fulfilment of God's covenant to grant them the Promised Land. These were in turn justified in Christian terms by their divine role in producing the Messiah. Christian writers could of course escape from these aspects of the Jewish tradition by claiming that the failure of the Jews to recognise the Messiah had caused them to pass on their special status as chosen people to the Christian community, and they had thereby forfeited their right to a promised land. But it nevertheless made it extremely difficult to produce a historical account that would enable Judaism to be directly compared with Greece and Rome. And Milman himself believed in the divine dispensation of human history; he ends with the declaration:

History, which is the record of the Past has now discharged its office: it presumes not to raise the mysterious veil which the Almighty has spread over the Future. The destinies of this wonderful people, as of all mankind, are in the hands of the All-Wise Ruler of the Universe; his decrees will be accomplished, his truth, his goodness, and his wisdom vindicated. (vol III p. 424)

Milman did his best to create a modern scientific version of history from the biblical tradition, explaining

---

① The preface to the 1863 edition lists a number of more recent writers that Milman has used (Everyman edn. pp.16-28).

the interventions of God on rationalistic principles and even playing down the historical significance of the Crucifixion to the same extent as the (interpolated) narrative of Josephus:

We leave to the Christian historian the description of this event, and all its consequences—inestimable in their importance to mankind, but which produced hardly any *immediate* effect on the affairs of the Jewish nation. Yet our history will have shown that the state of the public mind in Judaea, as well as the character of Pilate, the chief agent in the transaction, harmonize in the most remarkable manner with the narrative of the Evangelists. (vol. II p. 158)

The crucifixion, despite the earthquake and unnatural solar darkness that accompanied it according to the gospel narratives, created no more perturbation than the fall of Icarus in Brueghel's famous painting.

Milman had of course many fewer problems to contend with than either his predecessors or his twentieth century successors. He could leave behind the notion that the sufferings of the Jews in the Diaspora were a consequence of their refusal to recognise Christ, and admire the Jewish community for its tenacity and its ability to overcome persecution; he could welcome the new era of mutual tolerance and even assimilation of 19th century western Europe. The future, fortunately for him, as he says was 'in the hands of the All-Wise Ruler of the Universe'. To him classical history and Jewish history were indeed flowing together, and comparison was simply a question of selection from tradition. But how does Milman's problem seem now? What sort of Jewish history do we want to write today, and how far will it be compatible with the dominant conception of a secular Greco-Roman history? These are the problems with which my teacher Arnaldo Momigliano wrestled throughout his life.

Before we consider this question we need also to recall a quite different tradition of the writing of Jewish history, that which arose out of the needs of the Jewish community to understand its own past. In his early editions Milman had already recognised the importance, if only as a source, of the work of Isaac Jost, and he refers in the preface to the edition of 1863 (p.20) to other recent works of Jewish scholars. But he was scarcely aware of the profound reinterpretation of Jewish history that emerged in the age of Romanticism amid the struggles between the various traditions of German Judaism. In 1846 the young Heinrich Graetz published his famous manifesto 'Die Construction der jüdischen Geschichte' [1] and in 1853 began his multi-volume *History of the Jews* with volume 4 on the period 70–500 C.E.: 'Another history of the Jews' said Leopold Zunz, the eminent rabbinic scholar—'But this time a Jewish history,' Graetz replied.

In starting his enterprise from the destruction of the Temple by the Roman authorities, Graetz indicated a new interpretation of Jewish history based on the concept of the Diaspora, which made it fundamentally different from the standard histories of other peoples. His narrative was to combine the political story of the persecutions of the Jews with the history of their inner life, which in the spirit of Maimonides revolved around their moral or divine mission to uphold the true principle of monotheism against their Christian persecutors.

The Christian conception of history, as is well known, fully denies to Judaism any history, in the higher sense of the word, since the loss of its national independence, an event which coincided with another of great importance to the Christian world structure.[2]

In contrast, Graetz proclaims the idea of history as the story of a cultural or spiritual mission:

---

[1] Translated with an important preface and other material in Ismar Schorsch, *Heinrich Graetz, The Structure of Jewish History and Other Essays* (New York 1975), from which I take the following translations.

[2] *o.c.* p. 93.

There is scarcely a science, an art, an intellectual province in which Jews have not taken a part, for which Jews have not manifested an equal aptitude. To think was as much a characteristic feature of the Jews as to suffer.[1]

History still has not produced another case of a nation which has laid aside its weapons of war to devote itself entirely to the peaceful pursuits of study and poetry, which has freed itself from the bonds of narrow self-interest and let its thoughts soar to fathom its own nature and its mysterious relationship to the universe and God.[2]

And on the completion of his *History* in 1874 he reflected on the twin legacy of western history in Hellenism and Hebraism:

The classical Greeks are dead, and toward the deceased posterity behaves properly. Envy and hatred are silent at the grave of the dead; their contributions are, in fact, usually exaggerated. It is quite different with that other creative nation, the Hebrews. Precisely because they're still alive their contributions to culture are not generally acknowledged; they are criticized, or given another name to partially conceal their authorship or to dislodge them entirely. Even if the fair-minded concede that they introduced the monotheistic idea and a higher morality into the life of nations, very few appreciate the great significance of these admissions. They fail to consider why one creative nation with its rich talents perished, whereas the other, so often on the brink of death, still wanders over the earth having rejuvenated itself several times.[3]

Graetz concludes by characterising the Jewish tradition:

The history of the Israelite nation manifests, therefore, at the beginning a thoroughly irregular pattern. Two factors determine its rise and fall, a physical and spiritual one, or a political and a religious-ethical one.[4]

Thus Graetz's History has a dual structure, as a celebration of Jewish philosophy and learning, but also a history of a religious culture surviving persecution. Despite the romantic language of its formulation and the somewhat unsatisfactory nature of his essentially biographical narrative, this alternative vision of the meaning of ancient history surely deserves more attention than it is given today as a future direction for the study of world ancient history. At the start of the fateful age of the creation of national histories as national myths, Jewish history liberated itself; in this respect it stands alongside the earlier Enlightenment traditions of Greek and Roman ancient history, but it transcends them in offering a new sort of history based on the cultural life of the spirit. No wonder this escape from the political history so dominant in the second half of the nineteenth century earned in 1879 the wrath of the most extreme of the German nationalist historians, Heinrich Treitschke.[5]

What is revealed by reflecting on the presuppositions of the western traditions of ancient history is the extent to which the modern western world has continually developed a myth of the past in order to justify contemporary preoccupations. That is of course true of all history that is not pure antiquarianism, but it is important to know why we think in this particular way in order to understand that it is not the only way that world history can be structured. And when we westerners criticise other historical political traditions for

---

[1] Introduction to vol. 4 of the *History, o.c.* p. 126.
[2] Introduction to vol 5 of the *History, o.c.* p. 136.
[3] Introduction to vol 1, *o.c.* p. 175.
[4] *Ibid.* p. 187.
[5] Graetz's emphasis on the centrality of the Diaspora is perhaps no longer in fashion. In the modern post-holocaust world, Jewish history may be turning back from this cultural interpretation of the Jewish tradition to a form of nationalist historiography based on that evolved by its persecutors in the second half of the 19th century, in a search for a political myth based on the Promised Land.

their inability to translate, or understand or even to see as important, concepts like liberty and democracy, we should remember that these are not transcendental human values. The western traditions of ancient world history rest on the 18th century foundations established by the Enlightenment, that combined imperialism with democracy and the free market economy of Adam Smith to create a western interpretation of history; to this it married a Judaeo–Christian tradition of a religion capable of being translated into rational history because it was ultimately based on historical narrative rather than myth. But the example of Graetz suggests that this dominant western view is not the only way to structure ancient history. Perhaps the 21st century will enable us to construct a new vision of ancient world history that is inclusive of other cultures like China, India and the Near East, and is not based solely on traditional western European values.

Bibliography

These reflections are based on a number of previous studies:

'The Beginnings of Greats, 1800–1872. II. Ancient History', *The History of the University of Oxford vol.VI. Nineteenth Century Oxford, Part I* ed. M.G. Brock, M.C. Curthoys (Oxford, 1997) 520–542.

'Ancient History, 1872–1914', *The History of the University of Oxford vol.VI. Nineteenth Century Oxford, Part 2* ed. M.G. Brock, M.C. Curthoys (Oxford 2000) 333–60.

'In Search of the Key to All Mythologies', *Translating Antiquity* ed. Stefan Rebenich, Barbara von Reibnitz, Thomas Späth (Basel 2010) 119–29.

'Modern Perceptions of Ancient Realities from Montesquieu to Mill', *Démocratie athéniennes– Démocratie moderne: Tradition et Influences* Entretiens Fondation Hardt LVI (Vandoeuvres–Genève 2010) 137–66 and 'Conclusion' ibid. pp. 395–401.

'Niebuhr in Britain', *Historiographie de l' antiquité et transferts culturels: Les histoires anciennes dans l' Europe des XVIIIe et XIXe siècles,* ed. Chryssanthi Avlami and Jaime Alvar (Rodopi, Amsterdam–New York 2010) 239–54.

'Ireland invents Greek History: the lost historian John Gast', *Hermathena* 185 (2008; published 2011) 23–106.

'Momigliano on Peace and Liberty (1940)', *Acta Universitatis Carolinae–Philologica I Graecolatina Pragensia XXIII* (2010; published 2011) 81–96; reprinted in *The Annual of Texts by Foreign Guest Professors* (University of Prague) 4 (2010) 95–114.

'Ancient History in the Eighteenth Century', Afterword to *The Western Time of Ancient History*, ed. A. Lianeri (Cambridge 2011) 301–6.

Origins of Political Thought in the Ancient World: Interactions and Comparisons

Kurt A. Raaflaub，Brown University

Abstract：In the formative stages of their culture, from the eighth into the sixth century BCE, the ancient Greeks interacted intensely with cultures descended from the great Near Eastern civilizations (from Anatolia to Egypt) and absorbed an immense amount of outside impulses in all spheres of culture, including the intellectual. Strangely, with few partial exceptions, nobody has seriously investigated whether such influences affected the emergence of Greek political thought as well. There is no a priori reason to think that this was not the case, and my larger project aims at finding out whether, to what extent, and how it was.

This essay will focus specifically on reflections on politics and government. It will briefly summarize the early Greek evidence for such reflections in Homer's epics and the political conceptions underlying early laws as well as reforms enacted in the late seventh and sixth century in Sparta and Athens. The essay will then offer some explanations for the emergence of such reflections in their Greek context and examine the question of whether there exists evidence for comparable ancient Near Eastern thought that might have influenced Greek thought. In a final and very tentative section, the essay will address the potential for comparison with the emergence of political thinking in early China.

Introduction

My current research project investigates the beginnings of political thinking among the ancient Greeks in the intercultural context of the eastern Mediterranean.[①] Let me begin with a few explanations. In contrast to

---

① This is an expanded version of a paper I gave at the 2012 International Symposium on Ancient World History ("Contacts, Exchanges, and Comparison in the Ancient World: From the Mediterranean to the Yellow River") at Nankai University in Tianjin, June 16–18, 2012. I have kept the lecture format but added documentation. I am most grateful to Prof. Yang Ju-ping, Dr. Zheng Wei, and their assistants for the excellent organization of the conference and their generous hospitality. — Various earlier versions were presented at McGill University, the University of Southern California, Brown University, and the University of Tübingen. I thank colleagues and students at all these events for their thoughtful and helpful comments.

"political theory" which I take to be direct, systematic, and at least partially abstract thinking about political matters, by "political thought" I mean, more broadly, any reflection on politics, institutions, the community or state, and relations between citizens and among communities or states.[①] Why is it important at all to gain a deeper understanding of the *beginnings* of Greek political thought? Because it is this type of political thinking, with its specific contents, focuses, and modes of expression, that prompted the emergence of Greek political theory and philosophy which in turn exerted decisive influence on the development of political thought in all its forms among the Romans, in the Middle Ages, the Renaissance, early modern Europe, and even the modern western world. The political terminology the Greeks developed essentially is our political terminology, the political values they discovered and defined (justice, equality, and liberty foremost among them) are more important than ever in our own time, the constitutions they distinguished, systematized, and debated (monarchy, aristocracy or oligarchy, and democracy), are still at the core of our debates and aspirations, and the authors who contributed most intensely to these ancient efforts, Thucydides, Plato, and Aristotle, still stimulate the thinking of modern philosophers, political scientists, and historians. Without the Greeks, we would not think about politics the way we do. It certainly seems worth understanding why this tradition originated in a small, poor, and mountainous country beyond the reach of great civilizations and empires.[②] Or did it substantially originate even earlier, at the core of those great civilizations?

This is why we need to consider the "Mediterranean Context." From the eighth to the sixth centuries (often called the "Orientalizing Period"), the Greeks interacted intensively with Near Eastern civilizations (from Anatolia via Mesopotamia and the Levant to Egypt) that were the heirs to more than two millennia of cultural development. In this formative period of their culture, the Greeks absorbed a vast range of impulses in every aspect of material and intellectual culture.[③] There is no a *priori* reason why such influences should not have affected political thought as well. With a few partial exceptions, however, no one has seriously investigated whether and to what extent this was the case.[④] My project aims at filling this gap. In this essay, I shall very briefly summarize and higlight the main themes and nature of early Greek political thinking. I shall then offer some explanations for the emergence of such reflections in their purely Greek context and suggest some answers to the question of whether there exists evidence for comparable ancient Near Eastern thought that might have influenced Greek thought. In a final and very tentative section, I shall boldly address the potential for comparison with the emergence of political thinking in early China.

Early Greek political thought

From its very beginning, Greek literature paid close attention to politics and institutions and engaged in political reflection that focused, from a strongly communal perspective, on leadership, the role of institutions, and justice. Let me give a couple of examples from Homer's *Iliad*, dating to the late eighth century.[⑤] The

---

① On definitions of political thought and theory, see Rowe and Schofield 2000: 1–2; also Meier 1990: pt. I; Cartledge 2009: ch. 2.

② For Greek culture as a whole, Meier 2011 tries to answer this question. On archaic Greece, see also chs. in *CAH* III.3 (1982) and IV (1988); Snodgrass 1980; Osborne 1996; Morris 1998; Hall 2007; Raaflaub and van Wees 2009.

③ Eastern intellectual influences: e.g., West 1997; Burkert 1992, 2004. All dates are BCE.

④ Eastern influence on Greek philosophy: West 1971; on Greek thought in general: Vernant 1982. Political thought in the ancient Near East: see, e.g., chs. in Weber–Schäfer 1976 and Fetscher and Münkler 1988 (without attention to comparison or influence); in the Hebrew Bible: Oswald 2009. Attempts at comparison: Raaflaub 1993.

⑤ For the relationship between the society described in Homer's epics and early Greek society (the "historicity" of epic society), see Finkelberg 2011, s.v. "Historicity," "Society." On Homer, see Latacz 1996.

epic's opening notoriously does not announce great deeds of great heroes but the immeasurable misery brought about the community by the quarrel of its two greatest leaders. Agamemnon, who has caused this quarrel by making horrendous mistakes of judgement, suffers through a deep crisis of leadership—at one point, his men even desert him, despairing of their chances to win the war, and run to the ships, eager to get home. Yet he admits his mistakes, listens to the advice of his peers, does everything he can to achieve reconciliation, and succeeds in reintegrating the community. In the end he is honored as "more just," that is, for having reached a higher level of justice: everybody makes mistakes; the community recognizes the leader who is able to overcome division and achieve unity. Hector, the Trojan leader, offers a contrasting example: he is a perfect leader, making every effort to save his city; his name even expresses that: "the holder, the savior," and his fellow citizens honor him by giving his son the name Astyanax, "lord of the city," because, the poet explains, "Hector alone saved the city." But this man, led astray by ambition, makes a crucial tactical mistake that costs his army enormous losses. Standing alone outside of the walls and ashamed of his failure, he finds himself incapable of facing the criticism of the citizens. He compounds his mistake by deciding to fight Achilles alone, to win or die with honor, and thereby deprives his city of the only chance it has to survive the war. The epic's dramatic action is thus described from the perspective of the community and its well-being. This is a political perspective that is visible in many other details and narrative choices the poet makes.[1]

Another example: the *agora* (in Homeric Greek *agorē*), the public square, is the center of the community and the place where political actions take place. The poet pays extraordinary attention to what happens there, describing several assemblies in great detail and showing that the men who meet in assembly and fight the community's wars, matter. When booty is distributed after a successful military campaign, the leaders receive their share of honor, and the rest is distributed equally to all—by the leaders but on behalf of the community's men. The assembly does not vote and commoners usually do not speak, but the men express their opinion unmistakably by voice or feet. The leader is not formally obliged to heed their opinion but if he ignores it and fails he is in trouble, and occasional statements make clear that it is difficult to act against a firmly expressed opinion of council or assembly. A good leader listens to his peers' advice and follows the best proposal. The establishment of consensus and resolution of conflicts are important; hence the ideal leader is best in fighting and *speaking*; he does not rule but persuade, he performs leadership on the battlefield and in the assembly.[2]

Remarkably, the *agora* is even the object of explicit political conceptualization. The atomized "non-society" of the giant one-eyed Cyclopes, whom Odysseus meets in his adventures, has "no common norms, no meetings for counsels" (*agorai boulēphoroi*). In other ways too it is characterized as the extreme opposite of a civilized society. But contrast, the poet exemplifies a "super-civilized" society with the Phaeacians: they have an *agora* set aside for communal meetings; it is paved, with polished stones as seats for the council members, and leader, council, and assembly interact properly throughout.[3] In the conceptual design of the famous shield of Achilles, an arbitration scene, together with wedding and harvest, symbolizes the community

---

[1]　For Agememnon, see *Iliad* books 1, 2, 9, 19; for Hector: 6.402–3; 12.210–50; 18.243–313; 22.99–110, and Finkelberg 2011, *s.v.* "Hector." For details, see Raaflaub 2000: 29–32.

[2]　Finkelberg 2011, *s.v.* "Agora," "Boule," "Polis." Army: Raaflaub 2008a. On politics as performance: Hammer 2002.

[3]　Cyclopes: *Odyssey* 9.105–15, 125–30, 170–479. Phaeacians: Bks. 6–8, 13; they were once neighbors of the Cyclopes (6.4–6): juxtaposition of contrasts is also a means of conceptualization. Paved agora: 6.266–67; 8.4–7; cf. *Iliad* 18.503–4. For attempts at conceptualization, see also *Iliad* 18.483–608; Hesiod, *Works and Days* 225–47.

in peace. This suggests that in peace justice rules; conflicts are resolved through arbitration in public, amidst an assembly of people; although elite judges debate and propose solutions, ordinary people let their opinions on the proposed verdicts be heard.[1]

Several scenes indicate that the people play a potentially powerful role. It is clear, therefore, that the community the poet describes is an early form of the polis which soon came to dominate political and cultural developments in Greece. Moreover, already in the epics the *polis* is a citizen state (not a city state). "The men are the *polis*," says the historian Thucydides, anticipated by the early sixth-century poet Alcaeus.[2]

Moving beyond Homer, by the mid-seventh century we have the first extant law, inscribed on stone. It begins with "this was decided by the polis" and regulates rotation in the chief office of the town. Similar phrases occur elsewhere, indicating that the polis or demos, that is, the collectivity of citizens is the body that enacts laws dealing with several aspects of political life, including public funds, a council of elders, and a "popular council." Early lawgivers, attested in several poleis, even enacted clusters or collections of laws. Such laws reflect communities that acted with a communal will and voice. Laws were instruments to realize such collective will and to change the polis' order and institutions. They presuppose political reflection and an awareness of the conditions, power, potential, and consequences of thought and action in the political realm. Communities realized that they had gained control over their law and, with it, first in small, then in larger ways, over their political and social order, their way of life; they recognized law's significance for communal stability.[3] Political thought could thus be transformed through legislation into political action. This paved the way for constitutional creativity and reform, and this made it possible, later on, to postulate the sovereignty of law as a condition and guarantee of communal liberty (as Pindar and Herodotus did in memorable formulations): *nomos basileus*, law is the king![4]

And indeed, still in the seventh century, in a time of severe crisis that greatly enhanced the responsibility of the citizen army, the *polis* of Sparta adopted the first constitutional reform we know of (called the "Great Rhetra," Pronouncement). Among other issues, it institutionalized the assembly (with monthly meetings at a predetermined date and place), and regulated communal decision making: the council of elders (*gerousia*), limited to thirty members including the two leaders or "kings" (which implies an election), had to formulate proposals that were discussed in the assembly. The mass of the people was "to have victory (*nikê*) and power (*kratos*)," that is, to make the final decision, even if the gerousia apparently retained some kind of veto power.[5] This reform formally placed communal decision-making into the hands of the citizens who as soldiers defended the land and the citizens' privileges.

A few decades later in Athens Solon was given extraordinary powers as an arbitrator to resolve an urgent social and economic crisis. Such arbitrators played a crucial role at the time, representing a peaceful

---

① Arbitration scene: *Iliad* 18.497–508.

② Thucydides, *History* 7.77.7; Alcaeus, frag. 112.10; 426 in Campbell 1982.

③ "This was decided by the polis": law of Dreros on Crete (ca. 750 BCE): see Meiggs and Lewis 1988: no. 2; translation in Fornara 1983: no. 11. Early laws are collected in Koerner 1993; van Effenterre and Ruzé 1994. On early Greek law: Gagarin 1986. Law, writing, and monumentalization: Farenga 2006; Gagarin 2008; Hawke 2011. Security of Law: Eder 2005. Communal origin of legal culture: Meier 2011.

④ Pindar, frag. 169 Snell-Maehler; cf. Herodotus 7.104; Gigante 1956.

⑤ Sources for the "Rhetra": Tyrtaeus, frag. 4 in West 1992 (W); translated in West 1994: 23; Plutarch, *Lycurgus* 6 (van Effenterre and Ruzé 1994: no.61; Fornara 1983: no.12). Discussion: e.g., Cartledge 2002b: 115–17; Welwei 2004: 59–69.

alternative to civil strife or tyranny. They were closely connected with Apollo's oracle in Delphi (famous for advocating moderation), stood above the conflicting parties and as sages (*sophoi*) enjoyed far-reaching authority. Importantly, they were appointed and empowered by the community and thus acted from among the citizen community. Aristotle calls Pittacus of Mytilene, like Solon a sage and lawgiver, an "elected tyrant." [1] Solon speaks as an Athenian ("our polis") and addresses his fellow citizens, occupying a position between the conflicting parties (roughly, elite and demos) and preventing either from hurting the other or profiting unjustly.[2] He enacted a broad range of reforms in virtually every aspect of the community's life. He abolished debt bondage and guaranteed the citizens' personal freedom. His comment on his legislation, "I wrote down ordinances for low and high alike, providing straight justice fitted for each man (or case)," approximates the principle of equality before the law. His priority was to establish certainty of law, give all citizens access to justice, and involve large numbers of citizens in jurisdiction: a special assembly served as a court for communally important issues, and any person who wished was empowered to take legal action on behalf of an injured third party. In the political sphere, he introduced a "timocratic constitution," determining political participation and access to offices according to military and economic capacity, and a new annually elected "popular" council with 400 members which balanced the power of the old aristocratic council, enhanced the role of the assembly, and probably made some regulation of the assembly's meetings and procedures necessary. Finally, he protected the Athenian institutions from subversion by outlawing tyranny and making it mandatory for citizens to take sides in the event of civil strife.[3]

All these measures served three purposes: to stabilize the community by eliminating abuses and establishing a firm system of justice, to balance elite power by creating venues for political participation by nonelite citizens, and to prevent civil discord with the potential result of tyranny. They are the logical consequence of Solon's understanding of civic responsibility: if every citizen was to suffer from political abuses, the citizens had to assume responsibility for the common good.

After Solon a long interval of tyranny intervened, caused by excessive aristocratic rivalry. Paradoxically, by weakening aristocratic control and securing internal peace, this tyranny paved the way for a more egalitarian constitution.[4] When it was overthrown at the end of the sixth century, Cleisthenes enacted a complex set of reforms, based on sophisticated political thinking, that completely reorganized the structure of the citizen body and the political institutions. He created an institutional framework that made it possible for citizens from all over the large Attic territory to collaborate in cults and festivals, in the army, and in politics. In a dense system of representation, all citizens were, so-to-speak, made present in the *polis* center, the town hall where the 500 councilors met: about one per sixty citizens; since the office was limited to a year and could not be held more than twice, close to half of all citizens spent at least one year of their lives in this time-consuming office.[5]

Cleisthenes' reforms succeeded in overcoming aristocratic and regional conflicts and contributed

---

[1]　On arbitrators (*katartistēres, aisymnētai*), see Meier 1990: 40–52; Faraguna 2001; Wallace 2009. Pittacus of Mytilene: Aristotle, **Politics** 1285a35ff.

[2]　Solon, frag. 4.1–8, 30; 5; 36.1–2, 20–27; 37 W.

[3]　Solon's reforms: Aristotle, **Constitution of the Athenians** 5–12; Plutarch, **Solon**. Solon's poems are collected in West 1992: 139–65, translated in West 1994: 74–83, his laws in Ruschenbusch 1966, translated in Ruschenbusch 2010. For discussion, see Andrewes 1982a; Welwei 1992: 133–206; Raaflaub 1996c; Blok and Lardinois 2006; Wallace 2007. Personal freedom: Raaflaub 2004b: 45–53. Equality before the law: frag. 36.18–20 W.

[4]　On Athenian tyranny, see Andrewes 1982b; Stahl 1987; Lewis 1988.

[5]　On Cleisthenes' reforms, see Ostwald 1988; Meier 1990: ch.4; Ober 1996: ch.4; Anderson 2003.

crucially to integrating the community. He, and Solon before him, demonstrated that the polis not only provided the framework within which the citizens performed politics but that it had itself become the object of political action by the citizens: through legislation enacted in the assembly or the delegation of power to an elected lawgiver, they were able to change and improve their communal order, even profoundly and completely: the citizens were in control of their community. Feeling in charge, they felt responsible. Their newly found self-confidence expressed itself not least in their decision, a few years later, to resist the invading Persians and defeat them in the battles of Marathon (490) and Salamis (480).

These victories over the Persians changed everything. With the huge fleet Athens had built out of the proceeds of a newly discovered silver mine (rather than distributing this income among all citizens, as was done traditionally), it became a major military power. The fleet was rowed largely by lower class citizens—those who could not afford the equipment to fight in the heavily armed infantry army and therefore militarily and politically had not counted much before. This fleet became Athens' instrument of power and rule over a large number of other Greek poleis. Their changed military role enhanced the social prestige of the lower class citizens; as a result, equal political rights were extended to all citizens, regardless of their birth, wealth, or education. This was the breakthrough of democracy in the mid-fifth century: a development without precedent in the ancient world and not paralleled again for almost two-and-a half millennia.[1] (That this democracy reserved political rights only for adult male citizens, excluded women from political participation, and was based on slave labor, was normal under the conditions prevailing throughout the ancient world and far beyond.) Because this democracy was so unusual, it provoked resistance and intense debates; it provided an intense stimulus to cultural achievement and political and constitutional thought: much that followed, including the development of political theory by the sophists and political philosophy by Plato and Aristotle happened in reaction or resistance to democracy.[2]

I cannot pursue this further here but let me return briefly to Solon for two aspects that are crucial to understanding the development of Greek political thinking. One is that Solon essentially is the ancestor of political theory. In an extant poem, later entitled "Good Order" (*eunomia*), he explains his thinking. Humans, he emphasizes, are responsible for their own fate: the gods are not against but for them. The citizens, particularly the elite, driven by greed, commit abuses that cause civil strife with disastrous consequences for all. Based on empirical observation, Solon constructs a chain of cause and effect that links socio-political wrong-doing by citizens with harm suffered by the community; this causal relationship is necessary, inescapable, comparable to laws of nature (such as thunder following upon lightning). While earlier poets had found the punishment of human wrong-doing, imposed by the gods, in the realm of natural disasters, Solon places such consequences entirely on the socio-political level. Earlier thinkers believed hat justice is realized by the power of the supreme god, Zeus, through whom his daughter, Dike, the goddess of Justice, exacts her revenge. Solon sees Dike as an independent demon of revenge, acting on her own, almost as an abstract principle: "the silent one, who knows what is and has been done, and comes at last with certainty (*pantōs*) to seek her revenge." [3]

---

[1] On the breakthrough of democracy in the mid-fifth century, see Rhodes 1992; Meier 1999: chs. 6-7; Raaflaub, Ober, and Wallace 2007: ch.5. On the working of democracy: Hansen 1999.

[2] On debates about democracy: Raaflaub 1989. On the interaction between empire, democracy, and culture: Sakellariou 1996; Boedeker and Raaflaub 1998; Arnason et al. 2013. On political theory and philosophy: relevant chs. in Rowe and Schofield 2000.

[3] Solon's theory of socio-political causation; justice as an autonomous principle: frag. 4 W. Comparable to laws of nature: 9 W; cf. 11; 13.17-32. On Solon's political thinking: Jaeger 1966: 75-99; Raaflaub 2000: 39-42; Meier 2011: ch.21.

Justice will prevail with certainty! The entire city is affected, nobody can escape.

For the first time, a political process is here analyzed entirely on the political level. Understanding it, one can prevent the consequences by eliminating the causes, that is, by political intervention. Earlier thinkers had founded their conclusions on myth and belief; Solon proceeds from a theory based on empirical knowledge and political analysis. His advice therefore is compelling. The community, afflicted by "bad order" (*dysnomia*) and "taught" by the mediator, has the chance to re-establish "good order" (*eunomia*). Solon's ideas represent a thrilling breakthrough in political thought.

This leads me to the second aspect: constitutional thought and terminology. Several early poets emphasize the crucial importance of the concept of "good order" (*eunomia*) for communal well-being. Lawgiver and community, confronted with crisis and conflict (bad order, *dysnomia*), aim at restoring *eunomia*, which emerges as the focus of early Greek constitutional thought.[1] Dealing with the threat of monopolization of power by an individual (a usually unstable and shortlived form of monarchy which the Greeks called tyranny),[2] the Greek aristocrats discovered the importance of something they had previously taken for granted: equality. To formulate this value, they modified eunomia by the prefix iso- (equal) to produce isonomia (equal order, equality before the law, political equality). By the late sixth century, numerous polis constitutions, including Cleisthenes' new system in Athens, were based on isonomia in the sense of the political equality of at least the land-owning citizen-soldiers; to distinguish these egalitarian constitutions from fully developed democracy, we call them "isonomic." Equality was the political value that continued to drive constitutional development until it reached its fullest extent in fifth-century democracy: Herodotus says "democracy has the most beautiful name of all, equality (*isonomia*)," and he explains the Athenians' rise to power with the equality and liberty they gained after the expulsion of the tyrants. Liberty, however, was connected with democracy much later and as the result of different developments.[3]

The emergence of "isonomic" constitutions made people realize that there was not only order and disorder but a variety of orders that could be distinguished by the number and nature of those who ruled: one (*monarchos*, a king or *tyrannos*, a tyrant), a few (oligarchy) or the best (aristocracy), and rule by the people (*dēmo-kratia*) or the masses (*ochlokratia*). The distinction of three types of constitution occurs in the extant evidence for the first time around 470, and the term *dēmokratia* was probably coined only a few years later. These distinctions and democracy itself proved enormously stimulating for constitutional thought: the definition of constitutions, the discussion of positive and negative aspects of each and especially of democracy, the design of new constitutions from scratch (culminating in the "ideal states" discussed by Plato and Aristotle), the idea of a "mixed constitution," and much more. But these later developments lead us far beyond archaic Greece and the emergence of political thought.[4]

Let me sum up so far: From its emergence in the early archaic period, Greek literature paid attention to politics and institutions and engaged in political reflection that focused, from a strongly communal perspective,

---

[1]　*Eunomia*: Hesiod, *Theogony* 901-3; Tyrtaeus, frag. 4 W; Solon, frag. 4.31-39 W. Focus of constitutional thought: Meier 1990: 160.

[2]　See above n.18. On tyranny in general, see Murray 1993: ch.9; Stein-Hölkeskamp 2009.

[3]　*Eunomia, nomos*, and *isonomia*: Ostwald 1969. Modification to *isonomia*: Raaflaub 1996b. Egalitarian constitutions: Robinson 1997. Herodotus 3.80.6; 5.78. Liberty and democracy: Raaflaub 2004b: ch.6.

[4]　Generally on the development of constitutional terminology: Meier 1990: ch.7. Discussions about constitutions: Raaflaub 1989. Designing constitutions from scratch: Aristotle, *Politics* 2.7-8. Mixed constitution: von Fritz 1954.

on leadership, the role of institutions, and justice. Early written laws and "constitutions," decided upon or authorised by the assembly, regulated political processes. Political reforms, enacted by elected lawgivers, initially aimed at restoring an ideal "good order" that was based on justice, equitable distribution, and popular participation, then at realizing specific communal goals. The development leads from description of (informal) institutions and their problems to political conceptualization, analysis, regulation, theorization, and deliberate intervention for the purpose of correcting abuses, restoring an old ideal, and, eventually, realizing an anticipated new one. Greek thinking about politics and government reached a first high point in sixth-century Athens, first in Solon's theory of political causation and later in Cleisthenes' complex set of reforms aimed at thorough communal integration.

Greek explanations

It is certainly possible to explain the emergence of this kind of political reflection, as scholars have usually done in the past, by focusing on the conditions under which society and culture in archaic Greece were formed, and on the specific nature of the Greek polis as a community of citizens.[1] In pursuing this line of argument, we need to think, first of all, of three elements that did *not* exist in early Greece. (a) Due to the Aegean world's location outside the power sphere of major empires, and because of the deep rupture that separated archaic Greece from its magnificent Bronze Age past,[2] state formation did not take the path of centralized states, strong and religiously sanctioned monarchies, and vassal systems. (b) In their formative period, Greek poleis did not need to cope with strong external pressure or large and vital communal projects (such as water distribution), and war played an important but rather limited role; all this obviated the need for a strong and cohesive elite, strong leadership, or centralization.[3] (c) Until they were confronted with the expanding Persian Empire in the mid-sixth century, the Greeks were open to foreign influences and lacked attitudes that were hostile to the outside world and were common especially in both Egypt and Mesopotamia: a perception that a chaotic outside world needed to be conquered and tamed, and a strong sense of superiority over the inferior "barbarians."[4]

Second, Greek poleis developed in clusters, balancing each other and allowing for a degree of equality in international relations. Some large poleis emerged but were unable to create power formations beyond the level of alliances; the Greeks took the "imperial turn" only in the fifth century. Within the poleis, paramount leaders, first among equals, did not stand above their communities, let alone "rule" them. Members of an emerging aristocracy were essentially equal, separated by a relatively small gap from the majority of independent farmers who played an indispensable communal role in army and assembly. The leader's status and privileges were embedded in the community; elite and commoners depended on each other; hence the polis was built on egalitarian foundations.[5] Criticism of elite and leaders was possible and frequent. Moreover, elite competition was intense and often destructive; it mobilized resistance among the demos, temporarily opened the way to tyranny, and encouraged the search for alternatives.

Third, in a period of rapid change, the communal element in the polis was strengthened at the expense

---

[1] Explanations of the emergence of Greek political thought: Meier 1990, 2011; Raaflaub 2000: 57-59.

[2] On the Greek "Dark Ages," see Snodgrass 1971; Deger-Jalkotzy 2006; Dickinson 2006.

[3] In this respect, the different conditions that shaped Rome's development are illuminating: Raaflaub 1996a.

[4] Sharp antithesis between inside and outside in Mesopotamia: Nissen and Renger 1987; in Egypt: Moers 2010. Greek concept of "barbarian": Georges 1994; Mitchell 2007.

[5] Egalitarian foundation of polis: Morris 2000: pt. 3; Raaflaub et al. 2007: ch.2. See also Starr 1977, 1986.

of elite aspirations; power and political procedures were formalized. Overseas trade and emigration offered opportunities for gain and social mobility, challenging traditional values and leadership. Crisis and social strife made it necessary to find new ways of resolving conflicts—often through communally appointed lawgivers. Differences among poleis encouraged comparison, and the foundation of new poleis abroad, with settlers of different origins, made it necessary to experiment with new institutional solutions that in turn influenced developments in the "old world." As a result, a sophisticated culture of political thinking emerged that generated remarkably complex and sometimes radical solutions.

Fourth, whatever they thought of the power of gods and fate, the Greeks understood early that ultimately humans themselves were responsible for their misfortune—and fortune. As enforcers of justice too, the gods were needed only as long as no sufficiently powerful human agency existed. Legislation, backed by communal enforcement, and Solon's understanding of justice as a virtually abstract principle, pushed the gods more into the background in both the political and legal spheres—though not in that of politics and popular morality. The citizens collectively assumed control.[1] Hence "the polis" —itself or through lawgivers— enacted laws and engaged in communal regulation and reform. Government in Greece was not a suffered reality but a communal project, the object of political reflection, analysis, and action.

Fifth, the demos's role was potentially powerful early on. Intercommunal wars enhanced the commoners' communal importance. This trend reached a climax in Sparta where extraordinary conditions— an enemy (a large and coherent slave population) within the polis' own boundaries—facilitated the enactment of a constitution that *formally* placed communal decisions in the citizens' hands. Elsewhere, elite abuses resulted in civil strife that could only be resolved by enhancing the citizens' communal involvement and adjusting the institutions. The polis, placed on a broader foundation, was thus institutionalized and stabilized.

Institutions and their interplay, and constitutions in a broader sense, even *politeia* as the entire way of life of a polis, thus became the focus of political thought and action, even of first attempts at theorisation, and communal laws became the means by which such ideas could be realized.

Possible Near Eastern influences

The question remains what role outside influences played in this process, not only for the reasons mentioned earlier but also because scholars have observed vast amounts of eastern influences in the works of those very poets who provide the evidence for early political thought. I limit myself here to three aspects: law and justice, collective decision making, and wisdom literature.

First, then, law and justice. Although Greco-Roman "law codes" show many similarities with Mesopotamian ones and were probably to some extent influenced by them, there are decisive differences.[2] These begin with ideas about the origins of law and justice which in Mesopotamia lie in a primordial world order and are conveyed by the gods to the king whom they charge with administering them on earth.[3] Mesopotamian law thus is essentially conservative and static. It is controlled and maintained by the king and those placed in power by him. The inscribed codes, such as that of Hammurabi, are part of monuments serving the king's self-presentation. The king is supreme judge and supreme creator of norms, but these norms are

---

① See, e.g., Raaflaub 2005; Meier 2011.
② Influence of Mesopotamian on Greco-Roman legislation and law codes: Mühl 1933; Westbrook 1988, 1989; discussion: Raaflaub 2009: 41–48.
③ Origins of law in Mesopotamian thought: Lang 2008: 57–58, with ref. to Otto 2005: 58.

expressed not through laws but through decrees that are imposed from the top, as a demonstration of the king's care and benefaction (and an expression of the supreme god's will); the people are passive recipients.[1] Similar conditions prevailed in Egypt.[2] As a consequence, with a possible exception in Israel,[3] *communal* or *public* thinking about laws, constitutions, communal order, and related issues in Near Eastern societies remained underdeveloped. By contrast, we saw, Greek legal culture was rooted in citizen communities. Greeks did not derive their laws from the gods, even if they might characterize venerable traditions as "divine norms" or solicit the approval of Apollo's oracle in Delphi for incisive legislative actions. And Greek law was dynamic and adaptable.

Among royal qualities, all Near Eastern societies emphasized justice: the king was expected to be a defender of justice and protect the weak from oppression by the strong. Analogies with early Greek thinking are undeniable.[4] In Mesopotamia, however, this element is emphasized especially in almost formulaic contexts that primarily serve royal self-presentation. In epic narratives (such as the *Enuma elish*), it seems to rank far behind martial qualities. Although here too parallels with Greek epic (especially Hesiod) are obvious, the Greeks place much greater emphasis on the supreme god's justice.[5] Nor do Mesopotamian sources engage in conceptualization or theorization of justice. By contrast, Egypt did have a concept of justice but it was part of a far more comprehensive concept of world, social, and ethical order (*ma' at*) that was primordial, superior to gods, kings, and man.[6] This concept is widely attested in texts and images but there is no comprehensive discussion of it, just as the Egyptians generally "did not leave systematic treatises about their political ideas…, let alone engage in the formulation of political theories." This makes it difficult to assess the role of political thought in Egyptian society and its possible influence on archaic Greece.

Second, collective decision making. In Mesopotamia centralized kingdoms and empires came and went. Beside them and under their umbrella, cities and tribes with their own structures and institutions played important roles. In epics, councils and assemblies appear on both the divine and human levels (as they do in Homer).[7] But, in difference to Homer, institutions are mentioned occasionally, when the narrative demands it; they are not an object of close attention or explicit conceptualization. In documentary sources (such as inscriptions, letters, or legal texts) references to these collective bodies, which operated entirely on the basis of traditional norms, remain on a factual level, without political reflection, analysis, or conceptualization. It is hard to see what political impulses might have originated there. By contrast, in the archaic Greek poleis it was precisely the collective body of citizens that through its institutions of government and justice shaped social, political, cultural, and legal developments. Still, it seems worth pursuing this further, especially in Neo-

---

[1] Mesopotamia: royal decrees, not laws: Wells 2005: 188-90; see also Westbrook 2003: 12-23 (6: "The source most closely identifiable with what we think of today as statutes are royal decrees."); Streck 2007.

[2] Redford 2001: II 277-82; *Lexikon der Ägyptologie*, under "Dekret," "Gesetze."

[3] For a comparison between Israelite and Greco-Roman "law codes," see Burckhardt et al. 2007.

[4] Royal ideology and justice: generally, Irani and Silver 1995. Egypt: Weber-Schäfer 1976: 26-40; Assmann 1990, 1993; O' Connor and Silverman 1995; Mesopotamia: Garelli 1974; Kramer 1974; Hittites: Archi 1979; Bryce 2002: 31; Persia: Briant 2002: 126, 329-30, and ch. 6.

[5] Justice in *Enuma elish*: Foster 2005: 478; parallels with Hesiod: West 1997: 280-83; comparison: Raaflaub 2008b: 49-51.

[6] *Ma' at* : Assmann 1990; 1993; Morschauser 1995: 101; cf. Zibelius-Chen 1988: 118-24 (quote: 113).

[7] Institutions of collective decision making: Beckman 1982; Durand 1989; Liverani 1993; Schemeil 1999; Fleming 2004. Councils and assemblies in epic: Katz 1993; West 1997: 193-99. For critical discussion of Jacobsen's concept of "primitive democracy" (1970: 132-70), see Robinson 1997: 16-22.

Assyrian and Late Babylonian cities which claimed specific privileges and "civic rights," almost a "charter of autonomy," based on tradition, guaranteed by the king, and protected by the city deity.[1] I need to find out whether the arguments used in these texts go beyond the invocation of tradition, divine will, and the king's obligations.

Third, wisdom literature: This category of texts is abundantly attested in Egypt, Mesopotamia, and the Hebrew Bible.[2] It was long believed to have had a direct influence on Hesiod and other Greek poets but this view is probably too simple.[3] At any rate, such texts contain moral and practical advice intended to secure a happy and successful life *within the given hierarchical framework*. Advice to the powerful concerns their blameless conduct toward superiors and justice and generosity toward their inferiors.[4] The world of politics is almost completely ignored—Hesiod too mentions it only as something to be avoided—and of political thought there are hardly any traces.

One text that is to some extent political is a Babylonian *Advice to a Prince*, dating to the first millennium and claiming that royal injustice will prompt divine punishment in the form of natural disasters, enemy attacks, rebellion, and loss of wealth, rule, and life. In *Works and Days* too Hesiod insists that crooked decisions by aristocratic judges will be answered by divine punishment and "one man's wickedness" causes the ruin of an entire city, prompting Zeus to send famine and sickness, infertility of fields, animals, and women, war, and destruction of armies and fleets.[5] Neither the Babylonian text nor Hesiod relate the forms of punishment specifically to the acts of injustice provoking them; these both seem to be picked randomly from lists of frequent misdeeds by the powerful, and frequent disasters. Nor can the authors do more than exhort the powerful to avoid injustice, and trust that the gods will react as expected. The two authors think on the same generic and traditional level. A decisive step beyond such generic thinking was taken first by Solon: in his effort, described above, to establish a specific and purely political causal connection between evil deeds and disastrous consequences, and to draw the necessary consequences to restore and protect the good order. Of this step I have as yet to find evidence in Near Eastern thought.

Extant Egyptian texts comprise *Instructions to Princes* as well.[6] They do not envisage royal failure and punishment but contain catalogs of policies and behaviors a king needs to observe in order to demonstrate his care. These texts too seem traditional and generic, informed by ancestral wisdom. They reflect the kind of political thinking that must have been common in Near Eastern monarchies, focusing on the qualities of the king and the best means to secure his popularity and rule. Crucially, though, they do not make such thinking explicit but only *imply* it, distilling its results into lists of advice. In other words, such thinking is not stimulated by the need to react to current problems and crisis. A unique exception seems to be the *Instruction of King*

---

[1]　Civic privileges of Late-Babylonian cities: Kuhrt 1995: 610-21 with bibliog.

[2]　"Wisdom literature": represented esp. by Babylonian wisdom texts (Lambert 1960); Egyptian "instructions" or "didactic literature" of various kinds and periods (easily accessible in Lichtheim 1973-1980), and in the Books of Job, Proverbs, and Ecclesiastes in the Hebrew Bible.

[3]　See relevant chapters in Dornseiff 1959; Walcot 1966; West 1978; 1997: 324-32. Schmitz 2004 offers a recent discussion with rich bibliog., not least on Near Eastern wisdom literature.

[4]　Advice to powerful persons: e.g., *Instruction of Ptahhotep*, par. 5-6, 24-25, 28 (Lichtheim 1973-1980: I 64-65, 70-71).

[5]　Babylonian *Fürstenspiegel*: Lambert 1960: 110-15. Hesiod on the just and unjust city: *Works and Days* 225-47.

[6]　*The Instruction Addressed to King Merikare* (Lichtheim 1973-1980: I 97-109) or *The Instruction of King Amenemhet I for his Son Sesostris I* (ibid. 135-39).

Amenemhet, written posthumously under the impression of the king's assassination, and advising his son not to trust anyone.[1] Overall, I suspect that the stability, unchallenged authority, and religious implications of the Egyptian monarchy were not conducive to an open and public culture of political thought or debate, even in the first millennium when it could have influenced Greek thinking.

Conclusions

Let me draw a few conclusions. Since my work is still in progress, these can only be preliminary. In what I have seen so far, we do indeed find analogies to some of the early Greek evidence, mostly on the pragmatic and narrative levels, in the sphere of traditional or generic thinking, and concerning the qualities of kings or leaders, especially their responsibility for justice. But I am still looking for evidence showing that the political sphere received specific and detailed attention and that steps were taken toward explicit conceptualization, systematic reflection, and theorization, as we observed them in Solon's thought. In this and other respects the Hebrew Bible may offer closer parallels—a big topic that remains to be investigated. Even so, it is in Solon's thinking that we seem to grasp a crucial advance in Greek political reflection that decisively broke through age-old patterns common to many cultures. If so, this marks a first step on a separate path toward Greek originality.

If this is correct what were the conditions that made this first step possible? I listed above a series of factors that created an environment encouraging independent thinking and collective responsibility. In particular, I want to emphasize here two points. One is an early disposition that was fostered by the nature of the Greek polis as a citizen community—a disposition to focus on the political sphere and to discuss political phenomena publicly and critically and to define them conceptually. The other is the discovery of the potential offered by communally initiated and controlled legislation and reform. All this facilitated the step onto a new level of political thinking that was taken in a situation of deep communal crisis by an exceptionally clear-sighted and determined statesman.

At any rate, thinking about institutions, communities, government, and politics overall seems much less prominent in Near Eastern sources than it is in archaic Greek ones. I conclude—tentatively and as a thesis to be tested in future research—that Near Eastern influence on early Greek political reflection was much smaller than one might have expected.

Even as a tentative conclusion this calls for explanation. Obvious reasons lie in the fundamental differences between early Greek and Near Eastern societies, particularly regarding the conditions under which society and culture developed, the place of the individual in the social hierarchy, and the social conditions of political thinking. Different perceptions of human responsibility seem especially important here. Greek poleis were micro-states, essentially egalitarian face-to-face citizen communities, in which the collectivity of citizens had to work out their problems themselves.[2] Near Eastern communities and states, despite perhaps similar origins, soon developed starkly hierarchical structures in which the individual, whether high or low, was tied into a strictly vertical system of authority that determined values and norms. In Thorkild Jacobsen's words, "in Mesopotamia the 'good life' was the 'obedient life'."[3] In such a system one would expect the individual's thoughts and actions to

---

① *Amenemhet*: previous note; see, e.g., Burkard 1999. National crisis as a literary topos: Lichtheim 1973–1980: I 134–35.

② Micro-states: Davies 1997. Working out their own problems: Meier 2011.

③ Jacobsen 1946: 138–39, 202.

have been severely restricted; independence would not have been valued. With few exceptions, political thinking must have been limited to the ruling circles and focused on legitimizing the existing order and distribution of power in order to secure their stability and permanence. This is largely true for Egypt as well.

Perhaps typically, the early Greek poets, pathbreakers in political reflection, were not part of the ruling circles—not even Solon. Political thought was not limited to the top of society. The Greeks encountered the Eastern system in their confrontation with the Persians. Even if one-sided and distorted by chauvinism and misunderstandings, these experiences prompted them to conceptualize the difference in a fundamental contrast: between a world of slavery and one of freedom.① The Greeks' communal structures, their valuation of independence, and their early understanding that they all, not only their leaders, were responsible for individual and communal well-being, created conditions that were conducive for a broadly-based culture of critical and independent thinking and for increasingly focused reflection on politics, institutions, and community.

Further comparison: the emergence and nature of political thought in early China

Finally, the event at which this essay was presented invites further comparison. The roughly contemporaneous but, on current knowledge, completely independent emergence in China and Greece of philosophy and historiography, among other intellectual endeavors, has long attracted attention and prompted attempts at explanation, such as the "Axial Age Theory" developed by Karl Jaspers, Shmuel Eisenstadt, and others.② However that may be, the parallels include political thought as well, and it would be tempting to embark on a full-scale comparison between forms, contents, and functions of political thought in archaic Greece and early China as well as the social-political causes of its emergence. At this point I am far from qualified to undertake such a comparison—which would exceed the limits of this paper anyway. But perhaps I may be permitted to offer a few very general and preliminary observations.③

The old Zhou states, consisting mainly of a capital city and a number of fortified towns inhabited by ruler, elite, and garrison soldiers, and ruling over the rural population, have been compared to ancient Greek poleis: elite and soldiers in these states had civil and military obligations and were consulted in state affairs. Yet this comparison seems at best to be valid only for Sparta (and a small number of other Greek communities) where a relatively small citizen body controlled not only a large slave population (the helots) but a vast dependent but free population of *perioikoi* (those "living around," that is, in the outlying areas). By contrast, in the other poleis urban and rural citizens were not differentiated and the city did not rule over the country-side.

At any rate, Zhou feudalism with hundreds of small states soon gave way to increasing centralization and hierarchization and the ruthless competition for power typical of the Warring States, where an ever smaller number of polities strove to maximise power, control, and resources in order to survive and prevail over others. It was most likely these pressures that prompted the emergence and high valuation of a particular resource we might call "brain power." Members of an educated elite, long involved in service to the state (the *shi*),

---

① Greek views of Persian vassalage: e.g., Herodotus 7.135; Meiggs and Lewis 1988: no. 12; Fornara 1983: no. 35; see generally Raaflaub 2004b: ch. 3.

② Jaspers 1953; Eisenstadt 1986; Arnason et al. 2005.

③ I intend to pursue this comparison in a paper I am preparing for a meeting hosted by Robert Rollinger at the University of Helsinki in early May 2013. I refer here generally to a very selective bibliography on political thought in early China: Needham 1956; Hsiao 1979; Schwartz 1985; Obberborn and Weber–Schäfer 1988; Lewis 1999, and relevant chs. in Loewe and Saghnessy 1999. For earlier efforts at comparison of early Greek and Chinese thought, see, e.g., Lloyd 1990: ch.4; 1996, 2002; Shankman and Durrant 2000 and 2002. On freedom, see Lloyd 1996: ch.6.

often relatively low-ranking and uprooted, became itinerant scholars and experts, offering their services to the powerful. These services included specialized intellectual knowledge, such as expertise in military matters, diplomacy, persuasion (rhetoric), administration, and government. Presenting their programs in oral or written form, these experts were hired by the rulers to realize their ideas, as generals, administrators, reformers, diplomats, and so on. This is a rough sketch but it suffices for my present purposes. Clearly, much of this expertise concerned political matters and was based on political thought.

I wish to emphasize three points. One is that such political thought, although based on earlier foundations, emerged and became institutionalized, prominent, and influential precisely when an urgent need arose and the social and economic structures were in place to support it. It is not far-fetched to see here analogies with the emergence of the sophists in mid-fifth-century Greece. These were itinerant philosophers and teachers, who in contrast to the earlier "natural philosophers" focused on the human world, state, society, and social interactions and earned their living by teaching rhetoric, politics, and much else. Plato's dialogues have immortalized their visits to Athens and debates with Socrates, while his refutation of their ideas has largely caused the loss of their works. For various reasons they were attracted to Athens but it is clear that they were a panhellenic phenomenon, originating in many poleis from Sicily to the coast of Thrace, and offering their services all over the Greek world. They too therefore rose to prominence when there was a widespread need for expert and specialized training and teaching—not only in democratic Athens and not only to improve chances in political competition. In fact, rhetoric was in high demand for judicial purposes, irrespective of a city's constitution. Still, thinking intensely about political issues, they advanced to higher and more systematic levels of political reflection and developed a variety of political and constitutional theories.[1] Protagoras, invited by Pericles to design the constitution of a new panhellenic colony in Southern Italy, offers a particularly apt example. He apparently defined the subject of his teaching as "practical wisdom" (*euboulia*) concerning "one's own affairs, how best to run one's household, and the management of public affairs, how to make the most effective contribution to the affairs of the city both by word and action"—in other words, "the art of running a city" (*politikē technē*) and being "a good citizen."[2]

Second, in archaic and classical Greece political thought was not limited to the top of society. It was part of a widespread political culture that found expression in all forms of literature (from epic and lyric poetry to tragedy, comedy, and historiography).[3] Hence specialized political writings emerged late (only in the late fifth century). Moreover, political thought penetrated political life and rhetoric (in political debates in councils and assemblies). Like much else, in democracy political thought was popularized, so that Aristophanes could make fun of it in *Clouds* and other plays. Thucydides shows, though in a highly condensed and abstract form, how political theories were used to support political arguments in public debate. In Greece, political thought thus became an integral part of public culture.[4] In China political thought expressed itself in specifically political writings early on; this was a necessary condition for the thinkers' success. Yet experts in political thought were largely concentrated in the rulers' courts. They helped the rulers to maximize their resources, prevail in power struggles within and among polities, and solidify and justify their control. As philosophical traditions and

---

[1] On the sophists, see generally Guthrie 1971; Kerferd 1981a, 1981b; de Romilly 1992; Wallace 1998; on the origins of the "sophistic movement," see Martin 1976.

[2] Plato, *Protagoras* 318e–319a (trans. Taylor 1991).

[3] For example, on political thought in tragedy see Meier 1993; Boedeker and Raaflaub 2005; Raaflaub 2012.

[4] Thucydides: e.g., 5.84–112; 6.38–39.

"schools" emerged, they too appropriated strands of political thought. These conditions seem to encourage a comparison less with those in archaic and classical Greece than with those in the kingdoms and empires of the ancient Near Eastern or Hellenistic Greek worlds. There too, political thought was concentrated primarily, on the one hand, in the courts of kings and rulers and, on the other, in the "academic" settings of scribal schools (the universities of the ancient Near East) or the philosophical schools and traditions that succeeded those of Plato and Aristotle. As in China, this political culture addressed the needs of rulers and elites; it was neither public nor popular. Moreover, as we saw, in the extant ancient Near Eastern sources such political thought is more implicit than explicit, while in early China it is exuberantly explicit, allowing us (despite many problems of dating and authenticity) to reconstruct its main forms and contents in sufficient detail.

My third and final point concerns precisely the contents of political thought. As a result of the increasingly hierarchical and centralized structure of state and society in early China, the concentration of political thought at the top, and its focus on the needs and concerns of those on the top, political thought necessarily paid much attention to issues of government, administration, economics, and warfare, to the ideology of monarchy, and to moral values that supported rulership (including respect for tradition and ancestors, fairness, justice, virtue, etc.). The same, we saw, is true for ancient Near Eastern political thought. Yet, for the same reasons, neither in the ancient Near East nor in early China political thought was much interested in constitutional differentiation, the question of whether and to what extent the masses could and should be involved in political responsibility, the concept of citizenship, and those political values that rose to prominence in the egalitarian polis societies of Greece and retained their prominence in Western political thought until today: equality and liberty.

Abbreviations and Bibliography

CAH   *The Cambridge Ancient History.* 2nd ed. Multiple vols. Cambridge

W   West 1992

Anderson, G. 2003. *The Athenian Experiment: Building an Imagined Political Community in Ancient Attica, 508–490 b.c.* Ann Arbor.

Andrewes, A. 1982a. "The Growth of the Athenian State." *CAH* III.3: 360–91.

——. 1982b. "Thy Tyranny of Pisistratus." *CAH* III.3: 392–416.

Archi, A. 1979. "L' Humanité des Hittites." In *Florilegium Anatolicum. Mélanges offerts à E. Laroche,* 37–48. Paris.

Arnason, J.P., S.N. Eisenstadt, and B. Wittrock (eds.). 2005. *Axial Civilizations and World History.* Leiden.

——, K.A. Raaflaub, and P. Wagner (eds.). 2013. *The Greek Polis and the Invention of Democracy: A Politico-cultural Transformation and Its Interpretations.* Malden Mass. and Oxford.

Assmann, J. 1990. *Ma' at: Gerechtigkeit und Unsterblichkeit im Alten Ägypten.* Munich.

——. 1993. "Politisierung durch Polarisierung. Zur impliziten Axiomatik altägyptischer Politik." In Raaflaub 1993: 13–28.

Beckman, G. 1982. "The Hittite Assembly." *Journal of the American Oriental Society* 102: 435–42.

Blok, J., and A. Lardinois (eds.). 2006. *Solon of Athens: New Historical and Philological Approaches.* Leiden.

Boedeker, D., and K.A. Raaflaub (eds.). 1998. *Democracy, Empire, and the Arts in Fifth-century Athens.* Cambridge Mass.

——. 2005. "Tragedy and City." In R. Bushnell (ed.), *A Companion to Tragedy,* 109–27. Malden Mass. and

Oxford.

Briant, P. 2002. *From Cyrus to Alexander: A History of the Persian Empire.* Winona Lake.

Bryce, T. 2002. *Life and Society in the Hittite World.* Oxford.

Burckhardt, L., K. Seybold, and J. von Ungern-Sternberg (eds.). 2007. *Gesetzgebung in antiken Gesellschaften: Israel, Griechenland, Rom.* Berlin.

Burkard, G. 1999. "'Als Gott erschienen spricht er.' Die Lehre des Amenemhet als postumes Vermächtnis." In J. Assmann and E. Blumenthal (eds.), *Literatur und Politik im pharaonischen und ptolemäischen Ägypten*, 153–73. Cairo.

Burkert, W. 1992. *The Orientalizing Revolution: Near Eastern Influence on Greek Culture in the Early Archaic* Age. Cambridge Mass.

——. 2004. *Babylon—Memphis—Persepolis: Eastern Contexts of Greek Culture.* Cambridge Mass.

Campbell, D.A. (ed., trans.). 1982. *Greek Lyric*, I. Cambridge Mass.

Cartledge, P. 2002. *Sparta and Lakonia: A Regional History 1300 to 362 BC.* 2nd ed. London.

——. 2009. *Ancient Greek Political Thought in Practice.* Cambridge.

Davies, J.K. 1997. "The 'Origins of the *Greek Polis*': Where Should We Be Looking?" In L.G. Mitchell and P.J. Rhodes (eds.), *The Development of the Polis in Archaic Greece*, 24–38. London.

Deger-Jalkotzy, S., and I.S. Lemos (eds.). 2006. *Ancient Greece from the Mycenaean Palaces to the Age of Homer.* Edinburgh.

Dickinson, O. 2006. *The Aegean from Bronze Age to Iron Age: Continuity and Change between the Twelfth and Eighth Centuries bc.* London.

Dornseiff, F. 1959. *Antike und alter Orient.* 2nd ed. Leipzig.

Durand, J.-M. 1989. "L'assemblée en Syrie à l'époque pré-armorite." In P. Fronzaroli (ed.), *Miscellanea Eblaitica*, II: 27–44. Florence.

Eder, W. 2005. "The Political Significance of the Codification of Law in Archaic Societies." In K. Raaflaub (ed.), *Social Struggles in Archaic Rome: New Perspectives on the Conflict of the Orders*, 239–67. Malden, Mass. and Oxford.

Effenterre, H. van, and F. Ruzé (eds.). 1994. *Nomima: Recueil d'inscriptions politiques et juridiques de l'archaïsme grec*, I. Paris.

Eisenstadt, S.N. 1986. *The Origin and Diversity of Axial Age Civilizations.* Albany.

Faraguna, M. 2001. "La figura dell'aisymnetes tra realtà storica e teoria politica." In R.W. Wallace and M. Gagarin (eds.), *Symposion 2001: Papers on Greek and Hellenistic Legal History*, 321–38. Vienna.

Farenga, V. 2006. *Citizen and Self in Ancient Greece: Individuals Performing Justice and the Law.* Cambridge.

Fetscher, I., and H. Münkler (eds.). 1988. *Pipers Handbuch der politischen Ideen*, I: *Frühe Hochkulturen und europäische Antike.* Munich.

Finkelberg, M. (ed.). 2011. *Homer Encyclopedia.* 3 vols. Malden Mass. and Oxford.

Fleming, D. 2004. *Democracy's Ancient Ancestors: Mari and Early Collective Governance.* Cambridge.

Fornara, C.W. (ed., trans.). 1983. *Archaic Times to the End of the Peloponnesian War.* Translated Documents of Greece and Rome, 1. 2nd ed. Cambridge.

Foster, B. (trans.). 2005. *Before the Muses: An Anthology of Akkadian Literature.* 3rd ed. Bethesda Maryland.

Fritz, K. von. 1954. *The Theory of the Mixed Constitution in Antiquity.* New York.

Gagarin, M. 1986. *Early Greek Law.* Berkeley.

——. 2008. *Writing Greek Law.* Cambridge.

Garelli, P. (ed.). 1974. *Le Palais et la royauté. Archéologie et civilisation.* Paris.

Georges, P. 1994. *Barbarian Asia and the Greek Experience from the Archaic Period to the Age of Xenophon.* Baltimore.

Gigante, M. 1956. *Nomos basileus.* Naples.

Guthrie, W.K.C. 1971. *The Sophists.* Cambridge.

Hall, J. 2007. *A History of the Archaic Greek World ca. 1200–479 BCE.* Malden Mass. and Oxford.

Hammer, D. 2002. *The Iliad as Politics: The Performance of Political Thought.* Norman.

Hansen, M. H. 1999. *The Athenian Democracy in the Age of Demosthenes.* Expanded ed. Norman.

Hawke, J. 2011. *Writing Authority: Elite Competition and Written Law in Early Greece.* DeKalb.

Hsiao, K. 1979. *A History of Chinese Political Thought.* Trans. F.W. Mote. Princeton.

Irani, K. D., and M. Silver (eds.). 1995. *Social Justice in the Ancient World.* Westport Connecticut.

Jacobsen, T. 1946. "Mesopotamia." In H. Frankfort, H. A. Frankfort, J. A. Wilson, et al., *The Intellectual Adventure of Ancient Man*, 125–219. Chicago.

——. 1970. *Toward the Image of Tammuz and Other Essays on Mesopotamian History and Culture.* Cambridge.

Jaeger, W. 1966. *Five Essays.* Montreal.

Jaspers, K. 1953. *The Origin and Goal of History.* New Haven.

Katz, D. 1993. *Gilgamesh and Akka.* Groningen and Broomall PA.

Kerferd, G.B. 1981a. *The Sophistic Movement.* Cambridge.

——. 1981b. *The Sophists and Their Legacy.* Wiesbaden.

Koerner, R. 1993. *Inschriftliche Gesetzestexte der frühen griechischen Polis.* Cologne.

Kramer, S. N. 1974. "Kingship in Sumer and Akkad: The Ideal King." In Garelli 1974: 163–76.

Kuhrt, A. 1995. *The Ancient Near East c. 3000–330 BC*, II. London.

Lambert, W. G. 1960. *Babylonian Wisdom Literature.* Oxford.

Lang, M. 2008. "Zum Begriff von menschlicher und göttlicher Gerechtigkeit in den Prologen der altorientalischen Codices." In H. Barta, R. Rollinger, and M. Lang (eds.), *Recht und Religion. Menschliche und göttliche Gerechtigkeitsvorstellungen in den antiken Welten*, 49–71. Wiesbaden.

Latacz, J. 1996. *Homer: His Art and His World.* Ann Arbor.

Lewis, D.M. 1988. "The Tyranny of the Pisistratidae." *CAH* IV: 287–302.

Lewis, M.E. 1999. *Writing and Authority in Early China.* Albany.

Lichtheim, M. 1973–1980. *Ancient Egyptian Literature.* 3 vols. Berkeley.

Liverani, M. 1993. "Nelle pieghe del despotismo. Organismi rappresentativi nell' antico Oriente." *Studi Storici* 34: 7–33.

Lloyd, G.E.R. 1990. *Demystifying Mentalities.* Cambridge.

——. 1996. *Adversaries and Authorities: Investigations into Ancient Greek and Chinese Science.* Cambridge.

——. 2002. *The Ambitions of Curiosity: Understanding the World in Ancient Greece and China.* Cambridge.

Loewe, M., and E.L. Shaughnessy (eds.). 1999. *The Cambridge History of Ancient China: From the Origins of Civilization to 221 B.C.* Cambridge.

Martin, J. 1976. "Zur Entstehung der Sophistik." *Saeculum* 27: 143–64.

Meier, C. 1990. *The Greek Discovery of Politics.* Trans. D. McLintock. Cambridge, Mass.

——. 1993. *The Political Art of Greek Tragedy.* Trans. A. Webber. Baltimore.

——. 1999. *Athens: A Portrait of the City in Its Golden Age.* Trans. R. and R. Kimber. London.

——. 2011. *A Culture of Freedom: Ancient Greece and the Origins of Europe.* Oxford.

Meiggs, R., and D. Lewis (eds.). 1988. *A Selection of Greek Historical Inscriptions to the End of the Fifth Century B.C.* Rev. ed. Oxford.

Mitchell, L. 2007. *Panhellenism and the Barbarian in Archaic and Classical Greece.* Swansea.

Moers, G. 2010. "The World and the Geography of Otherness in Pharaonic Egypt." In K. Raaflaub and R. Talbert (eds.), *Geography and Ethnography: Perceptions of the World in Pre-modern Societies*, 169–81. Malden Mass. and Oxford.

Morris, I. 1998. "Archaeology and Archaic Greek History." In N. Fisher and H. van Wees (eds.), *Archaic Greece: New Approaches and New Evidence.* London and Swansea.

——. 2000. *Archaeology as Cultural History.* Malden Mass. and Oxford.

Morschauser, S. N. 1995. "The Ideological Basis for Social Justice/Responsibility in Ancient Egypt." In Irani and Silver 1995: 101–13.

Mühl, M. 1933. *Untersuchungen zur altorientalischen und althellenischen Gesetzgebung.* Leipzig.

Murray, O. 1993. *Early Greece.* 2nd ed. Cambridge Mass.

Needham, J. 1956. *Science and Civilization in China, II: History of Scientific Thought.* Cambridge.

Nissen, H.-J., and J. Renger (eds.). 1987. *Mesopotamien und seine Nachbarn: politische und kulturelle Wechselbeziehungen im alten Vorderasien vom 4. bis 1. Jahrtausend v. Chr.* 2 vols. 2nd ed. Berlin.

Ober, J. 1996. *The Athenian Revolution: Essays on Ancient Greek Democracy and Political Theory.* Princeton.

O'Connor, D., and D. P. Silverman (eds.). 1995. *Egyptian Kingship.* Leiden.

Ommerborn, W., and P. Weber-Schäfer. 1988. "Die politischen Ideen des traditionellen China." In Fetscher and Münkler 1988: 41–84.

Osborne, R. 1996. *Greece in the Making, 1200 – 479 BC.* London.

Oswald, W. 2009. *Staatstheorie im Alten Israel. Der politische Diskurs im Pentateuch und in den Geschichtsb ü chern des Alten Testaments.* Stuttgart.

Ostwald, M. 1969. *Nomos and the Beginnings of the Athenian Democracy.* Oxford.

——. 1988. The Reform of the Athenian State by Cleisthenes." *CAH* IV: 303–46.

Otto, E. 2005. "Der Zusammenhang von Herrscherlegitimation und Rechtskodifizierung in altorientalischer und biblischer Rechtsgeschichte." *Zeitschrift für Altorientalische und Biblische Rechtsgeschichte* 11: 51–92.

Raaflaub, K.A. 1989. "Contemporary Perceptions of Democracy in Fifth-century Athens." *Classica et Mediaevalia* 40: 33–70.

——(ed.). 1993. *Anfänge politischen Denkens in der Antike. Die nahöstlichen Kulturen und die Griechen.* Munich.

——. 1996a. "Born to be Wolves? Origins of Roman Imperialism." In E. Harris and R.W. Wallace (eds.), *Transitions to Empire in the Graeco-Roman World, 360–146 B.C.*, 273–314. Norman.

——. 1996b. "Equalities and Inequalities in Athenian Democracy." In J. Ober and C. Hedrick (eds.), Demokratia: *A Conversation on Democracies, Ancient and Modern*, 129–74. Princeton.

——. 1996c. "Solone, la nuova Atene e l'emergere della politica." In S. Settis (ed.), *I Greci*, II.1: 1035–81. Turin.

——. 2000. "Poets, Lawgivers, and the Beginnings of Political Reflection in Archaic Greece." In Rowe and Schofield 2000: 23–59.

——. 2004b. *The Discovery of Freedom in Ancient Greece.* Chicago.

——. 2005. "Polis, 'the Political', and Political Thought: New Departures in Ancient Greece, c. 800–500 BCE." In Arnason et al. 2005: 253–83.

——. 2008a. "Homeric Warriors and Battles: Trying to Resolve Old Problems." *Classical World* 101: 469–83.

———. 2008b. "Zeus und Prometheus: Zur griechischen Interpretation vorderasiatischer Mythen." In M. Bernett, W. Nippel, and A. Winterling (eds.), *Christian Meier zur Diskussion*, 33–60. Stuttgart.

———. 2009. "Early Greek Political Thought in Its Mediterranean Context." In R. Balot (ed.), *A Companion to Greek and Roman Political Thought*, 37–56. Malden Mass. and Oxford.

———. 2012. "Sophocles and Political Thought." In A. Markantonnatos (ed.), *Brill's Companion to Sophocles*, 471–88. Leiden.

———, J. Ober, and R.W. Wallace. 2007. *Origins of Democracy in Ancient Greece*. Berkeley.

———, and H. van Wees (eds.). 2009. *A Companion to Archaic Greece* (Malden Mass. and Oxford 2009).

Redford, D. B. (ed.). 2001. *The Oxford Encyclopedia of Ancient Egypt*. 3 vols. Oxford.

Rhodes, P.J. 1992. "The Athenian Revolution." *CAH* V: 62–95.

Robinson, E. W. 1997. *The First Democracies: Early Popular Government outside Athens*. Stuttgart.

Romilly, J. de. 1992. *The Great Sophists in Periclean Athens*. Oxford.

Rowe, C., and M. Schofield (eds.). 2000. *The Cambridge History of Greek and Roman Political Thought*. Cambridge.

Ruschenbusch, E. 1966. *SOLŌNOS NOMOI. Die Fragmente des solonischen Gesetzeswerkes mit einer Text– und Überlieferungsgeschichte*. Wiesbaden.

———. 2010. *Solon: Das Gesetzeswerk–Fragmente. Übersetzung und Kommentar*. Ed. K. Bringmann. Stuttgart.

Sakellariou, M. 1996. *Démocratie athénienne et culture*. Athens.

Schemeil, Y. 1999. *La Politique dans l'ancien Orient*. Paris.

Schmitz, W. 2004. "Griechische und nahöstliche Spruchweisheit. Die *erga kai hemerai Hesiods* und nahöstliche Weisheitsliteratur." In R. Rollinger and C. Ulf (eds.), *Griechische Archaik und der Orient: Interne und externe Impulse*, 311–33. Berlin.

Schwartz, B.I. 1985. *The World of Thought in Ancient China*. Cambridge, Mass.

Shankman, S., and S.W. Durrant. 2000. *The Siren and the Sage: Knowledge and Wisdom in Ancient Greece and China*. London.

——— (eds.). 2002. *Early China/Ancient Greece: Thinking through Comparisons* Albany.

Snodgrass, A. 1971. *The Dark Age of Greece*. Edinburgh.

———. 1980. *Archaic Greece: The Age of Experiment*. Berkeley.

Stahl, M. 1987. *Aristokraten und Tyrannen im archaischen Athen*. Stuttgart.

Starr, C.G. 1977. *The Economic and Social Growth of Early Greece, 800–500 B.C.* New York and Oxford.

———. 1986. *Individual and Community: The Rise of the Polis 800–500 B.C.* New York and Oxford.

Stein–Hölkeskamp, E. 2009. "The Tyrants." In Raaflaub and van Wees 2009: 100–116.

Streck, M. P. 2007. "Recht. A. In Mesopotamien." *Reallexikon der Assyriologie* 11.3/4: 280–85.

Taylor, C. C. W. 1991. *Plato*, Protagoras. *Trans. with Notes*. Rev. ed. Oxford.

Vernant, J.–P. 1982. *The Origins of Greek Thought*. Ithaca NY.

Walcot, P. 1966. *Hesiod and the Near East*. Cardiff.

Wallace, R. W. 1998. "The Sophists in Athens." In Boedeker and Raaflaub 1998: 203–22, 392–95.

———. 2007. "Revolutions and a New Order in Solonian Athens and Archaic Greece." In Raaflaub et al. 2007: 49–82.

———. 2009. "Charismatic Leaders." In Raaflaub and van Wees 2009: 411–26.

Weber–Schäfer, P. 1976. *Einführung in die politische Theorie*, I: Die Frühzeit. Darmstadt.

Wells, B. 2005. "Law and Practice." In D. C. Snell (ed.), *A Companion to the Ancient Near East*, 183–95. Malden

Mass. and Oxford.

Welwei, K–W. 1992. *Athen. Vom neolithischen Siedlungsplatz zur archaischen Grosspolis.* Darmstadt.

——. 2004. *Sparta. Aufstieg und Niedergang einer antiken Grossmacht.* Stuttgart.

West, M.L. 1971. *Early Greek Philosophy and the Orient.* Oxford.

——. 1978. *Hesiod, Works and Days. Edited with Prolegomena and Commentary.* Oxford.

—— (ed.). 1992. *Iambi et Elegi Graeci ante Alexandrum Cantati*, II. 2nd ed. Oxford.

—— (trans.). 1994. *Greek Lyric Poetry.* Oxford.

——. 1997. *The East Face of Helicon: West Asiatic Elements in Greek Poetry and Myth.* Oxford.

Westbrook, R. 1988. "The Nature and Origins of the Twelve Tables." *Zeitschrift für Rechtsgeschichte* 105: 74–121.

——. 1989. "Cuneiform Law Codes and the Origins of Legislation." *Zeitschrift für Assyriologie* 79: 201–22.

——. 2003. "Introduction: The Character of Ancient Near Eastern Law." In Westbrook (ed.), *A History of Ancient Near Eastern Law*, I: 1–90. Leiden.

Zibelius–Chen, K. 1988. "Das Alte Ägypten." In Fetscher and Münkler 1988: 113–34.

古代世界政治思想溯源：交流与比较（译稿）

库尔特·拉夫劳布（Kurt A. Raaflaub）布朗大学　杨巨平、徐朗 译 南开大学

摘要：在古希腊文化的形成阶段，即公元前 8 至 6 世纪期间，希腊人与一些源自大近东文明（从安纳托利亚到埃及）的文化之间产生了强烈的互动，并在各种文化领域受到了大量外来思想的冲击，其中也包括智力上的影响。但令人惊奇的是，除了极少数例外，目前还没有人认真研究过这些影响是否也促进了古希腊政治思想的产生。没有任何现成的理由（priori reason 来否认这一事实。我的宏大研究计划的目的就是要证明这种影响是否存在，影响到何种程度，以及它如何得以实现。

本文将主要集中探讨近东文明在古希腊政治和政府方面的影响。这些影响在荷马史诗和公元前 7 世纪后期至 6 世纪间在斯巴达和雅典出现的早期法律和改革中所隐含的那些政治概念中都有反映，本文将对这些希腊早期的证据进行简要的概括。本文还将对希腊背景之下所出现的这些影响做出一些解释，并审视是否有证据证明古代近东的相关思想可能影响了希腊的政治思想。在最后一节中，本文将力图揭示与早期中国政治思想的产生进行比较的可能性。

导　论

我当前的研究计划是探讨在东地中海不同文化交流的背景下古希腊政治思想的起源。[1]让我首先做几点解释。在我看来，"政治理论"是指一种对政治事务直观的、系统的、至少部分抽象性的思考，与此相对的"政治思想"的含义则比较宽泛，是指所有对政治，制度，共同体或国家，以及公民之间乃至不同共同体或国家之间关系的思考。[2]为什么说更深刻地理解古希腊政治思想的起源是相当重要的呢？因为正是这种具有其特定的内容，聚焦点和表达方式的政治思想推动了希腊政治理论和哲学的产生，从而对罗马时期、中世纪、文艺复兴时期，以及早期近代欧洲乃至现代西方世界各种形式的政治思想的发展起到了决定性的影响。古希腊人所形成的政治术语实则我们的政治术语；他们所发现并定义的政治价值观（特别值得一提的是正义，平等和自由）在我们现今的时代比以往

---

[1]　2012 年 6 月 16 至 18 日，我在中国天津参加了由南开大学举办的"世界古代史国际学术研讨会"（会议的主题是："古代世界的接触、交流与比较：从地中海到黄河"）。此文是我在会议上发言稿的拓展版。我在原发言稿的基础上补充了一些文献资料。在此我谨就会议的出色组织和主办方的热情好客向杨巨平教授、郑玮博士及其他会务组成员表示最衷心的感谢。我曾在麦吉尔大学、南加州大学、布朗大学和图宾根大学宣读过本文的早期版本。在此我也向历次讲演中各位同仁和学生们所提出的深邃而有益的评论表示谢意。

[2]　有关政治思想和政治理论的定义，详见 Rowe and Schofield 2000: 1–2; 也见 Meier 1990: pt. I; Cartledge 2009: ch. 2.

更为重要；他们所区分，系统化并争论的政体（君主制、贵族制或寡头制、民主制）仍旧是我们现代社会所争论或所追求的核心之所在；对这些古代思想成就贡献最大的几位作家，如修昔底德，柏拉图和亚里士多德，仍旧激励着当代哲学家、政治科学家以及历史学家去求索。如果没有希腊人，我们便不会用现在这样的方式去进行政治学的思考。理解这一问题显然具有重要的价值，即这种思想传统为什么会起源于一个地域狭小，贫瘠且多山且远离那些伟大的文明和帝国的国家之中。①或者就其本质而言，它的起源是否甚至更早，可以溯至那些伟大文明的核心区域呢？

这就是我们需要考虑"地中海背景"的原因。从公元前 8 到 6 世纪（通常称为"东方化时期"），希腊人与近东各文明（从安纳托利亚经由美索不达米亚和黎凡特地区到埃及）之间产生了紧密的互动，而上述近东文明则是该地区两千余年文化发展的结果。在这些文化的形成期内，希腊人在物质和精神文化的各个层面都吸收了大量的外来因素。②现在也没有任何原因来说明这类影响为何不涉及政治思想领域。然而，除了少数例外，没有人曾深入研究过这种影响是否存在及其影响的程度。③我的计划在于填补这项空白。在这篇文章中，我将非常简要地概述并强调早期希腊政治思想的主题和本质。然后我将对这类影响在纯粹的希腊语境中的出现做一些解释，并试图对在古代近东思想是否存在可比性的证据来证明它曾影响过希腊思想这一问题做出一些回应。在最后的、纯属尝试性的一节中，我将冒昧地论述与早期中国政治思想的产生进行比较研究的可能性。

早期希腊政治思想

自最早的时候起，希腊的文学作品便密切关注政治和社会制度，积极进行政治思考，即从一种强烈的公共视角来对领导权，制度的作用和正义这些概念进行重点思考。我首先从公元前 8 世纪晚期荷马的《伊利亚特》中提取几例予以说明。④这部史诗在开篇所讲述的并不是英雄们的英勇作为，而是两位伟大领袖的争吵给公众带来的不可估量的痛苦。阿伽门农因犯下可怕的错误而挑起这场争吵，使自己的领导权遭遇了一场深刻的危机——也正是由于这一点，他的同胞对胜利感到绝望，一度弃他而去。他们跑向各自的船只，急切地想返回故乡。然而他能承认自己的错误，接受贵族首领们的建议，尽其所能取得同胞间的信任，成功地使希腊联盟重归于好，团结如初，以致最后获得了"更公正者"的荣誉，即达到了一种更高层次的正义：人人皆可犯错，但有能力平息纠纷、保持统一的领袖还是会被公众所认可。特洛伊的领袖赫克托耳则恰恰相反：他是一个完美的领导者，竭尽全力挽救自己的城邦。他的名字甚至表达这样的含义："拥有者，拯救者"。他的同胞特洛伊人为了向他表示敬意，将他的儿子命名为 Astyanax，"城市之主"。诗人荷马解释说，这是因为"赫克托耳独自拯救了城邦"。但这个人由于雄心勃勃而误入歧途，战术上严重失误，致使他的军队遭遇了巨大的损失。当他独自站在城墙外，因自己的失败而感到羞愧时，他发现自己无颜面对公民们的指责。而错上加错的是他决定与阿喀琉斯决斗，要么获胜要么英勇地死去，但他的城邦也因此失去了从战争中幸存的唯一希望。这部史诗从城邦及城邦利益的角度来描述其中的戏剧性行为。这种政治性的

---

① 就希腊文化整体而言，迈尔（Meier, 2011）试图回答这一问题。关于古风时代的希腊，也见 chs. in CAH III.3 (1982) and IV (1988); Snodgrass 1980; Osborne 1996; Morris 1998; Hall 2007; Raaflaub and van Wees 2009.

② 东方文化的影响，可见 West 1997; Burkert 1992, 2004. 所有涉及的时间都是指公元前。

③ 东方对希腊哲学的影响，见 West 1971；对希腊思想的一般影响，见 Vernant 1982；古代近东的政治思想，可见 chs. in Weber-Schäfer 1976 以及 Fetscher and Münkler 1988（对比较和影响没有涉及）；希伯来圣经中的政治思想，见 Oswald 2009；一些比较的尝试，见 Raaflaub 1993.

④ 荷马史诗中描述的社会与早期希腊社会（史诗中社会的"历史真实性"）的关系，参见 Finkelberg 2011, *s.v.* "Historicity," "Society."；关于荷马，参见 Latacz 1996.

视角还体现在很多其他的细节和诗人的叙述选择之中。[1]

另一个例子: agora(荷马时期的希腊文为 agorē),即公共广场,是城邦的中心和政治活动的举办地。诗人对那里所发生的事表现出特别地关注,非常详细地描述了几次战士大会的实况,显示了那些聚集在会场,为城邦而战的人们的切身关注。当人们在一次成功的战斗之后瓜分战利品时,首领们获得了他们应有的一份,剩余的则在普通战士中平等分配——由首领们主持,但是以全体联盟成员的名义。战士大会并不投票,一般的参会者通常也不发言,但人们通过吆喝或跺脚来清楚地表达自己的观点。首领并非一定要听取他们的意见,但如果他忽视他们的意愿或者行动失败,他就会陷入麻烦。一些偶然的描述也表明,试图对议事会或战士大会上强烈表达的意见反其道而行之是很困难的。一位好的首领会虚心倾听他的贵族同僚们的建议并择其最佳者而行之。建立共识和解决冲突是很重要的,因此理想的首领最擅长战斗和演讲,他不是在统治而是在劝说,他在战场和战士大会上都行使着他的领导权。[2]

值得注意的是,agora 正是在政治上被明确地概念化了。奥德修斯在回国途中遇到的独眼巨人库克罗普斯(Cyclopes)部族,就是一个个体化的、各行其是的(atomized)"非社会"(non-society)群体, 其中"没有共同的规则和议事的集会"(agorai boulēphoroi)。就其他方面而言,它也具有文明社会极端对立面的特征。与此相反,诗人将费阿西安人(Phaeacians)作为"高度文明"(super-civilized)的典型,以此为例说明:他们拥有一个专门用于公共集会的场所(agora),广场平整,设有富有光泽的石座供议事会成员专用,议事会和公民大会在此进行正常的全面的互动。[3]在著名的阿喀琉斯盾牌的图案上,仲裁,婚礼和收获的场景都象征着城邦的和平安宁。这意味着在和平时期是正义在进行统治,冲突往往通过公开的,公民大会上的仲裁来解决。虽然贵族法官们进行争辩并提出解决方案,但普通民众也有权对判决结果当场公开发表意见。[4]

几幅情景暗示着民众所扮演的是一个潜在的、具有强大影响力的角色。因此,很显然,诗人所描述的社会是很快就要在希腊占据政治和文化发展主导地位的城邦(polis)的早期形态。此外,史诗中的 polis 已然是一个公民国家(citizen state)(非城市国家,city state)。历史学家修昔底德曾说过"人即城邦"(the men are the polis),而公元前6世纪早期的诗人阿卡埃乌斯(Alcaeus)早就意识到这一点。[5]

荷马之后,到公元前7世纪中期,第一条至今尚存的石刻法律出现了。开头开宗明义,"此法律由城邦决定",内容规定了这个城镇中主要官职的轮流更替。同样的说法也出现在其他地方,标志着城邦或德莫(demo),即公民集体,是制定法律的主体。这些法律涉及到包括公共基金,长老议事会和"民众议事会"在内的政治生活的几个方面。几个城邦还证明,早期的立法者甚至还制定了多部法律或法律集成。这样的法律反映出,共同体是依据公共意愿和话语来运行。法律是实现这种集体意愿,改变城邦秩序和制度的工具。它们的制定是以政治思考和对政治领域中的条件、权力、潜在的可能性以及思想与行动的结果的体悟为前提。这些共同体意识到,它们已经控制了自己的法律,并随之由小到大地控制了它们的政治和社会的秩序,以及他们的生活方式。他们认识到法律对

---

[1] 关于阿伽门农,见 Iliad books 1, 2, 9, 19;赫克托耳,见 6.402–3; 12.210–50; 18.243–313; 22.99–110, 以及 Finkelberg 2011, *s.v.* "Hector." 详见 Raaflaub 2000: 29–32.

[2] Finkelberg 2011, *s.v.* "Agora," "Boule," "Polis.";军队,见 Raaflaub 2008a. 关于表演性的政治,见 Hammer 2002.

[3] 库克罗普斯,见 *Odyssey* 9.105–15, 125–30, 170–479. 费阿西安人,见 Bks. 6–8, 13;他们曾是库克罗普斯的邻居 (6.4–6)。将这些对照物并列也是一种概念化的方式。铺设的广场,见 6.266–67; 8.4–7;参见 *Iliad* 18.503–4. 其他概念化的尝试,也见 *Iliad* 18.483–608; Hesiod, *Works and Days* 225–47.

[4] 仲裁的场景,见 *Iliad* 18.497–508.

[5] Thucydides, *History* 7.77.7; Alcaeus, frag. 112.10; 426 in Campbell 1982.

于共同体的稳定性所具有的重要意义。[1]因此，政治思想可以通过立法而转化为政治行动。这为政治制度的创新和改革铺平了道路，也使后来以法律至上作为公民自由的条件和保证成为可能（正如品达和希罗多德在其著名的构想中所设想的那样）：nomos basileus，法律即君王[2]。

事实上，仍然在公元前7世纪，在公民兵责任感得到大大加强的严峻危机时期，斯巴达城邦接受了我们所知晓的第一次宪政改革（被称作"大瑞特拉"Great Rhetra，意为"公告"）。除了其他方面的改革之外，它确立了公民大会制度（每月在预定的时间和地点举行集会），并制定了集体决策的规则：长老会（gerousia）人数限制在三十人，且包括两名领导人或"国王"（这暗示选举产生）在内。它须先提出议案，随后交由公民大会讨论。民众"拥有胜利（nikē）和权力 (kratos)"，即最后的决定权，即使长老会明显保留了某些否决权。[3]这场改革正式将城邦决策权赋予公民之手，他们同时也是保家卫国和维护公民权利的战士。

几十年后在雅典，作为仲裁者的梭伦被授予了特别的权力，以应对迫在眉睫的社会和经济危机。这样的仲裁者在当时扮演了重要的角色，代表了一种取代内战或僭政的和平选择。他们都与德尔斐的阿波罗神谕（以提倡节制而著名）有着密切的联系，超然于互相争斗的党派之上，以智者（sophoi）的身份享有广泛的权威。重要的是，他们得到城邦的委任和授权，从而以公民集体的名义行使权力。亚里士多德曾称呼密提林的皮塔库斯（Pittacus of Mytilene），一位类似于梭伦的智者和立法者为"民选僭主"（elected tyrant）。[4]梭伦以一位雅典人的身份（"我们的城邦"）向他的同胞们发表演讲，将自身置于彼此争斗的两派之间（大致可分为贵族和平民两派），阻止双方彼此伤害或不正当获利。[5]他所实施的是一场大范围的改革，实际上涉及到公共生活的各个方面。他废除了债务奴役，保证了公民的个人自由。他这样评论自己的立法，"不论地位高低，我的法令是为所有公民制定的，给每个人（或每件事）都直接提供适合于他们的正义"。这样的说法基本上体现了法律面前人人平等的原则。他首先考虑的是建立法律的权威，将正义赋予所有的公民，使广大民众能够参与司法审判：设立一种特别的陪审法庭，审理城邦的重大案件，任何人都可有权代表第三方受害者启动司法程序。在政治领域内，他创立了"以财产资格为基础的政体"（timocratic constitution），公民可依据自己的军事和经济实力来参政和任职。同时设立了一个新的、由每年选举产生的400人所组成的"公民"议事会，以制约古老的贵族议事会（元老院）的权力，强化了公民大会的作用。他还可能还对公民大会的召开和必要的程序做了一些规定。最后，他宣布僭主政体非法，要求公民们在内部争斗中必须表明立场，以保护雅典政制免遭颠覆。[6]

所有这些措施围绕着三个目的：杜绝滥用权力，建立坚实的正义体系，以维护城邦共同体的稳定；为非贵族阶层的公民参政创造空间，以制约贵族阶层的权力；以僭主政治的潜在威胁来防止公民之

---

[1] "此事由城邦决定"，语出克里特的德雷罗法典（law of Dreros，约公元前750年）。参见 Meiggs and Lewis 1988: no. 2; translation in Fornara 1983: no. 11. 早期法律集成，见 Koerner 1993; van Effenterre and Ruzé 1994. 早期希腊法律，见 Gagarin 1986. 法律、书写及碑记，见 Farenga 2006; Gagarin 2008; Hawke 2011. 法律保护，见 Eder 2005. 法律文化的共同起源，见 Meier 2011.

[2] Pindar, frag. 169 Snell-Maehler; cf. Herodotus 7.104; Gigante 1956.

[3] 关于"瑞特拉"的资料来源，见 Tyrtaeus, frag. 4 in West 1992 (W); 翻译见 West 1994: 23; Plutarch, *Lycurgus* 6 (van Effenterre and Ruzé 1994: no.61; Fornara 1983: no.12). 相关讨论见 Cartledge 2002b: 115–17; Welwei 2004: 59–69.

[4] 关于仲裁者（*katartistēres, aisymnētai*），见 Meier 1990: 40–52; Faraguna 2001; Wallace 2009. 有关密提林的皮塔库斯，见 Aristotle, *Politics* 1285a35ff.

[5] Solon, frag. 4.1–8, 30; 5; 36.1–2, 20–27; 37 W.

[6] 梭伦改革，见 Aristotle, *Constitution of the Athenians* 5–12; Plutarch, *Solon*. 辑录的梭伦诗歌，见 West 1992: 139–65, 翻译见 West 1994: 74–83, 梭伦的法律，见 Ruschenbusch 1966, 翻译见 Ruschenbusch 2010. 相关讨论可参见 Andrewes 1982a; Welwei 1992: 133–206; Raaflaub 1996c; Blok and Lardinois 2006; Wallace 2007. 个人自由，见 Raaflaub 2004b: 45–53. 法律面前人人平等，见 frag. 36.18–20 W.

间产生不和。三者都是梭伦从逻辑上对公民责任加以理解的结果：任何一个公民如遭受政治权力的滥用，公民们都必须为维护共同的利益而尽责相助。

梭伦之后是一段漫长的僭主统治时期，起因是激烈的贵族党争。但结局却出人预料，本意在于削弱贵族政治控制，保证内部和平的而建立的僭主政体，反而为一个更加平等的宪政铺平了道路。[①]当它在公元前6世纪末被推翻时，克里斯提尼基于精密的政治思考而实施了一套复杂的改革方案，全面重组了公民集体和政治制度的内部结构。他所设计的制度框架使得阿提卡广大地域上的所有公民都能够在宗教仪式、节庆、军队和政治上通力合作。可以说，在这种广泛的参与制度之下，所有的公民都会以议事会成员的身份出现在在城邦的中心——五百人会议的议事大厅，大约是每60位公民中就有一位担任此职。既然议事会成员的任期仅限一年，且任何公民一生中不得担任两次以上，所以几乎半数的公民都曾花费至少一年的时间来承担这份耗时费力的职责。[②]

克里斯提尼的改革成功地解决了贵族和地域的冲突，为城邦共同体的统一发挥了至关重要的作用。他和他之前的梭伦都已表明，城邦不仅为公民参政提供基本的框架，城邦自身也是公民政治行动的目标：借助于公民大会通过的法律，或把权力让渡给那些选举产生的立法者，公民们甚至深刻而彻底地改变和改进了他们的城邦秩序：他们成了城邦的主人。当他们感到自己在管理这个城邦时，责任感就油然而生。这种新生的自信不仅仅只是表现在几年之后他们决定抵御波斯入侵，并在马拉松战役（公元前490年）和萨拉米斯海战（公元前480年）中击败敌人。

这些反抗波斯人的胜利改变了一切。由于新银矿的发现，雅典建立起了一支庞大舰队（这笔收入并未按照传统在所有公民中分配），成为当时主要的军事强国。在这支舰队中担任桨手的主要是下层公民——他们无力承担重装步兵的装备，因而此前在军事和政治上无足轻重。这支舰队成为雅典凌驾于大量的其他城邦之上，确立霸权的工具。军事作用的变化提升了下层公民的政治地位，结果是所有公民不论出身、财富或受教育程度都获得了平等的政治权利。这是公元前5世纪中期民主政治的重大突破：这一发展不但前无古人，在近2500年的时间内也后无来者。[③]（这种民主政治只保留了成年男性公民的政治权利，妇女被排除在政治参与之外；它的基础是奴隶劳动。但在整个古代世界通行的历史条件之下，这是一种正常的社会现象。）这种民主制是如此的特殊，以致引起了抵触和激烈的争论。但它为随后诸多的文化成就、政治及宪政思想提供了强烈的推动力：其中包括智者学派对政治理论的发展，以及柏拉图和亚里士多德出于对民主制的反应和抵触而提出的政治哲学。[④]

在这里我不想对这些问题做进一步的探讨，但我想再简短地回到梭伦。他有两点对于理解希腊政治思想的发展相当关键。首先，梭伦实际上是政治理论的开山鼻祖。在一首现存于世，后得名为"好秩序"（Good order, eunomia）的诗歌中，他解释了他的想法。他强调说，人应对自己的命运负责：神明并不与人作对，相反却乐于造福人类。公民们，特别是那些贵族精英们为贪欲所驱使，胡作非为，引起内乱，为所有人带来可怕的后果。基于实际观察，梭伦建构了一种因果关系的链条，将公民们犯下的社会政治错误与城邦共同体所遭受的损害联系起来，这种因果关系是必然的，不可避免的，类似于自然法则（如闪电过后才打雷）。早期的诗人们常常从自然灾害的角度来解释神明对人类罪行所施加的惩罚，但与之相反，梭伦将这样的后果完全置于社会政治层面来理解。早期的思想家相

---

① 关于雅典僭主政体，可见 Andrewes 1982b; Stahl 1987; Lewis 1988.

② 关于克里斯提尼改革，参见 Ostwald 1988; Meier 1990: ch.4; Ober 1996: ch.4; Anderson 2003.

③ 关于民主制在公元前5世纪中期的突破，见 Rhodes 1992; Meier 1999: chs. 6–7; Raaflaub, Ober, and Wallace 2007: ch.5. 民主制的运作：Hansen 1999.

④ 关于民主制的争论，见 Raaflaub 1989. 帝国，民主制和文化之间的互动，见 Sakellariou 1996; Boedeker and Raaflaub 1998; Arnason et al. 2013. 政治理论和政治哲学，见 relevant chs. in Rowe and Schofield 2000.

信正义是通过至高无上的主神宙斯的权威实现的，他的女儿，正义女神狄克（Dike），正是通过她的父亲来实现她的复仇愿望。但梭伦却把狄克看作是一位独立的复仇女神，自行其事，正如一条抽象的原则所言："那位沉默者知晓事情的真相和人们的所作所为，最后必定（pantō）要来完成她的复仇。"①正义必将获胜！整个城市都受到影响，无人能从中逃脱。

这是人类第一次完全从政治层面来分析一场政治进程。理解了这一点，人们就可以通过消除原因，即通过政治干预阻止结果的发生。早期的思想家们根据神话和宗教信仰得出结论，但梭伦是从一种以经验知识和政治分析为基础的理论出发。因此他的建议更具有吸引力。遭遇"坏秩序"（dysnomia）的共同体在调停人的"教导"(taught by mediator)之下有机会重新建立起"好的秩序"（eunomia）。梭伦的观点代表着政治思想领域的一次巨大突破。

这使我转向第二个方面：政制观念和术语。几位早期诗人强调了"良好秩序"这一概念对于公众福祉的重要意义。当立法者和共同体遭遇危机和冲突时（即坏秩序），他们的目标就是恢复良好秩序，这也是早期希腊宪政思想的重点之所在。②在应对个人权力垄断的威胁时（一种通常不稳定且短命的君主制形式，希腊人称之为僭主制），③希腊的贵族们发现具有重要价值的反而是他们以前所轻视的那种观念，即平等。为了确切表述它的价值，他们在 eunomia 前加上一个表示平等的前缀 iso-，构成 isonomia 一词（平等秩序，法律面前平等，政治平等）。到公元前 6 世纪晚期，为数众多的城邦宪法，其中包括克里斯提尼在雅典实行的新宪法，都是建立在 isonomia 的原则之上，至少是在占有土地的公民兵之间政治平等的基础之上。为了将这些平等政体与完全发展的民主制相区分，我们称它们为"isonomic"。正是平等这种政治价值持续地推动了政治体制的发展，直至在公元前 5 世纪的民主制中达到顶峰：希罗多德说过，"民主制拥有所有体制中最美好的名声，即法律面前人人平等（isonomia）"，他也解释说雅典人正是凭借他们在驱逐僭主后所获得的自由和平等而跃居强国之列。然而自由与民主制的联系则要更晚，而且是不同发展的结果。④

"平等"政体的出现使人们认识到，不仅仅有根据秩序与混乱，还包括依据统治者的数量和本质而区分的多种政体形式：即一个人（一位国王或一位僭主），少数人（寡头制）或最好的人（贵族制政体）的统治，被平民（民主制）或民众（暴民）统治的政体。现存史料中对三种政体的首次区分大约出现于公元前 470 年，仅仅在几年之后，民主制（dēmokratia）这一术语可能就被创造出来了。这些区分和民主制自身的发展证明了它们对如下宪政理念的强烈刺激与推动：即各种政体的定义，对每种政制特别是民主制优缺点的讨论，从头开始的新的政制设计（最后成为柏拉图和亚里士多德所讨论的"理想城邦"），"混合政体"的理念以及其他更多的方面。但是，这些后来的发展大大超出了我们现在关于古风时期希腊和政治思想出现的讨论范畴。⑤

至此我要做一个总结：自古风时代早期出现以来，希腊文学作品便密切关注政治活动和制度，并积极从事政治思考。这种思考从一种强烈的公众视角集中于领导权，制度的作用，以及正义。由公民大会所决定或批准的早期成文法和"政体"调节着政治进程。民选立法者实施的政治改革的最初目的，是恢复一个以正义，平等分配和公众参与为基础的理想化的"良好秩序"，然后再实现特

---

① 梭伦有关社会政治因果关系的理论；作为一种自治原则的正义，见 frag. 4 W. 与自然法的可比较性，见 9 W; cf. 11; 13.17–32. 关于梭伦的政治思想，见 Jaeger 1966: 75–99; Raaflaub 2000: 39–42; Meier 2011: ch.21.

② *Eunomia*: Hesiod, *Theogony* 901–3; Tyrtaeus, frag. 4 W; Solon, frag. 4.31–39 W. 对政体思想的关注，见 Meier 1990: 160.

③ 见前引书注释 18。一般僭主制，见 Murray 1993: ch.9; Stein–Hölkeskamp 2009.

④ *Eunomia, nomos, and isonomi*, 见 Ostwald 1969. 对 *isonomia* 的修正，见 Raaflaub 1996b. 平等政体，见 Robinson 1997. Herodotus 3.80.6; 5.78. 自由与民主，见 Raaflaub 2004b: ch.6.

⑤ 关于政体术语的一般演变，见 Meier 1990: ch.7. 对政体的讨论，见 Raaflaub 1989. 新政体的从头设计，见 Aristotle, *Politics* 2.7–8. 混合政体，见 von Fritz 1954.

殊的公共目标。这一发展始于对（非正式）制度及其问题的描述，发展到政治的概念化、分析、调整、理论化，以及出于纠正滥用权力，恢复古老理想，最终实现一个预期中的新理想而进行的深思熟虑的介入。希腊人对于政治和政府管理的思考在公元前6世纪的雅典达到了第一个高峰，首先是梭伦的政治因果理论，随后是克里斯提尼为实现完全的城邦一体化而进行的复杂改革。

希腊人的解释

正如学者们以往所做的那样，通过聚焦于古风时代希腊社会和文化形成所具备的条件，以及希腊城邦作为公民共同体的特殊本质，[1]解释这种政治反思的出现是完全有可能的。在追寻这种争论的发展时，我们需要首先考虑三种并不存在于早期希腊的要素。（1）由于爱琴海世界位于主要帝国的统治范围之外，以及将古风时期的希腊与辉煌的青铜时代相分离的深刻时代断裂，[2]希腊的国家形成并没有走向中央集权制，强大的、王权神授的君主制以及封建诸侯制的发展之路。（2）希腊城邦在其形成时期，并不需要应付强大的外部压力，或大规模的、关乎国家命运的公共工程（例如水资源的分配），战争扮演着一个重要但又相当有限的角色。所有这一切避免了强大团结的贵族阶层，强大的领导权，或是中央集权制的出现。[3]（3）直到公元前6世纪中期遭遇向外扩张的波斯帝国之前，希腊人对外来的影响持一种开放的态度，他们对外部世界没有任何敌意，而这种排外态度在埃及和美索不达米亚却极为普遍。他们并未怀有这样的观念，即混乱的外部世界亟待征服和整治；对于所谓的劣等"蛮族"也没有如此强烈的高人一等的优越感。[4]

其二，希腊城邦呈集聚式发展，互相平衡且在国际关系中保持了一定程度的平等。一些较大的城邦虽已出现，但却不能发展出超越于联盟之上的霸权形式；希腊人只是在公元前5世纪才实现了"帝国的转型"（imperial turn）。在城邦内部，那些从平等的社会成员中脱颖而出的最高领导者并未凌驾于整个共同体之上，更不用说"统治"他人了。新兴的贵族阶层成员在本质上是平等的，与大部分独立的自耕农之间的区别甚小，后者在军队和公民大会中都发挥着不可或缺的集体作用。领袖的地位和声望与城邦息息相关，贵族精英与平民互为依托，因此整个城邦是建立在人人平等的基础之上。[5]对贵族精英和领袖的批判是完全可能且习以为常的。此外，贵族之间的竞争是激烈而极具破坏性的；它鼓动民众加以反抗，偶尔会为僭主制提供可乘之机，并促使人们寻求其他的政治选择。

其三，在一个急剧变革的时期，城邦的集体要素（communal element）以贵族精英的热望受到压抑为代价而得到增强；权力和政治程序定型。海外贸易和移民提供了追求商业利益和社会流动的机会，但也对传统价值观和领导权构成了挑战。危机和社会斗争迫使人们去寻找新的途径来解决冲突——通常是由公众委任的立法者来完成。城邦之间的差异促进了相互的竞争，由不同出身的移民者所组成的海外新城邦则使得人们有必要去试验一种新的制度性解决方案，这种尝试反过来也影响了"旧世界"的发展。结果是出现了一种高层次的政治思想文化，一些复杂甚至激进的社会解决方案也随之产生。

其四，无论希腊人如何看待众神和命运的强力，他们很早便明白，人类本身最后要为自己的不幸和幸运负责。以伸张正义为己任的诸神，只是在他们强有力地的人间代理人缺位时，才会得到人

---

① 对希腊政治思想出现的解释，见 Meier 1990, 2011; Raaflaub 2000: 57–59.
② 关于希腊"黑暗时代"，见 Snodgrass 1971; Deger-Jalkotzy 2006; Dickinson 2006.
③ 在这一方面，决定罗马发展的那些特殊环境颇具启示意义，见 Raaflaub 1996a.
④ 关于美索不达米亚内外尖锐的对立，见 Nissen and Renger 1987；埃及，见 Moers 2010. 希腊人对于"蛮族"的观念，见 Georges 1994; Mitchell 2007.
⑤ 城邦的平等主义基础，见 Morris 2000: pt. 3; Raaflaub et al. 2007: ch.2. 也见 Starr 1977, 1986.

们的吁求。以公众力量支持为背景的立法，梭伦将正义作为一种本质上抽象的原则的理解，都将众神更多地推向了具体的政治和立法行为的背后——虽然在政治学和流行的道德观念领域并非如此。公民们集体行使控制权。[1]"城邦"——无论是城邦自身还是通过立法者——因此制定法律，从事公共管理和改革。希腊的政府并非一个历经挫折的现实存在，而是一项公共工程，是政治反思、分析及行动的目标。

其五，民众早就是一个潜在的强有力的角色。共同体内部的战争加强了平民集体的重要性。这一趋势在斯巴达达到了顶峰，那里特殊的条件——城邦边界之内的敌人（一群数目庞大且聚居的奴隶）——促使它实行了一种将公共决策权正式交付于公民之手的政体。在其他地区，贵族的滥权引发了城邦的内乱，解决的办法只有加强公民的集体参与和制度的调整。因而，建立在一种更为广泛基础之上的城邦实现了制度化和稳定化。

各种制度及其相互影响，更广泛意义上的宪政，甚至作为城邦全部生活方式的共和政体（politeia），都因此成为政治思想及行动，甚至是早期理论化尝试所关注的焦点，而公共法律则成为实现上述理念的途径。

可能来自近东的影响

外来影响在这一进程所扮演的角色仍旧悬而未决，这不仅由于先前提到的那些原因，也因为学者们在那些为早期政治思想研究提供证据的诗人们的作品中发现了大量的东方文化的影响。这里，我把自己的研究限定在三个方面：法律与正义，集体决策，以及智慧文学（wisdom literature）。

首先是法律和正义。虽然希腊罗马的"法典"与美索不达米亚的法典有很多相似之处，并可能受到后者一定程度的影响，但两者之间还是存在着巨大的差异。[2]这些差异始于法律和正义的起源。在美索不达米亚，法律和正义存在于原始的世界秩序之中，诸神将其授予国王，让他在人间代为行使。[3]因此，美索不达米亚的法律在本质上是保守的、不变的，由国王以及那些被他赋予权力的人们所控制和维护。那些铭文法典，如汉谟拉比法典，就是国王用来自我炫耀的纪念碑的一部分。国王是至高无上的法官和规则的制定者，但这些规则不是通过法律，而是作为国王的关心和恩惠（也表达了最高神的旨意），通过自上而下强制执行的法令来表达，民众只是被动的接受者。[4]同样的情况也盛行于埃及。[5]除了在以色列情况可能有所不同以外，[6]集体或公开地对法律、政制、公共秩序和相关话题的思考在近东社会长期以来发展滞后。相反，我们看到希腊的法律文化与公民社会的联系则根深蒂固。希腊人并不是从诸神那里获得法律，即使他们可能将一些值得尊敬的传统视为"神的规则"，或为一些重大的立法行为而恳求德尔斐阿波罗神谕的支持。因此，希腊的法律充满活力和适应性。

在国王的诸多品行之中，所有的近东社会都强调了正义的地位。人们期望国王是一位正义的维护者，保护弱者免遭强者欺凌。不可否认，这一点与早期希腊的思想极为类似。[7]然而，在美索不达

---

① 参见 Raaflaub 2005; Meier 2011.

② 美索不达米亚对希腊罗马立法和法典的影响，见 Mühl 1933; Westbrook 1988, 1989; 相关讨论见 Raaflaub 2009: 41–48.

③ 美索不达米亚思想中的法律起源，见 Lang 2008: 57–58, with ref. to Otto 2005: 58.

④ 美索不达米亚的王室法令非法律，见 Wells 2005: 188–90; 也见 Westbrook 2003: 12–23 (6: "与我们今日的法规最为接近认同的文献资料就是王室的法令。"); Streck 2007.

⑤ Redford 2001: II 277–82; *Lexikon der Ägyptologie*, under "Dekret," "Gesetze."

⑥ 以色列和希腊罗马"法典"的比较，见 Burckhardt et al. 2007.

⑦ 关于王室的意识形态和正义，一般意义上的，见 Irani and Silver 1995; 埃及，见 Weber-Schäfer 1976: 26–40; Assmann 1990, 1993; O'Connor and Silverman 1995; 美索不达米亚，见 Garelli 1974; Kramer 1974; 赫梯，见 Archi 1979; Bryce 2002: 31; 波斯，见 Briant 2002: 126, 329–30, and ch. 6.

米亚，这一点在那些主要用来阿谀奉承王室的语境中尤其被反复地强调。在叙述性的史诗中（例如 Enuma Elish），正义似乎远远排在军事才能之后。虽然这与希腊史诗（特别是赫西阿德）具有明显的相似性，但希腊人更为强调最高神的正义。①出自美索不达米亚的资料也从未将正义加以概念化或理论化。与此相反，埃及确实存在着正义的观念，但它只是一个更广泛的世界概念的一部分，是原始的、超越诸神、国王和人类的社会伦理秩序（ma'at）的一部分。②这一概念在文本和图画中得到了充分的证实，但关于它的全面讨论尚未展开，正如埃及人通常"没有留下任何有关政治观念的系统论著…更不用说从事政治理论的创建了。"这就使得人们很难去评估政治思想在埃及社会中的作用及其对古风时代的希腊可能产生的影响。

其二，集体决策。在美索不达米亚，中央集权制的王国和帝国来去匆匆，频繁更迭。在它们之外或在它们的保护之下，具有独立结构和制度的城市与部落发挥了重要的作用。史诗中的议事会和民众大会都曾出现在诸神和人间的世界里（正如在荷马史诗中的那样）。③但与荷马不同的是，这些作品只是在叙述需要的时候才会偶尔提及这些制度，它们并不是受到密切关注或明确概念化的对象。在文献资料中（如铭文、书信或法律文书），这些完全以传统规则为基础而运作的共同体常被涉及，但这些记载依旧停留在事实的层面，缺乏政治上的反思、分析或概念化。很难看出哪些政治上的冲动能由此产生。相反，在古风时期的希腊城邦中可以明显地看出，恰恰是这个公民集体通过政府管理机制和正义推动了社会、政治、文化及法律上的发展。尽管如此，这个问题仍然值得进一步探究，特别是在新亚述时期和晚期巴比伦时期那些标榜拥有特权和"城市权利"（civic rights）的城市中；它们如同获得了一张以传统为基础，由国王所授予，并受到城市神明保护的"自治的特许状"。④我需要弄清这些文本中所使用的证据是否超出了对传统、神意和国王义务的诉求。

其三，智慧文学。这类作品在埃及，美索不达米亚和希伯来《圣经》中大量存在。⑤很长时间以来，人们一直相信它们对赫西阿德及其他希腊诗人产生了直接的影响，但这种观点可能太过于简单。⑥无论如何，这类作品中包含着道德和实际上的建议，目的是使人们在一个既定的等级社会结构中能够过上一种幸福和成功的生活。对于当权者的建议是，对上要使自己的行为无可指责，对下则要表现出正义和慷慨。⑦政治领域几乎完全被忽视——赫西阿德也只是把它当作某种唯恐避之不及之物——政治思想的痕迹也难以寻觅。

有一部作品在某种程度上说是政治性的。这是一个巴比伦人在公元前 1000 年间所写的"给王子的建议"（Advice to a Prince）。文中认为君主的不正义将招致神明的惩罚，其形式包括自然灾害、敌人入侵、叛乱，以及财富、统治权乃至生命的丧失。赫西阿德在《工作和日子》（Works and Days）中坚信，贵族法官所做出的邪恶决定会招来神明的惩罚，"一个人的邪恶"会引起整个城市的毁灭，促使宙斯给人间降下饥荒和疾病，田野荒芜，动物不蕃，女人不育，带来战争以及军队和

---

① *Enuma elish* 中的正义，见 Foster 2005: 478；与赫西阿德的相似之处，见 West 1997: 280-83；二者对比，见 Raaflaub 2008b: 49-51.

② *Ma' at:* Assmann 1990; 1993; Morschauser 1995: 101; cf. Zibelius-Chen 1988: 118-24 (quote: 113).

③ 集体决策制度，见 Beckman 1982; Durand 1989; Liverani 1993; Schemeil 1999; Fleming 2004. 史诗中的议事会和民众大会，见 Katz 1993; West 1997: 193-99. 对雅各布森"原始民主制"(1970: 132-70) 概念的批判性讨论，见 Robinson 1997: 16-22.

④ 晚期巴比伦城市的特权，见 Kuhrt 1995: 610-21 及参考书目。

⑤ "智慧文学"，特别体现于巴比伦的智慧文本 (wisdom texts, Lambert 1960)；埃及不同时期和种类的"教谕"（"instructions"）或"教谕文学"（"didactic literature"），在"Lichtheim 1973-1980"可以很容易地找到；智慧文学也存在于希伯来圣经中的《约伯记》（Job），《箴言》(Proverbs) 和《传道书》(Ecclesiastes) 中。

⑥ 参见 Dornseiff(1959) 的相关篇章；Walcot 1966; West 1978; 1997: 324-32. 最近的一次讨论见 Schmitz (2004)，书中有大量的参考书目，并不仅限于近东智慧文学。

⑦ 对当权者的建议，可见 *Instruction of Ptahhotep*, par. 5-6, 24-25, 28 (Lichtheim 1973-1980: I 64-65, 70-71).

舰队的毁灭。①不论是这位巴比伦人的作品还是赫西阿德，都未将惩罚的方式与引发惩罚的不义行为明确地联系起来，它们看上去就像是从当权者通常所犯的罪行和经常出现的灾祸中随机挑选出来的。作者们所能做的，也只是规劝当权者避免施行不义，相信神明会像所期望的那样做出反应。两位作者都是从一般和传统的层面去思考。梭伦率先跨出了超越这类一般性思考的决定性一步：正如前文所述，这体现在他努力在罪恶行为和灾难性后果之间建立一种特定的、纯粹政治性的因果联系，并得出必要的结论以恢复和保护良好的社会秩序。就这一步而言，我尚未在近东思想中找到证据。

现存的埃及文献中也包含着"给王子的教诲"（Instructions to Princes）②。它们并未设想到君王的失误和惩罚，但其中的目录却包括君王为展示其仁爱而应遵守的政策和行为规范。这些文献看起来同样显得具有一般和传统的特征，受到古人智慧的启发。它们反映出的这种政治思想在近东各君主国必然相当普遍，内容主要是国王的品格，以及他获得民众支持和施行统治的最佳手段。但关键的是，尽管它们对此并未明确表达只是暗示，但已经把思想的精华注入到了建议的内容中。换句话说，这些思想的动力并不是出于应对当前问题和危机的需要。唯一的例外似乎是"阿蒙尼姆赫特国王的教谕"（Instruction of King Amenehet），此文是受到国王遇刺的影响而在其死后写成的，规劝他的儿子不要相信任何人。③总体而言，埃及君主制的稳定、不可挑战的权威及其与宗教的关联使我怀疑，它并不利于一种公开的、大众的政治思想或政治争辩文化的产生，甚至在公元前 1000 年代，即它有可能影响希腊人思想的时候也是如此。

结　论

综上所述，我得出结论如下。由于我的研究仍在进行中，这些结论只能是初步的。就我目前所见而言，我们确实发现了一些与早期希腊证据相类似的线索。它们大多存在于实用与叙述的层面，存在于传统或一般性思考的范围之内，其内容涉及君主或领袖的品格，特别是他们对正义的责任感。但我仍在寻找证据以表明政治领域已获得了特别的、详细的关注，人们已经在明确的概念化、系统的反思和理论化等方面迈出了步伐，正如我们在梭伦的思想中所看到的那样。从这一点和其他方面来看，希伯来圣经提供了更为近似的对比——这是一个仍需研究的重大课题。即便如此，正是在梭伦的思想中，我们似乎发现了希腊政治反思中十分关键的一次进步，它彻底地打破了那些对许多文化来说习以为常的旧模式。果真如此，它就标志着希腊人与近东分道扬镳，开始了走向独创之路的第一步。

如果上述说法是正确的，迈出这第一步的条件又有哪些呢？我在上文列举了一系列因素，是它们创造了一种鼓励独立思考和集体责任感的环境。在此我想特别强调两点。其一是作为公民集体的希腊城邦的本性所培养出来的那种早期的政治倾向，即以政治领域为中心，公开地批评、讨论政治现象，并在概念上对其加以界定。其二是政治潜能的发现。它在公众发起并控制下的立法和改革中得到了体现。所有这一切都促使一位极为精明和果断的政治家在深刻的城邦危机之下迈出一大步，进入更高的政治思考层面。

无论如何，这种对制度、共同体、政府以及政治的总体思考在近东的文献中远不及古风时期的

---

① 巴比伦的"*Fürstenspiegel*"：见 Lambert 1960: 110–15。赫西阿德论正义与不正义之城，见 *Works and Days* 225–47.

② 《给国王莫里卡尔的教诲》（*The Instruction Addressed to King Merikare*, Lichtheim 1973–1980: I 97–109）或《国王阿蒙尼姆赫特给其子塞索斯特里斯一世的教谕》（*The Instruction of King Amenemhet I for his Son Sesostris I*, ibid. 135–39).

③ *Amenemhet*: 见前一注释，也可见 Burkard 1999. 作为文学传统主题的国家危机，见 Lichtheim 1973–1980: I 134–35.

希腊突出。我的结论是——尽管只是暂时的，还有待在未来的研究中接受检验——近东地区对早期希腊政治思想的影响远比人们先前推测的要少。

即使只是一种暂时的推论也同样需要解释。显而易见的原因是早期希腊和近东社会之间的根本差异，特别是在社会和文化发展的条件，个人在等级制度中的位置，以及政治思考的社会条件诸方面。二者对人类责任感的不同认识在这里似乎尤为重要。希腊城邦都是微型国家，本质上说是人人平等的面对面的公民共同体，公民集体不得不自己解决面临的问题。①近东的社会共同体和国家尽管可能有着相似的起源，但很快便形成了等级鲜明的社会结构，每个人无论高低贵贱都被束缚于一种严格的纵向权力体系。社会的价值观和规则就是由这一体系决定的。按照雅各布森（Thorkild Jacobsen）的说法，"在美索不达米亚，'好的生活'就是'顺从的生活'"②。人们可以想象到，个人的思想和行为在这样的体系中受到严厉的束缚，独立性受到压抑。除了个别例外，政治思考必然被限制在统治阶层之内，而且所关注的中心问题是现存制度的合法化和权力分配，以保证统治的稳定和长久。埃及的情况在很大程度上就是如此。

也许通常来说，早期希腊诗人作为在政治反思的开拓者，并不属于统治阶层——甚至连梭伦也不例外。政治思考并不仅仅局限于社会上层。希腊人在遭遇波斯人的时候接触到了东方的政治制度。即使希腊人对波斯的了解由于沙文主义和各种误解而显得片面化和扭曲，这些经历仍然促使他们将一种根本性的对比，即一个奴役世界和一个自由世界之间的对比中所体现出来的差异概念化。③希腊人的城邦制度，对独立的推崇，以及他们早期的认识——不只是领袖，他们中的所有人都应对个人和集体福祉负责——都为推动一种基础广泛的批判和独立思考文化的形成，推动对政治、制度和共同体越来越深入的集中反思创造了有利条件。

进一步的对比：早期中国政治思想的出现与本质

最后，本文所讨论的这个问题值得进一步的比较研究。根据我们目前的知识，哲学和历史学在中国和希腊虽然几乎同时产生，但却具有完全独立的起源。除了其他的智力方面的努力（intellectual endeavors）之外，这一现象长期以来引起了人们的关注，并促使人们试图提出某种解释，如雅斯贝斯（Karl Jaspers），艾森斯塔特（Shmuel Eisenstadt）等人所提出的"轴心时代理论"（Axial Age Theory）。④无论如何，这类对比也应该包含政治思想在内。对古风时代希腊和早期中国政治思想的形式、内容和功能及其产生的社会政治原因进行全面地对比确实也会颇为诱人。但当前我的能力远不足以完成这样一项比较——这无论如何都会超出这篇文章的范围。但我或许可以被允许提出几点非常笼统的初步看法。⑤

古老的周代国家，主要由一座都城及一些设防的城镇构成，国王、贵族和驻军居住于此，统治着乡村的农户。它们堪比古希腊的城邦。在这些国家中，贵族和士兵都身负民事和军事义务，并参

---

① 微型国家，见 Davies 1997. 自行解决问题，见 Meier 2011.
② Jacobsen 1946: 138–39, 202.
③ 希腊人对波斯臣民的认识，可见 Herodotus 7.135; Meiggs and Lewis 1988: no. 12; Fornara 1983: no. 35; 泛见 Raaflaub 2004b: ch. 3.
④ Jaspers 1953; Eisenstadt 1986; Arnason et al. 2005.
⑤ 2013 年 5 月初，罗林格（Robert Rollinger）将在赫尔辛基大学主办一次会议。我计划在提交会议的论文中就此做进一步的比较。我这里一般提及的是一份有关早期中国政治思想的精选书目，它们是 Needham 1956; Hsiao 1979; Schwartz 1985; Obberborn and Weber-Schäfer 1988; Lewis 1999, 以及 "Loewe and Saghnessy 1999" 中的相关章节。关于较早以前对早期希腊和中国思想的比较，可参见 Lloyd 1990: ch.4; 1996, 2002; Shankman and Durrant 2000 and 2002. 关于自由，见 Lloyd 1996: ch.6.

与国家事务的讨论。然而这种比较似乎只适用于斯巴达（以及少数希腊城邦）。在那里，相对少数的公民集体不仅统治着大量的奴隶（希洛人），而且还统治着数量众多的，具有依附性但仍是自由人的边民（Perioikoi，那些"住在四周的人"，意即住在边远地区的人）。与此相反，在其他城邦中，城市和乡村的居民都是公民，他们之间没有这样的区别，城市并未统治乡村。

无论如何，有着数百个小诸侯国的周代封建制很快便让位于日益增长的中央集权制和等级制，以及残酷的争霸局面。这种对权力的争夺以战国时代为典型。在这一时期，一直有少数诸侯国为了生存并胜过其他对手而最大程度地追逐霸权、统治权和资源。很可能出于这些需求的压力，一种或许可以称之为"智力"（brain power）的特殊资源（resource）悄然出现，并受到极高的重视。受过良好教育的社会精英（"士"），虽然长期以来为国效力，但通常地位低下，无根无基。此时他们成了游走各国的学者专家，为统治者贡献自己的聪明才智。其中包括专门的知识，如在军事、外交、游说、行政管理和国家治理诸方面的才能。这些饱学之士以口头或书面的形式提出自己的方案，以将军、执政者、改革家、外交家等身份为统治者所任用，从而实现自己的主张。上述只是大致的描述，但足以满足我当前的目的。很显然，这些专业知识大都与政治事务有关，并且是以政治思想为基础。

在此我希望强调三点。第一，这种政治思想虽然植根于早期，但却在需求迫切且社会经济结构足以提供支持之时出现并逐渐成型，一枝独秀，富有影响。在这种现象中发现与公元前5世纪中期希腊智者学派的出现有类似之处并非牵强之举。这些智者是游走各国的哲人和教师，与早期的那些"自然哲学家"不同，他们集中思考的是人类世界、国家、社会和社会的互动，以教授修辞学、政治学等其他更多的课程谋生。这些人在雅典的访问以及与苏格拉底的争辩借助于柏拉图的对话而名垂千古，但他们作品的遗失也在很大程度上归咎于柏拉图对其观点的驳斥。他们由于各种原因被吸引到雅典，很显然，他们自身就是一种泛希腊现象。他们来自于从西西里到色雷斯（Thrace）沿海的众多城邦，向整个希腊世界贡献自己的知识。这是一个普遍需要专家和某些特殊训练及教育的时代。这种需求不仅仅限于民主制的雅典，也不仅仅是为了在政治竞争中获得更多机遇。智者生当其时，自然声名鹊起。事实上无论城邦是何种政体，修辞术都因诉讼的目的需求大增。然而，正是由于对政治问题的深入思考，他们进入到了一个更高和更系统的政治反思层面，提出了各种各样的的政治和政体理论。[①]极典型的一个例子便是伯里克利邀请普罗泰戈拉（Protagoras）参与南意大利一处新的泛希腊殖民地的政体设计。普罗泰戈拉显然把自己教授的主题定为"实用之学"（euboulia），它所关注的事"个人的事务，如何最好地管理家务和公共事务，如何通过言行对城邦事务做出最有效的贡献"——换言之，即"管理城邦"（politikē technē）以及如何成为"一名好公民"的"艺术"。[②]

第二点，在古风和古典时代的希腊，政治思想并不仅局限于社会上层。它是一种广泛存在的，以各种文学形式（从史诗、抒情诗到悲剧、喜剧和历史编撰）表现出来的政治文化的一部分。[③]因此专门的政治学著述出现的比较晚（公元前5世纪晚期）。此外，政治思想渗透到政治生活和修辞学之中（如议事会和公民大会上的政治辩论）。就像在其他许多政体那样，政治思考在民主制度中相当流行，因而阿里斯多芬才会在《云》（Clouds）和其他剧作中把它作为取笑的对象。修昔底德的作品显示出政治理论是如何在公众辩论中被用来支撑政治观点的，尽管其形式过于浓缩和抽象。因此在希腊，政治思想成为公共文化的主要组成部分。[④]在中国，很早以来政治思想一直是通过专门的政治著述来表达的，这也是思想家获得成功的必要条件。然而政治思想方面的专家大部分集中在统

---

① 关于智者学派，参见 Guthrie 1971; Kerferd 1981a, 1981b; de Romilly 1992; Wallace 1998; "智者运动"（"sophistic movement"）的起源，见 Martin 1976.

② Plato, *Protagoras* 318e–319a (trans. Taylor 1991).

③ 例如悲剧中的政治思想，可见 Meier 1993; Boedeker and Raaflaub 2005; Raaflaub 2012.

④ Thucydides: e.g., 5.84–112; 6.38–39.

治者的宫廷之中。他们帮助统治者最大程度地利用自己的资源，在政治内外的权力斗争中占据优势地位，巩固其统治并为其正当性辩护。随着哲学传统和"诸子百家"（schools）的出现，这些专家也就掌握了全部的政治思想资源。这些情况似乎鼓励我们更多地是将中国与古代近东或希腊化世界中的王国和帝国，而不是与古风或古典时期的希腊进行对比。在那里，政治思想一方面主要集中于国王或统治者的宫廷之中，另一方面则集中于书吏学校（scribal schools，古代近东的大学）的"学术"环境之中，或是在继承了柏拉图和亚里士多德的那些哲学流派和传统之中。正如在中国，这种政治文化只满足了了统治者和贵族的需要，既不公开也没有被普遍接受。此外，正如我们所见，这类政治思想在现存的古代近东文献中更多是内含而非外露的，但在早期中国却是坦率直白的，这就使得我们可以非常详细地来重建其主要形式和内容（尽管还有许多年代和真实性的问题）。

第三点，也是最后一点，恰恰是关于政治思想的内容。在早期中国，随着国家和社会的结构日渐等级化和集权化，政治思想在社会高层的集中，且只对高层的需要和关切表现出关注，这结果必然是政治思想更多地关注于政府、行政管理、经济、战争的问题，关注君主制的意识形态以及支持其统治地位的道德价值（包括尊重传统、祖先、公平、正义、美德等）。我们看到，古代近东政治思想也同样如此。然而出于同样的原因，古代近东和早期中国的政治思想中都没有过多关注政体之间的差异，民众是否并在多大程度上能够和应该分担政治责任，公民权的概念，以及在人人平等的希腊城邦社会中占据主导地位，并在西方政治思想中保持至今的那些政治价值：平等和自由。

（文献缩写与参考书目同英文版，从略）

中国学者论古代文明和文明的发展与交往

王敦书　南开大学

摘要：什么是文明？文明的本质和特征为何？人类历史上存在过多少文明？其发展过程和相互关系为何？这一切都是研究人类的历史、社会和文化所必须回答的重要问题。外国学者，从达尼列夫斯基、斯宾格勒、汤因比到麦克尼尔及亨廷顿对有关文明的各个方面都进行了精深的研究。中国学者也不例外。本文介绍雷海宗、林志纯、吴于廑、胡钟达、刘家和、罗荣渠、彭树智、马克垚等著名史学家对古代文明和文明的发展与交往的看法，并最后简略说明作者的浅见。

关键词：古代文明；文明发展；文明交往；中国学者

Abstract：What is civilization? What are the nature and characteristics of civilization? How many civilizations have existed in human history? How did they develop and influence each other? All these are significant questions, which should be answered for studying human history, society and culture. Foreign scholars, from Danilevsky, Spengler, Toynbee, to McNeill and Huntington, have made profound research on various aspects about civilizations. So did Chinese scholars. In this paper the author will introduce the points of view on ancient civilizations and their development and communication by some distinguished Chinese historians, e.g., Lei Haizong, Lin Zhichun, Wu Yujin, Hu Zhongda, Liu Jiahe, Luo Rongqu, Peng Shuzhi and Ma Keyao. At last, the author will briefly explain his own opinion.

Keywords：Ancient Civilizations, Development of Civilization, Communication among Civilizations, Chinese scholars

什么是文明？文明的本质和特征为何？人类历史上存在过多少文明？其发展过程和相互关系为何？这一切都是研究人类的历史、社会和文化所必须回答的重要问题。外国学者，从达尼列夫斯基、斯宾格勒、汤因比到麦克尼尔及亨廷顿对有关文明的各个方面都进行了精深的研究。中国学者也不例外。本文准备介绍雷海宗、林志纯、吴于廑、胡钟达、刘家和、罗荣渠、彭树智、马克垚等著名史学家对古代文明和文明的发展与交往的看法，并最后简略说明作者个人的浅见。

雷海宗是上个世纪中叶驰名中外的史学大家。他引进德国历史哲学家斯宾格勒的文化形态史观，认为有特殊哲学意义的历史，在时间上以最近的五千年为限，历史是多元的，是一个个处于不同时间和地域的高等文化独自产生和自由发展的历史。迄今可确知七个高等文化（亦即文明——笔者），即埃及、巴比伦、印度、中国、希腊罗马、回教和欧西。这些时间和空间都不相同的历史单位，虽各有特点，但发展的节奏、时限和周期大致相同，都经过封建时代、贵族国家时代、帝国主义时代、大一统时代和政治破裂与文化灭绝的末世这五个阶段，最后趋于毁灭。在人类历史上，欧西文化与埃及、中国等其他六个文化相并列，并无高与下、中心与非中心之分，这就有力地破除了西欧中心论的谬论。雷海宗还多次批驳欧洲学者对阿拉伯的历史与文化的歪曲和诬蔑。

与斯宾格勒不同，雷海宗认为中国文化的发展有其独特之点。其他文化，除欧西因历史起步晚尚未结束外，皆按照上述五个阶段的进展，经形成、发展、兴盛、衰败一周而亡。唯独中国文化四千年来却经历了两个周期。以公元383年淝水之战为分界线，由殷商到"五胡乱华"为第一周。这是纯粹的华夏民族创造中国传统文化的古典中国时期。它经历了殷商西周封建时代、春秋贵族国家时代、战国帝国主义时代、秦汉帝国大一统时代（公元前221至公元88年）和帝国衰亡与古典文化没落时代（公元89至383年）。但中国文化与其他文化不同，至此并未灭亡，经淝水之战胜利后，却返老还童直至20世纪又经历了第二周。第二周的中国，无论民族血统还是思想文化，都有很大变化。胡人不断与汉人混合为一，印度佛教与中国原有文化发生化学作用，这是一个"胡汉混合、梵华同化"的综合中国时期。第二周的中国文化在政治和社会上并无更多的新的进展，大致墨守秦汉已定的规模；但在思想文艺上，却代代都有新的活动，可与第一周相比，共经五个时期，即宗教时代、哲学时代、哲学派别化与开始退化时代、哲学消灭与学术化时代、文化破灭时代。另一方面，南方的开发与发展则是中国第二周文化的一项伟大的事业与成就。中国文化之所以能有第二周，这是与吸收融合胡人的血统和印度的文化，以及由民族优秀分子大力发展南方分不开的（参见《断代问题与中国历史的分期》和《历史的形态与例证》）。①

新中国成立后，马克思列宁主义在中国的意识形态领域占支配的地位，是指导人们思想的理论基础。恩格斯采纳摩尔根的学说，在《家庭、私有制和国家的起源》一书中对文明作了明确的论述，认为人类的文化发展经过蒙昧时代、野蛮时代和文明时代三个阶段。文明开始于商品生产阶段，其经济特征是出现了金属货币、商人、土地私有制、抵押制和奴隶劳动。与文明相适应的家庭形式是一夫一妻制，男子对妇女的统治和个体家庭。国家是文明社会的概括，是统治阶级镇压被压迫被剥削阶级的机器。城乡对立和遗嘱制度是文明另一方面的特征。古代的奴隶制、中世纪的农奴制和近代的雇佣劳动制是文明的三大时期所特有的三大奴役形式。文明的基础是一个阶级对另一个阶级的剥削，它的全部发展是在经常的矛盾中进行的。最后，恩格斯引用摩尔根的话展望道："管理上的民主，社会中的博爱，权力的平等，普及的教育，将揭开社会的下一个更高的阶段，经验、理智和科学正在不断向这个阶段努力。这将是古代氏族的自由、平等和博爱的复活，但都是在更高级形式上的复活。"②

在上述论断的基础上，再根据列宁在《论国家》中的有关论述，斯大林进一步提出了五种生产方式说。他确定人类的历史发展必定经过原始社会、奴隶制社会、封建社会、资本主义社会和社会主义与共产主义社会五个阶段。新中国的学者基本上都接受了斯大林的五种生产方式的理论，雷海宗也不例外，但他认为奴隶制社会并不是世界历史和人类文明必须经过的一个普遍性阶段，因而受到了批判。

改革开放以来，我国史学家解放思想，实事求是，开拓创新，对古代文明及其发展与交往展开了广泛深入丰富多彩的研究和讨论。林志纯先生（笔名日知）在《世界上古史纲》（上、下册）、《古

---

① 雷海宗：《伯伦史学集》，中华书局2002年版，第132—158、243—258页。
② 《马克思恩格斯选集》中文第2版第4卷，人民出版社1995年版，第179页。

代城邦史研究》、《中西古典文明千年史》和《中西古典学引论》（1978—1996 年间论文集）等专著中对世界古代历史和中西古典文明做出了精辟深刻的论述，建立起博大精深的上古史体系。他提出，古代文明世界存在于三大地区（古代北非、西亚、南亚、中亚，古代欧洲，古代中国），构成为两大系统（中、西古典文明），发展分两大阶段（城邦—帝国）。

关于城邦，他认为城邦或邦是最早的政治单位，产生于旧社会转入新社会之初。新旧交替，除旧布新是城邦时期的特点。城邦是自由民、公民的集体组织。自由公民是城邦的主人和全权者，对于其他非全权者、无权者，尤其对于奴隶，是统治阶级。但公民内部逐渐分化，而有贵族与平民之分，富者与贫者之别。城邦的土地所有制是古典所有制，即公有和各家的私有并存，如中国的井田制。城邦的政治制度的出发点是民主政治。城邦首领邦君起初选任，后变世袭，由传贤而传子。城邦会议包括民众会和长老会议，原为民主机构，后来有的变成贵族会议，在古代中国是诸大夫和国人的会议。城邦首领起初偏重执行宗教任务，后逐渐加强政治军事的比重，或者邦君一身而兼祀与戎之职，或另选执政之人分掌。大体上说，有偏重宗教方面的君，偏重军事方面的王，和偏重政治方面的卿。城邦时代无专制君主，也不知专制政治为何物。城邦的政治形式经历了原始民主制、原始君主制、公卿执政制和向帝国过渡四个阶段。城邦发展中不时出现改革家和独裁者，有的是僭主式的人物，如乌鲁卡基那、伊尹和共伯和；有的为调停式人物，如梭伦、管仲和子产。孔子也曾是改革家和独裁者。城邦与城邦联盟并存，城邦联盟并不是国家，在中国古史上称"天下"。

至于中国古典文明，林志纯的看法可以大致归结为：东方专制主义为二千多年来误解说；中国早期国家城邦民主说；"周天下"城邦联盟说；"六经"皆"邦学"说；古典中国无西方所谓"黑暗时代"与排他宗教说；古典中国具有民主、革命传统与兄弟民族思想说；西方中世纪 Feudalism 不适用于中国古典时代，不宜译为"封建"说，等等。

吴于廑在《世界历史上的游牧世界与农耕世界》、《世界历史上的农本与重商》、《历史上农耕世界对工业世界的孕育》和《亚欧大陆传统农耕世界不同国家在新兴工业世界冲击下的反应》等重要论文中，高瞻远瞩而又细致透彻地探讨了游牧文明、农业文明、工业文明以及它们之间的相互关系。他更重视文明的传播与交往。在为《中国大百科全书·外国历史卷》所撰《世界历史》条目长文中，他明确提出了"世界历史的横向发展"的理论，说明这是"指历史由各地区间的相互闭塞到逐步开放，由彼此分散到逐步联系密切，终于发展成为整体的世界历史这一客观过程而言的。"由此，他确定世界历史的"内容为对人类历史自原始、孤立、分散的人群发展为全世界成一密切联系整体的过程进行系统探讨和阐述。"①随后，在"世界历史全局概览"一节中，他对世界历史和人类文明的纵向发展与横向发展过程展开了宏观而又具体的历史考察，对中国的世界史学科建设和文明史研究作出了重大的贡献。

胡钟达是改革开放后中国的历史学家中首先对五种生产方式说明确提出批评乃至否定的学者。在《试论亚细亚生产方式兼评五种生产方式说》一文中，他从理论上进行分析，认为亚细亚的、古代的、封建的生产方式代表的是同一社会发展阶段，是同一社会经济形态的不同类型或模式。只要把"封建主义"的含义和使用范围加以扩大，则不仅中世纪的欧洲社会是封建社会，整个古代东方社会、古代希腊罗马社会也都可以认为是封建社会。在另一篇《再评五种生产方式说》文章中，胡钟达结合中外历史，具体分析所谓奴隶社会和封建社会中的奴隶与农奴的实际状况，使用"前资本主义阶级社会"的概念，指出前资本主义阶级社会没有必要也没有可能分为奴隶社会和封建社会两个有前后高低之分的不同的社会经济形态。

胡钟达在《论世界历史发展的不平衡性》和《古典时代中国希腊政治制度演变的比较研究》两

---

① 吴于廑：《吴于廑学术论著自选集》，首都师范大学出版社 1995 年版，第 62—63、52 页。

篇长文中，通过观察人类各文明的兴衰和先进与落后交替更迭的过程，阐明了世界历史发展的不平衡性。更对古代世界的各个文明进行了比较研究，指出希腊古典文明是与古代近东以皇权专制主义和僧侣主义为特征的青铜文明相对立的古典理性主义和人文主义的新文明。希波战争的结局就判明了这两种文明的优劣。先秦华夏文明和古典希腊文明大体上是矗立在亚欧大陆两端的文明殿堂，都高举人文主义和理性主义的旗帜，冲破普遍笼罩古代世界的宗教迷雾。但在政治制度上，出现了王权专制主义和民主主义的鲜明对比。由于王权在起点上强弱不同，扩张方式不同，更因为商品经济发展的状况不同，中国西周春秋时期的封建王权，经战国时期的专制王权，到秦统一后转化为大一统专制皇权；而同期的希腊则由军事民主主义色彩的王权向贵族共和过渡，不少城邦又经过僭主政治，更进一步向民主政体发展，最后才由马其顿征服而结束城邦独立自由，接受专制王权统治。之后，两汉帝国和罗马帝国东西对峙，其经济基础大体类似，但上层建筑都存在明显差别，也就在相当大的程度上决定了它们未来的不同命运。在汉晋帝国，游牧民族的南迁最终导致了民族大融合和隋唐大帝国的出现，中华文明的发展迈上了新高峰；在罗马帝国，游牧民族的南迁导致了"西罗马帝国"的灭亡和"黑暗时代"的来临。"东罗马帝国"所保持的半壁江山逐步萎缩为拜占廷及其附近的一隅之地，苟延残喘约 1000 年后，也结束了生命。在上古、中古世界，只有中华文明一直保持持续发展的势头。[①]

刘家和对中外古史有精深造诣，更擅长比较研究，其力作为《古代中国与世界》一书。该书包括 22 篇学术论文，篇篇锦绣，精彩绝伦。这里只介绍其《论古代的人类精神觉醒》一文。刘家和采用雅斯贝斯的"轴心期"的概念，认为公元前 8—3 世纪之间世界主要文明国家在心智与文化的发展上都具有特色地经历了人类精神觉醒阶段，所谓人类精神觉醒是指人类通过对自身存在的反省而达到精神上的自觉。而产生这一人类精神觉醒的历史条件是铁器使用引起的社会经济新发展，早期国家血缘关系受到不同程度的破坏，以及小邦林立、竞争激烈和思想自由的局面。他着重比较古代印度、希腊和中国在人类精神觉醒上的特点：在人与天关系的觉醒方面，印度形成宗教传统，希腊形成哲学科学传统，中国形成人文伦理传统；在人与人关系的觉醒方面，印度提出虚幻的众生平等，希腊揭示出人类平等的内在矛盾，中国儒家则用具有礼的形式的仁使现实的有差别的人统一起来；在人的本质的觉醒方面，印度认为人是宗教的动物，希腊认为人是政治（城邦）的动物，中国认为人是伦理的动物。[②]

罗荣渠是在中国开辟和进行现代化理论研究的著名世界史学家，并不专门研究古代世界的历史与文明。但他从现代化理论出发，以生产力的发展和变革为立足点，认识到人类社会和文明发展的复杂性和多样性，称斯大林的五种生产方式理论为"一元单线说"，认为这种理论过度简单化、机械化，既不符合马克思、恩格斯的原意，也不符合人类历史的实际。他宏观地架构起一元多线的历史发展框架，提出人类社会生产力经历了三次大变革。第一次大变革是工具的制造与火的使用，从而产生了采集—渔猎文明和原始社会诸形态与发展阶段。第二次大变革是农业革命，相应产生了农业文明社会诸形态与发展阶段。第三次大变革是工业革命，因之产生了工业文明社会诸形态与发展阶段。

罗荣渠主张，自有文字以来的历史时期，文明的演进大约经过四个阶段：原始农业文明，古典农业文明，原始工业文明，发达工业文明。生产力发展是各文明发展阶段推动社会财富增长的根本动因。生产方式与交换方式的发展构成社会经济结构发展的基础。大致相同的生产方式与交换方式和其他因素相结合，在世界不同地区形成各种不同的经济结构，包括各种过渡形态和变异形态。政

① 以上诸文均见胡钟达：《胡钟达史学论文集》，内蒙古大学出版社 1997 年版。
② 刘家和：《古代中国与世界》，武汉出版社 1995 年版，第 571—599 页。

治结构在世界不同地区呈现更大的多样性，其发展落后于经济结构的变化。基本文化模式在世界不同地区又比基本政治结构呈现更大的多样性，文化传统具有更大的稳定性，成为影响历史动向的潜在的深层结构。人类从原始文明向发达工业文明演进的总趋势是：经济组织和社会组织由简单趋于复杂；各民族对自然力的支配由被动适应趋于主动支配；在每个社会系统，社会由一元趋于多元；在世界范围内则是从多元趋于一元，农业文明是地方性的，工业文明则是世界性的；归根到底，生产力愈发展，经济因素的能动作用愈大，人的能动作用也愈大，社会进步与经济发展的步伐就会愈加快。[1]

与罗荣渠相同，彭树智是世界现代史专家，但他在《论人类的文明交往》长文中对文明的交往作了全面的专门论述[2]。他指出，文明交往和生产力发展同为人类的基本实践，然而文明交往使生产力的潜在可能性变为实际上的可能性。文明交往形成的交往力，同生产力相互作用，分别组成人类社会发展进程中的横线和纵线，纺织成多样性的历史画卷。生产关系本质上是在生产和交换过程中形成的人与人之间的交往关系。交往不仅是物质交往，还包括人与人之间的感性和精神变换活动。文明交往是人类历史发展的动力，人类历史变革和社会进步的标尺，以及人类文明发展的里程碑。

彭树智认为，人类文明交往的基本内容是：物质文明、精神文明、制度文明和生态文明。不同文明之间的冲突和融合，构成文明交往史上的绚丽篇章。中华文明是人类历史上有数的独立起源的古文明之一，绵延流传，未曾中断，举世罕见。文明交往是一个双向或多向相互作用的过程。人类文明交往史是和平和暴力两种形式的交织史，也是和平交流日益深入人心的历史。在文明交往的诸多因素中，最重要的是：主体和客体、交通和科技、民族和国家、地缘和环境、宗教和文化、语言与文字、利益和正义。文明交往的基本属性包括实践性、互动性、开放性、多样性和迁徙性。人类文明交往的总链条中的基本环节有：冲突与整合、有秩与无秩、外化和内化、现代与传统、全球与本土、人类和自然。文明交往是人类智慧、善良和爱心的持续不断积累的结晶，其发展总轨迹是逐步摆脱人类的野蛮性而日渐文明化。文明交往所追求倡导的是不同文明之间的和睦共存、共处和在平等公平的基础上共同发展，是不同文明的感性同情、理性探索和深刻理解。

世界中古史与英国史专家马克垚先生主编的《世界文明史》（三卷本）于2004年问世[3]。在导言中，马克垚对全书的观点和体系作了提纲挈领的阐述。他指出：文明是人类所创造的全部物质和精神成果，从这个意义上说，文明史也就是世界通史。但另一方面，文明史又不同于世界史，即它所研究的单位是各个文明，是在历史长河中各文明的流动、发展、变化。把文明作为单位，就要区分不同的文明，划分不同类型的文明。文明是比较稳定的人类集体，有一个长期的发展过程，在发展过程中表现出阶段性。本书根据各文明生产力的发展变化和历史学界的习惯做法，将世界文明史划分为农业文明时代和工业文明时代。

农业文明时代各文明的共同点是农业成为文明社会发展的主要动力。人类生产使用的能源，主要是人力、畜力、风力和水力等可再生能源。农民是人口中的大多数。这一时代可再划分为初级农业文明阶段和发达的农业文明阶段，而以生产工具的铜器和铁器为划分的标志。全书第一卷即论述农业文明时代的历史，包括古代西亚文明、古代埃及文明、古代印度文明、古代中华文明、古代希腊文明、古代罗马文明，发达的中华农业文明——唐宋时期、中古伊斯兰文明、中古西欧的基督教文明、农业文明的相互交流等共10章。

工业文明时代的生产力开始以蒸汽机的使用为标志。能源多为煤炭、石油、天然气等不可再生

---

① 参见罗荣渠：《现代化新论》，北京大学出版社1993年版，第53—80页。
② 彭树智：《论人类的文明交往》，《史学理论研究》2001年第1期。
③ 马克垚主编：《世界文明史》上、中、下三卷，北京大学出版社2004年1月出版。

能源。科学技术在生产力中的作用日益重要。工商业逐渐取代农业成为人类文明发展的主要支柱，并改变农业的面貌和性质。人口快速增长，城市成为文明的中心。工业文明时代以 18 世纪下半期英国开始的工业革命为开端，又可分为工业文明的兴起和工业文明在全球的扩张两大阶段。

工业文明时代的到来，有一个长达几个世纪的酝酿时期，亦即原工业化时期，大约从 16 世纪至 18 世纪下半期英国工业革命。全书第二卷即探讨包括原工业化时期在内的工业文明的兴起阶段，直至 19 世纪末，共分原工业化时期亚欧诸农业文明的嬗变、科学革命与科学思想传统的确立、现代民主政治的兴起、工业革命、早期工业化时期西欧的文化、俄罗斯文化的主要特征，伊斯兰文明对西欧工业文明的吸收和冲突、印度教文明对西欧工业文明的吸收和冲突、中华文明同西欧工业文明的融会和碰撞、日本文明对西欧工业文明的吸收和冲突等十章。

工业文明在全球的扩张阶段从 19 世纪末、20 世纪初开始，迄今不过一百年，其间人类经历了空前的变化。这是全书第三卷的内容，由科技进步与持续的工业革命、欧美工业文明的新变化、俄罗斯的新文明——苏维埃文明、拉丁美洲向工业文明的过度、工业文明在南亚东南亚的演进、东亚文明的演变、世界现代化进程中的中东伊斯兰世界、非洲争取文明复兴的努力等八章构成。

以上概括地介绍了一些知名学者对古代文明和文明的发展与交往的看法。再极其简略地谈一下个人的浅见。

文明是有文化和组成为社会的人类摆脱野蛮状态后的一种存在或生存的状态。文明起源于农业革命，但诞生于城市冶金革命及其他一些生产技术的变革之后。文明的特征包括：农业、手工业和商业，城市和乡村及其对立，社会组织和阶级分化，国家政权和法律、军队，文字和科学知识，宗教和精神文化，大型建筑与艺术，等等。

由于地理（生存）环境和历史条件等方面的差异，不同地区的民族进入文明时代的时间不同；文明产生后，其生产方式、生活方式和思想方式也各有特色，从而形成不同类型或形态的文明。在古代，大体说来包括：东亚以黄河、长江为中心的中国华夏文明；南亚以印度河、恒河为中心的印度文明；近东以两河流域为中心的西亚文明和以尼罗河为中心的北非埃及文明；南欧地中海北岸的希腊文明和罗马文明。这些都是农业文明，但某些地区在某段时间工商业可以比较发达。此外，还有中亚草原的游牧文明。就社会性质来说，各古代文明都属于存在着剥削和奴役的阶级社会，但具体的剥削奴役方式多有差别不尽相同。奴隶制社会未必是普遍的必经阶段。这种社会称之为古代社会或前资本主义阶级社会或甚至封建社会未尝不可，但必须注意其以土地占有为基础对劳动者人身进行剥削奴役的共同性和具体剥削奴役方式因时空而异的多样性。

各地区文明之间，在经济、社会、政治、军事、文化各个层面，通过和平乃至战争的方式不断进行交往。随着生产力的发展和交往的扩大与频繁，人类的文明进一步发展和传播。各地区国家的文明有盛有衰，有的甚至由于外力或内部的原因而中断。但新的文明在产生，老的文明也在前进，哪怕是极其缓慢艰难而曲折。人类的文明存在和体现于各个地区的文明之中，各个地区的文明及其交往构成了整个人类的文明。随着世界各地区由分散孤立密切结合成为整体、工业革命和现代化的发生发展，以及资本主义工业文明和传统农业文明之间的相互作用，近五百年来人类文明有了巨大的发展，世界经济日益全球化和一体化，各地区文明之间更紧密频繁地展开多层面和全方位的交流。虽然存在文明冲突，但更多的是进行文明对话。人类是有理性和人性的高级生物，理性与人性也是文明所具有的根本特征。在 21 世纪，人类将根据理智和博爱的精神通过对话增进相互理解，和平公正地解决多种冲突。人类的文明、各地区民族的文明将空前繁荣昌盛。

【古典史学】

The Connection between Action and Consequence (Tun–Ergehens–Zusammenhang) in Ancient Chinese and Roman Historiography

Fritz–Heiner Mutschle, TU Dresden/Peking University

Abstract: The relation of doing (Tun) and faring (Ergehen),[1] i.e. the question of which consequences our actions have for our well being, is a fundamental problem of human life. Accordingly it has provoked a great amount of reflection which has found expression in religious, philosophical, and literary texts. In this paper I would like to present briefly what we find in two historiographical traditions, those of ancient China and Rome, concerning this problem. I will proceed in two steps. First I will look at how the general course of history, especially the rise and fall of dynasties and empires, is seen. Then I will investigate how the two historiographies deal with our problem on the level of individual lives.

I

In the section Shao Gao of the *Shangshu* Zhou Gong, the Duke of Zhou, speaks following sentences:[2]

We should not fail to mirror ourselves in the lords of Hia; we likewise should not fail to mirror ourselves in the lords of Yin. We do not presume to know and say: the lords of Hia undertook Heaven's mandate so as to have it for so–and–so many years; we do not presume to know and say: it could not be prolonged. It was that they did not reverently attend to their virtue, and so they prematurely renounced their mandate.

After this Zhou Gong goes on to describe with the same wording the fall of the Shang. The passage is

---

[1] The term, Tun–Ergehens–Zusammenhang " was coined in German Old Testament Studies in the fifties of the last century (cf. "Das wissenschaftliche Bibellexikon im Internet" www.wibilx.de sub voce "Tun–Ergehens–Zusammenhang"). Its English equivalent is used here in a generalized sense.

[2] *Shujing*, Shao Gao (Karlgren, p. 49, § 17, my underscore). As to the translations quoted see the end of the paper. The *Shao Gao* is an address of the famous Duke of Zhou to the people of the Shang/Ying after the overthrow of the Shang/Ying dynasty by the Zhou. I will not go into the question of the authorship and the transmission of the *Shangshu*. I take this passage simply as an early document of Chinese historical thinking and history writing which in one way or other it certainly is.

important because it presents us with one of the first formulations of the well know theory of "the mandate of heaven". According to this theory it is virtue which entitles a dynasty to rule. If the path of virtue is left heaven withdraws its mandate from the dynasty and confers it to another one which is more worthy of it. In our passage the transitions from the Xia dynasty to the Shang and from the Shang dynasty to the Zhou are explained in this way.[1] Obviously, we have here an interpretation of history which connects directly moral conduct and success and lack of morals with failure.

In the course of time the theory of the mandate of heaven became part and parcel of Chinese historical thought. Several hundred years later than the *Shangshu* the great Sima Qian, too, essentially follows it. According to the first chapters of his *Shiji*, the pattern in which the ruling houses follow each other is that of moral perfection of the early rulers of a dynasty, whereby the rule is stabilized and the realm made to thrive and prosper, and of moral degeneration of the late rulers, which causes heaven to withdraw its mandate and to transfer it to another dynasty, which then attacks the old one with the approval of the people and puts itself in its place.[2]

If we turn to Roman texts we find a comparable line of thought.

Already the fragments of the early historians and epic poets like the older Cato and Ennius show that these authors attributed the success of Rome to moral qualities, to virtues like manliness, reliability, piety etc.[3] In the writings of better preserved authors like Sallust and Livy we find full formulations of this view. Thus Sallust, in his first monograph on the conspiracy of Catiline, offers a concise survey of Roman history (c. 6–13), in which he ascribes the rise of Rome to its superior morals:[4]

> Hence at home and on campaign good behaviour was cultivated. There was the greatest harmony, very little avarice; justice and goodness thrived amongst them not because of laws but of nature. Quarrels, disharmony and conflict were what they conducted with the enemy; citizens competed with citizens in the area of prowess. They were lavish in supplicating the gods, sparing in the home, faithful to their

---

[1] There is no predetermined number of years for the duration of either of the dynasties. In each case the fall comes about because the rulers of both dynasties, the Xia and the Shang, from a certain point of time are not any longer concerned about virtue. The speaker Zhou Gong puts forward this theory for its actual significance: the Zhou leaders can learn from history and strive for virtue in order to extend their mandate as long as possible.

[2] Thus, concerning the end of the first dynasty, that of Xia, we read in chapter 2 (Nienhauser, I,38, my underscores): "From K'ung-chia's time to the time of Emperor Chieh, the feudal lords had revolted many times against the Hsia. Chieh did not engage in virtuous [government] but in military power and [thus] hurt the families of the hundred cognomens. The families of the hundred cognomens were not able to bear him. Tang, who later becomes the first Shang ruler, takes the lead of the insurgents, succeeds in toppling Jie, and ascends the throne of the Son of Heaven." At the beginning of chapter 3 the story is told once again, and here, before the decisive assault Jie explains to his supporters (Nienhauser I,43, my underscores): "I call upon you people to come. Listen to everything I say! It is not that I, this young man, dare to course disorder, but that the Yu-Hsia committed many crimes. I am in awe of the supreme deity and must chastise him. Now the Hsia has committed many crimes and Heaven [*tian*] has ordered [*ming*] me to condemn him. …" Endowed with this mandate, Tang is victorious and establishes the new dynasty. Later on the transition from the Shang to the Zhou is described in similar terms.

[3] Cf. F.-H. Mutschler, Norm und Erinnerung. Anmerkungen zur sozialen Funktion von Geschichtsschreibung und historischem Epos im 2. Jh. v. Chr., in: M. Braun / A. Haltenhoff / F.-H. Mutschler (ed.), *Moribus antiquis res stat Romana*. Römische Werte und römische Literatur im 3. und 2. Jh. v. Chr., München – Leipzig 2000 [= Beiträge zur Altertumskunde 134], 85–124.

[4] Cat. 9,1–3.

friends. By two qualities—daring in war and, when peace came, fairness—they took care both of themselves and of their commonwealth.

Livy expresses the same view already in his preface.[1]

But the interpretation of Rome's rise is only one side of the story. After the elimination of Carthage and the establishment of Rome's world-wide dominion, Sallust (and Livy) observe a general <u>decline</u> of morals. In Sallust's words:[2]

> Hence it was the desire for money first of all, and then for empire, which grew; and those factors were the kindling (so to speak) of every wickedness. For avarice undermined trust, probity and all other good qualities; instead, it taught men haughtiness, cruelty, to neglect the gods, to regard everything as for sale. ··· At first these things grew gradually, sometimes they were punished; but after, when the contamination had attacked like a plague, the community changed and the exercise of command, from being the best and most just, became cruel and intolerable.[3]

The possible or even probable consequence of this development is not made explicit in the immediate context, but it is apparent to authors and readers anyway: If Rome forfeits the virtues by which she gained and preserved her empire she will lose the empire as well.

The passages quoted so far refer only to the one case Rome. Already in the preface of the *Catiline*, however, Sallust had formulated the general rule, too:[4]

For command is easily held by means of the same quality as it was acquired initially; but, when toil is replaced by an attack of indolence, and self-control and fairness by one of lust and haughtiness, there is a change in fortune as well as in morals and behaviour. Hence command (*imperium*) is always transferred to the best from the less good.

Thus we can state that both Chinese and Roman historical thinking cherishes the idea that as far as the great political units are concerned there is a close link between "doing" and "faring", between "action" and "consequence" in so far as moral goodness is successful, while moral badness fails.

Now, in order not to draw preposterous parallels I point out that there are two differences which should not be overlooked. The first one concerns the concrete moulding of the respective morals. They differ in so far as on the Roman side the stress is on military competence and valour whereas on the Chinese side the ability of good governance is in the foreground. This first difference is connected with the second one that on the

---

① Thus he states e.g. (§ 9): "My wish is that each reader will pay the closest attention to the following: how men lived, what their moral principles were, under what leaders and by which measures at home and abroad our empire was won and expanded." In the course of his work it becomes clear that he attributes Rome's success to the same moral qualities as his predecessors.

② Cat. 10,3–4 and 6.

③ Livy sees things in the same way. In the second half of § 9 of the preface, in the first half of which he had talked about the specific ways of life and morals which had gained and preserved the empire, he states: "then let him [i.e. the reader] follow in his mind how, as discipline broke down bit by bit, morality first foundered; how it next subsided in ever greater collapse and then began to topple headlong in ruin – until the advent of our own age, in which we can endure neither our vices not the remedies needed to cure them.

④ Cat. 2,4–5.

Chinese side the rulership in question is internal rulership, i.e. the rulership of dynasties over one and the same realm, namely the All under heaven, whereas on the Roman side the rulership in question is that of one polity over others. That means that on the Chinese side the talk is about domestic, on the Roman side about foreign politics, to put it pointedly. Nevertheless–and this is the decisive point–the parallel of the idea of a direct connection between "doing" and "faring" remains.

How can we explain this parallel? I can think of two explanations which do not exclude but complement each other. The first one is that there may be some truth to the claim of a "doing-faring-connection" in macro-politics. All historical developments, to be sure, have a multiplicity of causes, but on the other hand it cannot be doubted that proper governance, regard for the people etc. are as good a fundament of stable domestic rule as military discipline and justice are for stable rule over an empire. Thus it could be that both historiographical traditions, at least to a certain extent, simply reflect a historical truth.

But apart from this another factor might play a role. I suspect that there exists something like a basic human desire for justice. It is easier to cope with the vicissitudes of life if we have the feeling that in these vicissitudes some law is operative and that in the end the course of events is a just one. As far as historiography is concerned the tendency towards such a view is probably particularly strong in histriographical traditions with a fundamentally moralistic outlook as it is characteristic for both ancient Chinese and Roman historiography. This is not to say that the claim we are talking about is made against better knowledge, but it is a claim towards which Chinese and Roman historians will be naturally inclined as long as they are not refuted by historical facts. So much for the level of macro-developments like the rise and fall of dynasties and empires.

II

But how about the micro-level of individual lives? Though it is always dangerous to make general statements of this kind, it can be safely asserted that in terms of individual lives history is not just throughout, i.e. that there are always cases in which a morally good person meets with failure and others in which a morally bad person is awarded success. In the second part of my paper I want to investigate how the ancient Chinese and Roman historians deal with this fact.[①]

I think that two strategies can be distinguished. The first one consists in concentrating on those cases in which on the level of individual lives, too, the connection between morals and outcome does seem to work. This concerns in particular individuals who belong to the uppermost layer of the socio-political hierarchy and whose affairs are therefore closely connected with that of the respective polity.

On the Chinese side, this applies e.g. to the *Shangshu*, whose texts deal almost exclusively with the affairs of the central rulers so that the distinction between the fate of individuals and that of dynasties, actually, does not make much sense. But it also holds for many stories of the *Zuozhuan*, where kings and princes are concerned. One case in point is in the section on the fourth year of Yin Gong that of the usurper Zhou Xu. Zhou

---

① One possible way out was, obviously not open to them: the belief in remuneration and retaliation for one's deeds in this life in another life after death, as it is manifested e.g. in the ancient Egyptian idea of a "Judgment of the Dead" and the Christian idea of a "Last Judgment". Both ancient Chinese and ancient Roman cultures were too matter of fact than that belief in a life of the individual after death would have found general dissemination. So how did the Chinese and Roman historians deal with the fact that the nexus between "doing" and "faring" on the level of individual lives does not hold in each case?

Xu murders his older brother, assumes power in the state of Wei and decides to attack the neighbouring state Zheng. These events are observed at the court of Lu, whose ruler asks one of his advisers whether Zhou Xu could be successful. The adviser answers decidedly to the negative.① In the next paragraph the narrative leads back to the state of Wei and describes how Zhou Xu, in consequence of his despotic behaviour, falls victim to a conspiracy. On the whole the *Zuozhuan*'s view of history is unambiguous. Man holds his destiny in his hands. Morally good behaviour leads to success, morally bad behaviour leads to failure. Thus it is fitting that the *Zuozhuan* has been called "an ethical treatise in historical disguise".②

Sima Qian's interpretation of history is–seen on the whole–certainly less naive than that of the *Zuozhuan*, but in the *Biography*–part of the *Shiji* we find quite a few cases where Sima Qian's interpretation follows a similar line. A good example is the biography of Shang Yang, the first reformer in the state of Qin. The reforms effected by Shang Yang as minister are geared towards centralisation and militarisation and actually lead to a considerable strengthening of the Qin state. But these reforms are interpreted by Sima Qian as a deviation from the old 'way', according to which the ruler is supposed to rule by example and not by laws; and correspondingly the rigorousness with which Shang Yang pushes through his policies of reform is criticised as lacking feeling and as being arrogant. That after the death of the ruler whose minister he was, Shang Yang meets his own death as a result of intrigue among the aristocrats that are envious of him seems to Sima Qian merely the just retribution for his morally reprehensible behaviour: "That he ended in such ill repute in the state of Qin is not without reason!"③

In the works of the Roman historians we can observe this interpretative pattern as well, even if, on the whole, more rarely. If we look e.g. at the first books of Livy we do find examples of men who either develop a fundamental viciousness or commit grave moral errors and who accordingly end badly. In Book 1 Mettius Fufetius, the leader of Alba Longa is a case in point. He tries to outmanoeuvre the Romans by devious schemes (1,27,1), but ends up being quartered (1,28,10). In Book 3 former consul, later decimvir Appius Claudius develops tyrannical traits (2,36ff.). Among other things he tries to get hold of a plebeian girl, young Verginia, who when his schemes are in the process of succeeding is killed by her father who sees no other way to preserve her integrity (3,44–48). This event, however, turns out to be the beginning of the end for Claudius. After unsuccessful attempts to extricate himself from the situation he has to face a trial and when it becomes clear that he has no chance to be acquitted he takes his own life (3,58).

More examples of the same or of the complementary kind, i.e. of good people rewarded with success, could be collected both from the Chinese and the Roman texts. But it is, nevertheless, clear that the wish to see in the course of events a consistent "action–consequence–connection" at work carries only so far. History is not always just. Sometimes the wicked do succeed and the good do fail. It is interesting to see that vis–à–vis this

---

① *Zuo Zhuan*, Yin Gong 4th year (Watson, pp.7–8): "I have heard of gaining the support of one's people through virtue, but I have never heard of doing so through violence. To try to do so through violence is like trying to straighten out threads by further tangling them. No Chou-hsü relies on military force and is quite ready to resort to cruelty. Relying on military force, he has few followers; ever ready to resort to cruelty, he has few allies. Anyone whose followers turn against him and whose allies desert him will find it difficult to accomplish anything. Military force is like fire–if it is not kept in check, it will end by consuming the user. Chou-hsü has assassinated his sovereign and used his people tyrannously. And yet he makes no attempt to practice true virtue by hopes to achieve success through violence–he will never escape."

② B.Watson, *Early Chinese Literature*, New York 1962, p.47.

③ *Shiji* 68 (Watson, Qin Dynasty, p. 99).

situation both Chinese and Roman historians develop a second strategy – apart from that of looking the other way. This second strategy consists in compensating the injustice of history by the justice of historiography: In history the wicked may be successful and the good fail, historiography will make up for it by calling the wicked wicked and the good good and by transmitting this judgment to posterity.

The situation in which cases of injustice of history occur most frequently is that of an autocratic regime where the ruler is able to decide on the spur of the moment about the fate of people and often enough does so with, in fact, fatal consequences. In ancient China – in contrast with Rome – the monarchical form of government is the norm. This may be one reason for that the articulation of just judgment, independent of external success of failure, is from early on considered as an important task of the historian. According to Sima Qian Confucius in his *Spring and Autumn Annals* made a critical judgment of the rights and wrongs of a period of two hundred and forty-two years in order to provide a standard of rules and ceremonies for the world. He criticized the emperors, reprimanded the feudal lords, and condemned the high officials in order to make known the business of a true ruler.[1]

In the *Zuozhuan* we read of four historian brothers the first of whom records dutifully the assassination of the Duke of the principality by his minister. For doing so he gets executed by the minister, only to be followed by two younger brothers, who record the event in the same way, get executed, and are followed by the fourth brother, who once agin records the event in the same way but whom the usurper finally lets have his way.[2] The image of the historian who is dedicated to nothing but the truth and who records what has to be recorded without taking into account even his own wellbeing is impressive. As to Sima Qian there can be no doubt that, especially in the biographical part of his work, he sees his task to a considerable extent as securing the just evaluation of the achievements of ministers and generals, but also of other individuals, and this especially in cases in which good men (or women) did not meet with acknowledgment and success. Certainly not by coincidence, an impressive example is Li Guang, who served under the three emperors Wendi, Jingdi, and Wudi in several military functions, in particular as general against the Xiongnu. He distinguished himself through strategic competence, leadership and personal courage, but also suffered defeats (though not because of his mistakes according to Sima Qian). At the end of his career he gets into a quarrel with a colleague whom he has been subordinated to by the emperor. After a victorious battle which concludes the campaign, but does not lead to the capture of the leader of the enemy, he is called in to report. Too proud to be questioned by petty officials, he commits suicide. In Sima Qian this reads as follows:[3]

> Then he went in person to headquarters and, when he got there, said to his officers, „Since I was old enough to wear my hair bound up, I have fought over seventy engagements, large and small, with the Xiongnu. This time I was fortunate enough to join the general in chief in a campaign against the soldiers of the Shanyu

---

[1]　*Shiji* 130 (Watson 1958, p. 50f.).

[2]　*Zuo Zhuan*, Xiang Gong 25th year (Watson, p. 147): "The grand historian wrote in his records: 'Ts'ui Shu assassinated his ruler.' Ts'ui Shu had him killed. The historian's younger brother succeeded to the post antd wrote the same thing. He too was killed, as was another brother. When a forth brother came forward to write, Ts'ui Shu finally desisted. Meanwhile, when the assistant historian living south of the city heard that the grand historians had been killed, he took up his bamboo tablets and set out for the court. Only when he learned that the fact had been recorded did he turn back."

[3]　*Shiji* 109 (Watson 1993, Han II, p. 126).

himself, but he shifted me to another division, and sent me riding around by the long way. On top of that, I lost my way. Heaven must have planned it this way! Now I am over sixty—much too old to stand up to a bunch of petty clerks and their list of charges!" Then he drew his sword and cut his throat. All the officers and men in his army wept at the news of his death, and when word reached the common people, those who had known him and those who had not, old men and young boys alike, were all moved to tears by his fate.

Other examples of the kind could be added. In addition, there are cases in which Sima Qian's judgment is neutral or negative, as well as cases in which certain persons in spite of their influence and power during life time are denied a biography of their own.

It is, finally in the same vein when Sima Qian's successor Ban Gu, the author of the *Hanshu*, presents his reader with a table in which he evaluates according to Confucian morals more than 2000 persons of all of Chinese history by putting them into three times three rubrics: top top, top middle, top bottom, middle top, middle middle, middle bottom, bottom top, bottom middle, bottom bottom.[1] However these persons fared in history, whether they succeeded or failed, historiography makes sure that posterity will appreciate them according to their true merits.

On the Roman side things are not as clear cut. If we leave aside the semi-legendary regal period we realize that in the representations of the republican period truly blatant cases of history's injustice are not so easy to find. But with the coming into being of monarchical rule during the dictatorship of Caesar things change. The most obvious case in point is that of the younger Cato. He is the exemplary good man who after Caesar's victory sees his cause lost and commits suicide. It is remarkable to see how well, in contrast with history, both historiography and historical epics took care of him.[2] Already his contemporary Sallust put him on one level with his opponent and conqueror Caesar;[3] Livy, as the experts assume, presented him in an even more favourable light;[4] Virgil attributed him the honorable place of a judge in the underworld;[5] Lucan, finally, made him one of the heroes, if not the hero of his epic poem.[6]

But it is under the fully established imperial regime, with problematic emperors like Tiberius, Nero, Domitian, that the possible discrepancy between "doing" and "faring" becomes most obvious. And it is the historian of this period, Tacitus, who from the beginning of his historical work makes the compensation of the injustice of history one of his foremost tasks. This concerns a whole series of men who proved themselves as able administrators and competent militaries. Tacitus considered it his duty to secure for such men, even

---

[1] *Hanshu* 20.

[2] For the most rrecent treatment of the subject see S. Wussow, *Die Persönlichkeit des Cato Uticensis-Zwischen stoischer Moralphilosophie und republikanischem Politikverständnis*, Diss. Düsseldorf 2004.

[3] Cf. the famous pair of speeches and the subsequent "syncrisis" in Cat. 51-54.

[4] Cf. e.g. Wussow (footnote 19), , esp. 7f., 237ff., 273f.

[5] Aeneid 8,666-670.

[6] Cf. already the famous line at the beginning of the work (1,126): *Victrix causa deis placuit, sed victa Catoni* - "The victorious cause pleased the gods, but the defeated one Cato".

though many of them finally had fallen from grace, the acknowledgment they deserved.[①] But the compensational function of his writing is even more clearly visible where he deals with the conduct of the senatorial elite in Rome. In almost daily contact with the emperor the majority of the senators, be it for fear or for greed, orientated their actions not towards the good of the *res publica* or general moral principles, but towards their own interest. That quite a number of them descended to shameless acts of flattery and malice, whereas many others kept a cowardly silence, was the depressing truth, which the historian had to confront. For a special topic, the discussions in the senate, Tacitus explicitly formulates the principle which guided his historiographical reaction to this situation (3,65,1):

> My purpose is not to relate at length every notion, but only such as were conspicuous for excellence or notorious for infamy. This I regard as history's highest function, to let no worthy action (*virtutes*) be uncommemorated and to hold out the reprobation of posterity as a terror to evil words and deeds (*prava dicta factaque*).

It seems to me that Sima Qian, could have described his practice in very similar, though more general terms.

On the whole, we can state that the parallelism between Chinese and Roman historiography exists on the level of the microstructure of the course of events as well as on that of macrostructure. Just as on the macro-level the Chinese idea of the mandate of heaven has its counterpart in Sallust's idea that authority/dominance (*imperium*) is always transferred from the less to the more deserving, so on the micro-level both Chinese and Roman historians, on the one hand, concentrate on cases were individuals seem to be rewarded and punished according to merit and, on the other hand, in cases where the injustice of history is obvious, attempt to compensate it through the justice of historiography.

However, it is clear that the observation of this kind of parallels is just the beginning. In a second step we would now have to take a closer look at the material and elaborate on the differences which undoubtedly exist within the parallelism, and in a third step one should try to put the parallels and differences in a wider literary and cultural context. Yet due to the special organisational framework within which this paper came into being we have to leave these undertakings to another occasion.

Translations Quoted:
Chinese Works
Shu Jing:
B.Karlgren, *The Book of Documents*, Stockholm 1950
Zuo Zhuan:
The Tso chuan. Selections from China's Oldest Narrative History, transl. by B.Watson, New York 1989

[①] Thus, already in his first work, the small biography of his father in law, he sees to that, in spite of Domitian's animosity, Agricola was recognized and acknowledged by the public as the man who completed the conquest of Britain. And in his major works he deals in similarly honorific fashion with many of the victims of Tiberius', Nero's, and Domitian's suspicion and jealousy, as e.g. with Cn. Domitius Corbulo, who under three emperors had served successfully in different parts of the world before I the end was forced to commit suicide at Nero's order.

Sima Qian, Shi Ji:

B.Watson, *Ssu—ma Ch' ien. Grand Historian of China*, New York 1958 [monograph with translations of individual chapters = Watson 1958]

Sima Qian, *Records of the Grand Historian*, 3 vols. (Qin, Han I, Han II), transl. by B. Watson, revised edition, Hong Kong – New York 1993

The Grand Scribe' s Records, transl. by W.N. Nienhauser et al., vol. 1, Bloomington 1994

Roman Works

Sallust:

Sallust, *Catiline' s War, The Jugurthine War, Histories*, transl. by A.J. Woodman, London 2007 (Penguin Classics)

Livy:

Livy, *The Rise of Rome. Books1–5. A new translation*, by T.J. Luce, Oxford 1998 (Oxford World' s Classics)

Tacitus:

Tacitus, *The Annals and The Histories*, transl. by A.J. Church and W.J. Brodribb, ed. by M. Hadas, New York 2003 (Modern Library)

Comparing ancient worlds: comparative history as comparative advantage[*]

Walter Scheidel, Stanford University

Abstract: Chinese historians of the Greco-Roman world can and should make a significant contribution to this field by promoting the comparative analysis of ancient civilizations in eastern and western Eurasia.

Keywords: Comparative History, History of scholarship, Ancient History

The 2012 International Symposium on Ancient World History in China served as a means of promoting dialogue between Chinese and western scholars working on the history of ancient western Eurasia. Chinese participation was strong: the official program lists 173 domestic participants, compared to 28 international scholars. A large majority of papers dealt with issues of 'western' ancient history without reference to the early history of China. 20 out of 107 presentations, or 19 percent, were explicitly comparative or cross-cultural in nature.[1] This represents an encouraging increase relative to the balance observed at the Third International Conference on Ancient History held at Fudan University seven years earlier: at that event, only 8 papers out of 62 (30 by Chinese scholars, 30 by Europeans and Americans, and 2 by Japanese), or 13 percent, fell in that category.[2] Even so, the continuing reluctance to engage more vigorously in comparative history is a reason for concern, given that both western and—especially—Chinese scholars stand to make significant contributions in this area. In this paper, I argue that for pragmatic as well as intellectual reasons, a comparative approach ought to be a priority for Chinese scholarship on the ancient world.

Academics in the People's Republic of China who wish to further our understanding of the ancient history of western Eurasia continue to face considerable obstacles. The most serious problem is that the study of the Greco-Roman world in particular is now a highly mature field. According to my own survey of the main bibliographical tool in this field, the periodical *L'Année Philologique*, publications in Classics

---

[*] This paper is a revised version of my earlier working paper 'Comparative history as comparative advantage: China's potential contribution to the study of ancient Mediterranean history', Princeton/Stanford Working Papers in Classics, Version 1.0, April 2006 (www.princeton.edu/~pswpc).

[1] Program, 2012 international symposium on ancient world history in China. 2012 congress of the society of ancient and medieval world history in China (SAMWHC), June 16–18, 2012, Nankai University, Tianjin, P.R. China.

[2] 3rd International conference on ancient history, Fudan University, Shanghai, 17–21 August 2005: Proceedings.

numbered approximately 750,000 between 1924 to 1992, and probably amount to around one million overall.[①] Every year, out of 18,000 publications in Classics, over 4,000 titles appear under the rubric of 'ancient history', accompanied by many more publications with a historical dimension. To this we must add the smaller but highly technical literature in Egyptology, Sumerology, Assyriology, Hittitology, Jewish Studies, and Iranian Studies, to name just the main branches of Early Near Eastern scholarship. Professional engagement with this enormous body of scholarship requires familiarity with a whole range of languages – my breakdown shows that English, German, French and Italian are of broadly equivalent importance, cumulatively accounting for some ninety to ninety-five per cent of all recent publications–, as well as access to substantial holdings of books and journals. The list of journals covered by *L'Année Philologique* now includes about 1,000 periodicals, several hundred of which are of immediate relevance to ancient historians. Another survey that I undertook over a decade ago, analyzing the background of ancient historians who held academic positions in anglophone countries in the late 1990s, yielded a total of 630 university-employed specialists in Greek and Roman history alone.[②] All this gives western scholarship a huge comparative advantage over newcomers that even substantial investments in the Chinese academic infrastructure are unlikely to reduce to any significant degree. Furthermore, the persistent intellectual stagnation of much of ancient history must make us wonder whether the emulation of the conventional efforts of most western scholars– by aiming to produce work in the same mold – should in fact be regarded as a desirable objective, let alone as the most promising way forward.

The practice of ancient history in Japan provides a real-life test case. Thanks to its post-war economic and political development, Japanese institutions of higher learning have been able to commit substantial funds to the acquisition of bibliographical resources in this field. At the same time, the ancient history of western Eurasia and North Africa has continued to occupy a rather marginal position in that country, at least compared to western academia. This places Japan in an intermediate position between the main western countries, with their thousands of academic positions, graduate programs, and historically grown libraries with relevant books numbering in the tens of thousands on the one hand, and China, with its emergent commitment to the study of foreign ancient history on the other. In a sense, one could say that ancient history in Japan is now where ancient history in China might one day be. This makes a closer look at Japan's overall contribution to the development of the discipline all the more interesting. This task is greatly facilitated by a comprehensive bibliography of work on the ancient Mediterranean and Near East produced by Japanese scholars in the twentieth century, published as a double issue of the journal *Kodai* in 2001/02.[③] This collection enumerates some 3,500 titles, half of them on the ancient Near East, an area in which Japanese scholarship has indeed made its mark in the international arena, and half on Greece and Rome. However, only thirty of the latter, or 1.7 per cent, were published in western languages, and more than half of those (eighteen) in a single conference volume.[④] This has seriously curtailed the impact of this work on scholarship outside Japan.

---

① W. Scheidel, 'Continuity and change in classical scholarship: a quantitative survey, 1924–1992', *Ancient Society* 28 (1997), 265–289.

② W. Scheidel, 'Professional historians of classical antiquity in the English-speaking world: a quantitative survey', *Ancient History Bulletin* 13 (1999), 151–156.

③ 'Bibliography: The ancient Mediterranean world. Studies by Japanese scholars in the 20th century', *Kodai* 11/12 (2001/02). I am grateful to Prof. Ryoji Motomura for a copy of this issue.

④ T. Yuge and M. Doi (eds.), *Forms of control and subordination in antiquity* (Leiden, 1988). Several others appeared in the Japanese journal *Kodai*, which is not well represented in western libraries.

Emergent Chinese scholarship faces a considerable risk of being trapped in a similarly marginal position. This trend is already in evidence in the survey of Roman studies in China prepared by Wang Naixin in 2002, which shows a similar picture of predominantly Chinese-language scholarship for domestic consumption.[1] To be sure, this is not to say that up-to-date presentations of Greco-Roman history for a Chinese readership is not a valid and indeed necessary endeavor: however, for present purposes, we are concerned in the first instance with China's potential to produce genuinely original research and participate meaningfully in international debates within this field. This is particularly relevant because ancient history, or Classics in general, has traditionally been a 'globalized' area of study that transcends national and linguistic boundaries, but has at the same time been permeated (and often sustained) by a strong eurocentric bias. More substantial contributions by East Asian scholars would not only enhance their own standing but also help to widen the ambit and horizons of the field as a whole.

This is why China's comparative advantage merits especial attention: its great potential to contribute to comparative world history. Comparative history has many benefits. In the most general terms, it makes it possible to distinguish historically common features from culturally specific or unique characteristics and developments, helps us to identify variables that were critical to particular historical outcomes, and allows us to assess the nature of a given system in the broader context of structurally similar entities (such as, for example, all city-state cultures or all agrarian empires). Comparisons may be employed in order to evaluate empirical evidence in relation to a predictive theory. This approach aims for the testing of general sociological principles or what have been called 'robust processes': the search for configurations of conditions that produce particular outcomes. A second major category of comparative historical research is sometimes labeled 'analytical comparison' or 'contrast of contexts'. This method focuses on comparisons between equivalent units for the purpose of identifying independent variables that help explain shared or contrasting patterns and occurrences. It applies comparisons to bring out the unique features of particular cases to show how these features shape more general social processes. Themes and questions serve as a framework for pointing out differences between cases. This approach helps to preserve the historical integrity of each case, and ultimately aims to define features of one system more sharply by comparison with conceptually or functionally equivalent features in another system.[2] Put more simply, we cannot really hope to understand developments in one system—say, the Roman empire, or the Han empire—unless we have some appreciation of how things turned out in broadly analogous cases: without comparisons, we can never know if particular outcomes were common or rare, and which variables were endowed with causative agency. To some extent, the historical study of a single case –a single empire, in our case–can only result in the antiquarian accumulation of data and untestable and therefore inherently arbitrary claims about significance and causality.

The early history of China and the Mediterranean is marked by initial convergence followed by ultimate

[1] N. Wang, 'A survey of Roman studies in China', *Kleos* 7 (2002), 319–334. I am grateful to Prof. Wang Naixin for a copy of this article.

[2] E. V. Bonnell, 'The uses of theory, concepts and comparison in historical sociology', *Comparative Studies in Society and History* 22 (1980), 156–173; T. Skocpol and M. Somers, 'The uses of comparative history in macrosocial inquiry', *Comparative Studies in Society and History* 22 (1980), 174–197. See also H.-G. Haupt and J. Kocka (eds.), *Geschichte und Vergleich* (Frankfurt, 1996); J. Mahoney and D. Rueschemeyer (eds.), *Comparative historical analysis in the social sciences* (Cambridge, 2003).

divergence. In the first two centuries CE, for the first time in history, two states controlled up to one-half of the human species: the Roman empire in the west and the Han empire in the east. At the most basic level of resolution, the circumstances of their creation were not very different. In the east, the Shang and Western Zhou periods created a shared cultural framework for the Warring States, with the gradual consolidation of numerous small polities into a handful of large kingdoms which were finally united by the westernmost marcher state of Qin. In the Mediterranean, we can observe comparable political fragmentation and gradual expansion of a unifying civilization, in this case Greek, followed by the gradual formation of a handful of major Warring States (the Hellenistic kingdoms in the east, Rome-Italy, Syracuse and Carthage in the west), and likewise eventual unification by the westernmost marcher state, the Roman-led Italian confederation.

By contrast, the most substantial differences occurred both before and after this period of convergent consolidation. *Before*, in that Mediterranean state formation was secondary to, and to some extent parasitical upon, much older traditions in the Fertile Crescent, where the first empire, Akkad, predated the Roman empire by 2,000 years. The Shang-Western Zhou tradition notwithstanding, China lacked any such precursors, and exemplifies primary imperial state formation on a grand scale. And *after*, with regard to the final fates of these two ancient super-empires. It is true that initially, destabilization occurred again in strikingly similar ways: both empires came to be divided into two halves, one that contained the original core but was more exposed to the main 'barbarian' periphery (the west in the Roman case, the north in China), and a traditionalist half in the east (Rome) and south (China). The more exposed halves experienced fragmentation into a small number of sizeable successor states that came under foreign leadership but retained imperial institutions. Eventually, however, their paths diverged quite significantly. In China, disunity lasted from the 310s to 589 CE, a bit over a quarter of a millennium, until the Sui regime achieved re-unification. This event spawned a series of regimes that have since maintained territorial cohesion with only relatively brief spells of fragmentation in the tenth, twelfth/thirteenth, and twentieth centuries. In western Eurasia, an attempt to bring about unification some 140 years after the formal division of the Roman empire in 395 CE was partly successful: in demographic terms, perhaps half of the core of the former western empire was recovered by the Eastern Roman empire, but was soon lost again, and this time for good. In the following century, the Arab invasions reduced the Eastern empire to a small fraction of its former size. In the West, Roman imperial institutions were gradually eroded during the second half of the first millennium CE, resulting in pervasive political fragmentation that reached a nadir around 1000 CE. In the eastern and southern Mediterranean, by contrast, imperial traditions were maintained by a series of Islamic regimes from the Umayyads to the Ottomans, for the most part up to 1918. Thus, the sixth and seventh centuries CE witnessed what I propose to call the 'First Great Divergence' between the eastern and western ends of the Eurasian land mass, when the first of several reunifications of China succeeded and that of the Roman empire failed. For the following 1400 years, this divergence created a lasting bifurcation and divergent tracks of path dependence: while the tradition of universal world empire continued to thrive in China, it survived only in diminished form in the eastern part of the former Roman empire, and de facto-if not ideationally-vanished from much of Europe. The long-term impact of this development on world history-and ultimately on the much more debated (second) 'Great Divergence' between modern growth in Europe and stagnation in later imperial China–has barely begun to be considered by contemporary scholarship.[1]

Overall, systematic comparisons between the Greco–Roman world and ancient China have been very rare (both in absolute terms and relative to the total amount of scholarship in either field), and moreover largely confined to the sphere of intellectual and cultural history. Over the last few years, a number of studies have focused on the nature of moral and scientific thought in Greece and China. The most active proponent of this line of inquiry has been Geoffrey Lloyd, with several books to date.[2] Further efforts in the same area have been undertaken by a number of other scholars.[3] However, there are no comparable studies of Roman and Chinese 'high culture', and, more importantly, virtually no similarly detailed comparative work on the political,

---

[1]　For this concept, see K. Pomeranz *The great divergence: China, Europe, and the making of the modern world economy* (Princeton, 2000). The literature on this topic is substantial and rapidly expanding. By contrast, the 'First Great Divergence' has yet to be properly conceptualized in history and historical sociology. I address this issue in forthcoming work.

[2]　G. Lloyd, *Adversaries and authorities: investigations into ancient Greek and Chinese science* (Cambridge, 1996); G. Lloyd and N. Sivin, *The way and the word: science and medicine in early China and Greece* (New Haven, 2002); G. Lloyd, *The ambitions of curiosity: understanding the world in ancient Greece and China* (Cambridge, 2003), *Ancient worlds, modern reflections: philosophical perspectives on Greek and Chinese science and culture* (Oxford, 2004), and *The delusions of invulnerability: wisdom and morality in ancient Greece, China and today* (London, 2005).

[3]　The excellent survey by J. Tanner, 'Ancient Greece, early China: Sino–Hellenic studies and comparative approaches to the classical world. A review article', *Journal of Hellenic Studies* 129 (2009), 89–109 provides the best starting point. Pertinent work includes L. A. Raphals, *Knowing words: wisdom and cunning in the classical tradition of China and Greece* (Ithaca, 1992); D. L. Hall and R. T. Ames, *Anticipating China: thinking through the narratives of Chinese and Western culture* (Albany, 1995) and *Thinking from the Han: self, truth, and transcendence in Chinese and Western culture* (Albany, 1998) ; F.–H. Mutschler, 'Vergleichende Beobachtungen zur griechisch–römischen und altchinesischen Geschichtsschreibung', *Saeculum* 48 (1997), 213–253; X. Lu, *Rhetoric in ancient China, fifth to third century B.C.E.: a comparison with classical Greek rhetoric* (Columbia, 1998); S. Kuriyama, *The expressiveness of the body and the divergence of Greek and Chinese medicine* (New York, 1999); D. Schaberg, 'Travel, geography, and the imperial imagination in fifth–century Athens and Han China', *Comparative Literature* 51 (1999), 152–191; F. Jullien, *Detour and access: strategies of meaning in China and Greece* (New York, 2000); S. Shankman and S. W. Durrant, *The siren and the sage: knowledge and wisdom in ancient Greece and China* (Albany, 2000) and *Early China/Ancient Greece: thinking through comparisons* (Albany, 2002); F.–H. Mutschler, 'Zu Sinnhorizont und Funktion griechischer, römischer und altchinesischer Geschichtsschreibung', in *Sinn (in) der Antike* (Mainz, 2003), 33–54; J.–P. Reding, *Comparative essays in early Greek and Chinese rational thinking* (Aldershot, 2004); F.–H. Mutschler, 'Tacitus und Sima Qian: eine Annäherung', Philologus 150 (2006), 115–135 and 'Tacitus und Sima Qian: Persönliche Erfahrung und historiographische Perspektive', *Philologus* 151 (2007), 127–152; M. Sim, *Remastering morals with Aristotle and Confucius* (Cambridge, 2007); J. Yu, *The ethics of Confucius and Aristotle: mirrors of virtue* (London, 2007); F.–H. Mutschler, 'Tacite (et Tite–Live) et Sima Qian: la vision politique d'historiens latins et chinois', *Bulletin de l' Association Guillaume Bud*é (2008/2), 123–155; H. J. Kim, *Ethnicity and foreigners in ancient Greece and China* (London, 2009) (cf. also M.–C. Poo, *Enemies of civilization: attitudes toward foreigners in ancient Mesopotamia, Egypt, and China* (Albany, 2005)).

social, economic or legal history of Hellenistic, Roman, and ancient Chinese empires.[①] For the first time, the Stanford-based 'Ancient Chinese and Mediterranean Empires Comparative History Project' has begun to put the comparative study of these areas on a more solid basis. A series of conferences brought together experts on ancient Chinese, Hellenistic, and Roman history and resulted in collaborative volumes centered on key aspects of state formation.[②] Further research will follow, and it is hoped that this approach will eventually be more widely adopted.

This is where China's comparative advantage comes into play. Comparative history is challenging at the best of times, as it requires practitioners to draw on evidence and secondary scholarship across the manifold narrow boundaries that so effectively compartmentalize historical training and research. Yet even by these standards, comparative analysis that involves early China proves unusually demanding. The double language barrier—for both ancient sources and modern scholarship—makes it very difficult for western non-experts to acquire more than the most superficial familiarity with the pertinent body of knowledge. The persistent shortage of translations even of principal early texts greatly exacerbates this problem. While Sima Qian's *Shiji* has by now been almost (but not quite) completely translated into western languages, two-thirds of the chapters of the *Hanshu* remain untranslated, as well as the entire *Hou Hanshu* and much of the later *Zizhi tongjian*. Less prominent works are often completely inaccessible to outsiders, and the same is true of the vast number of Qin and Han documents preserved on bamboo strips and wooden tablets which shed light on administrative practices and various other facets of daily life, as well as of early stone inscriptions.[③] This puts western scholars who attempt to utilize ancient Chinese evidence at a considerable disadvantage relative to Chinese scholars wishing to access Greco-Roman sources, which tend to be much more widely available in modern translation than early Chinese texts. Publication of secondary scholarship in Chinese and Japanese creates additional linguistic obstacles. Recent advances in archaeology are particularly hard to gauge for anyone who lacks close connections to Chinese researchers: even published material is available in the first instance merely in the form of brief abstracts in English.[④] At western universities, access to these resources is de facto controlled by a small

① Social history has most recently been covered by Y. Zhou, *Festivals, feasts, and gender relations in ancient China and Greece* (Cambridge, 2010). For Rome, Hsing I-Tien, 'Rome and China: the role of the armies in the imperial succession: a comparative study' (PhD thesis, University of Hawaii at Manoa, 1980), an unpublished thesis, seems to be the main exception in a western language (and cf. M. Custers, 'Balancing acts: comparing political and cultural unification and persistence in the Roman empire during the Principate and Western Han empire', MA thesis, Utrecht, 2008). See also G. Lorenz, 'Das Imperium Romanum und das China der Han-Dynastie: Gedanken und Materialien zu einem Vergleich', *Informationen für Geschichtslehrer* 12 (1990), 9-60, and R. Motomura, 'An approach towards a comparative study of the Roman empire and the Ch'in and Han empires', *Kodai* 2 (1991), 61-69, and now S. A. M. Adshead, *China in world history* (3rd ed. New York, 2000), 4-21 and *T'ang China: the rise of the East in world history* (Basingstoke, 2004), 20-29, and M. H. Dettenhofer, 'Das römische Imperium und das China der Han-Zeit: Ansätze zu einer historischen Komparatistik', *Latomus* 65 (2006), 880-897, for brief comparisons of the Roman and Han empires. On literary and ideological constructions of the Qin-Han and Roman empires, see now F.-H. Mutschler and A. Mittag (eds.), *Conceiving the empire: Rome and China compared* (Oxford 2008). V. T. Hui, *War and state formation in ancient China and early modern Europe* (Cambridge, 2005) ranges beyond antiquity.

② www.stanford.edu/~scheidel~acme.htm. W. Scheidel (ed.), *Rome and China: comparative perspectives on ancient world empires* (New York, 2009); *State power in ancient China and Rome* (forthcoming). See also W. Scheidel, 'Fiscal regimes and the 'First Great Divergence' between eastern and western Eurasia', in P. F. Bang and C. Bayly (eds.), *Tributary empires in global history* (Basingstoke, 2011), 193-204.

③ E. Wilkinson, *Chinese history: a manual* (revised and enlarged edition, Cambridge MA, 2000), esp. 780-807, 812.

④ *China Archaeology and Art Digest* 1- (1996-).

number of experts in early Chinese language, literature and material culture who are greatly outnumbered by scholars working on the Greco-Roman world and few of whom appear to be interested in explicitly comparative perspectives.

This bottleneck between the huge wealth of historical information about early China on the one hand and most students of western antiquity on the other puts Chinese scholars in a unique position to contribute to comparative study. Instead of striving to align their research with dominant scholarship in the West which is already bloated in volume and constrained by diminishing intellectual returns on conventionally self-contained (i.e., 'classical'-Mediterranean) lines of inquiry, Chinese historians of the ancient world ought to make the most of this exciting opportunity to be at the forefront of a much-needed conceptual expansion and re-orientation of their field. Thanks to native language skills and better access to domestic sources of pertinent information, they incur far smaller costs in incorporating Chinese history into their work on the earliest western civilizations than their European and American peers, and stand to reap considerable benefits. If China has any realistic hope of making a notable contribution to Greco-Roman or more generally ancient world history, it will be in the area of comparative study. In recent years, the People's Republic has made enormous strides by exploiting its comparative advantage in the world economy. The same approach can profitably be applied to the field of ancient history. Among ancient historians, comparative history is China's unique comparative advantage. Chinese scholars should make the most of it.

中西古代史学比较刍议

刘家和　北京师范大学

摘要：古代中国史学有着与希腊罗马史学不同的特点。《荷马史诗》虽有史影，但还不能成为史书，《书》《诗》也未能成为史书，但其中却有殷鉴不远等对历史发展的某种规律性的认识。希罗多德的《历史》和修昔底德的《伯罗奔尼撒战争史》都是当时人写当时事的断代史，总体上为编年体，富有时代精神，但缺乏历史反省。在中国，形式相近的有《左传》《国语》，但性质却不同。二书虽为断代，却记载大量前言往行以为当时之事的历史渊源，表现了通史精神。此后，色诺芬的《希腊史》、波利比乌斯的 HISTORIE，李维的《罗马史》（《建城以来》）和塔西佗的《历史》（HISTORIES）《编年史》（ANNALS），有的虽记载数百年史事，形式上近似通史，但与其他史书一样都缺乏通史精神。司马迁《史记》不但记载时间长，而且以"通古今之变"为职志，是形神兼具的通史。班固等的《汉书》虽为断代史，但具有通史精神，因为西汉时期的文明史是中国古代文明史中的一个不可分离的部分。历代正史都是如此，政治上分段，文明却是连续的，这就是中国古代史学连续性的存在的具体方式。古代中国在文明史层面上未曾发生断裂，在史学史层面上同样未曾发生断裂，原因就在于通史精神传统的确立。

Abstract：Ancient Chinese historiography has some different characteristics from those of the ancient Western one. *The Iliad* and *The Odyssey* have some historical elements, but cannot be ranked among the historical works. The Chinese *Shangshu (Ancient Books)* and *Shijing (Poems)* cannot be either. But in these two books can we see that the rulers in the early Zhou period do take the historical change of decline of the Yin Dynasty and the rising of the Zhou Dynasty as a good lesson through which people can find some historical laws and lessons. *The Histories* by Herodotus and the *History of Peloponnesian War* by Thucydides are of the works on contemporary events compiled by contemporary writers. So they are full of the spirit of their time, but lack of historical reflection. In China, however, *Zuozhuan* and *Guoyu* have the contrary characteristics though they share the similar compiling style. They can also be called the histories of specific periods, but they contain a lot of stories and words in the remote ancient times as the origins of the events in their own. Therefore they can be said to have a spirit of Tongshi(a Chinese expression for the comprehensive history, emphasizing in particular the history with the changes between the ancient and the modern times as one developmental process). Later on can we read *Hellenica* by Xenophon, *Historie* by Polybius, *Roman History* by Levy, *Histories* and *Annals* by Tacitus. These books are all lack of spirit of Tongshi. Meanwhile, the *Records of the Grand Historian* by Sima Qian not only records a long period history, but takes the principle to understand all changes of both ancient and modern times as his goal. So it is completely a Tongshi. And more than that, *the Book of Former Han* by Bangu is a dynastic history. But it has Tongshi spirit too, for in a sense, the Western Han Dynasty is a succeeding part of the whole Chinese civilization history and can only be explained clearly in the context of the comprehensive process. Therefore, all dynastic histories compiled by the historians after Ban share the same spirit. This is the existent style of the historical writing in ancient China: A dynasty has its beginning and end, and the civilization medium as its existence is continuous. In ancient China, civilization history is never gapped, nor is the history of historiography. The very reason lies in the establishment of the tradition of the Tongshi Spirit.

公元前 11 世纪，在西方的希腊，荷马时代取代了迈锡尼文明，接着就是前代的文明被遗忘，《荷马史诗》十口相传，其中虽不乏前代史影，究其实终不能成为史书；在中国，则出现了周之代商，《书》、《诗》与礼乐勃兴，难怪孔子会说："郁郁乎文哉，吾从周。"《尚书》（尤其其中的周初诸诰）作为原始史料是基本无问题的。《诗经》中有神话、有民歌，但也有史实之含蕴，作为原始史料也基本是无问题的。《书》、《诗》皆不能作为严格意义上的史书，不过其中却有宝贵的史识存在。如强调"殷鉴不远，在夏后之世"，这就涉及三代历史传统以及得民心者得天下、失民心者失天下这样的对于历史发展的某种规律性的认识。在古代世界，这既是难能可贵的重大创见，也为以后中国史学的连续性的发展奠定了深厚的基础。

公元前 8 世纪以后至公元 3 世纪，在西方，希腊、罗马迭兴，由城邦逐渐向罗马大帝国的方向进展。在中国，由东周之衰而"五霸"、"七雄"，而秦、汉一统帝国。中国之诸侯国与西方之城邦，皆为小邦，而体制不同。中国之秦、汉帝国与罗马帝国，皆为跨地区的泱泱大国，而体制殊异。希腊与罗马文明之间有断裂，而三代与秦、汉之间既有明显时代质变而又有历史之紧密相连。这一段历史的过程内容相当丰富，此处只作略微提示，是为了说明双方史学之所以不同之历史背景。

古希腊希罗多德与修昔底德开创了西方史学之传统，相对于《荷马史诗》而言，他们的著作可谓凿空性的呈现。《历史》（其核心实为希腊波斯战争史）、《伯罗奔尼撒战争史》皆为当时人写当时事的断代史，几乎"前无古人"。其体例为按年叙事，而年月标志并不突出，总体而言仍属编年之体。此等史书极富时代精神，而缺乏历史反省。故黑格尔称之为"原始的历史"。与古希腊史学发生大体同时，中国有"孔子作《春秋》"之说。《春秋》原为鲁国之编年史记，明确以日系月，以月系时（四时即四季），以时系年（鲁某公某年），故在叙述之体上为编年史。《春秋》仅记鲁十二公 242 年之事，故在划分时段上为断代史。孔子对于《春秋》，是作、是述抑或是讲习传授，至今聚讼纷纭，姑且不论。据近出出土简帛文书，谓孔子曾以《春秋》授弟子，大抵近是。孟子言孔子作《春秋》之说，似难谓之空穴来风。继孔子言《春秋》者，今所能见厥为三传，而《左传》以及《国语》叙事綦详。此二书，论形式与希罗多德及修昔底德之书相近，而论性质却大异其趣。《左传》、《国语》二书在时段划分上均为断代史，前者所叙述之时间略长于《春秋》（延续到孔子去世之后一些年），后者则分国叙述，表现为国别史体裁，而在时间划分上前展至周厉王时期，《吴语》《越语》又下延至《春秋》年代以后。又前者以记事为主、记言为辅，后者则以记言为主、记事为辅。此二书皆以记春秋时期之事为主，叙事者所反映出的基本是春秋时期的时代精神（如《左传》中所记的多种外交辞令、政治论辩与文化评说体现得尤为鲜明），显然与《尚书》（尤其《周书》）有别。不过，十分值得注意的是，此二书并非纯粹的断代史，其中大量记载前言往行及其与当时之事的历史渊源关系。这就说明其中原来是有着通史精神的，与古希腊的两部历史开山之作大不相同。这也不足为怪，当时人是把当代历史看作三代的自然延续的，不管他们对于三代持正面的肯定态度，还是持反面的否定态度。

在西方，色诺芬继修昔底德而撰《希腊史》，体例一如修氏，且等而下之。到希腊化时代晚期，希腊行将为罗马征服的时候，波利比乌斯作为希腊人质寓居罗马，作 HISTORIE。不少学者将其译为"通史"，看来不妥。因为此书主题所记仅为公元前 220- 公元前 145 年间之事，历时区区七十余年，恐难冠以"通史"之号。那么它是否具有某种通史精神呢？此书前二卷为引言，略述此前地中海世界分散纷争之大局，然后以七十余年之史实说明罗马必将统治整个地中海世界。借叙述罗马征服之历史趋势，以论证地中海世界必将归于罗马统治之下的结局。故其时代特色鲜明，罗马之所赖以战胜他邦之政治体制的优势背景亦鲜明，而于西方文明传统之渊源则似乎不在其视域之内。它与修昔底德之书一样，是一部出色的编年体的史书，但不是一部通史，也不能算具有通史精神的断代史。

罗马帝国前期（公元前 27 年至公元 192 年）是经济文化繁荣时期，也是史学的繁荣时期。此时曾有若干以拉丁文、希腊文撰述的史书，其中最为重要而著名者当推李维所著之《罗马史》（本名《建城以来》）与塔西佗所著之《历史》（HISTORIES）和《编年史》（ANNALS）。李维之《罗马史》述罗马建城以来之传说与历史，历时七百余年。就其时间跨度而言，此书不妨称为通史；但就其著史的价值取向而言，却似乎不具备作为"通史"的内在支柱的"通史精神"。从此书的简短前言中就可以看出，李维认为，历史是可以给予今人以教训的，罗马过去之所以能够从小到大、从弱到强，完全凭着道德与纪律的力量，而到了他的时代，这些风纪却在衰落之中。他的希望就在于罗马人能以史为鉴，重返往日的盛世（参见《建城以来史》卷 1，穆启乐等译，吉林文史出版社，1992 年，页 3-7）。有见于当时风纪衰落，而将过去笼统地看作一份纯粹的、无发展的道德风纪的典范，这种观念是缺乏历史意识的。黑格尔曾将此书置入"反省的历史"之列，这是不无道理的。塔西佗先写了《历史》，此书所记为公元 68-96 年（即弗拉维王朝）间的历史，皆为与作者同时近三十年之事，亦即地道的现代史。其书按年记事，于体例为断代编年史。他又写了《编年史》，此书所记为公元 14-68 年（即奥古斯都去世后的 4 个罗马元首或皇帝时期）五十余年之事，恰好与随后的《历史》相衔接，因此从时段上看，为近代史。此书亦按年记事，故于体例为断代编年史。既然这两部书体例相同，那么此二书的名称又何以不同？关于这个问题，我们看不到塔西佗本人的答案。看来他是把自己的"所见世"（当代）之历史称为"历史"，而把此前自己的"所闻世"以上之历史称为"编年史"的。这种说法倒与克罗齐说相似，而其"编年史"概念则与中国传统中的编年史概念颇不相同，因为中国的编年体是与纪传体、纪事本末体等并列而存在的。

李维（B.C.59-A.D.17）的《罗马史》记七百余年之事，司马迁（B.C.145/135-90）的《史记》自黄帝始至汉武帝太初止，即使从夏代开始所记也有约二千年之事。如果就时间长度而言，这两部书都可以称为"通史"，不过如上文所言，李维的书是缺乏通史精神的形式上的"通史"，而司马迁的书则是兼具形式与精神的通史。塔西佗（A.D.55-120）的两部书一共记载了八十余年的事，班固（A.D.32-92）的《汉书》记载了西汉一代二百二十年的事。塔西佗与班固的书，就其所记时间长度而言，都可以称为"断代史"而毫无疑义。不过，班固的《汉书》虽为断代史，而具有通史精神，这就是它与塔西佗书不同之所在。

　　就生存时间而言，司马迁早于李维两个世代有余，班固与塔西佗同时而年长一个世代，不过他们都生活于大帝国（汉与罗马）时期，总体时代背景大体是相当的。因此，对于这两对史家进行适当的比较研究，也是可能且应当的。

　　古代中国在文明史层面上未曾发生断裂，在史学史的层面上同样未曾发生断裂。其原因就在于通史精神传统的确立。《史记》是一部究天人之际、通古今之变的形神兼具的通史，为以后纪传体史书开了先河。《汉书》继《史记》为以后历朝断代纪传体史书奠定了初基。由此人们可能产生疑惑，《汉书》以下的所谓历代正史，都不过是不同线段之间的先后接龙（或按亚里士多德所言为"顺联"，请参拙作《论历史发展的连续性与统一性问题》，载《北京师范大学学报》，2009 年第 1 期）而已，岂能谓之为连续？其实，《汉书》作为断代史，仅仅是就其政治史层面的王朝兴亡来划分的，而《汉书》本身就是一部西汉时期的文明史，就这一层面而言，则是中国古代文明史中的一个不可分离的一部分（按亚里士多德的说法，《汉书》是"顺接"于《史记》的，亦请参阅同上拙作）。因此，正是《汉书》开了这样一个史学传统，这就是历代正史只是朝代史的分段，而不是中国文明史的断裂。分段而不断裂，这就是中国古代史学连续性（或变与常统一）的存在的具体方式。如果再来看古希腊、罗马的史学，那么我们就难以发现这样的情况了。

西方古典文献学的名与实

张 强 东北师范大学

摘要：以希腊文、拉丁文为载体的西方古典文献学，希腊文记作"philologia"。近代西方学界在根据各自的语言整理、研究古文献借以溯源其共同的"古代"过程中，西方古典文献学的名称与内容在不同历史时期、不同语境中均曾发生过变化，但总体上的沿革相类于中国古典文献学或传统文献学，即由校雠而校雠学而文献学，最终被冠之以"古典的"则意在强调"希腊、拉丁的"这一属性。

关键词：古典文献学；希腊拉丁文本；文献校雠学

Abstract：Philologia, the ancient Greek word, is utilized as the term to denote the study of the old texts written in Greek and Latin. In the process of modern western scholars' collations and researches of Greek and Latin texts in their own language in order to trace their common past, its name and nature kept varying from time to time and language to language. However, the general route of its evolution is under the direction of the critical activities to the textual criticism and the textual criticism to Philologie or philology, and finally the Philologie with klassische or the philology with classical as epithet to denote its dedication to Greek and Latin authors.

Keywords：Philologia, Greek and Latin Texts, Textual Criticism

《中国大百科全书》于"文献学"的定义是，"以文献和文献发展规律为研究对象的一门学科。研究内容包括：文献的特点、功能、类型、生产和分布、发展规律、文献整理方法及文献与文献学发展历史等"，所附英文为"documentation science"或"documentics"；在述及西方文献学时又称，

"西方文献学也有较长的发展历史。但汉语'文献学'在西文中没有确切的对应词"。①对此，米辰峰先生在《马比荣与西方古文献学的发展》（以下简称"米文"）一文中指出："从逻辑上讲，源于西方的'文献学'没有西文对应词是不可能的；现代文献学必然是从古代文献学嬗变而来"，"与广义校雠学类似的西学理应是 diplomatics 或者 paleography，虽然它们曾经分别译为'古文书学'和'古文字学'，其实现在都可以译为'古文献学'……"。②显然，"西方文献学……较长的发展历史"，米文认为是以"diplomatics 或者 paleography"为发端，时在十七世纪晚期。

作为"以文献和文献发展规律为研究对象的一门学科"，本文中的西方古典文献学是指对希腊、拉丁文献（下限至公元六世纪中叶的"晚期古代"）的整理与研究，其名称为"klassische Philologie"，为"classical philology"。③鉴于"'文献学'在国际上尚无一个为各国普遍接受的定义"，④《中国大百科全书》的界说也可用来定义西方古典文献学。米文所说的"校雠学"，若非"广义"层面上的，则可用来解读西方古典文献学沿革的早期阶段。继希腊文、拉丁文成为"死的语言"后，近代西方学界在根据各自的语言整理、研究古文献藉以溯源其共同的"古代"的过程中，西方古典文献学的名称（"对应词"）与所指在不同历史时期、不同语境中均曾发生过变化，均曾有过争议。但"文献学"若以"documentation science"或"documentics"为名作解，无疑偏离了"西方文献学……较长的发展历史"，而"古文献学"若仅仅限于与"古希腊文和拉丁文文本"⑤相关的"paleography"或"diplomatics"，则难以厘清"源于西方的'文献学'"的名称与概念。

在发生、发展过程中，西方古典文献学的名实变化错综复杂，下文所述难免挂一漏万，不当之处尚祈学界同仁多以教正。

一

英文中的"philology"，王力先生在《中国语言学史》一书的"前言"中译作"语文学"；"语文学在中国古代称为'小学'……是有关文字的学问。⑥词源学上言之，"philology"为"借自法文、德文的词"⑦，法文、德文中的"philologie"则从希腊文"philologia"演变而来。由"philos"与"logos"复合而成的"philologia"一词最早见于柏拉图的《塞阿埃特托斯篇》（Theaetetus，146 A）。"philos"

① 中国大百科全书总编辑委员会、《图书馆学、情报学、档案学》编辑委员会编：《中国大百科全书·图书馆学、情报学、档案学》，北京：中国大百科全书出版社，2004 年，第 490—491 页。另外，项楚、张子开在其新近出版的《古典文献学》（重庆大学出版社，2010 年版，第 8 页）一书中，引据袁翰青《现代文献工作的基本概念》（《图书馆》1964 年第 2 期）称，"无论是 date（按：似应为'data'）、documents 还是 literature，都无法完全与汉语'文献'相副"（按：原文大题应作《现代文献工作基本概念》，且通篇未见述及"data"一词的概念，在探讨"相应的外文名词"一节，论者也只是对"相当于文献"的俄文 [документ 和 литература]、英文 [document 和 literature]、德文 [Dokument 和 Literatur] 在用法上的些许区别进行了较为详尽的辨析），并认为"最好的英译方法莫如干脆以汉译拼音来表示这一系列词语：Wenxian（文献），Wenxianology（文献学），Wenxianier（文献学家）"[按：除"Wenxian"，"Wenxianology"与"Wenxianier"的表述准确说应为汉语拼音加英语词缀的构词方法]。

② 米辰峰：《马比荣与西方古文献学的发展》，《历史研究》，2004 年第 5 期，第 140 页注释 3 及第 141 页。

③ 其实，"古典文献学"足以传达"klassische Philologie"或"classical philology"之所指。冠以"西方"者，意在别于以"古典文献学"为大题的中文著述，如罗孟祯编著的《古典文献学》（重庆出版社，1989 年版）、陈广忠等编著的《古典文献学》（黄山书社，2005 年版）以及项楚、张子开主编的《古典文献学》等。

④ 中国大百科全书总编辑委员会、《图书馆学、情报学、档案学》编辑委员会编：《中国大百科全书·图书馆学、情报学、档案学》，第 491 页。

⑤ 米辰峰：《马比荣与西方古文献学的发展》，第 145 页。

⑥ 王力：《中国语言学史》，太原：山西人民出版社，1981 年，"前言"，第 1—2 页。

⑦ J. E. Sandys, *A History of Classical Scholarship: from the Six Century BC to the End of the Middle Ages,* Cambridge: Cambridge University Press, 1903, Volume 1, p. 2.

意指"爱或被爱",而同属动名词的"logos"则义项繁复,可为"字、词",也可为"知识、理性",等等。在柏拉图等古典著作家的笔下,"所钟爱者"虽无确切的指向,但与"有关文字的学问"——"对字或词的钟爱"——确实存在一定的关联,致使"在我国也有人称文字学、音韵学、训诂学、校勘学为语文学。现在往往将语文学包括在语言学内。"[①]然而,"语文学(philology)和语言学(linguistics)是有分别的",王力先生认为,"前者是文字或书面语言的研究,特别着重在文献资料的考证和故训的寻求,这种研究比较零碎,缺乏系统性;后者的研究对象则是语言的本身,研究的结果可以得出科学的、系统的、细致的、全面的语言理论。中国在'五四'以前所作的语言研究,大致是属于语文学范围的"。[②]

作为外来语,"philology"在中文语境中名实的上述差异与变化,实际上与"philologia"一词本身在西方不同历史时期、不同的解读视阈密切相关。从文献学角度讲,无论是"小学"、"语文学"还是"文献资料的考证和故训的寻求"抑或"校勘学"所反映出的仅仅是"philologia"在由校勘而校勘学或由校雠而校雠学的发展变化,即西方古典文献学的早期形态,但也仅仅限于狭义层面上的校雠一学。

至若校雠学狭义与广义的区分,胡朴安、胡道静在《校雠学》一书中指出:"自其狭义言之,则比勘篇籍文字同异而求其正,谓之校雠……自其广义言之,则搜集图书,辨别真伪,考订误缪,厘次部类,暨于装潢保存,举凡一切治书事业,均在校雠学范围之内"。[③]程千帆、徐有福亦认为:"狭义的仅指改正书面材料上的文字错误,广义的则兼指研究书籍的版本、校勘、目录、典藏等方面的问题。后人往往将狭义的校雠称为校勘"。[④]纵观西方古典文献学的发展历史,除古典时代的哲学家外,希腊化时代亚历山大城图书馆驻馆学者从泽诺多托斯、卡利马克斯、埃拉托斯特奈斯的校雠实践,至阿里斯多法奈斯而成一宗,[⑤]他们"对其所集确定善本的尝试"[⑥]以及"对真本所表现出的兴趣"[⑦]经后代尤其是文艺复兴时代人文主义者对新旧约圣经的校雠才渐成体系,即所谓的"狭义校雠学"。这一传统虽也关乎到马比荣在研读中世纪文书过程中所"规范"的古文字学(paleography),但其所完善的"文书学"与西方古典文献的整理并无任何关联。

让·马比荣(Johannis Mabillon,1632—1707),法国著名僧侣学者、历史学家。针对当时一份王室特许状的真伪所引发的教派之争,他"耗时数载研究中世纪特许状及写本,并首次系统地制定了一整套检视中世纪文书真伪的标准。其所述见于1681年完成的《文书论》(De re diplomatica)一书。现代英语中由此而来的'diplomatic'一词,即常为研究法律与官方文件之术语。"[⑧]《文书论》凡六编,所及辨伪方法具体到古文书的年代(veterum instrumentorum antiquitas)、书写材料(materia)、文本与文法(scriptura et stilus)、印玺(sigillum)以及后记(subscriptio)等项。[⑨]这些标准虽旨在辨伪中世纪的文书,但就古文字学而论,从希腊化时代到中世纪晚期等各代学人对书体风格等相关问

---

① 辞海编辑委员会:《辞海》,上海:上海辞书出版社,1999年版,第1068页。

② 王力:《中国语言学史》,"前言"第1页。

③ 胡朴安、胡道静:《校雠学》,商务印书馆,1934年,第1页。

④ 程千帆、徐有福:《校雠广义·校勘编》,齐鲁书社,1998年,第4页。

⑤ 在"考订"古希腊文献"误缪"的过程中,亚历山大城图书馆驻馆学者的实践虽也旁及到版本的遴选、收藏与编目,但所及范围有限,并未形成真正意义上的学科。他们的校雠方法代代相袭,故被称为"亚历山大城学派"。

⑥ G. Thomas Tanselle, "Classical, Biblical, and Medieval Textual Criticism and Modern Editing", in *Studies in Bibliography*, Vol. 36(1983), Bibliographical Society of the University of Virginia,p. 21.

⑦ *The Cambridge History of Literary Criticism, vol.1: Classical Criticism*, edited by George A. Kennedy, Cambridge: Cambridge University Press, 1989, p. 205.

⑧ L. D. Reynolds & N. G. Wilson, *Scribes and Scholars: A Guide to the Transmission of Greek and Latin Literature*, Oxford: Oxford University Press, 1989, p.171.

⑨ 详见 Johannis Mabillon, *De re diplomatica*, libri VI, Luteciae Parisiorum, sumtibus C. Robustel, MDCCIX。

题的研究传统①经马比荣的实践才成为专门之学。但是，除了"年代、书写材料、文本与文法"外，马比荣所措意的"印玺"等为中世纪文书所独有，未见古典文献写本。古文字学作为西方古典文献整理的重要研究手段，马比荣在使之成为一门学科的过程中所"发展"是文书学，而中世纪的文书并不属于古典文献的研究范畴。

由校雠而狭义校雠学，"philologia"的早期形态大体如此。其内涵与外延的变化发生在近代，始于欧陆学界。名称上则由"philologia"而为近现代西方语言中的"Philologie"、"philologie"或"philology"，被冠之以"古典的"意在强调"希腊、拉丁的"这一属性。

二

董恩林先生在《论传统文献学的内涵、范围和体系诸问题》一文中曾言："我国文史学界所称'文献学'都是以整理、研究古文献为目的的一门传统学问，过去称为'校雠学'"。②推及到西方古典文献学的名实变化，"philologia"的"过去"当指十八世纪以前，此后则为"文献学"，且常与古典学相提并论。

在西方古典学界，德国学者F. A.沃尔夫1777年4月8日在哥廷根大学成功注册为"文献学学生"（studiosus philologiae，当时并未设置的学科门类）通常被视作该学科的开端。在学期间，沃尔夫熟读荷马史诗，并完成了柏拉图《宴饮篇》的校订及注释。1783年，沃尔夫赴哈雷大学任教，始建文献学系。"因沃尔夫的创制，校雠学（philology）已不再是附属于《圣经》及《查士丁尼法典》的学科"。③在其后的二十三年间，沃尔夫先后完成了赫西俄德《神谱》、荷马史诗等古典文献的校订及评注。在1795年出版的《荷马引论》（Prolegomena ad Homerum）一书中，沃尔夫针对荷马史诗的成书年代、著者等问题提出了独到见解，从而引发了后世对所谓"荷马问题"的大讨论。除此而外，沃尔夫在哈雷大学文献学系经常讲授"古代研究通识教育与方法"(Encyclopaedie und Methodologie der Studien des Alterthums)，课程的拉丁文名称为"Encyclopaedia philologica"。④1806年，哈雷大学被迫关闭，沃尔夫在歌德建议下把该门课程的内容启述成文，次年以《古典学发凡》（Darstellung der Altert[h]umswissenschaft）为大题在柏林出版，1833年经S. F. W.霍夫曼整理后再版。该书中，沃尔夫把希腊拉丁文法、文献阐释学、校雠学、历史学、艺术史、宗教学、古钱币学、铭文学以及希腊拉丁文献学研究史（Litterarhistorie der griechischen und lateinischen Philologie）等二十四个部分均包括在其所创立的古典学（Altert[h]umswissenschaft）研究范畴之内。⑤由"Encyclopaedia philologica"而"Altert[h]umswissenschaft"，从沃尔夫所举各项来看，与文献学相关的诸学科——文法、校雠学、文献学史等——均列在了古典一学的名目之下。沃尔夫虽然也强调古典学的核心为文献学，但他并未对二者的从属关系加以区分，致使后世言人人殊，文献学与古典学所涵盖的内容往往混为一谈。例如，休·劳埃德－琼斯在维拉莫威兹《文献学史》（Geschichte der Philologie）英译本导论中就曾指出，"严格意义上

① 从希腊化时代起，古代西方的校勘实践已不仅仅限于对写本单个字母的正误，而是在广集例证的基础上通过比对书体的异同来确定写本的年代。详见 Bradley Hudson McLean, *An introduction to Greek epigraphy of the Hellenistic and Roman Periods from Alexander the Great down to the Reign of Constantine (323 B.C.– A.D.337)*, Michigan: The University of Michigan Press, 2005, pp. 40–45。

② 董恩林：《论传统文献学的内涵、范围和体系诸问题》，《史学理论研究》，2008年第3期，第44页。

③ Hermann Funke, "F.A. Wolf: 15 Feburary 1759–8 August 1824", in *Classical Scholarship：A Bibliographical Encyclopedia*, eds. by Ward W. Briggs and William M. Calder III, Carland Publishing, In., 1990, p. 524.

④ Fr. Aug. Wolf, Darstellung der Alterthumswissenschaft nebst einer Auswahl seiner Kleinen Schriften und literarischen Zugaben zu dessen Vorlesungen über die Alterthumswissenschaft, hg. von S. F. W. Hoffmann, Leipzig 1833, 6.

⑤ Fr. Aug. Wolf, Darstellung der Alterthumswissenschaft nebst einer Auswahl seiner Kleinen Schriften und literarischen Zugaben zu dessen Vorlesungen über die Alterthumswissenschaft, hg. von S. F. W. Hoffmann, 75—76.

讲，'文献学'不应包括对遗迹的研究，尽管应包括对历史与哲学的研究。但维拉莫威兹对此的叙述则包括考古学与艺术史，因为在他看来，'文献学'与此类学科不可分离"。①H. T. 佩克在其《古典文献学史》一书的导论中对文献学的界定，除了铭文学、古文字学、钱币学、校勘、哲学以及考古与宗教外，还涉及到语言学。②

特别需要指出的一点是，始于十九世纪的比较语言学在某种程度上初与文献学的指谓相去不远，关乎到的也是对古典文献与古典语言的研究。但在发展过程中，比较语言学逐渐脱离了文献学的范畴而成为一门新的学科，所关注的仅仅是对语言本身的研究，这便使得"philology"这一"借自法、德语文的词"在英国英语中出现了"模棱两可的寓意"③。"因为对大多数英国人而言，'philology'系指'comparative philology'，而'comparative philology'则意为'比较语言学'"。④故而在英国，与德文"Philologie"相对应的词通常用"scholarship"加以表述。德裔学者 R. 普法伊费尔在牛津大学出版社出版的 *A History of Classical Scholarship：from the Beginnings to the End of the Hellenistic Age* 一书，在德国出版时则译为 *Geschichte der klassischen Philologie von den Anfängen bis zum Ende des Hellenismus*。尽管美国的古典学传统与德国一脉相承，艾伦·哈里斯 1982 年还是把德国学者维拉莫威兹的 *Geschichte der Philologie*（1921 年）译作 History of Classical Scholarship 在英美两地同时出版。

综而言之，无论是"klassische Philologie"还是"classical scholarship"，从维拉莫威兹到普法伊费尔，西方古典学者有关的文献学著述除了内容上繁简不一外，体例上则多以文献学的发展历史为主线，与文献学相关的校勘学、版本学以及写本形态等均见于不同历史时期的叙述中。法国著名文献学家 A. 戴恩（1896 — 1964）在其《古典文献的写本》一书中断言称："不应忘记——事实亦显见——文献学（philologie）的所有发展均系围绕着文本的编订"。⑤

三

汉语中的"文献学"一词最早见于梁启超的《清代学术概论》。他在《中国近三百年学术史》中说："明清之交各大师，大率都重视史学——或广义的史学，即文献学。"⑥他在《读书法讲义》一文中，在回答为什么读本国书、读本国书有何用处时说："第二，为要知道本国社会过去的变迁情状作研究现在各种社会问题之基础，本国书应读"，并解释称："这种学问，我们名之曰'文献学'。——大部分是历史，但比普通所谓历史的范围更广……晓得本国文献，便是国民常识的主要部分。"⑦与其同时代的英国学者 J. E. 桑兹认为，"'古典文献学'……是对希腊、罗马语言、文学及艺术的确切研究，是对它们传授予我们有关人类本性与历史的一切的确切研究"。⑧比较而言，这两种界说均

① U. von Wilamowitz-Moellendorff, *History of Classical Scholarship*, translated from the German by Alan Harris, edited with Introduction and Notes by Hugh Lloyd-Jones, p.vii.

② H. T. Peck, *A History of Classical Philology：From the Seventh Century B.C. to the Twentieth Century A.D.*, New York: The Macmillan Company, 1911, p. 1.

③ J. E. Sandys, *A History of Classical Scholarship: from the Six Century BC to the End of the Middle Ages*, Volume 1, p. 2.

④ U. von Wilamowitz-Moellendorff, *History of Classical Scholarship*, translated from the German by Alan Harris, edited with Introduction and Notes by Hugh Lloyd-Jones, London and Baltimore: Gerald Duckworth & Co. Ltd and Johns Hopkins University Press, 1982, p. vii.

⑤ A. Dain, *Les Manuscrits*, Paris: Les Belles Lettres, 1949, p. 145.

⑥ 梁启超：《中国近三百年学术史》，北京：东方出版社，1996 年，第 97 页。

⑦ 梁启超：《读书法讲义》，载《〈饮冰室合集〉集外文》（下册），夏晓虹辑，北京：北京大学出版社，2005 年，第 1355 页。

⑧ J. E. Sandys, *A History of Classical Scholarship, from the Six Century BC to the End of the Middle Ages*, Volume 1, p. 2.

较宽泛。桑兹继承的无疑是沃尔夫的传统观点，但梁启超对文献学的认识是否受到西学影响，中文语境的文献学是否“源于西方的文献学”，就现有资料而言委实难做评判。

上世纪八十年代中期,《文献》杂志组织过“关于文献与文献学问题的讨论”,但对“文献的含义”、“文献学的界定”以及相关议题的讨论至九十年代初始终未臻一致。2008年，曾参与讨论的董恩林先生撰文称：“文史学科的文献学（笔者称之为‘传统文献学’）名称、内涵、范围、体系诸问题，到目前为止，仍然存在一些模糊认识”；而“以整理、研究古文献为目的的一门传统学问”的文献学，董恩林先生的界定明晰而确切：“……‘辨章学术、考镜源流’是其基本宗旨，保障传世文献文本的完整、理解的准确是其终极目标，注重研究文献文本价值与内容的真实是其基本特征。”①

在西方古典学界，1988年哈佛大学文献与文化研究中心也曾以“何为文献学？”（What is Philology？）为主题举办过一次研讨会。会后结集出版的《论文献学》（On Philology）一书中的论文及导论凡12篇，所及内容包括文献学与语言学、文献学与校勘学以及文献学与（结构）文献学理论的相互关系。至于文献学的概念，与会学者的论说虽各有偏重，但“研讨会上，已经完全摒弃了文献学等同于语言学的观点。”②故上文中把“philology”在英国英语中“模棱两可的寓意”名称上确切译作“文献学”。但是，鉴于文献学与古典学在西方的混用即已存在，“Philologie”、“philologie”以及“philology”还不能统一译作“文献学”，还要根据所及内容而定。例如，创刊于1880年的American Journal of Philology，我们只能译作《美国古典学杂志》，因为刊发的原创文章除了对古典文献的释读、校勘与校勘理论外，还涉及到对希腊罗马哲学、语言、历史、社会、宗教等领域的专题研究。另外，创建于1869年的The American Philological Association因其会旨涵盖了古代希腊、罗马文明研究的各个方面，所以也应该移译为“美国古典学学会”。

西方古典文献学作为古典学的一个分支学科，就其名实而言，日本学者江藤裕之在《文献学与语言学》一书中通过辨析十九世纪德国历史研究中文献学与语言学之间的关系问题，认为在名称上无论如何解读，建立在语言、文献以及历史研究基础之上的文献学（Philologie）是对一个国家、一个地区的文化研究。③值得注意的一点是，江藤裕之把文献学细化为以语言本身为载体的文献研究。由是而推，在历史上明显带有区域文化特征的西方古典文献，在语言上则可分为希腊文献、拉丁文献。对其形态、流布、校勘、版本等内容的综合研究为“klassische Philologie”，为“classical philology”，曰“西方古典文献学”。由于“‘文献学’在国际上尚无一个为各国普遍接受的定义”，江藤裕之的所论也可备为一说。比较而言，普法伊费尔在《古典文献学史》一书中对西方古典文献学的界定明晰而确切。他认为：“‘文献学’系为解读与还原文献传统之术。它源自公元前三世纪，经诗人们的艰难尝试而为一门独立的学科，目的是保存并利用他们的文献遗产——‘希腊、拉丁著作’（the classics）。因之，‘文献学’者现以‘古典’文献学为名矣。”普法伊费尔的这一观点亦与董恩林先生对中国传统文献学的界说相若，两端均明确了文献学的主旨与基本特征，或可摭为定说。

西方古典文献学由校雠而校雠学而文献学的阶段性演变，历经中世的几度“复兴”以及近代的“民族化”。这一演变反映出西方古典文献学作为独立学科的发生、发展以至完备的全过程。其名实在不同历史时期、不同语境中的解读虽有差异，但总体上与中国古典文献学或传统文献学的沿革相类。

---

① 董恩林，《论传统文献学的内涵、范围和体系诸问题》，第44页。

② Jan Ziokowski，“‘What is Philology？’：Introduction”，in *On Philology*, ed. by Jan Ziokowski, London: The Pennsyvania State University Press, 1990, p. 6.

③ 参见 Hiroyuki Eto, *Philologie vs. Sprachwissenschaft: Historiographie einer Begriffsbestimmung im Rahmen der Wissenschaftsgeschichte des 19.* Jahrhunderts, MÜnster 2003.

【东西方文化交流与比较】

Greek and Chinese Culture: Similarities and Differences

Elena Avramidou，The Embassy of Greece in Beijing and Peking University.

Abstract：This paper seeks to present the similarities and differences between Greek and Chinese culture; two cultures that are the origins of Western and Far-Eastern civilization and mark the development of two distinctive cultural examples.

It examines the distinct socio-economic environment, political system, language and religion that determined a different development of thought, which is wisdom from one side and philosophy from the other side.

However, beyond any differences, the two cultures converge to one point; the firm belief in moral values and the connection of ethics and politics, at least as this emerges through the thoughts of their two most representative thinkers, Confucius and Plato.

Finally, it is stressed the necessity of studying the two thoughts as well as of a dialogue, that can be beneficial for both parts.

Keywords：wisdom, philosophy, ethics, politics, language.

In this paper I will generally present the similarities and differences between Greek and Chinese culture; two cultures that, as it is known, are the origins of Western and Far- Eastern civilization, respectively, and mark the development of two distinctive cultural examples.

The reasons that influenced the different path that the development of thought followed in China and in Greece can be traced in the distinct geographical conditions (without however getting trapped in "an absolute geographical determinism", to quote Braudel[1]), in the financial, social and political conditions and the diversity of language.

However in this introduction I would like to point out that, beyond any differences, the two cultures converge to one point, fundamental for their development and the development of man as such: the firm belief in moral values and the connection of ethics and politics. At least as this emerges through the thoughts of two

---

[1] F. Braudel, *Grammaire des civilizations*, Athens, MIET, 2009, p. 241.

of their most representative thinkers, who had a profound influence on them and still influence them until today: Confucius and Plato. I often acknowledge the two thinkers as a reference point in this paper, due to their synchronicity and importance in the development of the two thoughts. Platonic or not, Confucian or anti-Confucian, we are still following their footsteps.

1. Socio-economic environment: China, as a continental country, has developed until recently an entirely agricultural economy. Consequently, the country's social, political and economic life was evolved around issues that were related to the use and distribution of land.

In the social scale of those times, the first to be mentioned were the scholars (usually landlords), followed by the farmers (the peasants who cultivated the land), the artisans and finally the merchants. Due to their education, the scholars expressed the farmers' emotional world, which the farmers themselves were unable to express, according to Feng Youlan. Art, literature and philosophy were born as expression of an agricultural society that did not only influence the context of Chinese thought but its methodology as well.

Both Confucianism and Daoism, the two main trends of Chinese thought, derive from this concept. Although they stand on two opposite poles, they are placed on the same axis, expressing the aspirations and inspirations of the agricultural spirit. Their difference is explained by the fact that they are a theoretical expression or the rationalization of its distinctive aspects. The Daoists emphasized what is natural and spontaneous in man and consequently dissociated the natural from the artificial. Confucians, on the contrary, emphasized the social responsibilities of man and thus provided a theoretical scheme and a rational interpretation of this social system. The Confucian theory therefore is the moral expression of the Chinese agricultural economic system's social organization. For this reason Confucianism became the orthodox philosophy and remained as such until the time when the economic foundations of the country changed, during the first attempt towards industrialization in the 19th century. According to Feng Youlan, "these two trends of thoughts rivaled one another, but also complemented each other. They exercised a sort of balance of power. This gave to the Chinese people a better sense of balance in regards to this-worldliness and other-worldliness" [1].

The contrast with the environment of the Athenian city is obvious. The progress of commerce and navigation, which involves the observation of nature (meteorological phenomena) and technical progress (measuring distance and calculating time), provided Athens with the material wealth and the possibility to develop a level of political constitution (democracy), social development (citizen equality) and creation of cultural works (poetry, theatre, philosophy).

The sea provided Athenians with the possibility to head towards different destinations, to travel, to meet people of other nations and different beliefs. According to Karl Popper, "perhaps the strongest reason for the collapse of closed society was the development of maritime communications and commerce (⋯). These two factors of shipping and trading were proven to be the major characteristics of Athenian imperialism (⋯). Commerce in Athens, its monetary economy, maritime policies and democratic tendencies were manifestations of a cohesive movement" [2].

The image of a philosopher, during the earliest period, is combined with the one who can predict the future, on the one hand, and the one who travels the world to encounter different historical realities, on the other hand. The travels of Solon, Thales, Pythagoras, Democritus and of course Herodotus are mentioned. Plato

---

① Feng Youlan, *A Short History of Chinese Philosophy,* New York, The Macmillan Company, 1960, p. 22.

② K. Popper, *The Open Society and Its Enemies*, Athens, Papazisi, 2003,vol. 1, p. 287.

also traveled to Egypt and South Italy by sea. For him the ancient biographers claim that he made his first trip to Sicily in order to study phenomena associated with the volcano in Etna.

In China though, from the times of Confucius until the end of the 19th century, thinkers had no experience of sea traveling and encountering unknown worlds. The whole world is identified with the Chinese world[1] which, as a carrier of culture, is dissociated from the other people who live in the border areas and are considered to be "semi–civilized" and "barbarian"[2]. Confucius did not live far away from the sea, however in the *Analects* he only mentions it once[3]. Very short is also Mencius' reference to the sea (7A.24).

Confucius, as well as other teachers, traveled but his goal was to get away from the anarchy of his own country and the aim for the implementation of his political program. Chinese sages do not travel forced by the need to relocate the limits of their knowledge, to encounter other historical realities, to doubt themselves comparing them with different societies and cultures. According to the philosopher Cornelius Castoriadis, this relativization of culture itself that emerges by encountering other cultures is a peculiarity of Greek culture. Indeed, the investigation of state institutions begin early, during the times of Herodotus, and it's worth mentioning that the Egyptians and Persians, who were barbarians, always charmed the Greeks; the first with their knowledge and the latter with their state power.

Certainly Zheng He carried out seven maritime expeditions, from 1405 until 1433, arriving in Indonesia, Malaysia, Arabia, India and East Africa. However this fact, as well as other facts (knowledge of mathematics, astronomy and medicine), remained limited within a circle of "experts" without causing the interest of scholars. The practical implementation of their knowledge was not associated with a theoretical reflection, contrary to what happened in ancient Greece and later in Western Europe with the combination of philosophical pursuits and scientific research.

2. Institutions and political system. In terms of political theory there are some interesting differences. The imaginary of two societies that are completely different to each other emerges on the surface. Considering Confucius as the carrier of a tradition, which is consolidated throughout the imperial period, we will acknowledge him as a reference point.

Therefore in order to constitute his political theory, a foundation of Chinese political theory until the 20th century, Confucius does not begin from the formation of the state, the principles that govern it, the relationships among the state and citizens and the citizens' participation, as the Greek tradition dictates. An absolute differentiation is documented between Chinese and Greek thought on the basis of the idea of constituting a state and the relationship between public and private.

The difference is defined by the Chinese perception of public as extension of private and the state as the expansion of family. The father–son relationship corresponds to the relationship between the ruler and the ruled, projecting the image of a moral ruler as a good father who takes care of his children with affection. Therefore filial piety (xiao 孝) becomes a fundamental virtue not only within the family but also in guojia (国

---

[1] The Chinese characters for *world* are 天下 tian xia "all beneath the sky" and 四海 si hai "all within the four seas".

[2] H. Fingarette, *The Secular and the Sacred*, Waveland Press, 1972, p. 58.

[3] "The Master said, The Way makes no progress. I shall get upon a raft and float out to sea. I am sure Yu would come with me. Tzu–lu on hearing of this was in high spirits. The Master said, That is Yu indeed! He sets far too much store by feats of physical daring. It seems as though I should never get hold of the right sort of people" (5.6), A. Waley, *The Analects: Confucius*, Beijing, Foreign Language Teaching and Research Press, 1996.

家 country-home, as the state is called in Chinese).

Thus for Confucius family is the basic social group and its constitution becomes the model for the structure and function of the state. This model, dated back to the Zhou dynasty, reveals that a continuum exists among the family and the state, which smoothens out the differences and establishes an environment of peace and harmony. A series of rituals ensure this order (between family and state) and so the stability of the regime is guaranteed. In a similar way moral feelings, which develop among the hierarchically positioned members of the family, extend towards the bearers of political power. As a result, it is ascertained that the meaning of politics in Chinese context is entirely different than the meaning it acquires in the Greek world.

In ancient Athens the centrality that is acquired by the *political* as such, as well as the way it acts, is immutably determined by the development of the *polis* and the meaning of the citizen. According to Hannah Arendt, "the foundation of the *polis* follows the destruction of any organized forms that were based on kinship, such as *clans and tribes*" [1]. She points also out that the appearance of the *polis* marks the transition from religion of family and household (Hestia) to the religion of the Olympian gods and Homer. According to Greek tradition, Hestia (Vesta) ceded her place in the assembly of the twelve Olympian gods (next to Zeus) to Dionysus.

Ancestor worship, as the only religion throughout the entire course of the empire, marks, and in this point, Chinese alterity, although "the word *religion* is of Western origin", as Schwartz observes [2]. According to Max Weber, strong family bonds that were based on ancestor worship are the reason that capitalism did not develop in China. Thus a political autonomy could not be developed and a different social class, which would bear the responsibility of promoting political rights, could not be specified.

However we must point out that in China there was never a theocratic clergy, which had control over power, knowledge and the progress of ideas, such as in other ancient civilizations (e.g. Egypt). Here knowledge becomes the only criterion in order to access higher ranks; writings exist and ideas circulate. Church does not exist; neither does clergy or any doctrine. There is worship, precisely as in ancient Greece, which appears through participation in rituals. Thus we observe an interpenetration of the religious, the social and the intellectual element and a superiority of ceremonial rituals, which strengthen the bonds among the members, equivalent to the ones that are recorded in archaic Greece. However at some point in Greece mythical speech eventually retreats and Aristotelian logic replaces logic of the ambiguous and the coexistence of opposites.

Returning to *polis* now, we observe that the meaning, which Athenians attach to this term, is indicative. It is a meaning that is expressed by Thucydides in the *Epitaph*: "For men are the *polis*", that is Athenians are the polis. As Castoriadis properly remarks, "Thucydides never talks about Athens or any other city. When he is referring to the city, he says: the Athenians, the Corinthians, the Mytilenians. He says: Athens, Corinth etc. when he refers to the location. *Polis is not a geographical attribution*". In other words, "Athens is an expression of geographical location. The Athenians are the city" [3].

Thus the city, as a collective form of life, becomes a source of identity for its residents. This collective action, which aims in the institution of society as such, is absent in Chinese perception and so documenting a basic difference in comparison to Greek perception. Moreover the cultivation of individual moral virtues

---

① H. Arendt, *The Human Condition* (vita activa), Athens, Gnosi, 2008, p. 42.

② B.I. Schwartz, *The world of thought in ancient China*, Harvard University Press, 1985, p.19.

③ C. Castoriadis, *The ancient Greek democracy and its meaning for us today*, Athens, Ypsilon, 1999, p. 38.

in ancient Greece is compared to the development of collective values that are cultivated within the Chinese system, including the absence of competition as it is manifested in Greece through the athletic games, the dramatic poetry and satyr plays.

The alterity of *polis* in comparison to the Chinese cities is expressed also through its very layout. The focal point of public life is the *Agora*, where the citizens meet and converse. Following this pattern, European cities are organized around public squares that extend in front of churches and town halls. On the contrary, the Chinese royal capital is not decorated with public squares. The absence of bourgeoisie, religious hierarchy (only the emperor had the right to sacrifice to Heaven) and communalism is reflected on the foundation, the layout, the role and the spirit of the city.

Furthermore the very act of founding cities seems to be placed on different basis in the Chinese world, since the centricity of the ancestors' tombs and their worship becomes fundamental on this aspect. Ancestor worship emerged, as already mentioned, as main religion and contributed to the development of the political order. It made the lineage an example of social class and defined family ties, along with the spirit of peace, harmony and ceremonial decency that distinguish them, as the standard of equivalent social relationships. People were not associated with community bonds but only family ties. Family becomes the field in which emotional, moral and religious bonds are developed and are also extended in social and political level.

3. Sages and wisdom: According to tradition, Chinese history begins with the seven sage-kings (sheng ren 圣人) the last period of the third millennium B.C. They are, as we learn from Confucius, the mythical kings Yao, Shun, Yu, Tang, Wu, Wen and Duke Zhou (Zhou gong).

In Greek antiquity we find, respectively, the seven Sages: Thales, Solon, Periander, Cleobulus, Chilon, Bias, Pittacus. Soon however wisdom (σοφία) is dissociated from philosophy (φιλοσοφία). Pythagoras was the first to self describe himself as a philosopher, "friend of wisdom", according to Diogenes Laertius in the prologue of *Lives* and *Opinions of Eminent Philosophers*. For him, besides god, there is no one else who is wise. However, as Hadot points out, it is Plato who establishes "an unreachable distance between philosophy and wisdom" [1].

Indeed philosophy is born with Plato and it acquires specific characteristics: questioning and notion. The Athenian philosopher searches for the meaning of a notion through its definition (what is). This search becomes the triggering event behind the beginning of Platonic dialogue. "The philosopher is the notion's friend, he is what he is according to the notion (···) philosophy is the discipline which is offered to *create* notions", Deleuze & Guattari point out [2].

The philosopher asks questions, wonders, admires; he knows that he knows nothing and this awareness of his ignorance or impossibility to conquer what he desires is his suffering. Hence he is standing in a tragic intermediate position which is neither specified by wisdom nor non-wisdom; which does not belong completely in the divine or the human world; which is found amongst gods and wises on the one hand, and foolish people on the other hand; two categories of beings that, according to Diotima, in Plato's *Symposium* (204b), do not philosophize. Gods and wises due to their wisdom and the foolish because they think they are wise.

The sage, on the contrary, does not consider the world as a subject of questioning; he does not face it with surprise; he does not feel admiration; he does not doubt. "*The Master said, He that is really Good can never be*

---

①   P. Hadot, *Qu' est-ce que la philosophie antique?* Athens, Indiktos, 2002, p. 75.

②   G. Deleuze & F. Guattari, *What is Philosophy?* Athens, Kalentis, 2004, p. 11.

unhappy. He that is really wise can never be perplexed. He that is really brave is never afraid" (9.28)[1]. If he had any doubts, if he had questions, he would not be a sage because, according to Jullien, "wisdom is inclusive, visualizing since the beginning (without dialectics) the opposite views"[2]. The sage has in front of him the entire reality in its sphericity and so he does not have any doubts, while the philosopher sees parts of it and not the whole of reality; for that, he is distinguished for his constant wondering gaze.

The difference between wisdom and philosophy pervades the connection of Greek and Chinese thought, but simultaneously they are also combined by the undisturbed unity of knowledge; the knowledge perceived as moral and political, as their two most brilliant exponents confirm. Confucius, with his sage-king theory (sheng ren 圣人) and Plato with his philosopher-king theory, assure the coincidence of knowledge (wisdom) and politics in combination with ethics. Both introduce a moral theory, new aspects on governance and ways to restore peace, order and harmony. We must say though, with Vernant, that, "ethics does not mean obedience to some compulsion, but a profound conformity of the individual with the world's order and beauty"[3]. What Vernant wrote, referring to ancient Greece, is absolutely valid for China too.

4. Language: The difference between Greek and Chinese language does not only lie in the apparent diversity of an alphabetic and an ideographic written language. In particular, according to Gadamer, the Greek language itself carries some specific theoretical and philosophical abilities that allowed the development of philosophy. The German philosopher names two "fertile features" of the Greek language. The first one is the use of neuter gender (a feature of the German language as well), which "allows (what is) an intentional object [intentionaler Gegenstand] of thought to be presented as a subject. (···). In this use of neuter gender the concept also becomes known"[4]. The second feature is the presence of the copulative verb to be which connects the subject with the predicate, although in ontology the conceptual analysis of *being* begins with Plato (427–347 BC) and perhaps with Parmenides (late 6th century BC).

Gadamer claims that without "the enigma of the Greek language and writing" Plato (as well as Homer beforehand) and the development of philosophy are unthinkable, due to its enormous deductive power[5].

Regarding the neuter gender, Jacqueline de Romilly and Monique Trédé point out that due to "the neuter gender and the use of the *nounificated* neuter, the Greek language precludes any kind of ambiguity"[6].

"The neuter-gender can actually *nounificate* any concept converting it into an abstract idea, which obtains a very usable form, as it is easily placed anywhere in the sentence, such as the good, the *just*, the *useful*, the *being*, the *non-being, etc*"[7]. "The neuter gender allows us in this way to isolate the concepts and use them as mathematical quantities, by comparing them, adding them up or multiplying them"[8].

This is exactly the point where the difference with the Chinese language resides. Because of Chinese characters, the Chinese language carries a large pictorial treasure (indeed a part of them are pictograms) and a tremendous suggestive power; a kind of magic, because of their beauty. Chinese characters are like a drawing and that is why the art of calligraphy was developed. Finally, because of their symbolic character, they function

---

①　A. Waley, *The Analects: Confucius*.

②　F. Jullien, *Entre la Grèce et la Chine*, Athens, Exantas, 2002, p. 77.

③　J-P. Vernant, *Entre mythe et politique*, Athens, Smili, 2003, p. 465.

④　H.G. Gadamer, *Der Anfang der Philosophie*, Athens, Patakis, 2005, pp. 22–23.

⑤　H. G. Gadamer, *Der Anfang der Philosophie*, p. 24.

⑥　J. de Romilly – M. Trédé, *Petites leçons sur le grec ancien, Athens*, Oceanida, 2008, p. 75.

⑦　J. de Romilly – M. Trédé, *Petites leçons sur le grec ancien*, p. 83.

⑧　J. de Romilly – M. Trédé, *Petites leçons sur le grec ancien*, p. 85.

as symbols, like emblems, and therefore they submit behaviors. However it does not contain genders and inflections (time, mood, number) nor does it contain the copulative verb; as Graham observes, "Chinese lacks anything exactly corresponding to the verb to be" [1]. Furthermore it does not formulate definitions and general concepts and it does not attain the concepts of subject–object because of the Chinese world outlook. It is not precise and "articulate, because it does not represent concepts in any deductive reasoning" [2].

Consequently, it did not experience the shifting of attention from the subject to the predicate, a fact that marks the transition of research in an ontological and logical level. The question "what is the Good?" (the Right etc.) was never raised in China. The interest was focused on "how will someone become good" (righteous etc.), because in ancient China everything is set up in terms of *becoming; the being* and *the truth* do not exist.

In Plato the tripartite cognitive condition (episteme/knowledge, doxa/ opinion and ignorance) is associated with the distinction of reality in three levels that correspond to the three ontological conditions of being, of becoming and of non–being. Thus the theory of knowledge "follows another path" [3] and ends in a theory of Being, which, by establishing the theory of Ideas, elevates thinking further up.

On the contrary, in Confucian epistemology there is nothing similar to this, because the development of ontology is absent. Chinese thought, as a whole, focused on ethical and practical matters. Questions about the nature of being and the chasm of knowledge–non–knowledge, which is kept vivid in Western thought, do not correspond to equivalent thoughtful efforts within the Chinese thought. Feng Youlan observes that, when a Chinese student of Philosophy studies Western philosophy he feels rather surprised to find that the Greek philosophers considered the non–being and the unlimited to be inferior to the being and the limited, since the exact opposite occurs in Chinese philosophy.

Thus we observe a disregard for detecting standards and invariable essences. Due to this insufficiency, any classification is impossible since any predicative cannot include its adversative condition. Besides "it is necessary for the predicate to refer to a non–linguistic object, which will exist autonomously and will express the consistent and invariable meaning. This object is in first approach what Plato calls *idea*", Vegetti quotes [4].

Therefore Confucian and the whole of Chinese thought was not interested in searching for an objective foundation of stability neither in juxtaposing a scientific criterion for establishing a system of predications with universal validity. For this reason science, which presumes definition and classification, did not develop in China. Only the latter Moists apprehended the accuracy of a definition, the means of predication and the notion of truth; they gave an abstract definition of space and time and interpreted dialogue as a confrontation of two opposite positions. It is the only movement of thought (developed during the 4th –3rd century B.C., prolonging the Mozi tradition) that is surprisingly close to Greek thought. Their rationality however could not find any fertile ground for development. Only in the beginning of the 20th century, when the Chinese discovered Western logic, were they interested in Moists.

In conclusion, I would like to emphasize that the diversity of the two thoughts does not mean that the one is insufficient compared to the other. On the contrary, it is precious wealth from which we can benefit.

---

[1] A.C. Graham, *Studies In Chinese Philosophy & Philosophical Literature*, Singapore, Institute of East Asian Philosophies, 1986, p. 331.

[2] Feng Youlan, *A Short History of Chinese Philosophy*, p. 25.

[3] F. Chatelet (editor), *La Philosophie*, Athens, Gnosi, 1989, vol. A′, p. 67.

[4] M. Vegetti, *Storia della filosofia antica*, Athens, P. Travlos, 2000, p.161.

The development of philosophy that occurred at some point of time in Athens does not mean earlier or elsewhere there was no reflection or thought. Simply Chinese thought is "another source" of thought[1] that had developed without pervading philosophy, at least in the very beginning; it had developed using other possibilities.

The study of both thoughts is undoubtedly of fundamental significance for the simultaneous study of the Western and Eastern world; two worlds that are still not adequately familiar with each other, but wish to do so and work towards this direction.

In order for this wish to come true, the study of the Greek and Chinese classical texts is necessary; texts which are dated in the beginnings of political thoughts in Greece and China. This knowledge can play a significant role in understanding the two worlds (Greek/Western and Chinese), which are mostly unaware of each other, as well as initiating an open and productive dialogue between them.

The necessity of such a dialogue is appointed today even more intense. A new encounter between Greek and Chinese thought can indisputably be greatly beneficial for both traditions.

---

[1]　F. Jullien, *Entre la Grèce et la Chine*, p. 22.

A Study of the (Western) Zodiac Signs in Medieval Asian Art[①]

Diana Y. Chou，Cleveland State University

Abstract：The focus of this paper is to draw a connection between East and West by tracing the travel of motifs and images of Babylonian astrological zodiac signs. This paper carefully exam the visual evidences, including mural painting and 3-D artifacts which dated from the 9th to 14th century CE, specifically from China. Such findings are further proofs that art and the visual representation of ideas are not confined by geographical boundaries but were spread by devoted believers, caravans, and other channels. In addition, the focus on the twelve zodiac signs suggests another possibility in connecting East Asia, South Asia, and Central Asia in a global context of the pre-Modern world.

Keywords: Astrological signs（星座）, Buddha Tejaprabha（大炽至佛）, Capricorn（摩羯）, Dunhuang（敦煌）, XuanhuaLiaomu（宣化辽墓）

My interest in this subject emerged during my first visit to the site of the Mogao caves at Dunhuang, in the Gobi Desert of China (Fig.1), in 2003. UNESCO has considered the Mogao Caves at Dunhuang to be a World Heritage site since 1987 on account of its exceptional significance to human history and creativity; the Mogao caves are also considered one of the earliest and most important surviving examples of Buddhist art in China.[②] One of the Mogao Grottoes will be considered in this paper. However, despite the challenge of limited materials (both primary and secondary sources) and extant artifacts relating to the "Western" zodiac signs, I would like to draw a connection between East and West via the route of the Silk Road, officially launched in the 2nd century BCE of the Han Dynasty (206 BCE–220 CE) in China, by tracing the travel and uses of motifs

---

① I would like to express my gratitude to Professor Yang Juping of Nankai University for his invitation and hospitality, to his faculty, staff and graduate student teams from their assistance at the Fourth Ancient World History International Conference in 2012; to Professors Roderick Whitfield (Emeritus Professor, SOAS, University of London), and Wang Huiming (Dunhuang Research Academy, China) for advising me on the uses of the images; Professor Gerry Guest for editing this paper.

② http://whc.unesco.org/en/list/440 (accessed on December 19, 2012); Roderick Whitfield, Susan Whitfield, and Neville Agnew, *Cave Temples of Mogao: Art and History on the Silk Road* (Los Angeles: The Getty Conservation Institute and the J. Paul Getty Museum, 2000).

and images of the Babylonian (or Western) zodiac signs. The visual evidence for this study includes mural paintings and three–dimensional artifacts from China, Japan, and India,[1] which date mainly to the 10th through 13th century CE. Such findings are further proof that art and the visual representation of ideas are not confined by geographical boundaries but were spread by devoted believers, caravans, and other channels. In addition, the focus on the Babylonian zodiac suggests another possibility for connecting East Asia (China and Japan), South Asia (India), and Central Asia (Iran and Iraq) in a global context during the pre–Modern world. In order to make these connections, I divide this paper into three major sections: the first considers the origins of the twelve zodiac signs; next will be a discussion of the sites of the discoveries of these zodiac signs in China and Japan; and lastly I will offer a scenario explaining the travels of these motifs/beliefs. Finally, I will conclude with some remarks regarding the interchanges and coexistences of these "Western" zodiac signs from various cultures in the pre–Modern world.

Origins

The history of astrology is mysterious and yet lengthy. Horoscopes, which are sometimes diagrams of astrological patterns and signs, have existed and been implanted in many ancient civilizations, including Mesopotamia and Greece.[2] In Greek horoscopes, two features are common: the presence of twelve signs and their arrangement in a circular pattern with the name of each sign inscribed.[3] This layout continues into medieval Europe, as evidenced by manuscripts,[4] and later in Asian civilizations.

In the case of China, the idea of applied astronomy and the study of constellations in the early era were documented in ancient texts, and occasionally sketches and diagrams of constellations are accompanied by difficult to decipher texts which were only understood by a very small group of professionals.[5] Before the introduction of the twelve astrological signs into China, twenty–eight stars or "houses" of astrology were used (Fig. 2).[6] These twenty–eight stars were divided into four groups, an idea of associated with the four directions (North, South, East and West) or with the four seasons; each direction (or season) corresponds to seven or eight stars respectively.[7] Chinese twenty–eight star astrology in its early stage was used mainly for predicting the seasons and the times of year for agricultural purposes, ritual practice, military combat, and other reasons; however, all of these event–predictions were also strongly associated with the destiny of kings and their

---

[1] Due to copyright issues, some images will not be provided here. However, for images which can be located online and in print, URLs and previous publications will be given.

[2] Johannes Thomann, "Square Horoscope Diagrams in Middle Eastern Astrology and Chinese Cosmological Diagrams: Were These Designs Transmitted Through the Silk Road?," in Philippe For ê t and Andreas Kaplony, ed. *The Journey of Maps and Images on the Silk Road* (Leiden/Boston: Brill, 2008), 97–117.

[3] Johannes Thomann, "Square Horoscope Diagrams in Middle Eastern Astrology and Chinese Cosmological Diagrams," 98.

[4] Johannes Thomann, "Square Horoscope Diagrams in Middle Eastern Astrology and Chinese Cosmological Diagram," 99.

[5] Xia Nai, "Cong Xuanhua Liaomu de xingtu lun ershiba xiu he Huangdao shier gong," *Kaogu xuebao*, No. 2 (1976): 35–58; *Da Xia xunzong: Xi Xia wenwu jicui* (Beijing: China Academy of Social Sciences Publishing, 2004), 75–80.

[6] Xia Nai, "Cong Xuanhua Liaomu de xintu lun ershiba xiu he Huandao shier gong," 35–58.

[7] Xia Nai, "Cong Xuanhua Liaomu de xintu lun ershiba xiu he Huandao shier gong," 36–37.

kingdoms, which became significant in Chinese politics after the 4th century.[①]

The records regarding the understanding and uses of astrology and the constellations can be traced back to one of the earliest ancient Chinese classics, *Xia xiaozheng*(夏小正), written in the (legendary) Xia Dynasty around 2000 BCE;[②] this knowledge was firmly recorded by ancient writers and scholars of post-Xia eras, between the 3rd century BCE to the 1st century CE).[③] However, the idea of twenty-eight houses or stars was not completely formulated when this ancient text was first written. Moreover, in addition to China, other ancient civilizations, such as India (which includes today's India, Pakistan and Bangladesh), Saudi Arabia, Iran, and Egypt, also recognized these twenty-eight, which will not be discussed in this paper.[④] Because of its geographic link with the South route of the Silk Road, some scholars have suggested that the notion of twenty-eight stars that developed in China was brought from India.[⑤]

The twenty-eight stars were later incorporated into astronomy and astrology, calendars, and rituals in China until the late Ming Dynasty (1369-1644 CE), circa the 17th century, when Western astronomy was introduced by Jesuit missionaries, such as Matteo Ricci (*Li Madou* 利玛窦 in Chinese, 1552-1610), Johann Adam Schall von Bell (*Tang Ruowang* 汤若望 in Chinese, 1592-1666), and Ferdinand Verbiest (*Nan Huairen* 南怀仁 in Chinese, 1623-1688), who introduced and demonstrated the accuracy of western astronomical technology in specific events that impressed the Emperors; the use of the twenty-eight star system was then gradually and completely abandoned at Court.[⑥]

However, the imagery of the "Western" zodiac, which traveled through ancient Persia and India,[⑦] emerged in China prior to the era of the Jesuit Missionaries. Unfortunately, for the use of the Babylonian or Greek astrological signs in China, no literary documents dating before the 7th century CE have been found.[⑧] However, with the flourishing and the imperial patronage of Buddhism, which originated in India, the nomenclature and understanding of the Babylonian zodiac was transmitted to China from the 7th to 10th centuries CE through Buddhist sutras.[⑨] In its original context of both Babylonia and Greece, the twelve zodiac signs had developed into images that resemble the current popular presentation of the zodiac and its attributes; these pictorial motifs survived in the "Chinese version" of the twelve astrological signs. Babylonian or Greek

---

① Xia Nai, "Cong Xuanhua Liaomu di xingtu lun ershiba xiu he Huangdao shier gong," 39-40.

② Xia Nai, "Cong Xuanhua Liaomu de xingtu lun ershiba xiu," 36-7; Dai De, *Da Dai Liji,* juan 2: 4-18.

③ Fu Songqing (ca. 11th-12th century CE) annotated, *Xia xiaozheng Daishi zhuan (Siku Quanshu* jingbu, juan 3); http://guji.artx.cn/article/47718.html (accessed on December 19, 2012).

④ Xia Nai, "Cong Xuanhua Liaomu de xingtu lun ershiba xiu," 40-41.

⑤ Xia Nai, "Cong Xuanhua Liaomu di xingtu lun ershiba xiu he Huangdao shier gong," 40-41.

⑥ David Mungello, *The Great Encounter of China and the West, 1500-1800* (NY: Roman and Littlefield Publishers, 2009); John Witek ed., *Ferdinand Veribest (1623-1688): Jesuit Missionary, Scientist, Engineer, and Diplomat* (Nettetal: Steyler Verlag, 1994); *Dunhuang Shiku Quanji*, 23: 20-21 (Hong Kong: The Commercial Press Ltd, 2001); Gauvin Alexander Bailey, *Art on the Jesuit Missions in Asia and Latin America, 1542-1773* (Toronto: University of Toronto Press, 1999).

⑦ *Dunhuang Shiku Quanji*, 23: 21; Needham, *Science and Civilization in China*, 3:257 (Cambridge: Cambridge University Press, 1954); Xia Nai, "Cong Xuanhua Liaomu de xingtu lun ershiba xiu," 49-50.

⑧ Zheng Shao zong, "Liaodai caihui xingtu shi wo guo tianwen shi zhang de zhong yao faxian," *Wenwu*, 8 (1975): 40-44.

⑨ Xia Nai, "Cong Xuanhua Liaomu de xingtu lun ershiba xiu," 52.

astrology was thus brought to China, in particular to Dunhuang and its environs, where pictorial records of the constellations and astrology are preserved today. Although the use of Western Zodiac signs is documented in 7th-century Chinese sources, very scanty visual evidence from this time period has survived to the present.[①] These few artifacts include metal objects, architectural fragments, and silk paintings, which were discovered in Inner Mongolia and in the Muslim Autonomous Region in northwestern China.

Furthermore, concerning the use or function of the Western zodiac signs in China, no other literary documents have been found.[②] Based on the extant pictorial evidence, some of the twelve astrological signs of Babylon were found in Buddhist caves and burial chambers where rituals were practiced and seasons were in play; perhaps we could assume that the use of Babylonian or Greek astrology was sometimes associated with the twenty-eight star astrology in ancient China.[③]

The Locations of Discoveries

Currently, images of the Western zodiac in Asian art can be found archeological sites (tombs and grottoes) and museum collections; these examples range from China, to Japan, to India, and to Iran and Iraq,[④] but my main focus here will be on China and Japan. In China, these astrological signs are surprisingly found in several sites, which date from the 7th to 13th century, Tang to Yuan Dynasties. These sites are largely confined to the Northwestern region of China, which included the Silk Road. This indicates again that the use of the twelve astrological signs was associated with travelers from the West (perhaps from Iran to India). Among these geographical sites, only two, the Xuanhua tombs (Hebei Province) and the Mogao caves (no. 61), have been studied with images being partially published.[⑤] A few objects, included here, are in the collection of the Xixia Museum in the Ningxia Muslim Autonomous Region, having been unearthed in recent years.[⑥] My selections in this paper focus mainly on mural paintings because of their state of preservation, visibility and colors.

a. Xuanhua site, Hebei Province, China (Fig. 3)

The Xuanhua site, discovered in 1971 with excavations completed in 1975, contains several tombs that share one family name, Zhang. Several members of the Zhang family were buried and identified in the

---

① *Dunhuang Shiku Quanji*, 23: 21 (HK: The Commercial Press, Ltd., 2001).

② "Liaodai caihua xintu shi woguo tianwenshi shang de zhongyao faxian," *Wen Wu*, no. 8 (1975): 40-44.

③ Xia Nai, "Cong Xuanhua Liaomu de xintu lun ershiba xiu he Huandao shier gong," *Kaogu xuebao*, No. 2 (1976): 35-58.

④ *Zhongguo Meishu quanji: Dunhuang bihua,* vols. 14 & 15 (Shanghai: Renming Meishu chubanshe, 1988); *Elegance, Virtue, & Ceremony: Buddhist Painting of the Heian and Kamakura Periods* (Japan: Kyoto National Museum, 1998).

⑤ Tansen Sen, "Astronomical Tomb Paintings from Xuanhua: Mandalas?," *Ars Orientalis,* vol. 29 (1999): 29-54; *Wen Wu, no. 8 (1975): 31-39; Tomb Murals of Liao Dynasty in Xuanhua*, Cultural Relics Publishing House (Beijing, 2001); *Xuanhua Liaomu (Excavation Reprot of the Liao Dynasty Frescoed tombs at Xuanhua,1974-1993)*, 2 volumes (Beijing: Wenwu Chubenshe, 2001); *Dunhuang Shiku quanji* (Hong Kong: The Commercial Press Ltd., 2001); *Zhongguo Meishu quanji: Dunhuang bihua,* vols. 14 & 15 (Shanghai: Renming Meishu chubanshe, 1988); Liu Haiwen, ed., *Xuanhua xiabali er qu Liao bihua mu kaogu fajue baogao* (Beijing: Wenwu chubenshe, 2008).

⑥ *Genghis Khan: The Ancient Nomadic Culture of the Northern China* (Beijing Chuben she, 2004); *Selected Treasures from Hejiacun Tang Hoard* (Beijing: Wenwu Chubenshe, 2003).

same location; three of these tombs, which are labeled M1, M2, and M5 by Chinese archeologists, feature the Babylonian (or Greek) zodiac signs on the ceilings of several tombs. M1 is the tomb of Zhang Shiqing, M2 is the tomb of Zhang Gongyou, and M5 is the tomb of Zhang Shigu. The star ceiling mural from these three tombs displays a combination of both Chinese twenty−eight stars and the Western (or Babylonian) zodiac respectively. Before fully discussing each tomb and its association with the twelve zodiac signs, some geographical and historical information relating to the Zhang family is necessary. Xuanhua of Hebei Province is in Central−North China of the Liao Kingdom, and later called themselves Liao Dynasty (907−1125 CE), established by the *Khitans* 契丹. The *Khitans* were nomadic minorities who resided in North China and who posed a severe political and military threat to the Northern Song Dynasty (960—1127 CE). Similar to the *Khitans*, the *Jurchens* 女真, a nomadic group neighboring the *Khitans* and Northern Song China, emerged in the 10th century. Finally in the year 1124 CE, Northern Song China was defeated and ended officially because of the invasion of the Jurchens, who later founded the Jin Dynasty (1115−1234 CE). The *Jurchens*, a fatal threat for both Song China and the Khitans, were not only responsible for pushing the imperial house of the Song to relocate to the Yangzhi River regions and to restructure as the Southern Song Dynasty; the *Jurchens* also defeated the *Khitan* Empire. Finally by the middle of the 13th century CE, the Mongols took over the Jurchens and other nomadic groups and further shortened the history of the Southern Song Dynasty. The Mongols not only unified China and its northern borders, but also established their own kingdom, the Yuan Dynasty (1279−1368 CE), in China.

Due to several shifts in ethnicities and political authority in northwestern and northern China, Xuanhua of Hebei was apparently not an exclusive "Han" Chinese community and society; rather, it exhibited a collision of ethnic and perhaps religious diversity. These factors might account for the complexity of the tombs in the Xuanhua site. The tomb owners, the Zhang family, were *Khitans*, and some of them were appointed officials during the Liao Dynasty, including Zhang Shiqing, who was buried in tomb M1. But with an adaption of a Chinese surname, *Zhang*, this family was likely *Sinicized* and assimilated to Chinese customs.[①]

In tomb M1 (Fig.4), the twenty−eight stars of the inner circle, depicted as a lotus, are Chinese and the twelve astrological signs of the outer circle are Babylonian. The master of tomb M1, Zhang Shiqing, died in 1116 AD, and was buried in the same year. The mural painting of the celestial ceiling is also likely to be dated around 1116 AD.[②] The most intriguing element of these celestial ceilings are not the twenty−eight stars, which were well−documented in China, but the twelve astrological signs are perhaps the earliest known complete zodiac in Chinese art. On the ceiling mural of tomb M1, the twelve astrological signs align with the Chinese twelve stars in an arrangement of four directions and four seasons—spring includes Aries, Taurus (which is missing in this mural painting and was probably destroyed by tomb robbers), and Gemini in the West, the summer includes Cancer, Leo, and Virgo in the South, the autumn signs are Libra, Scorpio, and Sagittarius in the East, and finally, the winter signs are Capricorn, Aquarius, and Pisces in the North.

The reason that the archeologists were able to identify these twelve signs was because of the pictorial

---

① Tao Jing−shen, *The Jurchen in twelfth−century China: A Study of Sinicization* (The University of Washington Press, 1977).

② "Liaodai caihui xingtu shi wo guo tianwen shi shang de zhong yao faxian," *Wenwu*, 8 (1975): 41.

similarities between the original Babylonian and "Chinese version" of the zodiac. The key features of some signs, particularly the animal signs, remain close, such as Aries, Cancer, Leo, Scorpio, and Pisces; however, some signs, at the same time, appear more "Chinese" or "localized" (Fig. 5). For example, a water−bearer as Aquarius was represented as the jar alone in this mural, and the design of the water jar was modified from a Greek high−neck amphora into a short−neck Tang style jar. The man and woman of Gemini are "Chinese" in customs and appearance, and Virgo is no longer singular, but is depicted as a pair of female figures in different dress and colors. The symbol of Libra, a scale, has become a Chinese scale, and the man's head with the horse body of Sagittarius has become a groom leading a horse. The most unexpected change is the sign of Capricorn, which is a mountain goat in Babylonian astrology, but becomes a mysterious water beast with wings and a dragon−like head. The changes in particular signs, such as Capricorn, remain unexplained in current scholarship.[1] In terms of artistic technique in tomb M1, the artisans generally created outline sketches and then applied the colors to the space, a common technique used in both wall and ink paintings. Some attempts at shading the volumes of the animals' bodies to create a sense of three−dimensionality are visible, but are not fully achieved.

The twelve astrological signs from the ceiling mural of tomb M2 survive intact as twelve distinct images displayed in an inner circle, surrounding the lotus at the center (Fig. 6). The constellation ceiling of tomb M2 adds the Chinese animal zodiac signs, locating them at the outer circle of the placement, something not included in tomb M1.[2] In terms of directional placement, attributes, and artistic technique, the signs are identical to those in the tomb M1. Unfortunately, the current published image from the M2 tomb is very blurry, and I have relied on the sketch to understand the placement of the twelve signs on the ceiling.

Tomb M5 lies south of tomb M1 and has been plundered (Fig. 7). The inclusion of all three systems of astrology (the Babylonian zodiac, the twenty−eight stars, and the Chinese twelve animal zodiac) is identical to tomb M2; and the placement of the directions of the signs is identical to tomb M1.[3] Among the Babylonian signs, four are missing because of the plunder. However, eight out of the twelve are visible on the ceiling mural. As for the style and representation of the signs, as well as the directional placement of the zodiac in both M2 and M5, they are similar to those in M1, so we could hypothetically suggest that both murals were done by the same hand or that the artisans shared a similar artistic tradition and understanding of astrology, although the dates for tombs M2 and M5 are not specified in the excavation report.[4]

b. Mogao Caves, Dunhuang, Gansu Province, China (Fig. 8)

The Mogao caves at Dunhuang of Gansu Province are comprised of North and South Cliffs, with about 1,000 caves in total number. Cave no. 61 is one of 492 painted caves of the South Cliffs. Its complexity, in terms of structural space, architectural layout, painting categories, and the iconography of its large mural paintings in

---

[1] The subject of Capricorn and its associations in Chinese art and culture is currently being studied by the same author of this paper.

[2] *Xuanhua Liaomu: 1974−1993 nian kaogu fajue* (Beijing: Wenwu chuban she, 2001), vol. 1: 268−277.

[3] *Xuanhua Liaomu: 1974−1993 nian kaogu fajue* (Beijing: Wenwu chubanshe, 2001), vol. 1: 257−259.

[4] *Xuanhua Liaomu: 1974−1993 nian kaogu fajue* (Beijing: Wenwu chuban she, 2001), vol. 1: 250−277.

the main hall, has received significant attention by scholars and art historians.[1] The surviving inscriptions on Cave no. 61 suggest that this cave was constructed sometime between 947 and 951 CE (Post-Tang Dynasty or the Five Dynasties) and that the mural painting in the main hall depict the pilgrimage to Mount Wutai, a very important site in the history of Chan (Zen in Japanese) and Pure Land Buddhism. The entrance pathway of cave no. 61, which has been touched, repainted, re-inscribed in different styles, time periods, and languages, has not been fully studied. Furthermore, the date for the entrance pathway is controversial. Some scholars consider it to be from the Xi Xia Kingdom (or the *Tangut* Empire, 1038–1227 CE), because it bears both Chinese and Tangut scripts, while on the basis of painting style, some date it later to the Mongol Yuan Era, because the Tangut Empire, a contemporary nomadic power of the *Jurchens*, was also defeated by Genghis Kahn in 1227 CE. However, evidence to support the Yuan dating is lacking. My focus in this paper is not to discuss the dating issue of the entrance pathway, but to consider how the Babylonian (or Greek) astrological zodiac signs were transformed and differ from the Xuanhua tomb murals discussed earlier. In addition, the depiction of the Babylonian zodiac in Cave no. 61 is the most unique feature among the Dunhang caves, because Cave no. 61 is the only cave at Mogao that bears the twelve astrological signs of Babylon.

All of the Mogao caves are erected facing the East, where cave entrances are located and the sun rises, to enhance the visibility of the murals. Due to this uniform architectural layout, the entrance pathway of Cave no. 61 naturally features north and south sidewalls. Both walls display both the twenty-eight stars and the Babylonian twelve-sign zodiac.[2] The key icon on the South Wall, which has been identified as Buddha *Tejaprabha*, will be the focus of this section (Fig.9). Buddha *Tejaprabha* is shown sitting in a chariot, which is surrounded Five Stars (Stars of the Four Directions and the Center), and the Sun and the Moon.

In the background is the Chinese twenty-eight stars astrology, with Babylonian astrological signs, grouped on the top, bordering the ceiling on both walls (Fig.10). Nine out of the Babylonian twelve signs remain on both walls, and six signs are repeated, namely Aries, Taurus, Virgo, Cancer, Scorpio, and Capricorn; overall they add up to a complete set of the twelve astrological signs from both the South and North Walls.[3] It is unclear the reason for the nine signs on each wall; however, my speculation is that the twelve signs were originally placed on each wall, and that some are now missing, probably covered by later designs and painting. It is also possible that artists/artisans intended to reflect the accuracy of the constellations in the seasons, and that the North and South walls represented the Northern and Southern hemispheres.[4] All stars on both walls, as well as the Sun and the Moon, are personified as human figures in Chinese costumes; the artistic technique of these personified constellations and their compositions are superior to those of the mural paintings of the Xuanhua Tombs. The

---

[1] *Zhongguo Meishu quanji: Dunhuang bihua,* vols. 14 & 15 (Shanghai: Renming Meishu chubanshe, 1988); *Dunhuang: A Centennial Commemoration of the Discovery of the Cave Library* (Beijing: Dunhuang Research Institute & Morning Glory Publishers, 2000); Jean-Pierre Drège ed., *Images de Dunhuang: Dessins et peintures sur papier des fonds Pelliot et Stein* (Paris, École fran aise d'Extrême-Orient, 1999); Zhao Shenliang, "Dunhuang wanqi yishi de shuoguo: Mogao ku di liushiyi ku nairong yu yishu," *Dunhuang shiku yishu* (Jiangsu yushu chubenshe, 1995); *Dunhuang Shiku Yishu: Mogao ku di liu shi yi ku* (Jiangsu Yushu chubenshe, 1995).

[2] *Tonkō Bakukōkutsu: Tonkō Bunbutsu Kenkyūjo hen* (Tokyo: Heibonsha, 1980–1982), vol. 5, 23; *Dunhuang shiku quanji 23: kexue jishu huajuan* (Hong Kong: The Commercial Press Ltd., 2001).

[3] *Dunhuang shiku quanji 23: kexue jishu huajuan* (Hong Kong: The Commercial Press Ltd., 2001), 20–22.

[4] This speculation requires a further study.

refined figures of Mogao Cave no. 61 display characteristics of Tang figure painting tradition, such as round faces with rosebud lips and almond–shaped eyes, full bodies with elaborate drapery that gives a sensuality and weight to the three–quarter profile of the figures; such characteristics were continuously adopted by artists of the Five Dynasties (907–960 CE).

On the walls of the pathway, most signs maintain their original identifiable elements; Capricorn, which was a water beast with wings at the Xuanhua tombs, is now completely transformed into a bird–like creature no longer associated with its original identity, a mountain goat.　The star murals in the Xuanhua tomb chambers function astronomically in a cosmic setting (perhaps from the perspective or viewing direction of the deceased), but the Mogao caves served as living prayer halls and temples in their time.　The astrological signs in Cave no. 61 may have been associated with rituals and religious practices.　No matter what function they provided, it seems clear to me that the twelve astrological signs were adapted in Northwestern China,[1] and were probably made known to the Chinese, and then traveled to Japan, where the Babylonian zodiac is also found, a topic to be briefly discussed later in this paper.[2]

c. Ningxia Muslim Autonomous Region, Xi Xia (Tangut) Museum[3]

Several painted silk banners, currently in the collection of the Xi Xia (*Tangut*) Museum, featuring Buddha *Tejaprabha*, the twenty–eight stars, and the Babylonian zodiac were unearthed in the 1990s (Fig. 11).　Although the condition of these silk banners is damaged and fragile, some of the twelve zodiac signs are legible, including Pieces (twin fishes), Aries (a goat), Gemini (twin figures), and Leo (a lion).　The details and composition of the banners are from skillful painters and the use of colors is vibrant.　In addition, their association with Buddha *Tejaprabha* is identical to the South Wall of Mogao Cave no. 61, even though their artistic styles differ, suggesting that the practice and belief of Buddha *Tejaprahba* may have prevailed in the northwestern regions under the rule of the *Tangut* Empire (*Xi Xia* in Chinese).

Another archeological excavation was conducted in the 2000s, and other materials were also discovered in this vast Ningxia Muslim Autonomous Region.　Among these architectural fragments (ceramics and sulfur glass) and metalwork, we found animals motifs attached; however, the number and variety of animal images among this group are limited and isolated.　The primary motif of the architectural decorations shares similarities with the modified shape of Capricorn from Mogao Cave no. 61—a mammal head with fish tale (Fig. 12).　This specific Capricorn–like creature appears on the ridge of roofs in Buddhist temples (possibly); the question of whether it had a religious function or was merely decorative awaits further study.

---

① Some scholars have suggested that Yulin Grotto no. 35 also displays the zodiac (*Dunhuang shiku quanji 23: kexue jishu huajuan*, 22); however, I have not included this cave in the current paper due to a lack published images and study.

② *Elegance, Virtue, & Ceremony: Buddhist Painting of the Heian and Kamakura Periods* (Kyoto National Museum, 1998).

③ *Da Xia xunzong: Xi Xia wenwu jicui* (Beijing: China Academy of Social Science Publishing, 2004), 176–185.

d. Horyuji and Kumeta Temples, Japan

Three Japanese paintings from the collection of Horyuji and Kumeta Temples relate to the present investigation.[1] Interestingly, these three Japanese paintings are in a format known as the "Star Mandala." A mandala (*mandara* in Japanese) is a diagram used in rituals, invoking the deity, expelling the evil spirits, or engaging with celestial powers for blessings;[2] it is one of the most important ritual devices in Esoteric (and Tantric) Buddhism.[3] The origin of Japanese Esoteric Buddhism derives from Tang China (670–906 CE) and can be traced back to Tandric Buddhism, an ancient tradition in India. When Tang China strongly impacted the linguistic and political formulations of the Nara Era (710–794 CE) of Japan, Monks Saichō (767–822 CE) and K ū kai (774–835 CE) brought Tandric Buddhism back to Japan and later founded the *Shingon* and *Tendai* sects respectively, which flourished under the imperial patronage of Emperor Kanmu (reigned 781–806 CE).[4] Today, the best known and the oldest surviving mandalas of Japanese Esoteric Buddhism, the *Diamond* and *Womb* paired mandalas, are housed in Toji (the East Temple) of Kyoto, Japan.[5]

These Star Mandalas are dated to the 12th century during the Heian Era (794–1185 CE), around the time of the Xuanhua tombs and Dunhuang Mogao Grottoes no. 61. In these extant pieces, unlike the earliest Japanese mandalas, which bear the Babylonian astrological zodiac signs, some of the motifs and symbols of each sign are identifiable and also maintain their Chinese influence, with greater elaboration in details (perhaps relating to patronage). The twelve Babylonian astrological signs were placed in either the second square or the middle circle from the center, where the major Buddha (or deity) sits; the third circle or the outer square displays the twenty-eight stars. The artistic styles employed here resemble the Japanese style instead of the "Chinese" style. The astrological zodiac signs on these Japanese Star Mandalas are personified as figures whose costume, headdresses, and hairdos reflect the style of the Heian court of the 11th and 12th centuries. In addition, most of the zodiac signs on the Horyuji mandalas also bear individual identifications with *kanji*, "Chinese characters," which confirm that they are the Babylonian signs.[6] The major signs in the Star Mandalas maintain their legible features, including Cancer (a crab), Libra (a scale), Aries (a goat), and Taurus (a bull), but we also see some transformations from those in China. Capricorn changes slightly but stays a mysterious creature with a pointy-nosed animal head and fish tale; Sagittarius is simplified into an archer's bow.

---

[1] Images of Star Mandalas from the Horyuji Temple can be located in the special exhibition catalogue, *Elegance, Virtue, & Ceremony: Buddhist Painting of the Heian and Kamakura Periods* (Kyoto National Museum, 1998), plates nos. 121 & 122, and www.artstor.org (accessed on December 27, 2012).

[2] Louis Frédéric, *Buddhism: Flammarion Iconographic Guides* (Paris/New York: Flammarion, 1995), 34–39; *Elegance, Virtue, & Ceremony: Buddhist Painting of the Heian and Kamakura Periods* (Kyoto National Museum, 1998), 351–352.

[3] The history and development of Japanese Esoteric Buddhism is very complex, please refer to publications by Japanese art historians and scholars. For instance, Elizabeth Ten Grotenhuis, *Japanese Mandalas: Representations of Sacred Geography* (University of Hawai'i Press, 1999).

[4] Penelope Mason (revised by Donald Dinwiddle), *History of Japanese Art* (Pearson/Prentice Hall, 2005), 122–123.

[5] Penelope Mason (revised by Donald Dinwiddle), *History of Japanese Art* (Pearson/Prentice Hall, 2005), 125–128.

[6] *Elegance, Virtue, & Ceremony: Buddhist Painting of the Heian and Kamakura Periods* (Japan: Kyoto National Museum, 1998), 238–240.

In the Esoteric Buddhist tradition, mandalas were mostly created or prepared by monks, who understood the doctrines of their religious practices and rituals. In addition, because of the nature and function of mandalas in Esoteric Buddhism, it clearly suggests that these Star Mandalas served ritual purposes. The function and use of these Star Mandalas perhaps follow the known practices in the Esoteric Buddhist tradition. Although the imagery or the knowledge of the Babylonian zodiac had spread to Japan (in format, function, display, and purpose), these examples align more precisely with the rituals of Tantric Buddhism, at least in the examples of the Horyuji Temple; furthermore, the Japanese examples clearly depart from those found in China, especially those in the Xuanhua Tombs.[①]

Scenario for the travel and transformation of the signs

How did the Babylonian (or Greek) zodiac signs reach the northwestern regions of China, and then Japan? Travel and cultural exchanges on the Silk Road are certainly a known fact. However, due to diverse cultural, ethnic, and even religious groups who were travelers on the Silk Road, images of the Babylonian zodiac were likely transported via objects, including diagrams, sketches, personal accessories, and other vessels and means. I suggest the path of the Babylonian (or Greek) signs mapping from Xuanhua and Dunhuang, to the east, connecting Xi'an, the capital city of Tang China, and reaching Japan; to the west, continuing to Kashgar, where the route splits West, leading to Iran (and neighbor nations), and South, leading to North India; and vice versa, from India (and West Asia), and arrived in Xuanhua and Dunhuang, China.

From the regions of Iran and Iraq, two silver/metal artifacts are included here, dating to the 13th century AD and bearing the Babylonian zodiac. One is the so-called "Wade Cup" (ca. 1200–1225 CE), currently in the collection of the Cleveland Museum of Art (USA), an Iranian work of the 13th century. The "Wade Cup" is made of brass inlaid with silver and the metalwork and engraving is exquisite. The astrological zodiac signs are treated with other designs at the exterior rim of the cup. Some individual signs share human figures with their identifiable attributes; some maintain their original Babylonian (or Greek) symbols; the sign of Leo is easily recognized by the shape of lion.[②] The other is a metal candlestick with Christian scenes, now in the Bibliothèque des Arts Décoratifs (Paris, France), from Mosul, Iraq of the Zengid dynasty (1127–1250 AD). With recent studies by scholars of various disciplines, they illustrate that uses of astronomy, cartography, and astrology, which spread into the regions of Arabic-Islamic cultures, then further throughout Asia. Other influences from China or Central Asia, and vice versa, via the Silk Route where Iran and Anatolia (Turkey)

---

① Although the function of mandalas is clear, why these Japanese mandalas incorporated astrological signs remains unclear. For example, the star mandala of Kumeta Temple suggests an association with Daoism and the School of *Yin* and *Yang*, but such suggestions require further study (Tokyo National Museum, *Elegance, Virtue, & Ceremony: Buddhist Painting of the Heian and Kamakura Periods*, 351). In addition, another star mandala, in the Metropolitan Museum of Art and dated in the 2nd half of the 14th century CE, also bears the twelve Babylonian zodiac signs and awaits a further study.

② This silver cup is currently on display at the Cleveland Museum of Art; unfortunately, its provenance is not known. In addition, this metal piece is dated to ca. 1200–1225 AD during the Seljuk Period, which ended by 1200 AD, except in Anatolia; the Seljuk Empire in Iran was defeated by Genghis Khan and later became a vessel of the Mongol Empire in 1220s. This artifact awaits further study. See http://www.britannica.com/EBchecked/topic/293359/Iran/32169/The-Seljuqs-and-the-Mongols?anchor=ref315798 (accessed on December 28, 2012).

connected, later entered Europe in the medieval period and later.[1]

Postscript

As I pointed at the beginning of this paper, this research is challenging and complicated due to its geographical scope and cultural/religious diversity; especially applications of the twelve zodiac signs in Islam and Judaism which are beyond my disciplinary. Here, I provide no conclusions, but rather raise questions in the study of cross-culturalism. A few final remarks regarding this research may perhaps add some insights; a few directions for further research are clear. One concerns the function of the astrological signs in the surviving artifacts; and the other is the symbolic purposes of these motifs.

The medium of the artifacts discussed includes mural paintings, silk banners, ceramics and metalwork; their uses range from ritual and religious practices to secular decorations and functions. Architectural fragments and ornaments, which were made of both ceramic and sulfur glass, were attached to the roof ridges found in the Ningxia Muslim Autonomous Region. Interestingly the motifs of these architectural pieces are identified as the Capricorn sign, *mojie* in Chinese, a beast head with fish body and tail.[2] Based on the extant scholarship and the presentation of this paper, the uses of the Babylonian zodiac signs were largely associated with religious/Buddhist practices in China. Do these architectural fragments suggest that astrological motifs are also associated with other contexts? If so, how did this transition occur? Or were perhaps pictorial motifs/symbols such as the Babylonian astrological signs, with various forms of humans and animals, not strictly defined as religious in these religious contexts? Or might these pictorial motifs have been always fully employed and operated in both secular and religious functions? Or were "foreign" pictorial motifs variable in their meaning and freely adapted from example to example after traveling from one place to another place, and one culture to another culture? It is logical and sensible that the Babylonian astrological signs should have been displayed in a sequence; the examples of artifacts that I have included in this paper confirm this practice. How can we explain the roof corner pieces and ridge ornaments featuring Capricorn or *mojie*, which were required in both quantity and scale, with respect to religious beliefs in medieval China? Or does the sign of Capricorn have a specific association in art or in other contexts that accounts for its popularity in Chinese visual culture?[3]

---

[1] Philippe Forêt & Andreas Kaplony ed., *The Journey of Maps and Images on the Silk Road* (Leiden & Boston: Brill, 2008); Paul Kumitzsch, "Celestial Maps and Illustrations in Arabic-Islamic Astronomy," *The Journey of Maps and Images on the Silk Road*, Chapter 9: 175-180; Songja Brentjes, "Revisiting Catalan Portolan Charts: Do they contain elements of Asian provenance?," *The Journey of Maps and Images on the Silk Road*," Chapter 10: 181-199; Ernest J. Grube, "Chinese Elements in Islamic Art, specificall in the Timurid Period," *The Phenonmenon of "Foreign" in Oriental Art*, ed. By Annette Hagedorn (Germany: Reichert Verlag Wiesbaden, 2006), 71-88.

[2] *Da Xia Xun Zong: Xi Xia Wenwu jicui*, 208-216.

[3] The confusion regarding the sign of Capricorn and other hybrid creatures in Chinese art is currently being studied by the present author for a future publication.

Appendix: Illustrations

Fig. 1: Mogao Grottoes, Dunhuang, Gansu, China (photography by the author)

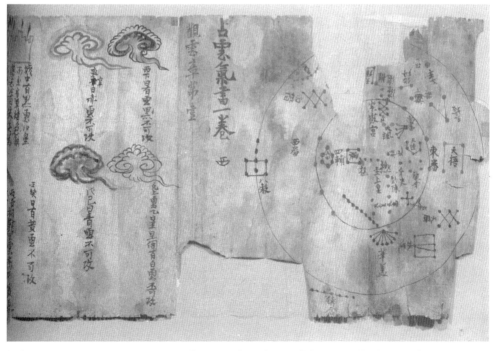

Fig. 2: Chinese twenty–eight stars astrology (Courtesy of *Dunhuang Shiku quanji*, The Commercial Press, Ltd., 2001)

Figs. 3 & 4: Ceiling mural from one of Xuanhua Liao tombs (Courtesy of *Xuanhua Liaomu*.

Beijing: Wenwu chubenshe, 2001)

Fig. 5: Aquarius & Gemini (Courtesy of *Xuanhua Liaomu*)

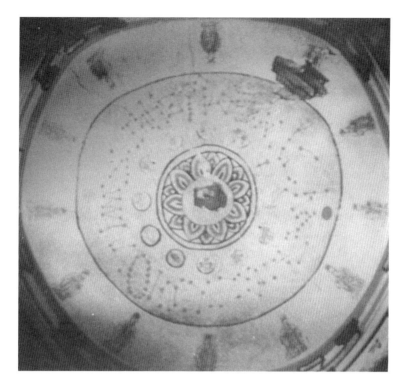

Fig. 6: Ceiling mural of Xuanhua tomb, M2 (Courtesy of *Xuanhua*)

u)

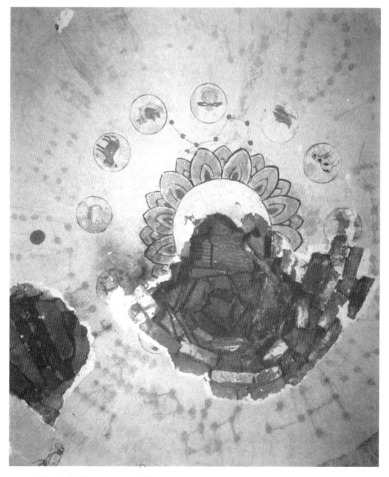

Fig. 7: Ceiling mural of Xuanhua tomb, M5 (Courtesy of *Xuanhua Liaomu*)

Fig. 8: Mogao Caves, no. 61, east wall of the entrance pathway (Courtesy of Dunhuang Research Academy)

Fig. 9: Buddha *Tejabrabha*, with deities of Sun and Moon, west wall of the entrance pathway of Mogao Caves, no. 61

(Courtesy of Dunhuang Research Academy)

Fig. 10: Details of East Wall of entrance pathway: Celestial Deities with Scorpion, Gemini, and Pisces

(Courtesy of Dunhuang Research Academy)

Fig. 11: Buddha *Tejaprabha* (Courtesy of *Da Xia xunzong: Xi Xia wenwu jicui*. Beijing: China Academy of Social Science Publishing, 2004)

Fig. 12: Capricorn, architectural fragment (Courtesy of *Da Xia xunzong: Xi Xia wenwu jicui*. Beijing: China Academy of Social Science Publishing, 2004)

Sailing the Ancient Silk Road of Western Central Asia

Jeffrey D. Lerner，Wake Forest University

Abstract: In the third century BCE, the Seleukid admiral Patrokles reported on large quantities of Indian goods that made their way from India and along a water route that connected the Central Asian country of Baktria to the Black Sea. Two centuries later Marcus Terentius Varro learned of the same route. Modern scholarship has tended to question the veracity of these accounts, even though the Han ambassador Zhang Qian in the mid-second century BCE likewise reported that Baktrian merchants regularly returned from India bearing Chinese goods. This paper seeks to establish the veracity of these accounts by examining the excavations conducted at the Hellenistic site of Aï Khanoum in Baktria (northeastern Afghanistan), which suggest that the city participated in regular commercial relations between Europe and South Asia.

Keywords: Aï Khanoum, Baktria, Oxos River, Kelif Uzboi, Black Sea, Caspian Sea

During the co-regency of Seleukos I and Antiochos I (c. 292–281 BCE), the Makedonian general and admiral Patrokles was appointed the task of exploring the Caspian Sea.[①] It is from him that Strabo understood the Caspian (i.e., Hyrkanian) Sea to have been an inland gulf of the Ocean with the rivers Oxos (modern Amu Daria) and Iaxartes (modern Syr Daria) discharging their waters into it.[②]

According to Patrokles, there were a series of interconnected water routes that were easily navigable between the river Oxos and the Black Sea city of Phasis, which were used by merchants journeying between Europe and India (Strabo 11.2.17 [507]). Thus the river Oxos, which formed the frontier between Baktria and Sogdiana, enabled merchants carrying Indian wares brought over the Hindu Kush Mountains to sail into the Caspian Sea, from where they were conveyed through Albania and along the Kuros River up to the Surami Pass and after a four day portage reached the city of Phasis by way of the river bearing the same name (Strabo 2.1.15 [73]).

[①]　Strabo 2.1.15 [73], 11.7.1 [508], 11.7.3 [509], 11.11.5–6 [518]; *cf.* Pliny 2.67 [167–168] and 6.21 [58] in which he seems to describe a sea passage that Patrokles took through the Caspian and Hyrkanian Sea to the Ocean and thence onto India.

[②]　Strabo 11.6.1 [507]; *cf.* 2.5.14 [118–119], 11.1.5 [491], 11.11.5 [518].

Some two centuries later during the third war against Mithridates VI in 65/64 BCE, Marcus Terentius Varro, while serving under Pompey, apparently learned of this same route. According to Pliny, it took seven days to reach the river Icarus in Baktria from India where it flows into the river Oxos and that Indian merchandise sailed from it through the Caspian Sea into the river Kyros where it *can be conveyed* by land to Phasis on the Black Sea in a journey lasting at most five days.[1] Moreover, we learn from Pseudo-Scymnos that in the city of Phasis there are barbarians from some sixty nations all speaking different languages, including those "from India and Baktria." [2]

It is clear that whatever direction Patrokles' voyage took on the Caspian he did not circumnavigate it, but instead seemed to have relied on informants for his description of the coast. Modern opinion remains divided on the feasibility that there was a trade route from India to the Black Sea as reported by Strabo (11.6.1 [507]) and Pliny (6.15 [36–37]) between those who maintain that such a route never existed and those who regard that it was of a "casual nature." [3] In other words, most dismiss the use of these waterways as a means by which trade of any significance was conducted and prefer instead to regard this highway as either unfounded stories believed by naïve explorers, or as exaggerations of an insignificant, irregular commercial exchange network involving small incidental items like coins and spices. Yet there is one significant factor that has been generally overlooked.

Aï Khanoum

From 1964–1978 in northeastern Afghanistan a Greek city known by its Uzbek name of Aï Khanoum, or "Moon Lady," (see map 1) was excavated by the French Archaeological Mission in Afghanistan. The site located along the Oxos River formed part of ancient Baktria in the Hellenistic Far East that had been conquered by Alexander the Great (329–327 BCE) during his Central Asian campaign, and remained under Greek rule until it was abandoned by its inhabitants in the middle of the first century BCE.[4] Inside the city at the palace treasury and the Temple with Indented Niches the mission unearthed a number of items imported from India, the Mediterranean and Black Sea, and the Near East as well as others produced locally in Central Asia.[5] Moreover, Zhang Qian, the Chinese envoy and diplomat sent by emperor Wudi of the Han dynasty to the Western Regions in 139 BCE[6] reported that he found the market of the main Baktrian city of Lanshi or Baktra to contain all sorts of goods that were bought and sold, including bamboo and cloth from China, and was told that merchants from Baktria journeyed to buy them in India.[7]

In the early stages of the site's excavations a group of five amphorae of Mediterranean or more probably Black Sea origin were unearthed, including a complete one from the city's southern residential quarter dated from the end of the fourth to the beginning of the third century BCE. Taken altogether the fragments of

---

[1] Pliny, *Natural History*, 6.19 [52]. Pearson (1960: 164), rightly argues that the use of *posse devehi* only serves to highlight the possibility that the trade route was in use at this time; it cannot be taken, however, as evidence that the route was no longer in existence; *cf*. Braund 1994: 41; Braund 2002: 291–295.

[2] *Ad Nicomedem regem*, 934 [F20]; *cf*. Johnston 1913: 260–262. On the city's founding, see Asheri 1998: 271 n.11.

[3] Lordkipanidze 2000: 30; *cf*. Lordkipanidze 1991: 135; Lordkipanidze 1996: 113–120; Gardiner-Garden 1987: 39–48; Braund 1994: 40–42; Braund 1999: 39–40.

[4] Lerner 2010: 66–72.

[5] See Rapin 1992: 143–256, 399–407.

[6] For a discussion on the problems of dating Zhang Qian's expedition, Hulsewé in Hulsewé/Loewe 1979: 209 n.774, and 13–39 on the transmission of Zhang Qian's account.

[7] *Shiji* 116 and 123; *Hanshu* 61 2B–3A.

these receptacles suggest that amphorae were used for storing (vintage?) wine and olive oil among other commodities.[1] It is speculated that wine was at least occasionally, if not rarely, imported from the West to Baktria and reserved perhaps for special occasions.[2]

Overland Routes

The presence of foreign made transport amphorae from the Black Sea or eastern Mediterranean poses the question of how they were brought to Aï Khanoum. After all, their shape, especially with a pointed base, was more practical for transport by ship than by pack

Map 1. Location of Aï Khanoum

animal, particularly given the long distance journey that the receptacle and its liquid contents would have endured. If in fact they were brought by pack animal, like camels, one can only imagine the impracticality of

---

①　According to Strabo 2.1.14, 2.73 and Herodotus 1.193, in Mesopotamia the use of olive oil is replaced by sesame oil. This practice thus explains the necessity of importing olive oil to Aï Khanoum. It also explains why it was stored as a luxury item in the palace treasury.

② 　A stamped amphora handle was noted among the objects unearthed from floor 1 of the propylaion (Inventory no.: Akh 407. Bernard consulted with Virginia Grace for much of the analysis of the piece, including the reading of the inscription, its provenance, and date (Bernard in Schlumberger/Bernard 1965: 635–639 no. 90, figs. 28–29; *Iscrizioni* 2004: no. 322). Opinions about the origin of this amphora like others found in the city at this time were divided: either it was made in Aï Khanoum or some other local Baktrian workshop, or it came from the Black Sea, perhaps from Sinope, or from a site located along the Near Eastern seaboard of the Mediterranean, such as from a city in Syria (Bernard 1965: 634–635, fig. 27 nos. 87 [AKh 140], 88 [AKh 390], and 89 [AKh 353]). Sinope was famous for its exports of wine and olive oil in amphorae (Doonan 1999: 42–45 for a concise overview). A compelling argument is made by Tsetskhladze and Vnukov (1992: 357–358, 363, 365, 380, 383–386) who identify amphorae produced in Kolkhis and designated as "Variant A" as the work of potters from Sinope in the mid–fourth to third century BCE. Thus it is possible that if these amphorae came from the Black Sea they may have been manufactured in a Kolkhian city like Phasis. Based on analogies, the amphora was tentatively dated to the High Hellenistic period of the third century BCE, although the fourth century was not entirely excluded. Finds of additional transport amphorae confirmed that the jar in fact had been imported from the west (Gardin 1985:460 n. 10). Among the finds made later in 1970 near stage III of the house in Aï Khanoum's southern residential quarter was a complete amphora. It, too, is of Mediterranean origin and has tentatively been dated between the end of the third and the beginning of the second century BCE (The amphora was found in room 26, see Bernard 1971: 411, figs. 11 and 14. On the chronology that was in use at that time to date it, see Gardin 1971: 447–452). Finally, store room 109 of the treasury yielded two fragments of another amphora identified as a *kermion* with an unreadable stamped handle (Rapin 1992: 113–114, pl. 57, 304, 327).

transporting these commodities given what must have been a high percentage of breakage. Yet the prevailing theory that seeks to explain how these vessels arrived at the site favors just such an overland journey of perhaps thousands of kilometers, although there is no consensus as to a specific route that might have been taken.

There are of course a number of well documented routes in antiquity that connected the Mediterranean world with Central Asia. For example, one of the most famous is the account preserved by Isidore of Charax who describes the overland journey from the Euphrates to Alexandropolis, modern Kandahar, in Afghanistan with numerous stations in between.[1] A similar route is described by the Roman merchant Maes Titianus who ventured from Asia Minor to western Central Asia, whereupon his agents completed the round-trip journey to the eastern city of "Sera Metropolis" in China.[2]

A third overland route ran north of the Iranian kingdom of Parthia and was controlled by numerous indistinct groups of nomads living in the region between the fringes of the Greek city-states of the Black Sea and ancient Khorasmia on the southern banks of the Aral Sea in Central Asia.[3] Another trade-route stems from an account in Strabo who states that nomads on the Black Sea and the western coast of the Caspian regularly imported on camels merchandise from India and Bablyonia by way of Armenia and Media.[4]

Aside from overland routes, goods were also shipped by sea to and from Indian ports. According to the Periplus of the Erythrean Sea, written probably shortly before 70 CE, Chinese goods, like silk, were transported on land through Baktria to the west coast of India from where they were then dispatched to Egyptian ports along the Red Sea, or through the Persian Gulf into Mesopotamia.[5]

Regardless of the route taken, however, each of these possibilities still leaves us with the problem of how to explain why amphorae better suited for transport by ship would have been brought overland to Aï Khanoum. Or better still, is there a viable route by ship to explain their appearance? After all, if the ceramic transport flask dating at least to the fourth century BCE from the Kurganzol fortress in Sogdiana (in modern southern Uzbekistan) is any indication, there were alternative receptacles better suited for long and short distances for overland journeys used by pack animals.[6] So the question remains: why do these western amphorae from the Black Sea or the Mediterranean basin appear in the archaeological record at Aï Khanoum?

Climate Change

Beginning in the middle of the ninth century BCE and continuing into the fifteenth century CE, the climate in northwest Europe and southern Siberia underwent a shift from the Subboreal to the Subatlantic due to a decrease in solar activity in which conditions became wetter and more humid, turning semi-deserts into lush stepped landscapes allowing for "a high biomass production, and therefore high carrying capacity." The

---

[1] Schoff 1914.

[2] E.g., Lerner 1998.

[3] The existence of this highway rests solely on the archaeological finds of nomadic and Greek pottery at Altyn-Asar in Khorasmia and on objects from India, the eastern Mediterranean, and of Sarmatian type, such as beads and a bronze mirror, found in the nearby kurgans at Tuz-Gyr dated from the fifth to the second century BCE. See, Толстов 1962: 186–200, esp. 187–189, 192–193 and Трудновская 1979: 106, 108–110, fig. 4; cf. Mutallib/Muxammedzon/ Rapin 2001: 57–59 esp. n.43.

[4] Manandian 1965: 50; cf. 30–33, 47–52, who traces the route according to the *Tabula Peutingeriana*; *cf.* Hewsen 2001: 62–65; Callieri 1999: 38–40. On trade in Sarmatia along the Caspian route.

[5] A number of recent works dealing with this topic have recently been published, e.g., McLaughlin 2010; Sidebotham 2011.

[6] As seen in Swertschkow 2009: 147 fig.6, 150.

onset of this climate change led to the increase of Scythian populations and their "expansion and migration" out of southern Siberia southward into Central Asia and westward into the Black Sea region.[1]

Central Asia in the eighth century BCE was marked by the pluvial period in which the Prisarykamysh delta at the mouth of the Amu Daria filled with water and overflowed into the Sarkamysh depression about 200 km southwest of the Aral Sea (Map 2). The result was the Sarykamysh Lake situated between the Caspian Sea and the Aral Sea. Throughout this period there was a regeneration of the steppe landscape with forests lining the banks of rivers and reservoirs. In the seventh century BCE to the fourth century CE the region witnessed a growth in river valleys, such as the emergence of the Uzboi River, while the entire deltaic region of the Aral Sea was filled with water. The emergence of the lake in the second half of the first millennium BCE allowed for intensive irrigation resulting in the blossoming of Korezm civilization on the southern shore of the Aral Sea. Not until the end of this period in the fifth century CE did the deltaic

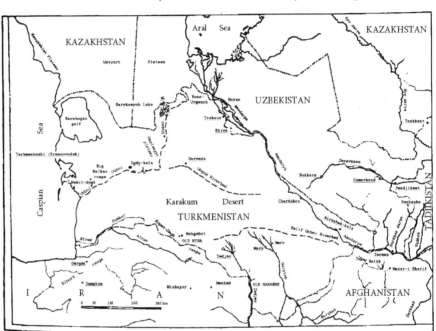

Map 2. Karakum Desert and the Uzboi Rivers (based on Bader/Usupov 1995, 29, fig.1).

channels begin to dry up and the Sarykamysh's water level likewise begin to drop significantly.[2] A similar climatic pattern throughout this period has also been detected to the east in the Ferghana valley[3] and to the south in the Merv oasis.[4]

In the last centuries leading to the Common Era, the Caspian Sea attained its maximum extent, causing vast territories in Central Asia to be inundated by its waters from the inflow of the Uzboi River which linked the Caspian Sea and the Sarykamysh Lake. Currently, the Amu Daria when it reaches Turkestan abruptly forms an oxbow from west to north, but at times in both the recent geological (Holocene) and historical past, the Amu Daria diverted itself (by sediment accumulation in its bed) or was diverted by humans westward, first filling the Sarykamysh Depression and then overflowing into the Uzboi depression where it emptied into the Caspian Sea. This channel of the Amu Daria depending on the route that it took was variously called the Unguz or the Sarykamysh Uzboi. Most of the time, the entire flow of the Amu was diverted, leading to the rapid desiccation

---

① van Geel/Bokovenko/Burova/Chugunov/Dergachev/Dirksen/Kulkova/Nagler/Parzinger/van der Plicht/Vasiliev/Zaitseva 2004: 151−158.

② Вайнберг/*Глушко*/*Цвецинская* 1998: 34−36, 39−41, especially the table on pp. 31−33.

③ Мокрынин/Плоских 2010: 37−38, 49−52, 98−99, 142−147.

④ Кошеленко/Губаев/Гаибов/Бадер 1994: 86−90.

of the Aral Sea into which the Amu normally flows. However, there were other occasions when the flow was bifurcated with one branch continuing to the Aral and another flowing into the Sarykamysh Uzboi.[1]

It was at the mouth of the upper Uzboi some 200 km northeast of the Balkhan Mountains that the Parthians between the second century BCE and first century CE founded their most northerly fortress at Igdy-qala on the border of Khorezm in order to safeguard the lucrative commercial waterways running from the west and south, and the overland caravan routes coming from the north and east.[2] Moreover, excavations of sites dating from the fifth century BCE along the lower Uzboi reveal that water flowed along this depression into the Caspian well into the first centuries of the Common Era.

The result is that what is now the Karakum Desert of Turkmenistan and Uzbekistan was in antiquity a completely different landscape marked by semi-desert, on the one hand, and immense forests along the Sarykamysh and Murgab valley on the other. An abundance of groundwater throughout the region, however, provided numerous pastures for nomads and their horses, including the Parni, a branch of the Scythian Dahae, from where led by their chief Arsakes in the mid-third century BCE they invaded the Seleukid satrapy of Parthia and founded the Arsakid or Parthian kingdom.

Finally, the ancient Kelif Uzboi channel, watered by the Amu and the rivers of Afghanistan, was not connected to the Sarykamysh Uzboi. Originating at the oxbow of the Amu Daria, this channel forms the southern most branch of the Amu near the Hellenistic site of Mirzabek kala.[3] The channel, however, is actually composed of a series of interconnected depressions that take the form of settling lakes, which when filled take on the appearance of a river. The Kelif Uzboi slopes in a westerly direction and empties into the Caspian. A line of seven Parthian fortresses situated at intervals of 50 km – a one to two days' march – along the Kelif Uzboi have been detected at the Merv oasis in the Murgab delta as part of the security afforded to travelers by caravan or ship.[4] During Alexander's campaign in Central Asia, it was along this same depression, known as the river Ochos by Greek and Latin authors, that he arrived at the Merv oasis where he founded Alexandria Margiana in 328 BCE.[5]

Conclusion

The excavations at Aï Khanoum suggest that the city participated in regular commercial relations between

---

[1] In c. 2000 BCE the Amu Daria ceased flowing directly into the Caspian, having changed its course to the current Akcha Daria channel (Boroffka 2010: 286–289, 294, 299). A concise hydrological and historical overview from the Neolithic to the Middle Ages is presented by Aladin/Plotnikov/Orlova/Filippov/Smurov/Pirulin/Rusakova/Zhakova 1996: especially 34–38.

[2] In one of its later incarnations, the fort has tentatively been identified as the capital of the Kidarites, known as Balkhan or Bolo-Balaam. Thus, Yagodin 2007: 51; *contra* Grenet 2002: 211. Vainberg supposes that the fortress Igdy-qala by the 4th century CE had ceased to exist (Ваинберг 1999: 257).

[3] Пилипко 1985: 47–60, 72–75, 177–178.

[4] Cerasetti 2004: 40–41.

[5] Notably, Curtius 7.10.15; Strabo 11.6.1, 7.3–4, 8.1–3, 9.2, 11.5; Pliny NH 6.18/49; 31.75/39; Ammianus Marcellinus 23.6.57; Polybios 10.48. For a discussion on the sources, see Walbank 1967: 261–265; Кошеленко/Гаибов/Бадер 1997: 66; Кошеленко/Губаев/Гаибов/Бадер 1994: 85–86; Košelenko/Bader/Gaibov 1996: 125–137; Koshelenko/Gaibov/Bader 1996: 308–317; Кошеленко/Гаибов/Бадер 2000: 7–10, 15; Olbrycht 2003: 114–117; Olbrycht 2004: 211–222; Олбрухт 2009: 86–90; Olbrycht 2010: 302–309; *cf.* Olbrycht 1998: 74. Juping has hypothesized that the formal opening of the Silk Road occurred as the direct result of Alexander's Central Asian campaign in which Aï Khanoum enjoyed a pivotal role (Juping 2009: 16–19).

Europe and South Asia and indirectly with China. Apart from the information gleaned from the ancient sources, the western end of this route has yielded very little in the way of objects from Central Asia and regions further east, apart from Graeco–Baktrian coins, albeit in extremely limited quantities, that have turned up in the Kura valley and other sites nearby, including Kabala and Tbilisi. Their presence, however, is not proof that they were brought by ship, since there was sufficient overland traffic and could thus easily have been transported by caravan. The imported Aï Khanoum amphorae, on the other hand, offer our best demonstration that water transport between the Black Sea and Central Asia was a regular, though somewhat limited, feature of the trade and commerce that was practiced throughout the Hellenistic Period.

One cannot help but to wonder if it was none other than the Indian merchants themselves who upon their return journey from the West brought with them amphorae filled with olive oil and wine for the Greek–Baktrians of Aï Khanoum. Unlike its overland counterparts, however, this route lacked the state formations that would presumably have provided the security needed for it to have flourished. Nonetheless, we need no longer imagine that when western imports arrived in Baktria they were brought on the backs of animals or men,[1] but in boats that sailed from ports on the Mediterranean and Black Seas to cities that lined the Oxus in Central Asia.

Bibliography

Aladin, N.V./Plotnikov, I.S./Orlova, M.I./Filippov, A.A./Smurov, A.O./Pirulin, D.D./Rusakova, O.M./Zhakova, L.V. 1996. Changes in the form and biota of the Aral Sea over time. NATO ASI Series, 2. *Environment 12. The Aral Sea Basin*, eds. P.P. Micklin/W.D. Williams (Berlin): 33-55.

Asheri, D. 1998. The Achaeans and the Heniochi. Reflections on the origins and history of a Greek rhetorical topos in: *The Greek colonisation of the Black Sea area: historical interpretation of archaeology*, ed. G.R. Tsetskhladze, Historia: Einzelschriften, H. 121 (Stuttgart): 265–286.

Bader, A.N./Usupov, Kh. 1995: 'Gold earrings from north–west Turkmenistan'. In Invernizzi, A. (ed.) *In the Land of the Gryphons. Papers on Central Asian Archaeology in Antiquity*, (Firenze), 23–38.

Bernard, P. 1971. La campagne de fouilles à Aï Khanoum (Afghanistan), *Comptes Rendus de l'Académie des Inscriptions et Belles–Lettres* 1971: 385–452.

Boroffka, N.G.O. 2010. Archaeology and its relevance to climate and water level changes: a review, *The Aral Sea Environment, Handbook of Environmental* Chemistry, 7: 283–303.

Braund, D. 1994. *Georgia in antiquity: a history of Colchis and Transcaucasian Iberia: 550 BC–AD 562* (Oxford/New York).

Braund, D. 1999. Indian traders at Phasis, *Trade on the Black Sea in the Archaic and Classical periods: historical perspective of the Silk Road*, ed. O. Lordkipanidze (Tbilisi): 39–40.

Braund, D. 2002. Indian traders at Phasis: neglected texts on Ancient Georgia in: *Pont–Euxin et commerce: la genèse de la Route de la soie: actes du IXe Symposium de Vani, Colchide, 1999*, eds. M. Faudot/A. Fraysse/É. Geny (Paris), 287–295.

Callieri, P. 1999. L'esplorazione geografica dell'Iran in epoca ellenistica e romana: il contributo della documentazione archeological, Ocnus 7: 31–43.

---

[1] Gardin 1985: 11 n.23.

Doonan, O. 1999. Trade in ancient Sinope: thoughts on the structure of intra-regional production and exchange, *Trade on the Black Sea in the Archaic and Classical periods: historical perspective of the Silk Road*, ed. O. Lordkipanidze (Tbilisi): 41-45.

Gardin, J.-Cl. 1971. C é ramique. In: Bernard 1971: 447-452.

Gardin, J.C. 1985. Les relations entre la M é diterran é e et la Bactriane dans l' Antiquité d' après des données céramologiques in é dites in: *De l' Indus aux Balkans: recueil à la mémoire de Jean Deshayes*, contributions rassemblées et édités par J.-L. Huot et al. (Paris): 447-460.

Gardiner-Garden, J.R. 1987. *Greek conceptions of Inner Asian geography and ethnography from Ephoros to Eratosthanes*, Papers on Inner Asia no.9 (Bloomington).

Grenet, F. 2002. Regional interaction in Central Asia and Northwest India in the Kidarite and Hephthalite in: *Indo-Iranian languages and peoples*, ed. N. Sims-Williams, *Proceedings of the British Academy* 116: 203-224.

Hewsen, R.H. 2001. *Armenia. A historical atlas* (Chicago/London).

Hulsewé/Lowe 1979. Hulsewé, A.F.P. 1979. *China in central Asia: the early stage*: 125 B.C. -A.D. 23: *An annotated translation of chapters 61 and 69 of the history of the former Han Dynasty, with an introduction by M.A.N. Lowe*. *Sinica Leidensia*, 4 (Leiden). *Iscrizioni 2004. Iscrizioni dello estremo oriente greco: un repertorio*, a cura di F.C. de Rossi (Bonn).

Johnston, H.A. 1913. The earliest colonizers of the Euxine Sea: II. The Hellenization of the Euxine, *Studies: an Irish quarterly review* 2/7: 247-282.

Juping, Y. 2009. Alexander the Great and the emergence of the Silk Road, *The Silk Road* 6/2: 15-22.

Košelenko, G./Bader, A./Gaibov, W., 1996. Die Margiana in hellenistischer Zeit in: *Hellenismus Beiträge zur Erforschung von Akkulturation und politischer Ordnung in den Staaten des hellenistischen Zeitalters (Akten des Internationalen Hellenismus-Kolloquiums 9.-14. März 1994 in Berlin.)*, Hrsg. v. Bernd Funck (T ü bingen): 121-145.

Koshelenko, G.A./Gaibov, V./Bader, A. 1996. Evolution of the settlement patterns in the Merv oasis (Turkmenistan) from Alexander the Great to Arab conquest in: *La Persia e l'Asia Centrale da Alessandro al X secolo (Roma, 9-12 novembre 1994)*, Atti dei Convegni Lincei, 127 (Roma): 305-317.

Lerner, J.D. 1998. "Ptolemy and Silk Road: From Baktra Basileion to Sera Metropolis," *East and West* 48/1-2: 9-26.

Lerner, J.D. 2010. Revising the chronologies of the Hellenistic colonies of Samarkand-Marakanda (Afrasiab II-III) and Aï Khanoum (northeastern Afghanistan), *Anabasis: studia classica et orientalia* 1: 58-79.

Lordkipanidze, O. 1991. *Archäologie in Georgien: von der Altsteinzeit zum Mittelalter*, Quellen und Forschungen zur prähistorischen und provinzialrömischen Archäologie, Bd. 5 (Weinheim).

Lordkipanidze, O. 1996. *Das alte Georgien (Kolchis und Iberien) in Strabons Geographie*, Neue Scholien, Deutsch von N. Begiaschwili (Amsterdam).

Lordkipanidze, O. 2000. *Phasis: the river and city in Colchis*, Geographica historica, Bd. 15 (Stuttgart).

Manandian, H.A. 1965. *The trade and cities of Armenia in relation to ancient world trade*, transl. from the second rev. ed. N.G. Garsoian (Lisbon).

McLaughlin, R. 2010. *Rome and the distant East: trade routes to the ancient lands of Arabia, India and China* (London/New York).

Mutallib, Kh./Muxammedzon, I./Rapin, Cl. 2001. La tombe d' une princess nomade à Koktepe près de Samarkand, *Comptes Rendus de l' Acad é mie des Inscriptions et Belles-Lettres* 145/1: 33-92.

Olbrycht, M.J. 1998. Parthia et ulteriores gentes. *Die politischen Beziehungen zwischen dem arsakidishen Iran und den Nomaden der eurasischen Steppen* (München).

Olbrycht, M.J. 2003. The Ochos river in the classical sources: a study in the historical geography of northeastern Iran and Middle Asia in: Центральная Азия. *Источники, история, культура*, под. ред. Т. Мкртычева (Москва) : 114–117.

Olbrycht, M.J. 2004. *Aleksander Wielki i swiat iranski* (Rzeszow, Poland).

Olbrycht, J.M. 2010. Some Remarks on the Rivers of Central Asia in Antiquity in: *Gaudeamus Igitur. Studies to honor the 60th birthday of A.V. Podossinov = Gaudeamus Igitur. Сборник статей к 60-летию А.В. Подосинова*, eds. T.N. Jackson/I.G. Konovalova/G.R. Tsetskhladze (Moskva): 302–309

Pearson, L.I.C. 1960. *Lost histories of Alexander the Great* (New York).

Rapin, Cl. 1992. *La trésorerie du palais hellénistique d'Aï Khanoum. L'apogée et la chute du royaume grec de Bactriane.* Mémoires de la Délégation Archéologique Française en Afghanistan 33, Fouilles d'Aï Khanoum 8 (Paris).

Schlumberger, D./Bernard, P. 1965. Aï Khanoum, BCH 89: 590–657.

Schoff, W.H. 1914. *Parthian Stations of Isidore of Charax: An account of the overland trade route between the Levant and India in the first century* B.C. (Philadelphia).

Sidebotham, S.E. 2011. *Berenike and the ancient maritime spice route*, The California world history library, 18 (Berkeley/Los Angeles).

Swertschkow, L.M. 2009. Die Grabungen im Fort Kurgansol im Süden Usbekistans – neue Daten zur Geschichte Zentralasiens am Ende des 4. Jhs. v. Chr. im: *Alexander der Grosse und die Öffnung der Welt. Asiens Kulturen im Wandel*, Publikationen der Reiss–Engelhorn–Museen, Bd. 36, S. Hansen/A. Wieczorek/M. Tellenbach, Hrsg. (Manheim): 145–153.

Tsetskhladze, G.R./Vnukov, S.Y. 1992. Colchian amphorae: typology, chronology, and aspects of production, *Annual of the British School at Athens* 87: 357–386.

van Geel, B./Bokovenko, N.A./Burova, N.D./Chugunov, K.V./Dergachev, V.A./Dirksen, V.G./Kulkova, M./Nagler, A./Parzinger, H./van der Plicht, J./Vasiliev, S.S./Zaitseva, G.I. 2004. The sun, climate change and the expansion of the Scythian culture after 850 BC in: *Impact of the environment on human migration in Eurasia*, NATO Science Series IV: Earth and environmental sciences v. 42, eds. E.M. Scott/A. Yu. Alekseev/G. Zaitseva (The Netherlands, 2004): 151–158.

Walbank, F.W. 1967. *A historical commentary on Polybius, vol. 2: commentary on Books VII–XVIII* (Oxford).

Yagodin, V.N. 2007. The Duana archaeological complex in: A*ncient nomads of the Aralo–Caspian region. The Duana Archaeological Complex*, eds. A.V.G. Betts/S. Blau (Leuven/Paris/Dudley): 11–78.

* * *

Ваинберг, Б.И. 1999. *Этнография Турана в древности, VII в. до н.э.-VIII в. н.э.* (Москва).

Вайнберг, Б.И./Глушко, Е.В./Цвецинская Е.А. 1998. Ландшафтно-археологическое исследование эволюции Присарыкамышской дельты Амударьи с использованием дистанционных методов, *Российская археология* 1998/1: 29-42.

Кошеленко, Г.А./Гаибов, В.А./Бадер, А.Н. 1997. О некоторых особенностях экологической ситуации в Мервском оазисе в древности и раннем средневековье, *Проблемы истории, филологии, культуры*, Межвузовский сборник, вып. 4/1. История: 57-72.

Кошеленко, Г.А./Гаибов, В.А./Бадер, А.Н. 2000. Александр Македонский в Маргиане, *Вестник древней истории* 230/1: 3-15.

Кошеленко, Г.А./Губаев, А.Г./Гаибов, В.А./Бадер, А.Н. 1994. Мервский оазис: динамика систем расселения и ирригации, *ВДИ* 1994/4: 78-91.

Мокрынин В./В. Плоских. 2010. *Археология и история Кыргызстана. Избранное, ред.*- сост. В.А. Воропаева (Бишкек: Илим).

Олбрухт, М.Я. 2009. Страбон и Ох: некоторые замечания по рекам античной Центральной

Азии в: *Дорога страбона как часть великого шелкового нути: Материалы Междынародной конференции (Баку, 28-29 ноября 2008 г.)*, ред. С.Г. Кляшторной/Ш.М. Мустафаев (Самарканд/Ташкент), 86-91.

Пилипко, В.Н. 1985. *Поселения северо-западной Батрии* (Ашхабад).

Толстов, С.П. 1962. *По древним дельтам Окса и Яксарта* (Москва).

Трудновская, С.А. 1979. Ранние погребения юго-западной курганной группы могильника

Туз-гыр in: *Кочевники на границах Хорезма, Труды Хорезмской Археолого-Этнографической Экспедиции*, под ред. С.П. Толстого, Т. 11 (Москва): 101-110.

China and the Mediterranean World:An international collaborative research project (SERICA)[*]

Samuel N C Lieu，Macquarie University

Abstract: The lecture draws attention to a relatively new international and inter-academy project on textual, epigraphical and archaeological sources relating to China's contacts with the Ancient Mediterranean World. The lecture will showcase a selection of its outcomes so far, viz. a series of monographs as well as a website containing on-line collections of texts and translations (both literary and epigraphical). It will also demonstrate how the compilation of a multilingual gazetteer for the project on 'Places and Peoples of Central Asia' has already helped to advance our ability to identify 'Western' toponymns (place-names) and ethnic terms in Chinese sources of the Han and Tang periods.

(1) About the Project

The theme of our conference, viz. "The Contacts, Exchanges and Comparisons of Ancient Civilizations", provides me with the perfect justification to introduce the participants to a relatively new international project on literary and epigraphical sources of China's contact with the ancient civilizations at the other end of the Eurasian landmass. "China and the Mediterranean World – archaeological sources and literary documents up to the 10th C CE (La Chine et le Monde Méditerranéen: sources archéologiques et documents écrits jusqu'au 10e siècle)" is an international and inter-academy research project adopted by the International Union of Academies (UAI = Union Académique Internationale) at the 78th session of its General Assembly held at Barcelona in May, 2004. The UAI is the over-arching organization for most of the major national academies in the world and plays an active role in fostering international research collaboration. The aim of this new project is to promote greater (and long overdue) collaborative research between scholars in China working on the history and archaeology of pre-Islamic Central Asia and on Hellenistic, Roman and Byzantine history, with their opposite numbers in countries in which research in these areas is more developed.

* The author is grateful to the financial support given to the SERICA project from the Australian Research Council and the Chiang Ching Kuo Foundation for International Scholarly Exchange.

Currently scholars from China are involved in only a handful of the sixty-five major international projects of the UAI and "China and the (Ancient) Mediterranean World" has therefore been given considerable priority by the Union as an international research project in the hope that major funding bodies like UNESCO will be interested in supporting it. The reason why the project has not been more in the public eye is that it is an inter-academy project and almost all the major participants are academicians representing their national academies. However, the collaborative research aspect of the project is open to all scholars as its main channels of publication are monographs and (unrestricted) on-line websites.

The official statement on the project is:

"The UAI has decided to launch this project (in collaboration with the Chinese Academy of Social Sciences and any academy who would like to participate). The aim of the project is to produce a series of volumes, which will demonstrate the mutual knowledge of the respective cultures during these periods, the mutual relations between them and influence they exerted on each other. The time frame shall be from ancient times until the Tang Dynasty in China.

Volumes shall be produced which document mutual contacts and influences, but there shall also be publications containing studies of more synthetic character.

Concrete tasks shall be (i) to collect a corpus of European, Chinese and Central Asian texts, which contain references to the other culture, and publish these in their original as well in translations into Chinese, English and French; (ii) to publish archaeological charts of objects from one culture found in another culture: silver and gold objects, pottery ceramics, silk, numismatic objects etc.; (iii) to produce synthetic studies of cultural, religious, philosophical, social and linguistic influence of one culture upon the other. This project was adopted by the UAI in 2004 as a category B Project."

The first joint-coordinators (i.e. directors) of the project were Prof. Lise Hannestad of the Danish Royal Academy and Prof. Bai Yunxiang of the Institute of Archaeology in Beijing. In 2011, the present author was invited to take over as the UAI co-ordinator of the project from Professor Hannestad. The first academy to provide funding for the project is the Royal Swedish Academy and this has enabled the project to have an official bilingual (English and Chinese) web-page detailing the project. The address for this bilingual webpage is:

http://www.vitterhetsakad.se/uai

The project co-ordinators realized from the outset that the greatest barrier to a deep and critical understanding of Old World cultural development in the early historical periods has been that of language. The primary Western sources are mainly in Latin, Greek, Syriac and Middle Iranian and these have been well studied by European scholars publishing mainly in English, French, German, Italian and Russian. The primary Eastern sources were written in Chinese and have been well studied mostly by Chinese scholars and only by a small number of specialists in the West. There have been a few notable scholars who have bridged the gap between the two but the depth of learning required has effectively prevented a wider field of study at a primary level. Most historians researching on East-West contacts have relied on secondary and tertiary sources for their writings. Provision of high quality translations of key texts with critical commentaries and accompanied by the texts in their original languages will be of great benefit to a much wider field of scholarship and in itself will go some way towards bridging the academic gap between East and West.

(2) Monograph publications

One of the most fundamental tasks of the research team(s) working for the project is to provide collections of texts and inscriptions in a variety of ancient languages in their original scripts together with reliable but not over literal translations in English in facing columns both in book form and in PDF files on the SERICA website (see below). The idea of producing an English version of the classic work of George Coedès, *Textes d'auteurs grecs et latins relatifs à l'Extrême-Orient depuis le IVe siècle avant J.-C. jusqu'au XIVe siècle* (Paris: Ernest Leroux, Éditeur 1910) as the first publication goal of the project was put forward to the co-ordinating committee by the late Professor Gregory Bongard-Levin at the UAI Assembly at Barcelona in 2004. It may seem odd to scholars that the provision of an English version of a collection of Greek and Latin sources published originally a century ago with a French translation should be the first major goal of a project which was about to enter the 21st C. The academic reason behind the suggestion, however, is sound. The collection of Coedès contains many of the better-known Greek and Latin texts on the Far East (incl. North India), and because all the Greek and Latin texts are given in their original, the book has been a standard work of reference for serious scholars throughout the 20th C. The present author immediately pointed out to the coordinating committee in 2004 that a substantial number of texts found in the work of Coedès had already been digitized by a research team under his direction at Macquarie University in Australia and first drafts of English translations of some of these texts had also been prepared by the same team. Dr John Sheldon, a key member of the Australian research team, has now produced the English version which appeared just over two years ago: G. Coedès, *Texts of Greek and Latin Authors on the Far East From the 4th C. B.C.E. to the 14th C. C.E.*, in the series Studia Antiqua Australiensia 4 published by Brepols (Turnhout, 2010, ISBN 9782503533667-1) and full details of it can be found at the publisher's website at:

http://www.brepols.net/Pages/ShowProduct.aspx?prod_id=IS-9782503533667-1

Dr Sheldon had also worked on a commentary to the texts that the original French work of Coedès lacked. Dr Sheldon's monograph-length commentary takes into account more recent scholarship on the historical geography of Central Asia as well as advances in our knowledge of the languages of the region in the pre-Islamic period. The commentary is now ready for publication as Volume 5 in the series Studia Antiqua Australiensia.

Future volumes in the texts and translations series of the project will include collections of Medieval and Byzantine sources on the Far East as well as Chinese Sources (both from Dynastic histories and Buddhist sources) on the Western Regions (esp. sources on Iran, Mesopotamia and Syria).

(3) On-line publications

The now widespread use of the inter-net has made possible collaborative research on a level unimaginable a decade ago. One of the very first pieces of research undertaken by two of a team of scholars, including Professor Nicholas Sims-Williams FBA (UK) and Dr Desmond Durkin-Meistererenst (Berlin, Germany) – both distinguished Iranologists-to show-case the genuinely collaborative nature of the project is 'Aesop's fables in Central Asia'. This fascinating mini-project which traces the transmission of a well-known set of stories from the original Greek to a variety of key Central Asian languages can now be viewed on-line at:

http://www.vitterhetsakad.se/pdf/uai/Turfan.pdf

"China and the Ancient Mediterranean World" was awarded a three-year (2010-2012) research grant by the Australian Research Council as part of its Discovery Project scheme. The Chiang Ching Kuo Foundation for International Scholarly Exchange has also given a support grant for most of the same period. The two awards have enabled the team working under direction of myself and Dr. Gunner Mikkelsen at Macquarie University (Sydney) to make a significant start on the establishment of a multi-purpose research and on-line publication website–SERICA (the Latin name for China, i.e. "land of Silk") as well as to continue the project's program of publications in the form of monographs (see above). The address for the SERICA website is:

http://www.mq.edu.au/research/centres_and_groups/ancient_cultures_research_centre/research/cultural_ex_silkroad/serica/

or simply Google™®: Serica Macquarie.

The SERICA website has a number of sub-sites and the ones which the present author would like to comment on briefly are the following:

(i) Texts and Translations:

This sub-site is designed to highlight on-going work by the Australian team on the translation of ancient and medieval authors on the Far East without jeopardizing the sale of the monographs like the already mentioned English version of the work of George Coedès. The present author has chosen to put on-line a handful of authors translated by the team along with the original Greek texts. These include a section of the *Perlipus of the Erythrean Sea*, a number of sections from Ptolemy's *Geographia* and a section of *Cosmographia Christiana* of Cosmas Indicopleustes, all dealing with Serica / Tzinitza and of proven value to scholars researching on sources on East-West contacts. This sub-site will also showcase the team's ongoing work to provide an English translation (with the hard-to-obtain critical Greek text by Darko) of the sections of *Demonstrations of Histories* by the Byzantine historian Laonicus Chalcocondylas which deal with lands, people and customs Central Asia and the Middle East. Although Laonicu-a native of Athens-wrote in the Early Ottoman period, his work is essential to our knowledge of the Mongols in Central Asia. Only the first three books of his work (which contains a total of ten books) are available to scholars in English translation in a published format.[1] An English translation (accompanied by the Greek text) of all the relevant passages (*excursus*) found in these and in the subsequent books will gradually be made available through the SERICA website and this should fill a significant gap for scholars of East-West contacts in the Mongol period.

(ii) Inscriptions:

An innovative aspect of the project is the provision through the SERICA website of a number of inscriptions (with both texts and translations) which are relevant to research on East-West contacts, both cultural and commercial. For this reason we have provided texts and English translations (by Dr. Gil Davis) of two panels of the Greek version of the multilingual inscription of the Edicts of Ashoka. Dr. Greg Fox and the present author has also compiled a collection of Palmyrene inscriptions (both in Greek and in Palmyrene Aramaic) on trade (*Inscriptiones Palmyrenae selectate ad commercium pertinentes*) based on a list given by

---

[1] N. Nikcoloudis, *Laonikos Chalkokondylas. A Translation and Commentary of the 'Demonstrations of Histories'* (*Books I-III*), Historical Monographs 16 (Athens: Historical Publications St. D. Basilopoulos, 1996).

Dr Gawlikowski in one of his many important publications on the subject of Palmyrene trade.[①] Inscriptions in Chinese have not been forgotten and the Australian team is currently working on a translation of both the Chinese and Syriac texts on the famous *Daqin Jingjiao* 大秦景教 (Nestorian) Stele from Xi'an (erected in 781 CE). As an inscription, the 'Xi'an Monument' as the text is known, is unique. Though a predominantly Chinese commemorative inscription, it includes a significant sub-text in Syriac – a language which was used in the eastern parts of the Byzantine Empire. The Chinese text also contains fascinating information on a bygone and utopian 'Roman' Empire (*Da Qin* 大秦) as the historical land of origin of Christianity.[②]

(iii) The (Multilingual) Geographical Gazetteer:

Work on the inscriptions for SERICA has led me to realize their value as sources on place- and ethnic-names in Central Asia as they often provide researchers with contemporary forms and spelling. Some inscriptions, like the famous trilingual (Greek, Middle Persian and Parthian) inscription of Shapur (discovered between 1936 and 1939 and popularly known as the *Res Gestae Divi Saporis*) at the Ka'ba-i Zarduš t,[③] which provides lists of the Sasanian provinces as well as names of Roman cities captured by Shapur I in his successful campaigns, is a major *onomasticon* in its own right. The material in this multilingual Gazetteer is organized around the standard forms of the place-and ethnic-names in English. Thus for Samarkand, one finds the material grouped under Samarkand and not Smarakanse or Maracanda or Samojian or Afrasiab although there will eventually be separate indices to all the ancient and medieval languages represented in the Gazetteer (i.e. Old Iranian, Middle Iranian, Parthian, Sogdian, Greek, Syriac, Chinese etc.).

The use of epigraphical material from Iranian sources as the basis of this Gazetteer has already led to the confirmation or rejection of older identifications of place and ethnic names as well as furnishing intriguing new discoveries. Take for instance the names for the Roman East now available in the Gazetteer:

ROMAN(AND BYZANTINE) EMPIRE, THE,

Greek: (1) · ῾ωμαίων · ρχή (lit. "the rule of the Romans" = the Roman Empire) *RGDS*(Gr.)7

(2) · ωμανία(late classical, <Lat. *Romania*) Athanasius, *Historia Arianorum* 35, PG 1.733C

Syriac: (ethn.) rhwmy' "Romans" *Doc. Addai* 1.10

Mddle Persian (1) hlwmy (Hrōm), *RGDS*(MPe.) 4, hrwm ' dyn štry (Hrōmāyīn šahr, lit. kingdom of the Romans") *RGDS*(MPe.) 16

(2) (Manichaean) hrwm (Hr ō m) M2 I R i 2, *MM* ii, p. 301.

Parthian: (1) prwm (Frōm) *RGDS* (Pth.) 3, prwmyn hštr (Frōmāy ī n šahr, lit. "kingdom of the Romans") *RGDS* (Pth.) 12

(2)(Manichaean) frwm (Frōm) *MMTKGI* 173 (p. 26)

Sogdian: (Manichaean) β r'wm– (cf. *βr'wm'yk* "Roman") *MMTKGI* 350 (p. 36)

Old Turkish: purum *KT* E4

---

① M. Gawlikowski, 'Palmyra as a trading centre', *Iraq* 56 (1994) 31–33.

② On this see S.N.C. Lieu, 'Epigraphica Nestoriana Serica' in W. Sundermann, A. Hintze and F. de Blois (eds) **Exegisti monumenta: Festschrift in Honour of Nicholas Sims-Williams** (Wiesbaden, 2009), 227–245.

③ See now the major edition by P. Huyse, *Die dreisprachige Inschrift Šābuhrs I. an der Ka'ba-i Zarduš t (ŠKZ)*, 2 vols = Corpus Inscriptionum Iranicarum, Pt. III Pahlavi Inscriptions Vol. 1 in 2 parts (London: Corpus Inscriptionum Iranicarum, 1999).

Chinese: (1) Da Qin 大秦 (lit. "Great Qin (Dynasty)" or "Great China") *HHS* 88 (N.B. the term might have originally been applied to the Seleucid Empire before it was transferred to the Romans)

(2) Fulin 拂林 *JTS* 198, also (Buddh.) Fulin 拂懔 *DTXYJ* 11, p. 37.9 (= *T* 2087, 938a25)

(3) Lumei 芦眉 (<Arab. *Rum*, i.e. former Roman Asia Minor) ZFZ, p. 231

While the list does provide us with an easy solution to the problem of Da Qin (Ta-ch'in), by contrast, the possibility of name *Fulin* as a transliteration for 'Rome' from a Middle Iranian language is now very high indeed.

Earlier scholars have suggested that *Fulin* is derived from the Greek *polin*, which has the indirect backing of Masudi who had originally explained the name Istanbul as a crasis of ε·ϛ·ν(or better τ·ν) πολί ν (*eis tēn/ tān polin*).[①] This is still widely cited because of the relative accessibility of the standard work Friederich Hirth on Chinese sources on the Roman East which mentions it.[②] Hirth also suggested that *Fulin* is a transcription of the Biblical city of Bethlehem (Hebr. *Bat-lim*).[③] This was rightly derided by the French scholar Blochet:[④]

Il serait bien étonnant de voir l'empire romain désigné sous le nom de pays de Bethléhem, car cet humble village de Palestine, où le Verbe s'est incarné par hasard, ne joue dans l'histoire du monde chrétien qu'un role tout à fait effacé qui n'a rien de comparable à celui de Jérusalem, la ville sainte des Hébreux et des Arabes, qui était encore pour Dante le centre de l'Univers, et il serait tout aussi insolite de trouver l'empire romain désigné sous le nom de royaume du Patriarche.

The well-known Japanese scholar on Nestorian Christianity in China, Saeki Yoshiro, suggested a different solution but also along Biblical lines. He was drawn to the fact that virtually the same two characters in Chinese (viz. 拂林) were used to transliterate the Syriac name for a Nestorian monk called Ephrem as it appeared in the bilingual list of names on the Xi'an Monument. 'Phrim' or 'Ephrim', as Saeki pointed out, was the ancient name for the land of Israel and *Fulin* must therefore have been the name for Palestine, the land of origin of the Christianity.[⑤] However, the same criticism Blochet made against Hirth's identification of Fulin with Bethlehem would automatically apply to the hypothesis of Saeki.

In the same study Blochet also made a strong case for *Fulin* as an indirect phonetic transliteration of the Greek name for Rome and for Byzantium, viz. ·ωμή (Rōmē).[⑥] He noted that the name for the Byzantine Empire which called herself Rome throughout her political existence appeared in forms which came very close to *Fulin* in a number of oriental languages, especially in Pahlavi (*Hrum*) and in Armenian (*Hrom*). He had little

---

① See arguments summarized in F. Hirth, *China and the Roman Orient – Researches into their ancient and medieval relations as represented in old Chinese records* (Shanghai and Hong Kong: Kelly and Walsh, 1885) 287–289, n. 2 and idem, 'The mystery of Fu-lin', 2.

② See e.g. J. Ferguson, 'China and Rome' in *Aufstieg und Niedergang der römischen Welt II. Principat* 9.2 (Berlin: Walter de Gruyter, 1978) 585.

③ Hirth, op. cit., 289–290 and idem, 'The mystery of Fu-lin', *Journal of the American Oriental Society* 30 (1909–1910) 17.

④ E. Blochet, 'Notes de géographie et d'histoire d'Extrême-Orient', *Revue de d'Orient Chrétien*, 2nd Ser. 3 (1908) 360.

⑤ *Xi'an Monument*, (Syr.) l. 28, ed. Saeki, *Documents* (text) 13, (trans.) 72. See also ibid. 109–11. Saeki's identification is regarded by Xu Jialing ('Narratives of the Roman-Byzantine World in Chinese Sources' in Burke, J. *et al.* (eds.) *Byzantine Narrative*, 503) as the most recent available to scholars in China at the time of publication.

⑥ Blochet, *op. cit.*, 359–366.

difficulty in demonstrating that both these forms were derived from the Greek ·· ωμή.[1] The main problem facing Blochet's identification, and of which he was certainly very conscious, was that *Fulin* as pronounced in Chinese suggests a phonetic transliteration of a foreign place-name beginning with a *f*- or a *p*, whereas there was then no known example of a name for 'Rome' in a Central Asian language which begins with either. A strong argument for directly linking *Fulin* with "Rome" through Middle Iranian intermediaries was made by Paul Pelliot in 1914[2] and in 1934, the eminent German Iranologist Heinrich Schaeder, drew our attention to the fact that in the then newly deciphered Manichaean texts the Roman Empire appears as *hrwm* (Hrōm) in Middle Persian, *frwm* (Frōm) in Parthian and βr'wm- in Sogdian.[3] Further confirmation for a phonetic link between Fulin and Rome via Middle Iranian is provided by the trilingual *Res Gestae Divi Saporis* in which the Greek term · · · ωμαίων ·· ρχή is rendered in Middle Persian as *hrwm 'dyn štry* (Hrōmāyīn šahr, lit. "kingdom of the Romans") and in Parthian as *prwmyn* hštr (Frōmāyīn šahr).[4] What is significant is that in the Parthian version of the Res Gestae, which is most probably the original of the three versions,[5] the "Romans" were no longer known as "Greeks" whom they had superseded, but because so many Romans were Greek-speaking the appellation "Greeks" lingered on in the minds of many Iranians who saw the Romans as successors to Alexander and his *diadochoi* (i.e. 'successors') as invaders from beyond the Hellespont.

Mention of the Greeks takes us appropriately to their entry in the Gazetteer:

GREEKS, THE

Greek:(1) ο · ·· · ωνες ("Ionians") Hdt. I.6.2; (adj.) ο · ·· · ωνικός ("Ionian") Hdt. I.56.2

(2) · · λλην, pl. ο · ·· · λληνες ("Hellenes") *CII (Gr.)* 5.5, *CISem.* 3924.3(Gr.)

Old Iranian: Yauna (a province of the Achaemenid Persian Empire consisting mainly of the Greek cities of the Aegean coast) DSm 10, ethn. Yauna, ethn. pl. as prov. Yaun ā

Aramaic (Palmyrene): *ywny*' *CISem.* 3924.4

Syriac: ywny' *DQJJLXZGB* Syr. l. 4

Bactrian: ιωναγγο Rabatak l. 3, IEOG, p. 204

Prakrit: Yona *IEOG* 409, p. 237

Chinese: Yuan 宛 (?) (as in Da Yuan 大宛)

As Thucydides (I,3,1-3) reminded us, the name "Hellene" (i.e. "Greek") used as a common ethnic term for Greek-speakers was a late phenomenon. The first major group of Greek-speakers whom the Achaemenid Persians encountered as their empire extended to the eastern shores of the Aegean were the Ionians and many Old Iranian proper names in Greek show Ionian phonetic peculiarities. While the Greeks who conquered Iran and Central Asia called themselves Hellenes, the Old Iranian name of Yauna (derived from Greek · ··ωνες "Ionians") had preceded them and derivatives of Yauna are found in almost all Semitic and

---

[1] Ibid. 362.

[2] P. Pelliot, 'Sur l'origine du nom Fou-lin', *Journal Asiatique*, ser. 11, 3 (1914) 497-500.

[3] H. H. Schaeder, *Iranica 1. Das Auge des Königs and 2. Fu-lin*, Abhandlungen der Gesellschaft der Wissenschaften zu Göttingen, Phil.-Hist. Klasse, 3. F., Nr. 10 (Berlin, 1934) 68-83.

[4] Cf, Huyse, *op. cit.* I, 39.

[5] On the textual and linguistic relations among the three versions see Z. Rubin, 'Res Gestae Divi Saporis: Greek and Middle Iranian in a Document of Anti-Roman Propaganda' in J.N. Adams et al. (eds.) *Bilingualism in Ancient Society* (Oxford, 2002) 267-97, esp. 270-77.

Central Asian languages. In compiling this list it occurred to the present author immediately that we may have here the origin of the term Da Yuan（大宛）, the ancient Chinese name for Ferghana famous for its 'Blood Horses'. The Chinese character *yuan*（宛）is rare and is found only in the name of a commandery (*xian* 县) in Henan（河 南）established during the Qin Dynasty and has no real literary meaning. The term Da Yuan therefore is most likely a phonetic transliteration for a foreign place-name. For several centuries Ferghana was the seat of the Indo-Greek Bactrian Kingdom. The latter was probably known in its time as the Yauana or Yavana (i.e. Greek) kingdom of Bactria[1] and the Chinese character *yuan*（宛）was therefore the phonetic transliteration of *Yauna*.[2] As *Yauna* could phonetically be comfortably accommodated by the single Chinese character *yuan*, the character *da* i.e. "great" was added as a prefix and compliment (i.e. "the Great (Kingdom) of the Greeks") or simply as a means to make it a two-syllable or two-character place-name—the minimum normally required in the transliteration and easy recognition of foreign ethnic and place-names in Chinese.

(4) Conclusion:

Although the project "China and the Ancient Mediterranean World" was officially launched in 2004, it was not until major funding from the Australian Research Council and the Chiang Chin Kuo Foundation was received in 2010 that the "scientific" aspects of the project could start to make serious progress. For such an ambitious project to fulfill its avowed intention, international and institutional collaboration is essential. It is hoped that the project currently sponsored by a group of European universities will be able to submit a major application for funding from the European Research Council in the not too distant future. The present author hopes that in the short time available for this presentation he has showcased the project sufficiently to demonstrate its long-term value and usefulness to all scholars who are actively engaged in research on East-West contacts.

Abbreviations

CII (Gr.) = G. Rougemount, *Inscriptions grecques d'Iran et d'Asie centrale*, Corpus Inscriptionum Iranicarum Part II, Inscriptions of the Seleucid and Parthian periods and of eastern Iran and Central Asia; v. 1, Inscriptions in non-Iranian languages (London, 2012).

CISem. = *Corpus Inscriptionum Semiticarum, Pars secunda. Tomus III: Inscriptiones palmyrenae*, eds. J.-B. Chabot et al. (Paris, 1926).

Doc. Addai = *Doctrina Addai*, ed. and trans. G. Howard, *The Teaching of Addai* (Chico, 1981).

DSm = Inscription of Darius at Susa (M), in R.G. Kent, *Old Persian, Grammar, Texts, Lexicon* (New Haven, 1952) 145-465

DTXYJ = *Da Tang Xiyuji* 大唐西域记 by Xuanzang 玄奘 (Kyoto 1911); also T 2087 (Vol. 51) 868a- 946c HHS

Hdt. = Herodotus.

IEOG = F.C. De Rossi (ed.) *Iscrizioni dello Estremo Oriente Greco*, Inschriften griechischer Städte aus Kleinasien 65 (Bonn, 2004).

---

[1] On the 'Yavana Kingdom of Bactria' in historical fiction and in history see esp. J. Wiesehöfer, 'Griechen, Iraner und Chinesen an der Seidenstraße' in E. Hübner *et al.* (eds.) *Die Seidenstraße*, Asien und Afrika. Beiträge des Zentrums für Asiatische und Afrikanische Studien (ZAAS) der Christian-Albrecht-Universität zu Kiel, Bd. 3 (Hamburg: E-B Verlag, 2001) 17-33, esp. 17-18.

[2] Cf. I. Lebedynsky, *Les Saces - les "Scythes" d'Asie, VIIIe siècle av. J.-C.-IVe siècle apr. J.-C.* (Paris, 2006) 61: 'Le nom Chinois pourrant cacher l'appellation iranienne ou indienne des "Grecs"'.

JTS = Jiu Tangshu 旧唐书 , ed. Liu Xu 刘昫 (Beijing, 1975).

KT = The K ü l Tigin Inscription, ed. T. Tekin, *A Grammar of Orkhon Turkic* (Bloomington, 1968) 231–242.

MM ii = F.C. Andreas and W.B. Henning, 'Mitteliranische Manichaica aus Chinesisch–Turkestan, II', *Sitzungsberichte der preussischen Akademie der Wissenschaften zu Berlin,* 1933.

MMTKGI = W. Sundermann, *Mittel–iranische manich*äische Texte kirchen–geschichtlichen Inhalts (Berlin, 1981).

MPe. = Middle Persian (language).

PG = Patrologia Graeca cursus completus, ed. J.–P. Migne (Paris, 1857–66).

Pth. = Parthian (language)

RGDS = Res Gestae Divi Saporis, ed. and trans. P. Huyse, *Die dreisprachige Inschrift* Šābuhrs I. an der Ka'ba–i Zardušt (ŠKZ), 2 vols. (London, 1999).

T = *Taishō shinshu daizōkyō* 大正新修大藏经 (Tokyo, 1936–)

DQJJLXZGB = Da Qin Jingjiao liuxing Zhongguo bei 大秦景教流行中国碑, , ed. Y.P. Saeki, *The Nestorian Monuments and Relics in China*, 2nd edn. (Tokyo 1951) 1–12 (Chinese texts section).

ZFZ = Zhu Fan Zhi 诸蕃志 , compiled by Zhao Rugua 赵汝适 , ed. Han Zhenhua 韩振华 , *Zhu Fan Zhi Zhubu* 诸蕃志注补 (Hong Kong, 2000).

Urbanization in Former–Han China and in the early Roman empire

L. de Ligt, Leiden University

The aim of this paper is to present a brief overview of levels of urban development in China during the Western Han period and in the Roman empire during the first two centuries AD. Before starting our investigations we must of course be clear what we mean by the terms 'city' and 'urban'. As is generally known, the scholarly literature abounds with definitions. From these I single out the juridical definition, which focuses on legal status and administrative functions; the economic definition, which centres on the occupational structures of populations; and the demographic one, which defines urban settlements on the basis of the size of their populations. In this contribution no detailed examination of these definitions will be attempted. Instead, I limit myself to the observation that shifting from one definition to another may produce a dramatically different urban network. To give just one example, if we use a strictly juridical definition, Roman Italy had about 430 cities. However, if we use a demographic approach focusing on settlements which are likely to have had at least 3,000 inhabitants, this number must be halved. With a higher threshold of 5,000, the lower limit used by Jan de Vries in his study of the urban systems of early–modern Europe, the number of 'genuine' cities would shrink even further, almost certainly to well under 100.[1]

In the case of Han China the defining feature of a city was the presence of a city wall. Most discussions of the urban system of early–imperial China, however, use an administrative approach. At the top of the urban hierarchy we find the capital city of Chang–an. The second tier of administrative cities is represented by the capitals of the 83 commanderies (*jun*) and the 20 kingdoms, 103 cities in total. The third tier comprised the central cities of the counties (*xian*). In the late western Han period there were 1,484 of these cities, or 1,577 if we include the administrative centres of the marquisates, estates and marches. The counties, in their turn, were subdivided into districts (*xiang*) each consisting of ten 'villages' (*ting*). Each of these villages was supposed to contain ten 'hamlets' (*li*). It must, however, be emphasized that this was an ideal arrangement which did not always correspond to practice.[2]

What level of urbanization is implied by this multi–tiered settlement system? In a recent study Chun–su Chang credits the intra–mural area of Chang–an with a population of over 500,000 and the city of Linzi (in Shandong) with no fewer than 650,000 inhabitants. In addition to these mega–cities there would have been

---

[1] Cf. De Ligt (2012), chapter 5. Threshold of 5,000: De Vries (1984).

[2] Loewe (2006), 46–47.

at least five other cities with more than 200,000 inhabitants, namely Wan (modern Nanyang), with 400,000, Chengdu, with 380,000, Handan, with 270,000, Luoyang, with 260,000, and Qufu (former capital of the state of Lu), with 230,000. For the Han empire as a whole (in Wudi's time) he posits the existence of twenty cities with populations ranging from 50,000 to 650,000, and of sixty cities with between 20,000 and 50,000 inhabitants.[1] Although he does not try to calculate the proportion of the total population residing in cities, there can be no doubt that the urbanization rate implied by these estimates is very high.

High estimates for the populations of former-Han China's largest cities also underlie Victor Sit's attempt to establish the proportion of the Chinese population living in cities at the time of the census of AD 2. His starting observation is that according to the census figures for AD 2 Chang-an had 80,800 households, implying a total urban population of about 246,200.[2] As a next step, he assigns an average population of 50,000 to each commandery capital, and a population of 10,000 inhabitants to each county seat.[3] These estimates result in an aggregate urban population of about 16.5 million. If we set the total Chinese population at 60 million, Sit's figure for the total urban population implies an urbanization rate of 27.7 per cent.[4]

Although Chang's and Sit's monographs contain many important insights, their staggering figures for the cities of the former-Han empire cannot be accepted. One reason for this is that their findings are completely out of line with reconstructed urbanization rates for later periods of Chinese history. It must be remembered, for instance, that during the final decade of the nineteenth century only 6 per cent of the Chinese population lived in settlements with 2,000 or more inhabitants. With a threshold of 10,000 inhabitants, this percentage drops to only 4.4%.[5] Of course there is a theoretical possibility that the intervening eighteen or nineteen centuries saw a dramatic change in the balance between urban and rural populations, for instance as a result of strong rural population growth.[6] However, if we move back to the period of the southern Song dynasty (13th century AD) from which we happen to have detailed tax records for at least some areas, we find that in this period only between 5% and 10% of the Chinese population lived in cities.[7] Interestingly, the thirteenth century is commonly seen as marking a high point in terms of economic development and urbanization.

---

[1] Chang (2007a), 85.

[2] Sit (2010), 129. The overall reliability of the census figures for AD 2 is confirmed by the documents from Yinwan which put the total population of Donghai commandery in c. 15 BC at around 1.4 million people in 266,000 households. These figures are reasonably close to the tally of AD 2 which gives the population of this area as 1.56 million in 358,000 households. See Loewe 2004, 60; Scheidel unpublished. The figures for AD 2 might derive from tax records rather than from population counts and may therefore be incomplete.

[3] The figures given in a recently found document from the county of Dongyang suggests that this county had a population of about 40,000. See Loewe 2010, 318–319. Starting from Sit's notional figure of 10,000 for the population of an average county seat, we obtain an urbanization rate of about 25 per cent, a very high figure. Cf. also Chang (2007b) 92, for the observation that the capital city of the frontier county of Chü-yen covered only 17.1 hectares.

[4] Sit (2010), 124, building on Zhou (2001).

[5] Skinner (1977), 229. Cf. Maddison (2007) 39: only 3.8 per cent of the Chinese population living in cities with populations of 10,000 or over around 1820.

[6] Rowe (2002) 537–538, suggests that long-term Ming and Ch'ing policies favouring the agricultural sector may have caused the urbanization rate in the lower Yangzi region to decline from approximately 10 per cent in AD 1200 to 7.4 per cent in 1843.

[7] I am relying here on the detailed investigations carried out by Liang Gengyao 1997, 507–37, and by Wu Songi 2008. While Bairoch (1988) 353, assigns 10–13 per cent of the population of twelfth-century China to cities with 5,000 or more inhabitants, these recent studies strongly support Rozman's view (Rozman 1973, 279–280) that only 6 to 7 per cent of the Chinese population of this period lived in cities with populations of 3,000 or over.

A much lower estimate of Han urbanization rates is to be found in Zhao's *Man and Land in Chinese History*. Building on various earlier studies, he posits the existence of 26,635 villages (*ting*) with an average size of 320 households or 1,660 persons. These figures imply a total rural population of slightly more than 49 million and an urbanization rate of 17.2 per cent.[1] Unfortunately, even this alternative calculation seems over-schematic and the estimated urbanization rate too high.

One problem which has not received enough attention is that the census figure for Chang-an and other cities clearly include the population of the countryside.[2] This means Chang-an may well have had considerably fewer than 246,200 inhabitants, and the same reasoning applies to the census figures for other large cities. On the rural side it must be emphasized that neither the approximate number of 'villages' nor their average populations can be established with any degree of confidence. This means that Zhao's input figures might well be too low.

In my view the only way to get to grips with this problem is by looking at taxation rates. When the dynasty was founded, the land tax was one fifteenth of the produce, but in 156 BC this was lowered to one thirtieth.[3] From a Roman perspective this is of course a ridiculously low level. However, in addition to the land tax Chinese peasants had to pay a poll tax which was rather more substantial. According to one estimate the poll tax amounted to about 4.3 per cent of net output. Cash payments to cover the costs of a substitute for garrison duty might also represent a considerable burden. Depending on the composition of the family, these payments could amount to another 4.3 per cent of the monetary value of net output.[4] In conjunction these tax impositions on the rural population may have amounted to between 10 and 12 per cent of net output and a somewhat lower proportion of gross output.[5]

A significant proportion of tax income is likely to have been used for military expenditure and to subsidize barbarian tribes.[6] It seems, moreover, a safe bet that a certain proportion of tax revenues was lost in transmission. If therefore expenditure of tax money and consumption of tax grain were the principal props of urban life in western-Han China, it is difficult to see how the overall urbanization rate could have exceeded 10 per cent.

This line of argumentation assumes that income from agricultural rents and division of labour between cities and rural areas made a relatively small contribution to urban incomes. In the case of craft production for rural consumers more research is needed, but the prevailing view is that the Chinese farmers of this period were also carpenters, masons, weavers and tailors.[7] In other words, they were largely self-sufficient. As far as income from land rents is concerned, it is possible to point to the current consensus that in the late second century BC tenants are unlikely to have accounted for more than one fifth of the total Chinese population.[8] Even

---

[1] Zhao 1986, p. 47–48.

[2] Thus correctly Wang Zijin 2007; Pirazzoli t' Serstevens 2010, 177.

[3] Hsu Cho-yun 1980, p. 72. Lee Swann 1950, 366–376., remains the best discussion of Han taxation.

[4] For these taxes see Hsu Cho-yun 1980, 79. Some peasants also paid monetary taxes to avoid corvée labour but since the revenue from this tax was used to hire rural labourers, it was not available for urban expenditure.

[5] In the second half of the second century BC the philosopher Dong Zhongshu pointed out that a simple tax system in which peasants had to hand over one tenth of the crops might be expected to yield sufficient revenue to cover all types of government expenditure See *Han-shu* 24a : 14b (Lee Swann 1950, p. 179).

[6] Scheidel (unpublished) suggest that the army absorbed between one sixth and one fifth of total state revenue. He argues that the Han state was less fiscally integrated and more locally entrenched than the Roman empire.

[7] Hsu Cho-yun (1980) 67.

[8] Hsu Cho-yun (1980) 64–65.

under these circumstances aggregate revenues from rural leasing might have made an important contribution to the incomes of city-based elites, thereby boosting urban expenditure and ultimately urbanization. While it seems certain that expenditure of elite income from privately-owned estates did create additional employment opportunities for city-based craftsmen, traders and servants, it must be borne in mind that this economic nexus also existed in later periods of Chinese history, when tenancy is believed to have been more important than in western-Han times. It seems significant that even in these later historical periods Chinese urbanization rates never exceeded 10 per cent.[1]

For all these reasons it seems a safe inference that in western-Han China the average urbanization rate fell within the same band as urbanization rates during the southern Song period, when between 5 per cent and 10 per cent of the Chinese population lived in cities.

What does all this mean for the role of inter-regional transportation and commerce in the urban economy? In the case of the capital city of Chang-an we happen to know that around 200 BC several hundred thousand *piculs* of grain were transported to the city (1 *picul* = 20 litres). This would have been enough to feed 11,000 to 16,000 persons. However, by 115 BC the amount of grain transported annually had risen to 4 million piculs and by 100 BC to 6 million.[2] This amount of grain would have been enough to feed about 335,000 people. As we have seen, however, we cannot be sure that all of these people lived within the walled area of Chang-an. Many of them may have lived in the suburbs or within a radius of 20 kilometres from the city.[3] According to many specialists the walled city had only some 80,000 or 90,000 inhabitants with a further 250,000 persons living distributed throughout the prefecture. One third of these 250,000 people can be assigned to smaller urban agglomerations.[4] The other two metropolitan prefectures had populations of about 280,000 and 180,000 respectively. Taken together, the central prefecture and the two other metropolitan prefectures may have had a

---

[1]　As Prof. Jin-yu Liu (DePaus University and Peking University) points out to me, there is a considerable amount of evidence (most of it unpublished) for wealthy urban residents not employed by the imperial government making contributions to the cost of various urban buildings, such as shrines. While these contributors certainly included retired officials, some of them are more likely to have been wealthy landowners living off the income of their rural estates.

[2]　The amounts are given in *Han Shu* 24a: 8b (c. 200 BC); 24b: 15b (c. 115 BC); 24b: 18b (c. 110 BC BC). Cf. Lee Swann (1950), 60; Schinz 1996, 113. The figure for 115 BC reoccurs in *Han Shu* 24a: 17a (c. 55 BC) where it is stated that 4 million *piculs* of grain for provisions for the capital were transported by water route from east of the pass (Hsien-ku).

[3]　Schinz (1996), 134. According to a poetical description of the early first century AD the city of Chang-an "was so full that it overflowed into the suburbs" (Schinz 1996, 134), but recent publications tend to play down the extent and relative importance of these suburbs. For a useful survey of the debate see Pirazzoli-t'Serstevens (2010), 176-177. The location of the extra-urban markets of Chang-an, between the capital and the mausoleum cities to the north and north-west, suggests that the powerful families living in or near the mausoleum cities obtained a significant proportion of their supplies from the capital.

[4]　Schinz (1996), 134 reasons that if each of the capital's 160 wards had 100 households, the walled area excluding the palaces must have had between 60,000 and 70,000 inhabitants. With an additional 20,000-30,000 residents in the palaces, the total urban population would have been of the order of 100,000. But we cannot be sure that the average city ward did not have more households than the canonical 100. Cf. Pirazzoli-t'Serstevens (2010), 180: 'The area of a walled city ward and the number of its inhabitants varied greatly'. The average figure of 105 households per ward indicated by the tax records from Donghai commandery refer to a combination of urban and rural wards. See also ibid., 177, for the view that the metropolitan district of Chang-an may have had a total population of between 350,000 and 400,000 (including residents not registered in the census of AD 2), of whom 20 to 30 per cent are likely to have resided *intra muros*. This would give the walled city between 70,000 and 120,000 inhabitants. Again the population of the suburbs remains a known unknown.

total population of 800,000 or 900,000, about half of whom may have lived in cities.[1]

While the surviving sources give detailed figures for the amounts of tax grain which reached Chang-an at various moments of its history, it is more difficult to determine to what extent the creation and existence of a very large capital city stimulated the growth of other cities in the empire which earned part of their keep by exporting manufactured goods to the political centre. In many publications on the Han empire six cities are identified as important centres of commerce: Chang-an itself, Luoyang, Linzi, Wan (or Ren), Chengdu, and Handan.[2] This conventional list is based on a famous passage in the *Han-shu* which states that in AD 10 offices for the supervision of markets were established in these cities.[3] Four of the cities listed in the *Han-shu*, namely Handan, Linzi, Wan and Luoyang are also found in the list of rich and famous cities at the beginning of the third chapter of the *Discourses on Salt and Iron*.[4]

Of course the presence of large urban markets need not indicate a high volume of production for export or even of entrepôt trade. It seems plausible, for instance, that the functions of the market of Chang-an included the commercial distribution of imported goods and that of goods produced in the city itself. The remaining five cities were not only commercial centres but also major administrative cities, the sites of ancestral temples and residences of feudal lords. In pre-imperial times they had all been capitals of independent kingdoms.

In assessing the relative importance of commerce and manufacturing in the urban economies of these cities we have to rely on a combination of literary clues and archaeological evidence.[5] Literary sources report that the city of Wan was home to an Iron Office, suggesting that it was an important centre of the iron industry. Excavations have revealed the presence of an iron foundery (covering some 28,000 square metres) in the central part of the city. These clues suggest that production for export made a substantial contribution to the urban economy. But about the city of Linzi the *Shih-Chi* reports that "because the land [that is to say, agriculture] was all important it was difficult to cause unrest and commotion".[6] Although this is an isolated clue, it shows that at least some of the six cities singled out in the *Han-shu* may have been regional markets rather than major players in trade on an empire-wide scale. It must also be emphasized that the so-called "Five Capitals" differed enormously in size. While in western-Han times the cities of Linzi and Handan covered an impressive 18 km^2 and 16.7 km^2 respectively, the corresponding figures for Luoyang, Wan and Chengdu are only 7.3 km^2, 2km^2 and 1.3 km^2.[7]

In some cases more detailed information about the areas served by commercial cities is available. In the *Shih-Chi* it is reported, for instance, that the city of Handan 'communicated' or 'traded' with the regions to its north and south and that Luoyang had commercial relations with the regions to the east and south.[8] About the people of Wan the same treatise says: "They were fond of new undertakings as well as business enterprises

① Schinz (1996), 134.

② *Han shu* 24b: 22b (Lee Swann 1950, 336-337). Cf. Lee Swann (1950), 67-68; Sit (2010), 127-133.

③ *Han shu* 24b : 22b (Lee Swann 1950, 336-337).

④ Gale (1931), 18.

⑤ For a very optimistic assessment of industrial and commercial growth and its impact on the development of cities see e.g. Chang (2007a), 81-85.

⑥ *Shih-Chi* 129: 9b (Lee Swann 1950, p. 443).

⑦ Linzi, Handan and Wan: Pirazzoli-t'Serstevens (2010), 178-179; Luoyang and Chengdu: Schinz (1996), 136 and 123. In eastern-Han times Luoyang expanded to 9.1 km^2. See Pirazzoli-t'Serstevens (2010), 177. Of course the low figures for Wan and Chengdu are incompatible with the high population estimates of Chun-su Chang (above, at note 3).

⑧ *Shih-Chi* 129: 8b and 9a (Lee Swann 1950, pp. 441-442).

and they were mostly tradespeople".[1] Some other cities, not included among the commercial top six, are identified as manufacturing centres. One illustration is the city of Sha-qiu (modern Guangzong in Hebei province) whose population is said to have "looked to profits from [mechanical] skill for their sustenance".[2] The same claim is made regarding the populations of the former states of Qi and Zhao, which are said to have "looked to their [mechanical] skill for profit".[3]

All in all it remains difficult to assess the proportion of urban populations sustained by regional or inter-regional commerce. What can be said with confidence is that the creation of a unified empire favoured trade over long distances. As Sima Qian writes in a famous passage: "When Han arose, all within the seas was united. Barriers and bridges were opened, restrictions were relaxed regarding the use of resources of mountains and marshes. Therefore, rich traders and great merchants roved around the empire. No commodity was not circulation so that each one was able to obtain what he desired".[4]

It also appears that private commerce played an important part in supplying the capital city with essential goods. One illustration is a passage from the first chapter of the *Discourses on Salt and Iron* where it is claimed that previously private merchants had made huge profits by transporting various goods to the capital. These goods were often found to be of poor quality. Therefore the government issued order to the effect that in the future tax money was to be used to buy goods in distant localities. New offices were to be set up to arrange their purchase and transportation to the capital. In short, the imperial government sought to cut costs and to improve the quality of purchased commodities by cutting out middlemen. The underlying assumption was clearly that private commerce had been important.[5]

Let me summarize my main findings on the urban system of former-Han China. If my interpretation of the census figures for AD 2 is correct, the capital city of Chang-an may have had about 200,000 inhabitants. However, the metropolitan region as a whole may have numbered as many as 900,000 urban residents and may have supported an urbanization rate of about 50 per cent. For China as a whole an average urbanization of between 5 per cent and 10 per cent seems most likely. The system as a whole was ultimately underpinned by expenditure of tax money.

It is time to turn to the urban system of the Roman empire. For the mid-second century AD the number of cities has been estimated at roughly 2,000. It must, however, be emphasized that this guesstimate is based on a purely juridical and administrative definition of 'city'. As is generally agreed, many Roman 'cities'

---

[1]　*Shih-Chi* 129: 11b (Lee Swann 1950, p. 446). Of course most or all statements about the relative importance of commerce belong to a moralizing discourse which extols the virtues of farmers. Cf. Shih-Chi 129 : 7a (Lee Swann 1950, 438) for the claim that the people of Qin are 'for the most part great merchants'. In a similar vein Chapter 2 of the *Discourses on Salt and Iron* (Gale 1931, 16–17) states that the merchants of Wan, Zhou, Qi and Lu spread all over the world and amass great fortunes. In *Shih-Chi* 129 : 9b (Lee Swann 1950, 443) we read that by Han times the regions of Lu and Zou had become decadent and that their people 'were fond of trading and running after [material] profits'.

[2]　*Shih-Chi* 129: 8b (Lee Swann 1950, p. 441).

[3]　*Shih-Chi* 129: 12b (Lee Swann 1950, p. 448). Chapter 3 of the *Discourses on Salt and Iron* (Gale 1931, 19) refers to Zhao and Qu as parts of the empire where commerce and luxurious living were deemed more important than agriculture. Two passages in the *Shih-Chi* (129: 8b and 129: 10a; Lee Swann 1950, 441 and 444) single out the districts of Zhong-shan (in Zhao) and of western Qu for the sterility of their soils. The latter passage mentions the city of Jiangling as a nodal point for east-west communication.

[4]　*Shih-chi* 129 : 6b/9; Lee Swann (1950), 437. The translation used here is that of Hsu (1980), 188.

[5]　Gale (1931), 9–10. Cf. Lee Swann (1950), 63–65; Sadao (1986), 604.

were tiny places. To give just one example, my own inquiries into the urban system of early-imperial Italy has revealed that of the roughly 430 Italian cities more than 200 covered fewer than 20 hectares, the average size of these settlements being only 10 hectares.[1] Although it remains difficult to put any hard figure on the populations of such agglomerations, it seems clear that few of them had more than 2,000 inhabitants. For this reason the 2,000 'cities' of the Roman empire cannot be compared directly with the roughly 1,600 commandery capitals and county seats of Han China.

If we try to look at the Roman empire through Chinese spectacles, we cannot fail to be struck by the enormous size of Rome. Even if the size of the population of Chang-an cannot be determined accurately, it is patently clear that Han China did not have any city with a population approaching or surpassing one million. On the other hand, it must not be forgotten that the metropolitan area of western-Han China had various other substantial cities beside Chang-an. As we have seen, the total urban population of the metropolitan region, an area of approximately 2,000 square kilometres, may have been as high as 450,000. The contrast between the two empires should therefore not be exaggerated.

The second tier of Chinese cities, the administrative capitals of the commanderies, may be compared to the provincial capitals of the Roman empire. In AD 14 the Roman empire numbered about 30 provinces. In AD 120 this figure had risen to about 45. In the scholarly literature some provincial capitals are credited with very large populations. Antioch, for instance, has been assigned 250,000 inhabitants, Carthage 300,000, and Alexandria half a million.[2] At least some of these estimates look far too high. To my mind it is extremely doubtful whether Carthage approached or surpassed the 100,000 mark before Late Antiquity.[3] The estimates for Alexandria fall into a wide range. While Scheidel credits Ptolemaic Alexandria with 300,000 inhabitants (around 200 BCE) and Delia Roman Alexandria with a population of 500,000 to 600,000, Stephens suggests 60,000–80,000 for the mid-third century BCE, while Sly offers an estimate of only 200,000 for the Roman city.[4]

Another large city in Wilson's tables is Roman Corinth, with an estimated population of 80,000.[5] The most recent data suggest that the Roman colony was laid out at about 240 hectares but also that it was replanned on 140 hectares within a few generations, almost certainly to match real population needs.[6] Why should a city which was about twice as large as Pompeii have had seven times as many inhabitants?

Other provincial capitals have been credited with much smaller populations. Examples include Lyon (Lugdunum) with an estimated population of 25,000, and Ephesos with a hypothetical population of 35,000.[7] Again, some of these estimates appear on the high side. The figure for Ephesos, for instance, is based on a figure of 224 hectares, but a recent study has shown that the city had a built-up area of 185 hectares of which only some 140 hectares were used as domestic space.[8]

The remaining cities of the Roman empire, numbering well over 1,950, were self-governing communities.

---

[1] De Ligt (2012), chapter 5.

[2] Wilson (2012), 184 and 186.

[3] See the cautionary remarks in Hurst (1993).

[4] See Delia (1989); Sly (1996) 44–48; Scheidel (2004) 12–15; Stephens (2010) 47. Early-Hellenistic Alexandria appears to have covered 200 to 250 hectares. The Roman city may have expanded to 825 or even to 1,000 hectares.

[5] Wilson (2012), 190. His estimate is identical to that of Engels (1990) 33 and 84.

[6] Bintliff (2012), 323.

[7] Wilson (2012), 187–188.

[8] Groh (2006).

Their sizes differed enormously. As we have seen, Roman Italy had a very large number of small cities. Judging from the archaeological evidence the smallest Italian agglomeration of urban status covered only one hectare. Viewed in this light, Pompeii, which covered about 65 hectares, was a very substantial city. Some other cities were much larger than this. Examples include Capua, with 200 hectares of built-up space, and Ostia, with about 130 hectares in the mid-second century AD.[1] Similar variations can be observed in the provinces.

It must be emphasized that, unlike most Chinese cities, the populations of most of the self-governing cities of the empire were sustained by private elite expenditure. This points to an important difference between the two empires. While in western-Han China taxation appears to have been the most important form of surplus extraction, Roman taxation does not seem to have captured more than 7 per cent of GDP, leaving ample room for additional surplus extraction through rents.[2] Another important difference is that the land-owning elites of the Roman empire appear to have owned or controlled a fairly large proportion of all landed property.[3] Since most Roman landowners were city-based, elite expenditure of revenues obtained from privately-owned landed estates may have help to push urbanization rates beyond contemporary Chinese levels.

This leads me to a brief discussion of recent attempts to estimate urbanization rates in the Roman empire. In a recent article Andrew Wilson has tried to work out Roman urbanization rate by compiling a catalogue of cities which are likely to have had 5,000 or more inhabitants. Taking into account likely variations in urban population densities and assigning estimated populations to each of the cities on his long list, Wilson arrives at the conclusion that by the mid-second century AD some 7.3 million people are likely to have lived in cities with 5,000 or more inhabitants. In fact, if the demographic threshold is lowered to 1,000, as many as 10.3 million people can be assigned to 'cities'. His next step is combine these hypothetical figures with Beloch's estimate for the population of the Roman empire as a whole, which amounts to 55 or 60 million for the time of Augustus. With a threshold of 5,000 and an urban population of 7.3 million the urbanization rate works out as 12 %. But with the lower threshold of 1,000 and 10.3 urban residents this figure rises to at least 17 per cent.[4]

While I warmly applaud Wilson's ambitious and innovative approach, I would like to make two critical observations. The first of these is simply that some of Wilson's input figures look unrealistically high. As we have seen, his figures for Carthage, Antioch, Alexandria and various other large cities are on the high side. His figures for Roman Italy also look over-optimistic.[5] But these are relatively minor quibbles. What is more important—and this is my second point—is that most of Wilson's estimates are based on data for city size during the mid-second century AD. In my view it is potentially misleading to confront these figures with estimates for the size of the empire's population in the time of Augustus. The obvious reason for this is that the first 150

---

[1]　De Ligt (2012), chapter 5.

[2]　Hopkins (2002), 201, followed by Scheidel unpublished.

[3]　For the scale of elite land-ownership in Roman Italy see e.g. Hopkins (1978), 55–56. Cicero, *Leg. Agr.* 2.78 famously claimed that the territory of Praeneste was owned by a few men; according to Pliny the Elder, *NH* 18.35 six men owned half of the province of Africa (until Nero got rid of them). Although such claims are highly rhetorical, it is generally agreed that Roman senators, *equites* and town-councillors had very high annual incomes and that most of their revenues came from landed property. For the relatively small size of elite-owned rural estates in the Han empire，See e.g. Lewis (2007), 115.

[4]　Wilson (2012), 192.

[5]　Wilson (2012), 182, assigns an estimated 1,547,000 inhabitants to Italian cities with 5,000 or more inhabitants. While his estimates for Rome, Ostia, Puteoli, Aquileia, Capua, Mediolanum and Patavium are likely to be of the right order of magnitude (at least for the mid-second century AD), his estimate for the total population of 25 additional 'major cities' looks too high. For the relative rarity of large cities in Roman Italy cf. De Ligt (2012), 242.

years of the empire are seen as a period of strong population growth. Even if we assume that the total population of the Roman empire increased by no more than 25 per cent in this period, the resulting population would be as high as 75 million. With this relatively minor adjustment Wilson's urbanization rates immediately drop to 9.7 per cent if we use a threshold of 5,000, and to 13.7 per cent if all settlements with 1,000 or more inhabitants are considered 'urban'. By lowering Wilson's estimates for Italy and some of his figures for provincial capitals the latter figure can easily be reduced to about 12 per cent.

It is time to pull some of the threads together. I have argued that current estimates of urbanization rates in western-Han China are much too high. In fact, the fragmentary surviving data suggest to me not only that in this period the capital city of Chang-an was much smaller than Rome but that western-Han China as a whole supported an urbanization rate which was substantially lower than the most reasonable estimates for the Roman empire in the mid-second century AD.

The discrepancy in size between early-imperial Rome and western-Han Chang-an might reflect the fact that Rome had easy access to food supplied arriving by sea whereas western-Han Chang-an depended heavily on food supplies being shipped over rivers and canals. The less favourable location of Chang-an in terms of transportation is likely to have curbed the expansion of its population, especially before the dramatic extension of the canal network which took place under the Sui and Tang dynasties.[1]

The relatively low urbanization rate indicated by various types of evidence relating to the commanderies and counties of western-Han China is less easily explained. I have argued that the cities of former-Han China were largely sustained by expenditure of state income from taxation. While state expenditure also helped to sustain a considerable proportion of the urban population of the Roman empire, the vast majority of Roman cities seem to have been supported by private income from landed property. As we have seen, China, too, had a land-owning elite which received large amounts of revenue from its rural estates. Nonetheless aggregate income from land rents in western-Han China is likely to have fallen short of Roman levels. This may tentatively be identified as one of the reasons why the city-dwellers of former-Han China accounted for a somewhat lower proportion of the total population than the urban residents of the Roman empire.

Bibliography

Bairoch, P. (1988). *Cities and Economic Development. From the dawn of History to the Present* (Chicago).

Bintliff, J. (2012). *The Complete Archaeology of Greece. From Hunter-Gatherers to the 20th Century* A.D. (Malden-Oxford).

Bowman, A.K. and Wilson, A.I. (eds.) (2012), *Settlement, Urbanisation and Population* (Oxford).

Chang, Chun-shu (2007a), *The Rise of the Chinese Empire, vol. 1. Nation, State, and Imperialism in Early China, ca. 1600 B.C.-A.D. 8* (Ann Arbor).

Chang, Chun-shu (2007b), *The Rise of the Chinese Empire, vol. 2. Frontier, Immigration, and Empire in Han China, 130 B.C.-A.D. 157* (Ann Arbor).

---

[1] Some of the logistical challenges posed by the food supply of western-Han Chang-an are highlighted in *Han shu* 24a : 17a-b, where it is stated that 60,000 conscript labourers were needed to supply the city with 4 million *piculs* of grain annually. The same passage reports that during the reign of emperor Xuan an attempt was made to scale down this logistical effort by purchasing grain within the three provinces of the metropolitan area and in four neighbouring counties. In the eight century Chang-an may have had a population of the order of one million. See e.g. Steinhardt (1999), 10.

Chao, K. (1986). *Man and Land in Chinese History* (Stanford, Cal.).

De Ligt, L. (2012). *Peasants, Citizens and Soldiers. Studies in the Demographic History of Roman Italy 225 BC–AD 100* (Cambridge).

De Vries, J. (1984). *European Urbanization 1500–1800* (London).

Delia, D. (1989). 'The population of Roman Alexandria,' *Transactions of the American Philological Association* 118, 275–92.

Engels, D. (1990). *Roman Corinth: An Alternative Model for the Classical City* (Chicao–London).

Gale, E.M. (1931). *Discourses on Salt and Iron. A Debate on State Control of Commerce and Industry in Ancient China, chapters I–XIX* (Leiden).

Groh, S. (2006), 'Neue Forschungen zur Stadtplanung in Ephesos', *Jahreshefte des Österreichischen Archäologischen Instituts* 75, 47–116.

Hopkins, K. (1978). *Conquerors and Slaves* (Cambridge).

Hopkins, K. (2002). 'Rome, Taxes, Rents and Trade,' (orig. published 1995/6), repr. in Scheidel, W. and von Reden, S. (eds.), *The Ancient Economy* (Edinburgh),190–230.

Hurst, H. (1993). 'Cartagine, la nuova Alessandria', in: Schiavone, A. (ed.), *Storia di Roma, vol.* 3.2 (Turin), 327–337.

Hsu, Cho–Yun, (1980). *Han Agriculture. The Formation of Early Chinese Agrarian Economy (206 B.C.–A.D. 220)*, edited by J.L. Dull (Seattle–London).

Lee Swann, Nancy (1950). *Food and Money in Ancient China. The Earliest Economic History of China to A.D. 25, Han Shu 24 with related texts, Han Shu 91 and Shih–Chi 129* (Princeton).

Lewis, M. (2007). *The Early Chinese Empires: Qin and Han* (Cambridge Mass.).

Liang Gengyao, *Songdai shehui jingji shi* (Taipei 1997).

Loewe, M. (2004). *The Men who governed Han China: companion to A biographical* dictionary of the Qin, Former Han and Xin periods, Leiden.

Loewe, M. (2006). *The Government of the Qin and Han Empires 221 BCE–220 CE*, Indianapolis.

Loewe, M. (2010). 'The operation of government', in: Nylan, M. and Loewe, M. (eds.), *China's Early Empires. A Re–appraisal* (Cambridge), pp. 308–319.

Maddison, A. (2007). *Chinese Economic Performance in the Long Run, second edition revised and updated, 960–2030 AD* (Paris).

Pirazzoli–t' Serstevens, M. (2010). 'Urbanism,' in: Nylan, M. and Loewe, M. (eds.), *China's Early Empires. A Re–appraisal* (Cambridge), pp. 169–185.

Rowe, W.T. (2002). 'Social stability and social change', in: Peterson, W.J. (ed.), *The Cambridge History of China, vol. 9, part 1. The Ch'ing Dynasty to 1800* (Cambridge), 473–562.

Rozman, G. (1973). *Urban Networks in Ch'ing China and Tokugawa Japan* (Princeton, N.J.).

Sadao, N. (1986). 'The economic and social history of former Han,' in: Twitchett, D., and Loewe, M. (eds.), *The Cambridge History of China, vol. 1. The Ch'in and Han Empires 221 B.C.–A.D. 220* (Cambridge), 545–607.

Scheidel, W. (2004). 'Creating a metropolis: a comparative demographic perspective,' in: Harris, W.V. and Ruffini, G. (eds.), *Ancient Alexandria between Egypt and Greece* (Leiden), 1–31.

Scheidel, W. unpublished. 'State revenue and expenditure in the Han and Roman empires', Princeton/Stanford working papers in Classics.

Schinz, A. (1996). *The Magic Square. Cities in Ancient China* (Stuttgart–London).

Sit, V. (2010). *Chinese City and Urbanism: evolution and development* (New Jersey).

Skinner (1977) 'Regional urbanization in nineteenth-century China', in: id. (ed.), *The City in Late Imperial China* (Stanford, Cal.), 211-249.

Sly, D.I. (1996), *Philo's Alexandria* (London).

Steinhardt, N. 1999. *Chinese Imperial City Planning* (Honolulu).

Stephens, S. (2010). 'Ptolemaic Alexandria,' in: Clauss, J.J. and Cuypers, M. (eds.), *A Companion to Hellenistic Literature* (Oxford), 46-61.

Wang Zijin (2007). 'Xi Han Chang'an jumin de shengcun kongjian', *Renwen zazhi* 2007.2, 150-158.

Wilson, A. (2012). 'City sizes and urbanization in the Roman empire,' in: Bowman and Wilson (2012), 161-195.

Wu Songdi 吴松弟, *Nan Song renkou shi* 南宋人口史 (Beijing: Renmin, 2008).

Zhou Changsan (2001). *Handai chengsi yanjiu* (Beijing: Renmin, 2001).

China in Ferdowsi's Shahnameh[*]

Hamidreza Pashazanous, University of Tehran.

Abstract: Ancient Iran, as a power which ruled over many lands, dominated peoples of different cultures, and was receptive in turn to their impact, had strong ties with her neighbors. In fact, the place of ancient Iran in the history of the world and her contribution to the history of mankind can be understood only in the light of her contacts and interactions with her surrounding major powers.

At that time, Iran had strong relations with many Eastern civilizations. Among the most prominent of them was China. Although the political relationship between Iran and China was negligible, both civilizations were in extensive contact with one another commercially and culturally. *Ferdowsi's Shahnameh*(Book of Kings) is one of our sources for understanding these relations between China and Iran in ancient times but despite the growing complexity of active foreign relations with China, Ferdowsi and early Iranian—Muslim writers' thoughts of China and her relations with ancient Iran were controversial. In fact, Ferdowsi like all his other contemporaries give us little information on China. If we divide *Shahnameh* into two sections: mythological and historical, it will be difficult to distinguishes between China as an historical country and as a mythical land. Ferdowsi rarely distinguishes clearly among eastern Turkestan, China and Far East. For this reason, the purpose of this study is to show where Ferdowsi's China exactly was situated and to distinguish between mythical and historical China in *Shahnameh*.

Keywords: Ferdowsi, *Shahnameh*, Iran, China, Mā chin.

The name "China" is by far the most popular name that Persians and many people around the world use to refer to the cultural complex known today as China. According to the traditional theory, suggested in the 17th century by the Jesuit priest Martino Martini, "China" is derived from "Qin" dynasty which ruled China from 221–206 BC. This theory was then supported by scholars such as Paul Pelliot and Berthold Laufer.

---

[*] I would like to mention here that this paper is based on my PhD dissertation entitled:" High culture or components of civilization: The Mechanisms of Contact and Interaction between Cultures of China and Iran in Parthian and Sasanian Period" at University of Tehran, Iran.

Although there are various scholarly theories regarding the origin of this word, the most popular theory tells us that the name "China" is derived from Chin (چین), a Persian name for China popularized in Europe. This name is also derived from its Sanskrit counterpart Cīna(Čīna).[1]

Paul Pelliot has shown us several samples from which it appears that even under the Han dynasty the Chinese people was known as men of Qin/Ts'in in central Asia.[2] As his theory holds that this name was common in Central Asia as a name for Chinese people, it leads us to accept that it was also a common name for China in the Iranian plateau because, historical and archaeological information suggests that Chinese merchants who came from Central Asia, influenced Persians under Parthian and Sassanid dynasties and popularized this name in Iran.

In the middle Persian texts we see "Saini" in the Farvardin Yaŝt and "Sini" in the Bundahiŝn, besides Chin and Chinastān.[3] It is difficult to understand where the Saini or Sini had to be situated according to these texts but as Ge Fangwen has suggested Cīna was a Sanskrit term for "the East".[4] From scholarly sources such as *Bundahishn* we understand that ancient Persians used the words Sini, Chin and Chinastān as references for Iran's eastern border.[5] Later, the words Chin, Chinistān, or Chinastān were frequently used by early Muslim historians and geographers to refer to eastern Turkestan, China and Far East.[6] These words were used as names for ancient China, were transferred into early Islamic sources by middle Persian works such as *Xvatāynamāk* "Book of Kings", a late Sassanid compilation of the history of the kings and heroes of Persia from mythical times down to the reign of ··osrow II (590－628 AD). Because after the defeat of the Persian Empire, this book was the main source for early Iranian-Muslim writers such as Ferdowsi in composing the history of ancient Iran and its contacts and interactions with the neighbors such as ancient China. However, as some scholars confirm from the primary sources of this period, we understand that in pre-Islamic times there were already established trade routes and contacts between the Chinese and Persians. This shows us after the defeat of the Persian Empire, these links and contacts were still kept, by which these names were popularized in Iran.

China or "Chin = چین" and its Combination words in Shahnameh

Ferdowsi's *Shahnameh*[7] or Book of Kings is one of our main sources for understanding the history of ancient Iran and her relations with her neighbors like China. Ferdowsi wrote this massive book between c.977 and 1010 AD. *Shahnameh*, which is comprised of some 50,000 verses, completed in 400/1010 and dedicated

---

[1] Berthold Laufer, *Sino-Iranica: Chinese Contributions to the History of Ancient Civilization in Ancient Iran*, Chicago, Field Museum of History, 1919. See p. 569.

[2] Ibid, p. 569.

[3] Ibid , p. 568. See also: *Bundahishn*, (Faranbagh Dadgee), Edited by Mehrdad Bahar, Tus Publications, Tehran, 1385, pp. 73, 83, 90, 128.

[4] Wade, Geoff. "The Polity of Yelang and the Origin of the Name 'China'", *Sino-Platonic Papers*, No. 188, May 2009. p. 11.

[5] *Bundahishn*, (Faranbagh Dadgee), Edited by Mehrdad Bahar, Tus Publications, Tehran, 1385, p. 128.

[6] Pulleyblank,Edwin G., "Chinese-Iranian Relations, i in pre-Islamic times", in Ehsan Yarshater (ed.), *Encyclopaedia Iranica*, vol. 5 (Costa Mesa, Ca.: Mazda Publishers, 1992), pp. 424-31, p. 431.

[7] All references to *the Shahnameh* are from the Khaleghi-Motlagh edition: Abu' l-Qaseme Ferdowsi, *The Shahnameh(Book of Kings)*, Edited By Djalal Khaleghi-Motlagh, Entesharat-e daeratolmāref-e bozorg-e eslāmi, 8 vols, Tehran, 1386.

to Ghaznavid sultan Ma・・mūd[1] (r. 388–421/998–1030 AD)[2] narrates the history of the Iranian people and the legends and histories of Iranian kings from the earliest times to the Islamic conquest of Persia in the 7th century AD. This book, a long poetic opus, is divided into three successive eras: the mythical, the heroic or legendary, and the historical.

The entire book is not only about the history of Iran and her Kings but also about her relations with neighbors to the East and the West. Although there is historical information in *Shahnameh* about Iranian relations with West and East, the quality of this information and reliability of the content in each of these three parts is different. In fact, Ferdowsi gives us various kinds of information about China and Eastern nations extremely variable and difficult to be assessed. In all of these mythical, the heroic or legendary, and the historical ages, he mentions the Eastern nations and Eastern lands by different geographical names; some are nouns and the rest are adjectives which describe a noun. He uses these words to refer to Eastern nations and Eastern lands: "Chin = چین" (China), " Chini" (Chinese), "Keshvar–e Chin" (the country of China), "Chīnistān", "Māchin", "the Turks of China", "Tūrān",[3] "Turks", "India", Khotan, Mokrān, Shaknān,[4] Shakni, koshani, Ghajghar,[5] Tarāz,[6] Hital.[7] There are some preliminary studies on some of these geographical names in *Shahnameh*. most of these names are opened up. Because there has not been any research about the conceptual differences between "Chin", "Keshvar–e Chin" (the country of China), Chīnistān, Māchin and the Turks of China in *Shahnameh* or at least about their geographical locations, the word "Chin" and its combinations in this part have been studied.

In addition to these combination names cited above, the word "Chin" is used in combination with other words in *Shahnameh*. They include the following:

---

[1]　Bosworth, C. Edmund., "Ma・mud B. Sebuktegin" in Encyclopædia Iranica, Online Edition, 2012, available at http://www.iranicaonline.org/articles/mahmud–b–sebuktegin

[2]　Both the Gregorian calendar and the Islamic Hijri calendar have 12 months. The two calendars differ, however, in that the Gregorian calendar divides its months into a solar year, while the Islamic calendar divides its months into a lunar year. The Islamic Hijri calendar correlates the number of days in each month to the regular lunar phases. When a new crescent moon is sighted every 29 or 30 days, a new lunar month begins. The result is a 12–month lunar calendar year with months synchronized to the lunar cycles. The Gregorian solar calendar, in contrast, adjusts the length of 12 months so that they are synchronized with a solar year and the seasons. This enables the Gregorian months to consistently fall within the same seasons each year.

[3]　In the Shahnameh, the term "Tūrān" ("land of the Tūrya" like Ērān, Īrān = "land of the Ārya") refers to the all the lands north and east of the Oxus, as far as China.

[4]　According to the oldest geographical book in Persian language, Mokrān, Shaknān were located in Tūrān.

[5]　Ghajghar was also located in Tūrān.

[6]　Tarāz was the name of a city which was located in Turkestan.

[7]　Hitāl or HEPHTHALITES, a people who formed apparently the second wave of "Hunnish" tribal invaders to impinge on the Iranian and Indian worlds from the mid–fourth century C.E.(Bivar, A.D.H., "Hephthalites", in Ehsan Yarshater (ed.), *Encyclopaedia Iranica*, vol. 12 (Iranica Foundation, New York, 2004), pp. 198–199.)

Table 1. List of key combination words used by Ferdowsi in *Shahnameh*

Combination words	meaning of words	Combination words	meaning of words
"Daryā-e chin"	The sea of China	"Faghfur of Chin"	A title applied by old Persian and Arabic writers to the Emperor of Turkestan
"Khaqan of chin"	The title for the "Kings of Turkestan"	"Khātoon"	Ferdowsi uses this title to refer to the wife and daughter of Khaghan
"Bozorgān- e Chin"	Nobles of China	"Dibā-e Chin"	Fine silk of China
"Dānā-e Chin"	Wise man of China	"Bāzargānān-e Chin"	Merchants of China
"Shāh-e Chin"	King of China	"Bāzār-e Chin"	Bazaar of China
"Sālār -e Chin"	Leader of China	"Asban-e chin"	Horses of China
"Sālār –e Tōrkān-ō Chin"	Leader of China and Turks	"Bot-e Chin"	Idol of China
"Shāhanshāh-e Tōrkān-ō Chin"	King of Kings of China and Turks	"Botkhane-e Chin"	Temple of Idols of China
"Gordan -e Chin"	Warriors of China	"Khame-e Chin"	Pen of China
"Taraef-e Chin"	Rare imported products of China	"Ghertas-e Chin"	Thick paper of China

The Narrative of Chinese–Iranian Relations in *Shahnameh*

In Ferdowsi's *Shahnameh*, the land of China, her people and products have been well presented. These relations sometimes have been depicted in the form of war and sometimes in some romantic love narratives. *Shahnameh* begins with the creation of the World. Throughout the book even in the mythical age and from the very old times, China plays a very important role in the history of Iran. Here we will try to study this role and its significance in Ferdowsi's thoughts in all of these three parts of *Shahnameh*.

The Mythical Age

The mythical part opens with the creation of the world and the first dynasty that has ruled the world, known as Pishdādian. This part contains over 2100 verses, which is four percent of the book. Although this part of *Shahnameh* is very short, it is very important because it narrates mythical and semi–mythical figures referring to some real persons and events in the history of ancient Iran. Ferdowsi tells us the mythical tales of ancient nations throughout the mythical part, except for his introduction that he refers to Ghaznavid sultan Ma·· mūd (r. 388–421/998–1030 AD) as a great king who is praised by all of the kings from Kashmir up to the sea of China.[1] As we first encounter the word 'Iran' in *Shahnameh* (at the part where the reign of Jamshid is mentioned), it is obvious prior to that Kioumars, Houshang and Tahmoures–who were referred to as kings of the world or just kings,– were the kings of Iran, China and other nations. there is information about

---

[1] Abu'I-Qaseme Ferdowsi, *The Shahnameh(Book of Kings)*, Edited By Djalal Khaleghi–Motlagh, Entesharat-e daeratolmāref-e bozorg-e eslāmi, vol 1, Tehran, 1386, p 17.

China in other sources such as *Hodud al-alam, Kush-nameh,*···.[1] In *Shahnameh* the first relation between Iran and China formed in the story of the sixth Pishdādi king, Fereydoon, who was a descendant of Jamshid. Before Kingship of Fereydoon, there is no mention of China except for his narrative of Jamshid who was killed by Zahak near "Daryā-e chin" (The sea of China).

Throughout the mythical Part, which is extending from the creation of the world and of man until Manuchehr's reign, the name "Chin" (China) is used 16 times. In addition to "Chin", the name "Daryā-e chin" cited above was used only one time and there is no mention of "Māchin", "Chīnistān" in this part. Ferdowsi uses the name "Chin" mostly, when he tells us the story of "Tūr", one of Fereydoon's sons became the King of "Tūrān" and China. In fact, according to *Shahnameh* and other Persian mythical and literary texts, Fereydoon, who was the king of the earth,[2] divides the earth among his three sons: Salm, Tūr and Īraj. He hands over Iran to Īraj (his beloved son) because in Ferdowsi's thoughts Iran was considered as the center of the world and the gracious land.[3] In *Shahnameh's* geographical divisions west of Iran was Rome which Fereydoon granted them to Salm while east of Iran was China and Tūrān which was granted to Tūr. Tūr dispatched a great number of troops, he took the throne there and the nobles granted him various gifts and declared him king.[4]

Three brothers lived peacefully together for a while but the two elder brothers, Salm and Tūr, were jealous of Īraj. They decided to take revenge as the father granted him Iran as well as the throne and the crown. Soon they kill Īraj but years later Fereydoon's grandson, Manuchehr, avenges his death by killing both Salm and Tūr. Throughout this part, these titles were also used to refer to Tūr: "Sālār -e Chin" (Leader of China),[5] "Sālār -e Tōrkān-ō Chin" (Leader of China and Turks),[6] "Shāh-e Chin" (King of China),[7] "Shāhanshāh-e Tōrkān-ō Chin" (King of Kings of China and Turks).[8] Since in *Shahnameh*, Fereydoon divided earth into three parts: West(Rome),Center (Iran), East (China and Tūrān) and since Ferdowsi considers Tūr as a king of kings of China, it may be supposed that in Ferdowsi's ancient mythology China and Tūrān were equivalent to the East of Iran as a whole. Especially while there is no mention of names: "Faghfur of Chin", "Khaqan of

[1] In some of these sources, one of the wives of "Jamshid", the fourth king of this dynasty, was the daughter of "Mahang", the Emperor of China. In one of the first and oldest geographical sources in Persian, i.e. "Hodud al-alam" written in the 10th century AD / 4th century AH, the Emperor of China is introduced as the child of Fereydoon, the sixth King of "Pishdādian" .(Unknown author, *Hudud ul-'alam min al-mashriq ila al-maghrib*, Edited by Manouchehr Sotoudeh, Ketābkhāneh Tahuri ,Tehran, 1362/1983, p.60.) In "Kush-name", a book written in verse in the late 11th century AD / 5th century AH, we read that: "After arriving to China Alexander encountered a large statue and the people told him that he can find the secret of this statue in a mountain where someone called Mahanesh was living; Mahanesh told Alexander that he was from the Jamshid dynasty and the wife of Jamshid was the daughter of Mahang the emperor of China, and this couple had two boys called Nunak and Farak. When "Zahak" conquered Iran, Jamshid sent his wife, children and relatives to China to hide in blue woods until the time when one of them can take Jamshid's revenge on Zahak." (Hakim Iranshāh b.Abi al-khayr, *Kush-Nāmeh*, Introduced and Edited By Djalal Matini, Enteshārāt-e Elmi,Tehran, 1370,pp. 182-189.).
for further reading, see: *Moj' malal-ol-Tavārikh val-Qesas*, Introduced and Edited By Malekoshoarāye Bahār, Enteshārāt-e Kolāleh-Khāvar, 1331, pp.41-42.

[2] *Shahnameh*, vol 1, p.116.
[3] Omid, Shiva., "Eastern nations in Ferdowsi thoughts", *Journal of American Science*, 2011;7(7), p. 374.
[4] *Shahnameh*, vol 1, p.107.
[5] *Shahnameh*, vol 1, p.116.
[6] *Shahnameh*, vol. 1, p.107.
[7] *Shahnameh*, vol. 1, p.108.
[8] *Shahnameh*, vol. 1, p.108.

Chin" and "Māchin" which is frequently used to refer to the kings and other parts of the east in other parts of *Shahnameh* (the legendary and historical ages).

The Heroic or Legendary Age

This Age begins with the story of Manuchehr's reign until the conquest of Persia by Alexander. Almost two–third of *Shahnameh* is devoted to the heroic or legendary age. The main characters and events described in this part are the romance of Zal & Rudabe, the Seven Stages (or Labors) of Rostam, Rostam and Sohrab, Siavash and Sudabe, Rostam and Akvan Div, the romance of Bijan and Manije, the wars with Afrasiab, the story of Goshtasp and Arjasp, and Rostam and Esfandyar.

In this part of *Shahnameh*, the name "Chin" has been repeated over 200 times In addition to the combined words cited above (in the mythical part), it must be mentioned that this name was sometimes used in combination with other words such as "Daryā–e chin" (The sea of China), "Khaghan of chin", "Faghfur of Chin", "Khodavand–e Chin" (Lord of China), "Gordan –e Chin" (Warriors of China), "Bozorgān– e Chin" (Nobles of China), "Danā–e Chin" (Wise man of China)," Taraef–e Chin"(Rare imported products of China), "Asban–e chin" (Horses of China), "Bot–e Chin" (Idol of China), "Botkhane–e Chin" (Temple of idols of China), "Ghertas–e Chin" (Thick paper of China), "Khame–e Chin" (Pen of China), "Dibā–e Chin" (Fine silk of China), "Shir–e Chin" (Lion of China), "Bāzār–e Chin" (Bazaar of China). Since these words have been used in the heroic or legendary age for the first time, there is no mention of them in the mythical age. In addition, –most important for the aim of this study –Ferdowsi uses other geographical names which were used in combination with "Chin". These names, used in variable meanings, are "Māchin", "Chīnistān" and "Chin–ō Barbar" (China and Barbarians). The first name, Māchin has been repeated over 15 times,[1] and the names "Chīnistān" and "Chin–ō Barbar", each one of them were used only one time.[2]

Although the heroic or legendary age begins with the story of Manuchehr's reign, there is little information about China in this story and this information is limited to some names and titles. In fact, the important information of China in this age can be found in following stories: Sīāvoš[3] and Afrāsīāb,[4] Kāmūs–e Kašānī, Rostam battle with Khaghan of China, the great war of Kay ̲kosrow and finally the story of Arjasp and Goshtasp. Since the main theme of these stories is the battles between kings of Tūrān and Iran and since the following lands and peoples: Turks of China, Khotan, Mokran, Shaknan, Shakni, Koshani, the sea of Kimak and Ghajghar were also designated as Tūrānian people located in Tūrān, we should consider that Ferdowsi mostly used the name "Chin" and its combination words to refer to the lands beyond Tūrān and the lands North and East of

---

① For example, **Shahnameh**, Vol. 1:pp. 398, 407, 422 and 449.

② **Shahnameh**, vol. 3, p. 333.

③ He was a son of Kay Kāvus, then Shah of Iran, and due to the treason of his stepmother, Sudabeh (with whom he refused to have sex and betray his father), exiled himself to Tūrān where he was killed innocently by order of The Tūrānian king Afrasiab.

④ Afrāsīāb was the mythical Tūrānian king and hero and Iran's archenemy in its legendary history. By far the most prominent of Tūrānian kings, Afrāsīāb is depicted in Iranian tradition as a formidable warrior and skillful general; an agent of Ahriman, he is endowed with magical powers and bent on the destruction of Iranian lands. (Yarshater, E., "Afrasiab" in Ehsan Yarshater (ed.), *Encyclopaedia Iranica*, vol. 1, (Routledge & Kegan Paul, London, 1985), p. 576.)

the Oxus, even as far as the borders of today's China.[1]

Although Ferdowsi has used the names "Chin", "Chīnistān", "Chin-ō Barbar" and "Māchin" to refer to the lands beyond Tūrān, from the meaning of his verses it becomes clear that in his idea there was difference between "Chin" and "Māchin". In his view, these two names were two separate geographical areas. However, the readers of *Shahnameh* have realized the vagueness of these names geographically. This geographical differentiation becomes clear especially in the story of "Kay kosrow", a legendary king of the Kayanian dynasty and a character in the *Shahnameh*, when he says it took one week for him to ride from "Chin" to "Māchin":

[2]به یک هفته از چین به ماچین براند   به چین زین مهمان رستم بماند

"Kay kosrow stayed in Chin and then decided to go to M ā chin it took one week for him to ride from Chin to Māchin."

So according to Ferdowsi or the sources that he had used, the distance between the two geographical areas of "Chin" and "Māchin" was one week of horse-riding.

"Khaghan of Chin",[3] "Faghfur of Chin"[4] are also the names that were mentioned in this part of *Shahnameh*. In the heroic or legendary age, these names, "Khaghan of Chin", "Faghfur of Chin", were repeated over 83 and 18 times, respectively. Barthold, however, says that this title (Khaghan) was firstly used by rulers of the earliest people who called themselves "Turk". It had been taken by them from their predecessors, the "genuine Awars" or the Žoan-Žoan of the Chinese. later a distinction was made between kan or Khān and kaghan or khākān and khākān used in the meaning of "Khān of Khāns", like the Persian Shāhānshāh…"[5] it seems Ferdowsi mostly used these names for the kings of China because he does not speak here of one king of China only, but of many kings of China. As we see in the following verse:

[6]چه افراسیاب و چه شاهان چین   بشتم همه نام تو بر نگین

"Afrāsiāb along with all kings of China put your name on their rings."

Since "Khaghan" was firstly used by the earliest people who called themselves "Turk"[7] and since

---

① *Shahnameh*, the story of Great War of Kay kosrow, vol. 4, p.279. When Afrāsiāb was defeated by the troops of Kay kosrow, he then sends to the Faghfur of China to ask for assistance. It shows that China and T ū r ā n were two separate lands. for further reading, see also: *Shahnameh*, vol. 2, p.449:

ازای ن رود ی تاچ ن و مامچی ن خور و مه و کی و نان و پروب ن رارست   نسارت ن

In this verse, HŌMĀN, who was, next to Pir ā n, the leading member of the Vēsa clan and the highest ranking Turanian commander, tells Afrāsiāb that the whole Tūrān as far as borders of China and M ā chin is under his command. This tells us again that China and T ū r ā n were two separate lands.

② *Shahnameh*, vol. 4, p.304.

③ this title first was used by rulers of Turks. It was the title of the rulers of certain Central Asian countries, especially Turkestan, meaning "king" or "King of Kings".

④ "Faghfur or Baghbur was a title applied by old Persian and Arabic writers to the Emperor of China, much in the way that we used to speak of the Great Mogul and our fathers of the Sophy. It is, as Neumann points out, an Old Persian translation of the Chinese title Tien-tzu "Son of Heaven"; Bagh-Pur= "The Son of the Divinity", as Sapor or Shā-Pūr = "The Son of the King." Faghfur_ seems to have been used as a proper name in Turkestan." (*The Travels of Marco Polo*, the Complete Yule-Cordier Edition, two volumes, reprinted by Dover, New York, USA, Volume 2,1993, p.148.)

⑤ Barthold, W., (1993 reprint) "Khākān" *E. J. Brill's First Encyclopedia of Islam*, 1913-1936, Volume 4, E.J. Brill, New York, p. 875.

⑥ *Shahnameh*, vol. 3, p.333.

⑦ Barthold, W., (1993 reprint) "Khākān" *E. J. Brill's First Encyclopedia of Islam*, 1913-1936, Volume 4, E.J. Brill, New York, p. 875.

"Faghfur of Chin" has been a proper name in Turkestan,[①] somehow, it makes us believe that these names were the titles for the kings in the Western part of China. Especially when we see that Ferdowsi uses the name "Chin" coupled with "Turks" such as "Sālār-e Tōrkān-ō Chin" (the leader of China and Turks), "Shāhanshāh-e Tōrkān-ō Chin" (King of Kings of China and Turks),…??? to denote the same thing.[②]

The legendary age ends with the story of Alexander, his journey to "Chin" through India. When Faghfur of Chin heard that Alexander intended to subdue him, in order to prevent war, he opened his treasures and presented Alexander with gifts of fifty crowns, gold, incense, fur, Silk, camphor, musk, squirrel, ermine, marten hair and finally "dibā-e Chin" along with 300 red-haired camels.[③] Ferdowsi calls these gifts: "Taraef-e Chin", which means rare imported products of China. This term refers to Chinese shipping goods, although later this term was used to refer to rare imported products.[④] Application of this term along with the name "Daryā-e chin" (the sea of China), throughout the legendary and historical ages, becomes of key importance to ensure that Ferdowsi used this term for products imported through the sea and actually from the Southern part of China.[⑤] This shows that he was well aware of China as a unique civilization which was known for its "aesthetic items",[⑥] culture, products and fine silk.

The Historical Age

Apart from its utmost literary importance, this part of *Shahnameh* is written with a good deal of accuracy, by which it is pivotal for understanding Ferdowsi's idea of China in a geographical sense. Here, Ferdowsi tells us the history of Iran, extending from the Parthian dynasty until the Arab conquest of Iran and the fall of the Sassanids. In the historical age, the names "Chin", "Māchin", "Daryā-e chin", "Khaghan of Chin", "Faghfur of Chin" have been repeated over 196, 3, 6, 230, 32 times, respectively. The important narratives are the following stories: story of Mani[⑦], story of Khaghan of Chin and Bahrām Gōr [⑧], story of Anōširavān [⑨], Hital and Khaghan of Chin, story of Bahrām Chōbīn[①] and Khaghan of Chin. These stories are of key importance for the purpose of this article. They are, however, instructive in another way as well, with regard to modes of

---

① Shahbazi, A. Sh., "Bahr ā m, vii. Bahrām VI Čōbīn" in Ehsan Yarshater (ed.), *Encyclopaedia Iranica*, vol. 2, London and New York: Routledge and Kegan Paul, 1987, p. 519.

② *Shahnameh*, vol. 5, pp. 88, 104, 128.

③ *Shahnameh*, vol. 6, pp. 110-111.

④ Yaaghubi, *Al-boldan*, Dar al-kotob al-elmi, Bairut, 1422, p.49 and also Ibn Al-faghih Hamdani, *Ketab Al-Boldan*, Alam Al-kotob, Bairut, 1416, p.70.

⑤ *Shahnameh*, vol. 6, pp. 107, 111; vol. 7, p. 236.

⑥ the phrase "aesthetic items" is intended to encompass a wide range of domains including works of arts, thought and literature. For further reading See, John Baines and Norman Yoffee., "Order, legitimacy, and wealth in ancient Egypt and Mesopotamia", in G. Feinman and J. Marcus (eds.), *Archaic states* (Advanced Seminar Series), Santa Fe: School of American Research Press, 1998, p. 235.

⑦ Mani was the founder of the religion of Manicheism in the 3rd century CE.

⑧ Bahrām V Gōr, a pre-Islamic Sassanian Iranian king who flourished in the fifth century, was son and successor of Yazdegerd I, reigned from 420 to 438. (Shahbazi, A. Sh., "Bahr ā m, v. Bahrām V Gōr, son of Yazdegerd I" in Ehsan Yarshater (ed.), *Encyclopaedia Iranica*, vol. 2, London and New York: Routledge and Kegan Paul, 1987, p. 516.

⑨ Kosrow I Anōširavān was a great king of the Sasanian dynasty who ruled the Sasanian empire from 531 to 579 and he is famous for his reforms.

① Bahrām VI Chōbīn was the highest ranking Sasanian commander under the Hormozd IV (579-590 AD) and king of Iran in 590-91. (Shahbazi, A. Sh., "Bahram, vii. Bahr ā m VI Čōbīn" in Ehsan Yarshater (ed.), *Encyclopaedia Iranica*, vol. 2, London and NewYork: Routledge and Kegan Paul, 1987, p. 519.)

identification based on proper names which allow us to set the land "Chin" geographically apart from the current China. In fact, in addition to the combination words and names cited above, when Ferdowsi tells us stories of these historical kings he gives us accurate information about China, including proper names such as "Sanjah", Parmoodeh and Maghātoorah.

Sanjah① and Maghātoorah② were the chief commanders under khaghan of chin during the reign of ··osrow I Anōširavān (531–79 AD) and Bahrām VI Chōbīn (590–91 AD) and Parmoodeh,③ who was a contemporary of Sasanian king, Hormozd IV (579–590 AD), was the name of Khaghan of Chin. Another name mentioned here is "Khātoon". It is the first time that we see Ferdowsi mentioning this name. Kh ā toon was the title given to the wife and daughter of Khaghan. It is used 31 times in two different stories: in the stories about Anōširavān and Hormozd IV they refer to the wife of Anōširavān and mother of Hormozd.④ Since Ferdowsi uses these names for Khaghan of Chin, his commanders and his wife and daughter while describing the war between Anōširav ā n, Hital and then the story of Bahrām Chōbīn and Khaghan of Chin, and since he uses the same Turkish names for the king of Turks and his commanders,⑤ it again shows us, that he means the people in the Western part of China. Especially from the story of Anōširavān, Hital and Khaghan of Chin, when Khaghan wished to send an envoy to make contact with ··osrow I Anōširavān (531–79 AD). But the king of Hital feared an alliance between them, and in order to prevent it, he insulted Khaghan by killing his envoy and stealing his tribute,⑥ it becomes even more evident that in his thoughts, "Khaghan of Chin" and "Faghfur of Chin" are the kings of the western parts of China.

Where was Ferdowsi's "Chin" situated? And where does "Māchin" in Shahnameh refer to?

As has been mentioned before, in three different parts of *Shahnameh*, the names "Chin" and "Māchin" are used 412 and 18 times, respectively (where is the third part?). Although the name "Chin" has been used frequently within this book, there is no mention of "Māchin" in mythical age. This is due to the nature of this book, in which as a national epic, "Chin" along with "Tūrān" mentioned to be the East as a whole and there is no need to mention "Māchin", because in mythical age, spatial and temporal dimensions are unimportant. In order to understand better Ferdowsi's idea of "Chin" and "Māchin", it is necessary to study the application of these names into the main Persian geographical literary sources. Although Ferdowsi does not speak of "Chin" and "Māchin" and their borders and boundaries and this vagueness regarding geographical names becomes a norm in his book, some of these sources and the sources of his contemporaries describe "Chin" and "Māchin" along with its borders and boundaries. In fact, the main feature of these sources is the geographical differentiation that they make between these two names. One of these sources is *Tārikh-e Yaghoubi* which was one of the first and oldest Islamic geographical texts in ninth century AD / third century AH (?). In the book in which Yaghoubi explained China and its borders, he states:

"China is a vast country, whoever wants to go to China by sea, he must cross seven seas, each one with

---

① *Shahnameh*, vol. 7, p. 237.
② *Shahnameh*, vol. 8, p. 173.
③ *Shahnameh*, vol.7, p. 562.
④ *Shahnameh*, vol.7, pp. 265–266.
⑤ *Shahnameh*, vol.7, p. 236.
⑥ *Shahnameh*, vol.7, pp. 235–237.

its own color and wind and fish and breeze, completely unlike the sea that lies beside it. The first of them is the Sea of Fars, which men sail setting out from Siraf⋯ The seventh sea is called the sea of Sanji, also known as Kanjli. It is the sea of China; one is driven by the south wind until one reaches a freshwater bay, along which are fortified places and cities, until one reaches Khanfu (Canton in China) ⋯and whoever wants to go to China by land route, along the Balkh river (Oxus River) he must pass through Soghd, Ferghana, Chach (Tashkent) and Tibet until he reaches China⋯" ①

And again he says:

"China has four borders including north western (the land of Turks), western (Tibet), south western, and southern borders (southern border of china is a sea border and it is the way that Muslims come to China)" ②

These passages show that in the first Islamic centuries, for Iranians the name "Chin" referred to the Western areas and Southern parts of current China, which could be accessed through the sea. Apart from Yaghoubi and Ferdowsi, who have used the name "Chin" as an equivalent to the Western and Southern parts of current China—and how does the sentence continue?. *Tarikh-e tabarestān*, written in thirteenth century AD / seventh century AH, is another source that applied "Chin" to the east (the Western and Southern parts of current China).③ Although the author of *tarikh-e tabarestān*, Ibn Esfandiar gives us little information about China. However, from one of his contemporaries, Mohammad Ibn Najib Bakran, a geographer in thirteenth century AD / seventh century AH, we may get to understand the differences between "Chin" and "Māchin". *It is important* to keep in mind that this is the main primary source of geography that tells us about "Chin" and "Māchin" and allows us to set "Chin" geographically apart from the current "Māchin". In his book *Jahān Nāmeh*, Mohammad Ibn Najib Bakran says:

"The country of Great China is an area with many villages and cities. And it seems that there are about three hundred big and prosperous cities in China, and there are two kinds of China: the first that is prosperous is called the Absolute China or the External China, and the second that is located in the East is called the Internal China or Māchin" ④

From this passage we may conclude that according to Najib Bakran, the Western borders of current China, which he calls the External China, was "Chin" and the Eastern part and internal China was "Māchin". This mention of internal China as "Māchin" has been already used by one of Najib Bakran's predecessors, Abū Rayḫān Bīrūnī (973–1048 AD) who also was Ferdowsi's contemporary. In his book when Bīrūnī speaks of the Himalayas, he mentions that beyond those mountains is "Mahachin".⑤ As some scholars conclude from the primary sources of this period, "Mahachin" is merely a contraction of "Mahachina" (Great China), the

① Yaghoubi, Ahmad Ibn Abi Yaghoub, *Tārikh-e Yaghoubi*, Translated by Mohammad Ebrahim Āyati, Bongah-e Tarjomeh va Nashr-e Ketab,Tehran, 1342, pp. 224–25.

② Yaghoubi, Ahmad Ibn Abi Yaghoub, *Tārikh-e Yaghoubi*, Translated by Mohammad Ebrahim Āyati, Bongah-e Tarjomeh va Nashr-e Ketab,Tehran, 1342, pp. 225–26.

③ Ibn Esfandiar -e Kātib, Baha al-Din Muhammad ibn Hasan., *Tārikh-e Tabarestān*, corrected by Abbas Iqbal, Enteshārāt-e Kolāleh-Khāvar,vol 1, 1330, p. 29.

④ Mohammad Ibn Najib Bakran, *Jahān nāmeh*, Edited by Mohammad amin Riyahi, Ebne sina, Tehran, 1342, pp.71–72.

⑤ Bīrūnī, Muḥammad ibn Aḥmad, taḥqīq mā le' l-Hend, Alam Al Kotob, Beirut – Lebanon, 1403, p.147. See also: Bīrūnī, Muḥammad ibn Aḥmad., Alberuni's India, an English ed., with notes and indices. By Dr. Edward C. Sachau, London: K. Paul, Trench, Trübner & Co., ltd. , 1910, p. 207.

name by which the Hindus anciently styled (?) the Great Empire.[①]

By comparing these sources we find that Since B ī r ū n ī has used the name "Mahachin" (Māchin) to refer to Great China and therefore Najib Bakran, Ferdowsi and his predecessors include Yaghoubi applied "Chin" to the Western and Southern parts of current China. Therefore, it may be conceived that in Ferdowsi's thoughts the name "Chin" referred to the Western and Southern parts of current China and the name "M ā chin" also referred to the central, Eastern and Northern parts of China

Conclusion

Throughout the *Shahnameh*, Ferdowsi, just as his contemporaries, considered China a very old and ancient civilization. Especially when we see that he uses the words such as "Gordan-e Chin" (Warriors of China), "Bozorgān-e Chin" (Nobles of China), "Danā-e Chin" (Wise man of China), "Botkhane-e Chin" (Temple of Idols of China), "Ghertas-e Chin" (Thick paper of China), "Khame-e Chin" (Pen of China), "dibā-e Chin" (Fine silk of China), "Bot-e Chin" (Idol of China), to refer to the Chinese civilization. In fact, in the early Islamic period according to Iranians, China was the first civilization in the East. This civilization, as described by Ferdowsi, reflected a belief that was accepted by Iranians.

Although one of the main features of *Shahnameh* is the major role played by China, this name was used in variable meanings for two different geographical parts. As a matter of fact, if we divide the three ages of *Shahnameh* into two parts: a mythical, an heroic and an historical part, in the first part China according to Ferdowsi was Eastern Turkestan, China and the Far East as a whole. This part of China was annexed to T ū ran and India. In this part "Chin" and "M ā chin" are interpreted as one region and China was considered as a mythical land. In the second part, the name "Chin" gradually finds its way as an entity separated from M ā chin and the Far East. In this part, as we already mentioned, China referred to the Western and Southern parts of current China, as an historical country with which the Iranians of the ancient and medieval times maintained cultural and economic relations.

References

In English

Barthold, W., (1993 reprint) "Khā·ān" *E. J. Brill's First Encyclop╵ of Islam*, 1913-1936, Volume 4, E.J. Brill, New York.

Bosworth, C. Edmund., "Ma·mud B. Sebuktegin" in Encyclopædia Iranica, Online Edition, 2012, available at http://www.iranicaonline.org/articles/mahmud-b-sebuktegin

Berthold Laufer, *Sino-Iranica: Chinese Contributions to the History of Ancient Civilization in Ancient Iran*, Chicago, Field Museum of History, 1919.

Bīrūnī, Muḥammad ibn Aḥmad., *Alberuni's India*, an English ed., with notes and indices. By Dr. Edward C. Sachau, London: K. Paul, Trench, Tr ü bner & Co., ltd. , 1910.

Bivar, A.D.H., "Hephthalites", in Ehsan Yarshater (ed.), *Encyclopedia Iranica*, vol. 12 (Iranica Foundation, New York, 2004).

[①] Cathay and the Way Thither, being a Collection of Medieval Notices of China, translated and edited by Colonel Sir Henry Yule. New edition, revised by Henri Cordier, London, Hakluyt Society, Vol. I, 1915,p. 150.

Cathay and the Way Thither, being a Collection of Medieval Notices of China, translated and edited by Colonel Sir Henry Yule. New edition, revised by Henri Cordier, London, Hakluyt Society, Vol. I, 1915.

John Baines and Norman Yoffee., "Order, legitimacy, and wealth in ancient Egypt and Mesopotamia", in G. Feinman and J. Marcus (eds.), *Archaic states* (Advanced Seminar Series), Santa Fe: School of American Research Press, 1998, pp. 199–260.

Omid, Shiva, "Eastern nations in Ferdowsi thoughts", *Journal of American Science*, 2011: 7(7).

Paul Pelliot, *Notes on Marco Polo*, 3 vols, Paris, Imprimerie Nationale, 1963–1973.

Pulleyblank,Edwin G., "Chinese–Iranian Relations, i in pre–Islamic times", in Ehsan Yarshater (ed.), *Encyclopaedia Iranica*, vol. 5 (Costa Mesa, Ca.: Mazda Publishers, 1992), pp. 424–31.

Shahbazi, A. Sh., "Bahrām, v. Bahr ā m V Gōr, son of Yazdegerd I" in Ehsan Yarshater (ed.), *Encyclopedia Iranica*, vol. 2, (London and New York: Routledge and Kegan Paul, 1987.)

The Travels of Marco Polo, the Complete Yule–Cordier Edition, two volumes, reprinted by Dover, New York, USA, Volume 2, 1993.

Wade, Geoff. "The Polity of Yelang and the Origin of the Name 'China'", *Sino–Platonic Papers*, No. 188, May 2009.

Yarshater, E., "Afrasiab" in Ehsan Yarshater (ed.), *Encyclopedia Iranica*, vol. 1, (routledge & Kegan Paul, London, 1985).

In Persian

Abu' l–Qaseme Ferdowsi, *The Shahnameh (Book of Kings)*, Edited By Djalal Khaleghi–Motlagh, Entesharat–e daeratolm ā ref–e bozorg–e esl ā mi, 8 vols, Tehran, 1386.

Bundahishn, (Faranbagh Dadgee), Edited by Mehrdad Bahar, Tus Publications, Tehran, 1385.

Ibn Esfandiar – e Kātib, Baha al–Din Muhammad ibn Hasan., *Tārikh–e Tabarest*ān, corrected by Abbas Iqbal, Enteshārāt–e Kolāleh–Khāvar,vol 1, 1330.

Mohammad Ibn Najib Bakran, *Jahān nāmeh*, Edited by Mohammad amin Riyahi, Ebne sina, Tehran, 1342.

Moj'malal–ol–Tavārikh val–Qesas, Introduced and Edited By Malekoshoarāye Bahār, Enteshārāt–e Kolāleh–Khāvar, 1331.

Unknown author, *Hudud ul–'alam min al–mashriq ila al–maghrib*, Edited by Manouchehr Sotoudeh, Ket ā bkh ā neh Tahuri ,Tehran, 1362/1983.

Yaghoubi, Ahmad Ibn Abi Yaghoub, *Tārikh–e Yaghoubi*, Translated by Mohammad Ebrahim Āyati, Bongah–e Tarjomeh va Nashr–e Ketab,Tehran, 1342.

In Arabic

Bīrūnī, Muḥammad ibn Aḥmad, taḥqīq *mā le'l–Hend*, Alam Al Kotob, Beirut – Lebanon, 1403.

Ibn Al–faghih Hamdani, *Ketab Al–Boldan*, Alam Al–kotob, Beirut – Lebanon, 1416.

Yaaghubi, *Al–boldan*, Dar al–kotob al–elmi, Beirut – Lebanon, 1422.

King Aśoka's Philanthrōpia[*]

Henk W. Singor, Leiden University

Abstract: King Asoka's inscriptions preaching the Dhamma to his subjects are well known. Some Greek influence may almost certainly be assumed. For instance, the very fact of these inscriptions having been put up at all, could be traced to the Greek epigraphic habit. As to the contents, these need not be characterized as so outspokenly Buddhist as is often assumed. Indeed, in this respect as well Greek influences are not at all to be dismissed. This paper surveys the Indian-Greek connections at the time of king Asoka and suggests how and in to what extent the king might have acted under Greek inspiration.

Keywords: king Asoka, Inscription,Greek Influence

Introduction

King Aśoka Maurya (ca. 270–ca. 234 BCE) is one of the most important and fascinating figures of Early Indian and Early Buddhist history. His reign is the first in Indian history that can be more or less accurately dated, thanks to the messengers he dispatched to five Hellenistic kings whose reigning years are known. Indeed, it is the links between Aśoka and the Hellenistic world that makes him such a tempting figure for anyone interested in cultural exchange and cultural interaction in the vast regions opened up by Alexander for Greek cultural expansion. Moreover, Aśoka must be considered one of the founding fathers of Buddhism. Whatever the Buddha himself taught or introduced, without the royal support of Aśoka, the convert-king, the new religion would never have attained the status and the geographical expansion that it eventually acquired. The dozens of inscriptions, set up by Aśoka all over his realm, are the oldest Indian written sources, and therefore also the oldest Buddhist texts we have. No king before Aśoka had ever bothered to address his people directly in writing, and thereby to divulge even some of his inner thoughts to his subjects. At least two of his inscriptions were in Greek, meant for the Greek-speaking populations of some cities in modern-day Afghanistan which had been annexed by Aśoka's grandfather Chandragupta Maurya, the founder of the realm and of the dynasty.

[*]　I wish to thank the participants of the 2012 International Symposium on Ancient World History in China, Tianjin June 16-18, 2012, for their remarks and criticisms. Especially, I want to thank Dr Jeffrey Lerner for his various critical observations which have led me to restate some of my views in a more subdued fashion. Needless to say, all possible errors of fact and all possibly unwarranted speculation remain my own responsibility.

Chandragupta, his son, and his grandson each in turn received Greek ambassadors sent by Seleukid and Ptolemaic rulers. What we have, then, is the sudden appearance of inscriptions in India; even inscriptions with philosophical, indeed with the earliest Buddhist content we know of; partial use of the Greek language; and messengers from and to Greek kings. All this makes for an intriguing mix of historical possibilities.

What I intend to do is first to survey briefly the various encounters of Greek and Indian cultures since the time of Alexander, or rather since his successor Seleukos Nikatōr had ceded Alexander's Indian conquests to the rising Maurya empire by his treaty with Chandragupta in 305 BCE. Further, to ascertain the character of Aśoka's inscriptions as an historical innovation. Then, to show briefly how these inscriptions relate perhaps even more to Greek texts and Greek ideas than to Indian or Buddhist ones. Finally, to venture just a little into the questions around Aśoka's position in the development of Early Buddhism. All this will doubtless raise more questions than answers. Speculative as especially the latter part of this exercise must necessarily be, the exercise itself, I hope, may not be wholly fruitless.

Historical overview

It is well known that from the time of Seleukos I Greek ambassadors made their way to Indian courts and Indian ambassadors were sent to Greek and later Roman courts. The first of these was the famous Megasthenēs, who stayed at the Maurya court at Pataliputra for at least a few months, probably a few years, at some time after the treaty between Seleukos and Chandragupta had been concluded in 305BCE. On his return he wrote his well known *Indika* in four books–fragments of which have survived–about the country, its political and social organization, its various peoples, flora and fauna and so on. He seems to have been particularly interested in Indian philosophers and wise men, and he was the first to notice the distinction between the *brāhmana* or official priests and the *śramana* or wandering ascetics. Whether he also mentioned the Buddha is not clear. Of course, Megasthenēs was not the first to have been so interested, for some twenty years earlier there had been Onēsikritos conversing, on behalf of his master Alexander, with the Indian ascetics outside the city–gate of Taxila, as related by Arrian. And there had been the Indian ascetic Kalanos who had accompanied Alexander all the way from Taxila back to Persia. Indeed, the conversation or rather the confrontation between ruler and wise man had become a topos in Greek discourse on kings and philosophers alike–perhaps starting with the famous encounter between Alexander and the Cynic Diogenēs outside the walls of Corinth–and as such it must surely have been at the back of Megasthenēs' mind when he noted his observations on the Indian philosophers, even correcting On ē sikritos' report on some point of detail.

We do not know the occasions on which or the reasons why ambassadors or envoys were sent other than to reestablish already existing friendly relations, and not even in the case of Megasthenēs do we know any further particulars. Be that as it may, some twenty years later another ambassador arrived from the Seleukid court at the Maurya court of Chandragupta's successor Bindusara. This man, a certain Deimachos or Daimachos, a Greek from Plataiai, must in his turn have had some philosophical interest as well, for he was the writer of a treatise *Peri Eusebeias* or On Piety. Of the same king Bindusara we are told in an anecdote by Athenaeus (14. 652–3) that he wrote to Antiochos, Seleukos' son and successor, asking him to send 'sweet wine, figs, and a sophist', a request that the Seleukid king could only partially fulfill, as he explained to his Indian counterpart, since sophists could not so easily be shipped abroad as wine and figs. The request of the king, Aśoka's father, is nevertheless revealing.

Possibly, another Greek philosopher, Klearchos of Soloi, arrived in India at roughly the same time (ca.

280 BCE) —that is: *if* this Klearchos was the man of the same name who left an epigram together with an inscription that had once contained around 147 maxims from the collection of maxims at Delphi on a stele in Aï Khanoum, only five of which have survived. And *if* that inscription can be dated to the years around 280 BCE. For if the date would be brought down by a few decades or more, the identification of that Klearchos with the philosopher from Soloi would indeed be impossible. The latter was a Peripatetic and it is known that he was particularly interested in maxims and sayings of wise men and more generally in the wisdom of 'barbaric' peoples like the Jews and the Indians. If the Aï Khanoum inscription does indeed date from his lifetime, which I still consider to be very plausible, the Klearchos mentioned there can hardly have been anyone else than the peripatetic philosopher, for two philosophers of the same name and interested in the same topic, living at the same time, strains credulity. And having arrived all the way from Greece to the Greek city on the Oxus river in Bactria it is practically inconceivable that he had not traveled further across the Hindu Kush into India, at least to the city of Taxila. Admittedly, an Indian visit by the philosopher Klearchos is nowhere mentioned in our sources, meagre as they are, but that silence does not carry much weight in my view. Nor does the fact that he seems to have been far from a truthful observer of Judaism, for his contemporary H ē kataios of Abd ē ra wrote a whole book on the Jews which also contained not a little nonsense.

As for Greek diplomats to India, we hear that Ptolemy II of Egypt, not to be outdone by the Seleukids, sent, in a moment of peace between the two rival kingdoms, an ambassador of his own to Pataliputra, a certain Dionysios of whom practically nothing is known.

The Maurya king Bindusara was succeeded by his son Aśoka around 270 BCE. The Maurya empire was in essence the creation of Aśoka's grandfather Chandragupta who had in 317 BCE or shortly after assumed power in the territories of the former Nanda dynasty, the kingdom of Magadha, that stretched over most of Northern and Central India. Chandragupta had added to this the regions of the Punjab and by his treaty with Seleukos I all the Greek conquests to the south of the Hindu Kush, thus incorporating Greek settlements like Alexandria-in-Arachosia (modern Kandahar) into his realm. His empire-building policy, the first of its kind in Indian history, is often seen as inspired by and as a counterweight to the Macedonian conquests and conquest-states of Alexander and his immediate successors. Chandragupta's son Bindusara consolidated Maurya rule but does not seem to have conquered new territory. Aśoka, on the other hand, waged a bloody and destructive war to subdue Kalinga in modern Orissa along the east coast of India, either as a new addition to his empire or as the suppression of a formerly incorporated region that had rebelled (this, like many other details of Mauryan history such as the exact borders of the empire, remains unclear). Tradition has it that Aśoka after his succession had to fight for his throne against his many brothers and half-brothers and that only after four years he was formally coronated. The Kalinga war took place a few years later, probably in 262 BCE. According to the king's own admission it was this bloody war—with, in his words, 100 000 people killed, another 100 000 dead as a further consequence of the war and 150 000 enslaved—that led him to embrace a policy of non-violence, of adopting the *Dhamma*, of supporting and arranging the affairs of the *sangha*, i.e. the Buddhist community of ascetics, and of preaching the *Dhamma* to his subjects. In short, the king converted to Buddhism and the testimonies of his new policy are to be found in the numerous inscriptions he set up all over his realm. We shall turn to these documents presently.

After Aśoka's death the Maurya empire sharply declined and not long after 200 BCE it completely desintegrated. The reasons for that are again not all too clear, but some historians have blamed Aśoka's policies of non-violence. In the meantime, the Greeks from Bactria had extended their rule south of the Hindu

Kush and inaugurated a new period of Greek dominance in Northwestern India in the second century BCE, which coincided with a further expansion of Buddhism in North West India and across the Hindu Kush into Bactria. Perhaps the most famous of these Greek kings was Menandros who reigned in the Punjab and in parts of the Ganges valley and who would figure as the main character in the later Buddhist dialogue *Milindapanha* ('Questions of Menandros), in which he is portrayed conversing with the renowned Buddhist monk Nagasena–another example of the topos of ruler and wise man–and, perhaps inevitably, being converted to Buddhism. In little over a century after Menandros the Greek political presence in India finally came to an end but Greek culture would go on exerting some influence for a few centuries more in the mainly Buddhist Gandhara art of North West India and Central Asia.

Ashoka's inscriptions as historical innovation

More than 160 inscriptions of Aśoka have been discovered, both complete and in fragments, containing at least 54 different texts, many of which were inscribed in various copies. Scholars divide the texts into several groups: 14 Rock Edicts, 7 Major Pillar Edicts, at least 18 Minor Rock Edicts, 2 separate rock edicts, minor pillar edicts, 3 cave edicts, and 4 edicts on stone slabs found in Kandahar and in Laghman in the vicinity of Jalalabad in Afghanistan. There are in all six inscriptions in Aramaic (one from Taxila, two from Kandahar, two from Laghman and one bilingual Aramaic–Greek text from Kandahar) and two in Greek (one from Kandahar and the bilingual text already mentioned from Kandahar). The 14 Rock Edicts have been found at 9 places, 5 of which yielded the complete version of all 14 edicts. In one of the Minor Rock Edicts the king complains of scribes who had not accurately written out what he had intended. We have to be careful, therefore, not to lay too much weight on every word of each text. Nevertheless, we can be confident that in the vast majority of cases we hear the voice of Aśoka himself. Perhaps the occasional tinkering with the text by a subordinate testifies to the novelty of the whole enterprise. For it is pretty certain that no one before Aśoka had ever set up inscriptions, let alone inscriptions of such a philosophical and moralistic character.

We can safely say that Aśoka began a tradition of royal inscriptions, an Indian epigraphic habit. Inscriptions in general appear in India only by the time of his reign; the handful of private inscriptions known, from caves and on copper utensils, can hardly predate Aśoka. The use of a script itself was surely older. The *Brāhmi* script had been derived, probably, from Aramaic and went back to the fifth century, the younger *Karosthi* had developed also from aramaic–and possibly under Greek literary influence as well– around 300 BCE. There are, however, no extant Indian texts in either of these alphabets from before the time of Aśoka. Further, as has been pointed out by others, the royal inscriptions of Aśoka's successors and especially those of later dynasties, differ greatly in style and content from Aśoka's texts. They are almost without exception not in the first person singular as many of Aśoka's inscriptions are and in their content they lack completely his modesty and care for the well–being of the common people. In their exaltation of royal virtues they resemble more the royal inscriptions of the Achaemenid kings.

The inspiration for Aśoka's first–person address has indeed been attributed to these Persian texts, for instance to the famous Bīsut ū n inscription of Darius I. But it is precisely this royal bragging, so to speak, that distinguishes starkly the Achaemenid texts from Aśoka's inscriptions–not to mention the fact that the Achaemenid inscriptions were placed at an height in the rock that made it impossible for passers–by to read the texts. There is, however, a resemblance between Achaemenid inscriptions and the ones set up by Aśoka in their multilingual character. The inscription of Darius just mentioned is in three languages and Aśoka took care to address his subjects in the languages which they could understand: the Prakrit and Maghadan dialects, Aramaic and Greek—albeit not in the Dravidian languages of the south of his empire. But to my mind this resemblance is not enough of an argument to assume Achaemenid inspiration for Aśoka's inscriptions. After all, by the time of Aśoka's reign the Persian Empire had already passed away for some sixty years and the great Seleukid kingdom, Aśoka's contemporary, also was acquainted with the practice of royal proclamations in other languages than the Greek of its ruling class. In any case, the idea to set up inscriptions in which the king addressed his subjects directly or indirectly—in the latter case by instructing royal officials to oversee the implementation of the king's directions—was a novelty in Aśoka's realm.

The king's inscriptions were not spread evenly across his empire but we find clusters in far apart regions as Karnataka in the South West and another one in the North West including the Aramaic and Greek texts. Why this is so, we do not know. In the North West the Indian texts are written in *Karosthi*, elsewhere in India they are mainly in *Brāhmi*. Many inscriptions are dated according to years after Aśoka's coronation (266 BCE?) or perhaps after his succession (270 BCE?). The major Rock Edicts are the most systematically dated and it is perhaps not without significance that the oldest of these is the Aramaic–Greek bilingual found at Kandahar that has a date of the eighth year of Aśoka's reign (263/2 or 259/8 BCE?). It is the language of this Greek text in particular that has made some scholars wondering—Western scholars, I should add, not their Indian counterparts—if not part of the contents of this inscription as well as of the other Greek text from the tenth year after the coronation (257/6 BCE?) too might be attributed to Greek ideas or if not even the whole enterprise of setting up these royal texts might be explained by direct Greek influence. In my view that was probably the case and that conclusion will be supported, I believe, when we now consider the contents of the king's messages to his people.

Greek and Buddhist contents of Aśoka's inscriptions

Four texts—minor Pillar Edicts—deal with the affairs of the *sangha* or recount the gifts that Aśoka's queen had bestowed on the ascetic community, the visit of the king to Lumbini, and his enlargement of a famous stupa in its vicinity. These, then, are solidly Buddhist documents. Further, in one of the so—called separate rock edicts Aśoka greets the *sangha* and exhorts monks and nuns to follow the teaching of the Buddha which he considers a truthful exposition of the *Dhamma*. This is the only mention of the Buddha in all of Aśoka's edicts. In another cave edict he mentions his gifts to the ascetic community of the Ājīvikas, a sect that resembled the Buddhists in its stress on non—violence. A few more inscriptions address the typically Indian situation by calling for respect for *brāhmana* and *śramana* and preaching the virtues of mutual tolerance and recognition between the various religious sects. All the other nearly fifty edicts contain moralistic proclamations and admonitions, preach non—violence, praise self—discipline and obedience towards one's elders and teachers. This vast majority of texts has usually been claimed as typically Buddhist and thus as 'Indian' as opposed to Greek in character. But the Greek texts from Kandahar just mentioned gives room for doubt.

The Greek inscription from Kandahar contained substantial parts of the Rock Edicts XII and XIII which are known in full from Brāhmi and Karoshti texts. In the first of these the king recommends *eusebeia* and *enkrateia*, that is: the *Dhamma* and self—control, in this case especially self—control in language: not critizising others and praising oneself but, conversely, praising others, i.e. the other 'schools' or 'sects', for that will bring enhancement of knowledge for everybody and make people steadfast in their *eusebeia*. In the second text it is related how the king in his eighth year conquered Kalinga and was shaken to remorse by all the bloodhed;

how since then he propagated the *Dhamma* and preached abstention from killing living beings, obedience and friendliness to one's elders, the mild treatment of slaves etc. In the other and slightly later Kandahar text, with its near-equivalent in Aramaic, the king 'shows' his Greek-speaking subjects the *Dhamma (eusebeian edeixen)*; tells them that he and his hunters and fishermen now abstain from the killing of living beings; admonishes them to stop being *akrateis* (i.e. without self-discipline), and to obey their parents and elders. The short remnant of Klearchos' inscription at Aï Khanoum dealing with the five stages of a man's life states that as a boy one should be well-behaved (*kosmios*) and as a youth self-disciplined (*enkratēs*). Terms like *enkrateia* or its opposite *akrasia*, and *Eusebeia*-Piety, but in Aśoka's texts used to render the concept of *Dhamma*-certainly refer to a well-known Greek philosophical vocabulary. Of course, this by itself would never be enough to suggest Greek inspiration for Aśoka's edicts. But the connections between the Indian king's texts and the inscription left by Klearchos in Aï Khanoum can be traced much further, as has been shown some twenty years ago by the Russian scholar V.-P. Yailenko in a little noticed article in the French journal *Dialogues d'Histoire Ancienne*.

Louis Robert, who had published and commented on some Aï Khanoum texts in 1968, dated our inscription to the years around 280 BCE and identified the Klearchos mentioned in it with the philosopher Klearchos of Soloi, had observed that this Klearchos must have set up a central stele on a base containing his dedicatory epigram and flanked on either side by another stele and all three of them in front of the *hēroön* of Kineas, the heroized founder of the city. Since Robert had identified the remnants of the inscription as maxims 46 and 47 of the collection of Delphic maxims assembled by the Greek author Sosiadēs he concluded that the three stelae together must have contained the whole collection of between 140 and 150 sayings. We know that these maxims from Delphi and others attributed to the Seven Sages enjoyed a renewed popularity and were published in several collections of which fragments have been preserved; the collection of Sosiadēs being the most complete (and preserved for us in the *Florilegium* of Stobaeus in the fifth century CE). In the small city of Miletoupolis in Asia Minor a similar stele on a base containing 56 Delphic maxims had been discovered in the beginning of the 20th century, and another collection of maxims is known from the gymnasium of Thera. Yailenko concluded that in Aï Khanoum likewise the stelae with Delphic maxims erected in front of the sanctuary of the city's founder must have served as the moral code for the inhabitants of this new *polis*. Assuming that all the maxims that we know from Sosiadēs' collection were thus engraved at Aï Khanoum-and had been in the possession of Klearchos who claimed to have meticulously copied them himself at Delphi -Yailenko then had the idea of comparing Aśoka's texts with the contents of this wider collection of Greek maxims. The results are, to my mind, very revealing.

In a series of his edicts Aśoka proclaims that to make people know the *Dhamma* and to admonish them to live according to its principles is the surest way to their happiness. The corresponding terms in a number of Greek maxims are *to dikaion* and *ho nomos*: live in obedience with the laws, live according to what is just. The obedience to parents, elders and superiors is repeatedly mentioned in Aśoka's edicts and the same idea of obedience and respect for the ancestors we find in the Delphic maxims. Aśoka advises to be courteous and generous towards one's friends and acquaintances; the Greek maxims contain many advices in the same spirit; only the king's recommendations that a pupil should respect his teacher and that a master should care about his slaves have no corresponding items among the Delphic maxims. General recommendations of Aśoka to be benevolent towards all people and to pity those in misery have their counterparts too among the Greek sayings, with the exception of his appeal to patience. Where the *Dhamma* prescribes a high measure of self-control, we find among the Delphic maxims several exhortations to self-discipline in various respects. Aśoka's stress on non-violence, on benevolence towards all living beings, including animals, has its corresponding admonitions from Delphi: do not resort to violence, do not use violence against a mortal man. Likewise, the vices to be avoided or suppressed are nearly all the same in Aśoka's edicts and in the Delphic maxims: dishonesty, bad temper, anger, arrogance, envy, inconstancy, obstinacy, cruelty.

For most scholars there has been no doubt that all of Aśoka's moralistic exhortations can be explained on the basis of the king's Buddhistic convictions. After his conversion the king, as so many converts to a new faith are apt to do, started to preach in order to let all his subjects share in the bliss of his newly found faith. And indeed it is not all too difficult to see in his edicts the spirit of Buddhism as we know it today. That his ideas might have been derived from another source, let alone in large part from a non-Indian source, seems inconceivable to most historians. Yet there is more to all this than appears at first sight. Twice Aśoka himself mentions a source for his maxims and it is not the preaching of the Buddha but the wisdom of the ancestors that he points to (in one of the minor Rock Edicts, where he advises that a pupil should respect his teacher, and that a man should behave well towards his family and relations; further in Pillar Edict VII where he notes that even the kings of old tried to teach the *Dhamma* to the people, but without success). As mentioned above, he only once refers to the teaching of the Buddha by considering it, as it were in passing, a just rendering of the *Dhamma*. All this does in my view not amount to very much. The single mention of the Buddha, the few references to the ancestors, and the overall presentation of the *Dhamma* as Aśoka's *Dhamma*, or rather an already pre-existing *Dhamma* to which the teaching of the Buddha only conforms, suggest to my mind that we do not have a sort of Buddhist ethical catechism here that the king was eager to spread among his people. Moreover, as Yailenko rightly pointed out, Buddhist literature that contains a similar ethical program as the precepts of Aśoka is all of later date, often centuries later. And then not even all of Aśoka's precepts can be found in that literature; certainly there is not one Buddhist work from India that contains all of them. And besides, *if* the whole of Aśoka's preaching would have been derived from the Buddhist teachings of his day, why would the king have gone to such extremes as to publish these moralistic precepts in a large number of inscriptions that few people could read instead of simply referring the people to the Buddhist monks and sages and exhorting them to listen to their sermons? In view of all this I am inclined to assume a Greek rather than an Indian-Buddhist source for the king's edicts, both for the fact of their existence and for most of their contents.

Aśoka's Philanthrōpia and Aśoka's place in the development of Buddhism

We have no reason to doubt Aśoka's conversion to Buddhism. His revulsion to the bloodbath of the Kalinga war was surely sincere. But to what sort of Buddhism did he convert? Certainly, it proclaimed non-violence, but so did other Indian sects like the Jainists and the Ājīvikas to which his mother is said to have belonged. What is less certain is what moral precepts the Buddhists of Aśoka's day preached and what metaphysics they taught. Aśoka's Buddhism, as expressed in his edicts, was of a peculiar sort, certainly not conforming to classical Buddhist doctrines. The concept of nirwana is lacking; instead, we find references to a blissfull paradise in the hereafter and even to the possibility of conversing with the gods for those people who fully practice the *Dhamma*. Earthly blessings, too, are the reward of the pious. Moreover, in the eyes of the king in principle *all* people could arrive at a state of ultimate happiness, if not in this life, then in the hereafter. Although the *sangha* of monks and nuns is mentioned a few times, it not clear what their status is, and the now classical Buddhist idea that only the ordained could achieve to enlightenment and that the common people had to hope for their chance only in a future life, is certainly absent.

It has been suggested, convincingly in my view, that where Aśoka speaks of the gods with whom the pious people would mix he is referring to an older idea expressed at the end of a Vedic hymn that exhorts the sacrificers to 'sit down, arrived in heaven, mixed among the gods'. What Aśoka meant, then, was that not only the brahmanic priest of old could reach this company of the gods, namely in a state of exstatic vision, but that even for the common people that exalting visionary experience had now become a possibility. We have here a substratum, so to say, of classical Buddhism, a substratum with shamanistic overtones that would lend itself to all sorts of magical practices against which, or rather against the misuse of which, various Buddhist tracts and rules would warn (I need not go into the vast subject of magical practices in Buddhism here). If this was part of the character of Aśoka's Buddhism we might even suppose that his Buddhism was mainly a doctrine of world-renouncement and non-violence; indeed, as tradition has it, a world-renouncement less extreme than the self-mortification practiced by some of the wandering ascetics, but nevertheless essentially a social and focused on the personal state of otherworldly bliss for the steadfastly striving individual. It is not at all clear that this early Buddhism would have engendered the set of moral codes typical of a harmonious society that we find in Aśoka's edicts.

This leads us back to the possible Greek inspiration for these edicts. The moral code as left by Klearchos in Aï Khanoum must have easily appealed to a king who had adopted a new, non-violent, worldview but who could as a king not simply side with the Buddhist 'sect', however much he may have admired its legendary founder. He made a pilgrimage to Lumbini, restored a famous stupa not far from there, and erected at least one of his well-known pillars-inscribed monoliths crowned with twin lions the significance of which is not altogether clear-in Sarnath, honouring the spots of the Buddha's enlightenment and first sermon and inaugurating a practice of Buddhist pilgrimages centred on these places. Nevertheless, other 'sects' were honoured by him as well and the king admonishes his people to respect all wandering ascetics and also the priestly *brāhmana*. The Greek maxims were well adjusted to his now at least in theory pacifistic kingdom. How exactly Aśoka came to know of this corpus of Greek wisdom will probably remain a mystery for us, but historical possibilities are not lacking. Klearchos himself may have gone on to India, a copy of these wise sayings in his luggage. Even if he did not go further than Taxila he might have left his precious specimens of wisdom there as a present for his Indian hosts just as he had done in the Greek city of Aï Khanoum. If the Klearchos inscription there would be dated a little later, say to 270-260 BCE, we might still assume a Greek traveler from that city bringing the text of these maxims across the Hindu Kush to Taxila. Aśoka is said to have been governor in Taxila for some years during the reign of his father Bindusara. It is perfectly conceivable that after his conversion to Buddhism he remembered the wise sayings of the westerners and had them brought to him again (and probably translated, although it is not impossible that during his stay in Taxila he had acquired a little knowledge of Greek himself) or that, as a newly convert, he was particularly open to such texts of wisdom if these were by then just brought into the land by some wise man from the world of the *Yona*. We may recall king Bindusara's request to king Antiochos to send him among other things a Greek sophist or wise man. We have to assume a genuine interest on the part of some Indians and of some Greeks in each other's ideas that had started already in the fourth century BCE and on the Greek side perhaps even earlier, ever since the first contacts between Greeks and Indians at the royal courts of Persia since the later 6th century BCE. And there was Deimachos, royal envoy and author of a book 'On Piety', coming to India at some time between 290 and 260 BCE and most probably by way of Aï Khanoum. *Eusebeia*, moreover, was not only used as a translation for

Dhamma, it was also in the Hellenistic world one of the cardinal virtues of a king.

Being a king it must have been clear or made clear by others to Aśoka that his missionary effort of setting up his edicts over vast stretches of his empire was an enterprise worthy of a king. Who better could have conveyed such an idea than a Greek royal ambassador! We must not forget the prestige, cultural as well as military, that the *Yona* or *Yonaka* enjoyed in the Indian world. It does not require an effort of the imagination to see before us, so to speak, a Greek ambassador expounding to his royal Indian host on the qualities of the ideal king. In the Hellenistic conception of kingship the king should reign for the well-being of his subjects, he should be a Benefactor and a Saviour from external foes. In bestowing all sorts of blessings on his subjects the king would manifest his superhuman nature and present himself as *philanthrōpos*. Originally, *philanthrōpia* or 'love of men' was a quality of the gods, but ever since Xenoph ō n in the fourth century it had become part of the ideology of idealized kingship, and in the Hellenistic world it even became a common place quality of a king. Inscriptions attest to countless royal Benefactors, Saviours, and *Philanthrōpoi*. This, I presume, triggered Aśoka's epigraphic program: to be *philanthrōpos* as the kings his contemporaries were and let his subjects know, in the Greek manner of inscriptions, how to obtain happiness in this life and in the hereafter. For, to be sure, the contents of Aśoka's *philanthrōpia* were not exclusively Greek. The moralistic maxims may have suited his non-violent conviction well, that conviction itself was rooted in Buddhism, in the early Buddhism of his day.

When Aśoka sent out his ambassadors or missionaries to Sri Lanka, to the westcoast of presentday Myanmar, to the lands of the *Yona* and the *Kamboja* (i.e. the Greeks and the Iranians in the North West of his realm) and, surprisingly, to the Hellenistic kings Antiochos II, Ptolemy II, Antigonos of Macedon, Magas of Cyrene and Alexander of (probably) Epirus, it is tempting to assume that he expected the same recognition of the *Dhamma* and the same willingness to act upon that recognition in a royal manner, that is by propagating the new doctrine, as he himself may have shown when he became acquainted with the Greek moral code and the Greek concepts of true kingship. If so, he must certainly have been disappointed in the lack of response from any of his counterparts in the Greek world.

Finally, as to the development of Buddhism, Aśoka certainly was responsible for a major expansion of Buddhism beyond the borders of India. Less certain, but in my view quite possible, may be a shift in emphasis, under the royal patronage, away from the individual ascetic and towards the community of the *sangha* and a more institutionalized division between monks and laymen, and also towards a more coherent set of ethical rules for society as a whole. Likewise, partly thanks to Aśoka and directly or indirectly under Greek philosophical, more precisely Epicurean influence, Buddhist metataphysics may have undergone a shift towards a materialistic worldview, towards atheism and the accompanying concept of nirwana. This may come as a surprise for those of us who believe that all these concepts stem from the Buddha himself who lived in the sixth century BCE. That dating, however, is certainly wrong, and the Buddha may have lived at any time between 500 and 300 BCE, even not so long before the time of Aśoka. Moreover, we know very little with any certainty about his life and his teachings. Greek influence on early Buddhist ideas is not at all far fetched. But to expound on that is another story.

Bibliography

Bechert, H., 'Die Datierung des Buddha als Problem der Weltgeschichte', *Saeculum* 39 (1988) : 24–34.

Chakrabarti, D.K., *The Geopolitical Orbit of Ancient India*, Oxford, 2010.

Falk, H., 'The diverse degrees of authenticity of Aśokan texts', in: P. Olivelle (ed.), *Aśoka in History and Historical Memory* (Delhi 2009) : 5–18.

Hagens, G., 'Syncretism and ancient chronology: can Democritus date the Buddha?', *Mouseion* 3 (2009) : 29–55.

Hamilton, S., *Early Buddhism: a New Approach. The I of the Beholder*, Richmond, 2000.

Holt, F.L., *Thundering Zeus. The making of Hellenistic Bactria*, Berkeley, 1999.

Karttunen, K., *India and the Hellenistic World*, Helsinki, 1997.

Karttunen, K., 'Aśoka and Mauryas: a Graeco–Roman perspective', in: P. Olivelle (ed.), *Aśoka in History and Historical Memory* (Delhi 2009) :103–108.

Kinnard, J.N., *The Emergence of Buddhism*, London, 2006.

Leoshko, J., 'Assessing evidence of Aśokan–period art', in: P. Olivell (ed.), *Aśoka in History and Historical Memory* (Delhi 2009) : 53–93.

Lorentz, S., *De progressu notionis* Philanthrōpias, Leipzig, 1914.

McEvilley, T., *The Shape of Ancient Thought. Comparative studies in Greek and Indian philosophies*, New York, 2002.

Merkelbach, R. & J. Stauber, *Jenseits des Euphrat: Griechische Inschriften*, Leipzig, 2005.

Pugliese Carratelli, G., 'Asoka e i re ellenistici', *Parola del Passato* 8 (1953) : 449–454.

Robert, L., 'De Delphes à l'Oxus. Nouvelles inscriptions grecques de la Bactriane', *Comptes Rendus de l'Académie des Inscriptions* (1968) : 416–457.

Salomon, R., 'Aśoka and the 'Epigraphic Habit' in India', in: P. Olivelle (ed.), *Aśoka in History and Historical Memory* (Delhi 2009) : 45–52.

Schlingloff, D., 'König Asoka und das Wesen des ältesten Buddhismus', *Saeculum* 36 (1985) : 326–333.

Schlumberger, D.S., 'De la pensée grecque à la pensée bouddhique', *Comptes Rendus de l'Académie des Inscriptions* (1972) : 188–198.

Scott, D.A., Ashokan missionary expansion of Buddhism among the Greeks (in N.W. India, Bactria and the Levant), *Religion* 15 (1985) : 131–141.

Talim, M., *Edicts of King Aśoka. A new vision*, New Delhi, 2010.

Thapar, R. *The Mauryas Revisited*, Calcutta – New Delhi, 1987.

Yailenko, V.–P., 'Les maximes delphiques d'Ai Khanoum et la formation de la doctrine de *Dhamma d'*Asoka', *Dialogues d'Histoire Ancienne* 16 (1990) : 239–256.

Imperial Highways and Ideology: China and Rome Compared

Richard Talbert, University of North Carolina

Abstract: Comparison of the highways of imperial Rome and China's Classical Era (323 BCE–316 CE) has typically focused on their length and geographical extent. This paper goes further to consider highway planning, classification, construction, maintenance, and usage; regulation of travel; and perception of highways as instruments of power and civilization from cultural, philosophical, and religious perspectives. Striking results emerge: Rome's minimal control of movement appears remarkable; by contrast, the highway's prominence as a ubiquitous leitmotif and metaphor in Chinese ethics and thought is hardly paralleled in Roman thought.

Keywords: China, ancient Rome, ancient emperor, highway, trade, transport, travel

Both scholars who study China's classical era (323 BCE–316 CE) and those who study the Roman empire have always been aware that highways were an important underpinning of each state. The total length of the highways in each, and their geographical extent, have often been compared. But otherwise research into China's highways and Rome's has varied notably in character and intensity, and there has been no cross-cultural comparison in any depth. In fact this lack of comparison applies more widely, too, extending to other pre-modern states worldwide known for their highways—among them, for example, Tokugawa Japan, the Maya in Central America, and the Inca in South America. On my initiative, therefore, with the support of Kurt Raaflaub, a conference was organized in 2008 to stimulate such comparison. This occasion led in turn to a collaborative volume entitled *Highways, Byways, and Road Systems in the Pre-Modern World*, published by Wiley-Blackwell (Oxford and Malden, Mass.) in May 2012.[1] It is a pleasure to report that the contributors responded positively to the call not to be content merely with traditional, largely technical description of road construction and traveling conditions, but to consider rather the significance of roads in the government, culture and self-identity of the peoples and states under consideration. The focus of my present paper is on findings that emerged concerning China's classical era and the Roman empire. For the latter, I draw upon my own contribution to the volume.[2] For China, I depend heavily and gratefully upon the pioneering contribution by

---

[1]　Co-editors Susan E. Alcock, John Bodel, Richard J. A. Talbert.

[2]　"Roads not featured: a Roman failure to communicate?," pp. 235–54.

Prof. Michael Nylan (University of California, Berkeley).[1]

Understandably enough, the variation in the degree of attention that scholars have devoted to China's highways and Rome's is in the first instance the consequence of stark differences in the contemporary records and in the survival rate of such materials. The number of inscriptions known from China's classical era relating to the construction of roads and bridges and to road deities is currently less than thirty. To be sure, this total is certain to increase, given the tens of thousands of archaeological discoveries for early China that continue to emerge. Nonetheless, the total is so small that we may fairly wonder just how much the Chinese in fact chose to commemorate roadwork in inscriptions. From the Roman empire, on the other hand, inscribed milestones survive in large enough numbers—over 7,000 are now known—for their study to be recognized as a specialism in its own right. Despite such quantities, however, the geographical distribution of these milestones is far from even. To date, only one survives from all of Sicily, for example, but over 150 from Sardinia, and several hundred from the north-west of the Iberian peninsula.[2] A further stark contrast emerges in the cultural sphere, concerning the role of the 'path' or 'way' or 'road' as a powerful metaphor. This notion is fundamental to Chinese historical, philosophical and religious thinking, and is extensively exploited, but it finds no corresponding match of such importance in the outlook of Romans.

Any student of the Roman empire who might hastily presume—without first checking—that on the ground highways commissioned by the authorities in Rome and in China were more or less similar in character is liable to receive a sobering shock. In China, a huge labor force—as many as twenty to thirty thousand men — could be assigned to constructing a highway and the bridges along it. In mountain country, if it was considered necessary to cut into sheer rock faces and run the course of a highway along trestles protruding from them for long distances, the work would be undertaken. The grandest imperial highways could be built as much as 70 metres wide, comparable to the width of a six-lane Interstate highway in the United States today. Moreover, numbers of roads were built for the exclusive use of the First Emperor and his close associates. These so-called 'corridor' roads were fenced with palisades or walls; in some instances they were also elevated, so that no onlooker could even glimpse who was traveling along them, or in what vehicles. In 212 BCE two hundred or so of these 'corridor' roads in the region of the capital district were deliberately consolidated into a single, interconnected system in order to reinforce the secrecy surrounding the Qin emperor's movements.

For those imperial highways not reserved for the exclusive use of the emperor, there was without question tireless concern on the part of the Chinese administrative hierarchy at every level, from various imperial ministries at the top down to local Controllers of Works. Everywhere, both in the empire's heartland and in its frontier zones, regular maintenance was prescribed, along with whatever measures were essential to ensure that bulk transport of such vital items as grain, silk and metals could continue smoothly, often over hundreds of miles. A fast courier service had also to be supported, furnishing relay riders and post-horses capable of covering 200 miles per day if required, and in a special crisis even over 300 miles in a 24-hour period. This government service conveyed legal and judicial documents, as well as alerting the emperor to rebellions, epidemics and environmental disasters in need of rapid relief.

Travel on China's imperial highways was heavily regulated. Axle-lengths were standardized so that

---

[1]   "The power of highway networks during China's classical era (323 BCE–316 CE): regulations, metaphors, rituals, and deities," pp. 33–65.

[2]   *See Barrington Atlas Directory*, pp. 709 and 736, with my entry "Maps," sub-section "Roman Milestones," in D. Clayman (ed.), *Oxford Bibliographies Online:* Classics (2012).

carts and carriages could run along the same ruts. For the sake of maintaining their dignity in a finely ranked society, high officials and nobles were obliged to make journeys in carriages, rather than merely on horseback. All travelers had to submit to inspections periodically, and to show a document or tally at checking–stations (when entering a pass, for instance) as well as at border control–points between administrative districts; it was common for payment of a toll to be required too. Travelers on official business could be accommodated overnight in the state guest houses situated along imperial highways; here again, a plethora of regulations governed what could be provided for them, their servants, and their horses or oxen.

Naturally, it would be naive to imagine that China's imperial highways always ran without fault or strain in any respect. In fact corruption did occur, while forced labor on road maintenance was liable to impose a heavy burden on already impoverished local populations. It would be equally mistaken to imagine that all highways were built, maintained and supervised by the imperial authorities. Rather, surviving testimony points to a remarkable mix of imperial and private initiatives. Trade and traffic were sufficiently profitable that merchants and great families could afford to build and maintain highways, as well as to offer their own haulage and courier services and to provide rest houses. There is no denying that the imperial authorities made a huge investment in developing, maintaining and exploiting highways. It is vital to recognize, however, that in China they were by no means the only providers of such an important resource.

Much of this outline about conditions in China can surely invite students of the Roman empire to see the situation there in a fresh–and, I suspect, unfamiliar–light. Most striking perhaps is the sheer freedom of movement that Rome allowed. With their constant concern to maintain a stable, productive agrarian society, China's ruling authorities actively sought to control–and thereby restrict–the movement of people, goods and ideas. The Roman authorities for the most part did not. Obvious exceptions to that general claim are readily accounted for. All movement by slaves, in particular, was controlled by their owners. So too, ironically, the movements of the empire's grandest inhabitants, the 600 or so Roman senators, were subject to the emperor's prior approval for almost all journeys outside Italy. Cassius Dio, himself a senator, informs us that this regulation–introduced by Augustus, no doubt in fear of potential rivals–still applied in his own day early in the third century (52.42.6). Also from Augustus' time onwards, exile became a standard sentence for a senator convicted of some high crime. In fact two levels were instituted–what might be termed a 'comfortable' exile (*relegatio*) potentially for a limited period only, and a harsher one (*deportatio*) in principle for life. At both levels the convicted senator was required to live on an island designated by the authorities. Not only could he be confined there under close surveillance, but also any visitors could be monitored more effectively than might be possible at a mainland location, especially if it was on a highway or near one. Augustus even seems to have deliberately kept the Aegean Sea area, with its many small islands, under his personal charge rather than assigning it to any of the provincial governors responsible for adjacent mainland territory.[1]

It is valid to assert nonetheless that, in general, civilians with the means and the motivation to travel were free to proceed–without any special documents–almost anywhere they pleased throughout the Roman empire. Such lack of restriction must indeed originate in the traditional Roman respect for personal freedom, and in the Roman state's aversion to interfering with the private lives of individuals or the internal affairs of communities. Over time, practical considerations no doubt gained weight too. The empire grew so vast in extent, the

---

[1]　For this claim, see Fred K. Drogula, "Controlling travel: deportation, islands and the regulation of senatorial mobility in the Augustan Principate," *Classical Quarterly* 61.1 (2011) 230–66.

Romans' limited administrative presence was thinly spread, and until the late third century CE they remained disinclined to enlarge it. There must also have been a realization that most people did not need restricting in any case, because they could never afford to travel more than locally.

There is no question that—by the standards of the Mediterranean world—the Roman authorities, like their Chinese counterparts, made a colossal investment in the construction of highways. Yet manifest differences from the Chinese experience stand out. There were never grand Roman highways of exceptional width, nor any built for the exclusive use of a privileged group. The Latin term *militaris via*—used loosely from the 50s BC onwards—does for certain mean a road made for the army, or by the army, or both. What it never signifies, however, is a road built for the army's exclusive use. Such highways did not exist in the Roman empire, nor were there ever highways privately constructed and maintained; private enterprise on that scale was unthinkable.

The claim could be advanced that there is a lasting, and perhaps characteristic, failure on the part of the Roman authorities to exploit the empire's highways, despite the praise offered by Greeks who assume an outsider's perspective. The strongest admiration is articulated by Aelius Aristides in the mid-second century CE (*To Rome* 101):

"… on the one hand you [Romans] have surveyed the whole world (*oikoumene*), on the other you have spanned rivers with all kinds of bridges. By cutting through mountains you have made land travel feasible; you have filled the deserts with way-stations, and you have civilized everything with your lifestyle and organization."

However, highway construction and control remain an imperial feat and a blessing to all the empire's inhabitants that emperors themselves appear persistently reluctant to boast about. Milestones at the local level aside, any such reference seldom occurs in inscriptions, let alone on coins; these obvious opportunities for an emperor to identify himself with the empire's roads are simply not acted upon. The "golden milestone" (*miliarium aureum*), a pillar set up Augustus in the forum at Rome in 20 BCE, commemorated only the commission he accepted to restore the roads of Italy, not of the entire empire (as modern commentators often mistakenly imagine). To be sure, no compelling means of representing a highway visually was ever devised, but that is not the heart of the puzzle. Equally, no subject ever praises the emperor explicitly as builder and controller of highways. It is exceptional that around 100 CE both the Latin court poet Statius (*Silvae* 4.3.20–23) and the Greek orator Dio Chrysostom (*Or.* 3.127) each happen to affirm in general terms to Domitian and Trajan respectively that one characteristic of a 'good ruler' is to build roads for his subjects (as both these emperors in fact did). But neither author then proceeds to develop the point, and certainly not with reference to imperial control of highways. Possibly, emperors feared that repeated boasting about the excellence of the highways would only alert enemies beyond the frontiers to the relative ease with which invaders could rapidly penetrate deep into the empire. At the same time, when highway maintenance was largely a burden imposed upon local communities rather than one borne by the Roman authorities, an emperor may have hesitated before presuming to celebrate the highways as all his own.

Indeed one might fairly query how far the Roman emperor, unlike his Chinese counterpart, did have a clear sense of being in control of the highways, and moreover of them cohering as a network. The one instance known to me where they are explicitly so conceived is poetic. Here Statius lists among the budgeting responsibilities of Domitian's deceased *a rationibus*, the father of Claudius Etruscus, the needs of *longe series porrecta viarum*, "the far extended series/network of roads" (*Silvae* 3.3.102). Conceivably, however, such a vision remained in effect confined to poetry. After all, no imperial Ministry with responsibility for highway maintenance existed. A few highways happened to be named, but randomly. There was never co-ordinated naming of them, let alone any numbering of the modern type; highways named after Roman emperors are surprisingly few. Any sign that comprehensive information about highways was readily available is lacking. The same may be said about maps tracing the principal routes. At least, the few extant references to Roman maps never mention roads as a feature marked, and they are ignored in turn by what is by far the largest surviving source of cartographic data, Ptolemy's *Geography* of the mid-second century CE.

Against this background it is all the more surprising that the one surviving Roman map of the empire and beyond the so-called 'Peutinger Map'—marks plenty of roads. Their prominence here calls for explanation, therefore. Even though the matter remains disputed, my own opinion is that the surviving incomplete medieval copy of the map does reproduce a Roman original (rather than, say, one of Carolingian date); and that this original spanned the entire world known to the Romans, from the British Isles and the Atlantic Ocean across to Persia and India, with the city of Rome moreover deliberately positioned to occupy the map's centerpoint (another controversial issue).[①] Ever since the map's 'rediscovery' around 1500, fixation with its road courses has remained the dominant preoccupation of interested scholars, and has allowed a pair of unwarranted assumptions to remain unchallenged for too long.

The first of these assumptions is that the network of roads truly was the primary concern of the map's designer, and that everything else marked—peoples, rivers, mountains, islands, spas, etc—is to be considered merely background. The second assumption is that the presentation of the road network was intended to be useful, a tool for planning journeys and actually making them on the ground. This evaluation of the designer's concerns, however, seems to me unduly arbitrary when the map's appearance makes it clear that the designer has by no means lavished special care on the road network alone. At the same time, scholars' insistence that the map should be useful to travelers is too characteristically modern. Practical use seems an implausible priority for a map that so severely distorts and remolds landmasses, and indeed virtually removes a North–South dimension. In addition, dispassionate inspection of the road data in detail reveals that it teems with errors, muddles, anachronisms and omissions—many no doubt the slips of copyists, but far from all.

In my view the map is best understood as a display object, an item of imperial propaganda created to reinforce Roman claims to world power. While the date of the original can only be a matter of speculation, I see good reason to link it with Diocletian's Tetrarchy around 300 CE, a regime eager to proclaim its strength along with its deep commitment to reunifying the empire and securing for it a peaceful and prosperous future. It was a stroke of brilliance on the part of the designer to recognize how aptly roads shown on a map could project imperial control. Conceivably, it was even a novel initiative to map the empire's highways comprehensively. In that event, given the apparent dearth of readily accessible information about them, the task of gathering the necessary data and collating it for presentation in map form may have proven an exceptional challenge. Even so, fullness and accuracy in every detail did not have to be vital concerns. Rather, to furnish an arresting overall impression of the highways would suffice to fulfill the designer's propagandistic purpose.

During China's classical era, the highways there are not known to have been explicitly represented as an embodiment of imperial power. On the other hand, in China the 'path' or 'way' or 'road' always

---

① See further my book *Rome's World: The Peutinger Map Reconsidered* (Cambridge: Cambridge University Press, 2010), with associated website presenting the map itself at www.cambridge.org/us/talbert/mapa.html

had a religious and metaphorical importance unmatched in Roman thought. In Chinese mythology it was the culture hero Great Yu who first laid out and opened up the main highways in China's Nine Provinces; in other words, it was he who thereby created this underpinning of civilization itself. Later, humans would be prudent to embark upon roadbuilding with caution. In both the spirit sphere and the human one, roads could be forces for good and bad. To be sure, by opening up wild, inaccessible regions, roads could tame them, making them safer and more 'domesticated'; the rulers and officials responsible for such construction might become the objects of a cult as a result. But equally, new roads could bring undesirable immigrants, bandits, undisciplined soldiers, unwelcome ideas. A road that required extraordinary effort to construct through impenetrable terrain could be thought to offend the gods by disturbing their homes and remolding the landscape to an unacceptable extent.

Any individual in China contemplating travel would do well first to gain the approval of a hierarchy of road deities by undertaking various rites and sacrifices, and by consulting 'daybooks' which would advise on the days when a journey would be auspicious and in which directions. On the road also, there were rites and prayers prescribed to protect travelers from the perils of all kinds to which they were prey; as an extreme, to die on the road was regarded as a terrible fate. Life itself was conceived of as a journey, with an appropriate way to be followed, and key choices of direction to be determined at a series of crossroads. The satisfactory functioning of the human body, too, was seen as the smooth operation of various communication channels—blood circulating through a network of canals, and the five senses of vision, hearing, taste, smell and touch termed the "Five Roads".

In conclusion, it is of course impossible for me to predict what interest such brief comparison of highways in the Chinese and Roman empires will hold for experts on China's classical era. For my own part, as a student of the Roman empire, I can at least affirm that this endeavor not only reinforces my resolve to gain a more informed understanding of China, but also impels me to re-evaluate fundamental features of Roman rule and of the Roman community's values. Finally, I am convinced that an enlargement of the scope of such comparison to include other pre-modern states worldwide noted for their highways offers the potential to produce further rewarding results.

Orbis Terrarum and Tianxia: The World–view and Universalism under the Reign of the First Emperors in Rome and China

Zhong–xiao WANG（王忠孝）, Leiden University

Abstract: From the perspective of macrohistory, this paper aims at examining the imagination of the world in Roman and Chinese cultures in the pre–imperial period. This study focuses on *Tianxia* and *Orbis terrarum* and analyses the manner in which these terms defined the Roman and Chinese conceptions of the globe. *Tianxia* literally denoted all under heaven. But Chinese chronicles suggest that in practice, it implied a more closed structure. Chinese rulers considered themselves to inhabit the centre of the world and their rule and military campaigns therefore followed the basic structure of the *center–sifang*–the centre and its four quarters. With the *orbis terrarum*, the Romans understood their position in the world in linear terms and before Augustus, Rome was never thought to be the center of the *oikoumene* in both geography and culture. This implies a more aggressive and open world system on the part of the Romans and was reflected in their policy of world conquest. These distinctive differences in conceptions suggest varying attitudes of the Roman and the Chinese societies to warfare which influenced practical policy making in imperial times.

Keywords: tianxia, orbis terrarum, center sifang

I

According to the research of the Taiwanese scholar Xing Yitian 邢义田 , *a reference to tianxia appeareared* for the first time in Chinese literature in the period of Western Zhou. This occurs in the *Announcement of Duke Zhao（Shao Gao）*召诰 , a short article quoted from the *Document of Zhou (Zhou Shu)* 周书 :

> *Only if the King has virtues and the king himself serves as a model followed by the masses under the heaven (tianxia), his prestige spreads far and wide throughout the lands.* 其

惟王位在德元，小民乃惟刑用于天下，越王显．①

The *Announcement of Duke Zhao* is a chapter preserved in the *Book of Documents (Shang shu)* 尚书，known as the earliest historical writing in Chinese history. According to Sima Qian, the book contains some advice from Duke Zhou 周公, the younger brother of King Wu (r.1046–1043B.C.) 武王 for his nephew, the successor King Cheng (r. 1042/35–1006 B.C.) 成王 on how to behave as a monarch with excellent virtues. In the above context, *tianxia* should be considered as the vast area under the authority of the Zhou state with the city of Luoyi (present-day Luoyang, Henan Province) 洛邑, or Chengzhou 成周 at its centre. To be specific, the geographical sphere implied by *tianxia* cannot be assumed to mean *all under heaven* literally, but should be considered as being comprised of two parts: *wangji* 王畿, the land managed directly by the royal house, and the surrounding multiple hereditary fiefs ruled by the nobles, most of whom were the close relatives of Zhou kings. Although *tianxia* had not emerged from the early Chinese literature until the period of Western Zhou, the idea that the world was a sort of quadrate or rectangular-like structure with a clearly defined center and four quarters (sifang) 四方 can be traced back to the period of Shang (1600–1064 B.C.).②

After the battle of Muye 牧野 (1046 B.C.), Zhou, a subordinate state located at the periphery of the Shang world in the Wei river plain, annexed large parts of its lands and established a new regime in c. 1045 B.C.③ Although the extent to which the geographical and cosmological views of the Western Zhou people were influenced by the former Shang dynasty is unknown, the characters 四方 (*sifang*) appeared on many excavated bronze vessels, thus, clearly illustrating that there are connections on this issue between the two dynasties. Furthermore, the inscription on the bronze vessel named Dayu Ding 大盂鼎, which can be traced back to the time of king Kang 康王 (r. 1005/3—978 B.C.) in the early Western Zhou period, contains the phrase 匍有四方 *extending to sifang* . The same characters appeared once again on Lai Pan 逨盘, dated to the time of the late Western Zhou. In *Shi jing* 诗经 (*Book of Odes*), the earliest existing collection of Chinese songs and poems containing 305 pieces, some of which were written in the Western Zhou period, we can also find that the term *sifang* appeared many times and carries a similar meaning as the term in the inscription of Dayu Ding and some other contemporary vessel inscriptions. At least by the early Western Zhou period, as we have seen, the basic

---

① *Shang shu* 5.1 On the term of *tianxia* and its use in Chinese chronicles prior to the Qin dynasty, see Xing Yitian, 邢义田，"Tianxia yi jia–Zhongguo ren de tianxia guan" 天下一家，中国人的天下观, in *Zhongguo Wenhua Xin Lun Genyuan Pian Yongheng de Juliu*, 中国文化新论根源篇：永恒的巨流, Beijing: Sanlian Shudian, 北京：生活·读书·新知三联书店，1991, 425–79. Japanese scholar Shinichiro Watanabe has offered detailed research on the term in Japanese scholarship during the last three decades. For the analyses of *tianxia* used in the pre-Qin literary sources, see Shinichiro Watanabe, *The Imperial Power and the Order of Tianxia in Pre-modern China* 中国古代的王权与天下秩序：從日中比较史的视角出发, trans. Xu Cong, Beijing: Zhonghua Book Company 北京：中华书局，2008, 3–17. Chinese scholar Zhao Tingyang 赵汀阳 has also published a series of articles on this issue. On Zhao's theory and criticism of it, see Zhang Qixian 张其贤，"*Tianxia* system on a snail's horns"，*Inter-Asia Cultural Studies*, Vol. 12, 2001, 28–42.

② For the geographic and cosmological ideas of the Shang people, see Wang Aihe, *Cosmology and Political Culture in Early China*, Cambridge: Cambridge University Press, 2000, 23–6; Ch'ang Kuwang-Chi 张光直，*Zhongguo Qingtong Shidai* 中国青铜时代, Beijing: Sanlian Shudian, 1990. 8; 16–7.

③ There is no scholarly agreement concerning the precise date of the Zhou conquest of Shang because scholars cannot find the coherent and exact information in the sources. Shaughnessy suggests that the year of the starting of the Zhou dynasty is 1045 B.C. See E. Shaughnessy, *Sources of Western Zhou History: Inscribed Bronze Vessels*, Berkeley: University of California Press, 1991, 217–36. On the general history of the Western Zhou, see Hsu Cho-yun and K. M. Linduff, *Western Chou Civilization*, New Haven: Yale University Press, 1988.

structure of the territory defined by the peripheries with four quarters and a clearly defined centre had come into the minds of the Chinese ancients.[1]

Furthermore, it is worth noting that the emphasis on *sifang* in some early Chinese sources was also closely related to another important term *Zhong* 中 or *zhongguo* 中国, which means centrality or central state. For instance, a poem titled *Min Lao* 民劳 quoted from *Shi jing*, contains the following:

> Let us cherish the center of the state (zhongguo) in order to secure the pacification of the four quarters (sifang)⋯Let us cherish the capital (jingshi) of the state in order to secure the pacification of the four quarters (sifang). 惠此中国，以绥四方⋯⋯惠此京师，以绥四方.[2]

Sifang appears twice in the above passage, referring to the vast regions beyond the center of the Zhou state. Zhongguo here corresponds to another term *jingshi*, both of which should be assumed to be the new capital of Zhou, the city of *Luoyi*. In addition, the term *zhongguo* also appeared in one of the chapters entitled Zi Cai 梓材 compiled in *Shang shu*:

> Heaven has given a mission to the people who are at the center of the state to open up new fields together with our forefathers. 皇天既付中国民，越阙疆土于先王.[3]

In the opening of the chapter, we are told by the author that the article was written in the time of Duke Zhao, when the project of the construction of Luoyi had just commenced. *Zhongguo* once again appeared, referring to the city of Luoyi, the new capital located in the Luo River valley. Firmer evidence also comes from an inscription cast on the bronze vessel named He Zun 何尊, excavated from present-day Baoji 宝鸡, Shannxi province, in the early 1960s. The value of the He Zun inscription is not only that it can verify that the eastern capital Luoyi was constructed in the fifth year of Duke Zhou, as recorded in *Shang Shu*, but it is also seen as the earliest evidence containing the characters *zhongguo* 中国 (China) in the Chinese literary account. Therefore, this famous inscription is often quoted by those scholars who study the origin of the Chinese nationality.[4]

Although there are rare examples of the appearance of *tianxia* and *zhongguo* in the early literary sources, it can be concluded, however, that the basic territorial concept implied by *tianxia* in the period of Western

---

[1] For the evidence of *sifang* appearing in above inscriptions, see Yu Shengwu, 于省吾, "Siguo duofang kao" 四国多方攷, *Kaogu Shekan* 考古社刊, vol. 1, 1935, 38–43. For the examples that the characters *sifang* 四方 appear in *Shi jing*, see *Shi jing* 270; 280; 315; 367; 373; 381; 387; 395; 397; 422; 418; 422; 433; 450; 454; 562; 465; 478; 480; 483; 506; 527; 533. Gao Heng 高亨, *Shi Jing Jin Zhu* 诗经今注, Shanghai: Shanghai Guji Chubanshe 上海：上海古籍出版社, 1980.

[2] *Shi jing* 422.

[3] *Shang shu* 4.4.

[4] For the full inscription of the He Zun, see Tang Lan 唐兰, "He zun mingwen jieshi" 何尊铭文解释 *Wenwu* 文物, 1976 vol. 1, pp. 60–1. Ge Zhaoguang's book, *Zai Zhi Zhongguo* 宅兹中国, published in 2011, is given the title from the famous piece of inscription of He Zun: *I built my home in Zhongguo* 余其宅兹中国. Zhongguo, as a term, has different meanings in various periods of Chinese history. For this inscription, it denotes the city of Luoyi, the capital of the Western Zhou. Sima Qian also mentions that since Luoyi is located in the center of *tianxia*, so the states in its four directions could give their duties to the royal house averagely. See Sima Qian, *The Grand Historian 4*. Ge Zhaoguang 葛兆光, *Zai Zhi Zhongguo: Chong Jian Youguan Zhongguo de Lishi Lunshu* 宅兹中国——重建有关中国的历史论述. Beijing: Zhonghua Shuju 北京：中华书局, 2011.

Zhou can be considered as an area composed of a centre and *sifang*. In other words, historically, the vast space is made up of two sections: the Luo River valley (modern Henan and south Shanxi province) as the heartland with a centre, Luoyi, and the areas extending towards four directions. It is worthwhile to note that *sifang* cannot be assumed to be what it literally denotes. There are two main reasons for arguing this. Firstly, the territory of the Western Zhou saw a large-scale expansion in the two hundred years following the conquest of Shang.[1] Secondly, the boundaries of the Zhou state cannot be seen as being a neatly geometric shape. It is well known that the most distinctive feature of the political culture in the Western Zhou period is the feudal system.[2] Approximately from the time of the Duke Zhou onwards, the Zhou kings established multiple vassal states throughout the alluvial plain around the Yellow River basin. The nobles who took over lands from the Zhou kings at the same time were endowed with the right to rule the indigenous people within their subordinate states, although they themselves had to be under the supervision of the central government. The sovereignty belonged to the Zhou king, while these subordinate states to a large degree were autocratic polities. Most of the dukedoms located on the fringes of the Western Zhou state were surrounded by barbarians with varying specific names such as Man 蛮, Yi 夷, Rong 戎 and Di 狄. Such names were in fact coined in the later period after the fall of the Western Zhou house. Why were many of the vassal states located in remote places? One presumption is that these states could play the role of watchdog, fending off barbarian invasions. In this sense, it was not the heartland, but the edges that defined the territory of the Zhou world. The concept of *tianxia*, thus, could neither be considered as a structure of square or rectangular-like shape, nor did it have well-defined boundaries.

Accompanied by the fall of the Western Zhou royal house and particularly with the eastward migration of King Ping 平王 (r. 770–720B.C.), an event marking the commencement of a new era, the Spring and Autumn period 春秋 (771–476 B.C.) in Chinese history, the concept of *tianxia* in literature gradually changed. Firstly, in some literary sources compiled during the Eastern Zhou period, it was found that the meaning of *zhongguo* no longer referred to the city of Luoyi, but rather was equated with *zhongyuan* 中原, the eastern plain located on the alluvial Yellow River basin. Needless to say that this change demonstrates that as time went by, the royal house of the Zhou became more humble. As a result, the capital Luoyi gradually lost its importance as the centre of the Zhou world, *tianxia*. In contrast, some of the dukedoms located in the east established by the scions and relatives of the Zhou royal family such as Jin 晋, Qi 齐, Lu 鲁, Zheng 郑, Chen 陈 and Yan 燕 developed into stronger states by the early Spring and Autumn period. Meanwhile, some states established by the non-Zhou people, such as Chu 楚, in the Han River valley, and Wu 吴 and Yu 越 in the area of Yangzi Delta also became stronger.[3] From roughly the early Eastern Zhou period onwards, they saw themselves as having a common ethnical and cultural origin, *Huaxia* 华夏, consciously distinguishing themselves from the

---

[1] For the topography and the history of the territorial expansion in the early Western Zhou, see Li Feng, *Landscape and Power in Early China, The Crisis and Fall of the Western Zhou, 1044–771 BC*. Oxford: Oxford University Press, 1–27.

[2] Li Feng, however, is against the use of the term feudalism when one attempts to investigate the unique political institutions of the Western Zhou. Instead, he suggests that the political system of the Western Zhou is a kind of Delegatory Kin-ordered Settlement State. See *Bureaucracy and the State in Early China: Covering the Western Zhou*. Oxford: Oxford University Press, 2010, 269–302. For the relations between the locals and the central government of Zhou, see Li (2010), 254–67.

[3] For the eclipse of the Western Zhou royal house and the rise of its dukedoms, see *The Cambridge History of Ancient China*, vol. 1, 1999, 547–551.

barbarians inhabiting the frontiers. Correspondingly, the structure of *tianxia*, by the time of the Spring and Autumn period, had shifted into a more closed system. Down to the late Spring and Autumn period, the ethnic groups mentioned in the early literary accounts such as Man, Yi, Rong and Di, had almost been excluded from the renewed system of *tianxia*.[①] With the consolidation of cultural identity in the Warring States period, the concept of *tianxia* had tended to be identical to the meaning of *zhongguo*, a more encapsulated structure.[②]

Yet the change did not happen overnight. By the seventh century B.C. at the latest, *Zhouyuan* 周原 (The plain of Zhou), the original settlement of the Zhou people in the Wei River valley had been thoroughly occupied by the barbarians Rong 戎 and Di 狄 who had hostilities with the Zhou people since the early Western Zhou period. Meanwhile, some major vassal kingdoms of the Zhou state, such as Jin 晋, Qin 齐, Zheng 郑 and Yan 燕 that lay in the east of the Zhou world now grew to be stronger than before. The geographical centre of Chinese civilization therefore gradually moved to the East Plain (modern Henan, north of Jiangsu and Anhui, west of Shandong and a small part of Hubei Province), whilst those "barbarian" groups such as Man, Yi, Rong and Di, originally dwelling in the periphery of *sifang*, had become more and more marginalised. As a result, the cultural differences between these groups and the states in the Central Plain (Jin, Qi and Zheng) grew larger. This complex issue was due to a combination of causes.[③] If we come back to the literary sources, two striking features of this period draw our attention. Firstly, for those who established their states in the early Western Zhou period and had lineages with the Zhou clans, such as the states of Qi and Jin, they preferred to state that they were the heirs of the Zhou culture. Culturally and psychologically speaking, they also chose to consciously demarcate themselves from non−Zhou people, including both the northern nomadic tribes and those who lived along the Yangzi River. There is abundant evidence in the documents of the pre−Qin period of the cultural and ethnic discrimination faced by the non−Zhou peoples such as the Man 蛮 and the Yi 夷. In the coming three hundred years, in order to seize hegemony 霸 (Ba) over the Central Plain, the main states of Qi 齐 in the east, Jin 晋 in the north and Chu 楚 in the south as well as Wu 吴 and Yue 越 located in the Yangzi River Delta campaigned against one another in the name of *Zun wang rang yi* 尊王攘夷 (loyalty to Zhou Kings, against the barbarians). Interestingly, although some states in the Spring and Autumn period were located in the remote places of the Zhou world and were surrounded by different ethnic tribes, they themselves

---

① For the locations of the Zhou people and the Non−Zhou in the Western Zhou and Spring and Autumn period, see Shi Nianhai 史念海, "Xizhou yu chunqiu shiqi hua zu yu fei hua zu de zaju jiqi dili fenbu" 西周与春秋時期华族与非华族的杂居及其地理分布, *Zhongguo Dili Luncong* 中国地理论丛, vol. 1, pp. 3–40; vol. 2, 57–84.

② For the rise of the identity of *Huaxia*, it can be attributed to the long−term historical evolution of the amalgamation between the Zhou people and their neighbours. See E. G. Paulleyblank, "The Chinese and their neighbors in Pre−historic and Early Historic Times" in D. Keightly (ed.), *The Origins of Chinese Civilization*, Berkeley: The University of California Press, 1983, 411–66; CHAC, vol. 1, 550. In the modern period, *Huaxia* is sometimes interchangeable with the English term Chinese. On the relationship between *Huaxia* and Chinese, see N. Di Cosmo, *Ancient China and its Enemies*, Cambridge: Cambridge University Press, 2002, 93–4.

③ Scholars have carried out in−depth research concerning the fundamental impact of climate change in the formation of the two cultural zones in the first half of the last millennium B.C. See Chu Coching 竺可桢, "Zhongguo jin wuqian nian lai qihou bianqian de chubu yanjiu", 中国近五千年来气候变迁的初步研究, *Kaogu Xuebao* 考古学报, vol. 1, 1972; B. Hinsch, "Climate change and history in China", *Journal of Asian History*, vol. 22, 1988. From the perspective of anthropology and archaeology, Wang examined the formation of the ecosystems in the areas of modern Qinghai, Ordos and the West Liao River from c. 2000 B.C. to 600 B.C. Wang Mingke 王铭珂, *Huaxia Bianyuan: Lishi Jiyi yu Zuqun Rentong* 华夏边缘——历史记忆与族群认同 Taipei: Yun Chen Culture 允晨文化, 1997, pp. 95–151. Di Cosmo has also examined the transition to pastoral nomadism in the Northern zone of China during the Western Zhou and Spring and Autumn period. See Di Cosmo, The Northern frontier in Pre−Imperial China, in *Cambridge History of Ancient China,* vol. 1, pp. 909–51.

never thought that they did not belong to *zhongguo* or were not a part of many Xia 诸 夏 . The most typical example of this point is the state of Qi.

By the Warring States period (481—221B.C.), many small states had been annexed and finally seven major states dominated the Chinese world: Yan 燕 , Qi 齐 , Zhao 赵 , Wei 魏 , Han 韩 , Qin 秦 and Chu 楚 . There are two noteworthy features of this period. Firstly, those non-Zhou barbarian groups such as Rong, Di and Yi who used to be active in the peripheries of the Central Plain had either been annihilated during wars with the central states, or had migrated to the hinterland and gradually been absorbed into the mainstream of Huaxia culture. Secondly, by the end of this period, *tianxia*, territorially speaking, was no longer confined to the drainage basin of the Yellow River. The most positive example of this is the state of Chu. By the time of the middle and late Warring States, *tianxia*, in many cases in the contemporary literature, referred to the territory dominated by the seven major states. This view is reflected in the *Zhanguo Ce* 战国策 (Strategies of Warring States period), the most important source compiled in the Han dynasty recording the events of the seven states taken place in the Warring States period.

In ancient times, there were tens of thousands of states within the boundary of sihai. Although the size of some cities was large, there was no one larger than 300 zhang. Although the population of some cities was big, there was no bigger than 3000 hu (household)… The tens of thousands of states in ancient times have been absorbed into the territory of seven major states nowadays. 且古者四海之内，分为万国。城虽大，无过三百丈者。人虽众，无过三千家者……今古之为万国者，分为战国七。[1]

As mentioned above, by the Warring States period, the Chinese world was composed of tens of thousands of states within sihai 四 海 (four Seas) which in ancient times was separated by the seven major states. In the same source, Su Dai 苏 代 , a politician and strategist living in the middle Warring States period, once commented on the complex international situation of the Yan state in this period:

In the tianxia that consists of the seven states, Yan is a weak one. 凡天下之战国七，而燕处弱焉。[2]

This clearly shows that in the minds of the elites in the Warring States period the world had been equated to the lands of the seven major states. By the time of the Qin Empire, the sense of *tianxia* had changed tremendously since the Western Zhou period. In summary, it saw an evolution from the model with a clear centrality and open but poor-defined boundaries to a more closed well-defined structure. After the Spring and Autumn and the Warring States periods, this term, originally no more than a geographical concept, had strong cultural and moral connotations. Furthermore, it appeared more frequently in the documents written in the Warring States period. Therefore, by examining the term used in those texts, we know that it either refers to certain individual states, or to the world composed of the seven major states. In the *Annals* of *Qin Shi Huang* 秦始皇本纪 , a section of the sixth-volume *Records of the Grand Historian* 史记 by Sima Qian 司马迁 , *tianxia* appears no less than ninety-one times. Only in a few cases, can the term be interpreted as meaning *all under heaven*. Moreover, it suggests a more closed world system, namely the lands of the old seven major states.

---

[1] *Zhanguo Ce* (*Zhao* 3.20.1). In the text, Zhang is the unit of length. In the Warring States period, 1 Zhang is about 2.32 meters.

[2] *Zhanguo Ce* (*Yan* 1.29.13).

II

It is common sense that the chronology of Roman history is much shorter than that of China (if we consider that Chinese civilization began with the Shang dynasty). In contrast to China, literary sources on the early history of Rome did not emerge until the period of the Middle Republic.[1] Only in the second half of the third century B.C., did Rome have its first historian, Fabius Pictor. Even so, writing in Latin was still not commonplace until the time of Marcus Porcius Cato whose *Origines* was the first historical work written in Latin.[2] Contrastingly, the Ancient Chinese had invented their writing system as early as the Shang dynasty. Therefore, if one attempts to examine the knowledge of the inhabited world and of the cosmos in the minds of the ancient Chinese living in the Yellow River basin at the early stage of the civilization, Oracle inscriptions 甲骨文 and Bronze inscriptions 金文 are indispensable research tools.[3] In contrast, however, the primary sources regarding the early history of Rome are much poorer. For the study of the early history of the Roman and the Latin peoples, scholars have to rely on works written by Greeks and by the Roman writers who lived in much later times. Thus, when we try to examine the same topic in the field of Roman studies, there are a lot less sources and it is more problematic.

Furthermore, the knowledge of space, cosmos and geography that Roman elites acquired, was largely influenced by ancient Greek thought since the time of Homer. I don't intend to discuss here the various theories of the world and the universe raised by Hesiod, Anaximander, Herodotus and other Greek thinkers in the Hellenistic period, for many scholars have already done excellent work on this issue in last thirty years.[4] What I would stress is that for most Romans, especially for Roman republican aristocrats, their knowledge of geography and the cosmos, was probably gained not through reading the works of the Hellenistic scholars, but by listening to stories related to their clans or families told by an elder when they were children, or, by the speeches given by politicians in the public space. Those stories and orations are often involved with the *mos maiorum* of the Roman people, closely relating to the history of the military expansion in the early age.[5] Although the first Latin historical work written by Fabius Pictor had been lost, it is still possible to make assumptions on his childhood upbringing in the third century B.C. Born into one of the noblest families in the city of Rome, he would not only have been familiar with the tales about the eastward expedition of Alexander

---

[1] On the sources used by scholars for studying the history of the early Roman republic, see T. J. Cornell, *The beginnings of Rome: Italy and Rome from the Bronze Age to the Punic Wars (c. 1000–264 BC)*, London and New York: Routledge, 1995, 1–26.

[2] For the text of the fragments of the *Origines*, see M. Chassignet (ed.), *Caton, Les Origines*. Paris: Les Belles Lettres, 1986; Cornell (404) n. 16.

[3] For Chinese writing system in pre-Qin period, see W. G. Boltz, "Language and writing" in *The Cambridge History of Ancient China*, vol. 1, 74–124. So far the most important research on the oracle inscriptions in the Shang dynasty is the monograph written by Chen Mengjia 陈梦家. See Chen Mengjia, *Yinxu Buci Zongshu 殷墟卜辞综述*. Beijing: Zhonghua Shuju 北京：中华书局, 1988. For the bronze inscriptions in the Shang and the Zhou dynasties, the most influential work is the 8- volume book compiled by the institute for Archaeology of the Chinese Academy of Social Sciences, see *Yinzhou Jinwen Jicheng (JC) 殷周金文集成*, 8 vols., 2007. Shaughnessy's book focusing on the vessel inscriptions in the Western Zhou dynasty is also an indispensible reference in this field. See Shaughnessy, *Sources of Western Zhou History*, 1991.

[4] On the issue, see C. Nicolet, *Space, Geography and Politics in the Early Roman Empire*, Ann Arbor: The University of Michigan Press, 1991, 57–85.

[5] For the close relation between military expedition and knowledge of geography in ancient Rome, see P. Mattern, *Rome and the Enemy: Imperial Strategy in the Principate*, Berkeley: University of California Press, 1999, 24–81.

the Great, but would also have known the history of the early Roman Republic and of his own clan, the Fabii. Immediately before he was born, Rome had just defeated king Pyrrhus of Epirus and dominated the whole Apennines peninsula (with the exception of Gaul in the north). Fabius Pictor also witnessed both the first and second Carthaginian wars. Particularly in the darkest days after the battle of Cannae, he was dispatched by the Senate to travel to Delphi requesting oracles. The case of Pictor is not an exception among Roman aristocrats in the middle-republican period. It is well known that almost all members born to aristocratic families had to serve in the Roman army for at least ten years before becoming magistrates.[1] The extension of the geographical knowledge among Romans of the Republic was closely linked to the tradition of militarism which was deeply rooted in Roman republican society.[2]

Therefore, we can say that for both the Zhou people of China and the Romans in the Republic, the territorial expansion benefited from the military successes indeed played a significant role in the shaping of their respective worldviews. However, the approaches to empire in both the cases of the Qin China and the Roman Republic were quite different. Compared to Rome, the cultural and historical backgrounds of China are much more complex. I am not saying that Romans encountered less exterior resistance than Qin China on the path of the formation of their empire. Instead, the latter inherited much heavier legacies from its former dynasties which can even be traced back as early as the legendary time of Yao 尧, Sun 舜 and Great Yu 禹. During the five hundred years from 771 to 221 B.C., the impact of the declined Western Zhou culture on the states throughout the Yellow River and Yangzi River basin might be even stronger than we considered. In this sense, although both Qin and Rome built sovereignty over their respective worlds in a short time and in similar ways, the models of their territorial expansion were quite different. For the state of Qin and other states in the Eastern Zhou period, their military expeditions were influenced more or less by the ideas of geography and the cosmos inherited from the Western Zhou and even from the far ancient times. Although *sifang*, *zhongguo*, *sihai*, *jiuzhou* and some terms which could reflect the geo-political concepts had been continuously given new connotations in the later historical phrases since the decline of the Western Zhou royal house, the basic framework of *tianxia* which is made up of a centre and *sifang* (four quarters) in the minds of the ancient Chinese did not dramatically change until the end of Warring States period.

Unlike Qin and other states in the Spring and Autumn period of China, Rome was no more than a tiny city-state with a small population lying in the Latium plain of Italy at the beginning of the fifth century B.C. In its first one hundred and fifty years, the Republic constantly fought against the Etrurians (Veii and Fidenae) in the north and the mountain peoples such as Vosci and Aequi in the south. The success of the Latin War (340 – 338B.C.) removed the threats coming from the neighboring Latin peoples and enabled Rome to concentrate on the wars against the Samnites. After the defeat of Pyrrhus and Hannibal, by the beginning of the second century B.C., Rome had nearly completed the unification of the Western Mediterranean world. Throughout most of the second century B.C., Rome paid more attention to the affairs of the Eastern world. In 168 B.C., L. Aemilius Paullus defeated Perseus, the son of Philip V, king of Macedonia in the battle of Pydna. By this year, according to Polybius, Rome has conquered most parts of the world. In 146 B.C., Carthage in North Africa and Corinth in Greece were sacked nearly simultaneously, announcing that Rome had established its hegemony over the whole Mediterranean world. Only thirteen years after, Attalus III, the last king of Pergamon, bequeathed his kingdom

---

[1] On Fabius Pictor, see Cornell 5-9.

[2] See W. V. Harris, *War and Imperialism in Republican Rome, 327-70 B.C.*, Oxford: Clarendon Press, 1979.

to the Roman state which gave Rome more opportunities to interfere with the affairs of Asia Minor. In the last century B.C., the war with Mithridates continued from L. Cornelius Sulla to Pompey the Great, the latter making Syria a Roman province after the defeat of Mithridates in the battle of Dastria. The Romans did not halt their linear eastward expansion until 53 B.C., when M. Licinius Crassus shamefully lost his legions at the battle of Carrhae against the Parthians in Mesopotamia. Not until the time of Augustus, could Rome reclaim the Roman standard that had been in Parthian possession for more than thirty years by diplomatic means.

Above, we briefly reviewed the history of the Roman military expansion from the early republic to the period of Augustus in the first century A.D. In contrast to Rome's linear method of territorial expansion which was influenced by Alexander the Great, [1] China employed a much different tactic. From some oracle inscriptions and the archeological evidence, we know that the idea of centre–*sifang* had come into being as early as the Shang dynasty. More importantly, the territorial expansion of both the Shang and Zhou dynasties had been affected by the ideology of centre–*sifang*. It is worth mentioning that the structure of centre–*sifang*, does not only refer to its central position in geography, but also has cultural and religious dimensions. This viewpoint can be clearly seen in *Yu gong* 禹贡 (*The Tribute to the Great Yu*), a classical text compiled presumably in either the late Spring and Autumn or early Warring State period.[2] Contrastingly, not until the time of Augustus had the city of Rome been imaged as the centre of the world in either a geographic or cultural context. At least, there is no solid evidence to suggest that throughout most of the time of the republic, did the Romans envisage the city of Rome as the geographical centre of the *orbis terrarum*. Culturally speaking, it has been commonly assumed that particularly after the second century B.C. onwards and for the next two hundred years, Greek culture exerted profound influences on the Romans, which was reflected in their literature, sculpture, architecture, music and nearly all aspects of daily life. Although Roman legions made a large–scale conquest of the Greek world after the second century B.C., at last making it a part of the territory of the Roman Empire, the consensus of Roman intellectuals was that they were students of Greeks in terms of culture.[3]

On the contrary, cultural superiority is usually closely associated with the domain of the people and lands in the pre–Qin society. A cultural centralism is deeply rooted in the political ideology of the ruling class in pre–Qin China. According to *Yu Gong*, the Great Yu (and his predecessors Yao and Sun as well) were considered to inhabit the centre of the *tianxia*, which was divided into five zones or *wufu* (five layers) 五服. The innermost layer was not only the centre in geography, but also symbolised the highest level of civilization among the five. Hence, the military conquest from the centre to the peripheries was not only involved with territorial expansion, but also seen as culture popularisation from the higher level to the lower ones. As Wang Guowei 王国维 explained, the fight between the dynasties of Shang and Zhou, was in essence a combat

---

[1]　Pietro Janni, *La Mappa e il Periplo: Cartografia Antica e Spazio Odologico*, Rome: Bretschneider, 1984. Janni's theory was developed by R. Talbert, C. R. Whittaker and K. Brodersen. See C. Whittaker, Rome and its Frontiers: the Dynamics of Empire, London & New York: Routledge, 2004, 63–87; R. Talbert, "Greek and Roman mapping-twenty–first century perspectives", in R. Talbert and R. W. Unger (eds.), *Cartography in Antiquity and the Middle Ages: Fresh Perspectives and New Methods*, Leiden: Leiden University Press, 2008, 9–29. Also, see especially K. Brodersen, *Terra Cognita: Studizen zur römischen Raumerfassung*, Hildesheim: Olms, 1995.

[2]　*Shang shu, Yu gong* 2.1. For the geographical thought of Yu gong and its profound influence on Chinese intellectual history see Tang Xiaofeng 唐晓峰 , *Cong Hundun dao Zhixu: Zhongguo Shanggu Sixiangshi Shulun* 从混沌到秩序——中国上古思想史述论 . Beijing: Zhonghua Shuju 北京：中华书局 , 2010, 260–81.

[3]　Despite its complexity, plenty of books have been published in this field. See especially E. Rawson, *Intellectual Life in the Late Republic*, London: Duckworth, 1985, 3–84.

between virtues and non–virtues.[1] While for Romans, despite that in the works of some Latin writers such as Sallust, *virtus* is seen as one of the most valuable and significant characters that resulted in the establishment of Roman dominance over the whole Mediterranean world, and the demise of the Republic was mainly attributed to the lack of *virtus* among the Roman aristocrats, it is worthwhile to note that in the early and middle Republic the term mainly carries connotations of valour, manliness and courage in battle. The admiration of military strength and individual valour can be seen in the writings of Cato the Elder, Sallust, Cicero, Livy, Virgil and of many other Latin writers in the period of the republic.[2] Here there is no need to stress the well–known fact that Roman *imperatores* since early republican times preferred to display their martial courage in public and to boast of the military achievements gained during their lifetimes. Those achievements are often highlighted in the works of the Latin authors who preferred to enumerate the concrete data such as the number of enemies killed or the number of towns and spoils captured in certain wars.[3] By the time of Augustus, *virtus* as one of the excellent qualities of the Principate was engraved on a golden shield displayed in the Curia Iulia.[4] Concerning the visible images on coins, architecture, sculptures, trophies etc. which represented the military achievements of the *imperatores* including Augustus in the later Republic and the early empire, P. Zanker and C. Nicolet have contributed a lot to this topic.[5] Especially Augustus, in his Res Gestae *Divi Augusti*, asserted that under his leadership, the Roman people as victor has extended the boundaries of all Roman provinces and established the sovereignty of Rome throughout the whole inhabited world.[6] For both nations, territorial expansion was mainly by means of military conquest. Yet the most significant difference between Rome and China is that as individuals and as a nation, the Roman people did not hide their military ambitions and preferred to show off their martial power to the public. Thus, it is not surprising that in the Res Gestae, Augustus prefers to list long names of peoples and lands that he had subdued, while the Chinese First Emperor had a much more defensive policy to deal with the barbarians in the northern areas.

In fact, as Nicolet points out, the phrase *orbis terrarum* did not appear in political terminology until the

---

[1] Wang Guowei, *Yinzhou Zhidu Lun* 殷周制度论. Beijing: Zhonghua Shuju 北京：中华书局, 1956.

[2] Sallust, *B.C.* 1–11; *B. J.* 4. On the moral or *virtus* of the republican Rome, see D. Eck, *The Moral and Political Tradition of Rome*, Ithaca and New York: Cornell University Press; E. Badian, *Roman Imperialism in the Late Republic*, Oxford: Basil Blackwell, 1968, 1–16. *Virtus* appeared in the above Latin writers' works and its meaning changes in the texts from the Republic to the Principate period, see M. McDonnell, *Roman Manliness, Virtus and the Roman Republic*. Cambridge: Cambridge University Press, 2006

[3] For the martial spirit in the traditional Roman society and its role in the making of the Roman Empire, see the last chapter of P. Mattern, *Rome and the Enemy*, 1999, 211–33. In the Roman Republic, military achievement played a very significant role in the competition between the Roman noble families. See N. Rosenstein, *Imperatores Victi, Military Defeat and Aristocratic Competition in the Middle and Late Republic,* Berkeley: University of California Press; H. Flower, *Ancestor Masks and Aristocratic Power in Roman Culture*, Oxford: Clarendon Press, 1996, 60–90.

[4] W. Eck, *The Age of Augustus*. trans. D. Schneider, Blackwell, 2003, 3.

[5] P. Zanker, *The Power of Images in the Age of Augustus*, trans. A. Shapiro, Ann Arbor: The University of Michigan Press, 1988; C. Nicolet (1991).

[6] *R. E.* headline: *Rerum gestarum divi Augusti, quibus orbem terra[rum] imperio populi Rom[a]ni subiecit, et inpensarum, quas in rem publicam populumque Romanum fecit, incisarum in duabus aheneis pilis, quae su[n]t Romae positae, exemplar sub[i]ectum:* Of the achievements of the deified Augustus, by which the whole of the world he subdued to the command of Roman people, and of the expenses, which he made for the state and people of Rome, inscribed upon two bronze columns, which have been set up at Rome, the copy below; 3.1: *[b]ella terra et mari c[ivilia ex]ternaque toto in orbe terrarum s[ape gessi], victorque omnibus v[eniam petentib]us civibus peperci:* Wars, both on land and sea, civil and foreign, I often conducted in the whole world, and as a victor I spared all citizens who asked for pardon.

early first century B.C. when the state of Rome established its hegemonic power throughout the world.[①] If we consider Polybius' assertion that not until the early 160s B.C., did Rome subdue most parts of the *oikoumene*, it is not surprising that in the formation of its empire, why this phrase comes into the mind of the Roman elites much later than that of China.[②] Rome was a traditional farming society. Differently from ancient Greece, it had little seafaring knowledge in its early age. Throughout the first two hundred years of the Republic, obsessing over warfare with the Italian peoples, they had few opportunities to develop their maritime force. Thus, their vision of the world was mostly confined to the lands of the Italian Peninsula. As late as roughly the middle of the third century B.C. when the war between Rome and Carthage began, the Roman Senate realised the importance of having a naval force. Thus, it was only at this time that Rome built its first fleets. Thereafter, especially from the Hannibalic War onwards, Rome put unprecedented effort into its affairs in the East. In doing so it enlarged the knowledge and the horizons of the world.

Therefore, by the last century B.C., the phrases *orbis terrarum* and *terra marique (terra et mare)* frequently appeared in Latin literature. The former mainly refers to the human inhabited world, while the latter denotes a more universal natural space.[③] In Augustus' *Res Gestae, terra et mari* appears twice, illustrating that Roman power has extended to every corner of the earth.[④] The concept of *imperium sine fine*, accompanied by continuous military expedition, became increasingly clearer by the period of Augustus. Such a view of the world was very different from the more closed structure of the world in the minds of the decision–makers of Qin and the subsequent Han Empire.[⑤]

---

① C. Nicolet, 31.

② Polybius, 1. 5.

③ A. Momigliano, "*Terra marique*", *JRS,* vol. 23, 1942, pp. 53–64.

④ *R. E.* 3.1 see note 30; *R. E.* 26.4: *classis mea per Oceanum ab ostio Rheni ad solis orientis regionem usque ad fines Cimbrorum navigavit, quo neque terra neque mari quisquam Romanus ante id tempus adit, Cimbrique et Charydes et Semnones et eiusdem tractus alii Germanorum popu[l]l per legatos amicitiam meam et populi Romani petierunt*: My fleet through the Ocean from the mouth of Rhine to the region of the rising sun as far as the limit of Cimbri I navigated, where neither land nor sea Roman before this time has ever approached, Cimbri and Charydes and Semnones and the same place of other German peoples sent through legates for friendship of mine and of Roman people.

⑤ Over thirty years ago, E. Luttwak published his magnificent book arguing that Roman policymakers in general took a defensive strategy after the death of Augustus. It attracted strong interest and criticism from many scholars after it was published, although as far as I know in the last thirty years more scholars have come to support the aggressive theory (H. W. Harris, P. A. Brunt, K. Hopkins, C. Whittaker , E. Grune) rather than the seemingly outdated defensive theory (Theodor Mommsen, Maurice Holleaux, T. Frank, H. H. Scullard). In contrast, I think that the Qin Empire took a much more obvious defensive strategy (if there was a grand strategy as Luttwak stressed in antiquity) in its policy–making.

古代经济与资本主义经济
——韦伯、芬利、马克思、顾准有关思想辨析

毕会成、付晓倩　辽宁师范大学

摘要：在欧洲历史上，古代奴隶制社会与近代资本主义社会究竟存在着怎样的联系？本文通过对韦伯、芬利、马克思、顾准四人有关思想的辨析，说明两种社会不仅在文物制度等精神文化上，而且在经济模式、经济关系等物质文化上，都存在着相当多的一致性，这种一致性足以让古代希腊列入"古代商业社会"的范畴。

关键词：原始派；现代化派；合理主义；奴隶制度；资本主义

Abstract：What connections existed between ancient slave society and modern capitalist society in European history? By analysis of concerned theory of these four scholars, namely Weber, Finley, Max and Guzhun, I prove that there existed much conformity between these two societies, not only in spiritual culture such as ideology and institution, but also in material culture such as mode of economy and economic relation. Viewed from these, ancient Greece is justified to be listed in the catalogue of 'ancient commercial societies'.

Keywords：Primitivist, Modernist, rationalism, slave-owning system, capitalism

———

　　众所周知，在古代希腊经济史的研究中存在着一个著名的公案，即所谓"原始派"与"现代化派"的争论。1893 年，德国经济学家卡尔·布彻尔 (Karl.Bücher) 在《国民经济的兴起》一书中，将世界经济史划分为家庭经济、城市经济、国民经济三大发展阶段，包括希腊在内的整个古代经济被划归以封闭性为本质特征的家庭经济阶段。两年后，他的同胞、古史学家爱德华·梅耶 (Eduard Meyer) 发表长篇论文《古代经济的发展》，对布彻尔的理论进行系统批判，由此引发关于古代经济特点的旷日持久的争论。1928 年哈斯布鲁克在《古代希腊的贸易与政治》中首次把争论的双方称为"原始派" (Primitivist) 和"现代化派" (Modernist)，布彻尔和梅耶分别成为两派的肇端。梅耶认为：公元前 8 世纪以降希腊工商业的发展以及城市化浪潮的出现，最终导向中产阶级的产生和贵族政治的结束。"在希腊历史上，公元前七至六世纪相当于近代世界的十四、十五世纪，公元前五世纪则相当

于十六世纪。"①

布彻尔不甘示弱，他以中世纪为基准，指出与作为生产中心的中世纪城市不同，古代只有消费城市，因为"希腊和罗马的城市居民是土地的所有者和利用者，即使他让这些劳动由奴隶或佃户来承担。"②索姆巴尔特 (W.Sombart) 对布彻尔的核心概念作了进一步的阐释："所谓消费城市，意思是它不必用它的产品来换取消费品，……确切地说，它是依靠法定的权力，比如税收和租金来支付消费，而不必作对等的交换。"③两人的结论给人以强烈的错位感，好象把得自古代东方的结论强加到希腊罗马身上。相形之下，梅耶在史料的运用和结论的表述上尽管多有商榷之处，仍显得瑕不掩瑜。这样，在贝洛赫等著名古史学家的支持下，"现代化派"在西方古史学界首先取得了正统地位。20 世纪上半期出版的古希腊史著作，几乎都接受了"现代化派"的立场和观点。乌尔 (P.N.Ure) 的《希腊文艺复兴》(The Greek Renaissance) 和《僭主的起源》(The origins of Tyranny) 把这两大事件置于公元前 8 世纪以来的工商业革命的背景下加以探讨；格兰迪 (G.B.Grundy) 的《修昔底德和当代历史》(Thucydides and the history of his age) 以及本特森 (H.Bengtson) 的《希腊史》(History of Greece) 都把伯罗奔尼撒战争的缘起归于希腊世界的商业竞争；弗兰奇的《雅典经济的增长》(A.French, The growth of the Athenian economy)，主要从工商业发展的角度阐述雅典得以建立并巩固提洛同盟的原因；杜丹的《古代世界的经济生活》(J.Toutain, The economic life of the ancient world)，葛洛兹的《古代希腊的劳作》(G.Glotz,Ancient Greece at work)，以及雅德的《希腊民族的形成》(A.Jarde, The formation of the Greek people)，都强调希腊经济的商业化特征。该派的集大成之作则是俄裔美国历史学家罗斯托夫采夫 (M.I.Rostovtzeff) 的《世界古代史》(History of the ancient world) 第一卷，在这里，工商业的经济活动成了理解全部希腊历史运动的基础和核心。

不过，一旦某派学术观点成了正统，它也同时把理论创新的宝贵权利拱手他让。正当"现代化派"在古史领域一统江山之时，著名的德国学者马克斯·韦伯抛出《经济与社会》一书。该书在结论上不过是布彻尔等人"消费城市"的老调重弹，但韦伯凭靠他作为社会学家的宏阔眼光，为"原始派"提供了全新的研究视角，即从城邦政策与城邦经济的关系入手探讨古代经济的运行规律，从而为一度消沉的"原始派"注入新的活力。

1928 年以后，哈斯布鲁克在接连发表的《古代希腊的贸易与政治》和《波斯战争前的希腊经济与社会史》(J.Hasebroek, Trade and politics in ancient Greece, Griechische wirtschafts und Gesellschaftsgeschichte bis zu den perserkriegen) 两书中，全面借用韦伯的理论模式对"现代化派"进行清算。指出，希腊城市不存在现代意义的商业政策，城邦所关心的只是作为消费者的公民，而不是作为生产者的公民。波拉尼进一步指出，较多地受到诸如城邦政策等非经济因素的影响，正是古代经济不同于近代经济的地方。后者已成为有自身独特规律、摆脱了非经济影响的独立实体。据此他反对将近代的经济概念应用于古代经济研究，而代之以他所创造的"贸易式交换"、"家庭经济"和"礼物经济"等术语。波氏理论被汉弗里、奥斯丁及维达尔—内奎特等人奉为至宝。汉弗里在《政治的人与经济的人》、《古典雅典的经济与社会》等论文中，认为希腊商业的目的不为赢利，而是为筹措金钱、购置重装步兵装备以取得充分的政治权利。换言之，是政治动机这类上层建筑决定了经济基础的状况，而不是相反。

奥斯丁 (M.M.Austin) 与维达尔—内奎特 (Vidal—Naquet) 亦步亦趋，他们在合著的《古代希腊社会经济史》(Economic &social history of ancient Greece) 中证明了充斥希腊人的观念的是对职业高低贵

---

① M.M.Austin, *Economic and social history of ancient Greece*, California, 1980, p.5.

② K.Bücher, *Die Entstehung des Volkswirtschafts*, Tübingen, 1906. pp.370–371.

③ W.Sombart. *Der modern Kapitalismus*, Munish&Leipzig, 1916. pp.142–143.

贱的区分以及对劳动的鄙视和对闲暇的追求，故希腊工业生产规模有限，不能形成近代意义的公司。换言之，是意识形态决定物质基础，而不是相反。

芬利是韦伯、哈斯布鲁克以及波拉尼诸家思想的大拼盘。这些思想主要集中于 1973 年推出的《古代经济》一书，该书的"主旨是强调古典社会的特殊性，……反对用现代的经济术语去分析古代社会。他认为古代并不知道什么资本、资本积累、产品、需求与供给等词汇，也不存在谋取最大利润或技术进步的观念，国家的经济政策目标是保证公民集团的消费，而不是发展生产或创造有利于工商业发展的环境，因而工商业在古代并不是占优势的产业。从古代的城乡关系来看，城市首先是消费中心，生产只处于次要地位，城市的命运取决于它所拥有的自然资源与政治地位，而不是经济因素。"[1]与芬利观点接近的还有德圣克罗阿，他在专著《伯罗奔尼撒战争的起源》(G.E.M. de Ste Croix, The origins of the Peloponnesian War) 中指出，希腊商业与贸易发展的程度十分有限，根本不存在什么商业战争。雅典与科林斯的冲突不是经济性的，而是战略性的。换言之，是为战争而战争。德圣克罗阿与芬利，尤其是芬利，堪称古史学界的重量级人物，据说，在他们的影响下，"原始派"在二十世纪六、七十年代以后的西方古史学界逐渐取代"现代化派"，成为新的正统。

不过，这种说法从一开始就带有一厢情愿的意味。事实上，七十年代后期以来发表的有影响的作品几乎都可归入"现代化派"的帐下。科德斯特瑞在《几何陶时代的希腊》(J.N.Coldstream, Geometric Greece) 中证明了，希腊文明的全部活力都来自对外联系与贸易；默里的《早期希腊》(O.Murray, Early Greece) 把工商业视为希腊经济进步的驱动器；奥斯邦 (Robin Osborn, Pots, trade and the archaic Greek economy) 认为希腊的制造业和贸易都是有明确自身目的性的经济活动。另一方面，"原始派"的"原始"特征被无限提纯，已接近不可理喻。在 1983 年出版的论文集《古代经济中的贸易》中，斯诺德格拉斯、卡特里奇等人完全否认贸易在古风希腊经济中的地位；克拉里等人认为希腊铸币的产生与商品经济的发展完全无关；加恩西强调希腊主要消费本土的谷物，雅典进口谷物的数量远没有人们想象得那么大，时间也比通常认为的晚得多 (P.D.A.Garnsey, ect., Trade in the ancient economy; Famine and food supply in Graeco-Roman world)。这些说法让"原始派"元老们也不敢苟同。奥斯丁在评论此书时指出，即使在希腊人自己的观念中，贸易与他们的文明也是密不可分的。芬利本人也确认古典奴隶制与工商业的共生关系。"原始派"的内讧使他们的"正统地位"大打折扣；而默里在《早期希腊》1993 年第二版中，则声称"现代化派"已得到相当多的学者的支持，有可能（事实上正在——笔者加）重新成为正统。一百年的争讼不已，希腊经济史研究似乎又回到起点。

在国内，对希腊经济史的专门研究起步较晚，要到八十年代中期以后。当时正值中西文化比较研究方兴未艾之时，这一背景不能不对该领域的研究产生投影。如果说国外主要是在历史的纵向度（西欧自身）上考察古代经济状况的话，国内则主要是在历史的横向（中西之间）坐标上加以考察。但也同样产生了认识的分歧：一派观点认为，希腊文明的特质之一是工商业的相对发达，它在当时的经济结构中占有重要的、甚至是主导的地位；[2]另一派观点认为，农业在经济结构中的主导地位是古代社会的普遍特征，希腊自然也不例外。[3]至于游移两者之间的学术"骑墙者"，这里暂不予考虑。大致说来，前一派观点相当于国际史学界的"现代化派"，后一观点对应于"原始派"。但又不尽然，尤其是后一对应，在"原始派"那里只是相对欧洲近世而言的"希腊农业论"，到他们的中国同行

① 晏绍祥：《古典历史研究发展史》，武汉：华中师范大学出版社，1999 年，第 179–180 页。
② 参见朱龙华：《世界历史·上古部分》，北京大学出版社，1991 年；晏绍祥：《古典作家笔下的古代希腊商业》，载《内蒙古大学学报》1992 年第 3 期。
③ 参见启良：《希腊城邦的主要经济形式也是小农经济》，载《湘潭大学学报》，1988 年第 1 期；李韵琴：《公元前 8–6 世纪希腊移民运动中的农商关系》，载《北京师范大学学报》，1987 年第 4 期；《试析公元前 8–6 世纪希腊殖民运动的主要原因》，载《世界历史》，1989 年第 4 期；黄洋：《希腊城邦社会的农业特征》，载《历史研究》1996 年第 4 期，等。

这里，却被泛化为普遍性的"古代农业特征"，即转换成东西方社会的一致性了。用黄洋的话说："希腊城邦社会同古代中国社会一样，是一个以农业而不是工商业为特征的社会"，从而将希腊嵌入古代农业社会的范畴。可见，尽管谈到这场争论，我们不得不提及国内的对应情形，但至少从各自争论的出发点来看，两者有很大的不同。因此，以下对争论的评述部分并不适用于国内情形。

站在新的世纪之交的关口，检视迄自上一个世纪之交的这场百年争论，我们惊异地发现，争论双方其实是在大致平行的两条线路上做着很难实质性交锋的争论。"现代化派"从上古的希腊看到了绵延不绝的欧洲商业传统的"始基"，因此以求同的思维方式强调希腊文明的商业性和与近代社会在经济模式上的一致性。而求同者必从技术上模糊细节，"现代化派"少有对古代经济生活的精致分析，多以粗线条的结论统领具体意义参差有别的史料，故常常在史料的运用上招致非难。相形之下，"原始派"对古代社会的研究更为深入，这表现为他们提出了针对古代社会的一系列概念、范畴和模式。这种具体而微的探讨既是他们的优势，同时也容易转化为劣势，因为这往往使他们纠缠于细节不放，从而妨碍他们从更宏阔的层面上对历史规律的总体把握。"原始派"常常自觉不自觉地割裂古代与近世的联系，并非偶然。

可见，求同的"现代化派"从技术上模糊细节，求异的"原始派"从技术上挑剔细节，这才是导致争论的方法论根源。本应为历史研究相反相成的两个方面不期因各执一端而成犄角之争。至于"原始派"学者赠予对手的那顶"古史现代化"的帽子，则完全可以回赠"原始派"本身，在以近现代资本主义作参照系这一点上，两派并没有区别，这也是使他们的交锋偶有意义的唯一契合点。

于是，我们就得到了化解这场争论的一个很好的角度。既然双方都以近现代资本主义作参照系，为什么问题不能归结为：一、古代社会与近代社会在经济行为或经济模式上究竟存不存在一致性？二、如果答案是肯定的，那么这种一致性是否大到足以使古代社会[1]冠以"商业社会"的称号？

或许，以下四个人物的思想将有助于我们对上述问题的回答，他们是：韦伯、芬利、马克思、顾准。

二

马克斯·韦伯 (Max Weber,1864–1920) 是一位以博学著称的德国社会学家，但对历史学也颇有造诣。他著述宏富，已出版的著作高达二百三十多种。对我们而言，他的《世界经济通史》《经济与社会》《新教伦理与资本主义》三书更为重要。三书各有侧重，但均旨在回答这样一个问题：为什么现代资本主义首先兴起、生长并成熟于西方？为什么对于东方各国来讲这种发达的资本主义只能是一种外来现象？

韦伯首先对资本主义做出界定："哪里有用企业方法来供应人类集团所需要的工业，哪里就有资本主义存在，而不管需要的内容是什么。更具体地说，一个合理的资本主义企业，就是一个附有资本会计制度的企业，也就是，根据现代簿记和结算的方法来确定它的收益能力的一个机构"。[2]但韦伯不认为资本主义只是现代社会的独有现象，因此他又提出"资本主义经济行为"的概念，即"以利用交易机会取得预期利润为基础的行动，却依赖（形式上）和平的营利机会而采取的行动"。根据这一概念，人类历史上的不同时期、不同地域都可能存在不同程度的资本主义，而"只有需求的供应已经按资本主义方式组织到了这样突出的程度，以致如果我们设想这种形式的组织一旦取消，整个经济制度的崩溃就在意料之中，这整个时代才可以称作为典型的资本主义时代"。这样的情形只出现于西方世界，之外，这些"资本主义现象"最终都归于湮没，成为永恒的"萌芽"。

---

① 为使问题更有说明性，这里的古代社会还包括了古代罗马在内。

② 马克斯·韦伯：《新教伦理与资本主义精神》，黄晓京、彭强译，四川人民出版社，1987年，本节引文未注出处者，皆引自该书。

现代资本主义的技术核心和前提是企业中的合理会计制度，而它的出现又要求：第一，生产资料的私有化；第二，市场的自由和经济生活的商业化；第三，便捷的计算技术；第四，形式法律调节下的经济生活的可预期性；第五，实际上被迫而形式上自由的劳动力。上述这些因素，一方面导源于西方的经济传统和文化传统，主要是源自古罗马的信用工具与股份公司、使用形式法律而不是即兴命令进行统治，以物权法为核心的罗马法体系，古希腊罗马的理性化经验科学，古希腊以降的市场自由、经济生活的商业化和可计算性；另方面又是西方社会步入近代以后创造性转换的结果，主要是宗教改革、实验方法与数理方法的结合、民法与商法的健全、西蒙·勘蒂文发明会计中的平衡法，圈地运动造成自由劳动力，等。这样，在韦伯看来，西方资本主义的产生表面上是一个经济现象，实则是一个文化现象，关键在于西方所独有的文化特质："只有西方懂得什么是现代意义的国家，它既有专职行政机关又有专业化官员和以公民权利义务的观念为基础的法律。……只有西方才懂得什么是法学家所制定并予以合理解释和适用的合理法律，只有西方，才有公民权和义务的观念，因为也只有西方才有那种特殊意义的城市。而且只有西方才有现今这个词义上的科学。神学、哲学和对人生的最终问题的思考，都是中国人和印度人所理解的，也许比欧洲人理解得更加深刻些。但是合理的科学和与之有关的技术却依然是这两种文明所不能理解的。最后，西方文明更因为有具备这样一种指导生活的道德标准的人，而与其他文明有所不同。巫术和宗教固然是到处都可以看到的，但是像这样一种生活有条理的宗教基础——而那种有条理的生活，只要能始终坚持不渝，就必然会引向明确的理性主义——则仅仅是西方文明所固有的。"

从自由城市中衍生的公民权，以形式法律为基础的科层组织，实验与数学相结合的科学，规范生活条理化的宗教——这些因素构成了韦伯所谓"合理主义"的基本特征。正是从这种"合理主义"趋向中产生了现代合理的资本主义。而这种"合理主义"的源头无疑在希腊罗马的古典世界。1）具有单一政治共同体意义的自治城市和以自己制定的法律调节内部关系的自由城市都发轫于希腊。希腊城邦制度对中世纪的城市自治运动和近代资产阶级民族国家的形成有巨大影响，是欧洲文明"基因"的定型时期；公元前六世纪，在希腊城邦产生发达的公民意识的同时，也萌生了最早的法治意识，并在体系庞大、结构严谨的罗马法中进一步具体化。罗马法的制定或是基于物质利益原则或是基于形式法律的原则，造成可资信赖的典章制度，为资本主义所要求的可预测性提供了坚实的基础。十二世纪以来罗马法复兴的内在原因在此。2）韦伯思想中的科层制概念，确指现代西方基于形式法律的国家管理体制，在该体制下，行政职务只是职业，而不再是身份的标志，从而确保了个人与权力（管理手段）的分离。每一个微小的管理行为都来自法律、规章的规定，排除了个人的偏好或专断；管理手段集中于法律，而不是控制在少数个人手中，每个人都得以公民的身份在法律面前享有同等地位。这种科层制的古代原型也可以到希腊的直接民主和抽签选举、轮流执政的做法中寻找。3）对韦伯来讲，基督教文化的合理性表现在它对巫术的敌视和由此体现出来的理性主义，这种理性主义是古典哲学支持的结果，基督教正是古典希腊哲学的庸俗化。

韦伯从作为经济现象的资本主义出发，深入到内在的文化层面，从而肯定希腊罗马传统对于现代资本主义的源流关系，这是他在经济史研究中的过人之处和深刻之处。但令人不解的是，当他重新回到经济的本体层面时，古代与现代社会间的这种联系却荡然无存。他在《世界经济通史》（上海译文出版社，1981年版）中开篇即探讨日耳曼人的定居制度，从而将资本主义经济演变的由来只推到中世纪。这样做自非偶然。证之以他在《经济与社会》中的观点："希腊城市是由武士、甚至是由水手构成的贵族共和体，是一个消费者的城市，而中世纪的城市则是一个生产者的城市。"①古代城市既与中世纪在类型上截然不同，自然也与近代资本主义毫无共同之处。

---

① M.Weber, *Wirtschaft und Gesellschaft*, Tübingen, 1956. p.748.

这样，对于本文所提的问题，韦伯的回答是：古代社会与近代资本主义社会存在一致性，但只限文物制度的精神传承。在经济行为上，古代城市是一种原始的"消费型"社会，商业传统只能溯至中世纪。

这样的答案显然是难以自圆其说的。韦伯"合理主义"的两大来源，即希腊城市的公民权和罗马法都不能独立于商业经济之外而产生。希腊公民权的实质是摆脱了繁复身份关系的纯粹财产形式，它标志以物的依赖性为基础的人的独立性，在许多城邦中都体现于民主政治的实践。而民主的核心是平等和自由，两者都只能是商品经济的产物。因为在商品交换中，交换的双方在生产和需要上的相互差别及由此产生的相互依赖，导致了他们在社会关系上的平等。这种经济人格的平等，是政治人格平等的基础；同时，在商品交换中，交换者"并不是用暴力去占有这个商品，……相反地他们互相承认对方是所有者，是把自己的意志渗透到商品中去的人。因此，在这里第一次出现了人的法律因素以及其中包含的自由的因素。"① "可见，平等和自由不仅在以交换价值为基础的交换中受到尊重，而且交换价值的交换是一切平等和自由的产生的现实的基础。作为纯粹观念，平等和自由仅仅是交换价值的交换的一种理想化的表现；作为在法律的、政治的、社会关系上发展了的东西，平等和自由不过是另一次方的这种基础而已。"②

罗马法则是商品经济的司法语言，其法权原则的逻辑前提是财产所有者权利的平等。"罗马法是简单商品生产即资本主义前的商品生产的完善的法，但是它也包含着资本主义时期的大多数法权关系。因此，这正是我们的市民在他们兴起时期所需要，而在当地的习惯法中找不到的。"③ "罗马法是纯粹私有制占统治的社会的生活条件和冲突的十分经典性的法律表现，以致一切后来的法律都不能对它做任何实质性的修改。但是，中世纪的市民阶级所有制还同封建的限制密切交织在一起，例如，这种所有制主要由特权构成。因此，从这个意义上说，罗马法比当时的市民阶级的关系要先进得多……在罗马法中，凡是中世纪后期的市民阶级还在不自觉地追求的东西，都已经有了现成的了。"④罗马法遂重新崛起，几乎被欧洲各国所接受。有的将罗马私法稍加修改，变成现行法使用，有的吸取罗马法的概念、术语和基本原则，融入本国法律。大体上，前者即后来的罗马法系（大陆法系），后者则形成英美法系。在法国，拿破仑以查士丁尼的《法学总论》为蓝本主持制订的《法国民法典》（即著名的《拿破仑法典》），经历两次王政复辟、两次帝制、五次共和，却一以贯之，不改初衷。我们今天打开它，仍然看到在第一页上赫然注明："一八〇三年制订"。有人说，罗马曾三次征服世界，第一次以武力，第二次以宗教，第三次以法律。此言极是，所谓资产阶级法权即是罗马法的法权原则。

可见，历史在时间维度上呈现出来的前后序列，并不必然标志社会发展水平由低到高的序列，"从粗野的原始状态发展而来的"中世纪在不止一个方面上都是从古代文明水平上的倒退；而古代与近现代资本主义社会则无论在经济形态（商品生产）还是在经济关系（法权关系）上都存在着更多的一致性。

令人遗憾的是，韦伯在探讨资本主义的起源时，一头扎进了所谓的"文化精神"不能自拔，文化传统的递嬗与传承成了无所依傍的抽象的精神运动，从而割裂了精神与物质的共生关系，陷入文化神秘主义的泥潭。资本主义也被解释为首先是一种精神上的态度，一种行为理想，甚至就是新教伦理。在这种思想的观照下，非宗教的世俗主义倾向不但不是古典文化的可贵之处，反倒成了妨碍其经济"合理化"的根源。

---

① 《马克思恩格斯全集》(46 上)，北京：人民出版社，1979 年，第 195 页。
② 《马克思恩格斯全集》(46 上)，北京：人民出版社，1979 年，第 197 页。
③ 《马克思恩格斯全集》(36)，北京：人民出版社，1972 年，第 169 页。
④ 《马克思恩格斯全集》(21)，北京：人民出版社，1965 年，第 454 页。

三

M.I. 芬利是继韦伯之后"原始派"的集大成者。他分别从生产关系和生产力两个方面对古代经济社会进行探讨。根据芬利的说法，1) 希洛特和债务奴役可以出现在较为原始的社会，不管是古典时代的克里特、斯巴达、色萨利，还是前梭伦时代的雅典，但真正的奴隶在发达的城邦里是关键性因素；2) 虽然对奴隶的剥削是人类历史上的普遍现象，但真正的奴隶制社会只有 5 个，它们是希腊、罗马、南部美国、加勒比、巴西。即使在希腊罗马，也并非所有时期所有地区均有奴隶制社会，而只是在希腊罗马的中心地区（希腊之雅典、科林斯、厄齐那等，罗马之意大利、西西里），在其古典时代（希腊从梭伦改革以后，罗马从公元前 3 世纪到公元 2 世纪），才存在过真正的奴隶制社会。3) 而奴隶制的必要条件是商品和市场的充分发展，至于市场是通常意义上的远距离的出口市场还是附近的城市中心，均无关宏旨。在理论上，希洛特和其他的依附劳动可以使用于非商品生产，奴隶则不行，因为奴隶要经常大量进口，就需要付款。[1]

可见，芬利对奴隶制的研究完全是开放式的。他跨越时空，将古典奴隶制与近代作为资本主义补充的美洲奴隶制放到同一范畴内进行探讨，并且把商品生产视作这种制度的前提，从而得出了"奴隶经济商业化"的结论。

但是，这一结论并不能从他对古代经济生活的描述中得到确证，他笔下的希腊经济呈现出与商业社会毫无二致的原始而素朴的表征。在 1951 年出版的《古代雅典土地与信用研究》(Studies in land and credit in ancient Athens) 中，他证明在古典及希腊化时代的雅典，土地及信用仍处于分离状态，借贷或为承担捐助或为置办嫁妆，与生产无关。在随后出版的《奥德修斯的世界》(The World of Odysseus) 中，芬利运用礼物交换理论解释荷马时代的经济往来。1970 年，他发表了《亚里士多德与经济分析》(Aristotle and economic analysis) 的长篇论文，宣称希腊人根本不懂得什么叫经济分析。经过这一系列的准备，他于 1973 年推出了《古代经济》一书，断言：在古代希腊，"制造业的作用是可以忽略的；那只是一个错误的模式驱使历史学家到它们无法被证明、也并不存在的地方去寻找。""强烈的获取财富的欲望并没有转化为积累资金的欲望；换言之，当时普遍的心态是占有性的，而非生产性的。""在古代，对土地的投资从来没有成为系统的、经过深思熟虑的经济策略，或韦伯称为经济合理性的那种东西。没有对资金费用和劳动力费用的明确区分，没有基于利润考虑的有计划的开垦，没有以生产为目的的长期贷款。""作为规律，古代国家没有现代意义的预算。""税收并没有用作经济杠杆，……只要想一想一个国际性港口的情形就可以了：在那里，征自进口和出口货物的税收比率都是一样的。人们没有想到应保护国内的生产，应鼓励重要物资的进口或维持贸易平衡；甚至对正常时期的谷物供应都不例外……"[2]显然，"合理化"的近现代资本主义成了衡量商业经济的唯一标准。芬利之所以要小心地把古代希腊从商业社会中分离出来，在他的研究视野中，之所以会出现发达的生产关系（奴隶制度）与落后的生产力基础共处的奇特组合，其认识论的根源在此。

但是，商业经济较之资本主义是一个大得多的范畴。市场和货币关系可以并已经存在于其他社会形态。马克思指出，各种社会经济形态都有劳动分工（不管它是否由商品交换间接地表现出来），资本主义生产方式只是在以手工工场为特征的劳动分工的水平上发生的。[3]列宁也指出，市场是一般商品经济范畴，而资本主义条件下的市场关系的特点则是它的普遍流行和充分统治。[4]

---

① M.I.Finley, *Economy&society in ancient Greece*, Penguin Group, 1983. p.99;102–103.

② M.I.Finley, *The ancient economy*, California, 1973. p.139;144;174;164.

③ 《马克思恩格斯全集》(23)，北京：人民出版社，1972 年，第 397 页。

④ 《列宁全集》(3)，北京：人民出版社，1984 年，第 17 页。

而且，我们探讨的是距今两千多年以前的希腊历史，颇费心力地证明古代比现代缺少什么，对于说明特定的古代经济状况并无太大的意义。走得太远，则可能导致历史虚无主义。从历史哲学的高度上讲，一切成熟的历史现象都必以萌芽的或原始的状态存在于既往的阶段。历史没有"无源之水"，把古代与现代截然断开，恐不是历史唯物主义的态度。正确的做法应当是依据古代确曾出现过的现象对其进行客观的分析与定性，不是说明它"不是"什么，而是说明它"是"什么。

即便承认韦伯式的"经济合理主义"对于资本主义生产的意义，但对财富的无止境追求和商业经济的发展却是体现人类本能的自然历史现象，正所谓"天下熙熙，皆为利来，天下攘攘，皆为利往"，倒是要压抑它的发展，使之永远驻足于自给自足的状态，却需要强有力的人为钳制。以中国论，一向认为中国古代的商业经济若有若无，实不尽然。在与希腊城邦时代同期的春秋战国时期，就出现了中国商业经济的第一次勃兴，傅筑夫甚至认为这时已出现资本主义萌芽。究其原因，并不在于列国采取了什么鼓励工商之举，而恰在于当时王权失去了对经济生活的强有力干预。其时周室式微，诸侯称雄，政由方伯，于是乎私商蜂拥，人们堂而皇之地追求财富积累。被称为希腊世界"活化石"的斯巴达也是如此。根据考古材料，公元前七世纪斯巴达输入象牙、琥珀、甲虫形宝石以及金银首饰，而斯巴达工匠在象牙器、骨器和陶器制造方面也可以同其他城邦之上乘者媲美；到公元前六世纪，输入渐停，但斯巴达陶器远销至小亚细亚的萨迪斯和意大利的伊达拉里亚，达到极盛，到公元前550年以后迅速衰落。[1]斯巴达工商业的衰落，是众所周知的来库古复古的结果。商业经济的强大自生力，还可证诸现代中国大割资本主义尾巴时屡割屡现的民间集市贸易。商业交换才是文明社会的常态。对于前资本主义社会的经济史，更有价值的研究似乎不是某一社会何以产生了商业经济，而是商业经济何以在另一社会中受到了压制、甚或湮没无存。

四

还是让我们把目光转向马克思。这位历史唯物主义大师在《资本论》中已经对古典奴隶制的经济运行及与资本主义的关系作了鞭辟入里的分析："在奴隶经济（不是家长制的奴隶经济，而是后来希腊罗马时代那样的奴隶经济）作为致富手段存在的一切形式中，因而，在货币通过购买奴隶、土地等等而成为占有别人劳动的手段的一切形式中，货币正是因为可以这样使用，所以作为资本可以增殖，生出利息。"[2]奴隶的存在和无产者一样，都是货币转化为资本的前提。"在奴隶制度下，投下来购买劳动力的货币资本，是当作固定资本的货币形态，不过要跟着奴隶的能动的生活期间的消磨，逐渐地予以补偿。在雅典人中，奴隶主由产业地而直接使用奴隶得来的利益，或将奴隶出租给别个业主（譬如租给采矿工业）而间接得来的利益，只是当作垫付的货币资本的利息（连带折旧在内）。——这完全如同在资本主义生产之下，产业资本家把一部分剩余价值加上固定资本的折旧，当作他的固定资本的利息及偿还来计算一样；也完全如同那些把固定资本（房屋、机器等等）出租的资本家的一般通则那样。"[3]可见，奴隶制与资本主义有着原理相同的经济运行法则。那么，"无产者以什么跟奴隶区别呢？奴隶是一次就完全卖掉，而无产者则每日每时也要出卖自己！"[4]但从纯粹经济的角度，经常性购买劳动力商品（雇佣关系）和一次性购买劳动者本身（奴隶制）并没有实质性区别。英国农场主在本土使用雇佣的农业工人，在美国南部则使用非洲贩来的奴隶。两者的区别与其说是经济的，不如说是法律的。

---

① *Cambridge Ancient History(III)*，Cambridge，1983，p.559.
② 《马克思恩格斯全集》(25)，北京：人民出版社，1972年，第672页。
③ 马克思：《资本论》（二），北京：人民出版社，1953年，第600页。
④ 《马克思恩格斯全集》(5)，北京：人民出版社，1958年，第467页。

这就难怪奴隶制在近代的北美大陆上再度兴盛，并与资本主义发生着紧密的耦合。在有着大量处女地可供自由垦殖的北美，奴隶制成了组织大规模棉花生产的唯一形式。"没有奴隶制就没有棉花；没有棉花，现代工业就不可设想。奴隶制使殖民地具有价值，殖民地产生了世界贸易，世界贸易是大工业的必备条件。"故而，"同机器、信用等等一样，直接奴隶制是资产阶级工业的基础。"①

这样的奴隶制经济当然只能是以市场为旨归的商业经济。"在美国南部各州，当生产的目的主要是直接满足本地需要时，黑人劳动还带有一种温和的家长制的性质。但是随着棉花出口变成这些州的切身利益，黑人所从事的有时只要七年就把生命耗尽的过度劳动，就成为事事都要加以盘算的那个制度的一个因素。"②美国奴隶制在后来的废除，除了自由主义的政治考虑以外，经济上的首要原因便是它的棉花市场因受到印度、埃及、巴西等国的竞争而日趋缩小。③古代罗马的情形也如此。公元前二世纪以后，当罗马军团的滚滚征服用无以计数的战利品和战俘淹没了意大利本土，中部意大利和坎巴尼亚使用奴隶劳动的葡萄、橄榄种植园开始取代了原来的谷物经营；南部意大利、西西里、萨丁尼亚和北非则发展起奴隶制的大牧场；与此同时，在西西里和北非，大规模的谷物种植也采取了奴隶劳动的形式，此三者都以供应意大利日渐扩大的寄生性市场为依托。到三世纪危机期间，当中部意大利重新恢复了自足式的谷物种植时，则不仅意味着市场的萧条，也同时意味着奴隶制的衰落。奴隶制与市场存在着绝非偶然的关系。

但是，经常有人引用马克思的下述论断作为否定上述结论的依据："奴隶制度——即使象发达的国家希腊和罗马那样，奴隶制度在农业、手工业、航海业等上面是生产劳动的支配形态——还保存着自然经济的因素。"但是，请注意，这里的"自然经济"并不是对经济本身的定性，其真实的含义在紧接其后的下一句话里揭示无遗："奴隶市场是由战争，海上劫掠等来不断地补充它的商品——劳动力，而这种劫掠则无须通过流通领域，因为它是用直接肉体强制方法对别人劳动力的自然的占有。"④可见，这里的"自然经济"仅指不通过市场、而是诉诸暴力的奴隶获取方式，就经济本身而言，奴隶进入生产过程在起点上就是一个市场行为——"奴隶的买卖，在形式上，也是商品的买卖。"⑤这意味着生产过程的终点也只能是一个市场行为，否则，这种以不断补充劳动力为特征的经济制度将无以维持。奴隶制度只能以商业经济的发展为前提，并成为商业经济的组织形式，这一点同资本主义并无二致。"在古代世界，商业的影响和商人资本的发展，结果往往是奴隶制经济；或视其始点，结果不过把奴隶制度，由家长式的，以生产直接生活资料为目标的，转化为以生产剩余价值为目标的。反之，在近代世界，它是归结为资本主义的生产方式。"⑥

进一步地说，正是古代文明与近代文明在上述经济模式上的同构性，构成了欧洲历史纵向统一性的最深刻的基础。"正象不同的地质层系相继更迭一样，在各种不同的社会经济形态的形成上，不应该相信各个时期是突然出现的，相互截然分开的……在这里起作用的普遍规律在于：后一个（生产）形式的物质可能性——不论是工艺条件，还是与其相适应的企业经济结构——都是在前一个形式的范围内创造出来的。"⑦"古代文明遗留给中世纪的几个城市，即威尼斯、热那亚、皮萨、佛罗伦萨，这些城市共和国，曾经为现代资本主义举行过奠基礼：现代银行和国际汇兑制度发源于此，近代物理学和实验科学滥觞于此。她们还是文艺复兴的故乡。"⑧

---

① 《马克思恩格斯选集》(1)，北京：人民出版社，1995年，第110页。
② 《马克思恩格斯全集》(23)，北京：人民出版社，1972年，第264页。
③ 《马克思恩格斯选集》(1)，北京：人民出版社，1995年，第110页。
④ 马克思：《资本论》(二)，北京：人民出版社，1953年，第600页。
⑤ 马克思：《资本论》(二)，北京：人民出版社，1953年，第16页。
⑥ 马克思：《资本论》(二)，北京：人民出版社，1953年，第600页。
⑦ 《马克思恩格斯全集》(47)，北京：人民出版社，1979年，第472页。
⑧ 马克思：《资本论》(一)，北京：人民出版社，1951年，第905页。

马克思主要依据欧洲的历史，创造性地提出了人类社会发展的五种形态学说；但他并没有因此而割裂历史各阶段间的联系。就本文所关注的问题而言，马克思不仅认为欧洲的古代与近代存在着联系，而且这种联系远不仅限于精神文化的前后传承——文艺复兴已经概括了这种传承——，更指作为这种传承的基础的物质一致性。基于这种一致性，他明确提出了"古代商业民族"的重要概念，而古典奴隶制的希腊正是古代世界少有的"商业民族"。①显然，比诸韦伯和芬利，马克思的回答更合于历史的逻辑与真实。

五

最后谈一下中国人顾准。顾准不是专业的史学工作者，但他由研究笔记辑成的《希腊城邦制度》却成为希腊史研究的经典之作；同时，作为杰出的马克思主义的理论工作者，他的希腊史研究完整体现了马克思主义的世界观和方法论的指导，从而成为历史唯物主义在具体历史研究中的深化与发展。

关于古代与近代的关系，顾准认为："欧洲文明的传统，离不开希腊。希腊的社会经济类型、希腊思想，被罗马几乎全盘继承。蛮族征服，给欧洲文明打上了日耳曼的烙印，可是罗马传统通过基督教会大部分保存下来了。13 世纪以后的文艺复兴运动，更使被基督教神学掩盖掉的那部分，欢乐的、世俗的人生哲学，民主主义的政治哲学，和具有强烈实证气味的理性主义学术思想，以新的面目恢复了它们的旧观。谁都承认，文艺复兴是世界近代化，亦即资本主义化的一个重要因素。外国人承认这一点，随而肯定，迄今的西欧文明可以名之曰希腊罗马文明。中国人也承认这一点，可是他们目光所及，以中世纪为限，不再上溯到希腊罗马时代。种种误会，可以说大部分由之而起。"不过，某些外国人尽管不会冒天下之大不韪而随意割裂近现代欧洲与古代希腊在传统文化上的一脉相传，却可以随意割裂它们在生产方式上的陈陈相因。但事实上，"假如我们把资本主义和希腊罗马文明两者的关系弄得十分紧密的话，我们未始没理由把资本主义定义为产业革命以后那种现代化的生产方式和生产关系，而把产业革命以前的工场手工业，有组织的金融方法，规模十分宏阔的航海、商业、殖民，都看作现代化资本主义的准备阶段。"②

可见，顾准将资本主义生产方式的形成视为一个不间断的历史过程，其起点则在希腊。因为泛海殖民和商业正是希腊史的根本特征，舍此则无法理解希腊的城邦制度。根据顾准的《希腊城邦制度》，③"海外殖民城市是城邦制度的发源之地"。多利亚人的入侵，进一步促进了迈锡尼时代业已开始的海外殖民活动，迈锡尼旧民纷纷到小亚细亚沿岸及附近岛屿殖民。殖民者为了防卫当地土著人的报复，也为了防卫频频发生的海盗劫掠，不得不"筑城聚居"——这就是城邦的起源。

航海活动的最重要最深远的后果，是打破了迈锡尼时代的以血缘为基础的组织原则，建立了"以契约为基础的政体"。航海的艰险和同舟共济的要求无形中消弭了人们之间的氏族身份界限，这种关系还因上岸后对付本地敌人的需要得以延续。超越血族情感之上的"同伙""战友"关系由此孕育，它的进一步发展则是公民意识和公民政治的诞生。正是在最初的海外殖民地小亚细亚，最先传诵起摆脱氏族意识的传统，抒发个人自由和自主情绪的"抒情诗"。公元前七世纪起，发源于小亚细亚的城邦制度又反馈回希腊本土，城邦制度遂大行其道。

"在古代技术条件下移居海外的人，总有些冒险家的气质。即使多里安人入侵时期出走的，显然也因为他们不愿屈居于被征服者的地位……希腊人这种自立门户的强烈愿望"，决定了殖民城邦

①　《马克思恩格斯全集》(2)，北京：人民出版社，1965 年，第 539 页。
②　顾准：《民主与"终极目的"》，北京：中国青年出版社，1999 年，第 239 页；扉页。
③　顾准：《希腊城邦制度》，北京：中国社会科学出版社，1982 年。

的"分裂繁殖"，不相统属。多数殖民城邦不得不走上农工商兼营发展的道路。而星罗棋布的殖民城邦同时又构成了希腊世界的海上贸易商站网，因此，正如近代的"殖民地产生了世界贸易"①一样，古代希腊的殖民地产生了地中海范围的世界贸易。如果考虑到近代的世界贸易是整个资本主义世界合力参与的结果，则由小小的希腊民族独力造就的地中海贸易如何不是一种奇迹？

在另外的场合，顾准还从奴隶制度的角度分析了希腊城邦的商业性。他说："奴隶要占优势成为'制度'，这唯有在商品货币关系十分发达的工商业城邦中才有可能。其条件是：具有可以拥有奴隶的自由民（相对于没有这样大的个人权利的王朝臣民）；商品货币关系发达，使财富有无限积累的可能，使自由民有把财富投资于奴隶这种"生产性固定资本"上的要求。没有这些条件，只会有鸳鸯、袭人这类奴隶，奴隶成不了制度。"②换言之，古典奴隶制本身正是希腊商业经济的高度概括。

由上可见，顾准和马克思一样，直截了当地确认了古代社会与近现代资本主义的源流关系，并把这种关系由文化传统的精神层次进一步落实到生产方式和生产关系的物质层次，从而克服了韦伯和芬利因割裂两者关系而产生的深刻矛盾。希腊文化自始便与奴隶制度、商业及殖民这些物质要素密不可分，因此当新的"奴隶制度"（资本主义制度）和航海殖民再度出现在欧洲历史时，便同时呼吁着希腊文化的复兴，尽管这种复兴不可避免地打上了新时代的烙印。

通过对以上四人有关思想的辨析，似乎可以得出这样的结论：古代社会与近代资本主义无论在精神文化上，还是在经济模式、经济关系等物质文化上都存在着相当的一致性，这种一致性足以让古代希腊列入"古代商业社会"的范畴。这也是对本文核心问题的回答。

---

① 《马克思恩格斯全集》(1). 北京：人民出版社，1956 年，第 110 页。
② 顾准：《民主与"终极目的"》，北京：中国青年出版社，1999 年，第 296 页。

19 世纪前期来华传教士对西方古典学的传播 *

陈德正 聊城大学

摘要：在 19 世纪前期西方古典学传入中国的进程中，以麦都思（Walter Henry Medhurst）、郭实腊（Gtzlaff, Karl Friedrich August）等为代表的来华传教士发挥了主导作用。他们出版《东西史记和合》等书籍，编辑《东西洋考每月统纪传》等杂志，向中国人介绍西方古典学知识。这些作品对当时魏源、徐继畬等产生了程度不同的影响，成为他们撰著外国史地著作的主要参考文献。

关键词：传教士；西方古典学；西学东渐

Abstract: In the early 19thcentury, Classics was introduced into China. In the process of its dissemination, missionaries represented by Walter Henry Medhurst and Karl Friedrich August Güttzlaff had played a dominant role. In order to introduce Classics into China, they published some books and magazines, such as Comparative Chronology（《东西史记和合》）and Eastern Western Monthly Magazine（《东西洋考每月统纪传》）. At that time these works had an influence on Wei Yuan, Xu Jiyu and so on in some degree, which became the main bibliographies of their books on foreign history and geography.

Keywords: Missionaries, Classics, Eastward Spread of Western Culture

西方古典学（Classics）是关于古希腊 – 罗马文学、艺术、哲学、历史、科技乃至建筑、雕塑、音乐、绘画、舞蹈、陶器等方面的知识和学问。[①]中国人对西方古典学的了解始于明末清初的西学东渐。当时耶稣会士为配合传教，向中国人译介了希腊罗马时代的自然科学和哲学知识以及零星的历史知识；苏格拉底、亚里士多德、梭伦、屋大维、托勒密以及众多的希腊罗马文化名人甚至古罗马的奴隶制都出现在中文书籍中。[②]迨至 19 世纪前期，以马礼逊、郭实腊、麦都思等为代表的新教传教士取代耶稣会传教士成为西方古典学传播使命的主要承担者。他们编辑《东西洋考每月统纪传》等杂志，出版《外国史略》、《东西史记和合》等书籍，向中国人介绍诸如"希腊国史"、罗马历

---

* 本文为国家社科基金项目《西方古典学在中国》（编号 10BSS001）的阶段性成果。

① 玛丽·比尔德、约翰·汉德森著，董乐山译：《古典学》，沈阳：辽宁教育出版社，1998 年，第 5—6 页。

② 金尼阁：《七克》，收入《四库全书丛书存目·子部·杂家》，济南：齐鲁书社，1995 年；利玛窦：《畸人十篇》，见朱维铮主编《利玛窦中文著译集》，上海：复旦大学出版社，2001 年。

代皇帝大事纪略以及古希腊罗马文学等西方古典学知识。在中国朝野上下普遍渴求西方知识情况下，这些书报遂变成了中国人获取包括西方古典文化在内的西学新知的教科书。

一

较早传播西方古典学知识的是中文月刊《天下新闻》（Universal Gazette）。该刊于 1828 年创刊于马六甲，创办人和编辑是英华书院①院长吉德（Rev. Samuel Kidd 1799 — 1843）。杂志的主要内容包括欧洲的科学、历史、宗教伦理等。其中最引人注目的是，它连载了麦都思编写的《东西史记和合》（这是麦都思于 1829 年在巴达维亚出版的小册子）的摘要。麦都思编写此年代对照表，目的是要告诉中国读者，西洋人早在公元前 4000 年已有历史的记载，从而纠正中国人的西洋观。②麦都思的这篇文章后来被《东西洋考每月统纪传》全文转载。

瓦尔特·亨利·麦都思（Walter Henry Medhurst，1796 年——1857 年），英国伦敦会最早来华传教士之一。他先在东南亚侨中传教，后在上海定居，并在此设立了中国第一个近代出版印刷机构———墨海书馆。当时书馆所印书籍主要是宗教书，但也有一部分科技书籍。麦都思著作极多，尤其中文造诣颇深，有 59 种中文著作。其他如马来文有 6 种，英文有 27 种。③

《东西史记和合》是麦都思的早期作品，不仅反映了当时传教士对中国文化的态度，也暗示了他们的来华动机。从内容来看，《东西史记和合》的作者希望通过"和合"达成两种愿望。其一，表明西方也和中国一样有着悠久的古代文明，借此改变当时中国知识分子普遍存在的华夷之见；其二，向中国人证明自己并非"残虐性情之民"，而是和中国人一样，具有"君臣父子之伦"、"仁义礼智之性"。这就不难理解麦都思的《东西史记和合》为什么西方历史从"亚大麦"(Adam 亚当）开始，东方历史只能从传说中的盘古开辟天地开始。熟知中国文化的麦都思知道，直接向中国知识分子布道、传播福音，存在着一个极大的文化障碍，那便是自孔子创立以后在中国发展演变了两千多年以至根深蒂固的儒家文化体系。为了有效地消除这种文化障碍，唯一的方法是和合耶儒。

《东西史记和合》采取东西历史对比的格式，书中并列两栏，一栏中国，一栏欧洲，对东西历史上重大的文明创造、历史事件相比较。中国史起自盘古开天地，迄于明亡；西史起自上帝造天地，迄于英吉利哪耳慢朝（诺曼王朝）。叙述的方法，上栏叙东史，为"汉土帝王历代"，下栏述西史，为"西天古历传记"。在文章中，与盘古开天辟地相对应的是关于亚当（亚大麦）的故事；而与夏商周相对应的西史记述，大多是《圣经》等传说中的故事，如"通天塔"以及关于摩西的传说。

具有重要史学价值的是麦都思文中对埃及托勒密王朝和古罗马历史的叙述。"百多利米（托勒密十二世）名善行者，亦好学，用千万银以买书看。又治国以仁以义者，在位二十五年。"托勒密十二世死后，其女克娄巴特拉七世和其子托勒密十三世即位。不久，托勒密驱逐克娄巴特拉，恺撒侵入埃及，拥立克娄巴特拉。麦都思对此没有详细讲述，只是做了简单的结论："草利阿巴得拉（克娄巴特拉）为妇人，极美而无谋④，故灭于罗马，如是厄利革王朝亡，在位二十一年。"⑤稍后，麦都思为读者叙述评论了历代罗马皇帝的政绩概况和在位时间，包括韦伯艿（腓士敝西安）、第度（弟多）、图密善（多米弟安）、涅尔瓦（尼耳瓦）、哈德良（亚得里安）、图拉真（得拉然）、安敦

① 英华书院（Ying Wa College）由苏格兰传教士马礼逊于 1818 年创立于马六甲，其后于 1843 年迁校到香港，以中等教育为主。
② 转引自卓南生：《中国近代报业发展史》，北京：中国社会科学出版社，2002 年，第 43 页。
③ 伟烈亚力：《基督教在华传教士回忆录》，上海，1867 年，第 25 页。
④ "无谋"之说有违史实。现代学者认为，克娄巴特拉是颇有才干的埃及托勒密王朝末代女王。参见埃米尔·路德维希著，汪德春译：《一个真实的埃及艳后：克娄巴特拉七世》，北京：东方出版社，2005 年。
⑤ 麦都思：《东西史记和合》，参见爱汉者纂、黄时鉴整理：《东西洋考每月统纪传》，北京：中华书局，1997 年，第 74 页。

尼（安多尼）、康茂德（哥毛道）、卡拉卡拉（加拉加拉）一直到克劳狄二世（革劳氏）、奥里略（阿礼里安）等。[1]这堪称最早的一部中文版罗马皇帝大事年表。

很多希腊罗马的历史人物和历史事件在《东西史记和合》中首次用中文向国人作了介绍，虽然现尚未发现国人对此反应的资料，但它们在中文文献中仍有重大的资料价值。诸如尼禄、荷马、亚历山大、特洛伊战争，《东西史记和合》中首载的内容很多，值得我们世界古代史学者作进一步研究。

如提到亚历山大："亚勒山得乃厄利革大王，最善用兵。"[2]罗马史中提到了罗马帝国的开创者以及暴君尼禄（尼罗）等。罗马朝"阿厄色土为罗马始皇，周围百国，皆为之灭，故此称帝王于西天矣。"[3]"阿厄色土"显然是指罗马元老院授予屋大维的"奥古斯都"尊号。罗马最大的暴君尼禄也出现在《东西史记和合》中："尼罗为人最恶，弑母刺妻，戏烧民屋而残害善人"。[4]在谈及耶稣时，指出他是"古往今来最大之大圣贤"[5]。

《东西史记和合》的最大特色是将东西方历史上同一时期不同地区历史发展进程中的人物事件进行对比叙述，如把罗马帝国与秦帝国相提并论。采用中西历史比较的方法，可以将世界历史的真面目展现给中国的知识界，从而改变中国传统士大夫长期形成的对西方历史的偏见。黄时鉴在《东西洋考每月统纪传·导言》中指出，该书"确可被认作中文著作中比较叙述中西历史的首次尝试。"[6]这种将东西方历史等量齐观的视角是对早期来华耶稣会士历史观的一种继承，而比较历史思想资源可能源自18世纪欧洲启蒙运动的旗手和统帅伏尔泰的史学论著。伏尔泰的《风俗论》不仅注意欧洲历史，而且注意到中国、印度、波斯和阿拉伯等东方国家的历史。麦都思在该书开篇序言中写道："世间之史，万国之记茫也。读者如涉大洋荒陆，故简删之，与读者观纲目，较量东西史记之和合。读史者类，由是可观之。……善读书，看各国有其聪明睿知之人，孰为好学察之，及视万国当一家也。尽究头绪，则可看得明白。"[7]

但麦都思并非专业史学家，因此在史事选择上，有明显缺憾。比如，以中西历史发展作比较，中国百家争鸣的春秋战国时代，恰逢西方历史上古典文化的黄金时代，这本是中西比较的最好时段，而麦都思却只字未提。这也说明，麦都思的文化活动以传教为主，古典文化和其他历史知识只不过是其附带提及的传教工具和手段。

二

《东西洋考每月统纪传》(1833 ~ 1837，简称《东西洋考》)是德国传教士郭实腊(亦译郭士立，Gtzlaff, Karl Friedrich August, 1803-1851)在广州创办的中国境内第一份中文期刊，1834年迁往新加坡，1838年停刊，共出 4 卷。该刊除宗教知识外，还刊载史地哲学等内容。郭实腊编纂这样一份杂志，跟麦都思一样，其目的十分明显，是要传西学入中国，向中国人展示西方文明的优越，表明西方文化是与东方文化并存于世的两大文化，而不是如中国人所想象的是蛮夷之邦。而这样做的最终目的，便是以此来开化中国人，使之不致影响到在华的外国人的利益。他在出刊前的一个多月就曾写过一

---

① 麦都思：《东西史记和合》，参见爱汉者纂、黄时鉴整理：《东西洋考每月统纪传》，北京：中华书局，1997 年，第 87 – 88 页。

② 麦都思：《东西史记和合》，参见爱汉者纂、黄时鉴整理：《东西洋考每月统纪传》，北京：中华书局，1997 年，第 55 页。

③ 麦都思：《东西史记和合》，参见爱汉者纂、黄时鉴整理：《东西洋考每月统纪传》，北京：中华书局，1997 年，第 64 页。

④ 麦都思：《东西史记和合》，参见爱汉者纂、黄时鉴整理：《东西洋考每月统纪传》，北京：中华书局，1997 年，第 87 页。

⑤ 麦都思：《东西史记和合》，参见爱汉者纂、黄时鉴整理：《东西洋考每月统纪传》，北京：中华书局，1997 年，第 64 页。

⑥ 麦都思：《东西史记和合》，参见爱汉者纂、黄时鉴整理：《东西洋考每月统纪传》，北京：中华书局，1997 年，序言，第 16 页。

⑦ 麦都思：《东西史记和合》，参见爱汉者纂、黄时鉴整理：《东西洋考每月统纪传》，北京：中华书局，1997 年，第 4 页。

份出刊缘起，明白无误地说："虽然我们与他们（指中国人）长久交往，他们仍自称为天下诸民族之首尊，并视所有民族为蛮夷。如此妄自尊大，严重影响到广州的外国居民的利益，以及他们与中国人的交往。……（本月刊的）出版是为了使中国人知道我们的技艺、科学和准则。它将不谈政治，避免就任何主题以尖锐言词触怒他们。可有较妙的方法表达，我们确实不是蛮夷，编者偏向于用展示事实的手法使中国人相信，他们仍有许多东西要学。"①

传教士们知道中国有着悠久的重视历史的传统，所以，编纂者从创刊号起，除了序、论，几乎始终将叙述历史的文章置于首位。从创刊号开始至乙未五月（1835年6月）号，转载了《天下新闻》首发的麦都思的《东西史记和合》。郭实腊如此重视该书，目的是要让读者明白西方的历史十分悠久，有源可寻，并不逊色于中国。

在丁酉七月号上，又刊出《史记和合纲鉴》，进一步说明："自盘古至尧舜之时，自亚坦到挪亚，东西记庶乎相合，盖诸宗族之本源为一而已。盖前后异势，疏密异刑，各族继私风俗，故史记也不同，但诸国之礼，如身之有四肢，血脉相通，而疴养相关。兹史记之和合，结其联络，及通疏远焉。"②

除了《东西史记和合》，《东西洋考》还发表了基督教观念上的西洋上古史，讲到以色列、麦西（埃及）、非尼基（腓尼基）、亚书耳（亚述）、巴比伦、希腊、犹太诸古国的历史，介绍了希腊罗马的文化名人。丁酉二月刊出《经书》一文，指出："中国经书已翻译泰西之话，各人可读；但汉人未曾翻译经书也，天下无人可诵之。从来有一代之治法，必有一代之治心。向来中国人貌视外国之文法，惟各国有其文法诗书，一均令我景仰世人之聪明及其才能也。"③此文称："大清民之经书有四有五，惟泰西人之经书不胜其数，各国各话自有矣。"作者叙述了希腊罗马时代的古典著述，希腊时代，"超群卓异之史者，系希啰多都、都基帝底、洗那奉；开谕民卓异者，帝磨士体呢兼伊所嘉帝；博物君子超群，裨拉多兼亚喱士多帝利。希腊列国衰，罗马国兴，作诗超群者，为谓之味耳治兼和喇士；纂史者，利味兼大西多；有口才者，西细啰；穷理超群者，乃西呢嘉、彼利呢二人。"④

以上所列十四人译为现今通常的译名应为希罗多德、修昔底德、色诺芬、德摩斯提尼、伊索格拉底、柏拉图、亚里士多德、维吉尔、贺拉斯、李维、塔西佗、西塞罗、塞纳卡、老普林尼。

需要特别指出的是，刊于道光戊戌年正月到二月的《希腊国史略》介绍了希腊的位置、自然环境，叙述了古希腊的历史发展进程。这是第一部用中文撰著发表的希腊简史："古时夏商年间，游牧猎夫跋涉，遍地树木杂丛，山川险峻，野人或食禽兽之肉，衣皮。""当是之时，居东之列国已经向化成人，务艺大兴，见识日广，经商远谋财利，巡驶地中海，竟抵希腊国。搬移人民，教土人耕田种五谷为食，植萄藤为饮，栽橄榄为油，作金铁为刃刀耒耜矣。"⑤这段叙述虽与事实略有出入，但基本反映了希腊半岛历史的初始状态。作者还谈到了多利亚人南下的活动及方向："希腊人类或托足于欧罗巴东南方，或迁徙于亚细亚西向，沿地中海立国邦。""虽创列邦，然论其宗族，犹水之有分派，木之有分权，虽远近异势，疏密异形，要其本源，则一宗族也。"⑥这段叙述点明了希腊城邦分立和邦际间关系的一个显著特点。

这篇短文还叙述了特罗呀（特洛伊）战争的前因后果和经过。特洛伊王子拐走海伦、木马计等情节都在文章中出现了。"其事在商朝帝乙七年（前1128年）"，特洛伊"居民闭城坚守十载，虽攻城而难护也。"提到了后人尤其是荷马对这场战争的记载："骚人儒客，取此围城之情节，高

① 转引自周振鹤：《一度作为先行学科的地理学——序〈晚清西方地理学在中国的传播和影响〉》，载《书屋》2000年第8期。
② 爱汉者纂、黄时鉴整理：《东西洋考每月统纪传》，北京：中华书局，1997年，第279页。
③ 爱汉者纂、黄时鉴整理：《东西洋考每月统纪传》，北京：中华书局，1997年，第204页。
④ 爱汉者纂、黄时鉴整理：《东西洋考每月统纪传》，北京：中华书局，1997年，第204-205页。
⑤ 《希腊国史略》，爱汉者纂、黄时鉴整理：《东西洋考每月统纪传》，北京：中华书局，1997年，第312页。
⑥ 《希腊国史略》，爱汉者纂、黄时鉴整理：《东西洋考每月统纪传》，北京：中华书局，1997年，第326页。

兴吟诗作赋。……所述之言美矣而无凭据。乃何马诗翁之文辞，卓然大雅，语译华言甚难焉。"[1]

<h1 style="text-align:center">三</h1>

概而言之，19世纪前期，来华传教士对西方古典学的引介传播规模很小。整个这一时期，中国的西方古典学仍处于开始引进阶段。翻译和介绍性的文章占绝大比例，没有研究性的原创作品。

尽管如此，麦都思、郭实腊等作为已经掌握了中文并受到过基本西方史学教育和汉学训练的学者传教士，通过《东西史记和合》和《东西洋考每月统纪传》等书籍杂志介绍的的古希腊罗马历史的基本知识对当时睁眼看世界的先进中国人如魏源、徐继畬、梁廷枏等产生了程度不同的影响，成为他们撰著外国史地著作的主要参考文献之一。仅此一端，已可看出传教士传播西方古典文化的重大社会意义和历史价值。魏源的《海国图志》引用《东西洋考每月统纪传》13期，引用文章24篇，引文文字达28处。[2]另一位近代开眼看世界的伟大先驱徐继畬的代表作《瀛环志略》是一部极其严谨的世界史地学著作，书中也同样引用了《东西洋考每月统纪传》的记述。魏徐之外，精研史学的林则徐幕僚梁廷枏也是《东西洋考每月统纪传》的读者，其名著《海国四说》也有来自《东西洋考每月统纪传》的内容。

---

[1]　《希腊国史》，爱汉者纂、黄时鉴整理：《东西洋考每月统纪传》，北京：中华书局，1997年，第326页。
[2]　爱汉者纂、黄时鉴整理：《东西洋考每月统纪传》，北京：中华书局，1997年，第24页。

古蜀金面具与迈锡尼金面具之比较

冯　亚　平顶山学院

摘要：在世界考古史上，古埃及和古希腊等文明古国很早就出现了黄金面具。而在中国，三星堆和金沙遗址也同样出现了令世人瞩目的黄金面具。古代中国与古代希腊，天各一方的两个文明中心，都有黄金面具的存在。它们的造型、用途，以及所表达的文化内涵，既有相同之处，又存在一定差别。其相同之处应该是古文明之间相互交流的结果，而不同之处可能源自不同的宗教信仰和文化传统。

关键词：古蜀；迈锡尼；金面具

Abstract：In the world archaeology history, the golden masks had appeared in both ancient Egypt and ancient Greece very early. In China, Sanxingdui and Jinsha Ruins discovered the Golden Masks also. Ancient China and ancient Greece, even far from each other, the golden masks existed in both of them. There are both similarities and differences in the shape, use, as well as the expression of cultural connotation. Its similarities should be the result of exchanges between the ancient civilizations, while the differences may because of their different religions and Cultural traditions.

Keyword：Ancient Shu Kingdom, Mycenaean, Golden Mask

面具作为一种文化现象，曾在世界许多国家和地区出现过，其中包括埃及、希腊、中国、墨西哥、哥伦比亚等国家和地区，地域上涵盖了非洲、欧洲、亚洲和南美洲。但是，黄金制成的面具在古代世界并不十分普遍，只存在于有限几个古文明中心，例如：埃及的图坦卡蒙法老墓出土的黄金面罩，希腊迈锡尼氏族首领墓出土的金面具，以及中国古蜀三星堆遗址和金沙遗址发现的金面具。其中最著名最精巧的当数埃及图坦卡蒙法老的金面罩，它是古埃及人在继承两千多年面具制作工艺的基础上形成的，其上镶嵌有宝石，是雕刻师和金匠技艺的一座丰碑。[①]而迈锡尼墓葬出土的是目前所知爱琴文明中最早的金面具；古蜀金面具则是中华文明中发现的最早的金质面具。后二者均出现于青铜文明后期，且在各自文明区域内呈现出独一无二的特征，它们并不像古埃及那样很早就有制作面具的传统。因此笔者认为，古蜀金面具与迈锡尼金面具之间似乎更具可比性，它们之间的比较或许能

---

① Fred S. Kleiner, Helen Gardner, *Gardner's Art Through the Ages: A Global History*, Boston: Cengage Learning, 2011, p.75.

为我们更多地了解早期东西方文明的发展脉络提供些许启示。

一　面具的造型和用途

古蜀金面具包括：1986 年广汉三星堆遗址出土的 4 件粘于青铜人头像上的金面具，和 2001 年在成都金沙村遗址发掘出的 7 件小型纯金面具。[①]迈锡尼金面具是 19 世纪 70 年代考古学家施里曼，在古希腊迈锡尼墓葬中发现的古代部落首领的金质面具。[②]虽然古蜀金面具与迈锡尼金面具比较相似，均使用一整片黄金制成，其上并不镶嵌其它宝石作装饰，但是二者在形式、制作工艺和用途方面还是存在很多差异。

首先，就面具的造型而言，古蜀金面具体现的是抽象风格，而迈锡尼金面具却更加写实。古蜀地区的三星堆金面具，均附着于青铜人头像上，与青铜人头像一样具有夸张的造型。其尺寸与真人相似，眉毛成刀型，眉眼部镂空，鼻部突出，双耳穿孔，嘴巴的线条也凹凸分明。[③]金沙出土的金面具基本上继承了三星堆面具的风格，但尺寸比真人小很多，只有 3.74 厘米高，4.92 厘米宽，眉毛略突起，好似新月，双眼镂空，形态如梭，鼻梁高直，大嘴镂空，略呈笑意。[④]虽然金沙面具较三星堆面具而言，更具体地表现了人物的面部特征，但就其写实程度来讲，还远不及迈锡尼的金面具。迈锡尼出土的几个金面具形态各异，完全没有程式化的表现手法，嘴眼鼻等处都不留孔，为一块近似圆形的整片金箔制成。它们有的浓眉大眼，有的淡眉微现，有的面带愁容，还有的微笑浅浅。甚至每根眉毛、睫毛、胡须都做了细致地处理，以至令人似乎能从这些面具看出其主人的音容笑貌。正如施里曼发现金面具时所感受到的："我正凝视着阿伽门农的脸庞。"[⑤]

其次，从制作工艺来看，东西方基本相同，都掌握了较高水平的黄金冶炼技术。黄金大都以自然金的状态存在，而所有的自然金都是不纯的，大概包含 10% 的银和 1% 的铜。[⑥]金矿分为砂金和山金两种，无论哪种金矿，都必须先将自然金熔化或熔合才能进一步加工。[⑦]因此，中西方的金制品都是在掌握了黄金开采技术和自然金的熔炼技术后才兴起的。黄金的熔点为 1063℃，而纯铜的熔点为 1083℃，青铜由于混合了锡、铅等其它金属，其熔点比纯铜要低。中国商代，青铜冶炼技术已经高度发达，而青铜冶炼是在纯铜冶炼技术之上发展而来的，此时的炉温足以将黄金熔化，换言之，商代的金属冶炼技术已经足以冶炼黄金了。在古希腊，人们也较早地掌握了金属冶炼技术。据《荷马史诗》，火神赫淮斯托斯把铜、锡、银、金放入他的熔炉，再加上温度不一的风力鼓吹，结果练成了阿克琉斯使用的盾牌。[⑧]这说明当时的希腊人也已经掌握了不同金属的熔点和其物理属性，金属冶炼已达到较高水平。此外，在金面具成型的加工工艺上，古蜀与迈锡尼略有差别。古蜀人制作金面具，先是将纯金锤锻成金箔，然后做成与青铜人像相似的轮廓，将双眉、双眼镂空，包贴在青铜人头像上，再经过锤拓、蹭拭、剔除、粘合等工序，才制成与青铜人头像浑然一体的黄金面罩。[⑨]迈锡尼部落首领脸上的金面罩，虽然也是用薄金板敲打而成，但面罩的五官刻画地栩栩如生，且表情各异。它们应该是按照逝者本人的面部特征仿制出来的。很可能是先按照死者面部拓下个模子，再

① 成都市文物考古研究所、北京大学考古文博学院：《金沙淘珍——成都市金沙村遗址出土文物》，文物出版社，2002 年。
② （英）列昂纳德·科特勒尔：《爱琴文明探源》，卢剑波译，成都：四川人民出版社，1985 年，第 67—74 页。
③ 四川省文物考古研究所：《三星堆祭坑》，文物出版社，1999 年。
④ 成都市文物考古研究所、北京大学考古文博学院：《金沙淘珍》，文物出版社，2002 年，第 22 页。
⑤ （英）列昂纳德·科特勒尔：《爱琴文明探源》，卢剑波译，成都：四川人民出版社，1985 年，第 74 页。
⑥ R. F Tylecote, *A History of Metallurgy*, London: Institute of Materials, 1992, p.5.
⑦ 段渝：《商代金制品的南北系统》，《考古与文物》，2004 年第 2 期，第 39 页。
⑧ Homer, *Iliad*,18.465–475, trans. A.T. Murray, Loeb Classical Library Series. London and Cambridge, Mass.,1924.
⑨ 黄剑华：《三星堆出土金制品探讨》，《西南交通大学学报》，2002 年第 1 期，第 20 页。

将薄金板锤拓成模子的形状，如此制成的金面罩就与真人面部极为相似了，就像死者的遗像一般。

最后，古蜀金面具与迈锡尼金面具在用途上存在较大差异。古蜀金面具都是贴附在青铜人头像上，其用途也也是附属于青铜人的，主要用于大型祭祀场合，或者被供奉于神庙之中。有学者指出："金箔的脸面与其说是戴了一副金面具，还不如说是装点了黄金的面皮。"[1]即，金面具只是起到装饰青铜人头像的目的。另一些学者认为，面具本身与巫术息息相关，原始人在祭祀、祈年、节日活动中，广泛地使用面具，以赋予自己与神灵沟通的能力。[2]三星堆出土的青铜人像或许本身就是古代巫师的形象，他们戴着金质面具以便更好地与神灵相通。[3]在古代蜀人的观念中，黄金制品似乎与丧葬并无关系，而与社会生活中占据主导地位的重大祭祀活动密切相关。[4]这与迈锡尼出土的金面具截然不同。迈锡尼金面具正是用在丧葬礼俗中的，并且有意模仿刻画死者的面容，将金面罩覆盖在死者的脸上，仿佛他的音容笑貌永远留在世间一样。[5]今人猜测，古人之所以要将面具刻画成死者的模样，可能是基于以下两点原因：一是逝者的灵魂可以按照面具的容貌特征找到自己的躯体；二是让后人永远铭记死者的威仪。[6]古希腊的金面具应该起到的就是这两种作用。苏格拉底曾说："死亡是两种境界之一，或是灵魂与肉体俱灭，死者对任何事物都无知觉；或者如世俗所说，死亡就是灵魂从一处移居到另一处。"[7]因此，按照苏格拉底的说法，多数古希腊人是相信灵魂不灭的，他们希望为灵魂找到一个寄居之所。另外，将面罩罩在逝者的面孔上，既可以罩盖和保护面部，又可以将此作为神人合一的不朽象征。尤其是在古希腊人的宗教观念中，伟大的领袖就是神的后代，黄金打造的面罩使他们的音容笑貌永存于世，成为神人合一的永恒符号。在面具的用途上，中西金面罩之间存在较大差异，这应该与其各自的宗教信仰和文化背景有关。

二　青铜时代黄金在中西文明中的地位

黄金拥有色泽鲜亮，不易氧化，化学性质稳定，数量稀少，不易获得等特点，因此作为财富的象征，受到古今中外世人的珍爱。但在中国商代的青铜文明中，黄金并不是代表至高权位的金属；而在迈锡尼文明中，黄金已经成为王权和财富的象征。同样是在青铜文明末期，黄金在中西文明中地位存在较大差异。

中国开采和利用黄金的时间相对较晚。在新时期时代末期，人们最喜爱的是晶莹润泽的玉石，在祭祀和大型礼仪活动中所使用的也主要是玉器。同时，玉器也是当时人们身份与地位的象征。即使到了冶炼技术已经比较发达的青铜时代，黄金在中国大地上的使用也不普遍。青铜铸造的某些礼器，既是沟通人神的中介，也是人们身份等级的象征，青铜铸成的鼎更成为王权与国家的象征。即便到了青铜时代，玉器不但没有退出历史舞台，反而有进一步发展的趋势。玉器不仅被广泛应用于祭祀、礼仪、丧葬、服装配饰等方面，还用来形容人的道德品质，成为高尚节操的代表，正所谓"君子于玉比德"。在青铜器和玉器的受到尊宠的时代，金器的发展始终受到一定制约，它仅仅作为青铜器和玉器的一种配饰，起简单地装饰作用。

中国从商代后期就出现了"金"字，和一些以"金"为偏旁的字，但这些字最初并不代表黄金，而是用来指青铜时代最重要的资源"铜"。黄金的古名为"璗"，其美者曰"璆"，正所谓："黄

① 孙华：《关于三星堆若干问题的辩证》，《四川文物》，1993年第4期，第9页。

② 成都文物考古研究所编：《走进古蜀金沙村——考古工作者手记》，成都：四川文艺出版社，2004年，第44页。

③ 四川省考古研究所编：《三星堆祭祀坑》，北京：文物出版社，1999年，第443页。

④ 黄剑华：《三星堆出土黄金品质探讨》，《西南交通大学学报（社会科学版）》，2002年第1期，第20页。

⑤ （英）列昂纳德·科特勒尔：《爱琴文明探源》，卢剑波译，成都：四川人民出版社，1985年，第71—74页。

⑥ 顾朴光：《面具与丧葬礼俗》，《贵州民族学院学报》，1997年第4期，第21页。

⑦ 柏拉图：《柏拉图对话集》，北京：商务印书馆，2004年版，第53页。

金谓之鎏，其美者谓之镠"①。"鎏"和"镠"都是带有玉字旁的，最初其含义应该指代美玉。很明显，在先秦人们的观念中，并没有把黄金放在很重要的地位。直至春秋时期，这种现象仍然没有改变，文献记载和青铜铭文上的"金"还是指代铜。例如《左传》僖公十八年，"郑伯始朝于楚，楚子赐之金，既而悔之，与之盟约：'无以铸兵'。故以铸三钟。"②这说明当时的"金"还是指代"铜"的。

从考古资料来看，先秦时代中国北方出土的金质品主要为一些装饰物，如金耳饰、弓形头饰等，其唯一功能在于人体装饰。而且这些金质品大多是从相同种类的铜制品脱胎出来的，它们是作为相同种类青铜制品的艺术补充被看待和使用的，可说是相同种类青铜艺术的新发展。在安阳殷墟和藁城出土的金箔制品，不论在地位上，还是作用上，都远在青铜之下。这些金箔都是用于大型器物的装饰，仅为附件而已。从出土位置看，这些金箔既不在墓葬的中心位置，也不能与墓葬内格式制作精良的青铜器物相媲美。到目前为止，尽在中下层统治者的墓葬内发现了金箔，而在上层统治着的大型墓葬内却无金质品出土。③在三星堆文化中，金箔也同样是作为青铜人像的附属品存在的，起作用应该只是用来装饰青铜人的面皮。而且出土的青铜人像较多，而装饰有金面的只占其中少数。虽然三星堆也有金权杖出土，但是在中国古代权杖并不代表王权，"九鼎"才是至高王权的象征。中国夏、商、周用"九鼎"作为"宝鼎"象征政权，并形成了一种传统。因此，黄金在中国先秦文化中并非是至高权利和财富的象征，也没有作为等价物作流通之用，其地位应在青铜和玉之后。即便是有大量金器出土的金沙遗址，其金器也都是其它器物的装饰。④

迈锡尼同样有大量金质品出土，它曾被荷马誉为铺满黄金的地方。据考古资料，施里曼曾在迈锡尼墓葬中发现了大量黄金制品。在其中一个墓穴中发现了19具尸体，有男有女，这些尸体大多数严密覆盖着黄金。妇女和她们的金匣、金首饰葬在一起，男人旁边则放着金杯和一些兵器。其中有的妇女头上戴有金冠，其上刻有复杂的圆圈形的、螺纹形的图案。另外还有一些金质的人和野兽的小雕像。⑤在六号墓中，施里曼发现了三具男尸，他们的胸前覆盖着黄金铠甲，脸上罩着沉重的金面具。⑥由此可见，迈锡尼金器大都独立存在，其数量和重量依据墓主人的身份而有所差别。金冠冕本身就是权力和地位的象征，某些妇女头上的金冕应该与她们生前的显赫地位相关。而多数学者认为，金面罩应该是部族领袖才具有的丧葬规格，即使施里曼在6号墓中发现的罩有金面具的男尸不是阿伽门农，那他也很可能是一位国王。⑦很明显，迈锡尼的黄器并非其它器物的附属品，而是作为权力和财富的象征独立存在，它在当时希腊人的心目中应该具有无与伦比的崇高地位。

据《荷马史诗》可知，当时希腊人对黄金十分崇拜，将其视作权力和财富的象征，它也是战争中被争夺的对象。"黄金未能阻挡住死亡，捷足的阿伽门农把他杀死在河里，并夺走了他满身的黄金。""这些战马会获得数不清的奖品，谁拥有了他们，谁就不会缺少黄金。""在分取战利品时，他会尽量地拿取黄金和铜。""从这里，我要带回更多的财富，有黄金、铜、灰铁和衣着美丽的女子。"⑧类似描述还有很多，在此不多赘述，但无一例外，黄金已经被认为是最珍贵的金属，成为财富的象征。

① 李学勤主编：《十三经注疏·尔雅·释器》，北京：北京大学出版社，1999 年版，第 148 页。
② 李梦生：《左传译注》，上海：上海古籍出版社，1998 年版，第 252 页。
③ 河北省文物研究所：《藁城台西商代遗址》，北京：文物出版社，1985 年版，第 146–149 页。
④ 成都市文物考古研究所，北京大学考古文博学院：《金沙淘珍》，文物出版社，2002 年，第 19 页。
⑤ （英）列昂纳德·科特勒尔：《爱琴文明探源》，卢剑波译，成都：四川人民出版社，1985 年，第 66–67 页。
⑥ （英）列昂纳德·科特勒尔：《爱琴文明探源》，卢剑波译，成都：四川人民出版社，1985 年，第 74 页。
⑦ Fred S. Kleiner, Helen Gardner, *Gardner's Art Through the Ages: A Global History*, Boston: Cengage Learning, 2011, p.94.
⑧ Homer, *Iliad*, 2.870; 9.265; 9.280; 9.328, trans. A.T. Murray, Loeb Classical Library Series. London and Cambridge, Mass.,1924.

此外，黄金也被制成权杖，成为至高权利的代表，雅典娜"手握金权杖端坐着，大声宣判。"①

迈锡尼时代的王权是一种权力高度集中的成熟的君主制，迈锡尼的国王类似米诺人的"祭祀王"，是集宗教和世俗权力为一身的神权君主。②迈锡尼墓葬中出土的大量黄金制品，应该是迈锡尼王权的象征。虽然希腊的青铜文明时代，青铜制品也大量存在，但黄金却拥有更高的权威和地位，也更被人们所珍视和追捧。

三　面具下的文化交流

中国商代遗址中出土的黄金制品很少，而且没有像三星堆遗址和金沙遗址那样，有金面罩、金权杖、金叶、金璋等工艺精湛且内涵丰富的金质品存在。尤其金面具和金权杖，在整个商代中国包括蜀文化区都是绝无仅有的。因此有学者认为，古蜀文化中的金面具、金杖等，很有可能是从域外传入巴蜀地区的。从古代的西南夷道、蜀身毒道、滇缅道，经云南、缅甸、印度、巴基斯坦、阿富汗等地区，采借吸收了西亚近东文明的类似文化因素，而由古代蜀人按照自身的文化传统加以改造而成的，它们反映了商代中国与其它古文明中心之间的交流往来。③但另有学者认为，将三星堆文化与域外文明联系起来，其根据十分牵强。三星堆的金面罩、金杖在制作工艺、造型风格、思想内涵、功能用途等方面都与域外的那些存在很大差别。而且在巴蜀与地中海之间，并不存在"空间连续分布"的文化传播通道，与四川临近的云南、甘肃等地就没有发现"黄金面罩"和"金杖"等物存在。④

以上两种不同观点，笔者认为前一种似乎更合乎常理。因为从青铜雕像、权杖、金面罩以及相关文化因素的起源和发展上看，近东文明中的文化因素相继出现在其他文明中，并非偶然，它们是具有传播学上的意义的，这一点早为文化史学界所公认。学者们大都认为在先秦时代，中国存在一条南方丝绸路。《史记·西南夷列传》及其他古籍也或多或少地反映了先秦时期巴蜀地区有通往西南边陲的交通，如《大戴礼记·帝系》云："黄帝居轩辕之丘，娶西陵氏之女……产青阳及意。……昌意降居若水。"类似记载还见于《史记·五帝本纪》、《山海经·海内经》、《水经注·若水》等古籍。⑤但总的来看，古代文献中关于先秦时期南方丝绸之路的记载的确是语焉不详，更不系统。这主要是因为先秦巴蜀地区的文明演进相对独立，再加上地处偏远，因此，今人对它的了解很少。虽然，目前还缺乏大量考古依据来说明古蜀与地中海、近东文明之间确有联系，但种种迹象使我们有理由推测，这种联系似乎是存在的。随着考古学的不断进展，人类认识能力的不段提高，可能会有新的证据来解释目前的疑团。

① Homer, *Odyssey*, 11.567–570, trans. A.T. Murray, Loeb Classical Library Series. London and Cambridge, Mass.,1919.
② 王以欣：《迈锡尼时代的王权：起源和发展》，《世界历史》，2005 年第 1 期，第 66 页。
③ 段渝：《商代金制品的南北系统》，《考古与文物》，2004 年第 2 期，第 37 页。
④ 孙华：《四川盆地的青铜时代》，北京：科学出版社，2000 年，第 201 页。
⑤ 邹一清：《先秦巴蜀与南丝路研究述略》，《中华文化论坛》，2006 年，第 4 期。

Representations of the Other in Early Greek and Chinese Historiography

黄 洋 复旦大学

The ancient Greek and Chinese perceptions of foreign peoples invite comparison at some point. As a Chinese studying Greek history I cannot help wondering if it is by sheer coincidence that two of the most distinctive cultures in the ancient world held strikingly similar views of surrounding peoples, dubbing them 'barbarians'. These views have of course been subjects of intensive studies in their respective fields, but comparing them may at least broaden our perspective. In this discussion I propose to have a look at the ways in which foreign peoples are described in early Greek and Chinese historiography and to see if we can draw some general conclusions from the comparison.

The main texts in question are the Histories of Herodotus and the Records of the Grand Historian of Sima Qian. Both stand at the beginning of the historical tradition within their cultures. Herodotus was writing about the Persian Wars nearly two generations after that event, in the late fifth century BC. At the beginning of his narrative he states his purpose,

The historia of Herodotus of Halicarnssus is here published, so that what happened of men may not fade away in time, and the great and marvelous deeds both of the Hellenes and of the barbarians may not become inglorious, including among others the cause of their waging war to each other.

The cause or aitie which Herodotus seeks to expound extends far beyond the immediate cause of the Persian Wars. For him the fundamental causes seemed to lie much deeper, in the different nomoi or customs of different peoples. It was not without reason that Herodotus should devote almost half of his Histories, to be exact, from book one through chapter 28 of book five, to the ethnography of various peoples. He painstakingly described the habits and customs of the peoples within and around the Persian Empire, always stressing the aspects that were opposite to or different from the Greeks. One particular aspect he seemed to notice often was marriage custom and the treatment of women. The nomoi or customs of the Lydians, at one time he tells us, were not unlike those of the Greeks except that they prostituted their daughter. In particular, all the daughters of the common people (demos) in Lydia prostituted to collect money for their dowries, and continued the practice until they get married, and they chose their own husbands instead of their parents or guardians (I. 93–94). On another occasion he explains that the nomoi of the Lycians were similar to the Cretans and the Carians, but they were unique in counting their descent by their mothers' side instead of their fathers' side. Also children born of Lycian women and slave men were considered legitimate, whereas those born of Lycian men and foreign or slave women illegitimate (I. 173). This seemed to imply that the Lycian society was dominated by women rather than men, which was the opposite of the male dominated Greek polis society.

The list of such nomoi can be a long one. The Babylonians had auctioned their daughters for marriage in the past, among other peculiar customs, and no man was allowed to marry his daughter to anyone he wished. The Eneti in Illyria had similar customs, Herodotus does not fail to notice. Although this Babylonian practice had fallen into disuse, they now prostituted all the daughters of the common people who had been ill-treated and brought to ruin (I. 196). Then he mentions one custom which he considered "most shameful" (aischistos), namely that every Babylonian woman, including wealthy women, had to prostitute herself once in her lifetime in the temple of Aphrodite (I. 199).

Burial customs and the worship of gods are another area that was of great interests to Herodotus. The Persians, he noted, did not erect statues of gods, nor did they build temples and altars, and anyone who did this was considered foolish. When sacrifices were made, none of the things that were familiar to the Greeks such as libation, flute-music, the garlands and the sprinkled meal was made use of by the Persians (I. 131-2). Similarly the Scythians did not build statues, temples or altars except for their war god Ares, nor did they light fire, offer first-fruit or pour libation when they made sacrifices (IV. 59-60). When it comes to burial customs, the Massagetai, who used their wives promiscuously, sacrificed their old folks together with cattle and then ate the flesh. This they considered the happiest way of death (ta olbiotata). But if one died of disease and was buried instead of sacrificed, he was considered unfortunate (I. 216). East of the Argippaioi, a nation of bald men, lived the Issedones, who again sacrificed their dead together with sheep and ate the flesh, but they gilded the head of the dead as sacred images and made sacrifices to them 'just as the Greeks commemorated their dead' (IV. 26).

The examples I give here may seem an arbitrary selection of evidence, and they are certainly among the more extreme examples of the different nomoi of the 'barbarians' Herodotus recorded. Often his narratives are balanced and sophisticated. For example, in his Egyptian narrative he talks of a number of religious practices that the Greeks learnt from the Egyptians, and of Egyptian customs similar to the Greeks. Yet the inversion and strangeness of Egyptian customs and habits were brought out clearly. I would argue that Herodotus seems to have carefully collected these nomoi precisely to show to his Greek readers that the 'barbarians' were different from themselves. This is shown, I believe, in a revealing discussion on nomoi. After criticizing Cambyses' assault on Egyptian customs, he went on to say,

If one were to offer all men to choose the best nomoi out of all the nomoi, they would examine carefully and each of them would choose his own; and each of them is so convinced that their nomoi are far better...that all men think so about their own nomoi may be proven by a lot of evidence, and indeed in the following. Darius, after he had established his rule, called up some Greeks who were present and asked for what they would be willing to eat their fathers when they die. They replied that they would not do such a thing for anything. After this Darius called up some Indians, called Kallatians, who did eat their fathers, and asked, while the Greeks were present and were learning what was said through an interpreter, what they would take to burn their fathers with funeral-fire when they died. They exclaimed aloud and forbade him to speak such language. Such are the beliefs of men, and in my judgment is right when he says in a poem that nomos is king of all.

To be sure, this serious discussion proves that Herodotus had deep respect for the nomoi of different peoples, but it is precisely this respect that adds seriousness to the matter. Like a tourist, as James Refield has put it, he set out to discover and collect the nomoi of the foreigner, and compared them with those of his own, only to be convinced of the superiority of his own. 'Thus cultural relativism becomes ethnocentric and serves to reinforce the tourist's own norms' (James Refield 1985). In a more systematic treatment François Hartog has come to the conclusion that Herodotus' ethnographic narrative amounts to 'a rhetoric of alterity' (une rhétorique de 'l'altérité), a mirror through which the Greeks could see themselves more clearly (Hartog 1980).

In the political arena the differences between the barbarians and the Greeks are also brought to light through narrating the various behaviour of barbarian kings. In particular the madness of Cambyses and the hybris of Xerxes must have startled the Greek reader.

Compared to Herodotus' Histories, Sima Qian's Records of the Grand Historian is more ambitious. It covers the history of the areas seen as the Middle Kingdoms from the beginning down to his own time, i.e. the end of the second and beginning of the first centuries BC, but it is much more than a narrative along the chronological line as it also includes detailed treatises on a variety of human activity such as rituals, music, law, the calendar, astronomy and the economy. Like Herodotus, Sima Qian was interested in the surrounding peoples, and wrote individual chapters of narratives on them in his monumental work. The peoples that received special treatment included the Xiongnu in the north, the Southern Yue, the Eastern Yue, the Koreans in the northeast, the Southwestern Yi ('Southwestern barbarians') and the Da Wan in the west. It is worth noting that the historian arranged these narratives in the category of 'biographies' (zhuan), which contained mostly biographies of individuals of secondary importance or statuses and which was separate from the categories of 'annals' (benji) or 'genealogies' (shijia). The latter were exclusively preserved for the history of the Middle Kingdoms. Unlike Herodotus, Sima Qian was not so much interested in the customs of these peoples, but was mainly concerned with their relations with the Middle Kingdoms, in particular with their political history and their diplomatic ties and wars with the Han Empire. However, he did apply the term "barbarians" to them generally, and he treated them somewhat differently according to their relations to the Han Empire. The Yue, the Southwestern barbarians and the Koreans were treated as less barbarous as they were brought into the Chinese world order through the double means of diplomacy and war, as vassals who paid tribute to the Han imperial court. Only those kings or rulers who rebelled or tried to break away from the Chinese world were treated harshly. The events were narrated in such a way as to convey the sense that it was natural for the barbarians to be subordinate to the Chinese. Hence the political and cultural superiority of the Chinese was established. For Sima Qian the archetypal barbarian was the Xiongnu, a nomadic people in the North of China, who repeatedly devastated the Chinese regions and who never submitted to the Chinese rule, and whose customs and habits he did describe in detail,

...They migrate following water and grass, and they do not build cities and do not live a sedentary life or engage in farming, yet each of them has his allotment of land. They do not make use of writing and use the spoken word as binding promises. Their children can ride sheep and shoot birds and rats with bows...Their soldiers can bend bows, and all of them are armed horsemen. Their custom is that when in abundance they follow their herds, but when in need everyone of them learns to fight in order to invade and attack, for this is their nature...They attack when in advantage and retreat when in disadvantage, and are not ashamed of fleeing. When there is profit they do not care about rites and morals. Everyone else under the king lives on the meat of the livestock, wears its hides and woven hair. The strong eat the best food, while the elderly eat whatever is left. They esteem the strong and despise the elderly and the weak. When the father dies, the son marries his step-mother; and when brothers die, they marry their wives. (《史记·匈奴列传》)

It is not difficult to see that the habits and customs that Sima Qian singled out were directly opposed to the Chinese ideal of living on farming and observing filial piety which for the ancient Chinese were perhaps two of the most important symbols of civilized life.

In rendering the surrounding peoples as barbarians both Herodotus and Sima Qian were following existing traditions in their own cultures. In Greece there are grounds to believe that image of the barbarian as opposed to the civilized Greeks began to be drawn from the beginning of the Archaic period, for example, in the description of the Cyclops in the Odyssey. If there is still some doubt about this then during and immediately after the Persian Wars the barbarian figure emerged clearly in the Greek mind. The Persian Wars, as one commentator puts it, produced 'a new definition of the difference between Greeks and barbarians' (Yvon Thébert 1980), and the Persians of Aeschylus, staged in 472 BC, staged the barbarian as opposed to the Greek to the Athenian public powerfully, and from the mid–fifth century BC onwards, the hostility between the barbarians and the Greeks became a favourite theme in the visual arts, displayed in public on the walls of temples and public buildings.

In China the picture is very much the same. The differentiation between the Chinese and the surrounding barbarians had already appeared in earlier writers. In the early third-century BC text Xunzi it is said that 'all the states of China (夏) share the same territorial zones (fu) and the same customs; the different barbarians (蛮、夷、戎、狄) share the same territorial zones, but have different institutions' (《荀子・政论》). The words for 'different barbarians' mentioned here were terms that originally denoted peoples of different regions surrounding the Chinese world, but came to denote 'barbarians' generally and were sometimes used interchangeably. They were seen as generally inferior to the Chinese politically and culturally. Thus Confucius (551 — 479 BC) said that 'even if the barbarians (夷 狄) had kings, they are still inferior to the several Chinese states (夏) when they do not have kings' (《论语・八佾》). Mencius (372–289 BC) was also unequivocal, 'I have heard of transforming the barbarians by Chinese, but never of transforming the Chinese by barbarians.' (《孟子・滕文公上》)

So what can we make out of this comparison, preliminary and superficial as it is? Both Herodotus and Sima Qian were writing at a time when repeated large- scale clashes with the outside world took place and when there was ever more urgent need to understand and to grasp this dangerous and largely unknown world conceptually. Through their historical writings Herodotus and Sima Qian presented to their compatriots for the first time a full picture of the world which was essentially divided into two parts, i.e. the Greeks or Chinese and the barbarians, whose geographical, political and cultural borders were delineated as clearly as possible. The barbarians were seen as fundamentally different from and sometimes directly opposed to the Greeks or Chinese with their different customs and habits and their aggressiveness (Persians and Xiongnu). It has been argued that Herodotus and Sima Qian were among the more enlightened of their contemporaries and were free from prejudice in their presentations of foreign peoples. They may appear to be so, but there can be no doubt that in their narratives of foreign peoples they chose to emphasize certain aspects and configured their narratives in such a way that what appeared to be results of inquiries and objective description was in essence more subtle representations of the other than blunt statements in other types of texts.

Conceptualizing and representing the other is of course essentially about the self, about constructing self– identity. Jonathan Hall has called this aspect of identity as 'oppositional identity' (Hall 1997). Through their writings, their narratives on foreign peoples, through knowing the outside world, Herodotus and Sima Qian had contributed to the ongoing process of the construction of ethnic and cultural identity in a way that could not be replaced by writings other than history.

略论西方古代自然法学说与《韩非子》思想之比较

刘　亮　北京师范大学

摘要：《韩非子》中法令因循道理自然的主张与西方古代自然法（Natural Law）学说设立高于人定法的原则，在结构上有相近之处，这一点已为黄裕宜先生强调。除此之外，两者在特征上差异显著。如西方古代自然法学说的更高原则能够评判现行法可否具备法律效力，含有永恒不变的确切内容及伦理道德上固定的价值倾向。《韩非子》的道理自然则不具备对现行法可否具备效力的评判力量，其学说仅将其作为无强制力的规劝，不含永恒不变的确切内容与伦理道德上固定的价值倾向等。这一定程度上反映了中国传统思维与西方逻辑思维的差别。

关键词：自然法；《韩非子》；永恒原则

Abstract：Both the thoughts of *Han Fei* Zi and Natural Law in the Greek and Roman period claim that the human-made laws should follow certain principles. But from other angels, there are many differences between them. For example, the theories of Natural Law in the Greek and Roman period claim that those human-made laws, which go against Natural Justice, should not have their validity. They also claim that Natural Justice is eternal. While *Han Fei Zi* suggests that "Dao", "Li" and the nature cannot judge the law's validity. Yet is there no eternal principle in the thought of *Han Fei Zi*. We can find the differences between the deductive inference from the Western and the historical reason in traditional China.

Keywords：Natural Law, Han Fei Zi, Eternal Principle

通过与法律实证主义（Positive Law）及自然法学作比较，探求《韩非子》法观念特点的方法，已为陈汉钦、戴东雄、陈弱水、耿云卿、黄裕宜等先生所采用[1]。耿云卿先生所著《先秦法律思想与自然法》中，认为先秦法家思想大体上"相当于西洋的'法律实证主义'（Positive Law）的主张，

---

[1] 参见陈汉钦：《韩非的社会思想》，《新社会科学季刊》1934年第一卷第2期；戴东雄：《从法实证主义之观点论中国法家思想》，台北：三文印书馆有限公司，1989，页41-47；郭沫若，王元化等著，傅杰选编：《韩非子十二讲》，北京：华夏出版社，2008，页232-233；耿云卿：《先秦法律思想与自然法》，台北：台湾商务印书馆股份有限公司，1982，页114-117，黄裕宜：《〈韩非子〉的规范思想——以伦理、法律、逻辑为论》，台北：花木兰文化出版社，2009，页132-143。

尤其与奥斯丁（John Austin）的分析法学派（Analytical jurisprudence）思想相近似，而与自然法思想正相冲突，完全立于反对之地位。"[1]耿先生将自然法与实证法比对下的一些相异之处，作为分析先秦法家的参照尺度。此尺度一端是自然法，另一端是实证法。有关法与道德的关系上，自然法强调法与道德必然联系，实证法则否认这种联系。在对法概念的称述上，自然法认为"法律乃应乎宇宙之自然，为人类理性之表征"[2]；实证法则认定法律为"统治者所制定公布的命令"[3]。有关现行法效力的评判上，自然法强调现行法之上有权威与效力更高的自然法，并以之作为评判现行法优劣善恶及是否有效的标准；实证法则主张只有国家确立的现行法才具有法律效力，而不问此现行法是否合于自然正义、天理人情或民族精神等，亦即"恶法亦法"（No Law is unjust）。耿先生看来，包括《韩非子》在内的先秦法家思想从上述这几个方面考察，都明显接近实证法那一端[4]。李增先生所著《先秦法家哲学思想：先秦法家法理、政治、哲学》中，则将主张"宪律制度必法道"与"道生法"的齐法家归入"自然法系"[5]，将包括《韩非子》在内晋法家思想，归入了与自然法相对极的位置上。就《韩非子》与自然法的关系而言，李先生与耿先生观点基本一致。

　　这一观点为黄裕宜先生质疑。黄先生在著作《〈韩非子〉的规范思想——以伦理、法律、逻辑为论》中，强调《韩非子》中法的"因自然"原则"符合自然法说以为法的存立之基础基于天道自然的条理意义"。黄先生看来，"《韩非子》的'道'类似于芝诺（Zeno）的'自然'概念"，韩非学说主张"立法必须考量'因自然'的客观基础"，所以"《韩非子》的法就其立法的客观基础或其学归本于黄老而言，确实为自然法的主张"[6]。

　　本文尝试于此基础上，讨论《韩非子》中法令因循道理自然的主张在与西洋古代自然法学说相比之下彰显的某些尚不引人关注的特点，并期望以此为途径，了解《韩非子》作者那个时代中国人法观念的某些特征。谬误之处，诚求斧正。

西方古代自然法学说的某些典型特征

　　这里所称"西方古代自然法"者，是指基督教及以其教义为基础的法观念兴起之前，那些被今人归为"自然法"的观念与学说。思想观念的流变具有相当的过程，故其时间边界难于作出清晰划分。从讨论的便利着眼，本文暂且将查士丁尼《国法大全》作为一个假定的界限，《国法大全》完成之后的自然法学说不再作为讨论的主要内容。此外，笔者有关西洋古代自然法的概括性讨论，并非主张这些不同思想家内容繁复各异的学说是一个统一的体系，或存在"一部历史能够描摹单一而统一的自然法传统"[7]。此处仅是试图在其各自的内容中选取有代表性者，归纳出其局部的某些典型特征。当然，这些特征应属"理念型"（ideal type）的存在。

　　有学者看来，古代自然法的思想渊源可以追溯到古代希腊剧作家索福克勒斯（Sophocles）的《安提戈涅》[8]。其剧本中有如下内容：

---

① 《先秦法律思想与自然法》，页114。
② 《先秦法律思想与自然法》，页2。
③ 《先秦法律思想与自然法》，页119。
④ 《先秦法律思想与自然法》，页118–120。耿先生认为法家思想于此尺度下具有四项特征：主张法律与道德的分离；主张法律是由政府公布；法律必有强制力及制裁性；法的权威性不容批评质疑。这些特征都更接近于法实证主义。
⑤ 李增：《先秦法家哲学思想：先秦法家法理、政治、哲学》，台北：国立编译馆，自序，页7。
⑥ 《〈韩非子〉的规范思想——以伦理、法律、逻辑为论》，页135–136，142–143。
⑦ 登特列夫：《自然法》，北京：新星出版社，2008，新版导言，页13。
⑧ 参见《自然法》，导论，页3；乔治·萨拜因：《政治学说史》上卷，上海：上海人民出版社，2008，页59–60。

正义，并不是出自于这些人定法的规定。

我也不认为你，一个尘世的凡人，

能够一下子就取消和践踏

永恒不变的不成文神法。

神法的存在非一天两天，

它们永不消亡，也无人知道它们是何时出现的。

　　他们认为这一段文字能够作为古代自然法学说的思想渊源，是因其已经涉及到能够作为其古代自然法学说构成要件的一些特征：一是将"法"一分为二，即人定法与"神法"的区分，并承认其两者可能存在冲突。二是主张两者出现冲突之时，"神法"的权威高于人定法。三是认为"神法"自它"不知何时"出现之后，即"永不消亡"。我们在斯多葛学派及其后主张"普世的自然法"（common law of nature）的诸多古代学说中，都能够寻得这些面向上的特征。

　　自然法与人定法分离，被以乔治·萨拜因为代表的学者们解释为一个步步为营的过程。海因里希·罗门（Heinrich A. Rommen）所著《自然法的观念史和哲学》中称："希腊人看来，所有的法律都盖有神的印章"①。罗氏将其用以描述人定法与"神法"未被清楚区分的时代。希腊化时代的斯多葛派提出法的两个层次，亦即"城邦的习惯法和更加完善的自然法"。乔治·萨拜因将这一贡献称为"斯多葛思想的增量"②。罗马法律人在这一方向上所作的贡献为后人所铭记。对他们而言，法可以被分为市民法、万民法与自然法，但自然法与万民法在相当长的一个时期内并无清楚的界限。如盖尤斯（Gaius）在著作中提到：

　　　每一个民族为他们自己创立的法是他们所属城邦本身所有的法，被称为市民法，也就是本城邦自己的法。相反，自然理性在所有人之间建立的法，由所有的民族平等遵守，被称为万民法，就像说所有民族所适用的法。③

　　在这一语境里，万民法之成立，基于自然理性，而非罗马法所能涵盖的范围；且其已经脱离了其作为实然的现世法律，进入了理想状态。如许特征同为斯多葛思想家眼中"普世的自然法"所具备。乌尔比安（Ulpiannus）的大著中则可发现对这两者试图加以区别的用意：

　　　万民法是全体人类使用的法。显而易见它与自然法相区别……

　　　根据自然法，一切人生而自由，既不知有奴隶，也就无所谓释放。但奴隶制一旦在万民法中建立起来，接着也就产生了释放的善举。④

　　上述乌氏关于奴隶制度的观点，为查士丁尼《法学总论》所继承。今天看来，将实际中所施行的人定法与理念中所设定的自然法（或高于人定法的正义观念等）加以区别，是古代自然法学说的第一项典型特征，也是其他典型特征得以彰显的基础所在。

　　"神法"的权威高于人定法的思想，与古代普世自然法学说主张 Ius naturale（有学者译为"自

---

① 海因里希·罗门：《自然法的观念史和哲学》，上海：三联书店，2007，页4。

② 《政治学说史》上卷，页195。

③ *Digest*. 1. 1. 9.；译文引自《学说汇纂》第一卷，北京：中国政法大学出版社，2008，页13。

④ *Digest*. 1. 1. 1. 4；Digest. 1. 1. 4. 参见《学说汇纂》，页6–8，译文有改动。

然法"，有译为"自然正义"）高于人定法，并得以评判人定法可否具备效力（validity）接近。后者则是其学说的第二项典型特征。西塞罗（Cicero）曾强调"国家实施'有害'的法规，理所当然不配称为法律，因为这种法规无异于一伙强盗在其集团内部所可能制定的规则"①。这与前文所引"我也不认为你，一个尘世的凡人，能够一下子就取消和践踏，永恒不变的不成文神法"有着极其相似的立场。其后法学家圣·奥古斯丁（St. Augstione）所倡世俗法律若与"上帝之法"相悖，则不具有任何效力②之主张，看上去似乎与之一脉相承。后人将其归为一句广为人知的成语：恶法非法。

第三项典型特征在于，Ius naturale 的恒久不变，以及此种永恒原则具备确定的内容，或确定的价值倾向。索福克勒斯在其另一部作品《俄狄浦斯》中写道："法律诞生于天堂的最高层，并非由凡人所创造，遗忘不会使之沉寂，因为上帝赋予它们强大的永恒力量。"③由此，在"普世的自然法"学说尚未成型之前，希腊人则有主张"神法"恒久不易的观念。斯多葛学派的思想家看来，普遍适用于所有人，并且永世不变的自然法中，包含着如"人人平等"等确切的内容。在其看来，"人在本质上是平等的；因性别、阶级、种族或国籍不同而对人进行歧视的做法是不正义的，是与自然法背道而驰的。"④西塞罗的思想中，同样可以发现对永恒规章的承认："真正的法律乃是……具有普遍的适用性并且是不变而永恒的。……任何时候任何民族都必须遵守它。"⑤这位伟大的法学家列举出反抗侵略的自卫规则与对欺诈行为的禁止等作为"真正的法律"的确切内容⑥。查士丁尼《法学总论》写道：

> 各民族一体遵守的自然法则是上帝神意制定的，因此始终是固定不变的。至于每一国家为自身制定的法律则经常变动，其变动或由于人民的默示同意，或由于以后制定的其他法律。⑦

与此同时，《法学总论》中的自然法，包含着正义、平等、自由及"给予每个人它所应得的"⑧等具体内容。

对西方古代自然法学说而言，其"自然"的意涵与我们今天日常用语中所称的"自然"有不同。它包含着某些道德法则。这些道德法则同样具备法的效力，其地位高于人定法，甚至能够评判人定法可否具备效力。对古代自然法思想家而言，此种自然法则超越了所有的地域与民族，也超越了时间的流变。不同时期，不同的思想家或许各自所主张的自然法则内容不同，但就其绝大多数而言，都有着确定的内容，以及确切的价值倾向。

"比较"语境下的《韩非子》思想

一般情况下，将诸如自然法与人定法的区分、普世的永恒原则径自作为研究韩非学说的观察角

---

① *De Legibus*, Bk. II. v. 13. 译文引自 E·博登海默：《法理学：法律哲学与法律方法》，北京：中国政法大学出版社，2004，页 19。
② *Basic Writings of Saint Augstine*, II. p.51. 译文同上书，页 29。
③ 约翰·梅西·赞恩：《西方法律的历史》，西安：陕西师范大学出版社，2009，页 94。
④ 参见《法理学：法律哲学与法律方法》，页 22。
⑤ *Republic*, III, 22. 译文引自《政治学说史》上卷，页 209。
⑥ *De Re Publica*, transl. C.W. Keyes（Loeb Classical Library ed.，1928），Bk. III. Xxii.；*De Inventione*, transl. H. M. Hubbel, Loeb Classical Library ed.，1913, Bk. II. liii. 61; *De Officiis*, transl. W. Miller, Loeb Loeb Classical Library ed.，1913, Bk. III. xvii; 参见《法理学：法律哲学与法律方法》，页 18。
⑦ 查士丁尼：《法学总论》，北京：商务印书馆，1989，页 11。
⑧ 《法学总论》，页 5。

度，可能会引起"此种讨论有何意义"的质疑。毕竟这些观念出自古代的欧洲。但是在"比较"的语境中，西方古代自然法如许典型特征的参照之下，《韩非子》的法观念中一些昔日未曾引人注重的性质特征，则会迅速地呈现于读者。这或许可以用来回答上述意义上的质疑。

一、关于法的层次

黄裕宜先生认为《韩非子》思想与自然法的相符之处，在于立法原则上对道理自然的因循。笔者以为这里面包含着两个重要的问题，一是《韩非子》中"道"、"理"与"法"的区分；一是其"法"与道理自然的关联。

就第一个问题而言，韩非学说中"道"、"理"与"法"的区分与古代自然法将 Ius 划分层次的作法有一定程度的接近。如果认为《韩非子》中的"道"指万物的情实及其渊源，"理"则之具体事物的情实及其性质状态，"法"是官府公布的规章与命令等，那么人类的活动规则与程式即被包括在三者的意涵之内。仅就这一角度，"道"、"理"与"法"构成了人类活动规则的不同层次，这是其与西方古代自然法接近的因素。但与西方思想家开始有意地对不同法则加以辨别相比，作为万物的状态、变动及其渊源总和的"道"、"理"实属迎合先秦诸子的流行用法，而非专指规则。故《韩非子》并无从事此种"专为规则划分层次"的自觉。这可以说是相似的结构之下两者的本质差异所在。这一点同样适用于韩非学说中法与势、术的关系。其势治、术治思想中同样包含规则的因素，这些"规则"与法又构成不同层次。但势、术绝不完全等同于规则。《韩非子》既从未提出法势术在规则这一角度上具有一定的同质性，也就无所谓自觉划分规则之间不同层次的意识。

第二问题则较为复杂。首先应当承认，《韩非子》中的"法"对道理的因循，与西方古代自然法也有接近之处。若主张韩非学说中"法"具备对道理自然的因循特征，则可以从两方面找到依据。其一，《韩非子》对此有明确的主张。如《大体》篇称：

　　守成理，因自然。……因道全法，君子乐而大奸止。[1]

其二是今天看来，《韩非子》中的"道理"观念与法观念具有某种因循关系。在"阶段性地变化"这一特征上就更是如此。《解老》称："短长、大小、方圆、坚脆、轻重、白黑之谓理。理定，而物易割也"[2]。又称："定理有存亡，有死生，有盛衰。夫物之一存一亡，乍生乍死，初盛而后衰者，不可谓常。"[3]文中所称"坚脆、轻重、白黑"方面，可理解为理在一定阶段内相对的稳定性，其所称述的事物若超越了这种阶段上内稳定，则体现出变化特征（如文中指出的存亡、生死、盛衰）。这一角度上，"法"同样表现出"理"阶段性的变化：《解老》称："故以理观之，……治大国而数变法，则民苦之。是以有道之君贵静，不重变法。"[4]可见其依据理阶段上的稳定特性，主张特定情势下应保持法的稳定。《五蠹》称："世异则事异"，"事异则备变"[5]指出事物之"理"超越阶段所出现的变化，以及应对此种变化的措施："不期修古，不法常可"[6]；《心度》篇亦称"法与时移而禁与能变"[7]。由此，《韩非子》中"法"应因循道理自然的主张不但存在，且已成为其道理论

---

① 陈奇猷：《韩非子集释》，上海：上海人民出版社，1974，页513。李增先生认为这一部分内容应属《慎子》，而非《韩非子》，参见《先秦法家哲学思想：先秦法家法理、政治、哲学》，页402。
② 《韩非子集释》，页377。
③ 《韩非子集释》，页369。
④ 《韩非子集释》，页355。
⑤ 《韩非子集释》，页1042。
⑥ 《韩非子集释》，页1040。
⑦ 《韩非子集释》，页1135。

与有关"法"的某些现实主张（如上述"定法"、"变法"等）相互关联的纽带。仅从这一点上，《韩非子》与西方古代自然法学说主张一切法规皆须符合普遍而永恒的"自然正义"在结构上有相近之处。

但只要进一步加以辨别，仍会发现两者的显著差别。西方古代自然法学家将"自然法"作为评判各类"人定法"可否具备法律效力的标准。韩非学说中"因自然"的法观念并无此种法律效力方面的评判力。其说明确提倡维护现行法的权威与强制力，认为对现行法令的批评质疑有害于君国，主张严惩。《问辩》篇称："明主之国，令者，言最贵者也；法者，事最适者也。言无二贵，法不两适，故言行而不轨于法令者必禁。"[1]《五蠹》篇称："儒以文乱法"[2]；又称："是故乱国之俗，其学者，则称先王之道，以籍仁义、盛容服而饰辩说，以疑当世之法，而贰人主之心。"[3]《韩非子》强调世俗的毁誉与法令赏罚之间在价值观上具有相冲突的部分。两者之间，它明确倾向于在其看来能够富国强兵的现行法令这一方。法律的效力只应该由君主以制定、废止与修改的方式决定。王邦雄、蔡英文等先生对此都有关注，蔡先生概括其为"价值一元论"[4]。遵守并承认法令具备完全的效力，无论何时都是全体臣民面对君主制定的法令被强迫保持之态度。另一方面，"因道全法"、"因自然"等主张，不能成为法可否具备效力的评判标准，而属无强制力的规劝，更倾向于法的效果（efficacy）。韩非学说虽未具有区分应然的效力与实然的效果，但从其"君子乐而大奸止"等描述可见，"因自然"之类主张更倾向于效果而非效力。换言之，其学说意在表达即使最为荒诞的法令都具备完全的应然效力，只是它们或许不会收到效果，或不会收到好的效果。比方说，即使最为恶劣的暴政法规之下，统治者也不能完全处于恣意妄为的状态——譬如强令治下的人民像天使一样长出翅膀。因为这违反了客观的自然律。综合看来，其学说中强制力是法令所具，规劝所无；"因自然"、"因道全法"则属后者。

二、关于永恒原则

西方古代自然法学说的典型特征提示我们，《韩非子》中含有如前者有关永恒不易的自然法则那般不会改变并且内容确切的原则吗？

首先，《解老》篇提出了近于恒定不变的"常"这一概念：

> 夫物之一存一亡，乍生乍死，初盛而后衰者，不可谓常。唯夫与天地之剖判也俱生，至天地之消散也不死不衰者谓"常"。而常者，无攸易，无定理。无定理，非在于常所，是以不可道也。圣人观其玄虚，用其周行，强字之曰"道"，然而可论。故曰："道之可道，非常道也"。[5]

文中的"常"是指一种有始无终的存在，这就与西方古代所谓aeternitas所指的无终始之永恒有差异。"常"出现以后，则具备了永恒不变的特性。只是《韩非子》并未将任何确切的内容放入"常"中。在其看来可以用语言描述的"定理"，其成立具有起点和终点，即阶段性；"常"有起点而无终点，不属于定理范围，不能为语言所表述。"至天地之消散也不死不衰者"即否认了所有随着人类同时出现，同时灭绝的概念（如"圣人"、"赏罚"等）具备"常"的性质。

---

① 《韩非子集释》，页898。
② 《韩非子集释》，页1057。
③ 《韩非子集释》，页1078。
④ 参见王邦雄：《韩非子的哲学》，台北：东大图书公司，1983，页123–124；蔡英文：《韩非的法治思想及其历史意义》，台北：文史哲出版社，1986，页29–35。
⑤ 《韩非子集释》，页369。

此外，《解老》中描述"道"的特点："稽万物之理，故不得不化；不得不化，故无常操"；其指明"道"的变化特征，否认其中存在恒定不变的因素，这也与前述内容一致。韩非学说的具备确切内容的因素皆属"阶段性地变化"——这也是其历史观的一项显著特点。

三、关于价值倾向

韩非学说中的道理自然，都是事物客观的性质与规律，不存在价值上的固定倾向。这与西方古代自然法学说将具有普遍力量的道德法则赋予"自然"之中又具有本质不同。首先，"道"不具备价值倾向。《解老》篇称：

> 道，与尧、舜俱智，与接舆俱狂，与桀、纣俱灭，与汤、武俱昌……凡道之情，不制不形，柔弱随时，与理相应。万物得之以死，得之以生；万事得之以败，得之以成。道譬诸若水，溺者多饮之即死，渴者适饮之即生；譬之若剑戟，愚人以行忿则祸生，圣人以诛暴则福成。故得之以死，得之以生，得之以败，得之以成。[1]

王晓波先生所著《道与法：法家思想和黄老哲学解析》中认为，"老子把好事都往'道'上揽，把坏事都推到'不道'，……韩非则将老子具有价值判断的'道'，改造成'不制不形'的客观规律的'道'，'道'是'道'，'不道'也是'道'"[2]。引文通过中将智狂、生死、成败、福祸等价值上相对立的内容同时归入"道"的支配范围，表达出作者或许意在强调其语境中的"道"不具有价值倾向。

其次，其学说中的"理"在这一点上与"道"一致。《解老》称："理，成物之文也"[3]，"凡理者，方圆、短长、粗靡、坚脆之分也"[4]，又称："短长、大小、方圆、坚脆、轻重、白黑之谓理。理定，而物易割也。"[5]理属具体事物不同角度下的客观性质、规范，本身并无价值与伦理上固定的规定及限制。

再次，《韩非子》语境中人好利自为的"计算之心"，同样被排除了固定的价值倾向以及伦理内容上的判断。韩非学说一方面主张对此种人性加以因循利用，建立有序的社会："凡治天下，必因人情；人情者，有好恶，故赏罚可用；赏罚可用，则禁令可立而治道具矣"[6]；另一面则希望同样通过法令赏罚对此种人性可能带来的危险（即好利自为可导致人的争夺，从而出现如《五蠹》所称"不免于乱"的状态）加以防止："正明法，陈严刑，将以救群生之乱，去天下之祸，使强不凌弱，众不暴寡，耆老得遂，幼孤得长，边境不侵，君臣相亲，父子相保，而无死亡系虏之患。此亦功之至厚者也。"[7]在《韩非子》那里，此种计算与避就行为无伦理价值上的具体内容。计算与避就行为的一个显著特点是随环境而变化（如《五蠹》篇反复列举的那样），排除了先验的、固定的善恶存在。这一点亦为高柏园、王晓波、蒋重跃等诸位先生所主张[8]。

韩非学说与西方古代自然法在有关自然的价值倾向上的区别，一定程度上仍是其相差异的历史

---

① 《韩非子集释》，页365–366。
② 王晓波：《道与法：法家思想和黄老哲学解析》，台北：国立台湾大学出版中心，2009，页10。
③ 《韩非子集释》，页365。
④ 《韩非子集释》，页369。
⑤ 《韩非子集释》，页377。
⑥ 《韩非子集释》，页996。
⑦ 《韩非子集释》，页248。
⑧ 王晓波：《儒法思想论集》，台北：时报文化出版事业有限公司，1983，页194；参见高柏园：《论劳思光先生对韩非哲学之诠释》，《淡江人文学刊》1999（4）；蒋重跃：《韩非子的政治思想》，页133。

观所致。《韩非子》主张一种阶段式的历史观，其将历史设定为不同阶段，阶段内的历史具有某种稳定性，超越了这一阶段，稳定则被变化所取代。如《五蠹》称"上古竞于道德，中世逐于智谋，当今争于力气。"[①]历史的总体，必涵盖着不同的阶段，故有明确的变化特征——《五蠹》称"世异则事异"[②]。这与道理论所描述的抽象的稳定与变化一以贯之：理"有存亡，有死生，有盛衰"，是阶段性的变化；道"稽万物之理，故不得不化；不得不化，故无常操"[③]，因其涵盖了不同的理，表现出明确的变化无常、"不制不形"[④]（即不受特定框架的限制）特征。假如《韩非子》中的"道"受到（如自然法所主张的那种）具有固定性的道德伦理[⑤]上的限制，则与其学说的历史观与道理论整体相悖。西方自然法思想则坚信变化不息的历史中存在着永恒不变的原则，而正是此种不变的原则，作为宇宙运行的规律，指导和评判着包括人类活动在内的各种具体事物的运动变化。永恒不变的原则被认为是真理，其成立不证自明，在特定角度上处于自然法理论的预设地位。

结　语

综上所述，《韩非子》中主张法因循道理自然的观念，虽与西方古代自然法为人定法设置更高原则的思想有某些相近的结构，但双方在法则的层次划分、道理自然（或 Ius naturale）可否用以评判现行法效力、是否含有永世不变的确切内容、是否含有道德伦理上的固定倾向这几个方面看来，都相去甚远。韩非学说一面强调现行法的权威地位与强制力，一面将法令因循道理自然的主张作为一种无保证的规劝；其认为法令随时代而变，视具体情势而定；制定法令既无不变的原则，又无固定的伦理道德限制。如此，立法者则可假"变化"之名，行其所欲——此即推导出如郭沫若所称"只要于人主有利，什么坏事都可以做"的观点[⑥]。"法"终沦为工具，用以贯彻反复无常而又恣无忌惮的君主意志。这与西方古代自然法思想所强调现行法之上永恒不变的更高原则，及其向此原则上诉的权利等理念冰炭难容。

这些特征上的差别的背后，有着传统中西思维方式的不同。古典时代及其之前的西方学者对于法学、历史的思考，多立基于演绎思维的传统上。此传统一项显著的特点在于逻辑的起点是不证自明的公理，而结论是由公理出发，按照符合逻辑（logic）的思路加以推求。西方历史上，逻辑思维在从数学到法学的诸多领域都有所贯彻。自然正义对人定法可否存在效力的评判，同样遵循此种"A"是"A"，"A"不是"非A"的思路。其另一项显著特点，是探求那些永世不变的存在（being），其认为只有这种永恒成立的才是知识（episteme）[⑦]，特定情势之下才得以成立的，则不能算作知识，只能称为"意见"（opinion）；而那些不证自明的公理（Axiom），其成立必不以时空或情势的变化为转移。自然法学中的核心原则永世不易，放之四海而皆准，同样是逻辑思维的表征。《韩非子》所表现出的思维方式则与之迥异。其"世异则事异"，"事异则备变"的命题，强调事物处于运动之中，处于一定的历史情势之下，故对于事物是非对错等的评判也是放在历史的眼光之下，考虑其所处的特定情势。所以上述《韩非子》与自然法学诸多特征上的差异，其根源之一即前者的法观念出于中

---

① 《韩非子集释》，页 1042。

② 《韩非子集释》，页 1042。

③ 《韩非子集释》，页 365。

④ 《韩非子集释》，页 366。

⑤ 本部分所用"道德"一词为现代意义的"道德"，即代表着社会的正面价值取向，起判断行为正当与否的作用。并非先秦文献中的"道德"。

⑥ 郭沫若：《十批判书》，北京：人民出版社，1954，页 332。

⑦ 例如，在其看来"A"是"A"，"A"不是"非A"，无论何时何地，都是成立的。

国式的历史主义思维，后者则出于是非不可混淆的逻辑演绎 ①。

　　此外，由古代自然法思想到古典自然法学说，诸多西方思想家将自然法与"理性"（reason，拉丁语作 rationalis）概念相关联。"理性"这一含义复杂的概念，不同程度上成为自然法各派思想的基础之一。其与《韩非子》中将人之性情作为制定法令赏罚所循的依据同样是既有结构上的相近之处，又存在诸多层面的显著差异。我们可将这些近似与差异进行梳理，以探讨这些不同地域不同时代法观念的特点；并可将其为作为途径，探求生长出这些观念的东西方社会在彼时的不同特征。

---

① 将法家思想与自然法的差别与逻辑思维、中国式的历史主义的差别关联起来的观点，是承蒙北京师范大学历史学院教授刘家和先生指教而得。先生的教诲令我终生受益，特此表达对先生的感激之忱。

亚里士多德与荀子法治思想之差异

徐跃勤　山西师范大学

摘要：古代的中国和希腊几乎同时出现文化的繁荣，荀子与亚里士多德就是其中的思想巨匠。他们都提出重视"法治"的治国方略。毕竟，二者生活的社会背景不同，造成二者对"法"的理解、立法执法主体、法治的目的等方面的诸多差异。荀子的"法"是统治者治国驭民、实现"王道"和"霸道"的工具；所谓"法治"就是统治者"以法治国"，实现统治阶级利益的途径。亚氏的"法"具有至高的权威；"法治"是"依法治国"，是实现城邦正义和保护全体城邦公民利益的途径。工具理性和价值理性是两者原则性的差异。

关键词：亚里士多德；荀子；法治思想

Abstract：The cultural prosperities of ancient China and Greece appeared largely at the same time. Both Xunzi and Aristotle are the great masters respectively in their civilazation. They all insist on the principle of "rule by law". But, because of the different social background, they had a lot of differences in the understanding of the law, such as the the legislative and executing body, and the purpose of ruling by law. Xunzi thought that the law is the means for the rulers to govern and administer a state and to realize their ideal of ruling by kings and powers. Aristotelian "law" has supreme authority; he considered that "rule by law" is the way by which the justice of city-state could be ensured and the civil benefits protected.

Keywords：Aristotle, Xunzi , "Rule by Law"

荀子和亚里士多德分别在"轴心时代"的中国和希腊大致同时形成各自的法治思想。"轴心时代"的中国和希腊几乎同时出现文化的繁荣，在两个不同的地域，群星交映，荀子与亚里士多德就是其中的思想巨匠。他们的法治思想对中西法律文明基本理论的构建和法律制度史、法律思想史的演进、流变都产生了不可替代的历史作用。

荀子与亚里士多德生活在"轴心时代"的不同国度，他们都提出重视"法治"的治国方略，并有诸多相似之处。都从"人性恶"的基本认识出发，论述法的重要性、平等性、教化性等。毕竟，二者生活在不同的国度，具体的社会背景不同，造成二者对"法"的理解、立法执法主体、法治的目的等方面的诸多差异，甚至有些差异是原则性的。多年来，学界对二者各自法治思想的研究成果丰硕，借此笔者拟就二者法治思想的差异，进行尝试性的梳理，以企"古为今用"、"洋为中用"，并求教于方家。

一 荀子与亚里士多德所讲"法治"内涵的差异

荀子，名况，约生于公元前 313 年，卒于公元前 238，战国时赵国伊氏人（一般来说，即今天山西安泽县），是战国末期儒家学派的大师，作为先秦儒家思想之集大成者，博采诸家之长。《荀子》一书系统反映他的思想体系。现存的《荀子》三十二篇大部分是荀子自己的著作，涉及哲学、逻辑、政治、道德、法治等多方面的思想内容。荀子作为先秦宏儒，结合战国末期的时代特点，改造了孔、孟等早期儒家思想的"德政"和"仁政"，形成了以礼法思想为核心，隆礼重法，明德慎罚的法治思想。

荀子重视"法治"，提出"法者、治之端也"[①]，"道之与法也者，国家之本作也"[②]。但是，他重法并不否认"礼治"。他把"礼"外在化、客观化，成为制订法律的原则。所谓"礼者、法之大分，类之纲纪也"[③]、"礼者，贵贱有等；长幼有差，贫富轻重皆有称者也"[④]、"礼者、人主之所以为群臣寸尺寻丈检式也"[⑤]、今废礼者，是弃表也。"[⑥]等等。因此，荀子的思想主要表现为一种"礼治"思想。荀子重法，实际上是援法入礼，隆礼重法。荀子虽然具有法治思想，但要把荀子归为法家似有不妥。在荀子的法治思想中，法治是礼治的强化。如果按照现代对"礼治"的理解，礼治本质上是属于人治范畴。另外，他又说"治之经，礼与刑"[⑦]，荀子的"法治"实际上是"刑治"。在某种程度上把"法"等同于"刑"，把刑治作为治理国家的手段。刑治实际上是受人（统治者）指导与影响的维护统治阶级统治秩序的刑律，是变相的"人治"。也就是说，荀子"法治"的内涵是"人治"，因而，他说"有良法而乱者有之矣，有君子而乱者，自古及今，未尝闻也，传曰：'治生乎君子，乱生于小人。'此之谓也。"[⑧]而我们所说荀子的"法治"思想，只是说明荀子"人治"思想中的法律因素而已。

亚里士多德生于公元前 384 年，卒于公元前 322 年，出生于希腊北部马其顿的斯塔吉拉城。但是，他一生的大部分时光是在雅典渡过的，因故，人们往往把他与古希腊的雅典联系在一起。他是古希腊文化集大成者，在哲学、政治、伦理学、诗学及自然科学诸多领域做出了卓越的贡献。他一生著述颇丰，他的代表作之———《政治学》是西方政治学和法学的奠基之作。在该书中，他论述了良法、立法、执法、法治目的等法治思想。

亚里士多德虽然不是法学家，没有专门的法律论著，并且，在他的系列论著中也没有给"法"下过一个明确的定义，但在《政治学》中讨论城邦政体时，他认为："法治比任何一位公民的统治更为可取"，对城邦的治理更有利。并指出："法治应包含两重意义：已成立的法律获得普遍的服从，而大家所服从的法律又应该本身是制订得良好的法律。"。他认为"法律是恰似没有感情的，人类的本性是谁也难免有感情"，"常人既不能完全消除兽欲，虽最好的人们（贤良）也未免有热忱，这就在执政时引向偏向，法律恰恰是免除一切情欲影响的神祇和理智的体现"[⑨]。因此，在亚里士多德看来，法律是理性的体现，正义的化身，良好的法律是法治前提，变态政体的法律是不合乎正义的，

---

① 《荀子·君道》。
② 《荀子·致士》。
③ 《荀子·劝学》。
④ 《荀子·富国》。
⑤ 《荀子·儒效》。
⑥ 《荀子·大略》。
⑦ 《荀子·成相》。
⑧ 《荀子·致士》。
⑨ 亚里士多德：《政治学》，吴寿彭译，北京：商务印书馆，1983 年，第 9 页。

服从恶法不是法治。有了良好的法律，任何人都服从法律，否则也不会实现法治。

二 "法治"目的的差异

在荀子的"礼法"思想中基本内涵是"以君为核心，实施"法治"的前提条件是认同礼治和专制统治，是和君主专制的集权统治联系在一起的。他说"无君子，则法虽具，失先后之施，不能应事之变，足以乱矣。"①封建统治者以礼为政可以王天下，以法为政可以霸天下，实行"礼法"的终极目的是实现统治者"上可以王，下可以霸"②的"王道"或"霸道"。法治是战国末期的封建帝王治国驭民，维护其统治秩序的工具，因而，帝王可以凌驾于法律之上，"刑不上大夫，礼不下庶人"也就顺理成章。实施法治在于强化君权，为维护封建集权统治提供治国的方略，而不在于为人民谋福利。也就是说，荀子"礼法"中的法是为统治阶级服务的，是统治阶级实行专制统治的工具。

亚里士多德所讲"法治"是为城邦的存在、为城邦的统治者提供治理城邦的模式。他强调法律是公共利益的体现，"法律是以合乎德性的以及其它类似的方式表现了全体的共同利益，而不只是统治者的利益"。③因为，他认为：城邦的存在是为了给公民提供"优良的社会生活"，促进善德，为达目的城邦必须"以正义为原则，由正义衍生的礼法，可凭以判断 [人间的] 是非曲直。正义恰是树立社会秩序的基础"④。而公平、正义恰是法律的目的。因而"要使事物合乎正义（公平），需有毫无偏私的权衡，法律恰恰是这一个中道的权衡"，"法律恰恰是免除一切情欲影响的神祇和理智的体现"⑤。因此，在亚里士多德看来，法律是理性的体现，正义的化身，为世人所公认的公正无偏的权衡，是最高的社会权威，任何人都必须遵守法律，没有人可以凌驾于法律之上，执政者应该"依法为政"，执行良法，以促进善德为目的。这样，"法律的实际意义却应该是促进全邦人民都能进行于正义和善德的制度。"⑥因此，法治的目的是城邦的存在，实现优良的社会生活，而优良的社会生活，就是道德的良善。

三 立法和执法的主体差异

作为儒家学派大师之一，荀子儒家理论中的法治思想，关于立法、执法，他认为，作为统治阶级的"人"决定治国的"法"。他说道："法者、治之端也；君子者、法之原也。"⑦"道之与法也者，国家之本作也。君子也者，道法之撮要也，不可少顷旷也。"因此，"有良法而乱者有之矣，有君子而乱者，自古及今，未尝闻也，传曰：'治生乎君子，乱生于小人。'此之谓也。"⑧经国治世从法开始，但是，法毕竟是"圣人"依据"礼"的原则制订，虽有"良法"存在，而国家依然混乱不堪的情况在历史上曾经出现过，但是，从来没有听说过，国家在圣明"君子"治理下仍然混乱的情况。因此，治国的首要是"人"而不是"法"。"有治人，无治法。"只有善于治国的"人"，没有善于治世的"法"，并且，他说"法不能独立，类不能自行；得其人则存，失其人则亡"⑨，"法"要

---

① 《荀子·君道》。
② 《荀子·君道》。
③ 亚里士多德：《尼各马可伦理学》，苗力田译，北京：中国社会科学出版社，1990 年，第 89-90 页。
④ 亚里士多德：《政治学》，吴寿彭译，北京：商务印书馆，1983 年，第 9 页。
⑤ 亚里士多德：《政治学》，吴寿彭译，北京：商务印书馆，1983 年，第 169 页。
⑥ 亚里士多德：《政治学》，吴寿彭译，北京：商务印书馆，1983 年，第 138 页。
⑦ 《荀子·君道》。
⑧ 《荀子·致士》。
⑨ 《荀子·君道》。

依靠人的执行，执法的"人"的德行决定"法治"的成败。总之，荀子认为立法、执法的主体是"圣王，即专制君主。

亚氏认为人天生是政治动物，且众人的智慧胜于单人的智慧，他主张全体公民参政。因而，在论述君主制、共和制、贵族制等政体时，得出贵族制是最好政体的结论。因为，贵族制能够实现善良公民的广泛参政，而众多"善良公民"的执政能够保证代表整体利益和意志的良法的制订和保证法律的实行，以及城邦正义的实现。显而易见，立法、执法的主体是全体公民或统治阶层的整体。如此制定和实施的法律自然不是某个人利益和意志的体现，而是整体性的利益和意志的体现。在此，暂且不谈贵族制的优劣，单从立法、执法的主体来看，亚氏认为，善良公民集体或统治阶层整体作为立法、执法的主体，是保证法律公正和实现城邦正义的最好途径。

综上所述，从法治的内涵、目的、立法执法主体比较来看，荀子的"法"是统治者治国驭民、实现"王道"和"霸道"的工具；所谓"法治"就是统治者"以法治国"，实现统治阶级利益。亚氏的"法"具有至高的权威；"法治"是"依法治国"，是实现城邦正义和保护全体城邦公民利益的途径。因此，荀子和亚氏的法治思想虽有诸多相同点，但工具理性和价值理性的差异是原则性的。

浅谈旅顺博物馆藏古代印度佛教造像

徐媛媛　旅顺博物馆

摘要：旅顺博物馆收藏的这批古代印度佛教造像为日本大谷光瑞探险队于1902年11月至1903年1月在印度、巴基斯坦、阿富汗等地进行的第一次探险活动所得。几经辗转，1917年收藏于旅顺博物馆。这批佛教造像多为石质，仅有少数几件为白灰膏质，按工艺可分为浮雕和圆雕（单体造像）两大类。由于这些造像均是通过所谓的考古探险活动所得，因而大多已经因为粗暴的文物劫掠行为失去了其完整性，从而丧失了其原有的艺术价值，然而这些佛教造像仍拥有很高的学术价值。

关键词：旅顺博物馆；古印度；犍陀罗；马图拉；佛教造像

Abstract: The Buddhist statues of Ancient India which kept in Lvshun Museum were derived from the first adventure of the Ōtani Kōzui. From November 1902 to January 1903, the expedition of Ōtani Kōzui came to India, Pakistan, Afghanistan where they got lots of Buddhist statues and some other historical relics. Some of the Buddhist statues was sent to Lvshun and kept in Lvshun Museum in 1917. Most of the statues were made of stone, and only a few were made of stucco. These statues can be divided into two parts, relief sculpture and single statue. Because of the so-called archaeological expedition, these statues lost their original artistic value, but they still have high academic value.

Keywords: Lvshun Museum, Ancient India, Gandhara, Mathura, Buddhist statues

旅顺博物馆始建于1917年，如今已有近百年历史。在馆藏的六万余件藏品中，涵盖了古代印度佛教造像，日本、朝鲜古代陶瓷和日本书画，以及六十多个国家的近代邮票和货币的"外国文物"藏品系列可谓是馆藏鲜明特色之一。其中，古代印度佛教造像更是馆藏外国文物的重点。

一　馆藏古代印度佛教造像的由来

馆藏古代印度佛教造像共106件（组），为日本大谷光瑞（Ōtani Kōzui，1876年12月27日—

1948 年 10 月 5 日）于 1902 年 11 月至 1903 年 1 月[1]在印度、巴基斯坦、阿富汗等地进行的第一次探险活动所得。

大谷光瑞，日本京都府人，日本西本愿寺第 22 代法主（1903 年），探险家，为西本愿寺第 21 代宗主明如（大谷光尊）的长男。十岁剃度，学习院毕业后，留学欧洲。1900 年，在伦敦留学的大谷光瑞闻知一些西方人在中国、印度等地进行探险所获颇丰，受此启发，他决定组织日本人进行探险。1902 年 11 月至次年 1 月间，大谷光瑞利用留学归国之便，组建"大谷探险队"，前往印度、巴基斯坦、阿富汗的鹿野苑（Deer Park）、佛陀伽耶（Bodh-Gaya）、灵鹫山（Griddhkuta Hill）、王舍城（Rajagaha）、哈达（Hadda）等地，考查古迹、搜集文物，是谓"大谷探险队"的第一次探险活动，也是大谷光瑞本人唯一亲自参加的一次。这次探险收获了不少古代的石雕佛像、佛龛构件等类型文物，这些文物一部分被放置于京都本愿寺内，另一部分则存放在京都恩赐博物馆（现日本京都国立博物馆前身）。1909 年，在大谷光瑞主持下，本愿寺于大阪和神户之间的武库郡须弥月见山新建一座别邸——二乐庄，作为存放、整理这批数量庞大的文物之用。1914 年，由于多年大规模的考察探险、修建二乐庄，以及资助日俄战争等一系列活动，西本愿寺财政耗费巨大，巨额的债务迫使大谷光瑞于 5 月 17 日辞职，开始了其海外游历和布教的生涯。1915 年 4 月，大谷光瑞到达大连，出席西本愿寺关东别院的落成典礼，并最终决定将中国的旅顺作为其后半生的居留地。

大谷在旅顺新市区买下了一所俄国式建筑，将其大量藏书经由上海运抵旅顺。1916 年，大谷将其保留的文物，主要是古印度佛教造像和发现于中国新疆、甘肃等地的古丝绸之路文物也一并运到旅顺。据说，这部分文物在 1916 年由满铁转到旅顺，大约是保存在满蒙物产陈列所，这个陈列所是 1917 年 4 月开馆的关东都督府满蒙物产馆的前身，也就是如今旅顺博物馆的前身。[2]据原旅顺博物馆工作人员、日本学者森修的回忆，大谷光瑞的这些文物资料大概先暂时运到帝俄时代俄清银行的旧址，当时叫千岁俱乐部的楼里。在那里清点数量，记录品名后才保管，时间是大正六年（1917 年）四月。[3]

虽然这批文物中的古印度佛教造像大多不太完整，成为了残片，丧失了其原有的艺术价值，然而它们仍拥有很高的学术价值。

二　馆藏古代印度佛教造像的分类

馆藏古代印度佛教造像集中在贵霜王朝（The Kushan dynasty）、笈多王朝（The Gupta dynasty）、波罗王朝（The Pāla dynasty）三个时期，多为石质，仅有少数几件为白灰膏质，按工艺可分为浮雕和圆雕（单体造像）两大类。

按石材分类

现存的雕刻于石头之上的佛教艺术品可追溯至孔雀王朝阿育王（Ashoka，约公元前 268—前 232 年在位）统治时期。在那一个世纪以后，中印度和朱木纳河谷（Jumnā valley）地区的雕刻家们也开始使用石料取代木料进行雕刻。石雕的发展往往同适合雕刻的石头的产地有一定的关系，通常产石发达的地区，石雕的历史也相对悠久。用以雕塑馆藏古代印度佛教造像的材料主要有石质和白灰膏质两类。石质造像的材质颜色可分为灰青色、青黑色以及红色三种。灰青色和青黑色石材出自

---

① 1903 年 1 月，大谷光瑞的父亲因病猝死。大谷返回日本，接任父职。

② 王宇、王智远：《旅顺博物馆藏大谷探险队收集品及其整理研究情况》，《博物馆研究》，2002 年第 3 期；王振芬：《旅顺博物馆与大谷光瑞》，《旅顺博物馆精华录·馆史篇》，大连：大连出版社，2011 年，第 27-32 页。

③ 森修：《旅顺博物馆的回忆》，姚义田译，《博物馆研究》，1990 年第 4 期。

犍陀罗（Gandhara）地区，其中灰青色片岩占多数；而红色砂石则出自马图拉（Mathura，旧译秣菟罗）地区。

（1）灰青色片岩

犍陀罗地区位于古代印度西北部边陲，在今巴基斯坦西北与毗连的阿富汗东部地区，其以巴基斯坦北部的白沙瓦（Peshawar）为中心，西北到阿富汗的哈达，东南到印度河东岸的塔克西拉（Taxila），北到斯瓦特（Swat）。境内西北多高山，东南是印度河谷地。地处于"中亚、印度和欧洲的夹缝之间"的犍陀罗是东西文化交汇的枢纽。

公元前 326 年，希腊 – 马其顿国王亚历山大东征进入犍陀罗地区，在军事征服的同时也带来了希腊化艺术。公元前 2 世纪以后，巴克特里亚希腊人（Bactrian Greeks）大举入印，在印度西北部建立了长达两个世纪之久的统治，并在全盛时向恒河流域扩张。希腊人在印度的长期统治，奠定了希印文化融合的基础。犍陀罗艺术开始萌芽。贵霜王朝第四代国王迦腻色迦（Kanishka）统治时期[1]，贵霜王朝中心东南移，犍陀罗地区成为统治中心。这位国王信奉波斯拜火教，同时也赞助佛教，被誉为"阿育王第二"。迦腻色迦时代，在希腊化文化和佛教文化的相互作用之下，佛陀的形象在希腊罗马神像基础上，首先在这里被雕刻出来[2]，形成了一种独特的佛教造像风格。

犍陀罗地区当地所产的适于雕刻的石材主要有灰青色和青黑色片岩、绿泥片岩和黄色皂石等等。我馆收藏的此地区造像由灰青色和青黑色片岩雕刻而成的，其中灰青色占多数。

丰收女神倚坐像，为半圆雕倚座女神造像，贵霜王朝（公元 2—4 世纪），高 19.3 厘米、底座宽 11.9 厘米、厚 4.9 厘米，出土于现巴基斯坦斯瓦特地区。女神头戴高冠，头光右边残，边缘有一道单弦纹。眼凹鼻直，嘴小而单薄，面庞丰腴，面目表情慈祥、朴实而自然。倚椅而坐，座两旁刻立柱。发式中分侧梳成两条长辫延耳部自然垂下。右手上举，左手于膝上握着丰饶角。乳房高耸，腰肢纤细，曲线优美。双脚踏束腰圆座，膝盖向两侧分开。上衣下裙，衣纹简约流畅。

释迦说法故事浮雕，贵霜王朝（公元 2—3 世纪），高 19.3 厘米，宽 19.5 厘米，厚 6 厘米，出土于现巴基斯坦斯瓦特地区。释迦身穿盘领通肩衣，结跏趺坐于方形台座上，表情肃穆。高肉髻，头光较小，周围放射状分布菩提树叶。佛陀右手已失，从现存的部分看来很可能是上举施无畏印，左手握衣襟。浮雕右边残损，仅余四人，似在听释迦说法，释迦头旁有一飞天。释迦、飞天、菩提树冠等磨泐严重。

（2）青黑色片岩

馆藏青黑色片岩制佛教造像均属波罗王朝时期，其质地坚固、致密，雕刻后颜色深沉而具有金

---

[1] 1993 年，著名的腊跋闵柯铭文（Rabatak Inscription）在阿富汗出土，上面明确提到了迦腻色伽以前三位贵霜国王的名字，分别是他的曾祖父 Kujula Kadphises、祖父 Vima Taktu、父亲 Vima Kadphises。参见杨巨平："'Soter Megas'考辨"，《历史研究》2009 年第 4 期。

[2] 马图拉地区制造佛像的时间与犍陀罗地区所差无几，因而也有学者认为马图拉是佛像的发源地。晁华山先生对此观点持怀疑态度。他认为从现存早期佛像和传统佛像分析，很难确定佛像首先产生于马图拉。首先，马图拉佛像自铭"菩萨"，表明这里不出现佛真形的思想根源很深；其次，马图拉佛像源于传统的夜叉像，表明这种初次制作的佛像是在外来思想推动下和传统造像结合的产物。晁先生认为这种"外来的思想"就是从犍陀罗传来的制作佛像的思想。晁华山：《佛陀之光：印度与中亚佛教圣迹》，北京：文物出版社，2001 年，第 58、130 页。

属光泽，但浮雕损毁严重，现可分辨的内容十分有限。

菩萨残像，高 12.3 厘米，宽 12.5 厘米，出土于现巴基斯坦马拉根德山口[①]（the Malakand Pass），现仅可见菩萨的两腿和肘部，腿部的衣纹和装饰雕刻细腻，写实。旁边有一尊较小的力士像，身呈 S 形，配有颈饰，双手微抬，下半身穿裙，衣纹清晰。

太阳车，浮雕断为两部分，之一长 11.4 厘米，宽 6.1 厘米；之二长 4.9 厘米，宽 4.7 厘米。浮雕中残存三匹骏马，一匹较为完整，其余两匹仅可见腿部。由于太阳车通常由两匹或四匹骏马拉动，因而原浮雕上应共雕有四匹骏马。工匠用细腻的手法刻画了这些骏马奔驰的姿态。

在馆藏古印度佛教雕塑中，属古犍陀罗地区的占大多数，其按时间可分为犍陀罗早期雕塑和犍陀罗晚期雕塑[②]两大类，其中属于犍陀罗早期的数目较多。早期犍陀罗雕塑可分为供养浮雕、单体造像、故事浮雕以及建筑饰件等四类。馆藏犍陀罗晚期雕塑的质量稍逊于早期石刻，可分为供养塔及其部件、有背屏的造像以及部分佛像底座、建筑饰件（主要为贴面装饰及柱头装饰）等等。

（3）白灰膏

馆藏白灰膏制佛教造像共 8 件，可分为佛头像、天人（Deva）头像、建筑浮雕等三类，由"石灰、石膏和细沙混合制成"[③]，出土于阿富汗哈达地区。这一地区缺乏优质的石料，因而使用石灰的混合物作为材料，这一材料显然要比陶土更为耐用。但由于白灰膏要比片岩等石材柔软、粗糙，在雕刻时很难保证精致度。在人物雕塑时，人物的面部用模子铸造，而躯干则按"石膏墁灰法"（指在用木框架绷紧的帆布上墁抹一层薄石膏的制作石膏制品的工艺）原理制成[④]。遗憾的是馆藏的这些白灰膏人物塑像都仅余头部。

佛头像，贵霜王朝（公元 1—3 世纪），残高 8.8 厘米、宽 7.1 厘米。眉心有白毫，眉际与鼻相连，凹目，眼睑低垂，表情安详肃穆。头发、耳朵、眼睛、鼻梁等多残泐，肉髻不显，似乎为波纹发式。嘴部以下已失，隐约可见凹陷的左嘴角。

天人头像，贵霜王朝前期（公元 1 世纪），高 14.15 厘米、宽 10.5 厘米。花式头发，前额较宽，眼睛微睁，鼻尖缺损，鼻孔清晰，嘴唇稍厚，面颊丰腴。脖颈虽然仅剩一小段，且部分缺泐，但不失真实可亲之感。

浮雕塔，贵霜王朝前期（公元 1 世纪），高 23.05 厘米、宽 25.9 厘米，厚 4.9 厘米。覆钵式，方形塔基不高，靠近下部有一圈栏楯。塔身有两层纹饰，下层是小天使肩扛波浪式花缆，上层是整齐的栏楯。塔顶中央有施禅定印的坐佛，边

---

① 位于斯瓦特地区东面，是守卫斯瓦特地区的门户，战略位置十分重要。

② 对犍陀罗地区艺术发展的分期学界还存有争论，笔者根据馆藏情况将其分为早期（主要是贵霜王朝时期雕塑）和晚期（主要是波罗王朝时期雕塑）两个时期。

③ 晁华山：《佛陀之光：印度与中亚佛教圣迹》，北京：文物出版社，2001 年，第 131 页。

④ ［英］加勒特（Garratt, G. T.）主编：《印度的遗产》，陶笑虹译，上海：上海人民出版社，2005 年，第 92 页。

缘有破损，可能为建筑贴面。

馆藏白灰膏塑头像比较粗糙，具有早期造像的特点。这些塑像的头部、鼻子、眼睛等部位的损坏十分严重，很可能是由于非佛教徒进入该地后大规模的毁佛运动造成的。浮雕塔做工相对细腻，时间稍晚。

（4）红色砂石

马图拉，位于印度北方邦恒河支流朱木纳河西岸，距现在的德里南约140公里，这里同样也是古代东西方交通的要冲。公元1世纪，马图拉成为贵霜帝国的冬都。婆罗门教、耆那教和佛教同时流行于这一地区，此外在民间还流行着生殖精灵药叉与药叉女（Yakshi）的崇拜。早在公元前3世纪左右，马图拉地区便已经出现了石雕艺术，但直到贵霜王朝时期，这里才开始了佛像的制作。马图拉地区的艺术家们参照印度本土的药叉形象，创造了一种印度式的马图拉佛像和菩萨像，早期佛像均为袒右肩造型，后来可能是受到犍陀罗佛像的影响，通肩佛像逐渐增多。马图拉地区早期佛像的眼睛为圆睁，这与犍陀罗佛像眼睛为半睁不同，大约是在笈多王朝时期，这一地区的佛眼开始呈半睁状。公元3世纪后半叶，马图拉地区的雕刻艺术曾一度因造型形式化而衰退。然而，大约在公元5世纪初，一种"洗练圆熟"的雕刻的产生，使其"居于印度雕刻史的领导地位"。这时的马图拉佛像眼睛半闭，"眉毛以立体隆起线表现"，"具有稳定与威严、着通肩衣紧贴身躯，以流畅纤细的阴刻线表现衣褶"，[①]这些塑像造型孔武有力。

马图拉地区的雕塑通常都按照古老的传统刻于当地带有米黄色或乳白色斑点的红色砂石之上。由这种红色砂石雕刻而成的雕塑我馆藏有两件。一为半身像，另一件为女性手部和腿部残件。

天人礼佛像，贵霜王朝中后期（公元2—4世纪），高17.5厘米、宽13.2厘米、厚6.9厘米，出土于印度佛陀伽耶。雕有一位头戴花冠天人。天人面部丰腴，眉目修长，鼻梁直接额头。他的双手合十于胸前，右手腕部以下已失，左手腕部佩有手钏，虔诚地礼拜。这一石雕具有鲜明的马图拉造像特点，从其布局看应为一浮雕的局部，现仅存有天人的上身，无法判断原件的全貌。

女性手部和腿部残件，贵霜王朝（公元1—3世纪），长23.8厘米、宽14厘米、厚13.6厘米，出土于印度佛陀伽耶。手部五指刻画得真实细腻，指甲表现逼真，小指带有一指环。从其造型及手指的颀长、皮肤的细腻以及佩戴指环可以判断此当为女性之手，但无法断定她是天人还是供养人。原件或许是一立像，此可能是自然下垂置于腿侧的左手。

按雕刻工艺分类

从雕刻工艺来看，馆藏古代印度佛教造像基本可分为两大类：浮雕和圆雕。浮雕是佛教建筑物——佛塔和佛教石窟的主要装饰手段，其雕刻内容主要为两种：一是佛传故事和佛本生故事；二是纹饰浮雕，多为莲花纹和藤蔓纹。而圆雕工艺主要用于单体佛像的雕刻。

（1）佛塔上的浮雕

佛塔，即"窣堵波"（梵语 stūpa，巴利语 thūpa），意译为"高显处"、"功德聚"、"方坟"、"圆冢"、"坟陵"、"塔庙"、"归宗"、"灵庙"等。窣堵波在印度、巴基斯坦、尼泊尔等南亚国家及东南亚国家比较普遍。

---

① ［日］宫治昭：《犍陀罗美术寻踪》，李萍译，北京：人民美术出版社，2005年，第44—52页。

在印度，窣堵波被视为清净、吉祥的事物，印度居民在经过窣堵波时需要施右绕行（pradaksina）之礼。窣堵波最初可能仅仅是一个简单的半圆形土堆或石头堆，堆放于逝去之人身躯上，用以表示纪念之意。后来，佛教徒为了更好地保存佛陀的遗骨或遗物，开始用堆土、石、砖、木等材料筑造窣堵波。最古老的窣堵波是用土坯建成的，巴尔胡特和桑奇的大窣堵波初期都是如此，现存的石头外壳是后建的。据说，佛陀涅槃在摩罗国（Mallas）的都城拘尸那揭罗城，并在那里火葬（Jhapita，荼毗）后。周边七国罗阇[①]（raja）的使者闻讯赶来，要求分得舍利。摩罗国人以佛陀圆寂于他们的土地而拒绝，由此引发了"争舍利之战"，后来经婆罗门陀罗那（Drona）的调节，舍利被末罗族人和七国罗阇平均分作八份，当做圣物，并于其上建窣堵波。除了最初为八份舍利建造了八座窣堵波，调节者的

婆罗门陀罗那为保存其得到的装舍利的瓶子（骨灰罐）建造了瓶塔，再加上迟到的孔雀族使者持香木余灰回去建造的炭塔，一共有十座窣堵波。阿育王发掘了其中的七座，将佛陀的舍利取出，分给治下各大城市，建起宏伟的窣堵波或塔婆[②]（Tope）。换而言之，在阿育王时代之前，窣堵波早已存在并具有神圣的意义，然而阿育王又赋予了其佛教所独有的神圣象征的地位，窣堵波代表着佛陀的般涅槃[③]（Parinirvana），即他从痛苦而虚幻的世界到达幸福并真实存在的世界的道路，意味着佛教理想的实现；同时，窣堵波也象征着每个虔诚的佛教徒的归宿。窣堵波是佛教礼拜堂——支提[④]（chaitya）的重要组成部分，甚至可以说是核心部分，建造窣堵波也视为一种功德。[⑤]

建造窣堵波是很有讲究的。在起塔前，要预先选好"作塔处"，"塔不得在南不得在西，应在东应在北；若塔近死尸林，若狗食残持来污地，应作垣墙；应在西若南作僧坊，不得使僧地水流入佛地，佛地水得流入僧地；塔应在高显处……"[⑥]，塔外有栏楯围绕，四方各设有入口，入口处建有一牌楼形的建筑，其上刻有种种装饰纹样以及本生、佛传等故事内容。此外，大乘佛教兴起后，人们开始在大窣堵波周围建造还愿窣堵波以积聚功德。还愿窣堵波通常是由石头、金属、灰泥建造，其中不一定有舍利子或圣物。然而无论是窣堵波还是周围的许愿塔，其体积巨大，建造需要花费大量的人力、物力、财力，并非人人都能够积此功德。因而，广大信众开始仿照窣堵波的形制，塑造了体积相对较小的供养塔。

窣堵波大都由台基、覆钵（台上半球形部分）、平台（harmica，诃密迦）、竿和伞盖（chattra，

①　氏族部落的军事首领或王。
②　应为巴利语 thūpa 的音译，一般认为是一种实心的、半球形高大建筑。
③　上座部佛教认为释迦在佛陀伽耶的菩提树下成佛也可以称之为涅槃（nirvana，有余依涅槃），并将肉体死亡、完全进入寂灭的状态称为般涅槃（无余依涅槃）以示区别。
④　支提，意为"礼拜的场所"，它可以是一座建筑物，一座窣堵波，一座祭坛，甚至可以是一棵树。因此，支提还曾一度被当做窣堵波同义语使用。然而，支提的功能更为多样，"佛在世时，他奉献给药叉和天人，后来，通过僧纳佛的用具、佛或先哲的舍利或遗骨、经典或造像以及仅仅对佛的一生重要事件之纪念，重新变得神圣起来。"显然，支提本身更偏重于"可供养处"。参见李崇峰：《中印佛教石窟寺比较研究·以塔庙窟为中心·》，北京：北京大学出版社，2003年，第27-28页；卢慧敏："从巴赫特窣堵波浮雕图像探讨佛塔建筑式样"，《中华佛学》第二十期；[日]宫治昭：《涅槃和弥勒的图像学：从印度到中亚》，李萍、张清涛译，北京：文物出版社，2009年，第17页。
⑤　[美]罗伊·C·克雷文：《印度艺术简史》（Indian Art: A Concise History），王镛等译，北京：中国人民大学出版社，2003年，第33页；[巴基斯坦]穆罕默德·瓦利乌拉·汗：《犍陀罗——来自巴基斯坦的佛教文明》，陆水林译，张超音摄，北京：五洲传播出版社，2009年，第285页。
⑥　[东晋]佛陀跋陀罗、法显译：《摩诃僧祇律》，《大正藏》第 22 册 No. 1425。

查特拉）五部分组成。早期窣堵波的基座是圆形的，后来由于受到希腊的影响，窣堵波的基座变成方形。在梵文文献中，覆钵被称为噶尔巴（garbha，胎）或者安达（anda，卵），将释迦的遗骨舍利——"种子"（bija）放入覆钵中收藏，象征着释迦脱离轮回转生而实现了寂灭、空的世界。①在窣堵波覆钵的顶部有一平台，其最基本的形态是非常简单的方形栏楯形式。覆钵顶部、平台中央竖起用以制成伞盖的竿。为保存佛舍利还出现了各种形状（较为常见的有圆形、圆柱形、窣堵波形）、材质（陶制、石制、金属制、象牙制等等）和制作工艺的舍利盒（relic casket）。舍利盒很少单独出现，通常是两个、三个、四个或六个套在一起。套装时，通常石制或陶制的舍利盒在外层，其次是铜制和银制的，水晶制和金制的在最里层。舍利盒通常被埋在靠近覆钵中心轴的位置。②

馆内收藏有数座供养塔，这些供养塔多为方形基座，圆柱形塔身，塔身四面各开一三叶形龛，拱形龛楣，龛中供有坐佛，手施禅定印、说法印或降魔印。塔身上方为一四方形平台，其上有数层伞盖。

窣堵波作为佛教宗教仪式的中心，随着佛教的信仰传到印度境外，在不同的国家和地区演变为不同的形式，如缅甸的尖顶宝塔、中国西藏的层叠灵塔（chorten）和中原的多层宝塔，以及所有佛塔中最宏伟的中爪哇婆罗浮屠（Borobudur）的大塔"世界之山"。

（2）佛故事浮雕

约在公元前2世纪时，在佛教建筑中便出现了以佛本生、佛传故事为题材的雕刻作品。

佛本生故事，取自佛《本生经》（Jatakas），这是佛经中最具文学性的作品之一，它不仅是一部宗教典籍，而且是一部时间古老、规模庞大、流传极广的民间故事集。其在广义上是指佛经中的一个部类，包括所有讲述释迦牟尼前生事迹的作品；狭义则是指南传巴利文佛典小部中的一部佛经，它将一些讲述佛陀前生事迹的故事编辑在一起，共有547个。这些故事描述释迦牟尼从入胎、出生、成长、出家、苦修、悟道、降魔、成佛以及涅槃等被神化了的传记性故事，主要有：乘象入胎、树下诞生、步步生莲、九龙灌顶、太子回城、阿思陀仙（Asita）占相、易三时殿、八岁就学、角技议婚、掷象入坑、箭穿七鼓、掷缧定亲、出游四门、树下观耕、夜半逾城、车匿还宫、降伏魔众、鹿野苑说法、涅槃寂静等等。

佛传故事是描写释迦牟尼一生教化事迹的，但是它的根据主要不是佛陀一生中真实地发生过的事，而是一些神奇的传闻。常见的佛传故事的构图方法有两种：一种是以佛陀一生中的某一事迹为主要雕刻内容，如"四相图"，刻画了佛陀"诞生、成道、说法、涅槃"四件事；"八相图"，刻画了佛陀"受胎、诞生、出游、逾城、降魔、成道、说法、涅槃"八件事；而"十二相图"则刻画了佛陀"从人间上生兜率天③（Tusita）、从兜率天降、入胎、出胎、善巧诸技艺、受用诸妃眷、出家、修苦行、降魔、成道、转法轮、入涅槃"十二件事。另一种是多幅连续的浮雕刻画出佛陀的一生事迹。其内容一般有：仙人布发掩泥得燃灯佛授记；菩萨在忉利天宫④（Trayastrimsa Heven）说法；白象形降神入胎；右胁而生；父王奉太子入天祠，天神起迎；阿思陀为太子占相；入学习文；比试武术；太子纳妃；太子田间观耕后，树下静观；太子出游四门，见老、病、死和沙门；太子在宫闱中

① 也有认为窣堵波的造型是"模仿佛钵，圆冢的基座是佛座垂下的袈裟"。但最为普遍的看法是窣堵波"由古代墓葬形式发展而来，象征佛的涅槃"。见谌：《佛教藝術中的佛塔及形式（一）》，http://www.ctworld.org/buddaart/04.htm。

② ［日］宫治昭：《涅槃和弥勒的图像学：从印度到中亚》，李萍、张清涛译，北京：文物出版社，2009年，第18-31页。

③ 兜率天（梵语Tuṣita），又称甘丹，意思是"具有欢喜"，意译知足天、妙足天、喜足天、喜乐天，佛经记载乃"欲界六天"（the six deva-worlds of the Kāmadhātu，即四天王天、忉利天、夜摩天、兜率天、乐变化天、他化自在天）之第四天，是弥勒成佛前之居处，这里的一昼夜，相当于人间四百年，其一年三百六十天相当于于人间十四万四千年，此天人寿命四千岁，相当于人间五亿七千六百万年。诸多即将成佛者在这里等待着他们最后一次尘世之行。此天有内外两院，外院是凡夫果报天宫，只管享乐，直到福报用尽，属于天界；内院是弥勒的净土，菩萨修功圆满，尽此一生，便可成佛，又名为"一生补处"。

④ 忉利天（巴利文Tāvatiṃsa，梵文Trayastriṃśa），又意译为三十三天（belonging to the thirty-three [devas]），是佛教世界中"欲界六天"的第二层天，因有三十三个天国而得名。忉利天位于须弥山（Sumeru）顶端。

的生活，见妇女姿态深可厌恶；逾城出家；六年苦行；降魔；成道；梵天劝请说法；鹿野苑初转法轮，度五比丘（manks）；降伏毒龙，度三迦叶；游化摩揭陀国①（Magadha）；还回迦毗罗卫，与父净饭王（Suddhodana）相见；给孤独园长者奉献祇陀树园；升天为母摩耶（Maya）夫人说法后下降人间；提婆达多②（Devadatta）以醉象害佛，佛调伏醉象；教化伊罗钵龙（Erpattra）；在双林入涅槃；迦叶来礼佛，佛从金棺现双足；八王分取舍利等等。

由此可见，佛本生故事与佛传故事在佛陀涅槃之前的内容很难区分，因为它们在很大程度上是重合的。

馆藏的佛故事浮雕数量较多，除有两块属于笈多王朝时期，其它皆属于贵霜王朝时期和波罗王朝时期。这些佛故事浮雕表现了不同的主题，主要有初转法轮、仙人占梦、舍利故事、礼拜佛陀或菩萨、佛三尊等等。

主题一：初转法轮

"成道"在佛陀一生中占有十分重要的地位，因而在佛故事中十分重视对这一事件的描述。在佛教壁画和雕塑中，为了强调佛陀思想的威力，往往将成道描绘成佛陀降服天魔军众的场面，即"降魔成道"。佛陀成道后准备将"自己体验出的真理传播给他人"，这就是所谓的"转法轮"，即将"自己体验出的真理传播给一切众生"。他首先想到了曾同他一起苦修的憍陈如（Kaundinya）等五比丘。于是他前往五比丘所在的鹿野苑，并在那里向他们宣讲佛法，五人相继请作佛陀的弟子。这就是"初转法轮"或"鹿野苑说法"。这五人的皈依标志着佛教和及其僧伽③（sangha）的成立。④馆藏初转法轮故事浮雕，贵霜王朝（公元2—3世纪），灰青色片岩，高16.1厘米、宽10厘米，出土于现巴基斯坦马拉根德山口。浮雕左部残损，现存一法轮，下端为三叉戟。法轮与三叉戟的组合成为佛教"三宝"（trishulas），即佛、法、僧的象征物。据说这一象征符号是从古老的"公牛"象征符号中演变而来的。法轮代表法（dharma），三叉戟代表佛，三叉戟中心原还有一个代表僧伽的盾形符号，一般会被省略。三宝标志下一只鹿跪坐台座之上，代表佛陀在鹿野苑初转法轮。法轮边雕刻有两位护法神，其一为右手握金刚杵（vajra）的金刚力士。在经书中关于这位金刚力士的描述很少，但在浮雕中他似乎是佛陀从迦毗罗卫国"出家修道"时的忠实随行者，因而其形象有时是年轻人，有时则为中年人，他一直到佛陀圆寂都陪在佛陀身边，其手中所持的金刚杵⁵便是他特有的象征。台座旁边一礼拜者单腿跪地、双手合十；另有一蹲坐者，以手支颐呈沉思状。这三个人物具身着袒右肩大衣。第四个人物立于金刚力士身旁，

① 位于恒河（Ganges）中下游地区，大体相当于今比哈尔邦的中南部，是古代中印度的一个重要王国，其都城为王舍城（Rajagaha，今拉杰吉尔 Rajgir），后迁至位于松河（Son）和恒河汇合处的华氏城（Pataliputra，今巴特那 Patna）。

② 出身刹帝利释迦族，释迦牟尼的堂兄弟，佛侍者阿难罗汉亲生兄长。他曾加入释迦牟尼领导的僧团，但是后来因为意见不合与权力斗争，离开释迦牟尼，另外成立教团。

③ 即僧团。根据传统，僧伽由比丘、比丘尼、在家男居士、在家女居士四种人组成。僧伽由佛陀所创，是世界上最古老的禁欲教团。佛、法、僧共为佛教三宝，为佛教基本信条。佛陀为男众建立了比丘僧伽，后来又为女众建立了比丘尼僧伽。僧人均不从事商业或农业活动，仅依赖大众的布施，现在僧团都依照律藏生活。

④ 晁华山：《佛陀之光：印度与中亚佛教圣迹》，北京：文物出版社，2001年，第9-10页。

⑤ 金刚杵是因陀罗（Indra，天帝、战神，司雷雨，在佛教中变成了佛陀的胁侍帝释天）传下来的武器，下宽上尖，为底部连在一起的双股叉。

头部已失，双手合十，左肩披帔巾，上半身几乎完全外露，腰间围有裙裾。浮雕手法写实，人物形象生动。

主题二：仙人占梦

仙人占梦故事浮雕，灰青色片岩，高23.1厘米、宽21厘米、厚6.5厘米，贵霜王朝中期（公元2—3世纪），出土于现巴基斯坦斯瓦特地区。浮雕上雕有六个人物，分别为佛陀、仙人阿思陀以及三位女性。佛陀跣足而立，身着通肩大衣，肉髻较大，扁平，头光较小，符合斯瓦特地区的造像特点。阿思陀，又作阿斯陀、阿私陀、阿私多、阿私或阿夷，他是迦毗罗卫国的仙人。据说释迦诞生时，阿思陀为他占相，预言其出家必成正觉，可得菩提，转无上最妙法轮。他顾念自己年迈，无法看到释迦成道，受其教化，便令他的侍者那罗陀出家，以待释迦成道。浮雕中的阿思陀位于左侧，坐于菩提树下的台座之上。左脚着地，右脚放在左腿上，右手托下颏，他的对面有三位女性，应该是请求他占梦的女信徒。其中两人坐在石凳上，一人呈回首状，二人似乎正在交谈，第三位女性站在一旁，双手交握，紧张地聆听仙人的话语。

主题三：舍利故事

舍利故事，即释迦荼毗之后发生的种种与佛舍利相关的故事，如"供养舍利"、"舍利争夺战"、"分舍利"（"舍利八分"）、"搬运舍利"等等，是佛故事浮雕构图的重要组成部分。馆藏搬运舍利和供奉舍利故事浮雕，灰青色片岩，高18.1厘米、宽33.3厘米、厚5.6厘米，贵霜王朝中期（公元2—3世纪），出土于现巴基斯坦斯瓦特地区。浮雕略呈弧形，分为三层。上层残存四坐佛，原来很可能雕有七尊佛，为过去在婆娑世界度众的七佛[①]；中层饰栏楯；下层是残存两组佛传故事。一是"分舍利"，一人骑于马上，领队在前，马后有一头大象，象身上绑着舍利盒，展现了信徒携带舍利返回故土的画面。另一图为"供奉舍利"[②]，画面中央为一

----

① "去在婆娑世界度众的七佛"，又称原始七佛，即释迦牟尼以及成佛以前的过去六位佛，过去七佛从右至左分别为毗婆尸佛（Vipasyin）、尸弃佛（Sikhin）、毗舍婆佛（Visvabhu）、拘留孙佛（Krakucchanda）、俱那含牟尼佛（Kanakamuni）、迦叶佛（Kassapa）、释迦牟尼。毗婆尸佛，又作毗钵尸、微钵尸、鞞婆尸，毗婆沙，维卫，为过去七佛的第一位。姓拘邻，出生于刹帝利家庭，据说其出世时间，距今有九十一劫（一劫为13亿4千万年），一日于波咤罗树（Patali）下得阿耨多罗三藐三菩提（"无上正等正觉"，即"至高无上的平等觉悟之心"，指佛教修行上的最高觉悟、最高感受境界）。尸弃佛，又作式弃、严那尸弃，过去七佛的第二佛。姓拘邻，名弃如来，出生于刹帝利家庭。一日于芬陀利树（Pundarika，意指白莲花）下得阿耨多罗三藐三菩提。毗舍婆佛，又作毗湿婆、毗舍浮、摄罗等。过去七佛的第三佛。姓拘邻，生于刹帝利家庭，据说其出世的时间，距今已三十一劫。一日于娑罗树（Cala）下得阿耨多罗三藐三菩提。拘留孙佛，又作鸠楼孙佛、拘留秦、迦罗鸠餐陀等，过去七佛的第四位。姓迦叶，出生于婆罗门家庭。一日于尸利沙树（Cirisha）下得阿耨多罗三藐三菩提。俱那含牟尼佛，又作拘那含佛、拘那含牟尼、俱那含等，过去七佛的第五佛。姓迦叶，出生于婆罗门家庭，两眉间有毫毛，洁白光净常放光芒，一日于优昙婆罗树（Udumbara）下得阿耨多罗三藐三菩提。阿弥陀佛的前身是他的弟子。迦叶佛为过去七佛中的第六位佛陀，婆罗门种姓，姓迦叶。人寿二万岁时坐尼拘律树（Nyagrodha）下成最正觉。

② 宫治昭在其《涅槃和弥勒的图像学：从印度到中亚》一书中（第149页）收入了一幅现藏于拉合尔博物馆的舍利故事浮雕的插图，该浮雕的构图与我馆收藏的这件浮雕十分相似，书中认为浮雕表现的是"搬运舍利"和"起塔"的画面。

窣堵波，两边各立两人，面向窣堵波，双手合十，躬身礼拜，是信徒们建窣堵波后供奉舍利的场景。两组佛传故事中间以科林斯式石柱隔开。这些科林斯式石柱的作用是将连续描绘的佛故事分割开来，同时也是使浮雕所叙述的故事具有连续性的一个连贯因素。

主题四：礼拜浮雕

佛教徒深信"通过没有罪过的人生，通过坚韧不拔地履行家庭和社会的义务，通过仁慈和善良，通过向僧人施舍，通过礼拜佛以其义务，通过两周一次的斋戒，一个人积得了功德，并在来世享有对这一功德的果报，成为神或有福之人。"[1]因而，在礼拜佛陀浮雕中，佛陀通常会被众多极具不同个性的较次要人物形象所包围，他们或单膝跪拜，或躬身行礼，似乎这些人无论出身情况如何都向佛陀表达了敬意，希望能皈依佛教。显然，佛陀接纳并承认了他们。一些出资聘请工匠进行雕刻的供养人甚至还会请工匠将浮雕中的供养人的脸刻成他们的样子，有些则在石头上刻下了他们的名字。

弥勒菩萨是艺术家们喜欢雕刻的形象之一。他原来的姓名是阿阇世（Ajatsatru），意为"不可战胜"。这位菩萨掌握了"灵性的实质"，但却许愿说不会涅槃，要留在世间消除黎民的痛苦，助佑众生。他是未来的佛。在礼拜弥勒菩萨浮雕中，弥勒头发对分，束于头顶，两端均做环状。直鼻凹目，青年面容。上身袒露，从左肩至右侧腰际装饰以圣绳，这是弥勒属于婆罗门（祭司、献祭者）种姓的标志之一。身上戴有珠串、手钏等珠宝，斜披璎珞，帔巾缠绕肩头和臂，下着围于腰间的裙裾，交脚坐于须弥座上。右手已失，很可能举于胸前，施无畏印或归命印[2]。左手置于左膝上，手中提一长颈圆腹的宝瓶[3]，宝瓶内装着永生的甘露。右边站一供养人，双手合十，一副正在礼拜弥勒的姿态。

主题五：天使与花缆

"天使扛花缆"这一主题也多次出现在馆藏浮雕上。浮雕中的童子形象源自古希腊罗马艺术，通常被用来表示"胜利"、"庆贺"以及"乐园"诸如此类比较欢庆的主题，后来在犍陀罗地区广为传播。在佛教艺术中，一般被装饰在窣堵波的基座、圆柱塔身中部或阶梯两侧。天使扛花缆浮雕中的天使赤裸着身体，身上通常都佩戴着项饰、

臂钏、手镯和脚钏等珠宝首饰，肩上扛着用花瓣和树叶组成的花缆，花缆呈波纹状，其间是露出上半身的供养人，花缆底部常常会缀饰有茂盛的葡萄叶和果实，有的还装饰着其他的花纹图案，或者飘卷的绶带，将佛陀的永恒世界（窣堵波）用丰饶乐园和再生图像装饰起来。

以上属于贵霜王朝时期的佛故事浮雕具备两个特点：一是每个故事都是独立的，即采用一图一

---

① [英]加勒特（Garratt, G. T.）主编：《印度的遗产》，陶笑虹译，上海：上海人民出版社，2005年，第185页。

② "归命印"，即掌心向内的印相，是菩萨对佛陀表示敬意，或第二位的神对主神表示敬意的印相。在犍陀罗，施右手举在肩上、结掌心向内印相的有弥勒菩萨、梵天（释迦"诞生"、"七步"场面，以及在由佛陀、二菩萨、梵天、帝释天组成的佛五尊像中）、婆罗门行者（年轻的仙人、新入门的弟子）。[日]宫治昭：《涅槃和弥勒的图像学：从印度到中亚》，李萍、张清涛译，北京：文物出版社，2009年，第242-243页。

③ 一般认为是水瓶，也有学者认为应是香油瓶。

景的单独构图，每一浮雕叙述一个单独的故事情节，其间多会用科林斯式石柱做间隔；二是几乎处处都有佛陀的形象，佛陀为画面的中心人物，其他人物以佛陀为中心，水平展开。

主题六：佛三尊

馆藏波罗王朝时期的释迦降魔成道坐像是佛三尊形式造像的典型代表。佛陀为主尊，居中，形象高大，分立于其左右两旁的胁侍菩萨应为观音菩萨和弥勒菩萨。佛陀右边的菩萨发髻冠正面雕有佛塔，身上佩有项饰、臂钏、腕钏、圣绳等装饰。右手施与愿印，左手执花茎。其花为四瓣圆形小花，应为龙华。手执龙华是波罗王朝弥勒菩萨图像的一贯特征①，从而可以判定右胁侍应为弥勒菩萨，左胁侍则为观音菩萨。与弥勒菩萨形成对尊的观音菩萨结发髻冠，项饰呈莲花状，佩有臂钏、腕钏，从左肩至右侧腰际同样披挂着连珠圣绳。右手施与愿印，左手执莲花茎。

（3）单体造像

馆藏单体造像有全身像（姿态大致可分为坐像和立像两种）、半身像以及已被损坏的造像的头、手、足等部位。其中的佛陀雕像都具备佛的"三十二相"中的几种，如足下安平立相、手足缦网相、顶髻相、白毫相等等。佛像的手印有禅定印、降魔印、施无畏印、与愿印、说法印、合掌印。部分佛像有头光，又叫"顶圆光"，是由眉间的白毫放出的，是佛"三十二相"中的"眉间白毫相"的体现，此光焰聚集在头后，多为圆形。佛坐像的姿态为结跏趺坐，又称"双盘"，双足相互交叉置于左右双股上，脚心向上。这种坐法四平八稳，身端心正，为圆满安坐之相，是修行坐禅者常用的坐法。②

释迦说法像，贵霜王朝（公元1—3世纪），灰青色片岩，高38.1厘米、宽31厘米、厚13厘米，出土于现巴基斯坦斯瓦特地区，为半圆雕释迦说法半身造像。佛陀着袒右肩式大衣，衣褶凸起较细密。高肉髻，肉髻较扁平且大，波纹发式，头部有头光。面颊饱满，燕式眉，双目平视，前额与鼻梁相连，鼻梁直挺，鼻下有八字胡须，凹目薄嘴，表情庄重。体态丰满，着袈裟袒右肩，双手于胸前结说法印。衣纹隆起呈波谷状。发髻、鼻梁、双手等均磨泐，头光缺失逾半，腰以下不存，根据现存状态判断，应是佛立像。

释迦禅定坐像，贵霜王朝（公元1—3世纪），灰青色片岩，高35.8厘米、宽19.8厘米、厚8厘米，出土于现巴基斯坦斯瓦特地区。佛陀身着通肩大衣，结跏趺坐于方台座上，双目平视，神情安详。波状发式，高肉髻，有圆形头光。凹目高鼻薄唇，耳垂丰满。双手于腹前，掌心向上，结禅定印。衣纹下垂隆起呈波谷状，立体感强。工匠在塑造佛陀像耳部时，往往会使其垂至肩部，耳垂丰满，且有孔，这是富贵的象征。释迦牟尼在出家前是古印度迦毗罗卫国净饭王的儿子，曾挂过豪华的耳环，于是出家之后，便留下了这个耳环孔。

---

① ［日］宫治昭：《涅槃和弥勒的图像学：从印度到中亚》，李萍、张清涛译，北京：文物出版社，2009 年，第 316–317 页。
② 徐华铛编著：《佛像艺术造型》，上海：上海文化出版社，2006 年，第 1–41 页。

佛头像，贵霜王朝（公元1—3世纪），灰青色片岩，长13.3厘米、宽8.5厘米、厚4.6厘米，出土于巴基斯坦贾姆勒—格里。发型呈波纹状，高肉髻，面部丰满，眉心有白毫，眉际与鼻相连，鼻梁平直，稍有磨损，凹目，眼睑低垂，嘴抿合，唇较厚，表情安详。佛的眼、鼻、嘴轮廓清晰，线条流畅，雕工娴熟，技艺高超。以两耳为线，头后半部、双耳缺，鼻梁残，是保存较为完好的典型的犍陀罗风格佛头像。

三　结语

印度的雕塑作品，尤其是阿旃陀、埃洛拉（Elura）的洞窟庙宇和古犍陀罗、马图拉等地区的著名古代文化遗址所留下的文化遗存，如今已成为我们辨析佛教在印度不同地区和时期的隆盛与衰败的重要见证。更为重要的是这些文化遗产中所蕴含的缕缕历史信息，为历史学家还原历史原貌，重现这个古老却不注重历史记录的国家的古代政治、经济、文化历史活动提供了线索。然而，这些重要的线索随着历史的变迁以及19世纪前后各国探险队、"考古学家"的"考古探险活动"仅余片片废墟，较为有价值的遗迹都被保留在印度、巴基斯坦以及欧美等国著名的博物馆中，主要有巴基斯坦白沙瓦博物馆（Peshawar Museum）、拉合尔博物馆（Lahore Museum）、塔克西拉博物馆（Taxila Museum）、巴基斯坦国家博物馆（National Museum of Pakistan），印度加尔各答博物馆（Indian Museum, Kolkata）、马图拉博物馆（Mathura Museum），法国巴黎吉梅博物馆（Musée Guimet），大英博物馆（British Museum），意大利罗马的东方艺术博物馆（National Museum of Oriental Art），德国柏林的印度艺术博物馆（Museum of Indian Art），东京国立博物馆（Tokyo National Museum）。我馆所藏的古代印度佛教造像虽然仅有百余件，但在国内却是极为少见的，"虽同样不甚完整，但并不因此而失其珍贵"①。

---

① 金培锟：《浅谈犍陀罗式雕刻艺术》，《旅顺博物馆论文集》，2006年。

两汉中印关系考——兼论丝路南道的开通

杨巨平　南开大学

摘要：印度（身毒）之名首次为中国人所知是在汉武帝时期张骞出使西域之后。随着丝绸之路南道的开通，印度的一些王国与西汉王朝逐渐开始了直接的接触和交往，印度西北部的罽宾甚至成了中国的藩属。东汉初年，月氏－贵霜帝国建立，印度与中国的关系得到进一步的扩大和加强，丝路南道与海上丝路的联通和佛教的传入就是最好的说明。这些关系的发展轨迹不仅在《史记》、《汉书》、《后汉书》等关于西域的记载中有所反映，而且在西方古典作家的笔下和近代以来在印度的考古资料中也有体现。二者的互证使古代中印文明之间的关系变得更加清晰与明确。

关键词：张骞；《史记》；《汉书》；《后汉书》；中印关系

Abstract：India was known as Shendu（身毒）firstly by Chinese in the former Han Dynasty after Zhangqian（张骞）'s mission to the Western Regions（西域）. With the opening of the southern Silk Road some kingdoms in India began direct contacts and associations with the former Han Dynasty. Jibin, a kingdom located in the northwest of ancient India, even became formally a vassal of China. After the founding of the Kushan Empire in the early period of the Later Han Dynasty, the relations between India and China had been expanded and strengthened, which was confirmed and justified by the connection between the southern Silk Road and the Silk Route on sea and the spreading into China of Indian Buddhism. The courses and developments of these relations were not only reflected in the records about the Western Regions in the *Shiji, Hanshu, Houhanshu* and other historical documents, but were indicated in the western classical literatures and the materials of archaeology discovered in the areas of ancient India since the modern time. The mutual corroboration surely makes the relation between ancient Indian and Chinese civilizations become much clearer and more explicit.

Keywords：Zhang Qian, *Shiji, Hanshu, Houhanhsu*, relation between ancient India and China

古代中国与印度何时开始发生关系，又通过何种方式发生关系，确实是个老问题。季羡林先生曾对此做过比较详密的考证。根据他的考证，至少在孔雀王朝建立时，专指中国的"Cina"（脂那、支那）和"中国丝"之意的复合词——cinapatta 已经在印度出现。[1]可见在公元前四世纪与前三世纪之交，中国及其特产"丝"已经被印度人所知晓。但中国方面对印度的了解始于何时呢？除了佛教文献中的夸大讹传之词以外[2]，真正有根据的记载实际上始于汉代张骞通西域之时。虽然张骞本人没有到过印度，但他曾派使者出使身毒。在他之后的两个世纪内，印度西北部的罽宾、高附、天竺以及与之相邻的乌弋山离和其后征服印度的贵霜（月氏）先后与汉代中国发生了这样或那样的直接联系。丝路南道的开通和发展就是中印两大文明接触、交往的结果和见证。虽然有关印度的记载在《史记》的《大宛列传》和《汉书》与《后汉书》的《西域传》中多有反映，但它们往往语焉不详。如何揭开汉代中印关系史上的种种谜团，仅仅依靠汉文记载显然难有大的突破。近代以来西方汉学家利用其语言优势，确实在人名、地名的考订上很有贡献，但涉及到复杂的中国历史背景和艰深的古汉语文献，他们也有力不从心之感，甚至以讹传讹。本文的目的就是试图借助于西方古典文献中有限的证据和新的考古资料以及近年来国际学术界的最新研究成果，对两汉三史中所反映的历史事实和中印关系做出进一步的证实和解读。

一　《史记》、《汉书》中的中印关系

《史记·大宛列传》中有关"身毒"的传闻应是中国史书中对印度的最早记载。在张骞向汉武帝汇报他耳闻目睹的诸国中，他没有单独介绍身毒，但却向汉武帝提到，他在大夏惊讶地发现了来自中国蜀地的"邛竹杖"、和"蜀布"。问从何而来，答曰身毒。他借大夏人之口，对身毒做了简单描述："身毒在大夏东南可数千里。其俗土著，大与大夏同，而卑湿暑热云。其人民乘象以战，其国临大水焉。"[3]这里的介绍与前面对大宛、大月氏、安息、條枝、大夏的记载不大相同：其一，是间接而为，说明只是偶尔传闻所知；其二，内容简单，只提到其大致方位，民俗。但其他的内容却真实地反映了印度的特征：气候湿热，产大象，有大河为界。大河当指印度河。既然蜀物是经身毒而来，那就意味着身毒与蜀地之间可通。根据张骞的建议，汉武帝令他在蜀地犍爲郡发四道使者，欲通西南夷，由此进入身毒，但均无果而还。但张骞并没有放弃通身毒的想法，他在第二次西域之行时，坐镇乌孙，派遣副使到包括身毒在内的西域诸国。[4]张骞之后，汉武帝为了扩大在西域的影响，更是多次派遣汉使到身毒。[5]可见，至少在汉武帝之世，中国和身毒已经发生了直接的接触。但身毒的使者是否来朝奉献，《史记》中信息并不明确。"其后岁余，骞所遣使通大夏之属者皆颇与其人俱来，于是西北国始通于汉矣"[6]，不知这些大夏之属者中有无身毒，来人中有无身毒人。而且"西北国"是否包括身毒，从地理方位上看也似有疑问。《史记》完成于公元前91年，此后直到班固之时，中国与身毒有无来往就不得而知了。

班固（32 –92 年）的《汉书·西域传》可以说是司马迁《史记·大宛列传》延续和补充。班固的弟弟班超经营西域三十一年，应该给班固提供了不少西域方面的第一手资料。在他的笔下，身毒

---

① 本文属教育部人文社会科学重点研究基地重大项目"丝路古国文明研究"（11JJD770024）成果。
参见季羡林：《中印文化关系史论文集》，北京：三联书店，1982 年版，第 74–78, 113–114 页。
② 汤用彤先生认为，佛教的真正传入，始于东汉永平求法。关于此前的种种说法，均为后世"转相滋益，揣测附会"，均为无稽之谈。详见汤用彤：《汉魏两晋南北朝佛教史》，北京：北京大学出版社，1991 年版，第 3–22 页。
③ 司马迁：《史记·大宛列传》，北京：中华书局，1982 年版，第 3166 页。
④ 司马迁：《史记·大宛列传》，第 3169 页。
⑤ 司马迁：《史记·大宛列传》，第 3170 页。
⑥ 司马迁：《史记·大宛列传》，第 3169 页。

消失了，葱岭之外的印度出现了一个新的国家：罽宾。该传对罽宾的记载极为详细，其中包含了对其国都、方位、人种、地理、气候、物产、建筑、织造、饮食、市场、钱币、家畜、奇物等方面的介绍。此外还特别对罽宾与汉廷的政治外交关系做了重点梳理。[1]

司马迁对罽宾没有记载，说明至少在《史记》完成时，中国方面对它还知之甚少，甚至无所知晓。与汉廷之关系，始于武帝（公元前141- 前87年）几经反复，大致可分为四个阶段。

罽宾王乌头劳之时：自以绝远，数次剽杀汉使。

乌头劳之子之时：愿意修好，遣使贡献，汉关都尉文忠受命送还其使。但该王欲加害文忠，文忠发觉，与容屈王子阴末赴合谋，攻罽宾，杀其王。立阴末赴为罽宾王，授印绶。

阴末赴之时：拘禁汉使军侯赵德，杀副使以下70余人，然后遣使谢。元帝（公元前48–33年）因其绝远，遣其使者于县度，断绝关系。

汉成帝（公元前32- 前7年）之时：罽宾复遣使者来献谢罪，但仍因绝远，道路艰难，其归属与汉无直接利害关系而谢绝。汉廷送其使节到皮山而还。其实，罽宾人通汉的根本目的是获得赏赐和与中国从事商贸的机会（"实利赏赐贾市"）。因此，后来虽无政治从属关系，但其使仍数年一至。

《汉书·西域传》记载了罽宾的一个属国：难兜国。此国"王治去长安万一百五十里。东北至都护治所二千八百五十里，南至无雷三百四十里，西南至罽宾三百三十里，南与婼羌、北与休循、西与大月氏接。种五谷、蒲陶诸果。有金、银、铜、铁，作兵与诸国同……"[2]在罽宾东北方向330里（约合今130公里），应该不算遥远。位置大致在罽宾与大月氏接壤之地，可能是一葱岭绿洲国家。出产与罽宾相似，可种五谷，可产葡萄瓜果，也有金银铜铁，可以铸造兵器，无疑也可铸造钱币。既然归属罽宾，大概也用罽宾钱币。此处虽然没有提到难兜的东邻，但在对乌秅国的介绍中却说它西邻难兜。难兜之东即乌秅可证。

据《汉书·西域传》："乌秅国，王治乌秅城，去长安九千九百五十里。……东北至都护治所四千八百九十二里，北与子合、蒲犁，西与难兜接。山居，田石间。有白草。累石为室。民接手饮。出小步马，有驴无牛。其西则有县度，去阳关五千八百八十八里，去都护治所五千二（百）【十】里。县度者，石山也，溪谷不通，以绳索相引而度云。"[3]这个乌秅显然是个山区之国，很可能位于现在中巴边境巴基斯坦一侧的罕萨地区（Hunza）[4]。Hunza 或与乌秅古代读音相近（据唐颜师古注，乌音古读一加反，秅音直加反[5]）。乌秅之西数百里，就是县度。这个"县"就是古代的"悬"，是"悬绳而度"的意思。县度就是"悬度"，现代汉语简写为"悬度"。而悬度是丝路南道通往罽宾的必经之地。正是由于悬度路程艰险，难以通行，所以，汉廷往往送其使者至悬度而还。罽宾也借此天险之利，多次杀辱汉使。"自知绝远，兵不至也"。汉成帝时，大臣杜钦力劝与罽宾断绝关系，也是以此为理由。"今县度之厄，非罽宾所能越也。其乡慕，不足以安西域，虽不附，不能危城郭。"[6]"县度"应是丝路南道最艰难的一段，大概即今中巴公路从红其拉甫山口经 Hunza 到吉尔吉特（Gilgit）这一段。

《汉书·西域传》在紧接罽宾之后，提到了另外一个与其西邻的国家——乌弋山离。[7]该国与

---

① 详见班固：《汉书·西域传》，北京：中华书局，1962 年版，第 3884-3887 页。

② 班固：《汉书·西域传》，第 3884 页。

③ 班固：《汉书·西域传》，第 3882 页。

④ 余太山：《两汉魏晋南北朝正史西域传要注》，北京：中华书局，2005 年版，第 98 页 [181]。

⑤ 班固：《汉书·西域传》，第 3882 页。

⑥ 班固：《汉书·西域传》，第 3886-3887 页。

⑦ 关于该国的记载，详见班固：《汉书·西域传》，第 3888-3889 页。

罽宾的不同之处在于后者的气候可能更热一些（地暑热莽平），有"桃拔、师子、犀牛"等特产。钱币亦不同，"其钱独文为人头，幕为骑马"。此地是丝路南道的终点。"绝远，汉使希至。自玉门、阳关出南道，历鄯善而南行，至乌弋山离，南道极矣。"据其四至，一般认为是今日阿富汗喀布尔以南和伊朗西南部以塞斯坦（Seistan）、坎大哈为中心的地区，即古代的阿拉科西亚（Arachocia）和塞斯坦。此地在古代史上，也可归入一般意义上的印度西北部。

从罽宾及其属国"难兜"以及东西相邻地区乌秅、縣度和乌弋山离的大致方位来看，它们皆可归为古代印度或身毒的一部分。《汉书·西域传》不提身毒，大概是把罽宾之属视为它的替代。至于此传中偶尔提及的那个位于疏勒西北方向的塞种国家"捐毒"，[1]尽管"捐毒"古通"身毒"，但此"捐毒"显然不是《史记·大宛列传》中那个临水之大国"身毒"。乌秅、縣度都在葱岭之中，是从塔里木盆地抵达罽宾的必经之地。《汉书·西域传》对罽宾、乌弋山离、乌秅、縣度的记载之所以如此详细，应归因于它们与汉廷的直接关系。罽宾虽然时绝时通，但它一度接受汉廷的印绶，应该说也是汉帝国的属国之一。正是由于汉廷与这些沿路国家和地区建立了不同程度的外交关系，丝路南道得以开通，从而大大加强了古代印度与中国的联系，为后来佛教的传入和贵霜－印度文化进入塔里木盆地奠定了基础。

二　《后汉书》中的中印关系

东汉时期，由于贵霜帝国的建立和海上丝路的开通，中国与印度交往的范围扩大了，印度文化对中国的影响加深了。交流的方式由原来的单向转为双向，交往的途径也由陆路变为海陆并行。这一切都在范晔的《后汉书》，尤其是在"西域传"、"班超传"中得到了反映。《后汉书·西域传》记载的是东汉建武以后西域诸国的情况，材料主要来自班固之子班勇。[2]班勇子承父业，曾在公元123年（延光2年）到公元127年（永建二年）担任西域长史。他对西域的了解既有其父亲的遗教，也有本身的观察以及各方的传闻，属于耳闻目睹的第一手资料，可信度较高。其中关于汉地与印度诸国的关系，由于其父班超是主要的当事人，更为详实可靠。根据《后汉书·西域传》，与东汉王朝有外交关系的印度国家主要是大月氏、高附、天竺三地。

此时（灭大夏之后"百余岁"）的大月氏已经由五部翕侯之一的贵霜所统一。贵霜开国君主丘就却"侵安息，取高附地，又灭濮达、罽宾，悉有其国"。贵霜帝国的版图扩至印度西北部。丘就却死后，其子阎膏珍代为王。复灭天竺，置将一人监领之。

高附是一个新出现的国家："在大月氏西南，亦大国也。其俗似天竺，而弱，易服。善贾贩，内附于财。所属无常，天竺、罽宾、安息三国强则得之，弱则失之，而未尝属月氏。……后属安息。及月氏破安息，始得高附。"高附位于天竺、罽宾、安息之间，大月氏西南，与《史记》中"身毒"处于同一方位，应在兴都库什山以南，与原来的罽宾相邻。安息盛时，曾扩张至兴都库什山以南至阿拉科西亚一带。高附与喀布尔（Kabul）发音相近，似乎应是以今喀布尔为中心的地区。[3]但《汉书·西域传》未有提及，但它所说的乌弋山离似乎应该包括此地。该地是亚历山大进入印度的必经之地，先后受孔雀帝国、巴克特里亚希腊人王国、印度希腊人王国和印度－斯基泰人王国统治，也一度受

① 班固：《汉书·西域传》，第3884页。
② 范晔：《后汉书·西域传》，北京：中华书局，1965年版，第2912–2913页。
③ 喀布尔是印度的一个古老地名，在《梨俱吠陀》中就已出现。其名Kabul可能来自梵语的Kamboja（*Kamboj*）。一些古典作品中称其为"*Kophes* or *Kophene*"。（http://en.wikipedia.org/wiki/Kabul#Antiquity（2013/3/14）此发音与汉语的"高附"（"Kaofu, Gaofu"）相近。汉语古无轻唇音，"附"fu可读为"bu"，"高附"也可读为"Gaobu, Kaobu"，因此将高附比定于兴都库什山以南的喀布尔河流域地区还是比较可行的。

帕提亚人控制，是安息的属地。所以月氏只有破安息后才能取得高附。

至于天竺，方位与司马迁笔下的身毒相似。它位于月氏东南数千里，"俗与月氏同，而卑湿暑热。其国临大水。乘象而战"，[1]应在古代印度境内。天竺是一大国，西邻月氏、高附南至海，东至磐起国[2]。未提到北邻，但显然是指帕米尔以东的中国西域都护辖地。因非外国，不必提及。天竺（身毒）"有别城数百，城置长。别国数十，国置王。虽各小异，而俱以身毒为名，其时皆属月氏。月氏杀其王而置将，令统其人。"[3]罽宾当不是此别国之一，应是一独立国家，如在前汉之时。它曾与天竺、安息争夺高附，但终被月氏所征服。天竺、罽宾、高附最终皆归于贵霜。对于东汉时期中国西域的官员而言，贵霜（大月氏）就是原来的身毒、罽宾之地新的统治者。身毒（天竺）在《汉书·西域传》未出现，大概是当时的西汉政府只和罽宾发生了外交关系而忽略了它的存在。此时出现，是因为贵霜征服其地，且与中国的西域发生了关系，所以顺便对贵霜征服的身毒加以说明。身毒既然有"别国数十"，其地理意义大概要超过其政治含义。身毒应是印度诸国的一个统称，是虚称，而非实国。

但《后汉书》中关于天竺的记载，还是提供了许多重要的、有迹可查的信息。

它首次提到佛教在印度的流行："修浮图道，不杀伐，遂以成俗"。[4]佛教的发祥地在印度的恒河流域。在孔雀王朝阿育王之时已传入包括今阿富汗南部在内的印度西北部。佛教戒杀生，阿育王接受佛教后，对以前的征服杀伐行为极为懊悔，不仅在国内到处勒石刻铭，宣扬佛法，以正法治国，而且派出传教僧团远到东地中海的五个希腊化王国或地区去弘扬佛法。[5]尽管结果不详，但其精神可嘉。为使印度境内滞留的希腊人能够接受佛教，他甚至命人将其宣扬佛法的诏令用希腊语译出发布。[6]到公元前后贵霜人统治之时，佛教再次得到弘扬，犍陀罗艺术也应运而生。因此，这里所反映的应是佛教在印度广泛传播、深入人心的实际情况。汉明帝永平年间（公元58-75年）"遣使天竺问佛道法"就是在这样的背景下产生的。佛教传入中土，当然非明帝为始。汉哀帝时（元寿元年，公元前2年），"博士弟子景卢受大月氏王使伊存口授浮屠经"[7]。楚王英（与明帝同为光武帝刘秀之子）曾"学为浮屠斋戒祭祀"，[8]由于他"始信其术，中国因此颇有奉其道者"。[9]明帝夜梦金人，以问群臣，有大臣（傅毅）向他介绍"西方有神，名曰佛"[10]，说明中原内地对佛教已有所知晓。但令人奇怪的是《后汉书·显宗孝明帝纪》中却无此记载。关于永平求法，汤用彤先生有详细考证。

---

① 此处沿袭张骞说，大夏改为月氏，因大夏已被月氏所灭。

② "磐起国"的方位说法颇多，印度学者 Mukherjee 主张在印度河下游东部或者在东信德附近。沙畹认为是指印度南端的 Pandya 王国。Hill 倾向于在孟加拉或印度河口；国内余太山说位于今缅甸。窃以为，既然是"东至磐起国，皆身毒之地"，恒河中游的 Panchalas 也有可能。各家说法参见 J. E. Hill, *Through the Jade Gate to Rome: A Study of the Later Han Dynasty 1ˢᵗ to 2ⁿᵈ Centuries CE*, Lexington KY, 2010, pp. 359-260; 余太山：《两汉魏晋南北朝正史西域传要注》，第 288 页。Panchalas 的方位见 W. W. Tarn, *The Greeks in the Bactria and India*, Cambridge: The Cambridge University Press 1951, Map 2.

③ 范晔：《后汉书·西域传》，第 2921 页。

④ 范晔：《后汉书·西域传》，第 2921 页。

⑤ Ven. S. Dhammika, *The Edicts of King Ashoka*, Kandy, Sri Lanka: Budhist Publication Society (The Wheel Publication No. 386/387), 1993, "the Fourteen Rock Edicts": No. 13.

⑥ 这些希腊语石刻诏令在今阿富汗的坎大哈发现。见 Mortimer Wheeler, *Flames over Persepolis*, New York: Reynal & Company, Inc, 1968, pp. 65-69; Susan Sherwin-White and Amelie Kuhrt, *From Samarkand to Sardis: A New Approach to the Seleucid Empire*, London: Duckworth, 1993, pp.101-102。其一英译文见 S.M. Burstein, *The Hellenistic Age from the Battle of Ipsos to the Death of Kleopatra VII*, Cambridge: Cambridge University Press, 1985, pp. 67-68.

⑦ 鱼豢：《魏略·西戎传》，见陈寿：《三国志·魏书》，北京：中华书局，1982 年版，第 859 页。

⑧ 范晔：《后汉书·光武十王列传》"楚王英"，第 1428 页。

⑨ 范晔：《后汉书·西域传》，第 2922 页。

⑩ 范晔：《后汉书·西域传》，第 2922 页。

他认为大致可信，应有其事。①

东汉和帝时（89–105 年），天竺数遣使贡献。后因西域反叛而绝。桓帝（147–167 年）时，多次从日南徼外来献，②与海上前来的大秦商人大约同时（桓帝延熹九年，166 年）。③此时的天竺商人或从印度的恒河口、印度河口或南部港口起航。可见，由埃及、印度到中国的海上丝绸之路最迟在公元二世纪中期就已经开通。

贵霜取得高附、罽宾、天竺（身毒）之后，势力达到极盛，成为中亚、南亚地区可与东汉帝国抗衡的大国，同时也就自然与汉朝发生了密切的接触。班超在西域期间，除了设法控制、羁縻葱岭以东的西域诸国，遏制匈奴势力的渗入之外，就是对付贵霜的介入。《后汉书·班超传》中详细记述了班超与贵霜的交往与抗衡。

班超与贵霜的关系，实则利用与被利用的关系，双方都没有多少诚信可言。贵霜建国之初，还是愿意和汉朝建立友好关系。章帝建初三年（78 年），班超曾上疏说，"今拘弥、莎车、疏勒、月氏、乌孙、康居复愿归附"。章帝元和元年（84 年），班超攻打疏勒王忠，康居派兵救援。由于月氏当时刚与康居联姻，班超就派使者带着大批丝绸给月氏王，求其转告康居王勿进兵。月氏果然出手帮忙，劝退康居兵。班超遂攻克疏勒王固守的乌即城。此为汉廷与月氏的合作。此前，月氏还帮助汉军攻打过车师，但具体时间不详。章帝章和二年（88 年），月氏遣使贡奉珍宝、符拔、师子，向汉公主求婚。班超谢绝，并拒还其使，由此引起月氏怨恨。和帝永元二年（90 年）月氏派遣一位名为"谢"的副王率兵七万攻打班超。班超知其越葱岭千里而来，难以持久，故据城坚守，以逸待劳。并在中途截杀了向龟兹求援的月氏使者。谢王大惊，遣使请罪，愿得生归。班超允准，月氏大兵退回。从此慑于大汉雄威，岁奉贡献。这是目前所知月氏大兵翻越葱岭侵入塔里木盆地的唯一记载，说明当时月氏与东汉政府的关系依双方在此地的实力而定。④

需要说明的是，天竺虽被月氏（贵霜）所灭，但月氏显然未能占领天竺全境，所以和帝时还能独立遣使来献，桓帝时也有海上来献。但是否商人诈称（像大秦商人那样自称是安敦王所遣⑤）不得而知。月氏的统治区域显然是在古代印度西北部，以犍陀罗为中心。贵霜统治之地大致上是原来巴克特里亚希腊人、印度－希腊人以及随后而来的印度－斯基泰人和印度－帕提亚人的故地，贵霜王朝文化具有强烈的多元性特征应该与此有关。

三　印度与西方古典资料的佐证

众所周知，印度没有留下像中国正史那样系统的历史记载。但这并不是说，印度的古代文献中没有历史信息的反映。经过近代以来国际上包括印度本土学者在内的几代学者的努力，古代印度的历史还是越来越清晰地显示出来其基本的轮廓和发展的路径。而且就两汉时期的印度而言，由于有钱币、碑铭资料和西方古典文献的参照，它的历史面貌要更为清晰一些。

这一段的印度历史是与一位远道而来的不速之客——希腊－马其顿的亚历山大是分不开的。他率军于公元前 327 年侵入印度西北部，325 年离开。之后，印度孔雀王朝（约公元前 321–前 185 年）崛起。公元前 305 年，已经成为亚洲主人的亚历山大的部将塞琉古一世，从巴克特里亚越过兴都库

---

① 汤用彤：《汉魏两晋南北朝佛教史》，第 3–22 页。
② 发生于延熹二年（159 年）、四年（161 年）。见范晔：《后汉书·西域传》，第 2922 页。
③ 范晔：《后汉书·西域传》，第 2920 页。
④ 详见范晔：《后汉书·班梁列传》，第 1575–1580 页。
⑤ 范晔：《后汉书·西域传》，第 2920 页。大秦，学术界一般将其比定为罗马帝国；安敦一般比定为当时在位的罗马皇帝 Marcus Aurelius Antoninus（AD.161–180）。

什山，试图收复原来亚历山大帝国的属地，但中途而返。[1]但印度的放弃并不意味着的希腊人的完全撤离。由于巴克特里亚希腊人王国的存在，希腊人与印度的联系并未中断。相反有不少的希腊人定居于印度，以至于阿育王 (Ashoka，约公元前 273- 前 232 年在位)在刻石勒铭弘扬佛法时，也没有忘记用希腊语向这批希腊人传教。公元前 250 年左右，巴克特里亚的希腊人总督狄奥多托斯(Diodotus)独立建国，大约与此同时，帕提亚人也宣告独立。塞琉古王国的国王安条克三世挥师东进，先后进入帕提亚和巴克特里亚境内，并与公元前 206 年再次进入印度宣示主权，但同样无功而返。[2]此时，统治巴克特里亚的希腊人王朝已经易主，取而代之的是欧泰德姆斯(Euthydemus)家族。据斯特拉波，在此人及其儿子德米特里(Demetrius)统治之时(约公元前二世纪初)，巴克特里亚的希腊人侵入印度，不仅攻占了原来亚历山大征服过的印度河流域，甚至还有可能向恒河流域进发。[3]他们还一度向巴克特里亚以东的 Seres 和 Phuryni 扩张。[4]如果此说属实，他们很可能进入了塔里木盆地。德米特里甚至获得了"印度王"的称号。[5]他的钱币上的头像戴上了表示印度的大象头皮盔。这是继亚历山大之后出现的第二位戴此类头盔的希腊人国王。[6]印度西北部从此成了巴克特里亚希腊人王国的一部分。公元前 170 年左右，巴克特里亚的欧泰德姆斯家族被另外一个名为欧克拉提德（ Eucratides，约公元前 170- 前 145 年 ）的希腊人所取代。此人也曾向印度进军，[7]大概目的是征服那些仍然忠于欧泰德姆斯家族的将领。这些将领早就开始割据称王，这从他们独立发行的有国王本人头像的钱币就可以看出。根据法国钱币学家波比拉赫奇的研究，在从今日阿富汗南部到印度的旁遮普地区，都有印度 –希腊人国王在统治。其中最有名的是米南德（ Menander, 约公元前 155-130 年 ）。他在势力全盛时几乎占领了整个印度西北部。[8]他的大本营应该是在犍陀罗地区。[9]张骞大约是在公元前 128 年左右抵达大夏，他所耳闻的"临大水"之国"身毒"应该就是米南德王国全盛时期的印度西北部。

　　大约在米南德在位之时，巴克特里亚的欧克拉提德王朝受到来自北方游牧部落南下的威胁。根据西方古典作家斯特拉波的说法，从希腊人手中夺取巴克特里亚的游牧民族是来自锡尔河北岸与萨迦人（ the Sacae ）和索格狄亚那人相邻的地区的四个最著名部落，他们是 Asii, Pasiana, Tochari, Sacarauli；根据《史记·大宛列传》的记载，是来自中国敦煌、祁连山一带的大月氏部落辗转迁徙至阿姆河北岸，臣服了"大夏"即巴克特里亚。有学者认为大月氏就是四部落之一的吐火罗人——"Tochari"。[10]但游牧民族对此地的占领似乎经历了一个较长的过程。在游牧民族的冲击下，大约在

[1] 据说是塞琉古一世与孔雀王朝达成协议，双方联姻，放弃了对印度的领土要求，孔雀王朝则送给他 500 头大象作为回报。Strabo, *Geography*, XV. 2. 9. Cambridge, Mass.: Harvard University Press, 1988.

[2] 据说，仅在一位印度王公那里获得 150 头大象和一些金银财宝。Polybius, *The Histories*, 11. 34. Cambridge, Mass.: Harvard University Press, 1993.

[3] Strabo, *Geography*, XI. 11. 1. 但进入恒河流域的可能是斯特拉波特别提到的另一位与德米特里并列的希腊人国王米南德。二者并非同代人。参见下文。

[4] Strabo, *Geography*, XI. 11. 1.

[5] Justinus, *Epitome of Pompeius Trogus'* "*Philippic Histories*", Translated by Rev. J.S. Watson (London, 1853), 41.6.4. 这个 Demetrius 是一世还是二世学术界仍有争论，但 Eucratides 遭到来自一位印度国王 "Demetrius" 的长期围攻有明确的记载。

[6] O. Bopearachchi, *Monnaies gréco-bactriennes et indo-grecques, Catalogue raisonné*, Bibliothèque Nationale, Paris, 1991. PL. 4 (Demetrios I, Serie 1); I. Carradice, M. Prince, *Coinage in the Greek World*, London: B. A. Seaby Ltd, 1988, p. 116; M. Bieber, "The Portraits of Alexander", *Greece and Rome*, 2nd Ser., Vol.12, No.2, *Alexander the Great* (Oct., 1965), p. 185.

[7] Justinus, *Epitome of Pompeius Trogus'* "*Philippic Histories*", 41.6.1–5.

[8] O. Bopearachchi, *Monnaies gréco-bactriennes et indo-grecques, Catalogue raisonné*, p.453.

[9] Plutarch, *Moralia*, 821D.Cambridge, Mass. : Harvard University Press, 1991.

[10] A. K. Narain, *Indo-Greeks*, Oxford：Clarendon Press, 1957, p.132. 塔恩认为，中国方面所说的月氏由 Asii 和 Tochari 二部合并而来，而且这种合并早在月氏人离开中国的甘肃时已经完成。W.W.Tarn, *The Greeks in Bactria and India*, pp.286–287.

公元前 145 年，欧克拉提德家族退至东面的兴都库什山区，偏安一隅。原来的大部分国土沦为大月氏的藩属。各地"无大君长，往往城邑置小长。其兵弱，畏战"①，这就是张骞当时所看到的大夏（巴克特里亚）。也就是在这里，张骞见到了来自中国蜀地的竹杖和布，听到了关于身毒的传言。应该说，此时的张骞对印度的了解是肤浅的，但关于其地理、气候、出产等方面的特征还是比较准确的。

　　大约在米南德之后不久，印度就迎来了两次大的外来民族入侵浪潮。一次是所谓的印度斯基泰人（Indo-Scythians）或曰"塞人"，一次是所谓的"印度 - 帕提亚人"（Indo-Parthians）。关于塞人南下印度，《汉书·西域传》中有记载。他们可能与波斯帝国时期的 Sakas 有渊源关系，活动于里海以东直到今日新疆伊犁一带地区。②公元前二世纪前半期，受到大月氏迁徙的影响，被迫南迁，一部分可能经锡尔河南下索格底亚那（Sogdiana），再经巴克特里亚，最后定居于现在伊朗西南部的塞斯坦地区。这批塞人可能就是斯特拉波所说灭亡了巴克特利亚希腊人王国的北方四部落之一的 Sacarauli 人。③他们的南下无疑给了巴克特里亚希腊人王国致命的一击。张骞所见证的大月氏应该是尾随其后而来。据中国方面记载，还有一批塞人向西南越悬度，进入印度的罽宾地区，这就是前面《汉书·西域传》中所说的罽宾。其余塞人小国则散居于葱岭之中。④

　　此传中关于罽宾与汉廷关系的几个关键人物引起了一些西方学者的注意。他们的观点在塔恩的《巴克特里亚和印度的希腊人》一书中得到了进一步的发挥。其一，所谓的罽宾国王"乌头劳"，并非他的本名，他应是此地的塞人国王斯帕莱利斯 (Spalyrios, Spalyrises)，他曾在钱币上自称"国王的兄弟（"αδελφου του βασιλεωs"）"⑤。结果汉关都尉文忠把其中希腊语的"αδελφου"（"兄弟"）错译为国王之名，"乌头劳"的音译即由此而来。其二，文忠结盟的那位"容屈王子阴末赴"也与印度 - 希腊人有关。容屈是"Yonaki"的音译，意为"希腊城"。此城即 Alexanderia-kapisa 城。阴末赴就是这个希腊城主之子 Hermaeus，（Hermaios）。⑥一般认为，他是巴克特里亚希腊人欧克拉提德家族在印度西北部残留的最后一位国王。如果接受此论，那 Hermaeus 就成为历史上第一个，也是最后一个被中国中原王朝"授印绶"的希腊人了，希腊人的罽宾王国也就成了中国的藩属。但塔恩等的比附不仅在上个世纪五十年代就遭到另外一位著名学者纳拉因的断然否认⑦，而且也受到当代印度 - 希腊人钱币学家波比拉赫奇的反对。根据后者的研究，Hermaeus 的在位年代是公元前 90- 前 70 年，⑧这样就与元汉帝（公元前 48- 前 33 年）之时阴末赴"遣使者上书"的时间不符。但无论阴末赴是否 Hermaeus，公元前一世纪的中国西汉王朝与印度西北部的印度 - 希腊人肯定有过接触，此地的希腊化信息还是较为清晰地传回中国。《汉书·西域传》说，罽宾"民巧，雕文刻镂，治宫室，织罽，刺文绣"，似乎反映了希腊人的雕塑造型艺术和中国的织造技术在此地的流行。班固还注意到了罽宾钱币的特征："以金银为钱，文为骑马，幕为人面"⑨。这是比较典型的希腊式钱币，既与

①　司马迁：《史记·大宛列传》，第 3164 页。
②　班固：《汉书·西域传》，第 3901 页。
③　Strabo, *Geography*, XI. 8.2.
④　班固：《汉书·西域传》，第 3884、3901 页。
⑤　此人可能曾担任过副王，此类钱币可见李铁生编著：《古中亚币》，北京出版社 2008 年，第 118 页。他在位大约是公元前一世纪中期，在位时间有公元前 60-57 年、50-47 年多说。
⑥　见 W. W. Tarn, *The Greeks in the Bactria and India*, pp. 339–342, 418.
⑦　但纳拉因并没有解决"阴末赴、乌头劳"的所指问题。见 A.K. Narain, *The Indo-Greeks*, pp.154–155.
⑧　O. Bopearachchi, *Monnaies gréco-bactriennes et indo-grecques, Catalogue raisonné*, p.453.
⑨　班固：《汉书·西域传》，第 3885 页。

曾经统治此地的印度－斯基泰人国王的钱币相似，更与所谓的贵霜无名王 Soter Megas 的钱币相似。[1]前者的特征是"文为骑马"，幕为站立之希腊神；后者是"文为人面，幕为骑马"，二者均与班固之描述不同。而且，罽宾与汉发生关系是在汉元帝在位（公元前48－前33年）之前和之时的一段时间，因此与贵霜的无名王钱币应无关系。[2]但考虑到无名王属于公元一世纪后期的人物，班固的弟弟班超此时正在西域，不时与贵霜交往，他获得贵霜无名王钱币的信息并传回内地也是可能的。[3]估计班固是把印度－斯基泰人和贵霜无名王的两种钱币搞混了。还有一种是巴克特里亚－印度－希腊人国王欧克拉提德发行的"国王头像／狄俄斯库里兄弟"型钱币，反面的图像是二兄弟持矛骑马前行。[4]如果反过来看，也极为吻合。但不管怎样，印度西北部希腊式钱币流行的信息还是传到了中国。乌弋山离或是塞斯坦地城"Alexandria（Prophthasia）"的汉文音译。[5]此地的钱币在班固看来也比较特殊："其钱独文为人头，幕为骑马"[6]。其实，这种钱币恰恰是巴克特里亚－印度－希腊人钱币的类型之一[7]，也是贵霜无名王（The Nemeless King, Soter Megas）钱币的基本类型。说明班固的信息来源还是注意到了罽宾和乌弋山离钱币的不同。但提供者似乎对各种类型的归类和发行地、发行人还是不太清楚，所以才会有时间和空间的错位。

公元前二世纪后期和前一世纪的印度，印度－希腊人王国分崩离析，各自为政。这给塞人的南下和东来，以及随后帕提亚人的侵入创造了有利的时机。当时的印度西北部，实际上成了三个外来民族的角逐之地。随着印度－希腊人势力的衰落以及本身印度化程度的加深，他们逐渐退出了历史舞台。取而代之的除了早就从悬度而来的罽宾之属外，还有从塞斯坦－阿拉科西亚（seistan-Arachosia）西来的另外一支"印度－斯基泰人"。公元前二世纪末期，他们从伯朗关（Bolan Pass）进入信德地区，由南向北向东逐步推进，将印度－希腊人小王国压缩于西北部的一些地区。这时，帕提亚人的势力也扩张到了阿富汗和伊朗的西南部。这些帕提亚的属国享有高度的自治。公元前一世纪末，这些帕提亚人也进入印度，从塞人手中夺取了对信德地区、印度河口的控制权，并占领了

[1]　关于印度－斯基泰人的钱币特征，详见上海博物馆：《上海博物馆藏丝绸之路古代国家钱币》，第 194 － 204 页（No. 1111 － 1176）；http://www.answers.com/topic/azes-ii（2013/3/13）；李铁生编著：《古中亚币》，北京：北京出版社 2008 年版，第 118－127 页。关于贵霜无名王 Soter Megas 的钱币，国外的钱币网站收录颇多。本文主要依据 http://www.anythinganywhere.com/commerce/coins/coinpics/indi-kushan. html; www.beastcoins.com/Kushan/Kushan.htm（2013/3/13）两个网站提供的图片。上海博物馆也有收藏，见《上海博物馆藏丝绸之路古代国家钱币》，第 211 － 212 页（No.1224 － 1229）。但这三处均将 VimaTaktu 与 Soter Megas 的钱币混同为一，这是需要注意的。

[2]　Soter Megas 在贵霜早期王系年代学中的位置，近年来主要有三类不同说法：第一类是将 Vima Taktu 与 Soter Megas 视为同一人，同意此说者比较普遍。在位时间从公元一世纪中期到后期，甚至二世纪初年不等。跨度在 20-55 年之间。第二类是将 Soter Megas 单列，纳入贵霜早期王系之中，在位时间暂定在公元 97-110 或 92-110 年之间。此说由波比拉赫奇提出。见 Osmund Bopearachchi, "Some Observations on the Chronology of the Early Kushans", *Res Orientales*. Vol. XⅦ (2007), p.50. 第三类不承认 Vima Takto 和 Soter Megas 的存在，而以 Sadashkana 代之，但又认为他未即位，或许担任过一段时间的共治者。见 B. N.Mukherjee, "The Great Kushana Testament", *Indian Museum Bulletin* 30, Calcutta (1995), p. 88. 笔者认为，Soter Megas 只是一个僭位者。他与阎膏珍（Vima Taktu）是同时代人，应该属于公元一世纪后期。

[3]　根据《后汉书·班超传》，班超于汉明帝永平 16 年（公元 73 年）使西域，到汉和帝永元 14 年（公元 102 年）归来，先后达 30 个年头。

[4]　O. Bopearachchi, *Monnaies gréco-bactriennes et indo-grecques, Catalogue raisonné*. Pl. 16-22 (Eucratides：Serie 1-2, 4-8, 11, 19-21).

[5]　孙毓棠："安息与乌弋山离"，载《文史》第 5 辑，中华书局，1978 年；余太山：《塞种史研究》，北京：中国社会科学出版社，1992 年，第 168-171 页。

[6]　班固：《汉书·西域传》，第 3889 页。

[7]　前述的"国王头（胸）像／狄俄斯库里兄弟"型钱币就是此类钱币的典型。印度学者 Gauranganath Banerjee 就认为，这种钱币的信息在公元前一世纪传到了中国，并留下了记载。（Gauranganath Banerjee, *India as known to the Ancient World*, Oxford University Press, 1921, p. 21.）但 Eucratides 是公元前二世纪前半期的巴克特里亚国王，与公元前一世纪后期的罽宾王不可混同。

印度西北部的高附。他们就是历史上所称之的帕拉瓦人（palava），即"印度－帕提亚人"（Indo-Parthians），他们在此地的统治大约延续到公元一世纪末。可惜的是，中国的记载却对这时印度的复杂政治格局缺乏明确的、及时的反映。但幸运的是，公元一世纪后期出现的由一位佚名希腊航海家兼商人所写的《厄立特里亚航海记》，却对这一时期的南亚次大陆的政治地理记述颇详。

根据他的记述，从波斯湾国家 Persis 往东前行，就进入了印度－帕提亚国王的统治区域，此地由西向东有两个地区，先是 Parsidai 人之地，接着是斯基泰人（即 Saka 人）之地。后者的大致方位就是现在巴基斯坦的信德地区，印度河口的 Barbarikon 是当地的主要港口。其都城是内陆的 Minnagar（可能也是印度－帕提亚人的都城①）。从 Little Rann 和 Kurtch 湾起，进入作者所谓的印度本身。当时由 Saka 人（另外一部）实际统治。以前他们的王国包括从印度河三角洲东到乌贾因（Ujjain）的印度西北部，但被入侵的帕提亚人驱逐出印度河三角洲地区。他们向印度的西南方向转移，到达以孟买为中心的地区，原来此地的 Andhran 王国被迫向南退却。这个 Saka 王国拥有印度主要的港口 Barygaza（位于今坎贝湾），都城 Minnagara，位于其东北方向。Saka 人之北是贵霜人之地，即作者所说的巴克特里亚人之地。南面是强大的 Andhras，两国经常交战。Andhras 之南的半岛南部有三个大国，分别是 Chera, Pandya, Chola。前两个位于印度半岛的西南，后一个位于东南。恒河地区，也应有国家，但未说明。②看来，《后汉书·西域传》所记天竺"有别城数百，城置长。别国数十，国置王"，确非虚饰之词。由此也可知，此时的贵霜人大概进入印度西北部不久。该作者只知巴克特里亚而不知贵霜（Kushan），或可为证。③

《后汉书·西域传》曾经介绍了天竺的出产与对外贸易："土出象、犀、玳瑁、金、银、铜、铁、铅、锡，西与大秦通，有大秦珍物。又有细布、好毾𭨳、诸香、石蜜、胡椒、姜、黑盐。"④但这些物产哪些是本地出产，哪些是外来"珍物"，似乎语焉不详。《厄立特里亚航海记》对于这一时期印度进出口物品记载颇详，可资比较。丝绸南路与海上国际贸易关系之紧密也由此可见一斑。

据该书第 6 节，印度的铁和钢、棉布都被贩运到了红海沿岸；据第 39 节，当时从埃及、阿拉伯运入印度河口 Barbaricum 地区的商品有：细布（thin clothing）、华丽的亚麻布、黄玉（topaz）、珊瑚（coral）、苏合香（storax）、乳香（frankincense）、玻璃器皿（vessels of glass）、金银盘（silver and gold plate）、葡萄酒（wine）。由此出口的物品有：香草（costus，又译"生姜"）、没药树脂（bdellium）、枸杞（lycium）、甘松香（nard）、绿松石（turquoise）、天青石（lapis lazuli）、中国皮革（Seric skins）、棉花布（cotton cloth）、丝线（silk yarn）、靛蓝色染料（indigo）。据第 49 节，当时输入印度 Barygaza 港（今布罗奇，Broach，位于坎贝湾）的外来物品包括：葡萄酒、铜、锡、铅、珊瑚、黄玉、细布、腰带、苏合香、草木樨（sweet clover）、无色玻璃、雄黄、锑（antimony）、金银币、油膏。专卖国王的商品有：银器、歌童（singing boys）、少女、美酒、精品服装、上等的油膏。此地的出口物则有甘松油、没药树脂、象牙、玛瑙、红玉髓、枸杞（lycium）、各种棉布、丝绸、麻布、纱（yarn）、长辣椒等。据第 56 节，在印度西南端的 Muziris、Nelcynda 等城镇，出产胡椒、三条筋树叶（malabathrum）。进口物品有钱币、黄玉（topaz）、细布（thin clothing）、华丽的亚麻布（figured linens）、锑（antimony）、珊瑚（coral）、天然玻璃（crude glass）、铜、锡、铅、葡萄酒、雄黄（realgar）、雌黄（orpiment）、小麦。出口的有：胡椒（pepper）、珍珠（pearls）、象牙（ivory）、

---

① 见 Lionel Casson, *Periplus Maris Erythraei: Text with Introduction, Translation, and Commentary*, Princeton University Press, 1989, p. 185.

② Lionel Casson, *Periplus Maris Erythraei: Text with Introduction, Translation, and Commentary*, Princeton University Press, 1989，pp. 46–47.

③ Lionel Casson, *Periplus Maris Erythraei: Text with Introduction, Translation, and Commentary*, pp. 81, 91.

④ 范晔：《后汉书·西域传》，第 2921 页。

丝绸，各种水晶、宝石、玳瑁（tortoise-shell）、甘松香等。第63节还提到恒河地区有一个金矿，可以铸币。[1]

从这几份进出口物品清单[2]中可以看出，它们与《后汉书·西域传》所列举的物品种类差异较大。可以证明的印度本地产品也不多，只有各种香料（"诸香"）、胡椒和铁、金、大象、玳瑁等。但《厄立特里亚航海记》清单的真实性和准确性要大于前者。其中提到的从印度出口的棉布、象牙、玛瑙等宝石、珍珠、甘松油、没药树脂、枸杞、玳瑁、胡椒、香草（姜）等肯定出自印度本土，但像丝线、丝绸织品、皮革、玛瑙、水晶石、绿松石、天青石各种宝石的原产地显然非印度，而是中国、今阿富汗和中亚草原。进口的商品主要来自西方和海上。苏合香、乳香等应该来自阿拉伯半岛。像葡萄酒就来自意大利半岛和叙利亚地区的劳狄凯亚（Laodiceia，今贝鲁特 Beirut）。钱币、粗玻璃、珊瑚、亚麻布等显然也是从地中海、埃及等地运来。至于从海外输入的"细布"（疑为一种"丝绸"制品）大概是埃及商人从安息人"交市于海中"[3]获得，再转运至印度的。

《后汉书·西域传》中只记载了的贵霜的两位国王，丘就却和其子阎膏珍。但新的钱币资料和新出土的腊跋闽柯铭文（Rabatak Inscription）证明，在迦腻色迦（Kanishka）之前，实际上存在三位国王，分别是丘就却（Kujula Kadphises）、阎膏珍（Vima Taktu）、Vima Kadphises。至于那位贵霜钱币中匿名的那位"Soter Megas"，有可能就是中国史书中所说的"监领"印度的那位将军。他的钱币具有明显的希腊化特征，使人推测他可能就是一位当地希腊人的后裔。[4]那个率7万军队逾葱岭而来的王"谢"是否与他有关还不得而知。贵霜前期诸王的在位时间仍是国际贵霜史研究领域中的难点和热点。但大致可定在在公元一世纪初到二世纪中期之间，也就是中国的东汉时期。贵霜王朝时期是中国与印度政治、经济、文化关系最为紧密的时期，不论是海上还是陆地的丝绸之路，贵霜帝国都发挥了关键的枢纽作用。印度的佛教在贵霜帝国时期开始传入中国，以贵霜文化为代表的印度本土和希腊化文化也是在这一时期开始进入中国的塔里木盆地。斯坦因在和阗等地发现的佉卢文木牍、希腊式的人物形象、犍陀罗风格的器物、含有中、希、印三种文化因素的和阗马钱（汉佉二体钱）就是最好的证明。

纵览两汉三史，可见中国对印度由耳闻到目睹，再到发生密切的政治、商贸和文化关系的大致过程。中国方面在其中始终处于主动地位，这是以汉武帝为肇始的开边拓土、开发经营西域的必然结果。印度作为中国的近邻，与不断西扩的中国发生这样或那样的关系，是不可避免的。西方古典学者的记述和印度本土的考古资料证明了二者之间文化与经济上的联系，事实上也就证实了丝绸之路南道和海上丝绸之路的存在。正是随着丝路的延伸，印度的物产、佛教、希腊化文化的信息传到了中国，从而实现了古代希腊、印度和中国文化的三流合一。这是人类文明交流史上的奇迹，这样的结果是亚历山大、张骞以及班超父子他们所绝对想不到的。

---

[1]　W.H. Schoff (tr. & ed.), *The Periplus of the Erythraean Sea: Travel and Trade in the Indian Ocean by a Merchant of the First Century*, London, Bombay & Calcutta 1912, Chap. 6, 39.49, 56, 63. 关于这些进出口物品清单，也可见 Lionel Casson, *Periplus Maris Erythraei: Text with Introduction, Translation, and Commentary*, pp. 55, 75, 81, 85, 91. 二者在个别物品的译名上稍有不同。

[2]　Casson 对各地的出产与物品做了详细的分地区和分类，详见 Lionel Casson, *Periplus Maris Erythraei: Text with Introduction, Translation, and Commentary*, pp. 16–17.

[3]　范晔：《后汉书·西域传》，第2919页。

[4]　关于贵霜前期四王的世系及无名王身份的考证，参见杨巨平：《"Soter Megas"考辨》，《历史研究》2009年第4期，第140–152页。

丝绸之路与北魏平城

王银田 暨南大学

摘要：早在建都平城之前，鲜卑族已与丝绸之路结缘。东汉以后，鲜卑渐次西进，直至魏晋时期，鲜卑占有草原丝路亚洲部分的大部，具有东端通过高句丽与朝鲜半岛，西端直接连接中亚的客观条件。十六国时期，随着柔然、高车和鲜卑势力的此消彼长，鲜卑逐渐南下，但仍据有阴山南北的广大地区。鲜卑与草原丝路的联系十分密切。

建都平城之后，拓跋鲜卑以今内蒙南部与山西北部为中心逐步扩张，太武帝拓跋焘时期，讨柔然，征夏国，占凉州，取北燕，十六国战乱以来拥塞的绿洲丝路再次打通，西域各国以及东端的高句丽、百济与北魏王朝的使节、胡僧频繁往来，相关历史遗存也在平城一带出现，成为今天我们探讨丝绸之路与北魏平城关系的重要物证，这些遗存包括金银器、鎏金铜器、玻璃器、银币、漆器、石窟寺及石雕、胡俑、壁画、以及装饰纹样和植物遗存等。形象地反映了公元五世纪平城文化的多元与繁荣。

在汉唐之间，平城时代的丝绸之路开启了北魏洛阳时代以及隋唐时代丝路文化的先河，在中西交通史上具有重要意义。在吸收外来文化的基础上充分发展的北魏平城美术，以及长江流域的建康建业美术，构成了中国隋唐以前美术的主流意识，也成为唐代艺术文化的重要基础，为唐代艺术的发扬光大奠定了雄厚的基础，成为中华民族文化的重要组成部分。

关键词：北魏；平城；丝绸之路；中西交通

Abstract：Early before making Ping Cheng city as its capital, the Xianbei people had some relation with the Silk Road. After the reign of Eastern Han Dynasty, the Xianbei expanded gradually westwards. By the period of Wei and Jin, the Xianbei had occupied a larger part of the Asia passed by the Steppe Silk Road, including Goguryeo and Korean Peninsula to the east, and the Central Asia to the west. During the period of the Sixteen Separatist States, the powers of Rouran, Gaocha rose and declined. The Xianbei began to expand southwards, but it still controlled the vast region in the southern and northern parts of Yinshan, and had a close relation with the Steppe Silk Road.

After making Ping Cheng city as capital, Tuoba Xianbei continued to expanded their lands around today's southern Inner Mongolia and northern Shanxi Province, During the reign of Tuoba Tao (Tai Wu Emperor), he conquered Rouran, Xia Country,

Liangzhou and Beiyan and reopened the closed Silk Road that resulted from the fierce warfare in the period of the Sixteen Separatist States. The countries in the Western Regions, as well as Goguryeo and Baekje in the east, had frequent contacts with envoys and monks from Northern Wei Dynasty. The relative historical relics have been discovered and unearthed in the area of Ping Cheng in recent years, which provide the essential material evidences for the further discussion of relation between Ping Cheng and the Silk Road. Various remains such as gold and silver wares, gilding bronze wares, glasses, silver coins, lacquerwares, grottoes, stone carvings, and figures of non-Han ethnic groups, frescoes, ornamentation and floral remains, clearly reflect the diversity and prosperity of Ping Cheng culture in thefifth century.

The arts of Ping Cheng in Northern Wei period, fully developing with the absorption of exotic culture, and the arts of Jiankang and Jianye in the valley of the Yangtze River, formed the mainstream of art before Sui and Tang Dynasties, and also provided the significant basis for the development of arts and culture in these two dynasties.

Keywords: Ping Cheng city, Northern Wei, the Silk Road, China-West Communication

"丝绸之路"是一个动态概念，其具体的行进路线和东方的起点往往随着朝代更迭，地方割据势力的消长，以及不同时代政治、经济中心的转移而有所变化。在中国境内，丝路的起点西汉为长安，东汉为洛阳，公元五世纪则是位于黄河中游和长江下游的两座都城——平城和建康。后者因濒临长江，得河海之便而以海上丝绸之路与海东、南洋、南亚和西方交通，平城地处内陆，陆上丝绸之路自然是其必然的选择。

北魏立国凡148年，建都平城96年，期间正处在北魏王朝政治、经济、文化的上升时期，在献文帝、孝文帝时期达到高峰。在汉唐之间，平城时代的丝路交通开启了北魏洛阳时代以及隋唐时代丝路文化的先河，在中西交通史上具有十分重要的意义。

一　北魏立国前后丝绸之路的开拓

早在建都平城之前，鲜卑族已与丝绸之路结缘。西汉时期鲜卑西与匈奴接壤，而匈奴西接西域和中亚，西南与乌孙接壤，占有北纬40—55度，东经80—120之间的广大地区，包括草原丝绸之路亚洲段，此时鲜卑与西域的接触以间接交流为主。东汉以后，鲜卑由大兴安岭急遽向西扩张，东汉后期鲜卑"兵马甚盛，东西部大人皆归焉"，首领"檀石槐……因南抄缘边，北拒丁零，东却夫余，西击乌孙，尽据匈奴故地，东西万四千余里，南北七千余里。"[1]已据有蒙古高原大部，西临今北疆地区，势力范围已接近西域和中亚，原来匈奴人占有的草原丝路已多为鲜卑人所据。至魏晋，鲜卑一度曾具有东端通过高句丽与朝鲜半岛、西端直接连接中亚的客观条件。这一时期鲜卑人甚至曾到达新疆塔里木盆地南缘的且末，据新疆民丰县尼雅发现略当魏晋时期的324号佉卢文书记载："鲜卑人到达且末，劫掠王国，抢走居民。"[2]十六国时期，随着柔然、高车和鲜卑势力的此消彼长，鲜卑逐渐南下，但仍据有阴山南北的广大地区。

---

① 《后汉书》卷九〇《乌桓鲜卑列传》，类似的记载也见于《三国志》和《魏书》。
② 王广智译：《新疆出土佉卢文残卷译文集》（初稿），中国科学院新疆分院民族研究所油印稿，转引自佟柱臣《嘎仙洞拓跋焘祝文石刻考》，《历史研究》1981年6期。

建都平城初期，拓跋鲜卑以今内蒙南部与山西北部为中心逐步扩张，"太祖初，经营中原，未暇及于四表。"①太武帝拓跋焘时期，讨柔然、征夏国，取北燕，灭北凉，逐步统一黄河流域，十六国战乱以来拥塞的绿洲丝路再次打通，西域各国以及东端的高句丽、百济与北魏王朝的使节频繁往来，这种状况一直持续到迁都洛阳，相关历史遗存也在北魏境内尤其是在平城一带出现，成为今天我们探讨丝绸之路与北魏平城关系的重要物证，这些遗存包括金银器、鎏金铜器、玻璃器、银币、漆器、石窟造像以及石雕、胡俑、植物和壁画、装饰纹样等。形象地反映了公元五世纪平城文化的多元与繁荣。

在吸收外来文化的基础上充分发展的北魏平城美术，以及长江流域的建康建业美术，构成了中国隋唐以前美术的主流意识，也成为唐代艺术文化的重要基础，为唐代艺术的发扬光大奠定了雄厚的基础，成为中华民族文化的重要组成部分。

二　太武帝及其之后平城时代与丝绸之路国家的交往

北魏平城政权与西域的交流主要出现在太武帝灭北凉政权之后，但此前已有交往。以下是《魏书·太武帝本纪》中太延五年（439年）九月灭北凉政权前与西域及海东国家交往的文献：

太延元年（435年）二月，"蠕蠕、焉耆、车师诸国各遣使朝献。"五月太武帝"遣使者二十辈使西域。"六月"高丽、鄯善国并遣使朝献。"八月"粟特国遣使朝献。"

太延二年（436年）二月，"遣使者十余辈诣高丽、东夷诸国，诏谕之。""八月丁亥，遣使六辈使西域。……甲辰，高车国遣使朝献。"

太延三年（437年）二月，"高丽、契丹国并遣使朝献。"三月"龟兹、悦般、焉耆、车师、粟特、疏勒、乌孙、渴槃陁、鄯善诸国各遣使朝献。"（此即《魏书·西域传》所记载的"太延中，魏德益以远闻，西域龟兹、疏勒、乌孙、悦般，渴槃陁、鄯善、焉耆、车师、粟特诸国王始遣使来献。"）十一月"破洛那、者舌国各遣使朝献，奉汗血马。"

太延四年（438年）三月，"鄯善王弟素延耆来朝。"

太延五年（439年）四月，"鄯善、龟兹、疏勒、焉耆诸国遣使朝献。"五月"遮逸国献汗血马。"太武帝灭北凉期间还曾有使者出使天竺和罽宾。

在这五年内，每年都有西域国家使臣来访，太武帝也曾两次派出使者出使西域，北魏与西域交往之频繁可见。在太延三年（437年）西域九国来访后，太武帝派遣王恩生、许纲等人西使，"恩生出流沙，为蠕蠕所执，竟不果达。"于是"又遣散骑侍郎董琬、高明等多赍锦帛，出鄯善，招抚九国。"董琬等在乌孙王的帮助下并访问了破洛那、者舌两国，琬、明东还后，乌孙、破洛那等西域十六国遣使俱来平城。"自后相继而来，不间于岁，国使亦数十辈矣。"②

董琬、高明这次出行，不仅与西域诸国家建立了直接联系，而且增进了朝廷对西域各国的了解，"始琬等使还京师，具言凡所经见及传闻傍国，云：'西域自汉武时五十余国，后稍相并。至太延中，为十六国，分其地为四域。自葱岭以东，流沙以西为一域；葱岭以西，海曲以东为一域；者舌以南，月氏以北为一域；两海之间，水泽以南为一域。内诸小渠长，盖以百数'。"董琬等人也带回了丝绸之路交通线路的详细情报，"出西域本有二道，后更为四：出自玉门，渡流沙，西行二千里至鄯善，为一道；自玉门渡流沙，北行二千二百里至车师，为一道；从莎车西行一百里至葱岭，葱岭西一千三百里至伽倍，为一道；自莎车西南五百里，葱岭西南一千三百里至波路，为一道焉，"③这对

---

①　《魏书》卷一○二《西域传》。
②　《魏书》卷一○二《西域传》。
③　《魏书》卷一○二《西域传》。

北魏王朝后续和西域的交流无疑具有积极的意义。

　　灭北凉后北魏与西域国家的交往更趋频繁，直至武帝被害身亡，期间最为活跃的是天山南北的诸西域小国。

　　太武帝是中国历史上一个杰出的的军事家和政治家，"世祖睿略潜举，灵武独断，以夫僭伪未夷，九域尚阻，慨然有混一之志。既而戎车岁驾，神兵四出，全国克敌，伐罪吊民，遂使专制令、擅威福者，西自流沙，东极沧海，莫不授馆于东门，悬首于北阙矣。"①在灭北凉之前，北魏使臣出使西域，"常诏河西王沮渠牧犍令护送，至姑臧，牧犍恒发使导路出于流沙。"然而处在柔然与北魏两个强敌之间的北凉政权难免左右为难，"牧犍事主稍以慢堕"，成为急于开拓西域通道的拓跋焘的绊脚石，太武帝的讨凉檄文列举沮渠氏十二大罪状，其中"知朝廷志在怀远，固违圣略，切税商胡，以断行旅。"②就与其妨碍丝路有关，太延五年（439 年）北凉终于被大兵压境的魏军所灭。

　　太武帝灭北凉前与西域交往的国家中，不仅包括了今帕米尔以东，位于天山南北的诸小国家，也有帕米尔高原以西的中亚国家，如粟特、破洛那、者舌、罽宾以及南亚的天竺等。此外，太武帝时期还曾遣使者韩羊皮往波斯，但具体时间不明。灭北凉后以上国家和北魏政权的往来更为频繁。太平真君九年（448 年），因焉耆国剽劫魏国使臣，太武帝派"成周公万度归千里驿上，大破焉耆国，其王鸠尸卑那奔龟兹。"于是又诏万度归，自焉耆西讨龟兹。③可见太武帝对西域丝绸之路的通畅格外重视。

　　不仅中亚各国来使，平城时代还曾有古印度诸国的通使记录，"太和元年（477 年）九月庚子，车多罗、西天竺、舍卫、叠伏罗诸国各遣使朝贡。"④迁洛后通使逐渐增多。

　　除了以平城为出发点向西伸展的丝路外，太武帝时期与朝鲜半岛的联系也是空前的。随着公元436 年北燕被拓跋焘攻灭，北魏与高句丽接壤，丝绸之路进一步向东延伸，从平城经由辽西重镇龙城（今朝阳）和辽东达到朝鲜半岛，极大地促进了中原王朝与东北亚国家的交流。

　　高句丽与北魏的关系始于太武帝拓跋焘时期，太延元年（435 年）六月高句丽首次"遣使朝献"，⑤次年北魏灭北燕之后，与高句丽隔辽河对峙，双方交流渐趋频繁。高句丽王高琏遣使者安东奉表贡方物，并请国讳。拓跋焘遣员外散骑侍郎李敖前往平壤探访，并"拜琏为都督辽海诸军事、征东将军、领护东夷中郎将、辽东郡开国公、高句丽王。……后贡使相寻，岁致黄金二百斤，白银四百斤。"后因冯文通败逃高句丽并得到收留，双方一度交恶，但双方的交流一直在持续。献文帝时期曾试图与高句丽进行政治联姻，前因高琏犹豫不决，后逢显祖病故而未果。"至高祖时，琏贡献倍前，其报赐亦稍加焉。"太和十五年（491 年）高琏死，"高祖举哀于东郊，遣谒者仆射李安上策赠车骑大将军、太傅、辽东郡开国公、高句丽王，谥曰康。又遣大鸿胪拜琏孙云使持节、都督辽海诸军事、征东将军、领护东夷中郎将、辽东郡开国公、高句丽王，赐衣冠服物车旗之饰，……自此岁常贡献。"文献关于北魏王朝与高句丽交往的相关记载很多，但多称"遣使朝献"或"遣使朝贡"，具体内容大多缺省，其中除正常的政府间外交往来，必然有经济方面的贸易行为。迁洛后双方仍然保持着密切的交往，"讫于武定（543~550 年）末，其贡使无岁不至。"⑥据韩昇先生统计，高句丽派使者前往十六国十二次，北魏七十九次，东魏十五次，北齐六次，北周一次，派使者去东晋三次，刘宋

---

①　《魏书》卷九五《匈奴刘聪等传》。

②　《魏书》卷九九《卢水胡沮渠蒙逊传》。

③　《魏书》卷一〇二《西域传》。

④　《魏书》卷一〇二《西域传》。

⑤　《魏书》卷四《世祖纪》。

⑥　《魏书》卷一〇〇《高句丽传》。

二十二次，南齐五次，萧梁十一次，陈六次，与北魏的使臣往来最为频繁。①

百济位于朝鲜半岛西南部，与我国山东、江苏隔海相望，北魏与百济的交往远不及高句丽。延兴二年（472年），百济王余庆遣使上表，希望北魏出兵协助其攻打高句丽，并答应"奉送鄙女"，"并遣子弟"，然而此时北魏无意染指高句丽和百济事务，孝文帝遣邵安与其使者"至高句丽，琏称昔与余庆有仇，不令东过，安等于是皆还。"延兴"五年（475年），使安等从东莱浮海，赐余庆玺书，褒其诚节。安等至海滨，遇风飘荡，竟不达而还。"北魏与百济之间因陆路有高句丽横亘其间，当时也可通过海路往来，百济与南朝宋齐梁朝的交往就是通过海路实现的。②

三　北魏王朝开通丝绸之路的目的

太武帝开通丝绸之路首先是出于军事方面的考虑，主要针对当时北魏最大的敌国柔然。柔然本出于鲜卑，③作为游牧民族，与鲜卑人一样，他们都有抢夺其他部族或邻国财产的风俗，"常与魏虏为雠敌，"④双方战争不断。"晋世，什翼圭（拓跋珪）入塞内后，芮芮逐水草，尽有匈奴故庭，威服西域。"⑤北魏建国伊始拓跋珪就曾大破柔然，之后柔然兼并高车、匈奴，势力日渐强盛，"西则焉耆之地，东则朝鲜之地，"穷瀚海，临大碛，凶猛强悍，屡次危及平城，给北魏政权造成很大威胁，直至孝文帝迁都洛阳，与柔然的战争一直持续不断。由于柔然的强大，西域"小国皆苦其寇抄，羁縻附之。"⑥448年，悦般国就曾遣使至魏，寻求与魏合攻柔然，于是拓跋焘大举北上征伐至受降城。⑦对河西和西域的争夺也是北魏与柔然军事较量的一部分，这里是柔然后方补给区域之一，控制河西走廊与天山南北有利于遏制柔然势力的发展，军事上有牵制柔然的作用。

北魏加强与西域国家的联系也是阻断柔然与南朝联系的重要手段。早在宋元嘉七年（430年），柔然就曾遣使与刘宋政权联络，结果在今浙江、丹江一带被土人误劫。⑧此后柔然依然不断出使江南，据唐长孺先生统计，从宋元嘉五年（428年）至升明三年（479年）宋亡，柔然使宋达十次之多，⑨南齐时仍在继续。柔然"岁时遣使诣京师，与中国亢礼。"⑩柔然与南朝的联系意在远交近攻，联合攻魏，而柔然人南下的路径正是通过西域、河南道抵达益州实现的。此路可由塔里木盆地南缘的丝绸之路南道经于阗或鄯善直接入吐谷浑境，或由高昌经焉耆到鄯善，再东入益州。由于北魏与吐谷浑多有不睦，吐谷浑常常借道给敌方与南朝联络。升明二年（478年）宋遣骁骑将军王洪范出使柔然，约剋期攻魏，其行经路线据《资治通鉴》记载，"洪范自蜀出吐谷浑，历西域，乃得达。"⑪南朝时曾有多位僧人西出求法，经由此路。甚至北魏洛阳时代胡太后遣僧人惠生、宋云赴西天取经也曾走这条道。⑫柔然威慑西域，假道吐谷浑，联合南朝必然使北魏腹背受敌，所以经营西域对北魏王朝的重要性是不言而喻的。

① 韩昇：《四至六世纪百济在东亚国际关系中的地位和作用》，韩国忠南大学校百济研究所《第七回国际学术会议·百济社会诸问题》，1994年。
② 《北史》卷九四《百济传》。
③ 《魏书》卷一○三《蠕蠕传》。周伟洲：《敕勒与柔然》，桂林：广西师范大学出版社，2006年。
④ 《南齐书》卷五九《芮芮虏传》。
⑤ 《南齐书》卷五九《芮芮虏传》。
⑥ 《魏书》卷一○三《蠕蠕传》。
⑦ 《魏书》卷四《世祖纪》。《北史》卷九七《西域传》。
⑧ 中国科学院历史研究所史料编纂组编：《柔然资料辑录》，北京：中华书局，1962年。
⑨ 唐长孺：《魏晋南北朝史论拾遗·南北朝期间西域与南朝的陆路交通》，北京：中华书局，1983年。
⑩ 《宋书》卷九五《索虏传》。
⑪ 《资治通鉴》卷第一百三十五，建元元年条。
⑫ 周祖谟：《洛阳伽蓝记校注》卷五，北京：中华书局，1987年。

灭北凉，占领河西走廊与太武帝经营西域的策略是相辅相成的，也意在经济。①拓跋焘伐北凉时曾罗列了对方的十二大罪状，其中"民籍地图，不登公府，任土作贡，不入司农"；"切税商胡，以断行旅"；"坐自封殖，不欲入朝。"②无不与北魏在河西与西域的经济利益有关。太平真君七年（446年），侍中刁雍上书以河西粮食经漕运支援六镇，"今求于牵屯山河水之次，造船二百艘，二船为一舫，一船胜谷二千斛，……一运二十万斛。方舟顺流，五日而至，自沃野牵上，十日还到，合六十日得一返。从三月至九月三返，运送六十万斛。"此建议得到太武帝的认可，诏曰："自可永以为式。"③可见经东汉以来的持续开发，河西走廊已然成为北方的重要粮仓。河西与西域又是良马的重要产地，在冷兵器时代马既是生产资料，更是重要的战略资源，文献记载平城时代北魏政权不仅从河西掠到大量马匹等畜产，而且西域国家也常有良马进贡，这对习惯于骑兵作战的拓跋鲜卑来说，不仅可以及时补充战马，而且对改良马种都起到了很好的作用。此外汉代"凿空"以来丝绸之路已成为中原王朝进行国际贸易的主要方式，丝路开通后的商税自然是一笔不小的收入。

继承、维护和开拓传统的华夏朝贡体系，创造"四夷来朝"、"万国慕化"的清平盛世是历代帝王的政治理想，拓跋鲜卑入主中原后即以华夏正统自居，随着太武帝时北方的统一，实现这一政治理想也成为这些游牧民族帝王的治国方略。太武帝以来积极与域外沟通，使这一理想初步得以实现。董琬、高明出使西域之后"东还，乌孙、破洛那之属遣使与琬俱来贡献者十有六国。自后相继而来，不间于岁，国使亦数十辈矣。"④至迁洛后与北魏通使的国家和地区甚至达到一百多个。⑤"自葱岭已西，至于大秦，百国千城，莫不款附。商胡贩客，日奔塞下。所谓尽天地之区已。乐中国土风因而宅者，不可胜数。是以附化之民，万有余家。门巷修整，阛阓填列。青槐荫陌，绿柳垂庭。天下难得之货，咸悉在焉。"⑥可谓盛况空前。

朝贡贸易是朝贡体系在经济方面的表现形式。与洛阳时代已大量出现民间的远途国际贸易不同，平城时代的贸易仍以官方的朝贡贸易为主，文献对于贸易双方交换的商品并无详细记载，但一般而言朝贡贸易进口商品皆以土特产、奢侈品或中土所没有的奇异动物为主，域外一方往往可以获得高额回馈。从《洛阳伽蓝记》有关记载可以看出，这种远途国际贸易对繁荣北魏经济确实产生了重要影响。

四 平城的胡人

北魏平城除来自各国的外交使节外，还有胡人定居，这些人包括官僚、商人、僧人、以及没有留下姓名的工匠和伎乐等，还有因婚配来平城的。如北京图书馆藏北魏延昌元年（512年）《魏故征虏将军河州刺史临泽定侯鄯乾墓志铭》拓片，⑦据志文记载，鄯乾乃鄯善王宠之孙，"自祖已上，世君西夏。"其父鄯视在太平真君六年（445年）归附北魏，鄯乾在北魏任员外散骑侍郎、左右辅国将军、城门校尉、征虏将军、安定内史等职，墓志所载鄯乾亡故年龄缺失，但从时间上推算应该曾在平城生活与工作，死后葬于洛阳。据林梅村先生考证，"鄯乾之父鄯视似即《魏书·西域传》提到的鄯善王真达，其祖父鄯宠似为同书所提到的鄯善王比龙。"⑧洛阳曾出土《大魏文成皇帝夫人

① 李向群：《北魏太武帝时期的西域经济战略》，《文史哲》2002 年第 3 期。
② 《魏书》卷九九《卢水胡沮渠蒙逊传》。
③ 《魏书》卷三八《刁雍传》。
④ 《魏书》卷一〇二《西域传》。
⑤ 石云涛：《北魏中西交通的开展》，《社会科学辑刊》2007 年第 1 期。
⑥ 周祖谟：《洛阳伽蓝记校注》卷三，中华书局，1987 年。
⑦ 赵超：《汉魏南北朝墓志汇编》，天津古籍出版社，1992 年。
⑧ 林梅村：《寻找楼兰王国》，北京大学出版社，2009 年。

于墓志铭》，据志文载，这位北魏文成帝的妃子于仙姬乃"西城（域）宇阗国主女也"，来自于阗国，享年九十，于孝昌二年（526年）葬于洛阳。[①]文成帝拓跋濬在位年代为公元452~465年，案志文于仙姬当生于437年，若以虚岁20嫁文成帝拓跋濬来平城，至太和十九年（495年）"六宫及文武尽迁洛阳"，仙姬在平城则近四十年。还有粟特人安同，其先祖安世高，汉时以安息王侍子入洛，安同因商贩偶遇太祖拓跋珪，于是任职北魏朝廷，其子孙亦有多人在北魏为官。[②]

严耕望先生指出："魏都平城时代，为亚洲盛国，西域诸国，相继来朝，从事朝贡贸易，僧徒亦乐东来宏法。魏之君主，或精诚信向，或为凝聚民心，而大崇佛法，凡所建制，规模宏丽，不但远过前朝，亦为南都建康所未闻。豪家大族，亦从而施舍，北魏高宦富室之有家僧盖不始于都洛时代也。"[③]孝文帝太和初，"京城内寺新旧且百所，僧尼二千余人，四方诸寺六千四百七十八，僧尼七万七千二百五十八人。"[④]高僧大德云集平城，其中必有大量胡僧，可惜僧皎《高僧传》详南而略北，平城时代高僧多已湮灭无闻。

赵郡有沙门法果，被太祖诏赴京师，任道人统，成为北魏朝廷管理僧众事务的高级僧官。至太宗时，弥加崇敬。"泰常中卒。未殡，帝三临其丧，追赠老寿将军、赵胡灵公。"[⑤]赵郡属定州，近中山，是魏晋以来中原地区佛教昌盛之地，法果去世后被追赠为"赵胡灵公"，此"胡"字必当有所指，他很可能是西域胡人。京师沙门师贤，罽宾人，少入道，曾东游凉州，太武帝平凉州后来到平城。历经太武帝灭佛而矢志不渝，任道人统。师子国胡沙门邪奢遗多、浮陀难提等五人，太安初奉佛像到京都。又有沙勒胡沙门，因擅长佛画，"赴京师致佛钵并画像迹。"天竺僧人常那邪舍，与昙曜翻译新经十四部，[⑥]此事也当发生于平城。另据《高僧传》记载，天竺僧人佛陀禅师，与道友游历诸国，于孝文帝时来到平城，"时值孝文敬隆诚至，别设禅林，凿石为龛，结徒定念，国家资供，倍加余部，而征应潜著，皆异之非常人也。恒安城内康家，资财百万，崇重佛法，为佛陀造别院，常居室内，自静遵业。"后随孝文帝南迁洛阳，并为之在少室山建造了著名的少林寺。[⑦]留居平城的胡人当远较记载的要多，这里不仅聚集了大量胡僧，从上文所引资财百万的康家来看，粟特商人也应当不少。

五　平城出土与丝绸之路有关的文化遗存

平城一带保留至今与丝绸之路有关的文化遗存十分丰富，即有出土文物如金银器、鎏金铜器、玻璃器、波斯银币等，也包括云冈石窟石雕造像，墓葬壁画以及其他物质遗存的装饰纹样等。这些遗物既有来自国外的，也有本地制作的。

金银器、鎏金铜器包括位于大同市区南部原轴承厂院内北魏遗址出土的鎏金錾花银碗和八曲银杯各一件，鎏金高足铜杯三件，墓葬出土器物包括正始元年（504年）封和突墓出土的狩猎纹鎏金银盘与素面高足银杯各一件，大同南郊北魏墓群出土的鎏金錾花银碗，鎏金錾花高足银杯，素面银碗和素面银杯。这些器物从制作工艺到装饰纹样都没有中土文化因素，应该是从国外输入的。对其具体产地虽有争议，但都认为产自萨珊波斯、东罗马或中亚一带，即中亚和西亚。对于以上器物的研究很多，本人曾有综述，[⑧]兹不赘叙。自古两河流域、古罗马、古希腊以及伊朗高原和中亚的交往

①　赵超：《汉魏南北朝墓志汇编》，天津古籍出版社，1992年。
②　《魏书》卷三十《安同传》。
③　严耕望：《魏晋南北朝佛教地理稿》，上海古籍出版社，2007年。
④　《魏书》卷一一四《释老志》。
⑤　《魏书》卷一一四《释老志》。
⑥　《魏书》卷一一四《释老志》。
⑦　释慧皎：《高僧传》卷一九，汤用彤校注本，北京：中华书局，1992年。
⑧　王银田：《北朝时期丝绸之路输入的西方器物》，张庆捷等编：《4—6世纪的北中国与欧亚大陆》，科学出版社，2006年。

就十分密切，伊朗至中亚一带曾经长期受到希腊、罗马文化的影响，而波斯与中亚各邻国的频繁交往，致使文化方面的影响十分明显，以至于两河流域、伊朗以及中亚的器物文化相互揉和，彼此渗透，难以辨认。需要指出的是，这些器物输入平城的时间都应该是在平城建都期间，即使是封和突墓出土的银器，虽然墓葬为迁洛之后的遗存，但平城迁都后虽仍称北都，孝文帝刚迁都时还曾巡幸，但实际上平城已沦为一个普通边镇，政府的对外交流已转移至洛阳，墓中出土的两件银器应该是墓主人家中的旧藏。其他器物从其组合关系来看也很清楚地表明是平城时代的。

已见诸报道的平城出土玻璃器共计 13 件，即方山永固陵玻璃指环，[①]湖东编组站 M21 圆锥形玻璃器，[②]大同南郊北魏墓群 M107 磨花纹碗，[③]大同七里村 M6 玻璃碗和 M20 玻璃瓶及一件残器，[④]东郊齐家坡迎宾大道工地 M16 玻璃壶和四件半球形泡饰件、M37 蜻蜓眼珠二件。[⑤]此外 2003 年位于市区北部的操场城一号建筑遗址曾出土一块绿玻璃残片，[⑥]另外近年来大同市近郊大规模基建施工中有大量北魏墓葬被挖，据传出土有不少玻璃器，皆已流入民间。以上玻璃器中以大同南郊北魏墓M107 磨花纹碗制作精良，保存完好而历来备受重视，据研究属萨珊波斯器，[⑦]其余器物极有可能是当地制作的，但也显示出与丝路有关的信息。七里村 M6 玻璃碗，更确切地说是玻璃钵，直口，圈足，器物外壁施凸弦纹一道，为典型的北魏器型，相同器型的陶器曾在永平元年（508 年）平城镇将元淑墓中出土，[⑧]该墓地的另两件器物的器型也明显具有本土特征。位于齐家坡的迎宾大道工地出土一件蓝色半透明玻璃壶，宽平沿，喇叭口，圆肩，弧腹，平底，相同器型的陶器在平城期墓葬中已多次发现，是平城时代墓葬陶器组合中的主要器型，[⑨]该玻璃壶色泽与大同操场城北魏一号遗址发现的玻璃残片相同。该墓地的半球形玻璃泡饰件，与平城时代墓葬常见的铜泡钉造型接近，[⑩]也是平城常见的器物。以上器物中七里村的三件玻璃器经检测为钠钙玻璃，属西方配方。[⑪]这类器物的出现显示了一个玻璃器制作工艺方面西方配方的本土化问题。据《魏书》与《北史》的《西域传·大月氏》记载：魏太武帝时"其国（大月氏）人商贩京师，自云能铸石为五色琉璃。于是采矿于山中，于京师铸之。"这些大月氏的工匠在北魏平城使用中国原料，利用西域配方和技术制作了玻璃器。以上几件玻璃器具有本土特征，造型准确，应该出自本土工匠之手，其中有的器物经安家瑶教授鉴定属于吹制玻璃，说明在与胡人的技术交流中，本地工匠已经掌握了钠钙玻璃的制作工艺，包括西域玻璃配方和吹制技术。这种配方和吹制技术的引进，是中国玻璃工艺技术和西方的一次科技交流的成功典范，它对于此后中国玻璃工艺发展的影响是巨大而又深远的。

大同市辖的天镇县曾发现 49 枚波斯银币，经张庆捷先生对其中 39 枚银币研究，37 枚为萨珊王朝卑路斯时期的，1 枚为阿卡德时期，另 1 枚为嚈哒仿卑路斯制品，年代皆属平城时代后期，是丝绸之路国际贸易最直观的反映。[⑫]

平城一带出土的另一种与西域有关的器物是铜下颌托。至今已出土 13 件，其中 12 件出自 1988

---

① 大同市博物馆 山西省文物工作委员会：《大同方山北魏永固陵》，《文物》1978 年第 7 期。
② 安家瑶、刘俊喜：《大同地区的北魏玻璃器》，张庆捷等编：《4—6 世纪的北中国与欧亚大陆》，科学出版社，2006 年。
③ 王银田、王雁卿：《大同南郊北魏墓群 M107 发掘报告》，《北朝研究》，北京燕山出版社，2000 年。山西大学历史文化学院等：《大同南郊北魏墓群》，科学出版社，2006 年。
④ 大同市考古研究所：《山西大同七里村北魏墓群发掘简报》，《文物》2006 年第 10 期。
⑤ 大同市考古研究所：《山西大同迎宾大道北魏墓群》，《文物》2006 年第 10 期。
⑥ 山西省考古研究所等：《大同操场城北魏建筑遗址发掘报告》，《考古学报》2005 年第 4 期。
⑦ 王银田：《萨珊波斯与北魏平城》，《敦煌研究》2005 年第 2 期。
⑧ 大同市博物馆：《大同东郊北魏元淑墓》，《文物》1989 年第 8 期。
⑨ 山西大学历史文化学院等：《大同南郊北魏墓群》，科学出版社，2006 年。
⑩ 王银田、韩生存：《大同市齐家坡北魏墓发掘简报》，《文物季刊》1995 年第 1 期。
⑪ 安家瑶、刘俊喜：《大同地区的北魏玻璃器》，张庆捷等编：《4—6 世纪的北中国与欧亚大陆》，科学出版社，2006 年。
⑫ 张庆捷：《民族汇聚与文明互动——北朝社会的考古学观察》，商务印书馆，2010 年。

年发掘的大同南郊北魏墓群，是到目前为止国内外出土该器物最多的地点。这些下颌托主要由扁平状铜条连接而成，上有环状头箍，固定在头颅，两鬓处与颊带组合在一起，颊带的下端呈勺状扣在下颌处。有的下颌托可能没有头箍，颊带加长，直接在颅顶处扣合在一起。大同南郊北魏墓群M107的下颌托出土时仍完整地扣合在墓主人的头骨上，恰好显示了下颌托的这种使用方法。该器物的功能主要在于固定下颌，以免人死后面部变形。1998年我们在整理M107发掘报告时首次开始关注该器物，在查阅大量资料的基础上对器物名称、时空分布、功能与传播等方面进行了初步研究。① 此后德国慕尼黑大学宋馨博士撰文《北魏下颌托：丧葬风俗向亚洲的传播》对下颌托进行了进一步研究。② 下颌托的使用至少可追溯至古希腊荷马时代（约公元前1200~前800年），在阿提卡和雅典地区的墓葬内就有金质或铅质的下颌托。这个传统在古风时期和古典时期（约公元前8—前4世纪）仍继续存在。古希腊文献称之为othone（复数othonai），原意是女性穿着用的白色亚麻布，推测古希腊大部分下颌托应属纺织品。古希腊公元前6至公元前5世纪时祭祀用的陶瓶上常绘有陈尸哭丧仪式的图像，死者头部从下颌到头顶使用布条绑扎，至今欧洲仍有此俗保留。这种下颌托与新疆发现的下颌托是一样的。新疆且末县扎滚鲁克二号墓，③ 民丰县尼雅遗址95MNI号墓地④以及公元一世纪阿富汗黄金之丘都曾发现下颌托。下颌托于公元五世纪中后期由新疆传入平城，这和北魏时期与丝绸之路的交通有关，而新疆的下颌托则是由希腊经中亚传入的。⑤

前述大同南郊北魏墓群M107曾出土15枚巴丹杏，果皮干枯，紧贴果核，已轻度炭化。这些巴丹杏与红枣、核桃等果品一起放置在一个铜盘内，盘内还有木盘和漆耳杯各一件，木盘内放置木勺一件，⑥显然这是一套食品系列的组合，说明巴丹杏在当时的中原也是作为坚果食用的，这是内地考古发现中的唯一一例实物遗存。此外，新疆吐鲁番阿斯塔那墓地北朝墓葬M320也曾发现一枚，现藏新疆维吾尔自治区博物馆。⑦巴丹杏，蔷薇科李亚科桃属落叶乔木或灌木，今称扁桃。⑧果核为食用的坚果。⑨巴丹杏原产于中亚和西亚地区，其野生种目前在中亚、小亚和新疆天山山区仍有分布。由于在中国古代巴丹杏一直被视为外来物种，这种植物遂成为中外文化交流的一个物证。中国古代文献最早在唐段成式《酉阳杂俎》中既有记载，⑩美国著名东方学者劳费尔据此认为中国从唐代开始人工种植巴丹杏，⑪北魏时期的巴丹杏显然是由西域带来的。

六　平城出土西域遗物的来源

平城出土的西域遗物大概有如下几种来源，首先是国外使节进贡。《魏书》和《北史》记载与北魏交往的西域国家很多，"魏德既广，西域、东夷贡其珍物，充于王府。"⑫这些国家常"遣使来

① 王银田、王雁卿：《大同南郊北魏墓群M107发掘报告》，《北朝研究》，北京燕山出版社，2000年。
② Mueller, Shing, "Chin-straps of the Early Northern Wei: New Perspectives on the Trans-Asiatic Diffusion of Funerary Practices," *Journal of East Asian Archaeology* 5, 1-4 (2003) [2006]。
③ 新疆博物馆文物队：《且末县扎滚鲁克五座墓葬发掘报告》，《新疆文物》1998年第3期。
④ 新疆文物考古研究所：《新疆民丰县尼雅遗址95MNI号墓地M8发掘简报》，《文物》2000年第1期。
⑤ 王银田：《再议下颌托》。
⑥ 王银田、王雁卿：《大同南郊北魏墓群M107发掘报告》，《北朝研究》，北京燕山出版社，2000年。山西大学历史文化学院、山西省考古研究所、大同市博物馆：《大同南郊北魏墓群》，科学出版社，2006年。
⑦ 伊斯拉菲尔·玉苏甫 安尼瓦尔·哈斯木：《西域饮食文化史》，新疆人民出版社，2012年。
⑧ 中国科学院中国植物志编辑委员会编：《中国植物志》第38卷，科学出版社，1986年。
⑨ 汪祖华、左思及主编：《中国果树志·桃卷》，中国林业出版社，2001年。
⑩ 段成式著、杜聪点校：《酉阳杂俎》卷十八，齐鲁书社，2007年。
⑪ 劳费尔著、林筠因译：《中国伊朗编》，商务印书馆，2001年。
⑫ 《魏书》卷一一○《食货志》。

献"，或来"朝贡"或"贡方物"，但具体记载所献贡物的较少，《魏书·世祖纪》载太武帝太延三年（437年）"破洛那、者舌国各遣使朝献，奉汗血马。"《魏书·高宗纪》文成帝和平六年（465年）"夏四月，破洛那国献汗血马，普岚国献宝剑。"《魏书·高祖纪》孝文帝太和二年（461年）"秋七月戊辰，龟兹国遣使献名驼七十头。……九月……龟兹国遣使献大马、名驼、珍宝甚众。"此外，献给北魏洛阳和南朝建康贡品的文献也可作为参考，如世宗宣武帝时，高车王弥俄突"复遣朝贡，又奉表献金方一、银方一、金杖二、马七匹、驼十头。"据《魏书·吐谷浑》记载，吐谷浑王国慕利延遣使刘义隆，"献乌丸帽、女国金酒器、胡王金钏等物。"由此可见，西域进贡的物品中当不乏金银器等贵重器物，这与中亚、西亚国家崇尚金银器的传统有关，平城的考古发现也证实了这一点，当然，彼时所进贡的东西可能远比我们现在所知道的要丰富。

战争掠夺也是西域物品的重要来源。登国六年（391年）道武帝破铁弗部刘卫辰，"收其珍宝、畜产，名马三十余万、牛羊四百余万，渐增国用。""自太祖定中原，世祖平方难，收获珍宝，府藏盈积。"[1]尤其是"世祖即位，开拓四海"期间，神䴥三年（430年）夏国"（赫连）定弟社于、度洛孤面缚出降，平凉平，收其珍宝。"[2]太延五年（439年）灭北凉，"收其城内户口二十余万，仓库珍宝不可称计。"[3]太平真君九年（公元448年），万度归率领北魏军大破焉耆三城，缴获了大量珍宝异玩。同年十二月又向龟兹国发动攻击，"举国臣民负钱怀货，一时降款。获其奇宝、异玩以巨万，驼、马、杂畜不可胜数。度归遂入龟兹，复获其殊方瑰诡之物亿万已上。"[4]五凉与赫连夏等西北地区各政权皆临近西域，府中必有大量西域珍宝，北魏平定西北各政权后这些珍宝必定有一部分流入平城，其中除入藏皇宫外，也会有部分赏赐功臣而流入民间。

除战争等国家行为以外，个人也可能通过一定渠道如民间贸易等途径获得西域物品，尤其是与西域公务有涉的官员更有近水楼台之便，这方面尚无直接证据，但北魏后期的一则案例或可说明一些问题，洛阳时期贪官河间王元琛[5]任秦州刺史时，曾"遣使向西域求名马，远至波斯国。……琛常会宗室，陈诸宝器，金瓶银瓮百余口，瓯檠盘盒称是。自余酒器，有水晶钵，玛瑙杯，玻璃碗，赤玉卮数十枚。作工奇妙，中土所无，皆从西域而来。"[6]元琛个人所拥有的波斯等西域金银器之类珍宝其数量多得惊人，可见当时对西域珍宝是何等崇尚，拥有这些珍宝是身份和地位的象征。大同南郊北魏墓群M107出土多件西域遗物，墓主人应该和西域有关。与匈奴人一样，鲜卑人也酷爱金银器，北魏太平真君十一年（公元450年）刘宋将领刘泰之率军袭击汝阳北魏军营时，见几个毡屋内"食具皆是金银。"[7]迁都前韩麒麟在其上高祖《陈时务表》中说平城"宝货盈于市里"，[8]现出土所见，不过万一。

七 平城的艺术遗存

公元五世纪，伴随着佛教文化的东传，西域各地的美术、音乐、舞蹈等域外艺术也东传平城。这类艺术首先集中表现在以云冈石窟为代表的北魏石窟寺中。"云冈石窟是新疆以东最早出现的大

---

① 《魏书》卷一一〇《食货志》。
② 《魏书》卷四上《世祖纪》。
③ 《魏书》卷四上《世祖纪》。
④ 《魏书》卷一一〇《食货志》。
⑤ 《魏书》卷二十《河间王若传附子琛传》。
⑥ 周祖谟：《洛阳伽蓝记校释》卷四，中华书局，1963年。
⑦ 《宋书》卷65《索虏传》。
⑧ 《全后魏文》卷三十一，严可均校辑：《全上古三代秦汉三国六朝文》，中华书局，1985年。

型石窟群，又是当时统治北中国的北魏皇室集中全国技艺和人力、物力所兴建。"①云冈石窟在吸收印度和中亚艺术的基础上又糅合了中国本土文化，创造出灿烂的东方艺术奇葩。

从根本上说，佛教属外来文化，佛教石窟寺所表现的题材也都是外来的。西域美术对云冈石窟的影响应首推犍陀罗艺术和新疆境内的早期石窟寺，除佛教题材外，云冈石窟中大量表现的建筑、服饰、伎乐飞天、音乐舞蹈、装饰纹样以及弟子像等包含了希腊、波斯、印度和中亚犍陀罗艺术的因素，形象地诉说着外来艺术在中土的茁壮成长。②

云冈石窟多见有帔帛，这种服饰也见于敦煌石窟，如莫高窟288窟和390窟北魏壁画女供养人及285窟西魏女供养人，之后在隋唐陶俑、墓葬壁画常见，成为隋唐妇女衣着的一个重要组成部分。帔帛状如飘带，缠绕于躯体和手臂间，轻盈飘逸，颇具美感。据《旧唐书·波斯传》记载：波斯人"丈夫剪发，戴白皮帽，衣不开襟，并有巾帔。多用苏方青白色为之，两边缘以织成锦。妇人亦巾帔裙衫，辫法垂后。"③新疆丹丹乌里克出土的早期木板佛画，波斯萨珊王朝银瓶人物都曾有帔帛出现，云冈石窟帔帛也应源于波斯。此外，云冈17窟南壁东侧胁侍菩萨头顶飘带颇具萨珊式样风格，而18窟北壁东侧的几个弟子像则直接雕刻成高鼻深目的胡人形象。④

在佛教艺术盛行的背景下，外来艺术式样在平城也影响到世俗艺术方面，具体表现在墓葬壁画、葬具、器物纹样、陶俑等方面。在装饰纹样方面，最常见的外来纹样当属忍冬纹，这种纹样起源于地中海地区，随着亚历山大大帝东征，希腊文化东传过程中忍冬纹开始在中亚流行，又随着佛教文化东传进入中国，公元五世纪在中国得到极大发展。北魏平城是此纹样最集中的地区，忍冬纹与伎乐、瑞兽、联珠纹等组合，幻化出多种不同的组合式忍冬纹，构图呈带状、二方连续、四方连续等，大量出现在石雕棺床、棺版画、墓葬壁画、模印墓砖、瓦当甚至普通陶器上，成为平城时代最为流行的装饰纹样，由此也可看到外来文化在平城已深深地浸润到世俗生活之中。此外流行的外来纹样还有葡萄纹和联珠纹等。

"移风易俗，莫善于乐。"⑤中土历来重视音乐的教化作用，由于深受中原汉文化影响，入主中原的拓跋鲜卑统治者对音乐同样十分重视，北魏建国之初"诏尚书吏部郎邓渊定律吕，协音乐。"⑥不久后即设置宫廷音乐机构太乐。"世祖破赫连昌，获古雅乐，及平凉州，得其伶人、器服、并择而存之。后通西域，又以悦般国鼓舞设于乐署。"⑦太和时"方乐之制及四夷歌舞，稍增列于太乐。"太和十五年（491年）冬，高祖诏曰："乐者所以动天地，感神祇，调阴阳，通人鬼。故能关山川之风，以播德于无外。由此言之，治用大矣。"太和十六年（492年）春，又诏曰："礼乐之道，自古所先，故圣王作以和中，制礼以防外。然音声之用，其致远矣，所以通感人神，移风易俗。"⑧《隋书·音乐志》对北魏宫廷音乐也有记载："西凉者，起苻氏之末，吕光、沮渠蒙逊等据有凉州，变龟兹声为之，号为秦汉伎。魏太武既平河西得之，谓之《西凉乐》。""《龟兹》者，起自吕光灭龟兹，因得其声。吕氏亡，其乐分散，后魏平中原，复获之。""《疏勒》、《安国》、《高丽》，并起

① 宿白：《平城实力的聚集和"云冈模式"的形成与发展》，云冈石窟文管所编：《中国石窟·云冈石窟》，文物出版社株式会社平凡社，1991年。
② 云冈石窟文管所编：《云冈百年论文选集》，文物出版社，2005年。云冈石窟研究院编：《2005年云冈国际学术讨论会论文集·研究卷》，北京：文物出版社，2006年。
③ 《旧唐书》卷一九八《波斯传》。
④ 宿白主编：《中国美术全集·云冈石窟》图150、151、158、159，文物出版社，1988年。
⑤ 《孝经·广要道章第十二》，《十三经注疏·孝经注疏卷六》，中华书局影印本，1980年。
⑥ 《魏书》卷一〇九《乐志》。
⑦ 《魏书》卷一〇九《乐志》。
⑧ 《魏书》卷一〇九《乐志》。

自后魏平冯氏及通西域，因得其伎。"①北魏宫廷音乐除保留下来的部分传统中土音乐外，还有来自西域各国以及高丽的音乐，②成为公元五世纪后期东亚音乐的集大成者。

北魏平城的音乐遗存主要集中于云冈石窟，其中有音乐图像的洞窟达22座，乐器雕刻不少于664件，乐器30余种。③这些乐器来自中亚、西亚和南亚印度以及高句丽。除中国本土或汉代传入中国的外来乐器外，也有北魏时期新近传入的乐器，如琵琶，仅云冈二期雕刻中就有44例，其中9例为用手弹奏，其余是用拨弹奏，比唐代文献记载"始废拨用手"的贞观年间大大提前；再如唢呐，云冈石窟所见为中原地区最早的资料。外来乐器的引进也丰富了中国本土乐器的演奏方法，如用拨子弹奏琵琶的方法被移植到阮的演奏上来，增加了乐器的表现力。④

音乐遗存也散见于出土文物，如司马金龙墓出土石棺床立面的伎乐雕刻，⑤雁北师院M2等。后者出土一组9个胡人俑和2个儿童俑组成的俑群，这些陶俑姿态各异，从其姿势判断，可能有吹笛子和演奏琵琶的，其中一个胡人和两个儿童俑正好还原出一组正在表演"缘橦"的场面。⑥此组陶俑似可称之为"百戏俑"。据《魏书·乐志》记载，拓跋珪天兴"六年（403年）冬，诏太乐、总章、鼓吹增修杂伎，造五兵、角抵、麒麟、凤皇、仙人、长蛇、白象、白虎及诸畏兽、鱼龙、辟邪、鹿马、仙车、高絙百尺、长趫、缘橦、跳丸、五案，以备百戏。"⑦百戏是北魏宫廷与民间都十分流行的艺术。近年发掘的大同云波里路北魏壁画墓在墓室东壁下层壁画中有胡人奏乐场景，五位胡人手持曲颈琵琶、横笛、排箫、细腰鼓和行鼓正在演奏。⑧大同雁北师院北魏墓M5出土一组四件胡人伎乐俑⑨此外，内蒙古呼和浩特大学路北魏墓也曾出土胡人俑，⑩这些胡人形象各异，服饰也有区别，当来自不同民族或不同国度，有的胡人俑与骆驼组合，在大同文瀛路北魏壁画墓还发现绘有高鼻、卷发的胡人牵驼图，⑪此类陶俑的出现是对平城时代丝绸之路国际贸易的形象注解。

随着佛教的传播，来自犍陀罗的石膏粘土模制佛像技术传入平城，在方山永固陵南侧的思远佛寺遗址⑫和大同城东北魏佛寺遗址大量发现，⑬此外也见于辽宁朝阳北塔和内蒙包头市固阳县北部的城圐圙古城址，前者据研究为冯太后所建思燕佛图遗迹，⑭后者既六镇之一的怀朔镇。⑮迁都后在洛阳永宁寺仍大量使用。⑯

① 《隋书》卷一五《音乐志》。
② 李方元、俞梅：《北魏宫廷音乐考述》，《中国音乐学》1998年第2期。
③ 林莎：《云冈石窟乐器图像补正与辨识》，云冈石窟研究院编：《2005年云冈国际学术讨论会论文集·研究卷》，文物出版社，2006年。
④ 肖兴华：《云冈石窟中的乐器雕刻》，《中国音乐》1981年第2期。项阳、陶正刚主编：《中国音乐文物大系·山西卷》，大象出版社，2000年。肖兴华：《云冈石窟——南北朝民族大融合带来的音乐繁荣的历史见证》。赵昆雨：《云冈石窟乐舞雕刻研究》，《敦煌研究》，2007年第2期。
⑤ 大同市博物馆、山西省文物工作委员会：《山西大同石家寨北魏司马金龙墓》，《文物》1972年第3期。
⑥ 大同市考古研究所：《大同雁北师院北魏墓葬群》，文物出版社，2008年。
⑦ 《魏书》卷一○九《乐志》。
⑧ 大同市考古研究所：《山西大同云波里路北魏壁画墓发掘简报》《文物》2011年第12期。
⑨ 大同市考古研究所：《大同雁北师院北魏墓群》，文物出版社，2008年。
⑩ 郭素新：《内蒙古呼和浩特北魏墓》，《文物》1977年第5期。
⑪ 大同市考古研究所：《山西大同文瀛路北魏壁画墓发掘简报》，《文物》2011年第12期。
⑫ 大同市博物馆：《大同北魏方山思远佛寺遗址发掘报告》，《文物》2007年第4期。
⑬ 出光美术馆：《中国の考古学展——北京大学考古学系发掘成果》，平凡社，1995年。
⑭ 辽宁省文物考古研究所 朝阳市北塔博物馆编：《朝阳北塔考古发掘与维修工程报告》，文物出版社，2007年。
⑮ 内蒙古文物工作队 包头市文物管理所：《内蒙古白灵淖城圐圙北魏古城遗址调查与试掘》，《考古》1984年第2期。
⑯ 中国社会科学院考古研究所：《北魏洛阳永宁寺1979~1994年考古发掘报告》，中国大百科全书出版社，1996年。

八　平城时代的交通路线

晋北地区历来就是中国北方的交通要冲，在东西方文化交流的舞台上扮演着重要角色，在中国最早的丝路文献《穆天子传》中，就已涉及到晋北。穆天子"绝漳水"，"至釾山"，"北循虖沱之阳"，旅途从东都洛阳出发，北行后过太行山进入山西北部，再折而向西，到达河套，最终进入昆仑山（今阿尔泰山）。马雍先生认为，从阿尔泰山中段的东麓越过山口，再沿黑水（今额尔齐斯河上游）西进，当时就存在着这样一条东方商道，而公元前五世纪的巴泽雷克古墓发现了铜镜、丝绸和漆器等中原遗物，遗迹地点正处在这条路线上。[1]公元前三世纪初，秦赵联军伐齐，齐王在一封给赵惠文王的信中说，（若秦军）"逾勾注，斩常山而守之，三百里而通于燕，代马胡犬不东下，昆山之玉不出，此三宝者亦非王有已。"[2]说假如秦国出兵切断山西北部恒山一带的交通线，昆仑山的玉石就无法运到赵国了，这封信证明当时的玉石贸易路线经过山西北部，与《穆天子传》描述的路线是一致的。

亚洲境内北纬40~50度之间的山脉多呈东西走向，为欧亚大陆间的交通提供了方便。由于欧亚草原地理的特殊性以及由此引起的游牧部落的东西向迁徙，欧亚草原丝绸之路成为最早开辟的东西交通线路。[3]从已发现的考古遗迹判断，拓跋鲜卑建立北魏政权前就已通过草原丝绸之路与西域建立了联系，平城时期则与绿洲丝路和草原丝路都有关联，平城成为公元五世纪沙漠丝路和草原丝路在中国北方的一个节点。

在巴基斯坦北部的洪扎河畔岩石上曾发现汉文题记"大魏使谷魏龙今向迷密使去"，据马雍先生考证，"迷密"即文献中始见于《魏书》与《北史》的西域国家迷密，隋唐时期昭武九姓中的米国，此为北魏题记，《魏书》迷密国遣使中国仅正平元年（451年）正月一次，谷魏龙的此次出访当在此前后不久。[4]这对考察唐代以前丝绸之路在中亚地区的确切路线颇为有益。北魏晚期宋云经过于阗时看到"悬彩幡盖，亦有万计，魏国之幡过半矣。幡上隶书，多云太和十九年（495年）、景明二年（501年）、延昌二年（413年）。"[5]尽管以洛阳时代纪年为主，或许也有平城时代的幡亦未可知。

北魏立国后，组建了以平城为中心的交通网，网络通达东西南北，并与周边国家以及更远的国度建立了联系。从平城向北经长川、牛川、阴山南麓的白道通往漠北；向南越句注山达晋阳盆地，沿汾河南下可进入关中或中原腹地；东经莎泉道或灵丘道沿滱水东南行，越太行山到中山，可达山东、中原或长江沿岸，或东出上谷、密云到三燕故都龙城，并经辽东进入高句丽及朝鲜半岛；西溯武州川水过盛乐、云中，经君子津过黄河，沿鄂尔多斯高原东南缘西行，经固原（高平镇）进入河西走廊，出敦煌，与西域绿洲丝路南、北路连接进入南亚、中亚和西亚。[6]或如前述经吐谷浑道西行进入绿洲丝路。吐谷浑曾占有若羌、且末等丝路中段南道部分地区，通过青海可以不经过河西走廊而西行直通丝路南道。沿途的西宁就曾出土萨珊波斯银币。太平真君年间鄯善反叛，北魏派韩拔为假持节征西将军、领户西戎校尉、鄯善王，在鄯善设置军镇。丝路南道过阳关，经罗布泊西南行可达鄯善，此路远离柔然，成为北魏通西域的主要道路。万度归出兵焉耆，曾驻军于此，此外北魏也曾经营中道。[7]北魏通西域的道路主要是汉代开通的南道和中道（汉代称北道），北道在448年道武帝联合悦

---

① 马雍、王炳华：《阿尔泰与欧亚草原丝绸之路》，张志尧编《草原丝绸之路与中亚文明》，新疆美术摄影出版社，1994年。

② 《史记》卷四三《赵世家》。

③ 余太山：《〈穆天子传〉所见东西交通路线》，上海社会科学院历史研究所：《第二届传统中国研究国际学术讨论会论文集》（一），上海人民出版社，2007年。

④ 马雍：《巴基斯坦北部所见"大魏"使者的岩刻题记》，《南亚研究》第3辑，1984年。后收入马雍《西域史地文物丛考》，文物出版社，1990年。

⑤ 周祖谟：《洛阳伽蓝记校释》卷五，中华书局，1963年。

⑥ 前田正名著，李凭等译：《平城历史地理学研究》，书目文献出版社，1994年。

⑦ 《魏书》卷一○二《西域传》。

般攻打柔然后也曾通行。

如何评价丝绸之路开通对北魏平城以及北朝隋唐文化的影响是一个复杂而有意义的课题，这方面深入、全面的研究尚需积累与时日。无疑这种影响是多方面的，持久的和有益的。由于中国地理位置与环境的特殊性，古代的中国一直处于东亚文明的中心，对中国有重要影响的域外文化主要来自广义的西域地区，这就注定了中国与西域国家的密切联系，这也是中国历代王朝重视开拓西域的内在原因。

丝绸之路开通对北魏平城首先具有经济方面的重要意义。平城政权获得了河西与西域大量的资源，如巨量的牲畜马牛羊等，这对改善北魏经济的落后局面大有益处。所获马匹有的可充作战马使用，中亚的良驹宝马对中土马种的改良十分有益，这又增强了北魏的军事实力，平城出土的大量陶马脊宽体长，硕健有力，或许与此有关。以平城为中心的交通网络的建设是拓跋鲜卑政权的重要贡献，它进一步完善了北方的交通架构，也被后代所继承。大月氏人在平城制作玻璃的记载是传统文献少见的工业技术交流的案例，对中国玻璃工艺技术的改进十分重要。据《南齐书·魏虏传》记载，"太后出，则妇女著铠骑马近辇左右。……坐施氍毹褥。前施金香鑪、琉璃钵、金捥，盛杂食器。"这些陈设、器具来自中亚、波斯或大秦，胡风尽显，形象的说明了外来文化对宫廷生活的影响。

丝绸之路带来的异域文化对平城时代以及公元五世纪中国的美术影响巨大而长久，不仅表现在宗教信仰，在艺术层面更直接地影响了国人的审美，此后各类艺术更具写实，在浓烈的宗教氛围中也常常显示出清新的现实主义风格。在大同南郊北魏墓群出土人骨的研究中发现，该墓地人群以东北亚蒙古人种为主，同时杂入带有欧洲人种特征的乌孙人种特征，这或许就与丝路开通以来不同种族人群间的通婚有关。太武帝以来丝绸之路的开通，使平城这座塞外边城一举成为公元五世纪的国际大都市。平城时代的各项成果都被洛阳时代所继承，于是直接促成了洛阳时代的繁荣，进而间接影响到隋唐。

（本文为国家社科基金项目《北魏平城考古研究——公元五世纪中国都城的演变》阶段性成果，项目批准号：12BKG011）

汉籍所载希腊渊源的"女人国"传说

张绪山 清华大学

摘要: 南北朝至隋唐时代的中国典籍,保留了与"拂菻国"有关系的"西女国"的记载。"西女国"的特点是无男,其女子与邻国男子偶配,生男不养而仅留女婴。这个故事本是希腊神话故事,后进入希罗多德的《历史》。这个版本的"女人国"故事流传于欧亚大陆的各个时代,与东方渊源的以无性繁殖为故事主干的"女王国"故事大异其趣。

关键词: 拂菻国;西女国;希腊神话;女人国

Abstract: In accounts of the Fu-lin country (the Byzantine Empire), ancient Chineses sources (especially in the Sui and Tang Dynasties) contain some records of "Women Kingdoms of the West", which were characterized by their pregnancy with men of Fu-lin, and leaving no male children in limits of their own conutry. The proto-type of the legend was found in Greek mythology and was introduced by Herodotus (484-425 BC) into his historical work, and was transmitted over to the Greeco-Roman World. The Greek version of "Women Kingdoms" had been passed down with little variance through all ages in Eurasian Continent, showing its differences in framework with the traditional "Women Kingdoms" of oriental origin.

Keywords: Fu-lin Country, Women Kingdoms of the West, Greek Mythology, Women Kingdoms

一

在南北朝至隋唐时代的中国典籍中,"拂菻"是一个新出现的名称。百余年来的研究证实,它指的是由罗马帝国演化而来的拜占廷帝国,即东罗马帝国。

在这一时期的汉籍记载中,颇有有一些与"拂菻"相关的事物,"女人国"传说是其中之一。《法苑珠林》三九云:

> 案《梁贡职图》云,(拂菻)去波斯北一万里,西南海岛有西女国,非印度摄,拂懔年别送男夫配焉。

《贡职图》亦作《职贡图》，乃南梁元帝萧绎所作。"拂懔"即"拂菻"。梁朝处于南方，此传说显然由海路传至中国。与此相应的是，《大唐西域记》记载，玄奘西域求法途中在北印度也听到了类似的"女人国"传说：

> 波剌斯国西北接拂懔国……拂懔国西南海岛，有西女国，皆是女人，略无男子。多诸珍货，附拂懔国，故拂懔王岁遣丈夫配焉。其俗产男，皆不举也。

《大慈恩寺三藏法师传》卷四记载大略相同：

> （波剌斯）国东境有鹤秣城，西北接拂懔国，西南海岛有西女国，皆是女人，无男子，多珍宝，附属拂懔，拂懔王岁遣丈夫配焉，其俗产男例皆不举。

《新唐书》卷二二一：

> 拂菻西，有西女国，种皆女子，附拂菻。拂菻君长岁遣男子配焉，俗差男不举。

《大慈恩寺三藏法师传》与《新唐书》所记"女人国"事，均取材于玄奘《大唐西域记》，故所记与《大唐西域记》完全一致。玄奘所记内容多取自梵文典籍或亲身见闻，他将拂懔国与女人国的记载附于"波剌斯国"条下，且明言"非印度之国，路次附见"，说明女国故事乃玄奘在中亚或印度所获闻。显然，在印度和中亚都流传着与"拂菻"相联系的"西女国"故事。

德国汉学家夏德（F. Hirth）在其名著《中国与罗马东边地》（China and the Roman Orient）中注意到玄奘关于女人国的记载多与古希腊史家斯特拉波（公元前58–公元21）著作关于女人国（Amazons）的记载相合，似注意到二者之间的渊源关系，不过，他对此似乎有些犹豫不决，难以断定，原因是两种记载中女人国位置的不同："斯特拉波笔下的女人国据说位于麦奥提斯湖（Lake Maeotis，即亚速海）岸边，而不是在拂菻西南，他们也不是生活在岛上，派遣男子与她们相配的邻人不是叙利亚人而是居于高加索山下的加加尔人（Gargareans）。"不管夏德态度如何优柔寡断，他联想到玄奘所记故事与希腊世界的"女人国"传说的关系，确实显示了他思维的敏锐。

夏德研究的不足之处在于：首先，他对希腊罗马世界有关"女人国"传说的考察仅上溯至斯特拉波，未能从根源上看到它的原型。实际上，希腊神话中的"女人国"故事，不仅远比斯特拉波更为古老，而且在传播范围上也比想象的更为广阔。其次，夏德不太了解民俗传说在不同地区传播的规则，所以要向人们指出两种记载显示的地点的差异。从民间传说显示的传播规则看，将故事发生地与讲述者母邦混为一谈，这一现象在世界各地的民间传说交流中十分常见，是一种普遍现象。由于当时的拜占廷帝国（即"拂菻"）在欧亚大陆是有相当知名度而又充满神秘感的国家，将一种带有神秘色彩的传说附会于其上，是完全可以理解的。

二

在希腊世界，"女人国"的传说可能产生于希腊人向黑海地区殖民时期，所以，在地理范围上，古希腊神话传说将"女人国"置于黑海（亚速海）沿岸或小亚细亚地区。根据希腊神话，女人国的女人们崇尚武艺，骁勇异常。为繁衍后代，她们与邻近的部落男子婚配，然后将男子送走，生下女婴便留下由母亲抚养，训练其狩猎和战争本领，培养成勇猛的女将，男婴则交还其父，或将其杀掉。

女人国的妇女自认为是战神阿瑞斯的后裔，热衷于战争，经常对他族发动战争。为便于使用弓箭，她们烧掉右侧乳房。女武士使用的武器有双面斧、弓、矛和半月形盾等。早期"女人国"传说有三个元素：一是女人国妇女的尚武；二是女人国妇女与邻近群体的男子婚配以繁衍后代；三是所生后代只留养女婴而不留男婴。在这三个元素中，又以后两个元素为基本核心元素。

与早期女人国传说相关的神话人物有大力神赫拉克利斯等。在赫拉克利斯建立的十二功勋中，其中之一是他从女人国取得金腰带。在赫拉克利斯神话中，女人国位于黑海边本都地区的特尔莫冬河两岸，女王拥有战神阿瑞斯赠送的金腰带。赫拉克利斯到达女人国后，女王对大力神很有好感，打算献出金腰带，不料大力神的敌人天后赫拉从中挑起事端，致使赫拉克利斯与尚武好战的女人国战士发生战争。赫拉克利斯打败女人国的军队，女王被迫交出金腰带。赫拉克利斯以力大勇武著称，大力神传说突出了女人国妇女的强悍和好战。

"女人国"主题除了见于神话传说，也进入历史著作。希罗多德在其著作《历史》（IV, 110–117）记载，女人国的女子曾与黑海沿岸的希腊人作战，希腊人打败了她们，准备把大量俘虏运到雅典，船到海上航行时，"女人国"战士杀死了押运她们的希腊人。但她们不会操纵船只，船只漂流到黑海东北部的亚速海（麦奥提斯湖）岸边，由此与该地的斯基泰人发生战争。斯基泰人从战死的女人国战士尸体上发现她们是妇女，决定不再以战争手段对付她们。他们派出大约数量相等的年轻男子，在她们的驻地附近安营扎寨，并模仿女人国战士的一切动作。如果女战士们前来交战，斯基泰男人并不迎战，而是逃跑；待女战士停止追击，则仍回到女战士驻地附近安营。当女战士看到斯基泰人并无伤害自己的意图时，就不再主动发起攻击，双方的营地也逐渐接近起来。起初，单个的斯基泰男子与单个的女战士交往，随后带来各自身边的伙伴彼此交往，最后双方的营帐合并在一起，每个斯基泰男子娶最初交往的女战士为妻，彼此结合在一起。新形成的群体并没有回到斯基泰男子原来的群体，也没有定居于女战士占领的土地，而是迁移到一个新的地区开始生活，这个地区位于塔奈斯河以东三日路程，从麦奥提斯湖向北三日路程。

在希罗多德的记载中，我们确实可以看到斯基泰人"遣丈夫配焉"这个情节，但不是每岁都派遣，而是派遣的男子与女战士结合成一个新团体；而且，希罗多德也没有提到"产男不举"的风俗。实际上包含了女人国妇女尚武和他族派遣男子婚配这两个元素。这体现出历史著作的的特点：神话传说母题在与历史事实结合时，只保留与历史实际相符的细节，并加以突出和强调，而改变或略去一些具体细节，一些人们熟悉的细节。正如在中国的帝王神话中，与"龙"的关系及由此获得的神圣性是不可缺少的核心元素，但如何表现"龙"与帝王的关系则形式各异。

三

"女人国"故事，在欧亚大陆各地经久流传，地点随时代不同而有所变化。阿拉伯故事集《天方夜谭》中，女人国位于第聂伯河中的若干岛屿上。马可·波罗游记中，女人国是印度辖下的一个岛屿，与男人岛相对，位于克思马克兰南海行 500 哩，两岛相距约 30 哩，每年第三月，诸男子尽赴女岛，居住三个月，与女子欢处，然后返回。"彼等与诸妇所产之子女，女则属母，男则由母抚养至 14 岁，然后遣归父所。"15 世纪初叶出使帖木儿汗廷的西班牙人克拉维约（Klaviyo）则将女人国置于中亚以东地区："由撒马尔罕向契丹行 15 日里程，有女人国（Amazons），迄今仍保持不与男人相处之俗，只是一年一度与男人交往。她们从首领们那里获得准许，携女儿前往最近的地区与男人交会，每人得一悦己之男人，与之同居住、共饮食，随后返归本土。生女后则留下抚养，生男则送其生父养育。女人国现属帖木儿统治，但曾经归辖于契丹皇帝。信仰基督教，属希腊教会。她们是守防特洛耶城的女战士的后裔，希腊人攻取特洛耶城后，乃移居于此地。"克拉维约所述显然是久已流行的版本，但仍突出了希腊渊源。

西班牙人门多萨（Juan Gonzalez De Mendoza，1545–1618）根据此前相关人员的东方消息，于1585年出版《大中华帝国史》，其中也有"女人国"的记载，不过，他笔下的"女人国"是在东亚海中："距离日本不远，近顷发现有女人岛，岛中仅有女人，持弓矢，善射，为习射致烧其右乳房。每年一定月份，有若干日本船舶，载货至其岛交易。船至岛后，令二人登岸，以船中人数通知女王。女王指定舟人登岸之日，至日，舟人未登岸前，岛中女子至港，女数如舟中男数，女各携绳鞋一双，鞋上皆有暗记，乱置沙上而退。舟中男子然后登岸，各着绳鞋往就诸女，诸女各认鞋而延之归。其着女王之鞋者，虽丑陋而亦不拒。迨至限期已满，各人以其住址告女而与之别。告以住址者，如次年生子，男儿应送交其父也。"这位西班牙人明言"此事乃诸教士闻诸两年前曾至此岛某人者，但日本之耶稣会士，对于此事毫无记录，余尚疑而未信云。"很显然，这里的东方"女人国"，是欧西人将希腊渊源的"女人国"传说移植到了东方背景中，虽其细节有所变化，而其整体面目仍是希腊传统的。这是民间传说随时代、地域变动而发生时空转化的又一例证。

类似的例证还有一例。1697年法国某传教士在马尼拉（Manille）写的书信中说："此种外人（假拟在 Mariannes 群岛南方某岛中之外人），谓彼等岛中有一岛，仅有女子住在其中，自成一国，不许男子羼入。女子多不婚，惟在年中某季许男子来会，聚数日，携其无需乳哺之男孩而归，女孩则留母所。"其核心仍是与外部男子婚配、生男不举的内容。

自古希腊以降，"女人国"传说的一个特点是婚配繁衍。希腊传统的"女人国"传说中，几乎看不到无性繁殖的实例。罗马传说中出现过无性繁殖的传说，如公元1世纪的罗马作家梅拉（Pomponius Mela）曾记载一地"女子独居，全身有毛，浴海而孕，其俗蛮野，为人所捕者，用绳缚之，尚虞其逃走。"杜环《经行记》说："又闻（拂菻）西有女国，感水而生。"依夏德的看法，杜环所说的意思可能是"生于水"，如塞浦路斯岛流行的维纳斯崇拜（Venus Anadyomene of Cyprus）。但这一传说传播不广，不占据主导地位。

在中国，女人国（或女儿国）传说也是历史悠久，连绵不绝。《山海经》记载女人国故事：女子国无男子；成年女子到黄池洗澡而致使怀孕，生育男婴，至多活三岁而死，唯女婴才能长大成人。就正史论，《后汉书·东夷列传》最早提到"女国"，其位置在东海："海中有女国，无男人，或传其国有神井，窥之辄生子云。"《梁书·东夷传》记"女国"："慧深又云：'扶桑东千里，有女国，容貌端正，色甚洁白，身体有毛，发长委地。至二、三月，竞入水则任娠，六七月产子。女人胸前无乳，项后生毛，根白，毛中有汁，以乳子，一百日能行，三四年则成人矣。见人惊避，偏畏丈夫。'"宋代赵汝适《诸蕃志》多采其前辈周去非《岭外代答》材料，其于"沙华公国"之后记"女人国"："又东南有女人国，水常东流，数年水一泛涨……其国女人遇南风盛发，裸而感风，即生女也。""沙华公国"不可定考。有人认为在加里曼丹岛。南宋末年建州崇安（今属福建）人陈元靓撰《事林广记》记女人国："女人国，居东北海角，与奚部小如者部抵界。其国无男，每视井即生也。"宋代的两位作者的作品中都贯穿无性繁衍的母题。而作为明代文学作品的《西游记》，其中的女人国的故事，也突出女人喝过子母河的河水而怀孕的主题。无性繁殖是"女人国"传说中远东系统区别于西方系统的最重要、最明显的元素。

可见，玄奘《西域记》中的"女人国"传说属于希腊传说系统，是希腊渊源的"女人国"传说的翻板。玄奘《西域记》记载中"拂菻"与"女人国"的联系，暗示着拜占廷帝国在这个传说流播过程中的作用；同时也反映了此一时期拜占廷帝国在欧亚大陆文化交往中的重要地位。阿拉伯伊斯兰势力兴起以后，女人国传说演化为伊斯兰教文化的一个内容了。

【古代亚非史】

古代两河流域印章雕刻工艺初探

曹明玉　大连大学

摘要：早期玉石器雕刻工艺一直备受相关学界的关注，古代两河流域较为发达的玉石印章制造业为深入研究该问题提供了丰富的材料。通过对雕刻工具遗留微痕的考察，可以复原和分析古代印章雕刻运用的工艺技术。两河流域凿、钻、锉应用广泛且历时较长，而具有划时代意义的砣具则出现较晚，可能首次应用于古巴比伦中晚期，普及于迦喜特晚期，其对砣具的接受是一个渐进的过程，对凿锉等在硬石印章雕刻局限上的突破、对钻等旋杆式转动工具的改进，以及对硬质石材的逐渐青睐是砣具得以发明的主要动因。

关键词：两河流域；印章雕刻；微痕分析；工艺技术

Abstract：Mesopotamian early jade-carving craft, for which the local seal manufacturing enterprises provide a wealth of materials, has always been the study focus in academic field. The technology utilized in the ancient seal engravings can be analyzed and recovered through micro-mark analysis. The tools, including chisels, drills and files, have widely been used since very earlier times. The significant one of them, cutting wheel, appeared in late Old Babylonia period and became popular in late Kassite period. The impulsion for its invention lies in the following three factors: the limitation of chisels and files, the improvement of drills as well as the preference for semi-precious stones.

Keywords：Mesopotamia, Seal carving, Micro-mark analysis, Technology

早期雕刻工艺是世界玉石器制作工艺研究中的一个备受关注的课题，中外许多学者纷纷撰文探讨其中的相关问题。作为人类文明的发祥地之一，两河流域在世界文明史上具有重要的影响。在玉石器具加工制造方面，这一地区的玉石制造业为我们了解和研究早期雕刻工艺的发展提供了比较丰富的材料。本文拟对在两河流域玉石制造业中占有重要地位的印章雕刻工艺的发展情况作简要的介绍和初步的探讨，从而为深入认识两河流域文明提供一个视角。

在古代两河流域地区，印章根据外在形态主要可以分为平印和滚印两大类型，其中后者在两河文明中占有比较重要的地位，与泥板、塔庙并称为该文明的三大标志。滚印顾名思义是以滚动方式使用的印章，这种印章呈圆柱体，柱面阴刻图案，其中一些刻有印文，整个印体通常为实心，但也有少部分钻有贯通的穿孔。在两河流域地区，平印属于印章的早期形态，其出现年代相对较早，大约首见于公元前6千纪初期的叙利亚布格拉斯（Buqras），滚印虽然年代稍晚，最早见于公元前4千纪中晚期的巴比伦尼亚和伊朗库齐斯坦（Khuzestan）地区，但其短时间内在广泛的区域普遍取代平印，成为伊朗、两河流域、叙利亚地区印章的主要形态，直到公元前1千纪中期平印重新占据历史舞台。根据即有的研究成果，滚印与平印之间并不存在承传关系。

印章具有多方面的史学价值和艺术价值。从其地理分布当中，可以看到不同时期和地区商贸交往的一些情况，从其异彩纷呈的雕刻图案中，可以窥见当时社会的宗教观念和文化交流状况，而从其所用原料和制作工艺中，又可以分析两河流域雕刻工艺的发展和变化。

一　微痕分析与早期工具的应用

两河流域制作印章的主要石材有石灰石、绿泥石、蛇纹石、天青石、赤铁石、石英等，不同历史时期在具体材料选取上存在一定差异。例如，阿卡德时期最流行的是蛇纹石，现存阿卡德印章几乎半数都以此为材料，在古巴比伦时期赤铁石则成为包括叙利亚和土耳其在内的整个近东地区印章制作的首选石材。总体而言，制印章材料选择的发展趋势是硬质石材比例不断上升，这种变化与雕刻工具的改进和工艺的革新有着密切的关系。

在制作印章的过程中，古代工匠通常会在雕刻面上留下工具的痕迹，通过比较形态学的方法观察和研究各种雕刻工具遗留的微痕，可以推测和复原古代印章雕刻运用的工艺。[1] 微痕分析注重实验，强调反复观察得到客观规律性认识，能从主观到客观，从经验到实证。在两河流域早期手工作坊遗址和相关工具遗物发现极少的情况下，微痕分析是一个重要的研究方法。一个多世纪以来，欧美各主要博物馆及相关研究机构通过考古发掘或购买等途径收藏了大量古代近东印章实物和印迹，其中一部分精雕细琢的滚印为探讨古代两河流域印章雕刻工艺的发展演变提供了可资利用的材料。

在众多收藏机构中，英国大英博物馆滚印藏品的绝对数量和年代分布具有一定的代表性。[2] 萨格斯（M.Sax）等学者对该馆2500多枚滚印进行了物相分析，鉴于低硬度石材很难对雕刻工具的发展变化产生重要影响，也难以引起雕刻工艺方面的重大变化，所以他们将研究重点放在高硬度石材印章上。两河流域容易获取的高硬度石材主要是石英和赤铁石，前者是制作印章的最坚硬的石料，后者是一种带有金属光泽的铁氧化物，硬度虽比石英低但相对而言仍然比较坚硬，其硬度为摩氏5.5-6.0。赤铁石这种石料适合制作印章，特别在公元前2000至公元前1600年期间，赤铁石成为包括叙利亚和土耳其在内的整个近东地区制作印章的上选材料。这些石材的使用可能刺激了雕刻工艺的革新。毋庸讳言，雕刻工艺的发展也在一定程度上限制了材料可供选择的范围。基于上述因素，

① M.Sax, J.Mcnabb and N.D.Meeks, "Methods of engraving Mesopotamian cylinder seals: experimental confirmation", *Archaeometry*, vol. 40(1998), pp.7-8, 19,21.

② D.J.Wiseman, *Catalogue of the Western Asiatic Seals in the British Museum, Cylinder Seals I: Uruk-Early Dynastic Periods*, London: British Museum Publications, 1962; D.Collon, *Catalogue of the Western Asiatic Seals in the British Museum, Cylinder Seals II: Akkadian, Post Akkadian, UrIII Periods*, London: British Museum Publications, 1982; D.Collon, *Catalogue of the Western Asiatic Seals in the British Museum, Cylinder Seals III: Isin-Larsa and Old Babylonian Periods*, London: British Museum Publications, 1986; D.Collon, *Catalogue of the Western Asiatic Seals in the British Museum, Cylinder Seals V: New-Assyrian and Neo-Babylonian Periods*, London: British Museum Publications, 2001; P.H.Merrillees, *Catalogue of the Western Asiatic Seals in the British Museum, Cylinder Seals VI: Pre-Achaemenid and Achaemenid Periods*, London: British Museum Publications, 2005.

经过筛选后他们集中分析了其中的 400 枚石英印章和 350 枚赤铁石印章，这些印章的年代在公元前 3100 年至公元前 400 年之间。

他们的研究方法是用低倍显微镜对印章雕刻痕迹进行初步观察，然后再将其中能够体现雕刻技术发展变化的印章挑选出来，使用扫描电子显微镜、X 射线衍射分析进行细致的检测，并使用硅树脂对印章做精细的印迹翻模，再现雕刻工具留下的微痕。[①]他们在研究中所使用的印章包括以下几个部分：54 枚古巴比伦时期印章，年代约在公元前 2004 年至公元前 1595 年之间；35 枚伽喜特风格印章，基本属于公元前 14 世纪；16 枚米坦尼风格印章，年代约在公元前 1500 年至公元前 1330 年之间；22 枚中亚述时期印章，基本属于公元前 13 世纪。此外，还有一少部分巴比伦尼亚周边地区的印章。

这些检测分析为研究印章雕刻工艺的变化提供了科学的依据，其结果显示这些印章在雕刻过程中使用了以下一种或多种工具：凿、锉、钻、砣具，其中砣具主要指用于细部雕刻的錾砣。这项调查虽然只是针对大英博物馆的相应藏品进行取样，但是从中得出的数据应该具有一定的典型性和代表性。

作为一种沿用至今的重要手工工具，钻的应用相当广泛，出现年代亦比较久远，两河流域地区一些旧石器时代晚期的贝壳和软石手工制品上就有钻孔的痕迹。[②]早期制作钻凿一类工具使用的应该是相对较硬的燧石块，操作方式主要是徒手使用，但也有可能安装在木柄或骨柄之上。稍后时期，人们发明了弓式手动钻，弓式手动钻主要有两种类型：一种钻杆呈弓形或几字形，使用时一手按钻杆上部末端施加压力，使钻杆下部末端的钻头固定在已经选好的待钻孔位置，另一手摇转弓形钻杆带动钻头工作；另一种钻杆呈直线形，用绳或皮条绕钻杆两三圈后将绳两端分别反向延伸，把两端固定在弓形杆或直杆上，使用时前后拉动弓形杆，就会带动钻杆反复作顺时针和逆时针转动，这样能产生每分钟近 700-800 转的转数。早期的实心钻头一般使用燧石磨制而成，有时也会用闪长石、石灰石或者玄武岩，后期则使用金属铜。除常见的实心钻外还有管钻，管钻与滚印关系也非常密切，制作滚印所用的圆柱石芯应该就是管钻应用的产物。早期滚印直径通常较大，其柱体可能是使用管钻在石罐、石瓶制作过程中完整套取的钻芯，从个别滚印表面遗留的钻痕可以看出管钻的使用。[③]弓式手动钻在两河流域印章制作中应用相当广泛，工匠们借助这种钻大大提高了雕刻的精确度和灵活度，公元前 3 千纪的印章在制作过程中基本都使用了这种工具。

公元前 3100 年至公元前 400 年期间两河流域地区印章雕刻中主要工具和技术应用变化情况基本如下：凿从公元前 4 千纪中晚期的杰姆迭特·纳塞尔时期到古巴比伦中期一直被广泛使用，此后 500 年间罕用；锉从杰姆迭特·纳塞尔时期到古巴比伦中晚期使用频率不高，应用亦不广泛，但是从古巴比伦晚期以后该技术被广泛应用，直至公元前 700 年左右式微；钻应用的情况与锉基本相同，只是使用年限较后者有所延长；砣具可能在古巴比伦中晚期被最初应用，但使用频率不高，其大规模应用始于公元前 14 世纪，至今仍在玉器加工中广泛使用。

具体而言，用工具凿剖出的凹痕两侧凿面多见细微崩裂痕，有的甚至会形成台阶状；用锉磨出的锉磨面不是很规整，常有波浪状起伏，遗留的线纹两端会有很多由锉碰蹭造成的细茬痕迹；实心

① M. Sax and N.D.Meeks, "The introduction of wheel cutting as a technique for engraving cylinder seals: its distinction from filing", *Iraq*,vol.56(1994),pp.154–155; M.Sax and N.D.Meeks, "Methods of engraving Mesopotamian quartz cylinder seals", *Archaeometry*,vol.37,no.1(1995),pp.26–27.

② Semenov,S.A. *Prehistoric Technology:an Experimental Study of the Oldest Tools and Artefacts from Traces of Manufacture and Wear*, London: Cory,Adams &Mackay, 1964,pp.74–78.

③ P.R.S.Moorey, *Ancient Mesopotamian Materials and Industries: the Archaeological Evidence*, Oxford: Clarendon Press, 1994, p.103.

锥钻或管钻的钻痕多表现为圆点或圆环状，其中规整平齐的钻痕通常是由弓式手动钻遗留的；砣具的剖割面中间宽深、两端尖浅，可见整齐平行的弧形线纹痕迹，同时剖割面也比较规整，有些甚至因砣具高速旋转切磨而出现光泽效果。

不过需要注意的是，不同工具留下的痕迹有时候比较相似，因此必须尽可能采用多重标准来清晰地辨别印章雕刻所应用的工具。平锉和砣具的区别较明显，使用这两种工具会留下完全不同的痕迹，同时工匠可以用直锉在印章弧形工作面上笔直地锉磨出水平和微斜的凹痕，但是无法锉出垂直的非贯通性短小凹痕。平锉和曲锉的锉痕区别也相对容易，但区分曲锉和砣具的痕迹有时候会比较困难，特别是使用金刚砂研磨料之后，这种区分更为不易，因为金刚砂造成的磨痕特点可能与砣具的磨痕特点相重合。砣具的弧形切磨面通常比较圆润，带有整齐的纵向平行切磨线，弧形剖面也比较深。

二　砣具的发展及其重要意义

随着技术的逐步发展，两河流域出现了在印章雕刻工艺中占有重要地位的砣具。砣具是一种利用简单机械原理旋转切片以切磨玉石的工具，它出现的时间相对晚近，情况也比较复杂。[①] 砣具的出现是玉石雕刻工艺发展的重要标志，其高速旋转时边缘产生的切磨效果前所未有地提高了硬石雕刻的效率。下文主要介绍和讨论从古巴比伦晚期即公元前18世纪中晚期至迦喜特晚期即公元前14世纪晚期砣具在两河流域印章制作中产生和早期应用方面的情况。[②]

砣具的发明和应用依赖诸多因素，与其他雕刻工具有着比较密切的关系。砣具的出现可能与弓式手动钻不无联系。在公元前19世纪中期后的赤铁石印章和公元前18世纪中期后的石英印章中，使用锥钻加工的比例明显逐渐增加，而砣具的发明可能正是从对钻的改造中生发出来的。大英博物馆藏编号为WA89181的古巴比伦晚期赤铁石印章，其上人物形象的轮廓由一系列圆点构成，说明其主体部分的雕刻使用了锥钻。人物下肢躯体由椭圆状点构成，椭圆凹痕纵向雕刻，实验表明这些椭圆凹痕不能使用简单的手动钻或弓转钻钻磨出来。该钻的钻头部分可能接近于球状，因此当钻杆与雕刻工作面呈倾斜或平行角度旋转时，钻头实际是以"砣具"的形式旋转工作。从上述痕迹中可以推断，将转动杆装在两个或多个复合轴承之间的旋转工具在古巴比伦晚期就已经使用，而圆轮类工具使用的一个必要技术前提就是对将转轴装在两个复合轴承之间的旋转工具的采纳。

另一个促成两河流域砣具出现的因素可能是对金刚砂一类研磨料的引进，金刚砂硬度（摩氏9.0）明显高于石英（摩氏7.0），它的采用让工匠运用铜质工具对石英等硬石印章进行纵向打孔和砣具

---

① 在公元前4千纪后半期，包括两河流域南部在内的近东一些地区在制造陶器时已经使用快轮等旋转工具设备。见 P.M.Rice, *Pottery Analysis:A Sourcebook*, Chicago: University of Chicago Press, 1987, pp.12,132–135。一些学者认为两河流域最早使用砣具的时间应该是公元前4千纪后半期，砣具的发明应该与制造陶器所用的快轮等旋转工具有一定关系。见 H.J.Nissen, "Aspects of the development of early cylinder seals", in Mc.Gibson and R.D.Biggs (eds.), *Seals and Sealing in the Ancient Near East*, Malibu: Undena Publications, 1977, p.16; A.J.Gwinnett and Gorelick, "Ancient lapidary: a study using scanning electron microscopy and functional analysis", *Expedition*,vol.22(1979),pp.25–27。

② 下限定在迦喜特晚期，是因为该时期砣具技术发展已相当成熟，成为印章雕刻工艺中一项重要的技术。与此同时，目前未发现早于公元前18世纪中期砣具应用的确凿证据。

切磨成为可能。在公元前 2 千纪，两河流域手工艺者主要使用金属工具。[①] 其中使用最广泛的是黄铜及其合金工具，黄铜质地较软，镶嵌金刚砂研磨料后使工匠在高硬度石材上雕刻和打孔变得更为便易。金刚砂的引进引发了雕刻工艺的一系列变化，其中之一就是促使较低效的石钻被镶嵌金刚砂的铜钻取代。两河流域所用金刚砂来源于纳克索斯岛（Naxos）和印度，目前所见最早的金刚砂研磨料发现于乌尔。[②] 戈雷利克（L.Gorelick）和格威内特（A.J.Gwinnett）发现了至迟公元前 2000 年印章钻孔时使用金刚砂的证据，在大英博物馆一枚编号为 WA28800 的后阿卡德时期水晶印章的穿孔内表面上，他们使用静电放射摄影技术观察到使用嵌金刚砂研磨料铜钻所留的平行环状痕迹。[③] 有研究表明，在公元前 2 千纪期间金刚砂一直被作为雕刻石英印章的研磨料。[④] 对钻这种旋杆式工具的频繁使用和改进，以及人们对硬石石材的偏爱可能促成了工匠对砣具的发明或引进。

在公元前 18 世纪至公元前 14 世纪时期，工匠们在印章制作过程中可能已经将砣具与钻和锉一同应用。大英博物馆所藏的一枚古巴比伦晚期印章为该时期砣具的应用提供了证据。这枚印章编号为 WA28794，由红白角砾岩状硬玉制成，图案中两个人物形象采用的雕刻方法比较相似，体形较大的形象有明显的纵向凹痕，这是锉磨遗留的痕迹；直锉常用来锉磨人物躯体中笔直、水平或近似水平角度的部分，例如国王的肩部，而曲锉则用来锉磨稍微弯曲的垂直部分，例如女神躯体的主干部分。躯体上较小的纵向凹痕，例如国王四肢和女神裙子的轮廓可能是使用砣具切磨或者曲锉锉磨而成。萨格等人将图像放大后在女神裙子轮廓右侧边缘部位发现了砣具使用的证据，其显示的痕迹与砣具使用的特征相吻合。[⑤]

伽喜特时期砣具的应用日益普遍。在大英博物馆收藏的 35 枚伽喜特印章中，有 12 枚清晰地表现出砣具使用的痕迹，同早些时期比较，伽喜特时期运用砣具雕刻的印章比例有较大的提高。另外有 5 枚印章几乎完全使用微凿技术雕刻完成，余下 18 枚印章情况比较复杂，人物雕刻带有砣具、锉或者二者结合使用的特征。辨识伽喜特印章上砣具使用证据的标准常常需要多重考虑，在这里仅举选三个例子说明其中存在的困难。有一枚编号为 WA89091 的伽喜特带纹光玉髓印章，其图案中构成神与山羊的纵向凹痕呈现为轻微的弧形，这些可能是使用圆轮或曲锉造成的，神的双肩和双臂部位可以初步看出砣具使用的证据。萨格等人使用直径较小的錾砣仅能复制山羊后肢的小块肌肉部分。从上述特征可以推断，这枚印章在雕刻过程中至少部分地使用了砣具。而另一枚编号为 WA89214 的伽喜特印章则很难准确判断出在雕刻过程中是否运用了砣具工艺。因为多色斑点硬玉石材的印章不易观察，特别是在印章有磨损凹痕和断裂的情况下更是难上加难，但是从神形象躯体上的圆形特征分析，这些部分最初应该是使用钻雕刻轮廓。从平面看神躯干上只有一个非常小的凹痕，

① 考古发掘发现了一些金属印章雕刻工具：考古学家在阿富汗蒙迪伽克（Mundigak）发掘到一个黄铜钻头，年代约为公元前 27 世纪。弗兰克福特（Frankfort）记载了发掘阿斯玛尔丘（Tell Asmar）时发现的一套阿卡德珠宝匠（约公元前 24 世纪）使用的工具，包括数柄黄铜刻刀、窄刃凿、小手柄钻，还有一个有抹刀状切刃的工具，其杆部横断面呈正方形，考古学家认为它是嵌在钉状砣具上的钻孔器。这些工具与一些滚动成品、半成品以及带孔珠、数根黄铜和银条一同被塞在小罐中。详细记载参看 H.Frankfort, *Cylinder Seals*, London: Macmillan and Co., 1939,p.5. 法国考古队在两河流域南部发掘拉尔萨（Larsa）时发现了公元前 18 世纪后期一位珠宝匠的工具，也是放在罐子里，包括一些带孔珠、印迹、印章、珠宝、砝码还有一块小砧骨和磨石。D.Collon, *First Impressions: Cylinder Seals in the Ancient Near East*, London: British Museum Press, 1987, p.104, n.15。

② L.Woolley,*The Royal Cemetery, Ur Excavations ii*, London: Oxford University Press, 1934,p.373,n.2.

③ Gorelick,L. and A.J.Gwinnett, "'Collars' in the holes of Near Eastern cylinder seals",*Archaeomaterials*,vol.3,no.1(1989), pp.39-46.

④ W.Heimpel et al., "Philological and archaeological evidence for the use of emery in the Bronze Age Near East", *Journal of Cuneiform Studies*, vol.40,no.2(1988),pp.195-210.

⑤ M.Sax, N.D.Meeks and D.Collon, "The early development of the lapidary engraving wheel in Mesopotamia",*Iraq*,vol.62(2000),pp.161-164.

因此不能轻易确定其使用的是砣具还是曲锉，但是神上臂的弧形纵向凹痕表明这一部分雕刻使用的是砣具。另外还有值得注意的是，印章上被捕食的飞鸟的羽毛呈现为倾斜和水平方向，这可能是使用直锉磨锉而成，但这些羽毛的弧形剖面痕迹与砣具使用的特征又是一致的，这一点不容易理解。与前两枚印章比较而言，编号为 WA89240 的玉髓印章上面砣具应用的痕迹则非常明显。在早期伽喜特印章雕刻中，工匠能够使用砣具切磨出人物形象的弧形以及线条性躯体部位。直线躯体特征可以通过使印章雕刻面与砣具弧刃呈平行角度即雕刻面与砣具的砣面呈垂直角度切磨出来，而曲线躯体特征则可以通过使雕刻面与砣具的切磨刃呈倾斜角度的方法切磨出来。呈坐姿的国王几乎所有雕刻较深的细部、楔形文字印文及栏框都呈现为精细的水平纵向凹痕，这些特征同砣具留下的磨痕特征非常相似。其中垂直的栏框似乎是使用能够连续快速旋转的砣具切磨而成的。①

砣具这种旋转类工具使用其边缘部位切磨时要比使用中心部位工作效率更高，其边缘部位的线性速度与工具直径成一定比例，当轴杆转速固定不变时，直径越大边缘的线性速度即旋转速度越大，所有圆盘状工具均适用这一原则。弓转砣具的边缘不但可以产生高速切割的效果，而且薄刃砣具还可以任何角度对印章进行切磨，不必受直锉垂直锉磨时的操作限制。因此，砣具的逐渐应用和普及前所未有地推动了两河流域印章制作工艺的发展，在整个近东地区手工艺发展史上占有重要的地位并产生了深远的影响。

三　余论

将雕刻技术的变化与印章中石英质料的比例变化情况进行对比，可以看出在公元前 2 千纪印章雕刻技术的发展过程中，以砣具为主要雕刻工具的出现和过渡与人们对石英需求量的上升有明显的同步性。借助砣具工匠易于对硬质石料如硬玉、玉髓和其他各种短石英石料进行雕刻。相对水晶和其他种类的长石英而言，上述石料硬度较高，而其他雕刻工具如钻凿等难以胜任。

砣具在制印中首次应用可能是在古巴比伦晚期，但直至伽喜特晚期才发展成熟，这表明两河流域对砣具的接受是一个渐进的过程，其间经历了近三百年的时间。萨格等人的研究结果也表明，从不同时期石英印章的雕刻工艺来看，砣具技术是逐步发展起来的。对钻锉等工具在硬石印章雕刻局限上的突破，对钻一类旋杆式转动工具的改进，以及对硬石石材的日益偏爱等因素，可能促成了工匠对砣具的发明或引进。但由于古巴比伦时期相关材料的详细年代证据的缺乏，我们无法对砣具逐步发展的过程进行细致入微的考察，更难以给出明确的结论。古巴比伦王朝与新巴比伦王朝之间的中间期属于"黑暗时期"，这期间雕刻工艺鲜有发展，甚至某些方面出现了停滞和倒退的现象。②

印章雕刻工艺上的这一重大变革发生在公元前 2 千纪的巴比伦尼亚，可以说在砣具产生之后，两河流域以之为基础的雕刻工艺发展观念基本未再出现重要的阶段性变化，这种状况一直延续到当代机械工业应用到手工制造业才有所改变。

---

① 值得注意的是，在古代尽管工匠可以给砣具弓转轴安装整速轮以使砣具能够连续转动，但最初的砣具旋转时可能仍旧会时断时续左右摆动，而现在砣具试验中使用的是电动车床，转轮可以连续不断的平稳旋转，这样两者的痕迹会出现轻微的差异。

② 虽然很多学者都赞同上述的观点，但库伦和马休斯却注意到了古巴比伦时期与伽喜特时期雕刻风格之间的连贯性，详细情况请参见 D.Collon, *First Impressions, Cylinder Seals in the Ancient Near East*, London: British Museum Press, 1987, p.58; D.M.Matthews, *Principles of Composition in Near Eastern Glyptic of the Later Second Millennium BC*, Ordis Biblicus et Orentalis, Series Archaeologica 8, Fribourg: University Press Fribourg, 1990, pp.55-57.

古代埃及文献中的沙苏人考

郭丹彤　东北师范大学

摘要： 术语沙苏是对巴勒斯坦地区南部和外约旦地区讲塞姆语的贝都因人的称谓，后来被泛指贝都因人。"沙苏"最早出现于古王国，直到新王国时期，这一术语才普遍出现在古代埃及社会中。在语源学上，这一术语的词根是 Vas "旅行，游逛"。沙苏不是一个种族，它是一个带有军事色彩的社会阶层，但是他们的生活方式却包含了各种形式，或定居，或游牧。埃及社会中的沙苏人一部分是战俘，而另一部分则是雇佣兵，或强盗。而古代埃及索莱布文献和西阿玛拉文献中提到的耶和华的沙苏人就是以色列人。

关键词： 沙苏；古王国；社会阶层

Abstract： The term "Shasu" designates "Bedouin" outside Transjordan, later generally refers to "Bedouin". The term "Shasu" was known as early as the Old Kingdom though it did not become common until the New Kingdom. Linguistic considerations indicate it was probably derived from Egyptian word "wander about". These people comprised a social class with military color which embraced varying modes of life, settlement or nomad, and did not constitute an ethnic unity. They appeared in Egyptian soceity partly as captives, partly as mercenaries or robbers. The term "Shasu of Yahweh" in topographical lists at Soleb and Amarah-West refers to Israelites

Keywords： Shasu, the Old Kingdom, Social class

古代埃及新王国时期（约公元前 1567 年—前 1086 年），被埃及人称为"沙苏"的人们不时地出现在埃及的文献中和神庙壁画上，但是我们对他们的认识却始终是模糊的。他们是一个种族吗？抑或是一个社会阶层？一个政治团体？一个分散的部落联盟？他们又与以色列人有着怎样的关系呢？为了解决这些问题，我们需从古代埃及文献中关于沙苏人的记述入手。

一　古代埃及文献中的术语沙苏

术语沙苏，埃及语形式是 Vasw，词根为 Vas "旅行，游逛"。①学界普遍认为，Vasw 一词首先出现于第十八王朝国王图特摩斯三世统治时期（约公元前 1479 年—前 1425 年），并且因为希克索斯人是来自亚洲的移民而推测这一术语应该首次出现于希克索斯王朝统治时期（约公元前 1786 年—前 1567 年）。然而一个来自古王国时期的证据却改变了学者们的观点，这就是第五王朝的最后一位国王乌纳斯（约公元前 2375 年—前 2345 年）金字塔建筑群甬道浮雕上出现了 "Vasw" 一词。这幅浮雕刻在一块岩石上，描述了埃及人和外国人之间的战斗。②浮雕的左侧是一名倒地的塞姆人，其上刻有象形文字符号 sw 和 w，这两个符号是 Vasw 这一单词的后半部分，而它的前半部分则随同浮雕的残破一同遗失了，但是残破处却足以刻下 Va 这一符号。据此，我们有理由推断，这幅浮雕是 Vasw 这一术语出现于古王国时期的证据之一。

上述证据表明，Vasw 这一术语的出现时间要比图特摩斯三世统治时期早得多。此外，时间被勘定为第十二王朝的诅咒铭文也曾出现过地名 Vwsw。③总之，我们有证据显示沙苏出现在古王国和中王国，尽管我们仍然缺少沙苏出现于新王国之前的十分明晰的证据。

学界通常认为，Vasw 是对巴勒斯坦地区南部和外约旦地区讲塞姆语的贝都因人的称谓，后来被泛指贝都因人。证据有三：第一个证据中的术语形式是 vais，即新王国后期的 Vasw，用来指代居于埃及东部的居民，根据上下文的联系，他们应该是阿拉伯人。第二个证据中的这一术语指代两河流域的米底人，后来泛指位于东部的埃及所有的敌人。④前两个证据皆来自埃德福，第三个证据则来自于二十王朝时期底比斯阿蒙神庙的书信，在这些书信中，Vasw 泛指居于距离巴勒斯坦南部和外约旦以远地区的居民。⑤根据上文的讨论，沙苏人的故乡应该位于约旦河谷东部的阿拉巴赫干涸河道（wadi arabah），在古代埃及文献中，这一地区被称为 ta-Vasw，"沙苏之地"。

此外，我们有另一种观点。古蒂克（Goedicke）曾对兰辛（lansing）纸草和其他两篇与该纸草同时代的文献中的单词 Vsa 进行过考察。在这些文献中，无聊的书吏被比喻成 Vsa，接着，他的几个特点被指出。大多数翻译者把 Vsa 译成 "狷羚"，但是关于他的特点的段落却让古蒂克得出了这样的结论："他们的一个主要特征是生活在沙漠中，与之相连的是他们对自由的渴望和对束缚的恐惧。他们的生活方式不是农耕，而是畜牧。而根据考勒（koller）纸草，Vsa 更应该被翻译成'沙漠的狩猎者'，'西方的迈扎伊'。所有的这些特征都不适用于狷羚，他们更像贝都因人，无论它是社会阶层还是种族，它都是与定居的农耕生活相对的。"⑥

古蒂克进一步指出，Vsa 应该等同于 Vasw，之所以出现差异，是因为拼写上的错误，或者是用一种动物来代表一个种族的章纹。

总之，古蒂克对兰辛纸草中出现的 Vsa 的释读是很有说服力的。Vsw 这一单词最初应该有一个中间音 a，新埃及语却经常把半元音或弱辅音省略，于是 Vsa 经常作为 Vasw 的一种非正式的书写。

① 关于术语沙苏，参见 K. R. Cooper, "The Shasu of Palestine in Egyptian Texts," Part One, *Artifax,* Vol. 21, No. 4, 2006, pp. 22–27; Part Two, *Artifax,* Vol. 22, No. 1, 2007, pp. 24–29。关于术语沙苏的原始含义，参见 R. O. Faulkner, *A concise Dictionary of Middle Egyptian*, oxford: Ashmolean Museum, p. 261; A. H. Gardiner, *Ancient Egyptian Onomastica*, Vol. I, Oxford: Oxford University Press, p. 193; R. Hannig, *Grosses Handworterbuch Agyptisch–Deutsch (2800–950 v. Chr.): Die Sprache der Pharaonen*, Mainz: P. von Zabern, 1995, p.870.

② W. S. Smith, *Interconnections in the Ancient Near East*, New Haven：Yale University Press，1965, fig. 13.

③ G. Posener, *Princes et Pays d'Asie et de Nubie*, Brussels: Bruxelles, 1940, p. 91。

④ R. Giveon, *Les Bedouins shosou des documents egyptiens*, Documenta et Monumenta Orientis Antiqui, Vol. 18, Leiden：E. J. Brill, 1971, pp. 165–66.

⑤ W. Helck, "Eine Briefsammlung aus der Verwaltung des Amun Tempels," *JARCE* 6 (1967), p. 140.

⑥ H. Goedicke, "Papyrus Lansing 3,9–3, 10," *JARCE* 7 (1968), pp. 128–130.

从这两个单词的含义看，Vasw 是贝都因人，而 Vsa 则是羚羊。然而，因一种人与某一动物的一些特征相近而用后者指代前者却是埃及人经常使用的一种修辞方法。

二 沙苏的属性

那么，沙苏究竟是一个种族还是一个社会阶层呢，他们的生活方式是游牧的还是的定居的呢。解决这个问题，需要从他们所从事的职业入手。我们发现，与沙苏有关的埃及文献几乎都是关于战争的。沙苏人或者与埃及人在叙利亚巴勒斯坦地区开战，或者以抢劫者的身份出现在该地区。[①]在埃及人看来，沙苏似乎是一群流浪者，他们来自外约旦，通常以雇佣兵或抢劫者的身份出现在迦南城镇和商队中。

早在拉美西斯二世统治之前，埃及人用一些非常泛泛的术语称呼从东部来到巴勒斯坦和叙利亚南部的数量众多的塞姆人。他们把来到死海北部地区的人称为哈皮如[②]，而把来到南部的那些人称作沙苏。塞提一世的卡尔纳克浮雕对沙苏的描绘与塞提一世的本特山（beth shan）石碑对哈皮如的描绘基本相同，这表明，在埃及人看来，这两个术语指的是同一种人。而哈皮如是一个职业军人的社会阶层，那么，我们有理由推断出沙苏也是一个社会阶层。对于埃及人来说，沙苏以战争冒险者的身份出现，他们游荡在叙利亚巴勒斯坦地区的主要目的是从事他们的或雇佣兵或强盗的生意。[③]

如果这种推断是正确的，如果我们把他们视为以正规战争或非正规的抢劫为事业的一种人，那么我们对沙苏的认识便开始清晰起来。没有任何证据能够证明沙苏人驻留迦南是为了定居于此。由于他们向西方移动的主要目的是去作雇佣兵或去抢劫，当进入巴勒斯坦地区的目的得以实现后，他们将返回他们的故乡。他们中的一些可能滞留并定居在迦南，这就同因服务于埃及军队而定居在埃及的那些人那样。但是大多数沙苏人，在大多数情况下，他们进入迦南的目的是为了寻找生意，所以他们一定会与他们位于东部的故乡保持着联系。

一旦我们把沙苏勘定为一个带有军事色彩的社会阶层，关于他们的一些谜团便能够得到解决了。一些学者将他们视为游牧或半游牧民族，当然，他们也不得不承认他们中的一些拥有他们自己的城镇。考古学家和历史学家普遍认为，东约旦是游牧民族的聚居地，自青铜早期文化结束到铁器时代的开始，这一地区就一直没有存在过定居生活。伴随着该地区考古发掘的不断深入，这一普遍被接受的观点受到了质疑。青铜中期二期的几座坟墓得以发掘，同时伴有大规模的聚址。青铜时代晚期，还出现了成规模的聚址以及坟墓和神庙。[④]故此，我们看到，一些沙苏人具有城市文明的背景。如此，一些沙苏人被描绘成生活在帐篷中以放牧为生的游牧部落的同时，另一些沙苏人却有着明显的城市

① 参见 Pap. Anastasi I, 19, 1–4 and 23, 7–8, in R. Caminos, *Late-Egyptian miscellanies*, London: Oxford University Press, 1954.

② 过去学者们通常认为阿皮如是一个种族，与希伯莱（Hebrews）有着千丝万缕的联系。然而莱德弗德认为阿皮如一词的原始含义是"灰尘的制造者"，即那些策马飞奔的人。青铜时代晚期他们居于巴勒斯坦社会的边缘，是一群与社会格格不入，被社会所抛弃的人。他们居住在巴勒斯坦各城邦的农村，处于一种半独立的状态。参见，D. B. Redford, *Egypt, Canaan, and Israel in Ancient Times*, Princeton: Princeton University Press, 1992, p. 195。在《以色列历史》中，布瑞特认为阿皮如一词并不是指一个种族，而是指一种社会阶层。任何种族都可能有阿皮如这个社会阶层。这个社会阶层没有公民权，没有固定的住所，处于一种半游牧的状态，间或以抢劫为生。偶尔他们也定居在城镇。在动荡的年代，他们常常组成一支临时军队，掠夺他们所需物资。当他们被原来所居之地驱逐的时候，他们通常会把自己卖到埃及，在埃及的各种王室工程中充当苦力。由此他断定拉美西斯二世统治时期的卖身为奴的阿皮如应该就是以色列的一个重要组成部分。参见，J. Bright, *A History of Israel: With an Introduction and Appendix by William P. Brown*, 4th ed., Louisville: Westminster John Knox Press, 2000. pp. 93–96.

③ W. Helck, "Die Bedrohung Palästinas durch einwandernde Gruppen am Ende der 18. und am Anfang der19," *VT* 18 (1968), pp. 477f.

④ E. Campbell and G. E. Wright, "Tribal League Shrines in Amman and Shechem," *Bibl. Arch.* 32 (1969), pp. 104ff.

居民的特征。但是，从词源学上看，如果 ssa 就是 šasw，那么，我们就应该把他们视为沙漠定居者。所有的描绘，如半牧民族，城市居民和沙漠定居者，都与把沙苏勘定为一个带有军事色彩的社会阶层相符合。一些沙苏人是定居者，而另一些人则不是，这与他们不是一个民族的论断相契合。事实上，埃及人对这一术语使用得如此地随便是有道理的，因为沙苏的构成成分十分复杂。从地缘上看，他们来自东部，但是他们的生活方式却包含了各种形式，或定居，或游牧。这些人走到一起的原因则是他们都有战争的意图，都是以获取财富为目的。

三　埃及社会中的沙苏人

学界通常认为，新王国时期，出现在埃及以及埃及属地巴勒斯坦地区的沙苏人是埃及推行"人口迁徙"政策的结果，即将被征服地的居民从他们原来的聚居地强行迁往其他地区。[①]其相关证据如下：一、拉美西斯二世的阿布辛贝勒神庙铭文揭示出埃及曾对努比亚人、利比亚人、亚洲人和沙苏人强行移民；二、沙苏雇佣兵出现于拉美西斯二世的军队是拉美西斯二世强行安置沙苏的结果；三、韦伯纸草提到了地名派尔恩·沙苏（pen shasu），与普恩·迈扎伊（Medjay）和普恩·奈赫斯（Nekhsy）相同，都是雇佣兵的聚居地；[②]四、其他文献揭示出新王国时期埃及曾实施过人口迁徙的政策。

新王国时期，生活在埃及的亚洲人主要有这么几种：战俘、平民、官员，以及作为人质被带到埃及的那些被征服地的王子们，他们在埃及接受纯正的埃及教育，然后返回本土成为亲埃的君主。阿蒙霍特普三世的底比斯神庙铭文对他们进行了详尽的描述："房间里满是那些被陛下征服的异邦首领的孩子们的男女仆人，……环绕着叙利亚人的居住地，哪里居住着与首领的孩子们一起来的随从。"[③]

这段文献告诉我们，被征服的异邦首领的孩子们作为人质带着他们的仆人来到埃及的神庙学校，进行埃及化的学习，至于亚洲人的军事殖民地和亚洲人口的迁徙则无法从这段文献中获取。人口迁徙观点的一个证据是拉美西斯二世的阿布辛贝勒神庙铭文："他把努比亚人带到北方，把亚洲人带到努比亚。他把沙苏安置在西方的土地上，把利比亚人安置在山地，他建立的要塞里装满了掠夺来的物品。"[④]由此，这一观点认为大量人口被迫向四个方向迁徙，努比亚迁徙到西亚，亚洲人被带到努比亚，而利比亚人和沙苏人则被安置在其他的地区，这里的沙苏成为埃及东部或北部敌人的代表。但是，本文却认为这段文献是埃及国王控制任何一方敌人的一种表达方式，它表达了埃及的帝国主义，或世界主义的意识形态。拉美西斯三世的一篇与之相似的文献集中反映埃及的世界主义，在这篇文献中，神列举了他所创造的奇迹，这些奇迹包括击败南方敌人、北方敌人、东方敌人和西方敌人，每一个方向都有一个代表，它们分别是南方的努比亚人，北方的沙漠定居者，东方的蓬特和西方的利比亚人。[⑤]而埃赫那吞统治时期的《阿吞颂诗》则是埃及世界主义意识形态的集中反映："他们都匍匐于被阿吞所爱的乌恩拉的脚下，"[⑥]"每一块土地上的人们都在称颂：噢，活着的太阳，奈菲尔

① R. Giveon, *Les Bedouins shosou des documents egyptiens*, Documenta et Monumenta Orientis Antiqui, Vol. 18, Leiden：E. J. Brill, 1971, pp. 73, 239.

② 迈扎伊（Medjay）和奈赫斯（Nekhsy）皆为努比亚部落名称。参见 R. Hannig, *Grosses Handworterbuch Agyptisch-Deutsch (2800–950 v. Chr.): Die Sprache der Pharaonen*, p. 402; p. 448.

③ J. H. Breasted, *Ancient Records of Egypt*, Vol. II, Chicago: the University of Chicago Press, 1906, §881.

④ J. H. Breasted, *Ancient Records of Egypt*, Vol. III, Chicago: the University of Chicago Press 1906, §457.

⑤ W. F. Edgerton and J. Wilson, *Historical Records of Rameses III*, Chicago, the University of Chicago Press, pp. 111ff.

⑥ M. Sandman, *Texts from the Time of Akhenaten*, Bibliotheca Aegyptiaca VIII, Brussels,1938, p.31, 1。引文中的"乌恩拉"为埃赫那吞的第四王名，而埃赫那吞则是他的第五王名。

海普如拉·乌恩拉，我们永远都臣服于你。"①"整个世界都归你所有，靠尔，库什和其他所有的土地。"②

由此，我们可以认为，拉美西斯二世的阿布辛贝勒铭文是在描绘国王遍布世界的权威，它并非是对人口迁徙的真实记录。

当然，我们在肯定文献的象征性的同时，也不否认在埃及存在着亚洲人的聚居地。新王国时期，居留在埃及的亚洲人数量是十分庞大的，他们来到埃及的方式和渠道各不相同，或者是战俘，或者是上文提到的作为人质的统治者们的孩子和随从们，或者是以个人的名义来到埃及，或者是官方的使节。亚洲人的聚居地同时带有军事和农业的性质，后者是为雇佣兵和永久性的定居服务的。③这样的聚居地是不需要强迫移民的，因为雇佣兵体系以及雇佣兵及其家庭的聚居地的基本特性是自愿的。

事实上，在古代世界，某一国家或地区外国人的聚居地早已有之，如公元前2千年代早期小亚的亚述人聚居地，公元前2前年代中期乌加里特的迈锡尼人聚居地，以及古王国时期巴比罗斯的埃及人聚居地。这些聚居地的建立绝不是强制性移民的结果。

根据阿纳斯塔斯纸草记载："我们不再允许伊多姆的沙苏人通过位于柴库（tcheku）的'美楞普塔·霍特普·霍尔·玛阿特'要塞，前往"美楞普塔·霍特普·霍尔·玛阿特"的派尔·阿图姆的池塘，以使他们和他们的牲畜生存下去。"④这段文献是驻守要塞监视外国人行动的官员呈给中央政府的官文，它直接告诉我们来自外约旦的沙苏人来到埃及的目的是为了水源和草场。但是，这段文献并没有告诉我们，这些沙苏人来到三角洲东部地区，并永久定居下来。相反，这段文献揭示出，允许沙苏暂时居于三角洲东部的政策，由于某些没有被说明的原因，而被停止执行。另一方面，在古代埃及文献中，沙苏人经常以埃及敌人的身份出现，故此，我们推断，一部分沙苏人是以战俘的身份被带到埃及的。而另一些沙苏也不是强制性移民的结果，与他们来到巴勒斯坦地区的目的相同，他们来到埃及，是为了寻找生意，或充当雇佣兵，或作强盗。

四　"耶和华的沙苏"

讨论沙苏人，一个无法规避的问题就是他们与以色列人的关系。长期以来，虽然埃及学者和圣经学者在以色列的起源上多有争议，⑤但是他们却一致认同最早提及以色列的历史文献是刻写于公

---

① M. Sandman, *Texts from the Time of Akhenaten*, p.81, 19。引文中的"奈菲尔海普如拉·乌恩拉"是埃赫那吞第四王名的全称。

② M. Sandman, *Texts from the Time of Akhenaten*, p.81, 11。引文中的靠尔(Khor)和库什（Cush）皆为地名，前者位于西亚，后者指的是努比亚，也即现今的苏丹。

③ A. H. Gardiner, "A Tax-Assessor's Journal of the Middle Kingdom," JEA 27 (1941), p. 40f.

④ A. Gardiner, *Late-Egyptian Miscellanies*, Bibliotheca Aegyptiaca VII, Bruxelles: Fondation Egyptologique Reine Elisabeth, 1937, pp. 76, 54–56.

⑤ 关于以色列起源的讨论，参见，F. J. Yurco, "Merenptah's Canaanite Campaign," *Journal of the American Research Center in Egypt*, 23(1986):pp. 189–215; Lawrence E. Stager, "Forging an Identity: The Emergence of Ancient Israel," in Michael Coogan (ed.), *The Oxford History of the Biblical World*, New York: Oxford University Press, 2001, pp. 90–129;M. G. Hasel, "Merenptah's Inscription and Reliefs and the Origin of Israel" in Beth Alpert Nakhai ed. *The Near East in the Southwest: Essays in Honor of William G. Dever*, Annual of the American Schools of Oriental Research 58, Boston: American Schools of Oriental Research, 2003, pp. 19–44.

元前 1208 年的古代埃及文献美楞普塔石碑。①。然而，以色列人的上帝耶和华却更早地出现于埃及语文献中，它们是除了《旧约》外，最早提及上帝耶和华的古代文献。

新王国时期的两个地名表提及了一个词组"耶和华的沙苏"。这两个地名表都刻写在神庙的墙壁上，一个在索莱布，一个在西阿玛拉。献给阿蒙·拉神的索莱布神庙由阿蒙霍特普三世于公元前 1400 年建造，位于今苏丹境内，尼罗河西岸哈尔法干河河道（Wadi-Halfa）135 英里处。西阿玛拉，也位于今苏丹境内，由拉美西斯二世于公元前 13 世纪建造。西阿玛拉地名表与索莱布地名表内容基本相同，它应该是索莱布地名表的复制品。这个地名表提及了 6 组沙苏人的土地：塞瑞尔的沙苏人之地、拉班的沙苏人之地、萨玛特的沙苏人之地、乌尔布尔的沙苏人之地、耶和华的沙苏人之地和皮斯皮斯的沙苏人之地。②

尽管学者们认为索莱布和西阿玛拉地名表中确乎出现了耶和华的名字，但是一些问题仍然存在，比如单词耶和华指的是谁或是什么？它就是以色列人的上帝吗？或者与上述 6 组短语中的 5 组那样，它也仅仅指的是巴勒斯坦地区的某一座城市或地区？

关于这些问题的答案，我们无从知晓。但是即使耶和华是一个地名，它也很明显是因《旧约》中的上帝耶和华而来，因为在叙利亚巴勒斯坦地区我们没有发现任何叫耶和华的或其他相近的地名，而《旧约》或其他古代文献也没有提到一个叫耶和华的地名。故此，与其他 5 组短语不同，短语耶和华的沙苏人之地（land of Shasu of Yahweh）应该被译为"信奉耶和华神的沙苏人之地"。

那么，谁是信奉耶和华神的沙苏人呢？事实上，耶和华的沙苏人就是以东人，耶和华首先是以东人的神。以东人的一个部落从以东人的主体中分离出来，向西北迁徙，成为以色列部落中的一支，同时把耶和华崇拜带给了以色列人。于是耶和华遂成为以色列人的神明。③

那么，古代埃及人是否也信奉以色列人的这位神明呢？众所周知，埃及人信奉外国神。新王国以前的第二中间期，也即希克索斯王朝统治时期，巴勒斯坦地区的暴雨神巴阿与埃及的塞特神几乎完全同化。新王国时期，尽管希克索斯人被驱逐出了埃及，但是他们的巴阿神却继续被埃及人崇拜着。除了巴阿之外，这一时期的埃及人对同样来自于亚洲的芮晒弗神、胡闰神、阿纳特女神、阿什塔特女神和卡代什女神加以崇拜。④这些来自异域的神明们完全融入到了埃及宗教生活之中，并被归于埃及官方崇拜的行列，也就是说，它们能够传入埃及是埃及国王倡导的结果。亚洲神之所以受到推崇，

---

① 美楞普塔石碑又称美楞普塔的诗体碑。该石碑原本属于第十八王朝后期的法老阿蒙霍特普三世，这位法老在该石碑的正面刻写了他的建筑活动。到第十九王朝时期，法老美楞普塔对其喜爱有加，遂把其置于他的丧葬神庙之中，并在它的背面刻写了这篇铭文，同时将这篇铭文的副本存放在卡纳克神庙里。该石碑记录了美楞普塔在他统治的第 5 年的一次对利比亚人入侵的成功抵御。在铭文的开始，美楞普塔被赞扬成成功抵御利比亚人入侵的伟大国王，而在结尾则进一步把他提升为埃及所有邻国，特别是叙利亚巴勒斯坦的征服者。关于美楞普塔对亚洲的征服，学者们一直存有疑虑。然而，在所有被征服地的名单中出现的"以色列"这一名称，却引起了学者们的高度重视，因为这是我们所能见到的古代埃及文献中最早提及的"以色列"的名称。故此，学者们把该石碑定名为"以色列石碑"。关于该铭文的原始文献，参见 K. Kitchen, *Ramesside Inscriptions: Translated and Annotated, Notes and Comments*, Vol. IV, Oxford, 1996, pp.12-19. 相关译文，参见 J. H. Breasted, *Ancient Records of Egypt*, Vol. III, Chicago, 1906, § § 602-617；M. Lichtheim, *Ancient Egyptian Literature*, Vol. II, Berkeley, Los Angeles & London, 1976, pp. 73-78；J. A. Wilson in *Ancient Near Eastern Texts*, ed. by J. B. Pritchard, Princeton, 1955, pp. 376-378.

② M.C. Astour, "Yahweh in Egyptian Topographic Lists," in *Festschrift Elmar Edel, Agypten und Altes Testament*, Vol. I, eds. M. Gorg & E. Pusch, Bamberg, 1979, p. 20ff. 塞瑞尔 Srr、拉班 Rbn、萨玛特 Simet、乌尔布尔 Wrbr 和皮斯皮斯 Pyspys 皆为埃及语中的外来语，它们都位于叙利亚巴勒斯坦地区，其中皮斯皮斯即为现代黎巴嫩里塔尼河（Litani）附近比卡河谷（Biqa）中的一座温泉；萨玛特位于腓尼基沿岸巴特闰（Batrun）南部 7 英里处；塞瑞尔就是《旧约》中提到的圣塞尔城（Mt. Seir）；而拉班则是叙利亚中部的一个城市国家。参见 R. Hannig, *Grosses Handworterbuch Agyptisch-Deutsch (2800-950 v. Chr.): Die Sprache der Pharaonen*, p.1184; p. 1162; p. 1183; p. 1131; p.1140.

③ D. B. Redford, *Egypt, Canaan and Israel In Ancient Times*. Princeton: Princeton University Press, 1992, pp. 272-73.

④ S. Morenz, *Egyptian Religion*, Ithaca: Cornell University Press, 1973, p.239.

是因为埃及国王的亚洲政策使然。较之于埃及的努比亚属国，埃及国王给予了他的亚洲属国更多的自治权，同时也给予它们的神明以最大限度的尊重。

然而，埃及人对叙利亚巴勒斯坦地区诸神的吸纳并不是把他们完全移植到埃及，而是把这些神明的某种力量融和到埃及神明身上，从而使这种力量得到最大限度的彰显。好斗是阿纳特女神、阿什塔特女神、巴阿勒、芮晒弗神和胡闰神的基本特征之一，这一点可以从他们的名衔和形象中得出：芮晒弗神被称为"力量之主"，因此，他通常与埃及战神蒙图合二为一而成为蒙图芮晒弗，并以勇猛的形象出现。为此，埃及国王经常在展示自己的勇猛时，会说自己就像芮晒弗那样。[1]阿什塔特女神，或阿纳特女神的形象通常是一位挥舞着弓箭的女骑手，这样，她们的其他诸如丰饶女神和爱神的形象便渐渐淡出埃及人的视野。新王国时期不断的对外战争需要强有力的战神的护佑，上述亚洲诸神恰恰满足了埃及国王在这一方面的需要。于是，对这些亚洲神祇的崇拜便在埃及社会悄然兴起。[2]

在这些来自于叙利亚巴勒斯坦地区的神明融入埃及宗教生活之初，他们并没有得到普通埃及民众的接受。因为战争通常是一种国家行为，尽管他们的好战特质迎合了埃及国王的口味，但却与埃及民众的生活相去甚远。然而，这些神祇并不是只有确保战争胜利的职能，他们还有治愈创伤的能力，这一点恰恰符合了埃及平民的要求，并因而使亚洲诸神崇拜得以在埃及民间传播。

有文献显示，普通埃及人在身受病痛折磨的时候，向伊什塔尔女神求助。而且埃及王室也曾求助于这位有着治愈和康复能力的亚洲神。米坦尼王国图什拉塔就曾把伊什塔尔的雕像借给第十八王朝的国王阿蒙霍特普三世，以此来减轻和治愈他的病痛。

从王室到民间，叙利亚巴勒斯坦地区的神祇已经如埃及本土神祇那样完全融入了埃及人的宗教生活，从而位列埃及众神。这主要得益于埃及人的宗教观。在埃及人看来，只要这位神祇能够满足他们的需求，无论是他来自何方，他们都会像崇拜埃及本民族的神祇那样崇拜他。

然而，出于某些原因，埃及人对同样是外来神的耶和华的态度有所不同。根据索莱布和西阿玛拉地名表，埃及人知道耶和华，但是他们对他并不崇拜，耶和华也没有像其他外来神那样等同于某位埃及神。埃及人既没有为耶和华建立神庙，也没有任何其他形式的艺术品，甚至也没有关于他的任何记录。一个可能的解释是埃及人视古代埃及人为敌对的神，是生活在埃及北部的被埃及人所僧恨的沙苏人中的一个敌对部落的神。

总之，古代埃及"象形文字 Yhw 与希伯来语神明 Yahweh 正好对应，它比迄今所知有神名出现的最古老的文献摩押石碑还要早 500 年。"[3] 被记录在美楞普塔石碑上的最后成为以色列人、并最终创建了以色列王国的人就是在某一历史时期被称为沙苏的那些人。"[4]

故此，古代埃及索莱布文献和西阿玛拉文献中提到的耶和华的沙苏人就是以色列人。到公元前 1400 年他们已经定居在迦南。对于埃及人来说，以色列人与其他沙苏人不同的之处就是他们是上帝耶和华的追随者。

---

[1] W. K. Simpson, "Reshep in Egypt," *Orientalia* 29 (1960), pp. 63–67.

[2] J. Cerny, "Reference to Blood Brotherhood among Semites in an Egyptian Text of the Ramesside Period," *JNES* 14 (1955), pp. 161–3.

[3] M.C. Astour, "Yahweh in Egyptian Topographic Lists," in *Festschrift Elmar Edel, Agypten und Altes Testament*, Vol. I, eds. M. Gorg & E. Pusch, Bamberg, 1979, p. 18.

[4] Redford, *Egypt, Canaan and Israel In Ancient Times*. Princeton: Princeton University Press, 1992.

《老子》：道的历史性

蒋重跃　北京师范大学

摘要：古汉语中"由"字与"道"相通，其意涵为我们分析《老子》的"道"思想提供了便利："由"含有生成过程的意义，"道"亦如此。"道"在内涵上可谓空洞，外延上泛指一切事物及其生成过程。"道"的历史性即体现在此生成过程中：其自身的变动性，令其得以表现事物的生成属性，亦即在时间维度上贯穿古今，包涵事物性质之历史变化。其变动性的成立原因，在于"道"所指向的事物因存在差异而出现相互的矛盾，矛盾又导致事物的发展。

关键词：老子；道；由；历史

Abstract: In ancient Chinese Language, the meaning of Chinese character "You" （由） and "Tao" （道）is similar, which offers convenience for analyzing the thought of "Tao" in *Laozi*. "You" means generation process, so does "Tao". The intension of "Tao" is empty, but its epitaxy refers to all the things and their generation process. The historicity of "Tao" is embodied in the generation process: the variability of "Tao" enables it to represent the generation character of things, i.e. the historical changes through past and present containing the nature of things. Its variability exists because the mutual contradiction which leads to the development of things occurs due to the difference between the things that "Tao" refers to.

Keywords: *Laozi*, Tao, You, historicity

公元前 5 世纪，古希腊的巴门尼德用"是"（το ον）表示世界的最高本体，从那开始，希腊人就把理论的关注点从"水"、"无定"、"气"等具体的世界本原（又译"始基"）转到普遍的世界本体上来。在中国，大约同时甚至更早，就有老子用"道"来代替"天""帝"等宗教性的最高概念，指万物的根据。但是，"道"究竟有怎样的意义呢？后来的古代中国学者习惯意会和描述，而不愿诉诸具有逻辑性的表达方式，所以他们的研究成果至今仍需继续解读。近代中国人学习了西方的哲学概念，并用以界说古代学术思想，由此引起老子的道究竟是"本原"还是"本体"、"唯物"还是"唯心"的争论。

经过这些年来的思考，我越来越感到把道做如此的理解是不妥的。为什么呢？因为这些概念来自西方哲学，它们所表达的东西，往往在范围上是片段的，在状态上是静止的，单纯哪一个都不足以表现道的真实情况。那么道的真实情况究竟是怎样的呢？以下略作说明。

按古汉语，"道"与"由"相通，这对理解道的含义具有十分重要的意义。《说文·辵部》："迪，道也，从辵，由声。"段玉裁注："道兼道路、引导二训。"①《尚书·太甲》上："旁求俊彦，启迪后人"。"启迪后人"，传曰"开道（导）后人"，"启迪"作"开道（导）"，至今犹然。"迪"常作"由"。《论语》"民可使由之，不可使知之。"（《泰伯》）"由"即"开导"，"知"即"知道""了解"。这句话意思是说，人民可以开导（以便他们自己去知），不可以勉强（他们接受某种观点）。《郭店楚墓竹简·尊德义》中有"民可使道（导）之，而不可使智（知）之。民可道（导）也，而不可强也"一句②，恰恰表明《论语》的这句话只能做如上解释，同时也证明"由"通"道"。其实，史上早有明证：孔子大弟子中有仲由，字子路，或曰季路，是"由"通"路"，"路"即"道"也。

"由"的本义和引申义大概如下。《说文·系部》：由，"随，从也"，或为本义，或接近本义。例如《诗·南山》："鲁道有荡，齐子由归。"诗中的"由"即有"从"的意思。再例如，《论语》"行不由径"（《雍也》）。"径"为小路，喻邪道，句中的"由"即有"遵"、"沿"之意。《论语》还有"谁能出不由户？何莫由斯道也？"（《雍也》）句中的"由"有"通过""遵循"之义。引而申之，"由"可作"由于""因为"解。例如《孟子·梁惠王上》："何由知吾可也？""道"为行路，当然可以由来，还可以表示何以至此的途径、方法或原因，这些都与"由"的基本含义相通。《韩非子》："人主不能明法而以制大臣之威，无道得小人之信矣。"（《南面》）句中的"道"可以直接换成"由"字。

上面两段文字显然是为了说明《老子》的道具有"由"的含义，实际情况是不是这样呢？回答是肯定的。《老子》曰：

> 孔德之容，惟道是从。道之为物，惟恍惟惚。惚兮恍兮，其中有象；恍兮惚兮，其中有物。窈兮冥兮，其中有精；其精甚真，其中有信。自古及今，其名不去，以阅众甫。吾何以知众甫之状哉？以此。（二十一章）

"德"说的是万物成就的过程。按这段话来理解，德只能是从（沿着）道而来。正是在这个意义上，后来《庄子》才能说出"道者，万物之所由也"（《渔父》），直接点破了主题。

不过，这里有一个问题，需提出来略作讨论。道是"万物之所由"，"由"又是"从来"，那岂不是说道早早地就存在那儿，供万物从它生长出来么？有人就是这样理解的。北宋王雱注《庄子》有所谓"大道……浑然为一而莫不由之"；"天地阴阳由道而生也"；"夫道无乎不在也，虽天地之大，由之而生，蜩鸴之小，由之而成"③。如果把这些话做机械的理解，那么道就成了某种既存的实体性的东西，也就成了神秘的存在物。事实上道家也的确有此一路，不足奇怪。

不过我并不这样理解。老子认为："人法地，地法天，天法道，道法自然"（二十五章），人、地、天、道，后面的比前面的越来越空灵，到了"道"就不可能再是任何具体的什物了。老子还认为："反者道之动，弱者道之用。天下万物生于有，有生于无。"（四十章）明明说"道"是"无"，即不是什么实有的东西，而只是某种运动方式或作用，或者说是万物的根本属性。道说的是万物以

---

① 段玉裁：《说文解字注》，上海：上海古籍出版社，1988年版，第71页下。
② 见荆门市博物馆：《郭店楚墓竹简》，北京：文物出版社，1998年版，第194页。
③ 王元泽（雱）：《南华真经新传》，卷二《齐物论》注，第18页；卷十四《则阳》注，第539页；卷七《天道》注，第262页。无求备斋《庄子集成初编》第6册，严灵峰编辑，艺文印书馆印行。

自己本然为法，道不是实体性的东西，而是空洞的，泛指一切事物。惟其为空洞，所以才能泛指一切。所谓"孔德之容，惟道是从"，万物获得自己的本质叫做德，这个德就是道，就是"所由"。所谓"道之为物"说的就是万物所由，也就是万物所从来，根本没有实体性的道预先存在那里。

道是由，指万物成为自己的过程，具体情况是怎样的呢？老子习惯于用生养或生成的譬喻来加以解说。例如：

> 道生一，一生二，二生三，三生万物，万物负阴而抱阳，冲气以为和。（四十二章）

道如果是"万物之所由"，那就一定要变化，变化的结果，就一定会从混沌中发展出"一"。世界上一旦有了有限的"一"，矛盾也就必不可免了，这就是"二"，阴阳就是"二"的代表。阴阳和合而生物，是为包含着"二"的第三者，于是就有了"三"。有了"三"也就有了万物。可见，万物成就自己的过程就是事物内在矛盾发展的过程。因为有矛盾，所以就要运动，就要发展。如今学术界已经达成共识：辩证的唯物主义一定是历史的唯物主义，两者是同一的，不会有两个。道也是如此，事物的"所由"，说的就是矛盾推动自身的发展，这是辩证的，同时又是历史的。

过去，学者往往强调道具有"生"的意义，却容易忽视"成"的意义，这或许是受了文献舛错的影响，请看这一段：

> 道生之，德畜之，物形之，势成之。是以万物莫不尊道而贵德。道之尊，德之贵，夫莫之命而常自然。故道生之，德畜之，长之、育之、亭之、毒之、养之、覆之。生而不有，为而不恃，长而不宰，是谓玄德。（五十一章）

从"道生之"到"势成之"，集中说明事物的生成过程。接下来，"故道生之，德畜之，长之、育之、亭（成）之、毒（熟）之、养之、覆之"一句，帛书甲乙本均做"道生之，畜之，长之，育之，亭之，毒之，养之，覆之"，中间没有"德"字。传世本"德畜之"与上下文不协调，有了这一个"德"字，读起来就感觉突兀。相比之下，帛书本则更顺，也更合乎老子思想的内容。按照帛书的文句，就可以这样理解本章的大意：万物有出生、有蓄养、有成形、有长成，从生到成，这个过程是开放的，历时的，动态的，动力不在别处，就在事物之内。所谓"道""德""物""势"，不过是说事物由内力推动的不同发展（生成）阶段而已。

道既然指事物的生成属性，那么在时间的维度中，它就一定是古今一体的，这在《老子》中不难读到：

> 视之不见名曰夷，听之不闻名曰希，搏之不得名曰微，此三者不可致诘，故混而为一。其上不曒，其下不昧，绳绳不可名，复归于无物，是谓无状之状，无物之象。是谓惚恍。迎之不见其首，随之不见其后。执古之道，以御今之有，能知古始，是谓道纪。（十四章）

《老子》指出：从感觉经验的角度看，道仍然不是实体性的，看不见，听不到，搏不得，因而是"无物"，无头也无尾，但它却贯穿古今，统一了古今。

《老子》关于"始"和"母"的譬喻同样说明了古今一体的思想。《老子》一章："无名，天地之始，有名，万物之母。"王弼这样解释："凡有皆始于无，故未形无名之时，则为万物之始，及其有形有名之时，则长之、育之、亭之、毒之，为其母也。言道以无形无名始成万物，以始以成，而不知其所以，玄之又玄也。"①道是无形无名的，它使万物有始有成，但却不知其所以，所以叫做玄之又玄。这种解释除了上面的引文以外，在《老子》中还可以得到印证，例如：

> 天下有始，以为天下母，既得其母，以知其子；既知其子，复守其母，没身不殆。（五十二章）

什么是"始"？《说文·女部》："始，女之初也。"由此看来，"始"是小女孩。可是小女孩会长大成人，会生儿育女成为母亲的。"始"和"母"可以是同一个人。子女之于母亲，除了出生，还有许多方面是需要哺养的，只有这样才能真正长成。如此看来，道既指物之始，更指物之成，生成之间的张力恰恰隐喻着事物的古与今之间的内在联系。老子用"始"和"母"来做譬喻，其实是用生育和哺养形象地表现事物的发展来历。王弼则把它解释为"始"和"成"的统一关系。这就是古与今的统一，这就是事物的发展史！

与单纯从价值角度断定道具有始的意义一样，若单纯从结果的角度，人们又容易只看到万物成就的一面，以为道只是万物已然的本质，从而忽略它的初始阶段，这就是为什么有人相信道具有本体意义的原因了：

> 无名，天地始；有名，万物之母。（一章）

只看到道的"无名"，因而称其为"本原"或"本根"；而只看到道的"有名"，就会认为道是万物本体，即万物的概念。这两者都不是道的全体。

> 昔之得一者：天得一以清，地得一以宁，神得一以灵，谷得一以盈，万物得一以生，侯王得一以为天下贞。（三十九章）

万物各有不同的属性，但最终的根据是相同的，那就是"一"，"一"作为最高的概念就是道。这样的道说的是万物的统一性，因而具有本体的特征。

道者，万物之奥。（六十二章）《礼运》"故人以为奥也"，郑玄注："'奥'，犹'主'也。"帛书本："道者，万物之注也。""注"通"主"。②

> 朴散则为器。（二十八章）
> 道常无名，朴虽小，天下莫能臣也。（三十二章）
> 天网恢恢，疏而不失。（七十三章）

道被认为是万物之主，统摄着万物；道的总名分散到具体之物，所以叫做"朴散则为器"，这样的朴不给任何人当"臣子"，其实还是万物之主。正因为是朴，所以才会像天网一样，恢宏而统摄万物。单纯看这点，自然容易把道理解为万物的本体。这样的看法仍然是片面的，不足为训。

总之，老子的道论是物的哲学，说的是万物的生成过程。凡物有始有成，有古有今，这个过程是由物自身的矛盾推动的发展运动过程。根据这样的辩证发展观，凡物皆发生在过去，持存于当下。

---

① 王弼：《老子注》，见《诸子集成》第3册，上海：上海书店出版社，1986年版，第1页。
② 高明：《帛书老子校注》，北京：中华书局，1996年版，第127页。

从发生的角度看它像是本原，从持存的角度看它又像是本体。从事实认识的角度看，它不是本原和本体中的某一个，而是始与成、古与今、过去与现在之间的一种张力。古希腊哲人的"始基"虽说也是世界的来历，但更主要的是要说明世界是由什么构成以及怎样构成的，强调的是横向的构成要素和构成方式。老子的道却不关心要素和方式，它只对世界万物如何成为现今这个样子的来历感兴趣，强调的是纵向的过程，虽然处在这个过程中的万物也会有其内在的构成要素和方式。由此可见，老子的道即物的根本属性具有鲜明的历史性，它不同于希腊人的"始基"之强调构成要素和方式，与希腊人后来重视"是"的传统更是不可同日而语。

古代中国人从来都把历史看作古与今之间的某种张力，在传统学术中史学一直享有崇高地位，这些都与老子开创的道论传统密不可分。今天，悉心体会老子之道的历史性，不但有助于深入理解中国哲学的本质特征，更有助于准确把握历史概念的基本内涵。

中古以来南北差异的整合发展与江南的角色功用

李治安　南开大学

摘要：东汉以后，中华诸地域子文明间相互关系的"主旋律"呈现南北整合发展。首次南北差异整合发生在南北朝隋唐。隋唐立国之本或入口诚为北朝体制，其演化趋势或出口则是南朝体制。某种意义上说，由"南朝化"起步的"唐宋变革"，就是革均田、租庸调、府兵等北朝三制度的"命"。元统一后的南北差异博弈整合，北制因素过分强大，总体占上风。朱元璋、朱棣父子的个人经历及政治文化心态等，致使明前期的整合再次以北制居主导。明中叶以后的另一次整合，改而以南制为重心。偏重革除徭役的"一条鞭法"，似为南制因素压倒北制的"里程碑"。5世纪以后的江南，充任中国经济重心和文化主脉所在，成为"富民"和农商并重秩序成长发展的"风水宝地"。尤其是宋元明清的江南长期代表着社会经济的发展趋势，依然是统一国家的条件下南北博弈整合中新兴动力的渊薮。在唐宋前后南北地域差异的上述三四次博弈整合中，江南地区的角色及能动功用，至为关键。大运河生逢其时，适应政治上北支配南、经济上北依赖南的错位需要，充当了南方在经济文化上支撑、带动、辐射北方，推动全国整合发展的特有水系通道。

关键词：南北整合发展；江南；一条鞭法；富民与农商并重；大运河

Abstract：After the Eastern Han Dynasty, the integration and development of the south and north of China became the "theme" of the relationship among those regions (sub-civilization areas) in China. It originated in the periods of the Southern-Northern Dynasties and Sui-Tang Dynasties. The systems of the Sui and Tang Dynasties were based on those of the Northern Dynasties. However, their developments led to reappearance of the system of the Southern Dynasties. In one sense, it is the "Tang-Song Transformation" beginning with "southernization" that abolished the three main governing policies in the Northern Dynasties, i.e. the systems of land equalization, the grain-labor-cloth tax, and the militia garrison. After the unity of China under the Yuan Dynasty, the Northern system generally prevailed in the course of integration between the south and north. Due to personal experiences, and political and cultural preferences of Zhu Yuanzhang and Zhu Di, the Northern system dominated once again in the integration during early Ming Dynasty. But in the mid-Ming dynasty the Southern system was accepted and became prevailed in integration between the South and North. The implementation of the single tax in silver could be regarded as a milestone of the trend. The regions south of the Yangtze River after the fifth century became most prosperous in China, where both agriculture and trade developed steadily and promptly. Such great social and economic developments in these regions during the period of Song, Yuan, Ming and Qing dynasties continued to promote the integration between the South and North. In the three or four integrations appearing around the Tang and Song Dynasties, the regions south of the Yangtze River played key role with the emergence of the Grand Canal linking the south and north of China.

Keywords: the integrations between the south and north and their own developments, the regions south of the Yangtze River, the single tax in silver, richening people and promoting the agriculture and trade equally, the Grand Canal

五千年的连绵发展，是中华文明独有的优长与特色。疆域广袤和地理风俗多样，又导致中华文明的长期繁荣很大程度上需要依赖于内部若干地域子文明间的碰触和整合。在若干子文明整合发展过程中，中原、关陇、海岱、江南等区域均在各个时期发挥了不可替代的历史作用^①。本文拟在前人研究的基础上，试从傅斯年"夷夏东西说"的贡献，东汉以后南北地域差异的博弈整合，南北地域整合中江南及大运河的角色功用等方面，予以进一步探索，就教于方家同好。

一　傅斯年"夷夏东西说"的贡献

鸟瞰五千年的中华文明，"共时性"地存在若干个地域子文明板块：以文明属性划分，可分为游牧文明和农耕文明两大板块；即使在农耕文明内部也存在东部与西部，黄河中下游与长江中下游等板块分野。"历时性"地纵观五千年中华文明，大致发生如下8次较大规模的地域子文明的整合发展：

（1）黄帝与炎帝"阪泉之战"、黄帝与蚩尤"涿鹿之战"——传说中华夏先民部落在黄河中游的初步整合；

（2）大禹治水创建夏朝与汤灭桀建商朝——第一次东、西地域的整合发展；

（3）武王克商与西周封邦建国——第二次东、西地域的整合发展；

（4）嬴政翦灭六国与秦朝郡县制统一天下——第三次东、西地域的整合发展；

（5）汉武帝征讨匈奴与汉地、漠北、西域的首次整合、融汇；

（6）魏晋南北朝和隋唐时期第一次南北地域的博弈整合；

（7）宋辽金元明清时期南北地域的进一步整合；

（8）民国"五族共和"为代表的多子文明整合与现代中华民族的形成；

1933年，傅斯年先生曾撰《夷夏东西说》，首次阐发了夏商周三代"夷与商属于东系，夏与周属于西系"，东西二系"因对峙而生争斗，因争斗而起混合，因混合而文化进展"的重要观点^②。此文堪称廓清上古东、西地域子文明共存整合的里程碑式的论著，首次解决了前述一至四次东、西

① 傅斯年：《夷夏东西说》，欧阳哲生主编：《傅斯年全集》第三卷，长沙：湖南教育出版社，2003年。萧启庆：《中国近世前期南北发展的歧异与统合——以南宋金元时期的经济社会文化为中心》，《清华历史讲堂初编》，北京：三联书店，2007年。拙稿《两个南北朝与中古以来的历史发展线索》，《文史哲》2009年第6期；《元和明前期南北差异的博弈与整合发展》，《历史研究》2011年第5期。
② 傅斯年：《夷夏东西说》，欧阳哲生主编：《傅斯年全集》第三卷，长沙：湖南教育出版社，2003年，第181—182页。

子文明相互关系的基本问题，拓荒开创，功莫大矣。美籍华人历史学、考古学家张光直教授对傅斯年和他的《夷夏东西说》推崇备至。认为："傅先生是一位历史天才，是无疑的。他的《夷夏东西说》一篇文章奠定他的天才地位是有余的。这篇文章以前，中国古史毫无系统可言。傅先生说自东汉以来的中国史，常分南北，但在三代与三代以前，中国的政治舞台，……地理形势只有东西之分，而文化亦分为东西两个系统。自傅先生夷夏东西说出现之后，新的考古资料全部是东西相对的：仰韶——大汶口，河南龙山——山东龙山，二里头（夏）——商，周——商、夷。……这样的文章可以说是有突破性的"。"他的东西系统成为一个解释整个中国大陆古史的一把总钥匙"[①]。而后虽然出现了少量试图质疑该说的文章[②]，但也仅是批评其有关夏文化地域的某些局部不足。如同任何经典宏论在阐发主流、本质的同时不可避免地舍弃偏枝末节的惯例，上述不足亦属正常。故而少量质疑，无关宏旨，也无法撼动"夷夏东西说"的基本立论及贡献。

二　东汉以后南北地域差异的博弈整合

对傅先生80年前业已指出的"自东汉末""常常分南北"的问题，即东晋和南宋南渡后各二三百年分裂对峙所导致南方、北方颇有差异的两大地域子文明或承载板块间的关系，笔者勉为"续貂"，试做初步探研。

先说南北朝与隋唐的"南朝化"。

1945年陈寅恪著《隋唐制度渊源略论稿》，揭示隋唐制度多半出于北朝，又受到南朝的部分影响，进而澄清了北朝制度的内涵、流变[③]。20世纪90年代，唐长孺《魏晋南北朝隋唐史三论》指出："唐代经济、政治、军事以及文化诸方面都发生了显著的变化……这些变化中的最重要部分，乃是东晋南朝的继承，我们姑且称之为'南朝化'"[④]。近年，阎步克、胡宝国、陈爽等又围绕隋唐"北朝化"、"南朝化"何者为主流，展开了小小的争论[⑤]。

以上争论都有史料依据和合理性，又相互抵牾对立，似乎单用其中一说难以涵盖隋唐时期的复杂历史情况。笔者拙见：南北朝、隋朝及唐前期的历史是循着"南朝"、"北朝"两种体制或线索来发展演化的。两者各有其赖以生存和实用的空间地域——南方和北方，又在并存发展中互相交融，互相影响。正如人们熟知的，随着秦汉"大一统"帝制的问世，黄河中下游东、西子文明的整合也基本完成。而东晋以后经济重心及文化精英的南移，以长江或淮河为界限的南北两大地域的差异转而上升和凸显。经历近300年的南北朝分裂对峙，特别是受"五胡乱华"等影响，南方与北方的制度状况或发展线索呈现异样，也是情理中事。"南朝"状况或线索，主要表现于东晋、宋、齐、梁、陈所沿袭汉魏西晋的体制。"北朝"状况或线索，主要表现在北魏、北齐、西魏、北周的体制。诚如阎步克教授所言，"隋唐王朝都是在北朝的基础上建立的"。故隋朝及唐前期基本实行的是"北朝"制度。而后，隋唐二王朝又在统一国度内实施了"南朝"体制与"北朝"体制的整合，到中唐

---

① 何兹全：《傅斯年的史学思想与史学著作》，《历史研究》2000年第4期。

② 杨向奎：《夏民族起于东方考》，《禹贡》第7卷，第6、7期。程德祺：《略论典型龙山文化即是夏朝文化》，《苏州大学学报》1982年1期。沈长云：《夏后氏居于古河济之间考》，《中国史研究》1994年3期。温玉春：《夏氏族起于山东考》，《河北师范大学学报》2000年4期。

③ 陈寅恪：《隋唐制度渊源略论稿·叙论》，北京：三联书店，2004年，第3页。

④ 唐长孺：《魏晋南北朝隋唐史三论》，北京：中华书局，2011年，第468页。

⑤ 牟发松：《略论唐代的南朝化倾向》，《中国史研究》1996年第2期，第55页。阎步克、胡宝国、陈爽：《关于南朝化的讨论》，《象牙塔》http://www.xiangyata.net 2003年6月2日。阎步克：《南北朝的不同道路与历史出口》，《国学论丛》http://bbs.guoxue.com 2004年8月24日。将无同：《关于南朝化问题》，《往复·史林杂识》http://www.wangf.net 2006年4月14日。揭胡：《"历史出口说"的"理论出口"》http://www.mzyi.cn 2007年3月。

以后整合完毕，国家整体上向"南朝化"过渡。笔者的看法大致可以找到三条证据支撑：贯穿北朝、隋朝及唐前期的均田、租庸调和府兵三大制度，均主要实施于北方，又都在中唐瓦解。替代它们的租佃制大土地占有、两税法和募兵制，正是整合后南朝因素转而占上风的结果。北制诚为隋唐立国之本或入口，南制则是其演化趋势或出口。从某种意义上说，由"南朝化"起步的"唐宋变革"，就是革均田、租庸调、府兵等三制度的"命"，也与上述南北地域差异的整合趋势，密不可分。

再谈元、明帝国南北差异的博弈整合。

继辽、金、西夏之后，蒙古铁骑南下，建立了统一南北的元王朝。元统一后"南不能从北，北不能从南"①等抵牾差异依然存在，甚至在国家制度层面亦呈现南、北制因素并存博弈的状况。蒙古草原制度与金朝后期汉法制度混合体的"北制"，更是始终充当元帝国的制度本位，在政治、经济、社会、文化各领域长期发挥着支配作用。相对于江南南制因素的北制表现为：职业户计制与全民服役，贵族分封制与驱口制，官营手工业的重新繁荣，儒士的边缘倾向与君臣关系主奴化。元朝社会经济整体上的发展进步，唐宋变革成果在元明的延伸，都有赖于国家统一条件下南、北制因素的融汇互动、博弈整合，唐宋变革和晚明清繁盛之间"过渡"或整合发展，同样是在此类融汇整合中逐步得以实现。不过，元统一后上述博弈整合，呈现为北制向江南的推广、南制因素遗留及部分上升且影响全国等较复杂的互动过程。由于元政权北制因素的过分强大，元统一后整合的结果，总体上是北制因素占上风，南制因素依然居从属。

朱元璋曾以"驱逐胡虏，恢复中华"为旗号，重建了汉人为皇帝的明王朝，也采取过定都南京，惩元末权臣和贪赃之弊，废中书省和丞相，以三司取代行省，创建卫所取代部族兵制，以及"黄册"及"鱼鳞册"等新制度，力图较多摆脱蒙元旧制，使国家体制恢复到汉地传统王朝的形态上来。但不容忽视的是，朱明王朝又自觉不自觉地继承了颇多的元朝制度。这与朱元璋、朱棣父子带有个性色彩的南、北政策及朱棣迁都燕京都有密切关联，客观上更是元朝覆灭后所遗留的社会关系、文化意识等潜在影响使然。如果说朱元璋实行的是半南半北的政策，眷顾中原北地的倾向尚带有偶然或不稳定性，朱棣就与乃父显著不同了。朱棣"靖难"，以燕京和北直隶充当根基地，其军旅精锐包含蒙古朵颜三卫等，又残酷镇压建文帝势力，自然容易站在建文帝南方本位的对立面，遂导致"欲定都北京，思得北士用之"等政策②，导致其封爵燕王、肇兴且起兵燕邸，最终迁都燕京等以燕京北地为基业所在的新体制。又兼他七次亲征大漠蒙古时难免反受草原习俗及主从关系等影响。其结果，朱棣实行北方本位政策，就形成政治驱动颇强，主、客观综合支撑等较为成熟、稳定的态势，就成为势在必行的了。明朝的军户制，"配户当差"户役法③，官府手工业和匠籍制，行省三司制，宗室分封及诛杀功臣士大夫，等等，都可以看到元制或北制的影子，都是被朱元璋率先多半保留变通，后又被朱棣等略加改造而长期沿袭下来。换言之，朱元璋、朱棣父子，特别是朱棣个人经历和政治文化心态等偶然因素，严重地影响了明前期南、北制因素的整合及走向，致使明前期的整合再次以北制占优势。明中叶以后较前期明显改变，南、北制因素开始实施另一次的整合，而且是改而以南制为重心。主要表现在：募兵制逐步占据主导，"一条鞭法"取代"配户当差"户役法，民营纳税淘汰匠役制，隆庆海禁开放，等等。尤其是万历九年（1581）的"一条鞭法"，应该是南、北制因素的再整合的关键。某种意义上，重在革除徭役的"一条鞭法"，亦是南制因素压倒北制的"里程碑"。然而，在某些领域内北制因素或改变无多，或依然如故。主要是伴当仆从隶属、籍没制及贱民遗留、

① 胡祗遹著，魏崇武、周思成点校：《胡祗遹集》卷21《论治法》，长春：吉林文史出版社，第440页。
② 张廷玉：《明史》卷177《王翱传》，中华书局，1974年，第4699页。
③ 参阅王毓铨：《明朝的配户当差制》，《中国史研究》1991年1期。

君主独裁与臣僚奴化等，这四者对明代朝野的影响长期而深刻①。

三　5—16世纪江南在南北地域整合发展中的能动角色

据唐长孺先生研究，南朝在孙吴豪门地主经济的基础上发展为大地主山林屯墅和田园形态，荫占佃客及其他依附民劳作。商业方面不仅建康城（今江苏南京）有4个市场及其与官廨、住宅的杂处，还出现了不少非官方市镇草市。率多从事商贾致富，泛舟贩运交易、海外商贸频繁及贵族官僚经商盛行，私人作坊出现和官府作坊的和雇、召募等萌生。估税、关津税、市税等名目的商税及包税，相继问世。②陈寅恪也说：南朝"国用注重于关市之税"③。东晋和刘宋主要沿用世袭兵制，刘宋中叶募兵增多，齐梁募兵完全取代了世袭兵制④。令人有些感叹的是，唐前期的地税和户税，实乃和南朝梁陈据田亩征租及据赀征调，一脉相承。而杨炎"两税法"的计亩征税及田亩归属户产的原则本来就是"南朝成法"。唐代不仅江南商业活动仍然沿袭南朝，诸如沿江草市和北方店铺兴盛，坊市制破坏，海外贸易发展，货币交换比重增长，行税、住税和盐、茶、酒税等商税征收，都带有南朝的因素。唐代商品经济和财税规制无疑是沿袭南朝的轨迹而发展起来的。开元二十五年以后取代府兵制的募兵，又能够从南朝募兵找到类同物⑤。足见，中唐发生的一系列社会变动，大多可以溯源于南朝。中唐以后之所以南朝因素占上风或以南制为"出口"，之所以租佃制大土地占有、两税法和募兵制成为中唐那次整合后的基本成果，就是因为均田、租庸调和府兵等北制大抵未在江南推行，南朝和隋唐江南较为先进的经济社会秩序一直未曾被改动。在这个意义上，中唐

诸多研究表明，忽必烈平宋战争以招降为主，较少杀戮。江南的先进农业、原有的土地、租佃、赋税、繁荣的手工业、商贸及海运、理学、科举等制，南宋所继承的唐宋变革的主要成果遂得以基本保留或延续发展。尤其是浙西一带圩田及沙塗田等能在人口稠密和土地偏少条件下追逐高于一般田地十倍的收获。⑥元末杭州丝织业等还出现了少量的自由雇佣劳动。⑦大土地占用和租佃关系在江南依然在发展。譬如延祐间松江下砂场"多田翁"瞿霆发"有当役民田二千七百顷，并佃官田共及万顷"。⑧二税制及差役亦在保留沿用。海外贸易的海港、贸易伙伴、中外海船的来往、基本贸易制度等，都承袭南宋。后又增添两个特别的因素：宫廷"中买"珠宝和斡脱商。漕粮海运亦由江南朱清、张瑄倡导主持，海外征伐的军士、船只及技术同样主要来自江南。故海外贸易、海运和海外征伐三者都算是南方航海技术、人力、财力等为元统治者所用的"典范"。尤其是元代海运和海外贸易的高度繁荣及其向东海、南海的开拓发展过程中，南制因素厥功甚伟。儒学与科举，是保留南制因素最多，并在南、北制因素博弈中最能体现南制优长的方面。理学北上及官方化，朱熹之学正统地位的确立，超族群士人文化圈的形成⑨，表明江南在儒学文化上处于绝对优势。而仁宗恢复科举，应是南制文化因素滋长并冲破蒙古旧俗束缚，得以跻身全国文官选举通行制度之列的突出成绩。尽管元代整体上南制因素依旧居从属，但经历上述兼容与初次整合，南北方之间的交流、沟通愈来愈频繁，

① 以上参阅拙稿《两个南北朝与中古以来的历史发展线索》，《文史哲》2009年第6期；《元和明前期南北差异的博弈与整合发展》，《历史研究》2011年第5期。
② 唐长孺：《魏晋南北朝隋唐史三论》，北京：中华书局，2011年，第100—106页，第125—141页。
③ 陈寅恪：《隋唐制度渊源略论稿》，北京：三联书店，2004年，第160页。
④ 唐长孺：《魏晋南北朝隋唐史三论》，第179页。
⑤ 唐长孺：《魏晋南北朝隋唐史三论》，第280页，第299页，第301—319页，第411页。
⑥ 王祯：《农书》卷11《农器图谱集一·田制门》，《影印文渊阁四库全书》，第730册，第416页。《洪武苏州府志》卷10《田亩》，《中国方志丛刊》，台北：成文出版有限公司，1983年，第432册，第424页。
⑦ 郑天挺：《关于徐一夔〈织工对〉》，《清史探微》，北京：北京大学出版社，1999年，第254—270页。
⑧ 杨瑀著，余大钧点校：《山居新语》卷4，北京：中华书局，2006年，第233页。
⑨ 萧启庆：《元代的族群文化与科举》，台北：联经出版事业公司，2008年，第20页，第62—68页。

相互依赖和彼此密不可分，更是大势所趋。忽必烈为代表的元朝统治者的可贵贡献，不仅在于首次完成了以少数民族为主角的空前规模的多民族国家大统一，还在于在南北整合中坚持北制本位的同时又实行南北异制，比较完整地保留了江南最富庶、最发达的经济实体，不自觉地继承了南方唐宋变革的成果，从而为 14 世纪以后南北进一步整合发展奠定了良好的基础。

尽管朱元璋父子在江南的"剗削"富民和"配户当差"，导致明前期江南社会经济结构的严重蜕变，南方唐宋变革的成果一度被毁坏大半。但明中叶以后江南农业、手工业和商业逐渐得到恢复发展，江南以富民为主导的农商秩序也逐步恢复重建。隆庆开放海禁，海外贸易迅速恢复发展，外贸入超颇丰所带来的大量白银流入，刺激了东南商品经济的再度繁荣①。张居正推行"一条鞭法"前，江西、南直隶、浙江等地已于嘉靖和隆庆年间率先实施，②根源又在于"一条鞭法"主要符合江南社会经济发展及社会关系的需要。晚明商品经济和城市商业化的发展较快，东南沿海城镇市民社会或有雏形，儒士世俗化非常明显，思想禁锢大大减少，等等，某种意义上可以视为南宋及元东南城镇社会的迅速重建与发展。李伯重所云"江南早期工业化"，也主要针对明嘉靖中叶的 1550 年至 1850 年的苏、松、常、镇江、江宁、湖、嘉兴、杭及太仓等八府一州之地。尽管此种工业化具有重工业畸轻而轻工业畸重的"超轻结构"特点，但毕竟属于因劳动分工和专业化能带来较高效率的"斯密性成长"，又兼江南与中国其他地区之间所构成的地区产业分工与专业化，使中国国内贸易充任着江南早期工业化的主要推动力量，最终造就了江南一度成为世界最发达的工业地区之一③。

生产力无疑是经济和社会发展的"火车头"。我们注意到，10 世纪以后手工业、农业等生产力方面的显著进步，大多是率先出现于江南。诸如宋元两浙涌现出专门从事丝织业的家庭机户，随之又有染色业独立和印花布风行。元黄道婆轧棉搅机、绳弦大弓等棉织工具改进及"错纱配色，综线挈花"等法，也发生在松江府乌泥泾④。陶瓷烧制方面，南宋官窑和龙泉哥窑的析晶釉，建窑兼有的分相釉和析晶釉，龙窑的普遍采用；景德镇以瓷石加高岭土二元配方，采用进口青钴料烧制的元青花瓷，以及烧制难度更大的釉里红等⑤。火器方面，"蒺藜火球"、铁火炮和"水底火炮"是南宋最先使用的陆地及水下爆炸性火器，寿春府等处制造的突火枪又是最早的管型火器和近代火枪的前身。造船技术在已有福船、沙船和广船等船型的基础上，率先采用世界上最先进的"水密舱结构"和"平行式梯形斜帆"⑥。护田挡水和水渠灌溉的圩田及相关水道疏浚，也集中于宋元频临长江的湖泊沿岸等低洼地带⑦。以上生产工具和生产技术的大幅度推进与提升，与这一时期以长江三角洲为首的早期工业化之间，似乎是互为因应的，同时也大大增强了整个江南地区经济繁荣及领先全国的原动力。

葛金芳还主张，宋以降长江三角洲等狭义的江南地区，属于典型的"农商社会"。此江南"农商社会"具有五个特征：商品性农业的成长导致农村传统经济结构发生显著变化；江南市镇兴起、市镇网络形成，城市化进程以市镇为据点不断加速；早期工业化进程启动，经济成长方式从"广泛

① 参见晁中辰：《明代海禁与海外贸易》，北京：人民出版社，2005 年，第 244—277 页。
② 参见白寿彝总主编、王毓铨主编《中国通史》第九卷《中古时代·明时期》上册，第 750 页。孙承泽：《春明梦余录》卷 35《户部一·一条鞭》载，庞尚鹏嘉隆之际在浙江奏行一条鞭，《影印文渊阁四库全书》，第 868 册，第 498 页。
③ 李伯重：《江南的早期工业化》，北京：社会科学文献出版社，2000 年，第 19 页，第 523 页，第 536 页，第 542 页。
④ 漆侠主编：《辽宋西夏金代通史·社会经济卷》，上，北京：人民出版社，2010 年，第 284 页。陶宗仪《南村辍耕录》卷 24《黄道婆》，北京：中华书局，1959 年，第 297 页。
⑤ 漆侠主编：《辽宋西夏金代通史·教育科学文化卷》，北京：人民出版社，2010 年，第 186 页。陈高华、史卫民：《中国经济通史·元代经济卷》北京：经济日报出版社，2000 年，第 318—319 页。
⑥ 李曾伯：《可斋续稿》后集卷 5《条具广南备御事宜奏》，《影印文渊阁四库全书》第 1179 册第 662 页。脱脱：《宋史》卷 197《兵志十一·器甲之制》，北京：中华书局校勘本，1977 年，第 4923 页。漆侠主编：《辽宋西夏金代通史·教育科学文化卷》，北京：人民出版社，2010 年，第 172—174 页，第 176—178 页。
⑦ 漆侠主编：《辽宋西夏金代通史·社会经济卷》上，北京：人民出版社，2010 年，第 220 页。陈高华、史卫民：《中国经济通史·元代经济卷》北京：经济日报出版社，2000 年，第 212—214 页。

型成长"向"斯密型成长"转变；区域贸易、区间贸易和国际贸易扩展、市场容量增大，经济开放度提高，一些发达地区由封闭向开放转变；纸币、商业信用、包买商和雇佣劳动等带有近代色彩的经济因素已然出现并有所成长①。上述观点可以得到斯波义信、李伯重、樊树志等诸多经济史学者一系列论著的有力支持，也与20世纪"资本主义萌芽"有关讨论相呼应。即使有人不愿意使用"农商社会"的说法，可谁也难以否认：宋元明清长江三角洲一带较多存在"农商并重"和"商业上升为社会生活繁荣的主要基础之一"的"世相"，进而悄然形成"农业和商业共同支撑社会经济的格局"。②诚然，广义江南地区内部的经济文化发展水平也呈现不平衡状态。长江三角洲等为中心的地区自5世纪以后的经济富庶和文化繁荣一直居全国之首，同时又是整个江南最发达的地区。湖北和湖南北部稍次之，16世纪长江三角洲一带"早期工业化"推进之际，农业重心逐步转移至湖广，随而出现"湖广熟，天下足"的局面。而江西和岭南尚处于晚近逐步开发的区域。

如果我们把唐宋前后的三四次南北博弈整合及唐宋变革的内容作一对照，不难发现北朝到唐前期的体制（科举例外）、元诸色户计全民当差和明前期的"配户当差"户役法等，大抵属于唐宋变革以前的旧形态。南朝统治下的江南经济及财税体制大抵是对唐宋变革的某种良好酝酿或准备。中唐两宋的江南无疑属于唐宋变革高潮中经济文化最先进和最具活力的区域。元代及明中后期的江南也属于承袭南宋"唐宋变革"成果最多的区域。就是说，5世纪以后的江南，逐渐成为中国经济重心和文化主脉所在，成为中国"富民"和农商并重秩序③成长发展的"风水宝地"。尤其是宋元明清的江南依然代表着社会经济发展趋势，依然是统一国家的条件下南北博弈整合中新兴的动力渊薮。在唐宋前后南北地域差异的上述三四次博弈整合中，承载着中国经济重心及文化精英的江南地区的角色及能动功用，至为关键。

四　大运河对南北社会经济整合发展的作用

中国古代都城发展，大体是依据帝国核心区、财赋及军事控驭等因素，自西向东逐步迁移的。周秦汉唐时期，中原王朝的国都主要在镐京、咸阳、长安和洛阳，北宋东移至汴梁。金元明清，北方民族南下又造成北移燕京。经济文化重心则是经历了前述东晋和南宋两次大规模的自北向南的转移，而且南移过程持续了将近七个世纪。在这两次南移之前，北方中原地区的经济文化是非常先进的。但在这两次南移之后，特别是唐后期五代和契丹、女真、蒙古南下或入主中原，战乱频仍，北方中原地区屡遭严重破坏，户口凋零，经济发展缓慢。因此，唐后期以降国家的财赋不得不主要仰赖东南。

与6世纪以后经济上北方依赖南方形成对应反差的是，政治中心长期在北方。隋唐北宋国都尚在黄河中下游，元明清三朝进而北移燕京。而经济命脉却远在江南。于是，在南北关系上便呈现了经济上北依赖南，政治上北支配南的新配置和新格局，且延续了近千年。

大运河的修筑，是中古经济文化重心南移和南方、北方经济政治中心错位的产物。大运河作为漕运命脉，不仅对多民族国家政治统一具有战略上的积极意义，而且在南北交通、经济文化交流等内容的南北差异博弈和整合发展过程中发挥了不可替代的作用。

第一，长期充任南粮北运的漕运黄金水道，有力支撑了千年以来政治上北支配南、经济上北依

①　葛金芳：《"农商社会"的过去、现在和未来——宋以降（11—20世纪）江南区域社会经济变迁论略》，《纪念郑天挺诞辰一百一十周年中国古代社会高层论坛文集》，北京：中华书局，2011年，第384—400页。

②　前揭葛金芳文第384页。赵轶峰：《明清帝制农商社会论纲》，《纪念郑天挺诞辰一百一十周年中国古代社会高层论坛文集》，北京：中华书局，2011年，第477页。

③　林文勋：《唐宋社会变革论纲》，《结论：中国古代"富民社会"的形成及其历史地位》，北京：人民出版社，2011年，第328—340页。另参见林文勋《中国古代富民社会——宋元明清的社会整体性》，载《宋元明国家与社会高端学术论坛会议文件》（打印本），2013年，第175—185页。

赖南的北南关系的新格局。自中唐设转运使总揽漕运，明清常设漕运总督于淮安，官至一、二品，位高权重，专门掌管跨省区的大运河漕运及河道事宜。大运河漕运及管理在 6 世纪以降诸王朝始终具有举足轻重的地位。大运河对维护大一统帝国的政治统一，也厥功甚伟。除了供给京师官民粮食之外，隋唐征高丽和经营东北，唐后期朝廷对付河朔三镇为代表的藩镇割据，元朝防御北方蒙古诸王反叛，明成祖朱棣"靖难"和迁都燕京后旨在防御蒙古的长城"九边"军事镇戍，清乾隆等经营蒙古、新疆、西藏的所谓"十大武功"，等等，无不仰赖大运河漕运。

第二，大运河首次将司马迁时代的燕、赵、魏、宋、齐、鲁、徐、吴、越等相对独立的自然经济区[1]自北向南连成一片，弥补了中国南北走向河流稀少和陆路交通常因山川阻隔而艰难等缺陷，有利于海河、黄河、淮河、长江、钱塘江五水系的东部地区的整合发展。

第三，大运河是沟通黄河中下游经济区与长江中下游经济区的商贸干道，为中古时期南北经济交流提供了极大便利。大运河既是海上丝绸之路与北方国都间的连通渠道，也是陆地丝绸之路和海上丝绸之路在国内的主要连通渠道。既有利于 5 世纪前后北方先进经济文化南传，又有利于发挥 7 世纪以后江南经济文化的带动和辐射作用，有利于促进北方社会经济的恢复发展。伴随着漕运，还催生了以扬州、淮安、济宁、聊城、临清、天津等一批运河城镇经济带的繁荣[2]。明李东阳"官船贾舶纷纷过，击鼓鸣锣处处闻"（《过鳌头矶》）的诗句，闻名遐迩。这种运河城镇当是唐长安和宋汴梁之外的另一类漕运商业城镇。自唐后期刘晏等盐铁使兼转运使以盐利补贴漕运，又因江淮、山东、长芦等盐场等都在运河沿线，大运河往往和官府榷盐及盐商经营联系在一起，成为历代盐商行盐贩运的南北通道。元明"开中法"以盐引招商运粮北边及丝绸、瓷器、茶叶等官民采购贩运等也需要依赖大运河通道。

第四，大运河还对南方、北方东部的社会文化彼此交流及结构优化带来了深刻影响。盐商、徽商、晋商等商帮常年在大运河一带贩运行商，山陕、广东、全晋等会馆林立。还形成了盐帮、漕帮等帮会组织。运河沿岸城镇还是元明以来回回人荟萃聚居之处，临清清真寺、扬州回回堂、杭州凤凰寺等就是历史见证。隋唐行科举制和元汉军镇戍、明卫所屯戍、清八旗绿营屯戍等推行之后，南方人游宦驻戍北方和北方人游宦驻戍南方的情况，频繁而普遍。千余年间，大运河又曾经是官员士人兵将等南北往返的主要通道，无形中对南、北方社会文化彼此交流带来了良好的影响。

五 余论

东汉以后南北差异的整合发展与江南的角色功用，很大程度上是游牧文明和农耕文明两大板块及农耕文明内东部与西部，黄河中下游与长江中下游等板块分野在五千年发展演进的产物。由于我国疆域广袤和地理风俗多样，20 世纪初蒙文通先生就曾提出江汉（炎族）、河洛（黄族）、海岱（泰族）的古史三系之说[3]。就是说，东周时代，地处江汉、江淮的楚、吴、越等文明发展水平，已仅次于河洛、海岱等中原文明核心地带，在华夏诸地域子文明中位列第三。其水利、气候、植被、文明传统等方面的良好基础，再开发和后来居上的潜力，又是其他地区无法比拟的。又兼，前述东晋和南宋两次南渡，造成中原文明南下且与江汉等文明的交融汇合以及若干次江南开发的浪潮，最终使江南后来居上成为现实。

10 世纪前后的航海技术的长足发展、海上丝绸之路和海外贸易的繁荣，使地处东亚大陆相对独立地理单元的中国，获得了与域外其他主要文明交流沟通的新的航海通道，同时也给江南特别是东

---

① 司马迁：《史记·货殖列传》，北京：中华书局，1959 年，第 3261—3270 页。
② 傅崇兰：《中国运河城市发展史》，成都：四川人民出版社，1985 年。
③ 蒙文通：《古史甄微》，载《蒙文通文集》第 5 卷，成都：巴蜀书社，1999 年。

南沿海带来了巨大的域外刺激。这在客观上促进了秦汉"头枕三河（河内、河东、河南）、面向草原"到唐宋以降的"头枕东南、面向海洋"经济趋势的重大转折[①]。在此形势下，江南在全国南北差异整合中的角色功用显赫，就是顺理成章了。而大运河也生逢其时，沟通南北水系交通，适应政治上北支配南、经济上北依赖南的错位需要，充当了南方在经济文化上支撑、带动、辐射北方，推动全国整合发展的特有管道。

我们还可以从更长的时段和更广阔的视野来观察思考：由于长城南北农耕文明和游牧文明两大板块的长期并存、冲突和融汇，东汉以后的中国，先后发生"五胡乱华"和女真、蒙古等南下入主，黄河中下游的华夏先进经济和文化曾经被基本中断两三次。万幸的是，华夏经济和文化，藉东晋和南宋南渡在江南得以延续，随着千年来江南的开发而不断扩展和提升，进而在唐宋前后数次南北博弈整合中积极影响全国，推动华夏经济和文化在南北统一国度下继续繁荣，不断进步。这就最终避免了欧洲五世纪日耳曼蛮族南下中断或暂时毁灭希腊罗马文明而整体步入黑暗中世纪的悲剧性道路。在这个意义上，中华文明五千年延续至今，总体上未曾中断，在世界范围独一无二，江南的历史性作用，功不可没。

---

① 葛金芳教授认为，秦汉和隋唐帝国以黄河中下游为政治经济文化中心，以自给自足农业经济为基础，特别是为防御匈奴、突厥等，故而主要是向西北开拓延伸其势力范围。此时期的基本格局可称为"头枕三河（河内、河东、河南），面向草原"。而中唐以后传统社会的经济重心已由黄河中下游转移到长江中下游。特别是长江三角洲为主体的东南沿海地区，以发达农业、手工业和商品经济为后盾，开始表现出向海洋发展的强烈倾向。此时期的基本格局又可称为"头枕东南，面向海洋"。（《头枕东南，面向海洋——南宋立国态势及经济格局论析》，《邓广铭教授百年诞辰纪念文集》，北京：中华书局，2006年，第219—220页）。就经济发展趋势而言，笔者基本同意葛教授的观点。

古埃及帝国时期王室女性"三位一体"现象研究[*]

王海利　北京师范大学

摘要：母后、王后、公主这三个王室女性群体在古埃及帝国时期（新王国时期）形成了牢不可破的"三位一体"现象，其中王后处于核心地位，发挥着承上启下的作用，该现象导致该时期成为一个王后权空前加强、王室女性地位空前提升的历史时期。作者认为，古埃及帝国时期王后权提升的背后其实正是王权得到加强的反映，或王权加强而产生的"副产品"而已。因为古埃及王权的观念源自神权，尤其与哈托尔女神密切相关，王后权与王权二者结合形成了一种牢不可破的伙伴关系。古埃及国王为了提升王权，则需要提升王后权。对古埃及帝国时期王室女性"三位一体"现象的研究，有助于我们更清楚地认识古埃及帝国时期王权的本质，同时也为我们深刻认识该时期的政治与社会提供了新的视角。

关键词：古埃及；王室女性；三位一体；王权；王后权

Abstract：This article makes a detailed survey on Egyptian royal women in the New Kingdom, and examines what kinds of roles that they actually played. Through the examination the author finds that the three groups formed a special triad of mother, consort and daughter. The queen lies, of course, at the central position in this triad. The queen-ship during the New Kingdom was highly promoted. The New Kingdom is a transitional period in the history of ancient Egypt, and the Egyptian empire eventually came into being. In order to strengthen the kingship, the king had to retrieve the mythology in which the kingship had a close connection with the goddesses, especially the goddess Hathor, who has multi-functional role as mother, wife and daughter. This study helps to shed some new light on the further understanding of the Egyptian kingship during the New Kingdom.

Keywords：ancient Egypt, royal women, trinity, kingship, queen-ship

　　学界对妇女史的研究是伴随着 20 世纪 60、70 年代西方妇女运动的兴起而出现的，至今仍方兴未艾。古代埃及是世界上最早进入文明的国家，对古代埃及妇女相关问题的研究自然吸引了国内外

---

[*] 本研究得到 2007～2008 年度，中国国家留学基金管理委员会、瑞士联邦政府基金会资助。（This study was financed by China Scholarship Council and Federal Commission for Scholarships for Foreign Students during 2007~2008 at the University of Basel, Switzerland. The author gratefully acknowledges the support of CSC and FCS.）

众多学者的兴趣，大量的研究成果陆续问世。①这些成果大大丰富了古埃及历史学研究的内容，也为古埃及史的研究提供了新的视角。尤其是近年来西方学界对古埃及帝国时期（即新王国时期，包括第18、19、20王朝，约1550—1069 BC）历史上比较著名的王室女性，例如泰伊②、奈弗尔提提③、奈弗尔塔丽④、哈特舍普苏特⑤等人物的个案研究，为我们全面审视新王国时期古埃及王室女性在当时社会所发挥的作用提供了可能。

本文拟结合近年来西方学者对新王国时期产生广泛影响的相关古埃及王室女性的个案研究成果，以新王国时期的整个历史和社会为背景，全面考察该时期母后、王后、公主三个王室女性群体在历史上所发挥的作用，分析这种现象背后的理论基础，阐释这种现象对新王国时期的古埃及王权产生的影响，揭示这种现象的本质。希望本文能为我们深刻认识古埃及帝国时期的政治与社会提供新的视角。

一 对母后、王后、公主群体的考察

首先，我们考察母后这个群体。在古埃及语中，"母后"是一个合成词 mwt nsw，直译为"国王的母亲"。根据德国埃及学者罗斯的考证，该头衔早在第1王朝时期就开始出现了。⑥历史地看，在古埃及社会中，母后是王室中一个重要的群体，她们经常对国王产生重要的影响，自然也格外受到国王的尊敬。阿赫霍特普是我们所知道的古埃及帝国时期第一位比较有影响力的母后，她是第18王朝国王阿赫摩斯的母亲。阿赫摩斯曾在卡尔纳克神庙里立下纪念碑专门纪念他的母亲，并写有祭文曰："她照顾埃及，她照看她的军队，她亲自领导，她带回俘虏，她安抚了上埃及，她平息了叛乱。"⑦阿赫霍特普死后被她的儿子阿赫摩斯国王进行了厚葬。19世纪中叶，埃及考古学家们发掘出了阿赫霍特普的坟墓，里面出土了大量的珍贵文物和阿赫霍特普的木乃伊，现被收藏于开罗埃及国家博物馆。另外，学者们甚至还认为，阿赫霍特普很可能曾经与她的儿子阿赫摩斯联合执政过几年的时间，直到阿赫摩斯长大成人。因为位于努比亚要塞上的一些铭文，常常同时刻有阿赫摩斯和阿赫霍特普

① 相关论著参见 S. Wenig, *Die Frau im alten Ägypten*, Leipzeig, 1967; S. Morenz, *Die Stellung der Frau im alten Ägypten*, Leipzig, 1982; B. Schmitz, *Nofret, die Schöne: die Frau im alten Ägypten: Wahrheit und Wirklichkeit*, Mainz, 1985; B.S. Lesko, *The Remarkable Women of Ancient Egypt*, Providence, 1987; Desroches-Noblecourt, *La femme au temps des pharons*, Paris, 1986; B. Watterson, *Women in Ancient Egypt*, New York, 1991; J. Tyldesley, *Daughters of Isis: Women of Ancient Egypt*, London, 1994; G. Robins, *Women in Ancient Egypt*, London, 1993; A.K. Capel *et al.*, *Mistress of the House, Mistress of Heaven : Women in Ancient Egypt*, New York, 1996。国内学界对古埃及妇女的相关研究，参见王海利著：《尼罗河畔的古埃及妇女》，北京：中国青年出版社，2007年。

② D. Arnold, *The Royal Women of Amarna: Images of Beauty from Ancient Egypt*, New York, 1996; J. Tyldesley, *Chronicles of the Queens of Egypt*, London, 2006, pp. 115–123.

③ C. Aldred, *Akhenaten and Nefertiti*, New York, 1973; J. Samson, *Nefertiti and Cleopatra: Queen-monarchs of Ancient Egypt*, London, 1985; J. Tyldesley, *Nerfertiti: Egypt's Sun Queen*, London, 1998. C. Aldred, *Akhenaten and Nefertiti*, New York, 1973; J. Samson, *Nefertiti and Cleopatra: Queen-monarchs of Ancient Egypt*, London, 1985; J. Tyldesley, *Nerfertiti: Egypt's Sun Queen*, London, 1998.

④ C. Leblanc, *Nefertari: Ausgrabungen im Tal der Königinnen*, Bechtermünz, 1998; H.C. Schmidt und J. Willeitner, *Nefertari: Gemahlin Ramses II*, Mainz, 1994.

⑤ P. H. Schulze, *Herrin beider Länder Hatschepsut: Frau, Gott und Pharao*, Lübbe, 1976; S. Ratié, *La Reine Hatchepsout*, Lugdunum Batavorum, 1979; J. Tyldesley, *Hatshepsut: the Female Pharaoh*, London, 1996; C. Desroches-Noblecourt, *La reine mystérieuse Hatshepsout*, Paris, 2002; C.H. Roehrig (ed.), *Hatshepsut: from Queen to Pharaoh*, New York, 2005.

⑥ S. Roth, *Königsmutter des alten Ägypten von der Frühzeit bis zum Ende der 12. Dynastie*, Wiesbaden, 2001, S.12.

⑦ T. G. H. James, "Egypt: from the Expulsion of the Hyksos to Amenophis I", in E. S. Edwards *et al.* (eds.), *Cambridge Ancient History*, 2 part 1, 3rd edition, Cambridge, 1973, p. 306; C. Vandersleyen, *Les guerres d'Amosis*, *Brussels*, 1971, pp. 129–196; Gay Robins, *Women in Ancient Egypt*, pp. 42–43.

母子两人的名字。①

古埃及帝国时期还出现了其他几位比较著名的母后，如阿赫摩斯—奈弗尔塔丽、泰伊等。她们的身份往往是双重的，如阿赫摩斯—奈弗尔塔丽既是国王阿赫摩斯的妻子，又是国王阿蒙霍特普一世的母亲；泰伊既是国王阿蒙霍特普三世的妻子，又是国王阿蒙霍特普四世（后来改名为埃赫那吞）的母亲。既然古埃及王位是父子继承的，那么，我们不难理解古埃及一些王室女性往往扮演着双重的角色，即她们往往既是王后，又是母后。

其次，我们考察王后这个群体。在古埃及语中，"王后"也是一个合成词，写为 emt nsw wrt，直译为"国王的主要妻子"，即我们中文语境中通常意义上的"王后"。显然古埃及文中并没有一个对应的专门的词汇，即没有类似英文中的 queen，德文中的 Königin，法文中的 reine。需要指出的是，古埃及国王不只有一个妻子，也就是说 emt nsw 可以有多个。但是，国王通常只有一个主妻，即王后。根据罗斯的考察，emt nsw 头衔最早从第4王朝开始出现②，emt nsw wrt 头衔则最早出现于第13王朝。③

王后在古埃及社会中发挥的作用就更为强大了，她们经常辅佐丈夫管理国家，处理国政。这样的例子很多，如哈舍普苏特就是一个典型的例子。哈舍普苏特是图特摩斯二世的王后（也是图特摩斯二世的同父异母姐妹），她常常辅佐丈夫处理政事。图特摩斯二世死后，哈特舍普苏特做了埃及国王，成为古埃及历史上著名的女王，统治国家长达20年之久。④古埃及帝国时期著名的王后还有第18王朝国王阿赫摩斯的王后阿赫摩斯—奈弗尔塔丽、第18王朝国王埃赫那吞的王后奈弗尔提提、第19王朝国王拉美西斯二世的王后奈弗尔塔丽等。阿赫摩斯—奈弗尔塔丽最早开始享有"两土地的女主人"（nbt tawy）这一头衔。⑤与该头衔相类似的另一头衔"两土地的女主人"（enwt tawy），最早出现于中王国第12王朝，最早由希索斯特里斯二世的王后奈弗尔特二世拥有。⑥学界对这两个头衔的具体区别不是很清楚。不过，我们确信 nbt tawy 这个头衔最早是从新王国时期开始出现并广为使用的。除了 nbt tawy 头衔外，另有一个头衔"所有土地的女主人"（enwt taw nbw)⑦，在第18王朝开始出现并陆续被广泛使用，泰伊是第一个拥有该头衔的王后。

"神之妻"（emt ntr）这个头衔最早也是从新王国时期开始使用的。⑧在新王国时期"阿蒙神之妻"是一个非常有权势的职位，它可以拥有大量的地产和财富，充任这一头衔的一般是国王的妻子或母亲，并且这一头衔世袭拥有。阿赫摩斯国王授予了他的王后阿赫摩斯—奈弗尔塔丽"阿蒙神之妻"这一头衔，即阿赫摩斯—奈弗尔塔丽是第一位拥有"阿蒙神之妻"头衔的女性，她对古埃及的政治产生过重大影响。在位于卡尔纳克的阿蒙神庙中，阿赫摩斯—奈弗尔塔丽被授予"第二代言人"的称号。⑨阿赫摩斯—奈弗尔塔丽将"阿蒙神之妻"头衔传给了她的女儿麦瑞特阿蒙。麦瑞特阿蒙，即法老阿蒙霍特普一世的王后（兼姐妹），把该头衔又传给了哈特舍普苏特。当哈特舍普苏特与阿蒙

① Shaw and Nicholson, *British Museum Dictionary of Ancient Egypt*, p. 18.
② Roth, *Königsmutter des alten Ägypten von der Frühzeit bis zum Ende der 12. Dynastie*, S. 38.
③ Roth, *Königsmutter des alten Ägypten von der Frühzeit bis zum Ende der 12. Dynastie*, S. 247.
④ 关于哈舍普苏特统治的确切时间学界有争议：1473–1458 BC, Ian Shaw, *The Oxford History of Ancient Egypt*, p. 223; 1472–1457 BC, A. Dodson, *Ancient Egypt*, London, 2006, p. 260; 1498–1483 BC, P. Clayton, *Chronicle of the Pharaohs*, London, 1994, p. 104; 1478–1458 BC, N. Grimal, *Histoire de l'Egypte ancienne*, Paris, 1992, p. 251; 1479–1457 BC, H. A. Schlögl, *Das alte Ägypten*, München, 2006, S. 199.
⑤ L. Troy, *Patterns of Queenship: in Ancient Egyptian Myth and History*, Uppsala, 1986, p. 134.
⑥ Troy, *Patterns of Queenship: in Ancient Egyptian Myth and History*, p. 134.
⑦ S. Roth, *Gebieterin aller Länder: die Rolle der königlichen Frauen in der fiktiven und realen Aussenpolitik des ägyptischen Neuen Reiches*, Fribourg und Göttingen, 2002, S. 14.
⑧ 参见 E. Graefe, *Untersuchungen zur Verwaltung und Geschichte der Institution der Gottesgemahlin des Amun vom Beginn des neuen Reiches bis zur Spätzeit*, Band II, Wiesbaden, 1981, S.101–112.
⑨ Robins, *Women in Ancient Egypt*, pp. 149–152.

霍特普三世联合执政时，她仍旧喜欢拥有"阿蒙神之妻"这个头衔。后来当她亲自当上埃及国王以后，便放弃了"阿蒙神之妻"头衔，并把它授予了她的女儿奈弗鲁拉。当图特摩斯三世独自控制国家大权成为上、下埃及的国王以后，便剥夺了"阿蒙神之妻"这一职位。到了阿蒙霍特普二世统治时期，这一头衔又被授予给了他的母亲麦瑞特拉。图特摩斯四世统治时期，该头衔又被授予给了他的母亲娣阿。从此以后，在第18王朝的历史中几乎再也看不到"阿蒙神之妻"这个头衔的踪影。到了第19、20王朝时期，"阿蒙神之妻"头衔再次出现。拉美西斯六世统治时期，他的女儿阿塞特被授予"阿蒙神之妻"头衔。在保存下来的墓碑上，阿塞特常被称为"国王的女儿、神圣的崇拜者、神之妻"。[1]

除了上面所述的这几个头衔外，古埃及帝国时期的王后还常常佩戴不同的饰冠出现在一些宗教场合。最早的例证是从阿蒙霍特普三世的王后泰伊开始，王后佩戴一种特殊的饰冠，即由一对牛角、两支羽毛，以及太阳圆盘组成的冠。因为牛角是哈托尔女神的象征，故我们不妨将这种冠称为"哈托尔冠"。[2]古埃及王后为什么要戴"哈托尔冠"呢？简言之，其目的显然是想将自己与女神哈托尔联系起来。其实，古埃及王后与神的联系已经不是什么新鲜事了。早在古王国时期（约 2686 — 2125BC）的一些壁画中，就有一些古埃及国王和王后手中常常握着一个象征"生命"的符号 2。如果王后手中握着象征"生命"的符号，旁边的铭文中一般都把她当作女神。[3]

在新王国时期，古埃及王后还常常伴随国王出现于各种仪式场合。王后泰伊是该时期第一位频繁伴随国王出席各种仪式的王后。[4]当然，并不是说新王国时期以前的古埃及王后就从来不伴随国王出席相关仪式，只不过从新王国时期开始，王后陪伴国王出席各种相关仪式似乎形成了一种约定俗成的惯例。[5]

王后泰伊有时还以斯芬克斯雕像的形式出现。女性斯芬克斯雕像最早开始出现于中王国时期（约 2055 — 1650BC），但是泰伊以王后的身份，作为践踏敌人的斯芬克斯形象出现在古埃及历史上还是第一次。她的脚下踩着两个女性敌人，一个是努比亚人，另一个是亚洲人。[6]德国埃及学者罗斯指出，从图特摩斯四世统治时期开始，直到拉美西斯二世统治时期止，古埃及王后常常作为国王的"痛击敌人者"的形象出现。[7]在来自叙利亚、巴勒斯坦地区的一个泥板上，出现了王后泰伊作为"痛击敌人者"的形象。[8]另外，在位于努比亚的斯坦恩格神庙上，泰伊被赋予"令人恐惧的伟大者"(oat nrwt)[9]这样一个头衔。

王后奈弗尔提提还作为外国贡品的接收者的形象而出现。在法老埃赫那吞的宫廷总管胡亚的坟墓的壁画上，奈弗尔提提作为国外贡品的接收者出现了。旁边的铭文这样记载说：

> 国王统治的第12年，第二个季节，第8天，……上埃及、下埃及的国王［埃赫那吞］，
> 愿他健康！长寿！富有！以及王后奈弗尔提提，愿她健康、长寿！他们出现在一个金轿上，
> 目的是接收来自卡鲁和库什地区的贡品。……他们向国王［埃赫那吞］王位呈献外国每个

① Robins, *Women in Ancient Egypt*, p. 153.

② Robins, *Women in Ancient Egypt*, p. 24.

③ Robins, *Women in Ancient Egypt*, p. 24.

④ Tyldesley, *Daughters of Isis*, p. 192.

⑤ R. Morkot, "Violent Images of Queenship and the Royal Cult", *Wepwawet: Research Papers in Egyptology*, vol. 2 (1986), p. 1.

⑥ Morkot, "Violent Images of Queenship and the Royal Cult", *Wepwawet* 2 (1986), p. 1.

⑦ Roth, *Gebieterin aller Länder*, S. 23.

⑧ Roth, *Gebieterin aller Länder*, S. 30, 31.

⑨ Roth, *Gebieterin aller Länder*, S. 19.

地区的贡品，伟大的国王赐予他们以生命！ ①

王后奈弗尔提提不仅拥有斯芬克斯雕像，而且还有作为"痛击敌人者"的画面。她手中握着一个半月形的镰刀正在挥向敌人。②值得指出的是，泰伊和奈弗尔提提是古埃及王室女性中拥有践踏敌人的斯芬克斯雕像的仅有的两位王后，新王国时期的其他王后都不具有这种雕像。③

拉美西斯二世的王后奈弗尔塔丽也拥有一系列的头衔和形象。阿布·辛拜勒神庙上的铭文中，奈弗尔塔丽被赋予了头衔"君主联合者"（enwt iti），伴随丈夫拉美西斯二世正在痛击敌人。④

考察新王国时期的古埃及王后的一系列头衔和形象，留给我们一个非常强烈的感觉是王后的重要性在古埃及帝国时期得到了很大程度的提升。同时我们发现，在新王国时期有不少的国王娶了自己的姐妹作为王后，例如，阿赫摩斯、阿蒙霍特普一世、图特摩斯二世等，以至于在埃及学界曾产生过"女继承人理论"说。该理论在20世纪60、70年代广为流行，这可以从当时出版的大量的相关论著中体现出来。⑤所谓"女继承人理论"，即认为在古埃及王权是通过女性来传承的，王后虽然不能直接行使对国家的统治权，但是统治权只有通过王后获得。也就是说，国王必须娶自己的姐妹为妻，尤其是对不具有王室血统的男性来说，若想继任王位则必须娶前任国王的公主为妻，这样他的登基才具有合法意义。⑥

事实上这种理论是错误的。因为按照这种理论，那么，古埃及的每位国王都必须娶自己的姐妹为妻，但是，只要我们仔细观察一下古埃及新王国时期的历史，就会发现事实上并不是每位国王都娶了自己的姐妹为妻。例如，阿蒙霍特普三世娶了平民出身的泰伊作为王后；埃赫那吞娶了非王室出身的奈弗尔提提为王后。另外，图特摩斯一世、图特摩斯二世、图特摩斯三世的母亲似乎都不具有王室血统。因此，"女继承人理论"是经不起推敲的。正如英国埃及学者罗宾斯指出的那样："女继承人理论"只不过是为了解释新王国时期古埃及王室中所发生的兄妹婚这一现象而提出的，而事实上古埃及文本中"女继承人理论"根本就不存在。⑦

尽管如此，我们也不能否认，在新王国时期的确有一定数量的古埃及国王娶了自己的姐妹为妻，这种现象在第18王朝尤其盛行。那么，古埃及国王为什么要娶自己的姐妹为妻呢？我们知道，科学证明近亲结婚会对后代产生不良影响。难道是古埃及人没有意识到这种不良影响？埃及学者们普遍认为，古代埃及王室之所以实行内婚制，其目的很可能是为了保持王室血统的纯洁性。不过，如果我们留意一下古埃及神话，内婚制倒是可以在古埃及神话中找到原型。在古埃及神话中，天神努特与地神盖驳结合，生下奥西里斯、爱茜丝、塞特和奈弗提斯四神。其中奥西里斯与爱茜丝结为夫妻，

---

① Roth, *Gebieterin aller Länder*, S.41–42; W.J. Murnane, *Texts from the Amarna Period in Egypt*, Atlanta, 1995, pp.134–135.

② Morkot, "Violent Images of Queenship and the Royal Cult", *Wepwawet* 2 (1986), p. 2.

③ Morkot, "Violent Images of Queenship and the Royal Cult", *Wepwawet* 2 (1986), p. 5.

④ Morkot, "Violent Images of Queenship and the Royal Cult", *Wepwawet* 2 (1986), 2; Roth, *Gebieterin aller Länder*, S. 24.

⑤ 参见 D. B. Redford, *History and Chronology*, Toronto, 1967, pp. 30–31, 71–74; S. Wenig, *The Woman in Egyptian Art*, New York, 1969, pp. 30–31; W. C. Hayes, in *The Cambridge Ancient History*, 3rd edition, 2 part 1, Cambridge, 1973, pp.315–317; E. Driton et J. Vandier, *L' Egypte*, Paris, 1975, pp. 336–338; M. Gitton, *L' epouse du dieu Ahmes Nefertary*, Paris, 1975, p. 15; B. Schmitz, *Untersuchungen zum Titel S3-NJSWT* "*Königssohn*", Bonn, 1976, S. 306–312; F. J. Schmitz, *Amenophis I*, Hildesheim,1978, S. 41–43, 66; S. Ratie, *La reine Hatchepsout: sources et problems*, Leiden, 1979, pp. 16, 23–31.

⑥ Robins, *Women in Ancient Egypt*, pp. 26–27; Tyldesley, *Daughters of Isis*, p. 197.

⑦ 参见 G. Robins, A Critical Examination of the Theory that the Right to the Throne of Ancient Egypt Passed through the Female Line in the 18th Dynasty, *Göttinger Miszellen: Beiträge zur ägyptologischen Diskussion* 62 (1983), p. 71; Robins, *Women in Ancient Egypt*, pp. 26–27.

塞特与奈弗提斯结为夫妻。①我们知道，在古埃及人看来，国王即神在人间统治的代理者，古埃及的每一位国王都被视为神灵受到崇拜，那么，我们则不难理解古埃及国王娶自己的姐妹为妻了。

再次，我们考察公主这个群体。在古埃及语中，"公主"也是一个合成词 sat nsw，即"国王的女儿"。这个名称本身也作为一个重要的头衔使用，一些王室女性常常拥有该头衔。在新王国时期，有一些公主经常伴随国王和王后共同出席一些仪式场合。例如，国王阿蒙霍特普三世和王后泰伊的四个女儿，莎塔蒙、赫努塔讷博、爱希斯、奈博塔赫的形象经常与她们的父母一起出现。②

在新王国时期，有的埃及国王甚至还娶了自己的女儿为妻，如第 18 王朝国王阿蒙霍特普三世娶了他的女儿莎塔蒙作为妻子。保存下来的一些雕刻和壁画上，莎塔蒙作为国王的妻子（emt nsw）伴随阿蒙霍特普三世频频出现，后来莎塔蒙还拥有了王后（emt nsw wrt）头衔。③阿蒙霍特普三世的王位继承者阿蒙霍特普四世（即埃赫那吞）也娶过自己的女儿为妻，甚至不仅一个女儿。埃赫那吞与王后奈弗提提生有六个女儿，虽然学界对埃赫那吞究竟娶过自己的几个女儿存在争议，但是，有充足的证据显示埃赫那吞曾娶了他的第三个女儿梅丽塔吞为妻。因为在埃赫那吞统治的后期，公主梅丽塔吞竟然取代了奈弗尔提提，成为了埃赫那吞的王后（emt nsw wrt）。④在接下来的第 19 王朝中，国王拉美西斯二世也曾娶过自己的女儿为妻。在拉美西斯二世的王后奈弗尔塔丽死后不久，拉美西斯二世娶了自己的女儿为王后。根据学者们的相关考证，拉美西斯二世的三个女儿宾特阿那赫、梅丽塔蒙、奈拜塔玮都曾拥有王后（emt nsw wrt）头衔。⑤其中，宾特阿那赫还为拉美西斯二世生下了至少一个孩子，这在她的坟墓里的有关铭文中体现得很清楚。⑥

二　母后、王后、公主结成"三位一体"

通过上面对古埃及帝国时期王室女性中母后、王后、公主三个群体的考察，我们发现在该时期，母后、王后、公主形成了"三位一体"的关系。这种关系很像一个链环锁，环环相扣，紧密相连。公主的身份是可以不断变化的，她年幼时作为公主，成年后（可能）成为国王的妻子——王后，年老后又（有可能）成为下一任国王的母亲——母后。在这个"三位一体"现象中，王后可以说处于中心地位，发挥着承上启下的作用。

在古埃及神话中也存在这样一个类似的"三位一体"，这个"三位一体"由太阳神拉、女神哈托尔、国王荷鲁斯三者构成。⑦哈托尔女神的名字在古埃及语中为 Ewt-Er，其字面意思是"荷鲁斯的房子"⑧。由于 Ewt（"房子"）一词有时也可以表示女性的子宫，因此，在古埃及神话中哈托尔常常被视为荷鲁斯的母亲。⑨在古埃及神话中，荷鲁斯是作为在凡世进行统治埃及的第一位国王，故古埃及国

① 参见王海利编著：《古埃及神话故事》，长春：吉林人民出版社，2001 年，第 82–98 页。
② Tyldesley, *Daughters of Isis*, p. 201.
③ Robins, *Women in Ancient Egypt*, p. 29.
④ Robins, *Women in Ancient Egypt*, p. 29.
⑤ K. A. Kitchen, *Pharaoh Trimphant: the Life and Times of Ramesses II*, Warminster 1982, pp. 100, 110–111; Robins, *Women in Ancient Egypt*, p. 29.
⑥ J. Tyldesley, *Ramesses: Egypt's Greatest Pharaoh*, London, 2000, pp. 133–134.
⑦ 参见 G. Pinch, *Ancient Egyptian Mythology*, Oxford, 2002, pp.137–139; P. Derchain, *Hathor quadrifrons: recherches sur la syntaxe d'un mythe égyptien*, Istanbul, 1972; G. Pinch, *Votive Offerings to Hathor*, Oxford, 1993; A. Roberts, *Hathor Rising: the Serpent Power of Ancient Egypt*, Devon, 1995.
⑧ Donald Redford, *The Oxford Encyclopedia of Ancient Egypt*, vol. 2, Oxford, 2001, p.82.
⑨ K. Sethe, *Urgeschichte und älteste Religion der Ägypter, Abhandlung für die Kunde des Morgenlandes*, Hrsg. von der Deutschen Morgenländischen Gesellschaft Band XVIII Nr. 4, Leipzig, 1930, S.67; C.J. Bleeker, "Hathor and Thoth", *Studies in the History of Religions*, vol. 26 (1973), p. 25.

王登基后常常自称"荷鲁斯的继承者",以此来加强自己王位的合法性。在古埃及国王常常具有的五个名字中,"荷鲁斯名"是古埃及国王名字中最为古老的一个。①由此看来,哈托尔女神与王权的联系便显而易见了。

德国埃及学者魏斯坦道夫指出,哈托尔女神位于古埃及王权观念的核心,她比任何其他女神更能表现王权的观念。②早在第1王朝古埃及国家建立之初,哈托尔便开始与王权联系起来了。在反映上、下埃及第一次完成统一,古埃及国家正式形成的考古发掘文物"那尔迈调色板"的正反两面上,都出现了女神哈托尔的形象。她呈一对牛角形象,将国王那尔迈的名字包围起来,即表示保护国王之意。我们知道,古埃及人常常把哈托尔描绘为长有一对奶牛耳朵的女神形象,有时也可以直接用一对牛角来代表。哈托尔女神在古埃及历史上对埃及王权观念的影响可谓源远流长,"从第1王朝开始,直到希腊—罗马统治时期,哈托尔女神都与古埃及的王权紧密相连。"③

古埃及是一个宗教色彩极为浓厚的国家,统治者往往从宗教和神话中寻找统治的依据来加强统治。西方埃及学者德奥伊指出,拉、哈托尔、荷鲁斯这个"三位一体",早在古王国时期的第5王朝就被确立了。④哈托尔女神具有多重功能,在古埃及神话中,她充当着创世神太阳神的母亲、妻子、女儿多重角色。⑤正是这种貌似混乱的多重角色影响了古埃及社会中王室女性的神性地位。由此我们则更容易理解为什么新王国时期的几位古埃及国王竟娶自己的女儿为妻。

哈托尔女神与王后权的关系可以通过几种方式体现,即"她既是国王的妻子,又是国王的母亲。她充当着中介的作用。"⑥既然哈托尔充当着如此重要而丰富的角色,那么,我们不难理解为什么新王国时期的王后们竭力将自己与哈托尔女神联系起来,从第18王朝国王阿蒙霍特普三世的王后泰伊开始,埃及王后们经常佩戴的"哈托尔冠"即是最典型的证明。显然,王后是想通过这种方式体现她们在王权中的重要性。新王国时期埃及王后拥有的一系列头衔,如"两土地的女主人"(nbt tawy, enwt tawy)、"所有土地的女主人"(enwt taw nbw)、"神之妻"(emt ntr)、"令人恐惧的伟大者"(oat nrwt)、"君主联合者"(enwt iti)等,以及埃及王后拥有的"痛击敌人者"的斯芬克斯雕像,都在说明一个问题——王后不仅是国王的保护者,而且还是国王的合作者,她们是古埃及王权不可或缺的一个方面。因此,正如西方学者所指出的那样:古埃及的"王后不一定是国王理想化的妻子,但她却是国王的匹配者和仲裁者。"⑦

从历史上看,在古代埃及社会中,王权是一个不面向女性开放的领地,而是男性的专属领地。那么,新王国时期王后权被大大提升的原因是什么?王后权被大大提升究竟又意味着什么?结合上文分析,我们认为,古埃及帝国时期王后权的提升,其实正是王权得以加强的表现,即王后权的加强是王权加强的"隐性反映"。换言之,古埃及帝国时期王后权的加强和提升只不过是埃及王权加强的"副产品"而已。

---

① 参见 James Allan, *Middle Egyptian: an Introduction to the Language and Culture of Hieroglyphs*, Cambridge University Press, 2010, pp.66–68.

② W. Westendorf, "Zweiheit, Dreiheit und Einheit in der altägyptischen Theologie", *Zeitschrift für ägyptische Sprache und Altertumskunde* 100 (1973), S. 138.

③ Troy, *Patterns of Queenship*, p. 54.

④ Troy, *Patterns of Queenship*, p. 55.

⑤ Pinch, *Ancient Egyptian Mythology*, p. 137.

⑥ Troy, *Patterns of Queenship*, pp. 54, 56.

⑦ Morkot, "Violent Images of Queenship and the Royal Cult", *Wepwawet* 2 (1986), p. 5.

三　结　语

新王国时期是古埃及历史上的鼎盛时期，同时也是一个巨大的转折时期。新王国初期历任法老的南征北战与开疆拓土，导致埃及版图空前（也是绝后的）扩大，横跨亚非两大洲的古埃及帝国逐步确立起来。为了应对一个如此庞大的世界帝国，古埃及国王必须加强王权，捍卫自己作为国家，甚至世界之主宰的地位。

在古代埃及，王权的观念源自神权，国王即神在人间的代理和媒介。同时，古埃及王权的观念是与女神，尤其与哈托尔女神密切相连。新王国时期的国王为了提升王权，显然必须提升王后权，因为王后不仅是国王的保护者，而且是国王的合作者，正如英国埃及学者提奥德斯莉所指出的那样，"王后权与王权的结合形成了一个完美的、牢不可破的伙伴关系，这种伙伴关系使得他们可以更好的服务神灵、统治国家，同时可以挫败混乱和无序。"[①]

古埃及帝国时期正是一个王后权空前加强的历史时期，从而导致王室女性地位的空前提高。由于当时内婚制的盛行，古埃及公主、王后、母后这三者间的身份的发展与变化则非常微妙。在当时情况下，古埃及公主长大成年后婚嫁对象有三种可能性。一、嫁给公主的（继任王位的）兄弟，成为王后，若婚后生下男性子嗣，那么她将来有望成为母后。二、嫁给自己的（已任国王的）父亲，身份由公主变为王后，若将来生下男性子嗣，她则有望成为母后。三、嫁给已经登上王位的非王室血统出身的篡权者（严格意义上说应该是篡权者主动迎娶前任埃及国王的公主为妻，因为这是促使其王位合法化的重要措施），成为王后，若将来生下男性子嗣，她则有望成为母后。因此，在古埃及帝国时期，公主既是潜在的王后，又是潜在的母后，公主、王后、母后三者环环相扣、紧密相连，共同构成特有的三位一体现象。

综上所述，本文通过对新王国时期王室女性"三位一体"现象的考察和探析，可以帮助我们更清楚地认识该时期古埃及王权的本质；认识为什么新王国时期是一个"女权高涨"、"群芳荟萃"的历史时期，同时也有助于我们理解新王国时期埃及公主不外嫁这一特有的历史现象。[②]总之，它为我们深刻认识古埃及帝国时期的政治与社会提供了新的视角。

---

① 　J. Tyldesley, *Chronicle of the Queens of Egypt*, London, 2006, p.22.
② 　关于新王国时期古埃及公主不外嫁这一历史现象及其原因的探讨，参见王海利：《古埃及"只娶不嫁"的外交婚姻》，《历史研究》，2002 年第 6 期；王海利：《论古埃及公主不外嫁》，《东方研究》（古代东方文明专辑），2007 年，第 295—306 页。

The Akkadian Armies in the Northeast Frontier of Ur III Dynasty at the Dawn of the Simurum Campaign of Ibbi-Sin *

吴宇虹　东北师范大学

摘要：通过研究乌尔帝国贡牲中心出土的苏美尔语楔形文字行政管理档案中各地将军和军队的名字和进贡牛羊的数量，识别出东北边疆各地（伊朗和土耳其邻接区）驻军的前后任将军和校尉的名字，并分析出各支军队的大致数量（总数约13万人）。根据贡牲中心在2年末3年初关闭的现象和3年的年名"席穆润国被打败"，得出帝国的这些军队在2年秋所进行的征服东北边疆强大的席穆润国的战役遭遇了失败，各边疆藩属纷纷重新独立，使乌尔第三王朝从一个西亚最强大的帝国下降到两河流域的中弱国家并在23年后被伊朗地区的埃兰人入侵所灭亡。

关键词：乌尔第三王朝；伊比辛；苏美尔语贡牲档案；阿卡德东北边疆各地驻军

Abstract：After the tributes were collected from 12 military towns in his 2nd year, King Ibbi-Sin launched his first campaign against the land of Simurum, the land destroyed by Šulgi for the ninth time at Šulgi 43rd year and the famous Ṣiluš-Dagan was installed by Šulgi as the governor there. In our list, this famous general now became the general of Išim-Šulgi, which implies that he had lost the control to Simurum. The 3rd year name of Ibbi-Sin proves that the campaign was launched in his 2nd year. The campaign must have not won a victory at all since the royal distributing center of animal tributes, Puzriš-Dagan, where all our texts came from, was closed in the end of Ibbi-Sin 2, with the last day of xii/23

Keywords: Ur III dynasty, Ibbi-Sin Animal Tribute Center, Akkadian Armies in Northeast

A tribute list as the income part of a ki-bi gi$_4$-a account balance tablet from Puzriš-Dagan, the animal

---

*　All the Ur III cuneiform texts over the world, copied or transliterated by various authors, in this paper are available to the present writer by using the search functions and photos, copies and transliterations computerized in CDLI http://cdli.ucla.edu/ mastered by B. Englund, and in BDTNS http://bdts.filol.csic.es/ by M. Molina; many thanks to the two great research databases and tools, but any mistakes here is own by the writer as of himself.

distributing center of Ur III dynasty (CT 32 19 BM 103398[1]), presents us the names and tributes of the 7 generals (ugula), as well as the captains (nu-bandà) and soldiers (érin) under them at the Northeast frontier cities of the empire during the first and second year of Ibbi-Sin (2026-2003 B.C.), the last king of the dynasty, who was captured by the Elam invaders in his 24th reign year. According to his third year name, Year of the Divine Ibbi-Sin, King of Ur, Destroyed Simurum, in his second year, he launched his northeast campaign against Simurum, a state in the area of Tigris, the Diyala and the two Zabs. The officers and troops in our list, dated by the last day, 29th, of the iv (4th Month) of the Ibbi-Sin 2, would soon depart against the rebel Simurrrum, a land on the Northeast Frontier, which had been conquered for 9 times by Šulgi, the most powerful king of Ur III dynasty and father of the two later kings, but rebelled again when the new king Ibbi-Sin came to the throne. The armies at the Northeast Frontier in our text must have been the main force in the campaign against the treacherous lands, launched by Ibbi-Sin in his second year to punish this stubborn country for the tenth time. The some Amorites, called Mar-tu by Sumerians, in the west frontiers of the Ur kingdom, came peacefully into the old cities of Sumerians and subjected to the Ur III dynasty as Naplanum, so that the main danger for the dynasty was the rebels and invasion of the other foreign people in the Northeast Frontier, which was located in the upper streams of the Diyala and the two Zabs Rivers, and the neighboring areas of modern Iran.

1. The Seven Northeast Military Zones and their Generals and Captains with the Akkadian Names

Our text is consisted two parts in two years: the first and smaller part is about the Ibbi-Sin first year's tributes (gú ma-da) from four generals and captains of five cities under them, who each sent one bull to the king. The second and main part is the list of the tributes from these four generals and other 3 generals, the captains under them and the troops under them. The four generals seemed to command only one city's garrison each: no 1. Ṣilua-Dagan at the fortress of Išim-Šulgi, nos. 4-6, Kurb-ilak at Maškan-ušuri, Humzum at Put-šadar and Ṣilua-'ulgi at Kiš-gati, but the three generals controlled two or three garrisons: the garrisons at Šami and Ibbal under the Lú-Nanna of Zimudar, the garrisons at Abi-bana, Puh-zigar and Kakkulatum under Ahuni, son of Irebum, and the garrisons at Maškan-abi and Tutub under the Lú-Nanna of Maškan-abi. All the geographical and personal names are Akkadian or none-Sumerian languages apart from the two Lú-Nannas, one at Zimudar and another at Maškan-abi and Tutub, but we can consider this name is the Sumerian logogram writing for the Akkadian name of *Awîl-Sin*, "the Man of the Moon God". These cities and their generals are listed below:

---

[1] Copied by King, L W. in 1912; transliterated by Maaijer, R. and de Jagersma, B., 2001 in CDLI P108667 and in BDTNS no. 002504 ; also in Politi, J and Verderame, L., Nisaba 8 019, 2005. The abbreviations here are from the two web projects.

Table 1 The Akkadian Named Cities and Generals on Northeast Frontier in Ibbi–Sin 2 iv (CT 32, pl. 19–22 BM 103398)

Cities	generals	towns and its captains	town and its army
1. Išim-Šulgi	Ṣilua-Dagan (gov. of Simuru before)	11 captains of **Išim-Šulgi**:	the army at **Išim-Šulgi**
2. Zimudar with Šami and *Íb -ba-al*	Lú-Nanna of Zimudar	3 captains of Šami with some **chief of 60 men and chief of the 20;1** captain of Íb--*ba-al* (not **Tum-ma-al**)	the army at Šami and army of **Ibbal**, the **ugula** (commander) is **Lu-Nanna of Zimudar**
3. Abi-bana **Puhzigar** and **Kakkulatum**	**Ahuni, son of Irebum**,	1 captain at **Abi-bana** and 1 captain at **Kakkulatum** (and **Puh-zigar**)	the army at **Abi-bana**; the army at **Puhzigar** and the army at **Kakkulatum**:
4. Maškan-ušuri	**Kurb-ilak: zero tribute**	1 captain at **Maškan-ušuri**	the army at **Maškan-ušuri**, ugula **Kurb-ilak**,
5. Put-šadar only in this text	**Humzum**	**3 captain at Put-šadar** and chief of 60 men and of 20 at **Put-šadar**	**the army at Put-šadar，ugula is Humzum**,
6. Kišgati:	Ṣiluš-Šulgi	**2 captains at Kišgati,**	the army at **Kiš-gati**, ugula is **Ṣiluš-Šulgi**
7. Maškan-abi and Tutub	**Lú-Nanna** on behalf of **Tutub and Maškan-abi**,	**2 captains of Tutub:** 1 captain at (**Maškan-abi**)	the army at **Tutub** and the army at Maškan- abi: ugula is **Lu-Nanna** of **Maškan-abi**

Siluš–Dagan was the most important and longest general of the Ur dynasty, who was active from Šulgi 43 vi /4 (OIP 115 152) to Ibbi–Sin 2 iv 29 of our text for 27 years. He was appointed possibly as the governor of Simurum about at Šulgi 44 when the land was at last conquered by the king after the nine campaigns. The seals in Umma naming him as the governor of Simurum are dated from AS 6 ii (BIN 3 627) to ŠS 3 vi (PDT 2 1355), ŠS 5 vi (PDT 1327) and ŠS 6 (UTI 6 3664). Siluš–Dagan had withdrawn from Simurum at the end of Šu–Sin and now became the commander of the troops of Išim–Šulgi in IS 2 iv/29, possibly because the rebel Simurum land drove him out of there. The army in the fortress of Išim–Šulgi was commanded by *Nu– ì –da* (ugula) at least from AS 5 ix/11 to AS 8 iii/13, according to 2 texts (SET 10, Studies Astour 369). He and his wife *Ru–ba–tum*, were active from Š 39 xi/20 (Princeton 2 130, OIP 115 042) to AS 8 ix/12 (JAOS 33 172 5). He might be the son-in-law of Šulgi since his wife and he often sent sheep to queen Šulgi–simti and received animal gifts from her (Š 46 iii/3+ PDT 2 1035; AS 4 ii/ 6 CUSAS 16 303) and sacrificed the throne of the past king Ur-^{d}Namma (AS 5 ix/28 TRU 125) and the dead Šulgi (AS 4 ix^2 /6, Nisaba 8 37). In a time after last quarter of AS 8, Nuida possibly retired and the army of Išim–Šulgi might be under S#ilua-Dagan who commanded them in IS 2. The three governors of Išim–Šulgi, Lugal–pa–è and other two, were colleagues during the Šulgi period (RSO 9 472 P368, AUCT 2 281) and after the three, Ur–sa6–sa6–ga and A–hu–wa–qar were its governors between AS 4 and 8 (AS 4 viii/3, JCS 35 177 2; AS 7 vi/ 22 NYPL 327; AS 8 iv/4, NYPL 327). However, the last two governors probably retired during the Šu–Sin reign, and Išim–Šulgi was under Siluš–Dagan till he became the general commander of the Ur army and led the 11 captains and their troops of Išim–Šulgi and other armies to launch the campaign against rebel Simurum in Ibbi–Sin's 2nd year.

Simurum possibly was free from Ur during the Šu–Sin period, since *Ki–ri/rí–ib–ul–me*, a man or ruler of Simurum from AS 8 ix/14 (BIN 3 173) to ŠS i/24 (BIN 3 217, once in SS 2 with xi/24 ZA 97 231), and *Tab/ Tab4–ba–an–Da–ra–ah*, another ruler of that land who and Kirib–ulme (2nd place), were together presented a ram gift each in ŠS 1 x/20 (SNAT 271). After Kirib–ulme, Tabban–Darah himself came to Ur from ŠS 1 iv/18 (PDT 1 567, 605) to ŠS 2 ix/23 (BIN 3 559). They were the allies of the Ur Dynasty and both seemed the semi-independent rulers. After 5 years' absence, in ŠS 7 xi/2 (MVN 18 044) Tabban–Darah with *Te–šup–še–la– ah* and lú *A–za–ma–an*^{ki} were under the command of Siluš–Dagan. Tabban–Darah's daughter possibly is a wife of Ur–Nammu since she was once sacrificed with the first king of the dynasty (1 udu–niga sá–dug4 ki–a–nag Ur–dNamma, 3 udu–niga sá–dug4~ dumu–munus~ *Tab–ba–an–da–ra–ah*, SACT 1 188 [Š 43–AS 4]). After ŠS 7, Tabban–Darah might died and Simurum began to rebel against Ur.

There are two ugula generals named Lú–Nanna[1] in our text: the general of Zimudar, which covered the cities of Šami and *Íb–ba–al*, and that of Tutub and Maškan–abi. During the Šulgi reign, there was a Lu–Nanna, the general (šakkana) of Nag–su near Umma (47 iii–iv, CST 098, TIM 6 36, TCL 2 5488) and a Lu–Nanna general mentioned without the city name (Š 47 vi–x MVN 18 150, MVN 13 641). Hence, possibly from Nag-su, the Lu–Nanna of was installed to Zimudar as general from ŠS 1 (ŠS 1 i in Ur UET 3 75; his seal in Nippur, SS 1 NATN 776) and he was mentioned with both his title and place in a text on Šu–Sin 8 v/19 (ASJ 4 140 02), which tells us that the goddess in his house was Haburitum connected with Dagan.

The predecessor o Lu–Nanna in Zimudar (ŠS 1–IS 2) was Zikru–ili, who was active from Š 45 viii/17 (CST 091) to AS 2 xi between the Urbilum campaign of Šulgi and that of Amar–Sin 5 years later. Twice, he and the captains and army of Zimudar appear in the tribute lists: on Š 47 xi/28 (OrSP 18 pl. 04 12: n[u–bandà]—me, [ugula] *Zikur–ili*). Four of the 6 captains under him in Š 47 xi, *Bur–*^{d}*Adad*, *Puzur4–*^{d}*Ha–Ià* (of Šami), *Šar–ru–um– ì –lí* and *Tá–hi–iš–še–en* (of Sitirša) occurred with him on AS 2 xi//14 (Studies Levine 115–119), and *A–ki–a* in the 2nd list was called lú~ *Zi–mu–dar*^{ki} in Š 46 xi (Rochester 231, Girsu). Among the five captains with him from the Šulgi reign, only *Puzur4–*^{d}*Ha–Ià*, the captain of Šami, survived to IS 2 iv and was in the army of Lu–Nanna, the new general.

The next general, who charged the troops in three towns, Abi–bana and Kakkulatum, as well as *Pu–úh–zi–gàr*^{ki}, was *Ahuni*, son of *Irebum*. The last town was governed before by general (šakkana) Amur–Ea (CST 121 Š 46 vii, AUCT 1 437) who was active from Šulgi 43 i/18 (PDT 1 102) to Amar–Sin 2 xi (Studies Levine 115–119) and made the troops send a normal tribute of 1 bull with 10 sheep on Š 47 xii/9 (PDT 1 448). On AS 7 xi/14, 2 bulls with 20 of flock were sent by *Šu–É–a*, lú~ **Pu–úh–zi–gàr*^{ki} (PDT 2 1237). Irebum, the father and predecessor of our Ahuni in Ibbi–Sin 2 was also the general of Abi–bana and Kakkulatum from AS 2 xi/12 (Studies Levine 115–119) to SS 5 i/10 (PDT 2 1073), and in the first text, he as ugula commander brought a tribute of 5 bulls with 50 of flock (1:10), and the troops (é rin) of *A–bí–ba–na*^{ki} under him sent 4 bulls with 40 of flock(1:10), and the troops of *Kak–ku8–la–tum*^{ki} 4 bulls, 40 of flock. The captain (nu–bandà) under him *I–gi4* sent a normal tribute, 1 bull, 10 sheep, but *Awil–šalim* and *Suhuš–ki–in* only presented 6 of flock each. This

---

[1] Other famous Lú–^{d}Nannas are the šabra majordomo of ^{d}Nin–sún in Ur and Ku6–a, Š 43 i –AS 6 ix/1, who is possibly the šabra Lú–^{d}Nanna without his deity's names in the texts, one dumu–lugal on Š 44 iv/5 (TRU 28) and the Lú–^{d}Nanna, šabra~^{d}Nanna, Š 48–AS 1–5, as well as others.

man who also was called I–re–eb was active from AS 2 xi to Šu–Sin 5 xi/16 (SET 091), and on SS 2 viii/17 he once was installed as the governor of Lulubu: 383 of flock was sent from *I–re–eb énsi*~ Lu–lu–bu[ki] (Ontario 1 132). During AS 8 v/5 –ŠS 1 xiii/16 (MVN 11 181, in the duty period of Zubaga), possibly his son Ahuni as a captain began to send a normal tribute (1 bull, 10 sheep) to the Ur dynasty and his captain *I–gi₄* was the commander (ugula) of two chiefs of lú~ [d]Za–ba₄–ba₄[ki] with a normal tribute each. In ŠS 5 i/20 (RA 49 87 05), *I–gi₄–a* sent a normal tribute as the majordomo (š abra) of his city.

The fourth general was Kurb–ilak of Maškan–ušuri, and this personal name was used by several official, but we believe he was the man or ruler of Ba–šim–e, who sent tributes in Š 46 vii/15 and Š 48 vii/19 and (RA 9 43 SA 25, OIP 115 287). On Š 48 viii/2, Arád–mu or Arad–Nanna, the secretary of state, issued 10 fat sheep to the house of *Tá–ra–am–[d]Šul–gi*, princess and wife the dam~ *Šu–Da–ba–ni*, the man of Ba–šim–e[ki], which shows that a daughter of Šulgi was married to the land of Bašime. Since Maškan–ušuri was only in our text in IS 2, so it might be the new name of Ba–šim–e. Note that Arad–Nanna in a later inscription once titled himself as *šakkana* Ba–šim[ki] (RIME 3/2.1.4.13). After the failure of the Simurum campaign in Ibbi–Sin 2nd year, the royal animal center in Puzriš–Dagan was abandoned, and in Girsu, in Ibbi–Sin 3 vii, a general *Iš–ku/ku8–un–É–a*, son of Kurb–ilak (ITT 2 00976), received large number of rations (532 gur of barley and 158 of emmer) from Gu–za–na of Gú–ab–ba of Girsu, for his troops when they marched against Amorites (érin~ugnim[ki]–ma–ke₄–ne ud– kaskal Mar–tu–––š è ì –re–ša–a Essays Gordon 1 135 3) and also in Gú–ab–ba, IS 3 ii (TÉL 129, ITT 3 5255). This general also appeared in Ur (UET 3 0719).

The fifth general was *Hu–um–zum* of town of *Pu–ut–ša–dar* and the person and the town occur only in our text, which shows that this was a new conquered place. This general in AS 6 vii (BPOA 6 0906) took 600 butchered sheep for the soldiers of Dukra (of *Nu–ga–ar* and *Ú–ṣa–ar–i–mi–AN*[ki]) from Turaya, chief of herdmen (kuš₇) in the city of Nimṣ ium of Amorites. *Nim– ṣi–um* is perhaps derived from Elam/Nim + *Sium* in Northeast since a text (MVN 5 233) mentions the *NIM–Si–ù*[ki]–me (the Elamites of Siu) among the subject Elamite cities of the Ur empire: NIM *Za–ul*[ki]–me NIM *An–ša–an*[ki]–me NIM *Á–NI–gi₄*[ki]–me, NIM *Ki–maš*[ki]–me, NIM D*uh–duh–NI*[ki]–me, NIM *Ši–ma–aš–ki/gi₄*–me, NIM Sa–bu–umki–me, NIM *Hu–hu–nu–ri*[ki], NIM *Gi–ša*[ki]–me and NIM *Ú–lí–ma*[ki]. The place was occupied by the Amorites since one text of *Tur–ra–a* (BPOA 7 3022+3023 AS 5 vi) is dated by the month of *Ni–iq–mu–um* (West Semitic "revenge"), the sixth month of the Amorite Eshnunna but as the first month of the Šamši–Adad's Autumn Equinox calendar, whose ancestor no. 5 is *Nam– ṣ u– ú* among the ten tribe–ancestor names (GHD JCS 20). Hence, Humṣ um might be a West Semitic chief near Nims)ium.

The sixth general was Ṣiluš–Šulgi of *Ki–iš–ga–ti*[ki], a place unknown to us. A senior soldier (agà–ús–gal) among the diplomats going to Susa is named *GIŠ–ga–ti* (vii–viii Nisaba 22 113, YOS 04 212) and he as captain sent 10 sheep tribute in AS 3 xi²/2 (BPOA 7 2960), so this place name may have derived from the Semitic person name. Before in this text, Ṣ i –lu–uš–[d]Šul–gi was listed in other tribute lists for 4 times from AS 5 x/9 to SS 3 iii/3, 23 (TCL 2 5504, SAT 3 1354, TJSASE 115, CST 435)

The last general was another Lú⁻Nanna, who commanded two garrisons, Tutub and Maškan–abi. In AS 8 iii/13 (Studies Astour 369), the troops (érin) of *Maš–kán–a–bí*[ki] was commanded by Inim–[d]Nanna (prince), troops of érin *I–šim–[d]Šul–gi*[ki] were under *Nu–i–da* and érin *Maš–kán–šar–ru–um*[ki] under *Na–ah–šum–BALA*. In SS 9 xi/15, the elders of Tutub was under Šamaš–ba–ni (general of Sippar; ASJ 03 068 01). On AS 8 iii/13, Inim–[d]Nanna (Prince) was the ugula general of Maškan–abi (Studies Astour 369), who was replaced by Lú–Nanna or renamed in IS 2. Prince Inim–dNanna, possibly son of Amar–Sin, married the daughter of *Hu–ba–*

a[①] on AS1 i/30 (TCL 2 5563 niĝ –mussa[sa]2 Inim–[d]Nanna[˜] dumu–lugal é[˜] *Hu–ba–a*––šè) and the daughter of Hubaya was named as royal bride (é–gi₄–a Hu–ba–a SS 8 ix/7 CST 448). During AS 2–3, Prince Inim–Nanna received monthly allowance from the court (2 iv BPOA 6, 82, 3 xii TRU 330) and then might go to Maškan–abi.

2. The Tributes from the Generals and Armies, Named the gú ma–da Tribute in Šu–Sin 3 to 9, from Troops at the Northeast Frontier

The tributes from the troops at the Northeast Frontier to the king of Ur listed in our texts are termed as gú ma–da, the tributes of (conquered or subject) lands. In the Puzriš–Dagan, the tributes or gú ma–da is consisted of bulls and rams, usually. The first list of the gú ma–da was dated to Šu–Sin 3. Apart from our text, we also collect the information of some generals and their fortresses from all the texts from Puzriš–Dagan.

The famous generals are Išar–ramaš of *A–ba–al* and Dašil, and after him, Adad–dani in Dašil in Šu–Sin 1, Šuruš–kin of *E–ba–al*[ki] in AS 4 xii–AS 7–Šu–Sin 1 ix, Hašipatal of Arraphum in AS 5 v, Tahšen of S/Šitirša in AS 5 vii, U_{18}–*ba–a* of Adamdun, *Il–ili*[li] of Bad3–an[ki]–(zi), Nir–ì–da–ĝál of Gàr–NE.NE and Tablala in AS 5 ix–8 iii, Nahšum–bal of Maškan–šarrum, Itib–šinat of Išur, Hubaya of Puttulium in AS 8 iii, who was replaced by Ibni–Šulgi of Puttulium in Šu–Sin 7 iii, Puzur–Šulgi of Arraphum who replaced his father Hašipatal in AS 8 v/8–ŠS 3, Šu–Šulgi of *Dur–maš*[ki], *Ki–na–mu–ša* of *A–gaz*[ki], Prince [D]a–da of *Lu–lu–bu*, Ur–[d]Iškur of *Ha–ma–zi₂*[ki], Iti–Dagan of Harši in Šu–Sin 1. Nir–ì–da–ĝál of Bàd–An/Der including *Gàr–NE–NE* and Tablala in ŠS 3 ix and Tahiš–atal of Daltum and Šurbu in Šu–Sin 8 (or 6) ix, Unap–atal of Urbilum in Šu–Sin 7 viii and Azaman under Ṣ_iluš–Dagan in Šu–Sin 7 xi.

Arad–mu or Arad–Nanna, the secretary of state, bore many titles, and one was the general of Ni–hi: Arád–Nanna, sukkal–mah, énsi Lagaša[ki]–ke₄, sanĝa–[d]En–ki–ka, šakkana Uṣar–Ĝar–ša–na[ki], šakkana Ba–šim[ki], énsi *Su–bu–um*[ki] ù ma–da Gu–te–bu–um[ki]–ma, šakkana Dì–ma–at–[d]En–líl–lá, énsi A–al–d*Šu–Sîn*, šakkana Ur–bí–lum[ki], énsi Ha–àm–zi[ki] ù Karà–har[ki], šakkana Ni–hi[ki], šakkana Šix–maš[ki]ki ù ma–da Kar–da[ki]—ka. (RIME 3/2.1.4.13). We have found in Š 48 viii, the troops of NI–HI[ki] under Arád–mu contributed 2 bulls and 60 of flock and the troops of Mahazum (for Hamzu?) under him is listed in UDT 91 ([AS 2–8]).

Table 2. A Concise List of the Places of Generals and Datings

Places	titles	names	Dating
?	šakkana	Hubaya ,	Šulgi 33 v:
Abal	ugula	Išar–ramaš	Š 4[x] xi/1
Abal		Išar–ramaš	Š 46 ix/11
(Abal and Dašil)		Išar–ramaš	[AS 2–8 ?]?/22
Abal	ugula	Išar–ramaš	AS 5 ix/24
***A–ba–al* [ki]**	énsi	*Ba–ba–ti*	ŠS 3 x
Abi–bana and Kakkulatum	ugula	Irebum; Suhuš–kin nu–bandà	AS 2 xi/12
(Abi–bana, Kakkulatum)	(general)	*I–re–eb*	[AS 2–8 ?]/21 Ireb
Abi–bana	érin troops	(general Irebum or Ahuni, his son)	AS 4 x/4

---

① Hubaya was the general of ***Dub/Dab₆–ru–um***, a northern Babylonian city and the god of which is Sin/Nanna, in TCL 5 6041, a text with many generals of Ur III discussed by A. Goetze in JCS 17 of 1963. D. Charpin in RA 72 studied the city of ***Damru*** or Du₁₀–ĝar[ki] in logograms of the OB period, a worshipping center of Sin. Damru in OB period should be the variant spelling of Dabrum or Dubrum in Ur III .

续表

Places	titles	names	Dating
Adamdun	ugula	Ubaya	Š 45 xii/6
Adamdun ;	ugula	U_{18}-ba-a =Ubaya	[AS 2-8 ?]/[28]
Adamdun	ugula	Ubaya *U_{18}-ba-a	AS 9 viii/26
Agaz	ugula	??Ki-na-mu-ša-ki	AS 8 v/8
***Ar-ma-an*^{ki}**	ugula	*Á-pi-la-ša*	ŠS 9 xi/15
A-ra-mi^{ki}	ugula	Abuni	Š 48 viii/3
(Arraphum)	ugula	*Ha-ši-pá-tal*	AS 5 v/4
Arraphum:	ugula	Hašip-atal/*Ha-ši!-pá-tal*	AS 5 v/25
(Arraphum)	(general)	*A-ši-ba-tal*= *Ha-ši-pá-tal*	AS 5 v/27
Arraphum	ugula	Puzur-Šulgi, son of Hašipatal Mar-ha-ši^{ki})	(lú AS 8 v/8
(Arraphum and *Mar-ha-ši*^{ki})	lú	*Puzur$_4$-^{d}Šul-gi* dumu *Ha-ši-pá-tal*	ŠS 3 0/00
Áš-nun^{ki}	ugula	Abuni	Š 48 viii/3
***A-za-ma-an*^{ki}**	ugula	Ș iluš-Dagan	ŠS 7 xi/2
Ba-a-bí	érin~	(under) Tahis-atal	Š 43 vii/2
Bàd-An^{ki}-zi	ugula	DINGIR-*li-lí* =Il-ili	AS 5 ix/11
Bàd-An/Der (with Tablala)	ugula	Nir-ì-da-ĝál	ŠS 3 ix/13
Balue	ugula	*Be-lí-a-rí-ik*	Š [39?] x/2
Balue	ugula	Šulgi-kalam-ma-me-te-bi	Š 47 xi/18
Bar-ma-an	érin	(under) Tahis-atal	Š 43 vii/2
Bašime	lú	*Kur-bi-la-ak* lú- Ba-šim-e^{ki}	Š 46 vii/15, 48 vii/19
***Ba-šim*^{ki}**	šakkana	Arád-Nanna	ŠS late years
Bidadun	ugula	*A-bu-ni*	Š 48 viii/3
***Bí-da-dun*^{ki}**	ugula	Apilaša	[(AS 7 iv/30)-ŠS]
Buhzigar	ugula	Amur-Ea	Š 46 xii/9
Daltum	general	Tahiš-atal	ŠS 6 or 8 ix/13
Dašil	ugula	Išar-ramaš	AS 5 ix/24
Dašil	ugula	Adad-dani	ŠS 1 ix/6
***Da-ši-bí-we*^{ki}**	troops	érin~ ***Da-ši-bí-we*^{ki}**	Š 43 vii/2
***Dì-ma-at-*^{d}En-líl-lá**	šakkana	Arad-Nanna	ŠS late years
Duh-duh-lí/Gabgabli	ruler	Hulibar	Š 48 vii/23
Dur-Ebla	man	Nur-ili	AS 5 ix/9
Dur-maš	ugula	*Šu-*^{d}*Šul-gi*	AS 8 v/8
(Ebal)？	šakkana	Suhuš-kin	Š 43 v
(Ebal)	general	*Šu-ru-uš-ki-in*	AS 2 xi/8
Ebal= *E-ba-al*^{ki}	ugula	Šuruš-kin	[AS 4 xii/7- AS 7]
Ebal	ugula	Šuruš-kin	AS 5 ix/11

续表

Places	titles	names	Dating
Ebal	[ugula]	Šuruš-kin	ŠS 1 ix/6
Erut	lú ruler	Ne-ne-a ugula Şiluš-Dagan	Š 47 x/25
*E-ru-ut*ki	érin	(under) Nigarx-[ki-du₁₀]	Š 43 vii/2
*Gáb-la-aš*ki	érin	(under) Tahis-atal	Š 43 vii/2
*Gá-la-aš*ki	ugula	*Ì-la-lum*	AS 8 v/8
Gàr-ne-ne	érin		Š 43 vi/30
Gàr-ne-ne and Tablala	ugula	Nir-ì-da-ĝál	Š 48 vii/22
(*Gàr-ne-ne* Tablala)	general	Nir-ì-da-ĝál	AS 2 xi/2
(*Gàr-ne-ne* Tablala),	general	Nir-ì-da-ĝál	AS 2 xi/4
Gàr-ne-ne and Tablala,	ugula	Nir-ì-da-ĝál (šakkana ÚR× A.HAki)	AS 5 ix/11
Hamazi:	énsi	ĝìr~ Ur-dIškur	AS 8 v/8
Hamazi	énsi	Ur-dIškur	[AS 4 xii/7- AS 7]
Harši	troops		Š 47 *xi/14
Harši	ugula	Hun-hab'ur	[AS?]
Harši	énsi, ugula	Iši-Wer and Iti-dDagan	ŠS 1 ix/6
Hubium	lú /ugula	Nu-nu, ugula Şiluš-Dagan	Š 47 x/25
Hubni	ugula	Iti-dSuen	Š 46 ix/11
Ibbal	érin	Íb-ba-alki	AS 7 viii/14
*Íb-*ba-al*[ki]	ugula	Šu-Da-da	AS 5 viii/15
Innaba	ugula	Sušanum	Š 46 xii/17
(**Išim-Šulgi**)	general	Nu-ì–da	AS 2 xi/12
Išim-Šulgi	(general)	Nu-ì-da	AS 5 ix/11
Išim-Šulgi	ugula	Nu-ì-da	AS 8 iii/13
Iš-ne-kal/dan	ugula	Ş iluš-Dagan	[AS?]
Išum = *I-šum-ma*ki	[érin]		[AS 4 xii/7- AS 7]
Išum	ruler/general	*Waşum-*dŠulgi,	ŠS [3-9]
Išur,	ugula	Itib-šinat	AS 8 iii/13
[A?]-šur₅ki	[ugula]	[N]ur-Ištar	ŠS 1 ix/6
Kismar	ugula	Nur-Ištar	Š 46 ix/00
Kismar	ugula	Išar-ramaš	Š 46 xii/17
Kismar	ugula	Išar-ramaš (near Maškan-šarrum TRU 144)	Š 47 xi/18
Lulubu	dumu-lugal	[ugula [D]a?-da	AS 8 v/8
Lulubu	governor	*I-re-eb* énsi~ Lu-lu-buki	ŠS 2 viii/17
Mahazum	ugula	Arád-mu	[AS 2-8 ?]/[28]
Marhaši	ugula	Abuni	AS 5 ix/24
*Már-ma-an*ki		*I-bí-it*-DINGIR?	Š 43 vi/30
Marman	ugula	Naram-ili	Š 47 vii/17
Már-ma-an	ugula	Naram-ili	Š 47 xi/18

Places	titles	names	Dating
[M]arman	[érin]		[AS 4 xii/7- AS 7] .
Maškan-Amar-Sin, Ur-Zababa	(general)	Dayyan (DI.KU₅)-ili in **Ur-ᵈZa-ba₆-ba₆**	AS 5 iv
Maškan-garaš	ugula	*A-mur*-DINGIR	ŠS 1 ix/6
Tutub, Dašil, Maškan-kalatum	ugula	Šamaš-bani/ᵈUTU-*ba-ni*	ŠS 9 xi/15
Maškan-šarrum	ugula	In-ta-è-a	Š 47 xi/1
Maškan-šarrum	lú	ᵈAmar-ᵈSuen-ha-ma-ti and BAD₃-ì-lí	AS 5 v/4
Maškan-šarrum	ugula	Nahšum-bala	AS 8 iii/13
Maškan-šarrum	šakkana	*Ba-ba-ti*	ŠS 3 x
Maškan-abi	ugula	Inim-ᵈNanna (Prince)	AS 8 iii/13
Me-a-bi	ugula	*I-šar-ra-ma-[aš]*	Š 48 viii/00
(NAG-su^ki)	general	Lú-ᵈNanna (šakkana TIM 6 36)	AS 2 xi/5
NI-amiš	ugula	Ur-Sin	Š 48 vii/23
Ni-hi^ki	ugula	Arád-mu	Š 48 viii/00
Ni-hi^ki	šakkana	Arad-Nanna	ŠS late years
(Ya)/Nidarašpi	[ugula]	Lugal-má-gur₈-re	[AS 4 xii/7- AS 7]
Neber-Amar-Sin	ugula	Arád-mu	AS 5 ix/9
Nugar	ugula	Du-uk-ra	AS 5 ix/9
(Puttulium)	general	Hu-ba-a	AS 2 xi/12
(Puttulium)	ugula	Hu-ba-a	AS 4 xi/3
Puttulium,	ugula	Hubaya	AS 8 iii/13
Puttulium	ugula	Ibni-Šulgi; Šarrum-bani nu-bandà,	ŠS 7 iii/25
Rabi	[érin]	Ra-bí^ki	[AS 4 xii/7- AS 7]
Salla-NE-wi	lú ruler	Šukubum, ugula Şiluš-Dagan	Š 47 x/25
(Sami)	captain	DI.KU₅-*[ì]-lí*	AS 8 v/8
(Sami)	(captain)	Dayyan-ili	ŠS 4 x
Si-um-mi^ki	ugula	Hu-ba-a	Š 48 viii/00
(Simurum)		Ş iluš-Dagan	AS 2 xi/2
(Simurum)		Ş iluš-Dagan	AS 2 xi/5
(Sitirša)	captain	*Tá-hi-iš-še-en* under Zikur-ili of Zimudar	AS 2 xi/14
S/Šitirša	ugula	Tahiš-en	AS 5 vii/11
Šitirša	ruler/captain	Tahiš-en	ŠS 7 viii/13
Šešel	ugula	Abi-kin	Š 46 vii/25
Ši_x-maški^ki *ù ma-da Kar-da*^ki	šakkana	Arad-Nanna	ŠS late years
	(ugula)	Nigar_x-[ki-du₁₀]	Š 43 vii/2
Šu-A-hi	(ugula)	érin under Nigar_x-[ki-du₁₀]	Š 43 vii/2
Šu-ah	troops	érin	AS 8 v/8
Šu-Ir-hu-um	troop	érin	Š 43 vii/2
Šu-Irhum	troops	érin	AS 8 v/8

Places	titles	names	Dating
Šurbu	lú	Šu-Tišpak, Ištar-kin, Dagi, Erra-bani *I-ti-ga*	Šu-Ištar ŠS 1 ix/6
Šurbu	ugula	Tahiš-atal	ŠS 6 or 8 ix/13
Šu-Suen-ì-du₁₀	ugula	Nanna-igi-du	ŠS 6 or 8 ix/13
Tag/šum-tium	ugula	Hubaya	Š 46 xii/17
Tiran	[érin]	*Ti-ra-an*ᵏⁱ	[AS 4 xii/7- AS 7]
Tiran	ugula	Šarrum-bani	[AS?]
Urbilum	ugula	Arád-mu, ĝìr~ Unap-atal	ŠS 7 viii/13
*Ur-bí-lum*ᵏⁱ	šakkana	Arad-Nanna	ŠS late years
Ur-gu-ha-lam	**ugula**	Amur-ili	ŠS 1 ix/6
URU×Aᵏⁱ	ugula	Šeš-kal-la	[(AS 7 iv/30)-ŠS]
<Ur>-ᵈZa-ba₄-ba₄ᵏⁱ	ugula	*La-la-a* and *I-gi₄*	(AS 8 v/5 - ŠS 1 xiii)
Uṣar-ᵈŠulgi ?	ruler general	*A-hu-ni*	(AS 8 v - ŠS 1 xiii/16)
*W/PI-il*ᵏⁱ	lú ruler	*Šu-ni-ki-ib*	Š [39?] x/2
W/Pil	[ugula]	Ṣiluš-Dagan	Š [39?] x/2
Zimudar	ugula	Zikur-ili	Š 47 x/10
(Zimudar)	ugula	Zikur-ili	AS 2 xi/14
(Zimudar)	(general)	Zikur-ili	AS 2 xi/17
Zibere	ugula	Má-sa₆-sa₆	AS 5 ix/14
Za₃-tumᵏⁱ	ugula	Šeš-kal-la	AS 8 v/8
	šakkana	Šulgi-ili	Š 47 ix
	(general)	Hun-hubše	AS 2 xi/3
	(Prince)	Ištar-il-šu	AS 2 xi/12

Table 3 the Tributes from Generals, Captains and Troops in the Northeast Frontier during Šulgi and Amar–Sin

Dating Places/general	and titles	names	tributes	Texts
Š 33 v:	general	*Hu-ba-a* šakkana,	1 bull, 10 of flock	CST 042
Šulgi [39?] x/4	general	[1 gud] *Be-lí-a-rí-ik*	[1+ bull]	AUCT 1 004
Balue under Beli-arik	troops	érin *Ba-lu-e*ᵏⁱ ugula *Be-lí-a-rí-ik*	[1 bull, 10 rams]	
x/2 **W/Pil** under ruler Ṣiluš-Dagan	under ruler	*Šu-ni-ki-ib* lú *W/PI-il*ᵏⁱ	1 bull 10 of flock	
	general	[ugula] *Ṣi-lu-uš-ᵈDa-gan*		
Šulgi [x] xi/1 1. **Abal** under	general	Išar-ramaš	6 fat bulls, 120 of flock	Wiseman Tablets W
Išar-ramaš	**troops**	érin *A-ba-al*ᵏⁱ, ugula Išar-ramaš	10 bulls, 240 of flock	22
2. **Hubni** Iti-Sin	**troops, general**	érin *Hu-ub-ni*ᵏⁱ ugula Iti-ᵈSuen	10 cattle, 100 flock	

Dating Places/general	and titles	names	tributes	Texts
Š 43 v	general	SUHUŠ-ki-in šakkana	29 cows	Princeton 2 1
Š 43 vi/30 Gàr-ne-ne	generals (mu-túm lugal)	Amar/Már-ma-an^{ki} é-du₆-la	6 bulls	CTMMA 1 09 (tribute to king for 30 day)
		Za-rí-iq (of Ashur)	12 bulls	
		I-šar-ru-um	14 bulls	
		I-bí-it-DINGIR	2 bulls	
	troops	érin Gàr-ne-ne	8 bulls	
		Šà-ba-na-sig and Ur-tilla₃	2 bulls	
	general?	Šu?-ᵈŠul-gi	6 bulls	
Š 43 vii/2 Šu-Ahi	general	Nigar_x-[ki-du₁₀]	8 bulls, 80 of flock,	OIP 115 158
	troops	érin Šu-A-hi^{ki} (also AUCT 3 484)	4 bulls, 40 of flock,	
Šu-Ir-hu-um	troops	érin Šu-Ir-hu-um^{ki} (AUCT 3 484)	6 bulls, 70 of flock,	
	captain	A-a <nu-bandà>	2 bulls, 20 of flock,	
E-ru-ut^{ki}	troops	érin E-ru-ut^{ki}	4 bulls, 40 of flock,	
	captain	Zé-ep-ra-am <nu-bandà>	2 bulls, 2=40 of flock,	
Gáb-la-aš Tahis-atal	under troops	érin Gáb-la-aš^{ki} (AUCT 3 484 ugula Ì-la-lum)	6 bulls, 80 of flock,	
Da-ši-bí-we^{ki}	troops	érin~ Da-ši-bí-we^{ki}	3 bulls, 30 of flock,	
	captain	dumu DINGIR-su-ra-bí^{ki}	1 bull	
Bar-ma-an^{ki}	troops	érin Bar-ma-an^{ki}	2 bulls, 10 of	
Ba-a-bí	troops	érin~ Ba-a-bí^{ki}	1 bull	
	(general)	Tá-hi-iš-a-tal	1 bull, 10 of flock	
Š 45 viii: Šulgi-ì-lí	general	dam-ᵈŠul-gi-ì-lí šakkana, mu-túm~ Šulgi-simtum	2 cows, 20 of flock,	RT 37 130
Š 45 xii/6 Adamdun troops Ubaya	and general	⸢erín⸣-A-⸢dam⸣-dun^{ki}, ⸢ugula⸣ U₁₈-ba-a	174 bulls, 1740 of flock	OIP 115 182
Š 46 vii/15, Š 48 vii/19	ruler	Kur-bi-la-ak lú-Ba-šim-e^{ki} (OIP 115 287)	5 goats; 11 of flock	RA 9 043 SA 25
Š 46 vii/25 Šešel by troops Abi-kin	and general	érin Še-še-il^{ki} ugula A-bí-ki-in	10 oxen	PDT 2 1163

续表

Dating Places/general	and titles	names	tributes	Texts
Š 46 ix/00 **Kismar** under Nur-Ištar	troops and general	érin *Ki-is-mar*^{ki}, ugula *Nu-úr-Iš₈-tár*	1 bull 10 of flock	VAMZ 3.s. 26-27 130
	majordomo	*Šu-É-a* šabra	2 bulls, 20 of flock	4
Š 46 ix/11 **Abal** Išar-ramaš		érin A-ba-al^{ki} ugula *I-šar-ra-ma-aš*	1 bull, 10 of flock	JCS 52 7 06
Š 46 xii/9 **Buhzigar**: troops Amur-Ea	general	érin *Bu-uh₂-zi-gàr*^{ki} ugula Amur-Ea	1 bull, 10 of flock	PDT 1 448
		ugula A-mur-é-a	1 bull, 10 of flock	Hermitage 3 188
Š 46 xii/17 **Innaba**: troops Sušanum	and general	érin *In-na-ba*^{ki} ugula *Su-ša-nu-um*	2 bulls, 20 flock 4 cows	OIP 115 195
Tagtim under Hubaya	troops	érin *TAG-t[i]-um*^{ki}, ugula Hu-ba-a	2 bulls	
Š 47 vii/17	troops	érin AMAR-ma-an^{ki}	10 of flock,	
Marman under Naram-ili	3 herdsmen under Naram-ili	*Ha-ar-bí-in* na-gada, *Ili-dan* na-gada, *Èr-ra-dan* na-gada, *Már/Amar-ma-an*^{ki}— me	5 rams, 2 of sipa flock, 2 of flock	MVN 13 868
Kismar Išar-ramaš	under herdsman	sipa *Ki-is-mar*^{ki} ugula *I-šar-ra-ma-aš*	4 goats	
Š 47 ix	general	*Šul-gi-ì-lí* šakkana, mu-túm- ^d*Šul-gi-sí-im-ti*,	2 bulls, 20 of flock,	OIP 115 113
Š 47 x/10 **Zimudar**: mayors Zikur-ili	general	ha-za-núm lú~ *Zi-mu-dar*^{ki}—me ugula Zi-kur-ì-lí	2 bulls, 17 of flock	CST 187
Š 47 x/25 **Hubium, Erut, Sallanewi** Š iluš-Dagan	3 rulers under and the general	*Nu-nu* lú~ *Hu-bi-um*^{ki}, *Ne-ne-a* lú~ **E-ru-ut**^{ki}, *Šu-ku₈-bu-um* lú~ **Sal-la-NE-wi**^{ki}, ugula	6 goats, 6 goats 10 goats	OIP 115 263
Š 47 **xi/1**, **Maškan-šarrum**	troops and chief	érin *Maš-kán-šar-ru-um*^{ki} ugula In-ta-è-a	9 bulls, 180 of flock	RO 11 96 02
			Hermitage 3 188	
Š 47 *xi/14	troops	among the delivery of érin *Ha-ar-ši*^{ki}	3 goats	BPOA 7 2603
Š 47 xi/18 **Balue** under Šulgi-kalama-me-te-bi;	general captain	*Nu-i₃-da*, 1 lamb; *I-bí-*^d*Suen* nu-bandà,	2 oxen, 1 deer 21 flock.	
Amar/Bur-man under Naram-ili	troops, general	érin *Ba-lu-e*^{ki} ugula ^d*Šul-gi-kalam-ma-me-te-bi*	7 oxen, 140 of flock	MVN 11 145
	3 herdsmen under Naram-ili	*Ha-ar-bi₂-in* na-gada, *Ili-dan* na-gada, *Èr-ra-dan* na-gada, *Amar-ma-an*^{ki} —me, ugula	5 rams, 2 of sipa flock, 2 of flock	
Kismar Išar-ramaš	under herdsman	sipa *Ki-is-mar*^{ki} ugula *I-šar-ra-ma-aš*	4 goats	

续表

Dating and titles Places/general		names	tributes	Texts
Š 47 xi/28 (see AS 2	érin	*Zi-mur-dar*^{ki} with 6 captains	13 bulls, 130 of flock	OrSP 18 pl. 04 12
xi/14)				
Zimudar under captain 1		*La-ma-ha-ar*	1 bull, 10 rams	n[u-bandà]
Zikur-ili				— me
	captain 2	*Tá-hi-(iš)-še-en₆* (of Sitirša AS	5 1 bull, 10 rams	[ugula]
		vii/11)		**Zikur-ili**
was general of captain 3		*Bur-^dAdad*	1 bull, 10 rams	
S/Šitirša)				
	captain 4	*A-bu-da-a*	1 bull, 0 rams	
Puzur-Haya, captain captain 5		*Šar-ru-um-ì-lí*	10 of flock	
of **Sami**				
under Lu-Nanna in IS 2 captain 6		*[Puzur₄-^d]Ha-là*	1 bull, 8 ram+ 2 goats	
iv				
Š 48 vii/22 Gàr-NE-NE troops		érin *Gàr-NE-NE*^{ki},	4 bulls, 300 of flock	SACT 1 065
and Tablala under				
Nir-ì-da-ĝál	troops	érin *Tab-la-la*^{ki}, ugula Nir-ì-da-ĝál	2 bulls, 120 of flock	
Š 48 vii/23 Yamiš, troops,		érin *Ià-a-mi-iš*^{ki}, ugula Ur-^dSuen	60 goats,	OrSP 05 53
under Ur-Sin, general				17 Wengler
Gabgabli under ruler		*Hu-li-ba-ar*, lú *Gab-gab(Duh-duh)-li*^{ki}	24 bulls, 187 of flock	25
Hulibar				
Š 48 viii/00 NI-HI^{ki}	troops,	érin *NI-HI*^{ki} ugula Arád-mu	3 bulls, 60 of flock	SA 001d
ugula Arád-mu	general			(Pl. 036)
	troops,	érin *Si-um-mi*^{ki} ugula *Hu-ba-a*	5 bulls, 50 of flock,	
	general			
	troops,	érin?- *Me-a-bi*, ugula	1 bull, 10 of flock	
	general	*I-šar-ra-ma-[aš]*		
Š 48 viii/3 Ašnunna, troops		érin *Áš-nun*^{ki}	6 bulls, 60 of flock,	OrSP 02 62
Arami, Bidadun				6 Wengler
(*Bí-da-dun* in BPOA 7 troops		érin *A-ra-mi*^{ki}	6 bulls, 60 of flock,	22
2350) under Abuni				
	troops,	érin *Bi-da-dun*^{ki}, ugula *A-bu-ni*	6 bulls, 60 of flock,	
	general			
Amar-Sin 2 iii/3	**šakkana**	**A-bu-ni**	1 lamb	BIN 3 374
AS 2 xi/2 (*Gàr-NE-NE*	general	Nir-ì-da-ĝál (šakkana ÚR×A.HA^{ki})	1 lamb	
Tablala) Nir-ì-da-ĝál,	general	*Ṣi-lu-uš-^dDa-gan*	2 lambs	
(Simurum):		Ur-^dIštaran	1 lamb	
Ṣ iluš-Dagan				Studies
(Išim-Šulgi): Nuida	general	*Nu-ì-da*	2 lambs	Levine
Amar-Sin 2 xi/3	general	*Hun-hubše* (1 lamb)	1 bull, 10 sheep	115-119

Dating Places/general	and titles	names	tributes	Texts
Amar-Sin 2 xi/4 (Gàr-NE-NE Tablala), (Simurum)	general	Nir-ì-da-ĝál	1 kid	
	general	Ṣi-lu-uš-ᵈDa-gan	1 kid	
		Gir₃-ir	1 kid	
		Id-da-a, I-pi₄-iq-na-ni	2 lambs	
		ᵈŠu-ᵈŠul-gi and ᵈNin-gal-du	2 lamb	
		Bur-Ma-ma	2 lamb	mu-túm lugal Ab-ba-sa₆-g a ì-dab₅,
(Simurum)	general	Ṣi-lu-uš-ᵈDa-gan	1 lamb	
		Ur-ᵈSuen	1 lamb	
		Ša-aṭ -ra-at	2 lamb	
(NAG-suᵏⁱ)	general	Lú-ᵈNanna (šakkana Š 46 iii TIM 6 36)	1 lamb	
		Lú~ ᵈNin-šubur and Šeš-zi-mu	2 lambs	
Amar-Sin 2 xi/8 (Ebal)	general	Šu-ru-uš-ki-in	1 lamb	
		Idin-ᵈSuen	1 kid	
	prince-general	kaš-dé-a Ištar-il-šu (Prince 3 lambs)	20 bulls, 200 of flock	
Amar-Sin 2 xi/12 1. **Abi-bana** and 2. **Kakkulatum** under Irebum	general	I-re-eb-um	5 bulls, 50 of flock	
	troops	érin **A-bí-ba-na**ᵏⁱ	4 bulls, 40 of flock	
	troops	érin **Kak-ku₈-la-tum**ᵏⁱ	4 bulls, 40 of flock	
	captain 1	I-gi₄ nu-bandà,	1 bull, 10 of flock	
	captain 2	Lú-ša-lim nu-bandà,	6 of flock	
	captain 3, general	Suhuš-ki-in nu-bandà, ugula **I-re-bu-um**	6 of flock	
		Šeš-sa₆-ga (1 lamb)	6 bulls 2 deer 60 flock	
		Suhuš-ki-in and Be!?(U)-li-be-lu-uk	1 lamb each	
(Puttulium)	general	Hu-ba-a (of Dabrum)	1 lamb	
	general	Nu-ì—da	2 lamb, 1 bear	
	general	Ištar-il-šu (Prince)	1 lamb	
Amar-Sin 2 xi/14	**general**	Zi-kur-ì-lí (ugula Zi-mur-darᵏⁱ)	10 bulls, 100 of flock	
Zimudar	captain 1	Ša-lim-ku-na	1 bull, 10 rams	

续表

Dating and titles Places/general		names	tributes	Texts
under Zikur-ili with 8 captains	captain 2	Bur-^dAdad	1 bull, 9 ram+ 1 kid	
(Puzur-Haya, captain of **Sami** was under Lu-Nanna in IS 2).	captain 3	**Puzur₄-^dHa-là** (of Sami) till to IS 2 iv	1 bull, 10 rams	
	captain 4	**Šar-ru-um-ì-lí**	1 bull, 8 ram+ 2 kids	
Tahiš-en in AS 5 vii/11 was general of **S/Šitirša)**	captain 5	**Tá-hi-iš-še-en** (of Sitirša)	1 bull, 10 rams	
	captain 6	Ša-lim-be-lí	1 bull, 7 ram+ 3 kids	
	captain 7	Ir-íb(tum)-DINGIR-šu	1 bull, 8 ram+ 2 kids	
	captain 8	**A-ki-a,** nu-bandà--me	1 bull, 10 rams	
	troops	érin Zi-mu-dar^{ki} ugula Zikur-ili	15 bulls, 150 of flock	
	(general)	Šar-ru-um-ba-ni	40 fallow deer, 1 ass	
AS 2 xi/17 (**Zimudar**) under Zikur-ili	general	Zi-kur-ì-lí	1 lamb	
	captain	Šar-ru-um-ì-lí	1 lamb	
AS 4 ii/25 Tutub	troops	érin **Tu-tu-ub**^{ki} (Lu-Nanna of Maškan-abi)	1 bull, 10 of flock	AUCT 2 278
AS 4 ix/1	**general** Dayyan-ili	DI.KUD-ì-lí, máš-da-ri-a ezem-mah	2 bulls 20 ram	HUCA 29 74 3
AS 4 x/4 **Abi-bana**	troops	mu-túm érin **A-bí-ba-na**^{ki} (general Irebum)	1 bull, 20 rams	MVN 11 182 = BIN 3
	general	é—uz-ga mu-túm Dukra	1 lamb	101
AS 4 xi/3	captain?, general	**Ba-ha-ar-še-en** ugula Hu-ba-a	10 of flock,	MVN 10 130
AS 4 **Susa**, AS 5 viii, xii	**šakkana**	**A-bu-ni** MDP 10, 74 126 Trouvaille 83		MVN 04 263
AS 5 iv Maškan-Amar-Sin, Ur-Zababa under Dayyan-ili	general	Dayyan(DI.KU₅)-ì-lí received the barley of Maš-kán-^dAmar-^dSuen^{ki} Ur-^dZa-ba₆-ba₆	346 gur of barley from the majordomo	Ontario 1 168
AS 5 v/4 (**Arraphum**)	captain general	/ Sar-ni-id nu-banda₃ ugula Ha-ši-pá-tal	1 bulls, 10 of flock	CDLJ 2007:1 16
Maškan-šarrum (under)	2 chiefs	^dAmar-^dSuen-ha-ma-ti	1 bulls, 10 of flock	Abba-sagga ì-dab₅
		BAD₃-ì-lí: Maš-kan₂-šar-ru-um^{ki}—me	lú~ 1 bulls, 10 of flock	
Amar-Sin 5 v/25 **Arraphum:** under Hašip-atal	general	kaš-dé-a Ha-ši-pa₂-tal	30 fat bulls, 70 goat	PDT 1 166; mu-túm
	troops	érin Ar-ra-ap-hu-um^{ki}	20 cattle, 300 of flock	Abba-sa₆-g a ì-dab₅

Dating Places/general	and titles	names	tributes	Texts
	captain 1	*Zu-zu* nu-bandà,	1 bull, 10 rams	
	captain 2	*Mu₆-ha-a* nu-bandà,	ugula 1 bull, 10 rams	
		Ha-ši!-pa₂-tal		
AS 5 v/27 (**Arraphum**)	(general)	*A-ši-ba-tal*= *Ha-ši-pá-tal*	1 lamb, 1 ewe	Nisaba 8 382
Amar-Sin 5 vii/11	general	*Tá -hi-še-en* (till Šu-Sin 7 viii/13)	1 bull	OIP 121
S/Šitirša under Tahiš-en	**troops**, general	érin *Si-ti-ir-ša*ᵏⁱ, ugula *Tá-hi-še-en*	5 bulls	092 Ab-ba-sa₆-g
mu-túm	general	mother (ama) of *Eš₄-tar₂ -il-šu* （Prince）	1 gazelle	a ì-dab₅,
AS 5 viii/15 **Ibbal** under Šu-Dada	captain	*Wa-wa-ti* nu-bandà,	2 bulls, 20 of flock,	CST 328 CDLI
	troops, general	*érin! Íb-*ba-al*[ᵏⁱ] ugula *Šu-Da-da*	3 bulls, 30 of flock,	107843 photo
[AS 2-8 ?]/21 Ireb	general	*I-re-eb* (**Abi-bana, Kakkulatum**): 1 lamb	2 bulls 20 of flock	UDT 091
?/22 (Abal/Dašil) Išar-ramaš	general	[*I*]-*šar-ra-ma-aš* (AS 5; Š 46 ix/11 JCS 52 7 06)	60 of flock,	UDT 091
?/[28] **Adamdun** under ruler Ubaya; a priestess of **Kismar**;	troops and general	érin *A-dam-DUN*ᵏⁱ Lugal-niĝ-si-sá-e dumu~ *Gu-še*, ugula *U₁₈-ba-a*	[60?] of flock 60 of flock	UDT 091
Mahazum under	noble	*Ši-me-a-ni* ereš-digir~ ᵈMes-lam-ta-è-a *Kismar*ᵏⁱ	1 bull, 10 of flock	
Arad-mu	troops	*érin! Ma-ha-zum*ᵏⁱ, ugula Arád-mu	2 bulls, 30 of flock	
AS 5 ix/9 **1. Neber-Amar-Sin**	general	ᵈNanna-i₃-gi?	6 bulls, 2 of flock,	MVN 11 140
under Arad-mu	troops	érin ***Ne-be₂-er-ᵈAmar-ᵈSuen***ᵏⁱ	35 oxen, 540 of flock,	
	captain?	*Ru-uš-dam* dumu *Ba-ak-ti Ši*ₓ-*maški*	200 of flock,	
	captain?	*Ga-ra-du* dumu gal-PI	6 bulls,	
	captain? general	*Na-he₂-zi* dumu *Ib-da-at;* ugula Arád-mu	4 bulls	
2. Nugar under Dukra	troops, general	érin ***Nu-ga-ar***ᵏⁱ ugula *Du-uk-ra*	2 bulls, 20 of flock,	
3. **Dur-Ebla** under man Nur-ili		*Nu-úr-ì-lí* lú *Dur-Eb-la*ᵏⁱ: 1 lamb	1 bull, 10 of flock	
AS 5 ix/11	general	*Šu-ru-uš-ki-in*: 44 asses,	5 bulls, 60 flock	SET 10
Ebal under Šuruš-kin	troops	érin *E-ba-al*ᵏⁱ ugula *Šu-ru-uš-ki-in*	15 bulls, 105 of flock	

续表

Dating **Places**/general	and titles	names	tributes	Texts
Bàd-An^{ki}**-zi** under *Il-ili^{li}* (see Nur-ì-da-ĝál on ŠS 3 ix/13)	general	DINGIR-*li-lí*: 10 asses, 7 bears	6 bulls, 100 of flock,	
	captain	*Ilšu-kin* nu-bandà,	1 bull, 10 rams	
	troops	érin Bàd-an-ki-zi^{ki} ugula *Il-ili^{li}*	17 bulls, 400 of flock	Ab-ba-sa₆-ga i₃-dab₅
Išim-Šulgi, under Nu-ì-da	**general**	*Nu-ì-da*	10 bulls, 100 rams	1873
	captain	^dNanše nu-bandà,	2 bulls, 20 rams	
	captain	*Šu-Èr-ra*	1 bull, 10 rams	
	captain	*Ú-bar*	1 bull, 10 rams	
	captain	*Za-rí-iq*	1 bull, 10 rams	
	captain	*I-pí-iq*-DINGIR	1 bull, 10 rams	
	captain	*Su-uk-su-uk*	1 bull, 10 rams	
	captain	*I-mi-íd*-DINGIR nu-bandà–me	1 bull, 10 rams	
	troops general	with **érin *I-šim-^dŠul-gi*^{ki}** ugula *Nu-ì-da*	17 bulls, 140 of flock	
Gàr-ne-ne and **Tablala,** under Nir-ì-da-ĝál (ÚR× A.HA^{ki} TCL 5 6041, AS 2; ŠS 3 ix/13 Bàd-An)	captain 1	*Šu-^dNin-šubur* nu-bandà,	1 bull, 10 rams	
	troops 1	érin~ ***Gàr-NE.NE*^{ki}**	4 bulls, 300 of flock	
	captain 2	*Hu-un~ha-ab-b*ur nu-bandà,	1 bull, 10 rams	
	troops 2, general	**érin *Tab-la-la*^{ki}** ugula Nir-ì-da-ĝál (šakkana)	2 bulls, 60 of flock	
Amar-Sin 5 ix/14 **Zibere** under Masasa	general	*Má-sa₆-sa₆*	2 bulls and 30 goats	JEOL 33 114 02
	troops, general	érin ***Zi-bi₂-re*^{ki}** ugula Má-sa₆-sa₆	2 bulls, 210 goats	
Amar-Sin 5 ix/24 1. **Abal,** under Išar-ramaš	**general**	**Išar-ramaš**	9 bull 150 of flock	
	captain 1	*Puzur₄-ma-ma*	1 bull, 10 of flock	MVN 15 350, 27
	captain 2	SI.A-a	1 bull, 10 of flock	bulls, 530 of flock:
	captain 3	*I-din-É-a*	1 bull, 10 of flock	
	captain 4	*Šu-ga-tum* nu-bandà–me	1 bull, 10 of flock	
	troops	érin *A-ba-al*^{ki}	6 bulls, 200 of flock	

Dating Places/general	and titles	names	tributes	Texts
2. **Dašil**, Išar-ramaš	captain 1	*Bur-dAdad*	1 bull, 10 flock	of goats are ¼ - 1/6 of
	captain 2	*Šu-dNin-šubur nu-bandà---me*	1 bull, 10 flock	sheep;
	troops general	**and** érin *Da-ši-il*ki ugula *Išar-ramaš*	*6 bulls, 60 of flock	
AS 5 ix/24 **Marhaši**: Abuni	soldiers general	and **agà-ús** lú *Mar-ha-ši*ki, ugula *A-bu-ni*	60 of flock,	Nik. 2 484
Amar-Sin 6 ii/19	captain general	and *Šu-ru-uš-ki-in* nu-bandà, ugula *Nu-ì-da*	1 bull, 10 sheep,	Ontario 1 072
AS 7 viii/14 **Ibbal**	troops	to Me-dIštaran, mu-túm érin *Íb-ba-al*ki	5 bulls, 50 of flock	OrSP 47-49 32
[AS 4 xii/7- AS 7]/ **(Ya(Ni)darašpi**		[...]-ar¹ kuš7	[1+] bull, [20] flock	sent to é-udu-niga of
under Lugal-má-gur8-re	captain	[...]-dŠul-gi nu-bandà,	0, [20] ram	**Eshnunna**
	troops, general	érin *NI-da-ra-aš-pí*ki, [ugula] *Lugal-má-gur8-re*	[1]40 of flock	PDT 2 0959 with
2. **Hamazi** under gov. Ur-Iškur	?	*I-gi4-ru¹-*mah?*	[1] bull	*Šara-kam, gov. of
	governor	Ur-dIškur énsi *Ha-ma-zi2*ki	116+ of flock	Girsu
3. **Rabi**	troops 1	[érin] *Ra-bí*ki	140 of flock	during AS 4 xii/7- AS 7;
	captain	**Ù-ne** nu-banda3	[2]0 of flock =160	
Rabi (BIN 3) AS 7 viii/13	troops 1	érin *Ra-bí*ki	5 bulls, 164 of flock	
4. **Arman**	troops 1	[érin] *Ar-ma-an*ki	140 of flock	and BIN 3 139
Arman (BIN 3)	troops 3	érin *Ar-ma-an*ki	5 bulls, 290 of flock,	AS 7 viii/13
5. **Išum**	troops 2	[érin] *I-šum-ma*ki	[14]0 of flock	
Išum (BIN 3)	troops 2	érin *I-šum-ma*ki	1 bull, 26 of flock	
	captain	**U4-ni** nu-bandà (Rabi and Išum),	1 bulls, 10 rams	
6. **Tiran**	troops 3	[érin] *Ti-ra-an*ki	[10]+10 of flock	
	captain	**[Lu]gal-ezem** nu-bandà,	[10]+ 10 maš2-gal	
Tiran (BIN 3)	troops 4	érin *Ti-ra-an*ki	1 bull, 18 rams	
	captain	**Lugal-ezem** nu-bandà,	1 bull, 10 rams	
7. **Ebal**, under Šuruš-kin	general	Šuruš-kin	30 of flock	
	troops	érin *E-ba-al*ki ugula Šuruš-kin	280 of flock	

Dating and titles Places/general		names	tributes	Texts
AS 8 iii/13 Išim-Šulgi, Nuida	1. troops/gener al	érin *I-šim-ᵈŠul-gi*ᵏⁱ ugula *Nu-ì-da*	17 bulls	Studies Astour 369
2. **Maškan-šarrum**, under Nahšum-bal; 3.	troops/gener al	érin *Maš-kán-šar-ru-um*ᵏⁱ, ugula *Na-ah-šum-BALA*	9 bulls	Nesbit A
Maškan-abi under Inim-ᵈNanna (Prince)	troops/gener al	érin *Maš-kán-a-bí*ᵏⁱ, ugula Inim-ᵈNanna	8 bulls	
4. **Išur**, under Itib-šinat	troops/gener al	érin *I-šur₆*ᵏⁱ (L Lxlagab), *I-ti-ib-ši-na-at*	ugula 10 bulls	
5. **Puttulium**, under Hubaya	troops/gener al	érin *Pu-ut-tu-li-um*ᵏⁱ ugula *Hu-ba-a*	8 bulls	
	ĝìr~ Lú–*ša-lim qar-du*, lú~ *kin-gi₄-a*~ lugal, mu-túm (4 udu *Bu-zi*)		total: 52 bulls	
AS 8 v/8 1. **Arraphum**: troops/ under Puzur-Šulgi, son general of Hašipatal		érin **A-ra-ap-hu-um**, ugula *Puzur₄*-ᵈŠul-gi dumu~ *Ha-ši-pa₂-tal*ᵏⁱ (lú *Mar-ha-ši*ᵏⁱ)	20 bulls	AUCT 3 484
2. **Durmaš** under Šu-Šul-gi	troops/gener al	érin~ *Dur-maš*ᵏⁱ ugula *Šu-*ᵈŠul-gi	5 bulls ₄	ki-bi [gi₄]-a Ab-ba-sa₆-a
[Amar-Sin 7 iv/30-ŠS] 1. **URU×A**ᵏⁱ under Šeš-kal-la	soldiers elder	agà-ús~ URU×Aᵏⁱ--me-éš, ugula Šeš-kal-la	1 bull, 10 of flock	BPOA 7 2350
2. **Bí-da-dun**ᵏⁱ under Apilaša;		ab-ba~ lú- *Bí-da-dun*ᵏⁱ, ugula *Á -pi-la-ša*	1 bull, 10 of flock	
6.1 **Šu-Irhum**	troops 1	érin *Šu-Ir-hu-um*ᵏⁱ	[x]+6 bulls	
6.2 **Šu-ah** and	troops 2	érin *Šu-ah*ᵏⁱ	[x]+3 bulls	
6.3 **Gáb -la-aš**: under **Ì-la-lum**	troops 3/general	érin *Gáb -la-aš*ᵏⁱ ĝìr~ *É-a-ra-bí*, ugula *Ì-la-lum*	[x]+2 bulls	
7. **Zagtum**: Šeš-kal-la	troops/gener al	érin *Za₃-tum*ᵏⁱ, ugula Šeš-kal-la	10 bulls '	
8. **Ebla** under **Nur-iii**	troops/gener al	érin Dur~ *Eb-la*ᵏⁱ, [ugula] *Nu-ur₂-ì-lí*	7 [bulls]	
9. (**captain** of Sami)	captain	DI.KU₅-[ì]-lí, (captain of Sami)	5 of flock	
AS 8	tribute of AS 8	gú mu en~ Eriduᵏⁱ ba-huĝ	1200 rams:	StOr 09-1 30
AS 9 viii/26 **Adamdun** under 9 Ubaya	tribute of AS gú **troops, general**	9th year (en Nanna Karzida) érin *A-dam-DUN*ᵏⁱ, ĝìr~ KAL-ᵈŠul-gi ra-gaba, ugula *U₁₈-ba-a	1200 of flock,	

Dating and titles Places/general		names	tributes	Texts
[Amar-Sin 7 iv/30-ŠS] **1.　URU×A**^{ki}　under Šeš-kal-la **2.　Bí-da-dun**^{ki}　under Apilaša;	soldiers elder	agà-ús~ URU×A^{ki}--me-éš, ugula Šeš-kal-la ab-ba~ lú- Bí-da-dun^{ki}, ugula Á -pi-la-ša	1 bull, 10 of flock 1 bull, 10 of flock	of BPOA 7 2350
[AS?]　**Tiran**　under (troops) Šarrum-bani		tribute (gú) Ti-ra-an^{ki}, ugula Šar-ru-um-ba-ni	1 bull, 18 of flock	of TAD 54
[AS?]　**Harši**　under captain Hunhab'ur　(šakkana general on **Š** 45 vii Trouv. 86)		ki Iq-bí-DINGIR-ma Za-rí-qum nu-bandà, ì-dab₅, ugula Hu-un-ha-ab-ur, šà Ha-ar-si^{ki}	11 oxen **Tablala** in 10)	(of TJAMC IES SET 337 (pl. 68)
[Amar-Sin　　　?] troops and **Iš-ne-ka**/dan　under **general Ş iluš-Šulgi**		[érin] Iš-ne-kal/dan^{ki}, nu-bandà, Ú-ni-ba-tal ugula Şe-lu-uš-^{d}Da-gan	1 bull, 6 of flock	Princeton 2 194

Table 4　the Tributes of Generals (ugula) and Troops during the Reign of Šu–Sin

(Amar-Sin 8 v/5 - ŠS xiii/16) **Zababa** under I-gi₄, **Uşar-^{d}Šulgi** under Ahuni?				
	1 captain 1	Ur-^{d}Nin-geš-zi-[da]	1 bull, 10 rams	MVN 11 181
	captain 2	Za-la-KA	1 bull, 10 rams	
	chiefs of 60 men lú ruler of geš₂-da-me, **Zababa**	ugula~　　geš₂-da-me,　　ugula~ ugula　　La-la-a　**lú~** ^{d}**Za-ba₄-ba₄**^{ki}--me ugula I-gi₄	18+3=21 rams	
	captain	Zu-la-lum	1 bull, 10 of flock	
	soldiers	agà-ús--me ugula DINGIR.KAL	20 of flock	
	general	A-pi-la-ša	2 lambs	
	ruler	I-za-nu-um lú **Ú-şa-ar-^{d}Šul-gi**^{ki}	1 kid	
	general	A-hu-ni (of **Abi-bana** and **Kakkulatum**)	1 bull, 10 of flock	
Šu-Sin 1 ix/6 1. **Ebal:** Šuruš-kin 2 **Harši:** Iti-Dagan	general troops/general governor general	Šu-ru-uš-ki-in érin E-ba-al^{ki} [ugula] Šuruš-kin / Iši-Wer énsi Ha-ar-ši^{ki} ugula Iti-^{d}Dagan	[1 bull 9]+1 of flock [11] bulls 1700 of flock, bears	MVN 03 338; 2 mu-túm, In-ta-è-a
3. **Šurbu** (érin Šu-úr-bu^{ki} AS men 4-5 YOS 15 158)	Tahiš-atal?) general captain	(under Šu-Tišpak, Ištar-kin, Dagi, Šu-Ištar Erra-bani I-ti-ga: lú Šu-ur₃-bu^{ki}-me or I-ti-^{d}Suen	8+4+2+2+2+2 = 20 ì-dab₅ of flock 1 bull, 10 of flock	
[Šu-Sin] 1. **Terqa:** Šeš-kal-la	troops/general	érin Ti-ir-ga^{ki} [ugula] Šeš-kal-la Zagtum)	(see [11?] ram 9 goats	
2. Dašil: Adad-dani (after Išar-ramaš on AS 5 ix/24)	general captain troops/general	[^{d}Adad]-da-ni (of Dašil) [...] x -tim érin **Da-ši-il**^{ki} ugula ^{d}Iškur-da-ni	[2 bulls], 20 of flock [1 bull, 10 of flock] [3 bulls 30] šà 60 flock	of Trouvaille 54

3. [...]	captain	x-si-ṣ um	10 rams šà 20	
	20 chiefs of 60	ugula~ géš-da-bí~ 20--me-éš	10 rams	
	[troops]	[érin xxxx]	2 bulls šà 4	
4. Ur-gu-ha-lam	troops/general	érin Ur-gu-ha-lam^ki	3 bulls, 30 of flock	
5. Maškan-garaš: Amur-ili	troops, general	érin Maš-kán-ga-raš^sar-ki A-mur-diĝir	ugula 1 bull, 10 of flock	
6. [A?]-šur₅^ki under Nur-Ištar	troops/general	[érin A?]-šur₅^ki [ugula Nu]-ú-Ištar	[1] bull, 10 of flock	
Šu-Sin 2 viii/17	governor	I-re-eb énsi~ Lu-lu-bu^ki	383 of flock	Ontario 1 132
Šu-Sin 3 0/00 (**Arraphum**)	general	Puzur₄-^dŠul-gi dumu Ha-ši-pá-tal (lú 1 sila₄ kišib~ Mar-ha-ši^ki and Arraphum)		CT 32 36
ŠS 3 ix/13 **Bàd-An/Der** (with **Tablala**) Nir-ì-da-ĝál	captain under general **gú~ ma-da**	Za-li-a nu-bandà, lú~ Bàd-AN^ki ugula Nir-ì-da-ĝál, mu-túm	1 bull and 10 of flock	SA 050a = SA 004
Šu-Sin 4 x (**Sami**) Dayyan-ili	captain	DI.KU₅-ì-li, gift of ezem-mah of Sin	2 bulls, 20 rams	HUCA 29 74 3
Šu-Sin [3-9], **Išum** under Waṣum-^dŠulgi	ruler/general troops **gú~ ma-da**, ĝir~ Iti-Erra lú~ kin-gi₄-a~ lugal ù Abi-li 12 bulls 400 rams	Waṣum-^dŠulgi érin I-šum^ki, ugula Waṣum-^dŠul-gi	8 bulls, 220 rams 4, 180 of flock	MVN 08 222
	kurušda			
Šu-Sin 6 or 8 ix/13 **1. Šu-Suen-ì-du₁₀** under Nanna-igi-du	general	Nanna-igi-du	2 bulls, 20 of flock	
	captain	x-me-x-ri? nu-bandà	1 bull, 10 rams	
	troops	érin ^dŠu-^dSuen-i₃-du₁₀^ki _____ ugula ^dNanna-igi-du	[8 bulls, 80 rams]	AUCT 3 198
2. Daltum under Tahiš-atal	general	Tahiš-atal	ugula	
	captain 1	Lugal-ezem nu-bandà,	1 bull, 10 rams	
	men (lú)	Išar-libbi lú Da-al-tum^ki-me-eš₂	5 rams	
"Tribute of Lands"	**gú~ ma-da**	(sum)	12 bulls,, 125 sheep	
3. Šurbu, under Tahiš-atal	soldiers general	**agà-ús** lú~ Šu-ur₂-bu^ki-me Tahiš-atal [In]-ta-e₃-a **ì-dab₅.**	ugula 52 of flock,	
Šu-Sin 7 iii/25 **Puttulium** under Ibni-Šulgi	captain	Šarrum-bani nu-bandà	10 rams	RA 09 054
	troops	érin Puttulium ugula Ibni-Šulgi	80 rams	AM 14 (pl.7)
	gú~ ma-da, mu-túm, ĝìr~ Ad-da-mu lú-kin-gi₄-a lugal		90 of flock	

	general ugula	Arád-mu	ugula	
Šu-Sin 7 viii/13	general/ruler	Unap-atal	30 bulls, 240 of	
gú~ ma-da			flock	CHEU 006 =
	captain 1	*Šar-ra-a*	1 bull, 1 ram	DoCu 006;
1. Urbilum	captain 2	*Da-še*	1, 1	
under Unap-atal	captain 3	*Gi-ib-la-ta-gú*	1, 1	115 gud, 248
	captain 4	*Ha-na-am*	1, 1	udu
with 8 captains	captain 5	*E?-ni-x-[x]-um*	1, 1	**gú~ ma-da**
110 bulls, 248 of flock	captain 6-7	x-x-[...]	1, 1, 1, 1	mu-túm,
	captain 8	A-da-x	[3] bulls, 1 ram	In-ta-è-[a]
	troops	érin *Ur-bi₂-lum*ki ĝìr~ Unap-atal	70 bulls	**ì-dab₅,**
2. Šitirša	ruler/captain	Tahiš-en (see AS 5 vii/11)	1 bull, 0	
under Tahiš-en	troops	érin Šetirša^{ki} ĝìr~ Tahiš-en,	4 bulls, 0	
	general	ugula Ṣ iluš-Dagan		
Šu-Sin 7 xi/2	man = ruler	Tabban-Darah	6, 80	MVN 18 044
	man = ruler	Tešup-šelah	1, 10	
Azaman	his wife	*Ad-du* dam-a-ni	1, 10	
under Ṣ__iluš-Dagan	captain under *U₃-zi* nu-bandà, lú ***A-za-ma-an***ki		1, 10	
	general			
	gú~ ma-da, mu-túm, In-ta-è-a **ì-dab₅**		(sum) 9 gud 110	
			udu	
Šu-Sin 9 xi/15	elders	[ab]-ba ***Tu-tu-ub***ki-meš	[1] bull, [10] of	ASJ 03 068
Tutub, Dašil,			flock	01
Maškan-kalatum (=abi?)	elders	ab-ba ***Da(tá)-ši-il***ki-me-eš₂	[1] bull, [1]0 of	mu-túm
under Šamaš-bani			flock	lugal
	elders,	ab-ba ***Maš-kán-kà(ga)-la-tum***ki-	1 bull, 10 of flock	
	general	-me-éš: ugula ᵈUTU-*ba-ni* (after		
		Išar-ramaš)		
Šu-Sin 9 0/0	captain	Lú-*ša-lim* nu-bandà,	1 bull	Trouvaille 50
	troops, general	érin *Ar-ma-an*ki, ugula *Á-pi-la-ša*	3 bulls	
Šu-Sin 9 **xi**/ 18	elders	ab-ba~ ***Gàr-NE.NE***ki-me-éš	2 bulls, 30 of flock,	MVN 08 195
Gàr-NE.NE and ***Tab-la-la*** elders		[ab-ba]~ ***Tab-la-la***ki-me-éš	[1] bull, 10 of flock	
under Ṣ__iluš-Dagan	general	Ṣi-lu-uš-ᵈDa-gan	5+ of flock, 3 bears	
Lu-Nanna	general	Lú-ᵈNanna and *Ilum-KI-ma-at*	1 lambs each	

3. The gú~ ma-da Tribute from Generals, Captains and their Troops on the Northeast Frontier during Ibbi-Sin 1-2/iv

The tributes from the armies on the frontier in our list are titled as "the tributes of the lands", (gú ma-da) and recorded as two parts: the first part in Ibbi-Sin 1 is possibly for the last part of the last year since it only includes 4 generals, only one of whom delivered 1 bull and 5 cities with their 7 captains each delivered one bull, and no troops are recorded.

Table 5 The Frontier Tributes (g ~ \<mada>) of the First Year of Ibbi–Sin (CT 32 19 = Nisaba 8 019 P108667)

Cities	Commanding generals (ugula) with tribute	town 1 and his captains' tribute	towns 2 and its captain's tribute	total
Abi-bana and Kakkulatum (see no 3 below)	**Ahuni son of Irebum** 1 bull	**Nur-Ištar** at **Abi-bana** with 1 bull	**Nabi-Suen** at **Kakkulatum** with 1 bull	3 bull
Išim-Šulgi (see no 1 below)	Ṣ iluš-Dagan zero	**Agu-ali** at **Išim-Šulgi** 1 bull		1 bull
Kišgati (see no 6 below)	**Ṣiluš-Šulgi**, zero	**2 captains of Kišgati: Šu-Mama** 1 bull, **Damqum** 1 bull		2 bull
Maškan-abi with Tutub (see no 7 below)	[ugula] **Lú-Nanna** of **Maškan-abi, zero** tribute	**2 captains of Tutub: Bar-ra**：2 cows for 1 fat **bull**, and **Šalim-ahum**, 1 bull		1 bull, 2 cows

The second part of the list records the bulls and flock delivered as the Tributes of the Lands (g ú ma–da) for Ibbi–Sin 2 i–iv and has more cities, officials and armies and more bulls and flock. It includes 7 generals, 4 of them appear in the next year's list recording 12 cities and 12 armies. The rate of bull and flock is 1:10, i.e. most deliveries consist of the times of 1 bull and 10 flock. In our text, and the 26 captains each delivers 1 bull and 10 of flock: 11 captains of Išim–Šulgi, 3 captains of Šami and 1 of Ibbal in Zimudar, 2 captains at Abi–bana and Kakkulatum, 1 captain at Maškan–ušuri, 3 captain at Put–šadar, 2 captain at Kišgati, 2 captains of Tutub and 1 at (Maškan–abi) in Maškan–abi. Among them, Agu–ali a captain, of Išim–Šulgi, 2 captains of Abi–bana and Kakkulatum, 2 captains of Kišgati and 2 of Tutub are listed in both Ibbi–Sin 1st and 2nd year.

Table 6 Armies with their Tributes in Month iv of the 2nd Year of Ibbi–Sin (and before)

Cities	generals/**ugula**	town, and captains and with tribute	town, army with tribute
1. **Išim-Šulgi**	Ṣ iluš-Dagan (at **Simurum**): 10 bulls, 100 rams	**11 captains of Išim-Šulgi: 1 bull 10 ram Ili-tappi I; 2 bull** 10 rams [..]-a;1 bull 10 rams **Puzur-abih**; 1 bull 10 rams **Šulgi-ili**; 1 bull 10 rams **Ili-şili**; 1 bull 10 rams **Nur-Adad**; 1 bull 10 rams **Agu-ali** (also in part of IS 1); 1 bull, 10 rams **Zariq**, 1 bull 10 rams **Zayanum**; 1 bull 10 rams **Ili-tappi II**; 2 bull 20 rams **Igihalum**:	**the army at Išim-Šulgi:** 17 bulls, 135 rams + 35 goats =170 of flock; the commander **ugula** is Ṣ iluš-Dagan
(SH46 **xi**/ 00)	*A-ki-a* lú~ Zi-mu-dar[ki]		Rochester 231 Girsu
(Š 47 **xi**/28)	**Zimudar** under , [ugula] Zikur-ili	6 captains: *La-ma-ha-ar* 1 bull, 10 rams, *Tá-hi-(iš)-še-en₆* 1 bull, 10 rams, ***Bur-ᵈAdad*** 1 bull, 10 rams, *A-bu-da-a* 1 bull, 10 rams, ***Šar-ru-um-ì-lí***, 1 bulls, 10 of flock, *[Puzur₄-ᵈ]Ha-là* [...] (captain of **Sami**)	11+2 bulls, 130 of flock **érin** *Zi-mur-dar*[ki] (OrSP 18 pl. 04 12)
(AS 2 xi) *Zi-mur-dar*[ki]	*Zi-kur-i-lí* 10 bulls, 100 of flock	1 bull, 10 rams ***Puzur₄-ᵈHa-là*** (of Sami) *Ša-lim-ku-na,* ***Bur-ᵈAdad, Šar-ru-um-ì-lí,*** *Tá-hi-iš-še-en* (of Sitirša), *Ša-lim-be-lí, Ir-íb*-DINGIR-*šu* and *A-ki-a,* nu-bandà—me **each** 1 bull, 10 rams	**érin** *Zi-mu-dar*[ki] ugula *Zikur-ili* 15 bulls, 150 of flock (Studies Levine 115-119)
2. **Zimudar** with **2a. Šami, 2b. Íb-ba-al**	**Lu-Nanna** of **Zimudar** with 2 bull, 20 rams: ugula of the two armies	3 captains of **Šami:** 1 bull 10 rams **Dayyani-ili;** 1 bull, 10 rams, **Puzur-Haya;** 1 bull, 10 rams, **Ikun-mišar**. **20 chief of 60 men:** 1 bull, 10 rams; 1 captain of **Ibbal: Lú -ᵈNin-šubur**, 2 bulls and 20 rams	**the army at Šami:** 4 bulls, 37 rams+3 goats =40 **the army at Ibbal:** 3 bulls, 25 rams+ 5 goats=30

Cities	generals/**ugula**	town, and captains and with tribute	town, army with tribute
3a. Abi-bana		1 captain at **Abi-bana**: [Nur-Ištar] with 1 bull, 10 rams, who is also in the part of IS 1	the army at **Abi-bana**: 4 bulls, 35 rams + 5 goats=40
3b. Puh-zigar **3c. Kakkula-tum**	**Ahuni, son of Irebum**, with 2 bull, 20 rams	1 captain at **Kakkulatum** (and **Puh-zigar?**): Nabi-Suen with 1 bull, 10 rams; (there is no captain here for **Puh-zigar**)	the army at **Puh-zigar**: 1 bull, 10 rams, **the army** at **Kakkulatum**: 3 bull, 25 rams+5 goats=40
4. Maškan-ušuri	**Kurb-ilak**: zero tribute	1 captain at **Maškan-ušuri**: 2 bull, 13 rams, 7 goats, **Amar-Mama**	army at **Maškan-ušuri**: 1 bull 10 rams,
5. Put-šadar	**Humzum**, 2 bull, 20 rams	3 captain at **Put-šadar**: 1 bull, 10 rams, **Zayanum**, 1 bull, 10 rams, **AN-[...]**, 1 [bull], 10 rams, **Arši-ah**; <u>The 20 chief of 60 men:</u> 1 bull, 10 rams	the army at **Put-šadar**: 4 bulls, 34 rams+6 goats=40
6. Kišgati:	**Šiluš-Šulgi** with 2 bull, 20 rams,	2 captain at **Kišgati**: 1 bull, 10 rams, **Šu-Mama II**, 1 bull, 10 rams, **Damqum** (both also in the part of IS 1)	the army at **Kišgati**: 8 bull, 61 rams+19 goats=80
(ŠS 5 xi/8)	**Šiluš-Šulgi** 1 lamb	1 lamb **Šu-Mama II**, 1 lamb, **Damqum** (of 2 captain at **Kišgati**); 1 lamb **Bar-ra** (of **Tutub**). 1 lamb **Laqip** (of **Maškan-abi**))	mu-túm~ lugal (TJSASE 115)
7a. Tutub **7b. Maškan-abi**	**Lu-Nanna** of **Maškan-abi** and Tutub 2 bull, 20 rams	2 captains of **Tutub**: 1 bull, 10 rams, **Šalim-ahum** and 1 bull, 10 rams, **Bar-ra**, both also in the part of IS 1	**the army at Tutub**: 6 bull, 47 rams+13 goats=60
		1 captain at (**Maškan-abi**): **Laqip**, 1 bull, 10 rams,	the army at **Maškan-abi**: 8 bull, 80 of flock
7' máš -da- ri-a **Lu-Nanna** of **Maškan-abi** behalf **Maškan-abi**		on The maš₂-da-ri-a tribute in ezem-mah (10th month), the delivery for the king is not of taken: 2 bulls for 1 fattened bull, and 10 rams, via AN-sukkal, ambassador of king and Suhuš-kin, fattener	

4. The Estimated Numbers of the Troops of Ur III Empire in 12 Military Towns of Northeast Frontier according to their Tributes: 130,800

Since in Zimudar and Put–šadar, the 20 chiefs of 60 men (ugula–géš 20–meš), who represented 1200 men, contributed 1 bull and 10 rams (or sheep and goats) and each captain delivered the same amount, we suppose that every 1200 men in the frontier should have contributed one norm, i.e. 1 bull and 10 flock to the king of the Ur III dynasty, as the tribute of the land (g ú ma–da), so that the 1 bull and 10 rams/flock is considered here as one tribute norm contributed by every 1200 men. Each captain who delivered 1 norm of animals might command 1200 men, i.e. 20 teams of 60 men. S#iluš–Dagan of Išim–Šulgi, a great general of a big military zone with his numerous captains and mass troops in the first place of the list, contributed more norms than the smaller generals: he himself delivered 10 norms, 10 bulls and 100 rams, which might be on behalf the troops of 12000 directly commanded by him, the 11 captains under his command paid 13 norms (2 captains paid 2 norms if they are not copy mistakes), which might represent 15,600 soldiers under them, and the army belonging to Išim–Šulgi contributed 17 norms of tribute, which might imply that their number was 20, 400 men, and the total of men at the Išim–Šulgi province is 48000. The second great general was Lu–Nanna of Maškan–abi and Tutub in the Diyala province, who was the last general in the list, and himself paid 3 norms for the two cities, 3 captains under him 3 norms of animals and the armies in two cities 14 norms, and total is

24000 men, a half of Išim–Šulgi. The third is Lu–Nanna of Zimudar, who governed two cities, Šami and Ibbal (*Íb–ba–al*), and he paid 2 norms, the 4 captains with 20 chiefs of 60 men 6 norms, and 3 armies of the two cities 7 norms, total 18000 men. The fourth is Şiluš–Šulgi of Kišgati who delivered 12 norms of bull and flock, which might represent 14400 men. The fifth is Humzum of Put–šadar who and 3 captains with 20 chiefs of 60 men and his army contributed 10 norms of animals, total 12000 men. The sixth and seventh generals are Ahuni, son of Irebum, of Abi–bana and Kakkulatum who might have 10800 men and Kurb–ilak of the new town of Maškan–ušuri who himself did not deliver tribute and might only command 3600 men. Note that general nos. 1 and 2 at Išim–Šulgi and Maškan–abi and Tutub, and no. 4 of Kišgati and no. 6 of Abi–bana and Kakkulatum are mentioned as the four area that also paid tributes in Ibbi–Sin 1, which may mean that the smallest military town as Maškan–ušuri might pay tribute less regularly.

In below, we have calculated how many men were led by a certain general and how many men were garrisoned in a certain city according to the tribute norms that he and they sent to the king. The total is 130800 men.

Table 7. Estimated Numbers of the troops in towns and under each genaral: Total 130,800

Cities	generals with tribute norms	convert to nos of men	captains with the tribute norms	convert to nos of men	army with tribute10800 norms	covert to men	total of men of a general
1. Išim-Šulgi	Ş iluš-Dag an (Simurum)1 0 bulls, 100 rams	12000	11 captains: 9 sent 1 bull 10 rams and 2 men sent 2 bull 20 rams=13 norms	15600	the army at Išim- Šulgi 17 bull, 170 of flock = 17 norms	20400	48000 men
2. Zimudar with Šami and Ibbal	Lu-Nanna of Zimudar with 2 bull, 20 rams = 2 norms	2400	3 captains of Šami: 3 bull 30 rams, 20 chief of 60 men: 1 bull, 10 rams: = 4 norms	4800	the army at Šami: 4 bull, 40 of flock	4800	12000 + 6000 = 18000
			1 captain of Ib₂-bal: 2 bulls and 20 rams	2400	the army at Ibbal: 3 bulls, 30 of flock	3600	
3a. Abi-bana	Ahuni, son of Irebum,	2400	1 captain at Abi-bana: [Nur-Ištar] with 1 bull, 10 rams	1200	the army at Abi-bana: 4 bulls, 40 flock	1200	2400+ 2400+60
3b Puh-zigar, 3c Kakkula-tum	with 2 bull, 20 rams		1 captain at Kakkulatum (and Puh-zigar?): Nabi-Suen with 1 bull, 10 rams	1200	the army at Puh-zigar: 1 bull, 10 rams, at Kakku- latum: 3 bull, 30 of flock	4800	00 = 10800
4. Maškan-ušuri	Kurb-ilak: zero tribute		1 captain at Maškan-ušuri: 2 bull, 20 rams and goats, Amar-Mama	2400	the army at Maškan-ušuri: 1 bull, 10 rams, Kurb-ilak,	1200	3600
5. Put-šadar	Humzum, 2 bull, 20 rams = 2 norms	2400	3 captain at Put-šadar: 1 bull, 10 rams Zayanum, 1 bull 10 rams AN-[...], 1 [bull], 10 rams, Arši-ah; The 20 chief of 60 men: 1 bull, 10 rams	3600 / 1200	the army at Put-šadar: 4 bulls, 40 of flock ugula Humzum,		2400 + 4800 + 4800 =12000

续表

Cities	generals with tribute norms	convert to nos of men	captains with the tribute norms	convert to nos of men	army with tribute10800 norms	covert to men	total of men of a general
6. Kišgati:	Şiluš-Šulgi 2 bull, 20 rams	2400	**2 captain:** 1 bull, 10 rams, **Šu-Mama II,** 1 bull, 10 rams **Damqum**	2400	the army at **Kišgati:** 8 bull, 80 of flock	9600	**14400**
7a. **Maškan-abi,** 7b Tutub	Lu-Nanna of Maškan-abi 2 bull, 20 rams for Tutub	2400	**2 captains of Tutub:** 1 bull, 10 rams, Šalim-ahum and 1 bull, 10 rams, Bar-ra	2400	the army at Tutub: 6 bull, 60 ram /goats = 6 norms	7200	**22800**
			1 captain at (**Maškan-abi**): Laqip, 1 bull, 10 rams,	1200	the army at **Maškan-abi:** 8 bull, 80 of flock,	9600	
7' maš$_2$-da-ri-a	Lu-Nanna		The **máš-da-ri-a tribute in ezem-mah** (10th month): 1 fattened bull, and 10 rams: on behalf of **Maškan-abi**				**1200**
total							**130800**

5. The Failure of the Simurum Campaign and the Falling of the Ur III Empire

After the tributes were collected from 12 military towns in his 2nd year, King Ibbi–Sin launched his first campaign against the land of Simurum, the land destroyed by Šulgi for the ninth time at Šulgi 43rd year and the famous Şiluš–Dagan was installed by Šulgi as the governor there. In our list, this famous general now became the general of Išim–Šulgi, which implies that he had lost the control to Simurum. The 3rd year name of Ibbi–Sin proves that the campaign was launched in his 2nd year. The campaign must have not won a victory at all since the royal distributing center of animal tributes, Puzriš–Dagan, where all our texts came from, was closed in the end of Ibbi–Sin 2, with the last day of xii/23[①].

The king could not launch any new campaigns in the next 11 years. Two years latter, in his 4th year (the 5th year name), he had to marry his daughter to the prince of Zabšali, a humble political marriage which never occurred in the Ur dynasty for 41 years since Šulgi 29th year (30th year name) when a princess of Šulgi was married to Anšan. Zabšali was defeated by Šu–Sin in his 6th year, eight year ago. In his fifth year (the 6th year name), Ibbi–Sin had to build the new city walls in both Ur and Nippur, which shows that the enemies were coming near to the political and religious capitals.

Only ten years latter in his 13th year, could king Ibbi–Sin launch his second campaign against Susa, Adamdun and Awan in the East Frontier in Iran, which must have been failure one again, since ten years later, the king was captured by the troops from Elamites from Iran, and his falling country came to the end. The year names which record the important events of the state under Ibbi–Sin are as follows.

---

① Puzur–Enlil's archive was finished on IS 2 xii/17 (BIN 3 608, P106415), that of Aba–Enlil-gin₇ on IS 2 xii/25 (AUCT 3 071; if AUCT 1 848 iti-{diri} is not a erase. he was in IS 2 xiii); Ur–kug–nun–na and In-ta-è-a on IS 2 xii/15 (Nisaba 08, 061,) Šulgi-uru–mu with Ur–kug-nun–na on IS 2 xii /23 (Akkadica 114–115, 102 32); In-ta-è-a on IS 2 xii/23 (AUCT 3 206= MVN 13 399). There are only 9 texts from Puzriš–Dagan certainly dated to IS 3 i–x in BDTNS, but apart from Za–zi in i/10, they do not belong to any known officials of the institute: Hermitage 3 399, IS 3 i/10 (Zazi), NABU 1996:131, ii/27, NYPL 322, iii/ 00, SET 290, iv/18, BIN 3 359, v/0, MVN 13 564, vii/0, NYPL 283, ix/11, MVN 11 151, x/0, BPOA 7 1747, IS 3 x/0.

Table 8 The Events after the Simurum Campaign till Ibbi–Sin 16th Year

3	mu ^dI-bí-^dEn.zu lugal~ Urím^{ki}-ma-ke₄ **Si-mu-ru-um**^{ki} mu-hul	Year Ibbi-Sin the king of Ur destroyed Simurum
4	mu **En-am-gal-an-na en-**^d**Inanna** ba-huĝ	Year En-am-gal-anna was installed as en-priest of Inanna
5	mu *Tu-ki-in-hatytyi-mi-ig-rí-ša* **dumu-munus-** lugal ensí~**Za-ab-ša-li**^{ki}-ke₄ **ba-an-tuk**	Year: the governor of Zabšali married Tukin-hatytyi-migriša the king's daughter
6	mu ^dI-bi-^dSin lugal~ Urím^{ki}-ma--ke₄ **Nibru**^{ki} **Urím**^{ki}-ma-ke₄ **bàd gal-bi mu-dù**	Year: Ibbi-Sin the king of Ur built for Nippur and Ur their great walls
7	mu **ús-sa bàd-gal Nibru**^{ki} ba-dù	Year: after the year the great city wall of Nippur was built
8	mu **ús-sa** bàd-gal ba-dù **ús-sa-bi**	Second year after the year: the great city wall (of Nippur) was built
9	mu ^dI-bí-^dEn.zu lugal~ Urím^{ki}-ma--ke₄ **Hu-úh-nu-ri**^{ki} sag- kul ma-da An-ša-an^{ki}- šè ... dugud ba-ši-in-gin ...-gin₇ bi ...	Year: Ibbi-Sin the king of Ur went with massive power to Huhnuri, the bolt to the land of Anšan and like ...
10	mu En-nir-si₃-an-na **en-**^d **Inanna** máš--e in-pàd	Year En-nir-sianna was chosen by means of the omen as en-priest of Inanna
11	mu En-nam-šita₄ ^dI-bí-^den.zu--šè šud₃-sag en-^dEn-ki **Eridug**^{ki}-ga maš-e in-pàd	Year: the šita-priest who prays piously for Ibbi-Sin was chosen by means of the omens as en-priest of Enki in Eridu
12	mu ^dI-bí-^dEn.zu lugal~ Urím^{ki}-ma--ke₄ **gu-za~ an** ^d**Nanna**--ra mu-na-dím	Year: Ibbi-Sin the king of Ur made for Nanna his divine throne
13	mu ús-sa ^dI-bí-^dEn.zu lugal~ Urím^{ki}-ma--ke₄ **gu-za:** an ^dNanna--ra mu-na-dím	Year after the year: Ibbi-Sin the king of Ur made for Nanna his divine throne
14	mu ^dI-bí-^den.zu lugal~ Urím^{ki}-ma-ke₄ **Šušan**^{ki} **A-dam-dun**^{ki} **A-wa-an**^{ki} ud--gim ka bi-in-gi₄ ud-1-a mu-un-gúr en--bi lú--a mi-ni-in-dab₅-ba-a	**Year: Ibbi-Sin, the king of Ur, overwhelmed Susa, Adamdun and Awan like a storm, subdued them in a single day and seized the lords of their people.**
15	mu ^dI-bí-^dEn.zu lugal~ Urím^{ki}-ma--ra ^dNanna-a šà~ ki-áĝ--gá-ni **dalla~ mu-un-na-an-è-a**	Year: Nanna the beloved of his heart manifested himself to Ibbi-Sin, the king of Ur
16	mu ^dI-bí-^dEn.zu lugal~ Urím^{ki}-ma--ke₄ ^dNanna-ar ^d**nun-me-te-an-na mu-na-dím**	Year: Ibbi-Sin the king of Ur made for Nanna the "the royal ornament of heaven".

古代世界区域整体史研究的一案例
——日本"古代东亚世界论"评介

徐建新　中国社会科学院

摘要：历史的纵向研究解释的是历史的发展问题；历史的横向研究解释的是历史的结构问题（刘家和先生语）。人类历史正是在空间范围不断扩大、结构上不断变化的横向联系中向前发展的。古代世界尚不存在真正意义上的世界史（"全球史"、"世界体系"），但古代世界存在着多个横向交往频繁、互动关系密切的区域。从实证的角度来讲，这样的区域大于某个古代民族生存的地区和某个国家存在的地域范围。从这样的角度探讨一个地区或某一古代民族和国家历史的研究视角，可以称之为"区域整体史研究"。上世纪六十年代以后日本古代史学界提出的"古代东亚世界论"就是这样一种区域整体史研究。本文拟就日本学界所提出的"古代东亚世界"的观点、所谓的"东亚世界"的结构、机制，以及这项研究的学术意义做一扼要的评介，以期为我国世界古代史学界关注这一问题的学者提供某些启发。

关键词：全球史；世界体系；区域整体史研究

Abstract：We can find two orientations in history study, i.e. diachronic study and contemporary or comparative study. The former deals with the question of development, while the latter explains historical social structure (quotation of Prof. Liu Jiahe). Human history evolves with the territorial enlargement and the continual change of structure. History of ancient world can not yet be considered as a real general world history (or so-called "Global history", "World system"), however, the close and frequent contacts and interactions between regions in ancient times could still be observed, in which its range usually exceeds a restricted people's area or a state. This research is the so-called "study of ancient regional history in general", in which "thought of ancient East Asia world" advocated by Japanese scholars since 1960s, should be included. The author intends to survey the relevant opinions of the study, then to analyze the structure, the mechanism and the significance of the thought.

Keywords：Global History, World System, Study of Ancient Regional History in General

古代世界不存在真正意义上的世界史（"全球史"、"世界体系"），但古代世界存在着多个横向交往频繁、互动关系密切的区域。汤因比把这样的区域称作文明圈或文化圈，有的日本史学家称之为"历史世界"。把这样的区域作为一个整体来把握和研究，或是以区域发展的历史作为背景研究一个古代国家或民族的历史，这样的研究视角，可以称之为"区域整体史研究"。

将东亚地区作为一个整体来研究，并以东亚整体的历史发展为背景，探讨日本古代历史的发展过程，这样的一种研究路数，是战后至今日本古代史学界的主要研究趋势。在日本，指导这类研究的学说，被称作"东亚世界论"。迄今为止，日本古代史学者在这方面的研究已经积累了不少的成果，并且也引起了国际学术界的注意。比如杰弗里·巴勒克拉夫就曾在《当代史学主要趋势》一书评价说，"日本史学家习惯于从国际格局中而不是从孤立的地位上来看待日本历史"。（巴勒克拉夫《当代史学主要趋势》201 页。）战后日本古代史研究中的"东亚世界论"在内涵上有一个逐渐变化发展的过程。日本学术界对古代东亚世界的看法与我国史学家的观点有相近之处，也有许多不同。梳理一下这一学说，对于了解战后日本古代史学的发展以及近年来我国学术界日渐兴盛的对古代中国的"天下观"、"华夷秩序"、"朝贡体系"等问题的研究，是有一定的启发的。

一 知识考古：从"東洋"、"东亚"到"東アジア"（东亚细亚）

日本学界的"東亚"一词是从十九世纪中后期的明治维新以后的"東洋史"概念衍生出来的。从"東洋"到"東亚"的转化，也反映了日本近代史学的重大变革。明治维新以后日本为了与西方历史学用语中的"东方"（Orient）和"东方学"相对应，提出了"东洋史"的概念。明治时期的日本史学家在对历史学进行学科分类时提出了西洋史、东洋史、日本史的三科目划分。日本史没有包括在东洋史中。东洋史概念的出现实与"中日甲午战争"的发生有着密切的关系，日本的历史教育按"东洋史"、"西洋史"、"日本史"三科目划分是为了显示当时"日本帝国"的与众不同，是为了与被西方和日本近代启蒙思想家们定位为"落后"或"停滞不前"的中国保持距离，即宣示日本不属于西洋人眼中"停滞、落后、野蛮"的东洋。当时日本的东洋史概念与西方的东方学概念的含义并不一致，这无非是想在西方面前确立日本与众不同的文化身分。可见，当近代以来的西方学者力图通过"东方"这一"他者"来寻觅自我历史与文化的根源和价值时，日本也开始努力从自己独创的"東洋"概念出发重塑本国的历史与文化记忆。（甘文杰《东洋史学与"东京文献学派"初探》，2009）

二战期间日本使用的"東亚"一词是日本帝国主义在侵略扩张时，对其施展帝国主义霸权的地理空间的称谓。日本的侵略战争使得"東亚"一词被理解为日本帝国的同义词。因此在战后，日文中的"東亚"一词不再为学术界采用，而改用"東アジア"一词，直译过来就是"东亚细亚"。我们今天从日文学术书翻译过来的"东亚"一词，原文都是"東アジア"（东亚细亚），而不是"東亚"这两个汉字。

二 日本的"东亚世界论"及其讨论

战后日本学界提出的"东亚"（東アジア）和"东亚世界"（東アジア世界）概念是在反省战前史学倾向的基础上提出的。战后最早谈到"东亚世界"的是日本的元史学者前田直典。他在1948 年发表的《东亚古代的终结》一文中说："一般以为，在近代之前，世界各地的历史史尚未有共同性时，中国是一个世界，印度又是一个世界，从文化史的角度来看，中国的世界可以视为一个包括满洲、朝鲜、安南等在内的东亚世界，这也是过去大家的看法。把日本放进这个世界中虽然多少有些犹疑，但我们亦曾考虑过这个可能性。"显然，在该文中前田没有明确地表示日本在历史上应当归入古代东亚世界。但是他明确提出了东亚的历史是一体的，东亚各民族并不是只进行其各自的历史发展，相互间存在关联性。

1961，日本筑摩书房相继出版了多卷本《世界的历史》的第六卷，其副标题为《东亚世界的变貌》。这卷中收入了日本中世纪史学者松本新八郎的《东亚史上的日本与朝鲜》一文，该文首次关注了唐代与周边国家的册封关系，认为在 8—10 世纪的东亚世界处在这样一种状态，即处于不同社会发展阶段的各国通过册封关系、国家层面的交往、贸易等方式相互影响、相互制约。该文是最早关注唐以前的东亚诸国的册封关系的论文。

战后日本学者对"东亚"一词的定义参考了美国汉学家费正清的观点。在日本学者西嶋定生看来，"东亚"一词具有多层含义，一是在地理上指亚洲被高山大漠一分为二的东部地区；二是在人种学上指蒙古人种(爱斯基摩人和印第安人除外)的栖居地；三是在文化上深受中国古代文明影响的地区；第四种含义所指最狭，即指中国、日本、朝鲜和越南。他并未把以下两个地区包括在内，其一为中亚地区，特别是蒙古、新疆和西藏，认为该地区游牧民族的历史是通过商业、战争和占领与中国的历史融为一体的。其二为东南亚地区，该地区似乎更多地受到印度的影响。

1962 年西嶋定生发表了《6～8 世纪的东亚》一文。(后来标题改为《东亚世界与册封体制—6～8 世纪的东亚》) 经过修改后收入《中国古代国家与东亚世界》(东京大学出版会，1983 年) 一书。西嶋的研究动机不仅来自对战后至五十年代日本社会的反思，也来源于对于近代以来以欧洲为中心的世界一体化的思考。他认为在一体化世界形成之前，存在着"东亚世界"、"伊斯兰世界"、"印度世界"、"欧洲世界"等多个历史世界。他在前文中提出中国、日本、朝鲜、越南乃至从蒙古草原到西藏高原中间地带的西北走廊地区，构成一个完整的、独立的、自律的"东亚世界"。西嶋特别强调了古代中国在东亚世界中的核心地位，他指出"东亚世界是以中国文明的发生及发展为基轴而形成的"，是"随着中国文明的开发，其影响进而达到周边诸民族，在那里形成以中国文明为中心，而自我完成的文化圈"，他认为，在东亚世界的文化圈内的各种文化皆源于中国，或者受中国的影响而成长。唐以前存在于对东亚诸国的册封在制约 6～8 世纪的国际关系上具有重要的意义。中国对周边民族实施册封所依据的政治原理是中国古代对天下的认识，即所谓的"天下秩序"、"天下观"。就是说，西嶋定生试图以中国的册封制度为杠杆，对唐以前的东亚世界中国际关系的结构作出概括。所以他的观点也被称作"册封体制论"。70 年代以后他还进一步论证了东亚世界中存在着的共同的基本文化要素，即汉字、儒学、律令制度和佛教。(后来台湾的高明士教授和上海的韩昇又主张还有两个要素，即教育制度和科学技术。) 西嶋定生的前述论文是日本的"东亚世界论"的奠基之作，他的观点在日本学界引起广泛的响应。60 年代以来的日本古代史研究基本上是在古代东亚世界的视野下展开的。

岩波书店 2002 年出版的《西嶋定生東アジア史論集、第三卷》中对东亚世界的册封体制论作了全面的归纳，其研究下限伸延到近代以前：即汉代是册封体制的产生期；公元 6 世纪前期是古代册封体制的完成期；从隋朝的建立到唐代是册封体制的全盛期；随着唐朝的衰退册封体制和古代东亚世界逐渐瓦解；宋元时期为以中国为中心的册封体制的复兴作了准备；明朝建立后册封体制再度复兴，清代把册封体制扩展到北亚和东南亚地区，但日本因实施锁国，没有进入中国的册封体制；十九世纪随着西方殖民主义的入侵，东亚的册封体制走向解体。

上世纪六十年代以来，学术界也在不同程度上对西嶋定生的东亚世界论提出了质疑和批评。例如，日本的隋唐史学者堀敏一从修正和补充完善西嶋观点的的角度提出了"羁縻体制论"，他认为以册封制度概括隋唐时期的东亚国际关系秩序并不妥当，在唐的西部和北部推行的是以怀柔和监视为目的"羁縻制度"。堀敏一认为中国的适用于日本、朝鲜的政策有许多也适用于处理同北亚各民族的关系。具体说，西藏高原、河西走廊以西的地区也应包含在东亚的历史世界中。按堀敏一的观点，中国周边除了与中国的关系不甚密切的东南亚外，几乎所有的地区都被纳入了东亚世界的范围。（金子修一《日本"东亚世界"论的回顾与展望》2011 年，徐建新、章林译。）另一方面，日本古代史学者认为西嶋过于机械地解释了东亚世界背景下日本民族的历史发展，似乎古代日本社会的变革都是被动的对日本列岛以外的国际格局的反应。在隔海相望的朝鲜、韩国学术界，人们用警惕的目光注视着日本的"东亚世界论"的研究，毕竟人们对二战期间日本推行的"大东亚共荣圈"、"大东亚新秩序"的政治构想仍记忆犹新，对于日本的"假共荣、真侵占"给朝鲜民族造成的巨大伤害难以忘怀。在朝鲜、韩国学者的论著中更多的是强调古代朝鲜文化对日本的深远影响，对于古代朝鲜半岛上的几个小国加入到中国的册封体制的问题，则认为是不过是当时人的一种生存手段。

上世纪八十年代以后西嶋定生等学者开始重视以日本为主体的东亚世界格局与变动的研究。这类研究强调古代日本在加入中国的册封体制的同时，还出现了谋求与古代中华帝国对等的"自我中心主义"的发展，指出日本和其他中国周边国家积极引进中国的"天下观"、"华夷观"，在周边小民族之间，构建自己的"小天下"，这就是所谓的日本"小中华帝国论"。

上世纪九十年代后期以来，一些日本学者将区域整体史研究范围进一步扩大，努力发掘包括中亚地区在内的亚洲东部地区历史发展中的互动关系，进而提出了"亚欧大陆东部世界论"的观点。例如 2011 年初，中国学者新发现了清代流传的南北朝时期梁元帝萧绎的《职贡图》的题记。新发现的题记（有 18 国的题记）比著名的国家图书馆藏北宋本题记（有 13 国的题记）多出了 5 个国家。此后有日本学者利用梁《职贡图》的新史料，力图证明亚欧大陆东部世界存在整体互动的国际秩序。（铃木靖民《从梁职贡图到"亚欧大陆东部世界论"》2011 年 8 月）

三　几点想法

1. 在汉唐时期，中国古代帝王依据儒家伦理学说，将国内政治统治中的君臣关系延伸到与周边国家和民族的关系中，构建起一套以华夷秩序为特点的古代国际关系体系。在这一体系中，册封国的职责包括封臣、回赐、德化等；受封国的义务包括朝贡、称臣、奉正朔（即遵从奉行册封国王朝的年号和历法）。册封和相关的制度（册封体制）是维护这一国际秩序的重要手段，除此之外，还有羁縻、和亲、征伐等手段。

中国古代的华夷秩序实施过程中，促进了东亚世界的区域一体化。东亚世界在华夷秩序下的整体性发展是历史存在，东亚世界不是一个从他者设置的概念而来的自我认同。早在"东亚"一词从西方传来之前，东亚世界的区域认同就已经存在了。（韩昇著《东亚世界形成史论》复旦大学出版社 2009 年 5 月）

2. 中国古代的"天下秩序"、"华夷秩序"包含了中国王朝统治者的政治统治理念和原理。台湾大学的高明士教授认为，天下秩序包含了四种原理，即"结合原理"、"统治原理"、"亲疏原理"、"德化原理"，针对构成天下的"内臣地区"、"外臣地区"和"暂不臣地区"这三类地区，所采用的统治和影响对策是不同的。（高明士：《天下秩序与文化圈的探索——以东亚古代的政治与教育为中心》上海古籍出版社 2008 年）对待"外臣地区"和"暂不臣地区"，征伐不是最终目的和唯一手段。在中国古代"华夷秩序"的原理中"德化原理"占有重要地位，强调"修文德，服远人"、"柔远人则四方归之，怀诸侯则天下畏之"的德化、感化政策。只有当周边民族（四夷）不履行臣的义务（"不臣"），或破坏天下秩序（不轨）时，才会考虑采用征伐的手段。

3. 东亚世界的整体互动关系（包括交流和征伐），导致古代东亚世界内部，人与物的大量流动，促进了区域内小国的社会经济发展，加速了区域内古代国家的形成和发展过程。如果只强调古代中国王朝与周边民族的矛盾和冲突，而忽视了在华夷体制下，中国文明对周边民族产生的积极且深远的影响，那么这种认识只能说是很不全面的。以日本为例，中国文明与国家的诸制度，如农耕生产技术、城市的规划与建设、文字的发明与使用、行政官僚制和法律制度的创建等等，是在非常漫长的数千年的历史过程中逐渐积累发展起来的。与中国相比，日本则是在较短的 1000—1200 年的时间里把这些在中国大陆和朝鲜半岛发展起来的先进文化成功地吸收进来，形成了古代国家。（徐建新《日本古代国家形成史研究中的几个问题》2010 年）实际上，日本学者前田直典也曾表达过同样的意思。他认为，在文明的形成期，中国比其周围各民族显示了 10 个世纪以上的先驱性发展；而伴随着自古代社会向封建社会的过渡，日本与朝鲜与中国社会的差距则缩小为 2—3 个世纪。而在向近代社会过渡之时，大体已没什么差距了。（前田直典：《東アジアに於ける古代の終末》1948 年）就是说，在东亚世界形成初期，中国与日本、朝鲜半岛等周边地区处在不同的社会发展阶段上，而到了中世纪，中国与上述地区的发展开始具有了平行性。这种让日本和朝鲜半岛的文明发展提速的原因，只是因为上述地区大量学习和引进了来自东亚世界核心地带的先进的文物制度和思想文化。

参考文献

前田直典：《東アジアに於ける古代の終末》（《历史》第 1 卷第 4 号 1948 年）。收入刘俊文主编、黄约瑟译《日本学者研究中国史论著选译》第 1 卷《通论》，中华书局 1992 年。

西嶋定生：《中国古代国家与东亚世界》东京大学出版会，1983 年。

堀敏一：《东亚中的古代日本》东京，研文出版社 1998 年。

堀敏一、韩昇等编译《隋唐帝国与东亚》昆明，云南人民出版社 2002 年 1 月。

李成市：《东亚文化圈的形成》东京，山川出版社 2000 年。

金子修一：《隋唐の国际秩序と东アジア》名著刊行会 2001 年。

金子修一著、徐建新、章林译《日本"东亚世界"论的回顾与展望》2011 年。

何芳川《"华夷秩序"论》，《北京大学学报》（哲学社会科学版）1998 年第 6 期第 30-45 页。

高明士：《天下秩序与文化圈的探索——以东亚古代的政治与教育为中心》上海古籍出版社 2008 年

韩昇：《东亚世界形成史论》复旦大学出版社，2009 年 5 月。

甘文杰：《东洋史学与"东京文献学派"初探》【网络首发】。

杨军：《中国与古代东亚国际体系》，《吉林大学学报（社会科学）》2004 年第 2 期第 34—41 页。

韩东育：《华夷秩序 的东亚构架与自解体内情》，《东北师大学报》（哲学社会科学版）2008 年第 1 期，总第 231 期

何新华：《"天下观"：一种建构世界秩序的区域性经验》，《二十一世纪》（网络版）2004 年 11 月号总第 32 期。

谢俊美《论历史上的"东亚世界"》，《江海学刊》2005 年第 2 期

古代两河流域神话的文化功能

张文安　陕西师范大学

摘要：神话是古代两河流域的重要文化现象，借助文化人类学中功能学派的神话理论，认为古代两河流域神话不是简单的艺术想象，而是神学集团有意创作服务宗教的，在社会生活中承担着宣传宗教观念、神化王权、强化社会礼仪和道德教化的重要文化功能。

关键词：两河流域；宗教；神话；文化功能

Abstract：Myth is an important cultural phenomenon in ancient Mesopotamia, with the help of fuctionism in the Cultural Anthropology I think the mythology of ancient Mesopotamia is not simple artistic imagination, but the workes created intentionally by theology groupes and act on religious services.It bears the fuction of propagandaing religion theology in social life,deifying kingship, strengthening social etiquette and moral indoctrination。

Keywords：Mesopotamia, Religion, Myth, Cultural fuction

宗教是古代两河流域文明的基石，在浓厚的宗教情绪驱使下古代两河流域祭司、歌手、书吏等神学集团创作了大量神话作品。世界上最早的文学目录发现于古代两河流域南部城市尼普尔废墟中，在两个盘状泥板上铭刻的 21 篇文学作品中有 7 篇都是神话题材，足见神话在公元前两千年时期的发展盛况。[①]两河流域神话经历苏美尔和阿卡德两个历史时期，时间跨度达 2500 年之久，神话无论在数量还是内容形式都堪称是该民族古代文化的重要遗产。英国功能主义人类学家马林诺夫斯基认为："神话在原始文化中有不可缺少的功用，那就是将信仰表现出来，提高了并加以制定；给道德以保障而加以执行；证明仪式的功效而有实用的规律以指导人群。所以神话乃是人类文明中一项重要的成分，不是闲话，而是吃苦的积极力量；不是理智的解说或艺术的想象，而是原始信仰与道德智慧上实用的特许证书。"[②]要理解神话何以在古代两河流域文化中呈现丰富发达的特征，必须从神话的文化功能入手，这点在古代两河流域宗教研究中长期被学者忽视。本文借助文化人类学中功能学派的神话理论，对此作一尝试。

---

① Samuel Noah kramer, **Sumerian Mythology**, Universty of Pennsylvania Press ,1972.
② 马林诺夫斯基：《巫术科学宗教与神话》，中国民间文艺出版社，1986 年。

一　宣传宗教观念的文化功能

古代两河流域神话中蕴含着丰富深刻的宗教观念，它们由一个个片面的主题共同组成了系统完整的宗教思想体系，这些宗教观念借助神话形式在广大民众中流行和传播，发挥着宣扬和统一广大民众宗教思想的文化功能，有效推动了神权政治文化机制的运行。

1. 宇宙世界和人类文明都是神灵创造和安排的

宇宙世界和人类文明都是神灵创造和安排的，这是古代两河流域宗教中的一个基本观念。这种宗教观念主要反映在苏美尔和阿卡德创世神话中。

宇宙创造神话解释的是天地怎样形成的问题。苏美尔神话"畜牧与谷物"编撰于公元前两千纪，开头两行是这样说的："在天和地的高山上，安神生出了安努那基（Anunnaki）。"从中可知天与地最初是连接成为高山的，其中顶部是天，底部是地；那么天地又是由谁创造出来的？在一块苏美尔神名的泥板上，女神纳穆（Nammu）被写成"大瀛海"的象形文字，形容为"一个诞生出天与地的母亲。"可知在苏美尔人看来，天与地是原始海的产物。既然天地最初是相连在一起的，后来又是被谁分离开来的？神话"鹤嘴锄的发明"序言这样写道："恩利勒从大地中带来土地的种子，计划把天从地上移开，计划把地从天上移开。"可知把天与地分离开来的创世主神正是大气神恩利勒。[1]宇宙创造神话也反映在公元前一千年阿卡德创世神话"埃努玛·埃利什"（Enūma eliš）中，该神话详细讲述了创世主神马尔杜克（Marduk）用咸水之神提阿玛特（Tiamat）的尸体上半身创造了天下半身创造了地的故事。

不仅是宇宙世界，很多神话还说明了人类文明是由神灵创造出来的宗教观念。

"伊南娜与恩基：文明的法则从埃利都转移至乌鲁克"神话出土于尼普尔，编撰时间在公元前2000年之际，由五片零碎的泥版组成。神话叙说乌鲁克的保护女神伊南娜（Inanna）为了提高自己城市的幸福和繁荣，前去苏美尔南部古老的文化中心埃利都拜访她的父亲水神兼智慧神恩基（Enki），恩基手里掌握着构成文明基础的神圣法则"美"（Me）。在迎接女儿的宴会上，恩基由于一时兴奋喝酒过度，三番五次地把一百多个神圣法则"美"都送给了伊南娜。伊南娜立即把这些法则装载在船上运回乌鲁克。这些"美"有110种之多，包括贵族身份、神道、尊贵永恒的王冠、国王的宝座、君权、神庙、牧师、国王、各种祭司官职、真理、上天入地、洪水、性交与卖淫、木匠、金属工匠、皮革匠、砖匠、智慧和理解、音乐、乐器等等。[2]该神话生动反映了古代苏美尔神学家宣扬的人类所有文明成果都是神所掌握和赐予的宗教观念。

"恩基与宁胡尔萨格"神话出土于尼普尔，铭刻在六个圆柱泥版上，编撰时间在公元前2千纪早期。神话叙述说智慧之神恩基巡游苏美尔、乌尔、麦哈鲁等五个城市，通过他的祝福这些城市拥有繁荣和富饶。他还创造出了世界万物并安排相应的神灵负责管理。具体有为底格里斯河和幼发拉底斯河注入新鲜水，并安排"懂得河流"的神恩比鲁鲁（Enbilulu）负责；为沼泽和藤丛赋予鱼和芦苇，派"喜欢鱼"的神负责；让生命之雨降临大地，派雷雨神伊什库尔（Iškur）负责；为大地提供犁、牛轭、锄等农具，并委派恩利勒的农夫恩基姆都（Enkimdu）负责；为耕地提供各种谷物和植物，委派谷物女神阿什南（Ashnan）负责；发明了鹤嘴锄和砖模，安排砖神库拉（Kulla）负责；建造房子，并安排"恩利勒伟大的建筑师"牧什达玛（Mushdamma）负责；为高原覆盖绿色植物，让牲畜繁殖，并委派"群山之王"苏姆干（Sumugan）负责；建造马厩和羊圈，为它们提供最好的肥肉和牛奶，委

---

[1] Samuel Noah kramer, *Sumerian Mythology*, Universty of Pennsylvania Press ,1972.

[2] Samuel Noah kramer, *Sumerian Mythology*, Universty of Pennsylvania Press ,1972.

派牧神杜牧兹（Dumuzi）负责；在各个城市和国家边界竖起界石来固定疆界，委派太阳神乌图（Utu）负责；委派衣服女神乌特图（Uttu）负责缝制衣服等。① "鹤嘴锄的发明" 神话讲述了大气神恩利勒发明出农业生产中用途广泛的农具"鹤嘴锄"，并把它交给"黑头"的人类使用。[6]51 这两个神话集中宣扬了人类文明的各种要素都是神灵掌管的观念。

苏美尔神话"夏天和冬天"叙述恩利勒神发愿要给大地带来树木和谷物，使大地富饶繁荣，为此他创造出了两个季节神夏天"埃美什"（Emesh）和冬天"恩藤"（Enten），在两个神互争高下争辩不休之际，最后恩利勒裁断"恩藤"作为众神的"农夫"，负责生产生命之水保证谷物生长，同时告诫二神要像兄弟和朋友一样一起尽心完成各自的职责。②

从上述神话可以看出：大瀛海神纳穆创造出天地合体的宇宙山，大气神恩利勒又把天地分离开来；智慧之神恩基掌握着众多人类文明的法则，他还创造出世界万物并安排相应的神灵负责管理；恩利勒神发明了农业生产的重要工具，还创造出两个季节神夏天和冬天为人类造福。总之这些神话都宣传并强化着一个宗教观念，那就是宇宙世界和人类文明都是神灵创造的。

2. 人类是神灵创造出来专门为神服务的仆役

人类是神灵创造出来专门为神服务是古代两河流域宗教中的一个基本观念，这一观念通过一系列"人类起源"主题的创世神话表达出来。

"畜牧与谷物"神话说天神安奴创造出"安奴那基"众神后，这些神灵为了应付生活，日子过得十分辛苦。开始的时候没有衣服穿没有谷物吃，只能啃树皮喝生水，后来家畜神拉哈尔（Lahar）和谷物神阿什南（Ashnan）在神灵创造室中被制造出来，神灵有吃有穿了但还不能心满意足，他们还要完成羊圈里的繁重工作，为了减轻神的劳动，于是人类被制造出来。③

"恩基与宁胡尔萨格"神话详细讲述了人类是神用泥土混合血液创造出来的过程，目的还是为神服务。神话开始叙述了神灵获取面包的艰辛和不易，尤其是女性神诞生以后。诸神开始抱怨他们生活的困难，他们希望水神和智慧神恩基能给他们提供帮助。恩基的母亲原始海神手捧诸神的眼泪从床上把儿子唤醒，于是恩基和生育女神宁玛赫（Ninmah）合作把人创造出来。后来由于在庆祝宴会上喝酒过量，宁马赫造出了六个不健全的人，恩基都他们在人类社会生活中找到了宦官等合适的职业。④

神灵创造了人类为神服务的宗教观念生动反映在阿卡德神话"阿特拉哈希斯"（Atarahsis）中，神话铭刻在公元前18世纪的古巴比伦泥版上。神话开始叙述神为了生计不得不负担繁重的劳动："神灵的负担很重，工作太艰苦，麻烦越来越多，安奴那基众神让小神负担七倍的重担，他们扛着很多篮子，不得不开挖运河，清理运河，不管白天黑夜地干着，他们痛苦地呻吟，彼此抱怨，抱怨挖不完的土地，终于其中一个神建议一起向神灵的顾问恩利勒诉苦，诸神烧毁了铲子等工具，包围了恩利勒的房子，以暴乱的激烈方式向恩利勒发起攻击"；恩利勒向天神安奴报告，安奴要打击暴乱的肇事者，这时智慧之神埃阿（苏美尔语"恩基"）提议让生育女神制造出人类以解除神的痛苦。后来埃阿提供泥土和肇事者尸体的肌肉给生育女神宁图，宁图终于通过十月怀胎生出了人类。⑤

---

① Samuel Noah kramer, *Mythology of the Ancient World*, Anchor Books, New York ,1961.
② Samuel Noah kramer, *Sumerian Mythology*, Universty of Pennsylvania Press ,1972.
③ Samuel Noah kramer, *Sumerian Mythology*, Universty of Pennsylvania Press ,1972.
④ Samuel Noah kramer, *Sumerian Mythology*, Universty of Pennsylvania Press ,1972.
⑤ Stephanie Dalley, *Myths From Mesopotamia*, Oxford University Press, 1989.

3. 神权至上的宗教观念

"大洪水"（又名"阿特拉哈希斯"）神话宣扬的主题就是神权至上的宗教观念。神话叙述说在神创造了人类后，过了600年，由于"国家越来越大，人口越来越多，国家产生出的噪音像一头怒吼的公牛一样。"面对人类的喧闹神灵无法休息，恩利勒终于发怒决定要毁灭人类。恩利勒先后采用了瘟疫、饥荒两种手段惩罚人类，但都被智慧之神恩基为人类出谋逃脱灾厄，最后恩利勒发愿采取最残暴的大洪水手段企图彻底消灭人类，幸亏智慧之神恩基授意人类国王阿特拉哈希斯建造方舟才得以幸免于难。① "大洪水"神话虽然以人类的幸存结束，但是其中对神毁灭人类以及人类所遭受的瘟疫、饥馑和洪水灾难的细节有详细叙述，其灾难的惨烈让人恐怖，今天读来依然心有余悸，很显然神学家这样设计的目的是为了彰显神意志的强大和威力，说明了神的利益高于一切，人类的活动如果影响了神的利益就要遭受毁灭性的惩罚，人类在神面前永远是无能和低下的。

4. 人类没有永生，死亡是人类与生俱来的定律

人类没有永生，任何人一生不可能逃脱死亡定律是古代两河流域早期宗教中的生命信仰，公元前三千纪流传并被记录下来的苏美尔神话"吉勒旮美什史诗"集中宣扬了这种宗教观念。

"吉勒旮美什史诗"最早是由五篇独立的苏美尔语版本的诗歌组成，在公元前2000年左右被用阿卡德语整合为一个完整的故事，其中一篇是"吉勒旮美什与胡巴巴"。神话中当吉勒旮美什的朋友恩基都反对他冒险去杉树林杀死魔怪胡巴巴（humbaba）时，吉勒旮美什说："恩基都啊，那个人能够登上天堂？只有神才能和荣耀的太阳神沙马什一样永生，对于我们人来说，生命的日子是有限的，我们拥有的一切就像一阵风一样短暂。既然人不能逃脱死亡的最后命运，那么我要到山地去，我要留名青史；能让人成名的地方，我定要前往；不能让人成名的地方，我也一定要和神一样出名！"朋友恩基都的死亡对吉勒旮美什打击很大，他决心要找到让人长生不死的药物，于是他开始了漫长艰辛的旅途。当他到达大海边的时候遇见了一个开酒馆的女老板思杜丽（Siduri），她得知吉勒旮美什此行的目的后说："吉勒旮美什啊，你想到哪里去？你要寻找的生命是永远找不到的。当众神创造人类的时候，同时也给人类创造了死，他们自己掌握着生死大权。你啊，吉勒旮美什，还是先把肚子填饱吧，日日夜夜，快块乐乐，每天都像过节一样，从早到晚，纵情玩乐，换上新衣，沐浴净身，看一看拉你手的小孩，拥抱你的妻子给她永远幸福，这就是人类生活的全部。"吉勒旮美什义无返顾，最后终于找到了他的祖先，那个加入神的行列的乌特那皮什提穆（Utnapishtim），他告诉吉勒旮美什说在大海的深处有一种药草，吃了它能使人长生不死。于是吉勒旮美什想办法潜入海底取出了那个药草，当他上岸洗澡的时候，一个蛇过来偷偷吃了这个草"返老还童"了，吉勒旮美什终于绝望地回到了他的城市乌鲁克。② 史诗通过吉勒旮美什历经艰难万险最后还是没能得到长生不死之药的悲剧，深刻地揭示了死亡是人类命中注定无法逃避的也即永生是不存在的生活哲理，这个哲理也构成了古代两河流域宗教思想中的一个基本命题。

以上四点是不同神话宣扬的宗教观念，把这些独立成篇的神话联系起来考察，不难发现它们共同揭示了一个完整系统的宗教思想，那就是：世界万物都是神创造的，人类也不例外；神创造人类的唯一目的就是为神服务；如果人类的行为影响了神的利益，神会采取一切手段毁灭人类；神在创造人类的时候就决定了人类的死亡，人类没有永生权利。这一系列宗教观念有力奠定了古代两河流域文明中神权至上的神本文化精神。

---

① Stephanie Dalley, *Myths From Mesopotamia*, Oxford University Press, 1989.
② N.K.Sandar, *The Epic of Girgamesh*, Penguin Books, New York, 1972.

二　神化世俗王权的文化功能

古代两河流域宗教认为国王是神在人间选派统治的代理人，国王的唯一义务是替神治理国家，如果国王违反的神的意志就会遭到神的罢免。乌尔第三王朝时期（BC2112–BC2004）编撰的《苏美尔王表》开篇就说："当王权自天而降，王权在埃利都"。古代两河流域的每个城邦都有自己的保护神，不同历史时期当某个城邦势力强大到足以臣服其他城邦的时候，该城邦的国王就会利用和编造神话来抬高自己城邦保护神的地位，借以神化自己政治上的霸主地位。苏美尔到阿卡德时期两河流域出现了众多版本的创世神话，其中充当创世主神的角色就依次经历了天神安、大气神恩利勒、巴比伦城神马尔都克以及亚述城神阿淑尔的转换，生动反映了创世神话为王权政治服务的宗旨。

编造神话以神化王权是古代两河流域国王惯用的伎俩。公元前三千纪后期拉旮什城邦国王古地亚这样宣称自己："牧羊者被宁吉尔苏（他的）心设想；被南筛坚定地认可；被宁达尔赋予力量；被巴巴认可的男人；贾图姆多格生出的孩子；被伊哥阿里马赋予高贵和令人尊敬的节杖；完全由敦沙旮尔提供给生命的气息；他的神宁吉兹达已经使他（高傲地）抬着头出现在议事会上。"国王阿淑尔纳西帕二世写给女神伊什塔尔的信中这样说道："你啊，众神可怕的女主人，你的确用你的眼光把我选出来了；你的确渴望看见我统治。你的确把我从山脉中带出来，你的确把我称为人类的牧羊人，你的确授予我正义的节杖。"[①]

神化王权统治的神话集中反映在巴比伦最著名的创世神话"埃努玛·埃利什"（Enūma eliš）中。神话生动讲述了巴比伦城神马尔杜克在接受众神赋予他至高无上的王权后，挺身而出杀死咸水神提阿玛特并用他上半身创造出天下半身创造出地，同时用提阿玛特的首领金古的血创造出人类来承担诸神劳役的故事。[14]233 神话编撰于公元前一千纪，出土于阿舒尔巴尼巴图书馆收藏的泥板文献，铭刻在七块泥板上。神话的形成可能更早，有学者推断最早形成于古巴比伦第一王朝（BC1894–BC1595），尤其在汉谟拉比（Hammurabi）统治时期。古巴比伦第六代国王汉谟拉比通过远交近攻灵活多变的外交策略，吞并伊辛、拉尔萨，征服马里和亚述，消灭埃什嫩那，统一了两河流域，这时巴比伦城由一个两河流域中部阿摩利国家的都城变成了统一的两河流域王国的都城，取得了政治上的霸主地位，马尔杜克也由一个城市保护神提升为全国性的主神。史诗就是为歌颂马尔杜克的丰功伟绩而创作的，在巴比伦一年一度的宗教节日"新年节"的第四天通过祭司吟诵演唱的，国王、祭司也在演出剧目中扮演马尔杜克和提阿玛特，借此神化和强化巴比伦王权自天的神圣观念，慑服所有城邦民众对巴比伦帝国王权的绝对顺从。

三　确定社会礼仪的文化功能

礼仪是人们约定俗成的行为规范，它顺应人们的心理和社会生活的需要，发挥着调节人们生活的作用，有它存在的必要性，为了使得这些社会礼仪不被人们破坏和疏忽，古代两河流域神学家有意通过神话的方式给以强化。

亲人死去是人类的一大悲哀，两河流域古代先民也用穿丧服的礼仪表达对死去亲人的哀悼，一些神话也强化了这种丧葬礼仪。

"阿达帕"神话中埃利都国王阿达帕按照智慧神埃阿的授意身穿丧服面见从人间离去的两个天庭守门神，果然赢得了两神的好感，两神在天神面前为阿达帕尽力说情，从而平息了天神的怒气被释放回人间。这个神话通过智慧之神埃阿劝说阿达帕穿丧服的说教确定了丧服礼仪在社会生活中的

---

① ［美］亨利·富兰克弗特著，郭子林译，《王权与神祇》，上海：三联书店，2007。

必要性，使得这种礼仪规范有了神话的神圣约束力。"吉勒呇美什、恩基都和地下世界"神话中当恩基都挺身而出要下地狱帮助吉勒呇美什寻找掉入地府的鼓和鼓槌时，吉勒呇美什告诫恩基都"不要穿干净的衣服，不要在身上涂油"等礼仪规范，因为冥府是死人集中的地方，不注意行为禁忌的话就要引起死神的攻击。但是恩基都没有采纳一意孤行，终于被冥府的鬼怪俘获。①这个细节宣扬了古代两河流域人们奉行穿丧服面对死者的行为礼仪。"伊南娜下冥府"神话也能看出对丧服之礼的强调。当伊南娜在冥府鬼怪监管下回到大地上的时候，她最先经过的是两个苏美尔城市温马（Umma）和巴德–提比拉（Bad-tibira），那两个城市的守护神沙拉（shara）和拉塔腊克（Latarak）见到伊南娜从地下世界出来，都纷纷穿上粗麻布丧服匍匐在地面上，伊南娜对他们谦卑的装扮感到满意，于是拒绝了冥府鬼怪要抓捕他们的请求。最后伊南娜让冥府鬼怪抓捕自己的丈夫杜牧兹的一个重要理由，就是杜牧兹在自己死亡的日子里不但不表示哀伤，反而衣着华丽吹着横笛满心欢乐。[16]109 这同样是对活人为亡人应穿丧服礼仪的神话确定。

古代两河流域南部多为沼泽地带，缺乏粮食，北部为农业产区，缺乏水产，这两个不同的经济区有互通有无交换产品的社会需要。苏美尔神话"南那旅行尼普尔"叙述南方城市乌尔的保护神月神南那为了使自己城市更加繁荣，用船装载很多树木、动物等礼物沿运河向北到尼普尔去拜访父亲众神之王恩利勒，请求得到恩利勒的祝福。后来恩利勒用农业产品饼和面包招待儿子，并让南那带回很多礼物，有田野的谷物，高地沙漠中的植物，森林中的雄鹿等。这个神话与"尼萨呇（Nisaga)船的春天仪式"有密切关系，该仪式的目的是把乌尔一年中最先出产的物品作为交换礼物带到尼普尔，满足北方农业区尼普尔对南方水产品的需求。同样，"南那旅行尼普尔"神话也具有确定这种经济交换社会礼仪的文化功能。②

四　道德教化的文化功能

人们的行为规范除了用国家制定的法律进行调节外，社会舆论和道德教化也是很重要和很必要的手段。古代两河流域一些神话行使着强化道德准则的文化功能。

强奸妇女一直是法律所严厉惩戒的，这也同样引起神话的关注。苏美尔神话"恩利勒与宁利勒"讲到恩利勒为了得到他喜爱的女人，在副使努斯库的协助下于河流中间的船上强奸了宁利勒，致使宁利勒怀孕。这个行为立即引起众神的愤怒，他们不顾恩利勒是众神之王，当他在自己宫廷漫步的时候，"五十位天神，其中有七个决定命运的神，俘获了恩利勒，说：'恩利勒，你这个无耻的家伙，从你的城市滚出去！'"于是众神就把恩利勒打发到地下世界接受惩罚。③另外，还有一个神话"伊南娜与园丁舒卡利图达（Shukallituda）"也揭示了这样的主题。神话叙述说从前有一个园丁叫舒卡利图达，他在园艺上的成功使得园林长满各种绿色植物，有个大树树冠遮天蔽日。一次女神伊南娜横越天空，疲惫的时候在距离大树不远的地方躺身休息，被园丁舒卡利图达发觉，园丁趁女神沉睡之际占有了她，伊南娜醒来之后发现自己受辱，发誓要惩罚苏美尔。第一个灾难是让洪水淹没棕榈树和葡萄园，第二个灾难是刮起大风和暴雨，第三个灾难由于泥版文献残损不得而知。园丁在父亲的帮助下隐藏在"黑头市民"中间，当伊南娜无力寻找羞辱自己的罪犯时，她又去埃利都求助智慧之神恩基，由于文献残损结局不得而知。④总之，这个神话也表达了奸淫妇女是神灵严重反对的行为，对现实生活中的男女关系也发挥着道德教化的文化功能。

---

①　Samuel Noah kramer, *Sumerian Mythology*, Universty of Pennsylvania Press,1972.
②　Thorkild Jacobsen, *The Treasure of Darkness – A History of Mesopotamia Religion*, Tale University Press,1976.
③　Samuel Noah kramer, *Mythology of the Ancient World*, Anchor Books, New York,1961.
④　Samuel Noah kramer, *Mythology of the Ancient World*, Anchor Books, New York,1961.

　　"埃塔那"（Etana）神话讲述的是住在同一个树上的两个鹰和蛇之间的恩怨故事。这个故事相当古老，在阿卡德时期（2390-2249BC）的圆筒印章上就有人骑着鹰飞上天空的图案。来自尼尼微的"标准"版本由三块泥版组成，文字共计有450行。[①]P188 神话前半部分叙述说在一棵白杨树上住着一个鹰和一个蛇，鹰和蛇为了彼此照顾，在太阳神沙马什面前发誓做朋友，保证当鹰出去觅食的时候由蛇负责看管两家的孩子，反之亦然。后来鹰因为自己的孩子已经长大不再需要蛇来照顾的时候遂生歹念，趁蛇不在家的时候偷吃了蛇的孩子。当蛇回来不见自己的孩子时痛苦不堪，并把自己的遭遇告诉了太阳神。为了报复鹰的背信弃义，太阳神沙马什给蛇想出了一个绝妙的计策，让蛇隐藏在一个野牛的腹中伺机报复老鹰。这个计策果然凑效，鹰被蛇咬伤了翅膀并拖入一个山洞。这个神话的设计遵循着古代两河流域的宗教信仰，由于太阳神有保护公正打击邪恶的司法官功能，所以神话中受屈之蛇向他诉冤，在太阳神乌图的帮助下做恶的老鹰终遭报应。这个故事取材于人们日常生活，通过鹰和蛇的恩怨故事宣扬了一个伦理准则，那就是朋友之间要讲究诚信，任何违背诚信的自私之举都要遭到神灵的惩罚。这个神话广泛流行在泥板印章上，对从事商业贸易的商人来说无疑起着诚信教育的文化功能。

　　古代两河流域神话不是没有意义的简单艺术想象，而是祭司等神学集团有意创作服务于宗教和政治的，在社会生活中承担着宣传宗教观念、神化王权、强化社会礼仪和道德教化的重要文化功能。

---

① Samuel Noah kramer, *Mythology of the Ancient World*, Anchor Books, New York, 1961.

【古希腊史】

泛希腊主义与帝国的统一——试论伯里克利的泛希腊政策

冯金朋　天津师范大学

摘要：倡议召开泛希腊大会、联合殖民图里伊和开放泛雅典娜节等三项政策是伯里克利的泛希腊政策的重要表现。尽管这些政策旨在维护雅典城邦利益，但实际上也惠及其他城邦乃至整个希腊世界，从而可以肯定其政策具有泛希腊主义的合理性。将其置于整个希腊主义历史之中，我们会发现，伯里克利将帝国统治和泛希腊主义有机地结合在一起，为实现泛希腊主义所主张的"普遍和平"提供了一条切实可行的途径，并被后世遵循。

关键词：泛希腊主义；帝国；伯里克利；泛希腊大会；图里伊；泛雅典娜节

Abstract：There were three important panhellenic policies of Pericles which were proposing the panhellenic convention, co-colonization of Thurii and opening the Panathenaic festival. These policies were designed to intention of maintaining the interests of Athens, but, in fact, they also did make beneficial to other poleis and even the whole Greek world; seeing which, it is reasonable to recognize them to be panhellenistic. Putting these policies into the development of panhellenistic history, we will find that Pericles integrated imperial rule and panhellenism harmoniously, which provided a practical way to realizing the general peace which the panhellenistic thinkers hoped; and this way became the model which the later political leaders would imitate.

Keywords：Panhellenism, Arche, Empire, Pericles, the Panhellenic Convention, Thurii, the Panathenaic Festival

公元前 500 年左右，积极扩张的波斯帝国对古希腊世界构成了严重威胁，这使得希腊诸城邦普遍产生危机感；他们迫切要求停止内部冲突、联合起来抗击波斯。在这种挑战与迎战的紧要关头，泛希腊主义（Panhellenism）①开始在政治层面活跃起来。公元前481年，31个希腊城邦在斯巴达和雅典的领导下组成了希腊同盟，并最终粉碎了波斯的侵略。公元前478年之后，雅典组织了提洛同盟，开始独自领导抗击波斯、解放希腊人的泛希腊事业。但是，随着时局的演进，提洛同盟的性质发生变化而最终转变成为雅典帝国。由于背负"帝国"②的恶名，雅典政治家们的泛希腊政策也就常常被定性为帝国主义政策，即使是那些认为它们带有泛希腊主义色彩的学者也认为其名为泛希腊主义而实为帝国主义。③对这些观点，笔者不敢苟同，拟在此文中以倡议召开泛希腊大会、联合殖民图里伊和将泛雅典娜节向所有提洛同盟成员开放等三项政策为论述对象来分析伯里克利在雅典帝国框架内为泛希腊主义事业做出的贡献及其历史意义，以期抛砖引玉。

一 召开泛希腊大会

自公元前463年登上雅典的政治舞台以来，伯里克利推行过诸多政策，其中有三项具有明显的泛希腊主义色彩：第一，倡议全体希腊人派代表来雅典召开泛希腊大会；第二，号召希腊人到南意

---

① 一般说来，泛希腊主义包括两层含义，第一层含义指希腊人之间的文化认同感，强调他们整体上有别于其他文化和民族；第二层含义指全希腊的联合与统一，一方面消除城邦分立带来的政治混乱局面，另一方面发动对波斯帝国的战争以报它对希腊的侵略之仇。（参见：Hornblower Simmon & Antony Spawforth ed., *Oxford Classical Dictionary*, 3rd ed., Oxford: Oxford University Press, 1996, p.1106; Michael A. Flower, "From Simonides to Isocrates: The Fifth-Century Origins of Fourth-Century Panhellenism", *Classical Antiquity*, Vol. 19, No. 1 (Apr., 2000), p. 65-66.）

② 本文中所使用的"帝国"、"帝国主义"，是现代术语在古史研究中的便宜用法。现代学界认为，帝国是"一个地域辽阔且具有强制性（作为一个原则）的国家，不一定必须是、但经常是由皇帝来统治"（引自：*Encyclopeadia Britannica—An New Survey of Universal Knowledge*, vol.8, 1956, p.402.）；换个说法，它是"一种政治组织形式，其中，由一个中央政权（a central authority）对广阔且又分散的领土、并且是多个民族行使主权"（引自：*Encyclopedia Americana*, vol.10, 1988, p.312.）。帝国基本上有三种类型，它可以是像德意志第二帝国那样的联邦，也可以是像沙皇俄国那样的单一制国家（unitary state），还可以是像大英帝国那样的由自由邦国组成的一个松散共同体与许多处于从属地位的领地联合起来组成的国家（详见：*Encyclopeadia Britannica—An New Survey of Universal Knowledge*, vol.8, 1956, p.402.）。从这些权威定义看，在马其顿帝国之前，古希腊世界不存在帝国现象。尽管这些定义是从近现代历史中总结出来的，但是，现代意义上的"帝国"（Empire），在古希腊语中却有对应的词汇，其拉丁化拼写为"arche"。在古希腊人眼中，提洛同盟便是"帝国"，这也是后世人将提洛同盟称为雅典帝国的最直接原因。西方古典学界，为了本领域的研究需要，对"帝国"作了一个专业性的定义；帝国是"因一个国家对其他国家进行统治而形成的一种国家"，其中的统治国不管实行君主制、贵族制还是民主制政体，都不会影响这种国家的性质，也即对这种国家的性质"造成任何本质性的变革"（引自[美]威廉·弗格森著：《希腊帝国主义》，晏绍祥译，上海三联书店2005年版，第1页）。不过，一些现代学者对将该古希腊语译为"empire"（帝国）的译法提出了质疑，因为两者之间存在着不对称性（日知、张强：《雅典帝国与周天下——兼论公卿执政制时代》，《世界历史》，1989年第6期，第113页；郝际陶：《伯里克利的民主与独裁》，《东北师大学报》（哲社版），1991年第5期，第59页）。笔者也认为这种做法有强译之嫌，但它在学界依然盛行，概因在现代语境中很难找到一个与其更为匹配并广为接受的词语。同时，本文中所使用的"雅典帝国"一词，并非承认提洛同盟具有帝国本质，而在于强调提洛同盟是一个强制性组织，是从国际同盟向国家实体过渡的一种途径或中间状态；例如，近代历史上德意志的统一便是在普鲁士帝国主义强力下完成的。

③ 在持这种观点的学者当中，伯尔曼（S. Perlman）最为著名；他曾发表论文详细探讨了伯里克利（Pericles）、吕西阿斯（Lysias）、伊索克拉底（Isocrates）和德谟斯提尼（Demosthenes）等人的泛希腊政策或构想，并得出结论，泛希腊主义不过是维护霸权和帝国统治的宣传工具（详见：S. Perlman, "Panhellenism, the Polis and Imperialism", *Historia: Zeitschrift für Alte Geschichte*, Vol. 25, No. 1 (1st Qtr., 1976), p.5.）。敦克尔（H. B. Dunkel）也有同样的观点。（参见：H. B. Dunkel, "Was Demosthenes A Panhellenist?", *Classical Philology*, Vol. 33, No. 3 (Jul., 1938), pp. 292-305.）其结论的预设中存在着一个根本缺陷，它们的立论是建立在帝国与泛希腊主义截然对立的假设基础上。这一假设，否认了希腊历史上泛希腊主义可以和帝国有机结合起来的史实，雅典帝国便是其中典型的例子。

大利建立殖民城邦图里伊（Thurii）[1]；第三，放松泛雅典娜节的资格限制，向雅典帝国内部所有城邦开放。

公元前449年，在伯里克利策划下，雅典派出四路使团，一路前往爱琴海诸岛和小亚细亚地区，一路前往赫勒斯滂、色雷斯以及拜占廷等地，一路前往彼奥提亚、佛西斯、伯罗奔尼撒、罗克里斯、阿开那尼亚和安布累喜阿等地区，一路前往优卑亚、马里斯湾、泰俄提斯和帖萨利亚等地区；使团代表"与所经过地区的人们谈判，劝导他们前来参加这个奠定安全和共同管理全希腊事务的讨论"。[2]这些事务包括，重建在希波战争中被毁掉的神庙、兑现当年战争中所许下的誓言并向诸神献祭牺牲、剿灭海盗以确保海上安全等，都是关涉希腊人共同利益的事务。[3]从邀请的对象和会议议程上看，伯里克利的提议具有强烈的泛希腊主义色彩。但是，这一倡议却因斯巴达等城邦的阻挠而无果而终。

伯里克利为什么要提出召开泛希腊大会，斯巴达等城邦却又为什么会反对呢？这应该从当时的历史背景找原因。公元前449年，雅典和波斯签订卡里阿斯和约（the Peace of Callias），停止了双方的敌对活动；波斯正式宣布退出希腊世界并放弃再次征服希腊的计划，而雅典则宣布终止反波斯战争、不再向波斯帝国的传统势力范围渗透。[4]此和约的签订某种程度上宣布，提洛同盟失去了其继

---

① 在现代学者经常使用三种拉丁化拼写形式的单词来指称"图里伊"，它们分别是"Thurii"、"Thurioi"和"Thurium"等；其中，"Thurii"最为常用，它的词源是希腊语中的"Θούριοι"。在《伯罗奔尼撒战争史》中，修昔底德用"Θουρία"表示图里伊城邦，用"Θούριοι"表示图里伊人民并由此也具有指称图里伊城邦的性质；像伪安多西德（Ps.–Andocides）、柏拉图、斯特拉波和普鲁塔克等古典作家，则是用"Θούριοι"来表示图里伊城邦。同时，有些古代作家也用"Θούριον"和"Thrurium"来表示图里伊城邦，但它更多地是用来表示新图里伊，而非通常所说的那个在公元前444/3年建立的图里伊。（参见：Victor Ehrenberg, "The Foundation of Thurii", *The American Journal of Philology*, Vol. 69, No. 2 (1948), p. 149.）

② Plutarch, *Pericles*, 17. 其中引文引自杨巨平先生所译的普鲁塔克《伯里克利传》，详见中国世界古代史研究会、内蒙古大学历史系（合编）：《世界古代史译文集》，内蒙古大学学报编辑部，1987年版，第213页。

③ Plutarch, *Pericles*, 17.

④ Diodorus Siculus, *The Library of History*, xii, 4. 4–5; Plutarch, *Cimon*, 13.4. 关于卡利阿斯和约的真实性，自古便存在着争论。普鲁塔克记载，卡利斯提尼（Callisthenes，公元前360–328年）否认雅典和波斯之间签订过这一和约，波斯人之所以按照"和约"的条款，长期未曾再次侵犯希腊人，是因为他们在塞浦路斯那场惨败使他们甚为恐惧，"远远避开，而不敢靠近希腊"。（参见：Plutarch, *Cimon*, 13.5.）同时，他还记载，克拉特鲁斯（Craterus，约公元前370–321年）曾经收集到过此项和约的一个副本；并且，雅典人还为此修建了一座和平祭坛。（参见：Plutarch, *Cimon*, 13.6.）与卡利斯提尼同时代的提奥庞普斯（Theopompus，约公元前380–420年），也认为卡利阿斯和约为虚构之事。（参见：Theopompus, F. 154, 转引自，David Stockton, "The Peace of Callias", *Historia: Zeitschrift für Alte Geschichte*, Vol. 8, No. 1 (Jan., 1959), p. 61.）与两派做法不一样的是修昔底德。作为"当代史的见证人"，修昔底德却没有提及此事；至于他为何没有提及此事，学界尚未做出确定的解释。大概是修昔底德惜墨如金的缘故吧，除了详细叙述伯罗奔尼撒战争及其根源外，他极少叙述其他事件。不过，大卫·斯托克顿认为，如果真有此事，修昔底德不会不记载；他没有记载，可以反证此事不存在。（参见：David Stockton, "The Peace of Callias", *Historia: Zeitschrift für Alte Geschichte*, Vol. 8, No. 1 (Jan., 1959), pp. 65.）卡根认为，斯托克顿对否定卡利阿斯和约存在的论证，是诸多反驳文章中最好的。相对于否定卡利阿斯和约存在的学者而言，肯定此条约存在的学者要多过他们许多。卡根对当代学者的相关争论进行了粗略的归纳和总结，并在最后赞成了大多数学者的观点。详见 Donald Kagan, *The Outbreak of the Peloponnesian War*, Ithaca and London: Cornell University Press, 1969, p. 107; p. 107, n. 25. 然而，这场争论，并没有随着卡根的总结而终结，它甚至一直持续到了现在。参见 Anton Powell, *Athens and Sparta: Constructing Greek Political and Social History from 478 BC*, London: Routledge, 1988, p. 49–54; A. B. Bosworth, "Plutarch, Callisthenes and the Peace of Callias", *The Journal of Hellenic Studies*, Vol. 110 (1990), pp. 1–13; Loren J. Samons II, "Kimon, Kallias and Peace with Persia", *Historia: Zeitschrift für Alte Geschichte*, Vol. 47, No. 2 (2nd Qtr., 1998), pp. 129–140. 而乔治·柯克威尔（George Cawkwell）对于对相关的学术史进行了最新且最为详尽的梳理，尤其值得一提的是，他提到了巴迪安（Badian）的一个独特观点。巴迪安认为，雅典曾经与波斯签订过两个和约，一个是公元前449年的卡利阿斯和约，另一个是在优里莫顿（Eurymedon）战役之后签订的。（参见 George Cawkwell, *The Greek Wars: The Failure of Persia*, New York: Oxford University Press Inc., 2005, pp. 281–289.）刘易斯（D. M. Lewis）认为卡利阿斯和约是真实存在的，修昔底德没有记载它是"一个严重疏漏（a serious omission）"。（参见 D. M. Lewis, "The Thirty Years' Peace", *The Cambridge Ancient History*, vol. V, Cambridge: Cambridge University Press, 1992, p. 121.）

续存在的合法性依据；因为，最初成立同盟的目的是惩罚波斯并将其赶出希腊①。和约签订之后，提洛同盟内部出现了危机，许多盟邦不愿意继续缴纳盟金，一些盟邦拒绝缴纳、一些盟邦只部分缴纳、一些则是延期缴纳。②此时的雅典，在用武力维持提洛同盟或雅典帝国存在的同时，仍需要论证其存在的合法性。伯尔曼认为，为了赋予雅典帝国以新的合法性，伯里克利才提议召开泛希腊会议的。③然而，提议召开泛希腊大会，并非仅出于此唯一目的。其次，斯巴达等城邦对雅典的崛起，始终存在着戒心和不满，并在五十年代发生过武装冲突；卡里阿斯和约使得雅典可以放心关注于它在希腊大陆的扩展，这更进一步加重了斯巴达诸城邦的恐惧感。④通过谈判来消弭斯巴达的误解和戒心，使其承认雅典的既得利益，与斯巴达和平分享希腊世界的领导权，⑤也是有必要的。此外，来自雅典内部的政治压力也让伯里克利有必要做出倡议召开泛希腊大会的抉择。在雅典，存在着两个削弱伯里克利政治影响力的因素。客蒙死后，贵族派不满伯里克利独自做大，便扶植起梅勒西阿斯之子修昔底德(Thucydides the son of Melesias)与伯里克利角逐，并很快在政治上形成对伯里克利的牵制。⑥同时，主张希腊城邦一律平等的雅典人也对伯里克利不满，他们对附属盟邦抱有同情，不相信任何举措能够使雅典的统治和斯巴达的暴政区分开来。⑦这些攻击是伯里克利无法回避的，它们也是民意的一部分；为了维持甚至提升在民众中的威望，伯里克利有必要采取新的、更受民众欢迎的政策。

从上面的背景分析看，伯里克利提议召开此次泛希腊大会的根本目的并不是为了解决所谓的修复神庙、献祭诸神、剿灭海盗等泛希腊事务，而是为了赋予雅典帝国以新的合法性、谋求与斯巴达共同分享希腊世界的领导权和巩固伯里克利在雅典城邦的政治地位。但是，我们不能因为其提议在一定程度上出于雅典和伯里克利的私利目的，就否定其中含有有利于整个希腊世界的效果，会议日程安排的事务的确是要处理一些泛希腊问题，共同的行动必定会增加彼此间的认同和信任。如果这次会议能够成功召开，或许会将希腊带入一个良性的发展轨道；它的召开，"或许会使得联合趋势（ converging tendency ）和分散割据的希腊人建立同盟具有新的可能性"，这是一个惠及包括斯巴达人和雅典人在内的所有希腊人的"普遍福祉"（ a comprehensive benefit ）。⑧但是，由于这一倡议胎死腹中，我们也就无法看到它会为希腊历史的发展带来何种影响。

二 联合殖民图里伊

尽管召开泛希腊大会的倡议遭到斯巴达等城邦的反对而受挫以及公元前447/6 年雅典又在希腊大陆遭遇惨重失败，但是这都未影响到伯里克利推行其泛希腊主义政策的热情；在公元前445 年

---

① Thucydides, *The Peloponnesian War*, II, 96.1; Plutarch, Aristeides, 25. 1; *Aristotle*, The *Athenian Constitutions*, 23.5.

② J. B. Bury and Russell Meiggs, *A History of Greece to the death of Alexander the Great*, London: Macmillan, 1975, p.225.

③ S. Perlman, "Panhellenism, the Polis and Imperialism", *Historia: Zeitschrift für Alte Geschichte*, Vol. 25, No. 1 (1st Qtr., 1976), p.7. 鲍尔策（ Balcer ）也有同样的观点，参见：Jack Martin Balcer, "Separatism and Anti-Separatism in the Athenian Empire (478–433 B.C.)", *Historia: Zeitschrift für Alte Geschichte*, Vol. 23, No. 1 (1st Qtr., 1974), p.34.

④ A. E. Raubitschek, "The Peace Policy of Pericles", *American Journal of Archaeology*, Vol. 70, No. 1 (Jan., 1966), p. 39.

⑤ 普鲁塔克在《伯里克利传》中提到，斯巴达因为雅典的强大而担心，伯里克利鼓励雅典人要迎难而上，建立一番伟大事业。（ 参见：Plutarch, Pericles, 17. ）照普鲁塔克看来，召开泛希腊会议，只是雅典与斯巴达争夺霸权的一个跳板，独霸希腊，似乎是伯里克利的最终目标。

⑥ Plutarch, *Pericles*, 11.

⑦ J. B. Bury and Russell Meiggs, *A History of Greece to the death of Alexander the Great*, London: Macmillan, 1975, p.224.

⑧ George Grote, *A History of Greece*, vol. 4, Bristol: Thoemmes Press, 2000, p. 511.

三十年和约签订后，伯里克利又策划了另一场泛希腊行动，他号召希腊人联合起来到南意大利的绪巴里斯（Sybaris）的旧址营建殖民城邦图里伊。

公元前443年，在伯里克利主持下，由雅典人兰博恩（Lampon）和色诺克利图斯（Xenocritus）率领，根据德尔菲神谕的指引，来自不同城邦的希腊人共同航海到意大利南部的绪巴里斯旧址建立了一个新的城邦——图里伊。这次联合行动带有显著的泛希腊色彩。在准备殖民活动期间，或许是基于召开泛希腊大会受挫的教训，伯里克利这次是向所有希腊人而非希腊城邦发出了邀请，从而获得了成功。从各方面来看，殖民图里伊的活动都带有泛希腊色彩。从殖民活动的参加者看，不仅有雅典人，还有与雅典交善的城邦公民如普罗泰哥拉（Protagoras）、希罗多德（Herodotus）和希波达摩斯（Hippodamus）等人，同时也包括来自敌对城邦的公民如伯罗奔尼撒半岛上的阿卡狄亚人、阿卡亚人和伊利斯人等，[①]这可谓是一次真正的泛希腊联合行动。城市规划的设计者是建设雅典比雷埃夫斯城（Piraeus）的工程师希波达摩斯，他是米利都人。城邦的政体是民主制，但不是仿照雅典的政体制定的，而是洛克里立法者札留库斯（Zaleucus）制定的政治制度。城邦使用的钱币，正面是雅典娜女神的头像，反面是象征和平的橄榄枝。可以说，图里伊的建立是全体希腊人的共同努力。当公元前434年图里伊派出使团向德尔菲的阿波罗神询问谁是这个城邦的建城者之时，他的回答则是阿波罗神自己应该是图里伊的建城者；由此可见，这泛希腊的殖民之神也承认了这个殖民城邦的泛希腊性质。[②]

然而，伯尔曼却仍然认为它是雅典为谋一己私利而筹划的，是披着泛希腊主义外衣的雅典帝国主义的表现；"建立图里伊是雅典在西方扩张其领导权的第一次实质性的尝试，它是雅典帝国主义政策的全新开始。"[③]至于这一观点是否能够成立，我们可以将其放进殖民图里伊的历史背景、历史结果和雅典人的态度中验证。

随着雅典的勃兴，它在西地中海的商业贸易活动开始频繁起来，并对这个地区产生了巨大影响；例如，西西里岛的许多希腊城邦采用了雅典的标准来铸造货币。[④]这便严重损害了科林斯在这个地区的商业利益。而科林斯又在西地中海有着广泛的优势，例如，它与叙拉古关系密切，它们联合制约着雅典在这个地区的渗透。雅典的确在这个地区不具备优势，既无殖民地，又无亲密且强大的战略伙伴。雅典想要在这个地区立足并发展起来，就必须寻找一个类似叙拉古的可靠盟友或建立自己的殖民地。早在数十年前，泰米斯托克利（Themistocles）便意识到雅典必定会扩张到西地中海，并为自己的两个女儿分别取名为伊大利娅（Italia）和绪巴里丝（Sybaris）；[⑤]这一带有谶纬色彩的行为向雅典人指明，要在这里首先取得突破。雅典在五十年代与厄基斯塔（Egesta）、瑞吉温（Rhegium）以及列文梯尼（Leontini）结盟[⑥]，便是有意或无意地执行了泰米斯托克利的遗嘱。公元前446/5年，绪巴里斯人的子嗣向雅典发出求助，请求帮助他们重建家园，此事正好为伯里克利继承了泰米斯托克利的战略思想和推行其泛希腊政策提供了新的契机。

同时，绪巴里斯人的子嗣此次求援的对象是斯巴达和雅典，并且他们首先求助了斯巴达，但遭

---

① Diodorus Siculus, *The Library of History*, XII, 11. 3.

② Diodorus Siculus, *The Library of History*, XII, 35. 3.

③ S. Perlman, "Panhellenism, the Polis and Imperialism", *Historia: Zeitschrift für Alte Geschichte*, Vol. 25, No. 1 (1st Qtr., 1976), p.16.

④ J. B. Bury and Russell Meiggs, *A History of Greece to the death of Alexander the Great*, London: Macmillan, 1975, p.238.

⑤ Plutarch, *Themistocles*, 32.

⑥ Victor Ehrenberg, "The Foundation of Thurii", *The American Journal of Philology*, Vol. 69, No. 2 (1948), p. 156; Donald Kagan, *The Outbreak of the Peloponnesian War*, Ithaca and London: Cornell University Press, 1969, p. 154–155.

到拒绝，这使得雅典可以独占这次扩张势力的机会。尽管可以单独进行殖民活动，但伯里克利还是赋予这次行动以泛希腊性质。[1]伯里克利这个做法也遭到了一部分雅典人的反对；例如，戏剧诗人克拉提努斯（Cratinus）便讽刺道，"伯里克利是否是忒修斯第二（a second Theseus），他将整个希腊人都统一在一起（synoecise the whole of Greece）"[2]。可见，这些雅典人的确意识到了联合行动很可能会损害雅典自身的利益。但是，伯里克利的做法却更为高明，与其他希腊人利益均沾是在希腊世界树立雅典领袖地位的一种必要代价。

尽管这次殖民活动是雅典组织的，并且在图里伊建立的是民主政体；但是，图里伊事实上并未成为雅典在希腊西部世界的势力中心，雅典始终没有将图里伊视为自己的殖民城邦，也没有与图里伊结盟[3]，甚至也没有干预图里伊的内政建设和内部冲突，协助雅典移民确立他们的优势[4]。由于雅典人在图里伊不占多数，同时也因为雅典的中立，导致图里伊和雅典的关系并不密切；在后来的伯罗奔尼撒战争中，图里伊保持了中立。从历史结果看，伯里克利主持的此次泛希腊殖民活动，并未实现所有预期的结果。

从这次泛希腊殖民活动的前后历史背景来看，伯里克利的这项泛希腊政策不能被定性为帝国主义；如果非要将其定性为帝国主义，它至多是一种利益均沾的帝国主义，因为它在很大程度上是基于希腊世界的整体利益而提出和实施的。伯里克利在这个问题上既没有严格贯彻泰米斯托克利的扩张主义，将图里伊纳入雅典的势力范围之内；所以，联合殖民图里伊所具有的泛希腊意义应该给予充分肯定。

三　泛雅典娜节泛希腊化

倡议召开泛希腊大会和联合殖民提议这两项政策是伯里克利针对雅典帝国外部推行的，同时，他还对帝国内部实行了一系列的泛希腊政策，以便加强帝国的向心力。由于雅典领导的反波斯战争不断取得胜利，从而使波斯的威胁逐渐减弱，进而使得抗击波斯的号召也逐渐失去它的说服力，一些盟邦甚至宣布脱离提洛同盟。面对这种情形，雅典一方面采用武力镇压的手段打击分离主义倾向，另一方面调整帝国的内部政策，从宗教上强化盟邦的文化认同感，其中的一个重要举措便是将泛雅典娜节向所有提洛同盟成员开放。

泛雅典娜节（Panathenaea）是为了纪念雅典城邦的保护神雅典娜的诞生而举办的节日庆典，它的出现甚至可以追溯到传说中的忒修斯时代。[5]每四年举行一次大泛雅典娜节（the Great Panathenaea），历时八天；其余三年，每年举办一次小泛雅典娜节（the Lesser Panathenaea）。从节

---

① 伯尔曼认为，伯里克利之所以将这次行动泛希腊化，是因为雅典缺乏足够的人力。（参见：S. Perlman, "Panhellenism, the Polis and Imperialism", *Historia: Zeitschrift für Alte Geschichte*, Vol. 25, No. 1 (1st Qtr., 1976), p.16.）但是，雅典当时正充斥着许多游手好闲、无所事事的游民，他们是雅典社会的不稳定因素；而殖民活动恰好是解决这个社会问题的良方；在此之前，雅典已经向其他地区陆续派出了两三千的移民。（参见：Plutarch, *Pericles*, 11.）但是，并不能根据雅典派出过这么多的移民，就能得出结论说，当时的人力资源匮乏。即便是雅典本身的人力资源匮乏，伯里克利同样可以从盟邦或友邦中招募志愿者共同移民，而不必向敌对城邦招募人员；同时，他还可以将殖民活动的时间向后推迟，等到储备够必要的人员后再进行殖民也未尝不可。

② J. B. Bury and Russell Meiggs, *A History of Greece to the death of Alexander the Great*, London: Macmillan, 1975, p.238.

③ 塞尔格叶夫认为，图里伊建成后是与雅典缔结了同盟条约的。（参见 [前苏联] В・С・塞尔格叶夫：《古希腊史》，缪灵珠译，高等教育出版社1956年版，第242页。）而事实上，笔者翻阅了所有相关原始史料，并未找到雅典和图里伊结盟的任何线索；并且，笔者所阅读的相关研究材料也没有提出过二者结盟的观点或信息。

④ Diodorus Siculus, *The Library of History*, XII, 10.4, 35. 3; Strabo, *Geography*, VI, 1.15.

⑤ J. A. Davison, "Notes on the Panathenaea", *The Journal of Hellenic Studies*, Vol. 78 (1958), p. 25.

日性质来讲，它是专属于雅典人的城邦庆典，不具有任何泛希腊色彩。但是，希波战争期间，普拉提亚人援助雅典人在马拉松战胜波斯军队之后，普拉提亚人被邀请参加了当年泛雅典娜宗教庆典，雅典人祈祷他们的守护神也同样保护普拉提亚人。[1]这一做法为泛雅典娜节成为泛希腊节日至少是整个提洛同盟的节日做了铺垫。公元前五世纪五十年代，泛雅典娜节又向帕罗斯(Paros)、普利尼(Priene)和克罗丰(Kolophon)等城邦开放，允许其公民以雅典的殖民者的身份在节庆期间向雅典娜进行献祭。[2]公元前447年前后，雅典颁布了克雷尼阿斯法令(the decree of Kleinias)，允许四年一度的大泛雅典娜节向所有同盟城邦开放，允许其青年公民穿着盛装参加节日游行献祭活动。[3]公元前566年左右，僭主庇西特拉图首次将体育竞技活动引入这个宗教庆典。后来，伯里克利扩充了竞赛的项目，在公元前442年的大泛雅典娜节上首次举行音乐比赛；在他主持下，进行了笛子、歌咏和竖琴比赛。这场音乐比赛是在他一手主持下完工的豪华音乐厅中举行的，此后的音乐比赛也都是在这个音乐厅里进行。[4]

泛雅典娜节的泛希腊化，或者将其贬抑为泛帝国化也可以；不过，有学者认为，此政策并非完全是雅典为了巩固帝国统治而采取的一种主动策略，它同样是各个盟邦的意愿促成的结果。[5]从历史作用上看，这一措施的确起到了加强雅典帝国内雅典与盟邦之间的宗教认同感，鲍隆(Barron)和鲍尔策(Balcer)甚至将此时的提洛同盟定性为了近邻同盟(amphictyony)，许多盟邦也愿意鼓励在当地公民信仰雅典城的保护神雅典娜(Athena the Protectrix)。公元前449年，雅典颁布货币法令(the Currency Decree)，禁止所有盟邦流通本地或外国的银币，一律采用印有雅典娜头像的雅典钱币；此举不仅仅是出于经济目的，也是为了在帝国内宣传雅典娜的"共奉神形象"(amphictyonic image)。[6]为了给提洛同盟敷上一层近邻同盟的色彩，雅典试图将提洛同盟从政治军事同盟转化为宗教同盟；此举旨在削减雅典帝国内盟主与盟邦之间的不平等色彩，在雅典的盟主身份之上再添加上一个母邦名份，以便减弱盟邦对帝国统治的抵触情绪；因为，"在希腊人中间，殖民城邦地位(colonial status)并不意味着卑下和耻辱，而是平等和荣耀"，"殖民城邦和母邦之间的关系通常是充满温情的和受到隆重庆祝的"。[7]

将泛雅典娜节向所有提洛同盟成员开放这项政策即便是雅典为了巩固帝国统治而推行的，但就其本身而言，则是一次历史性的突破。在古希腊，城邦内部的宗教是非常严密的，非本城邦公民不得参加其宗教仪式。[8]在希腊人心目中，对城邦保护神的祭祀活动必须保密，以防被其他城邦获得相

[1] Herodotus, *The Histories*, VI, 111.

[2] John P. Barron, "Religious Propaganda of the Delian League", *The Journal of Hellenic Studies*, Vol. 84 (1964), p. 47.

[3] Jack Martin Balcer, "Separatism and Anti-Separatism in the Athenian Empire (478-433 B.C.)", *Historia: Zeitschrift für Alte Geschichte*, Vol. 23, No. 1 (1st Qtr., 1974), p.34.

[4] Plutarch, *Pericles*, 13.6.

[5] 伯尔曼认为泛雅典娜节泛希腊化，其目的是为了"强化雅典的帝国地位"(参见：S. Perlman, "Panhellenism, the Polis and Imperialism", *Historia: Zeitschrift für Alte Geschichte*, Vol. 25, No. 1 (1st Qtr., 1976), p.13.)；而鲍隆(Barron)等人认为，这是雅典为了满足同盟城邦在这个节日上寻求认同感的渴望，"公元前454/3年，当同盟金库由提洛转移到雅典之后，盟邦渴望享有奉献一头牛和一套全幅盔甲的权利，以象征他们向母邦提供了食物和军事帮助"(参见：John P. Barron, "Religious Propaganda of the Delian League", *The Journal of Hellenic Studies*, Vol. 84 (1964), p. 47.)。而格罗特的观点又和上面的不同，他认为，雅典的依附盟邦对雅典的普遍态度，"既非忠顺亦非仇恨，而是对其霸权的一种简单的漠然和默认"(George Grote, *A History of Greece*, vol. 4, Bristol: Thoemmes Press, 2000, p. 518.)。

[6] Jack Martin Balcer, "Separatism and Anti-Separatism in the Athenian Empire (478-433 B.C.)", *Historia: Zeitschrift für Alte Geschichte*, Vol. 23, No. 1 (1st Qtr., 1974), p.34.

[7] Donald Kagan, *The Outbreak of the Peloponnesian War*, New York: Cornell University Press, 1969, p.102.

[8] Herodotus, *The Histories*, V, 72; VI, 81.

关信息；进而供奉此神以获得其欢心，从而降低他保护本城邦的忠诚度。[1]将本城邦的保护神信仰与其他城邦公民共同分享，这在希腊历史上极为罕见；由此可见，雅典的政治家和雅典公民的气度何等非凡。作为一个心态开放的民族，由她来领导泛希腊统一事业，不仅无可厚非，反而是明智之举。

从伯里克利的三项泛希腊政策看，尽管它们都带有维护雅典利益的目的，但是它们同时又惠及其他希腊城邦。可以肯定，在伯里克利的这些政策上体现了泛希腊主义和帝国统治的完美结合。不管学者如何批评伯里克利的泛希腊主义是其推行帝国统治的工具，但谁又能否认这种互惠双赢的"帝国主义"政策为古希腊的发展和繁荣做出了巨大贡献？在试图实现泛希腊统一的各种尝试中，又有哪一种尝试比在雅典帝国的框架内实现泛希腊统一的方案更可行、更有利于希腊的整体发展？

四　伯里克利泛希腊政策的历史意义

在希腊历史的发展进程中，存在着两种或两个层面上的泛希腊主义，一种是理念上的泛希腊主义，另一种是实践上的泛希腊主义；转言之，一种是泛希腊主义理想，一种是泛希腊主义实践。前者所要实现的目标是以保护城邦存在为目的的、多中心的泛希腊联合，而后者的逻辑发展结果是建立一种突破城邦体制的、只拥有一个权威核心的泛希腊统一；不过，两者有一个共同点，其目标都是为了实现希腊世界的和平与安全。如伯尔曼所言"古典时期，在政治实践中，泛希腊理念（the Panhellenic ideal）起的作用是充当一个城邦进行霸权统治或帝国统治的宣传工具（a tool of propaganda）"；[2]正是伯里克利领导下的雅典帝国的框架内，两种泛希腊主义才相互交融，共同推动着希腊历史的发展。

希波战争导致泛希腊主义实践与泛希腊主义理念分裂。在公元前500年之前，希腊人便普遍产生了泛希腊主义意识，这在希罗多德的《历史》中表达得非常清楚，"全体希腊人在血缘和语言方面是有亲属关系的，我们诸神的神殿和奉献牺牲的仪式是共通的，而我们的生活习惯也是相同的"。[3]但是，它们都始终停留在一个浅层次的层面，如泛希腊宗教信仰中心的出现和泛希腊赛会的形成等；而波斯帝国对希腊世界的征服活动彻底激活了潜藏在古希腊人心理底层的泛希腊主义观念，并促使其向着一个更高层面提升，反波斯的希腊同盟的成立便是其表现。然而，一般希腊人的泛希腊意识不过是文化上的认同：在非常时期如外敌入侵，全体希腊人应该联合起来保卫希腊世界的共同安全，这是每个希腊人应尽的义务和责任；而在和平时期，不同城邦的希腊人则应该和平相处、相安无事，更应该各自为政。所以，从历史上看，理念上的泛希腊主义，不管是《历史》中这段话的含义还是高尔吉亚（Gorgias）吕西阿斯（Lysias）、伊索克拉底（Isocrates）和德谟斯提尼（Demosthenes）等人的主张，其目标不是希腊世界长久性的政治统一，而是一种应付外敌入侵的短暂军事联合，以便希腊城邦能够长久存在。现代学者也意识到了这一点，"虽然泛希腊理念或许可以被视为救治希腊城邦制度（the Greek polis-system）的各种疑难杂症的灵丹妙药，但它从来都无意于统一希腊或建立一个各城邦一律平等的希腊合众国（a United States of Greece）。尽管对共同的起源、血缘关系、民族文化遗产等普遍认同，但希腊人并不希望为全希腊的民族统一或组织（an all-Greek national unification or organisation）放弃城邦。"[4]再加上，那些所谓的泛希腊主义者只是将其构想更多地停

---

[1] Herodotus, *The Histories*, V, 89; Plutarch, *Solon*, 9.

[2] S. Perlman, "Panhellenism, the Polis and Imperialism", *Historia: Zeitschrift für Alte Geschichte*, Vol. 25, No. 1 (1st Qtr., 1976), p.5.

[3] Herodotus, *The Histories*, VIII, 144.2.（中文译文来自 [古希腊] 希罗多德：《历史》，王以铸译，商务印书馆1959年版，第620-621页。）

[4] S. Perlman, "Panhellenism, the Polis and Imperialism", *Historia: Zeitschrift für Alte Geschichte*, Vol. 25, No. 1 (1st Qtr., 1976), pp.5-6.

留在语言上而很少付诸实践，尽管德谟斯提尼曾不懈地为其泛希腊理念而努力，但缺乏一套切实可行的方法和策略，以至于理念上的泛希腊主义不可能克服希腊世界城邦林立所造成的恶果、给希腊历史带来新的希望。

尽管古希腊人普遍抱守小国寡民的传统，但希波战争之后的古希腊历史却明显朝着泛希腊统一的方向发展。一批富有远见的希腊政治家通过各种努力来加速这一历史进程，其中，伯里克利的贡献尤其值得肯定。在伯里克利时代，提洛同盟在政治、经济、文化上实现了不同程度的统一。在政治上，同盟内部实现了较为长久的和平，雅典将同盟城邦的部分司法审判权剥夺，由雅典陪审法庭执行，以便公平处理盟邦间的公私纠纷；并凭借强大军事实力，对不服从裁决的城邦进行制裁和打击。在经济上，采取统一货币的政策，有利于加强同盟内部的经济交往，从而促进同盟的经济统一。文化上，雅典将原来只有雅典人才能参加的宗教节日对所有同盟成员开放，共同的节日庆典活动，有利于加强同盟内部的文化认同感，在文化上实现统一。同时，伯里克利的眼光并不局限于提洛同盟之内，他的战略眼光是泛希腊的；除了强化同盟内部的统一程度之外，他还在同盟之外积极推行和平外交政策，如倡议召开泛希腊大会和联合殖民图里伊，与敌对势力实现和解，以便实现泛希腊主义理念所主张的"普遍的和平"。总而言之，伯里克利的所有努力都服务于其泛希腊统一的构想，他所做的一切都是为了"使雅典更伟大，不仅仅成为一个拥有众多依附盟邦的帝国城市（an imperial city）"，[①]而且能够成为全希腊的政治经济文化中心；也即，在以雅典为核心的情况下，实现泛希腊的统一。事实上，伯里克利时代的雅典已经成为希腊世界的文化之都和经济中心，并且其政治军事影响力也在一定程度上超越了斯巴达，正向着希腊世界的政治军事中心演变。然而，由于伯罗奔尼撒战争的爆发以及雅典最终的失败，伯里克利这一旨在建立一个雅典领导下的泛希腊政治、经济、文化统一局面的历史进程，只能在逻辑上进行推理，而在历史现实中被阻断。

尽管伯里克利对泛希腊主义实践最终受挫，但是希腊历史发展的结果证明实践上的泛希腊主义战胜了理念上的泛希腊主义，腓力二世这位"雅典泛希腊政策的继承人"[②]和其子亚历山大大帝在一定程度上实现了希腊的统一[③]。但是，由于亚历山大大帝的注意力转移到了全力营造他的世界帝国的事业上以及他的早逝，致使他未能进一步采取及时的措施加强希腊的内部统一；亚历山大死后，这种统一局面便随之崩溃。尽管德米特里乌斯（Demetrius Poliorcetes）在公元前307/6年按照腓力二世的科林斯同盟的模式又一次重建泛希腊同盟，但是，他同样没有来得及改善希腊的政治局面，因为这个同盟仅仅存在了六年。公元前301年伊普索斯战役中，德米特里乌斯和其父"独眼龙"安提柯（Antigonus）遭遇惨败；它标志着，亚历山大继业者力图重新统一亚历山大帝国的尝试不仅遭到了最终的失败，同时泛希腊统一事业也随之葬送。在此后的历史上，尽管泛希腊主义理念余烬残存，但泛希腊主义实践却从此止步不前；最终，希腊世界经过罗马人的强力整合后实现了"被统一"。

---

① George Grote, *A History of Greece*, vol. 4, Bristol: Thoemmes Press, 2000, p. 505.

② S. Perlman, "Panhellenism, the Polis and Imperialism", *Historia: Zeitschrift für Alte Geschichte*, Vol. 25, No. 1 (1st Qtr., 1976), p.10.

③ 关于腓力二世和亚历山大对希腊的统治是否是对希腊的统一，这个问题在学界存在着争议。笔者认为他们的统治是对希腊的统一，不过是初级的、联邦式（或许，使用"邦联式"一词更为恰当）的统一。根据《大美百科全书》的定义，"联邦制度试图将那些渴望在不牺牲他们的认同感或地方自治的条件下实现一定程度上的统一的组成部分（component units）统一到一个共同的政府体系（a general governmental system）之下"；所以，联邦也是一种统一的模式，并且这种统一可以追溯到古希腊同盟，只是这些联邦不完全符合现代标准而已。（引自：*Encyclopedia Americana*, vol.11, 1982, p.77）同时，这种初级形态的统一有着进一步深化和强化的趋势；例如，美国便经历过从邦联体制到联邦体制的转变，"1787年宪法确立的美国统一（the American Union），将美国诸州（the American states）从（联邦条例下的）邦联同盟（a confederacy）转变为真正的联邦"（引自：*Encyclopedia Americana*, vol.11, 1982, p.77.）。现代学者爱德华·弗里曼认为，古希腊普遍存在着联邦或联邦式的统一并且这种统一还趋向于进一步的统一（参见：Edward A. Freeman, *History of Federal Government*, vol. I, London: Macmillan & Co. 1863, pp. 159–183.）。

愤怒，还是怜悯？——《伊利亚特》主题新论

蒋　保　江苏师范大学

摘要：荷马史诗《伊利亚特》的主题既非阿基琉斯的愤怒，也非阿基琉斯的愤怒和怜悯，亦非阿基琉斯的怜悯，而是怜悯，或者称之为荷马的怜悯。史诗是围绕从开始阿伽门农的拒绝怜悯到最后阿基琉斯的怜悯展开史诗的叙述。史诗中描述的阿基琉斯的愤怒既与阿伽门农的拒绝怜悯形成强烈对比，同时也更好地衬托出史诗最后阿基琉斯对普里阿摩斯的怜悯，从而突出了史诗的怜悯主题。

关键词：伊利亚特；愤怒；怜悯

Abstract：The theme of Homer's Iliad is neither the anger of Achilleus, nor the anger and pity of Achilleus, nor the pity of Achilleus, but the pity, or Homeric pity. The way of narration of the epic is from the refusing pity of Agamemnon at beginning to the pity of Achilleus at last. The anger of Achilleus contrasts sharply not only to the refusing pity of Agamemnon, but also to the Achilleus' pity to Priam, which shows the transition of Achilleus and highlights the pity theme of the epic.

Keywords：*Iliad*，anger，pity

一

　　国内外学者大多认为阿基琉斯的愤怒是《伊利亚特》的主题。史诗是围绕阿基琉斯愤怒的起因、愤怒的后果和愤怒的消解进行展开。王焕生说："《伊利亚特》虽然叙述特洛伊战争，但诗人并没有像历史叙述那样叙述它的全过程及其多方面，而是撷取其中的一段进行叙述，集中叙述了发生在战争进行到第十年时约五十天里所发生的事件。……对于发生在约五十天里的事情，诗人又使它始终围绕一个人——阿基琉斯，围绕一个事件——阿基琉斯的愤怒展开，叙述了愤怒的起因、愤怒的后果和愤怒的消解，把其他有关事件统统作为穿插，从而做到情节的整一性。"①晏绍祥指出："史诗以阿基琉斯的愤怒为中心，开篇即引出阿基琉斯愤怒的原因，然后是希腊军队败退，于是阿伽门农向阿基琉斯求和遭拒，然后是帕特罗克罗斯代阿基琉斯出战身亡，于是阿基琉斯与阿伽门农和解

---

① 王焕生：《伊利亚特·前言》，荷马：《伊利亚特》，罗念生、王焕生译，人民文学出版社1994年版，第4页。

重新参加战斗，并杀死赫克托耳。最后普里阿摩斯赎回赫克托耳的尸体，为之举行了葬礼。因此，全诗从头到尾，结构上相互照应，一气呵成，是一个完美的艺术整体。"①基尔克（G. S. Kirk）不仅认为阿基琉斯的愤怒是《伊利亚特》愤怒主题，而且他还进一步评价道："（荷马）选择阿基琉斯的愤怒作为史诗的主题是聪明的，因为除了其本身具有强烈的戏剧性之外，它还作为整部史诗的一个有效结构。"②

但是如果《伊利亚特》是围绕阿基琉斯的愤怒展开叙述，那么史诗为什么不在"阿基琉斯与阿伽门农和解怨"结束？如果说阿基琉斯的愤怒已由阿伽门农身上转移到赫克托耳身上的话，那么史诗也可以在"赫克托耳被阿基琉斯杀死遭凌辱"抑或在"为帕特罗克罗斯举行葬礼和竞技"结束。荷马为什么要增加"普里阿摩斯赎取赫克托耳的遗体"一卷，叙述阿基琉斯对普里阿摩斯的伟大怜悯？与《伊利亚特》主题"愤怒说"观点不同的是，莫斯特（Glenn W. Most）认为："《伊利亚特》的主题不仅仅是愤怒，而且还是怜悯"。③"从史诗的开头几乎到最后，怜悯和愤怒就交织在一起。"④因此他将史诗的结构划分为："首先是阿基琉斯对阿伽门农的愤怒，然后是对赫克托耳的愤怒，最后是对普里阿摩斯的怜悯。"⑤值得指出的是，在《伊利亚特》主题愤怒与怜悯的关系当中，莫斯特仍然认为愤怒处于核心的地位，因为荷马没有以歌唱阿基琉斯的怜悯来开始他的史诗。⑥程志敏也同样认为《伊利亚特》全诗围绕愤怒展开，愤怒是"固定低音"，贯穿全诗始终。……但是荷马还借愤怒这一主题宣传与之相对的另一面：怜悯。⑦

莫斯特等人的观点仍然没有摆脱"愤怒说"。他们只不过是在阿基琉斯愤怒的主题上再附加一个阿基琉斯的怜悯，以解释史诗最后一卷对全诗阿基琉斯愤怒主题的偏离。其实，如果诗人荷马宣扬的主题是阿基琉斯的愤怒，他没有必要增加阿基琉斯对普里阿摩斯的怜悯一卷。如果诚如桑顿（Agathe Thornton）所说，阿基琉斯的愤怒最后为阿基琉斯的怜悯所消解，⑧那么史诗最后所强调和突出的应该是阿基琉斯的怜悯，而不是阿基琉斯的愤怒。更令人费解的是：如果史诗的主题是阿基琉斯的愤怒，难道荷马在史诗中宣扬和提倡的是阿基琉斯的愤怒？荷马用他的史诗教育世世代代希腊人像阿基琉斯一样愤怒？即便如哈里斯（William Harris）所言，阿基琉斯的愤怒成为希腊教育的一部分。但是哈里斯认为荷马教育希腊人的不是阿基琉斯的愤怒本身，而是阿基琉斯愤怒的教训。⑨

与上述观点不同的是，在《阿基琉斯的怜悯》一书中，吉姆（Jinyo Kim）认为《伊利亚特》的中心主题不是阿基琉斯的愤怒，而是他的怜悯。吉姆分析指出：史诗开始叙述了希腊人的死亡，然后引起赫拉和阿基琉斯对希腊人的怜悯。由于怜悯希腊人，阿基琉斯召集士兵集会，随后导致与阿伽门农的争吵和退出战争。接着史诗叙述了阿基琉斯对朋友帕特罗克罗斯和欧墨洛斯的怜悯。最后，

① 晏绍祥：《荷马社会研究》，上海三联书店 2006 年版，第 13 页。
② G. S. Kirk, *The Songs of Homer*, Cambirdge: Cambridge University Press, 1962, p. 339.
③ Glenn W. Most, "Anger and Pity in Homer's Iliad", Susanna Braund, Glenn W. Most (ed.), *Ancient Anger: Perspectives from Homer to Galen*, Cambridge: Cambridge University Press, 2003, p. 54.
④ Glenn W. Most, "Anger and Pity in Homer's Iliad", Susanna Braund, Glenn W. Most (ed.), *Ancient Anger: Perspectives from Homer to Galen*, Cambridge: Cambridge University Press, 2003, p. 63.
⑤ Glenn W. Most, "Anger and Pity in Homer's Iliad", Susanna Braund, Glenn W. Most (ed.), *Ancient Anger: Perspectives from Homer to Galen*, Cambridge: Cambridge University Press, 2003, p. 62.
⑥ Glenn W. Most, "Anger and Pity in Homer's Iliad", Susanna Braund, Glenn W. Most (ed.), *Ancient Anger: Perspectives from Homer to Galen*, Cambridge: Cambridge University Press, 2003, p. 74.
⑦ 程志敏：《荷马史诗导读》，华东师范大学出版社 2007 年版，第 161—168 页。
⑧ Agathe Thornton, *Homer's Iliad: Its Composition and the Motif of Supplication*, Gottingen: Vandenhoeck & Ruprecht, 1984, p. 141.
⑨ William V. Harris, *Restraining Rage: The Ideology of Anger Control in Classical Antiquity*, Cambridge: Harvard Uniuersity Press, 2004, pp. 143—153.

史诗描述了阿基琉斯对普里阿摩斯的怜悯。正是由于阿基琉斯的怜悯，普里阿摩斯才得以赎回赫克托耳的尸体。因此，阿基琉斯的愤怒不仅一开始是，而且结果证明也是整部史诗的主题。[①]

可以说，吉姆以阿基琉斯的怜悯为中心将全诗统一起来，从而彻底颠覆了阿基琉斯的愤怒这一传统观点，为理解《伊利亚特》的主题提供一种新的视角。但是吉姆的观点存在以下几个问题：首先，吉姆没有对史诗开始句"阿基琉斯的愤怒"进行合理的解释。这恰恰是学者认为史诗的主题是阿基琉斯的愤怒的关键原因。其次，从表面上看，吉姆以阿基琉斯的怜悯似乎统一了全诗，但事实上史诗中阿基琉斯的怜悯彼此孤立，毫无关联。再次，吉姆虽然摆脱了阿基琉斯的愤怒，但是没有摆脱阿基琉斯这个人物。我们知道，史诗中不仅有阿基琉斯的怜悯，还有赫拉的怜悯，宙斯的怜悯。显然史诗中的怜悯不是阿基琉斯的怜悯，而是诗人荷马的怜悯。最后，史诗既描述了宙斯、赫拉对希腊人和阿基琉斯对普里阿摩斯的怜悯，也描述了阿伽门农对克律塞斯和阿基琉斯对希腊使团的拒绝怜悯。为什么说阿基琉斯的怜悯是史诗的主题？因此吉姆只看到阿基琉斯的怜悯，没有看到其他神、人的怜悯，只看到阿基琉斯的怜悯，没有看到阿基琉斯和其他人的拒绝怜悯。

二

其实，《伊利亚特》的主题既不是阿基琉斯的愤怒，也不是阿基琉斯的愤怒和怜悯，也不是阿基琉斯的怜悯，而是"怜悯"，或者说是荷马的怜悯。荷马是围绕"怜悯"这一整一性的行动——从拒绝怜悯到怜悯来展开史诗的叙述。

我们先来看看《伊利亚特》的开始。传统的观点认为《伊利亚特》的叙述开始于"阿基琉斯的致命的愤怒"。吉姆认为《伊利亚特》的叙述开始于阿基琉斯怜悯希腊人的死亡。[②] 笔者认为史诗叙述的开始既非"阿基琉斯的致命的愤怒"，也非阿基琉斯怜悯希腊人的死亡，而是阿伽门农对阿波罗祭司克律塞斯的拒绝怜悯。这从史诗第一卷叙述方法上可以看出。

"女神啊，请歌唱佩琉斯之子阿基琉斯的致命的愤怒，那一怒给阿开奥斯人带来无数的苦难，把战士的许多健壮英魂送往冥府，使他们的尸体成为野狗和各种飞禽的肉食，从阿特柔斯之子、人民的国王同神样的阿基琉斯最初在争吵中分离时开始吧，就这样实现了宙斯的意愿。"（Hom.Il.1.1–7）[③] 这是《伊利亚特》第一卷第一段的叙述。的确，荷马在史诗的开篇即歌唱阿基琉斯的愤怒，[④] 并指出阿基琉斯愤怒的后果和原因，即希腊将士死亡和阿伽门农与阿基琉斯的争吵。但是诗人马上用一个设问——"是哪位天神使他们两人争吵起来？"——转移了叙述的话题。原来是阿波罗对阿伽门农生气，使军中发生瘟疫，将士死亡。阿波罗为什么对阿伽门农生气，惩罚希腊人？紧接着，荷马进一步说明缘由，即阿伽门农侮辱了一个年迈的乞求者——阿波罗的祭司克律塞斯，拒绝怜悯老人。然后荷马从克律塞斯带着大量赎金向阿伽门农乞求怜悯赎取女儿正式开始史诗的叙述。接下来，阿伽门农当众拒绝并侮辱阿波罗祭司克律塞斯赎取女儿的怜悯乞求。结果，阿伽门农的希腊军队遭到阿波罗的惩罚。"天神一连九天把箭矢射向军队。"（Hom.Il.1.53）[⑤] 第十天阿基琉斯召集将士集会，商讨阿波罗惩罚希腊人的原因。遂与阿伽门农发生争吵，导致其愤怒并退出战争，从而给希腊军队带来更大的灾难，使得希腊"战士的许多健壮英魂送往冥府"。这正好与史诗开头部分阿基琉斯愤

①　Jinyo Kim, *The Pity of Achilles: Oral Style and the Unity of the Iliad*, Lanham: Rowman & Littlefield Publishers, 2000, pp. 71–74.

②　Jinyo Kim, *The Pity of Achilles: Oral Style and the Unity of the Iliad*, Lanham: Rowman & Littlefield Publishers, 2000, p. 71.

③　荷马：《伊利亚特》，罗念生、王焕生译，人民文学出版社 1994 年版，第 1 页。

④　黄洋、赵立行、金寿福：《世界古代中世纪史》，复旦大学出版社 2005 年版，第 123 页。

⑤　荷马：《伊利亚特》，罗念生、王焕生译，人民文学出版社 1994 年版，第 4 页。

怒的叙述吻合。然后史诗开始叙述希腊人在与特洛伊人战争中的溃败和伤亡。因此，在叙述方法上，《伊利亚特》是典型的倒叙方法。史诗开始的阿基琉斯的愤怒只不过是史诗叙述过程中的一个重要事件。诗人将阿基琉斯的愤怒提前作为全诗的引子至少具有两方面的作用：一方面，它可以引起听众或者读者的注意和兴趣；另一方面，它可以引出史诗叙述的内容。而阿基琉斯召集希腊将士集会，商讨阿波罗惩罚希腊人的原因只不过是阿伽门农拒绝怜悯克律塞斯事件叙述中的一个情节。即便我们能够从阿基琉斯召集希腊将士集会的举动窥探出他对希腊人的怜悯，但"阿基琉斯怜悯希腊人"的叙述也不是史诗的开始。

　　因此，从史诗开始部分的叙述来看，诗人采用的是典型的倒叙方法。虽然阿基琉斯的愤怒是史诗的开始句，但是它只不过是全诗的一个引子。史诗真正是从克律塞斯带着大量赎金向阿伽门农乞求怜悯赎取女儿遭拒开始叙述。

　　在以阿伽门农拒绝怜悯克律塞斯开始史诗的叙述之后，荷马又以阿基琉斯拒绝怜悯希腊使团进一步推进史诗的叙述，直至最后阿基琉斯对普里阿摩斯的伟大怜悯。这也就是说，荷马是以两个拒绝怜悯来展开史诗的叙述。我们知道，阿伽门农对阿波罗祭司克律塞斯乞求怜悯的拒绝使其遭到神的惩罚，进而导致阿基琉斯的愤怒和退出战争。然后史诗叙述了阿基琉斯退出战争导致希腊将士的伤亡和希腊军队的溃败。阿伽门农继续为其拒绝克律塞斯的乞求怜悯买单。在希腊军队不断溃败、将士大量伤亡的情况下，阿伽门农派遣一个3人使团带着大量礼物前往阿基琉斯的营帐乞求其怜悯希腊人，返回战场。对于希腊使团尤其是费尼克斯的乞求，阿基琉斯断然拒绝。阿基琉斯对希腊使团乞求怜悯的拒绝导致其好友帕特罗克罗斯决定代其返回战场作战并被赫克托人杀死。桑顿对此评价道："帕特洛克洛斯的死是宙斯对阿基琉斯拒绝使团乞求怜悯的惩罚，正如阿波罗对阿伽门农拒绝克律塞斯乞求怜悯的惩罚一样。"[1]帕特罗克罗斯的战死直接导致阿基琉斯重新返回战场，最终杀死赫克托耳。

　　因此，如果没有一开始的阿伽门农对克律塞斯乞求怜悯的拒绝，那么阿伽门农就不会遭受惩罚，希腊军队就不会受到阿波罗的报复。如果没有阿波罗对希腊军队的报复，也就不会有阿基琉斯召集士兵集会，也就不会引发他与阿伽门农的争吵和退出战争。如果没有阿基琉斯的退出战争，也就没有希腊军队的溃败和大量将士的伤亡，也就没有希腊使团前往乞求阿基琉斯的怜悯和阿基琉斯的拒绝。如果没有阿基琉斯对希腊使团乞求怜悯的拒绝，也就没有帕特罗克罗斯代其返回战场被杀。如果没有帕特罗克罗斯的被杀，也就没有阿基琉斯的重新返回战场和赫克托耳的被杀。荷马正是通过两个拒绝怜悯——阿伽门农拒绝怜悯克律塞斯和阿基琉斯拒绝怜悯希腊使团——展开史诗的叙述，使得史诗故事情节环环相扣，层层推进。

　　在完成两个拒绝怜悯的叙述之后，荷马以阿基琉斯对普里阿摩斯的伟大怜悯来结束史诗。在史诗最后一卷中，面对带着大量赎金乞求怜悯赎回自己儿子尸体的老人普里阿摩斯，阿基琉斯和老人一起痛哭，"怜悯他的灰白头发、灰白胡须"，并将赫克托耳的尸体归还老人，从而完成了从史诗开始和叙述过程中的拒绝怜悯到史诗最后的怜悯的转变和升华。所以珀斯特（L. A. Post）说："当阿基琉斯和普里阿摩斯一起哭泣的时候，怜悯又重新回到了它正确的位置。"[2]史诗一开始的阿伽门农对于乞求者的拒绝怜悯被史诗最后的阿基里斯将他眼前的乞求者搀扶起这一行为所颠覆。[3]第

[1]　Agathe Thornton, *Homer's Iliad: Its Composition and the Motif of Supplication*, Gottingen: Vandenhoeck & Ruprecht, 1984, pp. 135–136.

[2]　L. A. Post, "The Moral Pattern in Homer", *Transactions and Proceedings of the American Philological Association*, Vol. 70.(1939), p. 177.

[3]　Robin R. Schlunk, "The Theme of the Suppliant-Exile in the Iliad", *The American Journal of Philology*, Vol. 97, No. 3 (Autumn, 1976), p. 209.

24 卷代表怜悯的胜利，同时也是整部史诗一个内在的恰当的结局。①

三

《伊利亚特》以阿伽门农拒绝怜悯并侮辱克律塞斯开始叙述，以阿基琉斯拒绝怜悯希腊使团来展开和推进，以阿基琉斯对普里阿摩斯的怜悯和友善来结束。《伊利亚特》从拒绝怜悯到怜悯的叙述方式不是一种偶合，而是荷马为突出怜悯主题在史诗创造中的巧妙表现和精心设计。荷马的这种巧妙表现和精心设计不仅使得史诗故事情节环环相扣，层次推进，而且更为重要的是，史诗在开始和叙述过程中的拒绝怜悯更进一步衬托史诗最后的阿基琉斯的伟大怜悯，从而凸显了史诗的怜悯主题。诗人是如何通过对拒绝怜悯的描述来衬托怜悯的主题呢？

除了描述阿伽门农拒绝怜悯克律塞斯和阿基琉斯拒绝怜悯希腊使团这两个核心的拒绝怜悯之外，史诗中对拒绝怜悯描述最多的还是战争中希腊英雄拒绝怜悯特洛伊战败将士。比如阿伽门农和墨涅拉奥斯拒绝怜悯阿德拉斯托斯；狄奥墨德斯拒绝怜悯多隆；阿伽门农拒绝怜悯佩珊德罗斯和希波洛克斯等等。

对上述荷马史诗中拒绝怜悯的场面作进一步的分析，我们发现由于对乞求者克律塞斯拒绝怜悯，阿伽门农率领的希腊军队遭受阿波罗的惩罚。"天神一连九天把箭矢射向军队。" 由于对乞求者希腊使团拒绝怜悯，阿基琉斯失去了最亲密的伙伴帕特罗克罗斯。后者顶替阿基琉斯作战，被赫克托耳杀死。这也就是说，由于拒绝了正当的怜悯乞求，阿伽门农和阿基琉斯遭受到应有的惩罚，付出了惨重的代价。换句话说，阿伽门农应该怜悯克律塞斯，归还克律塞斯的女儿；阿基琉斯应该怜悯希腊使团，答应重返战场。但是，战争中希腊英雄对特洛伊战败将士乞求生命的拒绝则没有受到任何不利的惩罚和遭受任何坏的结局。荷马在史诗中给出了自己的答案。对于战争中希腊英雄对特洛伊战败将士乞求生命拒绝的原因，借用墨涅拉奥斯的话说就是："你们这些恶狗，曾经那样羞辱我，竟然也不怕激怒好客的鸣雷神宙斯，……我的合法妻子殷勤地招待你们，你们却把她连同许多财宝劫掠。"（Hom.Il.13.620–627)② 这也就是说，希腊英雄对特洛伊战败将士乞求生命的拒绝是作为对特洛伊人不义行为的一种惩罚。所以"没有一个将士会由于害怕宙斯而停止拒绝敌人对生命的乞求。"③

因此从某种意义上说，荷马在史诗中描述的拒绝怜悯和怜悯是一个问题。它们好像是一枚硬币的正反两面。硬币的正面是荷马赞颂和宣扬的怜悯；硬币的反面是荷马贬抑和斥责的拒绝怜悯。一方面，怜悯是一种受神保护的有正义的、选择的行为。这是荷马正面宣扬的。神作为乞求人的保护者形象的叙述在《伊利亚特》中先后出现 4 次。第一次是在第 1 卷中：阿伽门农警告阿波罗祭司克律塞斯离开，否则天神也保护不了他。第二次是在第 13 卷中：墨涅拉奥斯责骂特洛伊人竟然不怕激怒好客的鸣雷神宙斯。第 3、4 次是在第 24 卷中：普里阿摩斯乞求阿基琉斯怜悯时，他提醒阿基琉斯要敬畏神明，怜悯自己。阿基琉斯决定将赫克托耳的尸体归还给普里阿摩斯后，他提醒老国王不要惹其生气，否则他将会违反宙斯的命令而惩罚他。（Hom.Il.1.26–29;13.623–624;24.503–506;24.568–570)④ 但是诗人进一步强调神只保护那些值得怜悯的求助人。这也就是说怜悯是正义的、有选择的行为，应当怜悯那些值得怜悯的人，正如阿基琉斯怜悯普里阿摩斯一样。另一方面，拒绝怜悯值得怜

① Glenn W. Most, "Anger and Pity in Homer's Iliad", Susanna Braund, Glenn W. Most (ed.), *Ancient Anger: Perspectives from Homer to Galen*, Cambridge: Cambridge University Press, 2003, p. 71.
② 荷马：《伊利亚特》，罗念生、王焕生译，人民文学出版社 1994 年版，第 345 页。
③ Victoria Pedrick, "Supplication in the Iliad and the Odyssey", *Transactions of the American Philological Association*, Vol. 112(1982), p. 133.
④ 荷马：《伊利亚特》，罗念生、王焕生译，人民文学出版社 1994 年版，第 2 页，第 345 页，第 641 页，第 644 页。

恼的人的人将会受到神的惩罚，如阿伽门农拒绝怜悯克律塞斯。对于不值得怜悯的人则应当拒绝，如希腊英雄拒绝怜悯特洛伊战败士兵。因此拒绝怜悯将会受到神的惩罚是指拒绝怜悯值得怜悯的人将会受到神的惩罚。对于像特洛伊人那样不值得怜悯的人，对他们拒绝怜悯则是一种合理的行为。如果说拒绝怜悯和怜悯是一个问题，荷马对拒绝怜悯的描述更加突出了怜悯主题的话，那么史诗一开始阿基琉斯愤怒的描述同样也突出了史诗的怜悯主题。

四

如前所述，作为全诗引子的阿基琉斯愤怒的叙述是一种倒叙方法。一方面，它可以引起听众或者读者的注意和兴趣；另一方面，它可以引出史诗叙述的内容。但是从史诗的怜悯主题来看，史诗开始部分叙述的阿基琉斯的愤怒与阿伽门农的拒绝怜悯是同一个问题，两者形成强烈的反差和对比。可以说阿基琉斯的愤怒衬托出阿伽门农的拒绝怜悯。而当阿基琉斯完成从开始对阿伽门农的愤怒到最后对普里阿摩斯的伟大的怜悯这一伟大转变的时候，他实现自己对愤怒的控制，从而更加凸显了英雄的怜悯。

其实，史诗开始叙述的阿基琉斯对阿伽门农的愤怒可以看作是对阿伽门农拒绝怜悯克律塞斯的一种正常反应，是阿基琉斯对克律塞斯怜悯的另一种体现方式。众所周知，导致阿基琉斯愤怒的始作俑者是阿伽门农。当克律塞斯带着大量赎金来到希腊军营前恳请怜悯赎取女儿的时候，"所有阿开奥斯人都发出同意的呼声，表示尊敬祭司，接受丰厚的赎礼。"（Hom.Il.1.22–23）[1] 但是阿伽门农却拒绝怜悯祭司，没有将女儿归还于他。结果希腊军队遭受阿波罗的惩罚。"天神一连九天把箭矢射向军队。" 所以当阿伽门农决定归还克律塞斯的女儿，同时将阿基琉斯的战利品布里塞伊斯强行据为己有的时候，阿基琉斯心中早已压制的怒火终于爆发出来——阿基琉斯彻底愤怒了！因此从某种意义上说，史诗开始叙述的阿基琉斯的愤怒与阿伽门农的拒绝怜悯是同一个问题。从根本上说，阿基琉斯对阿伽门农的愤怒是源于阿伽门农对克律塞斯的拒绝怜悯，是对阿伽门农拒绝怜悯克律塞斯的一种正常反应。同时，阿基琉斯的愤怒又反映出他本人对克律塞斯的怜悯。这正如莫斯特评价所言："当我们对他人遭受不应受到的灾难怜悯的时候，我们既可以将焦点放在受害者身上，也可以将焦点放在迫害者的身上：在前者当中，我们感受到荷马的怜悯；在后者当中，我们感受到荷马的愤怒。"[2]

诚然，史诗开始描述的阿基琉斯的愤怒是阿基琉斯对阿伽门农的愤怒。阿基琉斯的这一愤怒不仅与阿伽门农的拒绝怜悯形成强烈对比，而且也体现了其本人对克律塞斯的怜悯。但是随着阿基琉斯的好友帕特罗克罗斯代己出战被赫克托耳杀死，阿基琉斯遂与阿伽门农和解释怨，阿基琉斯对阿伽门农的愤怒也转变成对赫克托耳的愤怒。即便在杀死赫克托耳并凌辱其尸体之后，阿基琉斯依然未能消除对前者的愤怒。直到面临前来赎取自己儿子尸体的老人普里阿摩斯时，阿基琉斯才抑制住心中对赫克托耳的愤怒，怜悯老人，同意其将赫克托耳的尸体赎回。因此史诗最后一卷在完成从一系列拒绝怜悯到怜悯的转变的同时，也完成了从阿基琉斯的愤怒到怜悯的伟大转变，阿基琉斯实现了对赫克托耳愤怒的控制和对普里阿摩斯的怜悯，从而最终突出了史诗的怜悯主题。这也就是说史诗中关于阿基琉斯愤怒的叙述其实也是为了更好地突出他最后的怜悯。当然，阿基琉斯从愤怒到怜悯的转变也体现了英雄自身的一种蜕变，即从一开始对阿伽门农愤怒的失控到史诗最后对赫克托耳愤怒的控制。清楚得很，当阿基琉斯怜悯普里阿摩斯老人的时候，他对赫克托耳的愤怒依然没有消除，

---

[1]　荷马：《伊利亚特》，罗念生、王焕生译，人民文学出版社 1994 年版，第 2 页。

[2]　Glenn W. Most, "Anger and Pity in Homer's Iliad", Susanna Braund, Glenn W. Most (ed.), *Ancient Anger: Perspectives from Homer to Galen*, Cambridge: Cambridge University Press, 2003, p. 61.

以至于在把赫克托耳的尸体处理好交给老人之后，阿基琉斯放声大哭，呼喊好友帕特罗克罗斯的名字。(Hom.Il.24. 582–598)[1] 因此史诗开始描述的阿基琉斯的愤怒也更好地衬托出阿基琉斯最后的怜悯和英雄的伟大，从而也形成了与阿伽门农拒绝怜悯的鲜明对比。[2]

综上所述，荷马史诗《伊利亚特》的主题既非阿基琉斯的愤怒，也非阿基琉斯的愤怒和怜悯，亦非阿基琉斯的怜悯，而是怜悯，或者称之为荷马的怜悯。诗人是围绕从开始阿伽门农的拒绝怜悯到最后阿基琉斯的怜悯展开史诗的叙述。史诗中以阿伽门农的拒绝怜悯为代表的一系列拒绝怜悯的叙述更好地突出了史诗最后阿基琉斯伟大的怜悯。史诗中描述的阿基琉斯对阿伽门农愤怒的失控和最后对赫克托耳的愤怒的控制既体现了阿基琉斯自身的蜕变，形成了与阿伽门农拒绝怜悯的强烈对比，同时也更好地衬托出史诗最后阿基琉斯伟大的怜悯，从而突出了史诗的怜悯主题。因此《伊利亚特》的主题是怜悯，史诗是围绕着从拒绝怜悯到怜悯来层层推进，展开叙述。

---

[1] 荷马：《伊利亚特》，罗念生、王焕生译，人民文学出版社 1994 年版，第 645 页。
[2] Simon Goldhill, "Supplication and Authorial Comment in the Iliad: Iliad Z 61–2", *Hermes*, Vol. 118, No. 3(1990), p. 373.

"rhētōr 述职审查"与雅典民众的政治认知
——以"腓罗克拉底和平协定"为例

李尚君 上海师范大学

摘要：作为案例研究，本文通过对"腓罗克拉底和平协定"演说的分析，研究演讲影响雅典民主时代民众的政治认知的方式。首先通过所谓的 rhētōr 述职审查，公民大会的演说同公共诉讼演说构成一种持续动态化的过程，成为民众形成他们政治认知的一种主要方法。其次，政治家在他们的演说中，总是诉诸于民众的集体回忆，依靠这种方法他们试图重塑对于政治事件的公共认知。一旦这种要求被集体记忆所肯定，这就意味着民众不仅会接受由政治家所给予的政治信息，而且也会接受由他们所构建的评价标准。在某种程度上，这种方式鼓励民众形成某种指定的政治认知，并因此影响在政治事务上的公众判断力以及他们对于政策的抉择。

关键词：德谟斯提尼；雅典民主；集体记忆；演说

Abstract：Taking the analysis of the speeches about the Peace of Philocrates as a case study, the author investigates the ways in which orations affected the political cognition of people in Athenian democracy. Firstly, through the so-called *euthuna rheētoroōn*, the Assembly orations and the litigation orations constituted a continuing dynamic process, which functioned as a major method for the popular to form their political cognition. Secondly, the statesmen in their speeches always appealed to the people's collective memory, by which way they tried to recast public cognition on political affairs. Once the appealing was confirmed by the collective memory, it meant that the people would accept not only the political information given by the statesmen, but also the criteria constructed by them. To some extent, it might prompt the people to form some designated political cognition, and therefore affect public judgments on the political affairs and their choices of the policies.

Keywords：Demosthenes; Athenian Democracy; Collective Memory; Oration

《金冠辞》中，德谟斯提尼自问道：作为政治家的 rhētōr 应该接受怎样的"述职审查"（hōng'

an ho rhētōr hupeuthunos eiē）？[1]这里的 hupeuthunos 是由前缀 hupo- 与 euthuna 构成的形容词，意思是"有必要接受 euthuna"，其中 euthuna 是雅典针对各类公职人员在卸任时进行的述职审查，但是，rhētōr 并非一种公职，因此，实际上并不存在"rhētōr 述职审查"（euthuna rhētorōn）这一制度。德谟斯提尼的表述其实是对作为政治家的 rhētōr 的公共职责所进行的考问。他自己给出答案：对 rhētōr 进行"述职审查"的内容应该包括"了解那些刚发生的事务，提前认识到它们并且把它们提前说给别人"（idein ta pragmat' arkhomena kai proaisthesthai kai proeipein tois allois）。[2]这正是政治家在公民大会演说中所肩负的职责。政治家通过公民大会演说向民众传播关于政治事务的信息，并指导民众形成对政治事务的认识，在此基础上，民众才可以进行政治商议，做出决定。因此，德谟斯提尼将公民大会演说与政治家的"述职审查"紧密联系起来，即，政治家是否能够在公民大会演说中及时正确地传播有关政治事务的信息，是对其进行所谓"述职审查"的最主要内容。

尽管针对政治家的"述职审查"是没有制度规定的，但是作为提议者的政治家往往又是公民大会决策的执行者，例如德谟斯提尼和埃斯基尼斯在雅典对马其顿的外交事务中担任使节。这时，雅典人就会要求他们接受针对使节的述职审查，考察其是否遵循民众的意愿公正地完成了任务。另外，关于政治家政治行为的公共诉讼在某种意义上也相当于一种"述职审查"。在这类诉讼演说辞中，我们可以看到，对政治家政治行为的考察主要集中在他的公民大会演说。所以，无论是对政治家所担任的具体职务的述职审查，还是对其一般政治行为的诉讼，都是政治家公民大会演说的某种延伸，都为民众获得关于政治事务的认识提供了机会，我们不妨将它们统称为"rhētōr 述职审查"。[3]

我们知道，《金冠辞》是公元前 330 年德谟斯提尼为自己的政治生涯进行辩护的公共诉讼演说辞，他在其中对自己的公民大会演说做出评价，如第 144 节中他声明自己的公民大会演说是使民众了解"事实"（pragma），获得"对公共事务的深入探讨"（historian tōn koinōn）并且认识腓力二世的"实力"（deinotēs）。第 169 至 187 节中，德谟斯提尼非常精彩的描绘了自己的一次公民大会演说，并且重申他是了解事实、了解腓力的人，他的公民大会演说可以使民众获得有关城邦未来政治生活的经验（pros ta loipa tēs pasēs politeias esesth' empeiroteroi）。[4]同时，德谟斯提尼还指出，自己在公共诉讼现场所阐述的政治事务并不是作为辩护的证据，[5]言外之意是，这些阐述同样也是为了民众更好地获得对政治事务的了解与认识。因此，我们可以说，从公民大会演说到"rhētōr 述职审查"构成了民众认识政治事务的一个基本动态过程。笔者将在本文中阐明这一动态过程的具体形式：政治家在公民大会中进行演说，传播政治事务的信息；对政治家的公民大会演说进行"述职审查"，以便民众能够获得关于政治事务的真实信息；为了确保"述职审查"本身的可靠性，政治家往往诉

---

① Demosthenes 18 (*On the Crown*), 246.

② Demosthenes 18 (*On the Crown*), 246.

③ 在针对政治行为的公共诉讼中，非常重要的一类就是"违法提议"案件（*graphē paranomōn*），这是对公民大会提议者所提起的指控，认为其提议违反了雅典法律（*nomoi*），我们可以将这类公共诉讼视为对政治家公民大会提议演说的最直接制约。关于"违法提议"诉讼以及针对各类公职人员的述职审查（*euthunai*），详见 Mogens Herman Hansen, *The Athenian Democracy in the Age of Demosthenes: Structure, Principles and Ideology*, pp. 208–212, pp. 222–224。另外，在存世演说辞中多次出现关于法律严禁政治家欺骗民众的说法，例如，Demosthenes 20 (*Against Leptines*), 100, 135、Demosthenes 49 (*Against Timotheus*), 67，赫斯克于是讨论了是否存在这类专门的诉讼程序的问题，他认为，演说辞中有关这类法律的说法更多的是具有一种象征意义，是一种修辞性的表述方式，是在民主观念和意识形态层面对政治家演说行为的制约，以及对民众权威的强调，同时也在提醒民众警惕政治家对民众权威的潜在威胁。见 Jon Hesk, *Deception and Democracy in Classical Athens*, pp. 51–57.

④ Demosthenes 18 (*On the Crown*), 173.

⑤ Demosthenes 18 (*On the Crown*), 211.

求于民众对公民大会演说的集体记忆，这种诉求作为一种重要的修辞策略实际上同时也在重塑着民众在认识政治事务方面的集体记忆。

德谟斯提尼与埃斯基尼斯在公共诉讼演说中关于腓罗克拉底和平协定制定经过的再现无疑是最能集中反映这一动态过程的经典案例。该和平协定的制定是一个重要的外交事件，涉及多次重要的公民大会商议过程。公元前 346 年德谟斯提尼与埃斯基尼斯共同参加了与腓力二世商议和平协定的第一次使团，又称"和平使团"，他们返回雅典后，雅典人于埃拉菲博里翁月（Elaphēboliōn）①18、19 日经过两次重要的公民大会商议通过了该和平协定，25 日由雅典盟邦在公民大会上对和平协定进行宣誓，而后选派第二次使团，又称"誓言使团"，前往马其顿获取腓力二世的宣誓，德谟斯提尼与埃斯基尼斯再次参加，返回雅典后先后在议事会和公民大会中进行汇报，时间分别为斯基罗佛里翁月（Skirophoriōn）②15、16 日。这就是和平协定制定的大致经过。当时的公民大会演说辞没有存世，但是，公元前 343 年（与和平协定制定相隔三年）德谟斯提尼控告埃斯基尼斯在出使马其顿期间受贿的起诉演说辞和埃斯基尼斯的申辩演说辞却完整保存下来，其中有很多关于商议和平协定的公民大会场景的描述，这些内容为我们分析从公民大会演说到"rhētōr 述职审查"这一动态过程提供了一个重要的"横截面"，有助于我们了解雅典民众在此过程中对政治事务的认识情况。

德谟斯提尼在起诉演说《使团辞》中要求埃斯基尼斯接受"述职审查"，既为了他在出使马其顿期间的行为，③更为了他的公民大会演说：埃斯基尼斯作为一个公民大会中的演说者（tōn en tōi dēmōi legontōn）而接受"述职审查"（euthunas hupheksei），并且为了受贿而接受审判（dikēn … hupekhoien）。④德谟斯提尼指出，对使节的控告就应该集中在考察他的演说；他同时强调演说对雅典民主政体的重要性："雅典的政体是建立在演说之中的"（en logois he politeia），说谎（pseudē legōn）是对民众犯下的最大罪行，如果演说不是真实的（mē alētheis），民众就无法安全的参与政治（asphalōs … politeuesthai）。⑤德谟斯提尼还告诉听众应该如何对埃斯基尼斯进行"述职审查"，并且直接质问埃斯基尼斯"你汇报了什么？如果讲了真话，就让你活；如果你说了谎，你就要接受审判。"⑥可见，无论是对使节的述职审查，还是公共诉讼，在名义上都是为了让民众获得关于政治事务的真实信息（talēthē）。

《使团辞》中，德谟斯提尼对埃斯基尼斯的指控从一开始就集中在埃斯基尼斯的公民大会演说上，针对埃斯基尼斯在"政治参与中的位置"（tina taksin en tēi politeiai），既包括他所做的事情又包括他所进行的公民大会演说（tois pepragmenois kai dedēmēgorēmenois），尤其是他的反腓力演说（logous kata tou Philippou dēmēgorein）。⑦第 10 和 11 两节用五个并列的分词结构表述埃斯基尼斯在受到腓力二世贿赂之前的一些列政治行为：在公民大会演说中宣称，最早识破腓力二世；与伊珊德（Ischander）一同在议事会和公民大会中进行演说；⑧说服雅典人派遣使团，准备对腓力二世的战争；出使阿卡迪亚（Arcadia）返回雅典后，复述自己在阿卡迪亚的演说；详细阐述那些受到腓力二世贿赂的希腊人所造成的危害。德谟斯提尼运用夸张的方式形容埃斯基尼斯在参加和平使团之前的这些

———————————

① 埃拉菲博里翁月（*Elaphēboliōn*）月是雅典历法的第九个月，相当于现在公历的 3 月中旬到 4 月中旬。
② 斯基罗佛里翁月（*Skirophoriōn*）月是雅典历法的第十二个月，相当于现在公历的 6 月中旬到 7 月中旬。
③ Demosthenes 19 (*On the False Embassy*), 17.
④ Demosthenes 19 (*On the False Embassy*), 182.
⑤ Demsothenes 19 (*On the False Embassy*), 184.
⑥ Demosthenes 19 (*On the False Embassy*), 82.
⑦ Demosthenes 19 (*On the False Embassy*), 9.
⑧ 伊珊德（Ischander）是演员尼奥普托勒慕斯（Neoptolemus）之子，据《论和平》的说法，尼奥普托勒慕斯后来被证实未被腓力二世所收买，见 Demosthenes 5 (*On the Peace*), 6–8.

演说："他那些美好而宏大的演说"（tous kalous ekeinous kai makrous logous）。①据德谟斯提尼所说，埃斯基尼斯受贿是在第一次出使马其顿返回雅典之后被发现的，其证据还是埃斯基尼斯在公民大会中的演说。13至16节叙述埃拉菲博里翁月18日和19日先后两次公民大会的场景。第14节直接引用埃斯基尼斯的演说内容，并且仍然使用强调的修饰语来形容他的演说：德谟斯提尼将埃斯基尼斯18日的演说称为"他那些简洁而谦逊的演说"（toioutous tinas brakheis kai metrious logous），到19日却变为"无比该死的演说"（pollōn akious thanatōn logous），②因为埃斯基尼斯一反之前的反马其顿政策，转而损害雅典盟邦。在14至16节叙述完两次公民大会的情况之后，德谟斯提尼表示将向听众讲述埃斯基尼斯在随后的第二次使团中如何拖延时间、损害雅典利益。但是，在进行这一说明之后，德谟斯提尼却并未叙述第二次使团的经过，而是从第17节开始直接转向第二次使团返回雅典之后于斯基罗佛里翁月15日在议事会和16日在公民大会中进行演说的情景。这一叙述延续到第56节，③其中，第17至24节是生动描述当时公民大会中的场景，45至46节叙述德谟斯提尼在公民大会中与腓罗克拉底进行的辩论。第57至63节进行总结，详细列举前后的事件经过，指出明确的日期，目的在于证明埃斯基尼斯等人与腓力二世合谋毁灭了弗基斯（tou tōn Phōkeōn olethrou）。④64至87节集中谴责埃斯基尼的上述罪行，并强调他给雅典造成的危害。第88至105节对埃斯基尼斯将进行的申辩演说加以反驳。第106至121节证明埃斯基尼斯被腓力二世收买，与腓罗克拉底同谋。第122节以后围绕对埃斯基尼斯的判决要求进行雄辩，直到第155节才开始正式叙述第二次使团的具体经过。这种叙述顺序即说明德谟斯提尼对公民大会演说重要性的强调，在此基础上，笔者将详细分析德谟斯提尼如何再现上述公民大会的场景，并且考察这种再现对民众认识政治事务具有怎样的意义。

在第17至24节描述了斯基罗佛里翁月16日的公民大会场景之后，25至28节解释为什么要复述这次公民大会中埃斯基尼斯的演说，德谟斯提尼给出两个原因：第一是因为埃斯基尼斯在演说中用虚假的许诺（tas huposkheseis）欺骗雅典民众，并且阻止其他人讲出真实情况（talēthē）；第二个原因则是要借此让雅典民众懂得怎样辨别埃斯基尼斯演说的真伪。第29节进一步强调，要让"事实"（pragmata）胜过民众向来对埃斯基尼斯所持有的认识（doksa）。这种"认识"在前面第12节中已经说明：当埃斯基尼斯参加第一次出使马其顿的使团时，雅典民众将他视为监督者，而不是出卖雅典利益的人。德谟斯提尼提醒听众，正是由于埃斯基尼斯以前所进行的演说（tous proeirēmenous logous），"你们所有人才会对他持有这样的认识（tēn doksan）"。在德谟斯提尼看来，民众的这种认识不但使他们相信埃斯基尼斯在和平使团中所扮演的角色，更会使他们相信埃斯基尼斯在公民大会演说中所呈现的政治事务，也就是那些所谓的许诺。因此，德谟斯提尼才要指导民众辨别埃斯基尼斯演说的真伪，他首先指出埃斯基尼斯的自相矛盾：在出使马其顿之前埃斯基尼斯如何不相信腓力二世，之后却又如何相信。此外，德谟斯提尼还提出反证，如果埃斯基尼斯的许诺成为现实，证明他讲了实情，对城邦有利，如果没有实现，他则是受贿而欺骗民众。⑤

从德谟斯提尼的以上表述中我们可以看到，再现公民大会演说在名义上的直接目的是要改变由政治家通过公民大会演说给民众造成的某些认识（doksa），而将民众的注意力引向真实的事实

---

① Demosthenes 19 (*On the False Embassy*), 11.
② Demosthenes 19 (*On the False Embassy*), 16.
③ 麦克道威尔也注意到德谟斯提尼这种叙述顺序，并给出一定解释，见 Douglas M. MacDowell, ed., *Demosthenes: On the False Embassy (Oration 19)*, pp.27–28.
④ Demosthenes 19 (*On the False Embassy*), 60.
⑤ Demosthenes 19 (*On the False Embassy*), 27–28.

（tal ē thē 与 pragmata）。因此，德谟斯提尼的叙述重点也就在于突出埃斯基尼斯如何在公民大会中用谎言排挤真实以便控制政治信息的发布，同时德谟斯提尼本人又是如何力争及时向民众传达实情的。在接下去的第 30 至 32 节中，德谟斯提尼提供议事会的一个议案作为证据，从该议案来看，第二次使团返回雅典后，议事会拒绝对使节给予肯定和奖励。德谟斯提尼提供该证据的目的在于表明，尽管埃斯基尼斯阻止他人在公民大会中讲出真实的政治事务，但是德谟斯提尼却通过其他渠道，在议事会中及时提出对其他使节的反驳，并且指出自己对事务的预见。在批评斯基罗佛里翁月 16 日公民大会中埃斯基尼斯对雅典民众的欺骗之前，德谟斯提尼首先强调了民众在公民大会中进行政治商议的正当程序：先要听取关于事实的演说（akousai peri tōn pragmatōn），然后商议（bouleusasthai），进而实施决策（prattein ho ti doksai）。这也就是说，民众了解"事实"（pragmata）是采取行动（prattein）的基本前提。但是，在斯基罗佛里翁月 16 日的公民大会上，由于埃斯基尼斯等人的欺骗，民众无法预先获知政治"事实"，当民众得知腓力二世已经到达温泉关的消息时，已经难以决定如何采取行动了。①前面提到的议事会议案并未提交公民大会，民众未能了解事实，而是由埃斯基尼斯向民众发布虚假的信息。其结果是，尽管雅典民众对腓力二世到达温泉关的消息感到惊讶，并且为使节没有向他们汇报而气愤，但是民众却仍然相信埃斯基尼斯给出的许诺是能够实现的，因而拒绝听取德谟斯提尼的演说。②第 40 至 43 节即讨论了腓力二世对雅典的虚假许诺：德谟斯提尼指出，在斯基罗佛里翁月 16 日公民大会上本来有可能"立即提出反驳"（euthus ekselegkhein），向民众传达信息（didaskein）并且防止雅典民众错失采取行动的机会（mē proesthai ta pragmat' ean），只要当时真实的信息（tēn alētheian）占据上风。但是，埃斯基尼斯却在演说中给出腓力二世的许诺：雅典宿敌忒拜将立即受到惩罚。③德谟斯提尼称埃斯基尼斯的目的是利用这些演说把雅典民众引向虚假的希望（phenakisthēnai tois logois toutois），同时阻止民众从德谟斯提尼这里听到实情（talēthē mē … akousai）。④德谟斯提尼的这些叙述集中体现了埃斯基尼斯如何利用公民大会演说来控制民众对政治事务的了解与认识，第 63 节又从弗基斯人的角度进一步强化了这种控制所造成的后果：埃斯基尼斯骗取弗基斯人的信任，并主导着弗基斯人"对一切事务的认识"（pant' eskopoun）以及和平协定的订立。与此同时，德谟斯提尼还指导听众如何识破埃斯基尼斯演说中的谎言：第 42 节指出，如果腓力二世的许诺是真实的，那么，这种许诺本不该被泄露出来。为此，他提出两个反证：首先，如果已经采取行动，不担心提前泄露，为什么没有看到实际行动呢？其次，如果因为泄漏消息而不能再采取行动，那么正是埃斯基尼斯泄露了消息。第 43 节给出结论，这些许诺本来就是骗局，根本不会实现。第 44 节中，德谟斯提尼再次说明自己是如何知道腓力二世的许诺是骗局的：一方面，如果真要保护弗基斯，那么在腓力二世宣誓和平协定时，雅典使节就本不该将弗基斯排除于和平协定之外；另一方面，只有埃斯基尼斯一人向雅典民众汇报腓力二世的许诺，而腓力二世的使节和腓力二世的信件中都没有提及这些许诺。

我们看到，为了让听众接受他自己所传达的"事实"（pragmata），并且摆脱由埃斯基尼斯的公民大会演说所造成的认识（doksa），德谟斯提尼在这里运用了多种修辞策略，包括批评埃斯基尼斯利用欺骗手段控制政治信息的发布，表明自己曾经力争及时让民众获得关于政治事务的真实信息，并且为了证明自己所讲的事实而提供各种证据。德谟斯提尼在关于斯基罗佛里翁月 16 日公民大会演说的叙

①　Demosthenes 19 (*On the False Embassy*), 34.

②　Demosthenes 19 (*On the False Embassy*), 35.

③　Demosthenes 19 (*On the False Embassy*), 42.

④　Demosthenes 19 (*On the False Embassy*), 43.

述中所引用的证据既有前文提到的议事会议案，也有公民大会决议、腓力二世的信件等。[1]此外，德谟斯提尼还以逻辑推理的方式指导民众如何辨别政治家演说内容的真伪，指出埃斯基尼斯公民大会演说的自相矛盾、有悖常理之处。这些就是对政治家的公民大会演说进行所谓"述职审查"的基本方式。

接下来，笔者将讨论这种"述职审查"所涉及的另一个重要问题，即，德谟斯提尼将关于公民大会演说场景的再现诉求于听众的记忆。《使团辞》第 9 节，在叙述埃斯基尼斯参与和平协定的政治行为之前，德谟斯提尼首先要求听众回忆（hupomnēsai）埃斯基尼斯曾经进行的公民大会演说（dēmēgorein），并且向听众强调，这些内容是"你们当中的大多数人都记得的"（mnēmoneuontas humōn … tous pollous）。在叙述完斯基罗佛里翁月 16 日的公民大会场景之后，德谟斯提尼又指出，埃斯基尼斯擅于否认自己做过的事情，这些事情包括汇报（apēggeilen）、许诺（hupeskheto）以及欺骗（pephenakike），显然都是指埃斯基尼斯的公民大会演说。德谟斯提尼为此特别向听众说明，埃斯基尼斯是"在你们这些了解一切的人们面前接受审判"（krinomenon … en humin tois hapant' eidosin）。[2]可见，在德谟斯提尼看来，政治家曾经在公民大会中的演说是为陪审员所了解并且记得的，听众的这种记忆可以证实德谟斯提尼关于公民大会演说场景的再现，从而确保了对政治家公民大会演说进行"述职审查"的可靠性。笔者将由此进一步分析德谟斯提尼在叙述中如何具体运用这种对听众记忆的诉求，以及这种诉求在民众认识政治事务方面所产生的作用。

前文已经列举，《使团辞》13 至 16 节、17 至 24 节和 45 至 46 节都是关于公民大会演说场景的生动描述，德谟斯提尼在这些地方均以直接引语的方式复述政治家在公民大会中的演说内容，我们来看他是怎样强调听众的记忆的。最值得注意的是，他在这些叙述中对第二人称复数的使用。13至 16 节："你们商议"（ebouleuesthe）和平协定，埃斯基尼斯"在你们面前"（en humin）演说，[3]"你们所有人听到"（pantōn akouontōn humōn）他的演说，"你们喜欢"（humōn boulomenōn）埃斯基尼斯的演说内容而"不愿听"（ethelontōn akouein）腓罗克拉底的演说；[4]17 至 24 节：使节"向你们进行演说"（pros humas edei legein），[5]"你们要试图共同回忆"（peirasthe sundiamnēmoneuein）当时公民大会的场景，埃斯基尼斯"向你们汇报"（apēggeilen pros humas），[6]"你们哄笑"（humeis d' egelate），"你们不愿听且不愿相信"（out' akouein ēthelete oute pisteuein eboulesthe）德谟斯提尼的演说；[7]45 至 46 节："你们要回忆"（anamimnēskesthe）公民大会中德谟斯提尼与腓罗克拉底的辩论场景，当时"你们不愿听"（hōs d' akouein ouk ēthelete）德谟斯提尼的反驳，[8]"你们嘲笑"（kai humeis egelate）。[9]

通过这一系列第二人称的运用，德谟斯提尼将公元前 343 年诉讼现场的听众表述为共同参加了公元前 346 年的公民大会。我们很难相信，这是对听众构成的真实记录，它实际上更是德谟斯提尼所使用的一种修辞策略。首先，在诉讼演说辞中，演说者会把诉讼现场的陪审员和其他听众视为雅

---

① 17 至 63 节关于斯基罗佛里翁月 16 日公民大会演说场景的叙述中，德谟斯提尼共举证 8 次，举证一是议事会预案（32），举证二、三、五是腓力二世信件（38、40、51），举证四是由腓罗克拉底提议的公民大会决议（47），举证六是弗基斯与雅典的同盟协定（61），举证七是腓力二世与弗基斯之间的协定，举证八是"近邻城邦同盟"议事会（*Amphiktuones*）在弗基斯问题上的决议（63）。

② Demosthenes 19 (*On the False Embassy*), 72.

③ Demosthenes 19 (*On the False Embassy*), 13.

④ Demosthenes 19 (*On the False Embassy*), 15.

⑤ Demosthenes 19 (*On the False Embassy*), 19.

⑥ Demosthenes 19 (*On the False Embassy*), 20.

⑦ Demosthenes 19 (*On the False Embassy*), 23.

⑧ Demosthenes 19 (*On the False Embassy*), 45.

⑨ Demosthenes 19 (*On the False Embassy*), 46.

典公民集体，[1]最典型的例子是，演说者在法庭陪审员面前将公民大会决议称为"你们的决议"。[2]其次，所有雅典成年男性公民均可参加公民大会，因此，在雅典人的观念中公民大会也就相当于公民集体，dēmos（民众）是 ekklesia（公民大会）的代名词。鉴于此，我们可以说，德谟斯提尼在叙述中使用的第二人称复数"你们"并非专指诉讼现场的一部分雅典人，而是雅典公民集体，这个公民集体在民主制原则上是任何一次公民大会和公民法庭的参与者，不受具体时空的限制。所以，德谟斯提尼所强调的听众的记忆其实是雅典民众的集体记忆，而公民大会就是这种集体记忆的来源。同时，我们还应注意到，"听"和"哄笑"等行为以及听众的某种"意愿"都明显带有某一次公民大会特定的场合特征，它们却同样被德谟斯提尼运用第二人称复数进行表述。通过这种方式，德谟斯提尼将某部分雅典人对某次特定公民大会场景的记忆转化为雅典民众的集体记忆。这种修辞策略根源于雅典民主政治原则及其意识形态，肯定并强化了民众政治参与的平等权利和掌控政治信息的权威，也为德谟斯提尼再现公民大会演说场景提供了有力依据。如前文所述，公民大会被视为雅典民众获知政治"事实"（pragmata）的最主要场所，而且，民众关于政治事务的"认识"（doksa）也被强调为形成于政治家的公民大会演说；此处我们又看到，这种认识的形成过程经由公民大会这一代表雅典公民集体的政治场合而被完全置于民众的集体记忆之中。也就是说，在德谟斯提尼的表述中，埃斯基尼斯曾经对政治事务的呈现及其对民众认识的影响通过公民大会场合而融入雅典民众的集体记忆。这种表述必然会激发民众去反思自身关于政治事务的认识，而德谟斯提尼对民众集体记忆的诉求在名义上为这一反思提供了保证。然而，我们却要问，既然这种诉求明显具有修辞策略的作用，那么，德谟斯提尼所谓的民众集体记忆果真是可靠的保证吗？

　　埃斯基尼斯的申辩演说有助于我们对该问题的讨论。首先，埃斯基尼斯同样强调民众关于公民大会演说场景的集体记忆。《论使团》12 至 19 节叙述第一次使团之前雅典人的商议过程，[3]埃斯基尼斯指出"你们所有人都记得"（hapantas humas … mnēmoneuein）当时公民大会的场景，同时使用第二人称复数的表述方式，优卑亚使节"在你们面前进行汇报"（humin apaggeilai），弗吕依（Phrynon）"请求你们"（edeito humōn）向腓力二世派遣使节，"你们被说服"（peisthentes d' humeis），[4]科忒西丰"向你们汇报"（apēggeile pros humas），[5]"你们所有人都了解这些"（tauth' humeis hapantes iste），[6]俘虏的家属"请求你们"（edeonto humōn）提供援助。[7]20 至 43 节叙述第一次使团期间德谟斯提尼等人的言行时，埃斯基尼斯强调这些内容曾经在公民大会中向所有雅典人进行汇

① 欧博尔在讨论公民大会与公民法庭各自的成员构成的时候，曾经注意到诉讼演说辞中叙述公民大会场景时所使用的第二人称复数，举例包括德谟斯提尼、埃斯基尼斯、伊塞乌斯、吕希亚斯等人的诉讼演说辞，欧博尔指出，不能根据这种表述方式而简单的认为公民大会与公民法庭在人员构成上是重合的，合理的解释是，演说者将陪审员视为雅典民众的代表。见 Josiah Ober, *Mass and Elite in Democratic Athens: Rhetoric, Ideology and the Power of the People*, pp. 145–147。Pelling 更为重视这种第二人称复数表述方式的修辞性，他指出，陪审员被视为城邦的代表，因此他们也就被认为是之前任何一次诉讼或公民大会场合的持续的参与者。见 Christopher Pelling, *Literary Texts and the Greek Historian*, Routledge, 2000, pp. 30–31.

② 例如，德谟斯提尼名下的演说辞《诉伯吕克里斯（Polycles）》同时使用"民众的决议"（*to psēphisma to tou dēmou*）和"你们的决议"（*tou psēphismatos tou humeterou*），分别见 Demosthenes 50 (*Against Polycles*), 15, 29，这两种说法的意思是相同的，而且，该篇演说辞 4 至 6 节论一次公民大会场景，同样运用第二人称复数的叙述方式。

③ 关于这一部分所涉及的史实以及埃斯基尼斯的叙述方式的分析，参见 E. Badian and Julia Heskel, "Aeschines 2.12–18: A Study in Rhetoric and Chronology", *Phoenix*, Vol. 41, No. 3. (Autumn, 1987), pp. 264–271.

④ Aeschines 2 (*On the Embassy*), 12.

⑤ Aeschines 2 (*On the Embassy*), 13.

⑥ Aeschines 2 (*On the Embassy*), 14.

⑦ Aeschines 2 (*On the Embassy*), 15.

报（en tōi dēmōi saphōs apēggeila pros hapantas Athēnaious），因此要求听众回忆（hupomimnēiskein）。[1]55 至 81 节叙述埃拉菲博里翁月 18、19 日的公民大会场景，也说明"所有雅典人和你们都记得"（pantes Athēnaioi kai humeis anamimnēiskomenoi）。[2]81 至 86 节叙述埃拉菲博里翁月 25 日的公民大会场景，仍然是"你们所有人都记得"（pantas humas mnēmoneuein）。[3]在此基础上，埃斯基尼斯对德谟斯提尼关于公民大会场景的再现进行反驳。根据德谟斯提尼《使团辞》的说法，埃拉菲博里翁月 19 日的公民大会中有许多雅典盟邦的使节在场。[4]但是，埃斯基尼斯援引公民大会决议，证明当时盟邦使节尚未到达雅典。[5]在这一反驳中，埃斯基尼斯不但诉求于民众的集体记忆：他对听众说，关于公民大会演说的场景，"你们是我的证人"（humeis este moi martures）。[6]而且，埃斯基尼斯还将公民大会决议作为民众集体记忆的保障，他认为，以公共文档的方式（en tois dēmosiois grammasi）保存公民大会决议（psēphismata）是雅典人一项最值得称道的举动，它可以杜绝有人在民众面前诋毁其他政治家。[7]但是，根据埃斯基尼斯的说法，德谟斯提尼却撒谎而无视这些公共文档，无视公民大会商议过程的事实（tōn dēmosiō n grammatōn … kai tōn ekklesiōn katapseudetai），因此亵渎了民众的集体记忆。既然如此，埃斯基尼斯进而批评道，德谟斯提尼关于出使经过的叙述更是毫无真实（alēthes）可言。[8]在埃斯基尼斯看来，是否遵循民众的集体记忆是衡量政治家关于政治事务的呈现是否真实的基本准则。

　　通过以上分析，我们不难发现，尽管德谟斯提尼和埃斯基尼斯都将自己关于公民大会演说场景的叙述诉求于民众的集体记忆，但是事实上这种集体记忆却并不完全可靠。无论二人当中谁的叙述更加符合公民大会的真实场景，他们都有可能在一定程度上进行歪曲。我们可以说，这种做法与其是对民众集体记忆的诉求，毋宁是对民众集体记忆的重塑。德谟斯提尼不按和平协定制定过程的先后顺序，而先行叙述第二次使团之后的公民大会演说场景，并且在 17 至 24 节和 45 至 46 节的场景描绘中使用第二人称复数来叙述当时公民大会参加者的行为，将公元前 346 年的这次公民大会场景表述为公元前 343 年诉讼现场听众共同的记忆，表述为雅典民众的集体记忆。德谟斯提尼为了突出雅典民众在获知和认识政治事务方面如何受到埃斯基尼斯的欺骗而试图重塑民众关于当时公民大会演说场景的集体记忆。同样的，埃斯基尼斯为了强调德谟斯提尼在和平协定制定过程中与腓罗克拉底的合谋，在《论使团》的 12 至 19 节中重点叙述了第一次使团之前雅典公民大会的商议经过，也将当时的公民大会参加者用第二人称复数进行表述。更明显的例子是《论使团》81 至 86 节关于埃拉菲博里翁月 25 日公民大会场景的叙述，在此次公民大会上由雅典各盟邦向和平协定宣誓。根据埃斯基尼斯的说法，德谟斯提尼在当天作为公民大会主席拒绝色雷斯国王科索布勒普提斯（Cersobleptes）加入和平协定，因而引发民众不满的哄闹。但是，对于这一说法，埃斯基尼斯并未提供当时公民大会允许科索布勒普提斯加入和平协定的决议作为最有力的证据。哈里斯认为，当时公民大会的真实情况很可能是民众赞成德谟斯提尼的做法，允许科索布勒普提斯加入和平协定的提议没有得到民众的通过。[9]我们看到，埃斯基尼斯虽然在这段叙述中依旧提醒听众"你们所有人都记得"（pantas humas mnēmoneuein），但是实际上却重塑了民众的集体记忆，这种重塑的集体记忆在

---

① Aeschines 2 (*On the Embassy*), 25.
② Aeschines 2 (*On the Embassy*), 64.
③ Aeschines 2 (*On the Embassy*), 84.
④ Demosthenes 19 (*On the False Embassy*), 16.
⑤ Aeschines 2 (*On the Embassy*), 61.
⑥ Aeschines 2 (*On the Embassy*), 56.
⑦ Aeschines 2 (*On the Embassy*), 89.
⑧ Aeschines 2 (*On the Embassy*), 92.
⑨ Edward M. Harris, *Aeschines and Athenian Politics*, p. 75.

内容上既包括当时公民大会演说的场景，更包括民众在当时公民大会中所形成的关于政治事务的认识（doksa）。

同时，我们还应注意到，埃斯基尼斯一方面强调公民大会决议是民众集体记忆的可靠保障，然而，他另一方面又将公民大会决议作为重塑民众集体记忆的工具。这些铭刻于石碑上的决议不但是政治家在公民大会中提议行为的部分记录，而且更是民众通过参与公民大会而获得的政治认识（doksa）的反映：公民大会决议的别名是 dogma，它在词源和意义上均与 doksa 相一致，指"观点、意见或者认识"；此外，公民大会决议铭文的开头多为 edokhsen tēi bolei kai tōi demoi（议事会与民众共同认为）这样的表述，①其中 edokhsen 也作 edoksen，是动词 dokeō 的一种过去式形式，dokeō 指"认识"，它就是 doksa 和 dogma 共同的词源。这些都说明，公民大会决议被视为雅典公民集体的政治认识。因此，埃斯基尼斯在再现公民大会演说场景时，有选择地提供公民大会决议作为证据，其目的仍然是重塑民众关于自身曾经的政治认识的集体记忆。针对埃斯基尼斯的这一举证方式，德谟斯提尼在公元前 330 年的《金冠辞》中有机会提出批评：埃斯基尼斯从时隔久远的公民大会决议中选出一些无人知晓更无人相信的说法，混淆事件的先后顺序，并且用谎言掩盖事实真相（prophaseis anti tōn alēthōn pseudeis）。②德谟斯提尼进一步向听众指出，埃斯基尼斯的这种欺骗手段在以前是不奏效的，因为那时"你们依然记得"（eti memnēmenōn humōn）事件经过，所有的演说也都是关于事实真相的（epi tēs alētheias）。③在德谟斯提尼看来，埃斯基尼斯对公民大会决议的援引非但不是为了保障民众的集体记忆，相反更是亵渎了民众的集体记忆。可见，无论是诉求于民众的集体记忆，还是援引公民大会决议作为民众集体记忆的可靠保障，在政治家的演说中都被作为重要的修辞策略来重塑民众在政治参与以及认识政治事务方面的集体记忆。在这种修辞策略的作用下，通过再现公民大会的演说场景，政治家试图改变民众在参与公民大会的过程中所形成的固有的政治认识，并且同时掌控民众对自身政治认识的反思。

正如笔者在本文开始曾经指出的那样，德谟斯提尼的《使团辞》和埃斯基尼斯的《论使团》为我们提供了一个颇具典型性的"横截面"，有助于我们详细了解从公民大会演说到所谓"rhētōr 述职审查"这一动态过程的具体展开方式。因此，我们现在有必要将前文分析结果重新放回它所属于的动态过程之中，也就是说，我们应该意识到，政治家在稍后的演说中再现之前公民大会演说场景的做法是被不断重复的。

这种再现不仅出现于本文所着重分析的诉讼演说当中，也同样被用于公民大会演说。例如，德谟斯提尼在其公民大会演说辞《第三篇奥林图斯辞》中就曾要求听众回忆（hupomnēsai）三四年前的一次公民大会场景，当时发布了（apēggelthē）关于腓力二世的哪些消息，"你们"是如何通过决议（epsēphisasthe），结果又是因为什么消息而错失了抵抗腓力二世的机会的。④在《第二篇反腓力辞》中，德谟斯提尼要求传唤参与制定腓罗克拉底和平协定的其他使节，并且向听众指出，"你们记得"（mnēmoneuete）这些人曾经在公民大会中向民众提供的腓力二世的欺骗性许诺，同时，德谟斯提尼还声明自己重提此事的目的是告诉听众事实真相（talēthē），让雅典人今后不再遭受腓力二世的侵害。⑤在另一篇公民大会演说辞《论和平》中，德谟斯提尼也曾向听众强调，"你们记得"（mnēmoneuete），在雅典民众为虚假的希望所欺骗而放弃弗基斯时，德谟斯提尼并未参与欺骗，

---

① 其中 *bolei* 的标准写法是 *boulēi*，*demoi* 的标准写法是 *dēmōi*。
② Demosthenes 18 (*On the Crown*), 225.
③ Demosthenes 18 (*On the Crown*), 226.
④ Demosthenes 3 (*Olynthiac III*), 4–5，其中 *epsēphisasthe* 是第二人称复数。
⑤ Demosthenes 6 (*Philippic II*), 29–32.

甚至不曾保持沉默，而是"预先向你们提出警告"（proeipōn humin）。①德谟斯提尼在这里指出，记得（mnēmoneusantas）他之前的公民大会演说是为了让听众更好地评判他现在的演说。②我们明显看到，成功的说服并不是通过某一次演说而单独实现的，相反，正是在一个不断回忆和再现之前的演说内容与演说场景的持续过程中，政治家才能逐步地呈现政治事务、阐述政策和说服民众。

如前文所述，在诉讼演说中，这种回忆和再现则更多的表现为批评政治家在公民大会演说中传播虚假政治信息以欺骗民众的恶劣行为。在公元前330年的起诉演说中，埃斯基尼斯对德谟斯提尼的攻击仍然集中于这一主题。例如，埃斯基尼斯称，德谟斯提尼为了与腓罗克拉底同谋，以出钱收买的方式成为公元前347/6年的议事会成员，③并且利用"手段"（ek paraskeuēs）取得当年埃拉菲博里翁月25日的公民大会主席之位。④再如，埃斯基尼斯指责德谟斯提尼在一次公民大会演说中诱骗民众与伯罗奔尼撒人结盟，特别强调德谟斯提尼的欺骗手段：不像其他说谎者那样含糊其辞，而是给出具体明确的许诺，用这种方式模仿说真话者（mimoumenos tous talēthē legontas），结果使民众甚至不再相信那些高尚诚实的表现（ta tōn khrēstōn semeia diaphtheirei）。⑤在另一次事件中，德谟斯提尼由于不能在公民大会中"公开"地（ek tou phanerou）实现其反对雅典城邦的行为，便去到议事会（eiselthōn eis to bouleuterion）驱赶在场的普通公民（tous idiōtas），通过暗箱操作向公民大会提交预案。⑥埃斯基尼斯甚至斥责德谟斯提尼等人向民众隐瞒政治事实，在自己的"私人家庭"（idiōtikas oikias）中操控政治事务，而无视公民大会与议事会（to men bouleuterion kai ho dēmos），却要在民众面前伪装成"民主的卫士"（phulakes tēs demokratias）和"城邦的拯救者"（sōtēres tēs poleos）。⑦政治家彼此之间的类似批评无疑会使参与公民大会的雅典民众提高警惕，对政治家的演说内容和演说方式持有批判态度。此外，前文还曾说明，在批评政敌欺骗民众的同时，政治家更会援引各类证据，并且以逻辑推论的方式指导听众如何获得符合理性的正确认识。埃斯基尼斯就曾在《诉科忒西丰》中明确指出，听众固有的认识是oikothen doksas，oikos是"家庭"的意思，代表私人领域，是与城邦公共领域相对应的⑧，因此，oikothen doksas直译为"来自于家中的认识"，也就是听众的个人认识。埃斯基尼斯断言这些个人认识是错误的（pseudeis oikothen doksas），而他自己在演说现场给出的则是"有关真实的理性论证"（autos ho tēs aletheias logismos）⑨。同时，oikothen一词也将这种所谓的"理性论证"（logismos）与听众的固有认识确立为"公共"与"私人"的对立关系，埃斯基尼斯意在以此说服听众接受他的"理性论证"并使之成为民众的共同认识。

以上这些修辞策略通过政治家对先前公民大会演说场景的反复再现而使民众不断增长着认识政治事务的经验。可以说，公民大会与公民法庭在很大程度上正是雅典民众认识政治事务乃至经历政治事件的主要场合，这种认识与经历的过程被政治家表述为民众集体记忆的来源。从前文的论述中我们看到，在公民大会演说到"rhētōr述职审查"的动态过程中，政治家对民众集体记忆的诉求同时也是对民众集体记忆的重塑。于是，对于雅典政治家来说，成功的说服便意味着成功的塑造了民众在认识政治事务方面的集体记忆，这种集体记忆在内容上不仅包括民众所共同了解与经历的政治

---

①　Demosthenes 5 (*On the Peace*), 9–10.
②　Demosthenes 5 (*On the Peace*), 4.
③　Aeschines 3 (*Against Ctesiphon*), 62.
④　Aeschines 3 (Against Ctesiphon), 73.
⑤　Aeschines 3 (Against Ctesiphon), 99；关于埃斯基尼斯对德谟斯提尼这一批评的分析，参见 Jon Hesk, Deception and Democracy in Classical Athens, pp. 232–233.
⑥　Aeschines 3 (Against Ctesiphon), 125.
⑦　Aeschines 3 (Against Ctesiphon), 250.
⑧　例如：tēn idian oikian 与 ta koina tēspoleōs的对应，见 Aeschines 1 (Against Timarchus), 30.
⑨　Aeschines 3 (Against Ctesiphon), 59–60.

"事实"（pragmata）以及对这些政治"事实"所形成的共同"认识"（doksa 或者以公民大会决议形式固定下来的 dogma）；而且它还提供了如下信息：哪位政治家在政治演说中曾经呈现过怎样的政治"事实"，其中哪些是真实的，哪些是虚假的，民众由此获知的政治"事实"及其相关"认识"中又有哪些是正确的，哪些是错误的。这种集体记忆之所以可能存在，是由于它建立在民众平等参与政治活动的雅典民主政治原则基础之上，故而在雅典人的观念中这种集体记忆成为民众权威的体现。因此，对于雅典民众来说，他们所接受的这种集体记忆便成为权威准则，用以判断政治家所呈现的政治事务是否真实。同时，雅典民众也在这种集体记忆中反思自身的政治认识与政治决定。

希腊"东方化革命"——想象的概念及其表述形式

李永斌　首都师范大学

摘要： 希腊"东方化革命"的概念最早于1990年由博德曼提出，伯克特的《东方化革命》使其广为人知。"东方化革命"的提出和影响的扩大其实是"东方化"和"东方化时代"这两个话题的延续和扩展。"东方化革命"本身不是一个纯粹历史性的概念，而是在历史的研究中混合了诸多想象的成分，实际上是对艺术史上"东方化时代"的扩大化理解，也是古典学与东方学、古典主义与东方主义在现代政治语境中碰撞的结果。

关键词： 东方化时代；东方化革命；古典主义；东方主义

Abstract： The concept of Orientalizing Revolution in Ancient Greece was first put forward by Boardman in 1990 and made well known by Burkert's book, *The Orientalizing Revolution*. In fact, the proposition of "Orientalizing Revolution" and the expansion of its impact were the continuation and extensions of two topics, namely "Orientalizing" and "The Orientalizing Period". The concept of Orientalizing Revolution itself was more of an imaginative than a historical concept. Indeed, it was the misunderstanding of "The Orientalizing Period" in the art history and the result of the clashes of Classical studies and Oriental studies, Classicalism and Orientalism in the context of modern politics.

KeyWords： The Orientalizing Period, Orientalizing Revolution, Classicalism, Orientalism

20世纪70年代以来，学术界掀起了一股东方研究热潮。这股热潮在世界古代史研究领域中也有较为迅速的反应。有学者提出古希腊"东方化革命"的命题，认为公元前750年—前650年这一时期，埃及、利凡特、[1]美索不达米亚等东方文明给予希腊文明以革命性的影响，根本上改变并决定了希腊文明的基本面貌。本文通过对具体史料的分析和对"东方"、"东方化"、"东方化时代"以及"东方化革命"等一系列概念的考量，得出的基本结论是：希腊历史上的"东方化"，是确实发生过的历史现象，但是其范围主要局限在艺术领域；文学、宗教、文字、语言等领域有一定程度

---

[1] 利凡特是是不同于埃及、美索不达米亚等古代东方文明地区的一个地理和文化概念，指的是土耳其和埃及之间的地中海东部沿岸地区，包括今天的黎巴嫩、叙利亚、以色列、巴勒斯坦、约旦、塞浦路斯，土耳其南部的哈塔伊省和其他地区，以及伊拉克和西奈半岛的西北部分地区。

的"东方化"。但艺术上的"东方化"并没有引起希腊社会的结构性变化，因而"革命"无从谈起。"东方化革命"是对艺术史上"东方化时代"的扩大化理解，更深层次背景则是古典学与东方学、古典主义与东方主义在现代政治语境中碰撞的结果；这种想象性构造在学术层面的表现则是激进化和简单化。

一

希腊"东方化革命"这一概念最早见于1990年，英国古代艺术史家和考古学家约翰·博德曼（John Boardman）在《阿尔明那与历史》一文中使用了 Orientalizing Revolution 这一术语。他在该文中指出，"希腊物质文化的东方化始于公元前900年左右，开始是零星的工匠移民和物件的引入。希腊大陆上真正的东方化革命，是公元前8世纪的一种现象，由北叙利亚及其他地方——而非（通常认为的）腓尼基——之技术和产物的出现而产生，东方化革命影响广泛而深远。"[①]博德曼此文的主要目的是补充关于阿尔明那考古发现的新成果，以此说明阿尔明那在东西交通中的地位高于腓尼基，顺便探讨阿尔明那这一交通要道在希腊物质文化的东方化革命中所起的巨大作用。但他没有意识到"东方化革命"这一概念会在此后的学术界引起如此强烈的反响和争论，因此也没有对"东方化革命"的内涵和外延进行阐释。

真正使这一概念广为人知的是瑞士古典学家沃尔特·伯克特（Walter Burkert），他于1992修订自己的德文著作《希腊宗教与文学中的东方化时期》[②]并与玛格丽特·E·品德尔（Margaret E. Pinder）合作将该书译为英文时，直接采用了这一术语并将其作为英译本的书名，即《东方化革命：古风时代早期近东对古希腊文化的影响》。[③]实际上，英译本《东方化革命》是一部标题大胆、行文谨慎的作品，伯克特并没有在"东方化革命"这个概念上过多纠缠，主要还是以翔实的史料对具体文化事项加以细致考证——如迁移的工匠、东方传往西方的巫术和医学、阿卡德文学和早期希腊文学的关系等。在全书正文中，并没有提到"东方化革命"这一术语。只在导论与结语中简单地提了三句：导论最后一句介绍性地说，"希腊文明的形成期正是它经历东方化革命的时代"；[④]结语则总结式地说："随着青铜浮雕、纺织品、印章和其他产品的输入，一幅完整的东方画卷展现在希腊人面前，希腊人在一个'东方化革命'的过程中如饥似渴地对其加以吸收和改造。"[⑤]对于"东方化革命"本身的含义，伯克特也没有进行定义式的阐释，只在一般意义上说明了这样一个时期的变革在文化发展方面的意义，"文化不是一株孤立地从种子里长出的植物，而是一个伴随着实际需求和利益、在好奇心驱使下不断学习的过程。愿意从'他者'、从奇异的和外来的事物中获取养分，尤

---

① John Boardman, "Al Mina and History", *Oxford Journal of Archaeology*, Vol.9, July, 1990, pp. 169–190.

② *Die orientalisierende Epoche in der griechischen Religion und Literatur*，最初发表于《海德堡科学院会刊》（*Sitzungsberichte der Heidelberger Akademie der Wissenschaften, Philosophisch-historische Klasse*）1984年第1期。

③ Walter Burkert, *The Orientalizing Revolution: Near Eastern Influence on Greek Culture in the Early Archaic Age*, translated by Margaret E. Pinder and Walter Burkert, Cambridge, Massachusetts: Harvard University Press, 1992. 中译本见：瓦尔特·伯克特著，刘智译：《东方化革命：古风时代前期近东对古希腊文化的影响》，上海：上海三联书店，2010年。伯克特在其英译本导论的注释中特别指出，Orientalizing Revolution 这一术语最早出自博德曼1990年的著作。见 Walter Burkert, *The Orientalizing Revolution: Near Eastern Influence on Greek Culture in the Early Archaic Age*, p. 156, note 17。

④ Walter Burkert, *The Orientalizing Revolution: Near Eastern Influence on Greek Culture in the Early Archaic Age*, p. 8.

⑤ Walter Burkert, *The Orientalizing Revolution: Near Eastern Influence on Greek Culture in the Early Archaic Age*, p. 128.

能促进文化发展；像东方化革命时期这样的变革阶段恰恰为文化发展提供了机遇，'希腊奇迹'不仅是独特天赋所产生的结果，还在于希腊人在西方民族中最靠近东方这一简单的事实。"[1]以上几处引文都不见于德文原文，而是在修订和英译过程中添加的内容，伯克特本人也没有就此展开论述。[2]换言之，作者由于自己在书中所列举的希腊人大量文化借用的事实而认为"革命"似乎是不言而喻的了。

尽管伯克特没有对"东方化革命"这一概念进行论述，但还是引起了巨大反响。[3]1994年，卡罗尔·G·托马斯（Carol G. Thomas）在《美国历史评论》发表关于《东方化革命》的书评。她充分肯定了伯克特严谨、出色的研究，认为伯克特"在没有否认自身天赋作用的同时，展示了这样一种希腊奇迹是在其他文明广泛的影响下成长起来的事实。尽管我们对他所认为是从其他文化借用来的某些特定实例仍然存疑，但是在伯克特修订自己德文版作品的严谨学术活动中，他已经在自己创建的体系中为我们建构了一座桥梁，使我们得以从不同角度去理解这一问题。"[4]尤其值得注意的是，托马斯看到了伯克特刻意强调希腊文明的东方背景，突出了希腊文明对"东方"文明的全面吸收与改造，意欲凸显希腊文明自身的优越性与包容力。同年7月，萨拉·门德尔（Sara Mandell）也发表了一篇书评，认为《东方化革命》是论述希波战争之前东方世界和西方希腊文化交互作用的作品之一，这些作品还限于较小范围，但是正在迅速增长。[5]她同样着眼于伯克特对不同文化间相互影响的研究，而没有强调"东方化革命"这一概念。

1996年，马丁·伯纳尔写了关于《东方化革命》的长篇书评，他认为这部作品的内容"比其中庸的标题所展示的要更为激进"。[6]伯纳尔认为，伯克特极力主张东方对希腊的影响主要来自利凡特和美索不达米亚，而非安纳托利亚，并且这种影响不仅仅像一些保守正统的学者所认为的那样限于艺术风格和字母。伯纳尔以其《黑色雅典娜：古典文明的亚非之根》[7]中的激进观点而著名，他自己

[1] Walter Burkert, *The Orientalizing Revolution: Near Eastern Influence on Greek Culture in the Early Archaic Age*, p. 129.

[2] 与英文版相比，德文版的导论没有最后两段，德文版也没有结语，英文版的结语将德文版第三章第七节最后段落单列出来，扩展成一个两页的结语，因此，德文版的最后一句与英文版的最后一句相同（Hellas ist nicht Hesperien= Hellas is not Hesperia= 希腊并非"西方之国"）。见 Walter Burkter, *Die orientalisierende Epoche in der griechischen Religion und Literatur*, Sitzungsberichte der Heidelberger Akademie der Wissenschaften, Philosophisch-historische Klasse: Bericht; Jg. 1984.1, pp. 7–14, pp.114–118.

[3] 实际上，该书的德文版就已经引起了学术界的关注和讨论，见 Günter Neumann, "Die orientalisierende Epoche in der griechischen Religion und Literatur by Walter Burkert" (Review), *Zeitschrift für vergleichende Sprachforschung*, 98. Bd., 2. H. (1985), pp. 304–306; P. Walcot, "Die orientalisierende Epoche in der griechischen Religion und Literatur by Walter Burkert" (Review), *The Classical Review*, New Series, Vol. 36, No. 1 (1986), p. 151; M. L. West, "Die orientalisierende Epoche in der griechischen Religion und Literatur by W. Burkert" (Review), *The Journal of Hellenic Studies*, Vol. 106, (1986), pp. 233–234.

[4] Carol G. Thomas, "The Orientalizing Revolution: Near Eastern Influence on Greek Culture in the Early Archaic Age by Walter Burkert; Margaret E. Pinder" (Review), *The American Historical Review*, Vol. 99, No. 1 (Feb., 1994), pp. 202–203.

[5] Sara Mandell, "The Orientalizing Revolution: Near Eastern Influence on Greek Culture in the Early Archaic Age by Walter Burkert" (Review), *The Classical World*, Vol. 87, No. 6 (Jul. – Aug., 1994), p. 517.

[6] Martin Bernal, "Burkert's Orientalizing Revolution, The Orientalizing Revolution: Near Eastern Influence on Greek Culture in the Early ArchaicAge by Walter Burkert; Margaret E. Pinder"(Review), *Arion*, Third Series, Vol. 4, No. 2 (Fall, 1996), pp. 137–147. 笔者前文的意见"标题大胆、行文谨慎"与马丁·伯纳尔的观点正好相反。对《东方化革命》一书风格的界定，正是理解学术界对"东方化革命"这一术语特性界定之关键所在，下文将详加论述。

[7] Martin Bernal, *Black Athena: Afro-Asiatic Roots of Classical Civilization*, Vol.I *The Fabrication of Ancient Greece, 1785-1985*, Vol. II *The Archaeological and Documentary Evidence,* Vol. III *The Linguistic Evidence*, New Brunswick: Rutgers Rutgers University Press, 1987-2006. 第一卷已有中译本。马丁·贝纳尔著，郝田虎、程英译：《黑色雅典娜：古典文明的亚非之根》（第一卷：构造古希腊：1785—1985），北京：吉林出版集团·北京汉阅传播，2011年。

的风格本身就是"标题新奇、观点激进",在《黑色雅典娜》招致尖锐批评,自己与学术界同行进行激烈辩论之时,①不免有在伯克特这里找到知音之感。因为实际上,伯纳尔是以自己的后殖民主义话语体系来考量伯克特的论述,他的体大精深的《黑色雅典娜》在古典文明研究领域确有创新之功,其基本观点与伯克特的"革命"是同气相求的。

当然,伯克特与伯纳尔的看法并非完全一致。他认为文明的发展并非遵循简单线性的因果论路线,多种文明间的交往是一种互动推进式的开放演进,单纯考察文明的影响是远远不够的,必须关注其内部与外部的互动与交流,因此他倾向于强调希腊文明产生时期的希腊社会本身,而将东方的影响作为背景来看待,因此将"东方化革命"的时间限定在公元前8世纪到前7世纪,范畴限定在具体文化事项方面。而伯纳尔并不同意这一点,他在另一部作品中批驳伯克特道,"这个世纪或者其他任何世纪,都没发生过东方化革命"。②当然,他的真实观点并不是否定"东方化"的存在,而是认为希腊一直处在东方化过程之中而非只经历了有限的一段革命。他的理由是:没有任何一个阶段存在一个"纯正的"希腊,正如任何一个阶段都不存在"纯正的"利凡特或"纯正的"埃及一样。任何试图标明闪米特和埃及对本土希腊影响的起始时间的努力都是根本不可能的,正如标明希腊对罗马的影响一样。希腊化或希腊本身不可能锁定在任何一个特定的阶段与空间之内——只可能将其视为一种风格或模式的延续,在这种模式下,希腊本土文化的发展与外来文化的介入相互交织或混杂在一起。

中国学界在20世纪90年代末开始关注古代近东文明对希腊文明的影响。③一些教材类著作涉及这一课题,④一些研究生也在学位论文中选择了这一题材,⑤近年来,一些具有国际学术视野的学者在这一领域进行了更为深入的思考和探究。⑥2009年,复旦大学思想史研究中心出版了专辑《希腊与东方》,⑦收录了布鲁诺·斯奈尔(Bruno Snell)的《〈精神的发现〉导论》(*Die Entdechckung des Geistes: Studien zur Entstehung des eurpäischen Denkens bei den Griechen*)、马丁·伯纳尔《黑色雅典娜》导论、马丁·韦斯特(Martin L. West)的《希腊化时期和罗马文学中的近东素材》(*Near Eastern Material in Hellenistic and Roman Literature*)等作品,系统地介绍了西方学界关于历史中的希腊与东方关系的再审视。

第一次介绍《东方化革命》的则是叶舒宪,他于2002年3月15日在北京大学东方文学研究中

① 关于《黑色雅典娜》的批评与辩论,见 Stanley M. Burstein, "The Debate over *Black Athena*",*Scholians*, Vol.5(1996)3-16, pp. 3-16; Mary R. Lefkowitz and G. M. Rogers eds., ***Black Athena Revisited***, Chapel Hill: University of North Carolina Press, 1996; Martin Bernal, ***Black Athena Writes Back: Martin Bernal Responds to His Critics***, eds. by David Chioni Moore, Durham & London: Duke University Press, 2001; 荷兰学者 Wim M.J. van Binsbergen 专门创办了一个讨论《黑色雅典娜》的网站 http://www.shikanda.net/afrocentrism,其中的长篇评论有: *Black Athena: Ten Years After; The continued relevance of Martin Bernal's: Black Athena thesis: Yes and No*,等。

② Martin Bernal, *Black Athena Writes Back: Martin Bernal Responds to His Critics*, p. 317.

③ 主要作品有:杨巨平:《希腊文明的形成、影响与古代诸文明的交叉和渗透》,《陕西师范大学学报》,1998年第3期;黄民兴:《试论古代两河流域文明对古希腊文化的影响》,《西北大学学报》,1999年4月第29卷第4期;王春红:《浅谈古代东方文化对希腊的影响》,《运城高等专科学校学报》,2001年第5期;徐宏英:《古代近东文化对希腊文化的影响》,《青岛大学师范学院学报》,2001年12月第18卷第4期;解晓毅:《古希腊文化的东方之源——试论古代东方文化对希腊文化的影响》,《乐山师范学院学报》,2005年4月第20卷第4期;张永秀:《试论古代东方文明对西方古典文化的影响》,《理论学刊》,2005年4月第4期等。

④ 如张广智主编《世界文化史》(古代卷),杭州:浙江人民出版社,1999年,第187-194页,黄洋撰文:"来自东方的影响";许海山:《古希腊简史》,北京:中国言实出版社,2006年,第12-15页,"古希腊文明的东方起源说"。

⑤ 主要作品有丁艳平:《东方文化对古希腊文化的影响》,硕士学位论文,湖南大学,2004年;解晓毅:《希腊历史上的"东方化时代"初探》,硕士学位论文,西南大学,2006年。

⑥ 主要作品有:陈恒:《略论古希腊文明中的东方因素》,《上海师范大学学报》(哲学社会科学版),2004年1月第33卷第1期;黄洋:《古代希腊罗马文明的"东方"想像》,《历史研究》,2006年第1期;黄洋:《古典希腊理想化:作为一种文化现象的Hellenism》,《中国社会科学》,2009年第2期。

⑦ 复旦大学思想史研究中心主编:《希腊与东方》,《思想史研究》(第六辑),上海人民出版社,2009年。

心网站发表《"东方"概念的话语建构之根——〈东方化革命〉读后》，介绍了伯克特的《东方化革命》一书的基本内容和主要观点，他认为该书"不仅较全面地论述了东方文学与古希腊文学的关系；还清楚地追溯出东方、西方概念区分的语源学与神话学背景。……多少受到后殖民理论思潮的影响，突出了西方文明起源中的东方文化成分及作用。……作者试图通过实证性地揭示西方文明起源中的东方化印记，来完成一种知识和观念上的'革命'"。叶舒宪的目的是"探究一下如今人云亦云、妇孺皆知的东、西方这样的空间语汇的话语建构背景"，认为这"对于不加思索地跟随着西方人使用这些语汇的我国学人而言，一定是有启示作用的"。[1]黄洋在《希腊史研究入门》一书中也介绍了伯克特作品的发表和修订情况以及基本内容，认为"第一个对希腊文化纯洁性进行深刻发反思的是著名瑞士古典学家伯克特……他首次全面论述了'东方'文化对古风时代早期希腊文化的影响"。[2]

对"东方化革命"这一概念做了进一步阐释的则是阮炜。[3]他在《东方化革命》中译本"导读"中将伯克特的论点总结为，"东方文化的输入极大提升了希腊的文明水平，使其得到'跨越式'发展。希腊人对古代东方文明的汲取如此之深，如此之广，完全可以说此时希腊发生了一场'东方化革命'"。[4]他基于希腊地理位置的特点，得出自己的结论，"正是由于希腊'蜷藏在滔滔大海和小亚细亚崎岖山峦背后的偏远角落'，[5]它才得以既保持政治独立，同时又能方便地从东方'拿来'，有选择地利用东方文明的一切成果。"[6]在此基础上，他对伯克特的原意做了一些更为激进的阐释，并将东方文明对希腊的影响拔高到"原生文明"与"次生文明"的角度："其实希腊之所以能方便地'拿来'，同时又无被吞并之虞，也凸显了这么一个基本事实：希腊文明并不是一个原生文明，而是建立在多个原生文明——主要是埃及和两河流域的古文明——基础上的一个后发或次生文明，一个大约在西元前7—前6世纪经历了'东方化'或'东方化革命'的文明"[7]阮炜的论述明显带有中国学者作为"东方"学者之一员的情感因素，甚至隐约有那么一点"东方优越感"或"中心文明优越感"。[8]他的结论并不是建立在原始史料基础上的考证与分析之上，而是将一种"口号式"的术语，从西方学者的著作中拿来，甚至加以进一步的演绎发挥。

这里还有一个有趣的现象值得一提。"东方化革命"在西方学术界热烈讨论了二十来年，却没

---

[1]　以上引文均见北京大学东方文学研究中心网站 http://www.eastlit.pku.edu.cn/show.php?id=6061，叶舒宪：《"东方"概念的话语建构之根——〈东方化革命〉读后》。

[2]　黄洋、晏绍祥：《希腊史研究入门》，第189页。

[3]　阮炜是较早关注"东方化革命"的中国学者之一，他于2006年12月在中国学术论坛发表了《西方两次东方化革命中的翻译》一文，第一次表述了"希腊文明是一个次生文明"的观点，见 http://www.frchina.net/forumnew/forum-viewthread-action-printable-tid-63166.html。

[4]　瓦尔特·伯克特著，刘智译：《东方化革命：古风时代前期近东对古希腊文化的影响》，"导读"第2页。

[5]　原文注释为 Chester G. Starr, *The Origins of Greek Civilization, 1100–650 B.C.*, New York: Alfred A. Knopf (punlisher), 1961, pp. 194–195、p.199、pp.200–201，及全书各处。

[6]　瓦尔特·伯克特著，刘智译：《东方化革命：古风时代前期近东对古希腊文化的影响》，"导读"第2–3页。

[7]　瓦尔特·伯克特著，刘智译：《东方化革命：古风时代前期近东对古希腊文化的影响》，"导读"第3页。此段引文中的"西元前7—前6世纪"应为作者之误。关于希腊"东方化时代"或"东方化革命"的时间阶段，学术界通常界定为约公元前750年—公元前650年，即约公元前8—前7世纪。见 Walter Burkert, *The Orientalizing Revolution: Near Eastern Influence on Greek Culture in the Early Archaic Age*, p. 6；奥斯温·默里著，晏绍祥译：《早期希腊》，第74页。

[8]　这一点在作者的其他论述中体现得很明显，如在《东方化革命》中译本"导读"中说："用通俗的话说，在与埃及和两河流域文明的关系上，希腊文明是一个子代文明，或者说埃及和两河流域文明是希腊的亲代文明。这就意味着，作为希腊（及叙利亚）文明的继承者，伊斯兰、东正教和基督教西方文明是埃及、两河流域文明的孙代文明。在此意义上，希腊与埃及、两河流域文明的关系跟日本、朝鲜与中国文明的关系相似，跟东南亚与印度、中国文明的关系相似，跟9至10世纪时的东斯拉夫人与拜占廷文明的关系相似，跟西元7世纪前阿拉伯半岛同两河流域、叙利亚文明的关系也相似。事实上，在相当长一段时期内，希腊与埃及、西亚的关系是一种边缘与中心的关系，是一种发展中世界与发达世界的关系。"瓦尔特·伯克特著，刘智译：《东方化革命：古风时代前期近东对古希腊文化的影响》，"导读"第4页。

有任何一位西方学者对这一概念有过完整清晰的界定。究其原因，多半是因为参与讨论的学者长于史实推考而不擅理论概括，似乎认为只要列出有限的考古学和其他学科的史料证据，便能自然而然地对这场"东方化革命"予以足够的证明，而无需再做定性分析。

人类在认识过程中，从感性认识上升到理性认识，把所感知的事物的共同本质特点抽象出来，加以概括，就成为概念。概念是反映对象本质属性的思维形式。学术研究的目的是为了归纳概括，为了这一目的往往需要创造一些特定的概念作为标识，这个标识应该能够较为准确地涵盖历史事项本身的基本特征。为了论述的方便以及一致性，也可以使用一些现代的词汇作为"约定俗成"的概念，这也是学术研究的需要，因为不同时代的人只能用自己时代的术语来表述特定的事物。"东方化革命"正是一个以现代术语来表述古希腊社会历史发展特定阶段的概念。虽然现代西方学者没有对希腊"东方化革命"的概念进行系统阐释，但博德曼、伯纳尔、伯克特等人从史料的角度进行具体考证，说明东方对西方的影响，萨义德等人则从另一角度，即以批评东方主义，重新认识东方来揭示历史上东方的影响和地位。我们从他们的论述中可以概括出"东方化革命"的基本内涵——大约公元前 750 年到公元前 650 年，埃及、利凡特、美索不达米亚等东方文明给予希腊文明革命性的影响，根本上改变并决定了希腊文明的基本面貌。

"东方化革命"不是一个孤立的概念，其提出和影响的扩大其实是"东方化"（Orientalizing）和"东方化时代"（The Orientalizing Period）这两个话题的延续和扩展。

"东方化"这一词被用作指代古希腊艺术的一种风格始于维也纳大学古典学教授亚历山大·孔兹（Alexander Conze）。他于 1870 年在《早期希腊艺术史》中提出这一说法，认为"东方化"这一术语可以用来说明 19 世纪前半期在意大利埃特鲁里亚墓冢中发现的瓶画风格。东方化风格瓶画的发展已经超越了与原型物件没有关系的几何风格，考古学家这些年在意大利中部以及 1845 年以来在亚述的发现——花卉旋纹和狂野的动物以及奇幻的怪物，都被认为是来自东方——尤其是埃及——的表达。这类东方化风格同样出现在希腊艺术中，尽管至 19 世纪中期在希腊只出现了少数考古证据。[1]自此以后，学术界对希腊艺术中东方因素的关注越来越密切。随着考古学的发展，越来越多的考古实物证据表明，古希腊文明中来自东方的因素不仅限于艺术领域。[2]

1980 年，英国学者奥斯温·默里（Oswyn Murray）在孔兹研究的基础上，第一次提出"东方化时代"

[1] Conze, A. *Zur Geschichte der Anfänge Griechischer Kunst*. Vienna,1870，转引自 Corinna Riva and Nicholas C. Vella, Eds., *Debating orientalizatio: multidisciplinary approaches to change in the ancient Mediterranean*, London · Oakville: Equinox Publishing Ltd, 2006, p. 4.

[2] 1980 年"东方化时代"提出以前的主要作品有：Right Hon. W.E. Gladstone, *Archaic Greece and the East*, London, 1892; William Stearns Davis, *Reading in Ancient History: Greece and the East*, New York: Allyn and Bacon, 1912; Hermann Wirth, *Homer und Babylon: ein Lösungsversuch der Homerischen Frage vom orientalischen Standpunkte aus*, Freiburg i. Br.: Herder, 1921; Gerorge G. James, *Stolen Legacy: Greek Philosophy is Stolen Egyptian Philosophy,* New Jersey:Africa World Press, Inc., 1st published in 1954, reprinted in 2001; Thomas James Dunbabin; John Boardman; John Davidson Beazley, *The Greeks and their eastern neighbours: studies in the relations between Greece and the countries of the Near East in the eighth and seventh centuries B.C*, London: Society for the Promotion of Hellenic Studies, 1957; M. L. West, *Hesiod, Theogony*, Oxford: Oxford University Press, 1966; M. L. West, *Early Greek Philosophy and the Orient*, Oxford: Oxford University Press, 1971. 等。

（The Orientalizing Period）这一术语，他的《早期希腊》①第六章即以"东方化时代"为章名②。默里借用了这个艺术史概念并且将其应用到整体希腊社会的研究。他认为，"与近东的接触，给公元前750年至公元前650年那一个世纪的希腊社会带来了大量的变化。"③通过考察希腊语借用的闪米特词汇的数量，尤其是在物质文化领域，例如陶器的形状、称呼服装的语汇、渔业和航海业的术语等，确认了希腊和腓尼基之间接触的密切。不过，他认为"这种传播发生的路径，以及它对希腊接受者的影响，最好通过对三个领域——艺术、宗教和文学——的研究来探讨。"④作者也正是凭借自己所掌握丰富的一手考古资料，在这几个方面进行了深入细致的研究。

默里提出"东方化时代"这一术语之后，西方古典学界的注意力开始逐步集中到东方化论题之上。1987年，马丁·伯纳尔的《黑色雅典娜》甫一面世便引起激烈争论，激发了学界对希腊文明中的东方因素的研究热情，相继发表了相关著述。

美国古典考古学家萨拉·莫里斯（Sarah Morris）在1992年出版的《代达洛斯与希腊艺术的起源》中提出，从青铜时代直至古风时代，东部地中海世界都是一个文化"共同体"，其内部的相互联系、相互影响是常态，而希腊也是这文化"共同体"的一部分，在公元前1100年之后并没有终止和东方的联系。⑤

1997年，英国古典学家韦斯特的《面向东方的赫利孔：希腊诗歌和神话中的西亚元素》面世，作者考察了爱琴地区与东方的来往和交流，包括贸易往来，希腊人对于"近东"艺术与工艺、词语、文学、天文学、音乐、宗教等多方面的借鉴，系统阐述了西亚文化对古风时代和古典时代早期希腊文化的影响。他认为，"在事实的冲击下，读者应该放弃、或至少大大减少对于早期希腊文化独立性所保有的任何幻想。我们不能把"近东"的影响贬低为边缘现象，只是在解释孤立的不正常现象时才偶尔援引。它在许多层面、在绝大多数时期都无处不在。"⑥

1998年，考古学家塔马斯·德兹索（Tamás Dezsö）在《不列颠考古报告》发表单行本长篇论文《公元前9—前7世纪爱琴海和东地中海头盔传统中的东方影响：东方化的模式》，⑦他将爱琴海和东地

---

① Oswyn Murray, *Early Greece*, Brighton : Harvester Press, 1980. 此书第一版还有 Glasgow: Fonnata Perss、Atlantic Highlands, N.J. : Humanities Press 等版本，另有1982年 Stanford, Calif : Stanford University Press 重印本。1993年，作者作了较多修订后出版第二版（London : Fontana Press），根据第二版翻译的中译本见：奥斯温·默里著，晏绍祥译：《早期希腊》，上海：上海人民出版社，2008年。

② 默里在1993年第二版序言中确认是他自己首次提出"东方化时代"这一术语，"有些章节变动很小……因为其基本结论似乎仍值得保留，而随后的研究已经从这里开始。我对其中的两章感到特别自豪……第六章即'东方化时代'，如今已经作为一个重要时期得到认可。首次借用了这个艺术史概念并且将其应用到作为整体的社会，正是本书。"（见奥斯温·默里著，晏绍祥译：《早期希腊》，第二版序。）国内学者普遍根据第二版认为"东方化时代"是1993年提出。如张广智：《西方史学史》，上海：复旦大学出版社，2000年第一版，第4页；丁艳平：《东方文化对古希腊文化的影响》，硕士学位论文，湖南大学，2004年，第36页；黄洋、晏绍祥：《希腊史研究入门》，北京：北京大学出版社，2009年，第191页。笔者核对了1980年 Harvester Press 版本，第六章即名为 *The Orientalizing Period*，见 Oswyn Murray, *Early Greece*, Brighton : Harvester Press, 1980, p. 80. 陈恒和谢晓毅根据1980年 Fonnata Perss 版本，也认为"东方化时代"这一术语是1980年首次提出，见陈恒：《略论古希腊文明中的东方因素》，上海师范大学学报（哲学社会科学版），2004年1月第33卷第1期；解晓毅：《希腊历史上的"东方化时代"初探》，硕士学位论文，西南大学，2006年，第2页。

③ 奥斯温·默里著，晏绍祥译：《早期希腊》，第74页。

④ 奥斯温·默里著，晏绍祥译：《早期希腊》，第74—75页。

⑤ Sarah Morris, *Daidalos and the Origins of Greek Art*, Princeton: University Press, 1992. 她在《荷马与"近东"》一文中也概括了希腊和东方的密切联系，见 "Homer and the Near East", in Ian Morris and Barry Powell eds., *A New Companion to Homer, Mnemosyne*, Suppl. 163, Leiden, E. J. Brill, 1997, pp. 599–623.

⑥ M. L. West, *The East Face of Helikon: West Asiatic Elements in Greek Poetry and Myth*, Oxford: Oxford University Press, p. 60.

⑦ Tamás Dezsö, "Oriental Influence in the Aegean and Eastern Mediterranean Helmet Traditions in the 9t h–7th Centuries B.C.: The Patterns of Orientalization", *BAR Internationl Series*, 691, 1998.

中海地区头盔传统中的东方影响分为四个层次：直接引入、对东方模式的模仿和形式上的重新解释、对东方模式的模仿和材料上的重新解释、塞浦路斯和希腊的头盔受到东方的启发。通过对具体文化事项的专题研究，德兹索为我们提供了一个关于东方文化对希腊文化影响的个案研究样本。

不仅学者们独立完成的专著聚焦于希腊文化与东方文化的关系研究，一些研究机构也以学术研讨会的形式进行集体探讨。

1990 年 3 月，纽约大学美术学院校友会（The Alumni Association of the Institute of Fine Arts）召开了一次主题为"希腊：东方与西方之间——公元前 10—前 8 世纪"的学术研讨会。1992 年，根据研讨会的议题出版了同名论文集。①2002 年 9 月，牛津大学圣约翰学院召开了一次以"古代的东方化"为主题的学术研讨会。与会学者不仅探讨了古代地中海某些特定地区或特定领域的"东方化"，还对"东方化"问题进行了一些理论上的思考与总结。2006 年，根据这次研讨会讨论的议题出版了《考量东方化：古代地中海地区变革的综合学科研究法》。其中尼古拉斯·珀塞尔（Nicholas Purcell）的《东方化：五个历史问题》和罗宾·奥斯本（Robin Osborne）的《东方化走向何方或消亡的东方化？》对学界热烈讨论的"东方化"进行了冷静的思考。珀塞尔认为，对"东方化"这一问题的讨论还缺乏足够的证据和理论支撑，"如果我们想要回应罗伯特·夏特里埃（Robert Chartier）所称'宏大历史'（Histoire à très large échelle）的挑战，将我们所理解的世界放入一个特定背景，就不应继续坐在一间暗室里，等待偶尔来自花园里一点火星的光亮，我们应该停止讨论'东方化'这一术语以及这一术语附带的沉重之物。" ②奥斯本在对"东方化"和"东方主义"（Orientalism）进综合对比分析后，得出与珀塞尔相反的结论，指出东方化论题的现实意义，"任何停止讨论'东方化'或者将'东方化'纳入'殖民主义'话语体系的动议，我们都应该坚决抵制。这两种做法都是会使得地中海地区政治共同体内部和广阔外部环境中的权力运行情况变得模糊不清而非更加明朗。希腊地区在吸收和改造其他文明因素的动态过程中，仍然保证了政治独立，这是一个独特的主题。厘清古代的'东方化'——正如本论文集竭力图所做的这样，不单单是为了古代的目的。" ③

在这样的背景下，一些学者将"东方化革命"的命题纳入希腊与东方文明交流的研究框架下，形成了"东方化—东方化时代—东方化革命"的话语体系。这一话语体系的基础就是"东方"以及东方文明对希腊文明的影响，因此，要理解和辨析"东方化革命"，前提是对"东方"、"东方化"以及"革命"等基本概念的考量。

三

许多现代语源学研究者将"东方"、"西方"两个词的词源上溯到腓尼基人传说中的卡德摩斯（Kadmos）和欧罗巴（Europa）甚至更为久远，④不过古代希腊人尚无"东方"的概念和意识。⑤我

---

① Günter Kopcke, Isabelle Tokumaru, eds.: *Greece between East and West, 10th–8th centuries BC*, Mainz, Franz Steiner, 1992.

② Nicholas Purcell, "Orientalizing: Five Historical Questions", Corinna Riva and Nicholas C. Vella, Eds., *Debating orientalization: multidisciplinary approaches to change in the ancient Mediterranean*, pp. 21–30. 珀塞尔所言之"沉重"，意指附加于这一话题的殖民主义、后殖民主义及东方主义等学术研究中的现实政治因素。

③ Robin Osborne, "W(h)ither Orientalization", Corinna Riva and Nicholas C. Vella, Eds., *Debating orientalization: multidisciplinary approaches to change in the ancient Mediterranean*, pp. 153–158.

④ 关于这两个词的词源解释及争论，参见 Walter Burkert, *The Orientalizing Revolution: Near Eastern Influence on Greek Culture in the Early Archaic Age*, p. 153, note 3.

⑤ 东西方对立的概念始见于罗马帝国时期，后被基督教拉丁文学采纳。直到十字军东征的时代，"东方"（Orient）才作为概念和术语，实际进入西方语言中。见 Walter Burkert, *The Orientalizing Revolution: Near Eastern Influence on Greek Culture in the Early Archaic Age*, p.1; p. 153, note 2.

们在论及这一主题时所使用的"西方"与"东方"（West and East）、"欧洲"与"亚洲"（Europe and Asia）、"希腊"与"东方"（Greece and Orient）这些二元对立概念都是现代的术语。尽管这些术语本身是现代性的，不过所指称的事项却是历史的具体存在。如前所述，不同时代的人只能用自己时代的术语来表述特定的事物。因此，现代人在研究公元前30世纪到公元前1世纪地中海地区的跨文化交流之时，必须仰赖于这些约定俗成的现代性概念。①

探讨这些概念首先要解决一个基本问题："东方"究竟是一个地域的还是文化的范畴，或者其他方面的范畴。关注古代地中海世界的学者倾向于将"西方"与"东方"和"欧洲"与"亚洲"看做两对同等概念，即东西方地缘文化的区分与欧亚大陆的自然分界线是重合的——从爱琴海到黑海，中间是达达尼尔海峡、马尔马拉海、博斯普鲁斯海峡。②部分希腊人居住的土耳其西海岸和沿岸岛屿被称为"东希腊"，在传统上属于"西方"或"欧洲"的范畴。然而这种地域的划分并不能准确表述文化或观念上的区别。一些学者甚至声称，"东方"是一个想象的地域，③或者"东方"在地域上是不存在的。④本文认为，地域上的"东方"概念是探讨其他范畴"东方"之基础，因此需要有较为明确的界定。在不同的历史语境下，地域上的"东方"也有不同的范围，本文大致以欧亚大陆的自然分界线作为地域上的西方与东方分界线。以此为基础，在涉及其他范畴的"东方"概念时进一步加以界定和阐述。

从希腊人的认知角度来说，尽管他们尚无"东方"的概念，但是文化认同范畴的"东方"在古典希腊时期已经出现了。波斯的入侵使得希腊人产生了一种联想，开始把波斯人和希腊人传说中的敌人联系起来，把他们一概视为来自亚细亚、对希腊产生巨大威胁的宿敌，因而也是对立于希腊方式的典型蛮族。正如默里所说，希波战争开创了一个新时代，但也终结了一个旧时代。希腊文化已经从东西方富有成果的交流中被创造出来。东方对抗西方，专制对抗自由，希波战争中创造的这种二元对立，在整个世界历史中回响。⑤希腊和波斯的对立与冲突从根本上改变了希腊文化的特性，希腊人开始意识到他们区别于其他民族的民族特性。因此，从文化和民族认同的角度来说，"希腊"与"东方"的对立实际上是希腊人关于"他者"的一种认识范畴，这一范畴中的"东方"可以泛指在文化方面与希腊人有一定联系但是又相区别的其他民族及其文化。

古典主义学者所关注的不仅仅是特定的地域或民族，而是人类知识的一部分，⑥故而我们在这里探讨的"东方"不仅是一个地域和文化的范畴，而是建立在地域、文化和民族基础上的综合研究领域。

第二个问题是关于"东方化"的界定。英语中的"东方化"有多重表述形式，有表过程的Orientalizing，表状态的Orientalization，表结果的Orientalized。这些表述形式在汉语中皆可译成"东

---

① 关于青铜时代的研究，Janice L. Crowley, *The Aegean and the East: an Inverstigation into the Transference of Artistic Motif between the Aegean, Egypt and the Near East in the Bronze Age*, Jonsered: Paul Åttröms Forlag, 1989. 使用了"爱琴"与"东方"的概念；Eric H. Cline, *Sailing the Wine Dark Sea: International Trade and the Late Bronze Age Aegean*, Oxford: Tempus Reparatum, 1994. 将爱琴地区从近东的引入称为"东方之物"（Orientalia），近东从爱琴地区的引入称为"西方之物"（Occidentalia）；此外还有 C. Lambrou-Phillipson, *Hellenorientalia: the Near Eastern Presence in the Bronze Age Aegean, ca. 3000-1100B.C.*, Göteborg: Paul Åttröms Forlag, 1990 等。

② Ann C. Gunter, *Greek Art and The Orient*, Cambridge: Cambridge University Press, 2009, p. 51.

③ Edward W. Said, *Orientalism*, London: Penguin, 1978, pp. 41-52.

④ Nicholas Purcell, "Orientalizing: Five Historical Questions", Corinna Riva and Nicholas C. Vella, eds., *Debating orientalization: multidisciplinary approaches to change in the ancient Mediterranean*, p. 25.

⑤ 奥斯温·默里著，晏绍祥译：《早期希腊》，第290-291页。

⑥ Edward W. Said, *Orientalism*, p. 50.

方化"。"化"的基本含义是变化，在名词和形容词后，表示转变成为某种性质或状态的情形。[1]因此，论及"东方化"时，必须考虑何种程度的性质或状态改变能够称之为"化"，还要考虑到"化"的过程、结果和状态。正如珀塞尔所诘问的："东方化"是否包括了关于程度和完整性的判断？是否意味着一个稳定但不断改变的时期，或者是完全的改变？换句话说，如果"东方化"是一个过程，是否意味着结果就"东方化"了？若不是，为什么不是？[2]早在1973年，博德曼就以黑格尔关于东方和西方"精神"对立的模式提出了一个关键的问题："东方化"是希腊人主动地、有自主意识地转变他们所接受的知识，还是被动地、因袭陈规地接受来自东方的产品？[3]

直到伯克特的时代，严谨的西方学者仍然侧重于从具体文化事项入手进行分析，拒绝在没有确凿证据之时贸然建构文明互动与交流的模式。伯克特在《东方化革命》前言中就明确表示："我有意侧重于提供证据，证明希腊与东方文化有相似之处，以及证明希腊可能采纳了东方文化。某些时候，当材料本身不能提供文化迁移的可靠证据时，确认文化间的相似也将是有价值的，因为这能使希腊和东方的文化现象摆脱孤立，为比较研究搭建了一个平台。"[4]而我们能够据以为证的主要是艺术、宗教和文学领域的比较研究。

在古风时代早期希腊艺术的"东方化"过程中，腓尼基人扮演着先驱的作用，尽管他们在艺术层面只是中转和媒介的角色。[5]亚述帝国和埃及的艺术被认为是希腊艺术最重要的原型。[6]从接受者的角度来说，塞浦路斯和克里特岛在东方对希腊产生影响的过程中有特殊地位；罗德岛在公元前8世纪时也十分重要；所有在公元前8世纪兴盛起来的重要朝拜地，即提洛岛、德尔斐，尤其是奥林匹亚，都发掘出了数量可观的东方工艺品；紧邻厄瑞特里亚的雅典也值得特别关注。[7]

希腊艺术中的东方因素首先体现在手工产品方面，最早的无疑是金属制品。从公元前9世纪后期起，克里特的腓尼基金属匠人已经开始生产锻造的青铜器物用于献祭，考古学家在伊达山的山洞中、[8]奥林匹亚、多铎纳和伊达拉里亚地区都发现了他们的产品。同时腓尼基的金匠正在克诺索斯工作，可能也在雅典工作。[9]腓尼基的青铜碗和银碗普遍被作为贵重物品交易，不仅在塞浦路斯，而且

---

① "化"，古字为"匕"。甲骨文上从二人，呈二人相倒背之形，一正一反，以示变化。汉代许慎的《说文》称"匕，变也"。段注曰："上匕之而下从匕谓之化。"《易·系辞传》称："知变化之道。"虞注："在阳称变，在阴称化，四时变化。"荀注曰："春夏为变，秋冬为化，坤化为物。"《礼记·乐记》称："故百物化焉。"《周礼·柞氏》称"欲其化也"，注曰"犹生也"。《荀子·正名》称"状态而实无别而为异者谓之化"，注曰"化者改旧形之名"。《国语·晋语》称"胜败若化"，注曰"言转化无常也"。《吕氏春秋·察今》称"因时而化"。

　　英语中还有一个与Hellenism相对应、表性质的Orientalism。Hellenism被中国学者译为"希腊化"，不过陈恒认为，一般来说，用Hellenism一词来表示希腊化的概念是不太合适的，但如今已为大多数人所接受，要想新造一个词来代替它已有困难，不过现今也有不少人在使用Hellenization来代替Hellenism一词（见陈恒：《从希腊化文化的传播看全球化之起源》，世界历史，2004年第3期）。同样，Orientalism也不适合译为"东方化"，中国学者一般译为"东方主义"，王宇根将其译为"东方学"（见爱德华·萨义德著，王宇根译：《东方学》，北京：三联书店，1999年），不过这种译法也不甚准确，不足为据。

② Nicholas Purcell，"Orientlizing: Five Historical Questions"，p. 26.

③ John Boardman, *Greek Art*, London: Thames and Hudson, 1973, p. 19.

④ Walter Burkert, *The Orientalizing Revolution: Near Eastern Influence on Greek Culture in the Early Archaic Age*, p. 8.

⑤ Walter Burkert, *The Orientalizing Revolution: Near Eastern Influence on Greek Culture in the Early Archaic Age*, p. 16; Glenn Markoe, "The Emergence of Orientalizing in Greek Art: Some Observations on the Interchange between Greeks and Phoenicians in the Eighth and Seventh Centuries B. C.", *Bulletin of the American Schools of Oriental Research*, No. 301(Feb., 1996), pp. 47–67; Ann C. Gunter, *Greek Art and The Orient*, p.65.

⑥ Ann C. Gunter, *Greek Art and The Orient*, p.66.

⑦ Walter Burkert, *The Orientalizing Revolution: Near Eastern Influence on Greek Culture in the Early Archaic Age*, p. 19.

⑧ 传说中婴儿宙斯的藏身之处。

⑨ 奥斯温·默里著，晏绍祥译：《早期希腊》，第75页。

雅典、奥林匹亚、德尔斐，甚至意大利南部的普勒尼斯特、伊达拉里亚等地都发现了这样的碗。上述地区发现的碗中至少有三个刻有阿拉米—腓尼基（Aramaic-Phoenician）铭文，一只法拉里（Falerri）出土的碗上还刻着楔形文字。①

"东方化"最为显著的是陶器。默里认为，陶器的东方化风格首先于公元前725年左右出现于原始科林斯陶器上，稍晚出现的雅典陶器也具有同样的倾向。②不过现在已经有学者确认其时间更早，几何陶后期即公元前750年左右，东方艺术的影响逐渐清晰起来。这一点在底比隆画家和他的工作室里装饰花瓶的动物图案中体现得尤为明显。③几何式的剪影画为灵活的黑画剪影与嵌入式细节的合成物（黑画技术）所取代，它是素描技法和附加涂色的混合……全套的东方装饰的主题被引入，如涡旋形、蔷薇花饰、棕叶饰、百合花和花蕾，以及复杂的"生命之树"等。④来自利凡特的艺术影响不仅体现在对装饰动物本身——如山羊和鹿——的选择，而且在与对动物姿势和形态的表达。从画家所使用的模型中确实能看到东方的输入。这些装饰对我们关于东方化主题研究有着特殊的意义。这不仅在于他们对动物形象的描述，而且在于他们包含了特殊的主题：正在捕食的猫科动物，经常以正在攻击其猎物的姿态呈现。⑤这些动物中最常见的就是狮子，不管是单独出现还是出现在捕食场景中的狮子，都在阿提卡陶瓶中能够看到。⑥然而对希腊人来说，狮子和豹子同斯芬克斯、塞壬、戈尔工以及其他有翼的怪物一样神奇。已经有学者精确地指出了这些动物模型的来源，例如，从形态上说，狮子首先是赫梯的，后来是亚述的。⑦

还有一些在希腊发掘出来的东方艺术品也值得注意。象牙雕刻——虽然这种技艺后来被希腊人采用——毫无疑问是来自东方，公元前7世纪出现的鸵鸟蛋和来自红海的砗磲贝壳也是如此。珠宝则更常见，如各式金饰、彩陶珠以及玻璃珠，荷马史诗中所提到的赫拉的三串桑椹状耳饰当属此类。宝石、印章的使用和传播更有力地证明了与东方的联系。伊斯基亚岛（Ischia）发掘出了近百枚叙利亚—西利西亚的印章。莱夫坎迪的陵墓中发现了叙利亚和埃及风格的类似护身符的饰品——葬于厄瑞特里亚英雄祠（Eretria Heroon）的王子佩戴着一枚镶嵌在黄金上的圣甲虫形护身符。此外，美索不达米亚风格的圆柱形印章在希腊的萨摩斯、提洛岛和奥林匹亚都有出土。⑧

希腊艺术的"东方化"，不仅是商人将东方的货物辗转贩卖到希腊，使得东方的产品在希腊出现，而且还有来自东方的工匠直接向希腊人传授技术，同时，希腊人也直接向对方学习。对此的直接证明就是希腊人在制造中吸取了种种新的技术性工艺，这不是简单地通过购买成品就能做到的。希腊手工业者们旅行到了靠近东方的某些地区，并在贸易据点建立起作坊。在那里，他们可能方便地见到东方的工人。艺术家的这类迁移从他们自己制造的物品中可以发现一部分，但主要是以专业的制作工艺传播到希腊作为假设前提，因为那些技术只能通过直接接触才能学到。金丝细工饰品和粒化

① Walter Burkert, *The Orientalizing Revolution: Near Eastern Influence on Greek Culture in the Early Archaic Age*, p. 19.

② 奥斯温·默里著，晏绍祥译：《早期希腊》，第77页。

③ Glenn Markoe, "The Emergence of Orientalizing in Greek Art: Some Observations on the Interchange between Greeks and Phoenicians in the Eighth and Seventh Centuries B. C.", p. 47.

④ 奥斯温·默里著，晏绍祥译：《早期希腊》，第77页。

⑤ Schweitzer, B. *Greek Geometric Art*. Trans. by P. Usborne and C. Usborne, London: Phaidon, 1971, pp. 186-200.

⑥ Glenn Markoe, "The Emergence of Orientalizing in Greek Art: Some Observations on the Interchange between Greeks and Phoenicians in the Eighth and Seventh Centuries B. C.", p. 47.

⑦ 奥斯温·默里著，晏绍祥译：《早期希腊》，第77页。

⑧ Walter Burkert, *The Orientalizing Revolution: Near Eastern Influence on Greek Culture in the Early Archaic Age*, p. 19; pp. 162-163. note 2-8.

技术、宝石的切割、象牙雕刻、赤陶模的使用和青铜的失蜡铸造法等，都是这类技术的例证。[1]这些技术都不是彼此进行远距离的接触能够学到的，而是至少有一段学徒过程，其间彼此曾密切合作，交流过种种细节问题。并且，工匠因有一技之长，与定居的农民和拥有土地的贵族截然不同，其流动性有着现实的基础，[2]这就为希腊手工艺者或者艺术家与东方的学习和交流提供了条件。

虽然研究者对艺术品地方风格的确定和单件物品的原产地鉴定仍在进行中，近东许多遗址尚未研究，或只是部分研究。但从现有的考古和艺术史研究成果来看，希腊艺术上的"东方化"已经得到证实。对于"东方化"这样一个综合性指标，已经有了众多地区的诸多样本，证明东方因素在希腊艺术中的影响成为普遍现象。

当然，我们还需要注意希腊人对东方艺术的改造以及在此基础上的再创造。面对各种外来模式，希腊工匠的反应是改造多于模仿。[3]浅层次的改造体现在技术层面，如东方失蜡铸造技术中的蜡芯以沥青为芯被改造成了以树脂和麸糠作芯。[4]更多改造过程则在对近东图像主题的转换中能够较为清晰地看到。例如，东方主题的牛或牛犊，在希腊的环境中则转换成马和马驹。同样，阿提卡艺术家借用了近东复合生物的观念，但是随即创造了希腊特有的风格。同样的借用和改造也体现在希腊艺术家对东方生命之树的描绘，将其以本土的几何陶形式展现出来。[5]这一改造过程还体现在对某些特殊主题的选择性借用，如围绕一个中心主题相对立的群组图像，是典型的东方风格，但是在阿提卡的后期几何艺术家那里，变成一种独特的风格——一位马夫被群马所包围，群马按两级或三角排列，然而又有两个人坐在中间的凳子或石块上面，这又是典型的本土风格，很少发现有近东的原型。[6]在所有这些例子中，东方原型的出现和影响主要体现在排列的顺序或形式结构方面，而在场景的风格和具体图像方面的影响则少得多。正如默里所说，希腊艺术从来不是东方的派生物，借鉴和采纳都是创造性的。正是几何陶的叙述与东方自然主义的结合，让希腊的艺术，因此也是西方的艺术，具有了它独特的方向：一种按照本来面貌描绘现实的兴趣，与那种风格和装饰、试验上的自由、对人的特殊关注以及人的作品乃艺术的主题等相对应。[7]

在艺术领域以外，学者们研究得较多的是文学和神话方面的"东方化"。荷马史诗和赫西俄德的作品与东方的关系尤为引人注目。荷马史诗虽于古风时代才最终成书，不过口头传颂已经有了数个世纪，在其传颂过程中，无疑吸收了多种文明元素。自古以来就有学者将荷马史诗与希伯来圣经相比较——二者都是在以宗教和语言为基础形成的社会单元中传播的历史、神学和叙述传统；二者在悲情主题（如以女儿献祭）、诗歌技巧（如明喻修辞）、宗教范式（如发誓与诅咒）等方面都有诸多共同之处。[8]布鲁斯·卢登在《荷马的〈奥德赛〉与近东》一书中通过对《奥德赛》与《创世记》、《出

① John Boardman, *The Greeks Overseas: Their Early Colonies and Trade*, 2nd edition, London: Thames & Hudson Ltd, 1980, p. 71；温·默里著，晏绍祥译：《早期希腊》，第75-76页。

② 荷马在其歌颂"为公众做工的人"的诗句中就明确表述了这一点："除非他们是懂得某种技艺的行家，或者是预言者、治病的医生，或是木工，或是感人的歌者，他能唱歌娱悦人。那些人在世间无际的大地上到处受到欢迎。"（Homer, *Odyssey*, 17. 383-385.）

③ John Boardman, *The Greeks Overseas: Their Early Colonies and Trade*, 2nd edition, London: Thames & Hudson Ltd, 1980, p. 78, 81; Benson, J. L., "On Early Protocorinthian Workshop and the Sources of its Motifs", Babesch: *Bulletin An-ticke Beschaving*, vol. 61 (1986): 13-14.

④ John Boardman, *The Greeks Overseas: Their Early Colonies and Trade*, 2nd edition, London: Thames & Hudson Ltd, 1980, p. 57.

⑤ Coldstream, J. N., *Greek Geometric Pottery: A Survey of Ten Local Styles and Their Chronology*, London: Methuen. 1968, p. 67, note 2.

⑥ Glenn Markoe, "The Emergence of Orientalizing in Greek Art: Some Observations on the Interchange between Greeks and Phoenicians in the Eighth and Seventh Centuries B. C.", p. 49.

⑦ 温·默里著，晏绍祥译：《早期希腊》，第78页。

⑧ Sarah Morris, "Homer and the Near East", p. 599.

埃及记》等近东文本的比较，得出结论：《奥德赛》融合了多种不同的神话传统，所有这些传统都能在近东找到对应物。尽管从近东内部来说，这些神话或传说又分属于不同地区，如美索不达米亚、埃及、乌加里特等地，但大量故事都集中在旧约圣经中。[1]默里认为，赫西俄德的《神谱》，其核心组织原则是"继承神话"，其结构和许多细节都与东方的继承神话严密对应，并对其中三个作相对详尽的阐释——即巴比伦的创始神话《恩努马·埃利什》（Enuma Elish）、赫梯的库马比（Kumarbi）神话和一部希腊人创作的《腓尼基史》。[2]赫西俄德的《劳作与时令》，虽然其中详尽的建议完全是希腊式的，但该诗篇的总体设想让人想起东方著名的智慧文字，核心神话的某些部分与东方类似。[3]伯克特也对希腊的宇宙神话与赫梯的库马比神话进行了比较，他还比较了希腊神话传说中最具传奇色彩的赫拉克勒斯形象与诸多近东神话的相似之处。[4]荷马颂歌与赫西俄德作品中的很多故事也被证明与美索不达米亚有着很多对应关系。[5]奥林帕斯12主神中，狄奥尼索斯、阿芙洛狄忒、阿波罗、阿尔忒弥斯都已证明与东方有着密切的联系。[6]

关于其他希腊文学作品，包括其他史诗、抒情诗、寓言，尤其是涉及神话传说的作品，都有学者从不同角度与东方传统进行了比较研究。[7]

但是，所有这些研究都面临一个核心问题：如何证明这些相似性之间存在着直接的影响，而不是按照自身的规则独立发展起来的。当然，学者们可以根据地理空间上的相互连接、年代时间上的先后关系做出一些推论。即便如此，也不能忽视希腊文学所具有的希腊本土性特征。荷马史诗的英雄传统是希腊社会的独特产物，其中人神同性的自由神学，体现的是希腊人独特的人文伦理观。[8]尽管赫西俄德借鉴了外来的模式，但他的思想有自己内在的逻辑，在希腊人的背景下，有它自己的关键之处。他对社会的关注如何让他通过创造世代的观念将神灵的世界和人类世界联系起来，并从神灵那里派生出抽象的政治概念，这种思想模型在东方并无对应。[9]

神灵起源的问题更为复杂，尽管某些希腊神灵在其发展过程中的确受到东方的影响，但是其源头显然并不只是唯一的，并且在最终成型之时，已经完成了对其他文明元素的吸收和改造，所彰显的主要是希腊特性了。以阿波罗为例，阿波罗显然是一个起源于希腊以外的神灵。笔者在另一篇文章中论证了阿波罗神名起源于北方，其神职主体起源于亚洲，这两种外来文化元素在传播和融合的过程中也吸收了希腊原住民族的某些崇拜成分。在人们对阿波罗崇拜的某一发展阶段，还吸纳了许

---

[1] Bruce Louden, *Homer's Odyssey and the Near East*, Cambridge: Cambridge University Press, 2011, p. 314.

[2] 奥斯温·默里著，晏绍祥译：《早期希腊》，第80-81页。

[3] 奥斯温·默里著，晏绍祥译：《早期希腊》，第83页。

[4] Walter Burkert, "Oriental and Greek Mythology: The Meeting of Parallels", in *Interpretations of Greek Mythology*, ed. by Jan Bremmer, London: Routledge, 1990, pp.10-40.

[5] Charles Penglase, *Greek myths and Mesopotamia: Parallels and Influence in the Homeric Hymns and Hesiod*, London and New York: Routledge, 1997, pp. 64-165.

[6] Martin Bernal, *Black Athena: Afro-Asiatic Roots of Classical Civilization, Vol. III The Linguistic Evidence*, pp. 453-464.

[7] 除了伯克特的《东方化革命》和韦斯特的《面向东方的赫利孔》以外，主要作品还有：Finkelberg, M., "The Cypria, the Iliad, and the problem of multiformity in oral and written tradition," *Classical Philology*, vol. 95 (2000): pp.1-11; Bollinger, R. "The ancient Greeks and the impact of the ancient Near East: Textual evidence and historical perspective(ca.750-650BC)," in *Mythology and Mythologies: Methodological Approaches to Intercultural Influences (Melammu Symposia II)*, ed. by Whiting, R. M., Helsinki: The Neo-Assyrian, 2001, pp. 233-264; Haubold, J., "Greek epic: a Near Eastern Genre?" *Proceedings of the Cambridge Philological Society*, vol. 48 (2001), pp. 1-19; Carolina López-Ruiz: *When the Gods Were Born :Greek Cosmogonies and the Near East*, Massachusetts: Harvard University Press, 2010 等。

[8] Sarah Morris, "Homer and the Near East", p. 599.

[9] 奥斯温·默里著，晏绍祥译：《早期希腊》，第84页。

多不同宗教元素和小的神祇，这些众多宗教元素和小神祇逐渐汇聚到"阿波罗"的名称之下。[1]关于这些汇聚到"阿波罗"名称之下的宗教元素和小神祇的具体情况，我们至少可以明确知道有三种成分：一种西北多利斯希腊（Dorian-northwest Greek）成分，一种克里特米诺斯（Cretan-Minoan）成分，一种叙利亚赫梯（Syro-Hittite）成分。[2]然而，希腊古风时代以来的艺术中，以阿波罗为原型的雕塑艺术形象的发展一直远胜过其他神祇，这种发展至少可以追溯到德勒洛斯的阿波罗神庙铸成那些青铜塑像之时（约公元前750年）。这些阿波罗塑像一般都是以年轻人形象出现，随着希腊艺术的不断成熟，这种形象逐渐上升到理想高度，经过后来的进一步净化和提升，这种理想明显具有神圣性，赋予希腊文化一种特殊的气质，而代表这种文化的神就是阿波罗。甚至有学者说，"阿波罗是希腊精神的具体体现。一切使希腊人与其他民族相区别，特别是使之与周围野蛮民族相区别的东西——各种各样的美，无论是艺术、音乐、诗歌还是年轻、明智、节制——统统汇聚在阿波罗身上。"[3]同样，其他与东方有着密切关系的神灵，在其发展过程中，也逐渐融合了多种文明元素，最终形成了希腊人所特有的奥林帕斯神系及与其崇拜相应的宗教。

还有一个领域是文字和语言。希腊文字的基础是腓尼基字母，这一点已经得到公认。希腊字母的形状是对腓尼基字母的改写；两种字母表的顺序基本一致，甚至绝大多数希腊字母的名称也是从腓尼基语接受过来的。腓尼基语向希腊语的转写几乎是机械的，只有在一个基本方面例外：元音。元音的发明正体现了希腊人对腓尼基字母创造性的修正。绝大多数希腊元音的形式源自腓尼基语的辅音或者半辅音字母，后者在希腊语中只是被视为简化过程的音节符号，而元音的发明则将这些音节符号转变成真正的字母符号。在希腊字母表中，主要的语言因素元音和辅音首次独立出来，各自单独表达。这一系统仍为绝大多数现代语言所使用。[4]马丁·伯纳尔考察了希腊语中外来语的现象，[5]提出了数百个他认为"可以验证的假设"，[6]当做希腊文明具有亚非之根的重要证据。然而，文字和语言领域的几百个案例仍然不足以构成文明整体特性。我们需要关注的应该是文字以及文字的运用对社会变革带来的影响。尽管有学者认为，文字应对古风时代的绝大多数变革负责，在走向民主、逻辑、理性思维的发展、批判的史学、法律的制定等方面起到了辅助或激励的作用。但是，文字的作用是加强社会中已经存在的趋向，而不是对其进行基本的改造。[7]希腊社会具有的独特性在文字到来之后并没有因此而消失，而是进一步朝着自己特有的方向前进，从而发展出于东方文明特征迥异的古典文明。

至此可以形成一个基本结论：希腊历史上的"东方化"是确实发生过的历史现象，但是其范围主要在艺术领域，文学、宗教、文字、语言领域有一定程度的"东方化"。在一些具体社会文化事

① 李永斌，郭小凌：《阿波罗崇拜的起源及传播路线》，《历史研究》，2011年第3期，第179页。
② Walter Burkert, *Greek Religion: Archaic and Classical*, translated by John Raffan, Oxford: Basil Blackwell, 1985, p. 144.
③ W. K. C. Guthrie, *The Greeks and Their Gods*, New York: Beacon PR Ltd., 1985, p. 73.
④ 奥斯温·默里著，晏绍祥译：《早期希腊》，第86—87页。
⑤ Martin Bernal, Black Athena: *Afro-Asiatic Roots of Classical Civilization*, Vol. III *The Linguistic Evidence*, pp. 90–299.
⑥ Martin Bernal, *Black Athena: Afro-Asiatic Roots of Classical Civilization*, Vol. I *The Fabrication of Ancient Greece*, 1785–1985, p. 73.
⑦ 奥斯温·默里著，晏绍祥译：《早期希腊》，第92—93页。

项方面，也能看到东方的影响，如哲学、[1]建筑、[2]还有如会饮等社会风俗，[3]以及一些实用的物品如钱币、[4]家鸡[5]等，至于是否能称得上"东方化"，还没有足够多的样本和确凿证据进行分析。但是在诸多领域，希腊人仍然保持了本土的独特性和创造性，如史学、抒情诗、舞台剧等。东方社会的许多独特事物也没有在希腊找到对应之物，如巨大的宫殿、强大的王权、连续性的王朝等。

　　"东方化"最初是一个艺术史的概念。艺术品方面的比较研究相对较易，因为有具体物件和作品作为证据。一旦将"东方化"从艺术史领域扩大到整个社会层面，难题就油然而生。艺术史术语"东方化"，其实是文化传播论者用以解释历史的方式，可能更适合于物质文化，而非观念的历史。具体文化事项层面的转换和改造比整个社会其他层面的转换更容易把握，然而以人工产品的流动为基础来建构文化交流甚至历史发展的脉络，还需要更多社会生活领域层面的分析。探讨一个诸如"东方化时代"这样的术语，并不是纯粹的概念与称谓的问题，而是涉及历史年代建构的问题。历史的时代划分是我们分析过去的核心方法之一。然而这不是一件简单"约定俗成"之事，其中的各个阶段并不是武断的划分，或者仅仅为了某种特殊的探究而任意选取我们易于处理的年限范围。选择某一社会中我们认为足够显著的特征，给予其一般特性并将其标注为一个时代，是历史学中最难以把握主题之一，并不只是提出一个概念这样简单的事情。因此，默里在提出"东方化时代"这一术语时指出，"艺术中的自然主义、宗教上的系统化、字母和文字，希腊人几乎都没有意识到，他们到底从东方借鉴了多少。像黑暗时代一样，东方化时代几乎从希腊人的视野中消失了，它需要在现代的研究中得以重新发现。"[6]

　　然而，关于这一问题的现代学术研究还只处于起步阶段，还远谈不上重新发现之时，一些学者就借用伯克特的"东方化革命"这一术语，试图以此为基础建构希腊文明和东方文明之间的宏观联系。

　　实际上，"东方化革命"是"东方化"和"革命"两个概念的合体。"革命"最初是一个政治学术语，指的是相对较短时间内权力或组织结构的根本性改变。[7]在世界古代史研究领域，"革命"一词也被引申到其他领域，其基本含义仍然指的是"结构性的变化"，如古希腊历史上的"公元前8世纪革命"，[8]指的就是城邦的兴起这一"结构性革命"。[9]因此，对"东方化革命"这一概念的辨析，关键在于"东方化"是否引起了希腊社会的"结构性变化"。就公元前750年—前650年的希腊社会来说，社会结构的基础是公民意识基础上城邦社会的兴起。尽管这一时期的希腊社会除了上述艺术等领域以外，在政治和社会结构方面也一定程度上受到了东方的影响，但是希腊人所汲取的总是适应于自己本土

① 前文所列 George G. James, *Stolen Legacy: Greek Philosophy is Stolen Egyptian Philosophy* 全书的主题是关于希腊哲学与埃及哲学的探讨，不过该书论据漏洞百出，论点简单偏激，在严谨的学术研究中并不足取。另有 M. L. West, *Early Greek Philosophy and the Orient*, Oxford: Oxford University Press, 1971 (reprinted 2002)，提供了诸多具体案例的比较研究。

② Erwin F. Cook, "Near Eastern Source for the Palace of Alkinoos", *American Journal of Archaeology*, vol. 108 (2004), pp. 43–77.

③ 奥斯温·默里著，晏绍祥译：《早期希腊》，第74页。

④ Alain Bresson，《吕底亚和希腊铸币的起源：成本和数量》，沈扬、黄洋译，《历史研究》，2006年第5期。

⑤ 奥斯温·默里著，晏绍祥译：《早期希腊》，第74页。

⑥ 奥斯温·默里著，晏绍祥译：《早期希腊》，第93页。

⑦ Aristotle, *Politics*, 1.1301a.

⑧ 1961年，美国古代史家切斯特·斯塔尔在其所著的《希腊文明的起源》一书中，首次提出了"公元前8世纪革命"的说法："公元前750—前650年这个革命的时期，是整个希腊历史上最为根本的发展阶段"。Chester G. Starr, *The Origins of Greek Civilization,1100 –650BC*, New York: Knopf, 1961, p. 160.

⑨ Anthony M. Snodgrass, *Archaic Greece: The Age of Experiment,* Berkeley：University of California Press, p. 15. 最近的论述见 IanMorris, "The Eighth-Century Revolution", Kurt A. Raaflaub and Hans van Wees eds, *A Companion to Archaic Greece*, Chichester, West Sussex, Malden, MA: Wiley-Blackwell, 2009, p. 65. 关于"公元前8世纪革命"这一概念的辨析，见黄洋：《迈锡尼文明、"黑暗时代"与希腊城邦的兴起》，《世界历史》，2010年第3期。

土壤的元素，因而在其发展过程中逐渐形成了与东方社会完全迥异的公民集体社会城邦体制。①

艺术上的"东方化"并没有引起希腊社会的结构性变化，"东方化革命"也只是一种想象的概念，实际上是对艺术史上"东方化时代"的扩大化理解。这种扩大化又源于对东方因素在希腊历史上的"公元前八世纪革命"中所起作用的评估。由于一些学者将"公元前八世纪革命"的时间界定为公元前750—前650年，②恰好与默里所提出的"东方化时代"吻合，而希腊城邦社会的兴起也确实和希腊与东方广泛而深刻的文化交流同时发生，这两股历史潮流对希腊社会的发展产生了深远持久的影响。但是，希腊城邦社会的发展，并不是在公元前750—前650年这一百年时间里突然发生的，而是源于迈锡尼时代以来希腊社会的缓慢发展。尤其是从古风时代到古典时代以城邦制度为框架的发展过程，决定了希腊文化的基本特质，在不同于东方的公共空间上所展开的自由辩论、智术师的公共话语等方面所带来的强烈转变，催生了不同于东方文化的希腊文化特质。东方的影响只是在社会的某些层面强化或加速了固有的趋向而已。然而，一些学者却着意强调这一时期东方影响的作用，甚至将这种影响夸大到"革命"的层面。

四

"东方化—东方化时代—东方化革命"的话语体系的深层次背景是古典学与东方学、古典主义与东方主义在现代政治语境中的碰撞。

18世纪中期，随着欧洲民族主义革命运动的勃兴和政治势力与版图的重新划分，在意识形态领域形成一股民族保护主义的风潮。加之学术上的日益专业化，西欧社会开始了一场将古希腊理想化的思潮和文化运动。③这一运动以理想化的古代希腊来寄托和抒发现代欧洲人的精神诉求和政治目的。温克尔曼、赫尔德、歌德、洪堡等文学巨匠和思想大家，将古代希腊理想化推向新的高潮。

与此同时，学术上的专业化趋势将这一潮流纳入学术领域。1777年，沃尔夫（Freidrich August Wolf）进入哥廷根大学，要求注册学习"语文学"或"文献学"（Studiosus Philologiae）。Philologiae一词被亚历山大里亚学者限定为文献研究领域，排除了文艺鉴赏，到了近代一般被等同于语言研究的科学，因此，沃尔夫用Alterthums-wissenschaft（意为"古典学"）一词来指称他所从事的研究，这标志着现代古典学正式确立。④古典学虽然以研究古希腊拉丁文献为基础，实际上不可避免地要表述欧洲人的现代价值观，因此很快与温克尔曼等人所倡导的新人文主义融为一体，并发展成为浪漫主义的民族主义思想。这种思想把文学或精神文化同某个独特的民族或部落、某个独特的人种联系在一起。独立起源与发展的概念取代了文化间相互影响的模式，成为理解文化的关键。⑤

语言学者对"印欧语系"——即大多数欧洲语言和波斯语及梵语都衍生自同一原始语言——的发现，强化了希腊、罗马、日耳曼之间的联系，就此把闪米特语世界排斥在外。但是为希腊人的独

①　关于希腊与东方在政治思想和体制方面的联系与区别，见 Christopher Rowe and Malcolm Schofield, eds., *The Cambridge history of Greek and Roman political thought*, New York: Cambridge University Press, 2000, pp. 50–59.

②　Chester G. Starr, *The Origins of Greek Civilization, 1100 –650BC*, p. 160.

③　关于这一主题，极为精彩的论述见黄洋：《古典希腊理想化：作为一种文化现象的Hellenism》。

④　R. Pferffer, *History of Classical Scholarship from 1300 to 1850*, Oxford: Oxford University Press, 1976, p. 173; John Edwin Sandys, *A History of Classical Scholarshi*, Cambridge: Cambridge University Press, 1921, p. 12. 桑兹提供了更明确的信息，即Ersch和Gruber主编的《科学与艺术综合大百科》中F. Hasse所撰词条"Philologie"，第383页注释29。

⑤　当然，自19世纪以来就已经出现了反对希腊奇迹说的学术思想，如人类文化学中的剑桥神话仪式学派学者，其中最著名者当属康福德（Cornford）。在古典学内部，从18、19世纪以来也有与温克尔曼思想相对的历史主义或希腊主义思想的存在，如道兹（Dodds）对希腊人与非理性的研究等。可以说，伯克特的学术特点体现了这几种思想潮流的集合。

立性辩护，还得否认他们在印欧语系的大家庭内与印度的亲缘关系，以确立一种观念，就是将古典的、民族的希腊理解为一个自成体系、自主发展的文明模式。①

在这样一种思想氛围的影响下，加之西方资产阶级革命和工业革命之后对东方的全面优势，以及近代以来"东方"的衰落和西方学界对东方衰落根源的解释——专制、腐朽、没落的景象，西方学者因此倾向于把古代东方对古代希腊的影响降到最低，甚至有意将东方因素从理想化的古代希腊文明中"驱逐出去"。维拉莫维茨（Ulrich von Wilamowitz-Moellendorff）的一段话对此颇具代表性，"闪米特以及埃及的民族和国家衰落了几个世纪，尽管他们有自己古老的文化，但除了少数手工工艺技艺、服装、品味低劣的器具、陈旧的饰品、令人厌恶的偶像崇拜和更令人反感的各路虚假的神祇以外，他们不可能对希腊人有任何贡献"。②

与这样一种自我膨胀的古典主义相对应的是差不多同一时期兴起的东方主义（Orientalism）思潮③。黑格尔在《历史哲学》中说："世界历史从'东方'到'西方'，因为欧洲绝对地是历史的终点，亚洲是起点。世界的历史有一个东方（'东方'这个名词的本身是一个完全相对的东西）；因为地球虽然是圆的，历史并不围绕着它转动，相反地，历史是有一个决定的'东方'，就是亚细亚。那个外界的物质的太阳便在这里升起，而在西方沉没的那个自觉的太阳也是在这里升起，散播一种更为高贵的光明。"④黑格尔从地理的角度来寻求或规定历史的起点，世界历史是世界精神从东方到西方的一次漫游，它起步于东方，向西经过小亚细亚到达希腊罗马。最后到达了充满活力的日耳曼民族所在的西欧。黑格尔认为"亚细亚是起点，欧洲是终点"，也就是说，他在一定程度上承认东方文明的先发性，但是他对东方的认识确实充满了想象。在黑格尔眼中，"蒙古"同"中国"一样，都是"神权专制"的形象，是"封建大家长主宰一切"的形象。而对于印度人，他也在《历史哲学》中说，由于"印度人天性的一般要素"就是"精神处于梦寐状态的特征"，印度人还没有获得"自我"或"意识"。同时，由于"历史"必须是"精神"发展上一个主要的时期，加之印度人并非能够有所行动的"个体"，印度文化的分布只是一种无声无息的扩张，也就是说，没有政治的行动。印度人民从来没有向外去征服别人而是自己常常为人家所征服。概而言之，"亚细亚帝国屈从于欧洲人便是其必然的命运"。⑤紧跟黑格尔论调的是琼斯、穆勒、沃德、马克思等人，他们笔下"野蛮的、闭关自守的、与文明世界隔绝的状态被打破"的东方世界，充塞着浓烈的"东方主义"色彩。萨义德认为，"东方主义"话语体系，通过对东方和东方人进行整体化、类型化、本质化和符码化，形成关于东方的集体观念、专业权威、话语体系和社会体制。其实它是一种想象视野和过滤框架，是对东方的"妖魔化"和"东方化"，是西方控制、重建和君临东方的一种方式，是一种殖民主义

---

① Walter Burkert, *The Orientalizing Revolution: Near Eastern Influence on Greek Culture in the Early Archaic Age*, pp. 4–5.

② Ulrich von Wilamowitz-Moellendorff, *Homerische Untersuchungen*, (1884)215. 转引自 Walter Burkert, *The Orientalizing Revolution: Near Eastern Influence on Greek Culture in the Early Archaic Age*, p. 5.

③ Orientalism 这一术语的"东方主义"内涵最早由爱德华·萨义德（Edward W. Said）于 1978 年提出。（见 Edward W. Said, *Orientalism*, London: Penguin, 1978, 中文译本有：爱德华·萨义德著，王宇根译：《东方学》，北京：三联书店，1999 年，不过译文诸多地方不甚准确，不足为据。从学理层面讲，Orientalism 翻译为"东方学"是可以接受的，也被很多学者所认同和采纳。不过，Orientalism 更多时候是一种思维方式和话语方式，因此，译为"东方主义"更合适。）在萨义德之前，已经有维克托·吉尔南（Victor Kiernan）、马歇尔·霍奇森（Marshall Hodgson）和布莱恩·特纳（Bryan Turner）等诸多学者对这一话题进行了探索性的研究。也有学者认为，"东方主义"在古代希腊罗马文明中业已形成了深厚的传统。（见黄洋：《古代希腊罗马文明的"东方"想像》，《历史研究》，2006 年第 1 期，第 123 页。）有学者认为，东方学作为一门学科，由"经典东方学"、"现代东方学"、"当代东方学"三个时期构成。黑格尔是其学理层面的始作俑者，萨义德是将其提升至当代话语机制层面的集大成者。（见费小平：《东方学：从黑格尔到萨义德》，《外国语文》，2009 年 12 月第 25 卷第 6 期。）

④ 黑格尔著，王造时译：《历史哲学》，上海：上海书店出版社，2001 年，第 106—107 页。

⑤ 黑格尔著，王造时译：《历史哲学》，第 141 页。

和帝国主义的工具和意识形态。①

　　20 世纪 70 年代以来，国际政治发生了剧烈变化，多数原殖民国家在经历了长期的斗争之后获得了独立，但是他们后来发现自己并没有最终摆脱殖民统治。西方国家，特别是前殖民统治国家，继续以种种方式对独立的国家进行控制。在这样的背景下，爱德华·萨义德的《东方主义》一书出版。萨义德指出，西方世界对东方人民和文化有一种微妙却非常持久的偏见，并决意以人文主义批评去开拓斗争领域，引入一种长期而连续的思考和分析，以期打破这一偏见，为东方正名。②以《东方主义》的出版和学该书的讨论为契机，学术界出现了东方研究的热潮。

　　带有浓厚孤立倾向的古典主义和具有强烈政治色彩的东方主义的合流，也曾在在西方学术领域引起质疑。19 世纪的几大重要发现，③使得西方部分研究者找到了克服古典主义和东方主义话语体系内在缺陷的重要工具，得以重新认识"东方"以及东方文明对希腊文明的影响。"东方化—东方化时代—东方化革命"这一话语体系正是这种重新认识过程的具体体现之一。这种重新认识自 19 世纪末叶开始，在 20 世纪晚期的后殖民主义时期由涓涓细流成为学术潮流，反映了西方学界在新的历史条件下的的自我反思与自发调整。从这个意义上说，东方化革命的提出具有合理的、积极的意义。伯克特是这一倾向在当代的代表人物，他的《东方化革命》的目的就是正本清源，抛弃传统观念："窃望拙著能充当一名打破藩篱的使者，将古典学家的注意力引导到他们一直太少关注的领域，并使这些研究领域更易接近，甚至非专业人士也能理解。或许它也能激励东方学者（他们几乎同古典学家一样有孤立的倾向）继续保持或重新恢复与相邻研究领域的联系。"④

　　然而，澄清希腊与东方的联系程度并不是一件轻而易举的工作。黄洋教授正确地指出，希腊和东方世界的联系仍然是非常值得期待的一个研究领域，更为充分的研究极有可能进一步修正我们对于早期希腊历史的认识，但是这也是一个非常艰深的研究领域，不仅需要掌握古代希腊文献，而且还要有比较语文学的训练，掌握古代西亚和埃及的文献以及多种语言之余，也要对考古材料有着充分的了解，目前只有少数学者有条件从事这个领域的研究。⑤虽然他的告诫对象是中国学者，但是笔者认为，这也同样适用于西方学者，适用于所有正在或者将要从事这一领域研究的学者。一旦脱离了具体文化事项的研究，忽视对"东方化"的具体考析，单方面强调"革命"，就不可避免渗入一些民族主义和文化本位主义的因素，陷于和东方主义一样的想象性构造。这种想象性构造在学术层面的表现则是激进化和简单化。

　　《东方化革命》的作者伯克特，是一位非常严谨的古典学者。如前文所述，他的这部作品"标题大胆，行文谨慎"，并没有简单纠缠于概念和术语，也没有带着先入之见去进行研究，而是侧重于提供证据，为比较研究搭建平台。"东方化革命"这样一个标题更多是吸引注意力。然而，在这一研究领域，带有明显价值判断的标题并不在少数。有些学者确实像伯克特一样，在内容上并没有简单处理，而是以翔实的证据来说明具体文化事项，如韦斯特的《面向东方的赫利孔：希腊诗歌和神话中的西亚元素》。即便是伯纳尔招致诸多批评的《黑色雅典娜》，如果说第一卷只是以知识社会学的视角来整理欧洲人对古典文明的观念变迁历史，因而可能只会被视为一种外在性批评的话，那么第二卷、第三卷中较为翔实的史料和论证就应该引起任何严肃的古典学者的注意了。但是，也

---

① Edward W. Said, *Orientalism*, p. 3.

② Edward W. Said, *Orientalism*, preface, xviii.

③ 伯克特认为这些发现一是楔形文字和象形文字的破译让近东文明和埃及文明重新浮现，二是迈锡尼文明的发掘，三是对古风时期希腊艺术发展中东方化阶段的确认。Walter Burkert, *The Orientalizing Revolution: Near Eastern Influence on Greek Culture in the Early Archaic Age*, p. 2.

④ Walter Burkert, *The Orientalizing Revolution: Near Eastern Influence on Greek Culture in the Early Archaic Age*, p. 8.

⑤ 黄洋、晏绍祥：《希腊史研究入门》，第 191—192 页。

有一些内容如标题一样不甚严谨的作品，如詹姆斯《偷来的遗产：希腊哲学是偷来的埃及哲学》。尽管希腊人自己认为哲学最早起源于埃及，希腊哲学家从埃及学习并带回了哲学。[1]然而，哲学思想毕竟属于观念范畴，想要从简单的人物活动或表象的相似特征归纳出哲学思想的传承，并不是一件容易的事情。因此，作者论证中的漏洞随处可见，如"埃及的神秘主义学说到达其他地方的时间要比到达雅典早了数个世纪"、"希腊哲学发展时期（公元前640—前322年）处于内外战患中，不适合产生哲学家"、"埃及和希腊体系的外部环境具有同一性"，[2]因而，希腊哲学是偷来的埃及哲学。这样简单偏激的论断，在严谨的学术研究中并不足取。如果说标题冠之以"偷来"一词是为了吸引眼球，尚可接受，但作者行文中也多次使用这一价值倾向和感情色彩浓厚的字眼，更是容易招致反感。[3]同样的道理，如果说"东方化革命"这一概念在纠正古典主义的孤立倾向、反对种族主义的欧洲中心论方面有一定积极意义，那么，对这一概念激进的理解和阐释则是矫枉过正，难免走入另一个极端。

一些学者不是建立在原始史料的基础上进行考证与分析，而是把"东方化革命"作为一种"口号式"或"标语式"的术语，从西方学者的著作中拿来就用，甚至大加发挥，以一些历史上并不存在或者并没有发生过的假设前提来论证预设的主题，出现了简单化倾向。如《东方化革命》中译本导读中的一段话，"不妨问一个简单的问题：如果没有埃及和两河流域的原生性文化积累，如果没有腓尼基人发明的字母，没有埃及人、苏美尔人、巴比伦人、叙利亚人等古代民族对希腊人方方面面的影响，希腊文明能够有它那惊人的表现吗？它在"哲学"、科学、艺术、建筑、法律等方面能够取得如此惊人的成就吗？它能够深刻影响西方基督教文化、西方世俗现代文化，以及全世界现代文化吗？"[4]对非专业人士来说，这种简单化倾向或可理解。然而，要从专业领域研究"希腊和东方世界的联系"这一课题，还需要暂且放下"东方化革命"这样想象性的预设前提，从基本史料和文献出发，深入探讨具体问题，才有历史的宏观建构之可能性。

---

① 伊索克拉底在《布西里斯》中说："在埃及的一次旅行中，他（毕达哥拉斯）成为埃及宗教的学生，并且第一次把所有哲学带给希腊人。"（Isocrates, *Busiris*, 28）希罗多德曾提及此事（Herodotus, *Histories*, II. 81），后来的拉丁作家西塞罗认为毕达哥拉斯自称是一个 *philosophos*，而不是一个 *sophos*（Cicero, *Tusculanae Disputationes*, V. 3. 9），狄奥根尼斯和亚历山大里亚的克莱门特认为最早使用 philosophía 这一词的是毕达哥拉斯（Diogenes Laertius, *Lives*, I. 12; Clement, *Stromateis*, I. 61）。伯纳尔认为 Σοφία 一词源于埃及语词根 –sb3（意为"教导、教学、学生"），见 Martin Bernal, *Black Athena: Afro-Asiatic Roots of Classical Civilization*, Vol. I, p. 104; Vol. III, p. 263.

② George G. James, *Stolen Legacy: Greek Philosophy is Stolen Egyptian Philosophy*, p. 9, 22, 28.

③ 这一点可从此书出版后的情况略窥管豹。《偷来的遗产》写于詹姆斯博士就职于阿肯色大学松崖分校（University of Arkansas at Pine Bluff）期间，据说，在此书发表以后不久，詹姆斯就神秘去世，没有任何一个关于他的年谱记载其去世的具体日期。时至今日，该校图书馆甚至没有一本此书的副本，校园里也没有任何詹姆斯的雕像或胸像，教室墙壁上也没有任何以詹姆斯为主题的装饰，甚至没有任何一纸可资证明他曾在此生活过的记录。见于 George G. James, *Stolen Legacy: Greek Philosophy is Stolen Egyptian Philosophy*, "Biography".

④ 瓦尔特·伯克特著，刘智译：《东方化革命：古风时代前期近东对古希腊文化的影响》，"导读"第4页。

从理想民主到理性民主
——当今西方大众政治与古雅典平民政治区别浅析

倪翠兰　泰山学院

摘要：古代雅典把民主制度演绎到了空前绝后的地步，它实行直接民主、政治绝对平等的平民政治，但这种理想的民主制度在实际运作过程中却出现了许多体制性的不足。当今西方的民主制度是对古雅典民主制度扬弃的结果，它通过混合民主、相对平等、精英政治等方式克服了古代雅典理想民主的不足，是一种理性的民主政治。

关键词：平民政治；精英政治；理性民主

Abstract：The ancient times deduced the democratic instutition Athens unique of situation, it practices the direct democracy, politics absolute equal civilian politics, but this kind of ideal democratic instutition is in actually operate process appear many system shortage, now west of democratic instutition is the result to the thou the Athens the democratic instutition abandon, it pass hybrid democracy, opposite and equal, elite political etc. the method overcame the ancient times Athens the shortage of the ideal democracy, is a kind of reasonableness of democracy.

Keyword：Civilian's politics, Elite politics, Reasonableness democracy

古希腊城邦雅典是世界民主制度的发祥地和民主思想的摇篮。古雅典城邦在自己的发展历程中，把民主政治发展到了空前绝后的地步，为后世探究出了民主的核心内涵，演绎出了民主制度的根本原则。雅典的民主制度成为了世界民主制度的标本而光耀史册。

雅典民主政治最本质的特点就是人民主权和直接民主：公民大众是国家的最高权力机关，人民直接行使立法权、直接行使行政管理权，也直接行使司法审判权。同时，雅典政治制度的主体是平民，雅典政治又是典型的大众政治。古雅典把平等、民主等政治原则发展到了极至，以至我们至今仍然想象不出更高境界的民主。

当今西方的政治制度是以古希腊、罗马为源头，从中世纪的西欧摄取了很多的民主滋养，在近代资产阶级反封建的斗争中逐渐形成的，现当代，又通过不断的调整和改革不断发展与完善。今天，西方政治制度已经由资产阶级的民主政治发展为大众政治。但当今西方的大众政治并不是古雅典民主政治的翻版与回归，而是具有鲜明时代特征的现代大众政治。究其原因，除时代因素外，雅典经典化的民主政治本身的缺陷也是重要因素。雅典的民主制度在当时的政治实践中就已经呈现出了许多体制性的弊端与不足，许多有识之士不仅对雅典的民主政治提出了质疑与批评，同时也对更合理的政治体制进行了探讨。今天看来，雅典的民主政治是一种理想化的政治，但在政治实践中却处处碰壁。正因如此，西方政治制度在形成与发展过程中，对古雅典的民主制度既继承又改造，最终形成了今天更理性、更现实的民主制度。当今西方的政治制度与古雅典民主制度的区别主要是混合民主与直接民主、相对平等与绝对平等、精英民主与大众民主的区别。

一　从直接民主到混合民主

雅典民主政治的典型特征是直接民主制。公民大会是雅典的最高权力机关，由雅典的全体公民组成。在雅典民主政治的鼎盛时期，公民大会每年定期召开四十次。每个公民在会上都有权提出议案和参加议案的讨论，国家的法令、政策和一切重大问题，如宣战、媾和、结盟、赋税等等都要在公民大会讨论、修改、批准，公民大会的决定具有最高的法律效力；公民大会还选举产生执政官、十将军等重要官职。全体公民直接参加的公民大会掌握国家的最高权力，体现了"主权在民"这一民主制的核心特征。

在雅典民主政治的鼎盛时期，行政权对全体公民开放。所有的官职均不受出身、门第、财产等方面的限制，官吏大多是通过抽签产生，一切职位任期短暂且不得连任。它使每个雅典公民都有机会担任公职，雅典政治也因此而具有了公民轮番为政的特征。如雅典每个年满 30 岁的公民都有机会通过抽签当选为五百人会议成员；雅典的许多高级官职包括执政官都是以抽签方式产生的。抽签保证了公职人员产生的公正性与普通公民当选的可能性，而任期限制则使更多的公民有机会从政。根据亚里士多德的估计，在雅典，大约每六名公民中就有一人在担任某种公职。可见雅典公民从政的广泛性。

雅典的公民也直接行使司法权。雅典有庞大的六千人组成的陪审法庭来行使司法权。陪审法庭的成员是从约四万公民中抽签产生的，任期一年，不得连任，任何公民都有机会成为陪审法庭的成员。审判过程中，陪审法庭的成员既是审判员，又是陪审员：他们首先判定相关成员是否有罪，然后再进行量刑判决。陪审法庭的判决是最终判决。因此，雅典的最高司法权也是由公民直接行使的。

雅典公民也直接行使监督权。雅典的政治权力机构没有明确的职权划分，其政治权力的制约不是表现为立法、行政和司法机关之间的监督和制约，而是表现为城邦公民集体对官吏的监督和制约。在雅典，所有通过抽签或选举产生的官吏在任职前都要经过陪审法庭的资格审查；每四次公民大会中就有一次是专门对官吏任职期间的表现进行审查；官吏任期结束后，也要由陪审法庭审核他任职期间的帐目，有问题立即移交法庭审判；每年春天，公民大会还专门对有专制倾向的危险分子进行投票，如果票数超过六千，就将他放逐出国。

总之，雅典公民不但有广泛而真正的参政权，还有实实在在担任各种官职的机会与可能，公民是国家权力的真正主体与核心。雅典的民主政治也因此成为典型的大众政治。而大众政治下，平民是主体，雅典的大众政治又更多地表现为平民政治。这种政治制度极大地激发了公民政治参与的积极性与创造性，促使了雅典政治、经济、思想文化的发展与繁荣。从理论上说，是一种非常理想而完美的政治制度。

但这种理想而完美的民主制度在实际运作过程中却出现了许多体制性的弊端，出现了理想民主与现实的矛盾。其弊端主要是公民在行使政治权力的过程中，经常以情绪取代理智，使雅典的政治决策经常出现原则性的失误与偏差，它集中表现在公民大会的决策和陪审法庭的判决上。

公民大会是雅典的最高权力机关，但在对法案和重大事情的讨论与表决过程中，雅典公民经常受一些演说家的鼓动、在缺乏对事情的理性思考和全面衡量而作出错误的决定，导致国家决策失误，给国家和社会造成不可挽回的最大损失。典型例子是伯罗奔尼撒战争期间公民大会对是否进行西西里远征的表决。当时公民并不了解西西里的真实情况，但主战派首领阿尔西比阿德为达到自己的目的，在公民大会上大肆鼓动，并动员了一些人为自己助威，于是，公民大会通过了远征西西里的计划。但计划实施受挫、远征军全军覆没后，受失败情绪的感染，公民大会又在主和派的煽动下通过了阿尔西比阿德犯有渎神罪并回国受审的决定。这一决定促使阿尔西比阿德叛逃到了斯巴达，向斯巴达泄露了雅典的军事部署并献计围困雅典城。这一围攻，使雅典丧失了精锐的海军，并从此丧失了雅典的海上优势。这一失败是雅典整个战争走向失败的转折点，而它在一定程度上可以说是由公民大会的错误决定导致的。在雅典历史上，公民大会受个别人物的鼓动而通过的错误决定有许多。

陪审法庭是雅典的最高司法机关。陪审法庭的成员都是由普通公民抽签当选的，他们不是专业司法人员，没有精深的法律知识，在审理案件与裁决过程中，都是凭借自己的主观认识去对案件做判断，加上判决前没有调查取证的程序，只是在法庭上听取涉案人员的辩解，做出错误的判断很难避免。而陪审法庭的判决又是最终判决，一旦出现冤假错案，连申诉的机会都没有。这种司法制度实际上存在体制性的弊端，在实践运作中，这种弊端经常显现。典型的例子是对苏格拉底的审判。苏格拉底被政敌以"慢神"与"蛊惑青年"罪指控，陪审法庭最终以281对220票的多数判处了苏格拉底死刑。14年后，有人认为这是一冤案，又追究当初起诉者的责任，陪审法庭又把当初的诬告者判处了死刑。这一事件往往被看作是雅典民主的耻辱。

正因如此，在希腊民主政治的顶峰期过后，就出现了对雅典民主政治的批评，这些批评者普遍认为，雅典的直接民主存在着混乱与立法的随意性。亚里斯多德把它定为"极端民主"，他说，"在这种极端形式的平民政体中，各自放纵于随心所欲的生活……"①。罗马共和末年的政治家与思想家西塞罗则直接对雅典的民主政治持否定态度，他指责雅典公民大会议事方式的无序与混乱，认为，民众判决不是经过深思熟虑的投票，而是"暴怒中的群民的举手和无约束的喊叫"，公民大会是"完全没有经验的人们支持了有害的战争"、"让那些制造麻烦的人负责公共事务"、"从城邦中驱逐了最能为它服务的公民"②等等。他认为，正是因为人民的过度自由以及公民大会的混乱，才使希腊失去了往日的辉煌、伟大与繁荣。在西塞罗眼中，直接民主意味着极端的无政府主义，是雅典走向衰落的重要原因。罗马共和末年的历史学家普鲁塔克则认为，在直接民主制下，希腊被一些政客与党徒煽起的内战搅得动荡不安，雅典的政治生活绝大多数是不正常的，雅典的政治家、尤其是那些演说家，都是只为自己谋利而不顾国家混乱的恶棍，"陶片放逐法不是对卑鄙行为的惩罚，而是散发仇恨情绪的一种温和手段"。③

这些批评者对雅典民主政治的批评虽然有时代与阶级的局限性，但却击中了雅典民主政治的要害。正因如此，如何充分发挥民主而又克服直接民主的弊端就成为后世民主政治建设需要克服的难题。

西方政治制度是在近代反封建斗争中建立起来的。在它建立的过程中，政治主体一直是资产阶级，它所谓的民主实际上是资产阶级的民主，所谓的平等实际上是以财富为基础的平等，近代的西方政治制度实质上是资产阶级的民主制度。

资本主义民主政治的主要内容是代议制度。这种制度起源于英国，后被资产阶级政治思想家认可并加以演绎，成为了资本主义政治制度的核心内容。这些构建资本主义政治制度的思想家普遍认

---

① 亚里士多德：《政治学》，北京：商务印书馆，1982年版，第191页。
② 转引自晏绍祥：《民主还是暴政》，载《世界历史》2004年第1期，第52—53页。
③ 普鲁塔克：《希腊罗马名人传》，北京：商务印书馆，1990年版，第319页。

为，直接民主有缺陷，近代的主体国家不适合实行直接民主制度。如英国的政治思想家密尔认为，所有的人都亲自参加公共事务是不可能的，完善政府的理想类型是代议制度。[①]美国的政治思想家潘恩也指出，直接民主制度是受幅员和人口限制的，领土过大与人口过多不适合直接民主，最好的政治体制是代议制，它可以把直接民主的缺陷清除，还能集中社会各部分和整体利益必需的知识，能够使政府始终处于成熟的状态。[②]他认为，雅典如果实行代议制，也会胜过原有的民主制。不仅如此，近代思想家们为了防止代议制下立法过程中出现情绪化与草率现象，还设计了两院制的议会。两院制、代议制，一定程度上可以说是借鉴雅典直接民主教训的结果。

伴随向现代工业社会的转化，在人民民主运动的不断推动下，西方各国的权力逐渐向社会大众开放，普选逐渐实现，它使普通大众获得了参与政治的资格与机会，资产阶级的代议制也逐渐发展成为大众的代议制。

但是，西方代议制的发展并没有杜绝直接民主，公民的直接民主权力不仅在某些层面上保留下来，并且伴随时代发展还有进一步加强的发展倾向。当今的西方国家，直接民主、半直接民主的政治参与形式普遍存在，主要表现为公民投票表决、公民复决、公民直接提案等。公民投票表决，是指通过全国公民直接投票的方式来批准法律和决定国家内外政策、政治制度、领土变更、国家独立等国家大事。而公民复决则是指立法机关已经通过的法律或决议，由于公众提出异议而提交公民重新表决，通过公民表决来决定这些法律与决议是否最终生效。公民直接提案是指一定数量的公民联合签名可直接提出法律草案。在意大利，宪法修正案如在两院二读后没有获得 2/3 的多数通过，可以由公民投票决定；有 50 万选民签名就可以提出法律草案；有 50 万公民提出要求，可以废除某项法律。1970——1985 年间，意大利有 50 万选民签名提出的法律草案就有 25 项，其中的 9 项通过公民投票而成为了法律。法国第五共和国宪法第 11 条规定，总统可以将一切有关公共权力机构的组织、批准共同体协定等的法律草案提交公民投票。在政治实践中，法国多次通过公民投票来决定宪法修改和重大立法问题。在瑞典，关于原子能的使用、禁酒、国家养老金计划等问题，都由公民投票决定。在美国，州及地方政治中广泛存在公民投票、公民罢免等制度。英国在二十世纪七十年代也通过公民投票解决了是否加入欧盟的问题。瑞士更是经常采用公民表决与公民倡议等直接民主形式。

这类直接民主、半直接民主的出现与发展，是当今西方政治制度发展的新现象，是当代民主与近代民主的一个明显区别，它使西方国家公民的参政程度加深，是西方政治制度发展的新趋势。

代议民主与直接民主、半直接民主的并行发展，使当代西方民主呈现出混合民主的特征，间接的代议制民主与直接民主相得益彰，形成了当今西方民主的新面貌，它既克服了直接民主的一些不足，同时又在很大程度了发扬了民主，有利于公民政治素质的提高。

二　从绝对平等到相对平等

雅典的民主制度是构建在公民绝对平等的原则之上的。梭伦改革开始削弱世袭特权、用财产差别取代出身差别，克里斯梯尼改革则取消了世袭特权、并按部落平等原则组织权力机关，伯里克利通过所有官职对所有等级的公民开放、官吏抽签选举与任期限制、公职补贴等方式实现了公民参政的绝对平等，使雅典民主政治发展到了最高峰。在伯里克利时代，公民大会每十天召开一次，所有的公民在会上都有平等的提议权、发言权、选举权、投票决定权，最后的结果都是以多数人的意见为准；五百人会议平等地分为十组，轮流担任主席团，团员之间彼此平等，通过抽签担任主席团的

---

① 密尔：《代议制政府》，北京：商务印书馆，1982 年版，第 55 页。
② 潘恩：《潘恩文集》，北京：商务印书馆，1987 年版，第 246 页。

主席；抽签产生各种公职，任何公民都绝对有可能、有机会担任公职，享有平等的公职津贴；陪审法庭的判决与量刑都以大多数人的意见为准。可以说，雅典的公民不仅有机会、有实际的可能担任各种公职，而且在担任公职期间也享有绝对平等而充分的权力。这是一种绝对平等的政治。

这种绝对平等是建立在这样的政治理念之上的——公民都具备很高的政治素养、都有行使专业政治权力的能力、并因有爱国之心而尽全力履行其政治责任。这样的政治理念强调了人的权力平等，并强调了人性的优点并将它理想化，但却忽略了人的能力与个性差异，更忽视了政治的专业性。因此，在现实社会中，这样的政治理念是行不通的，因为每个人的个性不同、能力不同、追求不同，并且从事公职需要一定的专业能力和经验积累，并不是每个人都适合从事并能够干好公职的。在公民绝对平等的政治原则下，雅典的公职由普通公民通过抽签担任，权力机构的组成确实有"业余"与"乌合之众"之嫌，权力机构运作过程中出现失误也在所难免。而从整个社会来看，这种绝对平等要求每个公民都要成为一个合格的公职人员，从事政治活动，普通公民为了参加十天一次的公民大会，就必须放下手中的工作，政治成为了社会生活的中心，既造成了政治肥大症，也扰乱了正常的社会生产秩序。从一个社会的正常运行来讲，全民来从事政治管理，雅典政治运作的成本太高，这种政治过于奢侈。

这种政治绝对平等的不足在雅典民主政治的顶峰时期就受到质疑。苏格拉底认为，人是有区别的，应分为智者、勇者、劳动者三类。政治需要智慧与专门的知识，不能随便选一个人来担当。就象没有人愿意抽签雇佣一位舵手或建筑师一样，用抽签方法选城邦的领导人是非常愚蠢的。[1]雅典的抽签民主导致了外行治国，它使雅典没有专门的立法人员、没有专门的法官、没有专职的政府人员，政治机构完全由外行操作。柏拉图认为，这是一种"使人乐意的、无政府状态的、花哨的管理形式，在这种制度下不加区别地把平等给了一切人，不管他们是不是平等者"。[2]罗马历史学家波里比阿则把绝对平等下的雅典比作一条没有船长的大船。[3]

在以上认识的基础上，柏拉图与亚里斯多德都对理想政体提出了自己的看法。柏拉图认为，民主制使社会处于无政府状态，当权者为讨好群众不主持正义，群众自由行事，民主政治是"恶政治"。理想的国家应由三部分人组成——统治者、武士、劳动者。理想的政治是由统治者用自己的哲学智慧和德行把握正义，进行统治。亚里斯多德则认为，平民政治是一种变态政体，最理想的政体是以中产阶级为主体的共和政体。可见，柏拉图与亚里斯多德都对雅典的民主政治进行了否定。而芝诺推崇的则是具有君主制、贵族制、民主制三种政体特点的混合政体。[4]

正因为政治绝对平等的不足，今天，西方政治制度的运作原则已经由公民的绝对平等发展到了相对平等，它是公民机会和权力平等基础之上的能力竞争。

首先，每个公民参政的机会和权力是平等的。宪法给予了公民平等的参政权，并通过普遍选举权、平等选举权（每个选民都以平等的地位参加选举、在选举过程中只有一次投票权、每张选票的效力相等）、直接选举（选民直接投票选出当选人）、秘密投票等原则来保证公民平等的参政权。法律也保障了参政程序的平等，所有公民都通过选举、竞争考试或资格考试等路径来参政，选举都要经过提名、预选、竞选、选民投票等相同的阶段，最终以投票的结果决定当选者。

但在实际的政治运作过程中，这种平等体现的只是一种机会、权力平等基础之上的能力竞争，而不是绝对平等。今天，公民从政的途径主要有竞选、竞争考试、职业资格基础之上的委任等，其中竞选与竞争考试是两种最基本的方式。目前，西方的议员、元首、政府首脑、地方行政首长等政

---

① 色诺芬：《回忆苏格拉底》，北京：商务印书馆，1984年版，第9页。
② 柏拉图：《理想国》第八卷（转引自：罗吉《释读古代雅典民主理念的不足》，载《西南民族大学学报》2004年7期）。
③ 波里比阿：《通史》第三卷（转引自：晏绍祥《民主还是暴政》，载《世界历史》2004年1期）。
④ 涅尔谢相茨：《古希腊政治学说》，北京：商务印书馆，1991年版，第47—48页。

务官员大多是选举产生的，而这些之外的文官大多是考试选拔的。在选举过程中，宪法给每个公民提供了平等的参政机会，但实际上，不论是政党提名还是选民推荐，参加者都要用一定的能力与实力去参与竞争，只有优胜者才能胜出。在考试竞争过程中，同样把机会给了每一个人，但最后都是以能力与技能来决定录用结果的。可以说，参与只是参政的前提，而能力才是参政的决定性因素，平等是能力相同基础上的平等。为了保证官员能力的充分发挥，西方各国的相关法律都规定了文官无过失不得被解雇、议员可以无限期连任，行政官员可以有一定的连任期等。这种相对平等既保证了从政人员的素质与专业能力，也保证了政治运作的高效率与高质量，有效克服了雅典绝对平等的不足。

三 从平民政治到精英政治

相对平等原则下，当今西方民主政治不再是古雅典式的平民政治，而是典型的精英政治。精英与平民相比，不仅文化素养高，而且有比较高的思想境界，有一定的专业能力与经验，在处理政治问题时，能够保持理性的认识，作出科学的判断与决策，保证政治运作的效率与质量。

代议制民主下，西方各国公民直接选举他们的代表（议员）组成立法机关——议会。这些议员都是通过预选、竞选而推出的，都属于社会精英。如美国，国会议员的选举要经过预选提名、竞选、大选三个阶段，在选举过程中，每一个众议员要代表50万选民，他们的资质、能力、政治素质是要经过50万选民的认可，一般人是不可能当选的。而在英国，一名保守党候选人当选平均需要4万张选票，一名工党候选人当选平均需要4.2万张选票。可以说，当选者都是公民选择出来的政治精英。目前，英国议会下院中的保守党议员有一半以上是公司的董事、经理，另一半则是律师、公职人员、专业人士，他们几乎都受过高等教育，都有比较高的政治素质，而工党的议员中许多是工会活动分子，也是本党的精英人士。

此外，议员的连选连任不受限制也助长了议员的精英化。也正因议员的连选连任不受限制，许多人把议员作为了终身追求的职业。现在美国的每一届议会中有80%的议员是连任的。议员连任的典型代表是卡尔·海顿，他1912年当选众议员，连任15年，1927年又连续任参议员42年，直到91岁退休。这种连选连任的规定使议员成为了一种职业，也使议员基本上成为了立法专业人士。

在行政机关，官员分政务官与文官两类，其中政务官都是政治专家。在内阁制国家，如英国，内阁大臣都是议员，首相是执政党的全国性领袖；在总统制国家，如美国，总统候选人一般都是有很高资质与能力及深厚政治背景的政治家，他们要先在五十个州进行预选，然后由政党推出本党最有实力的候选人参加全国竞选，在选举过程中，候选人个人的政见、能力、思想往往成为决定性的因素。而超高的政治见解、能力、思想本身就证明了他的政治精英属性。一定的能力与专业技能是文官被录取的前提条件，同时，文官被录用后，无过失不得被解雇，既保证了政治的连续性、稳定性与专业性，也保证了文官能力的有效发挥，并使得文官的专业能力与素质不断提高，成为了相关领域的专家。在司法领域，法官有的任命，有的选举，但任命与选举都是以比较高的专业资格为基础的，上任后一般都实行终身制度。终身制也使西方各国的法官成了为司法领域的专业人士。

总之，目前西方的政治基础是公民大众，但政治的主体却是社会相关领域的专业人士、专家，他们凭借自己的超众能力从大众中脱颖而出，来操纵国家的政治权力。可以说，目前西方的政治是由社会各方面专家与精英分子进行操作的，实质上是一种精英政治。这种精英政治克服了平民政治的不足，使政治运作更高效、更专业，是一种理性的民主政治。

古典时期雅典家庭中的夫妻关系

孙晶晶　潍坊大学

摘要：在古典时期，雅典家庭中的夫妻关系受到城邦性别观念的影响。在雅典人的观念中，男性居于统治和主导地位，而女性则处于被统治和依附的地位。在家庭中，丈夫是统治者，夫妻间的关系首先是统治与被统治的关系。夫妻间还有合作的伙伴关系，在养育孩子、监管奴隶、物品的储存与分配等家庭事务中，妻子与丈夫的协作对于整个家庭的繁荣和延续都非常重要。不过，这种夫妻合作关系必须以丈夫的掌控为前提。总体来看，古典时期雅典家庭中的夫妻关系是丈夫掌控下的夫妻合作关系。

关键词：古典时期；雅典家庭；夫妻关系

Abstract：The gender notion and sexual relations had effect on the spousal relationship. In Athenian's opinion, male was in dominant and drivers seat, female was subject. In Athenian family the relationship between the husband and the wife showed on tow aspects: one aspect was rule and ruled relationship; the other was partnership. In general, it was very important for the family that the husband cooperated with wife in the former's domination, however, this cooperation based on the domination of the husband.

Keywords：Classical Age, Athenian Family, Relationship between the Spouse

古希腊社会中的两性关系，特别是女性地位问题受到古希腊史学家和社会史学家的关注。不过他们的研究侧重于公共生活空间中的女性的地位问题。研究两性在家庭中的关系的人较少，并且大都强调丈夫对妻子的统治和妻子在家庭中的低下地位。裔昭印教授发表的《从家庭和私生活看古雅典妇女的地位》中谈到雅典的妻子在家庭中的地位，但家庭中的夫妻关系并不是她要谈论的重点，她认为妻子在家庭中的地位受到雅典人的性别观念的影响，同时，也受到来自妾和妓女的挑战，妻子在家庭中的地位较为低下。[①]虽然雅典家庭中的夫妻关系首先是统治和被统治的关系，但是，夫妻间协作也是夫妻关系的一项重要内容。因而，本文力图在前人研究的基础上，从丈夫对妻子的统治、夫妻在家庭中的分工与合作等方面对家庭中的夫妻关系进行探讨，以求教于学界同仁。

---

① 裔昭印：《从家庭和私生活看古雅典妇女的地位》，《历史研究》，2000 年第 2 期。

一 丈夫对妻子的统治

在古典时期，雅典的性别观念是男尊女卑，人们认为男性应该统治女性。在社会中，女性处于男性统治之下，地位低下。[1]在政治上，女性是消极公民，不能真正行使自己的公民权，无法参与城邦的统治、管理和大部分的公共生活，甚至户外的活动都受到严格的限制。她的公民权的全部意义就是能够嫁给公民，并生育合法的公民后代；在法律上，女性是无行为能力的人，她离不开男性公民的监护，她的一生只能在父亲（或兄弟）、丈夫，甚至是儿子的监护下生活。男尊女卑的性别观念无疑会影响家庭中的两性关系。未出嫁前，女性是在父亲或者兄弟的监护下生活；出嫁意味着对她的监护权由父亲转向丈夫，她必须委身于丈夫的监护与保护之下。在结婚后，如果离开丈夫的保护，女性的生活就无法保证。在德摩斯提尼演说中曾提到一个女性，在丈夫不在时，她无力保护家中的财产，甚至无法说服闯入者相信她的儿子不是奴隶。直到一个邻居——一个成年男性公民出面跟他们交涉，告诉他们这个男孩的身份，那些闯入者才肯罢休[2]。阿波罗多洛斯所说的关于女性对于男性的意义的一段话也充分表明了女性从属于男性的地位。在德摩斯提尼的演说中，阿波罗多洛斯说到："我们有妓女为我们提供快乐，有妾满足我们的日常需要，而我们的妻子则能够为我们生育合法的子嗣，并且为我们忠实地料理家务"。社会关系影响到了家庭中的夫妻关系，在家庭中，女性同样处于被统治和依附地位。

此外，女性的隐居生活和夫妻间的年龄差距，也使得女性在家庭两性关系中处于劣势。妇女在婚前受到的教育较少，她一直受着约束，尽量少看、少听、少说话。伯里克利在他的演说中提到：妇女们的最大光荣就是很少被男人谈及，不管是赞扬，还是批评。[3]也就是说，女子无名便是德。然而，她的丈夫则受到严格的训练，具有广泛的社会经验，因此她的能力和阅历很难与丈夫相匹敌。在刚结婚时，她只懂得怎样把交给她的毛布制成斗篷，只懂得给女仆们分派纺织工作。要成为家庭事务的管理者，她们还需要丈夫的管理和调教。在与克利托布勒斯的对话中，苏格拉底就将妻子比作羊和马，而将丈夫比作牧羊人和驯马师。[4]

在古希腊，男性和女性的结婚年龄差别较大，女性在出嫁时大约 15 岁左右，而她的丈夫则已经 30 岁左右。《经济论》中两个重要的人物（伊斯霍玛霍斯和克利托布勒斯）都承认自己的妻子结婚时还很小，还只是不懂事的孩子。年龄和阅历上的差异使得妻子从一开始就不可能同丈夫处于同等的位置。丈夫成为她们的教导者，担任起类似父亲的职责，这很容易导致妻子对丈夫的依赖和顺从。因此伊斯霍玛霍斯的妻子只能卑微的说"可是我怎样能够帮助你呢？我有什么能力？……我的责任就是顺从。"[5]伊斯霍玛霍斯与苏格拉底的对话也说明了丈夫要对妻子进行调教，而妻子则要听从丈夫的命令，愿意按照丈夫的安排管理家庭事务：

苏格拉底对伊斯霍玛霍斯说：

"那么，伊斯霍玛霍斯，"我说，"你的妻子愿意听你的话吗？"

"当然，苏格拉底，"他大声说，"她当时告诉我说：如果我认为叮嘱她必须照管我们的东西是给予她的一项困难的任务，那我就错了……"[6]

---

[1] *Demosthenes*, LIX, 122.

[2] *Demosthenes*, XLVII, 61.

[3] Thucydides, *History of the Peloponnesian War*, II, 45.

[4] 色诺芬：《经济论》，张伯健，陆大年译，北京：商务印书馆 1981 年，第 11 页。

[5] 色诺芬：《经济论》，张伯健，陆大年译，第 23 页。

[6] 色诺芬：《经济论》，张伯健，陆大年译，第 33 页。

由此看来，受到男尊女卑的社会观念的影响，在家庭中，丈夫是统治者，妻子则是被统治者，家庭中的夫妻关系明显地表现为统治与被统治的关系。

二　丈夫与妻子的合作与分工

然而，在古典时期雅典的家庭中，统治关系不是夫妻关系的全部，夫妻关系中还存在着合作的伙伴关系。亚里士多德就曾宣称，在 oikos（希腊的家庭）中，结婚了的男人和女人是伙伴关系或 koinonia（团队关系），它区别于家庭中的其它基本关系，例如主人和奴隶的关系和父母与孩子的关系。亚里士多德认为：一个主人对于奴隶的统治是专制统治；父亲对子女的统治是君主式的，因为年龄的关系，父亲既凭借着爱又凭借着尊敬而实施他的统治，体现某种君主式的权威。君主在本性上优越于他的臣民，但应当和他们是同一群体，这种关系也是长幼关系和父子关系。丈夫对妻子的统治则是共和制的统治，大多共和制的城邦中公民轮番为治，公民之间的关系本质上是平等的，但是一旦有人统治人，而另外的人被人统治，人们便会竭力使得外表、语言以及受尊重的方式有所不同，男女之间的关系永远都是这种关系。[1]亚里士多德的观点不免有点过于乐观了，从前文的分析中可以看出，在夫妻关系中，妻子轮到统治地位的机会几乎是没有的。但是，从他的观点中，我们至少可以看到：在家庭中，夫妻关系是一种特殊的统治关系——亦统治亦合作的关系，并且他们之间的合作对于家庭的意义不逊于统治关系。

夫妻之间的这种合作关系首先表现在为家庭生育合法的子嗣。在家庭生活中，男性与女性的关系主要包括丈夫与妻子的关系、男主人与妾的关系、男主人与女奴隶的关系。这三种关系的差别在于两性结合的方式，妻子、妾和女奴隶中，妻子的身份最高，她通过合法婚姻与男性结合在一起，而妾与奴隶则没有合法婚姻作保护。在雅典，婚姻的主要目的是为家庭和城邦生育合法的后代，合法的婚姻是后代合法性的保证，对于妻子对于家庭的意义在于，可以为她的丈夫生育合法的后代。在家庭中妻子的主要职责也是为家庭生育合法的后代，确保家庭的延续。苏格拉底曾对他的儿子说过："我们寻找妻子，她将为我们生育最好的孩子，并使他们结婚供养家庭。"[2]由此可见，妻子在生育孩子方面，对于丈夫和整个家庭都很重要。在孩子的养育方面，妻子是丈夫重要的合作者，正如伊斯霍玛霍斯对妻子所说：

神把男性和女性结合在一起，主要就是为了使他们结合成完美的合作关系，互相帮助。因为各种生物要传宗接代，他们就结成婚姻，好生儿育女。

法律也认可这些责任，因为它把男人和女人结合在一起。神使男人和女人成为他们养儿育女的合作者，所以法律也指定他们为家庭的合作者。[3]

对于雅典城邦、家庭和夫妻个人而言，共同生育和培养后代都是必需的。二者的合作不仅仅是能够为城邦提供合法的公民后代、为家庭的延续香火，也能给他们自己带来好处，在他们年老时能够得到最好的帮手和最好的赡养。因此，一对夫妻在组成家庭之后，丈夫首先要教给新婚妻子如何与自己合作，把孩子养育好。孩子（特别是儿子）是夫妻合作的产物，也是维系和调解夫妻关系的纽带。公元4世纪的尤菲利托斯在法庭上曾说："雅典人，当决定结婚，并将一位妻子带进我家时，在一段时间内，我不去打扰她，但她也不至于自由得为所欲为，我以一种合理的态度尽可能去观察她。但当我的儿子出生时，我便开始信任她了"[4]。尤菲利托斯因儿子的出生而开始信任妻子，孩子将夫

---

① 参见苗力田主编：《亚里士多德全集》，第九卷，北京：中国人民大学出版社，1994年，第25－26页。

② Xenophon, *Memorabilia*, II, 4.

③ 色诺芬：《经济论》，张伯健，陆大年译，第23-24页。

④ *Lysias*, I, 6.

妻二人紧密联系起来。一个古典时期雅典的瓶画上，描绘着一个父亲看着他的年轻的妻子鼓励他们幼的小儿子爬行的情景。[①]德摩斯提尼演说中也曾提到，一对夫妻会为了孩子而放弃他们之间的纷争。[②]

丈夫与妻子的合作除了生育与和培养后代之外，还表现在对家庭利益的关注以及对家庭经济事务的管理。夫妻在结婚后建立其共同的家庭，新建立的家庭的经济基础是二者共同建立起来的，妻子给新家庭的投资是嫁妆。嫁妆是新娘父亲给她的一笔财产，它一般是财物或货币。嫁妆占她父亲财产一定的比例，德摩斯提尼曾提到她的妹妹得到父亲 2 塔兰特的嫁妆，占其父亲财产总数的 14.2%。[③]而根据利杜斯的统计，嫁妆占支付者财产总额的最大的比例是 27.8%，最小的是 3.3%。[④]在结婚后，嫁妆与丈夫的财产一起构成新家庭的启动资金。因此，我们可以说，实际上，家庭的财产是夫妻共有的，故而二者在家庭经济利益上是一致的，妻子愿意照管她自己的财产，丈夫也应该与妻子合作，让她参与家庭经济事务的管理。前文提到的尤菲利托斯在妻子生了儿子之后把他所有的财产交给她掌管，并认为这是与妻子亲近的最好证明。[⑤]在德摩斯提尼演说中，演说者将妻子称作是"家里东西的可信赖的监管者"。[⑥]

色诺芬认为妻子在家庭管理中是必不可少的。他所关注的家政问题的重点就是讨论让妻子参与管理家庭事务，他强调丈夫与妻子共同协作，管理家庭经济事务，使财产得到增加并被有效地利用，对整个家庭经济和利益来说，能否获得妻子有效的合作是至关重要的：

> 目前我们共同享有我们这个家庭。因为我把我所有的东西都放到我们共有的财产里，而你也把你带来的一切都加了进去。我们并不要计算我们谁实际拿出来的更多，……对于家庭而言，谁能证明自己是更好的合作者，谁的贡献就更重要。[⑦]

有些人得到妻子的合作，因而增加了财产，另一些人却由于他们对待妻子的行为完全破坏了他们的家庭，我认为妻子如果在家庭中是一个好配偶，她对于家庭幸福的贡献和她的丈夫是完全一样的。[⑧]

在家庭中，夫妻有合作也有分工。实际上，以性别为基础的家庭自然分工早在原始时代就已经确立。在古典时期的雅典人看来，最好的分工方式是男主外，女主内。因为女性的特征适于室内工作，而男人的性情适于室外工作。正如伊斯霍玛霍斯对妻子说的：

> 神使男人的身心更能耐寒耐热，能够忍受旅途和远征的跋涉，所以让他们做室外的工作。而女人，由于他使她们的身体对于这种事情的忍耐力较差，所以，我认为，他就让她们做室内的工作。[⑨]

因而妻子的责任就是在家庭中照顾孩子和管理家庭事务：

---

① A. Powell, *Athens and Sparta*, p.364.
② *Demosthenes*, XL, 29.
③ *Demosthenes*, XXVII, 5.
④ C. Leduc, 'Marriage in Ancient Greece', in Stella Georgoudi, Georges Duby and Michelle Perrot eds. *A History of Women in the West*, vol. I, p.280.
⑤ *Lysias*, I, 6.
⑥ *Demosthenes*, LVII, 122.
⑦ 色诺芬：《经济论》，张伯健，陆大年译，第 23 页。
⑧ 色诺芬：《经济论》，张伯健，陆大年译，第 12 页。
⑨ 色诺芬：《经济论》，张伯健，陆大年译，第 24 页。

　　　而且神已经给女人创造了养育婴儿的任务，并使她们担负这一任务，所以他分给女人的对于初生婴儿的爱要比男人更多些。①

她应该：

　　　呆在家里，打发那些应该在外面工作的仆人出去工作，监督那些在家里工作的人；收受我们得到的东西，分配其中必须花费出去的部分，照管其中应该储存起来的部分；要注意不要在一个月内花掉留作一年使用的东西。有些专属于你的任务，做起来是很愉快的。使你高兴的事情是：教初来时不会纺织的女仆学会纺织，使她对于你有双倍的用处；照管不懂的管家和做事的女孩子，在教育她使她可靠和能够做事之后，发现她很有些用处；你有权力奖励家里小心谨慎和有用的人，惩罚那变坏的人。②

　　从这些对话中可以看出，妻子对家庭事务的管理首先是存储和管理粮食、衣物等家庭财产，主要是"把东西仔细地放在适当的地方"，因为在苏格拉底看来，"这也是财产管理的一部分"；其次，她还要适当地储存生产和生活用品；最后就是管理家中的男女佣人，监管和安排他们的日常工作。

　　丈夫的职责主要是管理家庭外部的事务，主要包括照料谷物和树林、在田间监督奴隶工作、训练战马、到市镇上进行贸易等。总之，收入大部分是丈夫勤劳的结果，而储存与支出则大半是妻子管理。两个人共同合作，各尽自己的本分，对家庭来说是最好的。

　　在生育和培养孩子方面对、妻子城邦、家庭和丈夫都很重要；在家庭经济方面，妻子做出自己的贡献；在家庭经济事务管理中，妻子对仆人的监管，对粮食、衣物等家庭财产的管理对于丈夫和家庭来说都非常重要。只从家庭分工和家庭事务的管理来看，妻子在家庭管理中占有重要的位置。

三　丈夫掌控之下的合作

　　在生育子嗣和家庭经济事务管理中，存在着妻子与丈夫的合作，丈夫甚至在家庭管理中几乎离不开妻子的合作，不过，事实上，无论是生育合法的孩子，还是在家庭经济事务的管理中，夫妻的合作关系始终不会改变丈夫与妻子的统治和被统治的关系。在妻子与丈夫的合作关系中，妻子都是丈夫被动的合作者，也就是说，她成为丈夫的合作者是因为丈夫的需要，而不是她主动的参与。夫妻间的合作关系始终以丈夫对妻子的统治关系为前提。

　　在生育合法后代时，妻子作为合作者往往被描述成一个被动接受这种生育义务的角色。在雅典的订婚仪式中，新娘的父亲要将女儿交给新郎，目的是让她为新郎生育合法的孩子。而丈夫选择与妻子的合作也并非是出于对妻子的亲密与爱。因此，在古典时代的雅典家庭生活中，夫妻的亲密与爱情并不是它的主旋律。虽然也不能否认夫妻间存在真挚的感情，但这却不是雅典人所倡导的。在许多文献中，对妻子表示太多感情，与她过于亲密被认为是低级趣味的，这种行为可能引来非议，别人可能认为这个妇女不是他的妻子而是一个妓女。③克利托布勒斯虽然将家庭事务交给妻子管理，但是妻子却几乎是他讲话最少的人。④与此相比，伊斯霍玛霍斯与妻子的关系似乎和谐得多，但是我

---

① 色诺芬：《经济论》，张伯健，陆大年译，第24页。
② 色诺芬：《经济论》，张伯健，陆大年译，第25—26页。
③ *Isaeus*, III, 13—14.
④ 色诺芬：《经济论》，张伯健，陆大年译，第10页。

们也没有发现夫妻间直接的爱的表达，而更多的是一个温顺的妻子对父亲般的丈夫的顺从。[1]丈夫与妻子之间存在的只有服从和责任，如果说顺从是妻子对丈夫最主要的美德的话，丈夫所给予妻子的则是责任。他要保护妻子，在妻子死后还要埋葬她，这是丈夫的义务。我们甚至可以说，男性对女性在生育合法子嗣过程中的合作或多或少是出于一种无奈。在男性为主导的雅典文化中，他们也曾企图避开女性强大的生殖能力，将她们排除在生育后代的行为之外。在雅典娜诞生的故事中，宙斯因害怕即将出生的孩子比自己更强大，设法把雅典娜的母亲墨提斯吞进了自己肚里，于是便从他的头里生出了雅典娜[2]。雅典娜为宙斯所生，这样一来，妇女专司的生育职能也被剥夺了。

同时，妻子在生育合法子嗣中的重要性给她们带来的是更多的限制和监控。妻子作为家庭合法继承人的生育者被单方面地要求保持对丈夫的性忠诚，她们的性对象只能是丈夫。如果她们有与人通奸的行为，就会被逐出丈夫的家门，不能在宗教庆典等重要场合露面。而她们的丈夫则不同，婚约无法束缚他们，他们不必对妻子保持对等的性忠诚。在家庭中，在男人身边的除了妻子之外，还有妾和女奴，在家庭外还有妓女，色诺芬在《回忆苏格拉底》中写到，大街上能够满足男人性欲的妓院很多，[3]此外，男孩也可以成为成年男子的性伴侣。

婚姻以生育合法后代为目的，加上夫妻间不对等的性忠诚，会导致丈夫与妻子之间性生活的缺乏。这一点我们也可以从雅典法律中得到验证。法律规定公民必须每月三次与妻子同房。虽然，法律保护妻子的合法权益，但是我们由此也不难看出，实际上，丈夫与妻子之间的性生活并不和谐，丈夫对妻子的漠视甚至引起的立法家的关注。因此，可以说在这种以生育为目的的婚姻中，丈夫和妻子之间的性生活可能成为一种只为了生育而进行的义务行为。而妻子在生育合法子嗣的行为中，只是一块被动地等待耕作的土地，而丈夫在其中则是一个耕作者和掌控者。

在家庭经济方面，妻子带来的嫁妆是她给新家庭的一笔投资，但这种投资在丈夫的家庭经济中所占的比例并不大，嫁妆的数量有可能只占丈夫财富的10%——20%，也有的少于这个比例，甚至有的少得不能维持她自己的日常开销。[4]无疑，嫁妆能够为妇女带来好处，它作为新娘对新家的投资，可能会提高新娘在家庭中的经济地位，嫁妆越多，她在新家中的经济地位就可能越高，而没有嫁妆的妇女在家庭中很容易成为一个被人奴役的囚徒。但是，实际上，妇女并非是嫁妆真正的主人。在结婚后，她的嫁妆一般由丈夫管理和使用，因为投资等经济事务要在公共领域中进行，而妻子的活动领域主要在家中，所以无法经营自己的嫁妆。经营嫁妆带来的收益能否为妻子所用，决定权在丈夫手中。塞奥夫拉图斯的妻子给他带来1塔兰特的嫁妆，还给他生了个儿子，但他不愿意用嫁妆带来的收益维持妻子的生活，只给她几个硬币，她在节日里只能用冷水洗澡。[5]

在家庭事务的管理中妻子的协作很重要，但是，这种合作处于丈夫的掌控之下。妻子在家庭事务的管理中是按照丈夫的教导和吩咐做事的角色，而丈夫则是教导者和掌控者，为了让妻子更好地完成自己的任务，丈夫应该首先教导妻子她应该管理哪些家庭事务，如何管理好它们：

> 我决定先把我们房子里可以放东西的地方指点给她看。……例如储藏室由于它的位置安全，应该存放最贵重的毯子和用具；几间干燥的屋子存放谷物；凉爽的屋子存酒；光线好的屋子存放需要亮光的艺术品和器具。……也要让她看到女佣人的住处已经用一扇上了锁的门同男佣人的住处隔开了，所以所有不应当搬动的东西都不会被人拿走，而仆人们没

---

① *Isaeus*, VI, 65.
② Hesiod, *Theogony*, 886 – 926.
③ Xenophon, *Memory*, II, 24.
④ Sue Blundell, *Women in Ancient Greece*, p.115.
⑤ Sue Blundell, *Women in Ancient Greece*, p.115.

有我们的许可也不会养孩子。

丈夫掌控加上夫妻合作才有利于家庭事务的管理，对家庭也更有利。色诺芬给出两个例子，克里托布勒斯和伊斯霍玛霍斯都将家庭事务交给妻子管理，但是结果却大相径庭，克利托布勒斯遭遇到经济问题，而伊斯霍玛霍斯的家庭却很繁盛。究其原因，克利托布勒斯只是将家庭交给妻子管理，而没有对其进行调教，不告诉她如何管理他的财产，同时他也放弃了对家庭事务的掌控。而伊斯霍玛霍斯的家庭管理模式则是丈夫教导妻子如何进行管理，然后再交给她管理，并且这一切都在他的掌控之下。二个家庭管理模式产生了不同的结果，而产生这种结果最关键的因素是丈夫是否对妻子参与管理家庭事务进行了掌控。

从社会学角度来看，男女通过婚姻组建的家庭具有组织生产和消费的经济功能、人口再生产的功能、满足性需要的功能和感情交流等诸多功能。[1]从上文的阐述我们可以看出，在古典时代的雅典家庭中，丈夫与妻子的合作更多的表现出社会性和功利性，妻子的合作更多的是为了完成家庭的后代繁衍和生产消费的任务，而夫妻之间更加私密、更加自然的性需求和感情交流则被搁置一旁。基于这一点，虽然在为家庭生育合法继承人和家庭经济事务管理的行为中，夫妻之间有合作和分工，强调了妻子对丈夫的合作及其对家庭的贡献。但是，实际上，在家庭中，妇女只是为了完成家庭的任务而被拉进夫妻合作关系中的，她始终是一个被动的合作者。同时她所做的一切都必须以丈夫的掌控为前提，丈夫的统治与掌控之下的夫妻分工和合作才是古典时期雅典家庭中夫妻关系的真实写照。

---

[1]　吴增寿等主编：《现代社会学》，上海人民出版社，1997 年版，第 137 - 141 页。

雅典被释奴地位刍议

孙艳萍　河北大学

摘要：尽管雅典奴隶制问题一直是学者们研究的热门话题，但对奴隶被释放后的处境却未引起学界足够的重视。许多学者直接把他们归入定居外邦人之列，也有少数学者主张将被释奴视为一个独立的阶层。他们在雅典社会的地位到底是完全等同于定居外邦人，还是另有区别？本文试图从经济、法律和社会三个方面分析和评价这一特殊阶层在雅典社会所处的地位。

关键词：被释奴；雅典；定居外邦人；奴隶

Abstract：Despite Athenian slavery has been the focus of western scholars, the question about Athenian was comparatively ignored. Some scholars equated the freedmen with metics and others supposed them as an independent estate. Analyzing their economic status, legal status and social status in Athenian society is the subject of the paper.

Keywords：Freedmen, Athens, metics, slaves

被释奴，作为从奴隶群体中脱胎出来的一个特殊阶层，在古代雅典社会占有独特的地位。古典作家虽然肯定了被释奴的自由身份，却在有意无意间将他们与奴隶混为一谈，而现代学者在讨论雅典奴隶制时又往往将他们直接归入定居外邦人（metics）之列。[①]他们的法律地位与奴隶、定居外邦人有何区别？他们对雅典经济与社会有何影响？鉴于目前国内鲜有文章涉及，笔者不揣冒昧，拟从经济、法律和社会三方面探讨被释奴在雅典社会的地位与影响。不当之处，敬请诸位方家批评指正。

一　从职业分布看被释奴的经济地位

在古代雅典，经济状况虽不是影响各阶层地位的决定性因素，但它对各阶层的生活方式和社会威望确实具有相当程度的影响。因此，要分析被释奴在雅典的地位，不能不考察他们所处的经济状况，而要考察被释奴的经济状况，又不能不分析他们的职业分布。1935 年发现的释奴银碗铭文（*phialai*

[①]　西方学者如菲舍尔（N.R.E.Fisher, *Slavery in Classical Greece*, London: Bristol Classical Press, 1993, p.68）、麦克道威尔（Douglas M.Macdowell, *The Law in Classical Athens*, London:Thames and Hudson Ltd, 1978, p.82）等，国内学者如李天祜（《古代希腊史》，兰州大学出版社 1991 年版，第 349 页）等。

exeleutherikai）恰好为我们了解雅典被释奴的职业分布提供了丰富的信息。根据英国学者路易斯的复原，①从这篇铭文中分辨出 81 名成年被释奴的职业，详情见下表：②

职业	编号	合 计
纺羊毛工（ταλασιουργός）	1、3、10、11、13、16、22、25、28、30、35、40、45、47、50、61、62、65、67、70、80、81、85–87、89–90、93	28
铜匠（χαλκεύς）	2	1
耕种者（γεωργος）	4、18、56、63、68、74	6
小商贩（κάπηλος）	5、38、39	3
金匠（χρυσοχόος）	6、66	2
宝石雕刻匠（ακτυλιογλύ-φος）	7、83	2
制床匠（κλινοπ-οιος）	8	1
商人（ἔμπορος）	9、41	2
厨子（μάγειρος）	12	1
皮匠（σκυτοτόμος）	14、19、46、57	4
卖芝麻饼的人（σησαμοπωλης）	15	1
缝鞋匠（ὑποδηματορράφος）	17	1
奶妈（τιτθός）	20、21	2
仆人（或信使）（διάκονος）	23	1
卖乳香的人（λιβανωτο-πολης）	24、52	2
清洗工（φαι-δρύντρια）	26	1
雇工（μισθωτός）	27	1
制造笛或萧的人（αὐλοποιός）	29	1
铁匠（σιδηρουργός）	31	1
煮胶人（κολλεψ-ος）	32	1
补鞋匠（νευρορράγος）	33	1
文书（γραμματεύς）	34	1
修葡萄树的人（ἀμπελουργος）	37、60	2
弹琴自唱的艺人（κιθαρῳδος）	42	1
卖咸鱼的人（ταριχοπώχεω）	43、59	2
赶驴人（ὀνηλάτης /ὀρεωκόμος）	48、51、88	3
修补破衣者（ἀκέστρια）	53	1
面包师傅（ἀρτοπώλης）	54	1
鞣皮匠（σκυλοδέψης）	55	1
卖豆子的人（ὀσπρίοπώλης）	69	1
磨坊主（μυλωθ-ρος）	75	1
吹笛手（αὐλη-τήρ）	76	1
木匠（τέκτων）	78	1
剃头匠（κουρεύς）	82	1
泥瓦匠（τειχιστης）	93	1
儿童（παιδίον）	36、44、49、58、64、71–73、79–80、84、91	12

---

① 参看 David M. Lewis, "Attic Manumissions", *Hesperia*, Vol. 28, No. 3. (Jul. – Sep., 1959), pp.209–226。

② 按照被释奴职业出现的先后次序，笔者为每位被释奴加上编号，其中编号 36、44、49、58、64、71–73、79–80、84、91，其职业一栏是"儿童"。这些人很可能是随父母一起释放的童奴。鉴于他们在铭文中占据着一席之地，在编号时未将其剔除出来。

从上表可以看出，被释奴从事的职业可谓五花八门，既有从事文职工作的文书，也有从事娱乐业的艺人、吹笛手；既有从事农业的耕种者和修葡萄树的人，也有从事零售业的小商贩（卖咸鱼的人、卖豆子的人、卖芝麻饼的人、卖乳香的人）；既有从事家政服务的清洗工、修补破衣者，也有从事运输业的赶驴人。不过总体看来，被释奴从业数量最多的领域是手工业。例如，在 81 名成年被释奴之中，有 28 名纺羊毛工、2 名金匠、2 名宝石雕刻匠、4 名皮匠，另有铜匠、制床匠、铁匠、补鞋匠、缝鞋匠、乐器匠、鞣皮匠、木匠、剃头匠、泥瓦匠、煮胶人、面包师傅各一名，共计 48 名，占全部成年被释奴的 59.3%，这一比例远远超过了其他领域。这说明"凭手艺吃饭"是被释奴首要的谋生途径。被释奴从事数量次多的领域是商业和零售业，共计 11 名，占成年被释奴总量的 13.6%。两者加起来，占全部被释奴总量的 73%，这一数字既反映出雅典被释奴的职业集中于工商业领域的特征，也反映出被释奴经济地位的相对独立性。当然，我们也注意到少数被释奴从事的行业仍具有很强的依附性，如奶妈、仆人等。据笔者推测，这些人很可能是无依无靠的家内被释奴。德谟斯提尼的演说词《控告埃沃尔格斯和奈斯布罗斯》（*Against Evergus and Mnesibulus*）可提供佐证。在其中发言人提到，他父亲释放的老保姆在丈夫死后因无人可依，只好又回到他家里服务。[1]

除了上述亚里士多德所谓的"奴性的活计"[2]外，上表中还有 6 位被释奴从事农业劳动，这似乎与被释奴不能拥有土地的雅典法律相悖，但事实上，两者并不冲突，因为被释奴耕种的土地应是租来的。关于这一点，同样有文学材料的佐证。吕西阿斯第七篇演说词的发言人提到，安提斯塞尼斯（Antisthenes）的被释奴阿尔基阿斯（Alcias）在第四年曾租种他的土地。[3]这说明被释奴并非像人们通常所认为的那样不能从事农业，他们只是不能占有土地，但可以通过租地的方式进行农业生产。当然，由于土地的所有权不在他们手中，所以他们的使用权会受到土地所有者的制约。

被释奴对职业的选择主要受两种因素的制约。首先是地域因素。从银碗铭文来看，可辨出户籍所在地的 4 名农业被释奴全部居住在平原和山地，[4]无一居住在海岸。很明显，平原和山地的地理条件更适合农业劳作，而海岸的地理条件更适合经商。因此，地域条件制约着被释奴的职业选择。其次，被释奴被释前所干活计对其职业选择也有重要影响。法庭演说词对此提供了有力印证。例如，帕西昂、福米奥（Phormio）和西图斯（Cittus）在被释放前都是银行职员，被释放后他们依然在银行工作并且做得有声有色。据说帕西昂死时已经成为富可敌国的大银行家，其财产总值高达 70 塔兰特，包括一家银行、一家制盾作坊、价值 20 塔兰特的地产和至少 39 塔兰特客户未付清的欠款。[5]而德谟斯提尼之父的被释奴米利阿斯在被释放后也在作坊里干着他的老本行。由此可见，很多被释奴在被释放后依然从事着以前的职业。之所以如此，既可能有职业惯性的因素，也可能是他们履行被释奴义务的结果。

总之，从职业分布来看，大多数被释奴在手工业、商业和服务业领域从事着与公民生活息息相关的各行各业，对国民经济起着举足轻重的作用。由于有一技之长，他们大多数人自食其力，经济

---

① *Demosthenes*, 47.55–56.

② 亚里士多德在《政治学》中说："奴役有多种形式，从而奴性的活计也是多种多样。例如手艺人就是其中的一种，正如其名称所示，用他们的手干活；工匠或技师也包括在内。由于这个缘故，古时候从事制造的人在有些民族中就不能参与行政统治，除非是在平民当政的极端情形下。所以，好的公民或政治家用不着去学做被统治者的活计，除非是为了自己的一时需要，如果常做这样的事情，就无从分辨主人和奴隶了。"（Aristotle, *Politics*, 1277a；亚里士多德：《政治学》，中国人民大学出版社，2003 年，第 79 页）

③ *Lysias*, 7.10. 演说词原文是："第四年，我将它出租给阿尔基阿斯，安提斯塞提斯的被释奴，他已经死了。"

④ 这四名被释奴分别是：Satyros，居于 Hagnous（山地）；Dionysios，居于在 Skambonidai（平原）；Antigon，居于 Pa-，"Pa-"代表的德谟可能是 Pallene 或 Paianiai 或 Paionidai，不过这三个德谟都位于山地；Eyklea，居于 Kol-，"Kol-"代表的德谟可能是 Kolonos 或 Kolonai，这两个德谟也都位于山地。参看 David M. Lewis, "Attic Manumissions," *Hesperia*, Vol. 28, No. 3. (Jul. – Sep., 1959), p.212, p.214, p.222, p.223。

⑤ Dem., 36.5. Cf. Jeremy Trevett, *Apollodoros the Son of Pasion*, Oxford University Press, 1992, pp.27–31.

独立，过着与定居外邦人类似的生活。极少数被释奴（如帕西昂、福米奥）凭借自身的努力和行业的特殊性，聚敛起巨额财富，成为雅典数一数二的富豪。当然，也有少数被释奴在被释放后由于各种因素依然从事着仰人鼻息的半奴役行业，不仅谈不上经济独立，连自身的自由都随时受到威胁。

二　从阶层比较看被释奴的法律地位

尽管德谟斯提尼说雅典存在两部被释奴法——"ἀπελεύθερος 法"和"ἐξελεύθερος"，[①]但由于缺乏史料，无从考证这两部法律的具体内容。有鉴于此，笔者试图借助古典文学材料和铭文，通过与奴隶、定居外邦人的比较，勾勒出雅典被释奴的法律地位。

（一）与奴隶相比较

韦斯特曼在详细考察了德尔菲释奴铭文后认为：被释奴一般享有"四种自由"：作为一个人的地位；免受非法掠夺或逮捕的权利；选择工作的自由（也就是'职业选择权'）；自由活动的权利（也就是空间流动权）。[②]笔者认为，这四种自由恰恰是被释奴区别于奴隶的四个标志。

首先，被释奴不再是一件财产或工具，而是一个人。不管他们享有的自由是有限的，还是完全的，其法律身份都已从财产变为人，这是奴隶与被释奴的本质区别；其次，雅典公民不能随意逮捕被释奴，对奴隶则可以。按照柏拉图的《法律篇》，如果被释奴的地位受到质疑，他可以通过说明自己的自由人身份来避免被捕；如果不是他自己而是第三方说出他的自由人身份并要求释放他，那么第三方提供三份保证金就能将其保释。[③]至于奴隶，柏拉图这样说："任何人，只要心智健全，都有权以自己喜欢的合法的方式对自己的奴隶动武，同样也有权抓获任何同胞或朋友的逃亡奴隶，为的是保障他的财产安全"；[④]再次，尽管被释奴迫于法律义务和职业习惯在被释放后往往还会继续从事原先的行业，但从法律上来说，他们至少有选择职业的权利，可以从事自己喜欢的工作。至于奴隶，则完全没有这种权利，他们只能遵从主人的吩咐，服从主人的需要；最后，被释奴有自由活动的权利，而奴隶则没有。对奴隶来说，他们最大的渴望莫过于人身自由。哲学家爱比克泰德《谈话录》中的对话也许反映了奴隶们的普遍想法："如果我被解放，一切都会立刻变好。我不用再唯唯诺诺，可以像其他所有平等的、地位一样的人说话，去我想去的地方，回我想回的地方。"[⑤]

此外，与奴隶比起来，被释奴参加的宗教活动更为广泛：他们可以和公民一起参加信奉外来信仰的团体，参加大多数祭祀、宴会、秘仪和节日；他们也可以参与泛雅典娜节的游行。而奴隶除某些宗教节日（如克罗尼亚节）及仪式（如厄琉西斯大秘仪）外，不能参加其他节日庆典，不能进入寺庙。

当然，我们也不得不承认，与完全释放的被释奴比较起来，有条件释放的被释奴不管是人身还是精神上依然受到前主人的束缚，这一点与奴隶并无二致。在服务期间，被释奴必须跟着前主人或受益人，他只有得到受益人的允许才能搬迁到他处。他必须尽可能地遵从受益人的命令，为他工作，给他提供一定的收入，偿清他的债务等等。如果被释奴没有履行他的义务，受益人有权对他进行惩罚或者将他出租给第三方。但需要指出的是，前主人在惩罚不履行义务的被释奴时必须有所节制，

---

① *Pollux*, 3.83. 转引自 R.Zelnick-Abramovitz, Not Wholly Free: *The Concept of Manumission and the Status of Manumitted Slaves in the Ancient Greek World*, Leidon, 2005, p.73.

② William Linn Westermann, *Two Studies in Athenian Manumission*, Journal of Near Eastern Studies, Vol.5, No.1, p.92.

③ Plato, *Laws*, 914E；参看《柏拉图全集》（第三卷），王晓朝译，中国人民大学出版社，第 681 页。

④ 同上。

⑤ *Epictetus*, 4.1.34.

因为他现在处理的是不再是一个奴隶，而是一个自由人。

（二）与定居外邦人相比较

迦兰在《古希腊的奴隶制度》中指出，"在公共法中，被释奴的地位即使与外邦人不完全相同，至少也是十分相似，与定居外邦人则更为相似。"[1] 这个判断不无道理。首先，被释奴像所有定居外邦人一样，归军事执政官管辖，军事行政官将有关被释奴的案件分配到各种各样的公民法庭。杀害被释奴的凶手通常被带到帕拉蒂昂法庭（Palladion），他所受的刑罚比杀害奴隶的凶手所受的刑罚重，但比杀害公民的凶手所受的刑罚轻；第二，被释奴的婚姻和外邦人的婚姻一样，在法律上得到承认。但是从公元前5世纪中期起他们的孩子被否认拥有公民权，即使其中一方是公民。后来这样的结合也被禁止，违者将重新沦为奴隶；[2] 第三，被释奴像定居外邦人一样，不能参加公民大会或者投票，也不能参加选举或从事公职；第四，两者都需要登记一名公民作为保护人（prostates），由保护人代为出面办理公共事务；第五，被释奴和定居外邦人都要缴纳一种叫做"μετοίκιον？的特殊税。[3] 男性每年缴纳12德拉克玛，单独居住的女性每年缴纳6德拉克玛。

尽管两者的法律地位十分相近，但绝非完全相同，我认为两者至少在四点上有着本质的区别。首先，被释奴只能将前主人登记为保护人（除非前主人是定居外邦人或被释奴），而定居外邦人则可以自由选择保护人。如果前主人发现被释奴登记别人为保护人，他就可以提起一种叫做"ἀποστασίου"的私人诉讼，被判有罪的被释奴将重新沦为奴隶，而被判无罪的被释奴则获得完全的自由。[4] 保护人的不可选择性不仅体现了雅典社会维护奴隶主利益的阶级本质，也反映出雅典社会等级制的不可动摇性；其次，雅典法律对定居外邦人的财产规模没有限制，但规定被释奴的财产不得超过第三等级被允许的限额（除非他取得公民权），否则，他必须在30天内离开雅典，无权要求当局延长他的居住期限；[5] 再次，雅典法律对定居外邦人的居住年限没有限制，但是被释奴在国内的居住时间不得超过20年；否则，他必须携带全部财产离开，除非得到当局和他主人的同意才可留下；[6] 最后，被释奴除了缴纳每年12德拉克玛（或6德拉克玛）的定居外邦人税外，还要另付3奥布尔的特殊税。[7] 至于这种小额税是一次性结清还是年年交付，我们不得而知。阿布拉莫威茨认为："这个费用是被释奴出身的标志，因为它将他们与其他自由居民区分开来，正如"μετοίκιον 将定居外邦人与公民区分开来一样。"[8] 当然，在现实生活中，通过职业、外表或住宅将被释奴和定居外邦人完全区分开来是不可能的。

总之，从法律上来说，雅典被释奴既不同于奴隶，也不完全等同于定居外邦人。换句话说，他们既拥有定居外邦人的权利，也肩负奴隶的某些义务。或许，克莱克（M. Clerc）的说法最恰当地说明了被释奴的这种地位："对城邦来说，被释奴是一个定居外邦人；对他的保护人来说，他则是一个被释奴。"[9]

---

① Yvon Garlan, *Slavery in Ancient Greece*, trans. by Janet Lloyd, Ithaca and London: Cornell University Press,1988, p.80.

② A.R.W.Harrison, *The law of Athens: The Family and Property*,Oxford:At the Clarendon Press,1968, p.184.

③ Harpocration, s.v. μετοίκιον. 转引自 A.R.W.Harrison, *The law of Athens: The Family and Property*, p.185.

④ Harpocration., s.v. ἀποστασίου . 转引自 R.Zelnick-Abramovitz, *Not Wholly Free*, p.248, p.274.

⑤ Plato, *Laws*,11.915b.

⑥ Plato, *Laws*, 11.915b.

⑦ Harpocration, s.v. μετοίκιον.

⑧ R.Zelnick-Abramovitz, p.311.

⑨ A.R.W.Harrison, *The law of Athens: The Family and Property*, Oxford:At the Clarendon Press,1968,p.188.

三 从演说词涉及个案透视被释奴的社会地位

要弄清被释奴在雅典社会所处的地位，不仅要探究被释奴的经济和法律地位，更重要的是观察他们是否真正融入雅典社会，是否为社会公民所认可和接受，他们的奴隶出身是否被人们所忽略或淡忘。但是，由于法庭演说词所涉及的被释奴大部分集中于中上层被释奴，[1]这在一定程度上决定了这项考察不可避免地带有片面性。即便如此，个案分析对于我们认识这一特殊阶层在雅典的社会地位仍具有重要价值。

在法庭演说词中，着墨最多、材料最丰富的被释奴是从事银行业的被释奴。他们往往因其巨额的财富和良好的声誉在社会上享有较高的地位。正如《关于银行家的演说词》（Trapeziticus）的发言人所说，银行家"交游甚广、手头宽裕并且因其职业而拥有诚实名声"，[2]发言人虽贵为博斯普鲁斯王国的贵族，也承认碰上这样的对手实在是件棘手的事情。尽管他的说法难脱夸大之嫌，但至少反映出作为银行家的被释奴容易在雅典公民中获得认同。伊塞奥斯残篇18便是最好的例证。这篇演说词中的发言人曾将一些钱存放在被释奴埃玛塞斯（Eumathes）处，后作为三列桨战船船长参加开俄斯附近的海战。当他在海战中阵亡的消息传到亲属那里时，埃玛塞斯不仅没有趁机霸占这笔钱，反而召集发言人的亲属和朋友并将整笔钱一分不差地转交给他们。发言人说："由于这件事情，我安全返回后，与他的关系更为亲密。"[3]因此当埃玛塞斯被起诉时，发言人虽然不是他的保护人，但还是义无反顾地出面为他代言。这说明埃玛塞斯已经与一些普通公民建立起亲密的友谊，较好地融入雅典公民社会。至于帕西昂、福米奥这样的大银行家，他们不仅在普通公民和定居外邦人中间拥有很高声望，还与政界的显赫人物关系密切。例如，公元前373-372年间帕西昂曾在没有证人和抵押的情况下向雅典将军提谟塞奥斯（Timotheos）提供四笔贷款，而后者则保证回报前者的服务。[4]显然，两者的关系是建立在利益基础上，如果说他们之间存在友爱，也应该是亚里士多德所说的"有用的友爱"。

我们也不应忘记，像帕西昂、埃玛塞斯这样富有的被释奴在雅典只是极少数，更多的被释奴还是生活在社会的中底层。这些被释奴的生活环境显然与前者有很大不同，他们或者独立地靠技艺谋生度日，或者继续与前主人居住在一起，从事被释放前的工作。普通的独立谋生者可能更容易融入公民社会之中，毕竟劳动阶级的被释奴与劳动阶级的公民在生活水平和生活环境上有着更多的相似点。租种土地以维持生活的阿尔基阿斯（Alcias）[5]可能就是这类被释奴的典型代表。而那些与主人呆在一起的被释奴，则继续处于实际上的依附状态，按照柏拉图的说法，"人们有权捕捉那些已经获得自由但对给予他们自由的主人不忠诚或不够忠诚的奴隶。"[6]在诉讼失败的情况下他们会再次沦为被奴役的对象。

尽管大部分被释奴能够被公民社会所接受和认可，在体貌特征和生活环境上与普通公民和定居外邦人没有什么区别，但是，他们的奴隶出身始终是无法回避的阴影，这种影响甚至会波及他们的后代子孙。这方面的例子可谓不胜枚举，例如，吕西阿斯的演说词《控告尼可马库斯》（Against Nicomachus）中发言人对被告父亲身世的一再提及，[7]德谟斯提尼的演说词《论花冠》中对埃斯基涅

---

① 据我所知，古典文学材料中所提到的雅典被释奴并不多，有名有姓的加起来不过几十个，而对其生平有所描述的则更少，其中包括帕西昂、福米奥、西吉努斯、埃玛塞斯、涅埃拉、米利阿斯、阿格拉图斯、阿尔基阿斯等人。

② *Isoc.*, 17.2.

③ *Isaeus*, fragment 18.18.

④ *Demosthenes*, 49.6–32.

⑤ *Lysias*, 7.10.

⑥ Plato, *Laws*, 915A；参看《柏拉图全集》（第三卷），王晓朝译，中国人民大学出版社，第681页。

⑦ *Lysias*, 30.2, 6.

斯父亲身世的描述，①目的都是唤起雅典公民对被释奴根深蒂固的偏见与歧视。而在吕西阿斯的另一篇演说词《控告阿格拉图斯》（*Against Agoratus*）中，发言人对阿格拉图斯的被释奴身份及其兄弟的劣迹不厌其烦地进行叙述，②意图显然是通过摆明他们的出身来凸显阿格拉图斯的品行从而引起陪审员对阿格拉图斯的恶感。

为了淡化自己的奴隶出身并获得雅典公民的支持和认可，富有的被释奴往往不吝资财，慷慨捐献。例如，帕西昂曾向雅典城邦捐献 1000 面盾，五次担任三列桨战船船长并"自愿花费自己的金钱来装备船只，配备船员"。③由于对雅典城邦贡献巨大，帕西昂和福米奥在生前都被赋予雅典公民权。④这是他们作为被释奴所获得的最大荣耀和权利。但是他们的例子不应误导我们。狄奥·克里索斯托曾说在雅典存在一条法律，法律宣称"天然奴隶"不能被授予公民权。⑤因此，通常情况下，被释奴获得公民权的机会极其渺茫。据笔者所知，古典文学材料中明确提到被释奴被赋予公民权的例子不过屈指可数的三个。⑥除帕西昂和福米奥外，剩下一例就是因参加阿吉纽斯海战而被释放的奴隶。不过在后种情况下参战奴隶被赋予的公民权并非完全的雅典公民权，而是普拉提亚公民权。⑦所以，被释奴要想获得雅典公民权、完全融入公民社会是一件非常艰难的事情。

总之，被释奴是雅典城邦的一个特殊阶层，既不同于奴隶，也不同于定居外邦人，更不同于公民。从原则上说，他们获得了自由，成为独立的个体，不再是别人的财产，但实际上，他们大多数仍然通过各种各样的义务与前主人联系在一起。不管是叱咤风云的大银行家，还是作坊里劳作的普通工匠，只要他曾经是某人的奴隶，就永远改变不了"自己是某人的被释奴"这一不争事实。被释奴在雅典社会的双重地位也在一定程度上反映了雅典公民对他们的双重态度。一方面，由于被释奴像定居外邦人一样在城邦的经济生活中起着重要作用，他们对前主人的持续服务使公民受益良多，因此雅典公民离不开被释奴，有释放奴隶的需求；另一方面，雅典公民集体仍是一个以血缘关系为纽带的集团，除特殊情况下，它不允许任何外人来污染这个集体的纯洁性。在雅典公民看来，被释奴始终是城邦的外人，排斥被释奴加入公民集体是他们的第一反应。因此，不管如何努力，被释奴要想在有生之年完全融入雅典公民社会绝非易事。

---

① *Demosthenes*, 18, 129.

② *Lysias*, 13.64–65.

③ *Demosthenes* , 45.85.

④ *Demosthenes* ,59.2; *Demosthenes* ,36.48; *Demosthenes* ,46.13.

⑤ *Dio Chrysostom*, 15.17.

⑥ 虽然狄纳尔科斯（ Dinarchus ）的演说词中提到银行家埃皮根尼（ Epigenes ）和科农（ Conon ）也被赋予了公民权（ Dinarchus, *Against Demosthenes*, 43 ），但是没有资料证明他们的明确身份。因此我没有将这两个例子包括进去。

⑦ Aristophanes, *Frogs*, 693–694. 参看罗念生译：《阿里斯托芬喜剧六种》，上海人民出版社 2004 年版，第 432 页。关于普拉提亚公民权，参看德谟斯提尼，59.104，59.92；伊索克拉底，12.93–94，14.51。

城邦背景下的古代奥林匹亚赛会

邢　颖　中国社会科学院

摘要：古代奥林匹亚赛会是希腊最著名的泛希腊节庆活动，其泛希腊的性质一直得到较多的关注。然而，作为祭祀宙斯神的重要的宗教活动，古代奥林匹亚赛会与希腊人的其他宗教行为一样，也离不开希腊文明最本质性的特征——城邦特征。

奥林匹亚赛会的创办及其声望的远播发生于希腊的古风时代，这正是希腊城邦共同体兴起、公民权观念形成的重要时段。在这样的大背景下发展起来的奥林匹亚赛会与城邦兴起时代希腊其他方面的显著变化一样，也具有深刻的城邦制度的印记。在创办之后不久，奥林匹亚赛会即开始由邻近城邦伊利斯管理，其管理机构与城邦的管理机构有相近之处，管理方式也与城邦的管理方式异曲同工，奥林匹亚的建筑及布局与城邦中心的结构也是相近的。此外，管理赛会的权力在赛会创办初期曾几次易手，对于奥林匹亚控制权的争夺反映了希腊几个大城邦的势力消长以及相互间的竞争关系。虽然赛会本身对比赛胜利者的奖励都是非物质性的，但获胜者所在的城邦会在其凯旋之后给予丰厚的物质奖励，这表明赛会上取胜不仅是个人层面的荣耀，更被视为整个城邦的巨大荣誉。

因而，奥林匹亚赛会不仅具有泛希腊的特征，其与城邦之间的关联也非常密切。这从一个侧面反映了希腊城邦与宗教之间的交融关系。即使是像奥林匹亚赛会这样并非属于某一城邦范畴内的宗教活动，也脱离不开城邦制度的框架背景。

关键词：泛希腊节庆；奥林匹亚赛会；希腊城邦

Abstract：As one of the most famous panhellenic festivals in ancient Greece, the Olympic Games have so far been emphasized a lot on the panhellenic characters. The Games, however, whose reputation spread rapidly with the rising of Greek city-states, were also closely associated with the cities.

Firstly, the way in which the Eleans managed the Games resembled the means by which they administered their own city. Secondly, the arrangement of Olympia's buildings were similar to that of a Greek city center. In addition, the conflicts over the control of the Games reflected keen competitions among Greek city-states. And a champion of the Games would get from his own city generous material rewards as well as spiritual ones, which further indicated that Greek cities regarded victories in the Games as great honors of their own.

In conclusion, despite being the most important panhellenic festival, the Olympic Games still took place within the framework of city-states, which, from one aspect, demonstrated how closely the Greek religion was interwoven with city-states.

Keywords：Panhellenic festivals, Olympic Games, Greek city-states

得益于现代奥运会的巨大影响力，古代奥林匹亚赛会近些年来也得到学界较多的关注。举办于伯罗奔尼撒半岛西部的奥林匹亚赛会是古希腊历史上最具影响力的宗教节庆活动，是希腊世界四大泛希腊节庆之一。其泛希腊的特征，以及与此相关的涉及希腊民族认同等方面的内容已为国内外学者普遍重视。然而，作为祭祀宙斯神的重要的宗教活动，古代奥林匹亚赛会与希腊世界的其他宗教仪式活动一样，与希腊文明本质性的城邦特征密切相关。

一　奥林匹亚赛会的早期历史与希腊城邦的兴起

对于早期奥林匹亚赛会兴起的历史，古代文献资料一方面数量不多，另一方面含有大量神话传说的元素，使用起来很容易引起争议。从目前的情况看，考古学方法是研究这段历史的重要手段。根据考古研究的成果，公元前9—8世纪，希腊的宗教崇拜中心数量剧增，分布范围更为广泛，大规模的神庙建筑在希腊本土及爱琴岛屿上的诸多宗教圣地兴起，新类型的供奉品也出现于这些崇拜中心，而且数量上大大多于从前。对奥林匹亚考古发掘的结果也呈现出相似的发展轨迹。日益深入的研究表明，奥林匹亚在迈锡尼时代就已是希腊世界的一个宗教崇拜中心，然而直到公元前8世纪，那里所举办的赛会的声望才逐渐提高到足以引起关注的程度，关于这一点最可靠的证据是考古发掘出的供奉品的数量及其出产的地域范围。罗宾·奥斯邦在《希腊的形成》（Robin Osborne, Greece in the Making）一书中指出，从公元前10世纪到前8世纪，奥林匹亚出土的供奉品呈猛烈增加的态势，如动物小雕像，出自10世纪的是18个，9世纪的160个，而8世纪的则达到1461个。另一方面，从供奉品的工艺传统来看，其中许多并非来自奥林匹亚及其周边地区，而是来自包括伯罗奔尼撒半岛其他地区、阿提卡、意大利和东地中海的其他地区。供奉品数量的剧增以及出产地域的广泛性足以说明奥林匹亚赛会在公元前8世纪的兴起以及影响力的扩大。

在谈到奥林匹亚赛会时，其泛希腊的性质以及由此带来的赛会的特征常常是研究者强调的对象。然而，虽然说奥林匹亚赛会在兴起之初就已具备泛希腊性质，但泛希腊主义的思潮以及相关的实践活动在当时却远未出现，因而也就不可能在奥林匹亚赛会发展初期起到重大的影响作用。奥林匹亚赛会勃兴于公元前8世纪，这也正是希腊城邦兴起的重要时代。在城邦兴起的背景下，奥林匹亚赛会各方面的变化更容易得到解释。在奥林匹亚出土的供奉品中有大量青铜三足鼎。从数量上看，奥林匹亚出土的三足鼎应该不仅仅是赛会获胜运动员的胜利祭品，同时也是其他到访者奉献给神的供品。而且从制作工艺来看，它们产自希腊多个地区。青铜三足鼎在早期希腊是身份与地位的象征，在《荷马史诗》中，它是极为贵重的礼物和奖品，有能力在奥林匹亚奉献三足鼎的应该都是具备一定身份地位和财富的人。除了三足鼎，其他青铜材质的供奉品也在奥林匹亚占据越来越重要的位置，青铜器本身在当时就具有特别的价值，其供奉者一般都是贵族。这些奢侈品过去都只出现在贵族的墓葬之中，而从公元前8世纪开始，贵族越来越多地将它们供奉给神祇。贵族群体之所以出现这样的转变，一是宗教上的虔诚，二是贵族也想借此展示身份、扩大自身在政治等方面的影响力。贵族的这种行为与当时的社会背景密切相关。

随着城邦共同体的兴起，城邦内部的等级结构确立起来。贵族作为一个群体，其身份地位以及财富的合法性得到确认；但同时，贵族群体内部的关系却愈发地紧张起来，相互间对于权力的争夺更为激烈。出于权力斗争的考虑，贵族们越来越乐于借助各种时机炫耀财富、扩大声望。奥林匹亚位于伯罗奔尼撒半岛西部的两条重要河流——阿尔菲奥斯河（Alpheios）和克拉迪奥斯河（Kladeos）的交汇处，可视为该地区的交通枢纽地带，在这里进行财富的展示显然可收到更好的效果。因而在这一时期的奥林匹亚，供奉品——特别是有价值的供奉品——数量剧增。另一方面，供奉品的贵重价值、供奉者乃至赛会参与者的尊贵身份等因素反过来又进一步提升了奥林匹亚赛会的声望。从这个角度上说，正是在希腊城邦兴起的大背景下，奥林匹亚赛会得以兴起并逐渐获得巨大的影响力。

二　奥林匹亚赛会与城邦的宗教和政治空间

在古代希腊，宗教权力属于全体公民，而不是掌握在祭司集团的手中。由公民组成的城邦共同体对于宗教崇拜及各种宗教祭祀活动进行管理和监督。奥林匹亚赛会在本质上是祭祀宙斯的宗教节日。在赛会历史上的绝大部分时间内，位于奥林匹亚西北约 36 公里处的城邦伊利斯承担着管理赛会的责任。由于奥林匹亚赛会的泛希腊性质，赛会的参与者及其奉献的供品来自于希腊各个地区的城邦，再加上伊利斯这个小城邦在希腊世界的影响力有限，因而其在奥林匹亚赛会中所扮演的角色常常被模糊化。由此奥林匹亚的泛希腊性得到最大程度的张扬，而它与希腊城邦之间千丝万缕的联系却容易被忽视。

奥林匹亚赛会的裁判被称为 Hellanodikai。"希腊人的裁判"这一称呼反映了奥林匹亚赛会的泛希腊性质。然而从这些裁判的选拔和设置的角度来看，他们与伊利斯城邦之间关系非常密切。根据波萨尼阿斯（Pausanias）的记载，从第 50 届赛会开始，两名裁判从全体伊利斯人中抽签选出，负责管理赛会；之后到第 95 届赛会，9 名裁判都是任命的了；下一届赛会变成 10 名；到第 103 届，裁判数目是 12 人，当时伊利斯一共 12 个部落（phylai），每部落选出 1 名；由于伊利斯人在与阿卡狄亚人的战争中失掉部分领土，伊利斯城邦的部落由 12 个缩减为 8 个，随之同期的第 104 届赛会上也只有 8 名裁判。直到第 108 届又恢复成 10 名，之后这个数目才固定下来。由此看来，赛会裁判的数目变化受多方面因素影响，而伊利斯城邦的行政区划结构则是其中重要的影响因素之一。

波萨尼阿斯在他的游记中详细描述了伊利斯城邦的建筑格局，这段叙述留给人最深的印象就是奥林匹亚赛会对于伊利斯城邦的重要意义。伊利斯最醒目的建筑之一即旧体育馆，除此之外还有两个体育馆。这些体育馆的功用都与奥林匹亚赛会有关。参赛运动员的赛前训练、裁判为一些项目的运动员分组等事宜都在伊利斯的这些体育馆完成。此外，伊利斯城邦议事会（Boule）的会场也设置在其中一个体育馆内。通向体育馆的道路有两条，一条连接浴室，另一条则连接裁判的居所和伊利斯的阿戈拉（Agora），裁判的居所与阿戈拉相邻。从波萨尼阿斯的介绍来看，与奥林匹亚赛会相关的建筑在伊利斯城邦占据中心地位。而伊利斯议事厅的位置也从一个侧面表明赛会与伊利斯城邦政治之间的联系。

在奥林匹亚出土了一些法律铭文，根据研究，这些铭文中的大部分都与赛会本身无关，是涉及土地使用、与其他城邦的和约以及与伊利斯社会结构相关的官方文件。由此可见，奥林匹亚圣地是伊利斯人放置城邦法律铭文的重要地点，而根据希腊人的传统，城邦的法律铭文要置于城邦的宗教中心，如雅典就将法律铭文保存在雅典卫城。这说明奥林匹亚本身就是伊利斯城邦的宗教中心。

在奥林匹亚圣地的建筑群中，一个建筑是议事厅（bouleuterion），不仅是解决赛会争端的地点，一些与赛会无关的民事案件也在此审判，如色诺芬从斯巴达获赠土地的案件。圣地中还有主席厅（prytaneion），也同样具有多重功能，里面有灶火女神赫斯提亚（Hestia）的祭坛。法国学者宰德曼（Zaidman）和潘特尔（Pantel）的研究指出，赫斯提亚祭坛中的灶火象征着城邦的生命力，通常都位于城邦主席厅或其他施行行政管理的地方。外国的使者通常都在灶火旁接受城邦的款待，雅典等一些城邦对于取得最高荣誉的公民给予的奖励即包括主席厅的公餐，也是在赫斯提亚灶火旁。从议事厅、主席厅以及赫斯提亚祭坛等元素来看，奥林匹亚虽然不是一个城邦，但其结构与希腊城邦的结构有相近之处。它可被视为是伊利斯城邦的一个政治与宗教中心。在希腊的城邦生活中，政治空间与宗教空间往往有重合之处，城邦的政治空间同时也是宗教空间，宗教空间也很可能还承担着政治空间的功能。

三　奥林匹亚赛会中的城邦博弈

奥林匹亚赛会与城邦的密切关联还体现在一些城邦对奥林匹亚控制权的争夺上。综合波萨尼阿斯、斯特拉波（Strabo）和色诺芬（Xenophone）的记载，我们大致可以理出早期奥林匹亚控制权争夺的历史过程。皮萨称自己是最早管理赛会的城邦，不久之后伊利斯就开始与其争夺控制权。公元前8世纪中期，阿尔戈斯国王斐冬（Pheidon）率军进入奥林匹亚，支持皮萨接管了第8届赛会。斐冬的势力很快从奥林匹亚撤出，赛会的控制权转回到伊利斯手中。到公元前644年的第34届赛会，皮萨国王潘塔雷翁（Pantaleon）又靠武力将赛会置于自己的控制管理之下。不过伊利斯很快再次收回控制权。到潘塔雷翁之后的第三代国王统治时期（大约6世纪中叶），伊利斯彻底摧毁皮萨，其对赛会的控制权固定下来。这方面的证据还包括上文提到过的在奥林匹亚出土的碑铭。从铭文来看，到公元前6世纪中晚期，伊利斯对奥林匹亚的管理权是无可争议的了。然而到公元前364年，阿卡提亚又旧事重提，以皮萨最早管理赛会为借口，试图取代伊利斯控制当年的第104届赛会，奥林匹亚圣地成为双方的战场，最终伊利斯方面取胜。根据波萨尼阿斯的说法，上述第8届、34届、104届赛会都被伊利斯人宣布为"非奥林匹亚"（non-Olympiad），排除于伊利斯人的"奥林匹亚赛会名单"之外。

对赛会管理权的激烈争夺一方面反映了奥林匹亚圣地以及赛会的巨大影响力，这种影响力最初也许还局限在伯罗奔尼撒半岛，但不久便扩大到希腊世界的其他地区。获得如此有影响力的赛会的管理权，对于伊利斯这样的小城邦来说是提高声望的绝佳机会。不过，奥林匹亚对于伊利斯城邦的意义或许还不止于此。法国学者波利尼亚克（Polignac）研究了希腊兴起时期的非城邦中心的圣地，揭示了这些边缘圣地对城邦边界的形成以及城邦共同体认同意识的发展所起到的巨大作用。但在谈到奥林匹亚、德尔菲、多多纳等泛希腊的宗教崇拜中心时，波利尼阿克却认为，这些圣地之所以从公元前8世纪开始逐渐发展出泛希腊的特征，恰恰是因为它们远离了标志着城邦形成的战争环境及其他因素。如果由这个角度出发，这些泛希腊圣地似乎与某一城邦的兴起没有太大关联。然而，从奥林匹亚的例子来看，这个观点有待商榷。

在奥林匹亚赛会举办期间，各方面的参与者都会参加富有典型希腊特征的列队游行仪式，从伊利斯城邦出发直至奥林匹亚，这段路程至少36公里。根据波利尼亚克对非城邦中心圣地的划定，即使是距离城市较远的圣所，远的也就在12到15公里之间。奥林匹亚显然比这还要远得多。但他同时也指出，"乡村圣所虽然不是人们日常宗教崇拜的地点，但在居民分散的地区，仍然成为住在附近的人们的集会地点，奥林匹亚对于伯罗奔尼撒西部的居民也正起到这样的作用。"那么我们可以想象，集会的盛大列队游行仪式以伊利斯为起点，这在某种程度上也是伊利斯城邦向其他周边国家展现其重要地位的好机会，这样的展示有利于城邦共同体认同的形成与强化。另外，从距离来看，奥林匹亚也许不能被看作是伊利斯的城邦边缘圣地，伊利斯对奥林匹亚管理权的争夺也不能被视为是其城邦领土边界的划定过程，但这一系列的斗争至少也是新兴的伊利斯城邦明确自身势力范围的历程。因而，即使是诸如奥林匹亚这样的泛希腊圣地，对其周边城邦的兴起也同样起到了促进作用。

除了伯罗奔尼撒半岛西部的城邦，其他城邦间的博弈也在奥林匹亚赛会中有所体现。赛会早期，伊利斯与皮萨的斗争背后有其双方的支持者斯巴达和阿尔戈斯的影子。在公元前420年第90届赛会上，伊利斯因领土问题与其一直以来的同盟领袖斯巴达反目，禁止斯巴达人进入圣地参加祭祀和比赛活动。值得注意的是，此时的伊利斯与斯巴达的对手阿尔戈斯和雅典却走得很近，甚至签订了三方的百年盟约，刻有盟约内容的铜柱就竖立在奥林匹亚。伊利斯这个小城邦利用奥林匹亚赛会作为筹码，周旋在几个大城邦之间，期望以此谋得更大的生存发展空间。奥林匹亚赛会虽然被赋予浓烈的泛希腊色彩，但城邦纷争的背景仍然显现于其中。

奥林匹亚赛会本身并不给予胜利者物质方面奖励，来自阿尔提斯（Altis）圣地的橄榄枝花冠几乎是唯一的奖品。然而，当这些取胜的运动员回到自己的城邦时，局面就大不一样了，城邦会给予这些胜利者慷慨的奖励：盛大的凯旋仪式、直接的金钱犒赏、城邦主席厅的免费公餐，等等。丰厚的奖品表明城邦对这个胜利的重视程度，这种重视与希腊文明所特有的崇尚竞争的精神有关，也与希腊城邦之间激烈斗争的大环境有关。赛会的胜利不仅是个人层面的荣誉，也为胜利者所属的城邦带来荣耀，运动员的竞争间接体现了希腊城邦间的竞争。

对于城邦与希腊宗教的关系，已有学者恰当地指出，当"城邦"——希腊政治组织最突出的形式出现之时，希腊的宗教信仰和仪式也被赋予了相应典型性的结构。这一观点充分表达了希腊城邦与宗教之间的交融关系。因而，即使奥林匹亚赛会具备充分的泛希腊特征，但对它的研究仍不应脱离开城邦制度的框架背景。

"神圣"与"世俗"之间
——试论古希腊奥林匹亚赛会的宗教性[*]

王大庆　中国人民大学

摘要： 奥林匹亚赛会是古代希腊最重要的宗教节日之一，也是现代奥林匹克运动的源头。这种古希腊人所特有的社会活动从一开始就与希腊的宗教结下了不解之缘，可以说，作为赛会重要组成部分的体育竞技正是古希腊宗教仪式活动的派生物和外在表现形式之一，其本身具有的"宗教性"和"神圣性"自不待言。不过，奥林匹亚赛会还带有"世俗性"的一面，并且经历了"世俗化"的过程，由此引发了关于奥林匹亚赛会的性质的争论。本文结合奥林匹亚赛会的历史发展过程和相关具体史实，从奥林匹亚赛会的"神圣性"、"世俗性"及其相关关系等三个方面，对奥林匹亚赛会中的这样两种相互对立的因素的具体表现以及如何能够有机地结合在一起等问题进行了尝试性的描述、分析和探讨，以期加深我们对奥林匹亚赛会的"宗教性"问题的理解和认识。

关键词： 古代奥林匹亚赛会；宗教性；神圣性；世俗性

Abstrcat： Olympic Games is not only one of the most important religious festivals of the ancient Greece, but also the birthplace of the modern Olympic Games. From the beginning, it has very close relationship with the Greek religion, i.e., as the necessary part of the festival, the sport games are surely the derivation and an outer display of the ancient Greek religious rituals. Its religiousness and sacredness is obvious. However, the ancient Olympic Games also has elements of secularity and has a process of secularizing. Therefore, there are different views of the nature of the ancient Olympic Games. The paper will try to discuss and make an analysis of the religiousness of the ancient Olympic Games from the sacredness, secularity and relation of the two factors through the history and practice of this social activity.

Keywords： ancient Olympic Games, religiousness, sacredness, secularity

　　众所周知，奥林匹亚赛会既是古希腊最盛大的体育比赛，也是古希腊人最重要的宗教节日之一。故而，希腊的体育竞技活动从一开始就与古希腊的宗教结下了不解之缘，希腊赛会活动所具有的"宗

---

*　本项研究得到了中国人民大学 985 工程第三期专项经费的资助。

教性"特征已经成为了学界的共识。但问题并非如此简单，希腊体育比赛实际上还有着十分明显的"世俗性"的一面，这既使希腊的竞技活动有别于作为纯粹的宗教仪式而存在的原始体育活动，也成为古希腊的赛会与现代奥林匹克运动的接合点。学者们虽然大都并不否认奥林匹亚赛会的"世俗性"因素的存在，但与其"宗教性"相比，则较少受到人们的关注。因此，在希腊体育赛会的性质上出现不同的看法就在所难免了。

　　大致说来，在这个问题上有三种代表性的观点。首先，大部分学者都认为，古希腊的赛会在本质上是一种宗教的活动。例如，多内指出："古希腊的奥林匹克运动会是一个神圣的运动会，在一个神圣的地点和神圣的节日举行，它们是一种向神灵表达敬意的宗教行为……奥运会植根于宗教中"。[1]这是一种比较传统的观点。第二种观点认为，古希腊的各类赛会，尽管其起源和内容与古典宗教有着千丝万缕的联系，但本质上却是世俗的，赛会满足了古希腊人的竞争天性、追求荣誉与利益、培养民族的团结精神和认同感以及审美等世俗的要求。[2]第三种观点是上述两种看法的折中，认为古希腊的体育和宗教的确有一些关联，但不能过于夸大，很多现象的解释依赖于我们的看法，宗教的影响力是很大的，但绝不是全能的。[3]

　　可见，在古希腊赛会的"宗教性"的问题上还是存在不同的看法的，之所以出现这样的不同，从根本上讲，还是由于希腊赛会中既有无可辩驳的"宗教性"的一面，也存在着不容忽视的"世俗性"的一面。那么，古希腊赛会中的"宗教性"有哪些具体表现？其"世俗性"又是如何体现出来的？这两种看似相互对立、互不相容的因素到底是一种什么样的关系，二者又是如何有机地结合在一起的？就古希腊赛会的"宗教性"而言，它在从原始体育到现代体育的历史发展中到底应该处于什么样的位置？本文就以古希腊的奥林匹亚赛会为主要的考察对象，结合古希腊体育竞技活动的具体方式和历史演变从以下三个方面对上述问题做出一些尝试性的回答，以期对古希腊赛会活动中的"宗教性"得到更为深入的理解和认识。

一　奥林匹亚赛会的"宗教性"

　　正如马克·戈顿所言："古希腊的节日把那些最能够表现出希腊宗教特征的行为集中在一起，是希腊宗教最重要的公开展现。"[4]作为古代希腊最重要的宗教节日之一，奥林匹亚赛会不论从起源和历史发展，还是从赛会本身的举办过程来看，随处都体现出其本身所具有的"神圣性"的一面，可以说，奥林匹亚赛会中的"宗教性"是贯穿始终和无所不在的。

　　在希腊人的观念中，奥运会的起源本身就与很多神灵或带有神性的英雄存在着十分密切的关系，而且在历史上有着很多个不同的版本。其中，关于来自于小亚细亚的王子珀罗普斯（Pelops）为赢得皮萨城美丽的公主在车赛中战胜了自己未来的岳父的故事最为家喻户晓，希腊人认为，正是在这次伟大的胜利之后，珀罗普斯创建了奥林匹亚的赛会，后来伯罗奔尼撒半岛（Peloponnesos）的名称就来源这位传说中的英雄。此外，奥运会还存在着赫拉克勒斯、宙斯等多种版本的神话起源说。从考古发掘上来看，大约在公元前7世纪末或公元前6世纪初，奥林匹亚最早兴建的是赫拉神庙。[5]后来随着奥林匹亚成为了宙斯崇拜的中心，在公元前460年左右兴建的宙斯神庙很快成为

① Ludwig Deubner, *Olympia: Gods, Artists, and Athletes*, New York,1968, p.24.
② 王以欣：《神话与竞技——古希腊体育运动与奥林匹亚赛会起源》，天津人民出版社，2008年，绪言，第2页。
③ Mark Golden, *Sport and Society in Ancient Greece*, Cambridge University Press, 1998, p.17, p.23.
④ Mark Golden, *Sport and Society in Ancient Greece*, p.15.
⑤ 王以欣：《神话与竞技——古希腊体育运动与奥林匹亚赛会起源》，第36页。

了圣域的中心。①

奥运会不仅在起源上与希腊的多神教传统的形成相伴随，在经历了一千多年的发展之后最终的衰亡也主要是由于宗教上的原因。正如米勒所言，奥林匹亚赛会的终结"不是因为基督教对体育的偏见，而是由于体育运动一直是附属于宗教的；每一位运动员都是为了向旧希腊的某位男神或女神表达敬意的。在新宗教的压力下，这些神灵不再受到人们的欢迎，运动也就衰亡了"。②因此，不论是从古代奥运会的起源还是其衰亡，都可以清楚地看出它与希腊宗教之间极为密切的伴生关系。

在每届奥运会举办的具体过程中，其"神圣性"的一面则体现得更为全面和充分。

在赛会举办之年的春天，赛会的主办者伊利斯城邦就会派出三位被称为"圣使"（theoroi 或 spondophoroi）的传令官，到各个城邦去通报赛会举办的消息，要求各邦遵守"神圣停战协定"（ekecheiria），即在赛会举办当月停止一切敌对行为，协议的有效期为一个月，后来延长到了两个月。

按照惯例，奥运会都在在每年夏至后的第二个或第三个满月之时举办，在希腊人看来，这个时间本身就带有不同一般的"神圣性"，奥运会举办期间，希腊人日常的"世俗"生活会被打破。有学者指出，在雅典，赛会之前120天的公民大会都是不正常的，但不是非法的。③更为重要的是，这个节日是希腊人特有的活动，只对希腊人开放。与此同时，奥运会的纪年使希腊人确定了一种时间上的坐标，他们通过这样一个节日来建构和记录时间，定位他们的历史。因此，对于每个希腊人来讲，"奥运时间"由于其自身所带有的这种"神圣性"而从"世俗时间"和"普遍时间"中被分割出来了。

奥运会不仅在一个"神圣的时间"（节日）里举办，而且也是在一个"神圣的空间"里举办的，奥运会举办过程中的各种仪式和规则无不体现出这一空间的"神圣性"。作为奥运会承办者的伊利斯（Elis）城邦位于奥林匹亚西北36公里的地方，陆上距离大约57到58公里。伊利斯在当时起到了现在的奥运村的作用，也是运动员的训练场所。因此，赛会举办之前，运动员、裁判员以及观众需要从伊利斯出发进入"圣域"。8月6日早晨，游行队伍从伊利斯出发，经过一夜的行程，7日早晨抵达奥林匹亚。在进入"圣域"之前，需要在一个叫皮里亚（pieria）地方停下来，在泉水旁边，由希腊法官主持举办一个净化仪式，然后才可以进入"圣域"。7日的主要活动是运动员在"发誓的宙斯"（Zeus Horkios）雕像前面宣誓，并核准身份，然后是参赛者个人的献祭，接下来就是第一项比赛，即吹笛手和传令官的比赛，比赛后还要举行一些献祭活动。8日早晨，举行点燃圣火的仪式，队伍中领头的是宙斯的祭司和身着紫袍、手拿鞭子的作为比赛裁判员的"希腊法官"（Hellanodikai），队伍要一一走过圣域中的63个祭坛，逐一献祭。接着就是马赛、车赛和裸体竞技的第一项"五项全能"的比赛，8日的最后一个活动是作为宙斯大祭前奏的向珀罗普斯的献祭活动。9日，也就是赛会第三天的月圆之日，宗教祭祀活动达到了高潮，要在宙斯神庙附近锥形的大祭坛举行盛大的"百牛大祭"（hekatombe），这是奥运会最重要的核心部分。当天下午是少年组的单程赛跑、摔跤和拳击比赛。10日是成年组的各项比赛。赛会的最后一天，所有比赛的优胜者会聚集在宙斯神庙的前面，等待希腊法官中的长者授予桂冠，当晚是主席厅的盛大宴会，赛会结束。④我们看到，在奥运会举办的过程中穿插了众多的祭神活动，这些活动无不通过各种方式告诉赛会的参加者，这是一个神圣的宗教节日，体育比赛正是这个节日的派生物和附属物，而不是相反，也就是说，体育竞技仅仅是祭神活动的一种外在的表现形式而已。

在比赛的过程中，这种"神圣性"也是无所不在的。比如，按照惯例，在奥运会上，除了德墨忒耳（Demeter）的女祭司之外，成年妇女既不允许参加比赛，也不允许观看比赛，原因并不在于参

① Stephen G. Miller, *Ancient Greek Athletics*, Yale University Press,2004, p.90.
② Stephen G. Miller, *Ancient Greek Athletics*,p.6.
③ Mark Golden, *Sport and Society in Ancient Greece*,p.16.
④ Stephen G. Miller, *Ancient Greek Athletics*,pp.113-128.

加比赛的男运动员是裸体的，有碍于妇女观瞻，而是因为奥林匹亚是宙斯的圣地，奥运会是男人们的节日，女孩们可以在自己的节日比如赫拉节上参加比赛。①可见，这一基本的规则无疑也是出自于奥运会的神圣性质。

再比如，奥运会上的奖惩规则也体现出了神灵的"在场"和"参与"。对于即将参赛的选手来说，在宙斯的神像面前发誓要遵守比赛的规则是必经的仪式。在体育场的入口处矗立着一排宙斯的铜像，这些铜像是用对收受贿赂者所处的罚金铸造的，宝桑尼阿斯（Pausanias）说，这些雕像是要告诫世人，"要明白奥林匹亚的胜利不是金钱得来的，而是靠腿脚敏捷和身强力壮"。②对于在严格遵守规则的情况下产生的各个项目的优胜者，赛会也会毫不吝惜地给予极高的荣誉。在比赛刚刚结束的时候，首先是在胜利者的头上系上羊毛缎带，最为激动人心的是在全部赛程结束之后授予橄榄枝编成的桂冠，这些橄榄枝不是一般的橄榄枝，而是取自于奥林匹亚宙斯祭坛背后的一片野生的橄榄林（其果实不能食用），并且需要一个父母健在的男孩用一把金质的镰刀砍下来的。之所以这样做，原因就在于，希腊人认为，这样的胜利不仅取决于运动员自身，更重要的是得到了神灵的助佑，授予橄榄桂冠的仪式就是人与神之间神秘交流的象征。除了桂冠之外，优胜者还会得到一般情况下只有神灵才能享受到的赞美诗和塑像的荣耀。总之，正如伽丁奈尔所指出的："运动被确定地置于神明庇护下，胜利的运动员会觉得，他是神明所钟爱的，他的成功有赖于神明。此外，运动员们会觉得，任何违反赛会规则的行为，尤其是不公正和腐败的行为，是一种渎神行为，是诸神所不悦的"。③

另外，有学者指出，对希腊人来说，即使是竞技运动本身也或多或少的是一种献祭行为，也就是说，竞技者既是贡献者也是贡献本身，④尤其是在奥运会创办的初期，很难把运动比赛和献祭活动清楚地分开。比如，作为奥运会最早设立的竞技项目，单程赛跑（stadion）最初就是一种祭礼行为，可能与点燃宙斯祭坛的圣火的仪式有关，后来才演变成为比赛项目。祭坛上摆满了大量的祭品，选手们站在克洛诺斯山上或东面约200米处，号令一响，大家就冲向祭坛，最先抵达的优胜者从裁判手中接过火炬，点燃了祭品。⑤此外，赤膊上阵的运动员都要在身上涂上橄榄油，这种涂油的做法既有诸如热身、护肤及美观等实用的功能，也具有宗教的功能，人们发现，古希腊人不仅在比赛和训练的时候往身上涂油，也在宗教仪式上为神像涂油。⑥如果这种宗教功能可以成立的话，也从另外一个角度印证了竞技者试图通过涂油将自己奉献给神灵的说法。

二　奥林匹亚赛会的"世俗性"

从以上的论述可以看出，奥林匹亚赛会首先是作为全体希腊人都可以参加的一个宗教节庆活动而出现在历史舞台上的，向神表达敬意的愉神仪式无疑是其中的重头戏和主旋律，贯穿其中的体育竞技活动或者最初本身就是祭神仪式，或者是从祭神仪式演变出来的派生物。总之，如果不了解古希腊的宗教，也就不能够对赛会中的竞技活动做出正确的理解和解释。但是，体育比赛和古代世界普遍存在的宗教祭祀活动毕竟存在着很多明显的差别，这主要表现在奥林匹亚赛会中还是存在着一些"世俗性"的因素，正是这些因素把奥林匹亚赛会与一般性的祭祀神灵的活动分开，从而带有了一定程度上的"现代色彩"。

---

① 王以欣：《神话与竞技——古希腊体育运动与奥林匹亚赛会起源》，第62页。
② Stephen G. Miller, *Ancient Greek Athletics*, p.93.
③ E. Norman Gardiner, *Athletics of the Ancient World*, Oxford, 1930, p.33. 转引自王以欣：《神话与竞技——古希腊体育运动与奥林匹亚赛会起源》，第29页。
④ Mark Golden, *Sport and Society in Ancient Greece*, p.17.
⑤ 王以欣：《神话与竞技——古希腊体育运动与奥林匹亚赛会起源》，第142页。
⑥ 王以欣：《神话与竞技——古希腊体育运动与奥林匹亚赛会起源》，第341页。

　　说到奥林匹亚赛会的"世俗性"，最重要的表现就是祭礼与比赛的分开了。前面讲到，奥林匹亚并不是一个城邦，而是一个希腊宙斯崇拜的中心和宗教圣地。负责承办奥运会的是它附近的一个小城邦伊利斯，包括赛会前的神圣停战通知、赛会过程中的各项组织工作都是由伊利斯承担的，包括祭司、裁判以及赛会需要的各种服务和工作人员都是从伊利斯人当中选拔或委派出来的。因此，伊利斯和奥林匹亚之间就存在了一种紧密的共生关系。近代以来，通过考古发掘，在奥林匹亚的"圣域"中发现了公元前6世纪中晚期制定的"圣法"。按照希腊人的习俗，法律铭文通常存放在神庙中，为的是让神明来见证和监督法律的执行。学者们发现，这些"圣法"的大部分内容是伊利斯城邦本身的法律，有些铭文自然就涉及了与节日和赛会有关的内容，但祭礼和比赛的规则是彼此分开的。[1]不仅规则分开，在赛会的组织工作中，神职人员和比赛的裁判工作也是泾渭分明，互不影响，有关的祭祀活动均由专门的祭司引领或主持，体育比赛的执法权则交给"希腊法官"全权负责，值得注意的是，这些"希腊法官"都不是祭司或神职人员，[2]也就是说，在体育比赛中，"希腊法官"完全按照事先制定好的比赛规则，仅仅根据运动员的比赛成绩来进行裁决，在这里，比赛的结果就完全取决于运动员个人的能力了，从而摆脱了宗教的管辖和约束。

　　有学者指出，奥林匹亚赛会的"世俗性"还体现在其神话的起源上面，这些众多的神话起源说实际上"反映了不同集团的各自利益和相互之间的竞争"。[3]更加值得注意的是，尽管有很多种版本，但珀罗普斯还是脱颖而出，最终成为了奥林匹亚的核心神祇，这是非常耐人寻味的，因为"一个有死的英雄占据了主导的定位，从而获得了不朽，并在其他的赛会中纷纷效仿。这些英雄及其崇拜代表了运动会的一个永远的目标，就是通过超人的努力而获得不朽，珀罗普斯为他们树立了一个榜样"。[4]也就是说，尽管奥运会的创办可以归功于某位神灵，但体育比赛毕竟是一种有死的凡人进行的活动，人还是要通过自己的努力而超越自我，成为比赛的优胜者，这种观念与赛场上的以运动成绩来决定谁将获胜的原则是相吻合的。此外，还有些学者从军事训练、教育和成年礼仪等角度论证了作为一个宗教节日的奥林匹亚赛会背后的种种世俗的或实用的功能。[5]

　　最后，对于奥林匹亚赛会，除了"共时性"的分析，我们更要看到"历时性"的演变，古代的奥运会在其延续了上千年的历史发展过程中，如果说创始之处带有十分明显和强烈的"宗教性"和"仪式性"特征的话，那么随着时间的推移，这种"宗教性"就开始逐步受到削弱，与此同时，"世俗性"则日渐增长，人们开始把越来越多的注意力集中在了运动和比赛上面。这种逐渐显露的"世俗性"最为集中也最为典型地体现在宗教圣域和体育比赛的赛场的逐步分离上面。近代以来，通过对奥林匹亚的全面发掘和系统研究，考古学家们发现，最早的体育场（一期）就建在奥林匹亚圣域的中心地区，靠近宙斯祭坛，而且二者并不存在明显的分界线。但到了古典时代，大约建于公元前450年的体育场（三期）与圣域的中心已经拉开了相当的距离，三期与它的建于公元前6世纪晚期的前辈二期相比，与"圣域"的距离之差距达到了75米。最终，在三期兴建的一百年之后，体育场与圣域中心区被一组柱廊完全隔开了（见下图）[6]。

① 王以欣：《神话与竞技——古希腊体育运动与奥林匹亚赛会起源》，第57页。
② Mark Golden, *Sport and Society in Ancient Greece*, p.15.
③ 王以欣：《神话与竞技——古希腊体育运动与奥林匹亚赛会起源》，第52页。
④ Stephen G. Miller, *Ancient Greek Athletics*, p.90页。
⑤ 参看王以欣：《神话与竞技——古希腊体育运动与奥林匹亚赛会起源》，第352 – 353页，第322 – 327页。
⑥ Mark Golden, *Sport and Society in Ancient Greece*,pp.21 – 23.图中显示，尽管体育场一期的位置还存在着争议，但二期和三期还是清楚的，从中可以明显地看出体育场与圣域中心区逐步分离的过程。我们看到，如果Dree复原的体育场一期成立的话，那么单程赛跑的终点就正对着宙斯祭坛，恰好符合了上文讲到的单程赛跑起源于祭祀仪式的观点。

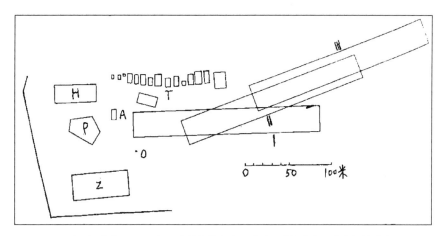

图（1）奥林匹亚圣域 H（赫拉神庙）P（珀罗普斯庙）Z（宙斯神庙）
T（财宝库） A（宙斯祭坛）O（奥诺玛斯柱廊）
I（Dree 复原的体育场一期） II（体育场二期） III（体育场三期）

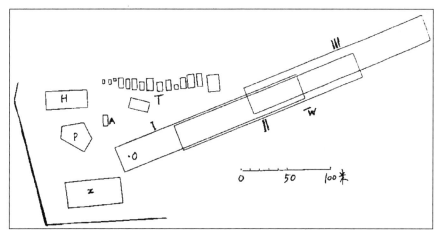

图（2）奥林匹亚圣域 H（赫拉神庙）P（珀罗普斯庙）Z（宙斯神庙）
T（财宝库） A（宙斯祭坛）O（奥诺玛斯柱廊）
I（Brulotte 复原的体育场一期） II（体育场二期） III（体育场三期）

　　有证据表明，这样一种分离的过程不仅仅出现在奥林匹亚，同时也出现在地峡赛会、尼米亚赛会等其他几个泛希腊赛会的举办地，虽然有人认为可能是由于观众的增加大有侵犯圣域之势，"出现这种趋势的原因可能在于，随着体育比赛越来越发展成为一种娱乐性的事业，需要为观众提供更大的和更完善的场地"，[①]但还是不能否认这种变化中所体现出来的希腊赛会的"世俗化"倾向。

三　"神圣性"与"世俗性"之间的相互关系

　　我们在上文中分别对奥林匹亚赛会中的"神圣性"和"世俗性"做出了具体的阐发。接下来我们要追问的是，这两种看似矛盾的倾向之间到底是一种什么样的关系，二者又是如何统一起来的呢？

　　著名的宗教史家伊利亚德（Mircea Eliade，1907–1986）在《神圣与世俗》一书中指出，"神圣和世俗是这个世界上的两种存在模式"。与被"去圣化"（desacralized）了的现代世界相比，"古代社会中的人们倾向于尽可能地生活在神圣之中，或者尽可能地接近已被奉为神圣的东西……对于

---

① Stephen G. Miller, *Ancient Greek Athletics*, p.105.

早期人类而言，神圣就是力量，而且归根结底，神圣就是现实。这种神圣被赋予到现实的存在当中。"这种被赋予了某种"神圣性"的"现实的存在"就是"显圣物"（hierophany）。①他还进一步指出，实际上这样一种宗教性的思维方式不仅存在于古代世界的宗教徒身上，也同样存在于现代世界的非宗教徒的生活和观念里，也就是说，不论古今，人们只有通过把"神圣性"赋予现实生活中的某种"显圣物"的方式才能够获得生活的意义。因此，"我们决不能找到一个纯粹状态的世俗存在。不管一个人对这个世界的去圣化达到多大程度，他根据世俗的生活所作出的选择绝不可能使他真正彻底地摆脱宗教的行为"。②

笔者认为，伊利亚德的上述观点对于我们理解古希腊奥林匹亚赛会中的"宗教性"和"世俗性"之间的关系是非常富于启发意义的。实际上，所谓的"神圣性"，是要通过现实中存在的"显圣物"显现出来的，而这个"显圣物"的出现则要通过人的主观选择和判断，也就是说，"神圣性"归根结底还是由人本身根据自身的需要创造出来的。因此，"神圣性"与"世俗性"之间不仅存在着相互对立和相互排斥的一面，也同样存在着相互统一和相互依存的一面，即具有"神圣性"的事物总是要通过"世俗性"的事物得到展现，而"世俗"的事物也可以通过人的赋予而成为"神圣"的事物，这就是所谓"即凡而圣"。作为最重要的宗教节庆活动之一的奥林匹亚赛会正是古希腊人打破世俗的日常生活而创造出来的具有"显圣物"特征的一种社会活动，在这个活动中，"通过对神圣历史的再现，通过对诸神行为的模仿，而把自己置于与诸神的亲密接触中，也即是置自己于真实的和有意义的生存之中"。③因此，跑步、跳远、投掷这些带有"世俗性"的体育竞赛活动也就被赋予了"神圣"的意义。

与此同时，我们也要看到，古希腊的宗教还处于比较原始的多神教时代，既没有统一的宗教经书，也缺乏系统和完备的教义，是一个行动的宗教，希腊人主要是通过带有仪式、表演特征的外在的行为（包括各种比赛）来向神表达敬意，神和人之间还没有拉开距离，在希腊人看来，神灵不但有着人的外观，还有着人的性格特征甚至七情六欲，同时，人也可以通过自身的努力追求卓越（arete）④而接近神性，所以"人性"和"神性"之间形成了一种"你中有我，我中有你"的交相辉映的关系。在公元前7到公元前6世纪前后普遍出现的用作神像的青年男子石头塑像（kouroi）中，我们看到的就是一个个体态健美的运动员的形象，而这些神像也的确是以赛会中取得优胜的运动员为模特雕塑而成的。通过这些雕像，我们看到了"神圣性"与"世俗性"的一种完美的结合。

最后，对于奥林匹亚赛会所具有的"宗教性"的定位问题，我们还可以把目光放得更为长远一些，看一看古希腊的赛会与在它前面的更为原始的体育比赛和其后发展出来的现代体育比赛之间的联系和区别。对于这个问题，美国学者阿兰·古特曼在他的《从仪式到记录：现代体育的性质》一书给出了很好的回答。

首先他认为，古希腊的赛会既包含了宗教性和世俗性两种因素，也经历了从宗教到世俗的演变过程，他指出，"奥林匹亚赛会和其他的桂冠运动会的确都是宗教性的，但我们也要看到希腊的体育运动或多或少也是一种世俗的现象。体育的世俗化并不是完全由一个宗教性的活动转变为世俗的，而是越来越集中于它的那些基本要素——游戏、锻炼和竞技。体育运动逐渐成为了城邦的普通公民

---

① 米尔恰·伊利亚德：《神圣与世俗》，王建光译，华夏出版社，2002年，序言，第2-5页。
② 米尔恰·伊利亚德：《神圣与世俗》，第3页。
③ 米尔恰·伊利亚德：《神圣与世俗》，第118页。
④ 米勒指出，在希腊文中，*arete* 一词的道德含义是与 *hubris*（傲慢）相对应的，经常被使用在体育运动的语境中，用来描绘运动员，常常被翻译成 excellence（卓越）或 virtue（美德），带有严格意义上的体育内涵。参看 Stephen G. Miller, *Ancient Greek Athletics*, pp.236-238.

日常生活的一个部分，这种活动同时也是宗教崇拜的一种方式。"①

第二，他认为，如果把希腊的赛会放到从古到今的体育运动的整个发展史上来看，我们就会发现，它既与原始时代的体育存在着明显的区别，带有更多的"世俗化"特征，同时，也与现代的体育运动有着本质上的不同，具体的表现就是带有强烈的"宗教性"特点。他指出，传统社会是一种"根据人们的身份来决定其地位"（the ascribed status）为主导的时代，而现代社会中，"根据人们的成就来决定其地位"（the achieved status）成为了基本的原则，体育运动由仪式（ritual）到记录（record）的发展变化正是这种转变的典型体现。不过，同样作为一种仪式行为，古希腊的体育运动还是与原始体育存在着明显的区别，这主要表现在，在原始体育中占支配地位的是"身份"或"地位"（ascription），而不是"成就"（achievement），也就是说，属于哪个阶层的成员比跑步的速度或手的力量更为重要，因为这样的体育在通常情况下完全不是什么真正意义上的竞赛，结果多是由宗教的需要决定的，而不是运动的水平，也就是说，在原始体育中，由于常常没有对胜负的关注，所以监管者通常是仪式的行家而非裁判员。对此，古特曼以印第安人的仪式性体育运动为例，来说明仪式本身比比赛的胜负更为重要。通过这样的比较，他指出，在古代希腊的赛会中，由于祭祀与比赛基本分开，比赛胜负由运动来决定，因而"成就"的因素比原始民族多，而"身份"的因素则比原始民族少。另外一方面，如果我们把古希腊的赛会与现代的体育比赛相比较的话，又会发现两者最大的区别就是希腊的赛会所带有的强烈的"宗教性"因素，也就是说，与现代的体育运动相比，古希腊的赛会虽然具有了"成就"的因素，但"身份"的因素还是较为明显的，这一方面表现为并不是所有人都可以参加比赛（仅限于成年和未成年的希腊男性公民），另一方面则是这种比赛仍旧带有宗教仪式的性质。在这个意义上，"尽管希腊体育被看作是现代体育的始祖，但奥林匹亚和德尔斐的比赛从文化中更接近它们的那些原始的祖先，而不是我们现在的奥运会。"不过，古特曼认为，希腊时代就已经出现的体育的世俗化趋势到罗马时代又有了进一步的加强，带有了更多的娱乐和表演的性质，越来越与宗教仪式拉开了距离，成为一种独立的社会生活。因此，"就世俗化而言，现代的体育运动更接近罗马而不是希腊的模式。"②

通过古特曼的上述分析，既可以是使我们能够用历史发展的眼光看待古希腊奥林匹亚赛会中的"宗教性"因素，同时也可以使我们更加准确地认识到它在整个体育运动发展史上的位置。

四　结语

在两千多年以前，古代希腊人开创了奥林匹克运动，这种古希腊人所特有的社会活动从一开始就与他们的宗教信仰存在着不可分割的密切关系，并且伴随着这种信仰经历了起源、发展和衰亡的过程。在希腊人看来，体育竞技既是一种向神灵表达敬意的宗教仪式，同时也满足了其超越自己、追求卓越的世俗需求，正是这种宗教性与世俗性的伴生和结合使得希腊人的体育运动走出了原始时代的纯粹的宗教仪式阶段，从而带有了一些"现代"特征，成为现代奥林匹克运动的先声。与此同时，作为宗教仪式活动的一个组成部分，其本身所带有的"神圣性"和"宗教性"又是现代的体育比赛所缺乏的，正如荷兰学者胡伊青加（Johan Huizinga）所言："运动与宗教仪式的这种联系在今天已被完全切断了；运动完全变成世俗的、'非神圣的'东西"。③在这个意义上，处于"神圣"与"世俗"之间抑或是正处于从"神圣"向"世俗"转变过程中的古希腊奥林匹亚赛会成为了我们认识和理解人类宗教与社会发展史的绝好个案。

---

① Allen Guttmann, *From Ritual to Record, the Nature of Modern Sports*, Columbia University Press, 2004, p.23.
② Allen Guttmann, *From Ritual to Record, the Nature of Modern Sports*, pp.17–28.
③ J. 胡伊青加：《人：游戏者》，成穷译，贵州人民出版社，2007年，第194页。

不过，正像上文中所指出的，"神圣"与"世俗"既是相互对立的，也是相互依存、相伴而生的，不论古代的宗教信徒还是现代的非宗教徒，一方面他们有着"世俗"的生活，另一方面他们都希望通过追寻某种"神圣"的东西而赋予生活以某种意义，在这一点上是共同的，因此，世界上既不存在纯粹意义上的"世俗的人"，也不存在纯粹意义上的"宗教的人"。在古希腊的奥林匹亚赛会中断了一千多年之后，1896年，在法国人顾拜旦（Baron Pierre de Coubertin, 1863–1937）的倡导和努力下，创办了现代奥林匹克运动，从而揭开了人类体育运动发展史的新的一章。与古希腊的奥林匹亚赛会相比，尽管宗教的背景没有了，但人们对体育运动的热情、期待和向往却不减当年，奥运会俨然成为了一种新时代的"显圣物"，正如古特曼所言，从原始仪式到世界记录，体育经历了世俗化的过程，但现代体育又创造出了"新的宗教"，人们开始崇拜现代的体育英雄，新闻界把体育称为"大众的宗教"，"世俗的宗教"，顾拜旦则恭敬地称之为"体育的宗教"（religio athletae）。[1]

---

① Allen Guttmann, *From Ritual to Record, the Nature of Modern Sports*, p.25.

古希腊人的合法竞争思想

王瑞聚 曲阜师范大学

摘要： 在古希腊城邦社会，无论是知识精英还是公民大众，有一种重要的政治思想，即与民主传统紧密相联系的合法竞争思想。特别是在雅典国家，关于合法竞争思想，形成了一种浓厚的社会氛围，成为处于主流意识形态地位的思想之一。本文从不同角度探讨了这一问题。

关键词： 合法竞争；荷马史诗；僭主政治；柏拉图；亚里士多德；梭伦

Abstract: The idea of legitimate competition was an important political thought in the ancient Greek society. It was intimately tethered to democratic tradition and prevalent in both the intellectual elite and the ordinary people. In Athens, in particular, legitimate competition formed a great social atmosphere and became one of the dominant ideologies. This paper attempts to discuss this issue from different angles.

Keywords: Legitimate Competition; Homa Epic; Tyranny; Plato; Aristotle; Solon

一 绪言

古希腊人相对系统化的政治学说主要体现在柏拉图和亚里士多德的著作中，可以称之为知识精英的相对专业的政治思想。除此之外，还有一般公民的非系统化的政治思想，包括史学家、悲剧家、喜剧家、抒情诗人、史诗作者、政治家等等，他们的政治思想一般都是零散的不成系统的。笔者在读书过程中发现，在古希腊城邦社会，无论是知识精英，还是公民大众，还有一种重要的政治思想，即与民主传统紧密相联系的合法竞争思想。特别是在雅典国家，关于合法竞争思想，形成了一种浓厚的社会氛围，成为处于主流意识形态地位的重要思想之一。

这里，首先引用首都博物馆为迎奥运于 2008 年 7 月举办的"公平的竞争——古希腊竞技精神"展览前言中的一段话，来概要说明古希腊人的合法竞争思想："在古希腊，'公平的竞争'理念体现在公民生活的方方面面。古希腊伟大的诗人荷马不断地教导希腊人，要'永远处于最佳状态并超越其他人'。这种主张与儿童和青年的教育联系在一起，引导人们强身健体、提高智力，成为好公民。在公平的基础上，在竞技场上的各种活动中，在决定国家大事的公民大会辩论中，在法庭的抗辩中，在节庆日的诗歌朗诵、戏剧表演中，甚至在战场上，古希腊人都表现出'比一比'的想法。"

　　竞争，是矛盾斗争性的表现形式之一。竞争有两种类型，即正当的竞争（公平竞争、合法竞争）和不正当的竞争（恶性竞争、不择手段的竞争）。正当的竞争体现公平、公正，有利于激发人的创造潜能和个体的进取心，调动人的积极性、主动性和创造性，有利于推动社会的进步和发展。不正当的竞争则破坏公平、公正的原则，恶化人与人乃至共同体与共同体之间的关系，扰乱正常的经济和社会秩序，阻碍社会的进步和发展。"同行是冤家"、"东方式的嫉妒"、出其不意突然袭击、为达目的不择手段，以及弱肉强食等等，都属于不正当的竞争。

　　合法竞争、公平竞争、和平竞争，用哲学的观点又可以理解为合法斗争、合法排斥、合法反对。这几个概念基本上同义，但合法斗争、合法反对一般用于政治斗争领域。无论是合法竞争还是合法斗争，前提都是存在相互对立的具有独立位格的矛盾双方——政治领域体现为不同的党派或派别——矛盾双方按既定的规则进行利益的角逐，体现和平、公平和正义的原则。[1]事事讲求合法（手段问题），"取之有道"，这标志着人类自身的一种文明程度。迄今为止，人类精神文明、政治文明所能达到的最高程度就是合法竞争，这是对立冲突的矛盾双方最理想的关系状态。

　　古希腊人对两种类型的竞争，早在古风时代（前 8 — 6 世纪）即已认识得非常清楚。继荷马之后的诗人赫西俄德指出："大地上不是只有一种不和女神，而是有两种。一种不和，只要人能理解她，就会对她大唱赞辞。而另一种不和则应受到谴责。这是因为她们的性情大相径庭。一种天性残忍，挑起罪恶的战争和争斗；只是因为永生天神的意愿，人类不得已而崇拜这种粗厉的不和女神，实际上没有人真的喜欢她。另一不和女神是夜神的长女，居住天庭高高在上的克洛诺斯之子（即宙斯）把她安置于大地之根，她对人类要好得多。她刺激怠惰者劳作，因为一个人看到别人因勤劳而致富，因勤于耕耘、栽种而把家事安排得顺顺当当时，他会因羡慕而变得热爱工作。邻居间相互攀比，争先富裕。这种不和女神有益于人类。陶工与陶工竞争，工匠和工匠竞争；乞丐忌妒乞丐；歌手忌妒歌手。"[2]

　　赫西俄德的意思是，竞争女神有两种：一种天性残忍，挑起罪恶的战争和争斗。人类社会的恶性竞争，就因这种不和女神所致。另一种不和女神则有益于人类：一个人看到别人因勤劳而致富，羡慕别人而变得热爱工作；邻居间相互攀比，争先富裕；陶工与陶工竞争，工匠和工匠竞争；乞丐忌妒乞丐，歌手忌妒歌手。这种不和女神象征的是良性竞争、正当竞争、公平竞争、合法竞争。赫西俄德赞同合法竞争，反对不正当竞争。他训诫他的弟弟"不要让那个乐于伤害的不和女神把你的心从工作中移开"。

　　赫西俄德的关于两种不同性质的竞争的思想，在人类思想发展史和政治发展史上具有重要意义。思想是行动的先导。早在两千多年以前，古希腊人就划分出了两种性质根本不同的竞争，并指出了正当竞争的积极作用，并且主张"不要压制对城邦有益的竞争"，[3]这对于传播合法竞争、公平竞争观念，并在全社会推动合法竞争、公平竞争行为，具有重要作用。反映到政治领域，则有助于形成合法斗争的机制和合法斗争的游戏规则。[4]

二　荷马史诗中的公平竞争思想

　　古希腊人是世界上最早具有成熟的合法竞争、公平竞争理念的民族，也是最早形成合法竞争和

① 据此看来，中国的政治领域不存在合法斗争、合法反对，没有对立面。
② 赫西俄德：《工作与时日》，商务印书馆，1991 年版，第 1—2 页。
③ 索福克勒斯：《俄狄浦斯王》，《古希腊悲剧喜剧全集》第 2 册，第 63 页，凤凰出版集团，2007 年版。
④ 这里的"合法斗争"，与"合法竞争"、"公平竞争"等概念同义，与近代以来建立在政党政治基础上的合法斗争有区别。

公平竞争机制的民族。早在荷马史诗中，公平竞争的现象就多次出现。在荷马史诗中，公平竞争不仅出现在希腊人处理内部矛盾的时候，也出现在处理外部矛盾的时候。套用今天的概念，希腊联军所面临的矛盾也是可以分为敌我矛盾和人民内部矛盾的。如他们远征特洛伊，在战场上，墨涅拉奥斯（希腊联军将领）与特洛伊王子帕里斯的矛盾，就属于敌我矛盾。但他们二人在特洛伊城下的决斗，就是一种公平竞争、文明竞争，不用计谋，不用暗算，也就是说不搞阴谋诡计，全凭膂力，刀对刀，枪对枪，按一定的规则，并且相互尊重对手。

《伊利亚特》第三卷生动地记载了这场人类历史上最早的有文字记载的决斗。先是赫克托尔代表帕里斯（"战争就因他引起"）向希腊人提出与墨涅拉奥斯单独进行决斗的建议——"他要求特洛亚人（即特洛伊人）和全体阿开奥斯人把他们的精良武器放在养育人的土地上，让他同阿瑞斯喜爱的战士墨涅拉奥斯在两军之间为海伦和她的财产而战斗，他们两人谁获得胜利，比对方强大，就让他把这个女人和财产带回家。其余的人就保证友谊，发出誓言。"——墨涅拉奥斯表示同意，但他提议把特洛伊国王普里阿摩斯"带到这里来起誓，免得有人破坏向宙斯发出的誓言，因为老国王的儿子们很是傲慢成性。年轻人的心变来变去，总是不坚定，但是老年人参与事情，他瞻前顾后，所以后果对双方都是最好不过。"

这样说了之后，阿开奥斯人和特洛亚人很是喜欢，希望结束这艰苦的战争。"他们把各自的战车停留在阵线里面，自己走出来，把武器放下，堆在地上，彼此靠近，中间只有很小的空地。""他们现在安静地坐下，停止战斗，依靠在盾牌边上，长枪插在身边。"请注意，这时候如果其中的任何一方背信弃义，发起对对方的突然袭击，消灭对方，将是非常容易的事情！接着，赫克托尔派两个传令官到城里去把普里阿摩斯国王请来。普里阿摩斯乘车来到了战场上，从车上下来，去到特洛亚人和阿开奥斯人中间。这时候，"阿伽门农立刻站起来，足智多谋的奥德修斯也跟着起立"。他们对普里阿摩斯国王很有礼貌，表示了应有的尊敬。试想，这时候如果希腊人不择手段，采取不正当的竞争手段，突然发起对普里阿摩斯的袭击，那他这特洛伊人的国王肯定也就没命了。擒贼擒王，王被擒，战争的结局也就基本上决定了。这时候是特洛伊战争的初期。如果那样的话，这特洛伊战争也就用不了打那么长时间了。

随后，联军统帅阿伽门农大声祷告："宙斯、伊达山的统治者、最光荣最伟大的主宰啊，眼观万物、耳听万事的赫利奥斯啊，大地啊，在下界向伪誓的死者报复的神啊，请你们作证，监视这些可信赖的誓言。如果帕里斯杀死墨涅拉奥斯，就让他占有海伦和她的全部财产，我们则坐上渡海的船舶离开这里；如果金色头发的墨涅拉奥斯杀死帕里斯，就让特洛亚人归还海伦和她的全部财产，向阿尔戈斯人付出值得后人记忆的可观赔偿。但是如果帕里斯倒在地上，普里阿摩斯和他的儿子们不愿赔偿，我就要为了获得赔偿而继续战斗，待在这里，直到我看见战争的终点。"

双方将士祷告："宙斯、最光荣最伟大的神啊，永生的众神啊，两军之一要是谁首先破坏盟誓，愿他们和他们的全体孩子的脑浆如同这些酒流在地上，妻子受奴役。"

仪式完毕，普里阿摩斯离开战场，返回特洛伊。赫克托尔（帕里斯的兄长）和奥德修斯（希腊联军方面的智囊）首先为即将进行的决斗量出地面，再把两只阄拿来，放在铜盔里摇动，决定两个对手谁首先投掷铜枪。这也属公平竞争。双方的将士同声祈祷："宙斯、伊达山的统治者、最光荣最伟大的主宰啊，他们两人谁给对方制造麻烦，就让他死在枪下，阴魂进入冥府，让我们保证友谊和可以信赖的誓言。"赫克托尔朝后看（即不能眼睛看着阄），摇头盔，帕里斯的阄很快跳出来。将士们一排排坐下（准备观战），在他们每个人身旁站着健跑的骏马，竖着精良的武器。随后，帕里斯披挂整齐，墨涅拉奥斯也武装起来，他们走到特洛伊人和阿开奥斯人（希腊人）阵前，在那块量好的空地上靠近站立，彼此怒目而视，挥舞手中的长枪。按照摇阄的结果，由帕里斯先出手。他投掷长枪，击中了墨涅拉奥斯的圆盾……决斗的最后结果，墨涅拉奥斯战胜了帕里斯，帕里斯被爱神阿芙洛狄特救出战场，才得以活命。

如果说，第三卷中帕里斯与墨涅拉奥斯这场较量还带有情敌决斗（争夺海伦）的因素，那么第七卷中赫克托尔对埃阿斯的挑战与应战，就纯粹是一种敌我矛盾的冲突了。但在这个过程中，不仅同样体现了"公平竞争"精神，而且过程更多波折，"他们曾经在吞食灵魂的战争中打斗，相逢作战，又在友谊中彼此告别。"①特别是在胜负难分的情况下，能够"文质彬彬"地休战，友好地握手告别，并且还互赠礼物，俨然是多年的老朋友分手。

大致过程如下：赫克托尔首先向希腊人发出挑战。在希腊联军"全都默不作声"的情况下，阿伽门农的弟弟墨涅拉奥斯起来应战，可是却被阿伽门农制止，阿伽门农不让他因为气愤去同比他强的人战斗。这时候希腊联军中的老将涅斯托尔站起来说了一番话，激起了9个人起来应战，他们是：联军统帅阿伽门农、军事将领狄奥墨得斯、大埃阿斯、小埃阿斯、伊多墨纽斯、墨里奥涅斯、欧律皮洛斯、托阿斯和奥德修斯（联军中最勇猛的阿喀琉斯因为女俘之争，与阿伽门农怄气，离开战场，躺在海边的弯船旁边）。"这些人全都乐意同神样的赫克托尔战斗"。然后，在涅斯托尔的提议下，通过"投阄"——这是希腊人内部的公平竞争——选出一个人来。于是每个人在自己的阄上作记号，然后投到阿伽门农的头盔里。涅斯托尔摇摇头盔。就这样，他们所盼望的阄跳了出来，这就是埃阿斯（大埃阿斯）的阄。传令官拿着阄穿过人群，从左走向右，交给阿开奥斯的首领们观看。埃阿斯见自己中阄，心里很是喜悦。随后披挂出阵，有如魁梧的阿瑞斯（战神）。埃阿斯把盾牌举在胸前，靠近赫克托尔身边站着，请他先出手。赫克托尔说："我不想偷偷地进攻，我要公开地刺中你，当心，看我的枪。"②他这样说，平衡他的有长影的枪杆，投掷出去，击中埃阿斯的盾牌。这时埃阿斯投掷他的长枪，也击中了赫克托尔的盾牌。随后两个人来回拼杀，很像好吃生肉的狮子或是野猪，它们都有不小的力气。赫克托尔还抓起地上的一块大石头，击中了埃阿斯盾牌中心突出来的部位。埃阿斯则抓起一块更大的石头，转身投出去，打瘪了赫克托尔的盾牌。他们在近战中挥剑砍杀。因为夜色降临，双方的传令官宣布休战，听从夜的安排。埃阿斯则回答传令官："你们把这样的话对他去说，是他向我们的最英勇的人提出挑战。他若同意这样，我也不斗下去。"头盔闪亮的伟大的赫克托尔说："埃阿斯，既然天神赋与你身长、力量、聪明才智，长枪赛过阿开奥斯人，现在让我们停止今天的战斗和厮杀，日后再打，直到天神为我们评判，把胜利的荣誉赐给你或是赐给我。你过来，让我们互相赠送光荣的礼物，……"③他这样说，把嵌银的剑连同剑鞘和精心剪裁的佩带一起取下来相赠；埃阿斯把发亮的紫色腰带送给赫克托尔。然后他们告别，一个到阿开奥斯人的队伍中，另一个到特洛亚人的人群里。

《伊利亚特》写的是希腊人和特洛伊人之间的战争，战争打了10年，双方少有使用谋略之处，基本上拼的是膂力，是实力，也就是人力和物力。如果说阴谋诡计，主要是第10年上的木马计。④但区区一个木马计，与古代中国人的"三十六计"，真可谓是小巫见大巫！对比中国，"兵不厌诈"

---

① 《伊利亚特》，罗念生、王焕生译本，人民文学出版社，1994年版，第181页。
② 《伊利亚特》，罗念生、王焕生译本，人民文学出版社，1994年版，第178页。
③ 《伊利亚特》，罗念生、王焕生译本，人民文学出版社，1994年版，第181页。
④ 《伊利亚特》中不择手段的情况当然也有，如第4卷：潘达罗斯射伤墨涅拉奥斯战事重起；说的是赫拉仇恨特洛伊人，想挑起战争，说服宙斯，宙斯让雅典娜怂恿特洛伊方面的潘达罗斯搞突然袭击，射了墨涅拉奥斯一箭。阿伽门农对弟弟墨涅拉奥斯说："特洛伊人却践踏他们的誓言，射中你，盟誓、羊血、纯酒的祭奠和我们信赖的双方的握手都没有产生应有的效果。"（92页）还说："如果奥林波斯神不立刻惩罚这件事——他迟早也会那样做——，敌人就要用他们的脑袋、妻子和儿女给我们作大笔偿付。"特洛伊"人们遭毁灭的日子定会到来，……这些事定会实现成事实。"（92－93页）他鼓励军队："不要削弱你们的勇气，父亲宙斯不会帮助赌假咒的人，对那些首先违反誓言而害人的人，秃鹫会去啄食他们的细嫩的肉，我们将在攻占他们的城市的时候，把他们的亲爱的妻子和儿女用船运走。"（95－96）来自克里特的军事将领伊多墨纽斯："我们好立刻参战，特洛伊人破坏了盟誓，死亡和苦难今后将临到他们头上，因为他们首先违反神圣的誓言。"（97页）希腊人对特洛伊人的谴责反映了重视公平竞争的思想。

成为千古名言，成为用兵者的座右铭和用兵之道。古代中国的兵家很少有在主观上想去进行纯粹的力的较量，亦即通过合法竞争以取胜的，大都是想出奇制胜。所谓出奇制胜，就是使用谋略。所谓使用谋略，就是通过非合法竞争的手段。"兵者，诡道也"（《始计篇》）是《孙子兵法》中的名言，一个"诡"字，道出了问题的实质。《孙子兵法》还说："百战百胜，非善之善者也。不战而屈人之兵，善之善者也。故上兵伐谋，其次伐交，其次伐兵，其下攻城。攻城之法，为不得已（也）。"（《谋攻篇》）意思是：拼实力，百战百胜，算不上是最高明的。不通过交战而凭谋略就能降服敌人的，亦即不战而胜，才是最高明的。所以，上等的军事行动是用谋略挫败敌方的战略意图或战争行为，其次就是用外交战胜敌人，再次是用武力击败敌军，最下之策是攻打敌人的城池。攻城，是不得已而为之的办法，是没有办法的办法。《孙子兵法》认为，用兵的关键在于真真假假，虚虚实实，即主力部队的正面作战和用奇兵出奇制胜相配合，也就是"实力"与"计谋"相配合，"拼实力"与"耍心眼儿"相配合。"以奇胜"（《兵势篇》），即出奇制胜，"兵以诈立"（《军争篇》），即战争靠以诈取胜。孙子①的这些思想与荷马史诗中的公平竞争思想可以说是大相径庭，双方对各自历史的社会的甚至各自民族的影响，当然也就也大相径庭。

司马迁《史记》（卷65）中记载的田忌赛马的故事，②同样也能说明问题。为了节省篇幅，这里只述其大意：

> 齐威王和手下大将田忌经常赛马。马分上、中、下三等，上等马对上等马，中等马对中等马，下等马对下等马。田忌每个等次的马都比齐威王的弱一些，因此每次比赛，三个回合下来，都是田忌失败。后来田忌的军师孙膑给他支招。于是在新一轮的比赛中，田忌先用自己的下等马对齐威王的上等马（败），然后再用自己的上等马对齐威王的中等马（胜），最后用自己的中等马对齐威王的下等马（胜）。结果三场比赛，一负两胜，总分第一。于是田忌赢了齐威王。

赛场上，表面上看，后来的比赛也是公平竞争，文质彬彬，但实际上却完全不是这么回事。田忌之所以最后胜出，靠的是（孙膑的）机巧，而不是实力。也就是说，他们这后来的比赛，在本质上是没有规则的，有的只是"耍心眼儿"的潜规则，是阴谋而不是阳谋。

尤其值得我们思考的是，在我们国家，《田忌赛马》的故事还被编进了教科书，成为六年级小学生——实际上也就是每一个中国的孩子——所必须要学习或熟悉的一篇课文。在我们的主导思想里，"田忌赛马"故事的价值，是中国历史上有名的揭示如何善用自己的长处去对付对手的短处，从而在竞争中获胜的事例。——即使笔者在给大学生讲哲学的时候，也把它作为量变引起事物质变的两种形式之一，来举例子的。在讲辩证法关于质量互变规律的时候讲到，量变引起事物的质变，有两种形式，一是单纯数量的增加或减少引起事物的质变。如，积劳成疾、集腋成裘、气球爆炸等等。二是数量没有发生变化，仅仅是构成成分的排列顺序和结构方式发生了变化，就能够引起事物的质变。其中笔者就举了田忌赛马的例子。马还是原来的马，由于孙膑的排列组合，亦即谋划，最

---

① 孙子（约公元前535年—？）即孙武，春秋末的军事思想家，齐国人，著兵家经典《孙子兵法》，被后世称为兵圣。
② "忌数与齐诸公子驰逐重射。孙子见其马足不甚相远，马有上、中、下辈。于是孙子谓田忌曰：'君弟重射，臣能令君胜。'田忌信然之，与王及诸公子逐射千金。及临质，孙子曰：'今以君之下驷与彼上驷，取君上驷与彼中驷，取君中驷与彼下驷。'既驰三辈毕，而田忌一不胜而再胜，卒得千金。"大意是，田忌经常与齐国诸公子赛马，设重金赌注。孙膑发现他们的马脚力都差不多，可分为上、中、下三等。于是孙膑对田忌说："您只管下大赌注，我能让您取胜。"田忌相信并答应了他，与齐王和诸公子用千金来赌注。比赛即将开始，孙膑说："现在用您的下等马对付他们的上等马，拿您的上等马对付他们的中等马，拿您的中等马对付他们的下等马。"三场比赛完后，田忌一场不胜而两场胜，最终赢得齐王的千金赌注。

后转败为胜。这说明，事物的质变，不但可以通过量的增减引起，而且还可以通过科学地调整内部而实现。——这是田忌赛马的故事提供给我们中国人的最大的智慧和学问。可是我们万万没有想到，当我们对这种智慧和学问赞不绝口、欣赏不已的时候，我们的思想观念于潜移默化之中便被"染黑"了：人人崇尚计谋，不以搞计谋为耻，并且实践中耻于去做，而以搞计谋为荣，认为这样的人有本事，而争相去效法。试想，在这种情况下，怎么有可能在全社会树立起并推行开来公平竞争的思想观念及相应的社会实践？在笔者看来，正确的做法，亦即真正的公平竞争，只能是这样子的，即田忌在前几轮的比赛失败（那是真正的公平竞争，实力不足者必败）之后，认真总结经验教训，退而采取科学的方法，养马、驯马、锻炼马，以争取下一次的比赛胜利。

我们中国人从来就缺乏合法竞争、公平竞争的思想观念，自古以来所崇尚的并且也是最为擅长的就是搞计谋（说白了就是搞阴谋诡计），穷根溯源，与上述这些耳熟能详的"传统文化"的长期浸染和熏陶分不开。无论是在战场上，还是在和平时期，都是如此。所以笔者认为，对小学课本中类似于"田忌赛马"的故事，我们应该进行批判性的教与学。在新的历史条件下，认清其消极的一面，剔除其糟粕，是十分必要的。

我们再接着说荷马史诗。战争是残酷的，"无数的盾牌、长枪和身披铜甲的战士冲突起来。……盾牌互相猛烈撞击，发出巨大的响声。被杀的人的痛苦和杀人的人的胜利欢呼，混成一片，殷红的鲜血流满地面。"[①]战争又是血腥的，战争更是不择手段。但在这残酷、血腥和不择手段的特洛伊战争中，却有这么几场文质彬彬的公平竞争，实在是难能可贵！实际上，竞争精神在荷马史诗，特别是在《伊利亚特》中，无处不在！[②]

尤其值得人们注意的是，由荷马史诗所发轫的这种文明风尚，直接或间接地影响了后来的西方社会，不仅表现在中世纪以及近代曾经非常流行的决斗（司法决斗和荣誉决斗），[③]形式上与荷马史诗中所描写的古希腊人的决斗一脉相承，而且还表现在其它领域的竞争中，如政治上的角逐、商场上的竞争等等。魏特夫曾经指出："欧洲中世纪，……封建的权力中心之间的冲突很多而且常常很激烈；但是敌对的力量之间常常是在战场上而不是在暗地里进行较量。而那些希望用阴谋诡计消灭他们敌人的人，宁愿采取伏击的方式，而不愿意进行法律上的诬陷。利用第一种手段的机会很多，而利用第二种手段的机会则是很少的。"[④]

所谓决斗，"简单地讲，就是'指按照预定的规则由两个带有致命武器的人为了解决争吵或某种荣誉而进行的格斗。它是诉诸于通常司法程序之外的另一种选择。'"[⑤]"诉诸于司法程序"当然是一种合法竞争，而"按照预定的规则"进行决斗，也属于合法竞争的范畴，原因就在于它是按预定的规则进行的。

当然，不择手段的非法竞争现象，无论是在古代的中国，还是古代的希腊，还是在后来的西方社会，都是客观存在的，这是人类社会因政治经济等利益冲突所必然会引起的一种现象。区别只在于，程度上有所不同而已。

---

① 《伊利亚特》，罗念生、王焕生译本，人民文学出版社，1994年版，第104页。
② 芬利：《希腊的遗产》，上海人民出版社，2004年版，第20页。
③ 参见董亚娟：《论决斗与近代西方社会》，《江汉大学学报》2009年第3期。
④ 魏特夫《东方专制主义——对于极权力量的比较研究》，中国社会科学出版社，1989年版，第72页。
⑤ 《简明不列颠百科全书》，第四卷，中国大百科全书出版社，1985年版，第474页。转引自董亚娟：《论决斗与近代西方社会》一文，《江汉大学学报》2009年第3期。

三　古希腊人合法竞争思想的几种表现

"一旦参加竞赛，丝毫不容客气。"[①]这是古希腊的一句俗语，反映了人们在各种竞赛活动中齐头并进、你追我赶、互相激励、互相促进、共同提高的公平竞争现实。英雄阿喀琉斯（阿基琉斯）的儿子涅奥普托勒莫斯说："宁愿光明磊落地失败，不愿用阴谋诡计取胜。"[②]这句话典型的代表了古希腊人合法竞争的思想。欧里庇得斯在悲剧中，通过色雷斯国王瑞索斯之口，表达了同样的思想："没有哪个勇士会偷偷摸摸去杀敌人，都愿意面对面地与敌人决斗。"[③]古希腊人的合法竞争，不仅表现在战场上，更表现在政治舞台上以及社会生活的其它领域。

在古希腊，那些实行民主制度的国家（甚至包括寡头政治的国家），通过选举或者抽签，或者其他规则，产生各种公职。各种公职均有一定的任期，任期内要受到一定的监督，任期结束时要受到审查。这些制度都属于合法竞争的形式。修昔底德说："在民主政治下，没有当选的候选人更容易接受其失败，因为被平等的人击败并不能使他感到羞辱。"[④]这里说的是，民主制度是一种合法竞争的制度，这种制度由于能够实现公平和公正，所以，即使竞争失败，也能够使人们心悦诚服。可以说，民主制度是古希腊人合法竞争思想的最重要的表现形式。

程序上通过民主选举，实现权力的有序更替，是民主制度的核心，也是合法竞争的精髓。古希腊人的这种民主精神和合法竞争思想，对后世西欧的中世纪市民民主以及近代资产阶级民主都有一定影响。而通过抽签或者拈阄产生公职，则是古希腊人的特有现象，是最为平民化的合法竞争形式，最能体现政治面前人人平等的原则。[⑤]在古希腊特别是雅典国家，政治领域合法竞争的游戏规则基本上处于主流地位。虽然也有政治暗杀（如公元前461年民主派代表人物厄菲阿尔特被贵族派暗杀、公元前411年民主派领袖安德罗克利斯被寡头党人暗杀[⑥]等等）和非法夺权（如庇西特拉图的僭主政治），但都是个别现象和短期行为，属于历史的支流，不占主导地位。

关于抽签或者拈阄，亦即遇事用抽签或者拈阄的办法来裁决，在古希腊有悠久的历史。荷马史诗、悲剧喜剧以及神话传说中，拈阄例子举不胜举，甚至连神界的分割，也实行这种办法。宙斯、波塞冬、哈得斯是三兄弟，他们就是通过拈阄划分"势力范围"的。"一切分成三份，各得自己的一份，我（波塞冬）从阄子拈得灰色的大海作为永久的居所，哈得斯统治昏冥世界，宙斯拈得太空和云气里的广阔天宇，大地和高耸的奥林波斯归大家共有。"[⑦]这是海神波塞冬的一段话。神界如此，遑论人间。这显然是人间的拈阄现象在神话中的反映，足见拈阄这种公平竞争方式在古希腊的盛行。这也反映了古希腊人公平竞争的传统。

---

① 柏拉图：《法律篇》（张智仁、何勤华译本），上海人民出版社，2001年版，第162页。
② 索福克勒斯：《菲罗克忒忒斯》，《古希腊悲剧喜剧全集》，第2卷，第622页。
③ 《古希腊悲剧喜剧全集》，第5卷，第38页。"偷偷摸摸去杀敌人"，却是中国人的擅长。
④ 修昔底德：《伯罗奔尼撒战争史》，广西师范大学出版社，2004年版，第474页。
⑤ 但也有弊端，即排斥了德才标准。曾受到苏格拉底、亚里士多德等思想家的批评。
⑥ 修昔底德：《伯罗奔尼撒战争史》，广西师范大学出版社，2004年版，第461页。
⑦ 罗念生、王焕生译《伊利亚特》，人民文学出版社，1997年版，第385页。

社会生活的其它领域最能反映古希腊人公平竞争思想和实践的是体育竞技①和戏剧比赛，以及其它文化赛事，如音乐比赛、②诗歌朗诵比赛等等，这里就不多说了。奥林匹克竞技不仅有严格的资格审查和比赛规则，而且比赛前全体选手还要在宙斯神像前宣誓："永不用不正当的方法从事竞赛"。竞技会期间还要进行和平休战。公平竞争精神不仅是奥林匹克竞技的灵魂，而且也因为它的巨大影响而渗透进希腊人的灵魂。在平等的条件下为获得荣誉而进行公平竞争，奥林匹克竞技为人们在社会的其他领域树立了一个独特而光辉的榜样。

在古希腊人的政治舞台上，著名政治家伯里克利与客蒙（约前512－449，又译西门）的角逐，是以和平方式进行竞争（斗争）的一个案例。客蒙是米泰亚得（马拉松战役指挥者）的儿子，贵族派领袖，是伯里克利崛起前雅典政治舞台上声名最为显赫的政治家。伯里克利"为了对抗客蒙的声望，尽量争取群众，他的产业和钱财比客蒙少。客蒙可以用他的钱财争取贫民，给雅典的穷人每天供应伙食，给老年人发寒衣，把自己庄园的围墙拆除，谁愿意进去摘水果就可以随便摘。在这些方面，伯里克利要想胜过他，只好转而把城邦的公款拿来分配。……他利用看戏津贴、陪审费，以及其他补助和津贴，很快就收买了民心，……后来，他靠埃菲阿特的帮助，剥夺了议事会的大部分权限，客蒙也被指控为亲斯巴达与仇视人民，而被流放（即陶片放逐）。……按照法律规定，流放的期限是10年。但这期间，斯巴达人以大军入侵塔那格拉城（前475年），雅典立即出兵抵抗。于是，客蒙便从流放中跑回来，参加他那乡区（自己家乡所在的地区）的队伍，打算用实际行动洗雪他的亲斯巴达罪名。他和同胞一起冒死奋战（对斯巴达人作战）。但是伯里克利的友人异口同声说他是流放中的人，联合起来把他赶走了。大概是由于这个原因，伯里克利在这次战斗中更加勇不可当，甘冒危险而奋不顾身（努力表现自己以与客蒙对斯巴达人的"冒死奋战"相比美）。而那些客蒙的友人，无一例外地全部战死。后来，雅典人在阿提卡边界一带大败，方才懊悔，他们展望来春的一场鏖战，更加怀念客蒙。伯里克利看到了这一点，他毫不犹豫立即迎合民心，亲笔下令召回客蒙。于是，客蒙从流放中归来，在城邦之间缔造了和平（前450年）。因为斯巴达人对他是极友好的，对伯里克利及其他领袖则十分痛恨。"③普鲁塔克的上述记载即反映了古希腊人合法竞争思想在政治舞台上的影响，反映了合法竞争思想在部分政治家那里所起的作用。

在古希腊，政治家同时也是演说家。政治家在政治舞台上表现自己，最重要的方式就是参加辩

---

① 柏拉图《法律篇》中关于第二理想国的体育竞赛问题作了许多制度性的规定，即反映了现实中的古希腊人体育竞技方面的合法竞争精神。如，我们的传令官要遵循习俗，宣布我们体育竞赛中的第一项是1斯塔狄亚全副武装赛跑。赛手要穿戴盔甲，徒手参赛的选手不能获奖。各项比赛的顺序是：第一，1斯塔狄亚赛跑，全副武装；第二，两斯塔狄亚赛跑；第三，战车比赛；第四，长距离赛跑；第五，比赛非常迷人，一边是被我们称作重装步兵的一名选手，携带全部沉重的装备，一直要跑到阿瑞斯神庙，然后折回，整个距离是60斯塔狄亚，另一边是他比赛的对手，弓箭手，也是全副装备，他必须穿山越岭，一直跑到阿波罗和阿尔忒弥斯的神庙，跑100斯塔狄亚。在比赛过程中，我们将在那里等候他们返回，奖品将授予各种比赛的胜利者。体育比赛分成三类，一类是少年男子的，一类是青年男子的，还有一类是成年男子的。青年男子的赛跑距离是全程的三分之二，少年男子的赛跑距离是全程的一半。至于女性，我们将安排1斯塔狄亚和两斯塔狄亚赛跑、赛车和长距离跑，参加比赛的妇女如果年龄还没有到青春期，那么必须完全裸体参赛，如果已经过了十三岁，正在等待婚配——她们的结婚年龄最小是十八岁，最大二十岁——那么就必须穿上适当的衣服参赛。膂力方面的竞赛，比如摔跤，以及类似的项目，这些运动当前非常流行，我们将举行的项目有穿盔甲格斗、单人格斗、双人格斗、集体格斗，每边人数最多可达十人。至于决定胜负的标准，我们将遵循先前已有的由权威们制定的格斗规则。以同样的方式，我们将请专家手持武器来协助纠正比赛中的犯规行为，击中对手必须记分，根据积分多少来决定胜负。这些规则同样也适用于那些不到结婚年龄的女性。我们将用一般的投掷比赛取代击手比赛，包括射箭、投标枪、用手掷石块、用投石器掷石块，在这些比赛中，我们也必须制定规则，奖励那些严格按照我们的规则获胜的人。关于赛马规则，参赛选手必须穿戴盔甲。不强迫妇女参加竞赛，但若她们在幼年和少年时期的早期训练已经使她们有了这种习惯和强壮的体力，并且不会带来什么不良后果，那么就允许她们参赛，不得加以阻止。

② 许多城邦都有音乐学校，都有专门的合唱队，如儿童合唱队、男女成年人的合唱队等等，用于参加节日和宗教活动的各种比赛。也有独唱和独奏表演。参看柏拉图《法律篇》第6、第8等卷。

③ 普鲁塔克：《希腊罗马名人传》，商务印书馆，1990年版，第470－471页。

论和发表演说，通过辩论和演说赢得民众的拥护和支持，使民众接受自己的而不是他人的提议和观点。在雅典国家，一切重大决策都由公民大会决定。在公民大会上每一个公民都可以自由发言，以自己的意见影响公众情绪和公共决策。在古希腊，一个公民或政治家，或外交使节，要使自己的意见获得支持，就必须利用演说和辩论的形式。修昔底德的史学名著《伯罗奔尼撒战争史》中，大约四分之一的篇幅是演说辞，这也反映了辩论和演说在古希腊人政治、军事、外交以及文化活动中的重要性和普遍性。这种辩论和演说，不同于命令和强制，是辩论者和演说者彼此之间对等的交流，是一种公平竞争。所以辩论和演说也是古希腊人合法竞争的重要表现形式，并且成为古希腊人合法竞争的重要手段（工具）之一。

四　反僭主政治与合法竞争思想的关系

在古希腊，能够反映合法竞争思想的另一重要社会现象和文化现象，就是人们对僭主政治的警惕、反对和批判，对反僭主英雄的崇拜和歌颂。僭主政治（tyrannia）是指通过政变或超越规定的权限等非法手段建立的独裁统治。僭主政治曾经在许多希腊城邦发生过，如阿尔戈斯、科林斯、麦加拉、西库昂、雅典以及小亚的米利都、西西里岛的叙拉古等等。古希腊最有名的僭主有阿尔戈斯的斐冬（公元前7世纪）、科林斯的柏利安得（？—前585）、[1] 雅典的庇西特拉图（约前600—527）、叙拉古的狄奥尼修斯一世（约前430—367）等等。

据认为"僭主"（tyrant）一词在古希腊最初并无贬义。[2] 在诗人（如品达）的作品中有时亦称为"王"。好多僭主在当时及后世，因为有所建树而留下了比较好的名声，或得到了某种程度的肯定。如柏利安得在古代就被列为古希腊"七贤"之一。庇西特拉图因为打击贵族势力，发展经济文化，在历史上也得到好评。狄奥尼修斯一世以希腊风格修建叙拉古城，奖励文学艺术，本人也是诗人和戏剧家，据说临死前其剧作还曾经在雅典上演获奖。但正如英国著名希腊史家安德鲁斯所指出的那样："问题不在于他们的统治是好是坏，而在于他们僭取政权的方式以及同原有政权决裂的手段。"[3] 所以，僭主不仅是实行强权政治的独裁者，更是通过非法手段上台的独裁者。

由于僭主都是野心家，都是通过非法手段取得政权实行独裁统治，所以僭主、甚至包括僭主的名字，后来（确切地说应该是始终）在古希腊便成为一个贬义词。古希腊"七贤"之一的克莱俄布卢（约生活于公元前600年前后，罗德斯岛林达斯人）在给梭伦的信中说："无论你走到哪里，你都会拥有很多朋友和一个家；但最适合梭伦的，是实行民主制的林达斯。这个岛屿地处远海，生活在这里的人用不着担心庇西特拉图。来自四面八方的朋友将会前来拜访你。"[4] 信中提到的庇西特拉图，就是含有贬义的明证。在古希腊，僭主政治被人们视为一种丑恶的政治现象，比君主制还不得人心。

---

① 关于科林斯僭主柏利安得（前625—585任僭主）有一个著名的故事，即他曾遣使向米利都僭主忒拉息布罗询问长久统治之道，后者将他的使者带到谷地里，不断砍掉身边那些长得最高的谷穗。使者回来告诉他之后，他明白了后者的意思，于是剪除身边一批最有势力的权臣。这是希罗多德的记载，见《历史》，Ⅴ.92。亚里士多德的记载则完全相反，说是米利都僭主向柏利安得求教，见《政治学》，Ⅲ.13。

② 《世界历史词典》，上海辞书出版社，1985年版，第713页。还有的学者认为，到公元前4世纪，"僭主"一词才具有贬义（蒋贤斌：《论贡斯当对僭主政治的研究》，《湖南科技学院学报》2006年第4期），这是没有道理的。实际上希腊人从什么时候开始反对僭主政治，或者说从什么时候产生了这个概念（公元前7世纪中叶或之前），就从什么时候开始赋予其贬义了。因为，即使在古希腊的早期它没有"暴君"的意思，但其含义仅是"指未经合法程序而取得政权的人"这一点就足够了（安德鲁斯《希腊僭主》中译本前言），就足以表明因为它的程序非法，人们对它的反感和憎恶了。至于个别诗人在诗中把"僭主"与"王"等同，那仅仅是个别诗人的做法，不具有普遍性。更多的情况是，人们反对僭主政治，鄙夷僭主行为。如萨福，如梭伦，等等，举不胜举。

③ 安德鲁斯：《希腊僭主》，商务印书馆，1997年版，第3页。

④ 第欧根尼·拉尔修：《名哲言行录》，吉林人民出版社，2003年版，第59页。一说克莱俄布卢后来成为林达斯的僭主。

公元前 6 世纪末，雅典的克利斯提尼改革，所制定的陶片放逐法，就是为了对付那些潜在的僭主，目的就在于防止僭主政治的重演。

马克思指出："僭主政治是建立在篡夺权力的基础上的，在希腊从来没有获得巩固的地位，始终被认为是非法的；杀害僭主被认为是一件功勋。"[①] 历史事实也是这样。公元前 514 年，两位青年哈墨迪（Harmodius）与阿里托格同（Aristogiton）因刺杀僭主希庇阿斯（约前 560 — 490；前 525 — 510），[②] 失败被害，雅典人尊他们为英雄，并在雅典广场树立了刺杀僭主的两英雄雕像，[③] 以永久纪念他们。还在广场和卫城上树立了记载僭主们的罪行的石柱。[④] 还在陶工区为他们修建了公墓。他们的家族获得了永久性的荣誉。[⑤] 时间过了一个多世纪以后，到了公元前 346 年，演说家埃斯奇涅斯（Aischines）在公共法庭的演讲中，还称他们的勇气"至今仍未被超越"，"凡赞美他们行为者都会感到，他们的赞美之词永远难以与两人完成的伟大事业媲美"。[⑥] 公元前 510 年，希庇阿斯被逐出雅典、结束了僭主政治之后，"雅典公民大会每次开会前都由传令人诅咒任何一个想做僭主的人"。[⑦] 关于这一点，周洪祥博士的《古代雅典公民大会研究》为我们提供了更为详尽的细节："公民大会开始时，首先要进行净化仪式。仪式上一只幼猪会被杀死，然后它的尸体由一名专职的官员拿着绕会场一周。古代雅典人认为猪血能够净化它所包围的地方。随后，传令官就会大声宣读对那些误导民众的演说家和其他人的诅咒。其中多为雅典人对可能在公民大会上欺骗人民、伤害人民的言行的诅咒，但也有一句涉及雅典人对独裁政体的极度憎恨：'让那些打算成为僭主或打算恢复僭主制的人及其整个家族痛苦地毁灭'。在同时，对其它一些希腊神的奉献仪式也要举行，结果由议事会的一位成员向公众宣读。"[⑧]

公元前 336 年，——这时候雅典人都已经沦入马其顿人的统治之下了，——雅典人通过了一项反僭主制的法律。其中规定任何人杀死企图在雅典建立僭主政治的人都属无罪。法律的内容被刻在一根保存下来的石柱上。石柱上半部的浮雕，是民主女神德谟克拉提亚（Democratia，"民主制"的化身），正在给"人民"的化身、一个长着胡子的成年男性雅典公民加冕。从法律的条文到浮雕的内容都反映了雅典人对民主制的强烈追求和向往，以及民主思想、反僭主思想在雅典人心中的根

---

① 《摩尔根〈古代社会〉一书摘要》，《马克思恩格斯全集》，第 45 卷，人民出版社，1985 年版，第 513 页。

② 希庇亚斯是庇西特拉图的长子。庇西特拉图死后继为僭主，与弟希帕库斯共同统治。亚里士多德说，哈墨迪和阿里托格同刺杀僭主的举动是为了报复，因为庇西特拉图家族当众羞辱了哈墨迪的妹妹，并羞辱了哈墨迪本人。哈墨迪的行为是为了他的妹妹，而阿里托格同挺身而出则是为了哈墨迪。见《政治学》第 5 卷第 10 章。具体情况是，哈墨迪与阿里斯托格同是同性恋关系，而希帕库斯也爱上了哈墨迪，但遭到拒绝，于是转而羞辱哈墨迪的妹妹。先是让她在泛雅典娜节作为持篮者，届时又拒绝她参加。持篮者在宗教仪式中是一个很光荣的职务，遭拒绝则被看作是对她家族的莫大侮辱。由此导致了哈墨迪和阿里斯托格同的报复行动。修昔底德则直接说他们二人是"制定计划，使出浑身解数，推翻僭主政治"。见《伯罗奔尼撒战争史》徐松岩译本第 350 页。希庇亚斯于公元前 510 年被逐出雅典后，先是到了小亚，后投靠波斯。在大流士第二次远征希腊时（前 490）随波斯军在马拉松登陆，进攻自己的祖国。时已老迈。马拉松战役波斯人大败，一说他死于此役，一说在马拉松战役后死于莱姆诺斯岛。

③ 见"百度图片"，又见《希腊艺术与考古学》（美国学者约翰·格里菲思·佩德利著，广西师范大学出版社，2005 年版第 206 页）等书。此为罗马时代的仿制品，大理石质地，高 1.95 米，那不勒斯国立博物馆收藏。原作为青铜雕像，作者为克里蒂乌斯和内西奥特斯，公元前 477 – 476 年左右创作，树立于雅典广场。一说该青铜雕像也属重新制作、并重新树立的，最初的原作在公元前 480 年波斯人入侵雅典时被运走。朱龙华编《古代世界史参考图集》第 330 幅图片"杀暴君者群像"与此略异。

④ 修昔底德：《伯罗奔尼撒战争史》，徐松岩译本，第 351 页。

⑤ 奥斯温·默里：《早期希腊》，上海人民出版社，2008 年版，第 208 页。该书还说，"刺杀僭主者雕像"被置于卫城之上；当雕像于公元前 480 年为波斯人移走后，雅典人立刻替换了雕像；被移走的雕像后来被亚历山大在帕赛波里斯（Persepolis）发现，并大张旗鼓地把它归还给了雅典。

⑥ 奥斯温·默里：《早期希腊》，上海人民出版社，2008 年版，第 208 页。

⑦ 《古希腊悲剧喜剧全集》，第 7 卷，第 307 页，注①。

⑧ 周洪祥博士论文：《古代雅典公民大会研究》，电子版，第 48 页。

深蒂固。①

　　亚里士多德（前384—322）记载："当时雅典所实行的关于僭主的法律……，特别是其中涉及建立僭主政治的那一条。条文如下：'这是雅典的法令和祖宗原则：任何人为了达到僭主统治目的而起来作乱者，或任何人帮助建立僭主政治者，他自己和他的家族都应被剥夺公民权利。'"②

　　亚里士多德还指出，在古希腊，"伟大的荣耀不会加于杀死一个窃贼的人，而会授予杀死僭主的人"，③这说明作为杀死僭主的英雄，在古希腊具有无上的光荣。这种光荣除了像指挥马拉松战役打败波斯侵略军那样的荣誉可以与之比美，其他则很难超过。④

　　前述古希腊抒情诗中那两篇无名氏的作品《哈墨迪与阿里托格同》和《山乡》，即反映了古希腊人普遍反对僭主政治和歌颂反僭主英雄的思想。在古希腊人的祝酒歌（酒令歌）里，还有赞美哈墨狄奥斯（哈墨迪）的内容，称作"哈墨狄奥斯歌"，即赞美刺杀僭主希帕库斯的英雄哈摩狄奥斯的赞歌。⑤不仅杀死僭主的人被视为英雄而无上光荣，就是曾经攻击过僭政的人也受到人们的怀念，被编入祝酒歌之中。据亚里士多德记载："早在阿尔克迈翁家族（在斯巴达的支持下驱逐僭主希庇亚斯）之前，喀东就攻击过僭政，因此人们在酒歌中也对他表示了纪念：

　　　　还要为喀东满斟此杯，孩子们！切莫忘却，
　　　　如果应当举杯敬祝善良的雄杰。"⑥

　　饮酒亦即会饮，是古希腊人的一种非常普遍而又频繁的活动。在这种普遍的频繁的身心均享愉悦的活动中，竟然包含着反僭主的思想内容，其影响和效果也就可想而知。

　　古希腊人的文学作品中涉及反僭主思想的内容也很多，笔者仅以戏剧为例，略作说明。

　　欧里庇得斯的悲剧《奥瑞斯特斯》（又译奥列斯特）中，主人公奥列斯特说阿伽门农"他配统治希腊，不是一个僭主，而是一个有神一样力量的人。"⑦揭示了僭主政治的非法性。在《请愿的妇女》一剧中，欧里庇得斯把雅典的先王提修斯看作是民主制度的创建者，借提修斯之口抨击僭主制度："对城邦没有什么比僭主更有害的了，城邦有僭主，首先就没有公共的法律，他一个人统治着，把法律掌握在自己的手里，于是平等不复存在。"⑧

　　阿里斯托芬的喜剧《地母节妇女》中，传令女一口气说出了10件在雅典妇女看来是罪不容赦、最值得诅咒的事情。其中第三件就是如果有谁"想当独裁僭主，想恢复僭主制度，……就诅咒他本

---

① 保罗·卡特里奇：《剑桥插图古希腊史》，山东画报出版社，2005年版，第156页、157页。魏凤莲：《古希腊民主制研究的历史考察》，山东大学出版社，2008年版，第7页。

② 亚里士多德：《雅典政制》，商务印书馆，1959年版，第20页。

③ 《亚里士多德全集》第9卷，中国人民大学出版社，1994年版，第50页。

④ 据希罗多德记载，马拉松战役前，雅典人内部关于战与不战问题，十将军意见各异。当不战的意见有可能占上风的时候，认为应当马上出战的米泰亚得找到十将军之一的当时担任军事执政官的卡利马库斯，对他说："卡利马库斯，现在的雅典，或者沦为奴隶，或者保持其自由，从而使人们世世代代都永远铭记你，甚至使你的声誉超过哈墨迪和阿里托格同，至于如何抉择就都取决于你了。……"米泰亚得的一番话赢得了卡利马库斯的支持。由于增加了这一票，所以最终作出了出战的决定。希罗多德：《历史》，徐松岩译本第337页。

⑤ 阿里斯托芬：《阿卡奈人》，《古希腊悲剧喜剧全集》第6卷第83页。另据【美】时代－生活图书公司《民主的曙光》（山东画报出版社2001年版）第87页说："会饮的活动最终以当时流行的一首劝酒歌而告结束。这首劝酒歌唱道：'和我一起饮酒吧，和我一起奏乐吧，和我一起相爱吧，和我一起戴上王冠吧；我痴迷时你同我一起痴迷，我清醒时你同我一道清醒！'"

⑥ 亚里士多德：《雅典政制》，见《亚里士多德全集》，第10卷，中国人民大学出版社1997年版，第23页。阿尔克迈翁家族是僭政垮台的最主要原因，克利斯提尼就是这个家族的，他成为平民的领袖，领导了著名的改革。

⑦ 《古希腊悲剧喜剧全集》，第3卷，第193页。

⑧ 《古希腊悲剧喜剧全集》，第4卷，第190页。

人和他一家人不得好死"。① 这时候歌队齐唱："我们也向神祈祷，愿这些愿望为城邦而实现，为人民而实现。"反映了古希腊人对僭主政治的痛恨。

阿里斯托芬的喜剧《吕西斯特拉特》中，男歌队长有两段台词②："我们生来是城邦公民，珍惜自由。快快脱下大氅，投入战斗，国事紧急，岂能高枕无忧！这里气氛紧张，乌云压城，形势比预料的严重得多。一个狡黠的计划已经出笼，僭主希庇阿斯的影子就在眼前晃动。" "这些女人想把僭主强加给我们，这光景岂能容忍！我要带上短剑，把它夹在香桃木树枝中间，全副武装，站在阿里托格同身边。" 阿里托格同即前述刺杀僭主希帕库斯的两英雄之一。行刺当天，他们把短剑藏在一捆捆香桃木（又译桃金娘）树枝中间，参加节日活动。这两段话深刻反映了古希腊人对僭主政治保持高度警惕、勿使重演的思想。

阿里斯托芬的喜剧《骑士》中，腊肠贩对德莫斯说讨好的话、做讨好的事，德莫斯问他："你是谁呀？是不是哈摩狄奥斯（又译哈墨迪）高贵的后代？③你的行为很高贵，人也真够朋友！"④言语中歌颂了反僭主的英雄，揭示了在古希腊作为反僭主的英雄的后代都是非常高贵的，也受到人们的敬仰和崇拜。

阿里斯托芬的喜剧《马蜂》中，更多次以否定的态度和抨击的口吻，提到"僭主行为"、"僭主统治"、"独裁僭主"，⑤表达了对僭主政治极端憎恶的思想。

众所周知，古希腊的戏剧表演规模是非常大的，几乎到了全民参与的程度，⑥公民的观剧热情非常高，为古代世界任何其它民族所不及。好多剧场都能够容纳一两万人。在这种全民观剧、盛况空前的气氛中，剧作家的剧本中能够见缝插针、不失时机地穿插一些对僭主政治的揭露、批判或者挪揄，并且通过舞台上的演员恰到好处地表演出来，这种宣传效果亦即政治影响，是非常大的。它在观众中引起互动，引起观众的思想共鸣，从而有助于形成一种崇尚民主、反对独裁、崇尚合法斗

---

① 《古希腊悲剧喜剧全集》，第 7 卷，第 307 页。
② 阿里斯托芬：《吕西斯特拉特》，《古希腊悲剧喜剧全集》，第 7 卷，第 211、212 页。
③ 哈摩狄奥斯是刺杀僭主希帕库斯的英雄。
④ 阿里斯托芬：《骑士》，《古希腊悲剧喜剧全集》，第 6 卷，第 172－173 页。
⑤ 见《古希腊悲剧喜剧全集》，第 6 卷，第 397 页、402 页、403 页。
⑥ 美国学者约翰·格里菲思·佩德利在《希腊艺术与考古学》一书中曾提出了一个问题："雅典的剧场：观众中有女性吗？"（见该书第 323 页，广西师范大学出版社 2005 年版）笔者认为，应该是有女性的。尽管雅典妇女的社会地位并不高，是一个有公民身份（伯里克利时代关于只有父母双方都是公民的人才能享有公民权的规定，反映了雅典妇女属于公民）但却并不享有充分公民权的群体，处于自古以来因自然分工影响所形成的男主外女主内的社会分工格局中，不能参加公民大会、陪审法庭等政治活动，甚至也不能参加体育竞技，基本上是以管理家务、生儿育女为天职，以家庭这个小圈子为活动范围。但是，雅典妇女也并不是完全不能抛头露面的，她们毕竟还能够走出家门，参加一些宗教活动，如泛雅典娜节、地母节、酒神节等等，从事一些商务或劳务之类的谋生活动，以及参加一些社交集会活动。从萨福的抒情诗中可以看出当时女子的自由程度。由能够参加宗教活动这一点，笔者判断，雅典妇女应该是能够参加观剧这一文化活动的。她们毕竟是自由人，属于公民群体中的一员，男性同胞似乎没有理由不让她们参加。关于妇女能够参加观剧，柏拉图的作品向我们透露出了些许信息。柏拉图在《高尔吉亚篇》中说："那么我们现在已经发现了一种修辞学的形式（指悲剧。——引者），是说给由儿童、妇女、男人、奴隶、自由人组成的民众听的，这种形式我们不能过分地加以崇敬，因为我们把它说成是一种奉承。"（对话人认为戏剧的目的也属于倾向于快乐、使观众满意一类，所以苏格拉底把这种活动说成是一种"奉承"。《柏拉图全集》第 1 卷第 395 页，人民出版社 2002 年版）据此看来，观剧的人群中，不仅有妇女，而且还有奴隶，亦即贴身侍奉主人的仆从。柏拉图在《法篇》中，就若干表演者，或者讲述史诗，或者表演竖琴，或者表演悲剧，或者表演喜剧，或者表演木偶戏，让不同的观众来评奖，对话的主角雅典人发表意见说："如果是儿童在做决定，他们无疑会认为表演木偶戏的人应该得奖，大一些的孩子会选上演喜剧的人，有教养的妇女、青年，他们也许是绝大多数，会选悲剧。"（《柏拉图全集》第 3 卷，第 406 页）可见，雅典妇女不仅能够参加观剧，而且很有可能还是观众中的主要组成部分之一。

争的舆论氛围。阿里斯托芬在《马蜂》一剧中说，独裁僭主"这名称已经有五十年没听说过了；[①]但如今它比咸鱼还贱地又在市场里流通了。如果有人想买大鲈鱼，不想买小鳀鱼，旁边的鳀（ti）鱼贩子立刻就会嚷道：'这家伙买鱼，像个独裁僭主！'如果有人要韭葱作为烧白杨鱼的佐料，那个卖菜的妇人就会用一只眼睛瞟（piao）他一下，说道，'告诉我，你要韭葱吗？你是不是想当独裁僭主，叫雅典给你进贡佐料？'"[②]连市场上的小商小贩都把挪揄"独裁僭主"当成了口头禅，这可能有些文学夸张的意味，但它在一定程度上反映了当时的社会现实，也是不容置疑的。

古希腊戏剧中的这些反僭主内容，应该说具有重要的现实意义，这就是影响到当时公民们的思想观念，使公民们加深了对僭主政治的认识。一方面，僭主政治是独裁统治，是暴政，连君主制也不如——这是僭主政治遭到人们唾弃的主要原因——另一方面，加深了对僭主政治的非法性的认识。僭主政治是野心家超出法律范围之外，凭借欺诈或暴力，不择手段攫取城邦权力的产物。不管僭主们施政效果如何，在取得权力时失去了程序正义，因此就是不齿的，所以遭到了诗人也好，一般平民大众也好，以及思想家们的口诛笔伐。这也意味着只有合法竞争、合法斗争、和平竞争，才是政治舞台上所应该遵循的。笔者认为，这应该是当时古希腊人的一个比较普遍的思想，只是没有明确地提出来，也没有上升到理论的高度来认识它罢了。

戏剧舞台上的反僭主政治宣传，影响到人们的思想观念，还包括形成这样一种社会舆论：谁通过非法手段上台，谁就是僭主，而不管他上台后干了多少好事。这种社会舆论直接有利于杜绝或减少那些想在政治上不择手段的人的产生，有利于迫使那些想在政治上有所作为的人在仕途上去走正道，最终结果有利于民主政治的巩固和发展。僭主实际上成为政治舞台上的一个反面典型，起着警诫世人的作用，正如"孔子作春秋，乱臣贼子惧"一样。

《早期希腊》一书的作者奥斯温·默里指出："僭主政治的经验创造出一种向往和仇恨，给希腊人反对君主制的政治态度以永恒的影响，直到希腊化世界庞大的领土国家建立为止。"[③]在笔者看来，古希腊僭主政治的出现不仅仅是影响了希腊人向往民主、反对君主政治亦即反对专制统治的政治态度，还应该包括影响了希腊人仇恨僭主、反对非法手段、追求程序正义的政治态度，只有这样理解才是全面的。也就是说古希腊人的反僭主政治不仅仅反对的是暴虐的统治即暴政，同时反对的也包括非法斗争的手段。

关于历史学家希罗多德和修昔底德的反僭主思想，以及思想家柏拉图和亚里士多德的反僭主思想，笔者在前文中已经或多或少有所提及，限于篇幅这里就不再赘述了。总起来说，笔者读他们的作品，发现也和戏剧作品一样，对僭主政治均持批判和否定态度，但是其着力点都在揭露和批判其暴政的一面，没有明确提出僭政非法的概念，也没有就僭政非法问题，亦即权力的正当性问题进行讨论。或许是这个问题太过于"常识"，对于古希腊人来说不言而喻了？修昔底德曾经指出，僭主政府"他们政策的主要目标是安全"，[④]亚里士多德曾经把僭主政治实行独裁统治的目的归结为"在于自卫"，[⑤]这在一定程度上都触及到了非法问题，或者说认识到了非法问题。因为僭主政治都是通过非法手段取得独裁权力的，非法性问题一定会像近代法国思想家贡斯当（1767—1830）所指出的那样，就像鬼魂一样纠缠着他们，[⑥]所以建立政权后如何维护自己的安全，亦即维护自己的统

---

① 庇士特拉图在公元前560年借民众的力量，夺取政权，成为雅典城的独裁君主（僭主），死后其子希庇阿斯和希帕库斯当权，很残暴，希帕库斯公元前514年被刺死，希庇阿斯公元前510年被放逐，公元前490年死于马拉松战役或莱姆诺斯岛。阿里斯托芬的《马蜂》于公元前422年上演。
② 阿里斯托芬：《马蜂》，见《古希腊悲剧喜剧全集》第6卷，第403页。
③ 奥斯温·默里：《早期希腊》，上海人民出版社，2008年版，第129页。
④ 修昔底德：《伯罗奔尼撒战争史》，徐松岩译本第11页，广西师范大学出版社2004年版。
⑤ 亚里士多德：《修辞术》，《亚里士多德全集》第9卷第370页，中国人民大学出版社1994年版。
⑥ 贡斯当：《古代人的自由与现代人的自由》，上海人民出版社，2003年版，第254页。

治地位，也就成了僭主们的第一要务。

五　政治学研究与合法竞争思想的关系

著名学者钱穆在《中国历史研究法》一书中指出："研究制度，必须明白在此制度之背后实有一套思想与一套理论之存在。"①其实，何止是制度背后有一套思想与理论之存在，就是研究者本人在研究的背后，也同样有一套思想与理论之存在。

政治学研究就是如此。其"背后"，亦即其内在前提和逻辑起点，就是为了实现公平竞争、和平竞争、合法斗争。在马基雅弗里主义者那里，是不需要政治学研究的，只需凭借和相信"为达目的不择手段"以及"丛林法则"就足够了。

政治学是什么？政治学就是研究政治体制、政治行为的学问，也就是研究国家及其活动的学问。亚里士多德研究政治学，主要是研究城邦政体，探寻城邦政体何者为佳。在亚里士多德看来，"一个政体就是对城邦中的各种官职——尤其是拥有最高权力的官职的某种制度或安排。"②那么，"制度或安排"是什么意思？毫无疑问，就是遵循一定的规则去设置和运转。规则是制度或安排的灵魂。体制要按一定的规则设置，行为要按一定的规则运转。且说后者。按规则运转，便必然表现为和平竞争、合法竞争、合法斗争。通俗地说就是和平、合法地去争（争权夺利）与斗（一决高下）。政治是经济的集中体现。参与政治，归根结底是为了实现（亦即争）本人、本家族或本集团、或本民族的名与利。利即经济的、政治的、文化的各个方面的利益。"公民政治依据的是平等或同等的原则，公民们认为应该由大家轮番进行统治。其更原始的根据是，大家轮流执政更加符合自然；……"③"法律也成了一纸契约，用智者吕科弗朗的话来说，法律是彼此间对公正的承诺"④这里无论是"原则"或"原始的根据"，还是"法律"、"契约"、"承诺"，其精髓无不都是和平竞争、合法竞争。

亚里士多德认为，"争取统治权力的凭据应该是定国安邦所依赖的要素。因此，只有良好的出身、自由人的身份和财富才可以用作竞争官职的理所当然的凭据。""担任官职的人必须是自由人和纳税人"，"财富和自由是必须的条件"，"没有前两种条件城邦就无法维持存在"。⑤"条件"成为"争取统治权力"和"竞争官职"必须遵循的规则和依据，这无异于说没有和平竞争、合法竞争的原则作支撑，城邦就不成其为城邦了。

亚里士多德在《政治学》第4卷第14、15、16三章中，讨论了政体的三个部分或要素（议事机构、行政官职、司法机构）的合理组合问题。⑥他认为，"一切政体都有三个部分或要素，一个好的立法者必须考虑什么样的组合才对个别的政体有利。……三者之中第一个部分或要素是与公共事务有关的议事机构，第二个要素与行政官职有关，它决定应该由什么人来主宰什么人或事，和应该通过什么样的方式来选举各类官员。第三个要素决定司法机构的组成。"（第148页）

在考察了作为政体主要构成部分的议事职能之后，亚里士多德接下来考察各种官职的分配问题。"因为这也牵涉到政体的一个部分或要素，并有着多种多样的差别——在官职的数目、权力的范围、官职的任期等方面都有很大差别；每一种官职都有一定的任期，有的为六个月，有的时间稍短；有的为一年，有的城邦的官职任期更长。应当研究，各种官职的任期应为终身制或长时期还是应为短

---

① 见中国世界古代史研究网《如何研究政治史？》一文（作者未知）。
② 《亚里士多德全集》，第9卷，第84页。
③ 《亚里士多德全集》，第9卷，第86页。
④ 《亚里士多德全集》，第9卷，第91页。
⑤ 《亚里士多德全集》，第9卷，第99页。
⑥ 《亚里士多德全集》，第9卷，第148页以下。

时期，应由同一些人多次担任同一些官职还是不应允许同一人两次担任同样的官职，而只能有一次任职机会。此外关于官员的委任也有多种差别，譬如官员应从什么人中产生，由什么人来任命，以及以什么方式任命等等。……"（第 152 — 153 页）

"让我们来详细研究官员的任用问题。以三方面的标准去衡量，所有不同的任用方式必然是出自这三个方面的相互关联。其中第一个方面是由什么人来任命各类官员，第二个方面是从什么人中间选拔官员，剩余的一个方面是以什么方式任命官员。上述三方面标准中的每一项又可以进一步分出三种差别来：（1）由全体公民或某一些公民来任用行政官员；（2）从全体公民或者从合乎财产、出身、德性等方面规定条件的某些公民中选用官员，或者规定诸如此类的其他条件，……；（3）或者通过选举或者通过抽签任用行政官员。上述差别还须归类合并，我是说有的官职由某些人任命而有的由全体公民任命，有的从全体公民中选举产生，有的从某些公民中产生，有的通过选举，有的通过抽签。（第 156 页）毫无疑问，亚里士多德所要研究和确定的官员的不同任用"方式"，就是规则。现实中如果把这些规则运用于官员的任命中去，那么城邦政治的运转必然是和平的、有序的，亦即合法的、公平的、公正的。

亚里士多德具体分析："以上每一种差别又可以分出四种方式。或者由全体公民从全体公民中选举产生行政官员，或者由全体公民从全体公民中通过抽签确定行政官员；又及，从全体公民中选用官员时既可以分部分进行，比如按部族、街坊和祠堂进行，直至所有公民都轮到为止，亦可以一直从全体公民中选用；有时以这种方式有时以那种方式进行（即是说以选举的方式或以抽签的方式进行）。再如，若是由某些人来任命行政官员，他们或者可以从全体公民中通过选举的办法来任命官员，也可以从全体公民中通过抽签的办法来任命官员；或者，从某些公民中通过选举任命官员，或从某些公民中通过抽签任命官员；或者，某些官员以这种方式产生而另一些官员以那种方式产生——我指的是某些官员从全体公民中选举产生而另一些通过抽签产生。于是，除去合二为一的数种方式外，我们一共举出了十二种任用官员的方式。"（第 156 — 157 页）

亚里士多德分析这些不同的任用方式与政体性质的关系，亦即对于政体性质的影响，如，"由全体公民从全体公民中通过选举或抽签的办法来任命行政官员，或者同时采用两种方法，即是说有些官员通过选举产生而另一些官员通过抽签产生"，就具有"平民性质"。"某些官职从特定的人选中选举产生和某些官职从特定人选中抽签产生（当然这种办法不见得会在寡头政体中出现，但性质还是一样的），是寡头政体的做法，或者由某些人从某些特定的人选中兼以选举和抽签两种方式任用官员。而由某些人以全体公民中或者由全体公民从某些人中选举产生官员的做法就具有贵族政体的性质"（第 156 — 158 页）等等。

亚里士多德进一步指出："任用行政官员的各种不同方式，它们分别对应于各种不同的政体形式。要想知道哪种方式对哪种形式的政体有利或应当通过什么样的方式来任命行政官员，就必须清楚各类官职的职权是什么。所谓官职的职权，我指的是诸如财政或防务方面的权力；例如将军的职权就不同于管理市场上契约的官员的权力。"（第 158 页）在亚里士多德看来，在一个城邦里，当规范了各类官职的职权、各类官职都在职权范围内行事，是实现政治上的有序状态的必不可少的条件。

接下来，亚里士多德考察城邦政体的三个部分或要素中的法庭审判。"法庭审判方面的差异也可以用三项标准去衡量：（1）法庭由什么人组成；（2）法庭审理什么事情；（3）法庭的成员以什么方式产生。"（第 158 页）根据法庭审理什么事情的不同，亚里士多德认为有八种形式的法庭。对于那些"审理细小契约讼案、凶杀和涉外案件的几种法庭"，他认为无须赘述，而"关系到城邦政治的法庭则须详加阐述"，认为"这些案件如果处置失当，就会在政体内引起分裂和骚乱"。他还分析了任用陪审员的方式，或者是由全体公民组成法庭，或者是只从部分公民中通过选举或者通过抽签产生陪审员，组成法庭，或者选举、抽签两种方式并用。亚里士多德分析了陪审法庭的组成方式与政体性质的关系，指出"从全体公民中选用陪审官员来审理一切讼案"，属于平民政体；"由某些公民组成的法庭来审理一切讼案"，属于寡头政体；"所有的陪审官员之中有的从全体公民中产生，有的从某些公民中产生"，属于贵族政体或共和政体。（第160页）由此可见，组成法庭的方式，亦即范式，或者说是原则，是多么重要。

亚里士多德关于城邦政体尤其是城邦政体三个部分或要素的组合问题的考察和研究，十分详细，以致笔者读来都有些繁琐之感。非常明显，亚里士多德是以现实中的希腊城邦特别是雅典为考察研究的对象，加上自己的理想和规划。即使从表面上，我们也能够觉察出，按这样的理想规划建设起来的城邦，一定是政治稳定、运作有序，一切遵循规则，一切按规则办事，和平竞争、合法竞争成为城邦的政治主流。而这些也恰恰是政治学研究的终极目的。

合法竞争是以规则为前提的，所以城邦政制的设计者无不殚精竭虑，制定规则。规则上升到法的高度，便成为法律和法则。这从柏拉图身上看得也很清楚。

柏拉图说："绝对服从已有法律的人才能对其同胞取得胜利（指国家对其委以重任），我们只能把诸神使臣的工作交给这样的人，让他担任最高职位，次一等的职位则通过竞选产生，其他职位也同样通过有序的选拔来确定。"[1]柏拉图说："建立一种体制要做两件事：一件事是把职务授予个人；另一件事是给官员提供一部法典。"[2]法典是什么？法典是系统、完备的法律、法则的汇总。如上所述，法则是上升到了法的高度的规则。

柏拉图在《法律篇》中为自己的第二理想国马格尼西亚设置了周密的法律、法则以及程序、规则等等，其中体现了他非常重视程序的正义，而程序正义本身就是一种合法竞争思想。

柏拉图强调，"要高度注意最初的官员任命，要尽可能使用最确定、最优秀的方法来做这件事"。[3]他设计的"最令人满意的程序"[4]就是：第一步，提名；第二步，初选；第三步，复选。其中还包括公示和审查。

以选举执法官为例。柏拉图说："要让这种制度（指第二理想国马格尼西亚——引者）能在时间的流逝中存活下来，就要按照这样一个过程任命这个委员会（即执法官——引者）。那些在骑兵或步兵队里携带武器，并在年纪许可的时间内上战场打仗的人都应在选举执法官时有自己的声音。选举应当在被国家认为最庄严的圣地举行。每位选举人都要把他的提名牌放在祭坛上，上面写着他提名的候选人，候选人的父亲、候选人的部落、候选人所属的居民区，提名人自己的名字也要写在牌子上，还要写上与被提名人相同的内容。任何人若是对提名牌的内容有疑问，只要他愿意，就可以把提名牌拿到市场上去公布，不少于三十天。提名的候选人可达三百人，由当局把候选名单向整个共同体公布，然后每个公民将根据自己的意愿对候选人进行初选，负责选举的官员会把得票在先的一百人公布。整个选举的第三步在两次献祭之间进行，公民们可以随意从这一百名候选人中选举自己喜欢的人，得票最多的三十七人将在接受审查后由官方任命为执法官。"[5]

柏拉图规定了"执法官的任期不得超过二十年，低于五十岁的公民不得当选。"[6]还规定了执法官的职责。

按照顺序，柏拉图任命马格尼西亚的其他官员，下一步为挑选军队的将领以及他们的助手，即主帅和副帅，以及各个部落的步兵指挥官，即统领。"首先是将军职位的提名，将军必须由我 们

---

① 《柏拉图全集》，第3卷，第475页。
② 《柏拉图全集》，第3卷，第493页。
③ 《柏拉图全集》，第3卷，第508页。
④ 《柏拉图全集》，第3卷，第509页。
⑤ 《柏拉图全集》，第3卷，第509页。此段引文中两处"执法官"原文皆作"执政官"，似不确。
⑥ 《柏拉图全集》，第3卷，第511页。

的公民担任，由执法官提名，由所有当过兵的人或正在服役的军人选举。若是有人认为某人不适宜被提名为将军候选人，那么他应该提出自己的候选人，并指出要用自己的候选人代替哪一位候选人，他还要发誓，然后把自己的候选人当作竞选者提出来，举手表决获得多数通过后才被列入选举名单。获得选票最多的三个人将被任命为将军，在通过与执法官相同的审查后掌管军事。当选的将军们可以提名步兵统领的候选人，共十二名，每个部落一名，整个选举过程和将军的选举一样，也要经过候选人复议、投票选举和最终审查。……将军和主帅由所有军人通过投票选举，统领由所有步兵选举，副帅由所有骑兵投票选举。……选举副帅的准备阶段与选举将军一样由执法官提名，复议候选人和投票选举的过程也和选将军一样。……副帅候选人要由骑兵们来投票，得票最多的两名候选人将成为整个骑兵部队的指挥官。"①

柏拉图还规定："在投票过程中有两次机会可以对选举结果表示异议，但若有人对选举结果第三次表示异议，那么整个选举无效，需要重选。"②

关于议事会的产生，柏拉图是这样设计的："要建立一个由三十打人组成的议事会——三百六十这个数字便于进一步划分——这些人将分成四组，每组九十人，即每一等级的公民选举九十名议员。首先要在最高财产等级的全体公民中举行强制性的投票，弃权者要交纳法律规定的罚金。投票结束后，当选者的名字要及时记录下来。第二天由第二财产等级按同样的程序投票。第三天由全体公民投票选举第三财产等级的议员，但第三等级的公民必须参加，而最低的第四等级的公民如果不参加可以免除罚金。第四天，这个最低的第四等级的议员要由全体公民投票选举，但对选择弃权的第三、第四等级的公民免除处罚，而那些第一等级和第二等级的成员如果拒绝参加投票就要受处罚，第二等级的罚金是先前罚金的三倍，第一等级的罚金是先前罚金的四倍。第五天，当局要向公众公布选举记录，对这些当选者再进行一次全体公民的投票，若有拒不参加者仍要处以原先数量的罚金。从每个财产等级中选出 180 人，③再根据抽签决定其中的一半送交审查，这些人将组成当年的议事会。"④

这里顺便再补充关于柏拉图的反僭主政治思想。柏拉图认为，在所有的政体形式中，最糟糕的也是最不正义的是僭主政治。僭主"在他早期对任何人都是满面堆笑，逢人问好，不以君主自居，于公于私他都有求必应，豁免穷人的债务，分配土地给平民和自己的随从，到处给人以和蔼可亲的印象。"⑤——这分明指的是庇西特拉图。但是随后，僭主"凶相毕露"，⑥"打倒了许多反对者，攫取了国家的最高权力"，⑦"控制着轻信的民众，不可抑制地要使人流血；他诬告别人，使人法庭受审，谋害人命，罪恶地舔尝同胞的血液；或将人流放域外，或判人死刑；或取消债款，或分人土地。最后，这种人或自己被人杀掉，或由人变成了豺狼"。⑧柏拉图指出，"僭主是杀父之徒，是老人（父和老人均指人民）的凶恶的照料者了"。这时候，"人民发现自己象俗语所说的，跳出油锅又入火坑；不受自由人的奴役了（指极端民主制），反受起奴隶（指僭主）的奴役来了；本想争取过分的极端自由的，却不意落入了最严酷最痛苦的奴役之中了。"⑨柏拉图的反僭主政治思想，

---

① 《柏拉图全集》，第 3 卷，第 511 – 512 页。此处引文中的"骑兵部队"四字原文为"武装力量"。今据张智仁、何勤华译《法律篇》第 167 页改。

② 《柏拉图全集》，第 3 卷，第 512 页。

③ 此处王晓朝原文为"来自各等级的一百八十人就这样选举出来"，含义模糊，今据张智仁译本改，见张译本第 168 页。

④ 《柏拉图全集》，第 3 卷，第 512 – 513 页。

⑤ 柏拉图：《理想国》，商务印书馆，1986 年版，第 347 页。

⑥ 柏拉图：《理想国》，商务印书馆，1986 年版，第 351 页。

⑦ 柏拉图：《理想国》，商务印书馆，1986 年版，第 346 页。

⑧ 柏拉图：《理想国》，商务印书馆，1986 年版，第 345 页。

⑨ 柏拉图：《理想国》，商务印书馆，1986 年版，第 351 页。

与他的追求程序正义思想是一致的。他对僭主政治的尖锐批评，被前苏联学者涅尔谢相茨认为"可能是全世界文献中最精彩的批评"。①

通过上述柏拉图和亚里士多德政治学研究中的部分内容，我们就可以清楚地看出，无论是研究的出发点，还是它的归宿，都是为了实现城邦的正义，亦即所谓善。柏拉图认为"幸福生活不可缺少的前提条件首先就是我们自己不犯罪，同时也不因他人的错误行为而受苦。要满足第一个条件不难，但要同时有力量避免伤害却非常难，确实，只有一个办法可以满足这些前提条件，这就是变成全善。对社会来说也一样，如果这个社会变成善的，那么它的生活就是一种和平；如果这个社会变成恶的，那么就会有内外战争。"②如何实现城邦的"全善"呢？毫无疑问，就是建立一个法制健全、并能够实现法治的社会，也就是建立一个具有完备的法律、法规并且避免了人治而实行法治的社会。法制的基本要求是社会生活的各个领域都法律化了、制度化了，就像柏拉图在《法律篇》中所面面俱到、详加规定的那样。实行法制的主要标志就是城邦从立法、执法、司法、守法到法律监督等方面都有比较完备的法律和制度，而实行法治的主要标志则是城邦的任何机关、团体和个人，包括国家公职人员，都严格遵守法律和依法办事。这是体现在柏拉图《法律篇》中的主导精神。如前所述，人们参与政治，归根结底是为了实现名与利，亦即参与全社会的名与利的分配和再分配。其中，权力是第一位的；争与斗是必不可少的手段和形式。但是这种对权力的争与斗，是有序的还是无序的，是和平的还是暴力的，是公平的还是不择手段的，亦即权力的获得是合法的还是非法的，是合法竞争，还是非法竞争，是在法制的框架内，还是不受法制的约束，则是区别城邦正义或非正义、进而达到善或非善的根本标志。柏拉图说："我刚才把权力称作法律的使臣，这样说并非为了标新立异，而是因为我深信社会的生存或毁灭主要取决于这一点，而非取决于其他事情。法律一旦被滥用或废除，共同体的毁灭也就不远了；但若法律支配着权力，权力成为法律驯服的奴仆，那么人类的拯救和上苍对社会的赐福也就到来了。"③所以，笔者认为，虽然柏拉图、亚里士多德这些睿智的思想家们在自己的政治学研究中没有提出合法竞争、合法斗争的概念，但他们的这一思想却是十分明显的，已经是呼之欲出了。

他们殚精竭虑，"设立行政职位和任命行政官员，决定恰当的职位数量和适当的任用官员的方式"，"等这件事做完之后，接下去就确定这些行政部门的法律，决定有多少个部门和行政官，每个行政官员要用什么样的适当方式来进行管理"，④他们还要"在我们的国家里制定这些选举规则和对当选者进行审查"，要"依法任命官员和审查当选者"。⑤总而言之一句话，他们要极力寻求"管理国家事务的合理方式"，⑥归根结底不就是为了要实现城邦政治生活中的合理有序的公平竞争、合法竞争从而实现理想国家的长治久安吗？

六　民主政治精英的合法竞争思想（以梭伦为代表）

一般认为，雅典国家的民主政治是从梭伦改革开始的，梭伦改革为雅典国家奴隶主民主政治的确立奠定了基础。

在雅典国家，之所以能够建成民主政治体制，与梭伦及后来的克利斯提尼、埃菲阿特、伯里克

---

① 涅尔谢相茨：《古希腊政治学说》，商务印书馆，1991 年版，第 141 页。
② 《柏拉图全集》，第 3 卷，第 587 页。
③ 《柏拉图全集》，第 3 卷，第 475 页。
④ 《柏拉图全集》，第 3 卷，第 506 页。
⑤ 《柏拉图全集》，第 3 卷，第 510 页。
⑥ 《柏拉图全集》，第 3 卷，第 515 页。

利等一代一代政治精英崇尚民主、反对专制、具有强烈的合法竞争思想分不开，或者说，雅典国家民主政治的大厦，就是具有合法竞争思想的雅典公民在一代一代政治精英的领导下，通过不懈努力精心构筑起来的。民主政治体制是合法竞争思想在政治领域实践和操作的必然结果，倒过来说，民主政治体制的实践和操作必定是以合法竞争思想为指导。

从合法竞争的角度看，民主政治就是一种合法竞争的政治体制，这是民主政治的最大优势。虽然梭伦本人并没有提出合法竞争或公平竞争的理论或概念，但细察他的改革措施及他本人的思想，确是隐含了这一精神的，他的改革是以合法竞争思想为前提的。如按财产多寡划分公民为四个等级：

> 500 麦第姆诺[①] 第一等级
> 300 麦第姆诺 第二等级 （又称骑士级）
> 200 麦第姆诺 第三等级 （又称双牛级）
> 200 麦第姆诺以下者 第四等级 （又称日佣级）

并且规定了四个等级相应的政治权利，一、二等级的公民可担任包括执政官在内的最高官职，第三等级只能担任普通官职，第四等级不能担任任何官职，只能参加公民大会和陪审法庭。这就等于明确界定了国家公职人员的任职资格，即财富标准。且不说担任国家公职需要一定的财富标准（后来还包括纳税）后来在西方成为担任国家公职的必要条件，并且形成一种牢不可破的传统，就单说在当时的雅典国家，从此也成为一种政治规则，不管是贵族还是平民，都必须遵循这个规则参与国家公职的竞争，这就体现了一种合法竞争的精神。

梭伦改革确立的另一政治规则，就是制定了民主的选举制度。梭伦规定，国家的官职先由各部落分别投票预选候选人——候选人要符合一定的财产标准——然后从这些候选人中抽签产生。以九执政官为例，每一部落先行投票预选 10 人，4 个部落产生 40 人，然后从中抽签产生 9 执政。到亚里士多德时（前 384—322），预选亦改用抽签法（时已 10 个部落，共 100 人）。[②]投票选举也好，抽签选举也好，这就是规则。遵循此路径登上政治舞台的，方为合法，否则即为非法，这里体现的仍然是一种合法竞争精神。

梭伦改革还使公民大会成为最高权力机关，决定战争、媾和，进行选举官吏，各级公民皆有权参加，贵族会议不能凌驾于公民大会之上。还设 400 人会议和陪审法庭。400 人会议由 4 个部落各选 100 人组成。除第四等级外其他各级公民都可当选。400 人会议类似公民大会的常设机构，为公民大会拟订议程，准备和预审公民大会的提案，并贯彻公民大会的决议。雅典的法庭，审判员叫陪审员，凡公民皆可当选为陪审员参与案件审理。陪审法庭成为雅典国家的最高司法机关。

这一系列的措施，在雅典国家创建了一种规范有序、合法竞争的政治体制和竞争体制，这反映了包括梭伦在内的当时的古希腊人就有了一种比较先进的而且是比较成熟的合法竞争思想，只不过没有把它们上升到理论的高度来加以概括和认识罢了。

梭伦还规定任何公民都有权为了自己或受害者的利益而对任何人提出控告，还对不关心公共事务的公民剥夺选举权，这实际上等于鼓励甚至强迫公民积极地去参与合法斗争（竞争）。

我们在评价梭伦改革的意义的时候，其中一点是说梭伦"提高了平民的地位"。其实，从合法斗争的角度说，就是使平民能够合法地参与国家政治了，政治舞台上采取的是合法斗争的方式。这一点至关重要，它规划了民主政治的游戏规则，为雅典奴隶主民主政治的确立奠定了基础。

---

① 1 麦第姆诺约合中国的 5.2 斗。
② 山东大学历史系世界史教研组：《世界古代史资料选辑》，1961 年版，第 247 页。

当然还有局限，如过分强调财富的作用，使财力不足者无力从政，从而难以享受平等的政治权利，以及氏族贵族在部落中操纵选举，仍有很大的势力等等。这一些，都需要后来的改革者不断去克服。后来的改革者如克利斯提尼、伯里克利等人，从合法竞争的角度看，都是推进和完善了雅典国家合法竞争机制的广度和深度，在此就不再赘述了。

关于梭伦在其他方面所反映出来的合法竞争思想，也值得一提。梭伦在改革之后，出国旅行达10年之久。回国后适值雅典国家正发生激烈的内部斗争，他的表弟庇西特拉图想当僭主，他曾进行过规劝，试图制止庇西特拉图的野心，但没有凑效。

据普鲁塔克记载，在梭伦改革之前，他的密友曾经责备他，说他不应该因为害怕僭主政治之名而拒绝绝对的权力，亦即不去当僭主，仿佛一旦夺取了这种权力，夺取者的品质就会使它不能立即成为合法的主权。他们说，以往在优卑亚，廷农达斯（Tynnondas）就证明了应该如此，现在米提利尼人（在列斯堡岛）也是这样，他们已经选出了皮塔库斯做他们的僭主。但所有这一切都不能使梭伦动摇他的决心。据说，他曾对他的朋友说，僭主政治是一个可爱的地位，可是没有一条路可以由那里走下台。在他写赠福科斯（Phocus）的诗里他这样说：

> 如果我保全我的故国，
> 不在僭主政治和无情的暴力中插手，
> 玷辱我的嘉名，
> 我就是无愧的；我这样做，只会使我的声名，
> 凌驾一切其他的人们。 [①]

由此可见，即使在他立法之前，梭伦就已经有了很高的声名。对于许多人因他拒绝僭主政治而给他的嘲笑，梭伦写了如下的诗句：

> 梭伦是一个没有头脑、没有主意的人，
> 神赐给他幸福，他自己不愿意接受；
> 网里已经装满了鱼，他吃惊，却不把它拉起，
> 一切都是由于没有勇气，也因为他已经失掉了聪明。
> 我当然也曾愿意获得这个权力，和无数的财富，
> 在雅典做不过一日的僭主，
> 然后我被剥皮，
> 我的后代被消灭。 [②]

通过梭伦的诗，我们可以看出，梭伦是一个头脑清醒、不愿冒天下之大不韪而一意孤行僭主之制的政治家。他虽然被认为奉行中庸之道，但反对僭主政治的思想却是十分明确的。梭伦不行僭主之制，堪称古希腊民主政治精英的表率。如果溯本求源，这与他的合法思想和合法竞争思想分不开。

笔者在上文曾经提到，梭伦本人并没有提出合法竞争或公平竞争的理论或概念。但实际上，已经是相当于提出了，因为在译成中文的梭伦诗中，我们发现梭伦不止一次地使用了"正当"、"公正"、"非法"以及"不正当"、"不公平"、"不公正"等概念。这里仅举两例。其一："我手执一个

---

① 普鲁塔克：《希腊罗马名人传》，商务印书馆，1990年版，第180页
② 普鲁塔克：《希腊罗马名人传》，商务印书馆，1990年版，第180—181页。

有力的盾牌，站在两个阶级的前面，不许他们任何一方不公平地占着优势。"①其二："我想有财富，但用不正当的方法取得它，我不愿意，正当的方法虽然慢，可是稳当。"②在"普布利科拉传"中，梭伦的这两句诗被浓缩为："我愿拥有财富，但不愿非法谋取。"③由此可见，在梭伦那里，合法以及合法竞争的思想，是非常明显的。

公元前594年，通过梭伦改革，在雅典国家建立起了民主政治体制，笔者认为这与包括梭伦在内的雅典人民所具有的合法竞争思想分不开。合法竞争思想是雅典国家之所以能够建立民主政治体制的最重要的法理依据和认识根源。

七　简短的结语

古希腊人的合法竞争思想，是人类思想史上最为宝贵的思想之一。这种思想对于达成良好的人际关系及共同体关系，尤其是对于形成人类社会经济和政治领域的最佳经营模式和斗争格局，激发个人的、共同体的乃至全社会的潜力和活力，推动社会的文明进步和快速发展，具有重要意义。合法竞争思想起源于古希腊，影响到古罗马，④影响到中世纪的西欧，进一步影响到近现代的西方，进而影响到全世界。最明显的例子莫过于中世纪的骑士决斗和近现代以来在全世界尤其是在西方普遍盛行的市场经济（如 WTO 的成立）和政党政治（亦即民主政治）。这种思想的理论意义和实践价值非常巨大，很值得我们去认真研究并加以全面借鉴，从而有力地推动我们国家现代化事业的建设和发展。

---

① 普鲁塔克：《希腊罗马名人传》，商务印书馆，1990 年版，185 页。又见《雅典政制》12 章。"不公平"一词有的学者译为"非法"（水建馥），有的学者译为"不公正"（林志纯、颜一）。
② 普鲁塔克：《希腊罗马名人传》，商务印书馆，1990 年版，167 页。
③ 普鲁塔克：《希腊罗马名人传》，商务印书馆，1990 年版，231 页。
④ 关于古罗马人的合法竞争思想，拙文《论罗马共和国保民官制度产生的社会根源和历史条件》（载《齐鲁学刊》1997年第 6 期，又见笔者《古希腊罗马论丛》一书第 427－442 页）曾有所涉及。

柏拉图学园有女学徒吗？

王正胜　南开大学

摘要：柏拉图创办学园实践自己的教育思想，中外学者基本上认为他在《理想国》中提出的男女平等接受教育的理念也得到了实现，具体表现在学园招收了女学徒。但也有人对此存在怀疑，认为是杜撰出来的。笔者从文献的角度结合当时的历史社会背景对此进行探究后认为：学园招收女学徒的可能性不大，但有女性通过其他方式学习柏拉图的教学内容。

关键词：柏拉图；学园；女学徒

Abstract: Plato established his Academy to practice his idea of education. Scholars at home and abroad think that in his Academy Plato achieved his idea that women have equal right to get education by going to school with men, which was showed by recruiting two women disciples. But some scholars have doubts about that. By probing into social background and literature ,this paper shows that there were no women disciples studying in the academy and it is possible for women to acquire knowledge from Plato by other means.

Keywords: Plato, Academy, Women Disciples

柏拉图被认为是西方第一个主张男女平权的思想家，在教育方面，他的《理想国》提出女性应和男性享有同等的受教育权。在柏拉图长期的教育实践中，学园是他教育理想和教育理论的实验园地，学园的教学内容和《理想国》等著作中所述基本一致，柏拉图在学园的教学方式也符合他本人的思想，但是关于男女平等的教育思想是否体现在实践中呢，本文将结合国内外的文献和当时希腊的社会情况进行考证。

一　国内学者的看法

国内学者对柏拉图是否在教育实践中体现男女平等的思想看法一致，即柏拉图在学园招收女学徒。如苏振兴、李立国提到早在古典时期的雅典，柏拉图的学园里就有两名妇女像男人们一样学习哲学。[①②]赵向红认为柏拉图不仅提出了男女教育平等的主张，而且他还是一个实践者……柏拉图在雅典城外西北郊，创建了名闻遐迩的阿卡德米学院。学院倡导男女平权，不仅招收男生也招收女子。[③]燕宏远，梁小燕更加肯定：为了孩子的教育，柏拉图还为他的"马革尼西亚"（《法律篇》中柏氏想象的城邦）设想了一座"中级学校"—为男孩和女孩的高等教育准备的一个永久学校。在学园中，柏拉图就招收了曼提尼亚的拉斯提亚和佛利乌斯的阿克西塞亚两位女性为弟子，这是对当时社会反对女性受教育最有力的抨击。[④]

从国内学者的论述来看，毫无疑问，《理想国》和《法律篇》中的教育思想在学园教育实践中得到了验证。

二　国外学者的看法

爱德华·J·鲍威尔（Edward J. Power）在他的一篇文中陈述：毫无疑问，柏拉图和其他教师把男学徒和两个据说是男扮女装的女学徒带到田野和森林去观察自然现象，对物种进行辨别、分类。[⑤]剑桥古代史在谈到柏拉图学园提到：学园向所有的人开放，还吸引了拉斯特尼娅和阿西奥西亚两位妇女。[⑥]弗里曼（Freeman）的叙述亦相类似：值得注意的是，《理想国》的作者承认，女子在阿卡德米的内部拥有与男子一样平等的权利，这是对雅典社会歧视女子的挑战。拉斯特尼娅（Lastheneia of Mantineia）和阿西奥西亚（Axiothea of Phious）这两位穿着男子衣服的女子是大学教育史上出现的第一批维护女权的斗士。[⑦]

上述几位国外学者对柏拉图学园招收女性也是持肯定态度的。当然肯定还有其他的研究会涉及到学园女性，但从目前掌握的资料和总体趋势来看，在学园招收女学徒方面基本上是趋于肯定的。

三　中外学者看法中存在的问题及事实追溯

我国学者对学园女学徒的陈述都没有做进一步的解释，没有说明该事实的出处，也没有说明是否是自己的论证。爱德华·J·鲍威尔和弗里曼以及《剑桥古代史》的说法都是引自一个出处，即狄奥根尼·拉尔修（Diogenes Laertius）的《名哲言行录》（*Lives of eminent philosophers*）一书，狄奥根尼·拉尔修是这样描述的：在柏拉图的学生中有两位女士，即 Lastheneia 和 Axiothea，据狄凯阿尔库斯（Dicaearchus）所述，她们的穿着像男士。[⑧]可以看出，狄奥根尼·拉尔修是根据狄凯阿尔库斯所述，狄凯阿尔库斯是谁目前不得而知，笔者认为有可能是柏拉图的学生。因为狄奥根尼·拉尔修的这本书不完全是个人独立创作的作品，更多的是转述性或引用性的资料汇编。正如英译者希克斯（Hicks）说："显然，他不是根据个人的知识，也不是源于事件的性质来写作，而是在借用、抄写，

---

① 苏振兴：《论古希腊教育文化》，《历史教学》2004 年第 9 期 69 页。
② 李立国著：《古代希腊教育》，教育科学出版社 2010 年版，73 页。
③ 赵向红：《柏拉图男女平权思想探析》，《学习与探索》2005 年第 6 期 190 页。
④ 燕宏远，梁小燕：《柏拉图：西方"女性主义"的先驱者》，《哲学动态》2005 年第 10 期 39 页。
⑤ Edward J. Power: "Plato's Academy:A Halting Step toward Higher Learning", *History of Education Quarterly*.1964,(3):156.
⑥ *The Cambridge Ancient History*, second edition, volume VI, *The fourth century B.C.* Edited by D.M.Lewis F.B.A, John Boardman F.B.A, Simon Hornblower, M.Ostwald.Cambridge University Press, 1994, p.604.
⑦ 《希腊的学校》（*School of Hellas*, Kenneth J. Freeman,1907,London)朱镜人译，山东教育出版社，2009 年版，第 160 页。
⑧ Mary R.Lefkowitz & Maureen B. Fant:*Women's Life in Greece & Rome, A Source in Translation*, second edition,The Johns Hopkins University Press, Baltimore, p.167.

在做摘录和引用。"①所以其中观点的真实性值得进一步推敲。

特米斯提乌斯（Themistius）在《演讲集》（Orations）用阿西奥西亚的例子来说明柏拉图哲学具有强大的吸引力：阿西奥西亚读了柏拉图的《理想国》后就离开了阿卡狄亚（Arcadia）的家来到雅典，她乔装后听柏拉图的讲座，没有人看出她的女性身份……②

据希波伯托斯（Hippobotus）所述：柏拉图去世后，拉斯特尼娅和柏拉图的学生斯佩乌西波斯（Speusippus）一起研习，然后又和埃略特里亚人麦涅德墨斯（Menedemus the Eretrian）一起学习。罗德岛的希埃罗尼墨斯（Hieronymus of Rhodes）在作品（on Physics）中也提到了她。逍遥学派的阿里斯托芬尼（Aristophanes）在著作（on Painlessness）中也讲了类似的故事，还说她是个不矫揉造作的美丽女孩。③

综上所知，柏拉图学园女学徒的依据是来自柏拉图学徒们的陈述，暂无明确的证据。另外学园明确男女平等并招收女性最初无人提及，柏拉图学徒们只是提到女扮男装混进学园学习的。由此来看，中外学者认为的学园男女平等并招收女性学徒是没有根据的，女学徒的真实性还需要进一步证实。所以朱丽娅·安娜斯（Julia Annas）有不同的看法：据说柏拉图学园里还有两个女学生：拉斯特妮娅（Lastheneia）和阿西欧提娅（Axiothea），她俩是在读完《理想国》后，女扮男装混进学园的。这个故事可能是有人读了《理想国》之后杜撰出来的，但无论是真是假，都说明在人们看来，柏拉图认为性别与思想发展毫无关系。④

四 对学园存在女学徒的疑问

由于柏拉图的教学是免费的，因此并不是所有求学者都可以获得入学的机会。柏拉图可以挑选学生，他希望他的学生有良好的几何学基础。他的学校一定有着某种入学考试（Freeman，1907,159）。他的继任者芝诺克拉蒂（Xenokrates）发现了一个学生在音乐、几何学和天文学方面一无所知，便让他离开了学校。他对学生说："因为你没有给哲学提供抓住你的机会"那么柏拉图是如何进行考试录取的呢？弗里曼只是说有女学生，也提到有入学考试，但没有说明女学生是如何通过考试进入学园学习的。⑤

按照当时的社会状况，女性受教育的程度较低，两位女性是如何被录取进学园的？既然柏拉图招收了女学徒，为什么在自己后来的作品如《法律篇》中没有提及。

按照希波伯托斯（Hippobotus）所述，学园的一个女学徒在柏拉图去世后继续和柏拉图的一个学生在一起学习，另外一个是读了《理想国》后来学园学习。应该说，两个女学徒在学园学习了很长时间，如果说开始是女扮男装，时间长了大家应该都知道了。学园有两个女学徒在当时应是一件轰动的事情，为什么其他的学徒没有提及，尤其是亚里士多德，他在学园学习了20年，而当时的学园人员并不多，他应该熟知此事，但他并未在自己的作品中提及这件事或表明态度。另外，时间长了，此事在社会上也应该有所影响，按照当时的社会情况，也应有所反应并有记录，但是其他方面并未发现相关的证据。

① 《名哲言行录》（Lives of Eminent Philosophers, Diogenes Laertius,Loeb Classical Library,Harvard University,1938）徐开来，傅林译，广西师范大学出版社，2010年版，第3页。

② Mary R.Lefkowitz & Maureen B. Fant, Women's Life in Greece & Rome, A Source in Translation, second edition,The Johns Hopkins University Press, Baltimore, p.167.

③ Mary R.Lefkowitz & Maureen B. Fant, Women's Life in Greece & Rome, A Source in Translation, second edition,The Johns Hopkins University Press, Baltimore, p.167.

④ 《解读柏拉图》(Plato: A Very Short Introduction, Julia Annas)，高峰枫译，外语教学与研究出版社2007年版。

⑤ 《希腊的学校》（School of Hellas, Kenneth J. Freeman,1907,London)，朱镜人译，山东教育出版社。2009年版，第159页。

再看看雅典当时女性的社会地位及教育情况：古典时代的女性的教育收到很大的压制，没有证据表明女孩能在家庭外的任何地方接受教育。有一个瓶画上的贵族妇女拿着一卷书，不过这画的也是在家里的情形。公开的社交聚会一般的公民妇女也是不参加的，如果一个女人跟随男人参加酒会等，这个女人一般被认为是高等妓女而不是男人的合法妻子。①

综上所述，我们很难想象有两个女孩在学园学习那么长的时间。

五　对柏拉图学园女学徒疑问的求证

可以说，柏拉图学园女学徒的说法都是来自于柏拉图学生的口中，其中一个学徒是为了说明柏拉图的学说具有吸引力，女性也加入学园。根据这一点，很有可能是学园学徒为了提高学园的影响而做的一种宣传，因为：毋庸讳言，雅典各派教育领袖人物之间存在尖锐矛盾。希腊不像文艺复兴时期的意大利那样容忍对手。伊索克拉底抨击柏拉图。柏拉图也抨击伊索克拉底。然后他们的学生又把争论带到下一代。所以入学前，学生十分为难，他们不知道应当选择哪位教师，因为每位教师都背有许多恶名和诽谤。②

当时雅典还有其他教育机构，如伊索克拉底学园，相互之间处于竞争状态，而柏拉图又是第一个在《理想国》提出男女平权的教育思想的，这在当时看来是荒谬和不可思议的，所以不排除有柏拉图学园的学徒以此作为提高声望的手段。

苏·布伦德尔（Sue Blundell）在谈到柏拉图的男女平等的思想时：男女在教育、工作机会、政治和军事权利方面的平等在今天来看已经在许多地方立法确认并被人们所接受，当然真正完全实现还有很长的路要走。但肯定的是雅典妇女根本就没有享受到上述的男女平等的权利。但不管怎样，柏拉图的思想在当时对女性争取权利方面还是一个巨大的进步。③

柏拉图在公元前 387 年创建学园，公元前 347 年去世，在公元前四世纪女性走出家门正式学习哲学是一件很难的事情，即使是在公元前 3 世纪，女性抛头露面从事哲学也是需要非凡的勇气，如狄奥根尼·拉尔修记载了公元前 3 世纪的一个女性希帕基娅（Hipparchia）爱上了一个哲学家克拉提斯（Crates），父母反对，她以自杀相威胁。克拉提斯也无法摆脱，最终两人结合。希帕基娅和克拉提斯穿着同样的陋衣四处漂泊游学，共同参加一些公开的宴会。而当时在宴会上出现的妇女（除了女佣人）通常被认为是高级妓女，而不是妻子。在公元前 3 世纪是如此，公元前 4 世纪的女性情况可想而知了。④

那么女性有没有可能成为柏拉图的学徒呢？这也是有可能的，因为雅典的年轻人完成了初等教育之后，如果希望师从柏拉图学习哲学，可以通过两种方式：一是在公共场所聆听讲座，二是进阿卡德米做学生。⑤所以女性完全可以通过乔装在公共场所学习，柏拉图学园的女学徒很有可能是乔装在公共场所听柏拉图讲座的女性。

---

① Sue Blundell: *Women in Ancient Greece*. Harvard University Press,Cambridge,Massachusetts.1995,P132,135.
② 《希腊的学校》（*School of Hellas*, Kenneth J. Freeman,1907,London），朱镜人译，山东教育出版社，2009 年版，第 165–166 页。
③ Sue Blundell: *Women in Ancient Greece*. Harvard University Press,Cambridge,Massachusetts.1995,P184.
④ Mary R.Lefkowitz&Maureen B.fant:*Women's Life in Greece & Rome, A Source in Translation*, second edition,The Johns Hopkins University Press, Baltimore, p.167.
⑤ 《希腊的学校》（*School of Hellas*, Kenneth J. Freeman,1907,London），朱镜人译，山东教育出版社,2009 年版,第 160页。

六 结语

对于柏拉图男女平等接受教育思想实践的研究还存在一些问题，具体表现在学园女学徒这一事例，柏拉图学生不太明确的说法被后人反复转引，已经大大偏离了原有的证据，多数学者为了论证自己的论点而对这一事例进行了夸大，如有的说柏拉图学园对所有人开放，有的说学园男女统招平等对待，藉此说明柏拉图是女性主义思想上和实践上的先驱。虽然柏拉图在理想国中提出的女性教育理论没有明确实践，但他的思想对以后的女性解放起到了重要的推动作用，到了希腊化时代，女孩可以和男孩在一起接受同样的教育了。[1]

---

[1]　Lesley Adkins and Roy A.Adkins : *Handbook to Life in Ancient Greece*. Facts On File,Inc. 1997.

论古希腊的疯狂仪式

魏凤莲　鲁东大学

摘要：古希腊的疯狂仪式是在祭祀狄奥尼索斯时由女性完成的一种仪式。疯狂仪式每两年一次发生在深冬时的荒山里，其高潮是被称为"狂女"（Maenads）的狄奥尼索斯信徒在激烈奔跑和舞蹈中进入迷狂或出神（ecstasy）状态。本文以解读五篇与疯狂仪式相关的铭文资料为基础，结合悲剧《酒神的伴侣》及古代作家留下的记载，试图构建古希腊疯狂仪式的具体内容，探析狂女们在城邦社会中的身份和地位。本文认为，疯狂仪式迥异于庄重肃穆的杀生献祭仪式，亦迥异于古希腊妇女封闭的日常生活，却是城邦尊重和支持的宗教活动，其原因在于，它不是破坏性因素，而是古希腊社会生活中的整合因素。

关键词：疯狂仪式；狄奥尼索斯崇拜；狂女；城邦

Abstract：Maenadism（or Maenadic ritual）is a kind of ritual in ancient Greece performed by Maenads who are the worshippers of Dionysos. Maenadic rituals took place in the rough mountains of Greece in the heart of winter every second year. Its climax is that the Maenads go into the ecstasy state stimulated by their running and dancing. This article tries to construct Maendic rituals in detail and analyze the Maenads' identities and their status in the polis, basing on the five epigraphic texts which related with Greek Maenadism, tragedy *Bacchae* and other writings by ancient writers. This article states that Maenadic rituals are different from the somber killing sacrifices and the secluded everyday life of Greek women. However, they are respected and supported by polis. So Maenadism is an integrated factor rather than a destructive factor in social society of ancient Greece.

Keywords：Maenadism, Dionysiac cult, Maenads, Polis

古希腊的疯狂仪式是祭祀狄奥尼索斯时由女性完成的一种仪式。疯狂仪式每两年一次发生在深冬的荒山里。被称为"狂女"（Maenads）的狄奥尼索斯的女信徒们离开城市，走进山林。她们奔跑着、舞蹈着，最终进入迷狂或出神（ecstasy）的状态，达到仪式的高潮。在欧里庇得斯的悲剧《酒神的伴侣》中，迷狂状态下的狂女甚至能徒手撕碎野兽，杀死忮拜城的国王彭透斯。

疯狂仪式迥异于庄严肃穆的杀生献祭，亦迥异于古希腊妇女封闭隔绝的日常生活，却是城邦尊重和支持的宗教活动，这一点引起了学者们的广泛兴趣。道兹（E. D. Dodds）认为疯狂仪式类似于已知的宗教疯狂行为（如萨满教的出神现象），具有净化的功能。人类学家则从疯狂仪式具有颠覆作用这一层面出发，认为疯狂崇拜是一种"间接的侵略的战略"，是"神秘力量对社会弱者的特殊馈赠"，能够帮助弱势群体或社会边缘因素短暂逃离社会的束缚，反抗占社会主导地位的法律权威。这些观点具有一定的理论基础，但并不足以解释疯狂仪式在古希腊城邦和女性生活中的特殊意义。因为参加疯狂仪式的人不是弱势群体，恰恰相反，只有贵族妇女或者至少女性公民才能被选为"城邦的狂女"（politai bacchae），代表城邦参加对狄奥尼索斯的祭祀活动，因此，妇女的疯狂仪式与城邦的利益是一致的。本文试图以解读五篇与疯狂仪式相关的铭文为基础，结合悲剧《酒神的伴侣》及古代作家留下的记载，试图构建古希腊疯狂仪式的具体内容，探析狂女们在城邦社会中的身分和地位，理清古希腊女性、宗教和城邦之间的密切关系。希望能通过这一问题的探讨，对古希腊城邦文明的实质有更深刻的理解。

一　疯狂仪式的具体内容

古代作家对疯狂仪式的记载散见于诗歌、游记和历史记述之中，但大多是零碎的历史片段，只有欧里庇得斯在悲剧《酒神的伴侣》中全面而细致地描绘了一幕令人惊心动魄的疯狂场面：

> 狂女们"把头发打散披在肩上"（688），"像在酒神的宴饮中一样，前后摆头"（930），"手握神杖，身穿兽皮"（835），"她们赤着雪白的脚跑出城"（665），"像飞鸟一样，腾空奔跑"，"把一切弄得天翻地覆，甚至把孩子们从人家家里抢走；所有的东西都放在她们肩上，没有绳子系住，却也没掉在黑色的地上；她们没有铜铁兵器，只是头发上有火，却又烧不着自己。……村民们的枪尖投过来不见血，而她们的棍子扔过去却见了伤……蛇用舌尖把她们脸上的血点舐干净"（747-768）。她们在山上奔跑，呼喊着，"追赶野羊，让它们流出血来，那生肉多么好吃啊！"（136）"整个山林和山中野兽都欢欣鼓舞，大自然也随着她们的奔跑而活跃起来"（727），最终，她们在狄奥尼索斯的魔力下，"嘴吐泡沫，眼珠乱转"（1122），进入疯狂状态，撕碎了忒拜城的国王彭透斯。

但是，在欧里庇得斯的这些描写中有多少是真实的疯狂仪式，学者们一直存有争议。古典学家拉普（A. Rapp）早在1872年就指出，传说中的疯狂仪式与历史上的疯狂仪式有着明显的区别。前者仅存在于艺术家和诗人的想象中，是一种艺术的创造。亨里奇（Albert Henrichs）认为，有关疯狂仪式的传说与仪式在《酒神的伴侣》中缠绕成一个复杂的网，几乎不可分割。而著名古典学家道兹认为欧里庇得斯所描写的就是真实的疯狂仪式，疯狂仪式中的出神现象，在现今世界的其它宗教经历里面都能找到相似的描述，都与真实的崇拜仪式有密切的联系。

所幸的是，从1890年到1968年，有5篇重要的希腊铭文出版，描述了从公元前3世纪到公元2世纪在希腊、小亚细亚和意大利举行的疯狂仪式，为我们了解疯狂仪式的历史真实提供了佐证。按照这些铭文的出版顺序，分别是（1）公元前200年左右的Magnesia铭文，复制了当地年代记中所引用的一则德尔斐神谕；（2）公元前3世纪晚期或前2世纪的Miletus铭文，是一篇挽歌体的碑文；（3）公元前276/275年的Miletus铭文，是关于出售狄奥尼索斯的女祭司职位的纪录；（4）公元2世纪的拉丁姆附近的Torre Nova铭文，是狄奥尼索斯神圣团体的成员名单；（5）公元2世纪的Physkos铭文，记录了有关狄奥尼索斯崇拜的规则。以这些铭文为基础，结合普鲁塔克（Plutarch）、狄奥多罗斯（Diodorus）、李维（Livy）等古代作家留下的相关记载，我们大致可以确定历史上的疯狂仪式应该有如下具体内容：

疯狂仪式开始于城邦内的某个地方。有一首诗歌提到仪式开始于饼的献祭（sacrifice of cakes），另据狄奥多罗斯记载，仪式开始时，女人们轮流吟唱，呼唤狄奥尼索斯的出现。这种呼喊能够帮助狂女们进入适当的狄奥尼索斯氛围。然后，她们离开城邦，呼喊着"eis oros"（意为"到山林里去"）走进山林。从家庭主妇转变为情绪激动的狂女是一种心理的转变，需要的不仅仅是呼喊，还必须借助于各种手段促成这种转变，如使用乐器扬琴（tympanon）、长笛（aulos），还有小手鼓等打击乐器。打击乐器在全世界各地的仪式上都有使用，能够带来"出神"（trance-like state）的效果。在疯狂仪式上，连续不断的小手鼓声，会大大刺激大脑中心的神经细胞活动，当外部的节奏与脑部运动同步时，声音和行动就会"迷住"或控制参与者。

生活在公元前1世纪晚期的地理学家斯特拉波（Strabo）认为，在狄奥尼索斯崇拜仪式中，疯狂的本质是在乐器伴奏下的舞蹈。狄奥尼索斯周围的信徒，有人手执低音的长笛，有人敲着古铜色的中空铙钹。竖琴（lyre）提升了喊叫声，庄严的公牛咆哮声从某些隐蔽的地方传出来，类似鼓、类似地下的雷声，带着最深的恐惧传了过来。

舞蹈会持续到深夜，其背景是深冬、寒夜和山间。连续不断的疯狂摇头、音乐的震荡、声嘶力竭的呼喊和舞蹈，都会降低血液对脑的供应，注定会出现晕眩的现象，或者得到类似于癫痫的反应，狂女们由此进入出神（ecstacy）状态。出神状态是仪式的最高潮，舞者会晕倒在地，这是狄奥尼索斯最终迷住信徒的标志。

最后，就像《酒神的伴侣》里歌队所唱的"这番劳累是甜蜜的"（66）那样，狂女们在精疲力竭之后，沐浴在愉悦和欢喜之中。然后，带着这种欣喜的心情回到家里，再由现实把她们带到枯燥和封闭的生活之中。

相对于这些可以确定的过程来说，在《酒神的伴侣》所描述的疯狂仪式中，有三个细节应该属于传说，而非真实的疯狂仪式。其一，吃生肉。米利都（Miletus）出土的铭文上确实提到了"ōmophagion"（生肉）这个词。铭文是这样说的：

> 当女祭司为了整个城邦的利益进行献祭活动时，在女祭司为了整个城邦的利益扔进一块献祭牺牲的生肉（ōmophagion embalmein）之前，任何人不准扔进生肉。也不允许任何人在一个公众的神圣团体（thiasos）前做引导。

道兹认为ōmophagion就是被狂女们生吃掉的肉，但很多学者都否定了他的看法。亨里奇认为这个词是指献祭牺牲的生肉，但并不是被崇拜者吃掉的。相反，它是被扔到一个专门堆积献祭物品的大坑里面的。在列斯堡岛，狄奥尼索斯被称为"食生肉者"，因此，这块生肉是要献给狄奥尼索斯的，而不是被信徒们吃掉的。"embalmein"的含义很确定，就是"扔进、投进"，并非"被吃掉"，让鲜血从狂女们的嘴里流出来。这一铭文足以证明传说夸大了仪式：狂女们食生肉只是在传说的层面上，而在现实中远不如这么令人窒息和不安。

但是在疯狂仪式中的确会设置进"一块生肉"。这是因为，在希腊人的意识里，食生肉是边缘宗派的典型特征，经常属于邻近的、被希腊人看成是野蛮的民族，是一种远离文明、具有破坏性和颠覆性的因素。在古希腊其他女性节日如地母节（Thesmophoria）、阿多尼节（Adonia）里，也有禁欲、乱交、不育和妇女离家等因素，表达的都是对日常秩序生活的破坏和颠覆。

其二，舞蛇。狄奥尼索斯崇拜与蛇有着非常密切的关系，古风时期的瓶画上经常出现狂女持蛇舞蹈的场景，但这些场景可能只是取材于传说或是想象。普鲁塔克曾提到，亚历山大的母亲奥林匹娅把一群驯服的大蛇弄进了神圣团体里，是为了摹仿传说中的狂女，令疯狂仪式更为夸张。演说家埃斯奇涅斯（Aeschines）的记载里提到在遥远的古代狂女是执蛇的，似乎更能证明在他生活的公元前4世纪，狂女恰恰是不执蛇的。

其三，狂女们具有刀火不入的能力。古希腊的狂女们在平常的日子里，都是居家妇女，只是在固定的节日里，才充当狄奥尼索斯的女性伴侣，从常理来判断，很难具有刀火不侵的能力。比较可能的情况是，在迷狂（出神）状态下，她们对疼痛不甚敏感。普鲁塔克记载说，大约在公元前3世纪中期，一群狂女们在寒冬的山上迷了路，人们组织了救援队去寻找，发现滴水成冰的天气里，女祭司们只穿着一层鹿皮衣，却不觉得特别寒冷。

尽管可以确定这些细节不属于历史上真实的疯狂仪式，只是传说，但是它们的作用却不容忽视。因为这些附着在仪式上的传说映射出疯狂仪式的内涵，甚至在更高层面上实现了仪式的意图。在现实中，狂女们无法具有刀火不入的能力，而传说却能赋予她们这样的能力，令疯狂仪式更加具有感召力。正是由于相信传说，相信神的魔力，古希腊人才能获得或增强某种宗教体验。公元前4世纪的杨布里克（Iamblichus）这样描述他看到的出神状态：

> 很多人，在神的感召之下，当火近身之时没有被烧伤，神的激励影响使火不能接触到他们。……还有一些人，尽管被射中了，但却没有意识到这一点；而其他那些肩膀上被斧子砍中的人、被刀砍伤胳膊的人，对自己身上发生的事毫无知觉。

传说还传达了社会对仪式的评价：通过女性离开家把孩子撕成碎片的传说，表达了男性对这种举动的恐惧；通过食生肉的传说，疯狂仪式表达了对文明社会的疏离；通过舞蛇的传说，表达了疯狂仪式与狄奥尼索斯之间的密切关系。所以，传说也是疯狂仪式的一部分，它从语言、想象等多个层面强化了疯狂仪式的特征。布莱默（J. Bremmer）认为，在考察疯狂仪式时不能仅盯住其中的一些细节，而应该全面系统地展现一个整体的画面，因为所有的已知因素都是多维度表演中不可分割的一部分。真实发生的疯狂仪式活动固然重要，对那些表达了仪式的目的、内涵和功能的传说也应给予分析和理解。

二　狂女（Maenads）

完成疯狂仪式的人是狄奥尼索斯的女信徒。对她们的称呼在不同地区、不同环境下有所差异。狂女们疯狂的舞蹈和迷狂的举止只在外人看来是疯狂的，大量的关于这种仪式的铭文显示，真正的信徒并不使用"疯狂的"（mania, mainesthai, mainades）来形容自己的仪式，而是使用跟仪式有关的中性词如"狄奥尼索斯的狂欢"（bakcheia, bakcheuein）。所以，"狂女"（Maenads）是外人对她们的称呼，她们自称为狄奥尼索斯的女信徒（Bacchae）或狄奥尼索斯的疯狂女信徒（Thuiads），Thiasos是这些女信徒组成的狂欢歌舞队，可译为"狂女们的神圣团体"。

狂女们的疯狂仪式迥异于女性的日常生活，但实施疯狂仪式的狂女并不是处于社会边缘的女性。恰恰相反，这些妇女通常是社会的上层妇女。马格奈西亚（Magnesia）出土的铭文讲述了这样一件事：曼伊安德河畔的马格奈西亚居民发现了松树里的面具，遂向德尔斐请求神谕，阿波罗的女祭司皮提亚让他们"去圣城忒拜去请狂女，她们是卡德莫斯（Kadmeian）家族中的伊诺（Ino）的后代。她们会给你们疯狂仪式以及尊贵的习俗，并将在你们的城市里建立巴库斯的神圣团体"。接下来，铭文还继续讲述了三个忒拜城的狂女被迎接到马格奈西亚以及最后被荣耀地埋葬在此处的故事。这个铭文显示出，即使在古典时代以后，狂女们仍然是集体中受人尊敬的成员，表演国家所支持的、被认为是高贵的仪式。

在雅典，每当德尔斐的Thuia节日（狄奥尼索斯的神圣节日）到来之际，雅典城邦会选出14名尊贵的女人组成神圣团体去帕纳苏斯山朝圣，允许她们外出进行对狄奥尼索斯的神秘祭祀活动，鲍萨尼阿斯（Pausanias）说她们在帕纳苏斯山顶为狄奥尼索斯和阿波罗疯狂舞蹈。在传说中，与疯狂仪式的起源有关的厄利斯（Elis）的 16 位女性、奥克迈诺斯的奥雷埃（Oleiai of Orchomenos）、明亚德斯（Minyads）的女儿们以及普罗托斯（Proitos），无一例外，都是公主，都有着尊贵的身份。

狂女们是受尊敬的一群人，在狄奥尼索斯的圣所里也会竖起她们的雕像。男人们会为他们曾做过狄奥尼索斯祭司的女儿、妻子和母亲制作雕像，并将其作为献祭的对象。艾瑞斯莱的斯摩（Simo of Erythrai）曾经是狄奥尼索斯（城邦的保护神）的女祭司，她在奉献的铭文中说她希望自己能被子孙后代记住。米利都出土的一块墓碑上也写着一个狂女的名字：

> 城邦的巴库斯官员，告别你们这些神圣的女祭司；对一个好女人来说，这是要做的正确的事情：她领导你们前往山林，她带着所有的献祭工具和圣物，在整个城邦面前游行。她的名字叫 Alkmeionis，Rhodios 的女儿；她知道自己受神护佑。

欧里庇得斯把忒拜的狂女分成三类：年轻的、年老的和少女。实际上，所有年龄段的女性都可以参加疯狂仪式。但按照狄奥多罗斯的记载，少女只扛着狄奥尼索斯的权杖（thyrsos）。布莱默认为，在传说里，狄奥尼索斯带来的疯狂常常在女性的婚礼中得到缓解和控制，因此疯狂仪式可能起源于婚前仪式——从少女到已婚妇女的过渡仪式，尽管这种仪式的痕迹在后来的疯狂仪式中已经不再明显。

狂女只是一种阶段性的和暂时的职务，并不排斥女性参与其他形式的狄奥尼索斯崇拜活动。例如，Alkmeionis 既是当地狂女的官方领袖，同时作为狄奥尼索斯的公共祭司，也具有非疯狂仪式的功能。一般来说，疯狂仪式只限于女性，至少到希腊化时代末期都是如此。希罗多德提到的斯基台人（Scythian）的国王司基勒斯（Scyles）所参加的狄奥尼索斯崇拜仪式是巴库斯入会仪式（telete），并不是疯狂仪式。而在《酒神的伴侣》里，卡德摩斯、先知特瑞西阿斯和彭透斯，尽管为了戏剧效果装扮成狂女，却从来没有加入到忒拜城的狂女队伍里。

从总体上看，希腊的仪式是一系列以动作为导向的，不断重复的、定型的、外在的和缺乏反思的活动，换句话说，是一种热心的回应规则，而不是内在感受和宗教感情的个人表达。所以，在古代文献里，我们找不到疯狂仪式中女性的自我反思或心理活动，也无法了解她们在进行疯狂仪式时是如何感受神和神圣的宗教的。古代和现代的学者都认为对酒的陶醉不是狂女疯狂的原因，尽管传说中的狂女经常举着酒杯或者神奇地创造溪流般的奶、蜜和酒，但是，她们只是在分配狄奥尼索斯的未经稀释的礼物，而不是自己饮用它。她们与酒的密切联系是她们对狄奥尼索斯的分享。借用结构主义的术语，生肉和未经稀释的酒反映了反常、他者和狄奥尼索斯经历的极限，那么，狂女们借助于疯狂仪式所要表达的也注定是一种反常，是对日常生活的颠覆，她们通过迷狂暂时与神合一，得到心灵的出神，借此逃离日常的平庸。

三 疯狂仪式的社会意义

古德里在《希腊人和他们的神》中写道："在希腊，由于日常的限制和乏味的生活，释放的诱惑对女人就有着强烈的吸引力"。他正确地指出了疯狂仪式对妇女具有吸引力的原因，那就是对日常生活的逃离。希腊妇女的传统职责是待在家里照看孩子、做琐碎的家务劳动。只有通过宗教节日，她们才有机会逃避日常的家务劳动，但专门为妇女安排的节日并不多，除了地母节之外，较大的就是狄奥尼索斯的节日和秘仪活动。狄奥尼索斯是城邦的神，他统治的领域很多，但疯狂仪式是最重要的，柏拉图甚至认为狄奥尼索斯崇拜的实质就是"疯狂的仪式"。只能由女性们完成的疯狂仪式无疑为妇女们暂时逃离家务劳动和枯燥的家庭生活提供了神圣的理由和必要的活动时间与空间。

在解释疯狂仪式何以存在于古希腊人生活中的原因时，一些学者把短暂逃离理解为一种反抗。近年来的研究表明，相当多的社会都存在着类似出神（ecstacy）或者是疯狂崇拜的现象，甚至在一些复杂和等级森严的社会里也能找到与疯狂仪式相类似的宗教现象。这些仪式的参加者通常属于社会的边缘因素。男女两性关系的不平衡、男性角色占优势的社会现实决定了妇女就是社会的弱者和边缘因素，也就成为仪式的主角。通过出神或者短暂的疯狂，女性能够达到两个目的：短暂逃离社会的束缚，反抗占社会主导地位的法律权威。

泽特林（Froma I. Zeitlin）从仪式的层面来考察这一问题，也得到了相似的结论。他认为仪式既是社会生活的反映也是对社会生活反面的反映，仪式行为所蕴含的信息可以加强社会规范，同时也提供了反抗这些社会规范的理由。疯狂仪式很显然是作为一种反抗的仪式存在的，在男女两性平衡关系这一问题上，疯狂仪式在深层次上更符合妇女的本性，因而也释放了妇女的紧张心理可能引起的攻击性行为。西蒙（Goldhill Simon）也认为"古希腊医学上所描述的歇斯底里症（hysteria）和狄奥尼索斯的疯狂仪式表达了并且可能矫正了存在于男女两性社会角色上的不平等。这种方式是为社会所包容和接受的，它是对社会内心不平衡的一种展示、妥协和重新调整。"

但是，仅仅把疯狂仪式看成是一种反抗，还不足以解释疯狂仪式在古希腊社会尤其是在古希腊城邦时代的存在意义。疯狂仪式很早就出现了，并被人们所熟知。荷马史诗在提到安德洛玛刻时，用到了"mainas"一词，即使这个词不是确指"狂女"，也具有"疯狂"的含义，在提到狄奥尼索斯时，说他是 mainomenos，即疯狂的神，吕库古斯（Lycurgus）被逼疯的传说，可能就是最早的疯狂仪式。公元前6世纪末，正是雅典政治改革的关键时期，在雅典人的瓶画艺术中，狂女们的舞蹈成为最流行的主题。古典时期是疯狂仪式发展的繁荣时期，公元前5世纪，除了欧里庇得斯的《酒神的伴侣》，悲剧作家埃斯库罗斯也在悲剧《酒神狂女》（Bassarai）中描写过疯狂仪式。城邦衰落之后，疯狂仪式也随之衰落，及至公元2世纪，疯狂仪式已经不再出现。可见，疯狂仪式是与城邦的发展和城邦的利益相一致的。只有从城邦和家庭关系的角度来分析疯狂仪式，才能窥见疯狂仪式的实质内容。

疯狂仪式与城邦的秩序密切相关。对女性来说，逃离与反抗都不是仪式的最终目的，回归秩序才是疯狂仪式的真正目标。在古代作家的笔下，妇女被禁锢在家庭中，生活在阴暗的、封闭的空间里，她的生活和兴趣天生地与房子和家务联系在一起。她的生活与其丈夫的生活是相对的：男人生活在公共空间，家庭是公民妻子存在的中心和界限。城邦中的女性，不管结婚还是未婚，都被想象成过分依附于家庭的利益而不是城邦的利益，也就被想象成与城邦相对立的群体。这一群体可能形成两种威胁：一种是对公共领域的拒绝，另一种是对公共领域的控制或颠覆。狄奥尼索斯的疯狂能够应对这两种威胁：狄奥尼索斯把女性从家里带出去参加集体的仪式，模糊了家庭与公共领域的界限，而疯狂仪式则让女性释放情绪，暂时地控制和颠覆了权力。有关疯狂仪式的传说旨在说明这样一个道理：如果女人拒绝跟随狄奥尼索斯，或者男人阻止女人跟随狄奥尼索斯，那么，狄奥尼索斯就会摧毁她们的房子连同她们的家庭。如果她们被允许与狄奥尼索斯共舞，那么女人的疯狂只是一种暂时的状态，当疯狂消除，她们就会回归家庭。因此，崇拜狄奥尼索斯，进行疯狂仪式就是致力于城邦秩序的建设。

在历史时期，疯狂仪式不是女性自发实施的，而是由城邦支持和管理的，这一点也能说明疯狂仪式与城邦之间的关系。雅典虽然没有关于举办疯狂仪式的文献记载，但狄奥尼索斯的仪式由城邦或德谟组织，而且被安排在官方的仪式日历中。每当德尔斐的 Thuia 节（狄奥尼索斯的神圣节日）到来之际，雅典会选专门的酒神女祭司（Thuiades）负责仪式，并选出14名尊贵的女人，作为狂女到帕纳苏斯山朝圣。在阿提卡的 Erchia 德谟，发现了一份属于公元前 4 世纪的祭祀日历，其中列出了每年一次对狄奥尼索斯和塞墨勒的祭祀。上面显示，仪式所需的费用由地方捐助者提供：12 德拉克玛用于为狄奥尼索斯购买山羊，10 德拉克玛用于为塞墨勒购买山羊。

除支持和管理疯狂仪式外，城邦还直接管理狄奥尼索斯的女祭司。在米利都，为狄奥尼索斯服务的女性是有层次的。城邦的女祭司在最顶部，是主要的，郊区的和乡下的女祭司处于她的管辖之下。把米利都的两个铭文放在一起，我们可以看到，城邦的女祭司的职责包括：主持献祭（公众的和私人的）、管理巴库斯庆祝的工具、引导城邦的巴库斯信徒前往山林、为整个城邦的利益参加公众游行、管理参加秘仪入会仪式的女性。其中一篇铭文是这样写的：

> 如果有人（无论男人还是女人）想为狄奥尼索斯献祭的话，就让献祭的人指定一个祭司为他主持，同时被指定的官员接受额外的补贴……
> 女祭司由妇女来担任……同时为妇女提供在庆祝活动中需要的设备。

在科斯（Kos），狄奥尼索斯的女祭司还调解城邦的管理机构和地方的女性崇拜团体之间的事宜。这里的女祭司在每个德谟都任命一个附属的女祭司，任何其他女性想要为狄奥尼索斯进行特殊的仪式（巴库斯秘仪）都是不可能的。如果女祭司发现有人没有遵守规则，她的主人（kurios）就会上报到地方议事会。

米利都的两篇铭文都提到，狂女是为了"城邦的利益"而履行仪式，游行要在整个城邦面前进行（paseis erksomenei pro poleos），必须由公众的神圣团体做引导，崇拜狄奥尼索斯的私人团体想要参加的话必须认可城邦的和公众的神圣团体的权威。这些都说明城邦和女性通过疯狂仪式找到了一个平衡点：通过支持疯狂仪式，城邦为女性提供了一个为城邦服务的机会，同时消除了女性可能会对城邦带来的隐性威胁。

因此，同其他女性崇拜一样，疯狂仪式是城邦时代希腊社会生活中的整合因素，而不是分裂的因素。城邦在政治生活中是排斥女性的，但狄奥尼索斯崇拜中的疯狂仪式却使女性成为主角，这是城邦通过宗教活动对女性低下地位的一种补偿。在古希腊，城邦就是公民集体，公民集体的利益就是城邦的最高利益。在城邦最高利益的要求下，疯狂仪式谋求的也是公共利益和安全，它以短暂的非常态超越了世俗的、既定的日常规范，宣泄了女性的情绪，平衡了古希腊男女社会角色上的不平等。这一过程可以视为一种"戏剧化表演"，它从既定秩序出发，到非秩序，消解秩序，进而再次建立新的秩序。而这一过程恰恰是符合城邦利益并为城邦所需要的，所以，它才能得到城邦的认可和尊重，并且要在城邦的管理之下完成。

雅典城邦的公民与公民权
——以造船区、德莫、三一区为中心

解光云　安徽师范大学

摘要：造船区、德莫、三一区是城邦的区域空间，是认知古希腊历史，尤其是雅典公民与公民权的基本语词。在古希腊历史语境下，造船区、德莫和三一区具有相对的时空意义。就地域关系而言，城邦的公民或"城邦的人"，属于造船区、德莫和三一区。公民权主要是男性公民所享有的，以造船区、德莫和三一区为基础的政治参与权力——投票权、陪审权和担任公职的权力，以及财产所有权。造船区、德莫、三一区是城邦公民的权力基础。本论文为教育部人文社科研究基地重大项目"西方都市史学的理论与方法"（项目批号：08JJD770086）的阶段成果。

关键词：城邦；造船区；德莫；三一区；公民；公民权

Abstract：Naukrariai, Tritemorin and Demos are suggested to be the regional space units of Athenian city-state, thereby they are the fundamental concepts for cognizing the history of Ancient Greece. In historical context of ancient Greek history, Naukrariai, Tritemorin and Demos have relatively time-space meanings. As for regional meaning, a citizen of the city-state or Polites belonged to a certain unit of Naukrariai, Tritemorin or Demos. Citizenship were primarily enjoyed by male citizens, which was characterized of suffrage, jury duty and government service, presumes the right of political participation basing on Naukrariai, Tritemorin and Demos. Naukrariai, Tritemorin and Demos therefore form the foundation of citizenship of Athenian city-state.

Keywords: City-state, Naukrariai, Demos, Tritemorin, Citizen, Citizenship

　　20 世纪 80 年代以来，随着对西方古典文明史研究的深入，更是得益于考古和铭文资料的发掘和解析，越来越多的欧美古史学者，开始关注古希腊历史上的德莫（demes）。其中，尤以古史专家罗宾·奥斯邦（Robin Osborne）和戴维·怀特赫德（David Whitehead）的研究最具影响力。罗宾·奥斯邦以"乡村结构与古典城邦：雅典社会的城乡关系（Rural Structure and the Classical Polis:Town-Country Relations in Athenian Society）"为题，完成其在剑桥国王学院（King's College, Cambridge）

的博士学位论文。后经扩充和完善，成为当今研究古希腊德莫的重要学术著作《德莫：古典阿提卡的发现》①。该著主要介绍文献和考古资料所反映的阿提卡的乡村居住方式，以及德莫的规模和财产。探究古典阿提卡土地所有制的形式、雅典德莫的乡村结构和民主政治的关系，以及德莫中的宗教因素等。

与奥斯邦一样，戴维·怀特赫德（David Whitehead）也专注于研究阿提卡的德莫，其代表作《阿提卡的德莫》②从克里斯提尼改革之前的阿提卡德莫入手，深入研究了克里斯提尼改革后阿提卡 139 个德莫的居民结构，村社大会的时间、地点和程序，公民大会的主要任务，村长及村社其他官职设置，村社的收支和宗教活动等。在此基础上，进一步探究德莫与城邦中央政权的关系。

此外，欧美学者詹姆森（M.H.Jameson）的《希腊乡村》③，安德尔（T.H.van Andel）的《卫城之外》④，奥斯邦（R.Osborn）的《古典历史图景》⑤，以及约翰·里茨（John Rich）等编著的《古代世界的城市与乡村》⑥，也为研究古希腊庇奥提亚、南阿戈利德、南优卑亚等地区的德莫，提供了极为珍贵的考古与文献资料。

在德莫研究深入的同时，造船区、三一区也被时常提及，并且成为认知古希腊历史，尤其是雅典公民与公民权的基本语词。那么，在古希腊历史语境下，公民和公民权的具体内涵是什么？作为城邦的区域空间的造船区、三一区和德莫，与城邦的公民权有何关系？本文试作探究。

一　πολιτησ——城邦的人（公民）

中文习惯于将古希腊语"πολιs"（波利斯）译为"城邦"，将城邦的人"πολιτηs"（波利忒斯或波利忒）译为"公民"。⑦

古希腊语中的"波利忒斯"一词在法律上最早出现于雅典的第一部成文法《德拉古法》，意为"城邦的人"。在其后的法典中，"波利忒斯"逐渐普遍使用。但是，意义不尽相同。即便是在古希腊城邦，同样很难给"πολιτηs"一个公认的定义。因为在民主政体中作为公民的人，在寡头政体中常常被排除在公民名籍之外。⑧

既然不是所有的人都可以成为城邦的公民，公民也非普遍意义上的通用概念。那么，什么样的人才可以称为"城邦的人"？为此，亚里士多德在《政治学》中用了较多的篇幅讨论公民的定义和概念。其基本结论可以概述为：

公民是属于城邦的人，而且是年满 18 岁以上的男性，具有同邦同种族的血亲关系。公民必须是"有权参加议事和审判职能的人"。⑨这三者的统一，才有资格被称为"全权公民"（或全称公民，citizen in full senses）。

首先，公民必须是属于城邦（πολιs）的人。

古希腊语中的"公民"是属于"城邦的人"（πολιτηs）。城邦是公民集体或公民共同体。判断

① Robin Osborne, Demos: *The Discovery of Classical Attika*, Cambridge: Cambridge University Press, 1985.
② David Whitelead, *The Demes of Attica*, Princeton: Princeton University Press, 1986.
③ M.H.Jameson, *A Greek Countryside, The Southern, Argolid from Prehistory to The Present Day*, Stanford:Stanford University Press, 1994.
④ T.H.van Andel, *Beyond The Acropolis: A Rural Greek Past*,Stanford:Stanford University Press, 1987.
⑤ Robin Osborne, *Classical Landscaps with Figurs*,London: George Philip,1987.
⑥ John Rich and Andrew Wallace-Hadrill, *City and Country in The Ancient World*, London and New York:Routledge,1991.
⑦ 与 polis 音译为"波利斯"一致，城邦的人πολιτηs音译为"波利忒"或波利忒斯似乎更为妥切。
⑧ Aristotle, *Politics*,1274b40;1275a1-3.
⑨ Aristotle, *Politics*,1275b19.

城邦的本质，关键是看其是否存在一个可以参与城邦事务、享有最高治权的公民团体。"城邦正是若干（许多）公民的组合。"①

早自荷马时代，"公民集体"的雏形已经产生。在《荷马史诗》中的"血缘集团"或部落，后来演化为公民集体。只是其原先尚没有任何直接的政治意义。直到古风时代（约公元前700年~前480年），以公民集体为本质特征的古希腊城邦普遍形成，公民共同体开始具有明确的政治意义。城邦的公民开始强调自身的特权以及与其他社会群体的区别。公民的集体意识和公民权观念也开始发展。只有属于本邦部落血统的成年男子才有资格成为城邦的公民。公民与城邦间的这种特殊的归属关系，是由氏族部落制向城邦演化过程中所形成的"历史权利"。②

第二，公民必须是18岁以上的男性，而且具有同邦同种族的血亲关系。

由于城邦的公民集体源自氏族血缘关系，而氏族部落中的本族人和外族人的界限非常严格。所以，作为"城邦的人"也沿袭这些严格的血缘界限。公民，首先是一种世袭身份，即父母都需要是本邦的自由人。从这个意义上说，城邦中具有公民身份的人，相互之间的关系是平等的，没有隶属和奴役的关系。

例如，雅典城邦形成之初的四个部落成年男子，罗马城邦形成中的拉丁姆地区的罗慕洛及其后代的成年男子等，都是基于血缘关系而获得公民身份或资格的人。公民内部是平等关系。城邦也努力通过不断改革和立法来调适和保护这种平等关系。

所以，即使在城邦居住，如果没有源自同氏族血亲关系的人，也不得为公民。诚如亚里士多德所言："一个正式的公民不应该由其住所所在而决定是当地的公民。侨民和奴隶有其住所，但他们不得称为公民。"③

这种世袭的血亲关系通过"登籍"程序而得以传承和维护。希腊文 πολιτο-γραφεω，意为"登记为公民"，就是指称这一登籍程序。

登籍有年龄要求。雅典儿童14岁时在其所属的德莫进行登籍。至18岁时为成年公民，④但这主要是一种资格，意味着有资格成为"全权公民"⑤。在《古希腊百科全书》中有这样的解释：城邦的"全权公民"是所有年满18岁以上的男子。他们的出生需要进行依据同种族血亲关系（registered with the traditional brotherhood）的登籍。无论其位居哪里，男性公民是城邦的核心，他们组成集团，遵从公民权法则。⑥

这就说明，城邦的公民，必须是18岁以上的男性，而且必须是具有同种族血亲关系。至少在雅典是如此限定的。

未及登籍年龄的儿童和已过免除兵役年龄的老人，不是"全权公民"。因为儿童是未长成的公民，老人是超龄的公民。"成年人是全权公民，儿童既未发育，要是也称为公民，就只是在含义上有所保留的虚拟公民。"⑦

关于公民登籍，亚里士多德在《雅典政制》中有较为详细的记载：

雅典儿童14岁时由德莫登籍于"德莫长保管的册籍"。17岁时为"及龄公民"。至18岁时为成年公民。公民18岁时在其德莫的名簿中登籍。当他们登籍之时，德莫成员对他们宣誓投票，作

---

① Aristotle, *Politics*, 1276b3.

② 丛日云：《西方政治文化传统》，黑龙江人民出版社，2002年版第36页。

③ Aristotle, *Politics*，1275a6-8.

④ Aristotle, *the Athenian Constituion*，ⅩⅬⅡ.

⑤ Aristotle, *Politics*，1278a5.

⑥ Nigel Wilson edt.,*Encyclopedia of Ancient Greece*, Routledge,2010,pp.164-165 "city-state" 词条。

⑦ Aristotle：*Politics*, 1278a5；1275a13-14.

出登籍资格决定。①

这段文本内容说明，公民登籍主要关乎公民身份的资格确认。

其一，确认是否达到法定年龄。如果认为没有达到法定年龄，将其重新归于儿童之列。

其二，确认是否为合法出生的自由民。这种合法性是世袭的血缘关系和地域关系的结合。一个雅典人的公民身份由他的源于父名的姓和德莫来确定，由此相异于异邦人。源于父名的姓，体现的是城邦的氏族 (genos) 因素。合法出生的自由民，必须具有同族的血亲关系。所有公民一定是属于一个氏族。这个氏族组织与合法、血统、继承等问题联系密切。氏族组织由此完全将异邦人排除在外。

至于登籍中的德莫，主要体现城邦公民集体的地域因素。源于父名的姓与德莫相结合，确定公民身份的血缘和地域关系。例如，登籍苏格拉底时，"苏格拉底，阿罗佩塞德莫的苏弗罗尼斯科斯之子"。

尤为重要的是，登籍必须接受德莫大会对其年龄和自由民身分等进行审核和投票表决。如果村社成员投票结果认为其没有合法的自由民身份，他可以向陪审法庭申诉。村民从同一氏族中选出五人对其辩论。如果判决其并无登籍权利，城邦便将其出卖。如果其胜诉，村民必须让其完成登籍。

接下来是议事会检查登籍者的名单，如果发现任何人未满18岁而登籍，允许其登籍的村民便要受到罚金的处分。罚金数额可能由议事会讨论议定。

完成登籍的合法男性自由民，或丁男（指雅典城邦18岁的男子，εφηβοι，*Ephebi*），他们的父亲便按照氏族部落举行会议，并在部落大会上宣誓。之后，各部落从部落中选定年龄在40岁以上并被认为是最好且最宜于监督这些丁男的部落成员3人。然后每个部落经过部落会议以举手的方式从各部落选定的3人中再选举1人为教练官，并从其他公民中推荐选举一个将军，统帅这些全体男丁。这些被推选产生的监督者、教练官和将军，把全体丁男集结成为队伍，在第一次巡行雅典娜神庙之后，开往比雷埃夫斯港作为守卫。

之后，部落大会为他们选出2个竞技教练和一些教师，教他们重装步兵操练和使用弓、投枪和投石器。在18岁至20岁期间主要进行守卫和军事训练。

部落会议给教练官分配口粮，每人一德拉克玛；丁男每人四个奥波尔。每一部落丁男的津贴费，由每一部落的教练官支领，教练官为部落丁男购备一样的食粮，按部落实行公餐。丁男至19岁时，民众通常在剧场开会。丁男们在部落民众面前举行一次操练表演，并从部落或城邦领到一只盾和一支枪；之后，丁男们在乡村中当巡逻兵，并驻在哨兵守卫所。

自18岁开始，丁男当巡逻兵2年。期间，"他们豁免一切赋税；他们不得被人起诉，也不得起诉别人"。2年期满后，便成为普通公民集团的成员。②

女孩达到登籍年龄，可能也经部落大会，被介绍和登籍在其父亲所属的氏族。但是，通常情况下，审查一个妇女是否具有资格获得公民身份，主要调查她作为一个男孩的母亲和一个男人的妻子的情况。

经登籍审查后具有公民身份的人，享有世袭的特权，如分享城邦共有土地、享受城邦对公民身份和权力的特殊保护政策等等。

至梭伦改革时期，确立财产等级与公民权的关系，将公民权与财产等级联系起来。梭伦按照财产等级在公民之间分配政治职务。鼓励公民参与政治活动，诸如出席公民大会，参与国家政策的制定；出席新创设的陪审法庭，参与司法审判。梭伦改革使雅典公民不仅是法律上的自由民，而且还具有

① 也有说公民年龄自17岁起。参见亚里士多德：《政治学》，吴寿彭译，商务印书馆1997年版，第111页注释②。在雅典，将17岁的男儿称作"及龄公民"或"年轻公民"。中译本第333页注释③。

② Aristotle, *the Athenian Constituion*, ⅩⅬⅡ, 1–5.

一系列的特权、荣誉和义务。

其后，雅典城邦的公民权不仅仅是世袭的身份特权，还因财产多寡而享有不同的政治、司法和军事权利。

此后，克里斯提尼的政治改革主要是公民权的裁定和适用。雅典创立了更加民主的新机构，为所有公民全面参与城邦的政治事务提供了新的机会。此时，异邦人移民雅典而获得雅典公民权变得十分困难。不管移民在阿提卡居住多久，这样的移民一律被正式称为"异邦人"（metics）。

克里斯提尼时代，德莫不仅登籍公民，也登籍定居在城邦的异邦人。但是，异邦人必须在其雅典保护人所属的德莫进行登籍。

值得注意的是，一个异邦人即使登籍了，仅仅属于他（或她）所定居的德莫，不享有公民的权利。不可以担任德莫的公职人员和祭司。而且，从公元前5世纪后半期开始，男性移民每年要缴纳人头税12德拉克马，女性6德拉克马。①异邦人只有通过公民大会的特殊投票，才能成为雅典公民。这主要是对那些为城邦作出特殊贡献的异邦人予以回报。但是，异邦人的特权较少或基本没有。异邦人之所以仍然聚集雅典，主要是受益于雅典成功扩张所取得的经济繁荣、民主政治以及其他方面所带来的实惠。

不过，定居在雅典德莫的异邦人，既然属于同一个德莫的居民，也就可以参加其所定居德莫的宗教生活，甚至分享献给这个德莫的部落英雄的牺牲。

雅典人将非定居在雅典的异邦人统称为Xenoi，不予以登籍。定居在雅典的异邦人（metics）与非定居的异邦人（Xenoi），虽然没有任何的公民权利，但是，有时经申请获准后，可以被召唤到公民大会上提供信息或代表自己的利益在公民大会上发言。

克利斯提尼改革之后，严格意义上的雅典公民是指在139个德莫（城邦最小的地域组织）中登籍的全体成年男性。②雅典公民权的裁定根植于德莫。克利斯提尼所创设的德莫体制一直延续了近200年的时间。③

需要说明的是，一个具有公民身份的妇女往往随丈夫或父亲而属于同一个德莫。例如，"阿雷马科，阿那基罗斯的卡利马科斯的女儿"。其意思是卡利马科斯的女儿阿雷马科属于其父亲卡利马科斯的德莫。

经过源自父名的姓与德莫裁定的雅典公民人数随时境变迁，学界说法不一。成年男性公民大约仅占阿提卡全部人口的15%左右。④公民权也仅限于成年男性。斯巴达公民最多的时候据说不超过九千人；⑤公元前6世纪末的雅典，虽然经历梭伦和克里斯提尼的改革，吸收不少异邦人甚至奴隶加入公民队伍，大概也不过三万公民；⑥号称希腊大邦的科林斯在普拉提亚战役中仅出动了五千名重装步兵；不少城邦如迈锡尼仅有几百名重装步兵。⑦柏拉图在《法律篇》中提出，城邦人口应当是五千多名农夫和他们的田产保卫者；理想城邦的公民数限于5040人，⑧并言明各家子女或多或少的应相

---

① [英] 保罗·卡特里奇：《剑桥插图古希腊史》，郭小凌等译，山东画报出版社，2005年版第92页。

② David Whitehead, *The Demes of Attica*, Princeton:Princeton University Press, 1986, pp.369–373; 同时参见 Robin Osborne, *Demos:The Discovery of Classical Attika*, Cambridge: Cambridge University Press,1985.pp.201–204. Tabel(2).The distribution of wealth by tribe and trittys.

③ David Stockton, *The Classical Athenian Democracy*.Oxford: Oxford University Press, 1991:58.

④ [英] 保罗·卡特里奇：《剑桥插图古希腊史》，郭小凌等译，山东画报出版社，2005年版第101页。

⑤ [古希腊] 普鲁塔克：《希腊罗马名人传》之《来库古传》，商务印书馆，1990年版第95页。

⑥ Herodotus, V, 97.

⑦ Herodotus, IX, 28–30.

⑧ Plato, *Law*, 740B—741A.

互调节，超额的人口应另谋出路，例如开辟海外殖民城市。①

亚里士多德的理想城邦没有具体人数，但认为人口不宜过多，以公民能够相互熟悉为好。②伦巴特认为，对于雅典平均每个部落的成年男性公民人数，仍是模糊不清的。一般认为公元前5世纪—公元前4世纪，雅典城邦的男性公民人数大约是2万或3万。③因此，在雅典城邦盛期的公元前5世纪，其公民人数应该大于此。戈麦和艾伦勃的估算说明了这一点。

戈麦和艾伦勃对古典时期雅典成年男性公民人数的估算④

	Gomme	Ehrenberg
c.480	35,000	25,000–30,000
c.432	43,000	35,000–45,000
c.400	22,000	20,000–25,000
c.360	———	28,000–30,000

经登籍和审定享有公民权的公民，有权参加村社德莫大会，城邦公民大会，选任官员和共同参与乡村德莫及城邦的各类行政、司法事务，在公民权的适用中体现了机会平等和轮流执政的雅典民主制原则。

第三，公民必须是管理城邦公共事务的人。

亚里士多德将全城邦的人分成两类：一为享有政治权利的公民，另一为有益于城邦经济生活的人，这些人是"虽为城邦所必需而不必享有政治权利的人们。"

第一类即是"凡得参加司法事务和治权机构的人们"，包括"公众法庭的审判员（陪审员）和公民大会的会员。"凡有权参加城邦的议事、司法和行政职司的人，都可以被称为是城邦的公民。⑤也就是说，公民与其权利结合在一起。公民与城邦的权力机构紧密相连。这些管理城邦公共事务的人都是城邦的公民。"人们如果一旦参加城邦政体，享有了政治权利，他们就的确是公民了。"⑥因此，公民不仅仅是18岁以上的男性和具有同种族的血亲关系，还必须是城邦权力机构的公职人员。公民直接参与城邦重大事务的讨论和决策。公民大会在各城邦都是最重要的权力机构。城邦一切重大问题必须由公民集体讨论决定。尽管城邦公职人员一般是非职业性的和业余性的，但是，公民担任官职是公民政治参与权的重要体现。亚里士多德最为强调的是公民的政治意义，而且，公民主要是指民主政体中参与公共事务的人。

此外，城邦的公民还具有排他性的约束条件。例如，异邦人、女性、奴隶以及卑贱职业者不得为公民。

异邦人不属于城邦。他们虽有自由身份，但没有政治权利。他们不能参加城邦的公共生活和宗教仪式，也不能分享城邦的土地。占公民人口半数的女性（妇女），即公民的配偶和女性后代，都属于自由人，但她们仅被看成是公民的家属，没有政治权利，也不属于公民。

城邦的自由人中，分为有公民权的自由人和无公民权的自由人（包括异邦人），其他则是奴隶。

---

① [古希腊] 亚里士多德：《政治学》，吴寿彭译，商务印书馆，1997年版第64页注释①。

② 同上，第354–356页。

③ S.D.Lambert, *The Phratries of Attica*. Michegan: The University of Michigan Press, 1993:19.

④ 戈麦的估算不包括60岁以上的男性。引自 P.J.Rhodes, *The Athenian Boule*, Oxford: Oxford University Press, 1985:3. Note 6.

⑤ Aristotle, *Politics*, 1275b18–20;1297b4–1298a3.

⑥ Aristotle, *Politics*, 1275a20–25.

奴隶属于主人，没有独立的人格和权利。

工匠和佣工属于"鄙俗的贱业"，被雅典公民所鄙夷。雅典技工多为异邦人。[①]在亚里士多德看来，"担任这些为维持城邦生存所必需的贱业者有二类——奴隶为私人服劳役，工匠和佣工（手艺人和苦力）则为社会劳作。"[②]

也就是说，只被作为有生命的财产看待的奴隶们，或仅仅赖以供应日用必需的工匠们，只能算是实现城邦生活的一些手段。这些人是城邦所必需的，有益于城邦经济生活，但不必享有政治权利的人们。

亚里士多德认为，最优良的城邦不应当把工匠作为公民。在容许工匠入籍的城邦中，就不可能每一公民都具备既能被统治也能统治的良好品德，仅仅一部分不担任鄙俗的贱业的人们才具备好公民的品德。

那么，好公民的品德是什么呢？这就是古代雅典公民的四德：（一）"节制"或温厚，相符于中国《论语》，"克己复礼"。（二）"正义"（公平正直）。（三）"勇毅"，谓其人有"丈夫气"。（四）"端谨"或"明哲"。[③]欲达到理想城邦的最大幸福，公民必须都具备四种美德。而工商和农业劳动者都不能具备好公民的"四德"，所以理想城邦不宜容许他们为公民。

柏拉图在《法律篇》中也说过：工匠没有闲暇从政修德。商贩牟利，多违四德，两者都不得入籍于亚里士多德所拟的次级理想国。[④]从政需要闲暇。农民缺少智慧。而智慧得自于教导和学习，学习必须有闲暇。农民少有闲暇，不能免于愚昧。所以，农民也不得入籍理想城邦为公民。[⑤]

由此可见，公民属于城邦，城邦也属于公民。城邦兴衰直接影响公民的权益。归属于城邦是公民的基本意义。

当然，各个城邦对于公民的认定，并非一成不变。众所周知，雅典在梭伦改革时期，许多奴隶因"解负令"而重获自由之身。成为自由人之后，以工艺和帮工（佣工）来养家糊口。[⑥]后来，雅典航海业和海军的强大就得力于这些技工和佣工。[⑦]雅典海军的桡手（ναυτης）大多是"船舶长老"（ναυκληρos）[⑧]从雅典城中和比雷埃夫斯港口招来的佣工。三层桨战舰每艘桡手150人。这些桡手服兵役后可以入籍为公民，所以，雅典从萨拉米海战（前480年）海军获胜以后，平民地位大大提高。从这个意义说，海权和平民政体有关。[⑨]

雅典公民也随政治变迁和人口增减而变更。雅典城邦人口增殖以后规定，"公民就是父母双方都是公民所生的儿子，但是父亲或母亲为公民，则其子不得称为公民。有时，这种条件还得追溯更远，推及二代、三代或更多世代的祖先。"[⑩]父母双方都是公民，其子为"正宗公民"。"凡是能够参与城邦官职和参与城邦光荣（名位）的公民（πολιτης o μετεχων των τιμων, *shares in the honours of the state*）[⑪]是最尊贵的公民"。[⑫]即担任城邦公职和为城邦争得荣誉的人是最尊贵的公民。

---

① Plato, *Law*, 848A.

② Aristotle, *Politics*, 1278a5–15.

③ Plato, *Republic*, Ⅳ, 428;433; *Law*, Ⅰ, 631.

④ Plato, *Law*, Ⅷ 846; Ⅺ 919.

⑤ Aristotle, *Politics*, 1328b25–40.

⑥ Plutarch, *Solon*, 24.

⑦ Diodorus Siculus, *The Library of History* Ⅺ, 43.3.

⑧ 雅典海军的每一艘三层桨战舰各规定由一户富室加以装备和管理，其人称"船主"或"船舶长老"（ναυκληρos）。希腊城邦富室捐献的著名人物多是为船舶捐献和剧团捐献。船舶长老基本上是船舶捐献者。

⑨ 参见 Aristotle, *Politics*, 1274a12; 1327a40–b17; 1341a29; *the Athenian Constituion*, ⅩⅩⅦ.

⑩ Aristotle, Politics, 1275b23–25.1278a30.

⑪ μετεχων, 分享、参与。τιμων, 荣誉、尊敬。

⑫ Aristotle, *Politics*, 1278a35.

二　πολιτεια——公民权

古希腊语"πολιτεια"，意为"公民权"，用以指称与公民的身份资格相关的共同体中的决策权（a power of decision）和参与权（a power of participating）。①公民权是古希腊人最为重要的一种社会权利。"城邦制度形成过程中的一个中心问题是对公民群体以及公民权的定义"。②

"权利"概念形成于罗马司法。古希腊人的历史时期尚没有明确的"权利"概念。古希腊人的公民权，首先只是公民依据血缘原则的一种身份或资格。③但是，公民身份不仅意味着政治上的统治权，也意味着占有土地的权利。土地是城邦和个人生活的重要基础，失去了土地就失去了公民的权利。公民的身份和军人的身份也是一致的。保卫城邦的独立和安全，出征侵夺土地和财富，是公民的义务。作战所需的武器装备由公民自备。公民所尽军事义务的多寡或在军队中的地位，往往直接决定其所享有的政治权力。

古希腊公民的这种资格或身份决定其为城邦担当的责任和贡献。在古希腊人心目中，"公民资格不是拥有什么，而是分享什么，这很像是处于一个家庭成员的地位"。④按照现代的权利与义务关系来理解，古希腊的公民权是以义务定权利。出席公民大会、参加陪审法庭、充任官职、从军作战等，这些都是城邦公共事务，既是公民的权利又是公民的义务。这些权利都是伴随着公民的身份而自然产生的，享有多少权利就要承担多少义务。在希腊城邦的历史上，很少见到有公民逃避义务。当公民为城邦尽较多的义务时，他们也期望得到较多的权力，并积极争取。

如果说公民权"是由公民身份或资格而产生的权力"，那么，包括哪些权力呢？按照亚里士多德对公民权的阐释，主要是根据人们在参与政治生活中的三种情况或方式来定义的，即在公民大会上的投票权（表决权）、担任陪审员的陪审权（司法权）、具有担任政治职务或公职的执政权。也就是说，公民权是基于公民身份或资格，参与城邦公共生活的权力。

这些权力是伴随城邦或国家的产生通过立法来确定和维护的。所以，公民权是宪法产生之后才有的，具有更鲜明的"宪政"（constitutional goverment）权利的特征。公民权是阶级社会的产物。具有阶级社会的不平等性。这种不平等性主要表现在两个方面。

其一，公民在城邦中担当的权力程度受财产资格等级的限制。城邦通过立法，按照每个公民不同的经济地位或承担义务的实力来分配相应的权利和义务。尽多少义务，就享有多少权力，依义务定权力。重要职权多属于财产富足的富室。因为富室比贫民能够为城邦承担更多的义务。而下层平民获得与公民身份相一致的公民权，往往只有在比较发达的民主制城邦才能实现。这就是公民之间的不平等。

城邦形成之初，往往只有贵族和具有一定财产基础的人才能真正实现与身份资格相一致的公民权力。而基于经济地位不同，男性公民的责任和权力——如在公民大会选举或发言、担任公职、出任法官、参军打仗等诸多方面，也不尽相等。在早期城邦，只有富人和贵族能够拥有完整的公民权。

---

① 　Simon Hornblower and Antony Spawforth, edt. *The Oxford Classical Dictionary*, Third edition revised, p.333, "citizenship,Greek" 词条。

② 黄洋：《古代希腊土地制度研究》，复旦大学出版社,1995 年版，第 65 页；第 11 页。

③ 在法律中，公民是自然人的一种身份或资格。自然人即依自然出生而成为的人。在法律中与法人身份相区别。在自然人获得公民身份的问题上，世界各国遵循不同的原则：出生地原则或血缘原则。所谓出生地原则是指，一个人出生在某国的领土内，就可以因其出生而获得其公民身份；而血缘原则是指，只要在一个人出生时，父母中的一人有某国公民身份，无论他出生在何处，都可以获得与父母相同的公民身份。

④ [美]G. 萨拜因：《政治学说史》，商务印书馆 1986 年版，第 25 页。

古风时代的政治史，就是中产阶层和下层社会奋力争取在城邦内获得平等权力的历史。①下层平民在城邦民主比较发达的时候才能获得充分的参与权。有时因贫穷等原因不能履行公民义务者还会失去公民权。当战争危机或公民人数不足时，也会吸收异邦人和被释放的奴隶加入公民团体。但是，人们仍然以传统的血缘关系的观念来看待城邦公民内部的关系，将所有属于"城邦的人"（公民）视为出于同一祖先。这无形中产生并加强了公民对城邦的归属感。梭伦立法的基本原则就是"雅典城邦必须由全体公民共同治理。"②

其二，公民权具有排他性。

公民权的排他性主要是指在行政、司法等领域，对女性、奴隶和异邦人的权利排除。自梭伦开始的立法者的法律，明确表达了对女性的要求。认为对女性的行为加以规范有益于国家统治。女性的活动范畴仅限于家庭生活，她们被排除在宗教事务以外。女人可以拥有公民身份，但她们没有参与政治的权利。不具有全部的公民权利。③成年男性"全权公民"的妻女所具有的公民身份，只是为男性公民之妻并合法生育公民的资格条件，并有权参加宗教祭仪。雅典女性既没有表决权，也没有从事公职的权利，但是，她们是唯一能生育雅典公民的女性。妇女被完全排除在政治、司法、军事事务之外。这些领域仅仅属于男性成年男子（18岁以上）的男子。

因此，城邦经常被看作是"男性公民俱乐部"或"男人俱乐部"。因为男人组成公民大会，在公民大会上做出影响整个社会的决策。男人是法庭陪审员；城邦的几百个公职人员全部是男人。只有在神话或喜剧情节里，妇女们才能进入公民大会。阿里斯托芬的喜剧《公民大会中的妇女》即是例证。

实际上，将公民权的排他性仅仅理解为对女性、奴隶和异邦人的排斥是不全面的。公民权还有对职业的排他性。从事工匠、佣工等卑贱职业的人不可以成为公民，不具有公民权。

公民权的排他性，还表现在以城邦公民集体利益为依归，排斥其他一切危害城邦公民集体的自私自利行为。公民权是在参与集体的职责中实现的权利与义务。公民权"是政治权利，只有同别人一起才能行使的权利"。公民权具有公共性和集体性。这种权利的内容就是参加这个共同体，而且是参加政治共同体，参加城邦或国家。④城邦对公职人员的资格审查、任期责任考核、卸任检查以及贝壳放逐法的适用，皆是以公民集体的权利维护和保障为目的。任何危害公民集体利益的人都是不良的"人民领袖"或"蛊惑者"（δημαγωγος，*demagogues*）。

伯里克利时期雅典公民对自身公民权利的珍视还表现在其对于裁定公民权的态度上。以前，庇西特拉图和克里斯提尼为了获取民众的支持而使很多出身不纯的异邦人获取了雅典公民权，而伯里克利时代，随着民主政治的繁荣和公民人数的激增，城邦对于异邦人取得公民权利有了正式的法律制度上的限制。公元前5世纪上半期，只要父母中有一方为雅典人的儿子，年满18岁时就自然成为雅典公民。然而到了公元前451年，经过伯里克利的提议，雅典公民大会通过了一项法律，规定此后可以享受公民权利的人只限于那些父母双方都是雅典人的人。⑤

---

① 根据亚里士多德《政治学》的贫富阶层定义，"中产阶层"介于"极富和极贫"之间，拥有一定数量的财产。属于既不富裕，但也不依赖富人生活的阶层。贵族阶层大致是"拥有足够多的土地以保证闲适的人"。"穷人阶层"属于没有足够土地养活自己的底层阶级。参见 Aristotle, *Politics*, 1297a–1297b.

② Sarah B.Pomeroy, Stanley M.Burstein, Walter Donlan, Jennifer Tolbert Roberts: *Ancient Greece:A Political, Social, and Cultural History* ,Oxford University Press, 1999, p.169.

③ Sarah B.Pomeroy, Stanley M.Burstein, Walter Donlan, Jennifer Tolbert Roberts: *Ancient Greece:A Political, Social, and Cultural History* ,Oxford University Press, 1999,169.

④ 公民权不同于人权（生存权、劳动权、教育权等）。人权自古就有，虽然那时可能没有得到充分保障。人权具有个体性、私人性、利己性等特征。

⑤ 参见 Aristotle, *The Athenian Constitution*, XXVI3; Plutarch: *Solon*, 37.3–5.

虽然这项措施出台的原因尚待考证，但是它无疑显示出了雅典城邦面对大量涌入的异邦人而采取的排他态度。[1]这种公民权的排他性也很快在现实中得到了印证。伯里克利的公民权立法实施四年后，埃及国王给雅典送来四万麦斗的麦子，城邦准备将其分配给城邦的公民，而这势必要对公民资格作一次彻底的清查。清查的结果是查出了很多以前被忽略的混入城邦的私生子，共有5000余人，而雅典人立即毫不客气地将其卖到了外地。

这项法案通过后还在城邦内部产生一些社会问题。为了保证子嗣拥有公民权，雅典男人只能跟雅典女人结婚，即便与外邦女子有很亲近的关系，也不能娶外邦女子为妻。伯里克利本人就面临这样的困境。因为对婚姻的不满，他和其合法的妻子离婚。随后与米利都女子阿斯帕西亚（Aspasia）生活在一起。据说，阿斯帕西亚聪颖过人，是当时为数不多的最有教养的女子之一。但是，伯里克利的两个有公民权的儿子死后，他祈求公民大会更改法案，使得他与阿斯帕西亚所生的儿子"小伯里克利"能成为雅典公民。后来，雅典人同情伯里克利，同意了请求。小伯里克利获得公民身份并在公元前406年当选"十将军"之一。之后，在爱奥尼亚的阿吉纽斯海战（Arginusae）中（公元前406年），由于未能将雅典海军战士从暴风雨中救出，他和其他八位将军被"人民"处死。

三　公民权的区域空间：造船区、三一区和德莫

尽管在较早时期，古希腊人并没有明确的权力概念。但是，以部落或区域空间表示义务或权力的行为很早就有。至少"造船区"可以被看作是这一区域空间的较早形态。

造船区（ναυκραριαι，naukrariai）是古希腊人的早期地方区划。古希腊人第一次联合外侵特洛伊时，造船区便是体现古希腊人义务和权利的区域空间。造船区是组织军事力量的基本区划。荷马史诗《伊利亚特》第二章中的《船表》，列出迈锡尼一方共派出29支舰队，派遣舰船共1116艘。其中阿提卡50艘，优卑亚40艘。船上水手数一般为50人，最多的达120人。这些船舰来自不同的造船区。

根据亚里士多德的记载，提秀斯时代的"统一运动"（Synoecism）之后，造船区划成为阿提卡用以征税的48个行政区。造船区的首领称"造船区长"（ναυκραρος/ναυληρος）。起初，每个造船区须为雅典舰队担负制备一艘战舰的费用。约在僭主政治时期，造船区被赋予行政管理职责，但仍包括征税。[2]

梭伦改革时，雅典有四个古老的部落，每个部落分为三个胞族，每个胞族包括三十个氏族。每个氏族三十户（家）。有四个部落王（φιλοβασιλεις，即巴塞勒斯）。每一个造船区设有一个官职，称为造船区长（ναυκραρος），职掌监督征税、开支及行政。[3]

克里斯提尼为"人民领袖"时，把所有的居民划分为10个部落，以代替原有的四个古老部落。每个部落包括5个造船区，共50个造船区。每个造船区提供战舰一艘，供城邦使用。造船区的领袖称为"船主"，"管理人"（ναυκραρος）。[4]但是，很难弄清楚50个造船区是如何与10个新的

---

[1]　关于此项措施出台的原因，学界尚有争议。西方多数学者一般都同意亚里士多德的说法，即认为是公民人数增加的结果，但是一些学者也提出异议。

[2]　Aristotle, *The Athenian Constitution*. Ⅷ.2–3.

[3]　值得注意的是，亚里士多德在《雅典政制》Ⅷ，3，提及梭伦时代的雅典四个部落，每一部落分为3个三一区和十二个造船区（复数ναυκραριαι）。如此，四个部落，应该有48个造船区。每个造船区必须担负制备一艘战舰的费用。不过，亚里士多德在这里可能不是指梭伦时代就有三一区。因为亚里士多德并没有明确此时的三一区是如何构成的。而在随后论及克里斯提尼时代，明确说明三一区是如何得名的。

[4]　罗念生、水建馥编：《古希腊语汉语词典》，商务印书馆，2004年版，第563页ναυκραρος词条。

地域部落及 30 个三一区相互融通地共存于阿提卡半岛（可能每个部落有 5 个造船区）。①

克里斯提尼还将阿提卡所有的德莫分为"三十区"（τριακοντα, thirty parts）。10 个在城郊，10 个在沿海，10 个城区。他称这 30 个区划为"三一区"（τριτημοριν, Thirds），意为"三分之一"。按地域组合的"三一区"是克里斯提尼的新创。每个"三一区"内包含若干个业已存在的德莫。德莫规模不等，共有 100 多个。每个三一区包含的数量不尽相等。

接着，克里斯提尼从城市、海岸和内陆三区各取一个"三一区"合在一起构成一个地区部落。如此一来，每个部落均由三个"三一区"组成，分别来自城市、海岸以及内陆。30 个三一区共组成 10 个部落。由此将不同区域的人混合起来。②居民以所在的行政区名互称，以取代其家族名称。③"人们不必再用祖上的名字相称，而正式以德莫的名字相称。雅典人自此在私人生活上也使用他们德莫的名字作为姓氏。而在之前，雅典人的姓氏用的是父名"。④传统世袭贵族所依赖的血缘关系被废除。所有按照新的划分而住在同一部落的人都是"德莫居民"（fellow—demesmen）。

克里斯提尼把雅典公民由氏族编制改为地区编制，突显了德莫和三一区等区域空间的政治地位与作用，由此分散和削弱了贵族寡头派所依仗的氏族血缘关系和势力。这种人为创设的行政区划，使得克里斯提尼的宪政得以实施。以德莫和三一区为基础的公民权力得到加强。

德莫（demos）既可指地域空间，也可指其间的居民。这两种意义的"德莫"出现较早。最早见于线形文字 B 的碑文中。⑤

荷马时代，以地域为界的德莫已经存在。在荷马史诗中，德莫与波利斯（堡垒或卫城 πολις, polis）相对，意指"乡郊"。"卫城"周围的地区称"市区"（αστυ, astu）。此时的德莫主要是地域概念。

荷马时代的德莫有两种"族群共同体"：伊达卡人（Ithacans）和派利安人 (Pylians)。二者膜拜的神祇是一样的。这些德莫里的族群共同体中"达到作战年龄的男子组成民众大会（the assembly）和议事会（the council of elders）。⑥此时，之所以还没有形成基于德莫的城邦，主要是因为并立存在的德莫尚没有在政治上正式达成一致，并建立中央政府（central goverment）。

公元前 7 ~ 前 6 世纪的"古风时代"，伴随贫富差距的扩大，在私有制、阶级和城邦的形成中，德莫之间的冲突和战争不断。其间，各地发生的"村镇联合"或"统一运动"就是指各个德莫接受同一政治中心的过程。⑦

居住在阿提卡地区的居民在"统一运动"后以雅典为中心城市，成立中央议事会等机构。起初，"巴塞勒斯"为王，后来为贵族（寡头）统治。雅典贵族议事会和民众大会等机构，成为统一的政治机构。各地居民皆称自己是"雅典人"（Athenians）。此时，德莫与城市基本重合。

因此，"统一运动"之后，阿提卡既有指"乡郊"的德莫，也有指"城区"的德莫。德莫内只有几百户人家，彼此距离很近，联系紧密，从而把古代的胞族和部落关系"统一"为以德莫为基础

---

① Aristotle: *The Athenian Constitution,* III2-3.

② Aristotle: *The Athenian Constituion* ⅩⅪ, 3-4.

③ Sarah B.Pomeroy, Stanley M.Burstein, Walter Donlan, Jennifer Tolbert Roberts: *Ancient Greece: A Political, Social, and Cultural History* ,Oxford University Press, 1999,p.176.

④ Aristotle: *The Athenian Constituion* ⅩⅪ, 3-5.

⑤ Simon Hornblower and Antony Spawforth ed., *The Oxford Classical Dictionary*, third edition revised, Oxford : Oxford University Press, 2003, p.446.

⑥ Sarah B.Pomeroy, Stanley M.Burstein, Walter Donlan, Jennifer Tolbert Roberts: *Ancient Greece: A Political, Social, and Cultural History* ,Oxford University Press, 1999,p.84.

⑦ "统一运动"，Σψνοεχισμ。原意为 ηαριν τηε οικοι τογετηερ, οικοι（οικοι）为 οικοσ 的复数，意指"房屋"、"居所"。"村镇联合"延续很久。可能始于前 9 世纪，至前 750 ~ 前 700 基本完成。

的包括城区及毗邻乡郊的新的共同体,这种新的共同体就是最初的城邦(πολιs)——以城市为中心的、结合周围乡村的公民集体。就地域而言,包括卫城、市区和乡郊。德莫成为城邦的基层组织,综合了土地、人民及其政治生活形态,赋有了"邦"或"国"的政治意义。德莫实际上就是一个投票机构,一个跟贵族阶层类似的利益集团。在后期的希腊历史上,民主制度的推行者将德莫定义为全体投票者。然而,反对民主制度的人继续认为德莫仅指全体穷人。[1]因为"德莫"一词用以指称"人民",最初是指郊区的庶民或平民,相对于城居的王族或贵族。

亚里士多德则把德莫更多的看作是邦内居民,认为德莫乃"自由而贫穷,同时又为邦内多数的人们。"[2]值得注意的是,德莫在指称"公民"时,尤指雅典有公民权的人,而在取意"平民"时,其意义不尽相同。亚里士多德在用指"平民"时,就有细微差异。或是指与"有产者们"相对的"无产者";[3]或与"富室"及"饶于资产的富人"相对的"薄于资产"的"平民";[4]或是指与"高尚人士"及"显贵之士"相对的"平民";[5]或有别于"重装兵"的"第四级公民"(事实上,重装兵也来自村落居民);[6]或包括艺工和商人在内的"群众",并非完全是"贫民"。[7]

克里斯提尼时代,重编阿提卡公民时(公元前 509 年),分城郊地区为 100 个德莫,嗣后,德莫遂为城乡通用名称。既有城市德莫,也有乡村德莫。德莫数量增加。[8]至克里斯提尼时代的后期,德莫总数 139 个。至公元前 3 世纪,已经有 176 个德莫。[9]编属于德莫的居民称为"德莫忒斯"(δημοτηs),都有资格成为"城邦的人",即波利忒斯 " πολιτηs ",享有公民权力。

德莫是城邦机制的权力基础。"德莫忒斯"为城邦的基本组成。公民(包括兵役)的登籍就在德莫办理。基于这种"德莫"而建立的政体,后世称之为"平民政体"或"民主政体"(δημοκρατια)。克里斯提尼因此被誉为"民主之父"。在民主制城邦,公民大会决议正式开头的一句话就是"人民决定"(The demos has decided)。

克利斯提尼时代的雅典公民,就是指在 139 个德莫(城邦最小的区域)中登记的全体成年男性。公民权的裁定始终决定于德莫的登记、审核、表决和军事训练。德莫的人口和土地登记为城邦的埃

① Sarah B.Pomeroy, Stanley M.Burstein, Walter Donlan, Jennifer Tolbert Roberts: *Ancient Greece:A Political, Social, and Cultural History* , Oxford University Press, 1999, p.166.
② 参见 Aristotle, *Politics*, 1290^b,17−20.
③ Aristotle, *Politics*, 1296^a,25.
④ Aristotle, *Politics*, 1297^a,11;1304^b,1.
⑤ Aristotle, *Politics*, 1274^a, 12.
⑥ Aristotle, *Politics*,1305^b,33.
⑦ Aristotle, *Politics*,1291^b,18; 1290^b,17.
⑧ [古希腊] 亚里士多德:《政治学》,吴寿彭译,商务印书馆,1997 年版第 129 页注释⑥。
⑨ Aristotle:*the Athenian Constituion* XⅪ, 4;同时参见中译本第 25 页注释④。但是,克里斯提尼所创的"三十区"中的每个区究竟包含多少个德莫,不得而知。大致所知,改革初始,每个部落有 10 个德莫。10 个部落共 100 个德莫。

非比制度 (ephebeia)、①非常财产税（eisphora）的征收、②公益捐制度（liturgies）等，也提供了必要的数据。③

克里斯提尼还曾一时许可若干异邦人和居留在雅典的外邦奴隶入籍于德莫，增加了平民人数。依照雅典和希腊各邦的传统观念，异邦人不应同本族等量齐观。奴隶更不可为公民。克里斯提尼的变革因而被亚里士多德指责为破坏了成规。④但是，亚里士多德同时也说，不管是否合乎陈规或道义，凡现实必须承认它是现实；凡已取得法定公民的身份者就得承认他是公民。而西塞罗等认为，如此法律是恶法，恶法就不成其为法律；他不承认恶法所赋予的权利，把它们看作是虚假的事物。⑤

近现代学者也认为，自克里斯提尼改革之后，德莫不仅是"地域"空间和"人民"的指称，更多了一层政治意义，德莫是民主制城邦的权力基础，意味着自治单位或人民的统治。雅典民主政治的组织结构与实践，例如，公民大会、五百人议事会和陪审法庭等公职人员的选举、任用与考核等，皆是以德莫为基础。诚如汉森所言，德莫有两种含义。一则是"人民"，意指(1)所有的雅典成年男性公民；(2)普通人或穷人；(3)人民的大会（即公民大会 ekklesia）；(4)人民的统治（即民主政治,demokratia）。一则是"自治单位"（municipality）。指克里斯提尼改革所划分的阿提卡的 139 个德莫。⑥

综上所述，德莫的基本含义是：①乡区，与 πολιs 城市相对；②民众或平民；③人民或公民（尤指雅典有公民权的人）；④民主政体。

四　德莫——民主政治的权力基础

享有公民权的公民，有权参加德莫大会，城邦公民大会，选任官员和共同参与德莫及城邦的各类行政、司法事务，"德莫体制确定同一类人聚居一起，彼此非常熟悉。共同管理村社及融为一体的城邦之事务。"⑦

因此，从制度上说，德莫是民主政治的基础。德莫为民主政治提供了最直接的组织方式和运行实践。"所有的德莫都有自己的政治生活。有些政治生活促进了城邦整体的政治管理"。通过德莫，公民可以被选入较大的城邦政治组织。"德莫和部落都是推选行政和军事组织公职人员候选人方便

---

① Ephebeia，是指雅典 15－20 岁男子的体育训练。埃非比教育制度始于前 335 年，由 Epicrates 首创。旨在对年轻人达 18 岁时进行更为有效的强制性军事训练。有 6 位老师和 4 个指导使用重装盔甲（heavy armour），弓（the bow），标枪（the javelin）和石弩（the catapult）等专项技能训练的教练。资助埃非比教育的人称为 sophronistai，10 个部落每个部落 1 人，共 10 人。这里可能是指征收用于埃非比教育、交给埃非比学院（Ephebic College）的款项。公元前 305 年之后，埃非比不再是强制性的教育。公元前 303 年以后，文献中很少提到 sophronistai。城邦不再支付给埃非比学员（ephebes）每天每人 4 个奥波尔的津贴。埃非比教育成为富人的教育，人数减少。教师的费用可能由城邦支付。详见 N.GL. Hammond, H.H.Scullard, *The Oxford Classical Dictionary*.Oxford: Oxford University Press, 1987, p.386. Epheboi 词条
② Eisphora，古代雅典、埃吉那、门德（Mende）、米利都、斯巴达、美塞尼等地对富有的人征收的非常财产税（an extraordinary property tax）。这里的财产包括土地和其它财产。征收的比例为估价财产的 1/100、1/50、1/12 不等。前 4 世纪的雅典征收的是可分配财产税（distributable property tax）。前 5 世纪，其它种类的财产税在雅典和别的城邦也提到。详见 N.GL.Hammond, H.H.Scullard. *The Oxford Classical Dictionary*,Oxford: Oxford University Press, 1987, p.376. Eisphora 词条
③ N.GL.Hammond, H.H.Scullard, *The Oxford Classical Dictionary*. Oxford: Oxford University Press, 1987, p.329. Demoi 词条。
④ Aristotle, *Politics*,1275b35.
⑤ [古希腊] 亚里士多德：《政治学》，吴寿彭译，商务印书馆，1997 年版第 115 页注释②。
⑥ 参见 Mogens Herman Hansen, *The Athenian Assembly in the Age of Demosthenes*, Oxford:Basil Blackwell Ltd., 1987,p.210.
⑦ David Stockton,*The Classical Athenian Democracy*. Oxford: Oxford University Press, 1991, p.66.

而有效的基层单位。"①"如果人们希望在城邦政治生活中充分发挥作用，就有必要了解自己的德莫，并被德莫所接纳。"②德莫还可以履行某些治安职责，占据土地，出庭为土地和宗教事务辩论，举行祭仪和推选官员等。有些政治家可能就是因为出自著名的德莫而获得荣耀，并因此进入城邦政治组织。③

古典盛期，德莫是公民大会、五百人议事会和陪审法庭等雅典民主政治的主要权力机构在地方上的"权力基础"（power-base）。德莫的主要行政功能有 2 个，一个功能是对年满 18 的雅典人作为全权公民进行登记。另一个功能是为五百人议事会选供候选人。④戴维·怀特赫德把村社与中央政权之间的这种关系称作是"地方政治与城市政治"（local politics and city politics），将德莫视为城邦"友好的合作伙伴"（companionable associates）和"政治权力的基础"（the deme as political power-base）。⑤公民权以德莫为基础而适用于中央权力机构的具体运作之中，主要表现如下：

其一，作为雅典城邦最高权力机构和立法机构的公民大会（*ekklesia, ecclesia*,the assembly），是以德莫为区域基础的全体公民的大会。

公民大会由议事会（council of 500,the *boule*）召集，每隔 10 天召开一次例会，一年大约 40 次，其中有 4 次是定期例会。公民大会主要讨论和决定由议事会提交的议案并负责立法，但不得随意颁布法令。诸如粮食供给、城邦防御、宗教问题乃至免除地方官员和将军等，皆是公民大会的重要议程。

从理论上讲，公民大会是经德莫裁定而享有公民权的全体公民的大会。参加公民大会的权力只限于雅典成年男性即 18 岁以上的男性公民。苏格拉底言及的公民大会与会人员有：漂洗工、制鞋工、木匠、铁匠、农民、商人和店主。⑥据现代学者的研究，一般情况下，与会人员主要是中上等阶层——重装步兵和战争税的纳税人。特别会议时，普通劳动阶层等更多的人员与会。⑦但是，无论与会人员多么复杂，公民大会始终面向所有的德莫和公民。

其二，五百人议事会是经由德莫抽签选举代表而组成的最高行政机构。

克里斯提尼创设的"五百人议事会"，每年抽签改选一次。⑧德莫中的"三一区"之重要作用，就在于选举议事会成员的程序上。选举中，"三一区"成为联结德莫和部落的重要桥梁。⑨选举议事会议员时，每个德莫按照既定的数额推选。⑩五百人议事会议员选自所有的德莫。首先由德莫选出候选人。每个德莫的议事会议员的人数是由德莫的成年男性公民人口的多少决定的。平均每个德莫可选出 3 ～ 4 个议员。但是，大约有 30 个德莫的议员席位每年只有 1 个。有 8 个德莫每年的议员席位为 10 个或更多。最大的德莫阿卡奈每年有 22 个议员席位。⑪然后，所有年龄达 30 岁以上的候选

① Robin Osborne, *Classical Landscape With Figures,The Ancient Greek City and Its Countryside*. London: George Philip, 1987, p.128.

② Robin Osborne, *Demos: The Discovery of Classical Attika*. Cambridge: Cambridge University Press ,1985, p.88

③ 见 Plut.Mor.843f.,cf,SIG³296.4; Robin Osborne, *Demos: The Discovery of Classical Attika*. Cambridge: Cambridge University Press ,1985, p.80; 88.

④ Mogens Herman Hansen, *The Athenian Assembly in the Age of Demosthenes*. Oxford:Basil Blackwell Ltd., 1987, pp.210-211.

⑤ 详见 David Whitehead, *The Demes of Attica.Princeton*:Princeton University Press, 1986, pp.291-326.

⑥ Xenohon, *Memorabilia*. Ⅲ .vii. 6.

⑦ A.H.M.Jones, *Athenian Democracy*.Oxford: Basil Blackwell Ltd., 1989, p.109.

⑧ R.J.Rhodes,*Athenian Boule*. London :Oxford University Press, 1972, p.12.

⑨ Robin Osborne. *Demos: The Discovery of Classical Attika*. Cambridge: Cambridge University Press ,1985, p.90

⑩ Robin Osborne,*Demos: The Discovery of Classical Attika*. Cambridge: Cambridge University Press ,1985, p.80; Aristotle, *The Athenian Constitution*, ⅩⅩⅠ ,3. 公元前 4 世纪以后，日佣等级的人也可以充任议事会议员。

⑪ David Stockton,*The Classical Athenian Democracy*.Oxford: Oxford University Press, 1991, p.58.

人按部落在提秀斯圣殿进行抽签。[①]雅典公民在一生中不能两次担任议事会议员。[②]即便是在城邦民主政治开始衰败的公元前4世纪，在议事会中同一人任同一公职两次的也只有16人。[③]如奥斯邦所言，"克里斯提尼改革所创设的五百人议事会是以德莫为基础的。"[④]

经选举产生的议事会议员起初并无薪，由第三等级以上的公民担任。伯里克利时期，此公职对全体公民开放。自公元前450年，议事会议员由抽签产生并给付生活费，为贫穷公民任职提供了条件。在一年的1/10时间内（36天～35天之间），分别来自10个部落的50名代表组成主席团或议事会执行委员会（the prytaneis）。主席团职位由10个部落轮流担任，其次序由抽签决定，前四个部落每一部落任职主席团的时限为36日，后六个部落每一部落任职主席团的时限为35日。[⑤]主席团公布议事会应办公事的通告、日常事务程序以及开会的地点等。每天从50名主席团成员中抽签选出一人任议事会各类会议的主席（president）和公民大会的主席，也叫"总主席"。总主席任职一日一夜，不得延长，也不得再度任职。任职期间负责保管国家的钱财、档案和国玺。当召开议事会或公民大会时，这个总主席就以抽签方式选出主席9人，每部落一人，唯担任主席团的部落除外。任何人不得在一年中两次担任总主席。[⑥]雅典议事会主席团有时在露天的市场举行公民大会，选举司令官、骑兵司令和其他军官。[⑦]

在大多数情况下，经德莫选举而成的议事会也参与其他官职的行政。例如，参与按部落经抽签选出的雅典娜神庙司库官（共10人）保管雅典娜像和胜利神像，以及其他的纪念品和基金的管理；参与按部落经抽签选出的公卖官（共10人）出租一切公共包揽事业、出包矿坑和赋税等事宜；参与按部落经抽签选出的收款官（共10人）之工作。[⑧]检查骑兵的战马、骑马的哨兵、骑兵等级内作战的步兵。检查体力衰弱不能从事任何工作者，且财产不足三明那的，由议事会从公众开支中供给其粮食津贴，每人每日2个奥波尔。[⑨]

此外，议事会还时常与陪审法庭一起，负责九执政官等重要公职的资格审查。起初，任何官吏未经议事会通过，不得任职。后来，可以向陪审法庭进行上诉，而资格的最后决定也以陪审法庭的判决为准。值得注意的是，审查资格的问题也是与村社、部落有关。诸如谁是你的父亲？属于哪个德莫？谁是你的父亲的父亲？谁是你的母亲？谁是你母亲的父亲？他们属于哪个德莫？等等。[⑩]

德莫除了主要选举五百人议事会的议员以外，在选举其他官职方面，德莫也发挥了作用。如选举执政官候选人、从60岁以上的人中推选公共调停人（public arbitrators）。这些人曾是重装步兵，

---

① 梭伦立法规定，只有五百斗者、骑士和双牛者可以充任议事会议员。Aristotle, *The Athenian Constitution*, Ⅶ,4

② David Stockton. *The Classical Athenian Democracy*. Oxford: Oxford University Press, 1991, p.84.

③ P.J.Rhodes. *The Athenian Boule*. London :Oxford University Press, 1972:242-243. Table B.Men serving twice in the Fourth-Century Boule. 西方学者 E.Ruschenbusch 和 R.F.Rodes 认为：很可能年龄在30以上的70%的雅典人至少参加一次议事会。参见 Robin Osborne, Demos: *The Discovery of Classical Attika*. Cambridge: Cambridge University Press ,1985, p.237, 注释56。

④ Robin Osborne, *Demos: The Discovery of Classical Attika*. Cambridge: Cambridge University Press ,1985, p.43

⑤ 雅典的年历按阴历计算，每月 29 或 30 日，全年 354 日，正好与各部落的任职之和相等：36 × 4 + 35 × 6 = 144+210 = 354 天。Aristotle, The Athenian Constitution,XLⅢ,2-3；另见 [古希腊] 亚里士多德：《雅典政制》，日知、力野译，商务印书馆，1959 年版第 48 页注释②；G.Glotz, *The Greek City and Its Institutions*.London: Kegan Paul, Trench, Trubner and Cc., Ltd., 1929,p.187.

⑥ Aristotle, *The Athenian Constitution*. ⅩLⅣ,3

⑦ [古希腊] 亚里士多德. 雅典政制. 日知、力野. 译, 北京: 商务印书馆, 1959 年版第 49 页注释②。

⑧ Aristotle, *The Athenian Constitution*. ⅩLⅦ,1-5; ⅩLⅧ,1-2.

⑨ Aristotle, *The Athenian Constitution*. ⅩLⅨ,1-4.

⑩ Aristotle, *The Athenian Constitution*. LⅤ,1-4. 同时参看 R.K.Sinclair, *Democracy and Participation in Athens*.Cambridge: Cambridge University Press,1993,p.77.

可能来自多个德莫。①德莫还要为军事服役提供合乎条件的人员名单，如提供可以服海军役的人员名单等。德莫也可以组织非正规的军事力量。这些都说明德莫在征召士兵和组织军事力量等方面具有某些权力。而军事服务既是社会的也是政治行为。因此，德莫作为城邦的组成部分，是社会和政治组织。②

其三，陪审法庭是经由德莫抽签选举而成的最高司法和监察机构。

陪审法庭（heliaea）也称陪审团或陪审会。它是由梭伦于公元前6世纪初改革时首创，以代替行政官员（magistrates）对案件的审理。公元前6世纪末克利斯提尼改革时，称迪克斯特里（dicasteria）。公元前5世纪中叶职权扩大，分享原属贵族会议的若干权力，成为雅典奴隶制民主政治的最高司法和监察机构。

古典时期，"陪审法庭布满了雅典城邦中的显著地方。"③不同的案件有不同规格的陪审团，人数从200人到1000人甚至更多不等。这些陪审员来自于德莫。凡30岁以上的公民均可被选为陪审员。陪审员最多达6000人，用抽签法在每个地区部落中以德莫为基础各选出600名，任期一年，不得连选。6000名陪审员按510人一组分为若干组，余作后备，遇缺即补，轮流审理各类司法案件。至公元前4世纪，陪审员的人数为单数，以避免投票表决时的平局。④几乎所有的司法权限（jurisdiction）都由陪审法庭掌控。执政官和其它一些官员可以作为具体案件审判的法庭负责人，但不得充任法官或审判员（judges），例如将军可以参与军事案件的审判，执政官可以参与宗教案件的审判，低职的官员可以参与诸如市场管理等方面的纠纷处理等。

总之，基于德莫的公民权及其在参加公民大会、选举议事会议员、出席法庭等具体适用中，都表现出机会平等和共同参与德莫及城邦管理事务的民主制原则。"公元前5世纪，雅典公民本身已经认识到自己的这些平等的参与权利"。⑤雅典公民在伯里克利的民主政治中所企求的，正是在法律、所有的政治权利和所提供的机会面前的一律平等。⑥"所有的成年男性公民有权选举官员和五百人议事会议员，出席法庭，参加公民大会。自由而公开的发表评论。任何一个雅典人都可以提交议案、修正案或参与辩论。"⑦"城邦的所有决策是公民大会中的大多数人决定的。公民大会的选举是非强制的自愿行为。"⑧由此，奥斯邦断言："经由德莫，理论上的直接民主制，于实践中得以最好的见证。"⑨

由此可见，在古希腊历史语境下，造船区、德莫和三一区是城邦的区域空间。尽管公民具有同邦同氏族的血亲关系，但是，公民的登籍，公民权的裁定和施用，离不开具体的地域关系和区域组织。造船区、德莫和三一区是构筑雅典城邦机制的基层组织，也是城邦公民施用公民权的权力基础。公民是属于"城邦的人"，同样属于造船区、德莫和三一区。雅典城邦的公民权主要是男性公民所享有的、以城邦区域空间为基础的政治参与权利——投票权、陪审权和担任公职的权力，以及财产所有权。

---

① Robin Osborne, *Demos: The Discovery of Classical Attika*. Cambridge: Cambridge University Press ,1985,p.81 同时参见 Aristotle, *The Athenian Constitution*, ⅬⅩⅡ,1.

② Robin Osborne, *Demos: The Discovery of Classical Attika*. Cambridge: Cambridge University Press ,1985,pp.82–83.

③ G.Glotz, *The Greek City and Its Institutions*. London: Kegan Paul, Trench, Trubner and Cc., Ltd., 1929,p.232.

④ L.Adkins and R.A.Adkins, *Handbook to Life in Ancient Greece*. New York: Facts On File, Inc.,1997,p. 37;著名学者、世界史专家王敦书先生也认为，一个集体由单数而不是由双数组成，以便投票结果不至于对等的做法，迟至公元前4世纪才在雅典实行。详见王敦书《贻书堂史集》，北京：中华书局，2003年版第563页。

⑤ R.K.Sinclair, *Democracy and Participation in Athens*, Cambridge: Cambridge University Press,1993,pp.21–23.

⑥ Donald Kagan, *Pericles of Athens and The Birth of Democracy*, New York: The Free Press, 1991,p.62.

⑦ Donald Kagan, *Pericles of Athens and The Birth of Democracy*, New York: The Free Press, 1991,p.15.

⑧ Donald Kagan, *Pericles of Athens and The Birth of Democracy*, New York: The Free Press, 1991,p.63.

⑨ Robin Osborne, *Demos: The Discovery of Classical Attika*, Cambridge: Cambridge University Press ,1985,p.92.

国外雅典的陪审法庭研究综述

张春梅 大连大学

摘要： 20 世纪 70 年代以来，西方学者针对雅典陪审法庭的起源和发展、构成和运行、职能和地位以及法庭与法律的关系等相关问题展开深入研究。制度考察和思想观念考察相结合，应是雅典陪审法庭研究的发展趋势。

关键词： 雅典民主；陪审法庭；制度

Abstract: Since the 1970s, Western scholars have studied the origin and development of Athenian Jury Courts, the composition and operation, the functions and position in Athenian democracy, as well as the relationship between the Jury Courts and the law. It will probably become the research trend of Athenian Jury Courts to combine the institution investigation and the ideas investigation.

Keywords: Athenian Democracy, Jury Courts, Institution

雅典民主一直都是学术界研究的热点问题，陪审法庭作为雅典民主政体的重要组成部分也相应地引起了学者们的广泛关注。20 世纪 70 年代以来，西方学者针对雅典陪审法庭的起源和发展、构成和运行、职能和地位以及法庭与法律的关系等相关问题展开研究。受学识所限，本文主要介绍英语论著的成果，以期对我国的雅典民主制研究有所启发，疏漏之处还请前辈和同仁批评指正。

一　陪审法庭的起源和发展

根据亚里士多德《雅典政制》的记载，陪审法庭由梭伦设立，这是学术界普遍认同的观点。但最初的陪审法庭的形式问题却引发了西方学者的争议：麦克道威尔等多数人认为梭伦改革建立的陪审法庭就是作为法庭的公民大会，也就是说，当召集起来的公民大会履行司法职能的时候，就称为陪审法庭（Heliaia），而不称作公民大会；丹麦哥本哈根研究中心的著名学者汉森则认为 Heliaia 是梭伦改革创建起来的一个单独的国家机构，和公民大会并列，并不附属于公民大会，由抽签选举的陪审员组成，Heliaia 能够被分成不同的法庭审理案件，到了演说家时代，Dikasteria（陪审法庭）这个术语才替代了 Heliaia。由于梭伦的司法改革措施没有留下直接的史料证据，西方学者的结论往往建立在词源学考据以及对铭文和演说词进行推论的基础上，所以这一问题仍无定论，有待进一步研究。

有关陪审法庭起源的第二个争议是陪审法庭的性质问题。约翰·索利认为梭伦改革建立的法庭是一个上诉的法庭，即当事人对司法官员的判决不服时可以上诉到陪审法庭。汉森则认为，梭伦时代国家的行政干预力量还不足以强大到迫使被告出席法庭的审判，所以很难说最初的陪审法庭就是上诉的法庭。汉森虽然对"上诉法庭"的说法表示质疑，但是也没有足够的证据能够证明。

大概在公元前5世纪中期以后，梭伦建立的陪审法庭的形式、职权和性质都发生了重大变革。《雅典政制》中对此次变革情况的记载模糊不清。究竟是谁推动了这次变革的发生？学术界对这个问题的看法并不一致，斯坦利（Stanley）认为是厄菲阿尔特和伯里克利创立了长久设置的陪审法庭（Dikasteria）。希格内特认为可能是厄菲阿尔特的同僚在他死后不久进行的这项变革，但是这样的变革和厄菲阿尔特在司法制度上的改革有着莫大的关系。哈蒙德认为是伯里克利完成了从Heliaia到Dikasteria的转变。约翰·索利则认为克利斯提尼改革促成了陪审法庭这种形式上的改变。虽然存在诸多的分歧，但是可以确定的是，雅典从一个Heliaia转变成多个Dikasteria大概是在公元前五世纪中期或者稍晚一点的时间，而且和厄菲阿尔特的改革有直接的关系。

二　陪审法庭的构成和运行程序

《雅典政制》是研究陪审法庭最为重要的古典史料。亚里士多德用了很大的篇幅（第63-69节）详细地介绍了公元前四世纪中后期陪审员的选举和分配办法，主持法庭的司法官员的分配办法，以及分配法庭的程序，这些都是我们还原陪审法庭的运行程序的主要依据。罗兹的《亚里士多德的〈雅典政制〉疏证》对《雅典政制》进行了逐字逐句的考证，他在广泛搜集古典文献和现代研究成果的同时，还发表了自己对有关问题的看法，展现了西方学者扎实的史料考据功底，其研究成果在西方学术界也得以广泛应用。除此之外，在雅典的美国古典研究院公布的由伯格霍尔德（Boegehold）等人合作完成阿戈拉考古报告《雅典法庭的地址、建筑、设备、程序以及证据》为陪审法庭研究主要提供了公元前五世纪和四世纪的考古证据。这份考古报告图文并茂，呈现了法庭的地点、庭审设备，并综合分析了陪审法庭的历史沿革。该报告的另一特色是用近一半的篇幅汇编了355条与陪审法庭相关的古典资料、批注以及铭文资料。这份报告是研究陪审法庭运行程序必不可少的工具书。

陪审员的阶层构成，即法庭的陪审员究竟是穷人多还是富人多？这一问题因涉及到雅典民主参与的广泛性问题而引起了较多的关注。学界对此仁者见仁智者见智，大致有三种观点。一种是以希格内特为代表的传统观点，认为陪审团的主体是又穷又老的人，就像阿里斯托芬在其喜剧《马蜂》中所描述的一群陪审员一样，他们以陪审津贴维持生计。圣克莱尔（Sinclair）在《雅典的民主与参与》一书中也认为：出席陪审法庭的大多数人是穷人、老人和没有工作能力的人，而富人更倾向于参加公民大会，因为公民大会消耗的时间要少。马克莱（Markle）认为：公元前四世纪，陪审员的主体既不是一无所有的穷人，更不是生活富裕的中等阶级，而是不得不自己从事劳动养活家人的没有闲暇的人。他虽然花费了大段的篇幅考证了"贫穷"和"赤贫"两个词的区别，但是可以看出，马克莱还是倾向于认为雅典社会的下层构成了陪审员的主体。第二种是以琼斯为代表的观点，他承认在公元前五世纪穷人占据陪审员的多数，但是公元前四世纪的陪审员主要是由较为富裕的中等和上层公民组成，他的理由是3个奥波尔的津贴太少，不足以养活一个家庭，许多人能赚取更多收入时，就不会积极出席陪审法庭。第三种观点是托德（Todd）提出的，他认为雅典社会不存在严格意义上的等级或者阶级的划分，整个公民集体是具有同一社会价值观念的统一体，所以他另辟蹊径，认为农民是公元前四世纪的陪审员主体。

除此之外，一些学者还对陪审法庭的构成和程序运行等细节性问题进行了深入探究。比如：马克莱分析了公元前四世纪陪审津贴低于公民大会津贴的原因；斯特林·道（Sterling Dow）和毕晓普

（Bishop）对亚里士多德记载的抽签机（kleroterion）进行了考证；有的学者考察了陪审员的身份牌；托德分析了法庭上诉讼人使用证据的目的；也有学者讨论了外邦人在雅典法庭诉讼中的地位问题。这些研究成果对准确还原陪审法庭的运行程序大有裨益。

三　陪审法庭的职能和地位

陪审法庭是雅典最为重要的司法机关，同时也是雅典民主制的支柱。公元前四世纪陪审法庭的职能发生了重大变化，除了履行主要的司法审判职能之外，还拥有了更多的政治权力。汉森认为公元前四世纪陪审法庭的监察职能越来越突出，法庭所拥有的政治权力不断攀升。他在《德谟斯提尼时代雅典的民主政治》一书中指出：有三种特别重要的起诉似乎构成陪审法庭的政治权力的基础：违法法令诉讼（graphe paranomon），告发（esiangelia），还有官员任职期满的账目审计（euthynai）。这三种类型分别针对特殊类型的政治领袖：违法法令诉讼，监控的是演说家，告发监控的是将军，任职期满的账目审计监控所有的行政官员。汉森在这本书中概括地介绍了这三个重要程序的源起、施行细则和产生的影响。

传统观点认为公民大会是雅典民主制的最高权力机关，近年来，汉森对此提出了质疑。他的另外两本书——《公元前四世纪雅典陪审法庭至高无上的权力和违法法令诉讼》、《告发：公元前四世纪雅典陪审法庭至高无上的权力和对将军以及政治家的弹劾》特别分析了"违法法令诉讼"和"告发"这两个程序。在第一本书中他对 39 起违法法令诉讼进行了分析，得出结论：既然陪审法庭可以推翻公民大会的决议，那么在公元前四世纪的雅典，拥有至高无上权力的机构不是公民大会而是陪审法庭。在汉森的第二本书中，他对文献中出现的公元前 493-322 年的 144 起告发案件进行梳理，并且对发生在公元前 432——355 年的 35 位将军的告发案件进行了重点分析，得出结论：在古典雅典是由陪审法庭对政治领袖，尤其是将军行使控制权。汉森对陪审法庭和公民大会的重新定位，在某种程度上引发了学者们对公元前四世纪的雅典民主政治进行重新审视，汉森也由此奠定了其在学术界的重要地位。

四　法律与法庭之间的关系

最近 30 年，古代希腊法律和法庭之间的关系问题引起欧美学者的浓厚兴趣，雅典因为其丰富的史料而尤其成为关注的焦点。学者们讨论的问题集中在雅典的法庭是否体现了"法治"（the rule of law）的理念，更确切地说，就是陪审员根据什么标准判案：根据法律还是其它的社会因素？法庭在雅典社会中究竟扮演的是政治角色还是司法角色？

学者们对这个问题的讨论莫衷一是，大致可分成两种对立的观点。一种是社会学派的观点：雅典的法庭并没有完全依法判案，法庭主要充当"社会竞技场"的角色。这一派的代表人物是科恩（Cohen）、奥斯邦（Osborne）、克里斯特（Christ）。他们认为法律在法庭判决中并不具有最高权威性，法律只是影响陪审员判决的因素之一，而且不是主导性的因素，法律对诉讼人和陪审员所起的作用微不足道，法律条文成为把世仇或竞争转移到公共舞台上来的工具，陪审员往往更多地考虑诉讼双方的个人品质和社会地位，还要考虑判决可能带来的政治和社会影响。在古典时期的雅典，诉讼不是为了揭示真相并最终解决纠纷，法庭成为诉讼双方进行政治角逐和社会等级斗争的竞技场，因此雅典的法庭具有强烈的政治性。约翰斯顿（Johnstone）的观点较为温和，认为：法律在法庭上仍旧处于核心地位，但是法律的意义存在着不同争议，诉讼人可以根据不同的意图对立法者制定的法律进行推衍，这就可以解释为什么在法庭上演说者习惯于引证不相关的法律。这一派学者的共同的特点是采用社会学的方法对雅典的法庭诉讼进行研究。

与之相反的观点认为：陪审法庭的陪审员做到了依法判案，贯彻的是"法治"的理念。认同这一观点的学者又因为他们研究方法的不同而分成两派：制度派和修辞派。制度派的代表人物之一汉森认为：通过公元前五世纪晚期和公元前四世纪初期一系列的立法和司法改革，雅典建立起了依法治国的制度体系。汉森的主要论据是雅典创立了立法委员会（Nomothetai），制定了新的严格的立法程序，有效防止法律被公民大会上的暴民推翻。西利也是从制度变革的角度考察了雅典人法律观念的变化，到了公元前五世纪末雅典人逐渐抛弃了习惯法，确立成文法为唯一的执法依据，从这个角度来说，雅典人实现了"法治"。奥斯瓦尔德（Ostwald）在专著《从人民主权到法律的主权》中系统地阐述了雅典社会由公民当家作主到法律主宰一切的历史演变过程，他认为从克利斯提尼改革开始公民的权力不断攀升，到厄菲阿尔特改革时达到顶峰；但是随之暴露的弊端迫使民主派调整政策，公元前五世纪末的改革确立了法律的最高统治地位。制度派的观点主要建立在对国家机关的运行程序和职能分配进行考察的基础之上，但是制度规定和实践操作之间显然存在差距，有的时候可能会相去甚远。修辞派致力于从诉讼辞分析入手，故此而得名，其代表人物哈里斯（Harris）发现：诉讼人在法庭上经常提醒陪审员不要忘记他们要"依法判案"的誓言；从诉讼辞的内容来看，诉讼人重视相关的法律条款的解释。修辞派的学者否定超出法律之外的因素在法庭上起主导作用，即使有这种情况，也是一种失常的行为而不是法庭惯常的表现。

陪审法庭是否依法判案的争论还在继续，需要注意的是我们在讨论这个问题的时候，不仅仅要从制度的运作入手，还要考虑诉讼演说所反映的雅典社会的公共道德和价值标准，切忌不能用现代人的"法治"观念来衡量古典时期的雅典社会，应当还原到当时的历史发展水平进行评判。

综上所述，西方史学界重视法庭与民主之间的关系，对陪审法庭的研究多分散在雅典民主政治的综合研究中，较少形成系统的专门研究。另外，从研究方法来看，制度派侧重从制度的层面强调法庭在民主制发展和法治发展过程中的地位和作用，修辞派和社会学派则从法庭演说辞入手，强调民众的思想观念对民主和法治的塑造作用。实际上，雅典民主的各种政治机构和雅典人的思想观念，都是雅典民主与法治建设不可分割的组成部分，过于偏重任何一方都难以全面的认识雅典的民主和法治。因此，制度考察和思想观念考察相结合，应是雅典陪审法庭研究的发展趋势。

色诺芬在《希腊史》中对泛希腊主义思潮的反思

张　凯　上海师范大学

摘要：前4世纪早期以伊索克拉底为代表的演说家在希腊努力宣扬一种狂热的泛希腊主义，力主希腊人在雅典和斯巴达的领导下结束内部纷争，将希望从希腊人内部获得的利益转而通过征服波斯而获得。色诺芬在《希腊史》中通过对城邦间霸权与反霸权的争斗和希腊人与波斯关系的叙述，实际上反思了这种狂热的泛希腊主义。他试图使人们认识到希腊霸权若不能与其他城邦建立起基于现实的正义关系，希腊人内部不可能结束纷争；波斯人利用希腊人内部的纷争成功地插手希腊事务并控制了小亚的希腊城邦，但希腊人也有自己切实可行的战略战术来对付波斯人；波斯人与希腊人一样有高贵的品质，希腊人与波斯人之间的关系同样不可以违反正义。

关键词：色诺芬；泛希腊主义

Abstract：In the 4th century B.C., orators such as Isocrates advocate a kind of fanatical panhellenism. They called on Greeks to end wars within and unite under Sparta and Athens, then to get benefits by conquering Persians than from within. In fact, Xenophon reflected this panhellenism by narrating struggles between the powers of hegemony and anti-hegemony, the relations between Persians and Greeks in Hellenica. He tried to let Greeks to know his reflections: if the Greek hegemonies failed to establish just relations with other city-states basing on the reality, wars within Greeks would never end; Persians exploited disputes among Greeks successfully and recontrolled city-states in Asia, however Greeks still had practical strategy and tactics to deal with them; Persians just as Greeks had noble qualities, and the relations between Greeks and them should conform to the justice as well.

Keywords：Xenophon; panhellenism

　　我们现代学者常说的泛希腊主义（panhellenism）这个词，源于古希腊语 *panhellenes*，它的意思是"所有的希腊人"。泛希腊主义是我们现代学者用以指称古希腊的这样一种思想：希腊各城邦之间停止战争，大家联合一致进攻波斯，希望从其他希腊城邦那里得到的利益，转而从蛮族那里得到。这种思想形成于希波战争之后，雅典将军客蒙曾经力图协调雅典与斯巴达两大希腊霸权，并有意推动反对波斯的行动。客蒙在前450年死后，雅典与斯巴达合作反对波斯的希望似乎也结束了。在前

5 世纪末和前 4 世纪的希腊城邦危机之中，泛希腊主义成为许多关心希腊问题的知识分子的诉求。前 408 年，高尔吉亚在《奥林匹亚演讲辞》中较早对泛希腊主义思想进行了全面的阐述。吕西阿斯在前 388 年奥林匹亚运动会上的演讲也号召对波斯发动泛希腊的远征。前 380 年伊索克拉底的《泛希腊集会演讲辞》似乎将泛希腊主义的思潮推向顶峰，他结合当时希腊的政治背景，希望斯巴达结束对希腊人的战争，与雅典分享希腊的霸权，进攻波斯，将希望从希腊人那里掠夺的，转而从波斯人那里掠夺。①伊索克拉底的思想可以说集以前泛希腊主义思想之大成，并明确地针对了当时希腊城邦内部战乱问题的解决，可以说在当时的希腊是颇有影响的。

如果说来伊索克拉底是泛希腊主义理论的鼓吹者，色诺芬常常被认为是泛希腊主义可行性的证明者。人们一般认为色诺芬的《长征记》叙述的希腊万人远征军能从波斯腹地成功撤离的故事，和《希腊史》中描述德西利达斯和阿格西劳斯在小亚成功地与波斯人作战的故事，是有意地在展现希腊人进攻波斯的现实可行性。而伊索克拉底在宣扬他的泛希腊主义思想时，对希腊万人军例子的重视，亚历山大对色诺芬《长征记》的推崇，更加容易使人确认这一点。当然也有不同的观点，有人认为《长征记》的描述恰恰是为了展现进攻波斯的难度，因为万人军在返回过程中确实经历了很大的困难，也经受了不少损失。但笔者以为，这两种观点都不足以认识色诺芬对泛希腊主义的思考。

色诺芬在写作《长征记》和《希腊史》的时候，②正是泛希腊主义思想在希腊很受推崇的时候，色诺芬本人自然对这些观点很熟悉，而他的两本著作，与泛希腊主义这样的话题又是直接相关的，他不可能不在著作中对此展现他自己的思考。而他的展现和思考又是非常特别的，因为以反思历史，来思考某个主题，他具有独特的优势。政论家善于用激动人心的演讲来鼓动人，而历史学家更善于通过全面的展现引发人们审慎的反思。

一　反思泛希腊主义之一：城邦之间霸权与反霸权

我们首先来看色诺芬对城邦之间关系的展现与思考。

希腊城邦之间的关系中一个重要的方面就是霸权与反霸权的关系。希腊的城邦内部由于一种长期的政治生活习惯形成了一种反僭主的思想，希腊城邦中的两个代表——雅典和斯巴达的内部都是反对僭主统治的。僭主统治在希腊的文化中一般被认为是个不名誉的称呼。但强大的城邦在对外关系中可以统治弱小的城邦，这在希腊被认为有其合理性。一个强大的城邦除了对外利益的欲求之外，还有就是对战略安全的考虑，雅典之所以努力控制爱琴海的制海权，一个重要的原因就是，她的粮食等运输通道需要有保证。斯巴达在伯罗奔尼撒的霸权也有相应的战略利益的考虑。

雅典这样一个典型的民主制城邦，在波斯战争之后，却渐渐成为一个推行霸权主义（或称"帝国主义"）的代表。③前 416 年，雅典使者为强迫弥罗斯（Melos）臣服，所依据的道理就是"正义的标准是以同等的强迫力量为基础的"，而"强者能够做他们有权力做的一切，弱者只能接受他们必须接受的一切"。弥罗斯人回答，强大的力量也不可能消除正义的原则，强大者也会有陷入危险的时候，那时他们不但会受到"可怕的报复"，也会受成为"全世界引以为鉴的例子"。但尽管如此，弥罗斯还是被雅典攻陷，城中的被俘的人或遭到屠杀，或被卖为奴隶。④

①　Michael A. Flower, "From Simonides to Isocrates: The Fifth-Century Origins of Fourth-Century Panhellenism", *Classical Antiquity*, Vol.19, No.1 (Apr., 2000), pp.65-101. 另见 Isocrates, *Panegyricus*, 17. (*Isocrates*, translated by George Norlin, Loeb Classical Library, Harvard University Press, 1991.)

②　这两部著作，前者可能早一些，但肯定不早于前 386 年，后者晚一些，但肯定不晚于前 350 年代。

③　在古希腊文中，*hēgemonia*（霸权或领导权）这个词既有带有帝国主义的性质的霸权的意思，也有受拥护的领导权的意思。参见罗念生、水建馥编：《古希腊汉语词典》，北京：商务印书馆，2010 年，第 366 页。

④　修昔底德：《伯罗奔尼撒战争史》，5.89。参见谢德风中文译本下册，北京商务印书馆 2008 年版，第 465-474 页。

　　如果说《伯罗奔尼撒战争史》重点展现了雅典霸权的兴衰，那么色诺芬的《希腊史》可以说展现了斯巴达霸权的兴衰。但《希腊史》对希腊城邦霸权的展现要丰富得多，在其中我们还可以看到雅典的第二次霸权企图，忒拜的霸权，及某些地区小邦昙花一现的霸权。在希腊城邦的霸权与反霸权的斗争史中，色诺芬试图向读者呈现正义在城邦间关系中强有力的存在。

　　在波斯金钱的有力支持下，斯巴达在前5世纪末最终打败雅典，赢得了伯罗奔尼撒战争的胜利。前404年，战败的雅典接受斯巴达的停战条件——拆毁部分长墙和比雷埃夫斯港的防御工事，只保留12条船，允许流放者返回雅典，成为追随斯巴达的盟邦。①此时斯巴达成为希腊唯一的霸主，也自我营造出希腊解放者的形象。在斯巴达霸权建立的同时，国内也成长起一个政治强人，即莱山德。他试图在一些斯巴达控制的城邦（主要在爱琴海东部）设立名义上服从斯巴达，实际上服从于他自己的"十人委员会"（dekarchies），以便自己做这些城邦的太上皇。②他在雅典支持的30僭主只是这种"十人委员会"的变体。莱山德的这种安排可以说是斯巴达霸权形象的一个污点。但稍后，他在斯巴达的势力受到了削弱和压制。先是在雅典30僭主的统治陷入困境时，莱山德试图拯救他们，但在国王保桑尼亚斯和几位监察官的计谋之下，帮助雅典城内贵族派政治力量与占领比雷埃夫斯的民主派政治力量和解，使逃亡埃琉西斯的僭主势力陷于孤立。③这使得莱山德控制雅典的企图破灭。他在其他城邦设立的"十人委员会"也被斯巴达废除了。之后他还曾试图通过扶植阿格西劳斯（他与莱山德有古典的同性恋关系），来恢复自己的势力，但阿格西劳斯排挤了他。④可以说，莱山德的失势延缓了斯巴达霸权走向激进道路的速度。

　　前401年—前400年，随着小居鲁士反叛其兄的失败，波斯开始重新着手控制小亚希腊城邦，小亚城邦向斯巴达求助。以维护希腊人自由自居的斯巴达开始向小亚派兵，以对抗波斯的势力。斯巴达的霸权也天然扮演了一种希腊人利益代理人的角色。先后派往小亚的统帅，有提布戎、德西利达斯和国王阿格西劳斯。提布戎因为曾率军劫掠小亚盟邦而被撤职流放，后两者都很好地处理了与盟邦的关系，一方面没有侵犯过她们的利益，另一方面尊重她们的独立，并获得了她们的积极支持。可以说斯巴达霸权的这一行动，与她所宣传的对小亚城邦的解放，基本是相符的。

　　但斯巴达霸权的另一面是在希腊打压任何可能威胁其地位的其他强大的城邦或地方霸权。而其他有实力的城邦也不愿处在斯巴达的打压之下，于是在希腊成功形成了霸权与反霸权的斗争。

　　约前402年，斯巴达王阿吉斯率军惩罚伊利斯。色诺芬提供了斯巴达之所以这样做的几个原因：伊利斯人曾在伯罗奔尼撒战争期间与斯巴达的敌人雅典等结过盟；在奥林匹亚运动会期间，斯巴达人曾遭受不公的待遇；（奥林匹亚就在伊利斯地区，运动会由伊利斯人主持）伊利斯人拒绝斯巴达人向奥林匹亚宙斯神殿献祭以求助对希腊人内部战争的胜利。⑤斯巴达人本来是为了这些关涉其自身利益的事决定教训伊利斯人，但斯巴达与之开战的借口却是要求伊利斯人给其控制的周边地区独立，而伊利斯人认为这是他们的战争所得，从而拒绝了斯巴达。⑥然而接下来的战争成为斯巴达及其盟邦阿卡亚人（Achaean）和阿卡迪亚人（Arcadian）对伊利斯地区的一次破坏和掠夺。以至于色诺

---

①　Xenophon, *Hellenica*, 2.2.20.（translated by Carleton L. Brownson, Loeb Classical Library, Harvard University Press, 1985.）

②　保罗·卡特利奇：《斯巴达人》，梁建东、章颜译，上海：上海三联书店，2010，第179页。

③　保桑尼亚斯等人这样做，一方面是为了防止斯巴达个人势力过大而出现僭主，另一方也是防止过分压制雅典，而主张在希腊形成一种"双霸权体系"，即斯巴达与雅典这希腊两大霸权进行合作。见保罗·卡特利奇：《斯巴达人》，上海三联书店，2010年，第185页。

④　Xenophon, *Hellenica*, 3.4.2, 3.4.7–9.

⑤　Xenophon, *Hellenica*, 3.2.21–22.

⑥　在希腊传统观念中，战争所得具有合理性，比如战争中的俘虏可以由胜利者处置。

芬不无讽刺地写道，"实际上这次军事行动本质上成了伯罗奔尼撒同盟储备给养的方式"。①后来在斯巴达的多次军事破坏和掠夺的威胁下，伊利斯人被迫接受了斯巴达的要求。但斯巴达人没有剥夺伊利斯人对奥林匹亚宙斯神庙事务的监管，因为他们比别人更适合。这一点在色诺芬看来显然是公正的，所以特别强调了一下。②

前395年，正当阿格西劳斯率军在小亚对波斯作战时，波斯在小亚的总督提斯罗斯特斯（Tithraustes）采取用金钱支持希腊本部反斯巴达势力的方式，来牵制斯巴达。忒拜、雅典、科林斯和亚各斯都积极响应，雅典没有接受波斯代表的金钱，但急切地想参加反斯巴达联盟。雅典参加的原因就是要恢复她的帝国。③同一年，忒拜设计挑起战争，斯巴达当局见此也感到高兴，因为早就想惩罚常与自己不合作的彼奥提亚人。④之后以斯巴达及其同盟为一方，以忒拜、雅典、科林斯和亚各斯及其同盟为一方，双方从海陆两方面展开了长期的战争，持续到前387年。这场战争因为其陆上主战场发生在科林斯附近，故又被称为科林斯战争。战争中双方各有胜负，斯巴达在陆上和海上整体上处于优势，而且在安塔尔奇达斯（Antalkidas，斯巴达人）的外交努力下，最终使波斯与斯巴达结盟。前387年，雅典的运粮通道再次被封锁，于是雅典感到恐惧，决定求和。战争给斯巴达造成的军费负担也很重，斯巴达也希望讲和。在这种背景下，波斯在小亚地区的总督提里巴祖斯（Tilibazus）召集希腊诸邦议和，并展示了之前安塔尔奇达斯与波斯大王商定的条约：

> 大王阿塔薛西斯相信以下安排是正义的：小亚的城邦、克拉佐门奈岛和塞浦路斯岛属于大王，其他的希腊城邦，除了雷姆诺斯（Lemnos）、音不洛斯（Imbros）和西罗斯（Skyros）岛如先前一样归属雅典之外，无论大小一律独立。两方面的任何一方若不遵守这一和平协议，我将与接受协议的成员一起，以战舰和金钱，从陆路和海路向其发动攻击。⑤

大部分城邦接受了这个和约，虽然忒拜主张代表彼奥提亚联邦缔约，科林斯在主战派的控制下主张保留亚各斯在科林斯的驻军，但两者都在阿格西劳斯的军事威胁下接受了和约。⑥这个和约显然表明，斯巴达为了维护自己在希腊本部的霸权，牺牲了小亚城邦的独立。通过这个条约，斯巴达粉碎了雅典的帝国梦，使忒拜领导彼奥提亚联邦的行为变得不合法，也使亚各斯无法与科林斯合并。和约使斯巴达的霸权得到巩固，而其他城邦受到削弱，她成为大王和约的实质保护人，可以以此为依据号令希腊了。

接下来的斯巴达又开始为其霸权利益，惩罚小邦，压制希腊崛起的地方霸权。前385/4年，斯巴达为了防止盟邦曼丁尼亚将来可能倒向敌方，同时惩罚她在以前对斯巴达的不忠，要求曼丁尼亚拆毁城墙，遭到拒绝后，对其进行围攻，最终迫使其拆毁城墙，并将其公民安置在四个村庄中。⑦前382年—前379，斯巴达经过艰难围困，使卡尔息底斯（Chalcidice）地区崛起的地方霸主奥林苏斯屈服，并使之成为追随斯巴达的盟邦。⑧

同一时期对待小邦夫利阿斯（Phleious）的措施，彰显了阿格西劳斯影响下的斯巴达当局从维护正义向维护本邦霸权利益的自然发展。小邦夫利阿斯的民主派当政，亲斯巴达者（贵族派）被流

① Xenophon, *Hellenica*, 3.2.23.
② Xenophon, *Hellenica*, 3.2.30–31.
③ Xenophon, *Hellenica*, 3.5.1–2.
④ Xenophon, *Hellenica*, 3.5.3–5.
⑤ Xenophon, *Hellenica*, 5.1.31.
⑥ Xenophon, *Hellenica*, 5.1.32–34.
⑦ Xenophon, *Hellenica*, 5.2.1–7.
⑧ Xenophon, *Hellenica*, 5.2.11–24, 5.2.37–5.3.9, 5.3.26.

放之后，夫利阿斯不再积极追随斯巴达。前384年，斯巴达当局要求夫利阿斯能够自愿允许以前被流放的人回城，并给予公正的待遇。夫利阿斯当局最终慑于斯巴达的武力，决定答应斯巴达的要求，发还给流亡者财产，若有争议，通过法庭审判解决。①这一安排自然是最好的处理方式，但后来夫利阿斯民主派当局违反了答应的措施，因为他们怀着侥幸心理，认为当时只有一个斯巴达王阿格西劳斯在国内，（另一位王阿格斯波利斯率军去征服奥林苏斯了）斯巴达不可能再派阿格西劳斯出兵攻打他们。（斯巴达的两个王按照习俗只派一个外出领兵）另外，当阿格斯波利斯率军出征时，夫利阿斯因为提供了大量给养而受到了他的赞扬。当回到夫利阿斯的流亡者对民主派的处理不满时，要求法庭审判，但法庭的法官就是由曾经对流亡者犯下罪行的人构成。这种情况下流亡贵族们再次求助于斯巴达，夫利阿斯城中一些同情流亡者的公民也随他们一起向斯巴达当局控告夫利阿斯民主派当局的不公。夫利阿斯民主派当局确实不义在先，这为斯巴达的干涉提供了借口。前381年，斯巴达当局决定惩罚夫利阿斯，阿格西劳斯由于与流亡者的私人关系亲自率军出征，并打出帮助受害者的旗号，蛮横地拒绝了夫利阿斯民主派的和谈请求。斯巴达军队经过对夫利阿斯一年零八个月的围困，迫使夫利阿斯屈服。前379年，阿格西劳斯安排了一个委员会，成员由50名流亡者和50名夫利阿斯城内同情流亡者的人构成。民主派与贵族派的争端由他们审判以决定谁生谁死，新的政治体制（显然是亲斯巴达的寡头制）也由他们来建立。阿格西劳斯还在夫利阿斯留下一队驻军，并给他们留下6个月的给养，令他们待上述委员会的任务完成后撤离。②色诺芬没有进一步叙述这个委员会后来的运作，但读者可以肯定，它与前述夫利阿斯民主派设立的那个法庭同样不公正。这里阿格西劳斯对夫利阿斯的安排表明，斯巴达与其说是为了维护正义而干涉，不如说是为了在夫利阿斯扶植亲斯巴达的寡头制政府而干涉。③

斯巴达当局更富有侵略性、更自私自利的霸权形象在占领忒拜卫城一事上表现更加明显。前382年，率军行径忒拜的斯巴达将领菲比达斯，在忒拜的亲斯巴达派将军利昂提阿德斯的引诱下占领了忒拜卫城阿卡德米，之后利昂提阿德斯等人建立了在斯巴达军队保护下的僭政。因为占领他邦卫城意味着该邦的独立失去了。菲比达斯的行为严重违反了大王和约中尊重各邦独立的规定。他本应受到斯巴达当局的严惩，但阿格西劳斯认为，是否惩罚菲比达斯，应该看他是给斯巴达带来了好处，还是伤害。利昂提阿德斯在斯巴达公民大会上的发言迎合了斯巴达的私利，力证菲比达斯此举对斯巴达的益处。结果斯巴达当局批准了这次占领，并与利昂提阿德斯进行合作，支持他们一伙人的僭政。④

至前379年，斯巴达在压服了曼丁尼亚、奥林苏斯，安置好了夫利阿斯的事务之后，其霸权也达到顶峰。忒拜、科林斯、雅典、亚各斯全都变得驯服而孤立，斯巴达的同盟中对她态度不好的，也受到了惩罚。"从各个方面来看，斯巴达对其统治（霸权）的安排，既强大又安全"。⑤然而就在此时，斯巴达的霸权开始走向疯狂（hybris）。

前379/8年，菲力达斯和梅农等人杀死了忒拜的僭主们，驱赶了驻扎在阿卡德米的斯巴达军队。斯巴达王克利俄姆布罗塔斯（Kleombrotos）奉命前去惩罚忒拜，无果而反。而稍后，斯巴达驻守在特斯匹伊（Thespiai）的将领斯福德里亚斯（Sphodrias）在忒拜人的撺掇下，（忒拜人此举是为了造成雅典对斯巴达的仇恨，进而与雅典结盟，共同对抗斯巴达）试图率军经过夜间跋涉在黎明时到达雅典的比雷埃夫斯港，趁港城的防御工事尚未修复占领该港。结果天亮时，他们只到达了离比雷埃

---

①　Xenophon, *Hellenica*, 5.2.8–10.

②　Xenophon, *Hellenica*, 5.3.10–25.

③　关于斯巴达对夫利阿斯的这次粗暴干涉，另见 N. G. L. Hammond, *A History of Greece*, Oxford: The Clarendon Press, 1959, p.468；保罗·卡特利奇：《斯巴达人》，第 200–201 页。

④　Xenophon, *Hellenica*, 5.2.25–36.

⑤　Xenophon, *Hellenica*, 5.3.27.

夫斯尚有较长距离的特里亚（Thria），在那里劫掠一阵后返回。[①]此举与菲比达斯一样没有经过斯巴达当局的授权，而且同样严重违反了大王和约。雅典人向斯巴达当局表示抗议，他们本来应该对此进行严惩。但阿格西劳斯认为在这个事上，斯福德里亚斯虽然是做错了，但他以前一直是个优秀的战士，为斯巴达做出了很大贡献，是不应当处死他的。结果斯福德里亚斯得到宽恕。[②]色诺芬在这里，一方面进一步反映了阿格西劳斯在斯巴达强大的影响力，（但不能说是僭主式的，因为他采取的是说服的方式，而不是强制性的，也不能说是非法的，因为在斯巴达，国王、长老或监察官有自由裁量权）另一方面再次承接对菲比达斯事件的处理，强调了斯巴达霸权的自私性。

之后，雅典加入忒拜一方与斯巴达作战，忒拜逐渐重新控制了大部分彼奥提亚城邦。雅典在伯罗奔尼撒沿岸进行骚扰，也颇有成就，但海战的军费令雅典难以承受，并且忒拜不但不给予雅典任何援助，还侵犯与雅典友好的城邦。忒拜的自私行为令雅典非常反感。于是雅典决定与斯巴达议和，同时也邀请了忒拜。[③]

前371年，在斯巴达的公民大会上，雅典的三位代表依次发表演讲。第一位讲话的是卡里亚斯（Kallias），他盛赞了斯巴达与雅典源远流长的友好关系；第二位是奥托克勒斯（Autokles），他严厉地批评了斯巴达侵犯他邦，违反大王和约的行为；第三位是卡利斯特拉托斯（Kallistratos），他认为斯巴达和雅典都曾犯过错误，两者若是能够以大王和约中对各邦独立的尊重为基础，在希腊世界实现密切合作，则无人能在陆上和海上对他们构成伤害。[④]之后，斯巴达人投票通过了和约的条款：

> 在他邦的驻军长官应该取消，陆军和海军力量应当解散，各城邦允许独立；如果有城邦受到了不公地待遇，其他城邦自愿决定是否给予受害城邦以援助。[⑤]

该条款秉承了大王合约的精神以处理各城邦之间的关系。很多城邦乐意接受，但在宣誓方式上出了问题。斯巴达是代表他自己和他的盟邦宣誓的，雅典也是如此，忒拜也坚决要求代表自己和盟邦宣誓，但被阿格西劳斯无礼地拒绝了。这样其他城邦都缔结了和约，但忒拜没有。雅典当时站在反忒拜的一方，认为可以借此机会惩罚忒拜。这次议和之后，"只有忒拜人自己怀着彻底失望的心情离开了"。[⑥]色诺芬对宣誓问题的描述，展现了斯巴达和雅典的双重标准，两者允许自己可以代表盟邦宣誓，却反对忒拜这样做。雅典和斯巴达为了自己的霸权利益很难容忍忒拜的崛起。彼奥提亚联邦在忒拜的领导下，此时已成为一个运行良好的政治组织，而且联邦下的各邦接受忒拜的领导不是单单因为被强制形成的，而是通过良好的政治经济架构。[⑦]后来的历史证明斯巴达和雅典这种不公的做法，给这个两个城邦的霸权带来了毁灭，也加重了希腊人的危机。所以色诺芬在描述忒拜人离开时的状态时，饱含一种叹息之情。

稍后，雅典执行了和约的规定，从他邦撤出了驻军。斯巴达尽管也撤回了大部分驻军，但却没有撤回国王克利俄姆布罗塔斯驻扎在福基斯地区的军队。尽管国内有人建议按照之前协议的规定撤回这支军队，但斯巴达当局不但予以拒绝，反而令克利俄姆布罗塔斯率军攻击忒拜，除非她允许其

① Xenophon, *Hellenica*, 5.4.20–21.
② Xenophon, *Hellenica*, 5.4.32.
③ Xenophon, *Hellenica*, 6.3.1–2.
④ Xenophon, *Hellenica*, 6.3.3–13.
⑤ Xenophon, *Hellenica*, 6.3.18.
⑥ Xenophon, *Hellenica*, 6.3.19–20.
⑦ P. J. Rhodes ed., *The Greek City States：A Source Book*, New York: Cambridge University Press, 2007, pp.229–230.

控制下的城邦独立。①色诺芬对斯巴达此项决定的描述，又一次展现了她的蛮横。她实质是在以一个美好的口号，公报私仇。

有趣的是，斯巴达的霸权就在这个时候，遭受了戏剧化的重创。前371年，在留克特拉一战中，克利俄姆布罗塔斯率领的斯巴达军队被忒拜军队打败，损失惨重，有接近1000斯巴达人战死，其中接近有400全权公民（当时参战的全权公民总共只有700人）。②斯巴达全权公民是其社会的核心，而他们的人数却因为斯巴达为维护霸权的不断征战和国内僵化的制度，而一直在减少。稍后，当伊帕美浓达率军兵临斯巴达时，阿格西劳斯可用来防卫的全权公民只有800人左右了。③全权公民的锐减对斯巴达的霸权是个致命的打击，但斯巴达的衰弱还没有停止。前370/369年，和前368年，伊帕美浓达两次入侵伯罗奔尼撒半岛虽然没有攻击斯巴达城，但导致了大量庇里奥西人和黑劳士叛逃；他解放了美塞尼亚，使美塞尼城重新独立，并推动了阿卡迪亚联邦中心城市麦加波利斯的建立，使斯巴达领导下的伯罗奔尼撒同盟出现瓦解的迹象。④色诺芬对这段历史的处理给后人留下很多疑问，他叙述了前370/369年忒拜入侵伯罗奔尼撒的情况，但显然故意回避了伊帕美浓达的领导；他叙述了庇里奥西人和黑劳士的叛逃，阿卡迪亚联邦和其他城邦与忒拜联合反对斯巴达的情况，但没有提及麦加波利斯的建立。⑤奇怪的是，美塞尼亚的独立、麦加波利斯城在他后面的叙述中都提到了。⑥

斯巴达的霸权在国内依靠对黑劳士和庇里奥西人支撑，在国外依靠伯罗奔尼撒同盟的支持，但此时两个方面都出了严重的问题。面对忒拜的迅速崛起和斯巴达的急剧衰弱，与斯巴达一样不能容忍忒拜强大的雅典决定加强和斯巴达的军事同盟关系。前369年，经过一番辩论，双方达成协议，由双方的将官轮流统率雅典和斯巴达的海陆军队。⑦

此时的忒拜拥有强大的军事实力和众多的盟邦，她像以前的斯巴达和雅典一样开始寻求希腊的霸权。前367年，希腊重要城邦的代表齐集苏萨的波斯王庭议和。忒拜代表培洛皮达斯（Pelopidas）与波斯大王关系密切，两者商定了议和条款：

> 美塞尼独立，不受斯巴达的控制；将雅典战舰拖到岸上搁置；如果斯巴达和雅典不服从，
> 大王将发动对她们的战争；其他各邦都要参与这样的军事行动，不从者将首先受到攻击。⑧

忒拜通过该议和条款可以与波斯大王结成密切联盟，并彻底终结斯巴达和雅典的霸权，而建立起自己的霸权。但这样的条款不但令斯巴达和雅典无法接受，而且令忒拜的盟友阿卡迪亚联邦无法接受。⑨相比于斯巴达和雅典的霸权，忒拜的霸权企图同样自私自利。

尽管如此，色诺芬并没有忽视忒拜霸权表现出来的正义之点。前面曾提到西息昂流亡者在忒拜刺杀了他们本国的僭主欧福荣，但因为流亡者的正义申辩，忒拜赦免了他们。⑩

另外关于忒拜对美塞尼的解放，色诺芬虽然没有正面描述，但我们可以通过联系色诺芬对两个

---

① Xenophon, *Hellenica*, 6.4.2–3.
② Xenophon, *Hellenica*, 6.4.15.
③ N. G. L. Hammond, *A History of Greece*, pp.496–497.
④ N. G. L. Hammond, *A History of Greece*, p.497.
⑤ Xenophon, *Hellenica*, 6.5.22–32.
⑥ Xenophon, *Hellenica*, 7.1.27, 7.5.5.
⑦ Xenophon, *Hellenica*, 7.1.1–14.
⑧ Xenophon, *Hellenica*, 7.1.36.
⑨ Xenophon, *Hellenica*, 7.1.38–40.
⑩ Xenophon, *Hellenica*, 7.3.4–12.

事件的关注来分析他的观点。一个是色诺芬对基纳东阴谋事件的描述，其中表现了黑劳士等下层民众对斯巴达全权公民的憎恨。[①]另一个是前370/369年，面对忒拜的入侵，斯巴达守城兵力不足，为了征召士兵，斯巴达许诺给所有愿意拿起武器的黑劳士自由，结果招到了6000名黑劳士战士。可是这些战士的聚集引起了斯巴达人（原文为拉西戴梦人，包括斯巴达公民和庇里奥西人[②]）的恐惧，直到斯巴达的盟邦派来援军时，他们才变得不那么担心。[③]由此可见，色诺芬有意展现黑劳士整体上与斯巴达人之间存在的一种深刻的矛盾。另外当美塞尼在忒拜的支持下取得独立，并与之结盟以后，斯巴达仍然念念不忘重新控制这个城邦。斯巴达人无法接受美塞尼独立的理由是，此地是他们从其父辈那里继承下来的。[④]这个理由会使读者想起之前的一个例子。约前400年，正当斯巴达的霸权蒸蒸日上的时候，她强迫伊利斯人放弃对一个小邦伊佩昂（Epeion）的占领。伊利斯人反对，理由是，那个小邦的土地是他们花了40塔兰特的钱买来的。但斯巴达对此予以反驳，认为当卖者比买者弱小，而买者强行买来的话，并不比强行占有更正义。于是斯巴达强迫伊利斯人允许伊佩昂独立。[⑤]伊利斯对于伊佩昂，斯巴达对于美塞尼，前后对比，读者便明白，色诺芬对斯巴达坚持要求美塞尼的心态确实含着一种巧妙的讽刺。这同时也表明，忒拜对美塞尼的支持，虽然有自身战略利益的考虑，但同样是件符合正义的事。

忒拜的将领伊帕美浓达是个与众不同的人，虽然他有许多伟大功绩，色诺芬似乎故意在叙述一些事件时没有提他的名字，（如前378年他参与推翻忒拜僭主统治，前370/379年率军驰骋伯罗奔尼撒）但他抓住了他的两个非常出色的表现。一个是他的军事才能，表现在他最后一次攻入伯罗奔尼撒和曼丁尼亚之战中。这一方面，读者一般都有共识，还有一方面，我们很容易忽视，那就是对他的政治才能的展现。在希腊城邦惯常采用的扩张霸权的手段，就是在其他城邦扶植对自己亲善的政治势力，以便使反对自己的政治势力被放逐，成为流亡者。这就是强大城邦为追求霸权相互争斗，同时伴随着弱小城邦内部民主派与贵族派之间相互争斗，民主制与贵族制轮换的一个重要原因。

伊帕美浓达对阿卡亚的政治安排却与众不同。约前366年，阿格西劳斯率军进攻阿卡亚人，以使他们成为忒拜的盟邦。按照通常做法，他应当在阿卡亚扶植民主派，（因为忒拜或彼奥提亚联邦是民主制的）流放阿卡亚的贵族派，使阿卡亚的民主派成为依赖忒拜的当政者。但伊帕美浓达没有这样做，他应阿卡亚贵族派的要求，依靠自己的威信，阻止了民主派对贵族派的放逐，也没有改变政制体制，但同样使阿卡亚人发誓追随忒拜的行动。但后来忒拜的盟友阿卡迪亚联邦反对伊帕美浓达的这种安排，说这样做有利于斯巴达人。忒拜政府于是向阿卡亚派遣了驻军长官（harmost），这些驻军长官在阿卡亚民主派的协助下流放了贵族派。但贵族派聚集在一起，又打了回来，重新控制了阿卡亚联邦的政权。然后，他们倒向了斯巴达一边。阿卡迪亚联邦因此也受到了阿卡亚联邦和斯巴达的双重压力。[⑥]色诺芬用这个富有戏剧化的历史情节，展现了伊帕美浓达独特的政治思想，及其不被奉行传统的霸权政策的忒拜政府所理解的困境。哈蒙德曾对伊帕美浓达的政治理想有高度的评价，认为他对其他城邦的政策不是像斯巴达和雅典那样分而治之，而是协调其他城邦内的两派，进而领导他们，并指出忒拜政府很难理解他的精神，这是他死后，忒拜急剧衰弱的原因。[⑦]

一种不正义的霸权，既会遭到外部的反对者，其内部的成员也会产生离心的倾向。前395年，

①　Xenophon, *Hellenica*, 3.3.4−11.
②　参见词条 "Laconia"，David Sacks ed., *Encyclopedia of the Ancient Greek World*, New York: Facts On File, 2005，p.187.
③　Xenophon, *Hellenica*, 6.5.28−29.
④　Xenophon, *Hellenica*, 7.1.27, 7.4.9.
⑤　Xenophon, *Hellenica*, 3.2.30−31.
⑥　Xenophon, *Hellenica*, 7.1.42−43.
⑦　N. G. L. Hammond, *A History of Greece*, p.510.

忒拜使节劝说雅典人跟他们一起联合反对斯巴达的霸权，在谈到不必害怕斯巴达及其同盟人多势众的理由时，这样说道：

> ……不要因为他们（斯巴达人）统治着这么多的人而感到害怕；相反，当考虑到你们统治最多的人口时，你们敌人的数量也达到最多，这一事实就会给你们更大的信心。只要这些敌人在他们叛离的时候，没有其他城邦支持他们，他们就掩盖对你们的仇恨，但只要斯巴达人成为反对你们的领导，然后那些敌人便表现出了他们对你们的真实情感。如果现在我们并肩战斗，反对斯巴达人，这也将是发生在他们身上的事：很多憎恨他们的城邦，将会表现出真实的自己。……[1]

忒拜使节的这段话也揭示希腊城邦中霸权的宿命——从强大走向不正义的霸权，随之而来的就是内外反霸权势力的出现，在这种打击下，霸权走向衰弱。

前362年，在曼丁尼亚，忒拜及其同盟的军队，与斯巴达、雅典及其同盟的军队进行决战。希腊主要的城邦都卷入了这场战争，她们要么站在忒拜一方，要么站在斯巴达和雅典一方。人们预测战争的结果便是一个统治全希腊的霸权的产生。但结果出乎人们的预料，每一方都声称自己是胜利者；但又在休战协议下取回自己一方阵亡者的尸体，这样看来显然又都是失败者。另外，敌对双方也没有在战争中获得更多的城邦、土地和统治权力。只是希腊社会比以前更加混乱了。[2]在色诺芬看来，希腊城邦之间缺乏正义、为了利益的争霸战争，只能是无休止的轮回，为希腊人徒增无数的苦难。但毕竟他从这些混乱的事件中看出了正义和希望。

二　反思泛希腊主义之二：希腊与波斯

我们再来看一下，色诺芬对希腊和波斯间关系的展现与思考。这在演说家的泛希腊主义思想中明确的表示是进攻波斯，那么色诺芬在《希腊史》展现了什么样的观点呢？笔者认为，首先色诺芬不是一个狂热的鼓动家，他是一个对希腊和波斯人关系进行冷静思考的人。

波斯人与希腊人在战略利益上存在矛盾，小亚沿岸的希腊城邦是这一矛盾的焦点。波斯希望控制富庶的小亚城邦，既可以获得贡赋，也可以增加自己的战略利益。[3]希腊的霸权力量——如雅典或斯巴达——也想插手此地，因为她们与小亚的城邦既有文化的共同性，又有在爱琴海的战略利益。希腊的霸权力量既然常常以维护希腊人的共同利益自居，那么保护小亚城邦免受波斯控制便成为这些霸权力量的正义的责任。

笔者认为，色诺芬展现的主要是波斯的基本战略，军事方面的优缺点，希腊人若与波斯人战争所应该采取的战略战术。色诺芬并没有明确贬低波斯人的意思，他对波斯人和希腊人表现出来的优缺点都有公正地对待。

波斯对待希腊的战略很简单，主要就是通过支持希腊一派攻打与自己利益有冲突的一派，最终使希腊保持衰弱，以致没有任何力量与之在小亚的霸权相抗衡。而希腊城邦间的战争中，一方为了打败另一方也常常争取波斯的援助。波斯的援助形式主要有金钱、骑兵、步兵和腓尼基舰队。其中金钱起

---

① Xenophon, *Hellenica*, 3.5.10–11.

② Xenophon, *Hellenica*, 7.5.26–27.

③ 波斯在希波战争失败后，已经没有入侵希腊本土的想法，她对希腊的干涉只是为了维护小亚的战略利益。参见词条 "Persian Wars：the Persian viewpoint", in *The Oxford Classical Dictionary*, Simon Hornblower and Antony Spawforth eds., third edition, New York: Oxford University Press, pp.1146–1147.

的作用常常更大些，因为随着雇佣兵的发展，和公民兵的雇佣化，金钱在战争中的作用日益加重。

伯罗奔尼撒战争后期，前412年，斯巴达以对小亚希腊城邦的牺牲，与波斯结盟，换取了波斯在金钱和军队方面的支持。雅典也曾试图通过亚西比德与波斯结盟，但没有成功。色诺芬对莱山德在前407年与小居鲁士会见，与他建立良好的私人关系，并获得他在金钱上的鼎力相助一事有生动的描述。①而小居鲁士与斯巴达密切合作，尤其是与莱山德密切合作的目的，就是希望能在他稍后（前401/400年）篡夺其兄之王位的战争中得到斯巴达的大力支持。斯巴达派了大量雇佣军由克利尔库斯（Clearchus）率领追随小居鲁士，还派了舰队提供支持。斯巴达之所以在得知小居鲁士反叛后仍支持他，主要是因为，小居鲁士在伯罗奔尼撒战争中对斯巴达的帮助，还有就是他对小亚城邦的宽松政策。但斯巴达此举也就意味着与波斯大王处于战争状态。

当小居鲁士的反叛在前401/400年被镇压后，波斯企图重新控制小亚城邦。前399年，斯巴达应小亚城邦之请，派军到小亚与波斯作战。在色诺芬的描述下，德西利达斯和阿格西劳斯对波斯的作战非常有希望。②但在此时，波斯总督提斯特罗特斯巧妙地运用金钱外交，化解了波斯的危险。前395年，他派人携带了价值约40塔兰特的金钱到希腊与忒拜、科林斯、亚各斯和雅典，与各邦反斯巴达的领袖们会见，在他们发誓带领本国反对斯巴达的前提下，他给他们金钱资助。雅典人没有收钱，但急切地想发动反斯巴达的战争。通过这种方式，波斯人将反斯巴达的几个大邦撮合在了一起。③稍后，科林斯战争爆发，波斯支持忒拜、科林斯、亚各斯和雅典与斯巴达及其盟邦作战。

波斯方面没有直接参与希腊本部的陆上战争，直接参与的主要是法那巴祖斯领导的腓尼基舰队和科侬领导的舰队，与斯巴达舰队在海上的战斗。④前394年，法那巴祖斯和科侬各自率舰队相互合作，在克尼杜斯（Cnidus）附近打败斯巴达舰队。前393年，法那巴祖斯和科侬率舰队前往伯罗奔尼撒海岸破坏拉科尼亚（Laconia）地区，占领拉科尼亚海岸对面的库特拉（Cythera）并留驻军队。然后他们还航往科林斯地峡，赞扬了在那里作战的盟邦，并留下一笔金钱。同一年，科侬以扶植雅典是对斯巴达最大的报复为依据，请求法那巴祖斯支持他率舰队回雅典重建被部分拆毁的长墙和比雷埃夫斯港城墙，后者不但允许，而且还资助了一笔重建的资金。⑤

当斯巴达得知科侬在用波斯的金钱修复雅典长墙，并维持海军后，担心雅典再次崛起，派安塔尔奇达斯前往小亚会见波斯的总督提里巴祖斯（Tiribazos），希望能阻止对雅典的支持。雅典、科林斯、亚各斯和彼奥提亚联邦也派了代表前往提里巴祖斯处。此时斯巴达代表安塔尔奇达斯为了使波斯从支持雅典等邦，转向支持斯巴达，向提里巴祖斯提出了这样的议和条款：如果波斯大王令所有的岛屿和希腊其他城邦独立，斯巴达放弃对小亚希腊城邦的控制。提里巴祖斯对此感到高兴，因为这样希腊便没有任何一个城邦可以跟大王作对了。但雅典、忒拜、亚各斯都反对，因为这将会使他们无法控制盟邦，而自己被削弱。结果议和失败。⑥

当雅典崛起的势头可能危害波斯在爱琴海的利益时，（雅典支持塞浦路斯的萨拉米斯王埃瓦格拉斯叛变波斯）波斯又根据自己的利益需求跟斯巴达开始接近。前392年，提里巴祖斯秘密资助斯巴达舰队与雅典作战，并逮捕了科侬。尽管前391年任小亚总督的斯特茹塔斯（Strouthas）因为个人对斯巴达王阿格西劳斯的憎恨而积极与斯巴达作战，但至前387年，安塔尔奇达斯与波斯大王谈

---

① Xenophon, *Hellenica*, 1.5.1–7.
② 在狄奥多鲁斯和奥克西林库斯史家的笔下看不到这种希望，对比 Diodorus Siculus, *The Library of History*, 14.38.2–3, 14.38.6–7,14.79.1–3. 和 *Hellenica Oxyrhynchia*, Fragment 14.3–6, 24, 25.
③ Xenophon, *Hellenica*, 3.5.1–2.
④ 科侬在前405年阿格斯波塔米战役后，没有回雅典，而是带领数艘战舰先到了塞浦路斯，后又投奔到法那巴祖斯麾下做海军将领，在科林斯战争中与斯巴达作战。
⑤ Xenophon, *Hellenica*, 4.3.10–12, 4.8.7–10.
⑥ Xenophon, *Hellenica*, 4.8.12–15.

妥了议和条款后，波斯明确转向了对斯巴达的支持，提里巴祖斯再次被任命为小亚总督以支持斯巴达，并推动议和之事。①前387/386年，当希腊对立的两派，都无力再继续战争的时候，提里巴祖斯召集各邦代表，公布了大王的议和约。（和约内容见第一部分）

最终希腊各邦或主动，或被动接受了这一条约。波斯大王显然是这一条约的最大受益者。通过该条约，他阻止了雅典在爱琴海势力的崛起，使斯巴达的势力退出了小亚，小亚城邦将再次处于波斯控制之下。同时希腊停战后，大量的雇佣兵将涌到他的麾下，成为镇压塞浦路斯埃瓦格拉斯（Evagoras）叛乱的工具。②波斯在科林斯战争中以支持雅典等邦开始，而以支持斯巴达结束，巧妙地利用了自己的金钱和希腊城邦间的矛盾。

大王和约表现了波斯在希腊打拉结合战略的新发展。这种发展表现在令各邦独立，以实现普遍和平（Koinē Eirēnē）的口号上。这样的口号迎合了大多数希腊城邦要求独立，要求和平的心理，自然是很容易受到到欢迎的。在此和约的推动下，以尊重城邦独立为基础的普遍和平成为希腊邦际政治的一股强有力的思潮。③波斯的此举毫无疑问占据了道义的制高点。而大王和约对波斯的实际意义是，保证除斯巴达之外的希腊其他城邦（尤其是雅典）的力量受到削弱从而使她们（特别是雅典）无力危害波斯在小亚的霸权；同时斯巴达承认了波斯在小亚的霸权。斯巴达由于热衷于在希腊压制其他城邦，自私地维护自身在希腊的霸权，这必然会造成与其他城邦，如雅典、忒拜的深刻矛盾。这样波斯依然保证了希腊本部紧张的矛盾，为她下一步根据自己的利益调整合作对象留有了很大空间。④

大王和约之后，斯巴达果然为了自己的霸权私利，四处报复压制对其不利的其他希腊各邦。她对忒拜卫城的占领和偷袭比雷埃夫斯的企图，没有采取惩罚措施，这使雅典和忒拜再次开始联合反对斯巴达霸权（前378/377年，忒拜以与雅典平等的地位加入第二雅典同盟）。前371年留克特拉之战，斯巴达大败，接着忒拜入侵伯罗奔尼撒，阿卡迪亚联邦崛起，美塞尼独立，加入到了反斯巴达联盟之中。面对忒拜的迅速崛起，雅典又与斯巴达联合反对忒拜。

当希腊政治格局发生变化，而矛盾依然尖锐、各方疲于战争的时候。前367年波斯又与希腊各邦代表议和，此时波斯开始与忒拜联合，新的议和条款仍然秉承尊重各邦独立，实现普遍和平的精神，只是忒拜取代了以前斯巴达的霸权角色，斯巴达和雅典都成为被削弱和打击的对象。⑤尽管这次和约，遭到很多希腊城邦的反对，没有像前386年的大王和约那样成功，但波斯这种战略的实际效果确是非常成功的，前362年的曼丁尼亚战争之后希腊陷入了更加混乱的状态之中。

波斯在整体战略上，为了自身利益，对希腊矛盾的利用，在色诺芬的历史叙述中昭然若揭。对于希腊的这种困境，色诺芬曾借卡里克拉提达斯（Kallikratidas）之口进行展现。前406年卡里克拉提达斯到小亚接替任期已满的莱山德担任斯巴达海军司令，他因与莱山德产生嫌隙，而莱山德与小居鲁士私交密切，所以他在向小居鲁士索要军费时，受到怠慢。卡里克拉提达斯无法忍受，便拂袖而去，并声称，希腊人受到了最严重的灾难，因为他们为了金钱而向蛮族人（指波斯人）献媚，如果他能安全返回，他将尽最大努力使雅典人和斯巴达人和解。⑥卡里克拉提达斯常常要么被称为一个

---

① Xenophon, *Hellenica*, 4.8.16, 4.8.17–19, 5.1.25, 5.1.28.
② N. G. L. Hammond, *A History of Greece*, p.464.
③ Paul Cartledge, *Ancient Greek Political Thought in Practice*, New York: Cambridge University Press, 2009. p.92.
④ 这方面与伊索克拉底的观点有些类似，见 Isocrates, *Panegyricus*, pp.175–178.
⑤ Xenophon, *Hellenica*, 7.1.36–37.
⑥ Xenophon, *Hellenica*, 1.6.6–7.

泛希腊主义的倡导者，要么被认为是一个无能的将军。①但无论如何，色诺芬之所以注意到他的这些话，原因就是这些话确实揭示了希腊人在波斯战略中的困境，同时也指出了摆脱这种困境的出路在于希腊城邦间的和解。

希腊人与波斯人之间的战争危险是长期存在的，那么针对与波斯作战的情况，希腊人应注意哪些战略战术呢？色诺芬在叙述斯巴达将领德西利达斯和国王阿格西劳斯在小亚与波斯作战时，及在他的其他著作中都有丰富的反映。

希腊人的重装步兵对波斯人有优势，而骑兵需要加强，并需借鉴波斯骑兵的经验。前396年，阿格西劳斯的骑兵被波斯骑兵打败，因为波斯骑兵在人数、战略战术上优于希腊骑兵，而且他们使用的矛也有优势。这种矛的杆是用山茱萸的木料制成，在打斗中可以将希腊骑兵的矛击碎。②阿格西劳斯认识到没有强大的骑兵，无法跟波斯人在平原上作战，便开始加强骑兵队伍。③与波斯人作战要有充足的军需贮备。做好军需贮备工作，可以使与波斯作战的希腊军队不必骚扰小亚的希腊城邦。这样希腊军队为解放同胞而战的口号便会与其实际行动相符合，这更能获得小亚希腊城邦的支持。前399年，德西利达斯在小亚与波斯作战时，将所获得的希腊城邦转交给民众管理的做法，得到了小亚城邦的拥护。④

另外希腊人与波斯作战需要在小亚建立一个士兵训练基地。阿格西劳斯在小亚作战时的大本营设在以弗所。希腊军队在此地进行勤劳地训练，呈现出一派繁荣的景象：

> 之后，当春天开始的时候，他（阿格西劳斯）将军队聚集在以弗所。正如他所希望的那样对军队进行训练。他在重装步兵中为那些被发现拥有最好身体素质的人设立奖品，也在骑兵当中为那些表现出最好骑术的人设立奖品。他也为轻装兵和弓箭手设立奖品，给予那些在专业技艺方面有卓越表现的人。由于这种政策的实施，人们可以看到，整个运动场上，满是进行训练的人，赛马跑道上满是练习骑术的人，标枪手和弓箭手也都在忙于各自的事务。实际上，阿格西劳斯使军队驻扎的整个城邦变成一个令人惊叹的奇迹！广场上摆满了要出售的各种马匹和武器，还有铜匠、木匠、铁匠、制革匠和漆工都在热情高涨地为战争打造武器，以致人们会认为整个城邦真得变成了为战争做准备的作坊。当人们看到阿格西劳斯带队，领着带花环的士兵，从运动场去给阿尔特弥斯敬献花环，也一定会很受鼓舞。那些尊敬神明，为了战争努力训练，并严格遵守长官命令的人，对任何人来说，都自然是充满希望的。……⑤

希腊人还要善于利用波斯总督之间的矛盾，及臣服于波斯的一些小国与波斯的矛盾。前399年，德西利达斯接替提布戎率领军队在小亚与波斯作战。当他得知法那巴祖斯和替萨弗尼斯之间有矛盾，相互不信任时，他与替萨弗尼斯达成休战协议，而后集中兵力进击法那巴祖斯的辖区。⑥前395年，阿格西劳斯在小亚带兵与波斯作战时，斯皮斯里达提斯（Spithridates，由莱山德策反投奔到阿格西劳斯这里的波斯贵族）对他说，自己可以使他与帕夫拉戈尼亚国王奥提斯（Otys）结盟。阿格西劳

---

① 持前一种观点的，参见 John Dillery, *Xenophon and the History of his Times, London*: Routledge, 1995, p.118, p.198, p.199. 持后一种观点的见 Gerald Proietti, *Xenophon's Sparta*, New York: E. J. Brill, 1987, p.15–16.
② 这一点色诺芬在《论骑术》里也强调了要求山茱萸木杆做标枪，见 Xenophon, *Art of Horsemanship*, 12.12.
③ Xenophon, *Hellenica*, 3.4.13–15.
④ Xenophon, *Hellenica*, 3.1.18–21.
⑤ Xenophon, *Hellenica*, 3.4.16–18.
⑥ Xenophon, *Hellenica*, 3.1.9.

斯很高兴，因为他早就想诱使一些波斯统治下的民族反叛波斯国王了。阿格西劳斯与奥提斯结盟后，后者送给他大量马匹和轻装兵。阿格西劳斯为了进一步巩固与斯皮斯里达提斯和奥提斯的联盟，还成功地使后两者联姻，斯皮斯里达提斯将自己的女儿嫁给了奥提斯。①

人们常常认为色诺芬对德西利达斯和阿格西劳斯在小亚与波斯作战的描述，和他的《长征记》一样，表现了波斯的孱弱，即可以征服并劫掠之的泛希腊主义思想。但色诺芬一贯是反对不正义之战争的。波斯企图控制小亚城邦，斯巴达为了小亚城邦的独立，出兵与波斯作战，并且确实尊重了小亚城邦的独立，这是正义之战。色诺芬进而在叙述这段历史中展现的对波斯作战正确的战略战术。但这不可以受演说家们那种狂热的泛希腊主义的影响，而对色诺芬的这段叙述的目的做歪曲的引申。②

前395年，科林斯战争爆发，前394年，斯巴达令与波斯作战很有希望的阿格西劳斯回援。这常被理解为由于"背后的一刀"，阿格西劳斯征服波斯的大业失败。这种理解确切的说是用演说家的思想来理解色诺芬，而不是按他自己的思维来理解他。③色诺芬两个有趣的描述反映了他的看法，一个是关于阿格西劳斯出征波斯的道路，他强调了阿格西劳斯模仿阿伽门农在奥里斯献祭，然后乘船启程，但阿格西劳斯走后祭坛受到了忒拜人的破坏；另一个是关于阿格西劳斯赶回斯巴达回援的道路，他走的与当年波斯大王薛西斯征讨希腊走的路一样。④这里显然含有这样的暗示，他出征波斯的行动尚有正义性可言，可斯巴达的行为已经在希腊引起了不满，而他回程的目的是为了维护斯巴达的霸权。所以说，色诺芬在阿格西劳斯被召回一事上，要表达的意思，不是简单的惋惜，而是要说，在希腊城邦中没有正义的安排，甚至也无法对波斯进行正义的战争。

狂热的泛希腊主义思想总是贬低外族人（Barbarians，带有贬义的中文译文为"蛮族人"），也包括波斯人。但色诺芬的著作中没有这种明确的贬低。《希腊史》中谈到，阿格西劳斯认为对波斯人的鄙视可以提高希腊人战斗的勇气，于是便找来一些孱弱的波斯俘虏，扒光他们的衣服，展示并出售，以便让希腊士兵们认为他们所与之战斗的敌人养尊处优，跟妇女差不多。⑤此处很容易被误解为色诺芬对波斯人的贬低，但从其语境来看，显然是在表现阿格西劳斯的一种鼓舞士气的技巧，并非波斯人真得是如此。在《长征记》中，色诺芬曾注意到这样一个例子。当小居鲁士在行军途中，看到一辆车陷入泥泞之中，他令几个希腊人前去帮忙，但他们做事慢慢腾腾，小居鲁士很不满，便令随行的波斯贵族前去。这些人虽然穿着华美的衣服，带着首饰，但马上甩掉紫袍，进入泥泞之中，并很快把车抬了出来。⑥实际上色诺芬对波斯人的描述跟对希腊人的描述一样，都是以他们做事所表现出来的技艺和美德来展现的。

色诺芬在叙述德西利达斯在小亚的征战时，特别插入了一段关于达达尼尔妇女玛尼娅（Mania）的故事。玛尼娅的丈夫达达尼尔人泽尼斯（Zenis）是法那巴祖斯之下统治爱奥里斯（Aeolis）等地的下一级总督。当她的丈夫去世后，玛尼娅带着礼品前去见法那巴祖斯，承诺她可以把以前他丈夫管理的地方管理得如他生前一样好，并向法那巴祖斯缴纳同样的贡赋，希望法那巴祖斯让她继承她丈夫的职位。法那巴祖斯欣然答应。事实上，玛尼娅比他的丈夫管理的更好，给予法那巴祖斯更多礼物；她通过一支希腊雇佣军征服了更多的城邦，并通过奖励的办法赢得了下属的拥护；她的雇佣军装备精良，她经常随法那巴祖斯一起出征，法那巴祖斯对她也特别尊敬，常征求她的意见。当她

---

① Xenophon, *Hellenica*, 4.1.1–16.

② W. E. Higgins, *Xenophon the Athenian: The Problem of the Individual and the Society of the Polis*, Albany: State University of New York, 1977, pp.97–98.

③ John Dillery, *Xenophon and the History of his Times*, London: Routlege, 1995, pp.115–117.

④ Xenophon, *Hellenica*, 3.4.3–4, 4.2.8.

⑤ Xenophon, *Hellenica*, 3.4.19.

⑥ Xenophon, *Anabasis*, 1.5.7–9.（translated by Carleton L. Brownson, Loeb Classical Library, Harvard University Press, 1992）参见崔金戎中文译本，北京商务印书馆1995年版，第18页。

被自己的女婿刺杀篡位后，法那巴祖斯甚至发誓要为她报仇。①色诺芬之所以插入这段故事，显然特别欣赏这位富有出色领导能力的外族妇女。

色诺芬对阿格西劳斯与法那巴祖斯议和场面的描述，表现了两个精明领导人的出色对话。前395年，在阿格西劳斯和法那巴祖斯的一个中间朋友的协助下，二人见面会谈。见面时，阿格西劳斯及其随从（30位斯巴达全权公民）衣着简单，坐在草地上。衣着华丽的法那巴祖斯本来要铺上精美的地毯才坐，但看到阿格西劳斯等人的简朴，便也靠近阿格西劳斯席地而坐。在交谈中，法那巴祖斯首先责备了阿格西劳斯恩将仇报的行为，因为法那巴祖斯曾帮助过斯巴达人攻打雅典人，现在却受到了他们的侵害。面对这些谴责，阿格西劳斯的随从都很羞愧，但阿格西劳斯灵机一变，回答说，若是出于个人原因，他是不会攻打法那巴祖斯的，但因为现在斯巴达与波斯处于交战状态，所以身不由己。接着阿格西劳斯以自由和财富，诱引法那巴祖斯叛离波斯大王，说如果他与斯巴达结盟，他便不会再向任何人卑躬屈膝，并且可以增加自己的财富，而不是为波斯大王增加财富。但法那巴祖斯回答，若大王派来另一个统治者，并让他臣服于这个人，那他会成为斯巴达的朋友和盟友；但如果大王让他继续统治他现在的王国，他认为这是大王给予他的荣誉和尊敬，他会以自己最大的努力来同斯巴达人作战。法那巴祖斯的回答表现了一个自由人的尊严和诚信，令阿格西劳斯非常敬重。②阿格西劳斯跟他议和，并撤出他的辖地，而且双方答应在将来的战斗中，尽量不侵犯对方。③

在这次会见中，色诺芬还特意叙述了一个小插曲。会见结束时，法那巴祖斯的儿子帕拉皮塔（Parapita）因对阿格西劳斯的爱慕，与之结成了客友关系，相互交换了礼物。后来帕拉皮塔被其兄弟流放，来到斯巴达，阿格西劳斯给予他很多关怀，甚至协助他的一位男青年密友（雅典人）参加了奥利匹亚运动会的比赛。④这个小插曲，展现了希腊人与波斯人在私人层面，有着美好的感情。⑤

所以在希腊人与波斯人的关系上，色诺芬在历史中的展现是冷静的，现实的，也是丰富的。

结 论

色诺芬在《希腊史》中通过对城邦间霸权与反霸权的争斗和希腊人与波斯关系的叙述，实际上反思了这种狂热的泛希腊主义。他试图使人们认识到希腊霸权（城邦）若不能与其他城邦建立起基于现实的正义关系，希腊人内部不可能结束纷争；波斯人利用希腊人内部的纷争成功地插手希腊事务并控制了小亚的希腊城邦，但希腊人也有自己切实可行的战略战术来对付波斯人；波斯人与希腊人一样有高贵的品质，希腊人与波斯人之间的关系同样不可以违反正义。

---

① Xenophon, *Hellenica*, 3.1.10–15.
② 关于法那巴祖斯在这次会谈中的出色表现，见 Vivienne Gray, *The Character of Xenophon's Hellenica, Baltimore*: The John Hopkins University Press, 1989, pp.52–56.
③ Xenophon, *Hellenica*, 4.1.29–38.
④ Xenophon, *Hellenica*, 4.1.39–40.
⑤ Vivienne Gray, *The Character of Xenophon's Hellenica*, p.57.

从派迪亚（paideia）到阿高盖（agoge）
——古代斯巴达教育制度的演变

祝宏俊　南京师范大学

摘要：古代希腊有两种教育模式，即派迪亚（paideia）模式和阿高盖（agōgē）模式，这两种模式都这是品德培养，但前者侧重于人文素养培养，是为培养合格公民而实行的全面文科教育，后者侧重于专业技能培养，特别是体育、军事技能培养，是为培养合格公民和合格战士而实行的专项教育。在斯巴达历史上，这两种模式都曾经存在过，前者主要存在于古风时期，后者主要存在于古典时期，它们都曾经为斯巴达的历史作出了积极的贡献；而到了罗马统治时期阿高盖制度则沦为一种带有血腥色彩的娱乐制度，失去了其原有的积极意义。

关键词：派迪亚；阿高盖；斯巴达；教育

Abstract：There are two education modes in ancient Greece: paideia and agoge, both aiming at moral cultivation, but the former, with an emphasis on humanistic quality, is an overall humanistic education for qualified citizens, whereas the latter, with an emphasis on skill training, especially on the physical and martial skills, is a specific education for qualified citizens and soldiers. In the ancient Sparta, paideia was prevailing in the archaic period and then was replaced by agoge in the classical time, both of which had made positive contribution to the history of Sparta; however, agoge deteriorated into a sort of bloody amusement in the Roman time.

Keywords: paideia, agōgē, Sparta, Education

派迪亚与阿高盖：两种不同的教育模式

派迪亚希腊文写作 paideia。在古希腊，教育一词大多用"paideia"，该词的词根是 paides（儿童），其词义是对儿童的培育与教导。在古希腊，教育的含义与现代教育有很大的不同，现代教育大多是技术教育、技能教育，而古希腊的教育主要是品德教育，是为培养自由的成年公民而实行的全面文科教育，是优雅艺术的教育与培训①。简言之，古希腊的教育主要是品德和人文素质之教育。柏拉图声称教育是从童年起所受的美德教育（*Law*，643E-644A），是善的获取（*Law*，653B）。所以，古希腊的 paideia 的主要意思更近似于现代的教化。但 paideia 一词主要是雅典作家立足雅典提出的一个范畴②，主要从"儿童的培育、教育"衍生而来的。因此，派迪亚教育的模式更主要的是从雅典的教育模式中抽象出来的。所以，有人又这样定义派迪亚：以参加公共生活为目的，旨在为学生提供全方位文化教育的雅典教育体制。

这种教育包括文化教育和身体锻炼两大部分，具体讲包括修辞、语法、数学、音乐、哲学、地理、自然史、体育。这种课程体系的目的不是传授赢利之道，不是传授经商或生产或经营管理方面的知识，而是为了培养合格的公民。古代雅典约在梭伦改革就开始建立民主制度，经过克里斯提尼改革，民主制度终于建立起来，到伯里克利时期，民主政治达到繁荣。在民主政治下，公民是天生的政治动物，作为公民的主要职责是参加公共活动，超群的演讲才能是其获得成功的必备条件。因此，派迪亚教育的主要科目都是围绕着如何提高演讲水平而设置的，修辞、语法不必说，就是哲学、地理、自然历史等等也都是围绕着这个目标。对于民主制下的公民来说，对个人的道德有着更高的要求，民主制赋予公民较多的权力，同时也需要权利主体能正确地行使权力，所以道德的修持是非承重要的，这样哲学，尤其是一个以个人修持为中心的哲学也是公民必须学习的。至于体育则在古代雅典具有特殊的意义，一方面，作为个人在群体生活中魁梧的身材、健康的体魄是吸引注意力、获得成功的重要条件，另一方面，公民的重要义务是为城邦充当公民兵，而充当公民兵也需要强壮的体魄。所以，派迪亚教育是以培育合格公民为目的的教育模式。

阿高盖

在古代希腊的大部分时间内，人们都是用派迪亚来指称"教育"，但到了希腊化时期之后，古希腊的思想家专用一个新的词 agōgē 来指称斯巴达的教育制度。agōgē 一词在希腊化时期之前并没有专门用于指斯巴达的教育制度，首次用来指称斯巴达教育大概在公元前 331 年，而最终定型专指斯巴达教育制度大概是在一百年之后。公元前 331 年，斯巴达国王阿基斯三世与马其顿王安提帕特（Antipater）发生战争，安提帕特获胜，命令斯巴达交出 50 名儿童作人质，斯巴达监察官厄提奥克勒斯（Eteocles）以这部分儿童不能通过 agōgē 为名加以拒绝。这是首次将 agōgē 用于特指斯巴达教育制度。但是首次用 agōgē 一词指称斯巴达教育制度的作家是大约生活在公元前 3 世纪的犬儒派作家特勒斯（Teles）。③

阿高盖的希腊文写作 àgwgh(agōgē)，该词的词根是 agon，原意是运动场、竞技场、体育锻炼。与它同一词根的词 agonia 意思是体育锻炼、角力、竞赛、争夺战斗胜利。因此，从词源学上看，阿高盖的核心是以体育锻炼、体育竞技为主。从斯巴达的教育实践来看，斯巴达的阿高盖教育主要是为了国家培养体质强壮、道德过硬的战士。训练的科目主要有各种战斗技能、狩猎、舞蹈、耐力训练、吃苦训练，如窃食、鞭打、秘密巡行（库普提亚制度）等。阿高盖制度也重视道德培养，但是阿高盖的道德主要是献身国家所需要的国家利益和群体利益至上的道德信条，是对国家、领袖的绝对顺从。

派迪亚和阿高盖教育作为两种教育模式，他们相似之处在于都是为了国家培养合格的公民。但是阿高盖更强调公民作为士兵的特性，而派迪亚更强调作为政治动物的秉性。亚里士多德曾经评价斯巴达的政治制度认为他们的制度的总体目的是培养军人武德，这种品德过分强调好强争胜、追逐

---

① R. S. Crane, *The Idea of the Humanities*, Chicago, The Universty of Chicago Press, 1987, p. 23. 转引自石敏敏：《希腊人文主义》，上海人民出版社，2003 年版，第 7 页。

② Paul Cartledge, *Spartan Reflections*, Duckworth, 2001, p.83.

③ Cf. Nigel M. Kennell, *Gymnasium of Virtue, Education & Culture in Ancient Sparta*, The University of North Carolina Press, 1995, p.114.

荣誉，不适合和平时期，不适合过休闲生活。

但是这两种教育模式也有巨大的不同。派迪亚教育等多地立足于儿童本身，尊重儿童的个性发展，所以这种教育主要是一种引导，更类似与苏格拉底的引导法、助产术，即在保护儿童个性的前提下用启发的方法引导儿童的个性发展。而阿高盖一词转化为教育学词汇后，具有"领导、指导、培训"等含义，这种教育是"按照一定的模式加以的培育"。这种教育模式更强调外在的指导和规约，是在一定目标制约之下、带有强制性的人才培养模式。

这种教育培养出来的儿童在人格上也有很大差别。派迪亚培养出来的儿童自由、独立、奔放、张扬。他们擅长演讲，演讲才能出众，其演讲洋洋洒洒，具有极强的感染力，部分学员为了自己的目的运用多种语言才能，成为类似于智者派的诡辩家。他们一追求自己的成功为人生目标，极力期望自己在社会上出人头地、飞黄腾达。其代表人物是克里昂、阿尔西比阿德。阿高盖培养出来的儿童节制、内敛、守法、保守。虽然他们具有一定的知识，但语言功能显然不及派迪亚制下培养的儿童。希罗多德、普鲁塔克称他们说话言简意赅，绝不多说一句话、一个字。他们将自己视为国家的一个组成部分，强调集体主义、整体主义，绝不会因为追求自己的荣誉、地位而置国家利益于不顾。

从更深层次上看，派迪亚和阿高盖并没有本质上的差别，它们的目的都是培养合格的公民，它们都将道德培养放在第一位，都注重培养履行公民义务所必须的才能、技能。所不同的是，它们培养的道德结构不一样、培养的公民技能不一样。就道德结构而言，前者更强调自我权益，而后者更强调整体利益，从公民技能来看，前者更强调政治才干，后者更强调军事才能。

古风时期的斯巴达教育以派迪亚模式为主

大多数希腊化时期及其之后的作家都把斯巴达教育模式归结为阿高盖。按照认为对阿高盖模式的归纳，这是一个以军事技能培养为主要内容的教育模式，它培养出来的人必定是一个缺少文化知识的一介武夫，斯巴达社会的文化生活也必定是一片荒漠。但是我们考之于历史，尽管斯巴达缺少雅典历史上的诗人、作家、哲学家、历史学家，但斯巴达的精神生活、文化生活和文化发展史并不是一直如此。

古代斯巴达实际上非常重视知识学习。斯巴达儿童与雅典儿童一样，7岁时就开始接受文化教育，只不过斯巴达儿童在公立学校由国家配备老师（官员）授课，而雅典儿童在私立学校由私人聘请的老师授课。斯巴达社会同样重视文化教育，经常派长老到操场上去关注他们体力和智力的竞赛[1]。这正因为这样，斯巴达人在青少年时期就学会了谈话辛辣而优美，言简而意赅[2]。整个斯巴达社会对知识、智慧都比较重视，戴玛拉托斯曾由于自己的许多成就和本身的智慧而博得了赫赫声名[3]。多里欧斯也以为凭自己的道德、才能应该应该成为国王[4]。这些都说明斯巴达社会是重视文化知识的。种种事实说明，斯巴达人并不全是一介武夫，正如雅典人并不都是饱学之士，事实上，在判处阿里斯提德流放的公民大会上，阿里斯提德就曾经帮一个文盲填写过选票。还是希罗多德说得对：说斯巴达人知识贫乏纯粹"是希腊人为了自己开心才凭空捏造出来的无稽之谈"[5]。

斯巴达的文化生活也不是死水一潭、荒漠一片。照弗格森说："公元前580年以前，斯巴达

---

[1]　Plut., Lyc., 17.1.

[2]　Plut., Lyc., 19.1.

[3]　Hdt., 6.70.

[4]　Hdt., 5.42.

[5]　Hdt. 4.77.

是诗人和艺术家的家乡"①。莫里也指出：第二次美塞尼亚战争之后，斯巴达曾经出现过文化的繁荣②。相传克里特诗人泰拉特斯（Thaletas）帮助斯巴达创立了 Gymnopaideia 节，将克里特诗歌传到斯巴达，并创作了大量的诗歌③。泰尔潘达是公元前 7 世纪中到 6 世纪初列斯波斯岛的著名音乐家，斯巴达曾经聘请他到斯巴达传授音乐。据说，斯巴达的琴原来只有四根弦，但泰尔潘达曾经用八弦琴表演④。吕底亚诗人阿尔克曼与泰尔潘达同时期，也曾经在斯巴达从事文化活动，《少女之歌》就是他在斯巴达创作的著名作品。在第二次美塞尼亚战争期间，提尔泰乌斯又来到斯巴达从事文化活动。

斯巴达音乐、舞蹈更是蜚声希腊。阿里斯托芬在公元前 411 年上演的喜剧《利西斯特拉》结尾处告诉我们：雅典青年男女为了感谢神灵，跳起了常在优拉托斯河边表演的歌舞⑤。可见，即使是在公元前 5 世纪，斯巴达的文化生活也不是一潭死水。据柏拉图、亚里士多德研究，斯巴达至少有三种不同风格的音乐：佛里基亚、多利亚和吕底亚音乐。相对而言，佛里基亚音乐更为古老，相传与佩罗普斯一起传入斯巴达⑥。多利亚音乐是在佛里基亚音乐的基础上发展起来的。这两种音乐都受到柏拉图和亚里士多德的赞赏⑦，但吕底亚音乐则受到他们的抨击，认为是格调低下的靡靡之音。斯巴达的音乐大多在各种节日上演出，在节日上斯巴达还会进行歌舞表演、歌曲对赛，普鲁塔克就曾经记下了部分歌曲的内容，而阿尔克曼的一首残诗则表现了当时赛歌的场景。

当然，上述材料反映的都是斯巴达早期的文化生活史。如此看来，我们有理由据此得出这样的结论：早期斯巴达教育实行的并不是阿高盖模式，而是派迪亚模式。当然斯巴达的派迪亚模式并不完全等同于雅典的派迪亚。

如前所述，阿高盖模式更侧重于培养具有军人特征的公民。这种模式只是到了古典时期中期才逐步形成。

古典时期阿高盖模式开始萌芽

古典时期前期，斯巴达遭遇了严重的地震，斯巴达人口急剧减少，斯巴达社会的人口结构发生了巨大变化，一直不满于现实处境的黑劳士在国外势力的支持下乘机发动起义。起义加剧了斯巴达人与黑劳士的矛盾。斯巴达人需要一支强大的军事力量维持自己的统治，在总人数减少的情况下，斯巴达人唯一的办法就是通过各种手段提高军队的战斗力。与此同时，迅速崛起的雅典对斯巴达的传统霸权地位提出了挑战，到公元前 446 年，雅典在传统的斯巴达势力范围内抢占了佩盖、厄庇道鲁斯、特洛伊曾等地，雅典海军还在斯巴达海岸线上耀武扬威。在这种情况下，斯巴达更需要强化军队的战斗力。而这一切只能通过严格的军事训练和军人品德的重塑来实现。

我们关于这时期的斯巴达教育的材料主要来自于修昔底德和色诺芬。伯里克利在葬礼演讲中说："在我们的教育制度上，我们的对手从孩提时代起就通过残酷的训练，以培养其英勇气概；在雅典，

---

① 弗格森：《希腊帝国主义》，晏绍祥译，上海三联书店，2005 年版，第 44 页。

② 奥斯温·莫里：《早期斯巴达》，晏绍祥译，上海人民出版社，2008 年版，第 163 页。

③ Simon Hornbilower and Antony Spawforth, *The Oxford Classical Dictionary*, Oxford Universty Press, Oxford New York, 1996, p.1491.

④ Athen. XIV, 625f.

⑤ 优拉托斯河是纵贯拉科尼亚的河流，优拉托斯河边的舞蹈则是指斯巴达表演的舞蹈。这说明当时斯巴达的歌舞在雅典也大受欢迎。——笔者注。

⑥ Athen. XIV, 625f–626a.

⑦ Plato, *Republic*, 399a; Arist. *Pol.* 1342a30.

我们的生活完全是自由自在的，但是我们也随时准备对付和他们一样的危险"①。这里伯里克利首先把斯巴达的教育模式和雅典的教育模式对立起来，显示出斯巴达的教育模式与雅典已经产生了巨大的差异；其次伯里克利还告诉我们，这个差异的关键是斯巴达实行了严格、残酷的训练，而雅典则是宽松自由的教育。我们设想这里的残酷训练与早期竞技体育的艰苦不一样，应该是因应当时斯巴达的形势需要而采取的一种军事性的训练。

此后阿高盖制度一直在不断强化。从伯罗奔尼撒战争爆发到公元前 330 年马其顿征服，希腊世界充满了战争。阿高盖制度为斯巴达培养了一批又一批勇敢的战士，为斯巴达赢得伯罗奔尼撒战争的胜利，建立希腊世界的霸权做出了巨大的贡献。阿高盖制度也不断强化，这反映在色诺芬的《拉凯戴蒙人政制》中，在这篇作品中，色诺芬提到斯巴达儿童能听懂他人的说话时就要求他们光脚走路、每年只有一件衣服，并实行饮食控制，鼓励儿童窃食以自己解决温饱问题，采取各种措施培养儿童的好强争胜、守纪服从的品性。这些都是后来普鲁塔克所称赞的阿高盖制度的内容。

阿高盖制度不仅为斯巴达建立霸权做出了贡献，同时赢得了国际声誉。在公元前 4 世纪曾经有不少非斯巴达的青年到斯巴达接受教育，色诺芬的两个儿子就是在斯巴达接受教育的，后来都参加了斯巴达军队，其中一个儿子在战斗中牺牲②。公元前 481 年，国王阿基斯波利斯率军远征北希腊，在这支军队中就有以养子身份在斯巴达接受教育的外国青年③。斯巴达在当时的希腊世界中文化建设远远落后于雅典，这些青年不可能来学文化知识，而且当时希腊世界战火纷飞，也没有人能够静下心来学习文化知识，他们只可能学习与战争有关的知识。

但是，这期间虽然斯巴达实施了阿高盖制度，斯巴达的文化生活并没有完全停止。古典时期，底比斯诗人品达、开俄斯的诗人西蒙尼德斯（Simonides）都曾经为斯巴达撰写诗作。戎马倥偬的莱山德不仅军事才华出众，而且在临死之前留下来一部构思斯巴达政治改革的作品，国王波桑尼阿斯流亡之际曾经对斯巴达的历史进行总结，这部书成为古代作家了解斯巴达历史的重要著作。公元前 5 世纪，克里特音乐家提摩特乌斯还在用八弦琴演奏，这说明吕底亚音乐一直在斯巴达流传。公元前 380 年，斯巴达士兵曾经从前线赶回去参加许阿肯托斯节。

亚里士多德一方面说斯巴达教育具有野性，同时也说他们能够理解音乐④。修昔底德声称伯拉西达绝不是一个拙于言辞的人⑤，确实他的演讲水平绝不亚于雅典的那些演说家，只是其内容更丰富，说服更有力。斯巴达也不乏智者派的活动，只不过人数不及雅典那么多，但这不能作为斯巴达不重视文化教育的依据，实际上，智者希庇亚曾经在斯巴达获得成功，他的成功之处就是适应斯巴达教育的需要及时调整教学内容，主要包括古代英雄和人的谱系，城邦的历史⑥。这些说明斯巴达的阿高盖制度还没有发展到典型状态。希罗多德曾经指出：所谓"斯巴达人不热心学习"只是希腊人为了自己开心凭空捏造出来的无稽之谈，实际上在希腊人当中只有拉戴蒙人在与人交谈时是十分谨慎的⑦。虽然普鲁塔克说斯巴达人的文化知识"只学到够用而已"。但他告诉我们一个更为普遍的情况：斯巴达少年说话辛辣而优美，言简意赅，普鲁塔克宣称：他本人发现斯巴达人的较短虽然简短，但确实有力、中肯，能抓住听者的思路。他还说：斯巴达人绝不信口乱说，绝不冒失地说出思想苍白或不能引人注意的毫无意义的言词。总之，热爱智慧胜过热爱健身运动是斯巴达人与众不同的特

---

①　Thuc. II. 39.

②　第欧根尼·拉尔修：《名哲言行录》（上），马永翔等译，吉林人民出版社，2003 年版，第 115 页。

③　Xen. *Hell.* V. 3. 6.

④　Arist. *Pol.* 1337a, 1338b, 1324b, 1339a–b.

⑤　Thuc. IV. 84.

⑥　Plato，《大希庇亚斯篇》，284a–286b.

⑦　Hdt. 4.77.

点①。这种言简意赅、一语中的比那些夸夸其谈、自我炫耀更有文化，更有涵养。

这种派迪亚和阿高盖交融的教育模式可能一直延续到公元前 3 世纪初。据普鲁塔克记述，公元前 244 年阿基斯四世实行改革提出要恢复斯巴达的传统制度②。这说明的当时的斯巴达已经中止了阿高盖教育模式。阿基斯曾经自称在不到 20 岁时就已经弃绝各种不良嗜好③，那么可以推测，他在 20 岁时才即位，在公元前 264 年斯巴达就不再实施阿高盖制度。公元前 272 年，皮鲁斯曾经声称要将自己的儿子在送到斯巴达接受教育④，我们还看到公元前 255 年一位接受过阿高盖教育的斯巴达人 Xanthippus 到迦太基军队的人军事指挥官⑤。这是我们在史书上见到的最后一位古典时期的接受过阿高盖教育的斯巴达人。可以想象，迦太基不可能要求一位刚刚年满 20 岁没有作战经验的人的人担任指挥官，如果我们假定这位指挥官应该至少有十年左右的从军经验，那么古典时期最后实施阿高盖的时间应该是在公元前 265 年左右。公元前 265 年左右，希腊南部各邦在埃及支持下发动反马其顿战争（公元前 267–261 年），斯巴达参加了这场战争。但战争的结果是城邦遭到失败。公元前 265 年，斯巴达国王埃瑞斯一世牺牲疆场，公元前 262 年，马其顿控制了雅典。可以想象，斯巴达也受到了马其顿的严厉惩罚。阿高盖制度可能就是在这一时期前后被取消的。

公元前 3 世纪之后，阿高盖模式形成

但是，战争点燃的寻求国家独立的火焰燃遍了斯巴达。公元前 244 年，年轻的国王阿基斯即位，揭开斯巴达改革救亡运动的序幕。教育体制的改革正是这次改革运动的内容。由于史料问题，我们不知道阿基斯改革中教育改革的具体内容，阿基斯改革的口号是"恢复旧制"，不过这种"恢复"不可能是原样照搬，首先其平分土地的份数只有过去的一半，其次公餐团的人数达到 400 人，那么教育制度也不可能照搬此前的教育模式。可以想见，对旧制修订的原则是适应当下的现实条件和需要。份地数量的减少显然是因为美塞尼亚地区的独立，而公餐团规模的扩大则是与军事组织的进一步趋同。教育模式的变化的原则那就是要为斯巴达锻炼一支能征善战的队伍，那么传统教育模式中的文化教育部分很可能被人为减少。

阿基斯改革失败后不久，克里奥墨涅斯再次发动改革。克里奥墨涅斯改革的范围更广、力度更大，涉及政治、经济、社会生活各个方面。与阿基斯改革相似，他也打着"恢复旧制"的旗号，甚至更严格，他为此专门设立维护传统的官职——patronomos。克里奥墨涅斯改革的根本目的是强兵强国，为此他征招了一支 4000 人的军队⑥。按照斯巴达的旧制，没有土地和公民身份的人不能当兵，在改革之前，据称斯巴达公民人数只有 700 人，其中只有 100 人能够真正履行公民的义务，即当兵。虽然经过阿基斯改革，但斯巴达的公民队伍并没有建立起来。可以想象，这支 4000 人的军队大多不谙战事，需要接受严格的训练。严格训练这支军队成为克里奥墨涅斯改革的主要任务。据普鲁塔克记载，克里奥孟尼斯改革的大部分措施都是在斯多噶哲学家塞法鲁斯协助下实施的。在塞法鲁斯的主持下，学校的演练和餐桌礼仪很快就恢复了。可以想象，在塞法鲁斯的主持下，斯巴达的教育体制迅速蜕变为严格和纯粹的军事教育，即典型的阿高盖制度，否则社会风气就不会很快发生转变。

塞法鲁斯的贡献不仅于此。塞法鲁斯作为斯多噶哲学的代表之一，深受斯多噶哲学的影响。在

---

① Plut. *Lyc.* 16; 19; 20.
② Plut. *Agis*, 4.
③ Plut. *Agis*, 4.
④ Plut. Pyrrh.
⑤ Poly. I. 32. 1.
⑥ Plut. *Cleo.* 11.

斯多噶哲学中，人的根本属性在于其道德品性，人的主要品德是智慧、勇敢、正义、节制①。勇敢成为位列第二的品德。塞法鲁斯作为斯多噶哲学的佼佼者一定会继承这些思想，也一定会把这些思想落实到具体的行动中。这样，斯多噶哲学的理论与克里奥墨涅斯的改革目标机缘巧合，发生的巨大效应就是在日常生活中针对勇敢品德或军人品德的训练大大强化了。这当中最突出的就是忍耐力的培养。

以忍耐力培养为宗旨鞭笞比赛是典型阿高盖制度的象征。但是这种鞭笞比赛不见于色诺芬的作品，色诺芬只是说在阿尔特弥斯祭祀活动中儿童们常常从祭台上窃取食物，而祭坛上则有人持鞭看护，孩子只要忍受短暂的疼痛②。这一仪式一直持续到普鲁塔克时期，普鲁塔克在《斯巴达政制》中用"现在时"记述了这一事件。这种鞭笞与作为忍耐力比较的鞭笞显然不一样，前者只是短暂的，而后者则会持续很长时间，甚至有人因此丧生。西塞罗就声称他曾经听到斯巴达儿童在阿尔特弥斯神坛上接收鞭笞的事，而且听说有的孩子宁可被打死也不肯呻吟求饶③。西塞罗生活在公元前1世纪，他所见到的残忍的鞭笞比赛应该是在公元前3世纪末期实施的、公元前146年恢复的、同时又在后来的历史中发展了的制度。

塞法鲁斯的改革还表现在阿高盖制度更为系统。在古典时期，斯巴达还没有形成细致的年龄组划分。色诺芬把斯巴达青年分为三组：儿童组（paides）、少年组（paidiskoi）和青年组（hēbōntes）。Paides被送进学校，学文习乐，演习体操，按照普鲁塔克的记述，这大概是7–12岁的儿童，hēbōntes是完全成熟的青年，应该是指20（或18）–30岁的青年，paidiskoi则是12–20（18）岁之间的少年，对应的正式阿高盖制度的教育对象。但色诺芬没有进一步的细分。但我们在亚历山大图书馆馆长阿里斯托芬尼的《论年龄组名称》中看到：色诺芬所称的少年组（paidiskoi）被分成了六组，每个年龄组都有特殊的名称，第一年称作rhōbidas，第二年称作promikizomenos，第三年称做mikizomenos，第四年称作propais，第五年称作pais，第六年称作meleirēn④。阿里斯托芬尼生活在公元前257–180年之间。他的这段话反映的当是他所生活的那个时代的情形，也就是说在塞法鲁斯主持改革时，斯巴达少年组的训练更加系统化了，原来整个少年组（paidiskoi）作为一个单位接收相同的教育，而现在每个年龄有不同的内容。

阿高盖制度的内容也更丰富了。波桑尼阿斯曾经记述在斯巴达城内的Platanistas举行的"模拟战争"⑤。模拟战争的雏形出现于色诺芬，色诺芬称刚刚通过阿高盖教育的青年汇选出三组，每组100人，彼此之间举行竞争，他们一见面就会彼此打斗，但必须接受长者的劝解。但是这种打斗是一种随意的偶发现为，国家的干预较少，只是在打斗比较激烈的时候有长者制止。但波桑尼阿斯的模拟战争却要经过精心的准备，这种"战争"更像是一种军事演练。不过笔者认为，波桑尼阿斯生活在2世纪，他所记述的模拟战争已经不是当初的情形。

总之，典型的阿高盖制度是在公元前3世纪后期的改革运动中才形成的。阿高盖制度的推行在短时间内迅速提高了斯巴达军队的战斗力，利用这支军队斯巴达重新确立在伯罗奔尼撒地区的优势地位。公元前192年，纳比斯凭借这支军队试图征服一度被分割出去的吉提乌姆，引起罗马和阿卡亚同盟的恐慌，在罗马支持下，公元前188年，阿卡亚同盟军队攻入斯巴达，杀死了纳比斯，取消了包括阿高盖制度在内的斯巴达主要制度。直到公元前146年，罗马打败阿卡亚同盟，斯巴达因为投靠罗马获得"自治城市"的身份，斯巴达得以恢复自己的管理制度。

---

① 第欧根尼·拉尔修：《名哲言行录》（上），吉林人民出版社，2003年版，第440页。
② Xen. *Lac*. Pol. II. 9.
③ Cicero, *Tusc*. 2. 34; 2. 46; 7. 77.
④ 拜占廷人，约生活在公元前257–180年，公元前194年曾任亚历山大图书馆馆长。参见《牛津古典辞书》，第165页。
⑤ Paus. III. 14. 8–10.

罗马时期被娱乐化的阿高盖制度

公元前 146 年之后，无论斯巴达如何自治，它终归从属于罗马。此时的斯巴达已经不再是一个独立国家了，历史的改变使得阿高盖制度的目也随之发生了变化。国家不再，斯巴达国家已经无需训练军队，阿高盖也不再是为了培养军队了，而是成为招徕各方游客的娱乐制度。作为娱乐的阿高盖与作为教育体制的阿高盖最大的不同在于前者的目的在于娱乐，而后者的目的是培养特殊的社会成员——公民。

科奈尔曾经形容，1 世纪的斯巴达已经成为一个理想的旅游胜地，游客到斯巴达到处可见健身场、浴室、剧院、市场和雕塑。而吸引游客的不仅有这些硬件设施，还有符合罗马游客喜好的旅游项目。鞭笞比赛就是一项重要的旅游项目。生活在公元 160–220 年的早期教父德尔图良说，当今斯巴达社会最重要的仪式就是鞭笞比赛，这已不是什么秘密 [1]。4 世纪的雅典修辞学家 Libanius 的记述非常形象地对此作了注释，他说他正赶往斯巴达观看鞭笞比赛，这是拉科尼亚的一个节日 [2]。显然，在稍晚的罗马作家看来鞭笞比赛已经成为一个节日。

其实这种性质在公元前 1 世纪就显示出来。西塞罗把斯巴达的这种鞭笞就奥林匹亚赛会上的青年选手、比武场上的蛮族人相提并论，称他们都一样接受严厉的打击并都默默地忍受 [3]。笔者认为，这里的比武场上的蛮族实际就是角斗场的角斗士。也就是说在西塞罗看来，这种鞭笞比赛与角斗性质一样。在埃利亚（Alea）有一个宗教节日——Sciereia，在这个节日上有妇女接受鞭打。波桑尼阿斯称这个活动与斯巴达的儿童接受鞭笞性质一样 [4]。波桑尼阿斯在解释鞭笞仪式起源时，称最初是两地的人们在阿尔特弥斯神坛祭祀时不断发生械斗，后来为了制止械斗，人们采用了活人祭，最后莱库古将其改为鞭打至出血，以此飨宴神灵 [5]。这里我们看到，波桑尼阿斯的解释不再是为了培养忍耐力，而是强调了活动的血腥性。众所周知，罗马文化中含有较为浓烈的血腥成分，角斗就是其中最典型的。在西塞罗等人看来，斯巴达城内的鞭笞与罗马城内的角斗一样，都是一种大型娱乐活动。

曾经的模拟战争现在也已经变成一种大型娱乐活动。据波桑尼阿斯介绍，这种活动固定在一个绿树成荫、四面环沟的类似小岛的地方，参加活动的青年分成两队，从两端跨桥入场。在活动开始的前一天晚上，他们抽签决定入场的地点，在战斗开始前，他们要在 Phoebaeum 神庙用宠物狗祭奠神灵，在祭神是他们还要举行斗野猪比赛。中午，双方入场，"战斗"开始。双方拳打脚踢、口咬手挖，有些人的眼珠也被挖出来，更多的人被推倒河里 [6]。这里呈现出来的是一个带有血腥味的、群体性的娱乐活动，看不到与战争有关的训练活动，倒是与罗马角斗场内的群体角斗和模拟战争非常相似。

罗马时期的阿高盖制度比此前明显增加了血腥味。西塞罗在逗留斯巴达期间不断听人们说有青年被打死，普鲁塔克曾经目睹许多斯巴达青年在阿尔特弥斯的祭坛下被鞭打致死 [7]，波桑尼阿斯称模拟战争中有人的眼睛被挖出来，有人被推到河里，可以想见，被打死、淹死的例子应该是司空见惯的。

总之，在克里奥墨涅斯时代神圣而严肃的以军事训练为主要特色以培养合格公民、合格军人为

---

① Tert. *Ad. Mart*. 4. 8. Cf. Kennell, *The Gymnasium of Virtue*, The University of North Carolina Press, 1995, p.155.
② Lianius, Or. 1. 23. Cf. Kennell, *The Gymnasium of Virtue*, p.158.
③ Cic. *Tusc*. 2. 46. Cf. Kennell, *The Gymnasium of Virtue*, p.149.
④ Paus. VIII. 23. 1.
⑤ Paus. III. 16. 9–11.
⑥ Paus. III. 14. 8–10.
⑦ Plut. Lyc. 18.

主要目的的阿高盖在制度已经成为具有罗马独有的血性色彩的群体性娱乐活动。但是曾经为斯巴达恢复国力、重塑辉煌的阿高盖制度依然留存在罗马人的记忆之中，这才有那么多的罗马人对这一制度充满敬意的回忆。

　　由此可见，斯巴达历史上以培养合格公民、合格军人为宗旨的阿高盖制度是在特定的历史条件下产生的。古风时期的斯巴达教育虽然突出了体育训练，但总体上除了国家办教育之外，在教学内容和教育宗旨上并没有特别之处。古典时期，为了应对战争的需要，斯巴达的教育中大量增加了体育训练和与军事相关的内容。典型的阿高盖制度成型于在公元前3世纪末期，大约实行了半个世纪，与公元前188年被取消。斯巴达的教育在绝大多数时间内都不具有军事化特征。

论荷马史诗中的波塞冬形象

朱毅璋 暨南大学

摘要：不管是在古希腊的宗教、神话还是文献中，波塞冬都是一位重要的角色。他的宗教职能、神话地位和文学形象，很大程度是由荷马史诗所奠定。波塞冬在荷马史诗中频繁出现，是其中重要角色之一。然而荷马史诗并未清晰介绍和归纳波塞冬的基本形象。本文指出，荷马史诗中的波塞冬既表现出神性的一面，但更多的是人性的一面，这暗示波塞冬的原型是一位世俗君主。

关键词：荷马史诗；波塞冬；形象；原型；影响

Abstract：Poseidon was an important role in religion, myth and literature of ancient Greece. His religious functions, and status in mythical image in literature were mainly established by *Homeric Epics*. Poseidon doesn't only appear frequently in the *Homeric Epics* but also influences the development of the plots directly; therefore, he could be seen as one of the most important gods in the *Epics*. But *Homeric Epics* do not introduce his basic image clearly. In *Homeric Epics*, Poseidon carries the deity and humanity aspect of the figure, and the latter was emphasized, which implied his archetype was a mortal wanax.

Keywords：Homeric Epics, Poseidon, Image, Archetype, Influence

波塞冬（Poseidon）是希腊宗教一位非常重要的神明，集海神、震地之神和马神于一身。在神话中，波塞冬也非常重要，他是宙斯（Zeus）的兄弟，是大海的统治者。此外，有关波塞冬形象的记载，古典作家的相关描述很多，大体集中在反映其外貌特征和神明职能上。我们不难发现，对波塞冬这个神明，包括其在宗教中的定位、神话的地位和文献中的形象，荷马史诗的记载都有奠基性的重要意义。可以说，荷马史诗对波塞冬的记载（包括神职定位和形象描述），深深地影响了希腊宗教和后世的文献。

在荷马史诗中，波塞冬频繁出现且形象鲜明。在《伊利亚特》里，波塞冬不仅加入众神的纷争，也参与了凡人的事务，他支持阿开亚人一方，坚定地与特洛伊①为敌。在《奥德赛》里，波塞冬却成为阻碍奥德修斯归家的主要敌人，而后者属于阿开亚同盟一方。尽管波塞冬是一位神明，但总体来说，史诗中的波塞冬形象可以归纳为五个方面，既展现出波塞冬"神"的一面，更反映其"人"的一面，其中前者反映在神明职能上，后者反映在外貌特征、性格特点、家庭角色和权力地位等四个方面上。本文依次考察这五个方面，对波塞冬在史诗中的形象进行归纳，进而揭示波塞冬在史诗中的形象原型，最后分析这些记载对后世希腊的重要影响。

1. 神明职能：能保护航海者安全航行或为其带来灾难，既管辖海洋、又能制造地震的海神。

波塞冬能制造地震，"震地之神"（Shaker of Earth，Ἐννοσίγαιος）是其在史诗中的称号之一，且为主要修饰语。该词在《伊利亚特》中最早出现于第7卷②，总出现次数不下30次，跟"Ποσειδῶν"③不相上下；在《奥德赛》中则被提及不下18次。此外，波塞冬毫无疑问是史诗中最重要的海神，因为他在三神分天下时得到大海，是大海的统治者，也是航海者的保护神。波塞冬在史诗中的另一称号是"绕地之神"（Enfolder of Earth，Γαιήοχος），其在《伊利亚特》出现了11次，集中在13到15卷，④在《奥德赛》中则为6次。⑤该称号突出了波塞冬作为海神的一面，因为古希腊人相信大地被海洋包围，"绕地之神"同样可以理解为"海神"。作为地位最高的海神，波塞冬能保佑航海者的安全航行，而航海者们也会因航海安全问题而向波塞冬献祭。当然，神明往往带有两面性，即既能赐福也能降灾以示惩戒，波塞冬自然不例外。史诗中最能反映波塞冬制造海难的一幕，莫过于他兴风作浪对付奥德修斯的场景了，只是由于海神女伊诺相救、波塞冬停手并离开以及雅典娜停息部分风浪，奥德修斯才得以存活。⑥波塞冬完全有能力杀掉奥德修斯，只是碍于其他神明的意志才作罢，转而让其远离故土、漂泊多年。⑦

因此，史诗中的波塞冬是一个既能够保护航海者平安，亦可以为航海者带来灾祸，既管辖海洋，也能制造地震的海神。

2. 外貌特征：身穿黄金铠甲、手持三叉戟、黑头发的强壮中年男子。

史诗并未对波塞冬的形象进行具体描述，相关信息存在于零散的资料中。总的来说，波塞冬在史诗作者头脑中的形象是一个穿金甲、握三叉戟、挺拔壮健的黑发中年男子。

3. 性格特点：在乎自己是否受到尊重、爱出风头、虚荣心强、度量极小。

波塞冬的性格特点，主要反映在其对凡人的态度上，这取决于他自己的想法。一方面，波塞冬特别在乎凡人对其是否尊重、不甘心被凡人冷落；另一方面，他的虚荣心很强，度量极小，并因此显得喜怒无常。从性格方面而言，波塞冬既在乎别人对自己是否尊重，也贪图虚荣且度量极低，而这主要基于他本身的情绪。在觉得风头被凡人盖过，或是受到凡人的冷落、不尊重甚至是侮辱时，波塞冬会发牢骚甚至采取极端手段去捍卫自己所希望得到的"尊严"。

4. 家庭角色：重视并宠爱后代、热衷帮子孙复仇的家长。

从作为家长的角度来说，波塞冬重视子孙们的情况，会为他们提供帮助。在他们受到伤害后，

---

① "特洛伊"中译自英文"Troy"，其希腊文为"Τροία"或"Τροίη"，直译英文应为"Troia"或"Troie"，因而有学者把该词音译为更靠近希腊语的"特洛亚"，如罗念生和王焕生。可参阅荷马：《伊利亚特》，罗念生译，《罗念生全集》第五卷，上海人民出版社，2004年；荷马：《奥德赛》，王焕生译，人民文学出版社，2008年。在本文中，笔者采纳更为常见的"特洛伊"。

② Homer, *The Iliad*, VII. 445.

③ 即"Poseidon"。

④ Homer, *The Iliad*, IX. 183; XIII. 43, 59, 83, 125, 677; XIV. 355; XV. 174, 201, 222; XXIII, 584.

⑤ Homer, *The Odyssey*, I.68; III.55; VIII.322; 350; IX. 525; XI. 241. 王焕生译本把第八卷350行处译为"震地之神"，疑误。可参阅荷马：《奥德赛》，王焕生译本，第142页。

⑥ Homer, *The Odyssey*, V. 282-387.

⑦ Homer, *The Odyssey*, I. 74-79.

他会尽量帮助报仇。因此，波塞冬在史诗中同样是一位对子孙非常关心的家长。

5. 权力地位：不满足已有权力且不甘受到宙斯约束，却因实力不济只能选择忍让和下意识地服从；就品性而言则是对宙斯时而阳奉阴违、见风使舵；"一神之下、万神之上"的主神。

波塞冬是史诗中的主神之一，海洋是他的领地，他是一位瓦纳克斯，海怪（κῆτος）是他的臣民[①]。但实际上，波塞冬的活动范围绝不限于其领地，他常常干预海洋之外的事务，如插手凡人的陆战。在史诗中，波塞冬的性格可谓"放荡不羁"，希望用手中的权力为所欲为，但他却常常受到宙斯的约束。波塞冬和宙斯的关系，是史诗的重要内容之一，相关记载不仅反映出波塞冬在众神中的地位，更重要的是暗示了波塞冬的形象原型。

波塞冬并不甘心受宙斯的约束，但在"宙斯比他强大"这个事实下，他只能无奈地接受。同样，由于不甘心受到约束，波塞冬选择了对宙斯阳奉阴违和见风使舵，这从其后来不惜违反宙斯的命令而为阿开亚人提供帮助中可见一斑。然而，波塞冬虽然讨厌宙斯的约束，但他也表现出对后者下意识服从的一面。波塞冬跟宙斯的关系同样侧面反映了他那"一神之下、万神之上"的地位，他在众神之中，地位仅次于宙斯，在史诗中处于一种"二把手"的地位。

史诗作者明显是按照自己对凡人君主的认识、对凡人社会的理解而塑造了众神的形象、性格和彼此关系。奥林波斯众神之间的关系，跟阿开亚联盟相似：即同盟之间的各方在经济上和政治上是相互独立的，他们有着各自的领地，而共同军事行动则由盟主来发号施令。但是，他们之间的关系是不稳固的，存在内讧的可能性。若把阿伽门农和阿喀琉斯的关系跟宙斯和波塞冬做一比较，我们不难看出这两种关系之间的相似性。不难想象，倘若波塞冬要比宙斯强大，那后者早就被推翻了。因此，宙斯和波塞冬之间理应是平等的关系，波塞冬认为他跟宙斯应有同一地位、后者不应该命令他的想法也是合理的。只是由于宙斯远比波塞冬强大，后者才无可奈何地接受前者的约束。

在荷马史诗中，众神虽然高于凡人，但又展现出人性的一面，显得更像是人类而非神明。如他们有着与凡人一样的性格和行为，甚至能被后者所伤或为凡人提供劳力服务。[②]神明的史诗形象虽与他们的神职有着联系，但彼此有着明显的区别：神明的史诗形象是作者基于自身对神明的认识（神明职能、已有传说等）并结合自己的理解和想象而成的文学产物。因而荷马史诗中的众神既有着神性，也有着明显的人性。就波塞冬而言，从"神"的角度来说，他既是海神，也是震地之神。而从"人"的角度来看，他的形象是一个强壮的中年男子，虚荣心强、心眼极小但对子孙非常看重；他还常常干预领地之外的事务，希望能为所欲为，但在宙斯更为强大的情况下，只能怨恨地表示屈服。此外，考虑到海怪们是波塞冬的臣民，史诗用"瓦纳克斯"来说明波塞冬对它们的关系，因此波塞冬的形象原型明显是一位世俗的统治者，是一位瓦纳克斯。

需要指出的是，虽然荷马史诗主要反映荷马时代，但其中也包含了迈锡尼时代的内容。瓦纳克斯虽然是迈锡尼时代的元素，带有专制王权的性质，但荷马笔下的瓦纳克斯更像是荷马所认识理解的世俗君主，也就是荷马时代的地方统治者。[③]荷马虽然知道以前曾存在过强大的王权，但他却不能理解这种王权有什么特点、强大到什么程度，因此在其笔下的瓦纳克斯，有时像专制暴君，有时像个普通的军事首领，总体来说则是权力不大。"权力无边"的波塞冬瓦纳克斯，乃是业已逝去的迈锡尼世界留给荷马的不朽记忆。

综上所述，笔者认为波塞冬的故事原型其实是一个拥有自己领地、势力仅次于盟主并受其宠信、喜欢干涉自身领地之外的事务、希望能为所欲为、关心子孙、心胸狭窄且爱好虚荣的一方统治者：

① Homer, *The Iliad*, XIII. 27–28. 史诗在此处用了"ἄναξ"（瓦纳克斯）一词来说明波塞冬和海怪们的关系，即波塞冬是它们的领袖、主人。
② 晏绍祥对此有着详细的论述，可参阅晏绍祥：《荷马社会研究》，第288–296页。
③ 晏绍祥对此有详细的论述，可参阅晏绍祥：《荷马社会研究》，第120–122页。

他权力广泛，有着独立的领地和臣民，但却喜欢干预领地之外的事务。在联盟中，他仅受制于一位比自己强大的盟主，而该盟主对其颇为尊敬且宠爱有加，不忍惩罚。他有多位妻子，且拥有众多后代。他很重视后代的情况，并能够不遗余力地为他们提供帮助或进行复仇。他心眼很小，总为某些事情耿耿于怀多年并进行报复。在报复时，他喜欢采用株连式的大范围处决。最后，他很在乎臣民对自己的态度，希望得到他们一贯的重视和尊重。在他觉得风光被臣民盖过、或得不到尊重甚至是受到侮辱的时候，就会采取极端手段进行报复，以维护自己所希望得到的"尊严"。

结　语

荷马史诗对后世希腊影响深远，这是不容置疑的。[①]就波塞冬内容的影响而言，其"神"性主要反映在宗教上、"人"性则主要反映在文献和美术作品中。在宗教方面，可以说荷马史诗对后世希腊人的宗教信仰和习俗有着奠基性的意义，希罗多德甚至认为众神由荷马和赫西奥德取名、决定地位、分配技能和描绘外貌[②]。史诗肯定了波塞冬那海神和震地之神的职能，[③]为后世希腊人所接受，他们往往把跟海洋有关的事情和地震归因于波塞冬，这在古典史家的笔下都能找到相关的记载。[④]在文献和美术作品方面，波塞冬形象经荷马史诗所设计后，已成为权威的定式和样本，被后来者模仿。总的来说，荷马史诗确定了波塞冬的基本形象，古风时代前期的作品加以继承并进一步补充，后世作家的相关描写往往基于这些已有的描述，或进行细化，或进行补充，除了因创作需要而加以修改外，他们更多的是表现出对波塞冬基本形象的传承和发扬。这同样反映在美术作品上。[⑤]此外，荷马史诗有关波塞冬的记载，在基于上述两点的基础上，更深层地影响着后世希腊社会。

有关荷马史诗的研究和争论，不管在国内还是国外，至今依然是古希腊史研究的一个重要组成部分，因此任何相关的研究都是值得的。以波塞冬的形象作为切入点，我们能够从中看出荷马史诗对后世希腊的深远影响，波塞冬的部分只是其中一个缩影；更重要的是，通过这个角度，有助于我们更深入地理解荷马史诗，这是对荷马史诗研究的一个有益补充。

---

① 可参阅晏绍祥：《荷马社会研究》，第 313–327 页。

② Herodotus, *Histories vol.1*, with an English translation by A. D. Godley, The Loeb Classical Library, Cambridge: Harvard University Press, 1926, II. 53.

③ 需要指出的是，波塞冬还是一位马神，但史诗中并未明确说明，只有朦胧的反映。

④ 希罗多德、修昔底德和色诺芬的著作均有记载，其中希罗多德的记载主要涉及波塞冬的海神职能，而修昔底德是海神和震地之神职能兼有，色诺芬则是主要反映波塞冬的震地之神职能。可参阅 Herodotus, *Histories*, VII. 129, 192; VIII. 129. Thucydides, *History of the Peloponnesian War vol.*1, with an English translation by Charles Forster Smith, The Loeb Classical Library, Cambridge: Harvard University Press, 1928, I. 128; II. 84, 92. Xenophon, *Hellenica*, with an English translation by Carleton L. Brownson, The Loeb Classical Library, Cambridge: Harvard University Press, 1918, III. III. 1–2; IV. VII. 4–5.

⑤ 这是笔者在博士论文《波塞冬研究》中根据洛布古典丛书多本著作中的相关记载进行研究所得出的结论

【罗马史】

Creating the Enemy: Ammianus Marcellinus' Double Digression on Huns and Alani (*Res Gestae* 31.2)

Diederik Burgersdijk, Radboud University

1. Introduction[1]

Since the very beginning of the expansion of Roman power over neighboring areas, images of the enemy threatening the rising empire were created. The Latins, the Etruscans, peoples of the Italian peninsula, and subsequently peoples farther removed by natural obstacles such as Gauls, Carthaginians and Persians, were —apart from military submission—all subject to an active creation of hostile reputation. Literary reports testify of terrifying peoples from abroad (mind the fourth century designations of *terror Gallicus or Punica fides*)[2] with corresponding habits and appearances. The portraiture of the enemy plays a crucial role in distinguishing what belonged to the own world and its civilization, and what belonged to the others, a process that was not alien to earlier empires such as the Persian and the Greek world.[3] In later Antiquity, this ongoing process of separating the world between own civilization and otherness began to acquire a world-wide scale, when peoples from the Eastern end of Asia entered the realm of the Roman empire.[4] This must have had a terrifying effect on the Mediterranean-centered Romans, whose main enemy had for a long time been the Persian empire.

By the time that the fourth-century historiographer Ammianus Marcellinus wrote his *Res Gestae* (finished about 390–2 AD),[5] hordes of savage horse-riding warriors from the far East were feared as the ultimate threat

---

[1] This article is an elaboration of the lecture held on the *Fourth International Conference on World History*, at Nankai University, Tianjin, China, on 16–18 June 2012. I am grateful to the participants for their comments. The research for this article was executed in the framework of the NWO (Netherlands Organization of Scientific Research) funded project *A Monument of Romanitas* (project number 275–50–012).

[2] Both terms occur in the *Historia Augusta*, a collection of imperial biographies from the later fourth century, more or less contemporaneous to Ammianus (following the date as proposed by Dessau 1889). *Punica fides occurs in the Vita Gordianorum* 14.1, 15.1 and 16.3, and *terror Gallicus* in the preface to the vita Probi (1.4).

[3] See for the Greek vision on a dual world of Greeks and barbarians and its historical origins (stemming exactly from the people that were later considered barbarians in Greek eyes, namely the Persians): Haubold 2013.

[4] The same people as attested as Xiongnu in Chinese literary records, see Kim 2013.

[5] See for a recent overview of the discussion about the date: Kulikowski 2012, 81–3.

to the empire's stability or even existence. In his thirty-first book, the last one of his work, Ammianus presents the reader with a horrifying portrait of the nomadic steppe-peoples of the Huns and the Halani, who threaten the empire on the brink of collapse. He does so by inserting a digression of this hitherto unknown people or peoples, about whose existence only rumour may have been spread, in the same vein as he earlier described Alamanni, Gauls, Goths, Moors, Saracenes and others.[1] Being an historiograper, Ammianus is keen on interweaving digressions in his historical narration, which in the case of book 31 is dominated by the battles at Ad Salices ('At the Willows' , near present-day Tomi on the Eastern coast of the Black Sea), where Romans were victorious, and the Thracian town of Hadrianople. Function and content of digressions in general have attracted due attention in scholarship, from an historical as well as literary point of view.[2] The obvious reason for inclusion of such a digression at this point, is to evoke the threat posed by the foreign danger within an internally weakened empire, that finally led to the largest defeat of the Romans since the battle of Cannae in

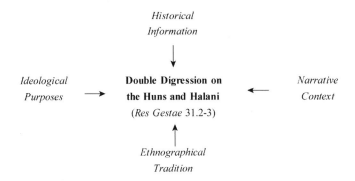

216 BC during the Punic wars.[3] The threatening danger and resulting defeat constitutes a dramatic highpoint in Ammianus' large-scale account of the tribulations in the Roman empire since emperor Nerva (reigning 96-98 BC).[4]

There may, however, be more to the last ethnographical excursus in Ammianus' work. It can hardly be imagined that the excursus only functions as a means to enhance the dramatic impact, and that the content of the digression, that so clearly distinguishes the educated world of the late Roman empire and the uncivilised barbarian, lacks any further meaning for the interpretation of Ammianus' entire work or his view on the surrounding world. In order to approach this question, the theoretical concepts of 'otherness' or 'alterity'

---

[1] A recent article by Kulikowski states that the Hunnic and Alans' digressions are dissimilar to the earlier ones, in order to use it as an argument for separate composition of book 31 of the **Res Gestae** (2013, 84).

[2] Richter 1974; Sabbah 1978; Rosen 1982; Matthews 1989, 333–42; Den Hengst 2010; Woolf 2011a; Vergin 2013.

[3] As Ammianus himself confirms, 31.13.19: *nec ulla annalibus praeter Cannensem pugnam ita ad internecionem res largiter gesta* ('The annals record no such massacre of a battle except the one at Cannae' , tr. Rolfe). Translations of Ammianus are by J.C. Rolfe 2001 (1939) vol. III, as all the translations below from **RG**.

[4] The first thirteen books of **Res Gestae** have been lost in textual transmission, but at the very end of the last book, 31.16.9, Ammianus reveals his scope: *a principatu Caesaris Nervae exorsus ad usque Valentis interitum* (beginning with the emperorship of Caesar Nerva up to the death of Valens, i.e. from 96 to 378 AD). Herewith, Ammianus choose to continue the work of his admired predessor Tacitus, whose **Annales and Historiae** from the early second century AD embraced the imperial history from Augustus up to Nerva (i.e. 14–96 AD).

will be used, a field that has been developed profitably in the past few decades.[1] Not the factual value of the sources are central to this field of research, but the image as presented by the author, regardless of the accuracy of the information. The approach has been applied to the mutual images of peoples like Persians, Egyptians, Greeks, Romans and others outside the borders of a well-defined state. For the Roman realm, the questions obtain an imperial dimension in the way that a distinction may be made between humans living within and those living outside the borders of the Roman empire, and their mutual relationships. These differences must certainly not be overstretched, as the Roman *limes* is a complex notion susceptible to interpretation, but the idea that a dividing line existed between civilization and barbary is a well attested idea. Recent studies have shown how Ammianus' fellow-Greek author Libanius uses the demarcation as an object of praise for his admired emperor Julian: the emperor had restored a clear separation of *oikoumenê*, in which the educated (*pepaideumenoi*) lived, and the uncivilized world of barbarians.[2]

In order to get a full picture of Ammianus' goals in describing the Huns, the digression will be approached from several angles. Firstly, we will closely examine the digression and its internal structure. The digression, composed from two separate parts consisting of a descriptions of the Huns (31.2.1–12) and one of the Halani (2.17–24) and separated by a geographical description (2.13–6). The digression is part of a strand, interwoven in the narration of the preceding books, of descriptions of foreign peoples well into the last book, there in its own specific context.[3] Beyond the scope of this particular work, this kind of excursus must be viewed in a long tradition of ethnographical writing. Finally, in the context of contemporary descriptions of foreigners, there may be detected an ideological layer of the narrative pertaining to the describe emperor's politics. The factors by which Ammianus' excursus has been informed may be presented graphically as follows:[4]

Figure 1: Factors in the Narrative of the Double Digression in Amm. RG 31.2.

By assuming that these factors, which supposedly did not weigh equally in the construction of the text, informed the writing of the digression, we will study the *exaedificatio* ('building up'), to use a term from Roman rhetorical theory, of the narrative material, clockwise beginning on top.

About the Historical Information, we may be brief. The content is deficient and almost full of fantasy.

---

[1] E.g. G. Woolf 1998 and 2011b, B. Isaac 2004 and 2009 (ed.); Eliav-Feldon 2009; specifically about Ammianus: Isaac 2011; Mutschler & Mittag 2008 and E.S. Gruen 2011a and 2011b. Books about the Huns in general are Bona 1991, Thompson 1995; Schmauder 2009; C. Kelly 2010 especially about the later Huns; still standard is Maenchen-Helfen 1973; about 'barbarians' in general, with very good chapters on the Huns: Heather 2009. Enemies in battle speeches, showing rhetorical techniques in creating enemy images: Adler 2005.

[2] See Libanius *Or.* 15.26: φρονεῖ δ' ὁ μὲν βάρβαρος μέγα λυττῶν καὶ ἀγριαίνων καὶ τὰ τῶν θηρίων μιμούμενος. (…) ἀλλ' ἡμῖν ἡ μεγίστη σπουδὴ τῶν θηρίων ὅτι πλεῖστον διεστάναι ('the barbarian, in his pride, rages and ravens like a wild beast; ···. But with us, our chief aim is to separate ourselves as far from brute beasts as we can···', cf. *Or.* 59.132, where the guidance of the superior is said to be naturally accepted by the inferior, 'having renounced their beast-like fury, they adopted human reason': τὴν θηριώδη λύσσαν ἐκβαλόντες λογισμοὺς ἀνθρωπίνους ἠσπάσαντο). See for the context of *Or.* 15 (to be dated in 363) Malosse 2014, 84 and *Or.* 59 (Libanius' oldest extant speech, 346–8) id. 87. For a treatment of the barbarians as beasts and related aspects in Libanius, see Quiroga Puertas 2013.

[3] See for a comprehensive analysis of the digressions on foreign peoples Matthews 2007 (or. 1989) chapter XIV 'Barbarians and Bandits', 304–382, and cf. the pertinent remarks on p.463–4 about the lengths and number of digressions, which particulartly figure in the Julianic part of the work, possibly in order 'to elevate this part of his work to a still higher level...'.

[4] Against the division as presented in the graph, one could object that historical fact, literary tradition and ideology are all part of the narration and left their marks in the text of the narrative. Apart from a narrator, however, there is also an author with his sources, knowledge and ideas about the surrounding world: this is why a distinction can be made between the worldview as presented by the author and the narrative proper.

At the same time, it is the first and most elaborate source for the dwellings and habits of the Huns. After Ammianus, other authors have provided more, and more accurate, information.[1] Ammianus suffered from a lack of sources, witness his introductory statement in 2.1 *Hunorum gens monumentis veteribus leviter nota*··· ('The people of the Huns, but little known of ancient records').[2] This is in concordance with other sources such as the sixth-century historiographer Zosimus, who took his information from Eunapius (a contemporary to Ammianus), who also appears to have had but little information.[3] Other sources about the Huns, such as Jordanes and Sozomenus are from later date and center on the Huns in the first half of the fifth century.[4]

2. The Double Digression

When having a closer look into the component elements of the digression, we pass to the level of the *inventio*, or the material out of which which Ammianus constructed his narration. The digression as a whole consists, after a brief introduction, mainly of a description of the Huns (2–11), and one of the Alans (17–25), interspersed by a geographical-ethnical description of the peoples of central-northern Asia which can be reckoned under the Alans (*et summatim omnes Halani cognominantur*– 'all, for short, are called Alans', 2.17). In the two main parts, which constitute a Double Digression, Ammianus touches upon the same motives. In the Huns' digression, their fighting habits take most of the narrative space, before nomadic life and morals;[5] in case of the Alans most attention is paid to their way of living and warfare.[6] In, or actually before, the passage about the Alans, most attention is paid to the geography and peoples in central Asia north of the Black Sea and the Caspian Sea (13–16, 171 words). So far in broad outlines the division of the themes in chapters. In short, the Double Digression contains: an introduction–the Huns–transition–geography and ethnography–the Alans, all rounded off with a variation on a traditional formula: *sed ad reliqua textus propositi revertamur* ('but let us return to what remains of our chosen subject').[7]

---

[1] E.g., relating to the conquests under the Huns' leader Attila († 452), which stay outside Ammianus scope. For a later, and historically better source, one can resort to the reports by Priscus, to be consulted in Blockley 1983, 222–400.

[2] Older sources are the scanty Dionysius Periegetes 5.130; Ptolemaeus 3.5.10; Eunapius *frgm.* 41. Kulikowski 2013, 100–1 and n.132 speculates that Ammianus reacted to Eunapius' attempt to describe the Huns.

[3] Zosimus 4.30.3 speaks about a φῦλόν τι βάρβαρον ... πρότερον μὲν οὐκ ἐγνωσμένον ('a barbaric people ··· not known before'), while his source Eunapius (*hist. fr. 41 / Exc. Sent.* P.84, 23) says that he hardly has any information at his disposal. The first version of Eunapius' works must have been finished just after the first invasions of the Huns in the years 376–78, see Paschoud 2003, 273; Barnes 1978, 116.

[4] Jordanes' *Getica* (50.261–2), Sozomenus' *Historia Ecclesiastica* (9.5) and Zosimus (4.20.3–5).

[5] Fighting habits 89 words, nomadic life 62 words, and morals 58 words. Following the order in which the elements occur (often, naturally, following chapter division), we encounter the introduction with a brief indication of the Huns' habitat (31.1), their outward appearance (2), diet (3), lifestyle (4), clothing (5–6), movements and horses (6), organization (7), fighting (8–9), nomadic life (10), morals (11), whereafter a transition to the people of the Halani is made (12).

[6] 72 and 59 words respectively. Nomadic life / unity (17), lifestyle (18), cattle (39), movements (20), outward appearance / degree of savageness (21), warfare (22), lack of religion (23), divination (21) and social organization (22). See also Richter 1974, 360–1 for another division.

[7] See Emmet 1981 for an analysis of this kind of formulas.

Let us first examine in what way the parts relate to each other as it comes to content. There are some remarkable similarities between the two main parts. Both peoples do not have houses or huts, but they live in wagons,[1] where they have intercourse, give birth and rear children. They are constantly on the move and do not practise agriculture, but instead are totally devoted to their horses. They don't fight or go easily on foot, the Huns because their clothing is unapt, the Alans because of their training experience. They eat flesh. The relevant quotes from the Latin texts are as follows:[2]

Figure 2: Similarities between Huns and Alans in the Double Digression in Amm. RG 31.2.

	Huns (2.1-11)	Alans (2.17-25)
houses	4: *nec enim apud eos vel* <u>*arundine fastigatum*</u> *reperiri* <u>*tugurium*</u> *potest*	18: *nec enim ulla sunt illisce* <u>*tuguria*</u> 23: *ne* <u>*tugurium*</u> *quidem* <u>*culmo tectum*</u> *cerni usquam potest*
wagons	10: <u>*carpentis*</u>, *in quibus habitant*	18: *velut* <u>*carpentis*</u> *civitates inpositas vehunt* 18: *et habitacula sunt haec illis perpetua*
sexual intercourse	10: <u>*coeunt*</u> *[sc. coniuges] cum maritis et pariunt et ad usque pubertatem nutriunt pueros*	18: *maresque supra cum feminis* <u>*coeunt*</u> *et nascuntur in his et educantur infantes.*
intercourse	10: *omnes enim sine sedibus fixis ...* <u>*dispalantur*</u>, *semper fugientium similes*	18: *per pagos (ut nomades)* <u>*vagantur*</u> *immensos /* 18: *et quocumque ierint, illic genuinum existimant larem.*
nomadism	10: *nemo apud eos* <u>*arat*</u> *nec* <u>*stivam*</u> *aliquando contingit*	18: *nec enim ulla sunt illis ...* <u>*versandi vomeris*</u> *cura.*
agriculture	6: *verum* <u>*equis*</u> *prope affixi*	19: *maximeque* <u>*equini pecoris*</u> *est eis sollicitior cura*; 20: *iuventus vero* <u>*equitandi*</u> *usu a prima pueritia coalescens.*
horses	6: *ad* <u>*pedestres*</u> *parum accomodati sunt pugnas*	20: *incedere* <u>*pedibus*</u> *existimat vile.*
going by foot	3: *semicruda cuiusvis pecoris* <u>*carne*</u> *vescantur*	18: *sed* <u>*carne*</u> *et copia victitant lactis.*
carnivorism	8: *ad pernicitatem leves et repentini*	21: *armorum levitate veloces*
swiftness		

Although Ammianus states that the Alans are in all respects somewhat like the Huns (21: *Hunisque per omnia suppares*), there are marked differences, that mainly relate to their degree of civilization. So, the Alans, in contrast with the Huns, do have cattle and flocks, training in fighting, some sort of leadership and a sense of religion. The Huns, who are untrustworthy and totally ignorant of right and wrong, do not have leaders at all, nor justice or religion, but only yearn for gold and booty,[3] while the Alans do have morals in their opinion of life and death in battle.

---

[1] Wagons are denoted by carpenta (10, 18), but also by *vehicula* (20) *and plaustra* (18).

[2] Verbal parallels underlined; note the change of perspective from women to men and to children in the last parallel sentences. Quotations from the Huns' and Halani's passages are divided by a double slash (//).

[3] A remarkable variation occurs in 2.11 *cupidine immense flagrantes* and 2.12 *aviditate flagrans immani*, both pertaining to the Huns, which underlines this particular habit has to be attributed to the more barbarian of the two.

Figure 3: Differences between Huns and Alans in the Double Digression in Amm. RG 31.2.

	Huns (2.1-11)	Alans (2.17-25)
cattle		19: *armenta prae se agentes, cum gregibus pascunt*
training		20: *et omnes multiplici disciplina prudentes sunt bellatores*
leaders	7: *aguntur autem **nulla** severitate regali;*	25: *iudicesque etiam nunc eligunt diuturno bellandi usu spectatos*
religions	11: ***nullius** religionis vel super-stitionis reverentia aliquando districti*	23: *eumque (sc. gladium) ut Martem ... verecundius colunt;* 24: *futura miro praesagiunt modo.*
morals	11: *per indutias **infidi inconstantes** ... perquam mobiles, ... quid honestum inhonestumve sit penitus ignorantes.*	22: *iudicatur ibi beatus qui in proelio profuderit animam, senescentes enim et fortuitis mortibus mundo digressos ut degeneres et ignavos conviciis atrocibus insectantur,....*
justice	10: ***abs**que lare vel lege aut victu; 11: adeo permutabiles ... ut... a sociis **nullo** inritante saepe desciscant, itidemque propitientur **nemine** leniente*	
booty	11: *auri cupidine immense flagrantes / 12: externa praedandi aviditate flagrans immani.*	

A passage on the geography and peoples of central–northern Asia connects the two parts of the digression (2.12–16). Ammianus advanced this passage in his introductory remark on the Huns: *Hunorum gens ... ultra paludes Maeoticas glacialem oceanum accolens...* ('The people of the Huns, dwelling beyond the Maeotic Sea near the ice–bound ocean···, 2.1); the Huns are neighbouring the Alans (formerly the Massagetae), whose regions are described in the following passage.

There is a line in Ammianus' reasoning, in that the Alans, living in Scythian regions, gradually incorporated neighboring peoples: the snowy Nervii, the exceedingly savage Vidini and Geloni, the Agathyrsi with blue–dyed hair, and the Melanchlaenae and Anthropophagi who feed on human flesh, until one comes to the *Seres* ('Chinese').[1] Apart from the latter people, whose land is famous for its fertile soil and amplitude, the first six are described in increasingly terrifying terms; the neighbors of the Anthropophagi have even fled to the outmost corners of the earth. The exposé fits into a line of discourse, that holds that the more remote people are also the less civilized: lack of knowledge inspires fear, resulting in fanciful descriptions. The same thought is found in Herodotus, by whom Ammianus may well have been informed as he often mentions the same peoples and

---

[1] Also mentioned in 23.6.64: *Vltra haec utriusque Scythiae loca contra orientalem plagam celsorum aggerum summitates ambiunt Seras, ubertate regionum et amplitudine circumspectos, ab occidentali latere Scythis adnexos,···.* ('Beyond these lands of both Scythias, towards the east, the summits of lofty walls form a circle and enclose the Seres, remarkable for the richness of their country. On the west they are bounded by the Scythians··· ').

details in his description of Scythia:① the farther the people, the more fantastic their appearance and customs.

Geographically, Ammianus shows more knowledge about the nearer-by people, whose regions are said to be disclosed in more recent times by learned men. When extending this idea to the people of the Huns, it may be stated that their remoteness, behind the Maeotic Sea (modern Sea of Azow) stretching to the *glacialem oceanum* ('ice-bound ocean'), beyond all the peoples who make up the Alans, is in accordance with their extremely low degree of civilization. By stating that all the mentioned peoples in the transitory digression can be reckoned to the Alans, Ammianus creates a problem. Generally, in ethnicological writing, a people is considered a unity based on similarity of physical appearance (like, for example, Tacitus' *Germania*② or similarity of language or customs.③ Although the second part of the digression cannot be harmonized with the data in the transitory part, Ammianus employs the degree of savageness (*ob mores et modum efferatum vivendi*, 'because of their savage mode of life) as an argument for unity.④ Earlier however, in 31.13, Ammianus had given a dynastic explanation (*crebritate victoriarum*, 'by repeated victories') for the unity of the different peoples.⑤ Moreover, in two different instances the Alans, who are also dwelling in the southern central Asian regions up to the river Ganges (31.16), are compared to the Persians (31.13 and 20), who are said to originate from Scythia. Both peoples, trained in fighting, have gathered many different tribes under their name, without necessarily sharing customs.⑥ It is hard to decide whether Ammianus wants the Alans to have grown towards a unity on a dynastic or an ethnic basis; probably he simply tries to decline the question by contradictory statements.

This leaves us with the question in how far the protagonists of the digression, the Huns and the Alans, have evolved into a united body. Immediately after the digression, the people of the Huns are easily fused with the already heterogenous Alans by a treaty of alliance, which is an ill-defined dynastic union.⑦ The binary excursus on Huns and Alans are shrouded in ambiguity, which is the aimed effect in order to veil a lack of information. Still, neither physical, nor moral behavior binds the two; there is only superficial likeness

---

① Matthews 1989, 333 *sqq.*; Sabbah 1999, 242n351. Nervi (cf. 23.8.40) are Herodotus' Neuri (4.105); the Vidini the Boudini (4.108-9); the Agathyrsi in 4.104; the Melanchlaenae in 4.107, the Massagetae in 1.204.

② Tac. *Germ.*4.1: *Unde habitus quoque corporum···idem omnibus: truces et caerulei oculi, rutilae comae, magna corpora et tantum ad impetum valida* ('Hence the physical type···is everywhere the same—wild, blue eyes, reddish hair and huge frames that excel only in violent effort', tr. H. Mattingly, Penguin Books 1948).

③ Tac. Germ. 46.1: *Peucinorum Venedorumque et Fennorum nationes Germanis an Sarmatis adscribam dubito, quamquam Peucini··· sermone, cultu, sede ac domiciliis ut Germani agunt* ('I cannot make up my mind whether to assign the tribes of the Peucini, Venedi and Fenni to Germany or Sarmatia. The Peucini, however, ··· in language, social habits, mode of settlement and dwelling are like Germans', tr. Mattingly).

④ *Halani···licet dirempti spatiis longis ··· aevi tamen progressu ad unum concessere vocabulum et summatim omnes Halani cognominantur ob mores et modum efferatum vivendi eandemque armaturam* ('The Halani ··· although widely separated from each other···yet in the course of time they have united under one name, and are, for short, all called Halani because of the similarity in their customs, their savage mode of life, and their weapons', 31.2.17).

⑤ *in inmensum extentas Scythiae solitudines Halani inhabitant, ··· paulatimque nationes conterminas crebritate victoriarum adtritas ad gentilitatem sui vocabuli traxerunt,ut Persae* ('the Halani ··· inhabit the measureless wastes of Scythia; and by repeated victories they gradually wore down the peoples whom they met and like the Persians incorporated them under their own national name', 31.13)

⑥ *omnes multiplici disciplina prudentes sunt bellatores. unde etiam Persae, qui sunt originitus Scythae,pugnandi sunt peritissimi* ('and by various forms of trainingthey are all skilled warriors. From the same causes the Persians also, who are Scythians by origin, are highly expert in fighting', 31.20).

⑦ 31.3.1: *Igitur Huni pervasis Halanorum regionibus···, interfectisque multis et spoliatis, reliquos sibi concordandi fide pacta iunxerunt···* ('The Huns, then, having overrun the territories of the Halani ··· killed and plundered many of them, and joined the survivors to themselves in a treaty of alliance···').

from Roman perspective, such as a nomadic lifestyle. The Hunni and Alans, though united, are said to be very dissimilar in outward appearance: while the Huns are deformed in their faces (due to the scars in their faces, deliberately applied in childhood to prevent growth of hair), their limbs are stocky and their necks thick. Their diet consist of roots of wild plants or grass (*radicibus herbarum agrestium*) and flesh (2.2–3). Both characteristics, in appearance and eating habit, are prompted to make the Huns similar to beasts, which is expressly stated with *ut bipedes existimes bestias* ('that one might take them for two–legged beasts' , 2.2) and Ammianus' introductory word for the digression: *Hunorum gens ··· omnem modum feritatis excedit* ('The people of the Huns ··· exceed every degree of savagery' , 2.1). Their clothing enforces the image of beasts, as they wear cloaks made from mice' s skins, and garments of goatskins on their legs.[1] The Huns are described as resembling beasts by a total lack of conscienceness about the difference between right and wrong.[2] The Alans, on the other part, are handsome and less savage in their manner of life.[3] It is, in the case of the heterogeneous Alans, a question of cultural determinism that the more remote the peoples live, the more savage they are, even to the horrible presence of Anthropophagi–with these horrible creatures, the savage Huns became one, 'guilty by association'.

3. The Narrative Context

At a first glance, it is remarkable that after the long digression on the Huns and their fellow–people of the Alans, the savages hardly seem to play a role in the rest of the last book of Ammianus' history. The digression is placed after an introductory passage, in which an impending disaster is predicted by dire portents, which primarily pertain to the historical narration that follows after the digression, which ends up in the terrible defeat of the Romans near the Thracian town of Hadrianople in 378. The grim description of the Huns may certainly add to the ominous atmosphere, but is presented in another light, namely a positivistic explanation of the disaster that was about to happen: *Totius autem sementem exitii et cladum originem diversarum···hanc comperimus causam* ('However, the seed and origin of all the ruin and various disasters ··· we have found to be this').[4] Then follows the Double Digression, beginning with the furrowing of little Huns' cheeks. In the historical narration (31.3–16), both the Huns and the Alans are only mentioned six times by name, four of which in combination, and especially in the chapter immediately following the digression, against thirteen times the people of the Goths, who had the largest part in the development of military affairs.[5] The following diagram shows the distribution of the peoples over the book:

---

[1] *indumentis operiuntur linteis vel ex pellibus silvestrium murum consarcinatis* ('They dress in linen cloth or in the skins of field–mice sown together'); *hirsuta crura coriis munientes haedinis* ('they protect their hairy legs with goatskins').

[2] *inconsultorum animalium ritu, quid honestum inhonestumve sit, penitus ignorantes* ('Like unreasoning beasts, they are utterly ignorant of the difference between right and wrong···' , 2.11).

[3] *Proceri autem Halani paene sunt omnes et pulchri, ··· Hunisque per omnia suppares verum victu mitiores et cultu* ('Moreover, almost all of the Halani are tall and handsome, ··· In all respects they are somewhat like the Huns, but in their manner of life and their habits they are less savage' , 31.21).

[4] And unreservedly copied by Stickler 2011, 502: 'The mass exodus of Gothic groups, ··· the catastrophic defeat inflicted on the eastern mobile army ··· and the formation of new barbarian entities ··· had all been ultimately caused by the Huns' appearance in Europe' – Ammianus' voice, loud and clear.

[5] The Huns (3.1, 3.3, 3.6, 3.8, 8.4 and 16.3), Alans (3.1, 3.3, 8.4, 11.6, 12.17, 16.3) and Goths (3.8, 6.1, 6.3, 7.8, 8.1, 9.1, 9.3, 11.4, 12.17, 15.7, 16.3, 16.6, 16.8).

Figure 4: Distribution of the occurences of Huns, Alans, Greuthungi and Goths in RG 31 in order of appearance; between brackets the relative amount (per thousand) in proportion to the total number of words in the passage.[1]

People	Digression (ch.2)	Narration (ch.3)	Narration (ch.4-16)	Total
Huns	2 (1,8 ‰)	4 (9,8 ‰)	2 (0,3 ‰)	8 (0,9 ‰)
Alans	6 (5,4 ‰)	2 (4,9 ‰)	4 (0,5 ‰)	12 (1,3 ‰)
Greuthungi	0	2 (4,9 ‰)	2 (0,3 ‰)	4 (0,4 ‰)
Goths	0	1 (2,4 ‰)	12 (1,6 ‰)	13 (1,4 ‰)
Total	8 (7,2 ‰)	9 (22,0 ‰)	20 (2,6 ‰)	37 (4,0 ‰)

It may be deduced that in two of the chapters (16 per cent of the total amount of text) 14 mentions (out of 20 in total, which makes 70 per cent) of the Huns and Alans occur, while the Goths prevail in the succeeding parts.[2] The question is what happened with the twin-peoples after the digression devoted to them.

In chapter 3, the Huns, unknown savages coming from the far ends of the earth,[3] drive the Goths, who take refuge at the other side of the river Hister ('Danube'), from their dwellings. Afterwards, sight is lost of the Huns and Alans for a while, until in 8.4, when the Goths east of the Danube are overwhelmed by the Roman army, they gained an alliance 'with some of the Huns and Alani'. The obvious conclusion is that the Huns and Alans in their turn merged into the people of the Goths, a fact that Ammianus nowhere explicitly mentions.[4] Just before the battle at Hadrianople, the Alans appear in an alliance with the Gothic leaders Alatheus and Saphrax (31.12.17).[5] Yet, a trace of their presence may be noticed before this event, when the enemies (i.e. the Goths) were seen in their encampment of wagons, perfectly arranged in a circle (31.12.11).[6] The same had occurred before the battle near the town Ad Salices, where the barbarian people *otio fruebatur et ubertate praedarum* ('were enjoying their rich booty at ease'), closedly watched by the Romans, who knew that the enemy moved their camps frequently.[7] The third occurrence of the habit of placing wagons in a circle is in 31.15.5, when the hordes of barbarians before Hadrianople return to their camp.[8] The circular form of the

---

[1] The number of words amount, for ch.2, to 1110; ch.3: 410 and ch. 4-16: 7650; the sum of these: 9170.

[2] Number of words in the digression (ch.2): 1110; and in the narration ch.3: 410; ch.4-16: 7650; total: 9170; in the introduction in ch. 1, no mentions of any of these peoples is made.

[3] an *invisitatum antehac hominum genus ···ex abdito sinu coortum–* 'a race of men hitherto unknown ··· arisen from a hidden nook of the earth ···', 31.3.8.

[4] See for discussion Lenski p.331 n. 67-332.

[5] *equitatus Gothorum cum Alatheo reversus et Saphrace, Halanorum manu permixta* ('the Gothic cavalry, returning with Alatheus and Saphrax, combined with a band of Halani').

[6] *hostium carpenta cernuntur, quae ad speciem rotunditatis detornatae digesta exploratorum relatione affirmabantur* ('they saw the wagons of the enemy, which, as the reports of the scouts had declared, were arranged in the form of a perfect circle').

[7] *unde haut longo spatio separatum vulgus inaestimabile barbarorum ad orbis rotundi figuram multitudine digesta plaustrorum* ('not far from there a countless mass of the barbarians had arranged their numerous wagons in the form of a circle', 31.7.5); *ut si aliorsum castra movissent, quod fecere creberrime* ('that in case the enemy moved their camp to any other place, as they frequently did', 31.7.6).

[8] *Reversique ad vallum dimensum tereti figura plaustrorum* ('but they returned to the circular rampart formed by their wagons', 31.15.5).

wagoncamp was also remarked in the digression on the Alans.[1] Although the Huns and Alans themselves are not frequently mentioned anymore after the digression and chapter 3, the habit of placing wagons in a circle, and frequently moving them, may be one of the elements that betray their presence in the Gothic bands.[2] The correspondence between digression and narration on this point may, however, also be explained the other way round: Ammianus may have used this particular habit of the nomadic enemies to embellish his description of the Alans. Only in 31.16.3, the three people, Goths, Alans and Huns, are mentioned as a triplet without reserve, when preparing to lay siege to Constantinople.[3]

The implication of the mentions of Huns and Alans is that the same happened to them what happened with the Greuthungi before, namely a merger with the Goths, after which they were only scarcely mentioned separately. There are other correspondences between digression and narration: The Huns' predilection for *praeda, merces and praemia* resonates in four different cases: this makes them a sort of mercenary soldiers, rebels without cause except booty. Huns are associated with or tempted by the promise of booty,[4] just as had been mentioned in 31.2.12 (*externa praedandi aviditate flagrans inmani*). In the battle near Ad Salices, the Romans are opposed to the Goths when raising their cultivated war cry (*Romani concinentes*) against a cacophony of barbaric voices (*clamoribus⋯inconditis*, 'with wild shouts'; *interque varios sermonis dissoni strepitus*, 'and amid this discordant clamour of different languages', 7.11).[5] Then, the forces challenge one another from afar with missiles (*verrutis et missilibus aliis utrimque semet eminus lacessentes*, 'after attacking each other from a distance with javelins and other missiles, they came together menacingly for a hand-to-hand conflict') and finally meat each other in a man-to-man battle, using swords. In the digression, a comparible process is described: *et pugnant nonnumquam lacessiti sed ineuntes proelia cuneatim variis vocibus sonantibus torvum. ⋯ eoque omnium acerrimos facile dixeris bellatores, quod procul missilibus telis,⋯ et distantiis percursis comminus ferro sine sui respectu confligunt* ('They also sometimes fight when provoked, and then they enter the battle drawn up in wedge-shaped masses, while their medley of voices make a savage noise. ⋯ then they gallop over the intervening spaces and fight hand to hand with swords, regardless of their own lives', 2.8–9). There are differences, and the descriptions may be typical. However, this may have been a source for

---

① *cumque ad graminea venerint, in orbiculatam figuram locatis sarracis ferino ritu vescuntur,*⋯ ('And when they come to a place rich in grass, they place their charts in a circle and feed like wild beasts⋯').

② As it is a characteristic of nomadic peoples or peoples on the move, also in war time: compare the habits of the farmer-soldiers in the Boer Wars (1880–1; 1899–1902) in South-Africa, or the cowboys from the American Mid-West, who all placed their wagons in circular form by way of encampment.

③ *At Gothi Hunis Halanisque permixti* ('But the Goths, joined with the Huns and the Halani'). It is worth remarking that in later times, the Huns, Goths and Bulgars indeed were presented as manifestations of Scythians, see Amory 1997, 18–33; 110–48.

④ 31.3.3: ⋯*rex Vithimiris creatus restitit aliquantisper Halanis, Hunis aliis fretus, quos* <u>mercede</u> *sociaverat partibus suis* ('Vithimiris was mad king, and resisted the Halani for a time, relying on other Huns, whom he had paid to take his side'); 31.3.9: *Huni* ⋯ *iam oppresserant adventantes, ni gravati* <u>praedarum</u> *onere destitissent* ('the Huns ⋯would have crushed crushed him at once on their arrival had they not been so loaded down with booty that they gave up the attempt'); 31.8.4: *Hunorum et Halanorum aliquos ad societatem spe* <u>praedarum</u> *ingentium adsciverunt* ('they gained an alliance with some of the Huns and Halani by holding out the hope of immense booty'); 31.16.3: *At Gothi Hunis Halanisque permixti*⋯, *quos miris* <u>praemiorum</u> *inlecebris sibi sociarat sollertia Fritigerni* ('But the Goths, joined with the Huns and the Halani ⋯ , whom the craft of Fritigern had won over to them by the attractions of wonderful prizes⋯').

⑤ Matthews (2007, 63) remarks the same with regard to *clamoribus dissonis* (Amm. RG 19.1.8), which is 'Ammianus' expression for 'confused' shouting ... used elsewhere to suggest the diverse cultures and languages of an army of Moorish rebels in north Africa.'

the content of the digression—anyways, the sound of voices in different languages provides us with another characteristic of the Goths annex Huns: an amalgam of peoples, untamed without encumbrances (*expeditum indomitumque*, 2.12).

4. The Latin Ethnographical Tradition

The digression is inserted in the narration on a most dramatic point: just after the portents predicting the defeat, and before the events that led to that catastrophic war. The Huns themselves were ominous enough: menacing, disordered and extremely dangerous and swift fighters. Although the Huns are not described as a multi-ethnic people (as the Alans are), they must certainly be considered so; their lack of kingly leadership made it, moreover, impossible for the Romans to define them. They were mercenaries, switching from one camp to another, with swift guerilla-methods, with whom no unequivocal battle could be fought, and with whom certainly no treaties could be made by lack of uniform organization (*per indutias infidi et inconstantes*, 2.11). The digression on the Huns, enlarged with one about the Alans, is entirely constructed to make this point clear: they were the *semen totius exitii and cladum diversarum origo* (2.1)

The elements from which the digression is made built up, possibly partly derived from material of the historical narration, contain typical elements from ethnographical writing, which stands in a long tradition in Roman historical and geographical literature. Let us just consider some examples from other parts of the *Res Gestae*, whereafter other sources will be taken into account. In 14.4, the description of the nomadic people of the Saracens, living in the region between Assyria to Egypt, contain some identical motives: no agriculture, no fixed dwelling places, no law. Their marriages differ, as the wives are hired as mercenaries; both men and women are arduous in their passions; which may be considered a question of geographical determinism, under the burning sun where they lived. They live on milk and plants, while being considered a *natio perniciosa* ('a dangerous tribe').[1] Another digression is on the Gauls, quite different in character, but with some comparable elements: morals, geography, appearance ('quasi-bestial').[2] Most of all, the digression is placed on a most dramatic moment, in order to add to the suspense of the narration: just after the appointment of the emperor Constantius' cousin Julian to Caesar and before his battle with the Alamanni in book 16. This shows how Ammianus may use, in the words of G. Woolf, the digression as a kind of 'punctuation mark' in the course of historical events.

It does not seem out of place here to compare the content of Ammianus' digression with comparable texts in the same tradition, for example one of his preferred models Tacitus, who wrote among other works a monography of the barbaric peoples in Germania, the *Germania*, referred to above.[3] This work ends with a

---

[1] Cf. Homer's description of the Thracians as breeders of horses (ἐφ' ἱπποπόλων Θρῃκῶν, Iliad 13.5) and nomad peoples as drinkers of Milk (γλακτοφάγων) and Hesiodus (fr. 217b, fr.97–98): 'milkers of horses' (*hippēmolgoi*). Milk and horses are traditionally associated with nomad an peripheral peoples, see Gracianskaya 1996. Matthews' remark (1989, 337): 'To call nomads 'drinkers of milk' may be a rhetorical stereotype, but milk is obviously characteristic of the diet of pastoralists, and there is no need to deny it to the Huns' nicely shows the nature of the problem of historiographical sources and literary motivation.

[2] This last characterization by Wiedemann 1986, 260. For the literary aims and the contemporary reader's perception, see Woolf 2011a.

[3] For Tacitus as a model: Kelly 2008; an historical commentary on the Germania: Rives 1999. Den Boeft et al. (2005, 215) remark that Ammianus may have used Tacitus' *Histories* as source for the Germans.

description of related people near the Roman frontier, among whom the Fenni and Veneti. In his considerations to assign these peoples to either the *Germans* or Sarmatians, Tacitus uses arguments of customs and race. As regards customs, sedentary or nomadic lifestyle is an important criterium: the Veneti do not live on wagons and horses like the Sarmatians.[①] The Fenni, who are characterized as beast–like creatures by their food and their clothing, are far more savage.[②] The Fenni's state of *feritas*, the substantive connected with *ferus* ('wild beast'), is among other things reflected in a lack of religion.[③] Some characteristic elements in ethnographical writing, as we have seen in the digressions on Saracens, Huns and Alans in Ammianus, are also present here: the mention of wives, children and the aged. Two elements ask for special attention, namely the case when honor is paid for the aged,[④] and the fact that they use arrows tipped with bones instead of iron.[⑤] Contrary to Ammianus, Tacitus does not speculate about the further removed peoples.[⑥]

Thus, Ammianus seems to draw on older templates of ethnographicalal writing. The specific aims he pursues may be different from earlier descriptions of barbaric peoples. Peoples living close to nature, in feral circumstances and mood, are more than once presented as more pure than civilized peoples. The primitive state of living, without law, luxury and sometimes agriculture or religion, may bring the advantage that crime, decadence and jealousy are also absent: although in descriptions of this kind the same elements are used to characterize these peoples, there is not just one state of primitivism. Primitivism is used as well for the pre–Roman (eventually Greek) way of living, often referring to an idealized and long–gone golden time (aurea aetas) as well as for the state of barbaric peoples.[⑦] For example, Ovidius in his Fasti (2.293) says about the primitive state of the *Arcades*, the Roman's ancestors: *pro domibus frondes norant*, *pro frugibus herbas* and for the *genus humanum* in earlier times in Ars Amatoria (2.475): silva domus fuerat, *cibus herba*, cubilia frondes. In these cases, the eating of herbs and grasses is not used to create a frightening portrait of savage peoples, but rather to the ancestor's untainted state of mind.[⑧] In much the same way, Seneca suggests the wearing of animal skins as sufficient for human needs (ep.90.16)[⑨] and names the Scythians as examples to follow–on which idea, of course,

---

① *Hi (sc. Veneti) tamen inter Germanos potius referuntur, quia et domos figunt et scuta gestant et pedum usu ac pernicitate gaudent: quae omnia diversa Sarmatis sunt in plaustro equoque viventibus* ('Still, they are more properly classed as Germani, because they have fixed homes and bear shields and take pleasure in moving fast by foot: all these things are at odds with Sarmatians, who live on wagons and horses').

② Tacitus, *Germania* 46: *Fennis mira feritas* (⋯); *victui herba*, *vestitui pelles*, *cubile humus* ('The Fenni are astonishingly wild. (⋯) They eat grass, dress in skins, and sleep on the ground').

③ *securi adversus deos*, ⋯ *ut illis ne voto quidem opus esset* ('they care for no god⋯ that they even do not need to prey').

④ RG 31.2.22: *iudicatur ibi beatus* ('there the man is judged happy⋯'); *Germ.* 46.3 *Sed beatius arbitrantur* ('but they are judged more blessed⋯').

⑤ RG 31.2.9: *acutis ossibus pro spiculorum acumine arte mira coagmentatis* ('with missiles having sharp bone, instead of their usual points'); *Germ.* 46.3: *solae in sagittis spes, quas inopia ferri ossibus asperant* ('their only hope is in arrows, which in the absence of iron they tip with bones').

⑥ *Cetera iam fabulosa: Hellusios et Oxionas ora hominum voltusque, corpora atque artus ferarum gerere* ('What comes after them is the stuff of fables – Hellusii and Oxiones with the faces and features of men, but the bodies and limbs of animals', 46.4).

⑦ The imagery of the degeneration is derived from Hesiod's narration in *Works and Days*; see for a recent treatment Edwards 2014.

⑧ In 31.2.3, Ammianus remarks that the Huns do no use fire, which 'may be intended as a symbol, to convey their lack of a basic resource of civilised life, rather than a plain statement of fact...' (Matthews 2007, 341).

⑨ *illi sapientes fuerunt aut certe sapientibus similes quibus expedita erat tutela corporis*. ⋯ *non pelles ferarum et aliorum animalium a frigore satis abundeque defendere queunt?* ('They were wise or at least acted like wise men whose bodily coverage was simple ... did not the skins of wild beasts and other animals protect them from cold abundantly?').

the romantic 'sauvage noble' is also based. Ammianus' *expeditum indomitumque hominum genus* of the Huns, however, points to exactly the opposite direction.

The positive assessment of a primitive and close-to-nature lifestyle is omnipresent in Latin literature. The idea of a Golden Age, as voiced in Catullus *carmen* 64 before the Argo was seabound on the Aegean waves, the Gods left the earth and the heroes died at the Trojan battlefield, holds that there was no seafaring, no agriculture and, consequently, no deteriorated morals among men. The idea, which later in different forms returns in Virgil's *Fourth Eclogue* (esp. the passages 4.31–45), is that culture is a threat to an uncivilised and morally unaffected state of living. As we have seen, this state of life is often presented as a positive feature, as, in ethical context, a sign of modesty and, in warlike situations, fortitude. Ammianus does not give such a positive assessment (at least not explicitly: the implication might be that primitivism is threatening), but follows the mode of ethnographical description in a different way. One of the characteristics in the description of barbarian peoples, is the formulation in the negative.[①] The ethnographical author describes what a certain people does not have, thereby implying the cultural standard. For example, Ammianus says about the Huns (2.4): *nec enim apud eos vel arundine fastigatum reperiri tugurium potest*; and about the Alans (2.18): *nec enim ulla sunt illisce tuguria*; The repeated *nec enim...* introducing a remark about the lack of houses (tuguria) shows that houses are a sign of civilisation up to the Roman standards. There are all kinds of negations (see for the quotes figure 2 and 3 above), with ne *quidem ...* (2.23): *sine* (2.10), *nemo* (2.10), *nec enim* (2.18), *nulla* (2.7), *nullus* (2.10),[②] *nullius* (2.11), or negating words such as *infidi* and *inconstantes* (2.11) or other constructions, such as *absque lare* (2.10).[③] By using negations, also Catullus and Virgil in the mentioned texts describe the situation before the iron race of men came into world, when the Golden Age was over.[④]

For the historiographer Ammianus, who is neither poet and philosopher nor romantic, foreign people's savageness is synonymous with terror, causing fear on the adversary's (Roman) side and providing bad omens for the nearby future. Not a trace of idealization of primitive living. Even Caesar, father of all war correspondents, in his *Bellum Gallicum* 1, makes compliments to the Belgians, who are good fighters because of their distance from the civilized province, where merchants do not trade with luxury goods by which the male spirit is effeminized. This positive reading of the enemy's uncultured spirit and concomitant brave behavior in the end does credit to the triumphant general. For Ammianus, who writes from the perspective of the people that soon will be defeated, this motive is absent, as it is not applicable to the situation in the narrative. Rather, the savageness serves as an omen and at the same time as an explanation for the terrible defeat, and discredits

---

① Quiroga 2013 in his analysis of Libanius' portraiture of the barbarian, rightly quotes Malosse 2003, 43 who stated that "pour peindre un barbare, il suffit de prendre le contre-pied des valeurs communément admises dans l'oikoumenê".

② *Nullusque apud eos interrogatus respondere unde oritur potest* ('None of their offspring, when asked, can tell you where he comes from'), not quoted in figure 1 and 2 (because not to be categorized in similarities and differences). There are other negations, but the principle may be clear.

③ In view of the point made here, it might well be that Bentley's deletion of *non in non numquam* (2.8) might be maintained: the negation numquam would be made undone by addition of non. The text would then read: *Et pugnant numquam lacessiti* ('And they never fight when provoked'); the implication is that the Huns do not fight for certain occasions, but simply attack according to their whims. The other nearby negations *incomposita acie* ('rushing about in disorder') and *nec invadentes vallum, nec castra inimica pilantes* ('they are never seen to attack a rampart or pillage an enemy's camp)' show the deviation from what is to be expected.

④ To show only one example from Verg. E 4.37–40: *cedet et ipse mari vector, nec nautica pinus mutabit merces* (...) *non rastros patietur humus, non vinea falcem*, etc. ('even the mariner will cede from the sea, and the seabound pinetree will not trade ... the earth will not bear the plow, and the vines will not suffer the blade').

the responsible emperor.

5. Greek Ethnographical Models

As a Greek, writing in the Latin language, Ammianus choose as his main model the ethnographical excursus about the Scythians by his fellow–Greek historiographer Herodotus (who lived ca. 480–425 BC, no less than nine centuries earlier) in his *Histories* book 4.[1] Numerous are the details that Ammianus borrows from the pater *historiae*, as Cicero (*De legibus* 1.5) had styled the author, as has been pointed out before; we will go deeper into this subject below. The borrowing from Herodotus may partly serve to hide a lack of historical knowledge about the contemporaneous Huns.[2] A more positive view may be that Herodotus' description may have been the best he could find about these people from the Asian steppes. In the antiquarian tradition, he esteemed old wisdom highly.[3] By lack of other sources, he took the text that served his goals best: if no other information is at hand, why not choosing the best possible source? Ammianus only drew on little actual knowledge about the newly arrived peoples, but on learned reading, at the same time envisaging to attain the maximum effect for the reader of his accounts. The question brought up in the introduction is whether literary effect on the base of scarce historical fact is the only reason for which this part of the narration–at a high peak of dramatic composition–was created. It would be poor if not disappointing to conclude that Ammianus took the easy way out by simply inserting a badly informed excursus on unknown peoples; or that he only choose his fellow Greek historiographer Herodotus in order to give him the honour of being the first and only source for the Scythians.[4] In the following, it will be investigated whether Ammianus may have envisaged other purposes, by implying an ideological and politically motivated program.

How does Ammianus actually gather the information about his subject? In the geographical part, he states to have heard or read it, without further specification, 2.15: *accepimus* and 2.16 *accepi*. This has all the appearances of being an imitation of Herodotus, who in his Scythian excursus (4.100) states, in the same geographical context, 'it has been said' (Ἀποκληίεται). In this same section, 2.13, Ammianus says about the Istros (present–day Danube): *Abundans Hister advenarum magnitudine fluenti* ⋯ ('the Danube overflowing by a streaming magnitude of feeding rivers'). Herodotus in *Histories* 4.50 speaks about the Istros, 'And so it is because of the rivers I have listed and many others, too, all contributing water to its volume, that the Ister becomes the greatest of all rivers, ⋯' (tr. Strassler 2007, 303; Τούτων ὦν τῶν καταλεχθέντων καὶ ἄλλων πολλῶν συμβαλλομένων τὸ σφέτερον ὕδωρ γίνεται ὁ Ἴστρος ποταμῶν μέγιστος). It seems that Ammianus followed Herodotus while quoting an unspecified source. One could speculate about whether Ammianus envisages a kind of double reading such as 'I read it (in Herodotus)', or that the formula is simply imitation of

---

[1] Ammianus names Herodotus explicitly in 22.15.28 (see also Den Boeft et al. 1995, 281, who, like Sabbah 1999, 247 –see note 71 –, suppose that Herodotus here is not used directly as a source).

[2] These studies differ in the degree in which Ammianus took historical truth as his guideline; Matthews and Thomson are quite positive about the historical information, while King 1987 and recently Kim 2013 present a far more negative picture.

[3] See also the pertinent remarks Woolf 2011b made about the use of old knowledge for a contemporaneous audience.

[4] Note Ammianus revealing remark in 31.2.20: *Unde etiam Persae, qui sunt originitus Scythae, pugnandi sunt peritissimi* ('This is why also the Persians, who are originally Scythians, are very skilled in fighting').

the model; but writing as *miles quondam et Graecus* (as the sphragis in 31.16.9 says), it could imply both.[1] We may tentatively conclude that Ammianus in his description of the Huns relied on Herodotus not only in content, but also in its presentation.

A comparison between the two text leads us to the question which peoples Herodotus counts among the Scythians, and which were mentioned by Ammianus as being Alans. The Scythians mentioned by Herodotus (4.100) are the Sauromates, the the Agathyrsi, the Nervi, and the Anthropophagi and the Melanchlaenae, while Ammianus mentions (31.2) the Sauromates (who do not belong to the Alans), the Alans, the Nervi, the Vidini and Geloni, the Agathyrsi, Melanchlaenae and the Anthropophagi. In other words, –apart from the Alans–all the peoples that Herodotus mentions recur in Ammianus, except for the Vidini and Geloni.[2] But also these appear to have been taken from Herodotus, because in 4.109 (nine chapters further on), they are treated seperately from the others: 'The Boudini are indigenous; they are nomads, and the only people in these parts that eat fir–cones; the Geloni are farmers, eating grain and cultivating gardens; they are altogether unlike the Boudini in form and in coloring. Yet the Geloni call the Boudini too Geloni; but this is wrong.'[3] This is a revealing text in Ammianus' model: the two peoples mentioned by Ammianus in his account of Steppe peoples that were initially not mentioned by Herodotus, recur later in the form of a Double Digression in a nutshell, in which the Boudini (*Vidini* in Ammianus) and Geloni are compared in eating habits, nomadism against agriculture and physical appearance (the traditional element of language, present in Herodotus, is left out by Ammianus). This may (among other models) have suggested the idea of a Double Digression in Ammianus, who also tries to distinguish character traits between the two peoples he treats. Herodotus' critical remark that the Greeks were not right to reckon the Boudini among the Geloni is not followed by Ammianus.

Herodotus is not the first one to distinguish between degrees of savageness. In the paragraph preceding the fragment above, he remarks that the Geloni originally had been Greeks, which leads to a comparison between the two related peoples, who share the same language, as to their lack of civilisation. An important example for the distinction in degrees of savageness is provided by Homer, who in a way binds together and at the same time compares the Cyclopes (*Odyssey* 9.105–15) with the Laestrygonians, e.g. *Od.* 10.112–5: whereas the first people do not have laws, do not grow crops and plow lands, and do not have councils nor (again) laws and live

---

[1]　Cf. Matthews 2007, 461: 'Ammianus is claiming a double qualification as a historian'. In his excursus on Egypt, Herodotus applies the same method, though more specified: Μέχρι μὲν τούτου ὄψις τε ἐμὴ καὶ γνώμη καὶ ἱστορίη ταῦτα λέγουσά ἐστι, τὸ δὲ ἀπὸ τοῦδε αἰγυπτίους ἔρχομαι λόγους ἐρέων κατὰ τὰ ἤκουον· προσέσται δέ τι αὐτοῖσι καὶ τῆς ἐμῆς ὄψιος (cf. 2.99: 'So far, all I have said is the record of my own autopsy and judgment and inquiry. Henceforth I will record Egyptian chronicles, according to what I have heard, adding something of what I myself have seen.', tr. Godley 1920).

[2]　Sabbah 1999, 247 supposes that there is an intermediate source between Ammianus and Herodotus, because the information in the two text are not entirely in agreement. It can, however, be supposed that Ammianus did not follow Herodotus too closely, quoting by heart, and making his own version of the ethnographical description.

[3]　tr. Godley 1920; 'οἱ μὲν γὰρ Βουδῖνοι ἐόντες αὐτόχθονες νομάδες τέ εἰσι καὶ φθειροτραγέουσι μοῦνοι τῶν ταύτῃ, Γελωνοὶ δὲ γῆς τε ἐργάται καὶ σιτοφάγοι καὶ κήπους ἐκτημένοι, οὐδὲν τὴν ἰδέην ὅμοιοι οὐδὲ τὸ χρῶμα. Ὑπὸ μέντοι Ἑλλήνων καλέονται καὶ οἱ Βουδῖνοι Γελωνοί, οὐκ ὀρθῶς καλεόμενοι.

in caves,[①] the Laestrygonians did have kingship, a council and a degree of civil organization.[②] Again, the lack of culture is, just like we saw in Ammianus and Virgil, described with many repetitions of ἀ–, οὔτε and οὐδε. Also, there is an element of remoteness in time, as the Cyclopes are the ascendants of the prehistoric Gigants, who are closer to nature and therefore more barbaric than the civilized race of men. They drink milk and eat flesh, likes the Huns and many other nomads do.[③] The Cyclopes are therefore remnants of an earlier epoch of World History, who still dwell in remote parts of the earth (Sicily in case), where the introduction of culture and the progress of civilisation has come to a standstill in the rapid movements of time.

6. Conclusion

When considering Ammianus' digression on the Huns from a literary viewpoint, there are two main functions within its immediate context: regarding content, the digression is meant to enhance the threat that menaces the Roman empire in the epochal years 376–8, for which reason the Huns are portrayed as uncivilized as possible, in order to enhance the menace to the stability of the empire; regarding structure, it is meant to mark the transition to the description of the military disaster, as a 'punctation mark' before the description of the collapse of empire. Ammianus uses the literary device of ethnography to create these effects, which has deep roots in classical literature, from the historiographers Herodotus in Greek to Tacitus in Latin language, not to speak of poets, philosophers and orators. While in the mentioned models a certain curiosity in its own right about barbaric peoples may be detected, Ammianus' description does not seem to be scientifically driven in the first place. Nor is there any trace of idealizing description of the barbarians' untainted state of living, rather the opposite. The framework in which the data are presented has a literary motivation, although the material may draw on some genuine information (which lies outside the scope of this article). Ancient ethnography provided the template in which the elements were presented, such as appearance, clothing, military affairs and customs, which together builds up towards an explanation of the disaster that befell the Roman Empire.

In order to enhance the threat of a hitherto unknown enemy by literary means, Ammianus uses traditional ethnographical elements. In doing so, he creates the image of an enemy that the Romans had not known before. The Romans were experienced in warfare with Goths, but the disaster of Hadrianople required a better explanation, which was provided by the appearance of the disorganized but extremely dangerous

---

① Κυκλώπων δ' ἐς γαῖαν ὑπερφιάλων ἀθεμίστων / ἱκόμεθ', οἵ ῥα θεοῖσι πεποιθότες ἀθανάτοισιν / οὔτε φυτεύουσιν χερσὶν φυτὸν οὔτ' ἀρόωσιν, / ἀλλὰ τά γ' ἄσπαρτα καὶ ἀνήροτα πάντα φύονται, / πυροὶ καὶ κριθαὶ ἠδ' ἄμπελοι, αἵ τε φέρουσι / οἶνον ἐρισταφυλον, καί σφιν Διὸς ὄμβρος ἀέξει. / τοῖσιν δ' οὔτ' ἀγοραὶ βουληφόροι οὔτε θέμιστες, / ἀλλ' οἵ γ' ὑψηλῶν ὀρέων ναίουσι κάρηνα / ἐν σπέεσι γλαφυροῖσι, θεμιστεύει δὲ ἕκαστος / παίδων ἠδ' ἀλόχων, οὐδ' ἀλλήλων ἀλέγουσι. ('..., and we came to the land of the Cyclopes, an insolent and lawless folk, who, trusting in the immortal gods, plant nothing with their hands, nor plow; but all these thins spring up for them without sowing or plowing, wheat, and barley, and vines, which bear the rich clusters of wine, and Zeus' rian makes these grow for them. Neither assemblies for council have they, nor appointed laws, but they dwell on the peaks of mountains in hollow caves, and each one is lawgiver to his children and his wives, and they have no regard for one another.' , tr. A.T. Murray 1995, 324–5, or. 1919 in *Loeb Classical Library* 104).

② The two peoples are a stock example in ethnography, recently treated by Saïd 2011, 165–70 in a clear analysis of degrees of civilisation, and similarities and differences between the two related peoples.

③ milk: Od.9.248–9; 297; flesh: 9.289, 311, 314: Saïd 2011, 67; Amm. RG 31.2.18: ... *sed carne et copia victitant lactis*. Also the Saracens eat flesh of wild animals and drink milk (Amm. RG 14.4.6 and cf. Matthews 2007, 337 and Shaw 1982–3).

Huns. Ammianus presented another people, namely the Alans, in a comparable template, by which a Double Digression is created, most probably prompted by a similar treatment of the Boudini and Geloni by Herodotus, and in line with the treatment of the Cyclopes and Laestrygones in Homer's *Odyssey* 9 and 10. Whether Ammianus consciously designed it this way or not, it adds to the confusion the Huns offered their baffled adversaries. Both peoples, Huns and Alans, were incorporated in the more familiar peoples of the Goths, but added an element of utter unpredictability. This was partly caused by the lack of regal guidance on the side of the Huns (so Ammianus suggests), so that they could never be offered an alliance. With his digression on the Huns, the longest of its kind, Ammianus provided, or rather created, an explanation (*Hanc comperimus causam*) for the largest defeat of a Roman army in imperial times.

Apart from historical information (which is tiny) and literary motivation annex narrative context, there may have been an ideological purpose in the extensive portraiture of the Huns. As a Greek in Roman service (*miles quondam et Graecus*–once a soldier and a Greek–as Ammianus states it in the sphragis of 31.16.9), Ammianus emphasizes his own Greekness, but also the blessings of Greek paideia that was part of the Roman successes. As Libanius indirectly praised the emperor Julian for his support of Greek culture by pointing out how the emperor drew a dividing line between culture and barbary, Ammianus shows how the blurring of this line ends in catastrophe, thereby criticizing the responsible emperor Valens. To underline this ideological program, the emphasis on the barbarians' otherness, Ammianus reached long back in ethnographical tradition, from the examples of Tacitus and Virgil towards the Greek foundations of ethnography by Herodotus and Homer. The Huns and Alans were instrumental in depicting the collapse of not only the Roman Empire and its Greek base, but of a whole culture. By the time Ammianus wrote his thirty–first book, more than a decade later, the empire was still under threat. The Huns and Alans served as the strongest possible warning for the reigning emperor.

Bibliography

Adler, E. *Valorizing the Barbarians. Enemy Speeches in Roman Historiography.* Austin 2005.

Amory, P. 'People and Identity in Ostrogothic Italy 489–554', *Cambridge Studies in Medieval Life and Thought: Fourth Series*, no. 33, Cambridge 1997.

Barnes, T.D. *The Sources of the Historia Augusta* (Collection Latomus 155), Brussels 1978.

Blockley, R.C. *The Fragmentary Classicising Historians of the Later Roman Empire. Eunapius, Olympiodorus, Priscus and Malchus II, Text, Translation and Historiographical Notes* (ARCA. Classical and Medieval Texts, Papers and Monographs 10), Liverpool 1983, p.177–82.

Bona, I. *Das Hunnenreich*, Budapest 1991.

Den Boeft, J., J.W. Drijvers, D. den Hengst, H.C. Teitler *Philological and Historical Commentary on Ammianus Marcellinus XXII*, Groningen 1995.

Den Boeft, J., J.W. Drijvers, D. den Hengst, H.C. Teitler: *Philological and Historical Commentary on Ammianus Marcellinus XXV*, Leiden 2005.

Den Hengst, D. 'The Scientific digressions in Ammianus' *Res Gestae*', in: 'Emperors and Historiography. Collected Essays on the Literature of the Roman Empire by Daniël den Hengst' (edd. D.W.P. Burgersdijk & J.A. van Waarden), *Mnemosyne Supplements* 319, Brill 2010, 236–47.

Dessau, H. 1889. 'Über Zeit und Persönlichkeit der Scriptores Historiae Augustae', *Hermes* 24, 337–92.

Edwards, A.T. 'The Ethical Geography of Hesiod's Works and Days', in: *Geography, Topography, Landscape: Configurations of Space in Greek and Roman Epic*, M. Skempis & I. Ziogas (edd.), Berlin

2013, 95-136.

Eliav-Feldon, M., B. Isaac and J. Ziegler (edd.), *The Origins of Racism in the West*. Cambridge/New York 2009.

Emmett, A. 'Introductions and Conclusions to Digressions in Ammianus Marcellinus', *Museum Philologum Londiniense* 5 (1981) 15–33.

Feeney, D. *Caesar's Calendar. Ancient Time and the Beginnings of History*, Los Angeles/Londen 2007.

Gracianskaya, L.I. 'Zentrum und Peripherie: Der Ethnopsychologische Befund und seine iderspiegelungen in der Literatur', in: B. Funck (ed.) *Hellenismus: Beitrage Zur Erforschung Von Akkulturation Und Politischer Ordnung in Den Staaten Des Hellenistischen Zeitalters*, Tübingen 1996, 475–90.

Gruen, E.S. (ed.) *Cultural Identity in the Ancient Mediterranean*, Los Angeles 2011.

Gruen, E.S. *Rethinking the Other in Antiquity*. Martin Classical Lectures, Princeton/Oxford 2011b.

Haubold, J. *Greece and Mesopotamia: Dialogues in Literature*, Cambridge 2013.

Haubold, J. 'Ethnography in the Iliad', in: *Geography, Topography, Landscape: Configurations of Space in Greek and Roman Epic*, M. Skempis & I. Ziogas (edd.), Berlin 2013, 19–36.

Heather, P. *Empires and Barbarians. Migration, Development and the Birth of Europe*, London 2009.

Isaac, B. *The Invention of Racism in Classical Antiquity*, Princeton/Oxford 2004.

Isaac, B. 'Ammianus on Foreigners', in: Kahlos, M. (ed.) 2011 *The Faces of the Other:Religious Rivalry and Ethnic Encounters in the Later Roman World* (Cursor mundi 10), Turnhout 2011.

Kelly, C. *The End of Empire. Attilla the Hun & The Fall of Rome*, New York 2010.

Kelly, G. *Ammianus Marcellinus. The Allusive Historian*, Cambridge 2008.

Kim, Hyun Jin The Huns, *Rome and the Birth of Europe*, Cambridge 2013.

King, Ch. 'The veracity of Ammianus' Marcellinus' Description of the Huns', *American Journal of Ancient History* 12 (1987) 77–95.

Kulikowsky, M. 'Coded Polemic in Ammianus Book 31 and the Date and Place of its Composition', *Journal of Roman Studies* 102 (2012) 79–102.

Lenski, N. *Failure of Empire: Valens and the Roman State in the Fourth Century* A.D., Berkeley 2002.

Maenchen-Helfen, O.J. *The World of the Huns*, 1973.

Malosse, P.-L. *Libanios, Discours, vol. IV: Discours LIX* (Collection des Université s de France, Budé), Paris 2003.

Malosse, P.-L. 'Libanius' Orations', in: L. van Hoof (ed.) *Libanius. A Critical Introduction*, Cambridge 2014, 81–106.

Matthews, J. *The Roman Empire of Ammianus Marcellinus*, Baltimore 2007 (or. 1989).

Mutschler, F.-H., A. Mittag (edd.) *Conceiving the Empire. China and Rome Compared*,Oxford， 2008.

Paschoud, F. (ed.) *Zosime. Histoire Nouvelle Tome II 2e partie: Livre IV*, Paris， 2003.

Quiroga Puertas, A.J. 'The Others: Cultural Monotheism and the Rhetorical Construction of 'Cultural Alterity' in Libanius' Panegyrics', *Talanta* XLV： (2013)： 55–66.

Richter, W. 'Die Darstellung der Hunnen bei Ammianus Marcellinus', *Historia* 23 (1974)： 343–77.

Rives, J.B. *Tacitus, Germania. Translated with Introduction and Commentary*, Oxford， 1999.

Sabbah, G. (ed.) *Ammien Marcellin Histoire tome VI livres XXIX–XXXI*, Paris， 1999.

Saïd, S. *Homer and the Odyssey*, Oxford， 2011.

Shaw, B. 'Eaters of Flesh, Drinkers of Milk, the Ancient Mediterranean Ideology of the Pastoral Nomads', *Ancient Society* 13-4 (1982-3) 5–31.

Schmauder, M. *Die Hunnen. Ein Reitervolk in Europa*, Darmstadt 2009.

Strassler, R.B. (ed.) *The Landmark Herodotus*, New York 2007.

Thompson, E.A. *The Huns*, Oxford 1995.

Vergin, W. 2013 *Das Imperium Romanum und seine Gegenwelten: die geographisch−ethnographischen Exkurse in den "Res Gestae" des Ammianus Marcellinus (Millennium−Studien 41)*, Berlin.

Wiedemann, Th. 'Between men and beasts: barbarians in Ammianus Marcellinus', in: I.S.Moxon e.a. *Past Perspectives: Studies in Greek and Roman Historical Writing*, Cambridge 1986, 189–201.

Woolf, G. *Becoming Roman. The Origins of Provincial Civilization in Gaul*, Cambridge 1998.

Woolf, G. 'Saving the Barbarian', in: Gruen 2011a, 255–71.

Woolf, G. *Tales of the Barbarians: Ethnography and Empire in the Roman West. Blackwell Bristol Lectures on Greece, Rome and the Classical Tradition*. Chichester/Malden MA, 2011b.

Honor or Embarrassment: a Case Study of Inscribed Public Munificence

Jinyu Liu, DePauw University

摘要：本文通过对 *AE* 1998.282（公元227—228年）的文字、事件进展、人物关系的细节分析，探讨罗马帝国时代基金捐赠与接受过程中的冲突与协商。AE 1998.282是出土于意大利拉维尼乌姆城的拉丁语碑铭，发现并整理出版于二十世纪九十年代。内容围绕一个总额为二万赛斯特斯的基金的设置。捐主为Servilius Diodorus, 是一名出身阿非利加行省的骑士，并兼具Laurentes Lavinates祭司团成员身份。捐主指定基金的最终受益人为拉维尼乌姆城的"抗树人"团体（通常和大母神崇拜相关联），但基金的托管机构则为拉维尼乌姆城。这个基金的设置可谓一波三折，最后还是通过一位元老的介入才告成功。整部碑铭对于我们重新审视罗马时代的捐赠行为和地方政治是不可多得的资料。作为公共性极为彰显的载体，罗马世界的碑铭，特别是关于捐赠和礼物的铭文，多侧重展示捐主的慷慨与美德，讲述正面故事。*AE* 1998.282所包含的多封通信却透露了类似事件背后的多方协商、迎拒、甚至挫败。整部碑铭为Servilius Diodorus所立，本应是替他歌功颂德的纪念碑，反而处处留下了尴尬印迹。

关键词：捐赠；慷慨彰显；拉丁碑铭；拉维尼乌姆城；"抗树"人团体

Abstract: Inscribed on three sides of a statue base, *AE* 1998.282 (for editio princeps, see Nonnis 1995) preserves a series of correspondences in 227—228 CE pertaining to the establishment of a perpetual endowment of HS 20,000 for the dendrophori of Lavinium. The donor was Servilius Diodorus, an *eques* of African origin (*domo Girba ex Africa*) and a member of the priestly college of the *Laurentes Lavinates*. It was through the intervention of a senator upon the request of Diodorus that the city accepted the endowment. While the city was to control the capital, the local *dendrophori* were to carry out the designated ceremonies and have banquets paid out of the annual income of the said endowment. In the letter responding to his being elected patron by the *dendrophori* out of gratitude, Servilius Diodorus included a clause exhorting his fellow Larentes Lavinates to emulate his euergetic deed. This remarkable dossier provides a rather rare glimpse into the (re)actions of the various interested parties (the donor, the city, the senator, the designated recipients, and the donor's peers) in the establishment of the gift. Several questions immediately arise: Why was the city so closely involved if the gift was intended to benefit the *dendrophori*? Why did Diodorus choose to convey his wish to give a donation through the senator? Was it because he had been turned down by the city initially? Or was it because he wanted to give the gift more prestige by taking a top-down approach? Was his non-native origin an aggravating factor in his dealing with the city, or the local elite? Based on a close analysis of the language of the correspondences, the chronological sequence of events, and the local politics, this paper addresses those inter-connected questions in the hopes to shed light on the conflicts, negotiations, and compromises in the euergetic politics in the Western cities in the early third century.

Keywords: euergetism, 捐赠 public munificence 慷慨彰显, Latin Epigraphy, 拉丁碑铭 Lavinium 拉维尼乌姆城, dendrophori "扛树" 人团体

Earlier studies of euergetism tended to see 'private liberality for public benefit' [1] as a one-way phenomenon, focusing on the status and deeds of the donors. Paul Veyne famously argued that euergetism served as a way for the elite to assert their social superiority, and that the benefactors' generosity was disinterested.[2] More recent studies, based primarily on the epigraphic evidence from the East, however, have emphasized the background negotiations behind the setting up of the gifts, the monitoring the donors received from their peers, the possible discrepancy between the expectations of the donors and the recipients, and the unease the imperial government and provincial cities sometimes felt toward munificence.[3] Based on a close examination of *AE* 1998. 282,[4] this paper contributes to this scholarship by shedding light on the tensions, negotiations, and compromises in the euergetic politics in the Western cities in the early third century.

Inscribed on three sides of a statue base, AE 1998. 282 preserved a series of correspondences in 227–228 CE pertaining to the establishment of a perpetual endowment of HS 20,000, of which the primary beneficiary would be the *collegium dendrophorum* of Lavinium.[5] The donor was a Gaius Servilius Diodorus, an otherwise unknown eques of African origin (*domo Girba ex Africa*; now Jerba, Tunisia) and a member of the priestly college of the *Laurentes Lavinates*, who were normally recruited from the equestrian order who did not themselves originate from Lavinium.[6] The sequence of events was set off by Diodorus' wife, Egnatia Salviana, who put up a statue (Text I), on September 7th, 227 (Text II), for her husband perhaps on the occasion of his

---

[1]　Paul Veyne's definition of euergetism (Veyne 1990: 10).

[2]　Veyne 1990: *passim*; eg. 148–49.

[3]　Rogers 1991a and 1991b: 91–100; Eck 1997: 326–31; Zuiderhoek 2007: 196–213.

[4]　For the *editio princeps* of the inscription, see Nonnis 1995: 248–62, which contains the images and transcript of the inscription, and a rich but primarily prosopographically oriented commentary. The numbering of the texts follows Nonnis 1995: 248–50.

[5]　For the *collegia dendrophorum* in the Roman Empire, see Liu 2009: 52–3 with further bibliography.

[6]　For recent studies of the *Laurentes Lavinates*, see Saulnier 1984: 525–31; Cooley 2000: 179.

appointment as a *Laurens Lavinas*.[1] On October 2nd, Diodorus wrote to senator Pontius Fuscus Ponti[anus], and asked him to order (*iubeas*) the praetors of Lavinium to take up the fund and to provide the *dendrophori* with the income of the said endowment for them to celebrate Diodorus' birthday and have a banquet along with his freedmen annually (Text IIIa). Pontianus then wrote to the praetors of the city of Lavinium concerning Diodorus' intention to establish the endowment, and urged them to make it happen (*ut… satis fiat*) (Text IIIb). Two days later on October 4th, the city of Lavinium notified Pontianus that it had accepted the endowment through the servile treasurer (*arkarius*) Asclepiades (Text IIIc). The dendrophori subsequently elected Diodorus as patron, and his wife mother of the collegium. The content of the patronage tablet, dated to August 18th, 228, was inscribed in full in our inscription (Text IV). So was Diodorus' letter responding to his being elected patron by the *dendrophori* (Text V), the last sentence of which seemed to suggest that the gift would inspire his fellow *Laurentes Lavinates* to emulate his euergetic deed.

Diodorus' gift itself was by no means unusual.[2] What is remarkable about this dossier is that it provides a rare glimpse into the (re)actions of the various interested parties (the donor, the city, a senator, the designated recipients, and the donor's peers) in the establishment of the gift, which makes it particularly valuable for a better understanding of the politics of munificence in the Roman cities. This paper attempts to suggest some ways of interpreting this dossier based on a close examination of the language of the correspondences, and the chronological sequence of events. It must be emphasized from the outset the difficulties involved. As David Nonnis mentioned in his *editio princeps* of the inscription, it provides the first attestations for several things such as a Laurens Lavinas making a donation to and putting up an inscription in the city of Lavinium, and the existence of a local *collegium dendrophorum*, which was closely connected with the cult of Magna Mater in many Western cities in the Empire. Valuable as this new information is, it also makes it difficult to ascertain the circumstances surrounding the benefaction.

- An immediately relevant question is "What role did the senator Pontianus play?" It is quite reasonable, with David Nonnis, to suggest that Pontianus the senator was acting in his capacity as *curator rei publicae*, although the inscription did not specify his title(s).[3] An intriguing position, the *curatores rei publicae* were not permanent appointments but their duties pertained fundamentally to the financial administration of civic communities including the general supervision of public funds and buildings.[4] It must be noted, however, that the overwhelming majority of the endowments in the Roman Empire did not mention any involvement of *curatores rei publicae* at all; nor was there any unequivocal indication in the literary, epigraphic or legal sources that benefactions, especially those that did not involve public property, normatively needed authorization of *curatores rei publicae*. In addition, legal sources seem to suggest that their tasks usually entailed the enforcement of promises (of money or public works) made to the cities, and protection of endowments from misuse rather than the establishment of foundations.[5] Therefore, even if Pontianus were indeed a *curator rei publicae*, it does not automatically explain why he was involved. It should be noted that a relatively large number of *curatores rei*

---

[1] Contr. Alföldy 2000, who suggests that the occasion might have been Diodorus' transfer from his procuratorship of Hispania Citerior (Inner Spain) to that in Hispania Superior (Upper Spain). But Diodorus' priestly status apparently received more emphasis in the correspondences (cf. Nonnis 2005: 261).

[2] For endowments, especially those for *collegia*, see Liu 2008: 231–56.

[3] Nonnis 1995: 259–60.

[4] *Dig.* 22.1.33.pr.–1; 50.12.1.pr.6, 50.10.5.1; 50.8.11.2, 50.8.12.2. Jacques 1984: 301–17; Burton 1979: 475; 2004: 337.

[5] Millar 1986: 316; Burton 2004: 337.

publicae, eleven altogether, have been attested in Lavinium from the mid–second century to fourth century CE. But what this means is not automatically clear. It may point to persistent or recurring financial mismanagement in the city.[1] If that were true, it may help explain why the curator's approval was important. But if the city's finance were indeed a mess, it would be puzzling why Diodorus wanted to entrust the fund to the city in the first place. The *Laurentes Lavinates* were not required to be stationed at Lavinium. Diodorus, however, apparently had estate or business operation(s) in the area of Lavinium, since he stipulated the participation of his freedmen in the annual ceremony funded by his endowment. It is not clear, however, whether Diodorus' wife, Egnatia Salviana, came from the same place as he did or not, as the *nomen gentilicium* Egnatia/Egnatius is widely attested in the Roman Empire. One may argue that since Diodorus, and perhaps his wife, did not originate from Lavinium, they may have had little knowledge of the city's financial crisis. Several scholars, however, have warned us that appointment of a *curator rei publicae* cannot be invariably taken as an secure indicator of the financial or political weakness in the city.[2] In Lavinium's case, the *curatores* rei publicae whose status is known were all senators of high rank with praetorian or consular status. Some of them even played the dual role, contradictory roles at that, of patron and *curator rei publicae*.[3] The consistently high status of these curators seemed "to be a reflection of imperial favour, and recognition of Lavinium's privileged position with regard to Rome".[4] But if we cannot see these *curatores rei publicae* as simply dispatched to intervene in local crises, further questions arise: Was Diodorus forced to seek support of the senator, because he was turned down by the city initially? Or did Diodorus choose to convey his wish to give a donation through the senator to give the gift more prestige by taking a top–down approach? We may never know the answer for sure. But circumstantial and internal evidence seems to suggest that Diodorus might have had experienced some difficulty or what he perceived as a delay in setting up the foundation, and at certain point he turned to Pontianus, whom he may know, which helped to expedite the establishment of the foundation. In what follows, I will elaborate on these points.

We must first note the absence of any praise or expression of gratitude from the city. The dossier contained mutual compliments between Diodorus and his wife, an economical but firm letter of support from Pontianus, and a highly formulaic and flattering decree from the *dendrophori*. But no direct correspondence between the city and Diodorus was documented. The letter from the city that was included in the dossier was addressed to the senator instead of Diodorus, and was brief, plain, and businesslike. This lack of interest on the part of the city was further confirmed by the fact that it was the donor, that is, Diodorus himself instead of the city that sent a letter to the senator. It was only after the praetors received the letter of the senator (*secundum praeceptum litterarum tuarum*) that the city accepted the money. In contrast, in the only other example that also involved a Western city, a benefactor, a *curator rei publicae*, it was the city that sent a letter concerning the benefaction to the curator.[5] In 113 CE, a Ulpius Vesbinus, an imperial freedman, sought permission from the city of Caere for a spot close to the basilica to build a *phretrium* for the local *Augustales* at his own expense. Before sending a letter to the curator on August 15, the local decurions had already agreed to grant Vesbinus the plot at a formal meeting on April 13, 113 CE. Sending the letter to the curator was more of a show of respect than necessity or

---

[1]　For the presence of **curatores rei publicae** as a sign of financial difficulties in the city, see, e.g., Duthoy 1979: 238.

[2]　D'Arms 1974: 106; Boatwright 2000: 76; Burton 2004.

[3]　*ILS* 6185; AE 1998. 280.

[4]　Cooley 2000:189. Cf. Duthoy 1979: 232–34; Camodeca 1980: 494–95; Jacques 1984: 196–97.

[5]　*CIL* 10.3614= *CIL* 10. 4347 = *ILS* 5918a.

procedural requirement. On September 12, the curator responded approvingly and praised the city's decision with highly rhetorical language. Returning to Diodorus' dossier, we find the city much more tacit and passive.

This is not to say, however, that the obligation to administer the endowment was simply imposed on the city out of the blue. Diodorus specifically requested Pontianus to write to the two praetors of Lavinium (Text IIIa). There were only two days apart between Diodorus' letter to Pontianus, and the praetors' response to Pontianus, notifying him of the acceptance of the endowment (Text IIIc). Are we to believe that the praetors could complete the transaction on such short notice without consulting the decurions? It is more reasonable to believe that Diodorus had already approached the city, that the matter had been discussed at the meeting of the decurions, but that the city had not made a definitive decision or taken any action in regard to the endowment. Was the city simply taking its time, for after all, it hadn't been even one month yet since the whole thing started with the erection of Diodorus' statue? Or was the city delaying because it had problems with the endowment? It may be relevant that very few endowments are known to have been entrusted to a third party, and very few endowments entrusted to the city left out the decurions as beneficiaries. I only know of one other inscription,[1] which recorded various gifts from a Manius Megonius Leo including a cash foundation of 10,000 sesterces and a vineyard dedicated/given exclusively to the *Augustales*. In that particular case, the donor had already made several donations to the city.[2] It would not be difficult to understand why he made the city the overseer of all of his endowments. Returning to Diodorus' case, the city may not be very thrilled by being merely entrusted the fund instead of being the direct beneficiary, but this factor alone should not constitute a strong reason for the city to turn down the offer. There were some general principles a city followed, or at least should have followed, in accepting gifts, among which the most important would be: first, the city was not to be burdened by the gift; second, the gift might enhance the status of the city.[3] The terms of Diodorus' endowment did not seem to contradict any of these two conditions. In fact, the terms seemed rather favorable to the city. 20,000 sesterces was a large amount to begin with, even at this date. In fact, 56% of all the perpetual endowments from the first three centuries were below HS 20,000. Noticeably, the interest rate, 5%, was set at the low end of the spectrum.[4] Duncan-Jones once suggested that the interest rate was in inverse correlation to the size of the endowment;[5] but there were too many exceptions to this 'rule' for it to account for the low interest rate of Diodorus' gift. For the same amount of 20,000 *sesterces*, for example, the interest rates could be as high as 12%.[6] The low interest rate may very likely have been the result of the negotiations between Diodorus and the city. Presumably, the city could even make a profit by lending out the money at higher interest rate than 5% but only providing the dendrophori with cash at the fixed rate of 5%, although we lack data from Lavinium to substantiate this point. If the terms were not unfavorable to the city, were there other factors such as Diodorus' non-native origin and/or the possible tension between the *Laurentes Lavinates* and the city that may have made the city uneasy? Again, we cannot answer this question with any certainty, but I will return to it later.

---

[1] *ILS 6469=CIL* 10. 114 (from Petelia, *Regio* III, Italy; dated to the reign of Antoninus Pius).

[2] For Manius Megonius Leo's benefactions, see Bossu 1982: 155–65.

[3] These were articulated in a number of inscriptions (e.g. *CIL* 10.3614= *CIL* 10. 4347 = *ILS* 5918a), and legal sources. For discussions on legal regulations, see Johnston 1985: 105–25; Zuiderhoek 2007: 197–200.

[4] For interest rates of endowments and further bibliography, see Liu 2008: 246–47.

[5] Duncan-Jones 1982: 134.

[6] E.g., *CIL* 6. 9254; 5. 1978.

Since Diodorus' birthday was November 12th, he was probably eager to have the foundation established before that date so that the celebrations could be carried out the following year. An impatient Diodorus, and a hesitant city: those factors may have combined to compel him to find a way out. Here is when Pontianus came to the scene. Ponitanus was probably in town at that time. This would not be surprising, especially since senatorial curators were often appointed to cities in whose territory they owned land.[1] He took particular interest in helping Diodorus, as suggested by the very fact that he wrote to Lavinium's praetors immediately after receiving Diodorus' letter. It is quite possible that they had known each other, as at one point of their careers, both of them served in Moesia Inferior. Pontianus was governor of Moesia Inferior from June/August to November/December 217.[2] Diodorus once served as *proc(urator) C(entenarius) Moes(iae) inf(erioris)*, the second of the five procurator positions he had served up until 227. Although the chronology is not entirely clear, the possibility of an overlap between Diodorus and Pontianus in Moesia Inferior cannot be excluded. The letter from Ponitanus can hardly be seen as superfluous. It made a difference: it sped up the setting up of the foundation, to say the least.

But why did Diodorus choose to set up an endowment for the *dendrophori*? In response to his cooptation of patron by the *dendrophori*, Diodorus wrote:

> I happily accept the bronze tablet presented to me on your behalf by Iulius Sabinus. I know that you are grateful of the gift that I gave you and that you will observe the provisions that I required especially since this gift would serve as an example for those of my priestly colleagues who desired the honor of the title of patron from you [*maxime cum ea res exemplo sit ceteris / consacerdotalib(us) meis optantib(us) a vobis honorem patronatus*].

The last sentence in Diodorus' letter to the dendrophori is full of intrigue. Here the *dendrophori* were emphasized as an honor-generating body. But more importantly, the wording seems to suggest that there was a special relationship between the *Laurentes Lavinates* and the *dendrophori* of Lavinium. Although the *dendrophori* in the Roman cities were frequently recipients of gifts,[3] no special relationship between *Laurentes Lavinates* and the *collegia dendrophorum* is known.[4] What we do know about the spheres of activities of the *collegia dendrophorum* in the Empire is that they were not only directly connected with the cult of Magna Mater but quite often also closely associated with imperial cult.[5] The *dendrophori's* participation in the emperor worship appeared to be more prominent than the other types of Roman *collegia*, as suggested by the their involvement in various religious rites such as ram-sacrifice (*criobolium*) and bull-sacrifice (*taurobolium*) for the well-being of the emperor (*pro salute imperatoris*),[6] and by such titles as *dendrophori Augustales*.[7] The *dendrophori's* roles in the imperial cult may account for the special relationship between the equestrian

---

[1] Eck 1979: 200-202.

[2] For Pontianus' career, see Boteva 1996: 248-52.

[3] E.g., CIL 10. 451; *AE* 1979. 140; 1987. 198.

[4] *AE* 1895. 120 may concern a priest of *M(ater) d(eum) M(agna) I(daea)*, who was also a *Laurens Lavinas*. But the fragmentary nature of the inscription precludes any certainty in the reconstruction of the inscription.

[5] Liu 2009: 52-4.

[6] *CIL* 8. 23401=*ILS* 4142 (Mactar, Africa; 284- 293 CE); *CIL* 8. 23400.

[7] E.g., *CIL* 13. 1937, 1961, 2026, 5154.

priestly group the *Laurentes Lavinates* and the *collegium dendrophorum* at Lavinum, especially since "the relationship between Lavinium and Rome was focused in part upon the person of the emperor himself."[1] The *dendophori' s* meeting place at Lavinium, for example, was specified as the Imperial cult building at the forum, *Caesareum quod est in foro*. This is very likely the site where a number of imperial portrait busts have been found. It may also be relevant that the *collegia dendrophorum* were particularly popular in the North Africa, where Diodorus came from.[2]

In the letter to the *dendrophori*, Diodorus also positioned himself as an inspiration (*exemplum*) for his priestly colleagues. Was this pure rhetoric? Or did it imply that the other *Laurentes Lavinates* had tried to earn the title of patrons of the *dendrophri* but failed? Although the dossier under discussion provides the first attestation to inscriptions put up by an individual *Laurens Lavinas* at Lavinium, Diodorus was not necessarily the first one who did it or who made a donation to the city. However, the scarcity of inscriptions put up by the *Laurentes Lavinates* either as a group or as individuals at Lavinium may point to the lack of connection or even tension between this *artificially* created priestly group and the town itself. If this were true, it could further explain why the city was not particularly enthusiastic in accepting the gift from Diodorus.

But then why did Diodorus entrust the fund to the city instead of directly to the *dendrophori*? David Nonnis suggested that Diodorus may have wanted to use the city as better guarantee for the effective uses of the fund.[3] As mentioned earlier in the paper, however, entrusting an endowment to a third party was not a common practice. In addition, unlike many of the inscriptions recording endowments, there was no emphasis on penalty of misuse in Diodorus' dossier.[4] Diodorus' anxiety for the moment seemed entirely focused on successfully setting up the foundation rather than ensuring its long-term viability. In my opinion, it seems more reasonable to find the explanation of entrusting the fund to the city in Diodorus' obsession with self-advertisement and self-glorification. In other words, he intended to give the gift a more 'public' or official appearance. This inclination can also be seen in his publication of the patronage tablet on the stone. The patronage tablets were normally inscribed metal plates intended to be displayed at the patron' s house.[5] He would have the actual plate hung on the wall of his house, but he also publicized it in a publicly accessible place. The inscription was found along with other honorific inscriptions in a colonnade building located near one of the main entrances of the city.[6] When the *dendrophori* offered the patronage tablet to Diodorus, they had not held the first anniversary meal yet, which was to be held less than three months later. Inscribing the correspondences between Diodorus and the *dendrophri* along with the other correspondences may also serve as a reminder to the city that the interest should be paid out to the *dendrophori* soon.

Conclusion

Centering entirely on Servilius Diodorus, the dossier paraded his dutiful wife, his priestly status as *Laurens Lavinas*, his own generosity, a senatorial friend, the gratitude of the dendrophori, his newly earned title of their patron, and a new endowment enabling the celebration of his birthdays by the *dendrophori* and his

---

① Cooley 2000: 180.

② For the geographical distribution of the *collegia dendrophorum*, see Liu 2009: 32.

③ Nonnis 1995: 259.

④ For examples of penalty clauses, see Liu 2008: 253.

⑤ For patronage tablets (*tabulae patronatus*), see Liu 2009: 235–38 with further bibliography.

⑥ Nonnis 1995: 235–36; Fenelli 1998: 110, 115.

freedmen. This entire business–correspondence–gone–public type of inscription was indicative of Diodorus' obsession with self–advertisement, and self–glorification. On surface, the dossier tells a positive story of generosity. Reading between the lines, however, the dossier also betrays tensions, negotiations, frustrations, and embarrassments. None of the honors that Diodorus received originated from the city. Although the inscription was found along with other honorific inscriptions in a public place, it was not one of the typical honorific inscriptions, where the city took an active role in granting honor.[1] The statue was put up by Diodorus' wife. His gift may not have met with enthusiasm by the decurions, and he had tü pull strings to speed up setting up the endowment. Being a new *Laurens Lavinas*, he may not have had knowledge of the history between the *Laurentes Lavinates* and the city. Yet, he was eager to claim his insider status, emphasizing repeatedly his status as 'priest' of Lavinium.[2] Diodorus' dossier seems to betray an outsider trying, with some frustrations, to enter the local network. It provides further testimony to euergetism as a site that showcased tensions, negotiations, compromises, and surprising twists and turns of events. This dossier, then, brings to light the many shades of public benefaction in the Roman cities. It serves as a reminder that most of the honorific inscriptions only recorded the end results of what may have been long processes, and tended to give a misleadingly rosy picture of private and public munificence.

Bibliography

Alföldy, G. 2000. *Provincia Hispania Superior. Philosophisch–historische Klasse der Heidelberger Akademie der Wissenschaften.* Heidelberg: Carl Winter.

Bossu, B. C. 1982. "M' Megonius Leo from Petelia (Regio III): a private benefactor from the local aristocracy." *ZPE* 45: 155 – 165.

Boteva, D. 1996. "On the cursus honorum of P. Fu⋯ Pontianus (PIR² F 496), Provincial Governor of Lower Moesia." *Zeitschrift für Papyrologie und Epigraphik* 110: 248 – 52.

Boatwright, M. T. 2000. *Hadrian and the Cities of the Roman Empire.* Princeton, N.J: Princeton University Press.

Burton, G. P. 1979. "The Curator Rei Publicae. Towards a Reappraisal." *Chiron* 9: 465–87.

——2004. "The Roman Imperial State, Provincial Governors, and the Public Finances of Provincial Cities, 27 B. C. –A.D. 235." *Historia* 53.3: 311–42.

Camodeca, G. 1980. "Ricerche sui curatores reipublicae." *Aufstieg und Niedergang der römischen Welt* 2.13: 453–534.

Cooley, A. 2000. "Politics and religion in the Ager Laurens." In Alison Cooley (ed.), *The Epigraphic Landscape of Roman Italy*, 173–191. London: Institute of Classical Studies (Bulletin of the Institute of Classical Studies Supplement 73).

Duthoy, R. 1979, "Curatores rei publicae en Occident durant le Principat. Recherches preliminaires sur l'apport des sources epigraphiques." *Ancient Society* 10: 171–238.

Eck, W. 1979. *Die staatliche Organisation Italiens in der hohen Kaiserzeit.* München: Beck.

——1997. "*Der Euergetismus im Funktionzusammenhang der kaiserzeitlichen Städte.*" In M. Christol and O.

---

[1]　The other honorific inscription whose text is complete and which was found alongside *AE* 1998.282 concerns a senator of consular rank, who had also served, among others, as patron and curator of Lavinium. The inscription, apparently put up by the city, only recorded his cursus honorum without any reference to his deeds or benefactions. (*AE* 1998. 280)

[2]　Text IIIa, line 4: *in civitate Laurentum Lavinatium ubi sacerdotalis sum* (in the city of Lavinium where I am a priest); Text IIIb, line 4: *sacerdotalis splendidissimae civitatis vestrae* (priest of your splendid city); Text V, lines 5–6: *ceteris consacerdotalib(us) meis* (my fellow priests).

Masson (eds.), *Actes du Xe Congrès international d'épigraphie grecque et latine, Nîmes, 4–9 octobre 1992*, 305–31. Paris: Publications de la Sorbonne.

Fenelli, M. 1998. "Lavinium." In *Scavi e ricerche archeologiche dell' Università di Roma La Sapienza*, 109–19. Rome: L'Erma di Bretschneider.

Jacques, F. 1984. *Le privilege de liberte: Politique imperiale et autonomie municipale dans les cites de l'Occident romain (161– 244)*. Rome: École française de Rome.

Johnston, D. 1985. "Munificence and Municipia: Bequests to towns in classical Roman Law." *Journal of Roman Studies* 75: 105‒25.

Liu, J. 2008. "The Economy of Endowments: the case of Roman associations." In K. Verboven, K. Vandorpe and V. Chankowski-Sable (eds.), 'Pistoi dia tèn technèn'. *Bankers, loans and archives in the Ancient World. Studies in honour of Raymond Bogaert*. Studia Hellenistica 44, 231–56. Leuven: Peeters.

——2009. *Collegia Centonariorum: the Guilds of Textile Dealers in the Roman West*. Leiden: Brill.

Millar, F. 1986. "Italy and the Roman Empire: Augustus to Constantine Italy and the Roman Empire: Augustus to Constantine." *Phoenix* 40. 3: 295–318.

Nonnis, D. 1995. "Un patrono dei dendrofori di Lavinium: Onori e munificenza in un dossier epigrafico di età severiana." *Atti della Pontificia Accademia Romana di Archeologia* 68: 235–62.

Rogers, G. M. 1991a. *The Sacred Identity of Ephesos*. London and New York: Routledge.

——1991b. "Demosthenes of Oenoanda and Models of Euergetism." *Journal of Roman Studies* 81: 91–100.

Sartori, M. 1989. "*Osservazioni sul ruolo del curator rei publicae*." *Athenaeum* 67: 5–20.

Saulinier, C. 1984. "Laurens Lavinas. Quelques remarques à propos d'un sacerdoce équestre à Rome." *Latomus* 43: 517–33.

Veyne, P., O. Murray, and B. Pearce. 1990. *Bread and circuses: Historical sociology and political pluralism*. London: Allen Lane, The Penguin Press.

Zuiderhoek, A. 2007. "The ambiguity of munificence." *Historia* 55: 196–213.

罗马边界与帝国极限

冯定雄　浙江海洋学院

摘要：罗马的"边界"观念是不断变化的。最初的罗马，以"边界"进行划分，由护界神保护。到共和国时代，罗马的理想"边界"是"已知世界"。帝国建立后，罗马人为自己编造了世界帝国"边界"理想的神话，这一神话一直延续到帝国的灭亡。表示罗马现实边界的术语 limes 在罗马国家发展过程中，意义不断发生变化，从最初的泥泞道路演变成一个军事、政治术语，体现了罗马从狭小城邦国家走向庞大帝国政治空间的变化。但是，罗马人的理想"边界"与 limes 所能包括的现实范围之间却存在着明显的矛盾，无限的理想"边界"只是罗马人的想像极限，而 limes 所包括的现实范围才是帝国的现实统治极限。

关键词：罗马边界；世界帝国；统治极限

Abstract：The boundary ideal of the Roman state was variational. At the beginning, Rome was divided by 'boundary', protected by *Terminus*, the boundary god. To the Repubic of Rome, Roman ideal boundary was the Known World. After the establishment of the Roman empire, the Romans were inventing a myth of the world empire 'boundary' for themselves and held it until the destruction of the empire. In the realization process of the Roman world empire ideal, meaning of the term *limes* which contained the significance of boundary was changing constantly. The original meaning of *limes* which means muddy road had been turned into a military and political term. This transition reflects the political space changes of Rome from narrow city state to the vast empire. However, there was an obvious contradiction between the Romans' ideal 'boundary' and the *limes* which contained the real boundary. The endless ideal 'boundary' was only the imagination, the real boundary limited by *limes* was the true limit of Roman rule climax.

KeyWords：Roman boundary, World empire, *Limes*, Roman rule climax

　　罗马人的"边界"观念经历了从建城以来到帝国时代的不同变化，其最终的理想目标是要建立一个统治全世界的世界帝国。表示罗马边界的术语 limes 也在随着国家的变化而不断变化，从最初指泥泞道路，后来演变成一个含义复杂的军事、政治概念，体现出罗马国家版图的扩大。国内学术界鲜有涉及罗马边界观念的论著，对 limes 这一术语的研究也往往只涉及到它的道路这一含义，对其它意义的研究几乎一片空白，[1]国外学者的研究也主要集中于罗马"道路"这一含义，[2]或者罗马"边境"这一含义，[3]对于罗马"边界"观念的变化、limes 含义的变化及它们所反映的罗马国家版图及其世界帝国理想的关系研究比较薄弱，本文拟就在这方面做一点尝试。

一　罗马人的"边界"观念

最初的罗马人生存环境非常恶劣，周边有很多强大的部落随时可能威胁到他们的生存。罗马建城以后，他们的首要任务是保卫罗马城，保住他们的生存空间。这时候的"（罗马）空间是以城市为中心的。"[4]罗马最早的城镇是所谓的方形罗马（Roma Quadrata），位于帕拉丁山上。据塔西佗说，城界是由罗慕路斯确定的："设置有青铜像的牛场是作为城界的犁沟的起点。"[5]因此，罗马人最初的"边界"观念是能够维持他们生存的"城界"。现代学术界一般认为罗马城的疆界是由第二位国王努玛·波皮利乌斯确立的，并由护界神特米努斯（Terminus）守卫。特米努斯神不仅划分领土范围，也划分财产范围，同时还是家庭保护神。[6]努玛颁布法令规定，任何破坏和移动奉献给疆界神的石头的人，都被认为是对神祇的亵渎。特米里亚节作为一种宗教仪式，一直延续了下来。[7]该神最初的地位并不高，其祭祀的地方位于山洞，奉献血、火灰及其它牺牲品，后来它的权力和地位才得到了加强。[8]尽管其地位并不突出，但据说当罗马修建朱庇特神庙的时候，在所有地位较低的众神中护界神特米努斯拒绝让位给朱庇特。这一传说显示了特米努斯神的牢固地位。[9]该神也成为罗马国家永不衰

① 国内研究罗马道路的文章主要有：宫秀华：《罗马帝国时期道路信息网的建设》，《常熟高等专科学校学报》2001 年第 1 期；冯定雄：《古罗马在非洲的道路建设》，《西亚非洲》2008 年第 3 期；《罗马共和国时期的道路建设》，《古代文明》2009 年第 3 期；《罗马道路与帝国统治》，《河北学刊》2011 年第 3 期。

② 国外学者研究罗马道路的专著很多，其中最具代表性的综合性著作主要有：Victor W. Von Hagen, *The Roads that Led to Rome*, Cleveland and New York: The World Publishing Company, 1967; Raymond Chevallier, *Roman Roads*, Translated by N. H. Field, London: B. T. Batsford Ltd, 1976; Romolo Augusto Staccioli, *Roads of the Romans*, Los Angeles and California: L'erma di Bretschneider, 2003. 区域性研究专著及论文更多，在此不一一列举。

③ 国外研究罗马边境线的著作比较多，这里择其要者罗列：Kennedy, D. L., *Archaeological Explorations on the Roman Frontier in North-East Jordan: The Roman and Byzantine Military Installations and Road Network on the Ground and from the Air*, BAR International Series 134, Oxford : British Archaeological Reports, 1982. Dyson, Stephen L., *The Creation of the Roman Frontier*, Princeton, NJ: Princeton University Press, 1985.A. D. Lee, *Information and Frontiers: Roman Foreign Relations in Late Antiquity*, New York: Cambridge University Press, 1993; Shape, M. E., *The Western Frontiers of Imperial Rome*, New York: Armonk, 1994.Cherry, Divid, *Frontier and Society in Roman North Africa*, Oxford: Clarendon Press, 1998. Jackson, Robert B., *At Empire's Edge: Exploring Rome's Egyptian Frontier*, New Haven & London: Yale University Press, 2002. "罗马边境学"（Roman Frontier Studies）已经成为西方学术界的一个专门学科分支，从 1949 年起，罗马边境研究国际学术会议多次在西方国家举行，每次会议后，都有论文集出版（仅第 4 次会议例外），这些论文集是其成果的集中体现。最近一次会议（第 21 届）于 2009 年 4 月 16–19 日在英国的达勒姆大学举行，其会议论文集《罗马世界的边界》（*Frontiers in the Roman World*）于 2011 年出版。

④ 唐纳德·R·凯利：《多面的历史》，陈恒、宋立宏译，上海三联书店，2003 年，第 88 页。

⑤ 塔西佗：《编年史》，王以铸、崔妙因译，北京：商务印书馆，1997 年，XII，24。瓦罗在《论拉丁语》中说："许多人按照伊特拉斯坎的仪节建立拉丁姆的城市。他们用牛、公牛、母牛联成一组沿着城域内部犁一圈沟（由于宗教方面的原因他们在选定吉日做这件事），这样他们就可以用一道沟和一道墙来保卫自己。他们把犁出了土的地方称为沟（fossa），而把抛到里面的土称为墙（murus）。"（Varro, *On the Latin Language*, Cambridge, MA: Harvard University Press, 1958, V, 143.）

⑥ H. H. Scullard, *Festivals and ceremonies of the Roman Republic*, London: Cornell University Press, 1981, pp.17–18.

⑦ Dionysius of Halicarnassus, *The Roman Antiquities*, Cambridge: Harvard University Press, 1937, II, 74.

⑧ Ovid, *Fasti*, II. (http://www.poetryintranslation.com/PITBR/Latin/OvidFastiBkTwo.htm#_Toc69367696)

⑨ Livy, *From the Founding of the City*, Cambridge, MA: Harvard University Press, 1976, I,55; Varro, *On the Latin Language*, L.L.v.74.

落的象征。①后人以此为依据，并从中得出推论，认为这是一种无可怀疑的朕兆，表明罗马国家的边界将绝不后退。这一预言的提出，对罗马边界的扩张起着极大的作用。②

到共和国时代，特别是到共和国后期，随着罗马国家版图的急剧增加，作为罗马"边界"的"城界"逐渐失去了最初的意义。罗马"边界"的观念延伸到了整个"已知世界"。生活在共和与帝制交替时期的科学家斯特拉波在其《地理学》一书中，把整个世界分为"已知世界"和可能有人居住的"未知世界"，并声明自己"为科学目的和国家需要，最重要的关心是要通过最简单的方式对落入我们版图的这部分地球的形状和大小予以说明。"③他所说的"落入我们版图的这部分地球"在很大程度上就是所谓的"已知世界"，而这个"已知世界"在很大程度上也等同于"罗马世界"，因此，到共和国后期，罗马人的"边界"观念在一定程度上已经延伸到了整个"已知世界"，而他们大规模向外扩张就是要不断地拓展他们的边界，即"未知世界"。

到帝国时代，罗马人的"边界"观念已经不仅仅局限于"已知世界"了，而是全世界（或整个领土世界 [Orbis terrarium]），其"边界"是整个世界帝国的边界。在罗马世界帝国边界的编织过程中，维吉尔的颂歌最具代表性。他在《埃涅阿斯纪》中"塑造"了罗马世界帝国边界的理想。埃涅阿斯在游历冥界时，他的父亲安奇塞斯明确指出："罗马人，你记住，你应当用你的权威统治万国。"④他还借主神朱庇特之口说过名言："对他们（即罗马人），我不施加任何空间或时间方面的限制，我已经给了他们无限的统治权。"⑤在为奥古斯都唱赞歌的同时，维吉尔也表达了罗马人建立世界帝国边界的理想，那就是没有任何"空间"和"时间"限制的"无限统治权"。

对于这一理想，奥古斯都本人在他的《功德碑》（Res Gestae）作了更详细和具体的解释。他极度自豪地宣称："我在全世界的陆地和海域进行内外战争，作为胜者，我宽免了所有请求饶恕的公民。"⑥在罗马的观念中，整个领土世界，即"全世界的陆地和海域"就是他们的罗马世界（Orbis Romanus），其范围是全人类、全世界。奥古斯都的这些话，不仅是他本人意志的写照，更代表了当时罗马国家的理想。这一理想与他们"祖先"制定的没有任何空间和时间限制的世界范围是一致的。当然，理论上讲，奥古斯都所说的"全世界"，只是指当时罗马人所知道的全部区域，尽管此时的罗马根本就没有统治它所知道的全世界，但这丝毫也不影响他们的世界帝国的理想边界。

帝国时代的罗马人事实上已经把奥古斯都视为全人类的统治者，奥古斯都本人也获得了无数关于他统治整个世界的赞誉。贺拉斯在《抒情诗》（Odes）中称奥古斯都是"人类保护者"。⑦奥维德在《罗马历书》中称奥古斯都是"人类之父和人类守卫者"。⑧公元12—13年，纳尔波城在建立奥古斯都的统治仪式时，规定在1月7日举行牺牲献祭仪式，因为这一天"奥古斯都已经宣布了他对整个世界的统治。"该城还计划在9月23日举行牺牲献祭仪式，因为"这一天，时代的福音已经给予奥古斯都作为世界的统治者。"⑨后来，皮萨城在其诏令中，提到奥古斯都时很明确地说，奥古斯都是"整个罗马帝国的守卫者和全世界的保护者"。⑩

① Sir William Smith, *A Classical Dictionary of Greek and Roman Biography Mythology and Geography*, Revisd throughout and in part Rewritten by G. E. Marindin, London: John Murray, 1932, p.928.
② 爱德华·吉本：《罗马帝国衰亡史》，上册，黄宜思、黄雨石译，北京：商务印书馆，2004年，第24页。
③ Strabo, *Geography*, Cambridge, MA: Harvard University Press, 1949, II. 5. 13.
④ 维吉尔：《埃涅阿斯纪》，杨周翰译，北京：人民文学出版社，1984年，第163页。
⑤ 维吉尔：《埃涅阿斯纪》，第10页。
⑥ 这里采用的是张楠、张强先生的译文，参见张楠、张强：《〈奥古斯都功德碑〉译注》，《古代文明》2007年第3期。
⑦ Victor Ehrenberg and A. H. M. Jones, *Documents Illustrating the Reigns of Augustus and Tiberius*, Oxford: Clarendon Press, 1955, no. 100.
⑧ Ovid, Fasti I–II.
⑨ Victor Ehrenberg and A. H. M. Jones, *Documents Illustrating the Reigns of Augustus and Tiberius*, no. 100.
⑩ Victor Ehrenberg and A. H. M. Jones, *Documents Illustrating the Reigns of Augustus and Tiberius*, no. 69.

奥古斯都的继任者延续着他开创的"世界帝国",走向真正的繁荣,特别是到"五贤帝"时代其世界帝国梦想达到了极致。这也难怪阿庇安在《罗马史》序言中难以抑制其洋溢之情:"自从皇帝出现到现在将近二百多年了,……他们占有陆地上和海洋上最好的部分,他们的目的,就整体来说,是以谨慎的办法来保全他们的帝国,……他们用许多军队驻守在帝国四周,把整个陆地和海洋上一带,好象一个完整的要塞一样地驻防起来。"①作为历史学家的阿庇安所阐述的思想,在很大程度上也是罗马人和罗马帝国的理想表达。

罗马人的世界帝国"边界"观念在罗马社会根深蒂固,他们认为自己的责任"更多地是要通过边界把原著民变成罗马人而不是要把自己的人民带到边界之外的荒野不毛之地。"②他们要承担的是世界帝国的责任,扮演的是世界帝国的角色。直到帝国晚期,这一观念仍然在罗马人心目中认为是理所当然的。据阿米阿努斯·马尔凯努斯记载,提奥多西称自己的皇帝瓦伦提里安是"世界之主"。③公元 417 年 10 月,路提利乌斯·纳玛提亚努斯在离开罗马前往其故乡高卢时,他含着眼泪告别这座城市,怀着敬畏的心情对它发出了由衷的赞美:"您把各俱特色的不同民族整合成一个单一的祖国……您一度把一个(罗马)城市变成了一个世界。"④罗马人的世界帝国"边界"观念一直持续到帝国的灭亡时(尽管这一边界理想从未真正实现过),他们才不得不面对残酷的现实。但即便如此,这一观念仍然保持在欧洲人的心目中,查士丁尼企图恢复罗马帝国的努力、"既非神圣、更非罗马"的神圣罗马帝国的出现、希特勒的世界帝国之梦、美国的世界警察角色都可以在罗马人的世界帝国观念里找到渊源。

二 罗马 *limes* 的演变

在罗马人"边界"观念随着国家的发展而不断变化的同时,表示"边界"的术语 *limes*,其含义也在不断地变化。在罗马军事史和边界史上,*limes* 是一个非常重要的术语,有学者认为它"是一个关于要塞、军营、殖民地、道路和运河等能组成边境防御网络的复杂体的普通术语。"⑤事实上,这一术语并不普通,它不仅含义比较多,而且衍生出来的意义也比较丰富,更重要的是,它与罗马人的"边界"观念相协调,从最初的实体概念演变成后来的抽象意义,反映出罗马国家的军事和政治特征。⑥

limes 来自于 *limus*(泥泞,泥浆),最初的意思是指光秃秃的泥路,通常指以泥泞道路形成的边界或者岔路。罗马帝国建立后,这一术语的用法开始发生了变化。首先,在公元 1—2 世纪,它的含义变成了军事道路。公元 10 年提比略在对外战争中经常在敌人的领土上建造军事道路,"他深入了更遥远的内地,建造了军事道路(*limites*)。"⑦塔西佗也多次在这一意义上使用这一术语,公元 14 年日耳曼尼库斯在征服莱茵河地区时,"罗马军队利用一次急行军穿过了凯西亚森林和提比略开始构筑的军事道路(中译本译为'边界')。他们在这条军事道路(中译本'这道边界')

① 阿庇安:《罗马史》,谢德风译,北京:商务印书馆,1979 年,序言,7。
② Stephen L. Dyson, *The Creation of the Roman Frontier*, New Jersey: Princeton University Press, 1985, p. 5.
③ Ammianus Marcellinus, *The Later Roman Empire*(A.D.354–378), 29.5.46.
④ Alan Cameron, "Rutilius Namatianus, St. Augustine, and the Date of the *De Reditu*." JRS 57, No. 1/2 (1967), pp. 31–39.
⑤ Steven K. Drummond, Lynn H. Nelson, *The Western Frontiers of Imperial Rome*, New York: M. E. Sharpe, Inc. 1994, p. 242.
⑥ 以色列著名古代史专家本杰明·伊萨克对 limes 及 limitanei 这两个术语进行过专文讨论,参见 Benjamin Isaac, "The Meaning of the Terms Limes and Limitanei", *JRS*, vol.78.(1988). 该文很有借鉴意义,但它讨论仅仅局限于这两个术语的具体含义。
⑦ C. Velleius Paterculus, *The Roman History*, Cambridge, MA: Harvard University Press, 1924, II, 120.

上筑营。"①公元 16 年，日耳曼尼库斯在莱茵河地区建造了新的军事道路："此外，从阿里索要塞到莱茵河这一整块地方，都用新修的各军事道路（limitibus）和堤道（中译本：一道壁垒和工事）被彻底地防御起来了。"②这里使用的是 limes 的复数形式，这说明，日耳曼尼库斯在这一地区建造的并不止一条军事道路，而是整个地区的军事道路网络体系，以方便在新入侵地区的军队运送。卡西乌斯·狄奥在《罗马史》中说，公元 9 年，昆提利乌斯·瓦鲁斯的军队遭到了日耳曼人的攻击，原因是罗马人不得不深入森林，在必要的地方建造军事道路和桥梁。③类似的情形还发生在图密善皇帝时期，"图密善皇帝在 120 英里军事道路的帮助下，不仅改变了战争的进程，而且还在他们的隐藏地牢牢地控制住了敌人。"④塔西佗在《日耳曼尼亚志》中也提到了高卢人在莱茵河地区建造军事道路的情形："那是从高卢去的一些鲁莽的冒险者，……接着修建了一条军事道路，卫戍部队也向前移来。"⑤以上这些关于军事道路的记载来源于公元 1 到 2 世纪早期的文献，由此可见，到公元 1 — 2 世纪时，limes 的含义由原来的泥路演变成了军事道路，这一演变与罗马的对外扩张有密切的联系。

在 limes 含义转向军事道路的时候，它也开始具有"边界"等含义。塔西佗在《阿古利可拉传》中记载："这时候，敌人所威胁的不只是帝国的边境和河岸，而是官军的冬营和国境之内的本土。"⑥在这里，塔西佗把"帝国的边境"与"河岸"相对比而提出，很明显，它指的应该是帝国的"陆地边界"。在《帝王传略·哈德良传》中，同样的提法再次出现："在许多不是通过河流而是通过陆上边界把野蛮人和罗马帝国相分开的地区，他（哈德良）都用高木桩打入地下并加固以便形成隔护栏。"⑦在《拉丁颂词》中，limes 一词既包括"边界"，也包括有"边境、边境线"的意思："在过去，沿莱茵河的自然障碍本身就是一条边界，保护罗马诸行省免遭野蛮人的残暴侵犯。"⑧在不列颠行省，其边界是用城墙来划分的，如著名的哈德良城墙。在希罗第安的《罗马帝国史》史中也有类似的提法："奥古斯都都通过障碍、河流、壕沟、山地及很难穿越的沙漠之地环绕帝国以加强其边境防御。"⑨从这里可以看出，limes 它的含义不仅仅是军事道路，而且还包括军事道路在内的边境线，其实体意义在逐渐发生变化，其所指范围也越来越广。

从公元 3 世纪末起，特别是 4 世纪以后，limes 这一术语又被作为"边境地区"的意义加以使用。如《拉丁颂词》在讲到公元 297 年的君士坦丁提乌斯时说："……日耳曼和拉埃提亚边境地区（limites）已经延伸到了远至多瑙河的源头。"⑩这里很明显是指边境地区，而不是单纯的边界线或军事道路。阿米阿努斯·马尔凯努斯说："曼德里克是后来的阿拉伯行省边境地区（Arabian limes）的长官。"⑪显然这里指的是边境地区。《帝王传略·三十僭主传》对伊索里亚描写道："尽管是在帝国的中部，

---

① Tacitus, *Annal*, Cambridge, MA: Harvard University Press, 1986, I, 50; 塔西佗：《编年史》, I, 50。

② Tacitus, *Annal*, II, 7; 塔西佗：《编年史》, II, 7。

③ Cassius Dio, *Roman History*, Cambridge, MA: Harvard University Press, 1924, LVI, 20–22.

④ Sextus Julius Frontinus, *Stratagems*, Cambridge, MA: Harvard University Press, 1925, I, 3, 10. 图密善于公元 83 年延伸了前线，并在道路上设置了障碍。

⑤ Tacitus, *Agricola. Germania. Dialogue on Oratory*, Cambridge, MA: Harvard University Press, 1960, 29.（这里的翻译与中译本有所出入，参见塔西佗：《日耳曼尼亚志》, 马雍、傅正元译，商务印书馆，1997 年，第 70 页。）这一地区原先为日耳曼人所占据，当日耳曼人东迁以后，由罗马人占据而拨给高卢人居住。

⑥ Tacitus, *Agricola*, 41, 2..

⑦ SHA, *Hadrianus*. 12, 6.(http://www.thelatinlibrary.com/sha/hadr.shtml)

⑧ *In Praise of Later Roman Emperors*, Translated by C.E.V. Nixon and Barbara Rodgers, Berkeley: University of California Press, 1994, x (II) 7, 3.

⑨ Herodian of Antioch's, *History of the Roman Empire*, Berkeley & Los Angeles: University of California Press, 1961, II, 11, 5.

⑩ *In Praise of Later Roman Emperors*, Translated by C.E.V. Nixon and Barbara Rodgers, Berkeley: University of California Press, 1994, VIII (v) 3, 3.

⑪ Ammianus Marcellinus, *The Later Roman Empire*(A.D.354–378), Selected and translated by Walter Hamilton with an Introduction and Notes by Andrew Wallace–Hadrill, London: Penguin Books, 1986, 3.5.

但它好像是在边境地区（*limites*）一样被一种新型的哨所包围。"①这里是把帝国中部地区与边境地区相对比。普罗柯比在《秘史》中也提到："到目前为止，罗马皇帝在帝国所有边境尤其是东部派驻了大批军队，以保卫帝国的边境地区（*limites*），抵御波斯人和萨拉森人的入侵。"②由此可以看出，到罗马帝国后期，*limes* 这一术语的含义已经发生了很大的变化，与最初的含义已经相去甚远，它代表的是一种行政概念，③是帝国政治空间范围的一种反映。

从 *limes* 这一术语本身的含义来看，它经历了一个变化过程，这个过程其实也是罗马人"边界"观念变化的过程，它是伴随着罗马国家的扩张而互动的。在 *limes* 上服务的士兵则被称为 *limitanei*（或者 *riparienses, ripenses*，即边境士兵），他们的长官称为边境长官（dux）。边境士兵与 *limes* 有着非常密切的关系。④

Limitanei 是君士坦丁及其后继者时代才有的一个关于边境军队的名称。它由骑兵（*cunei equitum*）和步兵（*legiones, cohortes, auxilia*）组成，由边境长官指挥。据《帝王传略·塞维鲁·亚历山大传》记载："（亚历山大）把从敌人那里获取的土地交给了边境地区的边境长官及士兵们。"⑤这些边境士兵常常驻守一个固定地方，但有时他们也被作为"伪宫廷卫队"（pseudocomitatenses）的野战军队组编成军团，有时甚至会晋升到宫廷卫队（comitatenses）。⑥根据琼斯⑦和伊萨克⑧的研究认为，*Limitanei* 是在边境长官指挥下的军事团体，是被分配到特定边境地区的所有军队。事实上，*limitanei* 这一术语只是在机动野战军出现后，为了把他们与前线军队相区才出现的，他们的主要任务是确保道路的安全，特别是边境地区的道路安全。他们控制帝国边界的行动，当边界地区发生骚乱的时候，他们要保持他们所在地区的安全。由此可见，边境士兵是在 *limes* 演变成边界、边境、边境地区等含义后才相伴生而出现的一个军事、政治概念。

从前面的演变中可以看出，*limes* 从罗马国家早期的泥泞之路，最后演变成一种比较抽象的军事、行政概念，它的演变实际上就是罗马国家从狭小城邦国家走向庞大帝国的演变。在这一过程中，罗马边界的发展演化更直接地体现罗马政治、军事统治主张的实现，体现了罗马人"统治万国"的军事霸权和政治空间范围，因为"与罗马人能力密切相关的是罗马人的空间观念，罗马人的空间观念主要是用边界来界定的。"⑨从 *limes* 这一术语的演变，不难看出，它的"演进反映了地方服务和权力归属被赋予了一种法律形式。"⑩这种法律当然是罗马的法律及其政治模式，适用范围包括其"边

① SHA, *Tyranni Triginta*. 26.(http://www.thelatinlibrary.com/sha/30.shtml)

② Procopius, *Secret History*, translated by Richard Atwater, Ann Arbor, MI: University of Michigan Press, 1961, 26. 英译本把 limites 译为 boundaries，中译本把它译成"边界"，这两种译法都没有问题。在中译本中，其"边界"也可以理解为边境地区，笔者在这里把它译为"边境地区"，是为了更准确地理解该术语的含义。中译本参见（东罗马）普罗柯比：《秘史》，吴舒屏、吕丽萍译，上海三联书店，2007 年，第 117 页。

③ Benjamin Isaac, "The Meaning of the Terms Limes and Limitanei", *JRS*, vol.78.(1988).

④ 与 limes 相关的另一个词语是 *limitatio*，通常指土地划分。（O. A. W. Dilke, *Greek and Roman Maps*, London: Thames and Hudson LTD., 1985, pp.89–90.）

⑤ SHA, *Seversu Alexander*. 58.(http://www.thelatinlibrary.com/sha/hadr.shtml)

⑥ N. G. L. Hammond and H. H. Scullard, *The Oxford Classical Dictionary*, 2nd edn. Oxford: Clarendon Press, 1970, p. 610. 宫廷卫队是君士坦丁皇帝组织的罗马野战军队两支部队中的一支，即被称为皇帝"卫队"（comitatus）的那一支。它由精锐部队（vexillationes）（由 500 人的骑兵队为单位组成）和普通军团（由 1000 人的步兵队为单位组成），由军事长官（magistri militum）指挥。

⑦ A. H. M. Jones, *The Later Roman Empire, 284–602: A social, Economic, and Administrative Survey*, Vol. I., Baltimore: The Johns Hopkins University Press, 1986, pp.649–654.

⑧ Benjamin Isaac, "The Meaning of the Terms Limes and Limitanei", *JRS*, vol.78.(1988).

⑨ A. D. Lee, *Information and Frontiers: Roman Foreign Relations in Late Antiquity,* New York: Cambridge University Press, 1993, p. 86.

⑩ Raymond Chevallier, *Roman Roads*, Translated by N. H. Field, London: B. T. Batsford LTD. 1976. p. 17.

界"内的"全世界"。

三 罗马"边界"与帝国极限

罗马人的"边界"观念在不断地变化，*limes* 的含义也在不断扩大，到帝国时代，罗马人的理想"边界"似乎已经通过其世界帝国边界范围确定下来了，从而使二者实现了内在的统一。但是，罗马人的理想"边界"却与 *limes* 所能确定的现实范围之间却存在着明显的矛盾性。

首先，罗马人的理想"边界"只是一种民族野心的极度膨胀，是想像中的理想范围，而 *limes* 所能确定的范围，无论是实体意义的指代还是抽象含义的表述，都是现实世界的表现，在理想与实现之间，二者不可能达到绝对完美的统一。在罗马人的理想"边界"中，他们的范围是"整个世界"、"整个人类"、"全世界的陆地和海域"、"没有任何空间或时间限制的统治权"。到图拉真时代，帝国的版图达到了整个罗马历史上的极致，罗马皇帝成为了"全人类主人"或"全世界主人"（*dominus totius orbis, or dominus orbis terrarum*）。"到公元 4 世纪，'全世界的主人'已经变成帝国题铭中的一个常用语。这一时期的写实作家们即使意识到'全世界'只是'罗马世界'，但他们还是很乐意使用这一术语。"①到了帝国后期，罗马人"慢慢竟然随便把罗马帝国和整个地球混为一谈了。"②

但是，在罗马语言中能真正书写出来的边界（*limes*）却远非罗马人想像中理想"边界"。图拉真时代，帝国版图达到最大，但它与罗马人想像中的"全世界的陆地和海域"范围却相去甚远。事实上，奥古斯都本人也承认还有"未归服于我们帝国的部族"，地理学家们更清醒罗马国家的版图不仅与整个世界范围相去甚远，就连罗马人"已知世界"的版图也远未达到。③现实中的 *limes* 能标示的仅仅是"罗马世界"与"非罗马世界"的界限而已，远非他们想像中的理想"边界"，阿米阿努斯·马尔凯努斯说，4 世纪，罗马在与利米干特人④谈判时，他们还请求罗马能够接纳这些遥远地方的居民，让他们能保留在"罗马世界"里。⑤这里再次明确地说明了"罗马世界"与"非罗马世界"的界限。理想"边界"只是罗马人民族野心极度膨胀的体现，而 *limes* 所能确定的范围，才是现实"罗马世界"空间的表现，二者是不可能达到完美统一的，只不过，为了帝国统治需要，罗马人想像与现实的矛盾好像从来就是合理的。

其次，罗马帝国所处的时代局限不允许它有无限制、超极限的能力保持其理想"边界"与现实范围的内在同一。不断对外扩张、版图无限制扩大的前提是无限制、超极限的经济、军事能力。这一方面表现在对边界扩张的征服上，另一方面则表现在对已征服边界的守卫上，无论是征服还是守卫，罗马国家都不可能具备无限制的能力。事实上，罗马的这种世界边界帝国之梦并不是什么新鲜事，早在罗马国家还仅仅局限于意大利半岛的时候，亚历山大大帝就曾做过世界帝国主人之梦。但是，"世界征服的梦想与古代技术实践局限性之间的冲突自亚历山大实现其梦想的时候就一直存在：正是他的成就使得世界征服看起来成为可能，但他的战争又同时使希腊地理学家意识到他所涉及的范围是多么的小！"⑥罗马帝国在东部的扩张，远不能与亚历山大相提并论，就连离罗马人的"已知世界"的版图也远未达到。按照吉本的说法，前现代经济是不能维持庞大帝国边境防御所需的数目庞大的卫戍军队的。⑦尽管罗马帝国通过它的军队已经获得并消融了被征服地区，但它并没有能力通过它的

---

① Clifford Ando, *Imperial Ideology and Provincial Loyalty in the Roman Empire*, p.320.
② 爱德华·吉本：《罗马帝国衰亡史》，上册，第 26 页。
③ C.R. Whittaker, *Rome and Its Frontiers: The Dynamics of Empire*, London: Routledge, 2004, pp. 63–65.
④ 利米干特人（*Limigantes*）是位于东匈牙利和西罗马尼亚一带的混杂民族，其名称可能来自于 *limitis gentis*（边境民族）。
⑤ Ammianus Marcellinus, *The Later Roman Empire*(A.D.354–378), 19.11.6.
⑥ Clifford Ando, *Imperial Ideology and Provincial Loyalty in the Roman Empire*, p.320.
⑦ 爱德华·吉本：《罗马帝国衰亡史》，上册，第 97 – 98 页。

军队来保持住帝国。[1]因此，无论罗马帝国如何扩张版图，它的世界帝国的理想"边界"都是无法实现的，理想"边界"与现实范围不可能达到内在的同一性。

从罗马人的理想"边界"与 limes 所能确定的现实范围之间的矛盾性中，我们可以看出，罗马人无限的理想"边界"只是他们的想像极限，罗马皇帝凭借其权威，把所征服地区的全体臣民都纳入了自己臆想的世界"边界"之中。在这里，权力的权威掩饰了事实的真相，帝国膨胀的虚荣心和统治者的现实需要缔造了罗马虚假的世界帝国和世界主人的神话，历史的真实不得不屈服于皇帝权力的重压和罗马人的遐想，但想像极限终究只是想像，它与现实有极大的差距。

罗马人的现实边界是由 limes 来确定的，它所包括的范围才是帝国的最终统治极限。早在阿庇安热诚地赞颂罗马，并以一种完全不同的方式解释罗马时，帝国的统治实际上已经到达了它的极限，"在他看来，罗马帝国主义已经达到了它的自然极限。"[2]哈德良皇帝即位后的第一件事就是放弃图拉真在东部占领的一切土地，放弃帝国的扩张政策。"护界神尽管曾抗拒过朱庇特的神威，却不得不屈服于哈德良皇帝的权势。"[3]哈德良皇帝的做法，实际上宣告了罗马人的理想"边界"的破产，也宣告了罗马统治极限的到来。这在罗马边疆史和政治史上都具有划时代意义，"哈德良从图拉真征服的新行省上的撤退，标志着'帝国极限'第一次在制度上得以承认。"[4]至此，罗马帝国终于从事实上承认了帝国边界的极限，承认了自己远非真正的世界帝国和全人类主宰。伴随帝国极限而来的是帝国的衰落，其版图上的变化是边界线上要塞和堡垒的不断丧失，联系边境地区的道路的废弛以及边界的不断缩小。罗马帝国最终盛极而衰，从不断向外扩张走向退而防守，最终在四周蛮族汹涌澎湃的入侵浪潮中走向四分五裂，罗马人的世界边界帝国理想也从想像到现实都彻底覆灭了。

---

① Edward Gibbon, *The History of the Decline and Fall of the Roman Empire*, edited by J. B. Bury, London: Methuen & Co., 1896–1902, chapter 2 (1. 70).

② Clifford Ando, *Imperial Ideology and Provincial Loyalty in the Roman Empire*, Berkeley, Los Angeles and London: University of California Press, 2000, p.332.

③ 爱德华·吉本：《罗马帝国衰亡史》，上册，第 24 页。

④ Clifford Ando, *Imperial Ideology and Provincial Loyalty in the Roman Empire*, p.330.

关于罗马—高卢"城市化"的几个问题

宫秀华、肖　丽　东北师范大学

摘要：罗马帝国统治下的高卢行省在城市化进程中表现突出，成为帝国西部地区城市化的典范。本文主要论述了高卢城市化研究中几个值得思考的问题，即统治者的政策引导、高卢贵族的主动合作、地方经济的繁荣和罗马化的特色，从而加深对该问题的理解与认识。

关键词：罗马；高卢；城市化

Abstract：Under Roman Empire, as a province, Roman Gaul showed its specialties in Western Urbanization. This paper discusses some questions about Roman emperors' policies, nobles' attitude, economic activity and Romanization in Gaul. It would be very helpful to understand deeply the nature of Urbanization in Gaul.

Keywords：Rome, Gaul, Urbanization

一　罗马统治者的政策引导

罗马帝国统治者极其重视帝国境内城市化的发展。

公元前 1 世纪，罗马已经成为统领地中海世界的霸主，如果仍以大规模许赐给行省居民公民权的方法来扩大罗马统治的基础显然是不可能的。因为这样做无利于罗马公民在整个帝国中所享有的特权优势地位，可见这是一种罗马公民不愿意接受的方法。而通过鼓励发展帝国境内城市生活的方式，来推动罗马化进程，不仅可以使罗马统治者从中获取巨大的经济利益，缓解罗马贵族与平民之间的矛盾，也可以得到各行省中那些生活提升到城市文明水准的居民们的支持。为此，共和末期帝国初期的统治者们都积极鼓励和支持行省的城市化运动，特别是对高卢城市的发展尤为关注。可以说，高卢许多地区的居民都是在这一时期开始步入城市生活的。

恺撒在高卢戎马倥偬九年（公元前 58- 前 49 年），"整个高卢，以比利牛斯山、阿尔卑斯山、塞文山、和莱茵河、罗纳河为界，周围约 3200 罗马里（约 3106 英里）范围内地方，除了同盟者和曾经给了他很多帮助的城市外——都被他并成一个行省。"[①]恺撒不仅将高卢作为扩展其政治势力与军事威望的战略基地，同时也把高卢经营成为其提供经济援助与扩展财源的物质基地。据苏维托

---

①　苏维托尼乌斯著，张竹明等译：《罗马十二帝王传》，北京：商务印书馆 1996 年版，第 1 卷，第 25 章。

尼乌斯记载，恺撒每年从高卢行省得到 400 万塞斯退斯的税金。[1]

奥古斯都继承和发展了恺撒的高卢政策，并使高卢行省的管理制度进一步规范化。公元前 27 年，奥古斯都依据恺撒对高卢土地和税收情况所进行的粗略登记，亲赴高卢行省首府路格敦姆城（Lugudunum，今里昂 Lyon），主持高卢地区的人口普查；[2]公元前 22 年，奥古斯都重建高卢行省。他将位于高卢南端海隅的那波嫩西斯行省划给元老院，将其以北的大面积的高卢地区划分为三个元首行省，由他亲自任命的三个特使和三个副手进行治理。[3]为加快高卢行省的城市建设，奥古斯都实施了许多重要的方针政策。例如，他对原有地区的文明采取保留、扶植、继承、改造和建设并举的政策，竭力地向高卢地区的部落推广城市生活；他"减轻了一些负债累累的城市的负担，重建了一些因地震而被毁灭的城市，并给予那些打算为罗马人民效力的城市以拉丁公民权或完全公民权。"[4]由于这个政策的结果，高卢许多地方的外貌几乎发生了彻底变化。原建于山顶上的村镇、市集和奥必达（Oppida，设防地，部落中心，镇子）逐渐消失，大河流域近旁的平原、沿海地区和交通要道则成为高卢人纷纷移居的新集聚地，他们在这里开始修盖房屋和建立通常的公共建筑物，从而吸引商人、工匠和水手们陆续来到这些地方经商、谋生，甚至定居于此地，"一个真正的城市就是这样形成起来的"。[5]例如，维埃奈（Vienne）地处交通要道，不仅控制着北部、东北部沿罗纳河 (Rhone) 和索恩河 (Saone) 的河道，还控制着通往罗依尔河 (Loire) 和通往大西洋沿岸的陆路，很快从一个小村庄发展成为颇具规模的城市。[6]

在奥古斯都的带动下，皇室成员也对高卢地区投以相当的关注：奥古斯都的女婿阿格里帕于公元前 19 年一整年都呆在高卢，亲自监督这一行省的治理；奥古斯都的养子提比略在公元前 16 年，公元前 9 年至公元前 7 年，公元 3 年至 5 年，9 年至 11 年多次奔赴高卢；提比略的哥哥德鲁苏斯于公元前 12 年至公元前 9 年到过高卢；提比略的儿子日耳曼尼库斯也于公元 12 年至 15 年到过高卢，他们频繁视察高卢的目的是一致的，即"加强对这块帝国要地的统治"。[7]

克劳狄于公元前 10 年 8 月 1 日诞生于高卢的路格敦姆（里昂），他常称这里为"故乡"。[8]他积极扩建城市、修筑新的道路、扩大罗马公民权，试图"让所有的高卢人都穿上罗马长袍"。[9]这一时期，"到处可见希腊人、高卢人、西班牙人和不列颠人统统身着罗马服装"。[10]塔西佗也详细地记叙了克劳狄为使高卢人能进入罗马元老院所进行的精彩演讲，他说："意大利本身扩展到阿尔卑斯山，这样就不仅仅个人，就是不少国家和民族也完全被包括到罗马人的整体里来了。当波河以北各地区的意大利居民取得了公民权的时候，我们在国内建立了巩固的和平，在国外取得了胜利；而我们利用我们的军团遍布于天下各地这一事实，把最强壮的行省居民加到他们中间去，这样就使这个凋敝的国家重新有了力量……现在高卢人已经在风俗习惯方面、文化方面并且通过婚姻关系而同化于我

---

① 苏维托尼乌斯著，张竹明等译：《罗马十二帝王传》，北京：商务印书馆 1996 年版，第 1 卷，第 25 章。

② Theodor Mommsen, *The Provinces of Roman Empire*, Edited by T.Robert S. Broughton, Chicago University Press, 1968,p.88.

③ Theodor Mommsen, *The Provinces of Roman Empire*, London,1909,vol.1,p.85.

④ 苏维托尼乌斯著，张竹明等译：《罗马十二帝王传》，北京：商务印书馆 1996 年版，第 2 卷，第 47 章。

⑤ Anthony King, *Roman Gaul and Germany*, Great Britain,1990,p.60. 也可参见 M. 罗斯托夫采夫著，马雍、厉以宁译：《罗马帝国社会经济史》上卷，北京：商务印书馆 1985 年版，第 80 页。

⑥ Edited by John Wacher, *The Roman World*, London,1987,p.29.

⑦ Theodor Mommsen, *The Provinces of Roman Empire*, Edited by T.Robert S. Broughton, Chicago University Press, 1968,p.88.

⑧ 苏维托尼乌斯著，张竹明等译：《罗马十二帝王传》北京：，商务印书馆 1996 年版，第 5 卷，第 2 章。

⑨ Barbara Levick, *Claudius*, London,1990,p.11.

⑩ W.T Arnold, *The Roman System of Provincial Administration to the Accession of Constantine the Great*, Revised by E・S.Bouchier, Roma,1968,p.144.

们了，让他们把他们自己的黄金和财富带到我们这里来，而不要留在我们的境界之外他们自己那里吧！"①这段讲话作为皇帝演说的范例被铭刻在铜匾上。1528 年至 1529 年期间，考古学家在里昂发现了其中的一块铜匾碎片，②为我们进一步解读这一时期的统治政策提供了珍贵的实证。在克劳狄倾斜政策的鼓励下，高卢中南部的爱杜依人率先取得了进入罗马元老院的权利，③其他高卢人紧随其后。克劳狄曾经说过："我的伯父提比略的愿望就是让殖民地和自治城市在帝国境内到处开花，也就是，所有站在罗马疆土上的人和他们所拥有的财富都应该属于罗马国家"。④克劳狄非常有远见地将高卢人选进元老院的举措，无疑对于罗马帝国的固本、强兵和扩展财源极其有利。

克劳狄加速了高卢城市建设，促使高卢部落早日接受城市生活。例如，在某场战争结束后，为了奖赏某座城市对罗马国家的忠诚，就把该城附近的一些土著部落拨归该城，使他们以被保护人资格附籍于该城，以此扩充城市人口、拓展城市规模，促使该地区的居民尽快地由部落生活转向城市生活。

韦伯芗继续推行扶植各行省发展城市生活的政策。韦伯芗的宗旨在于通过大规模授予行省居民以罗马公民权，加速城市化发展来扩大维护皇权所依靠的社会基础。四帝之争的血腥事件，表明了罗马公民，特别是居住在意大利的罗马公民所给予皇帝的支持是极其微弱的、不可靠的。尽管韦伯芗已经认识到将罗马公民权最大限度地扩及行省人民，以获取更广泛支持的迫切性。然而，他所面临的局势却很棘手：既不可能将罗马公民权一律平等地授予帝国境内所有的居民，这样会引起罗马人的不满，也不可能继续维持克劳狄时期有条件有限度地赐予部分行省居民以罗马公民权和拉丁公民权的政策，这样又加重了行省人民的不满。于是韦伯芗采用了一种折中手段。首先，对于那些多多少少已经罗马化了的行省，特别是那些主要的征兵地区，那些驻扎有罗马重兵的行省，他就加速其城市化运动，并扩大授予罗马公民权的范围。例如在高卢地区那些半开化的部落、氏族所在地建立新的自治市，将罗马公民权赐予拥护罗马统治的高卢贵族阶层，使他们统治当地的居民。这一时期，高卢城市化的发展意味着"把某些分子集中在城市里，使政府便于控制这些分子，并通过他们来控制广大的行省居民"；⑤其次，在罗马化程度较高的地区，韦伯芗将罗马公民权和拉丁公民权大规模地赐予当地居民，使他们所居住的城市成为帝国重要的征兵区域和依靠的基础力量；最后，对罗马化程度较低的地区，例如帝国的希腊地区不授予罗马公民权和拉丁公民权，至少在一定时期内暂时不授予或个别授予，⑥以便对这些地区的上层人物的傲慢与狂妄给以警戒，从而进行分而治之。⑦由于韦伯芗加快了城市化的建设，并逐步地扩大罗马公民权和拉丁公民权的授予范围，这一时期，无论在帝国的任何地方，"城市化运动都在迅速地推进，尽其实际可能的程度推进到极限。"⑧

二 高卢贵族的主动合作

高卢原有的氏族贵族阶层在恺撒征服高卢战争期间发生了极大的变化，有的因反抗罗马而遭到

① 塔西佗著，王以铸、崔妙音译：《历史》，北京：商务印书馆 1985 年版，第 11 卷，第 24 章。
② W.T Arnold, *The Roman System of Provincial Administration to the Accession of Constantine the Great*, Revised by E·S.Bouchier, Roma,1968,p.145.
③ 塔西佗著，王以铸、崔妙音译：《编年史》，商务印书馆 1983 年版，第 11 卷，第 24 章。
④ W.T Arnold, *The Roman System of Provincial Administration to the Accession of Constantine the Great*, Revised by E·S.Bouchier, Roma,1968,p.148.
⑤ M. 罗斯托夫采夫著，马雍、厉以宁译：《罗马帝国社会经济史》上卷，北京：商务印书馆 1985 年版，第 166 页。
⑥ M. 罗斯托夫采夫著，马雍、厉以宁译：《罗马帝国社会经济史》上卷，北京：商务印书馆 1985 年版，第 166 页。
⑦ 参见宫秀华："关于罗马–高卢城市兴起的几个因素"，《史学集刊》，2009 年第 1 期。
⑧ M. 罗斯托夫采夫著，马雍、厉以宁译：《罗马帝国社会经济史》上卷，北京：商务印书馆 1985 年版，第 166 页。

镇压，有的向罗马投降或主动与其合作而保持原来地位，并被赐予土地和奴隶，形成罗马 – 高卢新贵阶层。罗马在高卢建立统治政权后，这部分亲罗马的高卢贵族便理所当然地成为罗马统治者所依靠的地方势力。因而，高卢贵族的主动合作，亦是促进高卢城市发展的又一重要因素。

恺撒赢得高卢战争的胜利，使崇尚"勇武精神"的高卢人元气大伤，昔日的部落首领屡屡战败，声望极度下降，使其原有的稳固地位随之发生动摇。针对高卢的特殊情况，罗马人采取的措施主要有两点：一是，对那些顺从罗马统治的高卢贵族进行拉拢和诱惑，并在新政府内安排其适当的职位，构建罗马 – 高卢新贵阶层；二是，对那些骁勇善战的、但存有反抗情绪的高卢旧贵族送往罗马的辅助军团服役，通常是骑兵部队。使这些有潜在反叛意识的高卢贵族时刻处于罗马人的监督之下。此举对双方都有利：对于罗马人来说，不费分文，便可得到精兵强将，扩充兵源。因为，高卢人所在的整个辅助军团，均是由他们自己指挥和提供给养的；对于高卢贵族来说，也比较乐于"从军"，这样做既可以继续维护他们的社会地位和尊贵身份，也可以通过建立战功，延长其将领地位，荣获罗马公民权。当然，对于罗马而言，这种政策也存在着一定的风险。这些高卢将领们随时可能利用职权，率领麾下军队反叛罗马。但是，在严格的罗马式的军队管理体制下，高卢军官们指挥的辅助部队永远置于罗马将领的监控下，他们试图反叛罗马的"勇武精神"逐渐消失。他们虽然"还保留着个人的勇敢，但他们已不再具有公共的勇气"。[1]现时他们不得不接受罗马文化潜移默化的影响，在客观上加速了高卢的罗马化进程。同时，罗马公民权的赠予，对他们具有更大的诱惑力，在一定程度上弥补了他们因"勇武精神"的衰落所带来的心理落差。[2]

公元48年，克劳狄在位时授予高卢贵族以罗马公民权，以后又有选择地将一些贵族补充进罗马元老院。[3]正如上文所述，高卢爱杜依部落中的一部分贵族被选进罗马元老院，成为进入罗马政权机构的第一批外省人。这一时期，罗马政府还积极培植高卢贵族，让他们担任行政官员，在罗马的监督下管理地方事务。

公元73年，韦伯芗把高卢和西班牙行省的千余家显贵和奴隶主富户迁到罗马，将他们充实进元老院或列为骑士等级。允许他们在罗马正规部队中担任军职和担任财务官、督察官等政府高级职务。那些曾经与恺撒打过仗的高卢人的子孙们现在都是军团的指挥官、各省的总督，有的已经进入了罗马的元老院。"他们的野心并没有扰乱国家的安宁，相反，却和它的安全和伟大紧密联结在一起"。[4]罗马统治者的一系列举措，使被拉拢的高卢贵族愈加全力支持罗马在高卢的统治，以稳固他们自身的即得利益和特权地位，从而为城市化的发展创造了相对稳定的政治环境。

不可否认，高卢权贵在高卢城市化进程中扮演了最重要的角色。他们积极迎合罗马政治文化对行省文化的影响，支持扩建罗马殖民地、到处竖立和建设罗马风格的纪念碑和建筑物、推广罗马帝国崇拜等等，他们在罗马统治者的扶植下，积聚财富、扩展权势，逐渐完成自身罗马化过程，率先成为高卢 – 罗马人。但是，"这些贵族利用手中掌握的社会统治地位，建造了一个其他高卢 – 罗马人所被迫生活的物质和精神环境"。[5]在这样的环境里，尽管"行省精英阶层被认为是罗马化过程中的活动主体……却不能打破这些积极主动的、有权势的阶层与消极被动的被统治阶层之间的界限"。[6]从某种程度上讲，高卢 – 罗马化加剧了当地固有的社会矛盾。

---

① 爱德华·吉本著，黄宜思、黄雨石译：《罗马帝国衰亡史》上卷，北京：商务印书馆 1997 年版，第 55 页。

② Anthony King, *Roman Gaul and Germany*, Great Britain,1990,pp.64–5.

③ G.H.Stevenson, *Roman Provincial Administration*, Oxford University Press,1949,p.159.

④ 爱德华·吉本著，黄宜思、黄雨石译：《罗马帝国衰亡史》上卷，北京：商务印书馆 1997 年版，第 36 页。

⑤ Greg Woolf, "The Roman Cultural Revolution in Gaul", Edited by Simon Keay and Nicola Terrenato, *Italy and the West：Comparative Issues in Romanization*, Oxford University Press,2001,p.17.

⑥ Susan E. Alcock: "Vulgar Romanization and the Domination of Elites",Edited by Simon Keay and Nicola Terrenato, *Italy and the West：Comparative Issues in Romanization*, Oxford University Press,2001,p.202.

实际上，高卢的罗马化进程并非一帆风顺。随着罗马对高卢行省的统治，高卢社会的固有矛盾、新生矛盾进一步错综复杂。一些高卢权贵与平民联手多次发动反抗罗马的斗争。例如，公元 21 年，获得罗马公民权的高卢贵族优利乌斯·弗洛路斯和优利乌斯·撒克罗维尔分别带领特雷韦人和爱杜依人起义，[1]但起义很快被罗马统治者镇压下去；公元 68 年，担任要职的高卢贵族优利乌斯·文代克斯利用罗马皇帝尼禄统治不得人心，人民中普遍存在不堪忍受苛捐杂税的不满情绪，乘机发动兵变，宣称要把国家从暴君手里解放出来，但不久亦遭镇压。公元 1 世纪高卢境内的反罗马斗争，具有被征服者反抗征服者压迫斗争的性质，也有农民、城市贫民反抗新老贵族剥削的斗争内容。尽管这些斗争使罗马统治阶级感到惊慌，然而这些斗争在帝国境内毕竟属于局部动乱，并没有动摇罗马对高卢的整体统治，却促使统治者更多地采用怀柔安抚手段，加速高卢贵族与罗马奴隶主阶级逐渐溶为一体的过程，以获取高卢奴隶主对帝国政权的支持。同时，罗马政府给高卢地方政府一些有限的自主权，分批授予高卢居民以罗马公民权，以此缓和高卢人与罗马统治者之间的矛盾。通过这些措施，罗马扩大了在高卢的统治基础，建立了比较稳定的社会秩序。因此，罗马与高卢权贵阶层的合作，有利于政治的稳定，成为高卢城市化迅猛发展的重要条件之一。

三　地方经济的活跃繁荣

罗马征服高卢后，在农业上确立起奴隶占有制的生产方式。这一时期，土地主要有几种类型：罗马皇室领地；被保留的罗马－高卢贵族的土地；靠经营商业、手工业发财致富的外来移民在高卢购置的土地；罗马国家划给殖民者的土地；高卢小生产者的土地等。拥有大片土地的大农庄一般由监工管理，役使成批的奴隶，或租给佃户（自由农、破产农民和被释奴隶）耕种。中小规模的农庄主要由退役老兵、小生产者、手工业者和商人经营。高卢地区的气候、土壤条件比较适宜农耕，农业从先前种植谷物的单一生产方式逐渐发展为种植葡萄、橄榄和亚麻等多种经营的生产方式。罗马统治者鼓励商人从意大利引进葡萄、橄榄和亚麻等品种，使高卢的种植业迅速兴盛起来。[2]高卢生产的农副产品不仅销往意大利各地，甚至远销帝国的东方行省。

高卢手工业在罗马帝国经济生活中占据重要地位。高卢资源极其丰富，[3]除了蕴含金、银、铜、铁、铅等矿藏外，还盛产花岗石、大理石、石灰、石膏、沙子和木材等。采矿业、采石业、冶金业、制陶业和毛纺织业等部门均处于当时帝国境内的领先地位。[4]矿山和采石场大多属于罗马国家或皇帝的私产，它们或租给承包人经营，或由皇室奴隶和被释奴隶进行开采。帝国时期，大量石材的开采与加工，使高卢地区的建筑材料、建筑样式等发生了巨大变化。原有的泥坯草房渐渐消失，代之而起的是布局合理、式样独特、石砖结构的建筑物纷纷建立；传统的金属冶炼业，尤其是冶铁和青铜冶炼在罗马统治期间成为手工业中最活跃的部门。生产各种武器和工具的大小铁匠作坊遍布高卢各地，"高卢刀剑"是闻名罗马世界的名牌产品；高卢的制陶业在 2 世纪至 3 世纪期间无论在数量上还是质量上都有巨大发展，"高卢陶器"以独特的造型、新颖的几何图案或人物图像等脱颖而出，取代了意大利坎帕尼亚陶器在帝国市场上的独尊地位，畅销帝国境内；高卢还是罗马帝国重要的毛麻产品制造地。特别是羊毛外套、羊毛毯子、羊毛被等产品被认为是"最柔软、最保暖的极品"深受帝国境内居民的喜爱。[5]其他如木材、皮革、渔业加工等部门也有较大的发展。

---

① 　塔西佗著，王以铸、崔妙音译：《编年史》，北京：商务印书馆 1983 年版，第 3 卷，第 40 章。
② 　爱德华·吉本著，黄宜思、黄雨石译：《罗马帝国衰亡史》上卷，北京：商务印书馆 1997 年版，第 49—50 页。
③ 　Strabo, *Geography* 4.1.2. , Harvard University Press,1949.
④ 　J.E.Drinkwater, *Roman Gaul*, Cambridge University Press,1983,p.187.
⑤ 　M.P.Charlesworth, *Trade-Routes and Commerce of The Roman Empire*, Chicago University Press, 1926,p.182.

随着城市化的不断发展，高卢行省地区间的物品交换日益活跃，交换的种类也日益增多。不少水陆交叉地带成为重要的货物集散中心，例如，今日的索恩河上的马孔，卢瓦尔河上的奥尔良、里昂，塞纳河上的巴黎等都是昔日水陆贸易的重要地区，也是当时沟通南北高卢商贸线路上的重要关卡。

2世纪至3世纪初期，高卢的商业达到了空前未有的繁荣状态。[1]在商业竞争中，高卢商人赢得了极好的声誉，他们与意大利商人相比更熟悉高卢境内纵横交错的水道，并且手中掌管大量的河海船舶和其他运输工具，再加上他们熟知高卢市场行情，奔走于高卢本省和邻近各省集聚各类地方产品，然后再将其销往所需要的地区和军营中。值得一提的是，常年驻扎高卢行省的罗马军团是当地最大的消费群体，官兵们所需要的大部分物品例如木材、沥青、五金、皮革和毛麻制品等全部由高卢商人提供的。有时候，皇帝还亲自指定高卢商人专门供应帝国境内海陆军所需要的谷物、葡萄酒、橄榄油、木材、皮革、麻绳、五金、衣服、靴鞋、武器等物资。这一时期，不仅高卢商人富甲天下，高卢行省也在进入奴隶制社会后，凭借丰富的天然资源、方便的交通网和广阔的市场等诸多条件，逐渐地取代意大利而成为罗马帝国西方诸行省中的经济重地，成为行省城市发展的领头雁。

从里昂发掘的一些碑铭显示，路格敦姆城在高卢和整个罗马帝国的经济生活中地位突出，特别是从那些涉及各种不同商业行会的碑铭中更能看出这一点。罗马帝国时期，路格敦姆城不仅是谷物、葡萄酒、橄榄油和木材等方面交易的一个大的票据兑换所，而且它还是帝国制造业中负责分销高卢、日耳曼、不列颠等地大宗货物的中心地之一。

与路格敦姆城同等重要的是摩泽尔河上的城市特雷韦（Treviri，今特里尔 Trier），它既是一个重要的商业城市，也是一个工业中心。这里的商人与路格敦姆和阿莱拉特等城的商人一样，大多是帝国政府的经纪人。"他们在高卢收购各种货物，沿摩泽尔河用船运往莱茵河上诸城市和边塞上的城镇。他们主要是贩运羊毛制品和葡萄酒"。[2]摩泽尔河沿岸的一些墓碑，记载了特雷韦城在高卢的经济生活中所起的特殊作用。这些碑文和雕刻的场景详尽地描述了建碑者经营的事业和私生活等情形。从中我们了解到，这些建碑者大多是货物批发商。"公元3世纪初，在伊杰耳地方塞昆迪纽斯家墓地上建立的那座有名的墓碑上就详细地描绘了服装批发生意的情况以及这项买卖所使用的运输工具。一格连一格的雕图显示了塞昆迪纽斯家里的大帐房和帐房里的货样、铺面、货物包装以及货物在陆上用大型二轮运货马车运输的情景"。[3]同样，在其他一些地区还发现了墓碑碎片，上面铭刻的则是葡萄酒商人的状况。这些墓碑碎片反映了和伊杰耳的墓碑上次序相同的一组连环图画，只不过两者经手的货物不同，一个是经营衣物的，一个则是葡萄酒商人。[4]从这些墓碑上所反映的内容看，特雷韦城的富商们不仅把金钱投资于土地，还经营产品批发、产品中介和开设钱庄等业务，使该城的商业十分活跃。

罗马统治者在促进高卢行省城市化的过程中，注意发挥地方的经济优势，保护高卢商人的一些权益，鼓励地方商业的扩展，使帝国统治下的高卢行省出现了经济繁荣景象，为城市化提供了物质保障。

四　"罗马化"特色

罗马统治者在帝国境内大规模地推行城市化运动，不仅将城市作为地方行政管理机构、工商业中心和军事据点，也将城市作为扩展罗马文化、施加罗马政治影响的重要渠道，促进罗马文化向更广阔的地域传播。因而，在帝制强权政治下，许多行省城市在其发展进程中，都带有强烈的罗马色

---

① J.E.Drinkwater, *Roman Gaul*, Cambridge University Press,1983,p.198.

② M. 罗斯托夫采夫著，马雍、厉以宁译：《罗马帝国社会经济史》上卷，北京：商务印书馆1985年版，第243页。

③ M. 罗斯托夫采夫著，马雍、厉以宁译：《罗马帝国社会经济史》上卷，北京：商务印书馆1985年版，第243页。

④ M. 罗斯托夫采夫著，马雍、厉以宁译：《罗马帝国社会经济史》上卷，北京：商务印书馆1985年版，第243、244页。

彩，特别是高卢行省城市在宗教习俗、语言文化以及城市布局与建筑上均效仿罗马城，完全成了"罗马城的复制品"。从古典作家的记载到考古发掘的证明，"罗马化"在高卢地区的城市化进程中，表现的最为突出，产生的影响最为久远。事实上，高卢的城市化与罗马化是同构演进、并行发展的。或者说，两者互相影响、互为依存、密不可分。高卢城市发展的"罗马化"特征主要体现在文化教育、宗教习俗、社会生活、城市风貌等方面。

文化教育的罗马化 帝国早期，城市肩负着传播罗马文化的历史重任。通过城市的推介，拉丁语逐渐成为帝国境内的通用语言，罗马文化也以惊人的速度渗透至高卢地区。由于高卢人始终没有创造出自己的文字，这就为拉丁文化的传播提供了通道。它先是被高卢上层人物接受，然后又成为平民大众的语言。高卢地区的拉丁语经过长期演变成为中世纪的罗曼语，后来逐渐发展为现代法语。与罗马儿童一样，高卢儿童从小就要学习拉丁语，所受到的教育是典型的罗马式教育，其教育目的显然是为了培养忠实于并服务于罗马帝国的人才和顺民。帝国早期，马西里亚（Massilia，今马赛Marseilles）建有各类学校传播拉丁语，该城不仅成为罗马世界上层人物的集聚中心，也是不同身份、不同家庭背景、不同语言的人们向往和访问的学术圣地。"许多著名的演说家在这里演讲，宣传帝国文化和帝国精神"；[1]帝国晚期，奥古斯都鲁姆城（Octodurum）已经是一个享誉世界的大城市了，这里不仅是商业贸易中心，也是文化教育重地。在这里，年轻的高卢人从小就被教育成为一个地道的罗马人，他们竞相地为罗马帝国效力。同样，路格敦姆城也成为罗马－高卢文化中心，这里的人们热衷于学习拉丁语，以至于小普林尼的书供不应求，几次再版都一抢而空。[2]

宗教习俗的罗马化 罗马征服高卢之后，没有取缔高卢人的原始宗教——德鲁依德教（Druids）的信仰，而是把该教崇拜的众神祇搬到罗马神庙中，使其从属于罗马的大神，并让高卢人尊奉罗马皇帝为最高祭司。罗马宗教中虽然存在着对朱庇特(Jupiter)神的主神崇拜，但多神崇拜的观念仍长期存在，各地、各行业、各家庭都有自己的守护神。因此，德鲁依德的多神崇拜与罗马泛神基础上的主神崇拜具有某些共同的信仰特点。在高卢罗马化的过程中，这两种宗教很自然地结合起来，形成一种新的宗教形态，既保留了德鲁依德教对自然力量崇拜的观念以及在葬俗等方面的宗教仪式，又吸收了罗马宗教中的某些特征，在宗教上实现了高卢—罗马因素的融合。罗马在高卢宗教方面所进行的罗马化渗透是逐步展开的。恺撒征服高卢后不久，便根据高卢的一些重要神的职能，赋予了罗马式的称谓，例如，称一切技艺的创造者、一切道路和旅程的向导神为"麦邱利"（Mercury）、驱逐疾疫的神为"阿波罗"(Apollo)、战争神为"马尔斯"（Mars）、雷电和太阳神为"朱庇特"(Jupiter)和倡导技术和工艺之神为"米涅瓦"(Minerva)"等。[3]罗马还在高卢的主要城市建立罗马宗教中心。[4]例如，在路格敦姆城建造宏伟的罗马祭坛，使该城成为整个高卢宗教崇拜的中心地。[5]在罗马建筑风格的影响之下，各地的德鲁依德教的神庙由原先的木结构，方形、圆形或多边形的小型建筑，发展为大理石为主要建筑材料或砖石结构的、规模宏伟的、方形的罗马式神殿。公元前12年8月1日，奥古斯都派遣德鲁苏斯在路格敦姆城召集高卢三个行省64个城区（由原高卢地区的部落中心发展而来，斯特拉波列举的城区数目是60个，[6]本文采用的是塔西佗的说法[7]）代表参加的行省议会，举行崇拜罗马帝国和奥古斯都个人的宗教活动。根据蒙森的记载，64个城区分别是：阿奎塔尼亚行省

① Edited by John Wacher, *The Roman World*, London,1987,p.372.
② W.T Arnold, *The Roman System of Provincial Administration to the Accession of Constantine the Great,* Revised by E・S.Bouchier, Roma,1968,p.142.
③ 恺撒著，任炳湘译：《高卢战记》，北京：商务印书馆1997年版，第6卷，第17章。
④ Edited by John Wacher, *The Roman World*, London,1987,p.791.
⑤ G.H.Stevenson, *Roman Provincial Administration*, Oxford University Press,1949,p.159.
⑥ Strabo, *Geography* 4.3.2. ,Harvard University Press,1949.
⑦ 塔西佗著，王以铸、崔妙音译：《编年史》，北京：商务印书馆1983年版，第3卷，第44章。

17 个，路格敦西斯行省 25 个，贝尔吉卡行省 22 个。①在这次集会上做出了重要决定：今后每年的 8 月 1 日都要举行同样的活动来表达对元首和帝国的崇拜和忠诚，②也准许祭拜高卢众多的地方神灵，届时还举行节日庆典活动。虽然行省议会不是行省管理机构的组成部分，也无权干预行政事务，但它以宗教联盟和宗教活动的形式加强了帝国统治者对高卢人的思想统治。随着帝国对行省统治的加强，行省议会逐渐成为高卢行省城市与罗马政府、皇帝本人进行沟通的渠道之一。

社会生活的罗马化 高卢所有的城市，虽然面积大小、人口多寡不同，在政治经济等方面所处的地位也各异，却具备了某些共同特征，例如，这些城市全都尽其可能地致力于使它们的居民生活舒适与方便的各项建设活动之中。几乎所有的高卢城市，都像罗马城一样，有比较科学的输水排水系统，使净水源源不断地输入城内，甚至建设高架水道来保障高地上的人们用水方便，同时对排污水道也进行了建设；有规划合理的街道和广场，沿着街道两旁建有柱廊，替行人遮光挡雨，城市中心地区的街道汇合处建有宽敞的广场；有热闹繁华的市场，特别是鱼、肉市场遍布城内；有设备齐全的公共浴池，城市居民去公共浴池洗浴、解乏、交际和消遣已经成为他们日常生活的重要内容；有大型的剧场、竞技场和角斗演习所等公众娱乐场所；有公共图书馆和供辩论、演讲用的讲堂等公共教育场所；有行政长官的官邸，有供公众聚会的大厅，有审理案件的市政厅，还有关押罪犯的监狱等等。至于富人宅第则大多外观考究，内部豪华舒适，甚至像罗马人一样设有家庭浴室和自来水。罗马人喜爱的鱼汁、鱼酱、橄榄油烹调的食物和葡萄酒等均成为高卢人餐桌上的日常食品。③

城市风貌的罗马化 在罗马帝国城市发展中，高卢行省的城市居民在充分接纳罗马化生活方式的同时，也努力保持其特有的文化传统，以期达到高卢 – 罗马（Gallo-Roman）因素的和谐统一。④一方面，高卢在城市布局和建筑风格上充分吸收了罗马城的特点——具有统一的格式，一般有方正的围墙、十字交叉的道路，街道笔直、整齐，呈南北、东西走向。市中心有广场、政府机关、神庙、竞技场、大浴室在内的公共建筑，四周围以店铺、作坊、富人住宅和部分民房；另一方面，依照高卢地区的古老风俗，城市建筑的选址先由占卜官和祭司主持，在"神佑"下划定的地界。然后在选定的空地上，再按照罗马人的方法，进行丈量，标记出那些将要修建的各类建筑用地，另外在一些建筑中依然保留了高卢的原木结构。

高卢行省的城市外貌特征几乎全盘照搬罗马城，甚至街道上矗立的雕像都相差无几。例如，在各地修建的圆形竞技场、剧院、神殿、柱廊、凯旋门、浴场和上下水道等宏伟的公共建筑在选材、设计和风格上与罗马完全相同。其中今天仍然矗立在法国尼姆的奥古斯都城门、神殿、圆形竞技场等，都是典型的罗马式建筑。奥古斯都城门建于公元前 16 年至公元前 15 年期间，是当时这座城市的标志性建筑物，两个大拱门用于车马通行，两旁的小拱门供行人使用；尼姆神殿建于公元前 2 年——公元 4 年；圆形竞技场建于公元 1 世纪晚期。在该城的中心地区树立着奥古斯都雕像，城市大街小巷的规划布局、建筑风格与意大利北部的都灵和维罗纳极其相似。⑤另有奥顿的奥古斯都凯旋门（建于公元 1 世纪前后）、格兰努姆的大陵墓（建于公元 1 世纪初）、奥朗日的大剧院（建于公元 1 世纪）、阿莱斯的圆形竞技场（建于公元 1 世纪晚期）、阿莱斯的君士坦丁大浴池（建于 4 世纪）和随处可见的罗马高架水道、还在使用的罗马大道等等诸多的历史遗迹，至今依然向世人展示着高卢 – 罗马化城市发展的辉煌成果。

① heodor Mommsen, *The Provinces of Roman Empire,* Edited by T.Robert S. Broughton, Chicago University Press, 1968,p.100.
② Theodor Mommsen, *The Provinces of Roman Empire*, p.98.
③ T.Rice Holmes, *The Architect of Roman Empire*, Oxford University Press,1951,p.63.
④ Frank Sear, *Roman Architecture*, New York,1983,p.213.
⑤ Frank Sear, *Roman Architecture*, New York,1983,p.214.

被保护人与罗马早期社会的等级冲突

胡玉娟 中国社会科学院

摘要：罗马早期社会中的被保护人同贵族、平民的关系微妙。一方面，被保护人依附于贵族氏族；另一方面，他们的社会地位与平民接近。这种中间身份使被保护人阶层成为政治斗争中的一枚重要砝码。在某种意义上，贵族与平民的命运都取决于被保护人的立场。在等级冲突的初期（公元前 5-4 世纪前期），被保护人总是帮助贵族反对平民的保民官。公元前 4 世纪后期情况发生了变化，被保护人似乎逐渐摆脱了贵族的控制。一种学术假说认为在等级冲突中发生了一场被保护人的革命。本文旨在求证这一假说并做进一步的阐释。

关键词：被保护人；平民；贵族；早期罗马；等级冲突

Abstract：The early Roman clients had a very subtle relationship with the patricians and the plebs. On the one hand, they were dependents of the patricians' *gentes*, on the other hand, their social status was more close to the plebs. Such an intermediate identity made the class of the clients a crucial makeweight for the plebs as well as for the patricians. To some extent, both the patrician and the plebs' fates were decided by the clients' position. In the early two centuries of the Order Conflicts, the clients were always ready to help the patricians against the tribunes of the plebs. The situation changed in the second half of the 4th. century B.C. Since then it seems that the clients had gained more independence. It is assumed that there existed a revolution of the clients in parallel with the Order conflicts. This paper aims to detest this assumption and give further explanations.

Keywords：Clients, Plebs, Patricians, Early Rome, Order Conflicts

罗马共和早期（公元前 494 年—公元前 287 年）的等级冲突以贵族的妥协和平民获得了法律上的平等权利而告终。罗马贵族的妥协通常被认为是外因，或者说是外部战争压力造成的。

据李维（Livy）、哈利卡纳索斯的狄奥尼修斯（Dionysius of Harlicarnasus）关于罗马等级冲突的报道，保民官往往在外敌入侵关头，发动平民拒绝服兵役，迫使元老院接受他们关于土地、债务、开放高级职官等提案。但此举未必能奏效。因为贵族往往利用他们的被保护人在平民大会上对保民官的提案投以否决票，或率领氏族成员和被保护人出征。这种情况在公元前 5-4 世纪初的平民运动中屡见不鲜，后来情况则有所变化。

　　李维的《罗马史》自第 6 卷开始（关于公元前 4 世纪的历史叙事）少有贵族利用被保护人反对保民官和平民的报道①。这种变化被 19 世纪的法国历史学家库朗热（Fustel de Coulanges）解释为，罗马早期社会曾发生一场鲜为人知的革命——被保护人获得了解放②。脱离了贵族氏族的被保护人加入平民阶层，从而使政治天平向平民一边倾斜。

　　"被保护人革命"这一学术假说有助于揭示导致贵族妥协的内在原因。从等级结构来看，贵族、平民和被保护人三者的关系十分微妙③。被保护人从属于贵族氏族，却与氏族之外的平民的法律和社会地位接近。这种介于贵族与平民之间的中间角色使被保护人成为政治天平上的一枚重要砝码。从某种程度上说，被保护人阶层的立场决定着贵族和平民的命运。被保护人立场的改变从内部削弱了贵族集团的力量。平民的实力则相应增强。这应是导致贵族妥协的一个很重要的内在因素。

　　然而，被保护人在贵族与平民斗争中的重要作用长期以来未受到罗马史研究者的足够重视。罗马早期社会的"被保护人革命"仍是一个有待证明的学术命题。主要原因在于，近代以来，西方学术界弥漫着过度疑古的思潮。罗马早期文献传统真实性受到严重质疑，致使研究者往往对罗马早期史采取回避态度。关于保护关系的研究也大多以共和中、后期和帝国时代为背景④，涉足罗马早期社会的保护关系的研究者们一般态度比较谨慎⑤，许多问题还有待深入开展。

　　本文拟在有选择地利用传统史料文献的基础上，考察罗马早期被保护人在等级冲突中角色、地位的变化；尝试对平民中的被保护人进行身份识别，分析被保护人出身的平民政治家特殊的政治立场及利益诉求；重构罗马早期社会中的被保护人获得解放的途径和过程。

一　被保护人在等级冲突中的角色变化

　　关于罗马保护制度（clientela）的起源和早期发展情况，目前所知最早的文献史料出自公元前 1

---

① 必须谨慎对待李维提供的证据，因为他基本上只是通过二手或三手材料复述早期历史作品，并且在撰写时往往心怀偏见，缺乏批判性与学术性的思考，但早期历史的作品已不复存在，判断李维在多大程度上准确复述，以及这些资料在多大程度上提供了关于早期罗马历史的权威论述将是一项很有价值的工作。参见《剑桥古代史》第 7 卷第 2 分册（F.W.Walbank ed., The Cambridge Ancient History, Vol.7.Part 2, Cambridge University Press, 2002），第 9 页。

② 库朗热说："保民官的设立目的是使出走的被保护人获得保护，使平民地位得到某种程度的提高和趋于稳定，这就促进了解放的潮流。到公元前 372 年，被保护人已不复存在"库朗热：《古代城邦》（Fustel de Coulanges, *La Cité antique*, Champs Flammarion,1984），第 320 页。被保护人究竟如何脱离贵族氏族？这仍是一个有待探讨的问题。

③ 蒙森认为，原始的罗马共同体由公民与非公民构成，"起初公民实际上是保护人，非公民是被保护人"，王政时期，被保护人变为平民。《罗马史》第 1 卷，商务印书馆 1994，第 79，81 页。库朗热则认为，原始的罗马共同体由罗马人民和平民构成，前者包括贵族和被保护人，与平民对立。在平民运动中，被保护人逐渐获得解放，加入平民。《古代城邦》第 271-276 页。

④ 格尔泽 1912 年出版的《罗马显贵》（Matthias Gelzer, *Die Römische Nobilität*, Leipzig, 1912）以共和国末期的资料为基础，分析显贵如何通过保护关系操纵罗马政治、垄断高级官职。（参见英译本 Matthias Gelzer, *The Roman Nobility*, Oxford: Basil Blackwell, 1969）。闵采尔的《罗马贵族派系与家族》对于平民运动的某些联姻、联盟关系进行了分析（Friedrich Münzer, *Roman Aristocratic Parties and Families,* Baltimore and London: The Johns Hopkins University Press, 1999）。巴迪恩专论保护制在罗马征服与外交中的实践（E.Badian, *Foreign Clientelae*, 264-70 B.C., Oxford University Press,1958）。共和末期政治斗争中的保护关系见塞姆的《罗马革命》（Ronald Syme, *The Roman Revolution*, Oxford: Oxford University Press, 1960）。莫里森的《罗马共和晚期的平民与政治》（Henrik Mouritsen, *Plebs and Politics in the Late Roman Republic*, Cambridge: Cambridge University Press, 2001）等。

⑤ 阿尔弗蒂的《罗马社会史》简要提及早期被保护人的起源（参见英译本 Géza Alföldy, *The Social History of Rome*, Routledge, 1988）。布隆特的《罗马共和时期的社会冲突》（P. A. Brunt, *Social Conflicts in the Roman Republic*, New York: W. W. Norton & Company Inc., 1971）述及平民运动中的贵族及其被保护人的关系。华勒士—哈德里尔编纂的综合性研究著作《古代社会的保护制度》（Andrew Wallace-Hadrill ed., *Patronage in Ancient Society*, Routledge, 1989），书中有一篇论文《论罗马早期被保护人》（Andrew Drummond, *Early Roman Clients*, pp.89-115.），作者考证文献史料真伪，反思前人的研究方法，结合人类学理论思考，对罗马早期保护关系进行重构。

世纪晚期的希腊作家哈利卡纳索斯的狄奥尼修斯的《罗马古事记》①。

近代的研究者对于这段史料持辨证的批判态度,一方面认为狄奥尼修斯对罗马早期保护制度的概括和描述反映了他的政治理想,带有理想化色彩,某些细节具有时代错位之嫌,不能算是信史;另一方面,通过历史学和人类学的比较研究,认为保护制度在罗马早期社会的存在及其重要作用是无庸质疑的②。同时,"这些理论或多或少都认为,'起初'的保护关系与共和中/后期的保护关系相比,具有显著的不同特征和功能。"③早期的保护关系主要是氏族吸收外来者的一种形式,共和中后期的保护关系则主要是公民内部成员,奴隶主与被释奴,罗马征服者与被征服者之间的一种经济、政治荫庇关系④。保护人一般都属于罗马的政治精英阶层,被保护人的身份则比较复杂,既有社会底层的平民、被释奴和被征服者,也包括元老级和骑士级的上层人士。

罗马早期国家由氏族共同体演化而来,在血缘关系基础上形成了一种公民与非公民对立的等级、阶级结构。以自由民阶层而论,氏族内外的差别主要表现为"罗马人民"(populus Romanus)与"平民"(plebs)的对立。氏族之内的"罗马人民"又包含两种不同身份的成员:贵族(patricius)氏族成员及其被保护人(cliens)。平民则是站在氏族以外的,没有公民权的自由居民,他们大部分由于外来的被征服者组成。贵族、被保护人和平民这三个等级构成了早期罗马社会自由民阶层的基本结构。

王政时代的被保护人与平民的来源有相似之处,他们大都是外来的居民。但是两者的身份不同,其差别在于,被保护人在氏族之内,而平民在氏族之外。氏族制度对于外来人口的容纳性十分有限。一部分外来者被贵族氏族吸收,形成依附于贵族氏族的被保护人阶层;大部分外来人口则无法被氏族体系全部接纳,只能以王的名义加以收编,从而形成了依附于国王,或者说依附于城邦的平民阶层。

被保护人的另一个重要来源是被释奴(又称解放自由人)。王政时代后期奴隶制发展起来,被释奴现象随之出现。第6王塞尔维乌斯似乎就是王室被释奴出身。共和时代最初的一个世纪里,有记载的大规模奴隶暴动就有两次(公元前405年,公元前460年)。公元前460年,奴隶们一度占领卡皮托山,要求罗马人民释放全部奴隶⑤。公元前357年,执政官曼利乌斯(Gn.Manlius Capitolinus)颁布一条立法,规定被释放的奴隶必须向国库交纳赎身费。"这一举措使日渐匮乏的国库得到不少收入"⑥。按照罗马人的习俗,被释奴自身及其家属将成为主人的被保护人。

共和初期,平民集团形成,与贵族发生冲突。被保护人与平民的关系发生了微妙的变化。被保护人虽然属于贵族氏族,但是从一开始就参加平民的议事会,并且也接受平民保民官的庇护。贵族氏族中的被保护人在平民中占有很大比例⑦,并产生了一些著名的平民领袖。例如,公元前305年的保民官弗拉维乌斯(Cn.Flavius)原是贵族克劳狄乌斯氏族(Claudius)的被释奴,获得自由后成为平民领袖,他还担任过公元前304年的牙座营造官⑧。可以说,被保护人是平民集团的重要组成部分。

---

① "对于罗马王政时期这段历史,哈利卡纳索斯的狄奥尼修斯是一位严肃的研究者",他不仅和李维一样,借鉴早期罗马编年史家的作品,还引用了50种以上希腊人的历史著作,为我们提供了宝贵的、鲜为人知的材料。《剑桥古代史》第7卷,第2分册,第3页。

② 杜鲁门:"罗马的早期被保护人",载华勒士—哈德里尔编:《古代社会的保护制度》(Andrew Drummond, Early Roman Clientes, in Andrew Wallace-Hadrill ed., *Patronage in Ancient Society*, Routledge, 1989),第90–110页。

③ 参见杜鲁门:"罗马的早期被保护人",载华勒士—哈德里尔编:《古代社会的保护制度》,第95页。

④ "在氏族的内部存在一个真正的依附者阶层,即附庸阶层,即门客,……它是很古老的,并且注定会随着社会的发展本身以及由市民所组成的城邦的建立而消失。……并且在失去其古代特征的时候,催发了历史上存在的庇护体制"参见[意]弗朗切斯科·德·马尔蒂诺:《罗马政制史》,薛军译,北京大学出版社,2009年,第27页,第30页。

⑤ 李维:《罗马史》,III, XV, 9.

⑥ 李维:《罗马史》,VII, 16, 7.

⑦ 李维:《罗马史》(Livy, *History of Rome*, translated by B.O.Foster, Loeb Classical Library), V,32,8.李维提到,贵族卡米路斯(Camillus)的被保护人大部分属于平民(*magna pars plebis erat*)。

⑧ 李维:《罗马史》,IX, 46, 5–6.

不过，在平民运动初期（公元前5世纪），被保护人站在贵族一边反对平民。

公元前493年，部分平民士兵举行撤离，占领了"圣山"。贵族阿庇乌斯·克劳狄乌斯（Appius Claudius）提议，利用氏族中的被释奴和被保护人去镇压撤离者：

> 我们有足够的武装力量对付他们，只要我们选出一批身强力壮的奴隶，给予他们自由……我们不仅要动员自己的族人，还要率领我们的被保护人和留下来的平民出征，为了调动他们的积极性，我们可以替个别平民还债……①

被保护人在数量上与平民人口相当，他们是贵族氏族武装的重要组成部分。公元前5世纪前半叶，当保民官号召平民抵制征兵时，贵族合族出征，被保护人随行，似足以应付战争。例如，公元前455年，埃奎（Aequi）人来袭。平民拒绝作战。元老院下令由贵族率领其被保护人迎敌②。

被保护人还为主人提供法律援助。起诉贵族政敌是保民官惯用的政治攻击手法。被保护人往往在这种场合出现，身着丧服，聚集到法庭替主人申辩。例如，公元前473年，贵族弗瑞乌斯（Furius）和曼利乌斯（Manlius）受到保民官格努基乌斯（Cn.Genucius）起诉，当时有大批被保护人身着丧服陪同出庭，表示声援③。

公元前449年，第二个十人立法委员会的主要成员贵族阿庇乌斯·克劳狄乌斯因独裁统治被起诉时，他的伯父盖约·克劳狄乌斯（C.Claudius）带领族人和被保护人（cum gentilibus clientibusque）为他求情。他们身着丧服，在举行公民大会的广场上恳求公民们宽恕。④

被保护人在公民大会的选举和表决的投票过程中，始终受到贵族主人的影响。贵族操纵被保护人，干涉平民大会的选举和制订决议。李维说，"贵族利用其被保护人的选票把他们喜欢的人选举为保民官"。（per clientium suffragia creandi quos vellent tribunes auferre.）⑤公元前472年的平民部落大会改革就是针对这一现象的。当时"贵族及其被保护人云集会场，同保民官和平民争吵不休，直到当天会议结束仍无结果。"⑥

然而，从公元前5世纪中期开始，被保护人同贵族的关系开始发生变化。

首先，被保护人不再是贵族的军事支柱。公元前449年，当平民再次举行撤离时，贵族集团中已无人主张率领被保护人，以贵族私人的武装力量去镇压平民。⑦

公元前445年，保民官们利用干涉权，阻止征兵时，贵族无法靠联合被保护人，以氏族武装应付战争。克劳狄乌斯家族的盖约·克劳狄乌斯提出新主张，由两位执政官直接挑战保民官，对他们发动武力攻击，从而迫使平民参军。⑧

公元前387年，沃尔西（Volsci）人入侵，保民官抵制征兵。贵族无计可施。元老院只好妥协，承诺不再向平民征收战争税，战争期间暂停对平民的债务诉讼。⑨

其次，在法庭上，贵族身边再也没有大批被保护人支持者的身影。公元前362年，贵族曼利乌

---

① 哈利卡纳索斯的狄奥尼修斯：《罗马古事记》（Dionysius of Halicarnassus, *Roman Antiquities*, translated by Earnest Carry, Loeb Classical Library）VI, 63, 3. 狄奥尼修斯用 Peletas 一词对应 *Clientes*。
② 哈利卡纳索斯的狄奥尼修斯：《罗马古事记》，X, 43,2.
③ 李维：《罗马史》，II, 54, 2–55.
④ 李维：《罗马史》，III, 58, 1
⑤ 李维：《罗马史》，II, 56,3.
⑥ 李维：《罗马史》，II, 56, 1–5.
⑦ 李维：《罗马史》，III, 50.
⑧ 李维：《罗马史》，IV, 6, 7.
⑨ 李维：《罗马史》，VI, 31, 4.

斯（L.Manlius）受到保民官篷波尼乌斯（M.Pomponius）起诉。以致于其子提图斯（Titus）不得不亲自涉险闯入保民官府邸，拔刀相威胁，迫使保民官撤消起诉。①库朗热所谓"公元前 372 年已无被保护人"的说法大约根据这条史料而来的。②

再次，在公民大会和平民议事会，被保护人不再是贵族的傀儡。例如，公元前 367 年，保民官李锡尼乌斯（Licinius）和绥克斯图（Sextius）列举 9 年来贵族为阻止通过他们的法案而采取的各种手段，包括收买保民官；使平民外出作战；任命独裁官③，却惟独没提贵族操纵被保护人的选票否决其法案。

此外，贵族对待被保护人的态度也有很大变化。公元前 5 世纪，贵族尚能命令被保护人出征，操纵被保护人的选票。被保护人亦对主人惟命是从。到公元前 4 世纪，贵族却需要同被保护人商量，征求意见。而被保护人甚至可以拒绝主人的请求。

例如，公元前 391 年，贵族卡米路斯（Camillus）在审判他的平民大会召开之前，召集族人和被保护人到家中商议对策。他的族人和被保护人同意替他筹集罚金，但不愿帮助他开脱罪行④。

这差不多是李维最后一次提到被保护人对于贵族的作用。从第 6 卷以后，被保护人逐渐从李维的文字中淡出⑤，我们甚至无从得知被保护人在平民运动后期（公元前 4 世纪 – 公元前 3 世纪）的作用如何。"被保护人"的消失恐怕并非因为李维对此不感兴趣，或者是因为他所引用的古代文献缺乏这方面的记载所致⑥，而是由于发生了某种制度性变革，使贵族氏族中大量被保护人获得了自由，转变了政治立场，同平民一道反对贵族。从而使贵族与平民的力量对比发生变化。

关于"被保护人革命"，文献传统对此未置一词，似乎暗示这场革命未造成巨大的社会震荡，在不知不觉中就完成了。"被保护人革命"究竟是如何发生的？在考察这个问题之前，先要弄清谁是被保护人。在古代作家的笔下，被保护人一般是作为一个集体名词（clientis）出现的，这使我们有一种"只见森林，不见树木"的遗憾。众多被载入史籍的平民人物中有哪些人出身于被保护人？如何识别平民中的被保护人的身份？一个值得注意的线索是那些与贵族同姓的平民，他们很可能是出自贵族氏族的被保护人。下面对这个问题进行考证。

二 被保护人身份识别：与贵族同姓的平民

对比贵族执政官年表和平民保民官名单可知，罗马共和时期存在着不少同姓的贵族和平民⑦。

---

① 李维：《罗马史》，VII，5，1–8.
② 库朗热：《古代城邦》，第 320 页。原文为"公元前 372 年"，疑为"公元前 362 年"笔误。
③ 李维：《罗马史》，VI，39，7.
④ 李维：《罗马史》，V，32，8.
⑤ Clientis 一词在第 6 卷中仍有出现，但出现在显然是出自作者臆想的演说辞中，而且只具有比喻含义。据李维记载（《罗马史》VI,18,6）：公元前 384 年，贵族曼利乌斯同保民官们密谋推翻贵族统治，他说："你们平民在人数上远胜于对手。你们现在就应该像一群被保护人反抗一个主人一样，联合起来反对同一个敌人。"（Quot enim clientes circa singulos fuistis patronos, tot nunc adversus unum hostem eritis.）
⑥ 杜鲁门："罗马的早期被保护人"载华勒士—哈德里尔编：《古代社会的保护制度》，第 94 页。
⑦ 传世的《执政官年表》（Fasti）乃是奥古斯都时期的复制品，并非原件，因此有学者怀疑早期的执政官名单中有后来窜入的名字。然而，罗马人以执政官之名纪年，执政官名单属于最牢固的公共记忆部分，不大可能被轻易抹杀，亦不大可能被大规模篡改，不能因过度怀疑而置之不理。保民官年表参见 G. 尼柯里尼：《平民保民官》（Giovanni Niccolini, Il Tribunato Della Plebe, Milano: Editore Librario Della Real Casa 1932）；T.R.S. 布劳敦《罗马共和时期的职官》（T.R.S.Broughton, The Magistrates of the Roman Republic,Vol.1–2,supplement, American Philological Society, 1968）。

据粗略统计[①]，至少有 20 多个同名的贵族——平民姓氏（nomen gentile）[②]。某些平民氏族甚至与历史悠久、地位显赫的贵族氏族如科尔奈利乌斯（Cornelius），克劳狄乌斯（Claudius），瓦莱瑞乌斯（Valerius），帕皮瑞乌斯（Papirius），塞尔维利乌斯（Servilius）同姓[③]。一个令人深感困惑的事实是，在平民获准担任执政官之前，早期执政官名单（公元前509—公元前451）中竟然有三分之一左右是"平民姓氏"[④]。这些早期执政官当然不可能是平民，他们只是与某些平民同姓而已。

贵族与平民同姓不太可能是出于巧合。在古代罗马，姓氏与身份密切相关。罗马公民的姓氏，尤其是高贵的贵族姓氏绝不容许外来者冒用。公元 1 世纪，克劳狄皇帝曾颁布饬令："禁止外地出身的人使用罗马人的名字……他把那些冒充罗马公民的人斩首于埃斯奎林郊原"[⑤]。这段史料说明，直到早期帝国时代初期，氏族制遗风依然强大。可以推测，在共和前期一定也有这种规定，而且会更加严格，平民不得与贵族同姓。

贵族氏族也不太可能由于犯罪或经济原因降格为平民。在等级冲突时期，许多受到保民官攻击的贵族被判处罚金、流放甚至死刑，但在交纳了罚金、结束流放、被家族除名之后，受罚的贵族个人及其家族并未因此身份降等。共和末期也有不少贫穷的元老，但也并未降为平民。

共和晚期，贵族可以通过过继法，转入平民氏族，转为平民。例如，公元前 1 世纪，贵族克劳狄乌斯为了当保民官，自愿被平民封达纽斯（Fundanius）收养，从而取得竞选资格。但这个例子不足为证。正如西塞罗（Cicero）指出的，"尾随领养而来的，……就是被收养的一方继承领养者的名字、财产，以及他的领养者的家庭祭祀"。[⑥]这就说明，通过收养降为平民的贵族不可能继续保持原先的贵族姓氏。

许多平民姓氏带有外来者的特征。例如，著名的平民氏族李锡尼乌斯，其氏族名 Licinius 与埃特鲁里亚地区墓志铭中常见人名 Lecne 相似，很可能是王政晚期从埃特鲁里亚地区或图斯库伦城（Tusculum）迁来的[⑦]。享有执政官大权的平民军政官阿提利乌斯（Lucius Atilius Priscus，公元前 399 年）的姓氏（Atilius）出自希腊人名 Ateilios，可能是随老塔克文王迁入罗马的希腊人后代[⑧]。首任保民官之一阿尔比纽斯（Lucius Albinius Paterculus）的氏族（Albinius）可能来自古老的拉丁城邦阿尔巴·隆加（Alba Longa）。相传阿尔巴·隆加被罗马第三任国王图鲁斯灭国，其居民被迁至罗马。他们中的一部分人沦为罗马贵族氏族的被保护人，虽与罗马贵族同姓（nomen），但别名（cognomen）暗示其外来者身份和作为依附者的平民地位，罗马贵族氏族尤尼乌斯（Iunius）、博斯图米乌斯（Postumius）中以阿尔比纽斯（Albinus）或阿尔布斯（Albus）为别名的平民支系大概就是由此而来的。

据此推测，与贵族同姓的平民很可能出自贵族氏族中的被保护人。根据罗马人的姓氏法则，被

---

① 本文主要根据 T.R.S. 布劳敦《罗马共和时期的职官》第 1 卷列举的贵族和平民职官名单统计。

② 与贵族同姓的平民氏族：Antonius, Atilius, Aquillius, Cassius, Claudius, Cominius, Cornelius, Curiatius, Duilius, Furius, Genucius, Iunius, Lucretius, Manilius, Marcius, Menenius, Minucius, Mucius, Numicius, Oppius, Poetilius, Quinctius, Sempronius, Servilius, Sulpicius, Valerius, Verginius, Veturius, Volumnius 等。罗马氏族名单参见 http://en.wikipedia.org/wiki/List_of_Roman_gentes#I.

③ 威廉·史密斯：《希腊罗马人物传记与神话辞典》（William Smith, *Dictionary of Greek and Roman Biography and Mythology*, 1870），第 118，775，794，856 页。另见 http://en.wikipedia.org/wiki/Cornelia_(gens)；http://en.wikipedia.org/wiki/Claudius_(gens)；http://en.wikipedia.org/wiki/Valerius。

④ 与平民同姓的执政官家族：Iunius, Lucretius, Valerius, Menenius, Verginius, Cassius, Veturius, Sempronius, Minucius, Servilius, Furius, Claudius, Numicius, Volumnius, Curiatius, Genucius, Cornelius, Quinctius, Sulpicius。

⑤ 苏维托尼乌斯：《罗马十二帝王传》，张竹明、王乃新、蒋平等译，商务印书馆 1995 年，第 208 页。

⑥ 西塞罗：《西塞罗全集·演说辞卷》下，王晓朝译，人民出版社 2008 年，第 63 页。

⑦ http://en.wikipedia.org/wiki/Licinia_(gens).

⑧ 《新保利古典百科全书》（August Friedrich von Pauly ed., *Der Neue Pauly: Enzyklopädie der Antike*, Metzler Verlag, 1998），Atilii 辞条。

保护人中的外来自由人和解放自由人（被释奴）都有权与贵族主人同姓。罗马帝国时代的碑铭材料提供了最为直观的证据。

D(is) M(anibus) Sex(to) Val(erio) Sex(ti) lib(erto), Pal(atina tribu) Zotico, u(ixit) a(nnis) XLII, h(ic) s(itus) e(st).[①]

（释文：绥克斯图斯·瓦拉利乌斯·佐提库是绥克斯图·瓦拉利乌斯的被释奴，帕拉提纳部落公民，享年 42 岁，长眠于此。）

这位被释奴全名为绥克斯图斯·瓦拉利乌斯·佐提库。首名和中间的姓氏都与主人绥克斯图斯·瓦拉利乌斯相同，尾名是他做奴隶时的名字。他有部落籍贯，说明已成为罗马公民。这种姓名书写方式与生来自由的公民的名字写法不同。被释奴的姓名系统里只提主人的名字，不提父亲的名字。这是被释奴没有父权的表现。

在共和早期，某些与贵族同姓的平民似乎也没有父权。以弗吉尼乌斯（Verginius）为例[②]。关于公元前 450 年的第二个立法委员会的传说中有一个令人匪夷所思的故事情节：贵族阿庇乌斯·克劳狄乌斯企图霸占一位平民少女弗吉尼亚（Verginia），宣称她是自己家中的女奴隶。奇怪的是，这位少女的父亲弗吉尼乌斯在法庭上似乎无法证明他们的父女关系。最后，他亲手杀死了自己的女儿。这一举动与其说是为了保全女儿的贞洁，不如说是为了宣示他对子女拥有生杀予夺的"父权"[③]。倘若平民弗吉尼乌斯是一位生来自由的公民的话，他完全没必要这么做，因为可以在法庭上证明自己的父权。但如果他是一名被释奴或其后代的话，他的父权就成了问题，因为按照传统，被释奴的子女和财产将由主人继承。因此，我们可以把弗吉尼乌斯弑女的故事理解为被保护人迫使贵族承认其父权的一种激烈的表达方式。

自由人出身的被保护人亦采用贵族主人的姓氏。

C(aio) Iulio, C(aii) Iuli Ricoueriugi f(ilio), Vol(tinia tribu), Marino…[④]

（盖约·尤利乌斯·马利努斯是盖约·尤利乌斯·利库埃林古斯之子，沃提尼亚部落公民……）

这是一位获得了罗马公民权的高卢人盖约·尤利乌斯·马利努斯，他的名字已经罗马化了，只是通过其父亲的名字，我们才知道他具有高卢人的血统。马利努斯是通过罗马的贵族保护人盖约·尤利乌斯获得的公民权。因此，他的首名和族名与保护人相同。

最后，我们已知，公元前 4–3 世纪多次产生执政官的平民显贵家族克劳狄乌斯·马尔克卢斯（Claudius Marcellus）就是贵族克劳狄乌斯氏族中的被保护人[⑤]。这是与贵族同姓的平民是贵族的被保护人或其后代的最直接的证据。

罗马执政官年表显示，公元前 5 世纪，有 10 个与贵族同姓的平民家族产生，公元前 4 世纪有 8 个，公元前 3 世纪有 4 个，公元前 2 世纪有 3 个，公元前 1 世纪有 3 个，说明公元前 5–4 世纪是贵族氏族发生分裂的高峰时期。这与被保护人从李维笔下逐渐消失的时期相吻合，这种巧合绝非罗马作家所能伪造的，实际暗示在这个历史阶段确实发生了一场被保护人革命。

证实了与贵族同姓的平民是来自贵族氏族的被保护人及其后代之后，被保护人出身的平民政治家族及个人就逐渐浮出水面。据初步统计，这一时期（公元前 494—287 年）大约有 23 个与贵族同

---

① 让–马莉·拉塞尔：《罗马铭文学手册》（Jean–Marie Lassere, *Manuel D'epigraphie Romaine*, vol.1, Editions A.et J.Picard, 2007），第 1 卷，第 164 页。
② 弗吉尼乌斯氏族分为贵族和平民两支。公元前 5 世纪，贵族支系中产生了许多执政官，而平民支系中则产生了许多著名的保民官。
③ 李维：《罗马史》，III，48，5。
④ 让–马莉·拉塞尔：《罗马铭文学手册》，第 1 卷，第 173 页。
⑤ 西塞罗：《论演说家》，王焕生译，中国政法大学出版社 2003 年，第 119 页。

姓的平民家族①。籍此进一步探索隐藏在传统文献史料中的被保护人的行为事迹，考察被保护人阶层与贵族—平民集团的互动关系，分析其参政动机、政治立场与利益诉求。

三　平民运动与被保护人的解放

库朗热曾感叹罗马史家疏于记载"被保护人革命"这段历史：

> 　罗马在相当长的一段历史时期内充满了被保护人与保护人的斗争。李维不惯于深入探讨制度的变革，自然未说及此；并且李维翻阅古代史书，其材料皆采自祭司编年史记及同类史料，这些史记和史料皆不会述及氏族内部的斗争。
>
> 　……至于被保护人脱离贵族的时代，现在无确证可以知道。……似乎塞尔维乌斯时期，他们已是公民；……但不能立即说他们完全解放。……共和时期，平民以及保民官皆欲保护他们。许多被保护人如是脱离，氏族已无法维系。……大概保民官的设立，使逃出的被保护人得有保护，使平民地位可羡可靠，遂令解放的潮流加速。②

由于缺乏史料证据，库朗热只能推测罗马早期被保护人获得解放的基本过程。目前的研究表明，促使被保护人获得自由的一个原因很可能是贵族绝嗣③。共和前期，由于战争原因造成贵族氏族人口严重凋敝。据统计，公元前5世纪，罗马贵族氏族大约61族或53族，公元前4世纪只剩下29族或24族④。大批被保护人因贵族氏族衰败而获得解放，成为自由平民，在贵族氏族内部形成独立的平民家族支系。

有学者认为罗马早期的保护关系只是个人关系，即身而止。贵族保护人绝嗣后，氏族不能继承其被保护人的人身与财产⑤。但是，西塞罗时代的一些法律纠纷反映出氏族有权继承保护关系的古老风俗。而且，脱离了保护关系的被保护人何不建立独立的平民氏族，却继续被冠以贵族氏族的姓氏，只是通过别名表明其平民身份呢？这只能说明，早期的保护关系并非即身而止，与贵族同姓的平民家族受风俗和礼法的制约，与贵族氏族藕断丝连。这既是被保护人阶层加入平民阵营反对贵族的主要动机，也是贵族集团能够利用他们反对平民的原因所在。

其实，被保护人革命在罗马传统史料中并非完全无迹可寻，只不过出于史家的无心之笔。以下尝试重构这一过程。

一条线索是，在第一次撤离运动中（公元前494年），在"圣山"主持平民集体宣誓，订立神圣约法的卢西乌斯·尤尼乌斯·布鲁图斯（L.Iunius Brutus）就出自与贵族同姓的被保护人阶层。该家族成员随后两年继续担任平民职官。这是被保护人阶层从一开始就参与平民反抗贵族统治者的斗

---

① 即 Antonius, Atilius, Aquillius, Cassius, Claudius, Cominius, Curiatius, Duilius, Furius, Genucius, Iunius, Marcius, Menenius, Minucius, Mucius, Numicius, Oppius, Poetilius, Sempronius, Sulpicius, Verginius, Veturius, Volumnius.

② 库朗热：《古代城邦》，第317–320。参考李玄伯译文，《希腊罗马古代社会研究》，中国政法大学出版社2005年，第225–228页。

③ 阿尔弗蒂：《罗马社会史》（Géza Alfödy, *The Social History of Rome*, Routledge, 1988），第10页。

④ 卡瑞·斯卡拉德：《罗马史》（M.Cary & H.H.Scullard, *A History of Rome*, Macmillan,1986）第76页。奥莫：《罗马政治制度》（Léon Homo, *Roman Political Institutions*, Routledge, 1929）第35页。

⑤ 杜鲁门："罗马的早期被保护人"，载华勒士-哈德里尔编：《古代社会的保护制度》，第103–105页。

争的证据。此后（到公元前 287 年为止），共有 16 个与贵族同姓的平民家族产生了保民官。①

另一条线索是，被保护人出身的保民官强烈反对那些充当"平民保护人"的贵族。

公元前 491 年，贵族科瑞奥拉努斯（Coriolanus）自费从西西里购粮，分配给平民，结果遭到保民官的起诉、逮捕，经平民大会审判，以企图废除保民官制度的罪名被判处流放②。

公元前 384 年，贵族曼利乌斯（Manlius）拍卖自己的庄园，替 400 多个平民偿还债务，有两位保民官提出控告，罪名是"企图称王"，结果曼利乌斯被享有执政官大权的军政官判处死刑③。

两位被保护人出身的平民职官直接参与了这两起案件的审理：在第一起案件中，逮捕科瑞奥拉努斯的是平民营造官提图斯·尤尼乌斯·布鲁图斯（T.Iunius Brutus）。在第二起案件中，支持审判科瑞奥拉努斯的两位保民官中有一位名叫马库斯·美奈尼乌斯（M.Menenius）。他们都是与贵族同姓的平民，可见出身于被保护人阶层。这两起事件表明，被保护人出身的保民官强烈反对贵族利用保护关系支配平民，试图使保民官成为平民和被保护人唯一合法的"保护人"。这是被保护人革命的第一步。

被保护人革命的第二步是公元前 470 年的部落大会改革。塞尔维乌斯的百人团改革并没有赋予被保护人自主表决的权利，直到平民运动初期，被保护人在公民大会仍受到贵族主人的监督和操纵。直到设立平民部落大会，被保护人的投票自由才得到保障。

被保护人革命的第三步是通过立法限制贵族任意奴役、支配被保护人。公元前 5 世纪中期颁布的《十二铜表法》中出现了明确反映被保护人阶层利益诉求的法律。在第 8 表中有一条规定："保护人欺诈被保护人的，将受到诅咒（Patronus si clienti fraudem faxit, sacer esto）"④。促成这一立法的平民领袖中就有被保护人出身的弗吉尼乌斯（Verginius，公元前 461- 公元前 457 的保民官）。第二个立法委员会中也有被保护人出身的平民立法委员（Q. Poetilius、K.Duilius、Sp.Oppius）⑤。

这条法律颁布之后，立即产生效果。公元前 449 年，当平民举行第二次撤离运动时，贵族没有利用被保护人进行镇压；公元前 445 年，保民官阻止征兵时，贵族也不再动员被保护人参加战斗。这些现象表明，当被保护人不愿跟随贵族主人出征时，贵族不能滥用保护人的权威，强迫他们服从。此后，被保护人除了履行传统的义务以外（如经济上的义务），不必事事服从贵族主人。相应地，正如我们在前面看到的，公元前 4 世纪，当贵族需要被保护人的支持时，往往以商量的，而非命令的态度提出请求。

被保护人对贵族的依附性，在很大程度上是由于对贵族氏族土地的依赖。因此，在争取自由的过程中，被保护人必然要求拥有对土地的所有权。传统观点认为，平民运动中提出的一系列《土地法案》主要体现了氏族以外的无地的平民的意志。现在需要对此重新加以思考，因为试图脱离贵族氏族的被保护人同样有分配公有地和在被征服地区建立殖民地的要求。值得注意的是，《土地法案》

---

① 其中 Verginius 家族 4 人次；3 人次的家族有 Genucius, Iunius, Menenius, Poetilius；2 人次的家族有 Duilius, Marcius；1 人次的家族有 Cassius, Cominius, Curiatius, Furius, Minucius, Mucius, Numicius, Oppius, Sempronius。

② 李维：《罗马史》2, 33-35；哈利卡纳索斯的狄奥尼修斯：《罗马古事记》，7, 33, 1-66, 3; 8, 31, 4；普鲁塔克：《希腊罗马名人传·科里奥拉努斯传》（Plutarch, *Lives IV, Alcibiades and Coriolanus*, translated by Bernadotte Perrin, Loeb Classical Library），13, 1—21, 4。

③ 李维：《罗马史》，VI, 20, 1-12。

④ E.H. 瓦尔明登译：《拉丁古文献辑录》第 3 卷，《十二铜表法》（*Remains of Old Latin III*，"*Laws of the XII Tables*", translated by E.H.Warmington, Loeb Classical Library,1979）。参见《罗马法》，群众出版社 1985，第 369 页。

⑤ 李维说，第二个立法委员会的成员都是贵族（李维：《罗马史》3, 35, 9）。但狄奥尼修斯指出，其中有三人（Poetilius、Duilius、Oppius）是平民（哈利卡纳索斯的狄奥尼修斯：《罗马古事记》，10, 58, 4-5）。这种矛盾的说法恰恰说明，这三人是出自贵族氏族，与贵族同姓的被保护人。他们的身份具有模糊性，介于贵族与平民之间。

的制定者往往是被保护人出身的保民官——卡西乌斯（Cassius，公元前486①）、盖努基乌斯（Genucius，公元前476、公元前473）、美奈尼乌斯（Menenius，公元前409，《美奈尼乌斯法》Lex Menenia agraria）。他们代表了被保护人在土地所有权问题上的利益诉求。

被保护人革命最关键的一步是解除对贵族保护人的义务。被保护人究竟通过什么方式解除保护关系的？本人推测，使被保护人摆脱依附关系的一个重要契机就是平民职官的设立。有证据表明，被保护人可以通过担任公职获得免除被保护人义务的特权。普路塔克的《马略传》中有一则案例。公元前118年，时任平民营造官的盖尤斯·马略（Gaius Marius）遇到一起官司：

> 盖尤斯·赫兰纽斯（Gaius Herennius）作为证人受到召唤要出庭作证，律师提出抗辩，说是根据习惯，一位保护人不能出面指控其被保护人，法律豁免这种违背天理人情的义务，因为马略和他的父母一直都是赫兰纽斯家族的被保护人。法官接受律师的抗辩，马略自己加以反对，同时向赫兰纽斯说明，第一次授予官职就已不再是他的被保护人。②

马略第一次担任的官职是保民官。普路塔克对他的抗辩表示怀疑，他说："不是任何一种官职都可以免除被保护人的责任，身为后裔就可以对保护人不再尽自己的义务，按照法律的规定只有坐象牙椅的高官，可以获得这种特权。"③

普路塔克提到的这条法律非常重要，根据这条法律，被保护人一旦担任高级职官，就意味着保护关系的终止。普路塔克对马略的申辩也许存在误解。马略的说法与法律规定并不一定矛盾。马略说，他从第一次担任保民官起就不再是赫兰纽斯家族的被保护人，意思是，身为保民官，其人身神圣不可侵犯，自然不受保护人的支配。但这种人身自由只在任期内有效，一旦卸任则保护关系重新恢复。马略自保民官卸任后立即当选为平民营造官，继续拥有神圣人身，而且他是以现任营造官身份进行法律诉讼的，所以有权提出不受保护关系束缚，法官也接受了他的说法。

如果说，被保护人出身的平民通过担任保民官、平民营造官这类平民职官只能暂时获得解放的话，那么，通过担任高级职官则能永久地获得自由。这是公元前2世纪末的情况。公元前4-3世纪的情况不是这样。

西塞罗在《论演说家》中提到另一桩官司④。围绕平民家族克劳狄乌斯·马尔克卢斯中的一个被保护人或被释奴的遗产继承问题，同姓的两个克劳狄乌斯家族打起了官司。平民克劳狄乌斯·马尔克卢斯家族主张被保护人的遗产由本家族继承。但贵族克劳狄乌斯认为，平民克劳狄乌斯·马尔克卢斯家族本身就是贵族克劳狄乌斯氏族中的被保护人，他们的被保护人及其遗产都应归贵族克劳狄乌斯氏族所有。这桩诉讼令法学家左右为难。究竟百人团法庭判谁胜诉，我们不得而知。这桩官司发生的具体时间也不清楚。显然，这个案例触及被保护人及其后代对家族财产的所有权和继承权问题。而被保护人的后代若要获得充分的人身和财产的自由支配权利，就必须终止保护义务。很可能马略所提到的那条法律就是在这种社会背景下出台的。

---

① 公元1世纪的罗马作家瓦拉里乌斯·马克西姆斯（Valerius Maximus）提到一条史料：公元前486年，贵族执政官卡西乌斯（Sp.Cassius）之子担任了保民官，并制订了第一份《土地法案》（D.Wardle, *Valerius Maximus' Memorable Deeds and Sayings: Book* V,8,2. Oxford University Press, 1998）。贵族不可能担任平民保民官，故推断此人出自贵族卡西乌斯氏族的平民支系。
② 普鲁塔克：《希腊罗马名人传·马略传》（Plutarch, *Lives*, *IX*, *Pyrrhus and Gaius Marius*, translated by Bernadotte Perrin, Loeb Classical Library），5。
③ 同上。
④ 西塞罗：《论演说家》（Cicero, *On the Orator*, translated by E. W. Sutton and H. Rackham, Loeb Classical Library）1, 39。

由于平民马尔克卢斯家族未提到马略所说的那条法律，所以我们认为，该案件发生在公元前2世纪之前。既然平民马尔凯鲁斯能够拥有被保护人，说明该家族当时已成为拥有较高的政治地位和社会地位的显贵家族。公元前331年，马尔克卢斯家族产生第一位执政官（Marcus Claudius Marcellus）。公元前222年—公元前208年期间，另一位同名成员4度担任执政官。因此，这桩官司可能发生于公元前4世纪后半叶—公元前3世纪后半叶之间。

通过这个案例，我们明白了为什么被保护人出身的平民显贵需要挣脱保护关系的束缚。他们在政治、法律、宗教等方面已获得与贵族平等的权利，不再需要依赖贵族主人代理。但是，他们还要为享有合法的财产权同贵族氏族进行斗争。

那么，《李锡尼—绥克斯图法》中要求对平民开放执政官；公元前342年，被保护人出身的保民官盖努基乌斯制订了一条平民决议（Lex Genucia），要求两个执政官都可由平民担任[①]；以及后来要求开放牙座营造官、监察官等高级职官的动议，这些政治追求与被保护人阶层争取自由的利益诉求密切相关。那些与贵族同姓的平民政治家族的参政动机，很大程度上是为了解除被保护人世代因袭的义务。

公元前494年—公元前287年，参政的平民家族有73个，与贵族同姓的有23个，约占32%。这一时期65个保民官家族中与贵族同姓的有16个，约占25%。公元前366年—公元前287年期间产生了26个平民执政官家族，与贵族同姓的有11个，约占42%。被保护人出身的平民政治家在执政官中所占比例远远高于在保民官中所占比例。看来被保护人更热衷于谋求高级公职，其参政的动机与其说是同情、支持平民，不如说是出于个人家族利益的考虑——唯有通过担任高级职官才能解除保护关系，从而获得充分自由。

贵族为何容许被保护人脱离其氏族？我们知道，被保护人和朋友（amicitia）是共和中后期贵族政治的两大支柱，这一政治传统可追溯到共和早期的等级冲突。贵族解放被保护人，扶植其成为平民领袖，与之结成政治盟友，这既是贵族从内部分裂平民集团的一种手段，也是维护贵族家族政治利益的一种策略。

李维提到，贵族怂恿某些保民官反对其同僚，靠保民官的一票否决权使平民的改革法案流产[②]。有些被保护人出身的保民官似乎是贵族的代理人。例如弗吉尼乌斯（A. Verginius）。他在担任保民官期间（公元前395和公元前394年）屡屡否决平民的《土地法案》。公元前393年，他因支持贵族元老院受到平民大会的审判，被判处罚金1千阿斯[③]。

贵族尝试与平民分享政权时，被保护人出身的平民领袖成为理想人选。公元前450年第二个十人立法委员会中就有3位与贵族同姓的平民委员（Q. Poetilius、K.Duilius、Sp.Oppius）。公元前444年——公元前367年，在13个享有执政官大权的平民军政官家族中，有5个与贵族同姓（Antonius家族1人次、Atilius家族2人次、Aquilius家族1人次、Genucius家族3人次、Duilius家族1人次）。

被保护人家族亦跻身于最早的平民执政官家族之列。公元前366年，执政官对平民开放后，盖努基乌斯家族的成员于公元前365年、公元前363年、公元前362年连续当选。公元前366年—公元前287年，平民执政官出自被保护人家族的有Iunius（6人次）、Marcius（6人次）、Genucius（4人次）、Poetilius（4人次）、Atilius（2人次）、Veturius（2人次）、Volumnius（2人次）、Claudius（1人次）、Minucius（1人次）、Sempronius（1人次）、Duilius（1人次）。他们是新兴

---

① 李维：《罗马史》7，42，2。
② 李维：《罗马史》2，44，1–6。贵族利用保民官反对其同僚的事例见于公元前481年、公元前480年、公元前462年、公元前431年、公元前430年、公元前422年、公元前416年、公元前415年、公元前410年、公元前402年、公元前394年、公元前393年、公元前377年、公元前310年等。
③ 李维：《罗马史》5，24，11；25。

的平民显贵集团的主要成员，由此实现了自身解放。被保护人革命至此大功告成。

这场革命的真正意义在于使被保护人阶层找到了不依赖贵族保护人而获得自由的渠道。早期被保护人获得解放的根本原因在于，奴隶占有制经济的兴起使罗马统治阶级转向以占有奴隶劳动为主，以剥削自由民的依附性劳动为辅的生产方式。但是，保护关系依然存在，在共和中后期及帝国时代继续发挥重要的社会功能。只不过，平民显贵也充当起保护人的角色。被保护人则以被释奴（libertus或解放自由人）和贫困公民为主体。此外，那些为谋求仕途晋升而投身于豪门贵族荫庇的骑士，又如以整个王国、地方社会为单位托庇于罗马将军、权贵和元首的外邦臣民，他们构成了特殊的被保护人群体。

被保护人革命也对平民运动产生了深刻影响。被保护人独特的介于贵族和平民两者之间的"中间身份"使他们比较容易取得贵族和平民双方的信任和支持。这种双重身份赋予被保护人出身的平民政治家及其家族双重使命：他们既是本阶层的利益代言人，也是贵族与平民之间的调停人，这就促使他们不得不在两个对立的等级之间寻找妥协与合作的可能性，在很大程度上发挥了控制社会矛盾与冲突的作用。就这样，被保护人在等级冲突过程中，利用其中间者的身份，成功地实现了自我解放，同时也导致平民运动发生转向，逐渐由冲突走向和谐（concordia）。

迦太基共和政体的历史考察——对共和主义起源的思考

贾文言　枣庄学院

摘要：对于共和主义起源的认识，学界大多将之归结于罗马共和国，这彰显了罗马共和政体的实践对于共和主义思想形成所具有的巨大影响力。但是，与此同时，包括荷马、柏拉图、亚里士多德、李维、波里比阿、西塞罗、普鲁塔克等在内的古典作家皆对迦太基人及其政体有所涉及，而亚里士多德和波里比阿更是用大量的篇幅记述了迦太基的政体实践。与罗马共和政体相比，迦太基的政体在社会基础、对公民军事力量的依赖程度、政体的价值理念、组织结构以及灵活性等方面均有显著的差异。

关键词：迦太基；共和主义起源；政体实践

Abstract：Most people of the academic holds that Roman republic was the source of the republicanism, which reflecting the influence of the practice of the Roman republic acton the formation of republican ideology. Including Homer, Plato, Aristotle, Livy, Polybius, Cicero, Plutarch and other classical writers, all made the record of Republic of Carthage. Compared with the Roman Republic, it has significant differences in the social basis of government, dependence on civil military, regime values, the organizational structure of government and flexibility of regime and so on.

Keywords：Carthage, Source of the republicanism, Practice of regime

近年来，国内学术界对"共和主义"颇为关注，引进和翻译了一大批的国外相关文献。在英美史学界，伯纳德·贝林、戈登·伍德、J. G. A. 波科克、兰斯·班宁等人，对历史中的"共和主义"多有阐述，并引发了一场历时 20 多年的讨论。这对我国史学界也产生了深刻的影响，并促使一些学者对这些问题进行了大量的思考。在这些思考之中，涉及到共和主义的起源问题，由于受国外学者的影响，我们也普遍将共和主义的起源追溯到罗马共和国，而对于文明历史较之更长的迦太基的共和政体的实践普遍采取了漠视的态度。而本文的主旨则是以罗马共和政体为参照系来考察迦太基共和政体的具体状况。

一

作为一种社会政治理论意义上的"共和主义"而言，从古代的柏拉图、亚里士多德、波里比阿到最近的佩迪特，留下的论述相当丰富。对于共和主义起源的认识，学界大多将之归结于罗马共和国。例如美国普林斯顿大学教授菲利普·佩迪特认为："从起源和特征上看，共和主义是一种罗马传统……这一传统是与罗马共和制度同时诞生的，它被用来论证这些制度的合法性，并影响其塑造；它在波里比阿、李维、普鲁塔克、塔西佗和萨卢斯特这些历史学家的著作以及法学家、演说家兼哲学家马尔库斯·图利乌斯·西塞罗的 系列作品中得到阐述。"[1](314) 北京大学教授黄洋先生在考察古代世界的共和主义时，则将讨论的范围限定在了古代的希腊和罗马，他在文中特别声明不涉及印度，"如众所周知的，西文的'共和国'一词直接源出于罗马人的概念 res publica。不仅如此，在长达四五个世纪的时间里，我们所称的共和主义不仅在罗马稳固施 行，而且在希腊城邦世界也得到广泛施行"。[2] 这似乎表明他认为古代世界只有希腊、罗马以及古代的印度存在共和主义，或者说是共和主义的政体实践。与此同时，中国社会科学院研究院施治生先生也认为："共和国……以罗马共和制为其历史典范。"[3] 以上是三则关于共和主义起源的认识材料，它们表明了一个共同的基本认识，即罗马共和政体的实践对于共和主义思想形成所具有的巨大影响力。与这种认识相伴随的一个问题是，在希腊、罗马和古代印度以外的古代世界难道不存在共和政体的记述和实践吗？通过对历史事实的考察，我们发现与罗马同时代的迦太基也在施行共和政体。而实际上，迦太基的这种地位也是被认可的，例如在古代，波里比阿把迦太基和罗马、斯巴达一起看作是共和政体的典型；在近代，美国开国之父们在谈到历史上存在的共和国模式时，仍将迦太基与斯巴达、罗马并称为共和国模式的典型。[4](322) 虽然如此，学界对于迦太基共和政体实践的具体情况的认识却并不是很清晰。从严格意义上讲，我国学界只有王明毅在施治生先生主编的《古代民主和共和制度》中曾撰文专述迦太基的政体，他在肯定迦太基是混合政体或共和政体的同时，更强调了政体中的寡头制因素。[5](213-218) 在一些通史性的著作中，在谈及罗马的对外扩张时往往对迦太基的政体有所叙述，例如德国著名罗马史专家蒙森在其《罗马史》中就曾对迦太基的政体有所涉及，然多有贬损之意。[6](13-22)

二

在历史上，荷马、柏拉图、亚里士多德（以下简称亚氏）、李维、波里比阿、西塞罗、普鲁塔克等古典作家皆对迦太基人及其共和政体有所涉及，而亚氏和波里比阿更是留下了大量关于迦太基政体实践情况的记述。亚氏对于迦太基政体的记述集中体现在《政治学》中，他对希腊世界的 158 个城邦的政体进行了大量实地调查和研究，而在这些城邦中，迦太基是唯一的一个非希腊城邦。亚氏不仅对其进行了考察，而且对其进行了由衷的赞叹，他认为："迦太基在政体方面做得很出色，在许多地方超出其他城邦……迦太基的许多设置都比前两者（即斯巴达和克里特——引者）优良，其政体优良的一个证明是，尽管其政体制中保持着平民的因素，却一直很稳定，没有什么值得一提的动乱，也没有产生过暴君。"[7](64)

在对迦太基的政体展开论述时，亚氏注重将其与希腊世界最优良的斯巴达政体进行对比，在比较中突出其特色。在亚氏看来，迦太基政体的优势主要体现在四个方面：第一，人才的选拔主要依据是德能，不是依据同一个家族，也不是随便哪个人都可以当选。因为当权者都有极大的权力，假若是些无才无德之人，便会造成巨大的危害。第二，在政体中有平民因素，并在政体的运行过程中发挥相当作用。例如，当诸王和长老意见出现分歧时，平民可以就这些事情做出决定。对于他们提交的提案，平民并不只是听取，而是拥有判决的权力，这种情况在其它城邦是不存在的。第三，在安排政体时，迦太基根据品行优良和富有的选任官员，尤其是在选任君王和将军这类高级长官时更是如此。在这里，亚氏注意到了闲暇的重要性，但是他也对此提出了批评，认为这种做法使得财富胜过了德性，从而使得德性没有得到很好的尊崇，因此亚氏主张应该让那些最有能力治理的人当政。

第四，通过一人专任一个官职的方式在所有公民中贯彻管理与被管理的关系。迦太基人认为一个人兼任数职不是好办法，主张一人专任一个官职，从而使得政治更加制度化和平民化。[7](65-67)

而波里比阿也把迦太基和罗马、斯巴达的政体一起看作是混合政体的历史例证，并称赞迦太基的政制起初在最主要方面是很好的。[8](51) 虽然在他的书中不乏对迦太基的赞美，但是却把迦太基人说成是野蛮人。他在《通史》第六卷中，专门对罗马的政体、军事制度和传统习俗作了详细描述和评论，并将罗马与迦太基做了对比。他认为到汉尼拔战争时，迦太基已经渡过了它最为繁荣和稳定的时期，那里的人民已经掌握了国家权力，政体的平衡已经被破坏。就军事而论，迦太基人的海军固然强大，但它的陆军使用雇佣兵，效率远低于罗马。[8](51-52)

可以说，对于迦太基政体的描述，亚氏和波里比阿两人出现了诸多差异。亚里士多德记述迦太基政体的原因大体是出于对其政体的羡慕，并对其充分肯定。相比之下，波里比阿的记述则颇有一些被强迫的味道，因为在罗马对外征服扩张过程中必须要面对迦太基，并且，波里比阿记述的出发点或者说是视角则完全是罗马式的，因此对迦太基人的政体自然不如亚里士多德那样充满赞叹，而是多有批判。

三

在对迦太基政体的记述中，明显可以看出亚里士多德和波里比阿两位古典作家注重将其与其他政体进行对比，在比较中凸显其特色。但是这种符号化的比较，无助于认识迦太基政体的具体状况，因此笔者决定以罗马共和政体作为参照系，在比较中认识迦太基的共和政体。

学界一般认为迦太基是寡头制共和政体而罗马是贵族制共和政体，但是，正如英国学者戴维·赫尔德所认为的那样："相形之下，当代学者一般认为，罗马基本上是一种寡头体制。尽管罗马思想家的著作中（特别是西塞罗的著作中）包含了希腊的国家概念，尽管罗马的政治共同体包含了公民出身的农民和获得解放的奴隶，但是，精英人物稳固地支配着罗马政治的所有方面。"[9](34) 笔者认为，迦太基政体与罗马共和政体的区别并不仅仅是寡头制与共和制的区别，而是有着更为深刻的区别，因为两者在社会基础、对公民军事力量的依赖程度、政体的价值理念、组织结构以及灵活性等诸多方面均有较为显著的差异。

罗马共和政体建立的社会基础是自由而独立的小土地所有者。在罗马共和国时代，土地是罗马社会最为可靠的财产，小土地所有者是罗马共和国最有力的支柱，由此造成了其严正节俭的独特民族气质。由于罗马公民的土地情节，这使得他们对于土地是异常的珍惜，在经年累月的战争中，罗马人也曾经失败过，但是他们在媾和时从来没有割让过土地，正如美国圣母大学威廉·P.雷诺兹历史学讲座教授菲利普·费尔南德兹·阿迈斯托所评述的那样，"罗马人最初只是一群农民……军民迫于生计而变得好战。除了掠夺邻居之外，他们找不到其他获得财富的途径。罗马人按照战争的需要组织社会，并将胜利奉为最高价值。"[10](237)

相比之下，虽然迦太基人的所居之地适宜发展农业，其将军和政治家也不惜以科学方法管理农业和以之教人，但是商业永远是迦太基人心目中最为高尚的职业。因此，"在迦太基，富豪强于地主，……迦太基的农业家一概是大地主和蓄奴隶的人。……商业大城所独具的一切富豪现象已到处流行"。[6](17)表现在对战争以及土地的态度上便是，"争斗如果可以避免，他们总竭力妥协从事"、"他们的居留地只是商馆。由他们的眼光看，获得远方的广袤领地而在那里费力而持久地推行殖民实业，不如与土人交易的重要"。[6](4)

与罗马共和国所采取的公民兵制不同，迦太基人试图通过采用雇佣军避开公民兵制的方式去建立并统治其帝国。最初，迦太基同周边希腊城邦一样，也拥有一支公民军队，无论战备体系还是战术思想都带有浓厚的希腊风格。公元前 4 世纪晚期，亚历山大创建马其顿帝国以后，职业军队成为希腊化时代的主流。大约在此时，迦太基放弃了公民兵军事体制，但却未仿效希腊化王国建立职业军队，而是越来越依靠雇佣军。只有在敌军兵临城下时，迦太基公民才会应征入伍，保卫祖国，而这种情况在布匿战争之前几百年间只发生过一次。这在世界历史上是不曾存在的事情，哪怕是巴比伦早期的商业与城市帝国，统治与守护他们的也是一群来自南方草原的闪米特武士。迦太基人不像罗马人一样把战争当做日常事务的一部分，布匿战争爆发后迦太基人的准备明显地落后于罗马人。

至于缘何迦太基的公民在军队中角色会发生如此转化，这可能与迦太基人特殊的生存环境有着密切的关系，当时希腊人在意大利与西西里的殖民运动来势汹涌，而迦太基人则竭尽所能地寻找每一个潜在的盟友。原先，腓尼基人为了满足巴比伦统治者的勒索而远赴充满危险的海洋；而今天，他们为了获得贿赂土王蛮酋的财富而让自己的子民奔波在每一个危险与未知的地区——这也许是公民兵制消亡的最初原因。

在罗马共和政制中，波里比阿指出执政官代表王制因素，元老院代表着贵族制因素，人民代表民主制因素，这三者既分工合作又互相制约，使国家政体处于均衡状态，保证着国家长期稳定发展。但是，实际上执政官所代表的王制因素并不显见，因为在执政官为首的行政长官、元老院和公民大会三大政权机构 中，执政官等行政长官从属于元老院，卸职后进入元老院，不能算作独立存在的要素。而罗马共和国的直译国名"罗马元老院和人民 (Senatus Populusque Romanus)"似乎从另一个角度反映了罗马共和国的这种元老院和人民的二元政治结构的特色。就罗马共和国的政制而言，罗马贵族是共和政制的核心部分，构成了共和国的主导力量，他们通过元老院参与共和国的政体塑造，决定着共和国的命运。而人民虽然在罗马公民群体中占了绝大多数，并在军事和经济上对国家负有重大义务，但是他们在政治上并没有什么主导性的权力。

相比之下，迦太基的政体却不是简单的罗马式的"人民"与贵族分享权力的混合政体，而是注重防范部门专权和滥用权力分权制衡的政体，它的价值取向以及政体的变化形式都与罗马共和国的共和理念形成了明显的差异。在亚历山大·汉密尔顿那里，"republic"一词曾在多种意义上使用，他认为，迦太基与王制时代的罗马、设有任职终身的元老院的斯巴达一样拥有同样体制。[11]可以说，在迦太基的共和政体中确实含有一些分权制衡的理念和机制。而在罗马的共和政体中存在明确的等级之间的权力划分，并且侧重权力的功能和运作流程，却没有把这种划分置于相互制约以防止专权和滥用权力的框架中去，相反罗马共和国的共和政体所设置的独裁制为这种权力的集中和滥用大开方便之门。迦太基共和政体中的分权制衡理念和机制，可以防止迦太基政府的某一部分侵夺或者垄断权力，从而达到维护政体稳定的目的。在迦太基的政制中，分权和制衡的意义已经从罗马式的贵族与平民之间的分权均势转化为防范部门的专权和权力的滥用。

政治理念上的差异使得迦太基的政体在组织结构上有别于罗马的共和政体，这主要表现在如下几个方面：第一，它把政府的合理性和正当性建立在"人民主权"的基础上，并保障"人民"对政府的参与、信任和制约；第二，它消解了参议院的贵族性，没有采用参议员财产资格和任职终身制，而实行相对短期的轮换制，这在一定意义上使得参议院变成了一个"人民"的元老院；第三，它用代表制改造了迦太基的公民大会，使之成为"委托－代理"的"间接民主"的机构，可以说是一个精英化的民主分支；第四，它借鉴了君主制的好处，强化了行政权的功能和作用，并将它赋予单独一个人行使。从总体上来看，在迦太基，没有一个机构可以享有全部的绝对权力，元老院、执政官与公民代表大会互相制约，它的政体综合了贵族、寡头与平民体制的优点。可以说，迦太基的共和政体乃是在雅典的民主制与罗马的贵族制之间采取了一条中间路线：它固然比不上雅典政体那般民主，但同时也弱化了罗马共和政体的贵族色彩。政体组织结构的总体平衡使得迦太基建立并维持长达七个世纪的稳定，即使是经常贬损迦太基的罗马史家蒙森也不得不承认："迦太基没有值得挂齿的革命，无论是起于上流阶级或下流阶级的。"[6](15)

最后，迦太基的共和政体在政体变化形式以及灵活性上不如罗马共和国的共和政体。在探讨罗马对外扩张以及对外战争中成功的原因时，学者们往往将之归功于罗马共和国优良的混合政体，这一点尤以波里比阿最为典型。在罗马成功的众多原因之中，他最为强调政治体制的作用，认为罗马共和国优良的政体是其取得成功的根本原因。但是事实上，往往忽视了每每在罗马共和国最危急的时刻，它的独裁制所发挥的独特作用。考之于迦太基的政体，它没有类似的机构。相反，迦太基的制度有一种偏差却是特有的，即它的立国精神原本于贵族政体，或共和政体，可它有时偏向平民政体。亚里士多德认为："迦太基现行法制，并未消除一切乱源，倘使时运艰难，遭逢边警，平民是会反叛的。"[7](65)这种偏差在布匿战争中表现得尤为突出，不是元老院准备出卖人民的利益，就是人民置元老院的决策于不顾，彼此争执的结果，总是人民的鲁莽战胜元老院的理智，国家的毁灭即肇因于此。可以说，迦太基内部的政治斗争使它的政府在关键时刻难以保持足够的凝聚力，这正如孟德斯鸠在《罗马盛衰原因论》中所评述的那样："在迦太基得势的有两派，一派总是希望和平，另一派总是希望战争；结果迦太基把自己弄得既不能享有和平，又不能很好地进行战争。"[12](16)

综上，迦太基城邦的政体是完全建立在"人民主权"基础上的防范部门专权和滥用权力分权制衡的政体。它的社会基础、对公民军事力量的依赖程度、政体的价值理念、政体组织结构以及灵活性等诸多方面都与罗马共和国形成了明显的差异。其根本精神在于把大众民主、精英统治、领导决断三者进行混合，从而兼顾国家各个阶层的利益，做到尽可能的公正。相比之下，迦太基的政体比罗马的共和政体更为稳固，其政体的稳定性为希腊罗马古典作家所注目。比之于罗马共和政体，笔者认为迦太基的共和政体可能更贴近于现代共和主义的起源，迦太基共和政体更接近于现代西方的所谓民主政治，迦太基的诸王相当于其国家元首，迦太基的长老院相当于其议会，迦太基公民大会的职能则相当于其公民的投票权与选举权。这正如施治生先生在评述罗马政体时所说的那样，虽然共和国以罗马共和制为其历史典范，但是"这并不意味着古代的民主和共和仅仅限于古希腊罗马地区，单纯地把古代西方当作民主和共和的发源地。其实，东方文明古国并非所谓的东方专制主义一统天下，许多国家都留存了民主和共和的历史痕迹"。[3]这样看来，迦太基人所施行的共和政体比人们通常想象的都要重要得多，而它的重要性却往往被忽视。可以说，迦太基提供了一个很好的参照系，使我们能够更深刻地理解现代西方的所谓民主政治，有助于更加清晰地显现现代西方民主政治的一些特征。

参考文献

[1] 菲利普·佩迪特：《共和主义：一种关于自由与政府的理论》，南京：江苏人民出版社，2006.

[2] 黄洋：《古代世界的共和主义》，《史学集刊》，2010(5): 3–9.

[3] 施治生：《试论古代的民主与共和》，《世界历史》，1997(1): 3–13.

[4] 汉密尔顿：《联邦党人文集》，北京：商务印书馆，2004.

[5] 施治生，郭方：《古代民主和共和制度》，北京：中国社会科学出版社，2002.

[6] 特奥多尔·蒙森：《罗马史 (第三卷)》，北京：商务印书馆，2007.

[7] 亚里士多德：《政治学》，北京：中国人民大学出版社，2003.

[8] Polybius. *The Histories, the Loeb Classical Library*, vol. I, (Cambridge, Massachusetts: Harvard University Press, 2005.)

[9] 戴维·赫尔德：《民主的模式》，北京：中央编译出版社，2008.

[10] 菲利普·费尔南德兹·阿迈斯托：《世界：一部历史 (上卷)》，北京 : 北京大学出版社 , 2010.

[11] LEXANDER H. "New York Ratifying Convention, Notes for Speech of July 12, 1788," in Harold C. Syrett, ed. *The Paper of Alexander Hamilton*, New York: Columbian University Press, 1962, vol Ⅴ , pp.149–150.

[12] 孟德斯鸠 :《罗马盛衰原因论》， 北京 : 商务印书馆 , 2011.

印欧人迁徙与古罗马文明

孙振民 菏泽学院

摘要：印欧人的迁徙是历史上具有划时代意义的大事件，在一定程度上改变了世界文明的历史进程，不仅促使了同时代各种文明间的碰撞与融合，也推动了新的文明产生与发展。不断迁徙到亚平宁半岛各个地区的印欧人就发挥了这样的作用。他们与当地的和其他外来的文化相结合，不仅奠定了古罗马文明产生的基础，而且对其以后的发展产生了决定性的影响。

关键词：印欧人；古罗马；文明

Abstract: The Indo-Europeans migration is the landmark event in the history of ancient civilizations. To some extent, it changed the course of world civilization by promoting the collision and fusion of various contemporary civilizations and furthering the emergence and development of new civilizations. Those Indo-Europeans who continually immigrated into Apennine Peninsula should have plaid such roles. Having fused with other cultural elements they not only established the basis for the emergence of Roman Civilization but also had a decisive impact on its later development.

Keywords: the Indo-Europeans, Ancient Rome, Civilization

对于印欧人的研究一直广受国外史学界的关注，国外学者在印欧人的起源、[1]印欧语系的构成

---

[1] 对于印欧人的起源地问题，西方学术界争论颇多，大致可分为亚洲说和欧洲说两种，现在的主流观点是欧洲起源论。参看相关英文资料，以及龚缨晏：《关于印欧语系的起源问题》，《世界历史》，2000 年第 5 期，第 111—114 页。廖学盛：《苏联学者关于印欧语系诸族发源地的一些意见》，《史学理论研究》，1992 第 2 期，第 58 页。综合起来在国外学术界大致有最具代表性有两种的学术观点：第一种是伦夫鲁（C.Renfrew）提出的"小亚细亚说"，参见 Colin Renfrew : *Archaeology and Language: The Puzzle of Indo-European Origins*, Cambridge University Press, 1987. 第二种是吉布塔（M. Gimbutas) 提出的"黑海—里海说"，参见 M. Gimbutas ：*The Prehistory of Easten Europe*, Yale University Press,1956. 此外其他国外学者还持有"波罗的海—黑海起源说"、"中欧—巴尔干起源说"等学说，甚至有的学者认为就现在研究水平和资料而言，无法解决印欧人的起源地问题。

和传播、①印欧人的迁徙对其它文明的影响②等问题上展开了广泛的讨论，取得了一系列令人瞩目的学术成果。但国内的研究由于资料、语言等方面的原因，则显得比较薄弱。现有的成果大多是对国外学术界研究成果的介绍和评述，深入的研究并不多见，尤其是对迁徙到亚平宁半岛的印欧人更是很少关注，仅有个别文章稍微提及。③有鉴于此，本文试图从印欧人迁徙到亚平宁半岛的原因，特点以及与古罗马文明形成、发展之间的关系等几个方面探讨印欧人迁徙与古罗马文明之间的关系，以求教于学界，希望起到抛砖引玉的作用，引起学界对这个问题的关注。

一

18、19 世纪的欧洲语言学家经比较研究发现：古代的梵语、波斯语、拉丁语、希腊语在词根、语法形态、语音上也有许多相似之处，因此一些学者推断这些语言存在相似之处的语言很可能属于同一语系，有着共同的民族起源。④关于印欧人的发源地，一开始认为是来自中亚、近东或高加索，而在 19 世纪后，欧洲起源论逐渐成为主流，但具体发源地又有争论。因为"在亚欧大陆，宜于游牧的地带基本偏北，几乎和农耕地带平行，东起自西伯利亚，经我国的东北、蒙古、中亚、咸海里海之北、高加索、南俄罗斯，直到欧洲东境，也是自东而西，横亘于亚欧大陆的居中地带。"⑤作为一个游牧民族，印欧人的发源地应在这个区域范围之内。

出于生存本能的迁徙是印欧民族迁徙活动的主要特征。他们"牧牛，并从事少量的耕作。因为

---

① 对于印欧语系的研究在国外学术界备受关注，学术著作层出不穷，如 William Jones, *A Grammar of the Persian Language,1771,*Menston,Yorkshire：The Scolar Press,1969.；Thomas Trautmann, *Aryans and British India*, Berkeley and Los Angeles：University of California Press，1997；Stefan Arvidsson, *Aryan Idols：Indo-European Mythology as Ideology and Science*, trans. Sonia Wichmann, Chicago：The University of Chicago Press, 2006；Peter Wells, *The Barbarians Speak*, Princeton：Princeton University Press，1999；J. P. Mallory and D. Q. Adams, Encyclopedia of Indo-European Culture. 这些著作对于印欧语系的起源问题，印欧语系的各种语言之间的相同点与不同点等诸多问题阐述了自己的见解。

② 对于这个问题，国外学术界的研究从人种学、历史学、民族学、考古学等多个领域展开探讨，见 Barbara Katz Rothman, *Genetic Maps and Human Imaginations：The Limits of Science in Understanding Who We Are*, New York：W. W. Norton，1998；Stefan Arvidsson, *Aryan Idols：Indo—European Mythology as Ideology and Science*, trans. Sonia Wichmann, Chicago：The University of Chicago Press, 2006. Robert Drews, *The Coming of the Greeks：Indo—European Conquests in the Aegean and the Near East*, Princeton：Princeton University Press，1988. David Anthony, *The Horse, the Wheel, and Language: How Bronze-Age Riders from the Eurasian Steppes Shaped the Modern World*, Princeton: Princeton University Press,2007 等等。但这些著作侧重于印欧人迁徙对于亚欧大陆核心文明区印度、近东、希腊等地的影响，但对于印欧人迁徙对文明边缘区影响的研究则着墨不多。

③ 我国学术界对印欧人问题研究的文章主要有：刘欣如：《从雅利安人到欧亚游牧民族：探索印欧语系的起源》，《历史研究》，2011 年第 6 期；吴宇虹：《南方塞姆文明和北方印欧文明五千年的冲突与交融》，《东北师大学报》，2004 年第 2 期；龚缨晏：《关于印欧语系的起源问题》，《世界历史》，2000 年第 5 期；蓝琪：《印欧种人的第一次迁徙对世界历史的影响》，《贵州师范大学学报》（社会科学版），2003 年第 5 期；王欣：《印欧人的起源与吐火罗人的迁徙：学术史的回顾与方法论的思考》，《暨南史学》，2013 年.

④ Thomas Trautmann, *Aryans and British India*, Berkeley and Los Angeles：University of California Press，1997。在这部著作中作者认为：因为梵语和欧洲语言之间存在着相似之处，印度人和英国人很可能属于同一语族。同时在这部著作中提到的穆勒的文章也持有类似的观点，参见 Max Müiler，"On the Relation of the Bengali to the Arian and Aboriginal Languages of India，"（1847）.而柴尔德，安东尼则试图从物质文化的角度来论证这些语言上相似的民族属于同一语系的可能，参见 Gordon Childe, What *Happened in History*, Harmondsworth：Penguin Books, 1964；David Anthony, *The Horse, the Wheel, and Language: How Bronze-Age Riders from the Eurasian Steppes Shaped the Modern World*, Princeton: Princeton University Press,2007.

⑤ 吴于廑：《世界历史上的游牧世界与农耕世界》，武汉大学教务处编，《哲学社会科学近期学术论文选》，武汉：武汉大学出版社,1984 年，第 187 页。

主要靠畜牧为生，所以只要发现有更为理想的地方，他们就用大牛车载起所有行李，朝那里迁移。"①迁徙就这样与他们的生存需要紧密联系在一起，游牧和迁徙也就成了古印欧人的基本生活方式。

在迁徙到亚平宁半岛的印欧人中，他们保留了自己游牧文明中一些生活习惯，仍然以游牧作为重要的生存手段，这一点我们可以从与罗马相关资料中推测到，在罗马，牲畜（pecunia）是最早的罗马货币，拉丁语中"金钱"Pecunia 就来自于 pecus（牛）一字。曼德尔也写到："希腊人和罗马人直至公元前四——五世纪，仍以牛作为等价物。……这表明，在这个等价物形成的时代，畜牧业占着优势。"②根据在李维《罗马史》的记载，罗马城的建立者罗慕路斯兄弟是被牧人所收养，并且在牧人帮助下击败了阿穆略，建立了罗马城。③这表明在印欧人迁徙到亚平宁半岛以后相当长的一段时间内畜牧业仍非常重要，经济生活方式并没有发生太大变化，并没有像迁徙到东方的族人那样发生文明的裂变。

据相关资料考证，早在公元前 2000 年左右印欧人就来到亚平宁半岛的北部的，创造了巴拉菲特湖上文化，后陆续又出现了印欧人的特拉马拉文化、亚平宁文化、威兰诺瓦文化。虽然这些文化一直在发展，但与进入文明核心区的印欧人迅速进入文明时代不同的是，这里的印欧人始终在文明边缘徘徊，没有发生"化学反应"，进入文明时代。④

亚平宁半岛特殊的地理环境也是印欧人的"自然迁徙"的一个重要原因，亚平宁半岛三面环海，北面是高耸的阿尔卑斯山脉，亚平宁山脉贯穿全境。与希腊半岛相比，虽然亚平宁半岛航海条件不如希腊，但"意大利有肥沃之冲积平原与多水草之山坡地，宜于农牧"。⑤所以对于习惯游牧生活的印欧人来说，亚平宁半岛是非常理想的迁徙之地。阿尔卑斯山脉并没有阻断欧洲大陆与亚平宁半岛的交通往来与人口迁移，反而成为印欧人迁徙到亚平宁半岛的主要通道，从巴拉菲特文化创立者"从北面穿越阿尔卑斯山新移来的"⑥以后，印欧迁徙者就一批又一批来到亚平宁半岛享受这里温暖的气候与翠绿的山坡。

亚平宁半岛位于地中海的中心，地理位置对罗马后来的扩张非常有利，"意大利的创造，就是为了主宰地中海。"⑦也为其它民族通过海路来到亚平宁半岛提供了有利条件，伊特鲁里亚人、希腊人、腓尼基人等就是通过这种方式来到亚平宁半岛的。如果说，在前期原始印欧民族的迁徙是通过阿尔卑斯山口，那么"文明化了"印欧人来到亚平宁则是通过海路。由于海岸线比较平缓，缺乏天然良港，所以商业的发展要比农牧业发展的晚；无论怎样贸易的发展，给亚平宁半岛提供了接触比自己高级文明的机会，加速了古罗马文明的形成。罗马位于亚平宁半岛的中部，地处拉丁姆平原上的第伯河下游的东南岸，处于该河流渡口的位置，此地距海岸远近适中，土地肥沃。这样优越的地理位置"使罗马从一开始就比其他拉丁居留地更易于经营商业和接受外来影响"，通往意大利各地的商贸路线也就比较容易的汇集在此。罗马在意大利和地中海世界的地位也越来越重要了，"罗马是一支巨大社会威力的策源地，是中部意大利各种不同的人种的、经济的和文化的相互作用的中心。"⑧

---

① 斯塔夫里阿诺斯：《全球通史》（1500 年以前的世界），吴象婴 梁赤民译，上海：上海社会科学出版社，1999 年，第 51 页。
② 厄内斯特·曼德尔：《论马克思主义经济学》上册．廉佩直译，北京：商务印书馆，1979 年，第 43 页。
③ 参见 Livy, *History of Rome*, trans.B.O.Foster, The Loeb Classical Library ,London:Harvard University press,1996,Ⅵ.
④ 摩尔根认为在人类"文化"的发展可分为蒙昧、野蛮、文明三个阶段，参见摩尔根：《古代社会》，杨东莼，马雍，马巨译，北京：商务印书馆，1992 年，第 10—12 页。恩格斯也把文明定义为文化发展的高级阶段，并提出了"史前各文化阶段"这个定义，参见马克思，恩格斯：《马克思恩格斯选集》（第 4 卷），北京：人民出版社，1995 年，第 8 页。文章以此为基础把古文明产生之前在亚平宁半岛上存在的历史发展阶段，称为各文化阶段，以便区别于此后产生的古罗马文明。
⑤ 特奥多尔·蒙森：《罗马史》，孟祥森译，台北：远流出版公司，1982 年，第 4 页。
⑥ 李雅书，杨共乐：《古代罗马史》，北京：北京师范大学出版社，2004 年，第 4 页。
⑦ 埃米尔·路德维希：《地中海 传奇之海》，梁光严译，北京：国际文化出版社公司，2005 年，第 46 页。
⑧ 科瓦略夫：《古代罗马史》，王以铸译，北京：三联书店，1957 年，第 2 页。

不可否认，印欧民族迁徙到亚平宁半岛原因是多种多样的，甚至"文明化了"印欧语系的希腊人到来是为了进行海外殖民。但总的来说，"自然迁徙"是印欧人迁徙到亚平宁半岛的主导原因。正是这些印欧人推动了古罗马文明的最后形成，并对其后来的发展产生了重大的影响。

二

迁徙到亚平宁的印欧人与古罗马文明的关系主要体现在以下几个方面。。

其一，自然迁徙到亚平宁半岛的印欧人是古罗马文明的拓荒者。亚平宁半岛距离文明起源地或者核心地区远比地处东地中海的希腊要远得多，接受不到近东文明的强烈影响，因此在第一批印欧移民来到之前甚至此后相当长一段时间内都是落后的。但印欧人的到来预示着新的文明的到来，一个重要的标志就是城市的出现。在巴拉菲特湖上文化之前，就有一些人以茅屋取代穴居．集而为衬，出现了定居，但到了巴拉菲特和特拉马尔文化时期，出现了更大范围，排列更规则的摸泥草屋，则初步具备了城市的特征。

文明的另一个表现是金属器的使用，在亚平宁文化时期[1]青铜器工具在一定范围被使用；而到了铁器的维拉诺瓦时代，在亚平宁半岛上，从皮埃蒙特到普利亚广泛地分使用这一金属工具。作为人类文明产生的标志之一，金属工具的出现，不仅促进了亚平宁半岛社会生产力水平大大提升，而且使社会开始发生质的变革。在这一时期，根据考古发掘，一些墓葬里出现了大量的金银财宝，而且还有希腊的陶器和腓尼基的玻璃、象牙和金属制品，这说明一些比较富裕的家族出现，对外交往开始频繁，社会等级和阶级开始划分。而维埃遗址的发掘[2]，则证明了各个村落联合想组成城镇的趋势。这个时期虽然印欧人没有让亚平宁半岛过渡到文明时代，但经过印欧人和当地土著居民的不断努力，在亚平宁半岛这个蛮荒之地已经燃起文明的火种。

其二持续迁徙到亚平宁半岛的印欧人是古罗马文明的奠基者。与"其它早期迁移的民族一样这并不是一次大规模的移民活动，而是连续不断、逐渐累加的过程，小规模的群体在新的土地上定居下来，然后这里又成为他们进一步向外迁移的基地，最终造成了印欧人的扩张以及不同种族群体的出现。"[3]印欧人的迁徙是一批接一批地，一浪迎一浪地交错进入亚平宁半岛各地的。印欧人迁徙大抵有三次浪潮，第一次迁徙浪潮约始于公元前2000年左右的湖上草屋居民和陆地泥屋居民；第二次迁徙浪潮是公元前1000年左右威兰诺瓦文化的建立者；第三次迁徙浪潮是公元前8世纪左右以希腊人为代表的"文明化了"印欧人迁徙。

语言可以说是一个"民族的印记"，"历史比较语言学奠基人格林宣言"'我们的语言就是我们的历史'，认为语言比骨骼、武器和墓穴更能证明民族的历史，民族历史文化的碑铭。"[4]拉丁语原是是亚平宁半岛中部西海岸拉丁部族的方言，后来则成为古罗马文明通用语言，对于拉丁语的研究，可以让我们更加清晰认识到印欧人迁徙到亚平宁半岛过程中印欧人语言发展演变的历程，以及古罗马文明形成中各种文化因素的碰撞与融合的过程。

在公元前8世纪末，"南部的希腊殖民者已经把字母传到正处于铁器时代的意大利半岛并很快

---

① 亚平宁文化时期是指存在于公元1800年左右意大利半岛比较典型的青铜文化，主要分布于亚平宁山脉及其以东从博洛尼亚到阿普里亚的地区；实行的是土葬。参见叶民，王敦书：《伊达拉里亚人起源考》，《世界历史》，2001年第5期，第101页。

② 维埃是离罗马城比较近的一个城市，早在威兰诺瓦铁器时代就存在着许多农村，后来慢慢集合成一个城市，与罗马的关系时好时坏，后在公元前4世纪初被罗马人毁灭。

③ 杰里·本特利，赫伯特·齐格勒：《新全球史：文明的传承与交流》上册，魏凤莲等译，北京：北京大学出版社，2007年，第57页。

④ http://baike.baidu.com/view/1751851.htm

在整个半岛得到扩散。而用此书写的铭文也很幸运保存了那里大量不同的语言，其中很大一部分不久就灭绝了。"①在公元前七世纪，在亚平宁半岛定居的印欧人已经通过与希腊人进行商品交易的单据了解到各种商品的希腊文名字，"不久以后，罗马商人开始运用希腊字母来记事，并由此而演变成罗马字母，略加改变以后就成为拉丁字母。"②泰勒通过比较分析发现，拉丁语"包含了两个主要元素，第一个元素是与它有非常密切联系的希腊语，第二个则是奥斯坎语；对于前者，很大程度上，包括了所有表达艺术和与此有关系的文明生活的词语，而后者则是表达有组织社会之前人们愿望和想法的术语。"③无论是希腊语还是奥斯坎语都属于印欧语系。美国人类学家摩尔根认为文明社会"始于标音字母的发明和使用文字来写文章。"④拉丁字母普遍使用开启了古罗马文明时代。由此可以证实我们的一个猜测，拉丁人其实是一个融合的民族，它是在不断吸收其它民族优秀文化成果的基础上成长起来的，属于印欧语系的拉丁文的使用打开了古罗马通向文明的大门。同时随着希腊人和埃特鲁斯坎人的不断到来，他们开始建设城镇，大量生产古老的手工艺产品，劳动力集中于大农业庄园，出现了人剥削人的情况，这表明阶级社会逐渐形成。

其三印欧人迁徙方向的变化、成分的复杂导致了古罗马文明发展的不平衡性、多样性。印欧人持续不断来到亚平宁半岛，其迁徙方向大致有两类，一类是青铜器时代和铁器时代迁徙到这里原始印欧人，他们迁徙方向是由北向南，由东向西。经过长期的融合，原始印欧人"成为意大利主要居民，主体在意大利中部"⑤，这些人也是意大利人的祖先。根据现有资料，他们分为两大部族，一是翁波罗—萨博利安人，他们主要在分布台伯河中上游以及该地区以南的山区，他们有很多分支，有翁波罗人、萨宾人、伏尔西人、萨莫诺人，还有南部的布鲁提人等。另一大部族则是拉丁族，他们住在拉丁姆平原，有拉丁人、厄尔西人、马尔西人等，而罗马人则是拉丁人的一支。另一类是以希腊人为代表的"文明化了"带有更多殖民色彩的印欧人迁徙，他们迁徙方向是由南向北，由西向东。希腊在公元前8世纪开始了在亚平宁半岛南边的西西里岛开始了殖民活动，先是哈尔基季基人在西西里建立了纳索城，后科林斯人又兴建了叙拉古城。随后，希腊人又相继在亚平宁半岛的东南沿海地区建成了梅塔逢图姆、锡巴里斯、克罗托内、塔兰托等城。这些已经"文明化了"印欧人的到来为当地的发展注入了新的文明因素，加速了古罗马文明形成的步伐。

大约在公元前10世纪年左右伊特鲁里亚人出现在伊特鲁里亚平原，关于他们起源现在还有争论，他们应该不属于印欧人，但毫无疑问的是受到了印欧人影响，尤其是希腊文明对他们产生巨大的影响。作为古罗马文明的先驱，他们城市繁荣，能生产高质量的金属器具，各个城市之间也建立了联盟。更重要的是他们"设立了有权威的国王、强有力的政府和组织严密、善于使用马匹和两轮战车的军队"。⑥伊特鲁里亚人文化深深影响了罗马早期的发展。同"埃特鲁斯坎的城市一样，罗马城在早期阶段也采用君主制，并且好几位国王都是埃特鲁斯坎人。从公元前7世纪到公元前6世纪，国王是罗马城的统治者，他们拿出资金铺设道路、修筑防御城墙、建设大型神庙以及其他的公共设施。"⑦虽然伊达拉里人作为民族后来消失了，但他们的文化却一直影响后来古罗马文明。

此外，在亚平宁半岛西北部和东北部山区这些边缘地区还住着旧石器和新时期时代遗留下来的土著居民，以及出现在北部地区新的印欧移民—高卢人，还有在西西里岛西部活动的腓尼基人，他

---

① Mallory, J. P.：*In Search of the Indo-Europeans: Language, Archaeology and Myth*, London: Thames & Hudson,1989, pp.57–58.

② J.H. 伯利斯坦德：《走出蒙昧》，周作宇，洪成文译，南京：江苏人民出版社，2010 年，第 322 页。

③ William C. Taylor：*History of Rome*, Philadelphia:Thomas,Cowperthwait & Co.1851, p.12.

④ 摩尔根：《古代社会》，第 11 页。

⑤ 于贵信：《古代罗马史》，长春：吉林大学出版社,1988 年，第 9 页。

⑥ 皮特·斯特恩斯等：《全球文明史》，赵轶峰等译，北京：中华书局，2006 年，第 136 页。

⑦ 杰里·本特利，赫伯特·齐格勒：《新全球史：文明的传承与交流》（上册），第 280 页。

们带给了意大利奢侈品和奢侈的生活方式。由于不断迁徙，以及迁徙的方向变化，迁徙种族成分的复杂，使上古意大利的种族、语言、文化情况非常复杂，这也导致了古罗马文明以后发展的不平衡性、多样性。

其四在民族迁徙的过程中平和、渐进的方式使古罗马文明具有很强的包容性。在民族迁徙的过程中不可避免会发生冲突以及流血事件，还有现在也没有确切的史料证明印欧人到来给这里的土著居民带来了什么样的影响。但正如前面所提到那样，上古意大利的种族、语言、文化情况非常复杂，不仅有印欧移民，还有当地的土著居民，据此我们推测在迁徙的过程中很少甚至没有出现使旧有文化湮没的毁灭性征服事件。相关考古资料也证实：石器时代在亚存在各种不同的人种，有颅骨较长的．也有颅骨较短。青铜器时代，特拉马尔和亚平宁文化，虽都有印欧移民的身影，但也存在诸多差异，尤其是在丧葬方式的区别，更说明印欧移民与当地土著居民的和平共处，相互融合，而不是持续的相互残杀。

威兰诺瓦铁器文化也分为南北两个系统，而且考古发现有希腊人和腓尼基人制造的物品，这说明在当时民族融合和对外交流情况的出现。当希腊人迁入亚平宁半岛南部时，不是将未进入文明阶段的当地土著居民和原始印欧人迅速征服、奴役，而是共同在这里居住生息，逐渐相互融合，从而形成新的文明。其它迁入的亚得里亚海居民、腓尼基人、高卢人以及来源不明的伊特鲁里亚人等也没有给亚平宁半岛带来毁灭性的破坏，反而不断融进古罗马文明这个巨大的熔炉里。王政时代的七王来自不同的种族，更验证了古罗马民族融合的过程，以及古罗马文明巨大的包容性。而驱赶伊特鲁里亚人的方式是政变，而非战争。还有相比希腊人，"罗马乐于把公民权给予更多的人，在这一点上他们远比希腊人伟大。"[①]而当征服一个地方时，更乐于和当地居民和首领合作，而不是把对方彻底消灭。"海纳百川，有容乃大"，古罗马文明的辉煌与伟大深刻阐释这句话的真谛。"罗马文化在扩张之后成为一种广义的文化，普及到地中海世界……罗马文化与希腊文化比较而言，虽然创造性不及后者，但罗马文化兼容并蓄的特点使得它在世界文化史中占据着重要的一页……并对欧洲近代文化产生深远的影响。"[②]

文明一般是指一种先进的文化，很多学者用文明一词指与原始相区别的、较高的人类历史发展阶段，也就是阶级社会或者说是文明社会。文明是文化发展到较高阶段的产物，当某个阶段的文化，比较广泛的使用了文字，人文科学和自然科学已经初步形成，社会成员被划分成了阶级或等级，社会制度、政治制度、经济制度已经比较完备，出现了巨大的公用建筑甚至城市中心，那么发展到这种程度的文化，就可以称作文明。"在印欧人长达数千年的迁徙过程中，在不断的民族冲突与融合中，在各种文化与文明的碰撞与交流中，古罗马文明终于破茧而出，开启了一段属于自己的辉煌时代。

三

印欧人在亚平宁半岛的的民族迁徙同其在世界其他一些地区的民族迁徙的一样，对被征服地区带来不同程度的破坏；也同其它民族迁徙一样对各民族之间文明的交往、借鉴和融合起着促进作用。但与其它印欧人创造的文明相比，以印欧人的文化因素为主体而建立的古罗马文明又有自己的特色：完善的政治组织，成熟的政治手腕和内外政策，发达的法律体系，虔诚实用的多神教信仰，爱国务实守信的民族性格，以实用主义为核心的文化，具有世界主义的文明圈等等。

文明的形成绝不是孤立发展的结果，在古罗马文明形成过程中，汲取了多少外来文化的文明因

---

① 皮特·斯特恩斯等：《全球文明史》，第 135 页。
② 汪诗明：《罗马对外扩张的历史影响》，《史学月刊》，2000 年第 5 期，第 90 页。

子，实在难以具体衡量，有的文明甚至对古罗马文明的形成产生过非常重要的影响，公元一世纪的罗马诗人贺拉斯曾说过："罗马征服了希腊，文化上却反被希腊征服。"[1]的确如此，"它在保留希腊社会诸多特征方面扮演了非常重要的角色。罗马人使用并模仿了希腊的科学、建筑物的纪念形式以及希腊人的雕塑和戏剧……"[2]但古罗马文明绝对不是对古希腊文明简单抄袭，"罗马自身的拉丁传统和固有的伊达拉里亚背景已为它的文化奠定了固有的特色，何况为了适应内外发展的需要还不断有所革新和创造。更有甚者，罗马从蕞尔小邦建成空前帝国这件事本身，就是古罗马文明最大的成就"。[3]对古罗马文明影响更深远的则是印欧人迁徙，长达数千年民族、文明的碰撞、交流与融合在古罗马历史上打下了深深的烙印，影响到罗马社会的各个层面，刻在古罗马文明记忆的最深处，体现了古罗马文明最精髓的本质。因为"决定一个民族基本文化传统的，是它在民族文化兴起定型的早期所遭遇的一系列事变……民族的命运也像个人，所经历的事变与感受，将留下最深刻的记忆、最久远的烙印"。[4]

"罗马作为拉丁民族的一支，其文化渊源不仅可以上溯于拉丁，而且可追及于更遥远的祖先——孕育了从印度到欧洲许多同一语系民族的印欧语族的祖先。"[5]在原始印欧人的社会等级似乎有非常明确的阶层划分，"这一结论是对描述印度、伊朗凯尔特和日耳曼民族的社会组织形式的文献，以及对希腊和罗马证据中的某些片段比较而得出的，所有这些民族均表现出祭司、武士和老百姓（或者食物生产者）之间有一种独特的区别……"[6]在原始印欧人到亚平宁半岛时，毫无疑问作为印欧人的一支这种三等级划分应该是存在，而且在罗马的神话中，身份最高的神是朱庇特、马尔斯和基林努斯（他们的三个祭司是罗马地位最高的），"在这里他们行使印度—雅利安人三个等级的社会职能，即至尊的魔法和司法力、战斗力、繁衍力"。[7]"对三种主要祭司以及他们主持众神的细致考虑，令人想到那是前罗马人的等级观念在宗教和神话上的反映，这种等级观念和印度—伊朗人的等级观如出一辙"。[8]

罗马的起源在神话中有所表现的三分的等级观念，在现实中是否存在还有疑问。但根据传说记载罗木卢斯在帕拉丁山及其周围组成了三个部落，分别是拉丁人的纳姆尼部，萨宾人的梯铁部，其它人组成的卢库姆部；而杜梅兹勒更是推测：纳姆尼部是祭司阶层，梯铁部是武士阶层，卢库姆部则是农民阶层。这里我们可以得出这样那个一个结论：史前罗马部分历史只不过是"印欧祖先遗留给罗马人的传说、神话在人类的移植再现而已。……这三个部族实际代表'印欧人'的三个阶层，即前罗马社会的三个等级"。[9]

罗马的氏族"在一百年左右的时间内，就这样聚集于罗马而完全组织起来了，领导这个组织的是这时候称为元老院的酋长会议，当时称为库里亚大会的人民大会、以及一位军事指挥官勒克斯；"[10]这样，就初步形成了一个三个权力机构并列的政治体制。到了第六王塞尔维乌斯时期，他对公民注册进行登记、征兵和征税，并对罗马自由居民进行财产普查，按财产多寡把公民划分等级，此外，还以百人团会议取代库里亚大会的职权。"比较分析表明，塞尔维乌斯这一形象和他所起的作用应

① 贺拉斯：《诗艺》，杨周翰译，北京：人民文学出版社，1962年，第151页。
② 皮特·斯特恩斯等：《全球文明史》，第135页。
③ 朱龙华：《罗马文化与古典传统》，杭州：浙江人民出版社，1993年，第19—20页。
④ 谢选俊：《神话与民族精神》，济南：山东文艺出版社，1986年，第89页。
⑤ 朱龙华：《罗马文化与古典传统》，第23页。
⑥ 布鲁斯·林肯：《死亡、战争与献祭》，晏可佳译，上海：上海人民出版社，2002年，第5—6页。
⑦ 雷蒙·布洛克：《罗马的起源》，张泽乾等译，北京：商务印书馆，1998年，第24页。
⑧ 雷蒙·布洛克：《罗马的起源》，第23页。
⑨ 雷蒙·布洛克：《罗马的起源》，第26—27页。
⑩ 摩尔根：《古代社会》，第279—280页。

显存在于罗马并在印欧神话中出现过。"①

这次改革，最重要的成果就是，"任何一个百人团的每一个成员现在都是罗马公民了"，②罗马的公民权反映了个人与团体之间的关系，"每一个百人团都列在自己所属的阶级中，每一个阶级都自称一个团体"。③公民权"不只虚荣问题，其间有最实在、最宝贵的利益。凡非罗马公民不被认为丈夫、父亲；亦不能为合法的产主或继承人。非公民就在法外，有了这种资格，就进到正式社会。这就是罗马公民权的价值"。④公民权在罗马社会具有非常重要的作用，它不仅是一项法律和公民制度，更是与古罗马的荣辱兴衰紧密联系在一起，成为古罗马统治国家甚至世界的一种行之有效的方法。"公民权本身就是广义范围的罗马文化的一个重要组成部分，因为公民权的奠定，是罗马人民经过长期历史发展，特别是平民与贵族斗争而取得的成果，对于意大利和行省各地的居民来说，获得罗马公民权也就无异于获得了一张进入罗马文化大家庭的入场券。"⑤使罗马人最终"超越了希腊人创造的城邦狭隘性的政治框架和希腊人意识的局限性"，⑥创立了一个将地中海世界合为一体的大帝国。

在原始罗马时代，三个部族之间其实之间是不平等的，"卢策瑞部被接受为第三个罗马部落，属于这个部落的元老院议员有一个绰号，叫做'小族元老'，从这个绰号看来，旧氏族是不甘于承认同他们完全平等的"。⑦这种情况收反映了罗马旧氏族成员对接受新氏族成员的排斥，所以在第三个部落氏族的达到法定数额之后，罗马人便关闭了接纳新成员的大门。无族籍的人，还有三个部落之外的其它氏族的成员以及他们繁衍的子孙逐渐形成了罗马的平民阶级。由于被排斥在氏族之外，这些人无法得到罗马公民权，政治上、经济上处于被压迫被剥削的地位，尤其是在塞尔维乌斯改革后，"使贵族政治和特权大为突出，他们趁机大幅度地剥夺人民支配政府的权力，并将这种权力交给富人"。⑧

罗马平民为了反抗他们的政府制度中这时所混合的贵族主义和特权这两种新因素，在整个共和时期不断进行斗争，构成了罗马王政后期共和初期社会斗争的主要内容，是罗马社会发展的动力之一。平民与贵族的斗争也是"保持罗马自由的主要原因。每个城邦都分成平民和贵族两派，双方的冲突结果有利于城市产生自由的立法。正是平民保民官的设立才使罗马共和国更完美！"⑨从这里我们可以看出公民权问题不仅打开了罗马以后发展的大门，确定了其社会、政治框架，形成了一套以元老院、公民大会和行政长官的分工合作和相互制约为内容的政治制衡机制，保持了罗马这种混合政体的效率与活力；而且也在某种程度上决定了古罗马文明的发展方向，不断扩大的公民权加强了罗马人和其它民族之间的关系，增强了他们对古罗马文明的向心力，让古罗马文明影响的范围不断扩大，最终成为一种世界性的文明。

"我们所能知道的社会状态的雏形，来自三种记录—即观察者对于同时代比较落后的各种文明的记事，某一个特殊民族所保存下来的关于他们的原始历史的记录，以及古代的法律。"⑩值得注意的是，"这一种法律记录，几乎完全来自属于印度—欧罗巴种族的社会制度，其中较大部分是罗马人、

---

① 雷蒙·布洛克：《罗马的起源》，第 23 页。
② 摩尔根：《古代社会》，第 331 页。
③ Livy, *History of Rome*, Vi,I.44.
④ 古朗士：《希腊罗马古代社会研究》，李玄伯译，上海：上海文艺出版社，1990，第 316 页。
⑤ 朱龙华：《罗马文化与古典传统》，第 228 页。
⑥ 胡庆钧：《早期奴隶制社会比较研究》，北京：中国社会科学出版社，1996 年，第 101 页。
⑦ 摩尔根：《古代社会》，第 323 页。
⑧ 摩尔根：《古代社会》，第 332 页。
⑨ Marchiaviely, *The Discources*, London，1988,p.111.
⑩ 梅因：《古代法》，第 84 页。

印度人和斯拉夫人所供给的"①。人种学告诉我们，"罗马人与印度人来自同一个原始祖先，而在他们的原来习惯中，也确实有显著的类似之处。"②虽然现在关于西方法律渊源是"雅里安模式"还是"古代模式有所争论，但正如上面所涉及的那样，印欧人在罗马法的形成过程中无疑做出了巨大的贡献的，而"法是罗马人民天才的最高体现"。③威尔·杜兰也说："法律最足以说明罗马精神的特征。在历史上，罗马代表秩序就如同希腊之代表自由。希腊留下的民主与哲学成为个人自由的依据；罗马留下的法律与政绩，则成为社会秩序的基础。"④

罗马人这种法治观念与罗马社会长期以来印欧人遗留下来的崇敬父权家长制的权威有很大关系。在"这个'印欧语化'的过程中，欧洲从母系社会转变为父系社会。"⑤"在远东有一个和罗马人来自同一人种的支系也正在按照其最专门的细节重复施行"家父权"。但在公认为包括于罗马帝国内的各民族中，除了只在亚细亚加拉塔之外，该雅士不可能找到有类似罗马"家父权"的一种制度。⑥"在罗马传统的社会里，父系家长具有某些被习俗，继后被国家法律所认可的无上的权力。后来，当国家法律日渐完善，并取代习俗之后，父权虽消弱，但余威犹存，因此，通过对这种家长法权的强调与陈陈相因，逐渐形成了罗马人服从权威，遵纪守法的观念与民族特性，并进而找到了一条通向'伟大的罗马'的有效途径。"⑦"罗马人遵纪守法的观念除了表现在教育和日常生活中之外，罗马士兵对军纪的服从更是这种优秀品质的典型代表。新加入军团士兵都要立下誓言"坚决服从指挥，忠于自己的岗位职责。"⑧西塞罗在他的作品中也强调到："请注意，一切都处于法律之下。"⑨

同古罗马文明的一样，罗马法始终在不断的民族、文化交流与融合中吸收来自希腊与东方法律的内容与精髓，"通过联系外来法律观念，其产生业已充分证实，罗马法更新了自身。作为一种有机体，罗马法同化了这些外来因素，这些外来因素非但没有扭曲罗马法，相反却使它变得更年轻、更富有生命力。"⑩罗马法成为"以私有制为基础的法律的最完备形式"，是"商品生产者社会的第一个世界性法律"，"以至一切后来的法律都不能对它做任何实质性的修改"。⑪罗马人所创造的法律制度已经"给予几乎整个欧洲以法律概念的共同库藏、法律思想的共同文法，并且，在不断变化但不可轻视的范围内，提供了一批共同的法律规则。"⑫

创公民权，建混合政体、立罗马法都是"印欧人在长期迁移和随后的定居生活中，他们适应了各地的环境和接触到的其他民族的文化，不断有所演进，有所改变，终于发展为不同的文化。……但在突出适应性这一点上，罗马却充分发扬了祖族的固有特色，不仅在拉丁一支中堪称独秀，并终于凌驾于地中海各民族之上。"⑬这些成果的独特性和民族性使古罗马文明因它们的存在而更加耀眼和灿烂。但追踪溯源，罗马这些文明成果，都与罗马的宗教有着密不可分的关系。因为"从罗马王政时期到共和早期，原始宗教一直主导着罗马人的生活和法律。"

① 梅因：《古代法》，第 86 页。
② 梅因：《古代法》，第 14 页。
③ 朱塞佩·格罗索：《罗马法史》，黄风译，北京：中国政法大学出版社，1998 年，第 1 页。
④ 威尔·杜兰特：《凯撒与基督》，幼狮文化公司译，北京：东方出版社，1999 年，第 290 页。
⑤ 龚缨晏：《关于印欧语系起源问题》，《世界历史》，2000 年第 5 期，第 113 页。
⑥ 梅因：《古代法》，第 94 页。
⑦ 张广智：《论古罗马的政治文化：一项历史学的分析》，《江海学刊》，1995 年第 1 期，第 110 页。
⑧ Polybius, *The Histories*, Cambridge, Mass.: Harvard University Press, 1960, p.2.
⑨ 西塞罗：《论法律》，王焕生译，北京：中国政法大学出版社，1997 年，第 263 页。
⑩ 吉尔森：《有机同化论》，转引自刘金国，周丽：《西方法律传统的文化渊源》，《南通师范学院学报》（哲学社会科学版），2002 年第 3 期，第 30 页。
⑪ 马克思，恩格斯：《马克思恩格斯选集》第 21 卷，北京：人民出版社，1972 年，第 454 页。
⑫ 巴里·尼古拉斯：《罗马法概论》，黄风译，北京：法律出版社，2000 年，第 1—2 页。
⑬ 朱龙华：《罗马文化与古典传统》，第 24 页。

印欧人"无论到什么地方，这些印欧民族都努力吸收当地文化，不过在语言和宗教方面还是以印欧语和印欧宗教较占优势"。[①]印欧宗教"是一种有相当确切的证据表明原始印欧人集团已拥有一种由诸神、其崇拜仪式和讲述其神话的诗歌所构成的发达的宗教体系。"[②]印欧民族相信宇宙间有许多天神，这对他们的文化有很深远的影响。在罗马宗教中诸多天神中，我们知道最重要的有三个神，而这三个神在其它印欧语系力也能找到同种类型。其中，"天父"(*dieusPhater)印欧诸神中最重要的神，在拉丁文中则称为朱庇特(Jupitter)(事实上是 iov—pater，或"法父"之意)，事实上也是众神之首；诸神（Aser）这个字常见于各印欧文化地区，在拉丁文中为 deus . 在其它北欧的印欧语系中掌管万物生育、生长的神通称（vaner），而在拉丁文中则有代表生育之神的字 Venus(维纳斯)。但罗马宗教并不是单纯复制印欧宗教因素，在民族迁徙的过程中，罗马人对其他民族的宗教采取了"敬仰民族神明，宽容外邦神灵"政策，伊特鲁利亚人的宗教，希腊的宗教和神话，东方的秘传宗教和占星术都对罗马宗教产生过重要影响，他们把其它民族的神灵都请入罗马的神殿里，这就使"罗马的宗教传统具有鲜明的独特性和开放性"。[③]与此同时，"与神同在的直感，宗教仪式、活动把罗马人更紧密地联系在一起，鼓舞着他们的士气。虔诚、爱国、勇敢、荣誉和自我克制，是罗马人的民族精神，也是其由小而大战胜一个又一个敌人的重要原因"。[④]

"与古代其他大多数印欧语系的人们的制度一样，家族和氏族或家的集合，是至为重要的。家长把持着一切权力，也控制了日常活动中最重要的家庭崇拜。"[⑤]在罗马，民间也盛行多神教崇拜，其中最重要的对家族与氏族首长亡灵的玛纳崇拜和以万物有灵论为基础的拉尔（意为精灵）崇拜。罗马人对宗教这种虔诚的态度更反映"万物有灵"的观念上，"国家和民族、个别的自然现象、如同个别的心灵活动、每个人、每一地方和每一事物，甚至罗马法范围内的每一行动，无不再现于罗马神抵世界之中"，[⑥]这就造成了在罗马"神比人还要多"的现象、[⑦]罗马人的先祖创造了万神，同时也创造了对神的崇拜与服从。这种对神的敬畏和严肃态度，使"罗马人是世界上对誓约最虔诚的民族"。[⑧]他们对神是"言出必行"，"公民害怕违背誓约，更甚于害怕法律，就像有人敬重神的力量更甚于人的力量一样"。[⑨]这样，虔诚守信就成为这个民族的普遍信仰，强化了公民的社会道德。有人曾说："罗马管理大量金银财宝的官员保持廉洁之风，正是他们信仰对神明的誓言，因而忠于职守。"[⑩]

罗马人笃信神明，态度虔诚，但其敬神具有明显的目的性和实用性，"乃是一种肯定的意志目的的巩固，他们认为这些意志目的是绝对地存在于他们的神明身上，他们要求这些神明有绝对的权力。他们便是为了这目的而崇拜神明，为了这样的目的，他们就在一种有限制的方式下，从属于他们的神明。由此可见罗马宗教乃是一种完全不含诗意的、充满了狭隘、权宜、和利用的宗教"。[⑪]他们"只把拜神活动视为对契约的履行，他们认为，只要信神者尽了自己的职责，神就一定会保佑他。因此在宗教上，罗马人所遵循的只是一系列刻板机械的仪式，如供奉牺牲等，而这些活动是很容易

---

① 乔德坦·贾德：《苏菲的世界》，萧宝森译，北京：作家出版社，1996 年，第 199 页。
② 徐晓旭：《古代希腊宗教：一项长时段的考察》，《古代文明》，2007 年第 4 期，第 4 页。
③ 杨共乐：《早期罗马宗教传统特点》，《河北学刊》，2008 年第 2 期，第 97 页。
④ 郝际陶：《论罗马称霸地中海世界的宗教因素》，《东北师大学报》(哲学社会科学版)，2004 年第 2 期，第 13 页。
⑤ 蒙森：《罗马史》第一卷，李稼年译，北京：商务印书馆，2005 年，第 149 页。
⑥ 蒙森：《罗马史》第一卷，第 146 页。
⑦ Azbert Grenier: *The Roman Spirit: In Religion，Thought and Art*，London and New York，1996,p.84.
⑧ 孟德斯鸿：《罗马盛衰原因论》，婉玲译，北京：商务印书馆，1995 年，第 5 页。
⑨ 马基雅维里：《论李维》，冯克利等译，上海：世纪出版集团，2005 年，第 78 页。
⑩ Polybius, *The Histories*,Cambridge, Mass.: Harvard University Press,1960. 转引自朱龙华：《罗马文化》，上海：上海社会科学院出版社，2003 年，第 21 页。
⑪ 赵林：《神旨的感召：西方文化的传统与演进》，武汉：武汉大学出版社，1993 年，第 84 页。

完成的"。①这种功利性宗教是和政治紧密相连，在罗马人心中，国家就是他们信仰的最高宗旨。"罗马的宗教起先是家族的宗教，随后成为家族的延伸———国家的宗教。家族一旦神圣化，那么国家也就此变得神圣。"②而在"罗马共和国时期宗教与政治的一体化不仅是罗马宗教的最大特点，也是罗马政治的最大特点"。③

在长达数千年的印欧人大迁徙中，亚平宁半岛人员流动频繁，物品交换和文化技术传播也愈益增多，文明地区不断扩大，使古罗马文明最终形成。此后罗马人又通过征服又把古罗马文明传播到把当时的大半个世界，"使整个北非、西班牙、法国、罗马尼亚、今天英国的一些重要地区、低地国家和德国都受到希腊—罗马价值观和社会制度的影响，包括使用拉丁语为书面文字"，④甚至通过通商、宗教、文化等其它一些方式传播到巴比伦、印度甚至中国这些地区。文明的传播有助于打破各地的孤立闭塞状态，扩大国与国之间的联系，发展经济、文化交流，使人类社会逐渐从分散、孤立状态到逐渐融合成密切联系的整体。同时，因受到共同文明的影响，"罗马在西方人心目中的地位依然神圣不可侵犯，'西方'这个概念本身所指的乃是地中海盆地，而这个盆地是罗马人在这五十三年的时间中打下来的，西方人在内心里永远不会忘记这个事实，他们对罗马的感情是隐秘而永恒的"。⑤

印欧人是古罗马文明的拓荒者、奠基者，在千年的迁徙过程中，印欧人的文化、经历深刻作用于罗马民族的政治、经济、社会与文化等多个层面，形成了独具特色的古罗马文明，而且这种作用不是瞬时性的，而是潜在性与历时性的，对古罗马文明以后发展也产生了重要影响，决定了古罗马文明以后的发展轨迹，对近世以来西方社会产生了或直接、或潜移默化的影响。但古罗马文明绝对不是印欧人独自创造的，其它非印欧语系的人也作出了重要贡献，而且是同等重要的，古罗马文明是不同民族、文明碰撞、交流、融合的产物，它也反映了世界由闭塞、分散、孤立发展向开放、互相联系、整体世界发展的这一客观历史进程。

---

① 布雷斯特德：《文明的征程》，李静新译，北京：北京燕山出版社，2004年，第368页。
② R.H. 巴洛：《罗马人》，黄韬译，上海：上海人民出版社，2000年，第8页。
③ 吕波：《罗马共和国时期宗教情感对政治行为的影响》，《西北大学学报》（哲学社会科学版），2006年第6期，第111—112页。
④ 皮特·斯特恩斯等：《全球文明史》，第135页。
⑤ 林国荣：《罗马史随想》，上海：华东师范大学出版社，2005年，第139页。

罗马军队与帝国西部行省城市化 *

王　鹤　哈尔滨师范大学

摘要：罗马军队不仅是建立和平定西部行省的重要工具，同时还在西部行省的城市化和罗马化过程中发挥了不可估量的作用。罗马军队是帝国西部行省城市化建设的人力、技术资源储备库；军营、堡垒和要塞是帝国西部行省城市兴起的催化剂；军营设计与城市规划关系密切，许多罗马城市是从以前的罗马军营发展而来；大量老兵殖民地的建立也为西部行省提供了城市生活的样板。

关键词：罗马；军队；城市化

Abstract: Roman army acted as an important instrument in establishing Roman western provinces and it also played significant roles during the process of urbanization and Romanization of western provinces. Roman army was a reserve of manpower and technological resources. Camps ,forts and fortresses are catalysts of cities. The plan of Roman camps and cities had close ties and many Roman cities were developed from former camps. A large number of veteran colonies provided examples for the urban life of western provinces.

Keywords: Roman, army, urbanization

"在文化方面，罗马人的主要成就是把城市文化连同它所带来的一切扩展到中欧和北欧"。[1](p.237) 罗马帝国前期，统治者大力推行城市化运动，广泛建立新的城市，或将原先的部落、村庄、祠庙等发展成为新型都市。到 2 世纪中叶，城市化运动基本完成。帝国境内的城市星罗棋布，特别是在西部行省——如高卢、日耳曼尼亚、不列颠、西班牙等地区城市化运动表现更为突出，成果更为显著。罗马帝国时期有超过 2/3 的军队驻扎在西部行省，[2](p.267) 这些军队不仅是建立和平定西部行省的重要工具，同时还在西部行省的城市化和罗马化过程中发挥了不可估量的作用。

一　军队——城市化建设的人力、技术资源储备库

在罗马帝国初期，对内、对外战争相对减少。除了军事职责外，罗马军队"还履行了大量民事职能。

---

*　本文为国家社科基金项目"罗马军队与罗马化关系研究"（12CSS003）之阶段性成果。

它是帝国受过技能训练的人们——工程师、测量员、建筑师、各种行政管理人员的唯一的一个最大的储备库"。[3](p.370) 军队经常承担修建堡垒、开辟森林、清干沼泽、挖掘沟渠、筑路搭桥等任务。这一方面可以使士兵们充分发挥用武之地，防止闲极思变；另一方面也可以保持军队的强健和活力。特别是在"罗马和平"时期，从事工程建设活动对士兵们来说是一种司空见惯的差事。如克劳狄时期，下日耳曼军队统帅科尔布罗"为了使士兵有事可做，他要他们在莱茵河和摩撒河之间挖掘一道二十三英里长的运河"。[4](p.334) 尼禄时期，日耳曼军队统帅保里努斯"为了不使士兵无事可做，……要士兵们修筑一道制服莱茵河河水泛滥的大堤。[4](p.446) 公元106年，图拉真皇帝下令开通一条从叙利亚边境直到红海的公路。在佩特拉(Petra)附近驻扎的军队士兵可能参与了这条公路的修建。[5](p.123)

罗马军队在西部行省城市的基础设施建设和经济开发中发挥了突出的作用。在罗马军团的建筑成果中，最基本也是最宏大的就是公路的修建。公元2世纪时，罗马帝国的道路系统几乎遍及帝国全境，东起幼发拉底河，北达苏格兰低地，总计约5万英里的干道和20万英里的支线纵横交错，穿越不列颠、欧洲、北非、小亚细亚和阿拉伯、叙利亚及美索不达米亚的沙漠。罗马帝国四通八达的公路网大部分都是罗马军团的杰作。"罗马帝国的公路和桥梁系统，直到19世纪在欧洲是无可比拟的，其规划和建筑几乎完全是靠罗马军队"。[7](p.12) 公路网的修建主要是出于军事的需要，罗马军队的调动，给养的供应，以及弩炮等战斗器械的运输等都需要建立全天候的公路交通体系。同时，公路的修建也促进了帝国境内交通和贸易的发展，以及城市的兴起和繁荣。以不列颠为例，罗马帝国时期在该行省修建的道路系统总长度达5000公里。罗马军队的到来，使不列颠过去的坑坑洼洼的步行小道，变成了纵横交织、笔直宽阔的平坦大道，这些道路自伦敦向周围辐射，促进了当地商业贸易的发展，使伦敦由昔日的一个小村庄迅速发展成不列颠的行政首府。

除人力以外，军队还为西部行省城市的兴起提供了材料和技术支持。罗马军队中有自己的工场(fabrica)，生产部队所需的砖瓦、武器等等。① 这些由军队生产的建筑材料既用来供应军事工程，也可以用于民用。如位于莱茵河上的军事基地桑腾(Xenten)的砖场，制造了整个边境地区所使用的砖。罗马士兵既是战士又是工程师，每个军团都有一批掌握专门技术的士兵，他们被称作"免役者"(immunes)，如建筑师、勘测员、医务人员、水力工程师、造船工、铁匠、制箭者、铜匠、炮兵机械制造者等，据统计有100多种。免役者人数众多，至少占军团总人数的1/5。[8](p.68) 他们因具有专业技术，承担特殊的职责而被免除了普通士兵所要承担的艰苦的劳役和繁重的劳动。这些专业技术人员经常根据当地需要，受总督的调遣去援助驻地周边地区的民用工程建设，参与工程的设计和监督，提供技术支持。如公元137年，毛里塔尼亚的塞尔迪亚(Saldea)城居民在修建一条长达428米的隧道时，因角度计算错误，隧道无法在中间合拢。毛里塔尼亚总督向驻扎在附近的第三奥古斯塔军团请求援助，而该军团的一位老兵在服役期间曾负责这一工程的监督工作，他重新测量了角度并成功地使隧道汇合。

罗马军队在行省和边界地区的驻防，不但为当地经济与文化的发展提供了和平、稳定的环境，而且军队修筑的桥梁、道路等设施也为罗马文明的扩张和传播奠定了基础。军队的到来及其建设活动也为当地带来了新的技术（如拱券结构的运用）、新的建筑材料（如天然水泥和砖瓦）以及典型的罗马建筑风格和类型。军队还为西部行省城市的发展"提供了技术专家，大量的工匠，以及无限的劳动力"。[8](p.64) 罗马军队在边疆地区建筑公路、桥梁、船坞、港口和防御工事等，促进了军事设施周边地区城镇的成长，加速了当地的城市化进程。

---

① 在2世纪晚期位于今天英格兰的科布里奇的一个军营工场占地面积达560平方米，可供100—150人在其中工作，生产武器和铁制工具。军队还大量生产砖和瓦，一些私人的房屋使用了带有军团编号印记的砖，这表明了军队工场中所生产的砖有时被作为一种商品，用来交换当地的产品和服务。参见 Brian Campbell, *The Roman army 31BC—AD337, A Source Book*，London and New York，1994，p.121.

二　军营、堡垒和要塞——城市兴起的催化剂

在罗马帝国前期的城市化运动中，东西部行省的城市发展呈现出截然不同的特征。在东部行省，罗马人到来之前，高度发达的城市文明已存在并发展了达千年之久。罗马军队一般利用现有的城市作为军事基地，因此军队对东部行省城市发展影响很小；而在西部行省，"城市化是一个后来的现象，其本身部分是军队出现的结果"。[9] (p.36) 在西方，罗马式的城市往往在军事基地附近产生，或者是由老兵殖民地发展而来。在罗马军事征服过程中建立的大量的临时军营、永久性的军团要塞和辅军堡垒经常会促进城市的发展，成为西部行省城市兴起的催化剂。这些军队驻地大都经过精心挑选，位于战略要地，交通便利，在军队撤走后很容易为平民利用，发展成为新兴城市。"罗马帝国在西方最持久的遗产之一毫无疑问是城市制度的建立"。[10] (p.69) 许多现代欧洲名城均发端于古罗马军队所建立的堡垒或要塞，如米兰、佛罗伦萨、伦敦、约克、巴黎、斯特拉斯堡等。今天法国的里昂即是由帝国早期的军团要塞发展而来，其名称来源于拉丁语 Legio，意为"军团"。罗马军队是"广泛地传播罗马城市的机器"[11] (p.232) 莱茵河边境长期以来是罗马军队重兵防守之地。① 大规模的军队在莱茵河边境的出现促进了众多城市的兴起和繁荣，今天的科隆、美因兹、波恩等城市，其起源都可以追溯到罗马军团基地或辅军的堡垒。多瑙河上的维也纳、奥格斯堡、布达佩斯、贝尔格来德等城市也都是在以前的罗马军团基地的基础上兴起的。今天欧洲许多城市的名称仍能反映出罗马军队与城市之间的密切关系，如英语中以 caster、chester 结尾的城市名称源于拉丁语 castrum（"军营"）。

随着"罗马和平"的到来，特别是哈德良时代以后，罗马军队逐渐由"野战军"向戍边部队转变，军队的机动性日益缺失，[12] (p.118–119) 军队驻地逐渐长期化、固定化。军队的庞大需求所带来的获利可能性和士兵们定期发放的薪饷所带来的稳定购买力，如磁石般吸引了众多的军队追随者——如商人、工匠、士兵的家属、妓女，退役老兵等，在要塞和堡垒周围兴起了为军队提供各种服务的暂时性的平民定居点，被称为营市（canbae，或音译为"卡纳柏"，意为"棚子"）和威库斯（vicus，意为"庄子"）。如在罗马不列颠的卡厄列昂（Caerleon）有一处面积为 2296 平方米的罗马军团要塞遗址，营市从三面环绕着要塞，面积达 35 公顷。多数罗马士兵在军营中度过了一生的大部分时光。在此期间，许多士兵与当地的女子结合并组成家庭，将其家人安置在驻地周围的营市或威库斯中。辅军士兵在服役期满后，不但会获得罗马公民权，而且他们与当地妇女所缔结的婚姻也将合法化。对罗马士兵们来说，长达 25 年的军旅生活几乎已经割断了他们与故乡的联系，在退役时大多不愿返回故乡，而更喜欢在其曾经服役的地方定居下来，成为当地营市或威库斯的新居民，从而增加了这些平民定居点的人口和规模。而这些退役老兵所具有的罗马公民身份无疑也加强了营市和威库斯的地位。

随着这些营市和威库斯规模的不断扩大以及设施的日益完善，它们在外观、管理模式及居民的生活方式等方面都受到当地驻军的影响，逐渐演变成为罗马化的新兴城镇。许多营市的布局仿照罗马军营的棋盘状格局，当地驻军的军事指挥官负责营市的管理。营市大多位于官方指定的军团的领地内，处于军团长官的监督之下。退役老兵作为罗马公民，经常参与营市的民事管理，履行地方官员的职责。为了加强对这些新兴城市的管理，罗马政府经常会授予其正式的地位。它们有的获

---

① 约公元 6 年时，有 5 个军团驻扎在莱茵河中游和下游。加上配备的辅军部队，总人数可达到约 6 万人。到公元 20 年时，莱茵河军团的数量上升到了 8 个，加上辅军总人数达到 10 万。参见 Steven K. Drummond, Lynn H. Nelson, *The Western Frontiers of Imperial Rome*, New York and London, 1994, p.27.

得了自治市的地位，有的则地位进一步上升，发展成为罗马殖民地。①如位于多瑙河上的卡农图姆（Carnuntum）地处两条公路交汇处，战略位置十分重要。提比略时期首先在这里建立了一个军营。在图拉真统治末期，第十四 Gemina 军团在此驻扎。在军营周围的三面兴起了营市，建起了露天剧场、广场等建筑物。公元 124 年，哈德良授与卡农图姆以自治市的地位。194 年时塞维鲁又将该市提升为罗马殖民地。[6]（p.142）一份时间为 167–169 年的铭文表明，122 年，在毛里塔尼亚的 Rapidum 建立了一个辅军的军营，很快在军营周边兴起了一个平民定居点，3 世纪时发展成为自治市。[6]（p.148）罗马征服不列颠之后，于公元 49 年在 Corinium 建立了一个堡垒。到公元 1 世纪 70 年代晚期，在当地驻军撤走之后，以该堡垒为中心而形成的平民定居点发展成为一个正规的城镇。到 2 世纪时占地 101 公顷，约有 15,000 至 20,000 居民，成为英格兰地区除伦敦以外的第二大城市，即今天英国的著名城市 Circencester。

三　军营设计与城市规划的密切关系

整部罗马史基本上就是一部战争史，而和平只是战争间歇的小憩。在长期的战争中，罗马人克敌制胜的法宝之一是其高超的安营扎寨技术和卓越的军事工程建筑成就。罗马军队每到一处，即使只停留一夜也要修建一个临时营地。罗马人的军营设计在中医线是很难划分的，而特别适用于那些紧急项目实施时，军队必定至少在精确性、标准化和灵活性方面，都达到了完善的程度。罗马军营从广泛意义上来说包括战争期间建立的临时军营（camp）、永久性的军团要塞（fortress）和辅军堡垒（fort），其内部基本结构大体一致。军营整体呈长方形或方形，内部有两条主街，东西向的称为 Via Principalis，南北向的称为 Via Praetoria，两者呈"十"字型或"T"字型交叉。另有若干条辅路分别与这两条主街平行，从而形成正交网格状的街道网。在军营中心是军队指挥部（Principia）和指挥官的住所——帅帐（Praetorium）所在地，帅帐内设神龛（sacellum），部队的军旗和士兵的储蓄就存放在其中。早期帝国军团营地规模在 17 公顷至 28 公顷之间。[11]（p.161）如果驻扎一个军团的话，人数约为 5000 人。军营内部除了有精心规划的整齐街道以外，还设有市场、作坊、操练场、审判区、粮仓、医院、浴室和储藏室等设施以及官员住所和士兵的营房。因此，犹太历史学家约瑟夫形象地将罗马军营比喻为一座"行进中的城镇"。

安德斯·贝尔（Anders Bell）根据城市起源的不同将罗马帝国城市大体分为三种类型：A 型城市建立在早期的罗马军营基础之上，如不列颠的埃克塞特（Exeter）；B 型城市是作为殖民地（包括老兵殖民地和平民殖民地）而建立的城市，如北非的提姆加德（Timgad）；C 型城市则是在前罗马时代的居民点上发展起来的城市，如庞贝。其中前两种城市的产生都与军队有着密切的关系。这些城市一般都有两条主街在城市中心垂直相交，一条从北至南称为 cardo，另一条从东到西，称为 decumanus，广场就位于两条主街相交形成的一个拐角处。还有其他若干街道分别与这两条主街平行排列，形成以直角相交的格状街道网。

罗马军营与城市之间在规划、布局方面表现出惊人的相似性。军营的两条主街——Via Principalis 和 Via Praetoria 与罗马城市的两条主干道——decumanus 和 cardo 如出一辙，军团指挥部（Principia）和帅帐（Praetorium）所在位置往往是城市广场所在地，军营内的神龛的功能与城市神庙大体相当。关于二者之间到底谁起源于谁的问题目前还存在争论，但无疑罗马军营很容易演变成

---

① 为了加强对帝国境内城市的管理，罗马统治者根据各城市的重要性及其忠诚程度将其大致分为三个等级，其中级别最低的是行省当地原有的非罗马城市（civitates），级别最高的是那些被授予"殖民地"（colonia）称号的城市，其居民享有罗马公民权，可免除税收，如人头税（tributum capitis）和土地税（tributum soli）等。而界于两者之间的是"自治市"（municipium），其地方官员可获得罗马公民权，而其他居民享有拉丁权，实行内部自治。

一个城镇。有学者认为"许多罗马城市是从以前的罗马军营发展而来。"[13] 如公元前 23 年罗马人建立的城市阿奥斯达（Aosta）呈长方形，东西长 724 米，南北长 572 米，有两条主街呈十字形交叉，整个城市划分成 16 个长方形的主街区，再进一步划分为 64 个小街区，有四个城门两两相对，城市广场位于两条主街交叉点的东北方，神庙位于广场的北部，此外在城市的东北角还分布着浴场、竞技场和剧场。阿奥斯达的城市规划表明它"起源于一个古罗马兵营（castrum），当一个暂时的军营转变成为一个城市时，它被有计划地扩展了"。[14]（p. 152）

位于北非阿尔及利亚的提姆加德城约建于公元 100 年，是为驻扎在附近的第三奥古斯塔军团的退役老兵而建的殖民地。该城市最初也采用了军营的建筑形式。其城市规划近似方形，两条主街呈"T"字型交叉，其他街道分别与两条主街平行排列，将整个城市划分成东西 12 排，南北 11 列的网格状街区。在城市中心广场四周分布着公共图书馆、浴场、集市、会堂、神庙和一个可容纳 3500 人的露天剧场。这种由军营或殖民地发展而来的城市（包括 A 型和 B 型）被某些学者称为"营寨城"，它们在保留罗马军营基本布局的基础之上，增加了一些新的非军事功能的便利设施。

四　老兵殖民地——城市生活的样板

在罗马人到来之前，西部行省如高卢、日耳曼、北非和不列颠等地，除了以前的腓尼基人和希腊人建立的早期殖民地以外，只有少数大型的定居点，城市文明尚未产生或处于初始阶段。如在前罗马时代的高卢，典型的居住模式是被称为"奥庇达"（oppida）的小型设防的定居点，通常位于高地之上，俯视周边地区。面积大多只有几公顷。其主要特征是有城墙和城门建筑，有空间布局，有储藏设施和墓地，但大型纪念物、公共场所等相对较少。这些前罗马时代的奥庇达可被称为原始城市。而在"日耳曼人中，没有一个部落是居住在城郭内的，就是个别的住宅也不容许彼此毗连。他们零星散落地逐水泉、草地或树林而居。……在每座房屋的周围都留着一片空地，要不是为了预防火灾，就是不善于建筑。他们甚至不会使用石头和瓦：一切营造均用原木，不另加工，也没有装饰或娱目的地方。"[15](p.63)

在西部行省，真正的城市直到罗马帝国早期才出现，罗马军队的到来，为西部行省城市的兴起提供了前所未有的推动力。大量的军营、堡垒和要塞的建立促进了西部行省众多罗马式城市的出现。除此以外，"军事殖民地的建立是军队创造城市的最明显的方式"。[13] 早在第二次布匿战争期间，公元前 205 年，罗马统帅斯奇皮奥就在西班牙为其老兵建立了一个海外殖民地——意大利卡（Italica）。此后，在西班牙建立的老兵殖民地的数量也是相当惊人的。其中较为著名的如 Narba（今 Caceres，卡塞雷斯）、Tarraco（今 Tarragona，塔拉戈纳）、Caesar Augusta（今 Zaragoza，萨拉戈萨）、Emerita Augusta（今 Merida，梅里达）、Valentia（今 Valencia，巴伦西亚）、Corduba（今 Cordoba，科尔多瓦）等等。[16] 罗马共和国后期和帝国初期，为安置退役老兵，一些军事统帅进行了大规模的殖民活动，老兵殖民地在帝国西部行省普遍建立，如恺撒就在高卢、西班牙、阿非利加等行省建立了至少 40 个殖民地。奥古斯都统治时期为安置老兵建立的殖民地不少于 75 个。[17]（p.235）他因此被誉为"殖民地之父"。克劳狄在征服不列颠以后，在该岛建立了 3 个老兵殖民地——公元 49 年建立的科尔切斯特，公元 1 世纪时建立的格罗塞斯特和林肯。此外还有图拉真时期在北非建立的提姆加德，在下日耳曼建立的桑腾等等，建立老兵殖民地的作法一直到哈德良时期才逐渐停止。

老兵殖民地遍布各大行省，特别是西部行省，可起到多方面的作用：一是安置退役老兵；二是镇压当地居民反抗；三是同化土著居民。此外，由于老兵殖民地不但数量众多，而且设施先进，也为当地居民提供了城市生活的样板，使行省居民看到了"罗马城市是什么样的，罗马化的生活应该是什么样子。"[18](p.195) 老兵殖民地最初大多出于军事目的而建，而且在建立过程中往往有退役老兵的参与，因此在建城仪式和土地分配方式上也带有浓厚的军事色彩和罗马特色。殖民地大多按军营方式建立，以一军旗为标志，按古老的建城方式，用犁破土开地，先犁出市区范围，再以市区为中心把周围约50平方里的土地划为殖民地乡村范围，然后把这片土地分割成以200犹格（约折合800亩）为单位的方块地，称为森都里亚（Centuria，或译为"百户区"、"陌"）每个森都里亚又进一步细分成面积为25至50犹格大小不等的份地，根据每位老兵的军衔高低分给殖民者。有关土地所有权和位置等具体信息被刻在一张青铜地图上，供所有人观看。这些做法反映了皇帝对老兵殖民地的关注和重视。最后一步是由三人委员会颁发殖民地特许状，为殖民地未来的自治政府建立法律框架。

从外观来看，这些殖民地本身强烈地受到意大利模式的影响，具有典型的罗马城市的特征，殖民地"本身就是罗马城的缩影和翻版"。[19]（p.151）除了网格状街道设计以外，分区制是罗马式城市的另一个重要特征，城市的公共设施如道路、纪念碑和广场、神庙等大都位于城市的中心地区，生产区位于城市的边缘，墓地被排除在居住区域之外。

在殖民地的城市管理方面，也引进了罗马的自治市管理制度。殖民地设有城市议会和公民大会等自治机构，选举当地自治市政府的官员，采用罗马法，成立学校教授拉丁和希腊文化，建立罗马式的广场、公共浴室和露天剧场等公共设施，举行罗马式的竞技和表演，还任命祭司定期举行对罗马神的崇拜仪式。一些退役老兵由于拥有罗马公民权，在经济、法律和社会地位上享有某些特权，他们在服役期间积累了一定的财富，其退役金相当于一个城市议员的平均财富，属于当地居民中的上层。特别是退役的军官，如百人队长等经常成为城市的保护人或当地政府官员，或者通过对当地社会文化活动给予慷慨捐赠来获得声望，或者凭借自己的身份和地位为所在城市争得荣誉、地位和皇帝的赏赐，美化了城市的同时也刺激了当地经济和文化的发展和繁荣。如一位名为 Caius Vettius 的百人队长在退役后担任了殖民城市——乌尔索（Urso）的行政官（duoviri）。公元200年左右，一位曾在罗马军队中担任骑手的名为瑟丘斯的人，退役后在提姆加德建立了一个市场，他和妻子的肖像被用来装点这个城市。[20]（p.104）伴随着老兵殖民地的建立和老兵的到来，"他们在人口稀少的地区传播了城市化和罗马化"。[11](p.225)大量老兵殖民地的建立迅速增加了罗马式城市的数量，扩大了城市化运动的规模，推动了罗马城市化运动的发展和西部行省罗马化的进程。

参考文献

[1] [美] 斯塔夫里阿诺斯：《全球通史——1500年以前的世界》，吴象婴、梁赤民译，上海社会科学院出版社，2000.

[2] P.A. Brunt, *Roman Imperial Themes*, Clarendon Press, 1990.

[3] D. Brendan Nagle, *The Ancient World : A Social and Cultural History*, New Jersey, 1989.

[4] [古罗马] 塔西佗：《编年史》，王以铸、崔妙因译，商务印书馆，2002.

[5] Brian Campbell, *The Roman Army 31BC—AD337: A Source Book*, London and New York, 1994.

[7] Steven K. Drummond, Lynn H. Nelson, *The Western Frontiers of Imperial Rome*, New York and London, 1994.

[8] Roy W. Davies, *Service in the Roman Army*, Edinburgh University Press, 1989.

[9] Nigel Pollard, *Soldiers, Cities, and Civilians in Roman Syria*, The University of Michigan Press, 2000.

[10] Leonard A. Curchin, *The Romanization of central Spain: Complexity, Diversity and Change in a Provincial Hinterland*, New York, 2004.

[11] Yanne Le Bohec, Translated by Raphael Bate, *The Imperial Roman Army*, London and New York, 1994.

[12] 张晓校：《罗马军队与帝位嬗递》，中国社会科学出版社，2006.

[13] Anders Bell, "Castra et urbs romana:An Examination of the Common Features of Roman Settlements in Italy and the Empire and a System to aid in the Discovery of their Origins", from http://cac-scec.ca/concours-

essais/01Bell.html.

[14] J. P. V. D. Balsdon, *Roman Civilization*, Penguin Books，1965.

[15] [古罗马] 塔西佗：《阿古利可拉传 日耳曼尼亚志》，马雍、傅正元译，商务印书馆，1997.

[16] Frank Miranda， "Castra et Coloniae: The role of the Roman Army in the Romanization and Urbanization of Spain"，from http://en.wikipedia.org/wiki/Castra.

[17] 杨共乐：《罗马帝国社会经济研究》，北京师范大学出版社，1998.

[18] Kathryn Lomas，*Roman Italy 338BC-AD200*：*A Source Book*，New York, 1996.

[19] Paul Erdkamp，*A Companion to the Roman Army*, Blackwell Publishing, 2007.

[20] 戴尔·布朗主编：《罗马：帝国荣耀的回声》，陈俐丽译，华夏出版社、广西人民出版社，2002.

民族精神与罗马帝国的崛起 *

杨俊明 湖南师范大学

摘要：社会道德植根于一定的社会土壤。早期罗马公民崇尚冷静、勤劳、纪律和公民义务，将自己的道德规范、感情和习惯置于国家最高权力之下，公民的价值取向与国家利益紧密联系在一起。独特的传统美德，鲜明的民族精神，不仅为罗马民族增添了耀眼的光环，而且深刻影响了罗马历史的发展进程，使罗马在短短的时间内迅速扩张成为一个横跨欧亚非三大洲的大帝国。

关键词：罗马帝国；崛起；民族精神

Abstract: Social morality is rooted in certain social background. Early Roman citizens advocated calmness, diligence, discipline and civic duty and put their own code of ethics, feelings and habits under the country's supreme power. Citizen's value orientation and national interests closely link together. Unique traditional virtues, distinctive national spirit not only awarded dazzling aura for the Roman people, but also had great influence on the development of Roman. They made Roman rapidly expand into a large empire in a very short time, which located in three continents: Europe, Asia and Africa.

Keywords: Roman, Rise, National Spirit

罗马原本是意大利台伯河畔的一个小城邦，地不过百里，人不过数万。从公元前三世纪起开始向海外扩张，短短的一百多年里就成为一个横跨欧亚非三大洲、面积达数百万平方公里、人口达数千万的大帝国。究其原因就在于立国之初的罗马人保持了传统的公民美德。人们崇尚冷静、勤劳、纪律和公民义务，将自己的道德规范、感情和习俗置于国家最高权力之下，公民的价值取向与国家利益紧密联系在一起，从而铸就了罗马帝国的伟大功业。

罗马民族很早就认识到了道德建设的重要性，开始有意识地对公民进行道德教育。共和国的政治制度、教育制度、法律制度不仅稳固了罗马公民的社会道德，而且为之提供了保证和约束，从而有效地维护了公民社会道德的纯朴，铸就了勤俭、爱国、虔敬、诚信、守法和求真的民族精神。

---

* 本文系国家社科基金（批准号 07BSS002）和教育部人文社科规划基金（06JA770014）阶段性成果。

一 勤劳节俭的风尚

罗马民族视国人的贫穷、节俭为美德，为官为民者都恪守这一美德。在罗马人的心中，"道德远比知识重要，道德既是知识的目的，又是获取正确知识的必要条件。"[①]当时的罗马，"到处都表现出最大的和谐，人们几乎不知道贪欲为何物。"[②]由于罗马民族的农业特性，劳动光荣的观念深入人心。国家各级公务人员无论是元老贵族还是普通公民都从事农业劳动。公元前458年，埃魁人和沃尔斯奇人的进攻给罗马的安全造成了巨大的威胁，城内一片恐慌，元老院任命辛辛纳图斯为独裁官。派去请他上任的使者找到他时，他正在台伯河右岸的地里耕作，光着身子，浑身尘土，亲自扶着犁把。在接受元老院的委任后，他拭去灰尘和汗水，换好衣服，走马上任，前去解救被围困在阿尔基杜斯山的罗马军队。他成功解围，救出执政官弥努基乌斯，并在第16天就交卸了授权六个月的独裁权，解甲归田。[③]在赢得征服敌人、拯救罗马的巨大荣耀之后，他像一位普通的公民，重操旧业，扶犁耕作。辛辛纳图斯听从召唤、勤俭和纯朴的形象成为罗马人心目中的典范，受到了罗马不同时代民众的交口称赞，恩格斯更是称其为"真正的公民美德和异常质朴而高尚忘我精神的榜样。"[④]为了纪念这位英雄，美国俄亥俄州的人们以他的名字命名了一个城市（辛辛纳提市）。[⑤]

农业民族的特性铸就了罗马民族独有的崇尚清贫和节俭的社会风尚。罗马人对奢侈浪费深恶痛绝，贪图奢侈的人不仅遭到人们的唾弃，而且受到法律的严惩。曾任执政官的鲁菲努斯只因拥有一个超过10磅重的银盘，触犯法律而被逐出元老院。[⑥]在对待金钱诱惑时罗马人能廉洁自重，为官者更是大公无私，廉洁奉公。当时的官员"清廉寡欲，不贪财，不揽权，诚实节俭，公正质朴"，"不得收受或馈赠礼品。"[⑦]李维详细记载了曾四次担任执政官的普布利科拉的清廉，普鲁塔克更是称赞他使自己的一生达到了尽善尽美的境界。"他荣誉巨大，但家庭财产却如此微薄，甚至都不够葬礼费用，结果由国库提供"。[⑧]

这种崇尚劳动光荣、清贫节俭的道德风尚不仅保持了罗马社会良好的道德风尚，维持了社会成员之间的平等关系，巩固了国家的基础，而且增强了罗马民族的凝聚力和团结向上的精神。正是凭借这种由质朴的罗马古风哺育出来的巨大力量，罗马民族顽强地生存并逐渐强大，最终发展成为一支称霸地中海世界的主宰力量。

二 爱国奉献的精神

共和初期，为了生存与发展，逆境之中的罗马人在精神和意志上经受了严峻的考验，逐渐形成了一种勇敢坚韧、不屈不挠的民族性格和力挽狂澜的组织才能，形成了团结进取和随时准备为国捐躯的爱国奉献精神，培育了以爱国主义为核心理念的优秀品质。罗马人"把给公众作好事，有益于自己的祖国，看得远远胜过个人的不幸：儿子死在战斗中，父亲得到光荣，他为此而欢欣喜悦，胜

---

① 张斌贤等：《西方教育思想史》，四川教育出版社1994年，第163页。
② （古罗马）撒路斯乌提斯：《喀提林阴谋》，王以铸、崔妙因译，商务印书馆1995年，IX。
③ （古罗马）李维：《自建城以来》，王焕生译，中国政法大学出版社2009年，III，26—29。
④ 《马克思恩格斯选集》第4卷，人民出版社1965年，第260页。
⑤ （美）斯坦利·宾：《罗马公司》，张立梅译，中信出版社2007年，第50页。
⑥ （古希腊）普鲁塔克：《希腊罗马名人传·苏拉传》，席代岳译，吉林出版集团2009年，I。
⑦ （古罗马）西塞罗：《西塞罗三论·论责任》，徐奕春译，商务印书馆1998年，II，12。
⑧ （古罗马）李维：《自建城以来》，II，16，7。

过丧子之痛"。①执政官德西乌斯祖孙三代先后为国捐躯，其业绩在罗马传为美谈。②在公民的心目中，国家利益至上，个人德行、家庭利益都必须与国家利益保持一致。罗马民族非常强调个人对国家的忠诚，强调公民对国家的义务，于是"国亡我亡"、"国存我存"、"国兴我兴"的群体意识在罗马公民心中逐渐形成。"忠于罗马是至高无上的。为了国家的利益，公民不仅应该随时准备献出自己的生命，而且在必要时要牺牲家人和朋友的生命。"③真正的美德存在于一切与国家利益相符的活动中，并由此实现公民的个人价值。

罗马人对祖国的热爱从不计较个人得失，他们自觉地将个人活动纳入国家事务之中，将个人利益和国家命运紧密联系在一起，从而有效地维护和实现了公民内部的团结与合作，推进了国家的扩张进程。在长期的征服战争中，罗马人经常失败，但逆境之中的罗马人那里跌倒就在那里爬起，从不服输，在极为困难的条件下经常反败为胜。这种不屈不挠的顽强斗志，使罗马人能够勇敢面对各种威胁，对敌人发起更为猛烈的反击，其关键就在于爱国奉献精神激发了公民的高昂斗志。可以这样说："在勇敢、忍耐和艰苦奋斗方面，他们超过了所有其他的民族。在他们牢稳地巩固他们的势力之前，他们绝对不因为胜利而骄傲……也绝对不因为不幸而沮丧。"④强烈的爱国情感使罗马民族在险恶的环境中能团结一心，为保卫祖国而努力战斗。正如孟德斯鸠所说的那样："罗马人所以能够号令一切民族，不仅仅是由于他们的战术，同时也是由于他们的审慎、他们的贤明、他们的坚持、他们对荣誉和祖国的热爱。"⑤

罗马公民热爱祖国，勇敢善战是罗马民族崛起的精神动力，而战争中罗马公民所表现出的前赴后继、勇于牺牲的爱国奉献精神则为罗马国家的生存和发展提供了精神上的保障。

三　虔敬的宗教信仰

罗马宗教的主旨就是加强公民对罗马的忠诚。⑥在宗教信仰的虔诚性上罗马人比希腊人有过之而无不及。罗马人宣称帝国的伟大是诸神对罗马人虔诚的奖赏，"共和国之所以能够像今天这样伟大，完全是因为我们竭尽全力取悦于不朽的神祇的原因。"⑦罗马宗教中这种使宗教情感和公民义务感互相融合的精神植根并服务于以公民为主体的古代社会，当这种宗教渗透了人本主义思想时，它就进一步肯定了家庭宗教在培育公民道德素质方面的重大意义。

罗马宗教以原始宗教为核心，随着对外战争的胜利，罗马民族逐渐吸收其它民族宗教的因素，形成了虔敬的宗教态度。虔敬能确保神的持续保护，持续繁荣与幸福，它"是与道德有关的一种责任，以及与家庭、朋友、祖先、制度、公民和神之间良好关系的维护"。⑧在罗马，宗教情感与公民义务感互相融合，由于家庭宗教活动经常、直接而且责无旁贷，罗马人习惯于以认真执著的态度对待自己的宗教信念，就像他们遵纪守法、强调纪律性那样。罗马宗教中这种使宗教情感与公民义务感互相融合的精神，和罗马接受的希腊宗教的人本主义思想互为促进，不仅因为它们都植根并服务于以公民为主体的城邦社会，当罗马宗教渗透了人本主义思想时，它就进一步肯定了家庭宗教在培育公

① （法）比尔基埃等主编：《家庭史》第 1 卷，袁树仁、姚静、肖桂译，三联书店 1998 年，342 页。
② （古罗马）：西塞罗《论至善和至恶》，石敏敏译，中国社会科学出版社 2005 年，II，19。
③ （美）拉尔夫等：《世界文明史》上卷，赵丰等译，商务印书馆 2001 年，第 321 页。
④ （古罗马）阿庇安：《罗马史·序言》，谢德风译，商务印书馆 1985 年，XI。
⑤ （法）孟德斯鸠：《罗马盛衰原因论》，婉玲译，商务印书馆 1984 年，第 103 页。
⑥ （意）罗格拉：《古罗马的兴衰》，宋杰、宋玮译，明天出版社 2001 年，第 50 页。
⑦ 王晓朝：《罗马帝国文化转型论》，社会科学文献出版社 2002 年，第 99 页。
⑧ （英）阿德金斯：《探寻古罗马文明》，张楠、王悦、范秀琳译，张强校，商务印书馆 2008 年，第 543 页。

民道德素质方面的重大意义。①罗马人发自内心地尊重神祇，虔诚地进行各种宗教仪式。"罗马人是世界上对誓约最虔诚的民族，誓约永远是维护他们的军纪的动力。"②在神祇面前罗马人言必行，行必果。罗马"每一个重要决策都包含着宗教的因素，每一次改革和争论都与影响公共宗教活动或其它公开祭祀活动等宗教问题相关。"③罗马宗教"把国家熔化于与神那么密切结合的状态中，使对神的虔敬与爱国主义打成一片，养成了狂热的爱国心。"④

罗马传统的宗教信仰"提供了一个有助于爱国主义精神的源泉"，⑤它不仅激发和强化了公民的社会责任感和爱国精神，而且提高了罗马民族的凝聚力。对英雄和神祇的崇拜和虔诚信仰为罗马人提供了无穷的榜样和精神动力。

四　诚信的品德

古朴的风尚铸就了罗马人诚实正直的品德。罗马人弃恶扬善、诚实守约，形成了自己崇尚正直、诚信，忠诚誓言的传统美德。无论是处理人际关系还是国家关系，他们都谨守这一道德原则。现实生活中，即使是经商，卖者也会将自己商品的缺点告诉买者，因为这是诚信所必须的。对罗马人来说，诚信是一种非常重要的品质。罗马人深信"世界上没有什么比说假话更丑恶、更可耻的了"。⑥西塞罗强调罗马人"会不惜任何损失以坚持正义和诚信，不管损失有多大，也不会背弃正义和诚信，甚至面对死亡也在所不惜。"⑦即使在与敌国交战中罗马人也坚持光明正大，诚实正直的原则，鄙视为达目的不择手段的阴谋和不正当手段。皮洛斯战争期间，一个叛徒表示愿潜回军营毒死皮洛斯，元老院将他交给皮洛斯。"以此表明不赞成以奸诈的手段谋杀敌人"。⑧罗马人的正直比用武力征服更值得称道，因为这种胜利和征服使敌人输得心服口服，有利于以后罗马的统治。以至于罗马人的对手都称赞要"罗马人偏离诚信比太阳偏离自己的轨迹都难"。⑨

罗马人不仅遵守彼此之间的承诺，即使是因为环境所迫而对敌人许下的任何承诺，罗马人也会认真履行。第一次布匿战争中被俘的执政官雷古卢斯在宣誓决不去而不返之后，被迦太基派回罗马商谈媾和一事。雷古卢斯回去后立即向元老院提出，为了彻底打败迦太基，既不要与他们交换俘虏，也不要和他们讲和。当人们劝他不要返回迦太基时，明知回去必死无疑的雷古卢斯表示："宁愿回去后被敌人折磨至死，也不能违背自己的誓言，尽管这是对敌人的承诺。"⑩最终，迦太基人把他关在一个木板上钉满了长钉的木笼里面折磨至死。雷古卢斯此举得到世人的高度称赞，认为他忠实地履行了自己的道德责任。⑪奥古斯丁更是强调：在"所有著名的杰出公民中，罗马人找不出比他更值得宣扬的人来。富裕不能使他腐败，……敌人也不能使他屈服。"⑫罗马人正直、诚信到如此地步，以至于他们自己都为自己这种重信守约的民族特性感到自豪，李维说："我们的祖先决不用埋伏的方法打击敌人，决不在夜里向敌人发动袭击，也决不用假装逃跑然后突然转身的方法向那些还未作

---

① 朱龙华：《罗马文化与古典传统》，浙江人民出版社1993年，第27、第43页。

② （法）孟德斯鸠：《罗马盛衰原因论》，第4-5页。

③ Janet Lloyd, *An Introduction to Roman Religion*, Edinburgh :Edinburgh University, 2003, p.129.

④ （美）杜兰：《世界文明史·凯撒与基督》，幼狮文化公司译，东方出版社1999年，第93-94页。

⑤ 夏普：《比较宗教学史》，上海人民出版社1988年，第8页。

⑥ （古罗马）西塞罗：《西塞罗三论·论责任》，I，42。

⑦ （古罗马）西塞罗：《西塞罗三论·论责任》，I，25。

⑧ （古罗马）西塞罗：《西塞罗三论·论责任》，I，13。

⑨ （古罗马）尤特罗庇乌斯：《罗马国史大纲》，谢品巍译，上海人民出版社2011年，第17页。

⑩ （古罗马）西塞罗：《西塞罗三论·论责任》，I，13。

⑪ （古罗马）西塞罗：《西塞罗三论·论责任》，III，29。

⑫ （古罗马）奥古斯丁：《上帝之城》，王晓朝译，人民出版社2006年，I，24。

好准备的敌人发动进攻，更不以狡猾而以真正的勇敢为自豪。他们的习惯是在战前向敌人宣战，有时甚至让敌人知道他们发动战争的时间和地点。"①

诚信是罗马公民安身立命的基本要求，它不仅有利于罗马社会的和谐发展，而且也成为罗马迅速崛起的重要因素。

五　遵纪守法的模范

战争磨练了罗马人的坚强意志，培养了罗马人对国家的使命感。他们勇敢顽强，严守军纪，除了具有农民的勤劳质朴外，罗马公民还具有一个优秀士兵所必备的吃苦耐劳和忠勇卫国的优秀品质。当兵打仗不仅被看作是一种权利，更被视为一种社会荣誉而为世人所景仰。一个理想的罗马公民应该具备的重要品质就是英勇不屈和吃苦耐劳。为了保持这种品质和理想，罗马人极为重视严明的纪律、忍耐力、忠于职守的责任感、坚强的性格和不屈不挠的斗志。因为"纪律是罗马人获胜的秘诀。"②罗马军队之所以难以战胜，靠的是他们坚决服从的纪律和严格的训练。③在服从命令、严守军纪方面罗马军人成为了国家遵纪守法的典型。如果说卓越的战斗力是取胜的基础，那么服从命令与遵守军纪则是取得胜利的保证。在军纪严明的军队里，凡是不服从命令擅自行动者，不论官职大小，一律处以死刑。拉丁战争期间，执政官曼利乌斯之子由于受到敌人的挑衅而违背了不得与敌交战的命令，尽管得胜归来，但其父仍集合全军，当众宣布因为违背执政官的命令与敌交战，将儿子处以死刑。④

罗马人很早就有法律面前人人平等的观念。他们强调对于公民的审判应该遵循公开、公平、公正的原则，不论身份高低贵贱、不管其为国家作出的贡献大小都应一视同仁。这充分表明了罗马人对法律的崇敬，并对罗马社会法治理念的形成与发展起了重要的作用。罗马人遵纪守法，重视秩序的观念突出表现在他们看待法律与个人和政府的关系上。罗马人认为遵守法律与自由并不矛盾，遵守法律是一个公民应尽的义务和责任。因为法律存在的目的就是为了保证人民的自由和权利，国家权力必须依靠法律来行使，受法律的制约和约束。"罗马人是世界上最懂得使法律为自己的意图服务的民族"。⑤在拥有较为完善法律的基础上，利用法律的杠杆，以法治国。罗马人认为法律存在的目的就是为了保证人民的自由和权利，国家权力必须依靠法律来行使，受法律的制约和约束。任何官员，即使是国家高级官员的权力也绝对不能凌驾于法律之上。不管平民还是贵族，谁若触犯法律，都将受到严厉的惩罚。因为"如果不能对每一个人都一视同仁，那么法律就是一纸空文。"屡次在危难之际拯救罗马的卡米卢斯曾受到法庭控告，并处以巨额罚款。⑥这样一位战功卓著、身居高位的人也"难逃法网"，可见罗马人讲究法治，尊重法律之严格。

严明的军纪激发了罗马军人的斗志，造就了一支所向披靡、令敌人闻风丧胆的铁军，为征服战争的最后胜利奠定了坚实的基础。而在崇尚法治的罗马社会，法律维系着社会的正常运转，为创造良好的社会环境提供了保障，成为支配国家机构运行、社会关系和日常生活的基本准则。正是得益于强调法制，尊重法律，罗马享受着长期的稳定和繁荣。

---

① （古罗马）李维：《建城以来史》，王敦书选译，载吴于廑主编：《外国史学名著选》，商务印书馆1986年，XXXXII, 47。

② （英）斯托巴特：《伟大属于罗马》，王三义译，上海三联书店2011年，第39页。

③ （古犹太）约瑟福斯：《犹太战争》，王丽丽等译，山东大学出版社2007年，第111页。

④ （古罗马）李维：《自建城以来》，VIII, 7, 7-22。

⑤ （法）孟德斯鸠：《论法的精神》（下），张雁深译，商务印书馆1997年，第120页。

⑥ （古罗马）阿庇安：《罗马史·关于意大利》，谢德风译，商务印书馆1985年，，VIII, 2。

六 求真务实的楷模

现实的残酷、农民的本性和长期的征战培养了罗马人求真务实的品格。"虽然罗马人没有希腊人那样的天才，但却有丰富的实践经验，能够将质朴务实的理论常识运用到实践中的各个方面。罗马人解决实际事务的智慧，远远超出了希腊人。"①从现实出发既是罗马人思维模式的价值取向，又是罗马人谋求生存发展的必然选择。求真务实不仅成为罗马人崇奉的重要信条，也是他们坚持的一项重要原则。

在政治体制方面，罗马人的实用主义原则体现得最充分，表现了罗马人处理政务和人际关系的杰出才能。共和国时期的罗马形成了以执政官为核心的行政长官制度、以政界精英为基础的元老院制度和以全体公民为基础的公民大会制度。罗马公民廉洁奉公、道德自律、虔诚荣誉的社会风尚与这种相互制衡的政府权力体制不无关系。波里比乌斯认为罗马人之所以能够成功称霸地中海世界就在于他们拥有当时世界上最好的政治体制。这种由三方力量构成的政体结构具有制衡作用，平民制约执政官，执政官制约元老院，元老院制约平民。它们互相制约，互为补充，成为一个有机的整体，从而有效保证了国家的正常运转和政治稳定。②在社会生活中，罗马人非常重视技术改造，并将其应用于社会实践中。建筑家维特鲁威提出了"坚固、适用、美观"的建筑设计理论，③将坚固和适用置于重要地位。罗马人很好地遵循这个原则，并将其运用在诸如建筑、道路、引水渠等公共工程的修建上。医疗事业与人们的身体健康密切相关，适用性极强，罗马人对此倍加重视。以适用为特色的外科手术是罗马医学最发达的行业。教育方面罗马人的适用色彩更为浓厚。罗马民族需要培养的是具有严肃、虔诚和质朴品格的人，因此，"教导自己的孩子成为好公民，训练他们成为努力工作、服从、坚定和为了家庭、国家准备牺牲自己的人，是父亲的责任"。④

求真务实不仅成为罗马人崇奉的重要信条，也是他们坚持的一项重要原则。追求适用主义的罗马人在这种思想观念的指导下，不断将其融入到自己的生产和生活之中，从而对国家的政治、科学、文化产生了重大而深远的影响。它不仅给国家的发展打上了深深的适用主义烙印，而且创造了一种为世人所称道的适用主义的罗马文明。

公民社会道德的状况如何直接关系到一个国家的兴盛和长治久安。共和前期，严格的道德规范将罗马公民塑造成勤劳的农民、勇敢的战士、将国家利益置于首位的官员，从而成就了罗马帝国的伟大功业。

---

① （美）布雷斯特德：《文明的征程》，李静新译，北京燕山出版社 2004 年，第 366 页。
② Polybius, *The History*, Cambridge:Harvard University Press,1960, Ⅵ,15,18.
③ （古罗马）维特鲁威：《建筑十书》第一书，高履泰译，知识产权出版社 2001 年，Ⅲ, 2。
④ Jo-Ann Shelton, *As the Romans Did : A Source Book in Roman Social History*, New York:Oxford University Press, 1988, p.100.

【中世纪、拜占廷帝国史】

从雇佣军的作用看拜占廷帝国的衰亡

李秀玲 武警指挥学院

摘要： 拜占廷帝国史是一部胜败交加的战争史，军人具有举足轻重的影响力，其中由"蛮族人"组成的雇佣军发挥了不容忽视的作用。他们在帝国不同时期的作用和地位有所不同，经历了从辅助力量到支柱力量的转变，折射出帝国从强盛走向衰亡的历程。帝国晚期主要依靠雇佣军作战，巨额军费负担进一步加剧了国家的财政危机，雇佣军的不稳定性和易于哗变加速了帝国的衰亡。

关键词： 拜占廷帝国；雇佣军；兴衰

Abstract： The history of Byzantine Empire was annals of war cross defeat or victory, during which soldiers had crucial influence. Mercenary army played an important role as the part of them. Their effect and status were different in each phase. The change they were from subsidiary to backbone reflected the course which Byzantine Empire was from greatness to decline. In the terminal stage of Byzantine Empire, mercenary army became the main military force. Substantial military expenditure aggravated government finances. Furthermore, mutiny of the mercenary army accelerated the decline of the Empire.

Keywords： Byzantine Empire, Mercenary Army, decline

拜占廷帝国曾是中世纪欧洲存在时间最长的君主专制国家，在其千余年的历史中，几经盛衰沉浮，抵挡住了外敌的无数次入侵，但最终难逃灭亡的命运。国内外学者已经从经济停滞、政治腐败、精神颓废、宗教束缚等方面对帝国灭亡的原因进行了探讨，[1]但鲜有军事方面的分析。而拜占廷帝国的历史是在奥斯曼土耳其人的炮火中终结的，军事失败是其灭亡的直接原因。本文尝试从雇佣军在帝国军队中的地位和影响等方面，探究其衰亡历程。

---

[1] 崔艳红：《国内外学者对拜占廷帝国衰亡原因的研究》，载《世界历史》，2002年第6期，第82—86页。概述了国内外学者关于拜占廷帝国衰亡原因的几种观点，即阶级斗争论、小农经济破产论、社会机体腐败论、时代精神沦亡论、帕列奥列格王朝外交政策丧失独立论。

一　雇佣军在拜占廷帝国军队中的地位演变

拜占廷处于欧亚非三洲交界，都城君士坦丁堡处于东西南北多条商路的交汇点，扼守东西交通路桥和南北航道要冲，这种地理环境使帝国始终处于临战状态，深陷战乱的漩涡。哥特人、斯拉夫人、阿瓦尔人、波斯人、阿拉伯人、伦巴第人、保加利亚人、罗斯人、帕臣涅格人、斯基泰人、塞尔柱突厥人、诺曼人、西欧人、奥斯曼土耳其人等都是拜占廷在不同时期需要应对的劲敌，有些敌对关系甚至长达几个世纪，许多战争都是国家的生死存亡之战，例如，与波斯人和阿拉伯人对近东地区的争夺战绵延三个多世纪。[①]毫不夸张地说，拜占廷千年帝国史实际上就是一部胜败交加的战争史。战争的胜败不仅关系到疆域的变动，而且成为国内社会政治经济结构、军事体制编制和民族成分构成演变的直接动力，例如，7–12世纪期间实行的军区制，就是周边民族入侵的巨大威胁引发严峻边疆危机的产物。[②]因此，军人在拜占廷历史上具有举足轻重的影响，由"蛮族人"组成的雇佣军作为其组成部分发挥了不容忽视的作用，爱德华·吉本曾指出，近卫军的暴乱导致"蛮族"军官把持政权甚至取得帝位是构成帝国长期战乱和衰亡的重要因素。[③]雇佣军在帝国不同时期的作用和地位有所不同，从整体上看经历了从辅助力量到支柱力量的转变，在帝国早期和晚期的影响较大，而在军区制正常运行的五个世纪中作用微弱，这与他们在军队中的职务和地位高低、势力强弱相一致，折射出帝国从强盛走向衰亡的历程。

在拜占廷帝国，雇佣兵也称为"蛮兵"，一般在战时临时组建，拥有各自的军事首领和明确的军事任务，战事结束后便自行解散或离开拜占廷领土。在一般情况下，雇佣兵是拜占廷贵族的私人武装，由富有高官出钱雇佣，为其看家护院。当国家面临外敌入侵的威胁时，他们可能临时为政府服务，但由于人力资源短缺，兵力不足，国家经常被迫雇佣外籍士兵。拜占廷军队使用雇佣军的历史由来已久，几乎来自帝国周边的所有民族，例如，哥特人、保加利亚人、塞尔维亚人、西班牙人、伦巴第人、突厥人、瓦兰吉亚人、加泰罗尼亚人、诺曼人、罗斯人等都曾在帝国军队中服役。[④]帝国军队中的后备军作为战时紧急增援部队，属于临时性的军事组织，多由定居在帝国边境地区的"蛮族"组成，在帝国初期，这种"蛮族"军团由皇帝直接控制，作用日益增强。[⑤]甚至驻扎在君士坦丁堡及其郊区的皇宫御林军，最初由斯拉夫人和突厥人构成，后来增加了瓦兰吉亚人、加泰罗尼亚人、诺曼人和罗斯人。他们因为有机会与皇帝和朝廷高官接触频繁而获利不菲，军事仕途顺利，许多人担任高级军职。[⑥]帝国早期的许多皇帝都曾重用蛮族人。例如，君士坦丁一世（Constantine Ⅰ，324–337年在位）和塞奥多西一世（Theodosius Ⅰ，379–395年在位）均对哥特人采取安抚怀柔政策，在军队中建立哥特人兵团，4万名哥特人组成的"联盟者"在军队中拥有特殊身份，从帝国政府领取军饷。[⑦]许多哥特人将领担任军中要职，个别人甚至进入元老院。阿兰族雇佣兵阿巴斯甚至一度控制帝国军权，掌控皇帝废立。[⑧]当时的一位主教写道，"武装的蛮族将领使用各种借口窃取权力，成为罗马公民的统治者……这些外国人应该被赶出军队指挥岗位和元老阶层"。[⑨]不仅戍边部队中充斥着大量蛮族官兵，甚至连君士坦丁一世身边的宫廷卫队也由日耳曼人充任。有学者甚至认为"君士坦

①　徐家玲、崔艳红：《论拜占廷帝国灭亡的原因》，载《东北师大学报》（社科版），2001年第6期，第9页。
②　陈志强：《拜占廷军区制和农兵》，载《历史研究》，1998年第5期，第115页，第117页。
③　[英]爱德华·吉本（著），黄宜思、黄雨石译：罗马帝国衰亡史（下），北京：商务印书馆1997年版，第427页。
④　陈志强：《拜占廷帝国史》，商务印书馆2003年版，第438页。
⑤　陈志强：《拜占廷帝国史》，商务印书馆2003年版，第435页。
⑥　陈志强：《拜占廷帝国史》，商务印书馆2003年版，第439页。
⑦　[苏]科瓦略夫（著），王以铸译：《古代罗马史》，三联书店1957年版，第1936页。
⑧　陈志强：《拜占廷帝国史》，商务印书馆2003年版，第117页。
⑨　A. A. Vasiliev, *History of the Byzantine Empire,* Wisconsin, 1958, p.93.

丁对日耳曼军人的青睐导致帝国军队蛮族化。"[1]400 年 7 月，教俗各界希腊贵族在首都发动起义，大肆屠杀哥特将领和士兵，471 年被哥特人推上皇座的利奥一世（Leo I，457–474 年在位）也曾大规模清除宫廷中的哥特人。[2]这从侧面反映出在 4、5 世纪，哥特人拥有强大的军政势力。6 世纪，为了弥补兵力资源的巨大缺口，政府曾被迫招募大量日耳曼雇佣兵，莫里斯（Maurice，582–602 年在位）曾建立以矛手为主的后备军团，其中大部分士兵来自日耳曼部落和伊里利亚山民，他们尚武彪悍，战斗力极强，常常在两军对阵的关键时刻决定战斗的胜负。[3]

尽管雇佣军在帝国早期军队中的地位和作用非常重要，但基本上处于政府的有效控制之中，形成了积极的战斗力量。6 世纪以后，在军区制下，亦农亦兵的农兵阶层和自由农村公社的小农成为帝国防御力量的主体，[4]雇佣军的作用相对减弱。

从 11 世纪后半叶开始，随着军区制的瓦解，小农阶层几乎完全消失，被普洛尼亚土地上的依附农取代。[5]在普洛尼亚制度下，国家把一些大领地的税收权下放到一些修道院或世俗权贵手中，要求其按照占有土地和租税的比例提供相应兵力，他们取代农兵成为本土兵员的重要来源，但其战斗力远逊于农兵。此外，随着农兵阶层的大批破产，服军役成为一项极其沉重的负担，军人们开始采用交纳代役税的方法摆脱军事义务。[6]在这种情况下，原来以自由农兵阶层为基础的征兵体制和军事防御体制崩溃瓦解，帝国军队逐渐丧失了本国兵源，雇佣兵开始比在马其顿王朝强盛时代的帝国军队中占据更大的比例，起到更重要的作用，法兰克人、伦巴第人、罗斯人、阿兰人、保加尔人、达尔马提亚人、帕臣涅格人、库曼人和塞尔柱突厥人等都经常被征募，作为常备军或者临时辅助军队使用。

安娜·科穆宁娜[7]的记述表明了 11 中后期帝国军队的衰弱状况和兵力构成。阿莱科休斯一世（Alexius I，1081–1118 年在位）从前任者那里继承的军队，因为行政官僚机构的克扣而军费匮乏，又在米哈伊尔七世（Michael VII，1071–1078 年在位）和尼基弗鲁斯三世（Nicephorus III，1078–1081 年在位）统治期间频繁的内战[8]中遭到进一步破坏，其中的本国军队只包括来自安纳托利亚、色雷斯和马其顿地区的少量征兵。[9]他与诺曼人作战时，塞尔柱突厥人、瓦兰吉亚人和法兰克人军团都是其重要的依靠兵力。[10]军队中的塞尔柱突厥人雇佣军多次出现在安娜的笔下。[11]她也在著作中为我们提供了帝国在 11 世纪末的一些征兵细节：凯撒尼基弗鲁斯·迈里西努斯（Nikephorus Melissenus）被命令从保加尔人和游牧民中招募新兵，参加与斯基泰人（Scyths）的战争；阿莱科休斯一世从未放过征募外族将士的任何机会，卡斯托利亚（Castoria）被占领后，愿意为他服役的诺曼人被编入帝国军队。[12]11 世纪末，许多拜占廷将领接受过外族雇佣军宣誓的事实也体现了雇佣军的日益重要性。

① Arther Ferrill, *The Fall of Roman Empire, The Military Explanation*, Thames and Hudson, London, 1986, p.147.
② 陈志强：《拜占廷帝国史》，商务印书馆 2003 年版，第 440 页。
③ 陈志强：《拜占廷帝国史》，第 442 页。
④ 徐家玲、崔艳红：《论拜占廷帝国灭亡的原因》，第 11 页。
⑤ 陈志强：《独特的拜占廷文明》，中国青年出版社 1998 年，第 168 页。
⑥ G. Ostrogorsky, *The History of Byzantine State*, Oxford, 1956, pp.293–294.
⑦ 她是阿莱科休斯一世的长公主，被誉为西方史学史上第一位女历史学家，著有《阿莱科休斯传》（*Alexiad of Anna Comnena*）。这部希腊语传记共 15 卷，记录了阿莱科休斯一世的生平业绩，涉及 1069–1118 年间拜占廷帝国发生的重大事件，包括政治、经济、宗教、军事战争和外交等方面的内容，尤其关注了战争和外交事务，是了解 11 世纪中后期和 12 世纪初期拜占廷社会最重要的原始资料之一，具有很高的史料价值。
⑧ 两位皇帝在位时间共 9 年，期间大规模的军事叛乱就有 7 次，并且均被叛乱将领取代皇位。
⑨ Anna Comnena, *Alexiad of Anna Comnena*, Tr. by E.A.Sewter, London: Penguin Books, 1969, pp.38–39.
⑩ Anna Comnena, *Alexiad of Anna Comnena*, p.141.
⑪ Anna Comnena, *Alexiad of Anna Comnena*, pp.41–45, p.89, p.141, p.172, p.305.
⑫ Anna Comnena, *Alexiad of Anna Comnena*, p. 252, p. 182.

例如，尼基弗鲁斯·伯塔尼亚特斯（Nikephorus Botaneiates）在 1078 年的军事叛乱中，收到从米哈伊尔七世的军队中叛逃的塞尔柱突厥人首领呈献的象征忠诚的礼物，并举行正式的接收仪式，当他进入尼西亚城时，塞尔柱突厥人首领双手放在胸前，宣誓为他效忠。[1]冒充罗曼努斯四世（Romanus IV，1068–1071 年在位）儿子的士兵与同意帮助他夺取皇位的库曼人交换誓言；凯撒约翰用金钱收买路遇的塞尔柱突厥人首领宣誓加入科穆宁兄弟的军队，站在阿莱科休斯一边作战。[2]

阿莱科休斯一世统治期间，大量外族人进入其统治集团，其中许多人担任高级将领，例如，在科穆宁家族的军事叛乱中起过重要作用的乔治·帕库里亚努斯（George Pakourianos）和君士坦丁·胡姆伯特普鲁斯（Constantine Humbertopoulos）分别是格鲁吉亚人和诺曼人。阿莱科休斯一世登位后，任命帕库里亚努斯为西部军队总司令，胡姆伯特普鲁斯担任凯尔特人雇佣军团的指挥官，他们都曾参加对诺曼人和帕臣涅格人的战争；[3]拥有一半蛮族血统的塔提西乌斯，是掌握帝国军事大权的重要将领之一，以指挥官的身份几乎出现在安娜记述的所有重大战役和政治危机中；[4]因其勇敢而著名的萨尔马提亚人欧扎斯（Ouzas）[5]、优秀的士兵斯基泰人卡拉扎斯（Caratzas）[6]，都是深受皇帝器重的军事将领，分别在与帕臣涅格人和库曼人的战争中指挥帝国的联盟军队；具有一半塞尔柱突厥人人血统的莫纳斯特拉斯（Monstras）[7]和能力与忠诚都无可挑剔的拉丁人曼努伊尔·布图米特斯[8]是这些外族将领中深受皇帝信任和重用的佼佼者，均握有重要军权。也有许多外族人担任阿莱科休斯一世的外交使节和军事顾问，1108 年代表他与博希蒙德（Buhemond）签订《德沃尔条约》的 8 个使节中，塞巴斯托斯·马利诺斯（Sebastos Marinos）、罗杰、彼得·亚利发斯（Peter Aliphas）、胡伯特（Hubert，法兰克伯爵拉约尔的儿子）、普林斯皮特的理查德伯爵和根特的威廉（William of Gand）都是拉丁人，前三个人均曾担任阿莱科休斯一世的军事顾问。[9]

至 13 世纪初期，国家更是几乎到了兵不能战或无兵可用的地步，雇佣军成为御敌作战的主力，大量土耳其人、诺曼人、斯拉夫人、瓦兰吉亚人等充斥帝国军队。每当战事爆发，无论内战还是外战，皇帝和贵族都将命运交付给这些雇佣兵。在帕列奥列格王朝时期的皇族内战中，例如"两安德

---

① Shepard，"'Father' or 'Scorption'？Style and Substance in Alexius's Diplomacy"，Margaret Mullett and Dion Smythe，*Alexius I Comnenus, Papers* I，Belfast Byzantine Enterprises，1996，p.107.

② Anna Comnena，*Alexiad of Anna Comnena*，p.297，p.89.

③ Anna Comnena，*Alexiad of Anna Comnena*，pp.81–82，p.141，p.146，p.160，pp.212–213，p.257，p. 298.

④ 他在与诺曼人的战争中担任突厥人支队的指挥官，*The Alexiad of Anna Comnena*，IV，p.141；曾率领一支强大军队进攻尼西亚苏丹阿布·卡西姆（VI，pp.201–203）；在与帕臣涅格人的战争中，被委派带着大量军饷去亚得里亚纳堡为士兵支付年薪，从各地征募新兵，并在战斗中指挥右翼军队（VI，pp.213–216，p.224，p.232）；率领雇佣军与库曼人作战（X，p.299）；被命令和特兹塔斯一起带着 2000 轻盾兵，参加十字军对尼西亚的围攻（XI，pp.336–337）；被命令带领一支军队加入去安条克的十字军，为他们随时提供保护和帮助，并从他们手中接管攻占的城市（XI，p.341）；在与比萨人的海战中被任命为舰队总司令（XI，p.360）；在挫败尼基弗鲁斯·迪奥格尼斯的重大叛乱中是皇帝最重要的支持者之一（IX，p.279，p.282，p.288）。总之，几乎在所有重大战事中，我们都可以看到他的身影。

⑤ Anna Comnena，*Alexiad of Anna Comnena*，pp .172–173.

⑥ Anna Comnena，*Alexiad of Anna Comnena*，p.224，p.241，p.306.

⑦ 他是一名优秀的战士，在帕臣涅格人战争中率领精良骑兵偷袭敌人的战马并参加利乌尼乌姆战役（*The Alexiad of Anna Comnena*，VII，pp.240–241，p.257）；在与博希蒙德的战争中，带领骑兵占领了大量重要据点（XI，pp.365–366）；负责许多重要城镇的守卫（XI，pp.358–359; XII，p.372; XIV，p.445）；在与突厥人的战争中指挥前卫部队（XIV，p.455）；因为在将安条克的突厥人地方总督押送到皇帝那里去的过程中出现失误，受到皇帝的严厉谴责（XI，pp.338–340）。

⑧ 安娜称他是皇帝的密友之一，是值得委以重任的优秀将领。他曾率领帝国舰队进攻尼西亚苏丹阿布·卡西姆（*The Alexiad of Anna Comnena*，VI，pp.202–203）；率领帝国的精英部队占领西里西亚的一些地区（XI，pp.357–360）；在攻占尼西亚的过程中，代表皇帝与尼亚西城的突厥人进行了成功的谈判并被皇帝任命为尼西亚公爵（XI，p.331，pp.333–334, 336–340）；作为皇帝的使者被派去与控制安条克附近地区的伯爵们和耶路撒冷国王鲍德温谈判（XIV，pp.440–445）。

⑨ *The Alexiad of Anna Comnena*，p.434.

罗尼库斯之战"、"两约翰之战"和"约翰祖孙之战"，奥斯曼土耳其人、塞尔维亚人、保加利亚人等外国雇佣兵都是作战双方的主要借助力量。在保卫君士坦丁堡的最后战斗中，君士坦丁十一世（Constantine Ⅺ，1449–1453 年在位）能够指挥的军队只有奥斯曼军队的二十分之一，而且主要来自威尼斯和热那亚。从某种程度上说，拜占廷帝国晚期的军事历史已经不再是本国军队的历史，而是雇佣兵的历史。①

二　雇佣军的消极影响

在通常情况下，雇佣军主要为军饷而战，对雇佣他们的帝国不存在乡土观念，缺乏由此产生的保家卫国的情感和高昂的作战士气，背叛和逃跑在战斗中经常发生。这不仅加剧了国家的财政困难，并且为战争的胜败增加了更多的变数，在主要依靠雇佣军作战的帝国晚期，这成为加速国家灭亡的重要原因。

首先，雇佣军为金钱而战，巨额军费负担加重了国家的财政危机

随着军区制的瓦解，小农阶层几乎完全消失，被普洛尼亚土地上的依附农取代，致使国家税源枯竭。在帕列奥列格王朝时期，国家从农业征收的赋税收入逐年减少，在安德罗尼库斯货币改革以后，帝国年收入仅有 100 万金币，相当于盛期年收入的 2.18 %。②大量使用雇佣兵则导致已经捉襟见肘的国家财政更加吃紧，帝国政府被迫采取釜底抽薪的办法，加重税收或者没收大贵族和教会的财产，从而形成恶性循环，社会矛盾进一步激化，政治局面动荡不安。其实从科穆宁王朝开始，筹集军费，支付军饷，便存在持久的困难。根据安娜的记载，由于国库空虚，阿莱科休斯一世在位期间曾被迫先后征用家族成员和教会财产充当军费。③

雇佣兵完全为金钱而战，对他们而言，军事服役几乎完全是一种交易，利益分配经常被明确规定④。1071 年的曼兹克特战役中，拜占廷帝国的军队惨败，担任后卫的雇佣军的混乱无序难逃其责⑤。到了帝国晚期，雇佣兵的危害日益加剧。1204 年当君士坦丁堡处于危急之时，雇佣军因其提高军饷的要求未获满足而拒绝参战。14 世纪横行于希腊半岛的加泰罗尼亚雇佣军兵团给帝国带来极大破坏，这是一支由 6500 名加泰罗尼亚人组成的军队，首领是加泰罗尼亚贵族罗杰·德佛劳尔，13 世纪末至 14 世纪初驻扎在西西里，以被人雇佣作战为业。14 世纪初，拜占廷帝国的小亚细亚诸省受到奥斯曼土耳其人的侵扰，安德罗尼库斯二世（Andronicus Ⅱ，1282–1328 年在位）雇佣这个兵团前去援救，但事后没有如数付清许诺的高额军饷。这群亡命之徒便袭击了马其顿和希腊，在帝国境内的伯罗奔尼撒半岛建立了一个独立国家，在所占地区横征暴敛，发号施令，一直延续到 14 世纪末，才被另一支雇佣军逐走。⑥这并不是外国雇佣军在拜占廷帝国晚期割据称雄的唯一例子。这些目无法纪并且往往与入侵外敌相勾结的外族雇佣军，在城市和农村抢财掳人，进一步打击了拜占廷的工商业者和自耕农。城乡居民为了供应这些军队长期承受着沉重的负担，不得不为造船、筑垒、

---

① 陈志强：《拜占廷帝国史》，第 441 页。

② 陈志强：《独特的拜占廷文明》，第 168 页。

③ *The Alexiad of Anna Comnena*, pp.157–159, pp.185–186.

④ 库曼人和帕臣涅格人因为争夺战利品反目成仇，兵戎相见，从盟友变成敌人（*The Alexiad of Anna Comnena*, Ⅶ, pp.228–229）；在战争开始之前，作为同盟军的库曼人与阿莱科休斯一世达成协议，如果取得胜利，他们将分割一半战利品（*The Alexiad of Anna Comnena*, Ⅷ, p.254）；围攻安条克的十字军首领提前达成协议，一致同意将安条克的总督职位给与第一个成功赢取守卫城墙的蛮族人的将领（*The Alexiad of Anna Comnena*, Ⅺ, p.344）；为了赢得控制安条克附近地区的伯爵们和耶路撒冷国王对远征坦克雷得的支持，阿莱科休斯必须派使者给他们送去大量钱币和礼物作为交换（*The Alexiad of Anna Comnena*, ⅩⅣ, pp.440–444）。

⑤ 《中国大百科全书，军事卷》，中国大百科全书出版社 1989 版，第 35 页。

⑥ （美）汤普逊：《中世纪晚期欧洲经济社会史》，商务印书馆 1992 版，第 499 页。

架桥、修路提供物资和劳力，[1]从而激化了各种矛盾，致使国内的政治局面更加混乱。

其次，雇佣兵的不稳定性和易于哗变加速了帝国的灭亡

有学者将拜占廷帝国衰落的原因归结于其臣民缺乏爱国主义或民族主义，[2]有学者认为拜占廷人的战争都是为了保卫自己独特的希腊——拜占廷文明。[3]这实际上是一种情感上的归属感。对于雇佣军而言，这一点体现得尤其明显。

在军区制下，农兵参加战斗，为的是保护自己的土地，因此作战勇敢，战斗力很强。但雇佣军是为钱而战的军队，对他们而言，出卖自己的力气和性命只不过是维持生存的一种方式，谁给钱就会为谁服役。他们与国家之间是一种经济契约的关系，国家只负责给养和军饷，而不对他们负有明确的政治责任。[4]同样，他们也没有为国家和民族而战的概念，缺乏爱国精神，在作战过程中，如果对方出更高的价钱，极易倒戈相向，没有任何道义上的负担。那么，经济破败衰弱，税源枯竭，雇佣兵的军饷没有着落，就意味着兵源的枯竭。长期缺钱的君主不能牢靠地依赖一支仅仅因为欠薪就随时准备退出战场的军队。[5]马基雅维里认为雇佣军是危险的，如果君主以他们作为确保国家安全的主力，那么他不会安全，因为这些雇佣军队既不敬畏上帝，又毫无纪律，不讲忠义。[6]查士丁尼二世（Justinian Ⅱ，685–695，705–711 年在位）在位期间，曾一度迫使阿拉伯人求和纳贡，但最终因拜占廷军队中雇佣的斯拉夫士兵倒戈而失败。[7]

安娜·科穆宁娜认为塞尔柱突厥人是背信弃义，从不遵守诺言的傲慢种族；[8]凯尔特人对金钱的贪求总使他们不顾及任何理由地打破协议，[9]甚至为了一个奥卜尔（obol）[10]，卖掉自己最亲近和最爱的人。[11]不忠诚的现象在这些雇佣军中司空见惯。在阿莱科休斯一世的军队中服役的法兰克人在战斗中叛逃到尼基弗鲁斯·布林纽斯（Nikephorus Bryennius）那里[12]；守卫君士坦丁堡的纳米兹人（Nemitzi）将首都出卖给叛乱者[13]；好战的摩尼教徒在战败之后遗弃军旗，无视皇帝让他们返回战场的命令，后来加入帕臣涅格人（Pachenegs）进攻帝国；[14]斯基泰人天生倾向于抢劫和叛逃；[15]曾是帝国联盟军的库曼人是伪皇子叛乱的主要倚重力量。[16]鲁塞尔曾是帝国军队中的诺曼人雇佣军首领，1073 年在小亚细亚宣布独立，起兵反叛米哈伊尔七世，率领一支装备精良的庞大军队，几乎掠夺了所有东部省份。[17]帕列奥列格王朝时期的皇族内战，交战双方都主要依靠外国雇佣兵，这种行为无疑于引狼入室，为外敌入侵提供了充足的借口。后来成为拜占廷帝国掘墓人的奥斯曼土耳其人正是趁此侵入欧洲，在巴尔干半岛建立了桥头堡和军事基地。总体而言，今天通过巨额费用得到的雇佣军，

---

① 厉以宁：《论拜占廷帝国的灭亡》，载《北京大学学报》（社科版），2005 年第 5 期，第 142 页。

② Warren Treadgold, *A History of the Byzantine State and Society*, 3vols, Stanford: Stanford University Press, 1997, p.848.

③ 厉以宁：《论拜占廷帝国的灭亡》，第 141 页。

④ 徐进：《19 世纪欧洲强国的军队模式改革与公民军队的建立》，载《史学集刊》，2008 年第 5 期，第 73 页。

⑤ [美] 麦尼尔（著），倪大昕等译：《竞逐富强》，学林出版社 1996 年版，第 142 页。

⑥ [意] 马基雅维里（著），潘又典译：《君主论》，商务印书馆 1997 年版，第 57–58 页。

⑦ 陈志强：《拜占廷帝国史》，第 171 页。

⑧ *The Alexiad of Anna Comnena*, p.236.

⑨ *The Alexiad of Anna Comnena*, p.308.

⑩ 古希腊的小银币或价值 1/6 德拉克马的重量单位。

⑪ *The Alexiad of Anna Comnena*, p.193.

⑫ *The Alexiad of Anna Comnena*, p.43.

⑬ *The Alexiad of Anna Comnena*, p.96.

⑭ *The Alexiad of Anna Comnena*, pp.160–161.

⑮ *The Alexiad of Anna Comnena*, p.42, p.235, p.255, p.486.

⑯ *The Alexiad of Anna Comnena*, pp.296–304.

⑰ *The Alexiad of Anna Comnena*, pp.32–37.

明天可能就会变成敌人。

　　小农和城市工商业者曾是拜占廷帝国赖以生存和强盛的基石，在帝国晚期，他们的破产流失意味着帝国丧失了最可靠的支撑力量，在国内无兵可用、国外四面环敌的情况下，只能几乎全部依靠外族雇佣兵。[①]他们对战争胜负起着决定性的影响，因此也就成为了帝国衰亡的关键因素。但遗憾的是，雇佣兵没有也不可能成为帝国的救世主，相反却在一定程度上加速了帝国的灭亡。在拜占廷帝国灭亡的原因中，如果说军区制的瓦解是根本原因，奥斯曼土耳其人的军事进攻是直接原因，十字军的打击和基督教世界的分裂是外部推动力，那么，作为帝国晚期主要依靠的军事力量的雇佣军就是催化剂，在一定程度上加速了帝国走向灭亡的步伐。

---

① G. Ostrogorsky, *The History of Byzantine State*, Oxford, 1956, p.483.

公元6世纪拜占廷史料中政府的灾后救助

刘榕榕　南开大学

摘要：公元6世纪是拜占廷帝国境内城市及地区瘟疫、地震等灾害的高发期。鉴于灾害对经济、政治等方面造成了重大负面影响，以皇帝为中心的拜占廷政府在灾后对受灾地区进行了包括直接拨款、免税、派遣官员前往赈灾和举行纪念活动等积极的救助。一方面，这些救助措施对于经济的恢复和发展、稳定灾区的社会秩序、维护皇帝权威及抚慰受灾民众等方面均起到了积极的作用。另一方面，根据当时史家的记载，6世纪上半期政府的救助力度明显大于下半期，且在救助的过程中更侧重于对重要城市及教会建筑物的建设工作，这一特点体现了帝国在6世纪下半期经济与财政的困境。

关键词：中央政府；自然灾害；援助

Abstract: Plagues and earthquakes frequently happened in many cities and areas of Byzantine Empire in the 6th Century. In view of disasters bad impact on empire's economic and political aspects, Byzantine government centered on emperor carried on active help including funds allocation, duty free, sent officers to guide relieve people in a disaster areas and held commemoration activities. On the one hand, these help measures had an active impact on relief and development of economy, stabilization of the disaster area's public order, defendant of emperor's authority and consolation the people in the stricken areas. On the other hand, in the light of the historian's record, the relief situation of first part of the 6th Century was much better than the second part of it. The feature of this phenomenon reflected the dilemma of Byzantine Empire's economy and finance in later part of the 6th Century.

Keywords: Central government, natural disasters, Succour

公元6世纪拜占廷帝国正处于鼠疫、地震、水灾等灾害的高发期。541年，"查士丁尼瘟疫"首先出现在拜占廷帝国的埃及地区[①]，并于541–544年迅速蔓延至地中海沿岸和西欧的绝大部分城市

[①] Procopius, *History of the Wars*, translated by Dewing, H.B., Cambridge Mass: Harvard University Press, Loeb Classical Library, 1996, Book2, 22, 6, p.453.

及地区①。在 6 世纪余下的时间里，"查士丁尼瘟疫"曾于 558、573、590、599 年在帝国境内 4 次大规模复发②。除此之外，作为帝国核心区域的巴尔干、小亚细亚及叙利亚地区也在这一时期频繁受到地震、水灾等灾害的影响，其中首都君士坦丁堡曾于 532、543、551、554、557、582 年发生地震③。

鉴于 6 世纪帝国境内频繁爆发的自然灾害及其造成的不利影响，以皇帝为首的君士坦丁堡政府在灾害发生后对受灾地区采取了一系列救助与重建措施以期将灾害的破坏程度降到最低。部分国外史家对自然灾害过后，以皇帝为首的中央政府的灾后救助给予了关注，如唐尼在《古代安条克城》中就提到皇帝对灾难的救助措施④；斯科特则对当时拜占廷史家关于皇帝赈灾的相关记载进行了比较⑤；克里夫·福斯以安条克为例，对帝国的救灾情况进行了详细论述⑥；琼斯也注意到拜占廷皇帝在地震等灾难发生之后的重建工作⑦。但是，目前国内学界尚欠缺对 6 世纪拜占廷政府救灾措施的相关研究，本人希望通过对这一问题进行分析以收引玉之效。

一 直接经济援助

在实行中央集权制的拜占廷帝国内部，大权在握的皇帝及中央政府可以举全国之力对受灾地区进行救助。根据当时史家记载，面对 6 世纪多发的自然灾难，几乎每次灾难过后，拜占廷皇帝都会对受灾地区进行救助，以政府为主导的拨款与赈灾在灾后救助与重建工作中占据主导地位。当时史

① "查士丁尼瘟疫"的传播路线大致为：541 年 7 月，培琉喜阿姆；541 年 9 月，亚历山大里亚；542 年早春，耶路撒冷；542 年春、夏，安条克；542 年春、夏，米拉（Myra）；542 年 3/4 至 8 月，君士坦丁堡；542 年秋，美迪亚（Media）、阿特罗帕特纳（Atropatene）；542 年 12 月，西西里；543 年 1/2 月，突尼西亚（Tunisia）；543—544 年，意大利；543 年，伊利里库姆、罗马、高卢和西班牙。此后，瘟疫很可能于 544 或 545 年蔓延到爱尔兰。（Michael Maas, *The Cambridge Companion to the Age of Justinian*, New York: Cambridge University Press, 2006, pp.136–138.）

② 558 年春，"查士丁尼瘟疫"首次复发，复发的主要地点是君士坦丁堡。阿伽赛阿斯详细记载了这次瘟疫爆发的情况（*Agathias, The Histories*, translated by Joseph D. Frendo, Einband: Luderitz & Bauer, 1975, p.145.）；571—573 年，瘟疫再次袭击意大利、高卢辖区及君士坦丁堡。（马利乌斯记载 571 年一次可怕的瘟疫袭击了意大利和高卢（Marius of Avenches, *Chronica*, edited by T. Mommsen, MGH, AA, Berlin, 1894, 571, p.238.）；关于这次瘟疫的发生情况，格利高里也有相关记载，患者的腹沟处有类似于被毒蛇咬过的脓包（Gregory of Tours, *History of the Francs*, ed. B. Krusch and W. Levison(MGH SS Rerum Merovingarum I. Hannover 1884), Book4, 31.）。叙利亚人迈克尔则指出，573 年的君士坦丁堡每天大概有 3000 人因瘟疫去世（Michael the Syrian, *Chronicle*, edited by J.– B. Chabot, Paris, 1910, Book2, p.309.）；590—592 年，瘟疫在帝国境内第三次复发，在此过程中，罗马城首当其冲。图尔的格利高里记载，590 年 1 月，有"腹股沟出现脓包"症状的瘟疫出现在罗马城内（Gregory of Tours, *History of the Franks*, Book10, 1.）；"查士丁尼瘟疫"于 597 年在塞萨洛尼卡地区第 4 次复发，并在 2 年之后传播到君士坦丁堡（Michael the Syrian, *Chronicle*, Book2, pp.373–374.）。

③ 马拉拉斯记载下 532 年前后君士坦丁堡的地震情况（John Malalas, *The Chronicle of John Malalas*, a translation by E. Jeffreys, M. Jeffreys & R. Scott, Sydney: Sydney University Press, 2006, Book 18, p.282.）；塞奥发尼斯提到很多教堂及房屋都在 543 年君士坦丁堡地震中倒塌（Theophanes, *The Chronicle of Theophanes Confessor: Byzantine and Near Eastern History*, AD284–813, translated by Cyril Mango and Roger Scott, Oxford: Clarendon Press, 1997, p.322.）；阿伽赛阿斯则记载下 551 年君士坦丁堡遭遇强震打击的情况（Agathias, *The Histories*, p.47.）；《复活节编年史》记载了 554 年的地震令君士坦丁堡城墙倒塌（Michael Whitby and Mary Whitby translated, *Chronicon Paschale, 284–628AD*, Liverpool: Liverpool University Press, 1989, p.196.）；阿伽赛阿斯对 557 年强震对君士坦丁堡的情况进行了详实的记载（Agathias, *The Histories*, p.137.）。

④ Glanville Downey, *Ancient Antioch*, New Jersey: Princeton University Press, 1963, p.247.

⑤ Roger D. Scott, "Malalas, The Secret History and Justinian's Propaganda", *Dumbarton Oaks Papers*, V. 39, 1985, p.101.

⑥ Clive Foss, "Syria in Transition, A.D.550–750: An Archaeological Approach", *Dumbarton Oaks Papers*, V.51, 1997, p.202.

⑦ Jones, A. H. M., *The later Roman Empire 284—602: a Social, Economic, and Administrative Survey*, Oxford: Basil Blackwell, 1964, p.288.

家关于皇帝及政府赈灾的记载中，既有直接进行拨款以解灾区的燃眉之急，也有皇帝多次提供大笔款项以用于逐渐恢复灾区正常生活的记录。同时，在地震、水灾及海啸等灾害发生后，受灾地区的建筑物必定会遭到重创。作为民众的栖息及活动场所，及时修复建筑物是一项十分必要且紧急的工作，帝国政府对城市建筑物的具体修复工作给予了关注。马斯提到，自然灾难令城市中建筑物需要不断进行重建或修整。[1]因此，拜占廷中央政府的经济援助主要由直接拨款及修复受损建筑物构成。

从史家记录可以看出，中央政府在帝国境内自然灾害发生之后所实行的直接经济援助具有时间的差异性、地域的选择性及对教会和民用建筑物修复侧重点不同等特点。

首先，根据史家的记载，6世纪前期拜占廷皇帝对于受灾地区的拨款较之6世纪后期为多。6世纪初，位于美索不达米亚北部的埃德萨发生瘟疫并造成饥荒之后，尽管路途遥远，但阿纳斯塔修斯一世仍坚持运送金钱与粮食以进行灾后援助，并选择最近的港口来运送物资。[2]在6世纪20年代地震、水灾的高发期中，查士丁一世和查士丁尼一世给予灾区大量经济援助。在查士丁一世即位后不久，新伊皮鲁斯省（Nova Epirus）的迪拉休姆城（Dyrrachium）在520年发生地震。震后，查士丁一世为迪拉休姆的重建提供了大量的资金援助。[3]520年安条克大火，查士丁一世同样给灾区拨出大笔资金。[4]随后不久，埃德萨于521年发生水灾，查士丁一世随即对埃德萨拨款救济，同时为城市重新修建了很多华美的建筑和工事，并极力安抚幸存者，将其重新命名为"查士丁奥波利斯"[5]。524年的阿纳扎尔博斯地震之后，也有查士丁一世对其进行重建的记录[6]。在526年安条克发生地震之后，查士丁一世立即让卡里努斯（Carinus）携带款项前去赈灾，且在直接拨款赈灾后又拨出一大笔资金用于城市重建。[7]尼基乌主教约翰宣称，在安条克525年火灾及526年地震之后，查士丁一世拨出前所未见的巨额款项用于重建工作。[8]

查士丁尼一世在位前期，在拨款救灾上继承前人做法。塞奥发尼斯提到，在528年的安条克地震之后，刚刚继承皇位的查士丁尼一世同样为重建工作拨出资金。[9]528年，位于叙利亚北部的劳迪西亚在地震中损失惨重，查士丁尼一世和塞奥多拉对灾区给予了慷慨地救助。同年，小亚细亚城市庞培奥波利斯（Pompeioupolis）发生地震，查士丁尼一世下拨大笔款项赈灾，并着力重建城市。[10]529年米拉发生大地震后，皇帝同样拨出重金进行重建。[11]526与528年发生地震的阿帕米亚，也是在政府资金的支持下完成了重建工作。[12]

除了直接对灾区进行拨款及进行城市建筑物的修复工作外，据马拉拉斯记载，528年劳迪西亚地震后，查士丁尼一世还额外给予当地居民免税3年的特权[13]。同样的做法也出现在528年安条克地震发生之后。[14]这种拨款与免税相结合的救助措施可以减轻受灾民众负担，有助于灾区安定与恢复。

---

① Michael Maas, *The Cambridge Companion to the Age of Justinian*, p.71.

② G. W. Bowersock, Peter Brown, Oleg Gravar, *Late Antiquity: A Guide to The Postclassical World*, p.447.

③ John Malalas, *The Chronicle of John Malalas*, Book17, pp.236–237.

④ John Malalas, *The Chronicle of John Malalas*, Book17, p.236.

⑤ John Malalas, *The Chronicle of John Malalas*, Book17, p.237.

⑥ Theophanes, *The Chronicle of Theophanes Confessor: Byzantine and Near Eastern history, AD284–813*, p.262. 埃瓦格里乌斯也记载下皇帝以巨额资金重建受到地震打击的阿纳扎尔博斯（Evagrius Scholasticus, *A History of the Church in Six Books, from A.D.431 to A.D.594*, Book4, Chapter8.）。

⑦ Theophanes, *The Chronicle of Theophanes Confessor: Byzantine and Near Eastern History, AD284–813*, p.264.

⑧ John of Nikiu, *Chronicle*, Chapter90, 34.

⑨ Theophanes, *The Chronicle of Theophanes Confessor: Byzantine and Near Eastern History, AD284–813*, p.270.

⑩ John Malalas, *The Chronicle of John Malalas*, Book18, p.253. *Chronicon Paschale*, 284–628AD, p.195.

⑪ John Malalas, *The Chronicle of John Malalas*, Book18, p.262.

⑫ J.H.W.G Liebeschuetz, *Decline and Fall of the Roman City*, p.56.

⑬ John Malalas, *The Chronicle of John Malalas*, Book18, p.258.

⑭ John Malalas, *The Chronicle of John Malalas*, Book18, p.258.

从整个帝国的情况来看，很可能受到帝国财政状况的影响，6世纪上半期的赈灾情况明显好于6世纪后半期。在6世纪后半期的自然灾害发生后，当时史家似乎更侧重于刻画灾害的情况及程度等内容，而较少提及皇帝对受灾地的救助。像免税这类赈灾方式也只有在查士丁尼一世的早期阶段出现过，这种现象的出现很可能是因为帝国境内受到地震和瘟疫等自然灾害的侵袭过于频繁、帝国的财政状况每况愈下使然。不仅如此，中央政府的直接拨款的力度也逐渐减小。6世纪后半期灾害发生之后，史家的记载中仅提到了几个灾后救助的事例。551年，发生了影响帝国东部众多城市的大地震，查士丁尼一世下令拨款赈灾[1]。557年君士坦丁堡发生强震之后，查士丁尼一世将节约下来的钱财分给穷人。[2]588年安条克地震之后，埃瓦格里乌斯仅仅数语提到皇帝赈灾的情况。[3]马拉拉斯对君士坦丁堡在记载562年发生的旱灾及次年用水短缺和大火等灾害时，并未提到皇帝的救助。[4]未对救灾情况进行记载的原因除了史家没有对此给予关注外，很可能是由救助力度过小所引起的。

其次，除6世纪早期赈灾拨款力度明显强于后期这一特点外，相较于小城市与乡村地区而言，在财政状况逐渐恶化的6世纪后半期，帝国政府在救助中更为关注君士坦丁堡、安条克这类重要城市，首都君士坦丁堡更是最优先的救助对象。

从当时史家的记载可以看出，在这一时期，帝国境内自然灾害的影响范围较广。[5]其中，君士坦丁堡在查士丁尼一世时期就曾发生5次大地震[6]；帝国东部的小亚细亚和叙利亚地区也频发地震。在当时史家的记载当中很少提到查士丁尼一世在位后期对其他地震发生城市的经济救助[7]。作为帝国的首都，遭遇自然灾害的君士坦丁堡能够得到以皇帝为首的帝国政府的倾力援助，这是它能够从灾害中恢复并发展的重要原因。如在6世纪中，帝国东部受灾频率较低的埃及地区便在从查士丁一世直到伊拉克略一统治期间，向其输送了大量黄金以保证君士坦丁堡的恢复与发展。[8]里贝舒尔茨曾详述6世纪拜占廷帝国境内城市的衰落，他认为君士坦丁堡的恢复与发展是建立在小亚细亚其他城市牺牲的基础之上的。[9]

二 稳定灾区的社会秩序

首先，安抚受灾民众。除了直接拨款及免税外，在灾害发生之后，皇帝经常会派遣官员代表自己前往灾区指导救灾工作。通过这种方式不仅可以对受灾地区进行更加合理的救助和安抚，同时也可稳定灾区的社会秩序并增强皇帝在民众中的威信。根据马拉拉斯的记载，526年安条克地震发生

---

[1] Theophanes, *The Chronicle of Theophanes Confessor: Byzantine and Near Eastern History, AD284–813*, p.330.

[2] Theophanes, *The Chronicle of Theophanes Confessor: Byzantine and Near Eastern History, AD284–813*, p.339.

[3] Evagrius Scholasticus, *A History of the Church in Six Books, from A.D.431 to A.D.594*, Book6, Chapter8.

[4] John Malalas, *The Chronicle of John Malalas*, Book18, P.301; p.305.

[5] 如公元526、528年安条克发生地震之后，相距不远的劳迪西亚在528年、亚马尼亚和米拉于529年发生地震（Procopius, *History of the Wars*, Book2, 14, 6, p.383; John Malalas, *The Chronicle of John Malalas, Book18*, p.258; p.262.）。551年地震，影响遍及巴勒斯坦、美索不达米亚和叙利亚（Procopius, History of the wars, Book5, 8, 25, 16–18; Evagrius Scholasticus, *A History of the Church in Six Books, from A.D.431 to A.D.594*, Book4, Chapter34; John Malalas, *The Chronicle of John Malalas*, Book18, p.291; Theophanes, *The Chronicle of Theophanes Confessor: Byzantine and Near Eastern History, AD284–813*, p.332.）。

[6] 君士坦丁堡于公元532、542、550、554、557年发生地震。

[7] 从6世纪30年代后期开始，地震发生之后，很少提到皇帝对灾区的救助（Theophanes, *The Chronicle of Theophanes Confessor: Byzantine and Near Eastern History, AD284–813*, p.345.）。

[8] Thomas M. Jones, "East African Influences upon the Early Byzantine Empire", *The Journal of Negro History*, V.43, N.1, 1958, p.52.

[9] J.H.W.G Liebeschuetz, *Decline and Fall of the Roman City*, New York: Oxford University Press, 2001, p.409.

之后，查士丁一世命卡里努斯（Carinus）、福卡斯（Phokas）、阿斯特瑞奥斯（Asterios）前往安条克负责重建工作①。其中一部分官员负责废墟的清理工作，另一部分官员则肩负照顾幸存者并对安条克进行重建的责任；安条克在地震中受损的桥梁、浴池及排水系统很快得到了重建。②

其次，稳定居民情绪。为了防止自然灾害发生之后可能出现的混乱局面，皇帝还通过颁布政令的方式以稳定国内的秩序。在君士坦丁堡于532–533年发生地震之后，很可能因为惧怕异端教派趁机作乱，查士丁尼一世向所有城市颁布法令：确定正统的信仰并反对异端学说。③考虑到自然灾害发生之后，幸存者往往因失去亲朋而遭受到了巨大的心理创伤，包括查士丁尼一世在内的拜占廷皇帝经常会举行一些纪念活动来抚慰这些幸存者，并希望以此增强民众对帝国的信心。塞奥发尼斯声称，533年君士坦丁堡地震后，每年都要在固定地点举行纪念活动④。551年阿非利加省发生地震，受灾地民众于次年举行纪念活动。⑤557年君士坦丁堡地震后，每年都举行礼拜仪式以纪念遇难者。⑥而在君士坦丁堡于611年4月20日发生地震之后，同月22号进行公共祈福活动。⑦免税、颁布政令、搭建救灾帐篷及举行纪念活动等救灾方式对于稳定幸存民众的情绪起到了一定的作用。

最后，任命专人负责救灾工作以确保灾区社会秩序的稳定。鼠疫发生后不久，查士丁尼一世立即选派宫廷中的士兵，同时筹集并分配钱物，让塞奥多鲁斯（Theodorus）全权负责处理这次危机。⑧在得到查士丁尼一世的命令后，塞奥多鲁斯临危受命，迅速开始着手救灾工作，其主要措施之一便是对无人照料的尸体进行紧急处理。普罗柯比曾提到很多人将亲人的尸体随意丢弃的现象令君士坦丁堡城内各处出现了混乱和无序。⑨于是，通过掩埋尸体来恢复君士坦丁堡的社会秩序是十分必要的。在用尽皇帝的拨款之后，塞奥多鲁斯自掏腰包坚持将无人料理的尸体全体下葬。⑩因尸体过多，业已存在的坟墓全都被尸体填满，塞奥多鲁斯便命人在城内的各处挖洞来掩埋尸体⑪。塞奥多鲁斯作为帝国信息的上传下达者，经常向皇帝上报灾情及民众的请愿，并将皇帝的意旨下传给他们。塞奥多鲁斯控制灾情的举措对稳定君士坦丁堡鼠疫发生之后的社会秩序起到了一定的作用。

综上所述，拜占廷中央政府在灾难发生之后往往采取直接经济援助、派遣官员前往救灾和举行悼念活动等救助方式。拨款与免税相结合的直接经济救助不仅能够对受灾民众进行更好的安置工作，且使灾区在无税收负担的压力下能够更加快速且有效地得到恢复。由以上的赈灾记录可知，6世纪上半期的赈灾措施的力度明显强于6世纪下半期。

事实上，这种现象的出现与6世纪帝国的经济及财政的发展形势不无关系。在历经地震、鼠疫的洗礼和对外战争的失利之后，拜占廷帝国在6世纪中后期的经济状况已经十分困难，以致在查士丁尼一世统治后期出现了政府克扣前方军队军费的行为。⑫根据史家的记载，拜占廷帝国的财政收入在经受鼠疫和地震的轮番打击之后大幅下降。⑬特里戈尔德估计，541年帝国的财政收入与上年相比

---

① John Malalas, *The Chronicle of John Malalas*, Book17, p.242.
② Glanville Downey, *Ancient Antioch*, New Jersey: Princeton University Press, 1963, p.244.
③ John Malalas, *The Chronicle of John Malalas*, Book18, p.282.
④ Theophanes, *The Chronicle of Theophanes confessor: Byzantine and Near Eastern history, AD284–813*, P.332.
⑤ John of Nikiu, *Chronicle*, Chapter90, 82.
⑥ Michael Maas, *The Cambridge Companion to the Age of Justinian*, p.71.
⑦ Timothy Venning, *A Chronology of the Byzantine Empire*, p.148.
⑧ Procopius, *History of the Wars*, Book2, 23, 6, p.467.
⑨ Procopius, *History of the Wars*, Book2, 23, 3, p.465.
⑩ Procopius, *History of the Wars*, Book2, 23, 8, p.467.
⑪ Procopius, *History of the Wars*, Book2, 23, 9–10, pp.467–469.
⑫ Warren Treadgold, *A History of the Byzantine State and Society*, California: Stanford University Press, 1997, p.218.
⑬ Michael Maas, *The Cambridge Companion to the Age of Justinian*, pp.155–156.

可能下降了 20%。①同时，他提到不将地震、水灾等考虑在内，帝国单在瘟疫中的死亡人数和由此引发的经济和行政崩溃就缩减了至少 1/4 的财政收入，之后瘟疫的频繁复发使这种危机程度进一步加深。②曼戈也认为士兵和纳税人由于受到鼠疫周期性爆发的影响而大量死亡，拜占廷帝国的人员和财富都大幅度减少。③对此，埃文斯提到，从 6 世纪下半期起，帝国对教师和医生的工资进行缩减，并减少了很多公共娱乐活动的预算。④查士丁尼时代后期的经济发展没有延续早期的良好发展状况，逐渐出现了衰败的迹象。⑤与这种恶化的经济状况相对应，从 6 世纪中期开始，当时史家的著作中就几乎没有出现皇帝对灾区实行免税政策的记载。

即便如此，在实行中央集权制的拜占廷社会，皇帝和政府在灾后所采取的积极救助措施不仅对于恢复受灾地区的经济、社会面貌及民众的日常生活起到了至关重要的作用，同时也使帝国在危机之下能够较快地恢复并保存实力。救民于水火的拨款不仅可以用于安葬死者和安置灾民，也可以用来作为后续资金对受灾地进行修复，以此来促进经济的复苏与发展；派遣官吏前往灾区指导救援工作可令灾区的社会秩序得到较快恢复，并能增加皇帝在民众中的声望；而灾后在受灾地区进行的纪念活动则可起到平复灾民受伤心灵的作用。总体看来，拜占廷帝国的皇帝及中央政府所采取的救助措施仍然起到了一定的效果。

---

①　Warren Treadgold, *A History of the Byzantine State and Society*, p.276.
②　Warren Treadgold, *A History of the Byzantine State and Society*, p.216.
③　Cyril Mango, *The Oxford History of Byzantium*, New York: Oxford University Press, 2002, p.49.
④　J. A. S. Evans, *The Age of Justinian: the Circumstances of Imperial Power*, p.164.
⑤　John W. Barker, *Justinian and the later Roman Empire*, Wisconsin: The University of Wisconsin Press, 1966, p.192.

12 世纪拜占廷皇帝对西方的迎合及其后果

罗春梅　中南大学

摘要：第一次十字军东征导致阿莱克修斯一世和拜占廷帝国的形象被拉丁人丑化，为了应对西方的种种负面宣传，拜占廷皇帝们逐渐调整政策，迎合西方，他们极力表现自己分享十字军的理想，援助十字军国家，甚至承认教皇首位等。基本上，皇帝们对西方的迎合取得了一定的成功，但拜占廷为此付出了沉重的代价，12 世纪末拜占廷未能也无力迎合西方，这成为西方入侵的借口。

关键词：拜占廷；西方；十字军东征

Abstract: The First Crusade caused the images of Alexius I and Byzantium to be smeared by the Latins. To answer the negative publicity in the west, the Byzantine emperors adjusted their policies gradually and tried to curry favor with the Latins, for example, they tried their best to present themselves as sharing the ideals of the crusaders, gave aid to the Crusader states, and even accepted Rome's primacy, and so on. By so doing, they achieved some success but made Byzantium suffer a lot. In the end of the 12th century the Byzantine emperors didn't and weren't able to curry favor with the Latins, which became the excuse of the invasion of Byzantium by the Latins.

Keywords: the Byzantine Empire, Latin Europe, the Crusades

从 11 世纪起，西方开始对外扩张，主要表现为领土扩张、天主教扩大势力范围、以及意大利海上力量和商业贸易的扩张，其中一个重要方面是对拜占廷帝国的侵略扩张，主要包括诺曼人的侵略、十字军东征、意大利各城市共和国的扩张、匈牙利的侵略、德意志的扩张以及罗马教皇企图征服东正教、统治整个基督教世界。

西方的扩张对拜占廷产生了很多影响，其中之一是，第一次十字军东征导致阿莱克修斯一世（Alexius I Comnenus，1081 — 1118 年在位）和拜占廷的形象被拉丁人丑化。在这次十字军东征期间，拜占廷皇帝直接与十字军首领们打交道，由于利益、立场、目标、思想观念、处事方式等等都不同，双方的隔阂、冲突不可避免；特别是阿莱克修斯阻碍了十字军首领们的扩张野心，引起了首领们的不满。这种隔阂、冲突特别是不满被野心家波希蒙德（Bohemond）利用并加以宣传，于是阿莱克修斯的形象甚至拜占廷的形象逐渐被西方丑化。①结果，在十字军占领耶路撒冷 10 年内，西方普遍认为拜占廷背叛了基督教事业。②西方进行反拜占廷宣传：拜占廷分裂教会，阻碍十字军东征，未能援助十字军国家，等等。为了应对西方的种种负面宣传，拜占廷统治者们逐渐调整政策，迎合西方。本文旨在分析 12 世纪拜占廷皇帝们迎合西方的种种举动及其后果，以深化对 1204 年君士坦丁堡陷落原因的探讨。

一 12 世纪拜占廷皇帝对西方的迎合

为了应对波希蒙德的负面宣传，阿莱克修斯收买十字军的人心，期望他们能为自己说好话。据安娜（Anna Comnena，1083 — 1154 年，阿莱克修斯一世的长女）记载，在拉姆莱（Ramleh）一役十字军战败之后，阿莱克修斯一世派人带大量金钱去赎买十字军伯爵们，盛情款待他们，给他们大量金钱，送他们回到西方。③1105 年，波希蒙德溜回西方大力进行反拜占廷宣传。恰在这时，埃及俘虏了 300 个十字军伯爵。阿莱克修斯于是全力援救他们，派人带钱去赎买他们，款待他们，送金钱、衣服给他们，让他们康复身体。安娜说，这些人原来是拜占廷的敌人，积极反对拜占廷，违背曾对阿莱克修斯所发的誓言，这时认识到阿莱克修斯对他们极其宽容。阿莱克修斯送给他们大量礼物，送他们回家，一方面是他们自己想回家，另一方面是阿莱克修斯想让他们驳斥波希蒙德的诽谤。这些伯爵们于是出发离开君士坦丁堡，提供了不可辩驳的反波希蒙德的证据。他们指责波希蒙德是骗子，以自己为证据谴责他，在许多场合当面证明他有罪。④但这似乎只是安娜的自我欺骗，因为当时波希蒙德在西方的威望很高，他的宣传取得了极大成功，不仅娶法王的女儿为妻，而且获得教皇的支持，征募到一支规模庞大的军队。

后来的拜占廷统治者约翰二世（John II Comnenus，1118 — 1143 年在位）和曼努埃尔一世（Manuel I Comnenus，1143 — 1180 年在位）则迎合西方，竭力树立良好形象，改变西方的看法。

约翰二世继位后继续坚持对安条克（Antioch）的宗主权，⑤但由于安条克的拉丁人反对拜占廷的直接统治，约翰据说曾打算把西利西亚和安条克连同塞浦路斯岛和阿塔利亚（Attaleia）作为亲王封地授予他最小的儿子曼努埃尔。⑥约翰二世还极力表现自己分享十字军的理想。在死前几个月里，他写信给耶路撒冷国王，提出他去圣地援助国王驱逐异教徒并拜访圣地。为表明他希望朝圣的诚挚，他下令制作一盏巨大的黄金灯，准备送给圣墓教堂；他甚至可能声称对圣墓有监护权。⑦在临终前，据 12 世纪末拜占廷宫廷高官、著名史学家尼基塔斯·侯尼雅迪斯（Nicetas Choniates，1155 — 1217 年）

① 关于阿莱克修斯的形象被拉丁人丑化的原因，详见拙作《西方丑化阿莱克修斯一世形象原因探析》（载《西南大学学报》2009 年第 4 期）。本文所说的"西方"指的是信奉罗马天主教的欧洲国家和势力，"拉丁人"指的是信奉天主教的西方人，"希腊人"指的是拜占廷人。

② Steven Runciman, "Byzantium and the Crusades", *The Meeting of Two Worlds: Cultural Exchange Between East and West During the Period of the Crusades*, edited by Vladimir P. Goss, Kalamazoo, Mich.: Medieval Institute Publications, Western Michigan University, 1986, p.20.

③ Anna Comnena, *The Alexiad of Anna Comnena*, trans. by E. R. A. Sewter, Harmondsworth: Penguin Books, 1969, p.353.

④ Anna Comnena, *The Alexiad of Anna Comnena*, trans. by E. R. A. Sewter, Harmondsworth: Penguin Books, 1969, pp.369–371.

⑤ 安条克原属拜占廷领土，是拜占廷恢复对西利西亚地区（Cilicia，通往叙利亚的门户）统治的关键，1094 年被土耳其人占领，1098 年波希蒙德利用十字军为自己占领了这一战略重镇，创建了安条克公国。由于安条克地位很重要，拜占廷一直想要夺回。1105 年波希蒙德返回西方，大肆进行反拜占廷宣传，并于 1107–1108 年发动对拜占廷的侵略，但被阿莱克修斯一世打败，波希蒙德不得不求和，与拜占廷签订德沃尔（Devol）条约，承认拜占廷对安条克的宗主权。

⑥ Michael Angold, *The Byzantine Empire 1025–1204*, London; New York: Longman, 1984, p.158.

⑦ Michael Angold, *The Byzantine Empire 1025–1204*, London; New York: Longman, 1984, pp.158–159.

记载，约翰发表了一番讲话，谈到自己希望拜访圣地。[1]

曼努埃尔一世对西方的迎合极其明显。首先，他认同一些西方习俗，例如马上比武、崇尚单打独斗等。据尼基塔斯·侯尼雅迪斯记载，1151 年曼努埃尔攻打塞尔维亚人，其间曼努埃尔与塞尔维亚人援军匈牙利军队的指挥官进行决斗，取得胜利。1159 年曼努埃尔作为宗主在安条克（Antioch）举行入城仪式后，在安条克逗留期间，曼努埃尔曾举行马上比武大会，拜占廷人打败拉丁人，曼努埃尔表现突出，赢得拉丁人的崇拜，威望大大提高。[2]

其次，在十字军国家问题上，曼努埃尔成为安条克公国的宗主，与耶路撒冷王国联姻，与十字军国家关系日益紧密，并开始承担十字军国家保护者的角色，极力表明自己在推进十字军东征事业。他曾努力争取为安条克摄政康斯坦丝（Constance）寻找合适丈夫，但没有成功。1160 年他的第一位妻子去世后，他向十字军国家寻求新娘。1159 年，曼努埃尔准备攻打努尔·丁（Nūr al-Dīn Mahmūd），迫使后者释放大量拉丁人俘虏。[3] 1164 年，努尔·丁俘虏安条克统治者波希蒙德三世（Bohemond III，1163—1201 年在位）和许多拉丁人大贵族，企图征服安条克，曼努埃尔马上派大军去西利西亚，保住了安条克，还赎回了波希蒙德三世。为了把十字军国家与拜占廷帝国更加紧密地联系起来，曼努埃尔接受耶路撒冷国王阿马尔里克（Amalric，1162—1174 年在位）关于联合进攻埃及的提议，于 1169 年派出庞大舰队前去攻打埃及。[4] 1171 年阿马尔里克再次提议结盟攻打埃及，并承认拜占廷一定程度的宗主权，曼努埃尔派出 150 艘船组成的舰队于 1177 年到达阿克。[5]

再次，曼努埃尔极力表明自己分享十字军理想。1175 年他写信给教皇说他恢复了多里莱乌姆城（Dorylaion，该城是控制横过安纳托利亚高原的路线的关键），声称到圣地的路线对拉丁人和希腊人都安全了；并向教皇求助，决定对异教徒土耳其人发动战争。[6] 1176 年他率领大军攻打土耳其人，但在迈里欧科菲垅（Myriokephalon）遭到惨败。此外，曼努埃尔除了坚持拜占廷皇帝是正教教会在圣地的保护人这一传统角色之外，还帮助修建、装饰圣地的圣墓教堂，负责装饰伯利恒（Bethlehem）的耶稣诞生（Nativity）教堂等。

最后，曼努埃尔不断与教皇协商教会统一问题，1167 年曼努埃尔甚至作出让步，承认教皇首位，以换取教皇对他作为"罗马人皇帝"的承认。

二　皇帝们迎合西方的后果

基本上，拜占廷统治者们对西方的迎合取得了一定的成功，约翰二世和曼努埃尔一世因此在西方享有很好的名声。例如，尼基塔斯·侯尼雅迪斯说，"甚至到我们的时代，他（指约翰二世）仍

---

[1]　Nicetas Choniates, *O City of Byzantium, Annals of Nicetas Choniates*, trans. by H. Magoulias, Michigan: Detroit, 1984, p.24.

[2]　Nicetas Choniates, *O City of Byzantium, Annals of Nicetas Choniates*, trans. by H. Magoulias, Michigan: Detroit, 1984, pp.54, 62.

[3]　据约翰·金纳莫斯（John Cinnamus，约 1143–1203 年）记载，努尔·丁释放了图卢兹的贝尔特朗（Bertram of Toulouse）、圣殿骑士团首领贝特朗（Betrand of Blancfort）等许多贵族出身人士，他还释放了第二次十字军东征期间俘虏的普通十字军战士（多达 6000 人）。John Kinnamos, *Deeds of John and Manuel Comnenus*, trans. by Charles M. Brand, New York: Columbia University Press, 1976, p.143.

[4]　尼基塔斯·侯尼雅迪斯说共有 276 艘船，提尔的威廉（William of Tyre）说有 200 来艘船。Nicetas Choniates, *O City of Byzantium, Annals of Nicetas Choniates*, trans. by H. Magoulias, Michigan: Detroit, 1984, p.91. Michael Angold, *The Byzantine Empire 1025–1204*, London; New York: Longman, 1984, p.188.

[5]　John Kinnamos, *Deeds of John and Manuel Comnenus*, trans. by Charles M. Brand, New York: Columbia University Press, 1976, p.224.

[6]　Michael Angold, *The Byzantine Empire 1025–1204*, London; New York: Longman, 1984, p.189.

被所有人认为值得赞美。"①曼努埃尔在意大利和达尔马提亚深受怀念，人们认为他是很好的基督教皇帝，是强有力的将军，是慷慨赏赐的皇帝。②英诺森三世（Innocent III，1198 — 1216 年在位）在给阿莱克修斯三世（Alexius III Angelos，1195 — 1203 年在位）的信中，深情回忆曼努埃尔对罗马教会的忠诚。③甚至到了第四次十字军东征，一个普通的十字军士兵克拉里（Robert of Clari）也听说曼努埃尔声望甚高，认为他是一个非常值得敬重的人，是最富有、最慷慨的基督教徒，认为他非常热爱、信任法国人。④

但是，拜占廷付出了沉重的代价。1169 年、1177 年曼努埃尔先后派出庞大舰队攻打埃及，两次都因十字军国家的拉丁人不合作而失败，极大地削弱了拜占廷海军力量，特别是 1169 年远征。据尼基塔斯·侯尼雅迪斯记载，这次远征拜占廷损失惨重，276 艘船中许多毁于风暴，剩下不多的船回到拜占廷也遭到抛弃、忽视。约翰·金纳莫斯也记载了这次远征撤退途中遭遇风暴，丧失了许多船。⑤1176 年曼努埃尔率军攻打土耳其人，以证明自己努力推进十字军事业，但在迈里欧科菲垅遭到惨败。关于这一战败事件的影响，当时的拜占廷圣人利奥菲托斯（Neophytos the Recluse，1134 —约 1215 年）和塞萨洛尼基大主教埃夫斯塔西奥斯（Eustathios of Thessalonica）尽管歌颂曼努埃尔，但也承认这一战役是失败，造成了重大伤亡；⑥十字军史学家提尔的威廉认为，这一失败使得曼努埃尔不再有"思想的安宁和精神的稳定"。⑦一些历史学家由此认为这一失败同 1071 年曼兹克特（Mantzikert）失败一样，为帝国政治社会结构的瓦解开辟了道路。⑧朗西曼认为，曼努埃尔使帝国军队在迈里欧科菲垅战役中被土耳其人摧毁，后来拜占廷再也不能帮助叙利亚和巴勒斯坦的基督教徒，与拜占廷结盟不再有任何价值。⑨一些学者对这次战败的灾难性提出了质疑。例如，安戈尔德认为，除了一块真十字架圣物，曼努埃尔似乎所失甚少。保罗·斯蒂芬森认为，这一失败并不表明拜占廷东方前线的崩溃，也没有宣告曼努埃尔野心勃勃的外交政策的结束。马格达利诺也指出，它并非通常所认为的那么严重的一场灾难。约翰·哈尔登（John Haldon）认为，这一失败并非大灾难，但曼努埃尔丧失了围攻机械和辎重队，一度陷入绝望，再也不能召集这么昂贵庞大的远征军；然而，甚至在这一战败之后，帝国军队仍然完整无损，一年之后，仍然能够大败入侵的塞尔柱人军队，并

① Nicetas Choniates, *O City of Byzantium, Annals of Nicetas Choniates*, trans. by H. Magoulias, Michigan: Detroit, 1984, p.27.

② Paul Stephenson, *Byzantium's Balkan Frontier: a political study of the Northern Balkans, 900–1204*, Cambridge, U.K.; New York: Cambridge University Press, 2000, p.273.

③ An Anonymous Author, *The Deeds of Pope Innocent III*, translated with an introduction and notes by James M. Powell, Washington, D.C.: The Catholic University of America Press, 2004, p.93.

④ Robert of Clari, *The Conquest of Constantinople*, translated from the old French by Edgar Holmes McNeal, New York: Columbia University Press, 1936, pp.46–48.

⑤ Nicetas Choniates, *O City of Byzantium, Annals of Nicetas Choniates*, trans. by H. Magoulias, Michigan: Detroit, 1984, p.96. John Kinnamos, *Deeds of John and Manuel Comnenus*, trans. by Charles M. Brand, New York: Columbia University Press, 1976, p.209.

⑥ Paul Magdalino, *The Empire of Manuel I Komnenos, 1143–1180*, Cambridge [England]; New York: Cambridge University Press, 1993, p.458.

⑦ William of Tyre, *A History of Deeds Done Beyond the Sea*, translated by E. A. Babcock and A. C. Krey, New York: Columbia University Press, 1943, p.415. 参见 Michael Angold, *The Byzantine Empire 1025–1204*, London; New York: Longman, 1984, pp.192–193.

⑧ 参见 Michael Angold, *The Byzantine Empire 1025–1204*, London; New York: Longman, 1984, p.193.

⑨ Steven Runciman, "Byzantium and the Crusades", *The Meeting of Two Worlds: cultural exchange between east and west during the period of the Crusades*, edited by Vladimir P. Goss, Kalamazoo, Mich.: Medieval Institute Publications, Western Michigan University, 1986, p.22.

保持帝国在巴尔干地区的地位。[1] 约翰·伯肯迈耶则认为，尽管它事实上并非一些人所认为的军事灾难，但它摧毁了脆弱的外交结构，而这是曼努埃尔一世统治期间的主要成就。[2] 可见，人们一般认为这一失败给拜占廷造成了不良影响，只是对于影响程度的认识不一而已。

更严重的是，12 世纪末拜占廷未能也无力迎合西方，这成为西方侵略的借口。安德罗尼库斯一世（Andronicus I Comnenus，1183 — 1185 年在位）上台后，拜占廷开始试图脱离拉丁西方。1182 年安德罗尼库斯发动君士坦丁堡民众屠杀城中的拉丁人。但他很快发现他需要西方特别是威尼斯的援助，1183 年他开始对威尼斯表示友好。但面对 1185 年诺曼人西西里的入侵，威尼斯拒绝提供海军援助；他与萨拉丁（Saladin）结盟，而萨拉丁不能提供他所需要的援助。[3] 依沙克二世（Isaac II Angelos，1185 — 1195 年在位）巩固与萨拉丁的同盟关系，阻碍第三次十字军的通行，但在德皇腓特烈（Frederick I Barbarossa，1152 — 1190 年在位）攻打君士坦丁堡的威胁之下，依沙克不能指望得到萨拉丁的援助。依沙克恢复与威尼斯的关系，但他垮台后，阿莱克修斯三世与威尼斯关系恶化。[4] 但是，到这时拜占廷已经无法退出拉丁西方，西方要求拜占廷皇帝们以曼努埃尔一世为榜样，援助十字军东征，推动教会统一。例如，德皇亨利六世（Henry VI，1191 — 1197 年在位）向依沙克二世和阿莱克修斯三世勒索，借口他将要进行十字军东征，要求拜占廷为他提供金钱和船只。教皇英诺森三世则在给阿莱克修斯三世的信中，要求他以曼努埃尔一世为榜样，致力于援助圣地，推进教会统一。[5] 阿莱克修斯做不到，这最终成为西方侵略拜占廷的借口。在关于第四次十字军东征的拉丁人原始资料中，用来辩护十字军东征转向并攻打君士坦丁堡的理由基本上是拜占廷人不服从罗马教会、阻碍十字军东征、十字军为获得供给等。[6]

三 余论

11 世纪以后，拜占廷帝国陷入西方扩张势力的包围之中，处境艰难。而皇帝们未能认清西方的

[1] Michael Angold, *The Byzantine Empire 1025-1204*, London; New York: Longman, 1984, pp.193-194. Paul Stephenson, *Byzantium's Balkan Frontier: a political study of the Northern Balkans, 900-1204*, Cambridge, U.K.; New York: Cambridge University Press, 2000, p.269. Paul Magdalino, *The Empire of Manuel I Komnenos, 1143-1180*, Cambridge [England]; New York: Cambridge University Press, 1993, p.99. John Haldon, *The Byzantine Wars*, Stroud: Tempus, 2001, pp.143-144.

[2] John W. Birkenmeier, *The Development of the Komnenian Army 1081-1180*, Leiden; Boston; Köln: Brill, 2002, p.102.

[3] C. M. Brand, *Byzantium Confronts the West*, 1180-1204, Cambridge, Mass.: Harvard University Press, 1968 (reprinted by Gregg Revivals, 1992), pp.177,196.

[4] C. M. Brand, *Byzantium Confronts the West*, 1180-1204, Cambridge, Mass.: Harvard University Press, 1968 (reprinted by Gregg Revivals, 1992), pp.197-204.

[5] An Anonymous Author, *The Deeds of Pope Innocent III*, translated with an introduction and notes by James M. Powell, Washington, D.C.: The Catholic University of America Press, 2004, p.93.

[6] An Anonymous Author, *The Deeds of Pope Innocent III*, translated with an introduction and notes by James M. Powell, Washington, D.C.: The Catholic University of America Press, 2004, p.166. Robert of Clari, *The Conquest of Constantinople*, translated from the old French by Edgar Holmes McNeal, New York: Columbia University Press, 1936, p.94. "The Registers of Innocent III", *Contemporary Sources for the Fourth Crusade*, ed. and trans. by Alfred J. Andrea, Leiden; Boston; Köln: Brill, 2000, pp. 62-63,91. Geoffrey of Villehardouin, "The Conquest of Constantinople", *Chronicles of the Crusades*, by Joinville and Villehardouin; translated with an Introduction by M. R. B. Shaw, New York: Dorset Press, 1985, p.85. Gunther of Pairis, *The Capture of Constantinople: the Hystoria Constantinopolitana of Gunther of Pairis, ed.* and trans. by Alfred J. Andrea, Philadelphia: University of Pennsylvania Press, 1997, pp.90-91.

扩张性质，只是把西方人的侵略当作外敌对拜占廷帝国的无数侵略的其中之一，[1]他们没有客观权衡帝国自身的处境，没有对帝国做出符合国内外形势的正确定位，未能采取有效的应对措施，只是一味地迎合西方，结果给拜占廷自身带来不良影响。

拜占廷皇帝们作为当时基督教世界最强大国家的统治者，他们迎合西方，极力表现自己分享十字军的理想，援助十字军国家，甚至承认教皇首位等，主要是为了应对西方的负面宣传，树立良好形象，保持拜占廷皇帝在基督教世界最高统治者的地位，也反映了他们企图争夺十字军东征的实际领导权，表明拜占廷帝国实际上已经被西方牵着鼻子走。

然而，十字军东征是西方封建主在基督教旗帜下进行的对外扩张活动，但拜占廷帝国当时对外扩张的条件并不成熟。当时拜占廷帝国政策的重点也不应该是保持拜占廷皇帝在基督教世界最高统治者的地位，而应该着重发展国家的实力、完善国家各项制度、改善国内的民生，提出对抗十字军东征（圣战）的思想和舆论，使拜占廷帝国避免成为西方舆论和武力攻击的目标。

拜占廷皇帝们对西方的扩张性质认识不清，对拜占廷帝国的定位不正确，导致政策失误，国内人力财力浪费，为西方入侵制造了借口，把拜占廷自身拖入困境之中。

---

[1]　参见阿莱克修斯一世去世前不久写给儿子约翰二世的一首诗，见 Paul Magdalino, *The Empire of Manuel I Komnenos*, Ambridge [England]; New York: Cambridge University Press, 1993, pp.27–28.

浅论4-7世纪东地中海世界的军事变革

马锋　东北师范大学

摘要：4-7世纪是东地中海世界从古典时代向中古时代的过渡时期。继承了罗马帝国半壁江山的拜占廷帝国为了在持续的挑战中生存下来，主动或被动地进行了一系列的军事变革。这些军事变革从戴克里先时代开始一直持续到希拉克略改革完成时期。这些军事变革成为了大变革时代的重要组成部分。经过长时期的变革，拜占廷帝国完成了向中古时代的过渡。军事变革使拜占廷帝国屹立在欧亚大陆的中间千年不倒。

关键词：拜占廷帝国；军事变革；查士丁尼

Abstract：4-7 century is Eastern Mediterranean world from the classical era to the medieval period of transition. Byzantine Empire that inherited half of the Roman Empire to survive in the ongoing challenge and active or passive were range of military transformation. The military transformation from the Diocletian era lasted until Heraclius completion of the reform period. The military transformation has become an important part of the era of great change. After a long period of change so that the Byzantine Empire has completed the transition to the Middle Ages. The military transformation to the Byzantine Empire to stands in the middle of Eurasia thousand years do not fall.

Keywords: Byzantine Empire, Military Transformation, Justinian

4-7世纪是罗马文明所代表的地中海世界经历的前所未有的大变革时代。此前，罗马帝国通过不断的军事征服使得地中海世界都处于同一个政治和法律体制的控制之下。但是到4世纪初所有这些都开始发生了转变。帝国的中心已经转移到东方，皇帝和元老贵族居住在新罗马君士坦丁堡。罗马帝国的东部拥有帝国一半以上的规模，在接近一千年的时间里它的公民仍旧继续称自己为罗马人。虽然地中海世界还有古罗马文明的痕迹，但是在这个舞台上已经生长出新时代的萌芽，并且不断茁壮成长。学者认为这一时期是东罗马帝国拜占廷因素不断发展的历史时期。东罗马帝国通过自身的变革，越来越具有新的特点，与先前的罗马帝国有着明显的区别。帝国也由此走出大危机的时代。但是东罗马帝国仍旧面临着自己的危险。东罗马帝国承继了先前帝国面临的所有困境，却失去了先前的战略优势。帝国的规模、人口和资源以及战略性的地理环境都缩小了。[1]4-7 世纪既是罗马－拜占廷帝国历史上的一个大变革时期，也是罗马军队转型为拜占廷军队的关键时期。在这个时期里拜占廷的军队特征逐渐形成。这是一个军事历史上的变革时期。这一系列的军事变革从戴克里先 (Diocletian，284-305) 的改革开始一直持续到希拉克略 (Heraclius,610-641) 改革的结束。

一　戴克里先时代的军事变革

戴克里先提出"一切罪恶之至极，是去推翻一度已被我们的先人设定的事物。"[2]但是戴克里先进行的变革却违反了自己的原则。戴克里先的改革是对一个已经变化了的社会的回应，涉及到政治、经济、军事和宗教等各个方面。戴克里先最重要的改革就是把军事指挥权与行政管理权分开。戴克里先规定行省总督由文官担任，而军事长官 (duces) 则是几个行省军队的指挥官。这种军政分离的制度安排使得军事政变在没有行政官员支持的情况下变得很难成功。当然戴克里先并没有完成这种军政分离的过程，这要到君士坦丁大帝 (Constantine the Great, 324-337) 军事改革时期才得以完善。4 世纪时期东罗马帝国的军队不再成为谋杀皇帝的主角，这与西部形成了鲜明的对比。也可以说是 3 世纪混乱局面在东部结束的一个表现。东部世界的秩序得到恢复。[3]戴克里先重视完善国家的军事防御体系。在东方从埃及到波斯的边界，戴克里先将固定的营地成一线配置，每个营地有适当数量的驻防部队，派出军官负责指挥，供应所需的各种武器和给养，并且在安条克、埃米萨和大马士革设置新的军械库。从莱茵河口一直到多瑙河口的古老营地、城镇和碉堡，全部重新加以整修。在最暴露的地点，很技巧的建构新的防御工事，边疆的守备部队要求严密的加强警戒，运用各种可能的措施，使得漫长的防线更为坚固，成为无法飞越的天堑。[4]

戴克里先对军队进行了改组。戴克里先把军队分为边防军 (limitanei) 和野战军 (comitatenses)。边防军沿着边界驻扎在堡垒中，主要作用是对抗低烈度的敌人的侵扰，或者削弱敌人大部队的进攻锐气为野战部队的围歼争取时间。野战军驻扎在远离边境有军事交通线与边境相连的城镇。它的作用一方面是用来支持边防军，快速地对侵入本国境内的敌人形成包围的态势，歼灭敌人或者迫使敌人撤退。因此要求部队有强大的机动能力，增加骑兵的比重。另一方面镇压国内的动乱，维护城镇及其周边地区的安全。晚期罗马军队依赖卫戍部队作为屏障。卫戍部队阻击少量敌军的入侵，迫使入侵者为寻找粮食而分散，使他们变得脆弱易受临近野战部队的攻击。[5]这种战略被勒特韦克 (Luttwak)在《罗马帝国的大战略》一书中称为"弹性战略"。拜占廷史家左西莫斯谈到"在戴克里先统治下，依靠城镇和驻扎士兵的边境防御工事保护漫长的边界。当蛮族企图越过边界时，帝国能够提供足够的兵力来对抗他们的进攻。"[6]皇帝的宫廷卫队也属于野战军序列。但是边防军和野战军在待遇上有着天壤之别，这在征兵和报酬上有明显地差别。随着野战部队获得了重要地位，边防部队成为了次要军队。372 年的一项法律规定那些因为不够强壮或者身高达不到标准的而不能够进入野战部队的新募兵应当编入边防部队。（狄奥多西 (Theodosius The Great, 346-395) 法典Ⅶ .22.8.）[7]无论是边防军还是野战军都是步骑兵协同作战，但是骑兵取得了前所未有的优势。这时的军团士兵不再主要是徒

---

① Edward N. Luttwak, *The Grand Strategy of the Byzantine Empire*, Boston: Harvard University Press, 2009, pp.4-5.
② 【美】阿瑟·施莱辛格主编，【美】南希·津瑟·沃尔沃蒂著，林丽冠译：《君士坦丁大帝》，中国工人出版社 2010 年版，第 37 页。
③ Walter Emil Kaegi Jr., *Byzantine Military Unrest 471-843*, Adolf M. Hakkert-Publisher-Amsterdam, 1981,p.16.
④ 【英】爱德华·吉本著，席代岳译：《罗马帝国衰亡史》，吉林出版集团有限责任公司 2008 年版，第 295 页。
⑤ David Nicolle Phd, *Romano-Byzantine Armies:4th-9th Centuries*, Osprey Publishing Ltd, 1992,p.2.
⑥ Zosimus, Ronald T, Ridley, *New History, Australian Association for Byzantine Studies*, 1982, p.54.
⑦ Warren Treadgold, *Byzantine and Its Army,284-1081*, Stanford University Press, 1995, p.11.

步作战，而是跨上战马成为了马军弓箭手和长矛轻骑兵。罗马人开始向生活在黑海北岸大草原的哥特部落学习骑马技术、骑兵装备和战术。这些哥特骑兵首先在亚德里亚那堡通过给予罗马人惨痛的失败教训来宣示骑兵时代的到带来。罗马军队的失败不仅标志着重装步兵时代的没落，也标着罗马军队主要依靠公民兵时代的结束。帝国能够提供的精英部队遭受到沉重打击。帝国传统的由公民兵组成的部队是国家尚武精神遗留的支柱。这些精英部队的丧失，使整个帝国失去了尚武的文化。

戴克里先改革蛮族雇佣军的雇佣方式。罗马军队很早就有雇佣同盟军队 (Federati)①的做法。这是指帝国通过条约的方式雇佣蛮族人参加罗马的军事行动。但是先前的同盟军队没有这么庞大的规模。由于亚德里亚那堡战役使的罗马帝国失去了仅存的尚武精神的残余精锐队伍。帝国军队不得不依靠蛮族人来注入尚武的新鲜血液。②随着罗马人在 378 年于亚德里亚那堡惨败于西哥特人，一些低水平的卫戍部队被召集到野战部队，但是并不能担负此任务。帝国征募在他们自己首领率领下的蛮族分遣队同盟军队代替了先前对个人的征募。③狄奥多西和同时代的许多人都承认帝国没有能力消灭哥特人，如果能够善加运用，反而可以获得许多士兵和农夫，使衰竭的行省得以恢复活力。因此狄奥多西大帝把哥特人大规模的纳入军队中，这些同盟军享受优厚待遇和特权。④戴克里先之前的雇佣军是作为个体被帝国雇佣，它的军官是由罗马人担任，是罗马军队的组成部分。但是从戴克里先开始军队雇佣的蛮族雇佣军由他们自己本民族的首领统帅。这些雇佣军效忠于他们的领导人。由于他们并不是罗马正规军的组成部分，所以不遵守它的纪律。这些蛮族军队过去经常是从帝国外部招募，但是由于蛮族定居的进程现在发生了根本性的改变：同盟军队变得越来越多地从帝国内部招募，他们数量的增加达到这种程度，军队开始变得大体上有各种蛮族组成并且实际上变成了一支雇佣军的军队。⑤这种混合的复杂军队包含了严重的缺点和威胁。军队经常性的哗变成为司令官和帝国政府一直十分惧怕的事情。⑥由于本国臣民不愿意当兵，帝国不得不依靠大量的外族人来补充军队。日耳曼人具有身体强壮和人高马大的有时，罗马人着重于纪律严明和坚忍不拔。蛮族在帝国的旗帜之下服务，能把双方的优点结合起来。他们的蛮力发挥的效果，要依靠优秀指挥者的指挥。⑦在蛮族构成一定比例的罗马帝国军队中，军队被注入了新鲜的活力，同时具有蛮族战斗的特点和军团的特点，也突出了将道的作用。这是帝国早期的罗马军团向拜占廷特点的军队逐渐转变的过程。克劳维茨认为这种蛮族雇佣军是所有正规军的必要的补充。这些蛮族的战斗方式和观念来自于人类的早期时代。非国家甚或前国家人民的地方性战争，其中全无合法与非法武器持有者之间的区别，因为所有的男子都是武士；此乃人类历史的长时期里曾经一直流行的战争方式，此后仍在边缘上侵蚀文明国家的生活，并且确实通过征召其实行者为"非正规"轻骑兵和步兵这通常做法而被转供他们使用。文明国家的军官视而不见这些非正规武士在作战时用以犒劳他们自己的非法非文明手段，视而不见他们野蛮的战斗方法。所有正规军都征召非正规兵为自己从事巡逻、侦察和小规模战斗。他们的文明的雇佣者选择掩盖他们的惯常做法：抢劫、掠夺、抢劫、杀人、绑架、勒索和大规模野蛮破坏。这些

① 关于同盟军队在 Procopius of Caesarea, *History of the Wars*, The Loeb Classical Library, Oxford: Harvard University Press, 2006. 中被多次提及，有关这种军队的详细论述见 David Nicolle, *Romano-Byzantine Armies 4th-9th Centuries*, Oxford&New York: Osprey Publishing Ltd, 1992, p.35.

② Warren Treadgold, *Byzantine and Its Army,284-1081*, Stanford University Press, 1995, p.11.

③ David Nicolle Phd, *Romano-Byzantine Armies:4th-9th Centuries*, Osprey Publishing Ltd, 1992,p.4.

④ 【英】爱德华·吉本著，席代岳译：《罗马帝国衰亡史》，吉林出版集团有限责任公司 2008 年版，第 399 页。

⑤ Averil Cameron, *The Mediterranean World in Late Antiquity AD395-600*, London and New York: Routledge, 1993, p.50.

⑥ Anthony Brongna, *The Generalship of Belisarius*, Boston: Boston University, Master thesis, 1987.

⑦ 【英】爱德华·吉本著，席代岳译：《罗马帝国衰亡史》，吉林出版集团有限责任公司 2008 年版，第 108 页。

雇佣者宁愿不承认它是一种更古老和分布更广的战争方式。①对于蛮族而言战争不是政治，而是一种文化和生活方式。②罗马－拜占廷帝国雇佣的许多国内外蛮族都是这种"非正规"军队，他们在严阵以待的阵地战中面对强敌怯懦，但是面对弱者则表现的十分凶狠。所以帝国将军在战斗中不敢轻易地相信他们的忠诚和战斗力。由这些蛮族雇佣军组成的阵列的一翼，常常成为敌人打击的重点，也是敌人最容易冲破的阵线之处。另一方面帝国将军利用他们劫掠的天性，让他们在敌方领土内执行破坏的战术。这在贝利萨留入侵波斯的战争中被充分使用。蛮族雇佣军这种缺乏纪律和荣誉感把保持生命作为战争的第一准则的行为常常会毁灭一次战役，毁灭一支军队。如何驾驭和使用蛮族雇佣军是将军们面临的最大的难题之一。政府在雇佣蛮族问题上最恰当的做法就是把蛮族人群当作像是各个自由的武士社会一样对待，在其中响应征召的责任落在群体而非个人成员身上。这是一种封建、部分外交、部分雇佣的体制。差不多从有组织的战斗肇始时起，蛮族就以各种不同形式向国家提供训练有素的军事单位。③罗马－拜占廷帝国对于蛮族的雇佣方式从个体到群体的变化符合这种类型。单个的蛮族人是自由的追求者，他有自己的战斗理念和生存文化，因此与罗马－拜占廷帝国军队的严格要求格格不入。所以征召个体的蛮族参军无论是对于蛮族个人而言难以忍受，他们认为这是对他们自由的一种羞辱，而且对于帝国指挥官而言也无法让他们服从军队必要的纪律。但是作为整体，他们的本民族的指挥官只是为了完成与帝国缔结的协约关系，而在他们内部仍然执行他们武士社会的战斗要求，并没有把罗马－拜占廷的战争方式和文化强加给这些蛮族士兵。这样才能够达到双方相对比较满意的状态。但是戴克里先与狄奥多西大帝不同，他设法降低军队中雇佣兵的比重。这种情况是通过提供丰厚的新津贴来吸引大量的志愿兵，增加军队中公民兵的比重。戴克里先的这种改革的成效在后来或多或少地实现了，其措施被后代的皇帝所继承。5世纪的拜占廷军队虽然雇佣兵的人数仍然很多，但是重要性下降了。再没有新的蛮族将领尝试控制帝国，军队成为了一个更为有效的工具。④

戴克里先削弱禁卫军的地位。在罗马帝国晚期执政官和大公的显赫地位已经不复存在，只是一种荣誉头衔。执政官的名字虽然仍旧作为纪年的象征，执政官当选会接受隆重的仪式和人民的欢呼，但是这些都是来自于君主的恩赐。执政官和大公的权力来自于皇帝的授予，这反映了皇帝制的特点。但是禁卫军长官 (Praefecti Praetorio) 的地位却获得了逐步提高，成为了在皇帝之下代表皇帝行使罗马帝国行政和军事大权的首席大臣。他类似于东方的宰相地位。禁卫军长官的地位提高一方面是因为他是皇帝的亲信，另一方面是因为他掌握了精锐的禁卫军能够左右皇帝的废立。3世纪危机期间，皇帝的废立多有禁卫军的叛乱决定，地方军团的力量降为次要地位。这与禁卫军与地方军团力量对比发生的变化有着密切的关系。禁卫军长官掌握了三个方面的大权：控制皇宫和首都安全的权力，主导行政事务，统领全国军队。禁卫军长官成为了事实上的皇帝，因此皇权的大小取决于在位皇帝的个人能力和皇帝与禁卫军长官之间的博弈。禁卫军长官通过他直接掌握的禁卫军对皇权形成威胁，是3世纪军事政变一再发生的重要原因。戴克里先认识到禁卫军的危险，主动地削弱禁卫军的实力。戴克里先削减了禁卫军的人数，取消了他们享有的特权。禁卫军虽然仍旧驻扎在罗马城，但是由于君主很少幸临罗马城，因此禁卫军失去了保卫皇帝安全的职责。现在保卫皇帝安全的卫队是来自以勇敢善战著称的伊利里亚。他们一个名为约维乌斯军团，另一个是海克力乌斯军团。⑤禁卫军的士兵

---

① 【英】约翰·基根著，时殷弘译：《战争史》，北京：商务印书馆2010年版，第5页。
② 【英】约翰·基根著，时殷弘译：《战争史》，北京：商务印书馆2010年版，第7页。
③ 【英】约翰·基根著，时殷弘译：《战争史》，北京：商务印书馆2010年版，第8页。
④ Warren Treadgold, *Byzantine and Its Army,284–1081*, Stanford University Press, 1995, p.14.
⑤ M. Grant, *The Collapse and Recovery of the Roman Empire*, London and New York: Routledge,1999,p.37;【英】爱德华·吉本著，席代岳译：《罗马帝国衰亡史》，吉林出版集团有限责任公司2008年版，第310页。

长期来自于意大利本土，由于长期驻扎在罗马城与罗马城的社会各阶级和元老院形成了利益联盟。从戴克里先的角度看，禁卫军既是维持共和传统的元老院的支持者，又是威胁皇权和帝国安全的头号敌人。因此他为了实现君主专制的转型必然要削弱禁卫军的地位。除了从人数上和禁卫军的特权方面予以打击外，戴克里先还从禁卫军的外在支持力量上下手。戴克里先一方面把意大利降为行省，取消它的特权，把罗马城交给一名市政长官领导，独立于禁卫军长官之外。另一方面架空元老院，使其变成一个有名无实的空谈机构。

二 君士坦丁时代的军事变革

君士坦丁大帝统治时期帝国军队的组织仍旧延续戴克里先的改革。在戴克里先削弱禁卫军的基础上君士坦丁大帝解散了禁卫军。在君士坦丁大帝在位时，禁卫军长官不再对皇帝的人身安全负责，失去对整个宫廷各个部门的管辖权。他们不再直接指挥罗马军队的精锐部队，被君士坦丁大帝剥夺了统领军队的指挥权。最后他们变成各个行省的行政长官，永久失去了军事权。君士坦丁大帝解散了作恶多端威胁皇权的禁卫军部队。[1]君士坦丁创立了一支新的骑兵部队作为自己的卫队。这支卫队一部分来自于对手机动部队组成的野战军，另一部分是从边防部队中严格选拔出来。[2]帝国军队分为皇家卫队、野战军和边防军。野战军驻扎在内陆城市中，边防军主要由驻扎在边境上和边境要塞中的部队组成。拜占廷历史学家左西莫斯尖锐地批评驻扎在大城市的野战军，理由是边境上的防卫被剥去一半，以致向蛮族打开门户，而城市受到不必要的痛苦压榨，军人自己却学会从剧场和锦衣玉食中找寻乐趣。他接下来说，在戴克里先统治下，帝国的防卫截然不同；所有的部队驻扎在边境上，因此任何蛮族进攻都可及时击退。[3]军队驻扎在城市中或者城市附近而不是像从前那样大量地驻扎在边境，这种变化的事实直接反映了经过戴克里先和君士坦丁的改革，晚期罗马军队需要靠近各种税收来源地，从那里获得他们报酬的主要来源。[4]

君士坦丁大帝实行军民分治的原则。君士坦丁大帝进行了一系列加强君主专制中央集权制的措施，在中央集权方面，一是把戴克里先的十二个大区和一百多个行省组合成四个大辖区。中央直辖地方层面的数量的减少有利于中央对地方事务加强控制和管理。另一方面是地方军事权与民事权分离。原来的禁卫军长官只是东方、伊利里亚、意大利和高卢四大辖区的最高行政长官。而每个大辖区都有两名主将来分享最高统帅权，分别是骑兵长官 (magister equitum) 和步兵长官 (magister peditum)。这两位将领的职责不是按照地域而是按照骑兵和步兵划分。后来君士坦丁又在莱茵河、上多瑙河、下多瑙河和幼发拉底河四个边区各设置一名骑兵长官和步兵长官。这样帝国的军队就由八位步兵长官和八位骑兵长官来统领。在他们下面又设立三十五位军事指挥官，配置在个行省，其中三位在不列颠，六位在高卢，一位在西班牙，一位在意大利，五位在上多瑙河，四位在下多瑙河，八位在亚细亚，三位在埃及，四位在阿非利加。[5]但是到了4世纪末骑兵长官和步兵长官结合为军事长官 (Magister Militum)，至少在帝国的东半部分是如此。[6]在行省层面也对民事权和军事权进行了分离。以前的行省长官代执政官 (proconsul)、代大法官 (propraetor)、指挥官 (rector) 等在其统治区域内握有军

---

① 【英】爱德华·吉本著，席代岳译：《罗马帝国衰亡史》，吉林出版集团有限责任公司 2008 年版，第 21 页。

② Warren Treadgold, *Byzantine and Its Army,284-1081*, Stanford University Press, 1995, p.10.

③ 转引自【瑞士】雅各布·布克哈特 著 宋立宏 熊莹 卢彦名译 宋立宏 审校：《君士坦丁大帝时代》上海三联出版社 2006 年版，第 279-280 页。

④ Averil Cameron, *The Mediterranean World in Late Antiquity AD395-600*, London and New York: Routledge, 1993, p.50.

⑤ 【英】爱德华·吉本著，席代岳译：《罗马帝国衰亡史》，吉林出版集团有限责任公司 2008 年版，第 28-29 页。

⑥ David Nicolle Phd, *Romano-Byzantine Armies:4th-9th Centuries*, Osprey Publishing Ltd, 1992,p.5.

事指挥权，只与他们的副官 (legate) 分享，常常成为动乱的主体。这种体制安排使得地方军队对中央的威胁大大减少，军队叛乱如果不解决骑兵与步兵的协调，不解决地方行政结构与军事机构的配合问题不可能取得胜利。君士坦丁通过地方分权的方式，使地方的权力操控在中央政府手里。

勒特韦克在《罗马帝国的大战略》一书中把罗马帝国大战略的第三个阶段概括为纵深防御战略。纵深防御战略要求主力军和边防部队之间有明确的分工与合作，也要求边疆地区有广大的纵深地段能够用来削弱敌军的锐气，用土地换时间，赢取主力部队集中的时间，进而为主力部队围歼来犯之敌提供条件。[1]勒特韦克认为纵深防御战略阶段是由戴克里先开创的，但是钮先钟则认为它是开始于君士坦丁大帝时期。[2]后者的观点可以从原始文献的记载和后人的研究成果中得到印证。边境体系的逐渐衰弱可以看着是地方居民成分、经济和社会变化长期改变的一个部分。在当时的人看来边境的概念已经成为了一个引起强烈感情的事项；保持边境防御的失败等同于把边境"出让给蛮族人"。戴克里先通过建造和修复要塞明显地增强了边境，但是君士坦丁通过将军队撤销编入到一支机动的野战部队而"削弱了"它们：君士坦丁通过从边境转移大部分军队并使他们驻扎在不需要援助的城市破坏了这种安全〔戴克里先强调的强固的边境防御〕，这种条块的保护受到蛮族的干扰而且在城市的士兵由于暴行而激起义愤使得他们孤立了，因此都进一步使事情变得更糟。[3]纵观拜占廷军事战略和战术，帝国军队的布局仍旧体现了纵深防御的特点，只是这种战略是缩小化的。无论从规模上还是从程度上都是缩小的。这种纵深防御战略是在敌我力量对比中自身不处于优势，在攻防战略中总体处于守势的一方正确的选择。拜占廷帝国延续了这种纵深防御战略的思想。纵深防御战略多用于拜占廷军队面临大规模的敌人入侵而不得不采取的守势战略。这些战例主要使用于拜占廷长期据有的疆土，主要是位于与波斯有争议的东方战线和面对蛮族蜂拥而至的多瑙河战线。

纵深防御战略的实行是与帝国的实际情况紧密相关的。在君士坦丁大帝统治时期以及其后的大部分时间里，帝国军事实力下降无法进行扩张，并且面对各个方面的外敌入侵没有军事实力全面地阻挡敌人与国门之外，不得不放弃了戴克里先时代仍旧实行的弹性防御战略。即便是在戴克里先时期已经显示出国家的情况不能够完全实行弹性防御战略了，戴克里先的四帝共治从军事战略的角度来讲就是人为的捍卫这种战略。一个皇帝已经无法保卫所有的边境，只有通过四位皇帝各自负责一段边境的办法来维持弹性防御战略的继续实行。其实这种一个皇帝无法维持漫长边境的问题在狄奥多西大帝时期就已经存在，狄奥多西大帝不得不考虑用东西方分治的办法来维持弹性防御战略的运行。君士坦丁大帝推行君主专制中央集权制的措施，不可能再延续戴克里先为了维持弹性防御战略而分割皇权的做法，因此弹性防御战略必然要被一个新的战略所代替，这就是纵深防御战略。与弹性防御战略相比，纵深防御战略对于保卫国内安全而言无疑是一个巨大的退步，但是这种牺牲却换来了君主专制中央集权制的进一步完善，这也是一种历史的进步。但是纵深防御战略仍旧是建立在罗马－拜占廷帝国军队在一定程度上对入侵的敌军占有优势的基础上，这样罗马－拜占廷帝国主力军在能够围歼入侵之敌或者迫使敌军退出帝国领土。纵深防御战略与前者相比对民众财产和安全造成更大的伤害，受到左西莫斯和普罗柯比的批评。

三　查士丁尼时代的军事变革

在查士丁尼一世 (*Justinian the Great, 527—565*) 统治时期，帝国经历了军事动荡问题的关键性的

---

①　【美】爱德华·勒特韦克著，时殷弘、惠黎文译：《罗马帝国的大战略》，北京：商务印书馆 2008 年版，第 136 页。
②　钮先钟：《西方战略思想史》，桂林：广西师范大学出版社 2003 年版，第 56 页。
③　Averil Cameron, *The Mediterranean World in Late Antiquity AD395—600*, London and New York: Routledge, 1993, p.51.

改变。5世纪晚期似乎带来一些麻烦的的兵变到查士丁尼统治初期暂时地销声匿迹了。在520年通过暗杀的方式已经解决了最危险的将领。尽管有一些抱怨，军队在527年并没有对政府构成威胁，它表面上被控制住了。军队在反对政府问题上十分谨慎。但是到查士丁尼逝世后，政府失去了对士兵和军官逐渐增加的不安定的情绪和独立思想的控制。①

军队实行募兵制，现在有蛮族自愿兵和本土罗马士兵构成，而不再是由作为部落群体的蛮族人构成。②军队的主体基本上是雇佣兵，而古罗马军队的基础旧的公民阶级现在都已经完全消失了。它仍旧分为卫戍部队（边防军）和野战军。由于缺乏足够的军饷，查士丁尼统治时期边防军的经济情况进一步恶化，他们的消费支出减少了，像农民那样养活自己。③边防军是固定下来的，经常是兼职性的部队驻扎在边境的一个特别堡垒里面。野战军是帝国军队的机动部队，包括同盟者轻骑兵并配有重装骑兵。马上弓箭手在北非和意大利构成战斗的核心拥有很强的战斗力。野战军中一个重要的组织是军队中核心领导人的私人家兵。拿贝利萨留来说，在他的事例中被人们所知的他的家庭骑兵增加到超过7000人的力量。这些私人家兵由他们的主人付薪、训练和装备；他们向两个对象宣誓效忠，一个是他们的主人另一个是皇帝。私人家兵都是精心挑选的是战场上最好的部队。④这种私人家兵是日耳曼王公在3世纪从罗马人那里学到，它现在被查士丁尼和他的将军贝利萨留（*Belisarius*）和纳尔西斯（*Narses*）借回。由于他们向雇主而不是向国家宣誓，⑤他们自然地成为了对皇帝的一种威胁；然而这样职业性地，在一个长久基础上的征兵，会形成一个拥有重兵的核心。他们会轻易叛变，他们的忠诚几乎完全依赖于他们雇主的财富、影响和领导能力。⑥但是与其他军人相比，私人家兵的忠诚度更加可靠。在尼卡暴动中大部分军队都处于动摇状态，抛弃了他们的将军和皇帝。贝利撒留只能依靠他的私人家兵平定了叛乱。⑦贝利撒留受命进军北非时，他率领的军队包括众多的骑兵而和他自己的私人家兵。虽然军队的主体是雇佣军，⑧但是战斗力最强的是他的私人卫队。私人卫队的勇士常常被贝利撒留作为临时分遣队的指挥官，也常常成为他打开战斗僵局的主要依靠力量。

查士丁尼时代骑兵确立了在军队中的主导地位。在罗马帝国的军队中，步兵仍旧是主力兵种，而骑兵还是和共和国时期一样，只是辅助兵种。随着与外部蛮族军队的征战，罗马帝国的军队从战争的交往中学会了许多骑兵知识。尤其是漫长的边防线与军队数量有限，精锐部队数量更加有限的矛盾迫使在边防防御上投入比较大型的机动兵力，在军队中增加骑兵的比重。但是这种骑兵比重的增加受到多种因素的制约，既有农业社会人们远离骑射的原因，也有罗马人对古老的罗马重装步兵为主的军团报有深厚的感情，始终作为帝国安全和稳定的军事基石。从广义的历史时段来看，骑兵为主的军队代替步兵为主的军队，是古典时代向中古时代发展的大环境决定的。在这种新事物的发展过程中不可能不遇到阻力。但是378年，传统的罗马军团在亚德里亚纳堡惨败于骑兵为主的哥特军队是这种进程的得到了加速。阻碍军队变革的力量减弱了。尤其是罗马人主观上不再认为重装步兵军团战无不胜，而不得不接受了骑兵时代来临的现实；冶铁技术的提高和铁器供应量的增加为骑兵武器装备的多样化提供了基础；拜占廷缺乏人口和丰富的兵源但是商业发达，人口受教育水平较

① Walter Emil Kaegi Jr., *Byzantine Military Unrest 471-843*, Adolf M. Hakkert-Publisher-Amsterdam, 1981,p.41.

② David Nicolle Phd, *Romano-Byzantine Armies:4th-9th Centuries*, Osprey Publishing Ltd, 1992,p.6.

③ Warren Treadgold, *Byzantine and Its Army,284-1081*, Stanford University Press, 1995, p.165.

④ Anthony Brongna, *The Generalship of Belisarius*, Boston University, Master thesis, 1987.

⑤ 普罗柯比和一些研究者认为私人家兵既对雇主宣誓效忠，也宣誓效忠皇帝。见 Anthony Brongna, *The Generalship of Belisarius*, Boston University, Master thesis, 1987.

⑥ David Nicolle Phd, *Romano-Byzantine Armies:4th-9th Centuries*, Osprey Publishing Ltd, 1992,pp.6-7.

⑦ Lawrence Herbert Fauber, *Harses, Hammer of the Goths*, St. Martin's Press, p.36.

⑧ Theophanes Confessor, translated by Cyril Mango and Roger Scott, *The Chronicle of Theophanes Confessor-Byzantine and Near Eastern History(284-813)*, Oxford: Clarendon Press, 1997, p.288.

高，形成了富而不强的特点。因此军队珍惜兵力，利用策略是战略的合适的选择。拜占廷人知道和平是战争暂时的中止，因此在冲突的消耗中失去稀少和宝贵的士兵是不可挽回的损失。拜占廷拒绝旧罗马军队极力进行最大消耗的做法，强调对士兵的保护。无论在何时只要可能，拜占廷都极力避免前沿攻击和冲突的死板标准以及高昂的伤亡代价，依靠策略赢取战争而不是毁灭敌人。他们倾向于更加机动和更为复杂的骑兵而不是步兵，因为骑兵能够更好的适应各种形式的策略；[1]中世纪战争中骑兵取得了在冷兵器时代最大的优势，成为军队的主导力量。拜占廷军队中骑兵比例的增加只是适应了这个历史潮流。[2]亚德里亚纳堡的惨败使得罗马帝国失去了最后一支有尚武精神的军队。军队中一批有远见的皇帝和将领积极推行增加骑兵的计划。在狄奥多西大帝时代通过大量的增加蛮族人补充到元气大伤的帝国军队中，加速扩充了骑兵构成的机动部队。[3]以后，这个招募的比例终于获得了某种程度的平衡，于是才发展为一种有体系的新型组织。[4]并不清楚这种变化是何时和如何发生的，但是到查士丁尼开始掌权的 527 年，拜占廷军队最有效的武装确实是马军弓箭手。即使他们缺乏最完备的骑术和草原骑手的忍耐力，他们仍然拥有自己的优势：他们配置的弓更有弹性，一杆长矛挂在背后他们能够抽出发起冲锋。我们可以从凯撒里亚的普罗柯比的记载中找到亲眼所见的证据，新的投射骑兵从不良装备的危机中脱颖而出。[5]骑兵部队分为重装骑兵和轻装骑兵，同时与之配合的还有重装步兵和轻装步兵。这种轻重装结合，步骑兵协调一致的军队配置体现了拜占廷军事制度的科学性。重装步兵穿着铁甲衣，所使用的兵器由弓弩和长枪。[6]在原理上，它是想兼有机动"火力"和机动"冲力"两者之长——匈奴和波斯的骑弓手显示出了第一方面的价值，而哥特的骑枪兵也显示出了第二方面的价值。作为重骑兵的辅助兵力，又有轻骑兵的组织，那便是轻装的骑弓手。无论从组织上或战术上来看，这两者的结合都可以算是近代轻重（或中型）两型坦克联合使用的先例。步兵也同样分为轻重两型，但是后者却使用重矛和密集的队形，只是当作会战中的一个固定枢纽使用，而骑兵则环绕它做各种运动。[7]6 世纪罗马军队中步兵的主要目标包括守卫堡垒，作为弓箭手使用，作为围攻战的劳动力，根据罗马司令官的意愿在骑兵进行演习中充战场上的敌对力量。6 世纪拜占廷帝国的军队已经实现了专业化分类，军队有战斗人员、工程人员、后勤人员、医疗人员和随军传教士构成。[8]

拜占廷帝国军队的装备和战略战术在 5-6 世纪时期都得到了改进和完善。如果说罗马帝国的胜利是由于军队的纪律和操练，那么拜占廷帝国的胜利则是由于战略战术和将才。[9]查士丁尼时代的罗马士兵习惯于马上作战。罗马人也雇佣蛮族人充当轻骑兵或者重骑兵。这些蛮族作为马背上的民族，具有优越的骑兵作战条件和天赋。拜占廷将军在战斗中十分注意发挥各个民族自身的战术特点。拜占廷本国的士兵虽然没有这些天然条件，但是他们在新兵训练期间不断地接受各种技战术的演练和熟悉各种武器的使用方法。这使得士兵能够在战斗中自如地按照战地指挥官的意图完成战略战术的

① Edward N. Luttwak, *The Grand Strategy of the Byzantine Empire*, Harvard University Press, 2009, p.58.

② 有关骑兵的战术和编队情况见 Text, Translation, and Notes by George T. Dennis, *Three Byzantine Military Treatises*, Washington, D.C.: Dumbarton Oaks Research Library and Collection, 1985, pp.57-59.

③ 【英】爱德华·吉本著，席代岳译：《罗马帝国衰亡史》，吉林出版集团有限责任公司 2008 年版，第 399 页。

④ 【英】李德·哈特著，钮先钟译：《战略论：间接路线》，上海人民出版社 2010 年版，第 37 页。

⑤ Edward N. Luttwak, *The Grand Strategy of the Byzantine Empire*, Harvard University Press, 2009, p.57.

⑥ 有关 6 世纪拜占廷帝国军队的装备情况见 Text, Translation, and Notes by George T. Dennis, *Three Byzantine Military Treatises*, Washington, D.C.: Dumbarton Oaks Research Library and Collection, 1985, pp.54-55.. 也可以参考 Anthony Brongna, *The Generalship of Belisarius*, Boston University, Master thesis, 1987.

⑦ 【英】李德·哈特著，钮先钟译：《战略论：间接路线》，上海人民出版社 2010 年版，第 37 页。

⑧ Text, Translation, and Notes by George T. Dennis, *Three Byzantine Military Treatises*, Washington, D.C.: Dumbarton Oaks Research Library and Collection, 1985, p..46-47.

⑨ David Nicolle, *Romano-Byzantine Armies 4th-9th Centuries*, Oxford&New York: Osprey Publishing Ltd, 1992, p.3.

要求，在战斗中他们比其他人表现的更加多才多艺。[1]拜占廷建国之初，处于四面皆敌的恶劣环境之中，其统治者以自保为第一优先，在战略上是完全采取守势。直到查士丁尼即帝位后，始企图收复失地，重振帝国雄风。于是在贝利撒留和纳尔西斯等名将率领之下，拜占廷部队曾经收复意大利南部和中部，并远征北非，此种胜利并非由于拜占廷享有数量优势，而是武器、战术和将道都比敌人高明。[2]纽先钟在《西方战略思想史》一书中谈到了查士丁尼时代贝利萨留将军在军事活动中采用了防御进攻性战略[3]。这种战略在后来就成为了拜占廷军事战略思想的传统部分。防御进攻性战略是拜占廷在西方进行征服活动中所采用的基本的战略艺术。"他之所以能被称为名将的理由，有两点：（一）他的兵力真是少得可怜，与他的工作简直不成比例；（二）他经常使用守势的战术。在一连串的征服之中，竟完全缺乏攻势的行动，这种奇迹也可以算是史无前例的。而最大的特点，却是他所率领的军队，其基础完全是机动部队——主要是骑兵。贝利撒留并不缺乏胆量，但是他的战术都是设法引诱对方先动手进攻。他这种作风的理由，一方面是因为他在数量上总是居于劣势的缘故，但另一方面也表示他在战术和心理两个方面，都有极精密的计算。"[4]防御进攻性战略出现的背景中很重要的一点是查士丁尼时代君主专制中央集权制的加强，军队动乱处于一个低谷时期，查士丁尼的能力能够驾驭那些桀骜不驯的将领，把罗马帝国军队劣根性造成的危害降低到很低的程度。但是由于长年的军队在外征战，远离拜占廷本土，造成帝国行政机构对军队的监督鞭长莫及，为帝国军队潜伏的习惯性的弊病提供了复苏的温床。[5]军民对立之下的军队最难驾御。除粮饷充足外，将才是必不可少的。当然任何的军队都需要有才的人率领。但真正的民兵，即或主将不得人，顶多也不过是打败仗，决不至直接祸国殃民。流浪军却非有才将才率领不可，否则不止要战败辱国，并且要行动如土匪，甚至公开的变成土匪。[6]整个6世纪，查士丁尼统治时期的最主要的军事动荡是陷入既要为积极的长期军事行动提供充足的补给和军饷又要不会因为征用毁灭国内民众和农业的困境。查士丁尼和他的继任者并没有能够想出解决军民需要之间最明显的冲突的一种现实的办法，导致士兵的挫折感不断累积到世纪之交时达到最大化引起莫里斯皇帝的毁灭。[7]

四　莫里斯时代的军事变革

查士丁尼时代的攻势战略是拜占廷帝国历史上的一个特殊阶段，是帝国历史上整体防御战略构架下的一个特殊的反动。这只能用当时所具有的特殊的历史条件来说明。但是查士丁尼时代的军事行动挥霍了这些千年一遇的历史机遇，长期战争使得帝国国力受损严重。在查士丁尼驾崩后，他的继承人在军事和经济上都面临难以收拾的残局。查士丁尼统治的晚年无视军队的存在，因此受到历史学家阿加西阿斯（Agathias）对他的严厉批评，"因此防御和军队被忽视，被食物的缺乏所压迫，他们放弃了坚守岗位的斗争，他们分散到任何地方寻求能够维持生活的其它方式。军事基金被用尽，

① Edward N. Luttwak, *The Grand Strategy of the Byzantine Empire*, Boston: Harvard University Press, 2009,p.11.
② 纽先钟：《西方战略思想史》，桂林：广西师范大学出版社2003年版第64页。
③ 关于贝利萨留使用的防御进攻性战略（defensive-offensive strategy）见 B. H. Liddeel-Hart. *Strategy*, London: Fabaer and Faber, 1967,pp.56-69. 转引自纽先钟：《西方战略思想史》，桂林：广西师范大学出版社2003年版第64页。
④ 【英】李德·哈特著，纽先钟译：《战略论：间接路线》，上海人民出版社2010年版，第36页。
⑤ Walter Emil Kaegi Jr., *Byzantine Military Unrest 471-843*, Adolf M. Hakkert-Publisher-Amsterdam, 1981,pp.51-52.
⑥ 雷海宗：《中国的兵》，中华书局2005年版，第51页。
⑦ Walter Emil Kaegi Jr., *Byzantine Military Unrest 471-843*, Adolf M. Hakkert-Publisher-Amsterdam, 1981,pp.42-43.

大部分被用于无秩序的妇女，赛车手和卑贱的柔弱的人……身上。"①帝国没有能力统治扩大了的帝国，不能够在新征服的地区建立有效的民政统治机构，只能任由军队在新征服地区劫掠，政府官僚结构只能在拜占廷帝国原来的本土范围内部良好的运行，导致帝国本土和新征服地区出现完全不同的秩序局面。帝国的征服行动为军队潜伏的劣根性的爆发提供了机遇。军队动荡再次成为威胁皇权和帝国安全的一个重要因素。②到莫里斯 (Maurice, 582—602) 时期他根据国家的实际情况重新确立了国家战略的基本观念。莫里斯的战略构想是使用各种手段来避免战争，最好是能够使敌人知难而退，不敢进犯。这就是所谓的守势吓阻战略③，换句话说，就是用防御的手段来达到吓阻的目的。而这种观念也成为了此后 5 个世纪帝国的主体战略思想。莫里斯的守势吓阻战略的基本观点十分简单明了。对当时的拜占廷而言，其国力是攻则不足而守则有余。国内工商业发达，人民安享高水准生活，对侵略和征服早已丧失兴趣。领土的扩张不仅要付出重大成本，而且在管理上和防守上也会增加无穷的烦恼。所以，拜占廷对于不能消化的领土实无寻求之必要，拜占廷的唯一目的即为确保其现有的领土和财富，并永远过着富强康乐的生活。所以，其战略构想为企图使用各种手段以避免战争，最好是使敌人知难而退，不敢进犯。此即所谓守势吓阻战略，换言之，就是用防御的手段来达到吓阻的目的。④

莫里斯根据这种构想，建立了一套完整的国防体系，其主要目的就是实现"长治久安"：一方面企图用最小的成本来维护最大的安全；另一方面又可以预防国内军阀叛乱的危险。概括而言，可分为四点：（1）健全人事制度，使军事人员的升迁调动之权都直属中央，部队指挥官不得擅专；（2）减少佣兵人数，并对其任务加以严格限制，只用来组成中央战略预备队和充任边防部队的骨干；（3）建立民兵制，并依赖他们来防守边疆，同时建筑要塞网来增强防御；（4）对于民兵采取免税和授田的措施，在边区逐步推行兵农合一的制度。⑤

五　希拉克略时代的军事变革

莫里斯守势吓阻战略中的民兵制类似于中国唐朝的府兵制，这种制度一方面能够增强国家抵御入侵的武装数量和保持一定程度军事水平，但是另一方面这也说明了拜占廷帝国面临的外部威胁和内部承受能力之间的关系与之前出现了变化。这种关系从拜占廷建国一直是处于一个帝国军事优势逐渐丧失而敌方总体劣势逐渐转变为优势的过程，外敌的威胁从重点地区到边境沿线再到边疆大片区域。这种点线面逐渐深入的入侵不仅说明了外敌在不断地提高战斗能力和战略水平，更重要的是拜占廷帝国的国力和军事水平不断地在衰落。拜占廷的军事制度改革是在这种大背景下不得不进行的历史选择。守势吓阻战略发展为军区 (theme) 制是历史的必然。守势吓阻战略实施的环境已经是外敌入侵突破了线性防御，不断地深入边疆内地。从军事力量角度看，它是对纵深防御战略的一种弱化，到了 7 世纪，帝国国力和军力的衰落，以及阿拉伯势力的崛起，使得这种敌我双方相对均势状态下的军事战略失去了主导意义，帝国的军事战略不得不扩展为边疆更为纵深的全局防御，甚至是国家整体作为边疆，加强内地的军事存在才能够保持战略的平衡。这与唐朝府兵制发展为藩镇割据有着相识的背景。所以，守势吓阻战略发展为军区制是历史的必然。因为帝国几乎可能从任何方向上受

①　转引自 Walter Emil Kaegi Jr., *Byzantine Military Unrest 471—843*, Adolf M. Hakkert–Publisher–Amsterdam, 1981,p.59.

②　Walter Emil Kaegi Jr., *Byzantine Military Unrest 471—843*, Adolf M. Hakkert–Publisher–Amsterdam, 1981,pp.54–55.

③　莫里斯的守势吓阻战略见钮先钟：《西方战略思想史》，桂林：广西师范大学出版社 2003 年版，第 65 页。

④　钮先钟：《西方战略思想史》，桂林：广西师范大学出版社 2003 年版，第 65 页。

⑤　钮先钟：《西方战略思想史》，桂林：广西师范大学出版社 2003 年版，第 65 页。

到奇袭，假使敌军穿透了帝国的外围，则不设防的内地省区就会受到无情的蹂躏，而中央预备队也可能来不及救援，于是国家元气必将受到伤害。设立军区的目的即为保持一种区域性的高度戒备。[1]拜占廷军区数量不断变化，总体上是在不断增加。一方面说明边疆威胁不断增强，外敌入侵造成的全国整体的压力不断增强，另外一方面军区制数量的增多与中央政府通过削减军区的规模防止军阀割据和军队叛乱有关。除此之外，此时拜占廷帝国的有效抵抗能力更多的是依靠每一个军区的自我抵抗能力和相邻军区的协作能力，军事的重心已经由中央转变为地方。以前主要由中央控制的战斗力强大的野战部队也逐渐大部分被分配在军区内部管辖。每一个军区都是把有限的野战部队、边防部队和民兵部队结合起来进行联合防御。所以这一时期的军事冲突虽然频繁但是主要是低烈度的，在地方层面进行解决。与军区制的推广相适应，军队的具体战略战术也发生了变化。拜占廷帝国的军事指挥官根据实践的需要发展了游击战和前哨战 (Skirmishing)[2]。这在实战中效果极佳，有效地阻击了穆斯林加奇运动的冲击。穆斯林加奇运动不受中央政权的控制，具有突发性，分散性和随意性，一般规模较小，是一种非正规军战斗。而游击战和前哨战则很好地克制了加奇运动的特点，它把正规战和非正规战的战略战术相结合。在东部与萨珊人战斗时拜占廷演化出一种游击战略，依靠著名的"影子战斗 (Shadowing Warfare)"战术，后来用它来抵抗穆斯林阿拉伯人。[3]拜占廷军队数量少是当时拜占廷战略首先考虑的因素。军力小的原因，可能是由于生活安逸的平民不愿意当兵，而军户由于长期战争的破坏无法继续履行当兵义务，尚武精神的丧失使民众当兵热情降低。帝国国力下降无法像早前那样获得大量的募兵——雇佣外族兵和社会闲散人群。而"影子战斗"是失去了主力军支持的地方层面的抗争，是纵深防御战略被破坏的表现。

军区制是由总督制发展而来。总督制最早是在意大利和北非建立。著名的有拉文纳总督区和迦太基总督区。这两个总督区统治的范围都是查士丁尼时代军事远征的成果。但是这次远征遗留的问题是在被征服领土上始终没有建立与拜占廷帝国本土相同的军民分治制度，行政治理的能力很弱，一般都是由军事力量主导。[4]在这些新征服地区拜占廷帝国面临外敌入侵，内部民众不满和军队动荡的三重威胁。因此保持强有力的军事力量主导的政权是环境的需要。（在总督制之下拜占廷在北非和意大利的统治被分为几个军事长官管辖[5]）军队的招募和供给方式日益地方化。4-5世纪东罗马帝国没有出现成功的军事政变，一方面是3世纪危机的结束，政治秩序的获得新的稳定，另外一方面后期的行省的军事化还没有完成。[6]而到7世纪，拜占廷帝国埃及地区和东方边境环境的恶化，逐渐增加了这一地区面临外敌入侵和军队动荡的程度。这些地区的统治越来越带有迦太基总督区和拉文纳总督区的影子。随着帝国其他地区陷入同样的困难，帝国统治者不得不把在迦太基和拉文纳的总督制稍加改变的运用到埃及和东方，最终推广到全国。军区制虽然有利于维护国家的安全，是当时的一种相对优秀的选择，但是军区制却造成了民政体系的衰落和军阀割据的不断加深。帝国军队的分化导致了在帝国内部世界很快出现了众多的私人军队。许多都是由当地的财阀资助，们向他们的雇主而不向政府宣誓效忠，他们被认为是和平的威胁。[7]在修道院和地主的支持下拜占廷领土内的地

---

[1]　钮先钟：《西方战略思想史》，桂林：广西师范大学出版社2003年版，第65-66页。

[2]　关于前哨战见 Text, Translation, and Notes by George T. Dennis, *Three Byzantine Military Treatises*, Washington, D.C.: Dumbarton Oaks Research Library and Collection, 1985, pp.137-143.

[3]　David Nicolle Phd, *Romano-Byzantine Armies:4th-9th Centuries*, Osprey Publishing Ltd, 1992,p.13.

[4]　日耳曼努斯对北非的统治情况见 Theophanes Confessor, translated by Cyril Mango and Roger Scott, *The Chronicle of Theophanes Confessor-Byzantine and Near Eastern History(284-813)*, Oxford: Clarendon Press, 1997, p.298-299. Lawrence Herbert Fauber, *Harses, Hammer of the Goths*, St. Martin's Press, pp.42-151.

[5]　David Nicolle Phd, *Romano-Byzantine Armies:4th-9th Centuries*, Osprey Publishing Ltd, 1992,pp.7-8.

[6]　Walter Emil Kaegi Jr., *Byzantine Military Unrest 471-843*, Adolf M. Hakkert-Publisher-Amsterdam, 1981,p.19.

[7]　David Nicolle Phd, *Romano-Byzantine Armies:4th-9th Centuries*, Osprey Publishing Ltd, 1992,p.5.

方武装进一步兴起。一些旧皇族仍旧在西部帝国灭亡后幸存下来并且仍旧控制大面积的庄园；现在他们开始恢复长久失去的尊严、头衔和军事角色。[1]这对帝国深层次的影响是打破了帝国建立初期维持国家良好运行的官僚机制，削弱了君主专制中央集权制，使拜占廷帝国的历史轨迹发生了不可挽回的变化。从罗马帝国后期到拜占廷帝国，国家的历史是逐渐走向以官僚贵族统治为基础的专制主义中央集权制度。从领主制封建社会向地主官僚制的封建社会发展是历史发展的一条必然规律。但是军区制的发展反而逐渐削弱了拜占廷帝国早期建立的官僚贵族统治的基础，使得帝国的历史倒退回领主制封建社会。

军区设有司令（strategos）一人，不仅指挥军事，而且兼理民政。通常每个军区的常备兵力都是一个军(thema)，每个军下辖两到三个师(turma)。基本战术单位为营(numerus)，员额为300到400人。一个师所辖的营数为5到8个，可见其编制相当具有弹性。在其正常状况时，拜占廷的常备陆军总数约在12万人到15万人之间。[2]以如此少量兵力防守那样辽阔的边区实非易事，其常能完成任务似应归于下述两点理由：（1）有设计极佳的战略防御体系；（2）常备兵力虽少但素质极佳，而且又有民兵的支援。每个军区都有若干战略据点（要塞），其间有良好的道路交通和相当有效的通信联络（例如烽火台）。[3]另有高度机动化兵力（通常为重骑兵，相当于现代装甲部队）供紧急救援之用。通常入侵的异族都无法攻陷那些据点，因为他们缺乏攻城的能力。同时，由于缺乏适当的后动组织，他们又必须分散兵力去抢夺给养。于是拜占廷的机动兵力就会乘机反击，并把他们逐出界外。因为有要塞的掩护，再加上高速的行动，遂常能以寡敌众，以少胜多。[4]

军队的装备来源于军户自身，经济实力决定了只有富裕军户才能够装配骑兵的装备。所以骑兵就成为了一个贵族阶层。[5]在7世纪开始时大部分帝国轻骑兵来自蛮族民众。然而，莫里斯征兵花名册上却包括来自帝国安纳托利亚的伊苏利亚人和卡帕多西亚人，来自拜占廷巴尔干的伊利里亚人、亚美尼亚人、俘获的萨珊人，以及境外的匈人、保加尔人和伦巴德人。俘获的萨珊人被遣往西方，保加尔人分布在包括北非在内的众多地区。但是，希拉克略军队的核心是来自安纳托利亚的本都(Pontus)和伊苏利亚地区的说希腊语的人，尽管来自高加索的亚美尼亚人和格鲁吉亚盟友也存在。几乎所有的军官都是希腊人。[6]

六　总结

晚期罗马帝国面临着与以前不同的历史环境，帝国面临的不是扩张问题，而是生存问题，由于帝国领土、人口和经济资源的不断减少，帝国外部又面临蛮族大入侵的时代危机。这种完全不同的内外环境迫使帝国在各个方面发生了变化。西罗马帝国灭亡后，东罗马帝国继续面临着先前的困局，在这种情况下，生存成为了第一位的需要，帝国的体制都围绕这一主题而改变。拜占廷帝国的军队发生了巨大的变化。军队不得不修订了罗马帝国晚期的纵深防御战略，不得不改变了罗马军团的一系列战略战术以适应中古时代战争的要求。骑兵在军队中的重要性增强了，罗马帝国引以为豪的重装步兵下降到次要地位。

---

① David Nicolle Phd, *Romano-Byzantine Armies:4th-9th Centuries*, Osprey Publishing Ltd, 1992,p.8.

② 有关拜占廷帝国各个时期军队规模变化的统计见 Warren Treadgold, *Byzantium and its Army, 284-1081*, Stanford: Stanford University Press, 1995,pp.44-68.

③ Text, Translation, and Notes by George T. Dennis, *Three Byzantine Military Treatises*, Washington, D.C.: Dumbarton Oaks Research Library and Collection, 1985, pp.25-27.

④ 钮先钟：《西方战略思想史》，桂林：广西师范大学出版社2003年版，第66-67页。

⑤ David Nicolle Phd, *Romano-Byzantine Armies:4th-9th Centuries*, Osprey Publishing Ltd, 1992,p.15.

⑥ David Nicolle Phd, *Romano-Byzantine Armies:4th-9th Centuries*, Osprey Publishing Ltd, 1992,p.16.

在这个大变革时代，罗马－拜占廷帝国不得不被动的发生改变来适应环境的挑战。从戴克里先开始，到查士丁尼的军事变革都是这种被动改变的体现。这种变革既有军事方面，也有与军事制度相适应的其它方面的变革。为了解决军队的军饷问题，多个皇帝不得不进行变革。支付士兵的装备和费用一直是困扰军队和国家关系的重大问题。戴克里先实行分配制。在拜占廷帝国早期军队的供给方式既有实物供给又有货币供给。[1]到了阿纳斯塔修斯一世(Anastasius Ⅰ, 491–518)时期，他进行的财政改革首先就是废除了分配制，取而代之的是发给士兵装备津贴由士兵自己购买武器装备。[2]查士丁尼时代军队是以实物的方式或者是以货币的方式进行供给仍不稳定。一方面查士丁尼禁止士兵从纳税人那里要求和获得礼物，禁止要求获得在一个特定省份不存在的东西，禁止接受一笔现金支付代替各种物品的配给。[3]另一方面金钱作为军队装备的津贴在军队中仍旧使用。"士兵热爱贝利撒留因为他会用金钱来慰问受伤的士兵，把项链和手镯作为奖品赏赐给勇敢者，当士兵在战斗中失去马匹和弓箭时会立即得到补充（一种迹象表明士兵通常希望能够从国家那里得到现金津贴自己购买战马和武器）。"[4]但是经过查士丁尼时代的大肆挥霍，帝国的财力岌岌可危。到了莫里斯时期帝国出于财政困难企图取消津贴的做法因为东部军队的叛乱无果而终。在616年希拉克略把军费砍掉一半，虽然仍然像莫里斯统治时期那样供给货币津贴由士兵购买武器装备，但是减少了他们的收入使其只能够维持生计。[5]

如果考察4-7世纪大变革时代的军事发展状况，人们可以看出从戴克里先时代到查士丁尼时代是统治者面对军事危机和社会环境不得不进行的被动变革的时代，到了查士丁尼时代这种变革达到一个顶峰。此时的军队已经基本具备了成熟的拜占廷军队的特点。查士丁尼的大肆征伐是检验这种军事变革成就的实践活动。通过战争的考验，统治者不断审视军队的特点和不足。到了莫里斯统治时期统治者则根据这些实践的反馈信息进行主动的变革，这种变革更应该说是一种在前人基础上的完善。莫里斯改革的最大成就是将4世纪以来的军事变革理论化，上升为一种行之有效的制度。此后希拉克略进一步修订。因此从这个意义上说，希拉克略改革完成时期是军事意义上的大变革完成时期。这种拜占廷军事制度最终定型，为帝国在将近一千年的时间里屹立在欧亚大陆的中心立下了汗马功劳。这些改革都有它各自的特点，它们所确立的战略思想构成了拜占廷帝国军事战略的丰富内容。4-7世纪拜占廷帝国军事战略的内容既有君士坦丁大帝开创的纵深防御战略，又有贝利萨留推行的防御进攻性战略，同时也包含了莫里斯完善的守势吓阻战略。这些丰富的战略思想奠定了拜占廷军事战略的基础，奠定了帝国军事制度的基础。

---

① Warren Treadgold, *Byzantine and Its Army,284–1081*, Stanford University Press, 1995, p.179.

② Warren Treadgold, *Byzantine and Its Army,284–1081*, Stanford University Press, 1995, p.14,p.180.

③ Walter Emil Kaegi Jr., *Byzantine Military Unrest 471–843*, Adolf M. Hakkert–Publisher–Amsterdam, 1981,p.44.

④ Walter Emil Kaegi Jr., *Byzantine Military Unrest 471–843*, Adolf M. Hakkert–Publisher–Amsterdam, 1981,p.50.

⑤ Warren Treadgold, *Byzantine and Its Army,284–1081*, Stanford University Press, 1995, pp.19–20.

论拜占廷帝国对官办工厂的管理

毛欣欣 东北师范大学

摘要：为了满足帝国的财政与安全需求，以及皇帝与贵族的奢侈品需要，拜占廷帝国开办了为数众多的官办工厂，其中主要包括锻币工厂、军械制造工厂以及丝绸生产工厂。这些官办工厂的管理形式随帝国国力的强弱而变化。官办工厂在一定程度上保证了帝国的财政稳定与军械供应，但这种模式不利于推动社会生产的进步，很大程度上遏制了社会经济的生机与活力，这也是拜占廷帝国与西欧在中世纪晚期发展中出现巨大分野的根源之一。

关键词：官办工厂；锻币工厂；军械制造工厂；丝绸生产工厂

Abstract：In order to meet the fiscal and security needs, and the needs of emperor and nobilities, Byzantine Empire monopolized the most important manufactures of imperial factories. Imperial factories included mints, weapons manufacturing factories, and silk factories. Imperial factories reflected the variation of the imperial central autocratic system. The monopolies of imperial factories ensured the financial stability and weapon supply. But the monopoly prevented the progress of social production, which was the distinction about Byzantine Empire and Europe in the Middle Ages.

Keywords：imperial factories, mints, imperial factories for arms, imperial factories for silk textiles

三世纪危机以后，罗马帝国的社会经济趋于崩溃，工商业急剧衰落，手工业者大量失业，民生凋敝。为了恢复工商业生产秩序，戴克里先（Diocletianus，公元 284-305 年）当政之后，就开始实行城市经济的二元政策。即一方面加强对私人工商业的管制，另一方面在某些领域内采取国家垄断措施。[①]国家垄断的实质是指对于关系国家命脉的工商业，禁止私人经营，由国家直接垄断经营，即

---

① 厉以宁：《罗马—拜占廷经济史》（下编），北京：商务印书馆 2006 年版，第 491 页。

官办工厂①。然而，并没有确凿的证据能够证明在戴克里先之前官办工厂就已经存在。②显然，为了恢复帝国经济，戴克里先开创了国家直接经营工商业的官办工厂。395 年罗马帝国分裂之后，东罗马帝国继续实行戴克里先的经济政策。

官办工厂主要包括锻币工厂、军械制造工厂以及丝绸工厂，这些工厂关系到国家财政收入、国家安全以及皇室贵族的奢侈品需求。为了便于帝国中央政府能够直接控制和管理，官办工厂主要集中在君士坦丁堡。本文试图分析帝国对钱币锻造、军械制造和丝绸生产等三个方面的管理，探讨拜占廷帝国政府在工商业管理中的作用和影响，以及官办工厂这种生产模式的利弊得失。

一

3 世纪末，为了强化专制皇权，完善官僚政治，戴克里先改革了行省与财政制度，将原来 47个大的行省重新划分为 100 多个规模更小的行省，以分散地方势力，并在行省之上设置 12 个大区（dioces），由皇帝直接任命"大区总督（praetorian prefecture）"管理这些大区，大区总督直接受皇帝的控制。帝国的财税系统由"圣库伯爵（comes sacrarum largitionum）"、"皇产司伯爵（comes rei privatae）"和大区总督三元化的管理体系组成。③与此同时，戴克里先改革了罗马锻币工厂的管理，增加了锻币工厂的数量，并将锻币工厂设置于大区中，由帝国中央财政部门的最高官员圣库伯爵负责控制与管理。圣库伯爵向大区派遣专门的"圣库监察使（comes largitionum titulorum）"，负责管理本区的钱币锻造。圣库监察使在钱币锻造工序的每个环节（冶炼、洗涤、锻造）指派技术熟练的工头（praepositus monetae）负责指导生产，并在每个环节派遣专门的监督官（officinatores）监督生产。锻币工厂的劳工是奴隶，没有人身自由，不允许随便脱离锻币工厂，只有间接经过皇帝或直接经过圣库伯爵的允许，劳工才可以离开工厂，但不能带走家眷和财产。④

除此之外，皇帝将其巡行或战争驻扎地的锻币工厂交付于其随行的侍臣（comitatus），授予这些锻币工厂锻造金银钱币的权力，以供皇帝和随行人员所用，这些锻币工厂遂成为拥有锻造金银钱币特权的"御用锻币工厂"（comitatensian mint），这表明只有"御用锻币工厂"拥有锻造金银钱币的权力。如果驻扎地区没有锻币工厂，皇帝将临时设置一所"御用锻币工厂"。它们锻造的钱币拥有统一的标志，即"comitatensian"的缩写"COM"以标示其来自"御用锻币工厂"。⑤"御用锻币工厂"拥有专门的金匠（aurifices）从事锻造工作，由圣库伯爵直接负责管理，并受皇帝的庇护。"御用锻币工厂"的管理非常严格而苛刻，尼古拉斯·梅萨里特斯（Nicholas Mesarites）描述了帝国锻币工厂的工作情况："穿着黑色衣服的男人，他们的脸上和脚上都布满灰尘和汗水，他们不分昼夜地工作，

---

① "官办工厂"的英文是（imperial factories），也可翻译为"帝国工厂"，希腊文为"ergodosiα"，是由国家直接控制经营的"工厂"，此处的"工厂"与资本主义时代的"工厂"的概念不同，前者是由国家直接控制经营，且有奴隶身份的劳工，后者是现代意义上的大规模制造厂，有国家控制的，也由私人经营的，其工人为自由人。同时它也有别于中世纪的"工场"（workshops），罗马－拜占廷时期的"官办工厂"除了国家控制以外，还是一个封闭的、特定的生产场所，中世纪的"工场"是一个开放的场所。参见徐家玲：《早期拜占廷执事官职能探析》，《史学集刊》，2003 年第 4 期，第 56 页。

② [英]M. M. 波斯坦主编，钟和等译：《剑桥欧洲经济史》（第二卷，中世纪的贸易和工业），北京：人民出版社经济科学出版社 2003 年版，第 98 页。

③ 徐家玲：《早期拜占廷查查士丁尼时代研究》，长春：东北师范大学出版社 1998 年版，第 35－36,70 页。

④ C. H. V. Sutherland, eds., *The Roman Imperial Coinage, Vol. III*, London: Oxford University Press, 1984, pp. 22-23.

⑤ Hendy, Michael F., *Studies in the Byzantine Monetary Economy c. 300-1450*, Cambridge: Cambridge Unibersity Press, 1985, pp. 380-394.

在没有阳光的黑暗中不停地敲打着。"①这些"御用锻币工厂"不是固定在某一地区，而是伴随着皇帝及其随从人员进行转移。皇帝及其随从离开后，原锻币工厂锻造金银币的特权也将被收回。但在特殊时期，如帝国庆典之时，它们仍有锻造特殊的、纪念金币的权利。戴克里先时期这些金银锻币工厂主要存在于意大利半岛与非洲等地。

395年以后，由于东部帝国的皇帝很少离开首都，遂将"御用锻币工厂"固定于君士坦丁堡，垄断着帝国金银钱币的锻造，成为"帝国锻币工厂（moneta auri）"，仍由圣库伯爵负责监督管理，君士坦丁堡成为帝国锻造金银钱币的中心。②除此之外，君士坦丁堡也存在铜币锻造工厂，而其他地区的锻币工厂则主要锻造铜币，被称为"普通锻币工厂（moneta publica）"。5世纪中期，伴随着蛮族入侵和西罗马帝国的灭亡，西部的锻币工厂相继落入汪达尔人和东哥特人之手。帝国东部锻币工厂的数量也因蛮族的入侵而减少。498年，阿纳斯塔修斯一世（Anastasius I，491-518年在位）进行钱币改革，发行优质的铜币"弗里斯"（follis）以完善戴克里先和君士坦丁一世确立的货币体系，③这标志着拜占廷帝国开始使用不同于罗马帝国的钱币。6世纪中后期，查士丁尼一世（Justinian I，527-565年在位）对巴尔干、北非、意大利和西班牙部分地区再征服以后，收回了汪达尔人和东哥特人统治下的迦太基和拉文纳金银锻币工厂，允许其作为"帝国锻币工厂"的附属而继续存在。④显然，在查士丁尼统治时期，拜占廷帝国的锻币工厂数量增加了，这反映了拜占廷帝国国力的强盛。

7世纪，拜占廷帝国与波斯人和阿拉伯人之间相继爆发了旷日持久的战争，帝国失去了大片疆域，行省的锻币工厂遭到严重破坏。为解决国内危机，希拉克略一世（Heraclian I，610-641年在位）于610年至615年间在塞浦路斯、伊苏利亚建立临时的锻币工厂，生产铜币以满足军队的需要，但因国力衰微，这些临时开办的锻币工厂很快关闭了。⑤因此，拜占廷帝国的锻币工厂仍然主要集中在君士坦丁堡，这种状况一直持续至11世纪。这一时期，除了位于君士坦丁堡大皇宫（Great Palace）的帝国锻币工厂以外，在君士坦丁堡的其他地区还存在一个专门生产铜币的工厂。⑥长期的对外战争与锻币工厂的减少造成了严重的财政危机。为了缓解危机，帝国政府加强了对战争中幸存下来的锻币工厂的管理，所有的锻币工厂皆由国家中央财政机构直接管理。而这一时期拜占廷帝国财政机构也出现了显著的变化，发展起多个独立的、具有不同职能的财政机构（sekreta）。相应地，钱币锻造的管理也分别由这些不同的财政机构来负责，其中皇产司（eidikon）负责贵金属的熔炼，国库（vestiarion）负责管理钱币的锻造，财库（sakellion）负责监管钱币的重量和质量。11世纪财政改革以后，皇产司消失了，12世纪，财库也停止工作，锻币工厂开始由国库单独负责管理。⑦锻币工厂管理机构的变化，一方面体现了帝国的财政状况，另一方面也体现了不同时期皇权和国力的强弱变化。

1092年，阿列克修斯一世（Alexius I，1081-1118年在位）进行财政改革，在塞萨洛尼基

---

① Cecile Morrisson, "Byzantine Money: Its Production and Circulation", in A. Laiou (ed.-in-chief), *The Economic History of Byzantium*, Washington: Dumbarton Oaks Research Library and Collection, 2002, p. 916.

② Hendy, Michael F., *Studies in the Byzantine Monetary Economy c.* 300-1450, Cambridge: Cambridge University Press, 1985, p. 398.

③ [南斯拉夫]乔治·奥斯特洛格尔斯基著、陈志强译：《拜占廷帝国》，西宁：青海人民出版社2006年版，第47页。

④ Hendy, Michael F., *Studies in the Byzantine Monetary Economy c. 300-1450*, Cambridge: Cambridge University Press, 1985, pp. 399-400.

⑤ Cecile Morrisson, "Byzantine Money: Its Production and Circulation", in A. Laiou (ed.-in-chief), *The Economic History of Byzantium*, Washington: Dumbarton Oaks Research Library and Collection, 2002, p. 913.

⑥ Hendy, M., "Aspects of Coin Production and Fiscal Administration in the Late Roman and Early Byzantine Period," *NC (1972)*, p. 131.

⑦ Hendy, Michael F., *Studies in the Byzantine Monetary Economy c. 300-1450*, Cambridge: Cambridge University Press, 1985, p. 433.

（Thessalonica）新开办两个铜币锻造工厂，以补充君士坦丁堡的锻币工厂。随着地方贵族实力的增强，少数贵族也开始建立私人锻币工厂，如塞浦路斯的伊萨克·科穆宁（Isaac Komnenos）和特拉比松（Trebizond）的加伏拉斯（Gabras）家族等。有资料显示，12世纪，君士坦丁堡的钱币兑换商将他们的工作场地——君士坦丁广场，提供给私人作为锻造钱币的场所。其后不久，钱币兑换商也开始参与锻造钱币。[1]国家对锻币工厂的垄断经营被打破，作为官办工厂的补充，私人锻造钱币有了合法性，并一直存在到1453年。不过，帝国的钱币主要还是来源于君士坦丁堡的官办锻币工厂。

在拜占廷帝国历史中，国家对锻币工厂的管理具有一定的连续性，与罗马帝国管理钱币生产不同，拜占廷帝国以皇帝为中心的中央政府对钱币锻造控制的权力没有授予地方。虽然在12世纪以后允许私人有部分钱币锻造权，但整体而言，拜占廷帝国的钱币锻造主要掌握在官办工厂手中，而官办工厂的控制权始终属于以皇权为中心的帝国政府。这种状况反映了拜占廷帝国的中央集权体制，而关系帝国安危的军械制造则更加鲜明地反映了这一点。

二

罗马帝国晚期，皇帝非常重视军械物资的供应，国家控制着军械制造。因为军队是国家安全的保障，而军械制造又是保证军队战斗力的重要因素。同时，国家通过控制军械物资以更好的控制军队。为了保证军械物资的供应，帝国政府以税收的方式征收军队中所需的各种物资，如军人服装、马匹、以及制造军械的原料等，并雇佣劳工对征收的原料进行加工，制造各种武器，之后将这些武器售予士兵。[2]

拜占廷帝国早期，随着皇权的加强，国家对军械制造的控制更为强化。国家的财政部门负责征收和储存用于制造各种军械的材料，如皇产司负责管理铁与木材等材料的储存；国库负责海军物资的储存；军械长官（archon tou armamentou）经营管理军械工厂，负责生产各种防御性与攻击性的武器，将生产的武器存入军械库。[3]士兵可以用国家发放的薪酬购买这些武器，在钱币不足的情况下，士兵也可以用实物交换武器。贸易税收官可以将这些实物出售或自己保留。[4]由此可见，国家控制着武器的整个生产和流通过程。

为了使得军队能够及时获得军械物资，避免军队物资供应不足；同时为了节省运输的费用，国家在各地军队附近建造了许多官办军械工厂。在罗马法令中，有15个军械工厂遍布整个帝国东部。[5]这些官办军械工厂直接由帝国中央政府的控制。官办军械工厂的劳工大多为奴隶和罪犯，他们以劳动换取一定的实物报酬。国家对他们进行强制管理和监督，监督官员在劳工胳膊上打下烙印，以防止他们逃跑，且法律对窝藏逃犯者给予严厉惩罚。但由于他们的工作是为军队服务，被视为是一种执行军务的行为，因此，他们有时也被作为军事化的武装部队，比其他官办工厂的劳工地位相对高一些。[6]

---

① Klaus Peter Matschke, "Mining", in A. Laiou (ed.-in-chief), *The Economic History of Byzantium*, Washington: Dumbarton Oaks Research Library and Collection, 2002, p. 120.

② Haldon, John, *Warfare State and Society in the Byzantine World 565-1204*, London: Taylor & Francis e-Library, 2003, p.140

③ Haldon, John, *Warfare State and Society in the Byzantine World 565-1204*, London: Taylor & Francis e-Library, 2003, p. 141.

④ Warren Treadgold, *Byzantium and Its Army, 284-1081*, California: Stanford University Press, 1995, p. 181.

⑤ [英]爱德华·吉本著、席代岳译：《罗马帝国衰亡史》（第2卷），长春：吉林出版集团责任有限公司2008年版，第35页。

⑥ [英]M. M. 波斯坦主编，钟和等译：《剑桥欧洲经济史》（第二卷，中世纪的贸易和工业），北京：经济科学出版社2003年版，第100页。

6世纪中期至7世纪中期，帝国遭受了瘟疫，并且与波斯人以及阿拉伯人之间爆发了长期的战争。因此，帝国人口锐减，国力严重削弱。帝国各地的军械制造工厂消失殆尽，军械制造转移至君士坦丁堡，君士坦丁堡成为拜占廷帝国重要的武器生产中心，在皇城内设有"希腊火"制造作坊，在修道院内也建立冶铁高炉，[①]由皇帝任命的御林军长官（spatharios）管理君士坦丁堡的军械制造工厂。[②]

7世纪末至9世纪初，帝国处于恢复期，国家没有足够的财政来供应军队的需要，士兵的薪酬减少了。为了解决士兵的物资供应问题，也为了增强帝国的军事力量，国家开始设置军区制度。在军区制下，军队要长期驻守在某一地区，每位士兵则分配到一块份地，他们可以建立家庭，世代耕种这块份地。当战争来临时，他们必须立即上阵杀敌，并世代为国从军。在军区内，军事首长的权力高于一切。[③]在军区制度下，士兵可以从其土地上获得食物和其他生活资料，如果是骑兵，还要负责饲养自己的马匹，并且需要购买武器和服装。这一时期，国家甚至没有足够的财力来支付士兵的薪酬。有资料显示，659年之前，士兵的薪酬是10诺米斯玛[④]，659—840年之间，仅仅是5诺米斯玛。[⑤]因此，士兵的薪酬不足以购买武器，军队中武器变得非常缺乏，出现了士兵偷窃武器的现象。为保证士兵的武器配备，国家对武器生产的管理更加严格。利奥三世时期颁布法令规定偷窃士兵武器和马匹的人，将被处以严重惩罚。在继承其父亲的武器之前，士兵通常要受到审查，如果已经拥有一定量的武器，其将失去武器的继承权。由于骑兵的武器装备包括马匹与盔甲，价值昂贵，因此国家对骑兵的审查更为严格。[⑥]

随着军区制的发展，9世纪以后地方军事力量逐渐增强，对武器的需求也日益增加。为此，国家放松了对军械制造的垄断，允许地方军事长官组织地方工匠制造各种武器，如长矛、箭头、弓和盾牌等，[⑦]以增加武器和军备。军械制造的主体变得多元，这促进了军械制造技术的提高，工匠的劳动环境也有所改善。国家对军械制造的垄断被打破了。但是，国家军械工厂仍是集中提供大批军械的中心，如塞萨洛尼基军械工厂接到中央命令，要求提供20万支箭、3000支长矛和"尽可能多的"盾牌。[⑧]

12世纪以后，随着地方军事力量的增强，军事贵族势力发展起来。为限制地方军事贵族的实力，皇帝削减了军队的经费，"扩大地方行政首脑的权力，以减少来自军队的政治危险。"[⑨]拜占廷军队遭到削弱，本国士兵数量越来越少，雇佣兵成为帝国主要依靠的军事力量。与此同时，帝国遭受周边各族力量的入侵而逐渐衰落，无力支持雇佣兵的各种费用，遂将武器制造其转交于各地军队，由各地军事长官自行解决士兵的武器装备。至此，国家完全失去了对军械制造的控制与管理。对军械制造控制的逐渐弱化在一定程度上反映了中央集权的式微，也标志着拜占廷帝国的国势日渐衰微。

---

① 陈志强：《拜占廷帝国史》，北京：商务印书馆2006年版，第448页。

② Gilbert Dagron, "The Urban Economy, Seventh-Twelfth Centuries", in A. Laiou (ed.-in-chief), *The Economic History of Byzantium*, Washington: Dumbarton Oaks Research Library and Collection, 2002, p.430.

③ 徐家玲：《拜占廷文明》，北京：人民出版社2006年版，第222页。

④ "诺米斯玛"，希腊文为"νόμισμα"，它是拜占廷时期的一种金币，与罗马帝国时期的金币"索里达"（solidus）等值，1诺米斯玛等于1/72磅金子，等于4.5克。

⑤ Warren Treadgold, *Byzantium and Its Army, 284-1081*, California: Stanford University Press, 1995, p. 182.

⑥ Warren Treadgold, *Byzantium and Its Army, 284-1081*, California: Stanford University Press, 1995, p. 181.

⑦ Haldon, John, *Warfare State and Society in the Byzantine World 565-1204*, London: Taylor & Francis e-Library, 2003, p. 141.

⑧ 陈志强：《拜占廷帝国史》，北京：商务印书馆2006年版，第448页。

⑨ 陈志强：《拜占廷帝国史》，北京：商务印书馆2006年版，第440-441页。

三

6世纪中期之前，拜占廷帝国的生丝主要来自东方的中国，由波斯商人在缴纳一定关税后转运至君士坦丁堡。负责进口生丝的拜占廷帝国官员贸易税收官从波斯商人手中收购生丝，然后将上好的生丝留给国家官办丝绸工厂，将普通的生丝卖与国内私人生产者，并有权保留生丝交易中获得的部分利润，其余部分上缴国家。[①]这一时期，拜占廷帝国的丝绸纺织业由官办工厂、私人丝绸作坊以及大贵族家庭手工作坊三种形式，其中前两种是主要的丝绸生产方式。而大贵族的家庭手工作坊主要集中在庄园中，由家庭奴隶生产丝绸，其中生产的极少的上好丝绸送与皇帝，少量剩余投入市场。但他们不以出售为目的，主要是满足自身需要。[②]官办工厂生产的丝绸不进入市场，专门为皇室、贵族及上层官僚提供丝绸制品，"最好的锦缎给皇帝和皇后做衣服，或者可能作为礼物送给外朝官员，其他的则给宫廷贵族或行政官员的上层人士做制服。"[③]可见，质量好的丝绸成为皇室、贵族专门享用的奢侈品。因此，皇室和官僚贵族居住的君士坦丁堡成为官办丝绸工厂的主要城市。

由于生丝主要依靠进口，生产的丝绸稀少而昂贵，皇室贵族希望控制丝绸为其所有，因此试图将私人手工作坊排挤出丝绸生产领域，使官办工厂能够垄断丝绸生产。查士丁尼皇帝实现了皇室贵族的这一愿望，他通过提高生丝进口贸易的关税，使得私人手工作坊高价购买生丝，同时又要按照国家规定的原价格出售丝绸，私人手工作坊逐渐入不敷出，最后不得不退出市场。但官办工厂却不受这一政策的影响。[④]基于此，官办工厂逐渐控制了国内所有的丝绸生产。

丝绸官办工厂由圣库伯爵负责管理，皇帝对其进行监督。[⑤]圣库伯爵将官办工厂依据丝绸生产的程序分为三个部分：纺织与裁剪、染色、刺绣与镶金边。[⑥]女工负责技术含量较低的生产环节，拥有熟练技术的男性劳工负责技术含量高的工作。[⑦]圣库伯爵设置专门的官员严密监督丝绸生产的每个环节，为防止向外部泄漏丝绸生产技术，监督官员在劳工胳膊上打上烙印标志其身份，以限制其人身自由。[⑧]官办工厂的劳工身份大多为奴隶，他们不得随便脱离其工厂，他们的职业世代相传，即职业世袭制。如365年在米兰颁布一条法令：任何自由出身的妇女只要与纺织奴隶结婚就必须成为织工，除非她在结婚前公布了有关其地位的详细情况。[⑨]

官办工厂垄断丝绸生产以后，大量私人作坊倒闭，丝绸工人失业，许多丝绸生产地区经济衰落。帝国境内市场上流通的丝绸数量减少，价格飞涨，越来越少的丝绸不能满足皇室贵族的需要。而且，6世纪中叶，生丝生产技术传入拜占廷帝国，使得越来越多的个体也希望生产丝绸。因此，国家开始放松对丝绸生产的垄断，允许私人开设丝绸手工作坊进行生产，以解决丝绸产量的不足。虽然私

---

① Nicolas Oikonomide, "Silk Trade and Production in Byzantium from the Sixth to the Ninth Century: the Seals of Kommerkiarioi", *Dumbarton Oaks Papers*, Vol. 40 (1986), p.38.

② Gilbert Dagron, "The Urban Economy, Seventh-Twelfth Centuries", in A. Laiou (ed.-in-chief), *The Economic History of Byzantium*, Washington: Dumbarton Oaks Research Library and Collection, 2002, p. 442.

③ [英]M. M. 波斯坦主编，钟和等译：《剑桥欧洲经济史》（第二卷，中世纪的贸易和工业），北京：经济科学出版社2003年版，第129页。

④ [美]汤普逊著、耿淡如译：《中世纪经济社会史》（上册），北京：商务印书馆1997年版，第209页。

⑤ [英]M. M. 波斯坦主编，钟和等译：《剑桥欧洲经济史》（第二卷，中世纪的贸易和工业），北京：经济科学出版社2003年版，第98页。

⑥ [英]M. M. 波斯坦主编，钟和等译：《剑桥欧洲经济史》（第二卷，中世纪的贸易和工业），北京：经济科学出版社2003年版，第128页。

⑦ Robert Sabatino Lopez, "Silk Industry in the Byzantine Empire", *Speculum*, Vol. 20, No. 1 (Jan., 1945), p. 7.

⑧ [英]M. M. 波斯坦主编，钟和等译：《剑桥欧洲经济史》（第二卷，中世纪的贸易和工业），北京：经济科学出版社2003年版，第100页。

⑨ [英]M. M. 波斯坦主编，钟和等译：《剑桥欧洲经济史》（第二卷，中世纪的贸易和工业），北京：经济科学出版社2003年版，第128页。

人手工作坊获得了生产的许可，然而由于养蚕和抽丝技术复杂而精密，国内生丝的生产仍然处于初级阶段，不能满足官僚贵族的需要，国家仍然需要进口大量生丝以维持贵族对奢侈丝绸服装的需求，而且官办丝绸工厂在国内丝绸生产中仍占主导地位。①

7世纪时期，阿拉伯人侵占了埃及和叙利亚等行省，拜占廷帝国的疆域缩小，丝绸官办工厂也逐渐向西北转移，"君士坦丁堡成为帝国丝绸生产的集中地区"②。这一时期，君士坦丁堡丝绸官办工厂的管理发生变化，首先，随着国家财政机构的变化，官办工厂的管理权由圣库伯爵转移至皇产司伯爵手中；③其次，由于早期的职业世袭制度，劳工被禁止脱离工厂，这使得丝绸工厂的劳工数量逐渐增多，越来越多的无专业技能的人员参杂其中，官办丝绸工厂中劳工的生产技能参差不齐。为了提高官办丝绸工厂的效率，希拉克略一世重新制定法律规范丝绸工厂的管理，精简劳工人员，将原来劳工的世袭制转变为选拔制，管理官员可以辞退官办工厂中的劳工，劳工也可以申请退出官办工厂，而想进入官办丝绸工厂的劳动者要经过熟练技工和相关官员的审查，符合条件的人员才可以进入丝绸工厂劳动。这样，"丝绸工厂的劳动由最初的强制义务转变为一种特权，国家亦不再强迫劳工进入丝绸工厂，而是对希望进入工厂的候选人进行限制。"④官办工厂对劳工有了一定的技术要求，劳工的身份逐渐发生了变化，他们有了一定的自由和地位。国家对丝绸官办工厂控制强度减小了，管理更为灵活有效。希拉克略一世制定的关于丝绸官办工厂管理的政策一直持续至10世纪，官办工厂中的劳工逐渐变成为具有娴熟技术的工匠，而且丝绸工匠的身份也成为一种荣誉的象征。

9世纪以后，随着拜占廷帝国官僚体系不断膨胀，宫廷和上流社会对丝绸的需求量不断增加，丝绸官办工厂的供给不能满足宫廷贵族的需求。同时，私人丝绸生产规模也随着养蚕技术的发展而得以扩大。为顺应这一形势，帝国放宽了私人开设丝绸作坊的限制，缩小了官办丝绸工厂生产的范围，管办工厂只负责生产皇室贵族所穿戴的紫色丝绸和带有金银刺绣的丝绸，法律严禁私人作坊生产上述丝绸，即便"丝绸的颜色为接近紫色的红色，制造者也要向主管官员汇报，否则将受到惩罚。"⑤因此，虽然官办丝绸工厂生产范围缩小了，但国家对其管理却没有放松。

纵观拜占廷帝国丝绸生产的发展，君士坦丁堡一直是帝国丝绸生产的重要城市，国家非常重视对君士坦丁堡丝绸生产的管理。形成这种格局的原因更多是出于政治的考量，而非经济或市场的因素。官办工厂对丝绸生产的垄断，不仅阻碍了帝国丝绸生产技术的进步，而且严重制约了管办工厂自身的生产效率。希拉克略一世的改革改善了官办工厂的劳工管理，打破固有的世袭制度，引入竞争，提高了官办工厂整体的生产水平。及至后来，帝国为了应对丝绸供需失衡的局面，放开了对私人开办丝绸作坊的限制，这弥补了官办工厂生产的不足。

拜占廷帝国对钱币、军械、丝绸等工厂的控制与管理，是为了满足帝国的财政与安全需求，以及皇帝与贵族的奢侈品需要。这些官办工厂的兴衰直接反映了帝国的国势，帝国兴盛之时，官办工厂也能够得到很好地发展，而且国家对它们的控制与管理也非常严格，完全排斥私人开办生产同类产品的作坊。帝国处于动乱或危机时期，官办工厂也相应地会出现衰退的境况，私人作坊就有了生存与成长的空间，这在一定程度上能够促进社会生产的进步。然而，处于动荡与危机之下的私人作

---

① Anna Muthesius, "Essential Processes, Looms, and Technical Aspects of the Production of Silk Textiles", in A. Laiou (ed.-in-chief), *The Economic History of Byzantium*, Washington: Dumbarton Oaks Research Library and Collection, 2002, p. 159.

② Nicolas Oikonomide, "Silk Trade and Production in Byzantium from the Sixth to the Ninth Century: the Seals of Kommerkiarioi", *Dumbarton Oaks Papers*, Vol. 40 (1986), p. 44.

③ Robert Sabatino Lopez, "Silk Industry in the Byzantine Empire", *Speculum, Vol. 20*, No. 1 (Jan., 1945), p. 7.

④ Robert Sabatino Lopez, "Silk Industry in the Byzantine Empire", *Speculum, Vol. 20*, No. 1 (Jan., 1945), p. 1.

⑤ Leo VI, *The Book of the Eparch*, Freshfield, E. H., trans. & notes, London: Variorum Reprints, 1970, p. 240.

坊又很难具备持续发展的条件，这就是在帝国中央政府与其控制的官办工厂夹缝之中，私人作坊生存与发展面临的两难境地。整体而言，官办工厂是帝国专制皇权的一种体现，国家对官办工厂的垄断经营，在一定程度上保证了帝国的财政稳定与军械供应，但这种模式不利于推动社会生产的进步，很大程度上遏制了民间社会的生机与活力。因此，拜占廷帝国官办工厂这种看起来刚性的生产结构实质上很脆弱，因为其存在的基础是源于帝国的全面掌控，缺乏内在的生命力，即无法实现持续再生产的机制。不仅如此，官办工厂的长期而刚性的存在也扼杀了民间生产的活力，这也是拜占廷帝国与西欧在中世纪晚期的发展中出现巨大分野的根源之一。

试论克尔特教会特点

苏 静 太原科技大学

摘要：克尔特教会，作为基督教传播过程中的一个本土化例证，是拉丁文化、基督教文化与爱尔兰克尔特文化的综合产物。在特定的地理环境和历史条件下，克尔特教会形成了与罗马天主教会有所区别的，如以修道院为核心，极富宣教热情，个人色彩深厚等特点。

关键词：克尔特教会；基督教；爱尔兰；英国

Abstract： Renate Celt Church, as a local example of Christianity propagation, is Latin, Christian culture of Ireland Celt integrated product of culture. In the specific geographical and historical conditions, Celt formation and the Roman Catholic Church will differ, such as monasteries as the core, enrich the missionary passion, deep personal and so on.

Keywords： Celt Church, Christian, Ireland, the United Kingdom

克尔特教会，顾名思义是区别于罗马教会的一种含有克尔特文化因素的基督教组织形式。这一名称随着爱尔兰传教士的足迹所至，也适用于苏格兰、威尔士和布列塔尼亚的教会。作为基督教传播过程中一个很典型的本土化例证，克尔特教会是拉丁文化、基督教文化与爱尔兰克尔特文化的综合产物，而其产生得益于当时当地特定的历史文化条件。与不列颠相比，爱尔兰在中世纪早期拥有相对较为隔绝的自然地理环境，使强大的罗马帝国和英勇善战的盎格鲁—撒克逊人都对此处鞭长莫及。相对安定的爱尔兰成了战乱时期人们的避难所，同时也成为克尔特本土文化的保留之地。当罗马的统治崩溃，盎格鲁—撒克逊人蜂拥而至移居于不列颠英格兰后，爱尔兰便与欧陆失去了联系，在一段相当长的时期内形成了一个较为闭塞的空间，而传入此地的基督教也就很难与欧陆和罗马教会互传消息，这种情形持续了近一个世纪，于是爱尔兰基督教拥有了一段相当长的独立发展的时期。

没有了罗马教廷的指导和各种条条框框，帕特里克及其后继者们并未变得无所是从。他们一面遵循着基督教最基本的信条和规制，一面又依据当时当地的实际情况，对某些习俗规定作出了让步。这显然与奥古斯丁在不列颠英格兰传教时的情况大不相同。比德的《英吉利教会史》中引用了大量的奥古斯丁在创建不列颠教会时与教皇格雷戈里的来往信件内容。这些信件所涉及的内容，大到主教的权限和如何对待当地宗教信仰等重大事情，小到怎样处理偷窃教会财产的小偷以及教徒们的各种生活细节，教皇都对奥古斯丁作了非常细致的解释说明[1]。不仅如此，教皇还会从千里迢迢的罗马寄来象征着教廷权威的物品，诸如披肩之类，同时，也会致信给邻近地区的主教要求他们协助奥古斯丁的工作。由此可见，罗马教会与各地教会的关系是非常紧密的，一个地区教会的建立一般都是在教廷的严格指导下进行的。然而历史给予了爱尔兰不一样的机遇，这也是克尔特教会得以形成的一个重要条件。

另一个重要条件是克尔特文化因素在爱尔兰的根深蒂固。关于克尔特文化在爱尔兰的积累和延续的历史因由在本文中已多次提及。无论是遍布乡村田野的神祇，还是身处高位与王室过从甚密的督伊德祭司，亦或备受人尊崇的知识阶层"菲利"，处处都留下了克尔特文化的烙印。在这种情形下，虔诚的教士们不得不入乡随俗，以当地人可以接受的方式传播基督的福音。在这样的历史背景下，克尔特教会终于在爱尔兰成长为一种有别于罗马教会的颇具特色的教会组织形式，而它的特别之处主要表现在以下几个方面：

一 以修道院为核心，强调隐修主义

克尔特教会在组织形式上实行一套与罗马教会不同的修道院制度，即不是以主教教区为准则，而是以修道院为核心，建立修道院管区。这种修道院制度可以追溯至公元1、2世纪时，一些为了逃避宗教迫害而逃到埃及的基督徒，在埃及严酷的沙漠之地所过的社团生活。到4世纪，曾为罗马士兵的帕科米乌(Pachomius，约290—340)建立了第一座修道院，并建立起一套管理机制。他让僧侣们象士兵一样，大约每40个人组成一个团体，并让他们遵守各种规定。这些规定非常细致，涉及日常生活的方方面面，如每天祈祷的次数、进餐的时间及数量和睡眠的时间。[2]与早期埃及相比，克尔特教会以修道院院长为中心的管理模式更为严谨。[3]一些远离城市的大修道院，集中于如艾奥纳和林第斯凡(Lindsifarne)这样的岛屿上，从这里向爱尔兰各地以及不列颠英格兰，甚至于欧陆派出传教士。这些传教士在各地又建立修道院，后来建立的修道院又从属于原先的大修道院。如此以来，大修道院的院长便拥有了教会的司法权，有权对整个地区的百姓进行管理，而主教由修道院培养和派出，作为修道院的一员，自然也就归院长管辖。这一点是克尔特教会与罗马教会最大的不同。

在内部管理和信仰上，克尔特教会与不列颠教会相比更强调隐修主义。

一座大修道院往往又是一个自给自足的经济单位，在这里所有的生活必需品大多都由僧侣们自己生产。在具体的管理细则上，每个修道院都有不同的规定，有些非常严厉。无论宽严，僧侣们的生活都是非常艰苦的，所有的时间除了睡觉吃饭以外，大多用于劳作，然后就是祈祷。当然，僧侣中也会有一部分分离出来，专门从事抄写经书的工作，这在修道院中是受人尊敬的工作。这种单调简朴、严格苛刻的生活方式，为克尔特教会培养出了许多品行优秀的教士，从而为爱尔兰基督教赢得很高的荣誉。

在这种远离尘世的生活中，爱尔兰的僧侣们逐渐在由来已久的隐修主义之中加入了尊重自然的成分。[4]这很显然带有克尔特文化的痕迹。"对爱尔兰的凯尔特人来说，迷信的世界和自然的天地是不可分的"，[5]对于大自然的敬畏，充斥于社会生活的各个层面，大到部族国家之间的战争议和、小

---

[1] 比德：《英吉利教会史》，陈维振，周清民译，商务印书馆1997年版，第47-82页。

[2] Henry Mayr-Harting, *The Coming of Christianity of Anglo-Saxon England*, The Pennsylvania State University Press, 1991, p.79.

[3] Ibid, p. 82.

[4] 参见 Henry Mayr-Harting, *The Coming of Christianity of Anglo-Saxon England*, The Pennsylvania State University Press, 1991. 著者认为"爱尔兰（教会）的一个最为引人注目的特性，就是他们对自然的敏感。"(p.88)

[5] 时代—生活图书公司编著：《祭司与王制·凯尔特人的爱尔兰》，第15页．

到农家的婚丧嫁娶，春耕秋收。自然界的所有事物，从高山大河到某一口水井都由各自的神灵守护。时至今日爱尔兰在世人的眼中依然是精灵所居住的一片葱郁之地。而在爱尔兰占据统治地位的督伊德教也是"一种仪式严重的信仰，植根于对自然界的崇敬"①。

基督教在传入爱尔兰以后，无论从组织形式上，还是神学思想上，都与原先有所不同。应该说一方面是爱尔兰政治地理上的分隔林立，以及与欧陆和罗马教会的疏离，促成了克尔特教会所特有的以修道院为核心的管理模式；另一方面，积蕴多年、精致发达的克尔特文化，也一点一点地渗入到了基督教文化之中。虽然最终爱尔兰本身所有宗教、语言等文化都为基督教文化所代替，但克尔特教会的存在却将这些文化的很多因素保留了下来，并将它们融入到基督教中，从而成为文化交流融合的一个很好的例证。

二 极富宣教热情

大规模传教活动是普世宗教的共同特征，基督教自出现伊始，其传教活动就一直未曾间断。但相对于不列颠的基督教会而言，爱尔兰的克尔特教会作为一个地方教会，在没有罗马教廷的指示下，以自身的努力四处传教，其足迹遍及英国，甚至于欧陆。

克尔特教会的宣教热情，在科伦巴和艾丹 (Aidan) 的身上体现得非常明显。前者将克尔特教会从爱尔兰带至不列颠，并在不列颠北部建立根据地；后者则将克尔特教会继续向南传播，其中最重要的成果是诺森伯利亚的皈依。②由于这个国家在公元 7、8 世纪时是不列颠的霸主，因而对基督教的传播起到了非常重要的作用。在诺森伯利亚的影响下，一向桀骜难驯的麦西亚皈依了基督教③，埃塞克斯也恢复了放弃多年的基督教信仰④。至此，不列颠的诺森伯利亚、麦西亚、埃塞克斯，以及苏格兰、爱尔兰的大部分地区都信奉了基督教。很显然，克尔特教会在古代英国的宣教事业上，与同时期的罗马不列颠教会相比更为成功。

克尔特教会不仅仅只是在不列颠和爱尔兰传教，有时候他们中间的一些人也会离开这里，到欧洲大陆去建立修道院。比德就曾提到一位名叫富尔萨的僧侣。富尔萨 (Fusra/Fuseus)，出身于爱尔兰贵族家庭，在本地颇具声望。他在 631—634 年间带领一批信徒到东盎格鲁传教，当时的国王西格伯特 (Sigbert the Learn，631—634 年在位) 赐予他一块土地，他便在这里修建了一座修道院。这座修道院备受王亲贵族们的青睐，在他们的扶持下，修道院的规模迅速扩大。富尔萨的传教工作进展得很顺利，此后，他便将修道院交给跟随他的僧侣管理，自己则过起了隐居的生活。这种情况一直持续到东盎格鲁受到麦西亚的进攻⑤，局势动荡不安。富尔萨遂离开东盎格鲁，前往欧洲大陆的法兰克

---

① 时代一生活图书公司编著：《祭司与王制·凯尔特人的爱尔兰》，第 27 页。
② 诺森伯利亚皈依基督教的过程曾出现过反复，这种情况在当时很常见，该国首次信奉基督教是第二位国王爱德文在位时期 (Edwin，617 — 633 年在位)。诺森伯利亚的第四位国王奥斯瓦尔德 (Oswald，634 — 641 年在位)，是第一位国王埃塞尔弗里思之子。当第二位国王爱德文继承王位后，奥斯瓦尔德和他的兄弟们一起被流放，"住在苏格兰人和皮克特人中间"，即不列颠北部的苏挤兰地区。在这里，他和他的兄弟们一起接受了克尔特教会的洗礼和教育，爱德文死后，他们回到了诺森伯利亚并先后取得了王位，也将克尔特教会带入了诺森伯利亚。奥斯瓦尔德为王后，他便从爱尔兰邀请艾丹来当本国主教。
③ 麦西亚的皈依：到公元 7 世纪时，随着诺森伯利亚势力的增长，麦西亚的威名大不如前。到品达 (Peada，655 — 658 年在位) 即位时，麦西亚已基本处于诺森伯利亚控制之下。品达向奥斯维 (Oswy，651 — 671 年在位) 请求联姻，欲娶他的女儿阿尔奇弗莱德 (Alchfled) 为妻，以此为契机，品达被要求接受基督教。653 年，品达及其随从首先在诺森伯利亚皈依了基督教，然后他回国后，基督教便随之传入了麦西亚。
④ 埃塞克斯，首次皈依基督教是在其国王萨伯特 (Sabert，约 600 年一约 617 年在位) 时期。萨伯特死后，信仰荒废，主教被驱逐。到"良善的"西格伯特 (Sigbert the Good，653 年前一约 657 年在位) 即位，他与诺森伯利亚国王奥斯维是好友，两人来往频繁。在奥斯维的影响下，西格伯特最终接受了洗礼，仪式由主教菲南 (Finan) 主持。
⑤ 公元 634 年左右，麦西亚国王彭达率兵攻入东盎格鲁，西格伯特和其继任安纳先后被杀，国家一片混乱。

王国。在法兰克，富尔萨受到当地贵族上层的欢迎，在此修建了一座修道院，并最终逝世于此。由此可见，克尔特教会不但在不列颠和爱尔兰地区影响深远，在欧陆的法兰克也颇受尊崇。

当然，除了以上所提到的几位主要传教人士之外，爱尔兰基督教在各地传教的成功还应归功于众多克尔特教会僧侣孜孜不倦的努力。仅仅在《英吉利教会史》所提及的爱尔兰教士就有很多位，而没有在历史上留下姓名的僧侣就更是不计其数了。

三　重视学术文化

基督教是注重文本记录的宗教。在中世纪，它是保存文化遗产，推动文化发展的中坚力量，克尔特教会完全承袭了这一传统，并将它发扬光大。同时它还从爱尔兰的本土宗教，如督伊德教中，汲取了富有特色的文化气息，如前文所提到的，督伊德教的祭司们在爱尔兰社会中享有很高的地位，他们除了从事宗教活动外，还身兼教师、学者、法官、医生、天文学家等职。当他们作为一种旧宗教的代表，从爱尔兰逐渐消失之后，他们的种种职能却被基督教徒和学者们继承了下来。克尔特教会自形成之初，就在文化学术方面享有盛名。不管是以科伦巴扬名的艾奥纳岛，还是菲南建造林迪斯凡修道院的法恩岛，都在建成后成为古代英国的文化学术中心。慕名而来的人们蜂拥而至，到这些远离尘世的岛屿上学习、修行。众多优秀的人才汇聚于此，再加上学识渊博的导师，以及既锻炼身体又陶冶情操的周边环境，克尔特教会的修道院培养出很多品行皆优的教士和学者，如著名的艾丹、埃格伯特。同时，这里还出产了很多制作精良的宗教书籍和图画，为世人所瞩目。

四　个人传统色彩浓厚

与罗马基督教会相比，克尔特教会的个人传统色彩更为浓厚。

这一点首先是由克尔特教会的修道院制度所决定的。到各地去传教的主教，都是由修道院培养，并由院长派遣的。每到一地，主教们就会将他们在原先修道院中所学到的一切，运用到自己新建的修道院中。所以，从这一点上来讲，克尔特教会中的规章制度，生活习惯，都是由上一代人言传身教而来的。

因此对于克尔特教会而言，他们所遵循的各种规定中，包括与罗马基督教会不同的复活节日期[①]等，都是从传教先驱们那里一代一代继承下来的。在科尔曼(Colman)与威尔弗里德(Wilfrid I，也可称为威尔弗里德一世)的辩论中[②]，这一点表现得非常明显。

科尔曼说："我所习惯遵守的复活节是我从派我到这里当主教的先辈们那里接受的。"

而威尔弗里德的论据则是："我们已经看到，我们所遵守的利源节是所有罗马人所信守的，……我们注意到，整个意大利和法兰西都采取与此相同的守法，……我们还发现，在非洲、亚洲、埃及、希腊和世界上其它凡有基督教会存在的国家里，不管他们用的是哪一种语言，都毫无例外地按同一时间顺序，采取这种守法。"

将以上两方作一比较，可以看出，克尔特教会在独立发展的过程中，基本上是以个人为榜样和模板的，他们所遵守的，不是书上的记载，而是先人的具体行为。这一方面导致后辈对前辈的无比尊崇，这种尊崇甚至让他们敢于与世界为敌，而另一方面，也就要求开拓者和后来的领导者们谨言慎行。

---

① 　克尔特教会把复活节定在 3 月 25 日，罗马基督教会则定在 3 月 21 日。
② 　指在惠特比宗教会议上的辩论。

其次，这也可能是受了克尔特文化的影响。当地督伊德教僧侣的传承，就是依靠口口相传，而不是用书籍。克尔特教会受其影响，也特别看重教士本身的修养和品德，以教化后人。

久而久之，这也就造就了克尔特教会浓厚的个人色彩。从帕特里克，到科伦巴，再到艾丹、菲南，我们可以清楚地感受到他们强烈的个人魅力。这种魅力来自于他们自身的修养和渊博的学识。对于这一点，比德在《英吉利教会史》中曾颇费了些笔墨：

> ……艾丹给教士们留下了不少生活方面的经验教训，……他和他的兄弟们所过的生活与他教给别人学问相一致……他既不想得到也不迷恋今世上的任何东西。把世上国王和富人赠给他的一切东西立即分送给遇到他的穷人，这就是他的乐趣。除非偶然有什么重要的事情迫使他不得不骑马，他外出到城里或乡下时总是步行。……此外，他过的生活根本不象我们现在这样懒散。那时跟他同行的，不管是发誓修道的人还是普通的俗人，都需要读书。……他从不把钱送给世上有权有势的人（他招待任何富人时只备些好菜），相反，……他总是把有钱人慷慨赠送给他的诸如金钱之类的礼物，要么用作施舍物救助穷人，要么用于赎回被不正当地卖掉的那些人。[1]

以上就是克尔特教会的几个特点。如果说罗马教会给人印象最深的，是它无处不在的权威和严密的组织结构，那么克尔特教会留给世人的，则是它刻苦坚毅、热情强韧的精神风貌。从这一点来看，克尔特教会倒也正合了那句"成也萧何，败也萧何"的中国古语。由于它着重于隐修主义，强调通过自省来完成信仰，从而在基督教史上画上了独具色彩的一笔，也以此为基础对基督教世界产生了深远的影响。但是克尔特教会的这些特性，也是它后来败于不列颠教会的重要原因之一。对于正处在转型重组中的盎格鲁—撒克逊社会而言，代表着秩序和权威的罗马教会显然比管理松散的克尔特教会要显得合适。面对政治的实用选择，即使是经历了长年累月艰苦生活磨练的爱尔兰僧侣们也显得软弱无力。幸运的是，克尔特教会与不列颠罗马式教会的矛盾并不激烈，两者冲突的焦点仅止于宗教会议上的辩论。最终温和的解决方式，使克尔特教会与不列颠教会得以取长补短，相互借鉴，和谐共处。

---

[1] 比德：《英吉利教会史》，第 159–160 页。

中世纪后期华瓷在亚洲的传播和影响

孙锦泉　四川大学

摘要：中世纪后期，华瓷向亚洲传播主要通过四种方式：馈赠、朝贡贸易、官方贸易和民间贸易。华瓷外传的主要途径是海路输出，并导致了中国造瓷技术的向外传播。一些亚洲国家对中国瓷器纹饰和造型的模仿，认识、吸收并且传播了中国文化。华瓷在亚洲的传播，促进了亚洲各国对中国物华天宝、人文地理、历史文化的了解和国家之间的文化交流。

关键词：中世纪；中国瓷器；纹饰；仿制

Abstract：During the late Middle Ages, the Chinese porcelains spread throughout Asia mainly by four ways—gifts, tributary trades, official trades and nongovernmental trades. The chief way for Chinese porcelains' export was through sea route, which led to the outward spread of the Chinese porcelains techniques. Some Asian countries imitated the decorations and shapes of these porcelains, thus knowing, absorbing and spreading Chinese culture. The spread of Chinese porcelains throughout Asia helped other Asian countries understand Chinese treasures, human geography and history, and facilitated the cultural exchanges between these countries.

Keywords：Middle Ages, Chinese porcelain, decoration, imitation

在中世纪，中国不仅以其悠久的历史文化闻名于世，而且也以其内涵丰富的物质文化著称，中国制造的瓷器便是物质文化内容之一，也是中国的重要发明和对世界的重大贡献之一。中国瓷器的传布和影响，远远超越了作为一种器物存在的价值和意义，因为在中世纪，没有哪一种装饰艺术能够像中国的陶瓷装饰艺术那样异彩纷呈。随着华瓷的大量外销，尤其在亚洲市场的销售，实际上是以视觉艺术的形式，在向亚洲国家系统地介绍中华民族的文化精华，并为亚洲国家的人民熟悉、接受和喜爱。从文化交流的角度来看，华瓷在亚洲的传布与中国陶瓷制作技术的传播一样具有深远的影响。

近些年的考古发掘证明，中国陶瓷向亚洲的传播，至少可以追溯到公元前1世纪的西汉。此后，直到中世纪晚期，尽管华瓷的传播受限于中国的外交政策以及对外关系的变化，很不稳定，譬如，明初洪武年间实行海禁，华瓷出口大幅萎缩，但一千多年来从来断绝，中国瓷器以不同的方式和途径向外传布。华瓷向亚洲传播主要通过四种方式：

一、馈赠

明朝政府以瓷器为礼物赠予亚洲一些国家。如洪武十六年（1383 年）就曾赠予占城、暹罗和真腊瓷器各一万九千件。①三年以后，又"遣行人刘敏、唐敬偕中官赍磁器往赐"真腊。

二、朝贡贸易

入贡国家的使臣返程时买走华瓷。如永乐二年（1404 年）琉球的山南使臣在处州（今浙江丽水县）购买瓷器，携带回国。对贸易使臣进贡到京者购买瓷器，明朝政府有时还作了限制，如弘治时期，只允许每人购买青花磁器五十付。②

三、官方贸易

比较典型的是郑和船队大规模的远航贸易，许多中国瓷器通过这种途径销往国外。占城、瓜哇、锡兰、天方等国都非常喜爱中国瓷碗、瓷盘，在郑和下西洋期间，以金和珍珠宝石或其他本地异物与中国官员交换中国瓷器。③

四、民间贸易

中国瓷器的外传，大部分是通过民间贸易完成的。到了明代，民间贸易在份量和价值方面远远超过官方以及朝贡贸易而占绝对优势。④特别是中国民间的海外贸易兴盛的 16 世纪，华瓷大量输往亚洲各地。16 世纪后半期，当欧洲商人到达印度支那时，Cochin-china (the present south Annam) 的国王允许中国人在他们的版图内选择合适的位置建立一座城市，便于他们控制定期集市，这座城市被称为 Faifo，位于今日安南中部。中国的各种瓷器也运抵这里销售。⑤

华瓷外传的主要途径是海路输出，也有由陆路输出的。据《野获编》记载："鞑靼、女真诸部及天方诸国贡夷归装所载，他物不论，即以瓷器一项，多至数十车。"

从宋元时期的青瓷到此后的青花以及白瓷、彩瓷，根据考古发掘的资料显示，历代华瓷的分布范围很广，包括日本、朝鲜、越南、泰国、缅甸、菲律宾、马来西亚、新加坡、印度尼西亚、斯里兰卡、印度、巴基斯坦、巴林、南也门、文莱、阿富汗、伊朗、伊拉克、叙利亚、黎巴嫩、土耳其等国。与中国交往甚密的国家，华瓷的传入是很多的，如日本。在瓷器转运的中转地，如菲律宾，华瓷也不少。以菲律宾的马尼拉为例，据不完全统计，在马尼拉的藏品中发现了大约 4000 件完整或复原的中国陶瓷器皿，它们的年代从宋一直延续到清。⑥中国瓷器，以其瓷质的精细、造型的精巧、纹饰的精彩而走俏于亚洲市场，并且支配着亚洲瓷器市场。

中国瓷器在亚洲的走俏，导致了中国造瓷技术的向外传播。明代便有入华求艺的异国匠人，为学艺而来，学成便归。1511 年日本五郎太夫瑞祥入华学习陶瓷的烧制技术，1513 年归国后，在肥前的有田附近开窑，并在奈良附近的鹿脊山中烧制彩陶。⑦将中国的陶瓷烧制技术带到日本。也有中国陶瓷工匠到异国他乡传艺的。江户初期的宽永（1624—1643 年）末年，在中国人的教授之下，有田的柿右卫门烧制成红、黄、绿三色花纹的瓷器，称"伊万里瓷"，以后成为日本瓷器的名品。⑧对泰国陶瓷艺术研究有素的雷金纳德·李梅（R. Le may）认为，在素可泰（Sukhotai）时代，一批中国

---

① 　《明史》第 329 卷；同时参见《明太祖洪武实录》，第 156 卷。

② 　《大明会典》正德刊本，第 102 卷。

③ 　参照：[明] 黄省曾：《西洋朝贡典录》，中华书局 1982 年版，第 119 页；[明] 巩珍：《西洋番国志》，中华书局 1982 年版，第 4 页、第 10 页、第 24 页。

④ 　Edited by D. J. Steinberg, *In Search of Southeast Asia, A modern History*, University of Hawaii Press 1985, p.52.

⑤ 　参照 V. Purcell, *The Chinese in Southeast Asia*, Oxford University Press, 1951, p.222.

⑥ 　戴国华：《东南亚古陶瓷研究综述》，载《海交史研究》，1990 年第 1 期。

⑦ 　木宫泰彦：《日中文化交流史》，商务印书馆 1980 年版，第 609 页。

⑧ 　参照：夏应元：《相互影响两千年的中日文化交流》，载周一良主编：《中外文化交流史》，河南人民出版社 1987 年版。

制陶工匠就曾到过暹罗。15 世纪以后，又有一批华侨移居泰国，带去了中国的陶瓷烧制技术。[①]同一时期，朝鲜的青花瓷器在中国的影响下烧制成功。越南也在此时直接聘请中国的制瓷工人烧造青花瓷器。[②]这些在中国工匠具体操作或指导下生产的瓷器，其色泽、纹饰、式样、风格大多都是仿照华瓷制作的，这种定式在一些国家往往在陶器制作技术的引进时期就已形成。陶器模仿中国，使人想到元代中国陶工到暹罗形成的传统。安南陶器按中国的淡灰色陶体的釉底兰装饰。[③]

11 世纪以后，叙利亚、波斯等国大量生产的青釉陶器，很明显是仿中国青瓷而制的；14 世纪以后还生产了元青花瓷、明青花瓷的仿制品。[④]

中国瓷器在亚洲的影响并不仅仅在于传播了一种器物或是一种技术，还在于通过一些亚洲国家对中国瓷器纹饰和造型的模仿、认识、吸收并且传播了中国文化。

中国悠久的历史和深厚的文化底蕴集中体现在瓷器的纹饰上，中国的外销瓷除了一部分按销地的纹饰风格和造型艺术制作或订做以外，都具有浓郁的民族文化色调。中国的名山大川、历史人物、传说、典故、世风民俗、物华天宝、动物、植物等都浓缩到瓷器上，通过瓷器的图案纹饰展现中国几千年的文明精华和丰富的自然资源。

在暹罗的瓷器成品中，中国传统的龙凤图案屡见不鲜，还有一种容器，作柿形，盖柄为柿蒂状，这显然是受中国影响，因为暹罗并不产柿。[⑤]朝鲜的龙纹瓷罐寿纹图盖碗、安南的花叶图云纹瓷罐，都是中国瓷器图纹的仿制。安南瓷器仿制水平很高，产于 1450 年的牡丹图长颈瓶的纹饰可以与同时代中国御瓷纹饰媲美。[⑥]仿制华瓷纹饰最典型的是日本，龙、凤、麒麟都在日本瓷具中用作装饰，其意义与中国相同。尽管龙在日本不像中国那样风行，但仍然经常使用，日本龙是三爪的，对四爪、五爪的并不熟悉。[⑦]

在日本瓷器上有中国的观音菩萨、罗汉、普提和尚的变形，日本柿右卫门瓷器的某些图案花纹，如"井边顽童"取自中国宋代传说"破缸救友"。[⑧]日本的青花瓷器除了对华瓷纹饰的模仿，有时甚至还使用中国的年号，特别是宣德、成化和万历，一些堂名款和吉言款也被使用。

暹罗和安南的仿瓷在东南亚一带很受欢迎，日本仿瓷不仅在亚洲销售，还大量远销欧洲。

事实上，这种华瓷的仿制器或"再版的华瓷"保持着中国瓷器的式样和风格，有的仿制得足以乱真。以致于当 17 世纪中国的外销瓷减少时，许多国家毫不犹豫地采用了安南瓷器。在当时的情况下，显然，许多人是误以华瓷购买的。这些沉淀着丰富的中国文化的瓷器的销售，扩大了中国瓷器在亚洲的影响。通过瓷器上的图案纹饰或器物的造型，促进了亚洲各国对中国物华天宝、人文地理、历史文化的了解和国家之间的文化交流。

① 葛治伦：《1949 年以前的中泰文化交流》，载周一良主编：《中外文化交流史》。
② 中国硅酸盐学会主编：《中国陶瓷史》，文物出版社 1982 年版，第 412 页。
③ 参照 George Savage, *Porcelain through the Ages*, p.121.
④ [日] 三上次男：《冲绳出土的中世纪中国陶瓷——求证中世纪冲绳与中国陶瓷贸易的接点》（译文），载《海交史研究》1988 年 2 期。
⑤ 金雨雁：《明代中暹关系初探》，载《东南亚历史学刊》1983 年 1 期。
⑥ 参照 Harry Garner, *Oriental Blue and White*, Faber and Faber Limited，关于安南的论述。
⑦ George Savage, *Porcelain through the Ages*, p.116.
⑧ George Savage, *Porcelain through the Ages*, p.112.

论十字军骑士与突厥人在近东的军事交往和互动
——以阿尔伯特对第一次十字军的记载为中心

徐家玲、王向鹏 东北师范大学

摘要：第一次十字军是西欧基督教世界对伊斯兰教的塞尔柱突厥人发动的军事征伐。阿尔伯特的《耶路撒冷史》对这场战争有着翔实可信的记述。十字军为应对塞尔柱弓骑兵以及迥异的战场环境，在武装、战术层面上做出了各种调整和改变。他们从对手那里获得了新的知识和经验。在战场之外，十字军还以谈判、交易的形式实现了同突厥人的交往。

关键词：十字军；塞尔柱突厥人；军事；交往和互动

Abstract：First crusade was an expedition launched by the Christian Western Europe to the Seljuk Turks of Islamic Orient. Albert's *Historia Ierosolimitana* gives an extraordinarily detailed account of the military campaigns concerned. Faced with Seljuk horse-archers and alien battlefield environment, crusaders were obliged to change themselves in arms and tactics. They learnt more from their opponent. Besides battle, they also established some contact with Turks through the negotiation and political deal.

Keywords：Crusade, he Seljuk Turks, Military, Contact

第一次十字军东征（1096 — 1099）是在罗马教皇乌尔班二世的号召下，以"收复主的圣墓"为名被组织起来的、基督教西欧对信奉伊斯兰教的塞尔柱突厥人发动的军事征伐。这场漫长的远征，使得处于地中海两端、代表不同文明的两股强大的武装力量，首次在近东相遇，爆发了激烈而残酷的冲突。塞尔柱突厥人以强悍的战斗素质，诡异多变的战术风格，令法兰克人不寒而栗，陷于鏖战。[①]在迥异的战场环境下，十字军被迫对自身的武装和战术风格做出了适应性的调整和改变。他们尝试性地同突厥人在军事层面上实现了互动。

[①] 十字军与突厥人的军事冲突主要集中于小亚和叙利亚以北，先后历经围攻尼西亚，多里拉埃姆（Dorylaeum）之战，征伐乞里齐亚。在安条克，双方的冲突达到了顶峰。安条克之役历时近9个月，十字军先后击败了大马士革、阿勒颇的强援，通过收买城中叛徒攻占了城市，随即被摩苏尔总督率领的突厥联军围困在城内，最终突围决战而胜。此后，十字军再未遭遇任何顽强抵抗，最终攻占了耶路撒冷城，取得了战争的胜利。

阿尔伯特所著《耶路撒冷史》，是关于十字军战争的篇幅最长、记载最为详细的史著之一。[1]阿尔伯特是亚琛的一位教士，作为第一次十字军的同代人，他曾准备参加十字军，却因"各种阻碍"未能成行。为了弥补缺憾，他着力要将自己所听到的"那些在世的亲历者们的回忆告知世人"。[2]该书著于12世纪初，多数记述来于亲历十字军战争的德意志、佛兰德战士，对军事的描述可谓细致入微。阿尔伯特的记载，还原了十字军战争的历史面貌，从基督教军队的视角，彰显了法兰克人在这场大战中所受到的"异教徒"军事文化的冲击和震撼，显露了军事交往和互动的端倪。

一　武装的变化

突厥人武装的核心是弓骑兵。他们携带复合弓及多个箭袋，有软甲护身。这些弓骑兵臂力惊人，开弓力道超过60磅（相当27公斤），甚至会达到100磅（相当45公斤），并且能在快速运动中、或者飞驰的战马上保持拉满弓的状态。[3]此外，突厥人对弓骑兵的骑术和箭术要求甚高，他们射术精湛，驭马技术高超，灵活机动，配合协调。他们可驾驭马匹做8字形运动，能使马匹平稳地做出各种机动，在运动中能连贯地完成复杂动作；还能在不同的战术条件下采取不同的射击方式。[4]突厥弓骑兵的机动力、远距离的射杀能力，直接或间接地对十字军乃至整个西欧武器装备的发展产生了显而易见的影响。

马匹的进化

最显著的改变来自于马匹。欧洲此时尚未形成系统的育马体系，马匹普遍较矮，一般为12掌，至多14掌高，体轻，负重能力有限。[5]突厥人曾经生活于其中的东方草原则有着悠久的育种传统，培育了大量血统纯正的优种马。塞尔柱突厥人的马匹速度快、灵活矫健，耐力极强。亚洲热血马对欧洲冷血马的优势显而易见。阿尔伯特不禁感慨，突厥人骑的马匹"有风一样的速度"。[6]

同时，欧洲马在12世纪末以前没有任何防护措施，其负重能力更无法支撑铁质罩甲，而穆斯林世界在7世纪就已经有了给马匹披护甲的传统。因为缺少防护，十字军的马匹在弓骑兵的箭雨中损失惨重。依照阿尔伯特的记述，突厥人"射出箭矢伤害他们的马匹，使极其强悍的基督教斗士变为步行"。[7]在安条克最终决战前，他们仅剩下200匹马尚有战斗力。[8]

随着十字军战争运动的发展，中世纪西欧的马匹终于获得了改良，育马的显著改良很大程度上得益于东方的影响。12世纪，从巴克特里亚（大夏）和阿拉伯的种群中培育出来的战马已经达到17掌高，品性极佳。[9]以诺曼底为例，它的多个区域很早就是欧洲的优良牧场，如圣埃夫罗（St Evroul）和拉佩尔什（La Perche）。在十字军时期，这里大量引入东方血统的优良马匹进行饲育，

① 苏珊·B·爱丁顿对这部史著的拉丁文本重新进行了校勘，于2007年出版拉英对照本。本文所引《耶路撒冷史》全部来自于苏珊的拉丁文校勘本。
② 亚琛的阿尔伯特：《耶路撒冷史》（Albert of Aachen, *Historia Ierosolimitana*），牛津大学出版社2007年版，第1页。
③ 安·海兰：《从拜占廷到十字军战争的中世纪马匹》（Ann Hyland, *The Medieval Warhorse from Byzantium to the Crusades*），萨顿出版社1996年版，第109页。
④ 安·海兰：《从拜占廷到十字军战争的中世纪马匹》，第119页。
⑤ 安·海兰：《从拜占廷到十字军战争的中世纪马匹》，第86页。
⑥ 亚琛的阿尔伯特：《耶路撒冷史》，第214页。
⑦ 亚琛的阿尔伯特：《耶路撒冷史》，第40页。
⑧ 亚琛的阿尔伯特：《耶路撒冷史》，第332页。
⑨ 凯利·德弗里斯 & 罗伯特 D. 史密斯：《中世纪武器：其影响的插图史》（Kelly DeVries and Robert D. Smith, *Medieval Weapons: An Illustrated History of Their Impact*），美国文献中心/克利俄出版社2007年版，第92页。

培育出了纯种的佩尔什马。①总体来看，12—13世纪的欧洲战马，身高普遍达到了15—16掌，体重约为800到1000磅（360到455公斤）。②相应的，马匹的负重能力提高了，在13世纪可负重40公斤之多，与11世纪的马匹相比，提高负重力三分之一。③12世纪后期起，欧洲马披上了铁制护甲，13世纪普遍罩上马衣。现代人印象中的欧洲高头大马的形象此时才真正建立起来。

在拉丁东方，马对十字军至关重要。东方有着比欧洲更为广袤开阔的旷野，更适于骑乘作战。十字军必须依靠马匹来遏制塞尔柱弓骑兵的机动力。然而，当时的船只无法支持长距离、大批量运输战马，加之水土不服和疫病，东方的十字军国家很难从欧洲获得足够数量的马匹补充。虽然欧洲战马经过了引进东方品种的改良，但欧洲的育种环境与东方的草原显然大相径庭，因此，相对于近东的战马，其身躯之高大、骨密度之欠缺，显然不能适应炎热的荒漠环境，显出其耐力、速度的弱势。因此，叙利亚的法兰克人更愿意通过购买、俘获、赎买，甚至偷窃的方式来获取亚洲马。圣殿骑士团尤其重视马匹的饲养和训练，在其规章中，不仅明确规定了其成员拥有马匹的数量，还对马匹的饲养，战时的保管，乃至粮食与草料的搭配，都做了细致且严格的规定。圣殿骑士团规定，战争期间，圣殿兄弟们外出寻找草料和水源，必须要首先征得许可，且必须在有限的、听力所及的范围内活动。在骑士兄弟归营后，由扈从照管其马匹，并有专人监督。团务会还严格规定了饲养战马的草料配比，各骑士兄弟必须使用专有的容器和草料筛，按照规定给马匹补充饲草和大麦，不得随意增减，也不得随意改变麦秸、牧草和大麦的混合配比。对行为懒散的马匹，则严格控制进食量，以避免出现氮尿。④叙利亚的法兰克人在饲育和驾驭马匹方面，得益于与塞尔柱人更为频繁的冲突及更为密切的接触，显现出了较欧洲更为明显的进步和改观。

远程武器价值的凸显

除了马匹的机动力外，突厥弓骑兵还有射程的优势。突厥弓骑兵复合弓的最远射程可达365米远。⑤阿尔伯特在记述基利什·阿尔斯兰同十字军在尼西亚的激战时，曾如此描述道："他们乘着迅捷、善战的战马，手持角骨所制的弓，开弓满弦，以作击发。"⑥他们的密集射击被形象地称为"箭雨"。这种远程攻击，对人和马匹都是致命的，对士气和秩序的破坏尤为可畏。因此，十字军必须充分挖掘己方远程武器——弓和弩的战场潜力。

在攻城、争夺隘口，特别是反制弓骑兵时，十字军都适时地发挥己方射手的功效。十字军射手的功能主要是防御性的。他们有效地维持了阵型，使宝贵的骑兵阵列免受敌人箭矢的损害。在安条克的决战中，十字军将弓和弩的威力发挥到了极致：他们前所未有地将所有的弓箭手放到了全军阵列的最前方，以遏制突厥弓骑兵。在弓和弩的掩护下，十字军抢先从桥门突围而出，夺取了战略的主动，这种安排成为了致胜的关键。⑦远程武器在十字军战争中的价值凸显了出来，被置于了以往任何战役中都未曾有过的重要位置。某种意义上，突厥人对弓广泛而娴熟的应用，加深了十字军对这种武器的理解和认识，使得它成为了在近东战场上必不可少的重要武器。

此外，在东方战场上，弩境遇的改变更为显著。弩早在9世纪就在欧洲出现，但直到十字军战

① 安·海兰：《从拜占廷到十字军战争的中世纪马匹》，第84页。
② 安·海兰：《从拜占廷到十字军战争的中世纪马匹》，第114页。
③ 约翰·法郎士，《十字军战争时代的西方战争，1000—1300年》，（John France, *Western warfare in the age of the Crusades,1000—1300*），伦敦大学学院出版社1999年版，第24页。
④ 安·海兰：《从拜占廷到十字军战争的中世纪马匹》，第115页。文中所谓氮尿，即牲畜喂养得太精心，不活动，会造成机体内能量物质代谢紊乱而致乳酸在肌肉和血液中大量蓄积，引起腰部和臀部肌肉肿胀和变性的一种代谢障碍性疾病。
⑤ 安·海兰：《从拜占廷到十字军战争的中世纪马匹》，第120页。
⑥ 亚琛的阿尔伯特：《耶路撒冷史》，第106页。
⑦ 亚琛的阿尔伯特：《耶路撒冷史》，第324—326页。

争时才被正名。《阿列克修斯传》的著者，拜占廷公主安娜对这种陌生的武器印象深刻：它威力惊人，可以射穿城墙，是恶魔的机械。[1]阿尔伯特在夸赞戈德费雷（Godfrey）的武功时，显露出了弩的应用和威力："他拿起弩，站在两名同伴的盾牌后，射穿了这个突厥人的心脏。"[2]突厥弓骑兵始终在很远的距离游弋和射击，可能就是忌惮弩的强大穿透力。

弩的传播过程富有戏剧性。首先，它因巨大的威力、使用简便、提前上弦便可随时击发的优点而受到交战双方的广泛青睐。此后，突厥人将十字军的单木弩改造为了复合弩。然后，这种改进过的弩流传到了欧洲，被普遍采用。至12世纪末，欧洲南部的热那亚等地，受十字军影响，学会了这种复合短弓的制造工艺，因生产复合弩及输出雇佣弩手而闻名。[3]甚至，东方的制弩工匠被引入了欧洲宫廷，为王室服务：英格兰国王约翰的制弩者是"萨拉森人"彼得，国王路易九世的制弩人是"亚美尼亚人"约翰。[4]从12世纪到14世纪初，弩的军事价值超过了传统的弓箭。12世纪末，出现了执弩骑手，在1230年的文献中，对这类骑士的提法是"执弩大师"。[5]因为难于抵御弩的穿透力，锁子甲于12世纪末被逐渐淘汰，板甲重新流行。弩的杀伤力极大，以至屡遭教皇的反对和禁用：先是在1096–1097年间，然后是在1139年的第二次拉特兰公会议上。[6]

突厥武器装备的采纳

十字军也会直接采用突厥人的武器装备。位于地中海东岸的安条克，夏季气候炎热干燥，加之战时补给不足，饥渴难耐的十字军战士被迫卖掉其盔甲和武器。但为了继续战斗，他们接受了轻便、易于行动的突厥武器和护具：依照阿尔伯特的记载，如伯爵哈特曼这样身份显赫的人也持着突厥人的圆盾和剑上了战场。[7]为了适应东方的战场环境和机动多变的对手，叙利亚的法兰克人逐渐在不自觉中借鉴或使用了塞尔柱人的武器装备，显示出了西欧封建武装原本不具备的特征。十字军骑士开始采用芦苇杆或竹竿制成的轻矛；[8]像其穆斯林对手一样，他们在盔甲外套上了罩袍，在13世纪，这种穿着习惯在欧洲推广开来；[9]同时期，十字军迅速地推广了带有衬垫的盔甲（aketon），以及由羊毛、皮革、亚麻制成的软甲（Gambeson），这些同样来自于他们的异教徒对手。[10]

更为显著的变化体现在特科波佣兵（Turcopoles）的使用上。特科波佣兵意为突厥之子，阿尔伯特认为他们是混血儿，"由突厥人的父亲和希腊人的母亲所生"。[11]他们在拜占廷和十字军的部队中都占据着重要的位置。他们中多数人都有着类似于突厥弓骑兵的装备和作战习惯，阿尔伯特称他们为"擅长弓箭的特科波佣兵"。[12]到了13世纪，法兰克人也加入到特科波佣兵的行列之中，使用突厥骑兵的武器装备，至少部分　是弓骑兵。这时，特科波佣兵体现的只是武装的特征，而非民

---

① 安娜·科穆宁娜：《阿列克修斯传》（Anna Comnena, *Alexiad*），企鹅出版社1969年版，第316–317页。

② 亚琛的阿尔伯特：《耶路撒冷史》，第118页。

③ 大卫·埃奇＆约翰·迈尔斯：《中世纪骑士的武器和盔甲：中世纪武器插图史》（David Edge and John Miles Paddock, *Arms and Armor of the Medieval Knight: An Illustrated History of Weaponry in the Middle Ages*），克雷森特1991年版，第19页。

④ 伊恩·希思：《十字军的军队和敌人，1096–1291年：组织、战术、衣着和武器》（Ian Heath, *Armies and enemies of the crusades, 1096–1291: Organization, tactics, dress and weapons*），战争演习研究集团1978年版，第86页。

⑤ 大卫·尼科尔：《十字军时代的武器和盔甲，1050–135年：西欧和十字军国家》（*Arms and Armour of the Crusading Era, 1050–1350: Western Europe and the Crusader States*），格林希尔1999年版，第20页。

⑥ 凯利·德弗里斯＆罗伯特 D. 史密斯：《中世纪武器：其影响的插图史》，136页。

⑦ 亚琛的阿尔伯特：《耶路撒冷史》，第332页。

⑧ 大卫·尼科尔：《十字军时代的武器和盔甲，1050–135年：西欧和十字军国家》，第274页。

⑨ 伊恩·希思：《十字军的军队和敌人，1096–1291年：组织、战术、衣着和武器》，第69页。

⑩ 伊恩·希思：《十字军的军队和敌人，1096–1291年：组织、战术、衣着和武器》，第71页。

⑪ 亚琛的阿尔伯特：《耶路撒冷史》，第342页。

⑫ 亚琛的阿尔伯特：《耶路撒冷史》，第310页。

族的差异了。如约翰·法朗士所言，"他们表明了法兰克人的思想意识对叙利亚环境的适应"。①

二　战术的调整和强化

突厥人机动灵活、变化无常的战术风格，使得战场情势瞬息万变，不分昼夜的骚扰、伏击、挑衅和偷袭，更是无时无刻地困扰着十字军。这种多变、机动的战争在欧洲战场上是不曾有过的，身处其中的十字军在漫长的实践中，强化了以往已有的战斗特质，磨砺出了新的、特有的战术风格。

密集的行军阵型，更强的组织和纪律

首先，是更为密集的阵型，更强的组织和纪律性。十字军的威力来源于集群，依赖于完整的阵型和井然的秩序。突厥人擅于对行进中的队伍发动突袭，通过骚扰和挑衅来寻觅战机。行军是任何封建军队都难以避免的薄弱环节，军队的前卫，特别是尾部尤其缺乏保护。因此，十字军首先强化了行军，特别强调阵型的密集和严格的纪律。主教阿泰马尔特别强调，行军中不得冒进，要行动一致。②夜袭安条克的时候，戈德弗里发布命令，"严禁喧哗，违者处死"。③他们将阵型组织得紧凑严密，依靠盾牌铁甲形成有效的防卫，细致部署前锋和后卫。④密集而谨慎的行军是拉丁东方武装力量的优良传统，圣殿和医护骑士团总会在重大的军事行动中担负前锋和殿后的重责。

同时，十字军非常重视战斗中的组织和纪律。纪律是中世纪的封建武装普遍缺失的。骑士精神、个人英雄主义，贵族的荣誉感，都与纪律感和组织性相悖而行。然而，在长时间的残酷冲突中，十字军逐渐产生了相当的克制力和忍耐力，学会了节制。在面对敌人袭击时，他们首先会稳固阵型，保持秩序，而非盲目出击。取得胜利后，他们也不会过度追击，以免陷入伏击，给对手可乘之机。在船桥之战取胜后，阿尔伯特记载，胜利的十字军并没有追得太远，以免附近的安条克城内的突厥人出城袭击他们。⑤有时，他们所表现出的克制力和把握战机的能力，甚至令突厥人汗颜。据阿尔伯特记载，在突厥弓骑兵的一次挑衅中，十字军不仅没有冒进，反而有意识地利用适当的兵力击溃了这些散兵，并未追击。⑥他们可以做到忍耐、不冒进、在恰当的时机出击，适度追击，并在胜利的情况下保持理智。这是经历了长期的艰险和战争磨砺的结果。可以说，克制、忍耐、纪律是十字军在付出了极大的战争代价后所获得的宝贵资源。此后，宗教骑士团将这种品质和传统维系了下来，他们总是能在强悍的对手面前表现出极大的克制和耐心。

骑兵冲锋以及骑步兵间的配合协作

在战斗中，十字军尤其重视骑步兵间的配合协作。重装骑兵的集团冲锋是十字军对轻装的塞尔柱武装最有效的杀伤手段，是决定战争胜负的关键。据阿尔伯特记载，在反击阿勒颇的援军时，十字军就是依靠着 700 骑兵的集团冲锋，瓦解了敌人的阵线，取得了以少胜多的重大胜利。⑦但是，骑兵想要形成真正有效的集团冲锋，不仅需要时间组成密集队形，还要等待战机以最大程度地发挥威力。中世纪的指挥官普遍缺乏对战场的控制力，加之骑士的个人英雄主义精神，使得这种战术的效

---

① 约翰·法郎士，《十字军战争时代的西方战争，1000–1300 年》，第 219 页。
② 亚琛的阿尔伯特：《耶路撒冷史》，第 190 页。
③ 亚琛的阿尔伯特：《耶路撒冷史》，第 272 页。
④ 亚琛的阿尔伯特：《耶路撒冷史》，第 196–198 页。
⑤ 安娜·科穆宁娜：《阿列克修斯传》，第 194 页。
⑥ 亚琛的阿尔伯特：《耶路撒冷史》，第 214–216 页。
⑦ 亚琛的阿尔伯特：《耶路撒冷史》，第 236 页。

力受到很大的限制。同时，突厥弓骑兵的突袭、骚扰及远程打击，也会严重妨碍骑兵的组织和协调。

因此，十字军的骑兵必须要有步兵的协同配合。步兵阵线最大的作用在于确保骑兵阵线不受敌人攻击的损害，尽可能地为骑兵的冲锋提供保护，争取时间。盾墙、弩、弓箭是他们最有效的防护手段。骑步兵间的这种配合和保护是至关重要的。在安条克，随着十字军马匹的大量战损，步兵甚至开始成为战场上的主导力量。在安条克的最后一战中，十字军将弓箭手放到了队列最前方，率先突围而出，并利用步兵阵线使得突厥联军陷入了近距离的混战中。最终，少量的骑兵抓住时机，成功发动了冲锋，击溃了突厥人。期间，戈德弗里和休在增援博希蒙德的时候，主动放慢了骑兵前行的速度，以避免步兵阵列掉队。[1]此外，在近东，马匹的匮乏迫使众多叙利亚的法兰克骑士不得不步行作战，加入步兵阵列，这也在一定程度上增加了后者的战斗效力。骑步兵的紧密配合，集团冲锋的精于计算，成为了后世拉丁东方的军事特征，如约翰·法朗士所论，"常规的法兰克人的战术，强调大集群和密集队形，伴随着步兵和骑兵之间的合作，这种战术，在圣地达到了新的高度"。[2]

伏击、诱敌深入战术的使用

最后，十字军也借鉴了突厥人的战术，适当采取了伏击的策略。西欧的战斗传统是正面冲突、短兵相接，个人英雄主义是封建骑士的战争气质，设伏和偷袭都是罕见的。然而，为了反制对手的伏击和突袭，在常规的小规模冲突中，十字军也开始充分地利用气候和地势等有利条件，设伏、诱敌深入、甚至佯装撤退。这些策略在安条克之战期间使用得尤其频繁。圣波勒伯爵休曾率家族武装，昼伏夜出，在峡谷设伏，以步兵引诱突厥人出击，在敌人返回时予以伏击，取得了胜利；[3]雷蒙德夜间设伏，在破晓的时候成功偷袭了围攻十字军堡垒的突厥骑兵；[4]坦克雷德曾藏在安条克城的双重城墙之间，伺机突袭了挑衅的突厥弓骑兵。[5]甚至于在大规模的战斗中，十字军为了扭转敌众我寡的不利局面，也会采取伏击的战术。在获悉阿勒颇的援军即将到来后，十字军秘密集结，深夜行军，破晓发动突袭，以少胜多。[6]这些战例生动地表现出十字军在战术上的适应力和灵活性：他们在冲突中，从突厥人那里借鉴并获取了自己可以利用的资源和手段，并迅速成功地将它们付诸于实践。

三　战争中的交往和互动

十字军战争不仅是血腥的杀戮，它还有着更为丰富的内容。交战双方在一定程度上恪守着封建战争的基本规则，他们会谈判协商，乃至于会互相结盟，互为利用。尽管十字军与突厥人在近东是初次交锋，但其身后的两个文明在此前的数百年间，从伊比利亚半岛、普瓦提埃、到西西里岛，乃至整个意大利南部，都曾进行过长久的战争和冲突。法兰克人对强大的穆斯林对手早已心怀敬畏，反之亦然。这种对手的意识，也就使得双方在战场上可能保持一定的理性，达成相当的共识。

俘虏和赎金

在十字军战争中，存在着至少适用于贵族之间的战争规则。在一场冲突或战斗之后，会有人被俘虏，而非斩尽杀绝。在基利什·阿尔斯兰围攻被大众十字军中的斯瓦比亚人所占据的堡垒的时候，

---

① 亚琛的阿尔伯特：《耶路撒冷史》，第 324-330 页。
② 约翰·法郎士，《十字军战争时代的西方战争，1000-1300 年》，第 219 页。
③ 亚琛的阿尔伯特：《耶路撒冷史》，第 212-214 页。
④ 亚琛的阿尔伯特：《耶路撒冷史》，第 224-226 页。
⑤ 亚琛的阿尔伯特：《耶路撒冷史》，第 294-296 页。
⑥ 亚琛的阿尔伯特：《耶路撒冷史》，第 232-238 页。

突厥人就俘获了其中 200 名"年轻俊俏"的人。[①]尽管军事上的连续胜利所造就的乐观、高亢的情绪，外加基督教著者们的刻意掩饰，使得与战俘的交换和赎买相关的记载寥寥，但某些文字仍然能显露端倪。阿尔伯特提到了巴内维尔的罗格，赞扬"他是在突厥人中享有名望的人，经常受命在基督徒和突厥人间的俘虏交换及其它交涉中，充当中间人。"[②]他的褒奖意味深长，传递了不容忽视的信息：十字军与突厥人存在着俘虏的交换和赎买，并有专人担当中介。正如约翰·法朗士所论，"尽管这是一场宗教信仰之间的斗争，然而在一定程度上来说，至少某些战争的协议是被双方所遵守的"。[③]这种为金钱和政治利益而进行的俘虏赎买交易，此后在近东变成了约定俗成、根深蒂固的习惯：圣殿骑士团的一项重要任务就是同穆斯林交换、赎买战俘，这也是他们收入的重要来源。

战争中的谈判和交涉

与封建战争相同，十字军战争同样是最大的冒险，随时可能会招致无可挽回的毁灭。因此，在复杂、困难的形势下，军队统帅总会谋求战斗之外的手段和方法实现己方的军事诉求。宗教的虔诚和狂热并不能阻碍双方间寻求战斗之外的解决方法。战争的根本一定是利益之争，它始终是在谨慎的态度下被理性主导和推动的。在第一次十字军战争中，十字军一直寻求避免武力冲突的办法。即使在战事最为激烈的时候，他们也从不拒绝与其穆斯林对手谈判和交易。

首先，在尼西亚，尽管拜占廷皇帝背着十字军人与突厥人秘密达成了接收该城的协议，且不允许十字军人进城劫掠，令十字军人极其不满，但十字军还是接受了这个既成事实。此后，鲍德温和坦克雷德分兵向乞里齐亚进发，针对乞里齐亚这片疆土，其兵力显然不足，但他们还是取得了显赫的胜利，其原因，一方面得益于亚美尼亚人的鼎力支持，另一方面也由于突厥人的妥协退让。塔苏斯城的突厥人也是在坦克雷德压力下不战而降。[④]至此，十字军开始显现出愈发灵活多变、巧妙机智的外交策略和技巧。阿尔伯特记载，许多突厥人向坦克雷德进贡，"与他结交"，"为的是能与他相安无事"，坦克雷德接纳了这些礼物，迅速征服了整个地区。[⑤]鲍德温在入主埃德萨（Edessa）成为伯爵后，迅速迫使主要的穆斯林对手，萨莫萨塔（Samosata）的埃米尔巴杜卡（Balduk）同他结盟，并将其招纳为封臣。[⑥]此后，鲍德温利用奥托齐（Ortoqid）王公巴勒·伊本·巴赫拉姆（Balak Ibn Bahram）和萨鲁吉（Saruj）城的矛盾，同巴杜卡结盟，占领了这座城市。[⑦]显然，十字军充分地意识到了穆斯林世界内部的分崩离析和错综复杂的矛盾，恰当而适时地利用了这样的外交良机为己谋利。

在安条克，法兰克人同穆斯林的互动达到顶峰。他们非常清楚法蒂玛王朝同塞尔柱帝国间的敌对关系，皇帝很可能在君士坦丁堡就对此做出过中肯的建议。十字军没有坐失分裂、削弱对手的良机。按照阿尔伯特的记载，十字军率先派出了使者，向法蒂玛王朝示好，后者随即来到安条克与基督徒交涉谈判。[⑧]尽管交涉的实际内容不得而知，但双方至少达成了某种程度的默契和共识。法蒂玛使者甚至参加了基督徒对阿勒颇的战斗，并带着被杀突厥人的首级返回了营地。[⑨]随后，十字军领袖馈赠给这个使团慷慨的礼物，"真心诚意地"护送他们乘船返回。[⑩]这次成功的交涉为十字军赢得了宝贵

---

① 亚琛的阿尔伯特：《耶路撒冷史》，第 34–36 页。
② 亚琛的阿尔伯特：《耶路撒冷史》，第 234 页。
③ 约翰·法郎士，《十字军战争时代的西方战争，1000–1300 年》，第 227 页。
④ 亚琛的阿尔伯特：《耶路撒冷史》，第 150 页。
⑤ 亚琛的阿尔伯特：《耶路撒冷史》，第 180 页。
⑥ 亚琛的阿尔伯特：《耶路撒冷史》，第 176 页。
⑦ 亚琛的阿尔伯特：《耶路撒冷史》，第 176–178 页。
⑧ 亚琛的阿尔伯特：《耶路撒冷史》，第 230 页。
⑨ 亚琛的阿尔伯特：《耶路撒冷史》，第 236 页。
⑩ 亚琛的阿尔伯特：《耶路撒冷史》，第 238 页。

的生存空间，法蒂玛王朝不仅没有帮助突厥人，反而趁势于巴勒斯坦展开攻势，征服了耶路撒冷。这种外交手段，也为十字军兵不血刃地取得最终的胜利奠定了胜机。此后，依照伊本·阿西尔（Ibn al-Athir）的记载，十字军甚至曾向大马士革和阿勒颇派遣使者，谋求和约，权作缓兵之计。[1]阿勒颇的里德万（Ridwan）也确实没有参加随后摩苏尔总督发起的突厥联军。各个埃米尔间的隔阂和对立，他们自保、丢卒保车的心理，为十字军提供了施展外交手腕的空间，进而使困局有了转机。

在安条克之役后，十字军同的黎波里等地的埃米尔达成和约，几乎不受阻碍地通过了叙利亚，直捣巴勒斯坦，并最终攻占了耶路撒冷城。十字军充分地利用了对手阵营间清晰可见的裂痕，诡诈而狡黠地将所有对手逐一击破。如约翰·法朗士所言，"他们旋即估量了自己的敌人的能力，以老练的外交手段将自己的力量最大化，赢得了盟友，并通过随时准备撕毁的友好协约收买了敌人"。[2]

结　论

综上，十字军来到近东后，在同塞尔柱突厥人的战争冲突中，为适应新的对手和战场环境做出了种种适应性的改变。这些武装和战术上的变化，有些影响了后来西欧封建军事的发展，更多的是形成了东方十字军国家及宗教骑士团独有的军事风格。同时，人们也应对这种变化及其带来的影响做出更为理性的认识和估计。武器上，十字军乃至整个西欧封建社会对弓箭的鄙视态度并未改变，武器所附有的阶级性决定了世人对不同武器所具有的迥异态度和评判。在战争风格上，十字军的核心仍然是骑士精神，近战搏杀是其永远不变的战争理念和英雄主义的价值观。十字军并非颠覆，而是强化了以往传统的战术风格和理念，做出了适当的调整和改变。不过，尽管如此，这样的变化仍然是有意义的，诚如 RC·斯梅尔所言，十字军战争的形式是西方封建军事史必不可少的组成部分。[3]

从更广泛的意义上看，自阿拉伯帝国 8 世纪于普瓦蒂埃败于法兰克，到西班牙再征服运动，十字军东征，1453 年君士坦丁堡的陷落，直至 18 世纪奥斯曼土耳其的衰落，基督教欧洲和伊斯兰东方间一直充斥着战火和硝烟，双方共同见证了武装、军事技术、战略战术的复杂变化。显而易见的是，欧洲为了应对日趋复杂的军事形势，在不断地调整和进化中获益更多。

更远处着眼，十字军战争不仅是一场单纯的野蛮屠戮，它更是一次 11 世纪欧洲扩张大背景下的军事拓殖。它是欧洲殖民主义的最早范例。[4]来自西欧的武装朝圣者们，以军事冲突的方式实现了地中海的两个文明间的互动和交互影响。在第一次十字军后建立起来的，维系了近 200 年的十字军国家使得这种交往和融合成为了常态，在相当长的历史时期内改变了双方的关系，影响着历史的进程。在十字军时期，叙利亚法兰克统治者同他们的穆斯林臣民在朝夕相处中，彼此间达成了一定程度的认同和理解。虽然这种融合和交往更多的是表面化的，但它也在动荡不安的地中海世界，传递出了两种不同文明间相互认知、学习，乃至融合的积极信息。

参考文献

1. Albert of Aachen, edd. and trans. Susan B. Edgington, *Historia Ierosolimitana, History of the Journey to*

① 伊本·阿西尔：《伊本·阿西尔十字军时期的编年史：部分 1，491–541 年 /1097–1146 年》（Ibn al-Athir, *The chronicle of Ibn al-Athīr for the crusading period from al-Kāmil fī·· l-ta·· rīkh. Part. 1, The years 491–541/1097–1146: the coming of the Franks and the Muslim response*），阿什盖特 2006 年版，第 15 页。
② 约翰·法郎士，《十字军战争时代的西方战争，1000–1300 年》，第 209 页。
③ RC·斯梅尔：《十字军战争，1097–1193 年》（R. C. Smail, *Crusading Warfare, 1097–1193*），剑桥大学出版社 1995 年版，第 2 页。
④ 雅克·勒高夫：《中世纪文明：400–1500 年》（Jacques Le Goff, *Medieval Civilization: 400–1500*），布莱克韦尔 1988 年版，第 67 页。

Jerusalem[M]. New York: Oxford University Press, 2007.

2. John France, *Victory in the East: a military history of the First Crusade*[M]. New York: Cambridge University Press, 1994.

3. Ann Hyland, *The Medieval Warhorse from Byzantium to the Crusades*[M]. Conshohocken: Combined Publishing, 1996.

4. John France, *Western warfare in the age of the Crusades, 1000–1300*[M]. London: UCL Press, 1999.

5. Jim Bradbury, *The Medieval Archer*[M]. Woodbridge: Boydell Press, 1985.

6. David Edge and John Miles Paddock, *Arms and Armor of the Medieval Knight: An Illustrated History of Weaponry in the Middle Ages*[M]. New York: Crescent, 1988.

7. Anna Comnena, edd. and trans. E. R. A. Sewter, *The Alexiad of Anna Comnena*[M]. London: Penguin, 1969.

8. Ian Heath, *Armies and enemies of the crusades, 1096–1291: Organization, tactics, dress and weapons*[M]. Cambridge: Wargames Research Group, 1978.

9. Kelly DeVries and Robert D. Smith, *Medieval Weapons: An Illustrated History of Their Impact (Weapons and Warfare)*[M]. Santa Barbara: ABC–CLIO, 2007.

10. R. C. Smail, *Crusading Warfare, 1097–1193*[M]. New York: Cambridge University Press.

11. Jacques Le Goff, trans. Julia Barrow, *Medieval Civilization: 400 – 1500*[M]. Oxford: Blackwell Publishing, 1988.

12. Ibn al–Athir, edd. And trans. D.S. Richards, *The chronicle of Ibn al-Athīr for the crusading period from al-Kāmil fī 'l-ta'rīkh. Part. 1, The years 491–541/1097–1146: the coming of the Franks and the Muslim response*, Ashgate, 2006, p. 15.

论狄奥多拉对查士丁尼对内政策的影响

赵瑞杰　东北师范大学

摘要：查士丁尼时代是早期拜占廷的强盛时期。皇帝查士丁尼是一位杰出的、唯贤是用的君主，在他的统治下，拜占廷逐渐扩大了疆土，收复了罗马帝国的昔日版图，重振罗马神威。但是，在其成功的光环下，他的妻子——狄奥多拉功不可没。在其执政时期，皇后狄奥多拉被赋予共治的权利。查士丁尼对她的宠爱以及时代的需要，为狄奥多拉铺就了施展才华的历史舞台。从一位普通的女性到登上皇后宝座的这段时间，狄奥多拉在苦难的生涯中造就了果断、坚强、有远见的性格，这成为她日后统治政策中的一个屏障。

本文力图从普通女性的角度去剖析狄奥多拉在当时的心理活动及个性，并通过狄奥多拉对查士丁尼统治帝国政策的影响展开论述，再现狄奥多拉对查士丁尼时代皇权的统治所起的作用。

关键词：拜占廷皇权；查士丁尼；狄奥多拉；权力

Abstract：Justinian's era is the most brilliant during the period of the early Byzantine Empire. As a Emperor, Justinian is more outstanding and intellegent, especially respectful for the talents. Under his reigning, he has gradually expanded the domain, recovered the territory of the former Rome Empire, and made the Rome stronger than before. However, his success will never be lack of his wife-Theodora's support for him. During the period of his ruling, he also conferred the rule rights on the Queen—Theodora. It is the deepest love from Justinian to Theodora, and the characteristics at that time that Theodora can display her talent on this stage of history. During this period, stepping from an ordinary woman into the Queen's throne, Theodora has trained her decisive, strong and visionary personality, which has become the policy barriers for her rule. These personalities mainly resulted from her youth career.

This paper tries to analysize the psychology and mentality of Theodora who was at that era from the angle of the ordinary women. At the same time, I want to make a demonstration through the following aspects: the impact of Theodora's policy to an Empire, so that it can reproduce that Theodora had a great impact on the imperial power of Justinian era .

Keywords：Byzantine Imperial Power, Justinian, Theodora, Power

在查士丁尼的内政改革中，狄奥多拉功不可没。特别是在尼卡暴乱中，狄奥多拉临危不惧，以她突出的表现，巩固了查士丁尼的皇位，延续了查士丁尼时代的发展。至此，在史书关于有名的尼卡暴乱的记载中，使后人永远记住了拜占廷历史上一位坚强聪慧的皇后—狄奥多拉。

一　尼卡暴乱与查士丁尼皇位的巩固

在君士坦丁堡，一直保持着马拉战车比赛的传统。吉本曾经记载，此项比赛通常是由罗马共和国的行政官员或皇帝亲自出资兴办，并由专人负责管理。驾车手分别穿着红色和白色的制服参加比赛，后来又增添了蓝色和绿色，因此赛场也划分为红、白、蓝、绿四个主赛区，各区的观众可以为本区赛车呐喊助威。这四种颜色分加代表四个季节的自然现象：夏日天狼星的红色、冬雪银装素裹的白色、深秋的蓝色和春天的新绿；另一种看法认为蓝与绿的竞争是陆地和海洋的冲突，把各自的胜利看成是预示农业丰收或海运昌盛，从而引发农牧民和水手的敌对情绪。

竞技党派中蓝党和绿党日趋居于首要地位。无论是蓝党还是绿党，经常发生对抗的行为。因此，普罗柯比认为，究其本质，两党都是暴徒。他们时常在街道上群殴、杀人放火、奸淫劫掠。查士丁尼家族曾倚赖并支持的蓝党尤为严重，普罗柯比对此党也深恶痛绝，并在《秘史》中予以大力批判抨击。他们差不多一开始就公开身怀利刃，白天把它藏在斗篷内，一到天黑就聚到一起，在露天广场或狭窄的巷中抢劫富人，还有一些人遭劫后被杀。最初他们只反对自己的死对头，但随着事态的发展，他们还加害那些无辜的人。所以普罗柯比提到，在这种情形下，没有人能指望活得长久，因为大家都在担心他是否会成为下一个被害的目标。没有哪个地方是安全的，白天也没有任何时刻能够提供安全的屏障，因为谋杀即使在最神圣的教堂圣地也会继续。亲戚朋友已无信任可言，因为许多人正是死于家庭成员的阴谋。法律和条例已无约束力，因为在混乱中，凡事都要通过暴力加以解决。同时普罗柯比还陈述，有些女主人为奴隶所迫去做自己不愿做的事，还有些幸福的已婚妇女也遭遇到了不幸。他详尽地记载了一段史料：据说，一位颇具姿色的少妇和她的丈夫乘船到半岛大陆对面的京都城郊；几个蓝党人在水上与他们相遇后，就跳进她的船，将她的丈夫粗暴地拖入他们的船舱。她低声向丈夫起誓：要丈夫相信她，对任何责难都毫不惧怕，她会保护自己的清白。然后，在丈夫哀怨的目光中，她则纵身跳入博斯普鲁斯海峡，就此从人世上消失。这就是该党在君士坦丁堡的所为。而且，他还在《战记》中加以补充："他们（党徒们）除了在斗争中征服对方外，对什么神事人事都不关心……当祖国面临困境或受到不公正的待遇时，只要与党派无关，他们就漠不关心，所以称他们为帮伙，妇女们也参加到他们的竞争中，尽管她们从不参加公开比赛……所以我认为这些人都有一种灵魂疾病，他们必定会遭到麻烦。"从这些言辞中我们看出，普罗柯比对查士丁尼所支持的蓝党的所作所为可谓义愤填膺、恨之入骨。

事实上，在查士丁尼统治期间，他和皇后密切的合作就已经约束了两党的行为，面对蓝党的暴行，他不再袒护，而是下令对违法之徒一律惩罚，这导致了蓝党与查士丁尼的决裂。在查士丁尼早期实行的改革措施的实施中，也不乏一些帝国官员和政府的假公济私、贪污受贿现象，对首都民众的压迫就激化了以蓝党和绿党为代表的民众与朝廷的矛盾，矛盾激化的结果必然转化为反抗。绿党首先挑起事端，对帝国官员无情压榨穷苦人民提出控诉，并严厉指责查士丁尼在新法中所赋予的贵族特权。基于共同的利益，原本在赛场引发的蓝绿两派的冲突很快转变为一致批评指责查士丁尼一世的财政措施，抱怨政府的横征暴敛，并否定查士丁尼一世的中央集权化措施。因此，查士丁尼下令逮捕了闹事分子，并予以惩罚，但是小骚乱的背后隐藏着更大的暴乱。

公元 532 年 1 月，皇帝按照惯例在竞技场主持战车赛时，两派群众借机联合行动，请求皇帝释放其中的两名罪犯，在遭到查士丁尼的拒绝后，全场爆发出"蓝党和绿党万岁"的口号声，并一致提出"尼卡"的口号，表明两党的共同合作。尼卡 (nika) 是希腊语，代表"胜利"。两党党徒包围了市政官府，声讨市政官。在声讨无效的情况下，愤怒的暴乱者冲进监狱，放出囚犯并放火烧了监狱。1 月 14 日，蓝党和绿党继续纵火闹事，并要求皇帝罢免市政官尤戴蒙·卡帕多西亚的执政官约翰和大法官特里波尼安。他们三人因为贪污受贿、滥杀无辜而被群众所憎恨，面对暴乱者的压力与威胁，查士丁尼被迫撤消他们三人的职务。但是，暴动并没有因查士丁尼的妥协而停息，反而愈演愈烈。来自外省的穷人因不满帝国的横征暴敛，所以借着竞技党暴乱提出自己的要求；元老阶层也因无法控制查士丁尼，而其又影响了他们的利益，所以他们力图借暴乱之机改朝换代，拥立普罗布斯 (Probus) 为皇帝。帝国上下一片骚乱，局面已经无法控制，情急之下，查士丁尼一世从地道逃离大赛场，准备弃城逃走。

此时此刻，作为女人，狄奥多拉也同样怨恨丈夫此时的软弱怯懦，但是这些年的风雨历程使她无论面对多大的困难，都能够镇定从容地去应付，如同一个成人去处理幼童的琐事。面对着臣民暴乱、国家危亡，查士丁尼皇帝又企图弃位逃走，经历了生活磨练的狄奥多拉，这时候就成了夫君查士丁尼的主心骨。她的气色悠闲、冷静果断无疑给查士丁尼吃了一颗定心丸，而且她的果断镇定更使查士丁尼羞愧难当，也使在场的朝臣无不钦佩。她对查士丁尼说：

> 我的皇帝陛下，你可以为自救离开。喏！大海就在那边，船只也已准备起航，您也有足够的盘缠。但，我要留下！我认为凡穿上帝王紫袍的人就再也不应把它脱下，当人们不再称呼我皇后时，我不会苟且偷生。我喜欢那句老话：紫绸可做最好的衣服。

正是这样一位既平凡又高贵的女人，在关键时刻，力挽狂澜，挽救了国家危亡。曾经，几乎所有人都唾弃她的出身及品德败坏。但是，她以实际行动向人们证实这个皇后她当之无愧，因此而获得人们的仰慕和赞叹。在尼卡暴乱中，她不仅以坚强勇敢震撼朝臣上下，而且更以独到的见解和洞察问题实质的能力被人们深深折服。

在她看来，"解铃还需系铃人"。查士丁尼曾经一度信任、支持蓝党，而她的父母又是绿党的支持者，所以他们更了解两党的本质和特点。两党素来不和，经常争斗，只是在这次暴乱之前因某种利益而走到一起。且又因达官贵人的教唆利用才掀起了大暴乱。因此，她建议查士丁尼首先从乱党身上下手，挑拨离间，激化其内部矛盾，并派贝利撒留和蒙顿将军率领军队武力镇压竞技场的暴乱，在这场血腥的大屠杀中，死伤无数。据普罗柯比记载，约有三万民众被杀。伊帕提乌斯和庞培乌斯被处以死刑并将尸体抛入大海。尼卡暴乱就这样被平息了。所有参与此事的元老贵族及后代被取消封号，予以流放，全部财产充公。徐家玲教授曾在其著作《早期拜占廷和查士丁尼时代研究》中评价：这次血腥屠杀，标志着查士丁尼与古典时期共和传统的彻底决裂，以皇帝为中心的中央集权政府得到了巩固。同时，它宣告了大贵族们企图控制查士丁尼政府之举的彻底失败，作为一个有绝对独立意志的专制君主，查士丁尼不是任何一派势力的傀儡，他只是他自己。

在拜占廷帝国，所实行的是君主专制体制，正如前文所述，皇权是这个体制的核心，所以统治者所实行的内政改革、外交政策都是为了维护皇权的根本统治。虽然在召开民议时，君士坦丁堡民众有参与政治的传统，且元老院也有做出一些决策的权利，但是真正的决策权也掌握在皇帝的手中，而皇帝则是皇权的象征，任何对皇权和王朝统治构成威胁的力量也不允许存在。所以皇后在尼卡起义中的表现以及她所做出的决策则正体现出皇权与公民利益的对立。如果拜占廷帝国的皇权采用的是绝对的民主制，仅凭一个人态度的坚决也扭转不了事实。但是，不可否认，狄奥多拉的坚强优秀，并不是因为她贵为一国之母，或尊为共治皇帝，就表明她会有一颗坚定、不妥协的心。自古以来，有很多帝王和皇后贵妃，当大敌叛乱、国难当头时，反而扔下江山社稷不管，至天下百姓疾苦于不顾，只命令将士拼杀前敌、血战疆场，自己却带着后宫仓皇避难，找一处清新雅静之处继续逍遥快活。所以，狄奥多拉个性的锻炼与培养都与她少年时代的经历有关，这种个性同时也对她成为皇后以后，对帝国的统治都起到一定的作用，产生一定的影响。

前文已经提到，狄奥多拉的父亲属于绿党，但不幸因病早逝。最初，姐妹三人穿着求乞的服装，戴着桂树花环，被母亲带到竞技场坐在场地上对民众肯求。绿党民众无动于衷、冷漠鄙视的神情深深刺伤了狄奥多拉幼小的心灵，当时她还不到七岁，就已经初步体味到了人间冷暖；而蓝党民众寄予的同情才能如此深刻地印在狄奥多拉心中，但是在尼卡起义中，蓝党和绿党民众的联合暴动迫使狄奥多拉毫不留情地进行血腥大屠杀，因为对统治者而言，不管下层民众对他有多少恩惠，他绝不允许任何人动摇皇权的地位。据普罗柯比介绍，当姐姐沦为交际花时，她像女奴似的穿着短袖束腰外衣侍候姐姐，肩上经常扛着木凳，这是姐姐在公众聚集的地方坐的。这时狄奥多拉还年轻，还不懂男女之事的时候，她就在妓院中遭到了强暴。虽然普罗柯比没有也无法详述当时的情形，但是，就大多数女性而言，在其青春年少时期，如花似玉的年龄中也有无数美好的梦想，任何女性都不愿让"强暴"的惨剧发生在自己身上。狄奥多拉作为女性，当然也如此，但是当时卑微的社会地位、困苦的生活环境使她即使遭到这样的待遇，也没有反抗的可能，这就造就了她性格中隐忍的一面。当她终于足以登上社会的舞台后，她出色的哑剧表演赢得了观众的掌声，而且她的美同时也引起了大多数人的百般恭维。因为普罗柯比也不加掩饰地描绘了狄奥多拉如何借用美色放纵淫荡、自甘下贱。从本质上而言，狄奥多拉十分在乎尊严的，否则最初她又怎会选择忠于阿非利加总督。虽然后来因种种原因再次离弃！与她的闺中密友安东尼娜有所不同的是，嫁给查士丁尼后，狄奥多拉一直都洁身自爱、忠贞不渝，这点普罗柯比也极其赞赏。

狄奥多拉离开非洲总督后，她在亚历山大里亚陷入十分悲惨的境地，过着相当落魄的生活，后来在一性派教徒的帮助下，她历尽艰辛，回到君士坦丁堡。这一路颠沛流离的生活使她性格中坚强干练的一面得以培养。特别是在她的名声和境地处于低谷的时候，据说她做了一个梦：她注定会成为一个强有力的君王的皇后。怀惴着这种梦想，回到君士坦丁堡后，她一反常态，装成一个出色的女演员，过着端庄正派的日子；住在一间狭小的房子里，并时而纺纱卖线，一副贞洁、孤傲的仪表。曾有一句古老的格言如此形容："女人与力量结婚，男人与美丽结婚。"为了获得强有力的社会地位，找到坚实稳定的靠山，狄奥多拉工于心计的性情得到了良好的发挥，一次偶然的机会，查士丁尼遇到她，便被她的美貌所深深吸引，而狄奥多拉巧夺天工的欲擒故纵发挥得淋漓尽致，使查士丁尼迷恋上她便无法自拔。但是最初查士丁尼也只是视狄奥多拉为情妇，当查士丁尼的热情渐渐趋于平静时，她则凭温柔的性情及对查士丁尼的了解，从而扎根于查士丁尼的心中，使他心甘情愿地将财富堆积在她面前，并破例修改法律，使其成为皇后。应该说，虽然狄奥多拉经历了屈辱的开始，但是她并没有让查士丁尼失望，在这样的暴动面前，她的果断坚决稳定了朝中诚惶诚恐的局面，她所说出的话直言不讳，也体现出她与查士丁尼之间亲密无间的关系。但普罗柯比却借这次暴乱尖锐地批判了查士丁尼的内阁，并通过展现狄奥多拉并不适当的男性气质进而批判了当时的政治体制。这说明在当时的社会环境中，尽管女性享有很高的地位，而且狄奥多拉也取得了至高无上的王位，但是在社会中，居于主导地位，占主要力量的还是男性，这才是被社会所公认的。米德指出，妇女可以通过具备男性气质而成为富有开拓创新精神的人，攻击性恰恰是重要的男性气质。大多数妇女由于对攻击性的抑制，而成为成功的障碍。攻击性本身，存在着竞争的成分。一个好争斗、富有攻击性的人，必然有着较强的竞争意识。这种攻击性，竞争意识的强弱，往往表明自我成功期望的高低。尽管普罗柯比不欣赏狄奥多拉在此次暴乱中所表现出来的男性气质，但是他本人也不得不承认狄奥多拉在这场暴乱中所表现出来的勇气以及她所起的关键作用。没有国家，更谈不上皇权至上、皇帝至尊。狄奥多拉凭借自身的能力、凭借对皇帝和朝臣的影响，挽救了国家危亡，同时也就保全了皇权的存在，所以自始至终，在对皇权的影响中，她始终是一个不可或缺的关键人物；也由此向所有人证实了她身为皇后的真正实力所在。

二　罗马法中的女权

　　狄奥多拉对查士丁尼时代对内政策的影响，不仅表现在尼卡暴乱中她突出的表现与贡献，同时，在查士丁尼对罗马法的制定中，由于她的深刻影响，致使查士丁尼在罗马法中大力强调对女性权力的保护，她和武则天都成为中西方开创女性保护的第一人。中国古代皇后武则天成为中国历史上第一位女性天子，她用鲜血铺开通往天子宝座的道路，尽管她因改朝换代、谋权篡位而遭到史学家的批判、百姓的质疑。但是她也是第一位为女性谋取地位的皇后。在她成为皇后以后，改革了后宫，除保留皇后外，取消四妃、九嫔、美人、才人等，新设为数不多的服务性宫人如赞德、宣仪等，这就等于限制了皇帝对后宫三千女人的绝对统治，放松了对女性的束缚，使大多女性不必束缚在宫内，成为皇帝一人玩乐的工具。另一方面，她还规定，父在母丧，要为母亲服丧三年。这些措施都在不同程度上提高了妇女的地位。武则天在一定程度上改变了女性的地位，狄奥多拉也利用自己的政治权利，尽力保护女性。正是她的影响和干预，才将无数卖淫女拯救出水深火热之中。她与武则天虽然做法、政策不同，但是她们的相同之处在于身为女人，更了解女人，也更同情女人的遭遇。

　　古代的罗马社会，是一个父权制的社会，女性所具有的柔弱、轻浮兼备的个性，使罗马法规定妇女必须处于男人监护之下。妇女享有非常少的权利。在孩提时代，女儿处于家庭中父家长的控制之下，后者掌握着家庭中所有成员的生杀大权，任何年龄的男性后代都要服从于他的权威。在父家长死时，成年男性可以自动脱离他的控制；而女性却不行，惟一能够脱离父家长控制的办法是变成保持贞洁的修女。女子出嫁后，则由父权转为夫权，处于夫权的支配下，有夫权婚姻是当时市民法上的婚姻形式，直至共和国晚期，才普遍实行了"无夫权"的婚姻形式，在这种形式下，妇女有了更多的自由。相比较而言，上层社会的罗马妇女，则拥有更多的自由和选择。她们不必拘泥于家中，可以陪同丈夫出席晚宴，虽没有真正属于自己的政治职务，但是她们可以通过丈夫施加影响，与此同时，还可以接受到一定的教育以参加男人们的智力活动。尽管古罗马时期女性地位有所提高，但是与拥有更多自由权的上层妇女相比，下层社会的妇女在贫困生活的压迫下，自由权并无多大改变。皇后狄奥多拉正是由贫苦阶层步入上层社会，不能用"一跃而至"简单的词语来形容她成为皇后的经过，因为在她由普通妇女，也可以说妓女登上皇后宝座毕竟经历了艰难困苦的历程。舞台的阿谀献媚、色场的左右逢圆、旅途的颠沛流离、初识查士丁尼的装腔作势，隐忍、屈辱、艰辛、善变的生活经历改变了她的一生，塑造了她的个性。正是这样的生活经历，才使她深深理解并同情着下层社会女性的疾苦，对女性问题也极其关注。林达·加兰曾在其著作《拜占廷皇后》中评价狄奥多拉与当时罗马社会的女性地位，并猜测：可能她对免除首都下层妇女的不利因素感兴趣，在某种程度上，她过去的经历对这种社会状况产生了深刻的影响。

　　如第一部分所述，查士丁尼于529年颁布了《查士丁尼法典》。在法典的制定及编纂过程中，狄奥多拉虽未起完全决策的作用，但是她却影响了查士丁尼的社会立法。也正是受狄奥多拉的影响，查士丁尼为女性地位的改善立法。在首都君士坦丁堡，卖淫是一个既定的生活现象，在查士丁尼以前，大多数皇帝也曾试图通过法律控制它，虽然我们没有必要把狄奥多拉视为阻止卖淫的驱动力量，但是，毕竟狄奥多拉曾亲身经历过面临下层妇女的这种邪恶，所以她对这个问题的关注更大于其它，也因此为阻止或解放这些妇女卖淫作了大量的工作。狄奥多拉对于妇女的功绩也不完全在于作为一个"妇女解放者"，而在于她为她们争取获得和男性同样的法定权利，达成真正的男女平等；而且她也在以法律形式保护着女性的安全和荣誉，诸如：

CJ1.4.33（AD534）禁止强迫任何女性登台演出，曾为演员的自由民女性可以未经皇帝许可嫁给任何男性。

Nov.J.5.2(AD535)在上帝面前人人平等，既无男女性别之分，也无自由人和奴隶之分。

Nov.J.14.1（AD535）禁止妓院老板或淫媒者利用女孩卖淫

Nov.J.22.3（AD535）因双方感情缔结婚姻，不严格要求嫁妆。

Nov.J.22.18 禁止抛弃无嫁妆的已婚女性。

Nov.J.51（AD537）允许女性放弃她们的舞台生涯，并对试图扣留她们或威逼利诱的人处以罚款

Nov.J.117.6 允许元老与妓女通婚。

Nov.J.134.9（AD559）女性不因欠贷而被监禁，责任由担保人承担；如果某位女性必须承担主要刑事责任，则需送往修道院或由值得信赖的女性予以保护。

从她参与查士丁尼对立法编纂的这些规定中，就可以看出她对女性问题用心良苦，费尽心思地考虑到了对女性的各种保护。而且她更倾向于帮助不幸的妇女，普罗柯比曾提到皇帝的侄女普雷埃克塔（Praeiecta），她爱上了亚美尼亚人阿塔巴尼斯（Artabanes），虽然这桩婚事得到了查士丁尼的首肯，但是当阿塔巴尼斯的妻子来到宫廷乞求狄奥多拉的帮助时，她就竭力阻止此事，并将普雷埃克塔嫁给阿娜斯塔修斯的亲戚约翰。虽然到狄奥多拉死后，阿塔巴尼斯才解除婚约，但是毕竟在一段时间内，狄奥多拉暂时保护了阿塔巴尼斯与其妻的婚姻。

普罗柯比在《建筑》中记载这对夫妇把宫殿装修成华丽的修道院，给先前那些不是出于自愿，而是因为家穷在色欲逼迫下被迫堕入青楼卖淫的女子居住。而且，普罗柯比也在《秘史》中记载了狄奥多拉对妓女的救赎。她在首都广场抓到了五百多个妓女，她们靠出卖肉体，每次仅换取三个银币来维持悲惨落迫的生活。狄奥多拉将她们送到了博斯普鲁斯海峡对面的一个"忏悔修道院"，强迫她们改变生活方式，然而，有些人不愿意接受这样的安排，夜间翻墙逃走。不管采用什么手段，狄奥多拉都在用心关注着这些妓女的命运，她是她们的救星和解放者。

由于皇后狄奥多拉对女权的大力保护，在这一时期，使宫廷女性更加有恃无恐，背着丈夫在外偷情，这是狄奥多拉未曾预料的，即使她后来有所耳闻，却也未大力制止。从当时普罗柯比在《秘史》中愤慨的言语，就足以说明在那一段时期对女性地位的重视，以及当时贵族妇女生活作风的靡烂。宫廷中夫人们可以不必为自己对丈夫的不忠行为承担任何风险，即使被抓到，她们的丈夫也不会胜诉，反而会被处以罚金，偶尔还会遭到鞭笞和监禁。所以，笔者认为，在某种程度上，狄奥多拉对女性权力的过于保护，反而给当时的社会造成了不利的影响。

尽管狄奥多拉英明善助，为女性地位的提高做出了突出的贡献。但是狄奥多拉作为女性，必有其弱点。所以我们在评价每一位伟大的历史人物时，必须要从人性的角度去剖析、立意。狄奥多拉虽贵为皇后与君主双重角色，但是她同样拥有人性的弱点。她的随心所欲的个性则给许多女性也带来了灾难。也许她认为自己作为女性的解放者，就可以利用上天赐给的权力包办所有婚姻。她时常根据自己的喜好去匹配婚姻，而且，几乎没有任何新人会对自己婚姻的稳定性抱有幻想和希望，因为新郎和新娘可能随时就会被迫离开自己的洞房，与皇后安排的另外的人成婚。普罗柯比在《秘史》中特别提到了总理大臣赫摩根尼斯(Hermogenes)的儿子萨图尼乌斯(Saturnius)，他就是最鲜明的例子。原本他已经同自由人家庭出身且品性良好的表妹订婚，新婚前夕，就被狄奥多拉拘禁，带到了另一

个洞房，与艺妓克利索玛罗 (Chrysomallo) 成婚。新婚花烛夜过后，当他把妻子不是处女的事实告诉一个朋友，被狄奥多拉得知后，严厉地惩罚了他，并警告他不允许再做这种蠢事。尽管普罗柯比用随心所欲来斥责狄奥多拉安排婚嫁时的种种行为，但是从普罗柯比的叙述中，如果我们仔细推敲琢磨，反而让我们捕捉到了深一层的信息：大多数时候，狄奥多拉并不是凭借其心情的好与坏，违背很多人的意愿，拆散每一对情侣，而是她所安排的大多数婚姻都带有一定的政治目的，因为她所安排的许多人当时或日后都成为她的心腹、得力的助手。

从表面上看，皇后在罗马法中提高了女性地位，似乎对查士丁尼时代的皇权并无多大关联，而皇权的巩固几乎都与扩大疆域、保护国家稳定、国土统一、宗政和谐息息相关，但是皇权的稳定同样也离不开群众的支持。无论社会如何发展，推动社会进步、开拓文明空间的主体仍然是人。虽然当时罗马社会的女性地位从属于男性，但是作为国家的信众和公民，皇权依然不能脱离女性的支持。狄奥多拉并非完全周密地考虑到了她做此举动的影响，只是由于自己曾经的遭遇，在心底对女性有一种怜悯与同情，才使她极力保护女性的权利，然而，她的这种无意的举动反而为自己赢得了更多的支持者，也基本维护了社会的稳定，这当然可以称为维护皇权的另一种贡献。

拜占廷帝国毁坏圣像运动的影响

赵法欣 西南民族大学

摘要：历时百余年之久的毁坏圣像运动对拜占廷帝国产生的影响是多方面的，它甚至影响了拜占廷帝国在随后几个世纪里的发展。一些学者的相关论述已经就这场运动对于帝国军事、对西方君主国和教会外交、封建化及文化等问题作了有益的探讨，但是关于东正教会及各个修道院势力在运动前后的消长、拜占廷在东地中海地区的商贸地位与威尼斯崛起的关系和文化上某些具体问题的分析尚不够深入，或是有些结论值得进一步推敲。本文拟就以上问题进行一番梳理并作一定的分析，以期对这场运动有一个更为全面、深入的认识。

关键词：毁坏圣像运动；东正教会；威尼斯；拜占廷文化

Abstract：The Iconoclasm had its impacts on the development of the Byzantine Empire in the ensuing centuries that followed this movement. Some scholars have discussed several aspects, as its impacts on the imperial military actions, on its diplomacy, and on the feudalization of the empire and so on. However, this essay is focused on some different issues, as the fate of the orthodox church and monasteries after the movement, the rising of Venice in the East Mediterranean region and cultural activities of Byzantium.

Keywords：Iconoclasm, Orthodox Church, Venice, Byzantine culture

历时百余年之久的毁坏圣像运动是拜占廷帝国历史上一件重要的历史事件，是 8、9 世纪拜占廷教、俗统治集团发动的禁止和崇拜圣像的社会斗争。[1]它虽然以宗教的形式表现出来，但运动的背后却蕴涵着深刻的社会政治、经济因素；也正因为此，这场运动所带来的影响自然是波及到拜占廷帝国的诸多方面，其中有些是立竿见影的，而有些则是长期而持久的。可以说，毁坏圣像运动在某种程度上改变了拜占廷帝国的历史发展轨迹，其影响尤为突出地体现在教会及修道院地位的变化、外交重心的转移和文化生活等几个方面，本文拟就对这些方面的内容作一些粗浅的探讨，以期能对这场运动有更为深入的认识。

---

[1] 陈志强：《拜占廷帝国史》，北京：商务印书馆 2006 年版，第 209 页。

一

毁坏圣像运动对教会与修道院产生了相当的影响。在毁坏圣像运动之前的几个世纪里，拜占廷帝国经历了数次重大的教义问题争论，先后出现了若干影响深远的异端派别，如阿里乌派、聂斯托里派、一性论派等等，教会与国家之间的关系受其影响每每发出不和谐之音。但是，毁坏圣像运动的结束，标志着大规模的神学教义之争在拜占廷帝国内消失了，并由此带来国家与教会之间的关系发展的新阶段，二者的合作越来越密切，教会受到国家力量的庇护。[1]一些学者认为毁坏圣像运动后帝国教会的地位得到加强，更多地是体现在政治层面；但笔者认为除此之外，教会在经济方面的实力在运动之后也迅速恢复甚至较运动之前更为加强。

正如有学者指出的，毁坏圣像运动有着深刻的经济背景，运动之前东正教会和各修道院已经占有着大量的地产和人口，在经济上严重地削弱了国家的实力。[2]因此毁坏圣像派的皇帝们大多采取打击东正教会及其各修道院的政策，致使运动中教会和各修道院的土地和财产被大批的没收，许多修道士被迫还俗，教会实力受到了严重的削弱，这些现象特别突出地表现在君士坦丁五世在位时期（741—775年）。但是随着运动的结束，修道院的数量和它们所拥有的财产又迅速地增长起来。为此皇帝尼基弗鲁斯二世（963—969年在位）不得不于964年颁布法令，限制修道院地产的增长。该法令禁止新修道院的建立，同时对于维持修道院、医院和旅馆的捐赠以及献给都主教和主教的礼品予以禁止。[3]但由于该法令在帝国境内引起强烈不满，无法得以有效施行，因此很快便被皇帝瓦西里二世（976—1025年在位）废除了。所以笔者认为，"毁坏圣像运动虽几经反复但被没收的教会土地并没有回流"[4]的说法是不准确的；相反，毁坏圣像运动一结束，教会和修道院便收回了大部分在运动中被没收的土地和财产，与此同时，大批修道士重新回到修道院中。因此可以说，在毁坏圣像运动结束后的一段时期甚至是更长时间里，教会和修道院在经济上的地位得到了恢复和巩固，它们在帝国的社会生活中又开始发挥起重要的作用。

不仅如此，拜占廷帝国东正教会和君士坦丁堡教区的势力范围也相应地扩大，表现在它控制的地区增多，信仰的民族增加了。早在毁坏圣像运动刚刚开始之时，毁坏圣像诸帝的政策就遭到西方教会和罗马主教的强烈反对，双方由此展开激烈的斗争。为了与罗马主教相对抗，利奥三世皇帝（717—741年在位）将原属罗马主教教区的西西里、卡拉布里亚和伊利里安三个辖区置于君士坦丁堡主教区的管辖之下，并开始对西西里和卡拉布里亚两地征收人头税。君士坦丁堡主教区的辖区在原来的基础上又增加了巴尔干半岛诸省和希腊化的南部意大利。[5]

随着毁坏圣像运动的结束和教会势力的恢复，东正教会对帝国周边地区的影响逐渐加强。至瓦西里一世（867—886年在位）时，俄罗斯和伯罗奔尼撒半岛上的斯拉夫部落都先后皈依了东正教，甚至是帝国内部的许多犹太教居民也被迫改宗。[6]这里虽然有政治、外交等其它因素，但是在毁坏圣像运动时期打下的基础亦不容忽视。君士坦丁堡教区地位的提升，标志着东部教会势力的崛起，从此开启了与罗马教会分庭抗礼的时代，东西教会之间的斗争愈演愈烈。

还有一点需要指出，即基督教会的分裂。一方面基督教会的分裂表现为东、西教会的分道扬镳。由于文化传统、历史背景和居民成分上的种种不同，东西教会之间的分歧早已有之，之后又随着罗

① G. Ostrogorsky, *History of the Byzantine State*, translated by J. M. Hussey, Oxford, 1956, p.195.
② 参见陈志强：《拜占廷毁坏圣像运动的原因》，载《世界历史》1996年第3期，第51–59页；及其《拜占廷学研究》，北京：人民出版社2001年版，第190–206页。
③ A. A. Vasiliev, *History of the Byzantine Empire*, Vol. 1, Wisconsin, 1952, p.336.
④ 参见祁颖：《再析圣像破坏运动的影响》，载《学术交流》1997年第5期，第126–127页。
⑤ Ostrogorsky, *History of the Byzantine State*, p.146.
⑥ Vasiliev, *History of the Byzantine Empire*, Vol. 1, p.332.

马和君士坦丁堡之间的竞争而加剧。毁坏圣像运动则像一剂催化剂使得教皇和南部意大利脱离了拜占廷帝国，转而投向法兰克王国。这也为 1054 年东西教会正式分裂埋下了伏笔。自此，东、西两部分各自走上截然不同的发展道路。拜占廷帝国先是在宗教上进而是在政治和外交上被西方大大地孤立了，这也成为此后帝国衰落甚至是灭亡的一个重要原因。1204 年第四次十字军赤裸裸地洗劫君士坦丁堡，理由之一便是惩罚东方的教会分裂者。而当 15 世纪上半期土耳其人的进攻日益急促、拜占廷皇帝向西方求援之时，得到的全是来自天主教会和西方君主的空头许愿，而并无实际的援助行动，其中很重要的一个原因就是罗马教皇看到了把东部教会统一过来已经不可能了。[1]

教会的分裂另一个表现则是东正教会内部诸多派别之间的对立斗争。毁坏圣像运动结束后，在东方教会内部，"基督教早期发展过程中形成的教区在神学论战的同时也积极进行争夺最高宗教地位的角逐，形成大大小小的宗派，使基督教会长期陷于分裂。9 世纪以后，各教会之间的斗争更带有个人色彩。"[2]较著名的事件有斯都底奥斯修道院院长塞奥多利与大教长美塞迪乌斯（843 — 847年在任）、大教长伊格纳条斯（847 — 858，867 — 877 年在任）与弗条斯（858 — 867，877 — 886年在任）之间的斗争，他们攻击对方的武器虽都是神学教义问题，但实质上任何一方都没有提出什么新的理论。他们真实的目的是借此无情地打击异己分子，树立自己的权威，这使得东正教会内部的分裂日趋严重。[3]因此，东正教会始终没能像西方教会那样形成一个稳定的宗教中心，分裂造成了教会内部力量的分散，各地各民族教会的独立性十分强烈。不仅如此，东正教会内部的斗争还常常与世俗集团之间的政治斗争错综交织，最具代表性例子当属围绕皇帝利奥六世（886 — 912 年在位）的第四次婚姻事件所展开的激烈斗争了。更有悲剧性的是，这种教会参与皇室斗争的习俗延续到了拜占廷末代王朝统治时期，宗教争论与统治集团内部的纷争加剧了拜占廷社会的解体。当土耳其军队兵临城下、围攻君士坦丁堡之时，拜占廷教士们还在圣索非亚教堂里喋喋不休地争论着，一些主教甚至公开宣扬宁可欢迎伊斯兰教也不要天主教。[4]这些举动大大动摇了民心士气，削弱了本已不够强大的抵抗力量，延误了战机，加速了帝国的灭亡。这些无疑都是毁坏圣像运动对教会的消极影响。

二

从外交方面的影响来看，由毁坏圣像运动引起的教义之争使拜占廷帝国与西方渐渐疏远，罗马教皇将共同对抗伦巴德人的希望寄托在法兰克王国之上，拜占廷的地位愈发孤立。发生于 800 年的查理加冕一事更是对拜占廷帝国"大一统"观念的沉重打击。这些无疑都严重降低了作为罗马帝国正统继承人的拜占廷帝国的国际威望，使它在西方世界的势力遭受重创，只能将注意力专注于东方。这些已有学者作过专门论述。[5]但有一件事对拜占廷帝国此后几个世纪的发展产生了重要影响，可是似乎尚未有人涉及，那就是威尼斯共和国的崛起和壮大。可以说正是毁坏圣像运动和受其影响下的东西方关系，给威尼斯逐步摆脱东、西方两大帝国的双重束缚、走上独立发展的道路提供了契机和可能。

威尼斯在 8 世纪以前的相当长一段时期内受拜占廷帝国拉文纳总督区的管辖。727 年，威尼斯参加了意大利境内反对利奥三世毁坏圣像饬令的叛乱，虽然叛乱被镇压，但利奥却任命了威尼斯人自己的总督，并封赠给他以皇家头衔。这是威尼斯摆脱拉文纳总督区走向独立的第一步。751 年，

---

① 参见 J. Godfrey, *1204: The Unholy Crusade*, Oxford, 1980, p.11.
② 陈志强：《拜占廷学研究》，第 172 页。
③ 参见 J. M. Hussey, *The Orthodox Church in the Byzantine Empire*, Oxford, 1986, pp.69–86.
④ 陈志强：《拜占廷学研究》，第 178 页。
⑤ Ostrogorsky, *History of the Byzantine State*, p.193.

拉文纳总督区被伦巴德王国攻陷，威尼斯遂由自己的总督直接管理。丕平献土和教皇国建立后，教皇与法兰克人的联合使得拜占廷在南部意大利的统治受到挑战，查理曼于774年征服伦巴德王国后，这一地区只剩下威尼斯还属于拜占廷，但还是受到法兰克人的支配。此后威尼斯就这样在东西两大国之间的夹缝中谋求生存。812年，拜占廷帝国与法兰克王国在亚琛订立条约，规定威尼斯名义上属拜占廷管辖，但需继续向意大利的法兰克王国纳贡。该条约保证了威尼斯在大陆上可以免遭侵略，他们的商船自由航行进行贸易的权力也得到了承认。由此，威尼斯以最微小的代价获取了独立于东西两大国之外自由发展的良机。独立后的威尼斯迅速发展其海上贸易和海军，并逐渐控制了亚得里亚海的商贸。随后因向拜占廷帝国提供海上援助，威尼斯人从拜占廷皇帝那里获得了大量贸易特权，这更进一步促进了它海上势力的发展，使其在东地中海地区的贸易中处于极其有利的地位。①

正是由于毁坏圣像运动，使得本来就有很大差异的拜占廷与威尼斯按照各自的传统走上了不同的发展道路，对拜占廷来说它损失了一个可以观察、控制西方的前哨，而威尼斯则逐步走上自由发展之路。威尼斯的崛起和独立，对后几个世纪拜占廷帝国的命运造成了极为严重的后果。首先，它使拜占廷帝国传统的贸易格局遭到严重的破坏，拜占廷作为地中海世界贸易中心的地位逐渐被威尼斯所取代。10世纪末，亚得里亚海已经完全被威尼斯人所控制，帝国大量的商业贸易收入落入威尼斯人的手中，这无疑切断了拜占廷帝国一项重要的经济收入来源，瓦解了帝国的一个经济基础。而且，帝国长期维持的一系列金融、财政和海关制度也被打乱，帝国经济体制遭到严重破坏。此后拜占廷帝国再也没能从这中贸易衰落中恢复过来，它在某种程度上奠定了帝国灭亡的经济基础，正如有学者指出的，拜占廷帝国的历史"从根本上说是它的金融财政政策和贸易的历史"，"拜占廷灭亡的悲剧其实就是它的金融贸易的悲剧"。②其次，过分地依赖于来自威尼斯的海上援助，减弱了拜占廷人发展壮大本国海军的热情。在拜占廷历史上，海军建设从来未被给予足够的重视。正式的海军建设真正始于伊拉克略王朝诸帝，后因阿拉伯人海上势力的瓦解而被皇帝削弱；毁坏圣像运动后帝国海军力量曾一度复兴，但因为担心海军司令权力坐大会威胁皇权而再度被罗曼努斯一世裁减。③更为重要的原因，则在于威尼斯海上舰队已承担起了保卫海防的重任，拜占廷人自认为可以高枕无忧了！但正是因为他们忽视海军建设这一重大失误，遂将帝国海上防务完全托付他人，从而把帝国的海上大门向外人大开。一旦有外敌入侵，帝国既无能力组织足够强大的海军进行有效的抵抗，同时又早已将自己暴露在敌人面前。第四次十字军攻陷君士坦丁堡即印证了拜占廷帝国忽视海防的重大失误，也表现了威尼斯商业共和国的本性——只要有利可图，便可以抛弃一切信义和盟约。自毁坏圣像运动开始的威尼斯共和国的崛起，是对后期拜占廷发展的重大威胁。

三

对精神文化生活所造成的冲击，可以说是毁坏圣像运动对拜占廷帝国影响最为深刻的一个方面。毁坏圣像运动之后，拜占廷帝国的文化才正式形成了古典传统、基督教精神与东方因素三者并驾齐驱共同发展的局面。可以说，真正意义上独特的拜占廷文化是在此后才逐步发展起来的，之后兴起了拜占廷的文化复兴运动。④此外，有学者就这场运动对拜占廷教俗文化格局的改变、拜占廷艺术创作风格的变化等问题都作了有益探讨，笔者此处不再赘述。但是有一个方面的问题似乎尚未引起学者们足够的关注，即毁坏圣像运动对9世纪之后拜占廷文学发展的影响。

① D. M. Nicol, *Byzantium and Venice: A Study of Diplomatic and Cultural Relations*, Cambridge, 1988, p.50ff.
② S. Runciman, *Byzantine Civilization*, London, 1959, p.163, p.178.
③ Runciman, *Byzantine Civilization*, pp.150–152.
④ 参见邹薇：《论12世纪拜占廷的文化复兴》，载《现代企业教育》2008年第323期，第132–133页。

843 年塞奥多拉女皇恢复圣像的崇拜，标志着 8、9 世纪毁像派统治者政策的失败，也深刻说明他们的政策违背了帝国大多数基督教臣民的宗教习俗与情感，因而毁像政策不但未能禁止帝国境内崇拜圣像的行为，反而激发了民众对圣像的热情，致使崇拜圣像的原则一经重新确立，便以更炽热于以往的程度爆发出来。这虽然与毁坏圣像运动的初衷相抵牾，却可以被视作这场运动所带来的重要影响之一。这种热情波及至拜占廷文化生活的许多方面，体现在文学创作领域尤为明显。

毁坏圣像运动结束后的几个世纪里，拜占廷文学创作几乎呈现了"一边倒"的局面。由于崇像派最终取得胜利，大量毁像派人士创作的文学作品在运动中及运动结束后被销毁，我们只能通过崇像派人士的某些作品来了解这些被毁作品的有限信息。不仅如此，由于 843 年之后崇拜圣像重新获得合法地位并成为拜占廷人的正统行为，毁坏圣像的理念受到压制，之后的文学作品几乎毫无例外地宣扬圣像崇拜的合理，这些作品自然而然地成为支持圣像崇拜的旗手。这一观念最鲜明的结果便是圣徒传记作品的大量涌现。

圣徒传记作品的传主往往都是那些在毁坏圣像运动中因坚持圣像崇拜而遭受迫害的基督徒，这些人的虔诚行为在运动结束后受到热情歌颂，这种写作模式与风格影响了毁坏圣像运动之后几个世纪里圣徒传记的创作。从毁坏圣像运动期间直至运动结束后，一些拜占廷作家创作了大量活跃于毁坏圣像运动中的圣徒传记，这一势头在 843 年之后更为一发而不可收。[1]到了 10 和 11 世纪，圣徒传记这种文学形式更是迎来了自己的繁荣期。[2]可是这个时期几乎没有能够体现毁像派观点的圣徒传记作品，关于毁像派人士的传记也难觅踪影。[3]这种局面的出现表明，在毁坏圣像运动结束后，拜占廷民众宗教情感的整体趋势偏向于对圣像的崇拜，那些与之不符的原则与实践统统被排斥，因此我们今天见到的圣徒传记几乎清一色的代表了崇拜圣像人群的呼声。正是毁坏圣像运动中对这种具有古老传统的宗教情感的压制，才造就了运动结束后它的再一次爆发。

如果说圣徒传记作品因其题材特点能够与帝国宗教局势产生密切关联尚不足为奇的话，那运动之后许多拜占廷史学作品也都体现出明确的崇拜圣像立场，则更加生动反映出这场运动对拜占廷知识分子所造成的影响。无论是 9 世纪的"忏悔者"塞奥发尼斯、尼基弗鲁斯牧首，抑或之后的"执事官"利奥、尼基塔斯·侯尼亚迪斯等人，[4]许多拜占廷历史学家都在自己的史学著作中流露出对圣像的崇拜之情。如"忏悔者"塞奥发尼斯在其《编年史》中完全以对待圣像的态度作为评价历史人物的首要标准，支持圣像崇拜的人通常会受到褒扬，他们的恶行也会被隐而不宣，而反对圣像崇拜之人即便有所作为也会因其信仰不"虔诚"而遭受贬斥，他们的功绩也会受到作者的漠视甚至被完全抹杀。[5]塞奥发尼斯本人因为坚持崇拜圣像而在毁坏圣像运动期间遭受迫害，正是这种特殊的个人经历使他的《编年史》具有鲜明的宗教和政治立场，也使该书具有旗帜鲜明的单一评价体系。由于毁坏圣像运动伤及了许多拜占廷知识分子的宗教情感，所以迫使这些人拿起笔来反抗帝国当局的毁像政策，以自己的作品为武器向毁像派宣战。以塞奥发尼斯《编年史》为代表的拜占廷文学作品集中体现了这一点，而且这种导向性也深刻影响了随后几个世纪里拜占廷文学创作的风格。

---

① I. Ševčenko, "Hagiography of the Iconoclast Period", in *Iconoclasm, Papers given at the 9th Spring Symposium of Byzantine Studies*, ed. A. Bryer & J. Herrin, Birmingham, 1977, p.113.

② R. Morris, *Monks and Laymen in Byzantium, 843–1118*, Cambridge: Cambridge University Press, 1995, p.65.

③ Ševčenko, "Hagiography of the Iconoclast Period", p.113.

④ 分别参见 *The History of Leo the Deacon: Byzantine Military Expansion in the Tenth Century*, introduction, translation, and annotations by A.-M. Talbot and D. F. Sullivan, Washington, D.C.: Dumbarton Oaks Research Library and Collection, 2005; Niketas Choniatēs, *O City of Byzantium, Annals of Niketas Choniatēs*, translated by H. J. Magoulias, Detroit: Wayne State University Press, 1984.

⑤ *Chronicle of Theophanes Confessor, Byzantine and Near Eastern History, AD 284–813*, Translated with Introduction and Commentary By C. Mango and R. Scott, Oxford: Clarendon Press, 1997, passim.

综上所述，无论是宗教色彩浓厚的圣徒传记，还是相对世俗化的史学作品，毁坏圣像运动结束后的拜占廷文学作品呈现出思想观念的某种一致性，具体而言就是基本上反映的都是崇像派的立场与观点，毁像派自从慢慢销声匿迹。这一现象的出现，毫无疑问是毁坏圣像运动自身所造成的逻辑结果。

一场持续百余年轰轰烈烈的毁坏圣像运动带给拜占廷帝国的并不仅仅是动荡与破坏，它也在一定程度上帮助帝国摆脱了内忧外乱的困扰，逐步走向强盛，奠定了马其顿王朝盛世的基础。更为重要的是，运动结束后，拜占廷帝国走上了一条较以往发生了许多显著变化的发展道路。所以我们有理由认为，毁坏圣像运动是拜占廷历史发展中的重要转折点，它的影响深远而持久。

13—15 世纪欧洲的华瓷收藏

邹 薇 四川大学

摘要：欧洲收藏中国瓷器的早期阶段是 13 至 15 世纪。这一时期的藏品有的完整保存至今，有的成为残片通过考古出土，还有的已经失传只存在于中世纪的各种文献资料中。收藏特点：一是在来源上的非单一性；二是数量上的有限性；三是在欧洲收藏界的珍贵性。

关键词：13—15 世纪；欧洲；华瓷；收藏

Abstract：The early stage of European collecting Chinese porcelains is 13th to 15th centuries. Some of the collections have been completely preserved till now. Some of the Chinese porcelains were excavated as pieces. Others have been lost, and only exist in medieval documents. Characteristics of European collecting Chinese porcelains: extensive collection sources; limited number of collections; preciousness.

Keywords：the 13th to 15th centuries, Europe, Chinese porcelain, Collection

13—15 世纪是欧洲华瓷收藏的早期阶段。华瓷在 13—15 世纪的欧洲较为稀有，加之坊间盛传其有解毒等神奇功效，因此，华瓷在这时的欧洲很多地区，尤其是西欧，是财富、身份和地位的象征，被欧洲上层争相收藏。在 13 世纪以前，欧洲通常从地中海东岸的穆斯林国家那里获取华瓷。14 世纪时流入欧洲的华瓷数量仍旧不多。直到 16 世纪以后，葡萄牙人在东方海域建立起商业网络后，华瓷收藏才逐渐在欧洲普及开来。

一 保存至今的华瓷

13—15 世纪时能传入欧洲并能保存至今的华瓷是比较罕有的。这些华瓷现分布在欧洲各国博物馆和收藏家手中。

在欧洲，最早有记录的华瓷被称为甘尼尔凡提尔壶[①]（Gagnieres-Fonthill Vase）。这是一只元代的青白釉玉壶春瓶[②]，制成的时间大约是 1300 至 1330 年间，产地是景德镇。甘尼尔凡提尔壶高约

[①] 又被译为丰山瓶。

[②] 玉壶春瓶造型定型于北宋时期，以撇口、细颈、圆腹、圈足为特征。元代前期的玉壶春瓶多袭宋制，敞口、颈部瘦长，颈一下渐广，至底处内收，腹呈椭圆状，圈足微外撇。参见中国硅酸盐学会编：《中国陶瓷史》，文物出版社 1982 年版，第 347 页。

28.3 厘米，是硬质瓷器，釉色为白底的、略带蓝色的青白釉。瓶身为梨形，饰有浮雕类的花卉和叶子。[1]

甘尼尔凡提尔壶原是匈牙利国王拉约什一世（Lajos I of Hungary）[2]的藏品。传说是拉约什一世从前去觐见教皇本笃十二世（Pope Benedict XII）的中国使团那里获得。欧洲人在这个玉壶春瓶上加了一个银质的手柄、壶嘴、壶盖和基座[3]，将它变成一个执壶。1381 年，拉约什一世将它赠送给了同家族的那不勒斯的查理三世（Charles III of Naples）。后来又转手给了法国的贝瑞公爵（Duke of Berry）金恩·德·法兰西（Jean de France）和法国路易十三的王储。17 世纪晚期，甘尼尔凡提尔壶成为弗朗索瓦（François Lefebvre de Caumartin）的财产。他让人用水彩在瓶身上作画。其后，该瓷器被售予[4]拥有英国丰山大隐修院（Fonthill Abbey）的威廉姆·贝克福德（William Beckford），并一直安置在该宅邸中。后来甘尼尔凡提尔壶又卖给了曾一度拥有丰山大隐修院的英国武器商人约翰·法科（John Farquhar）。19 世纪时底座被取下，1882 年拥有此瓶的贝克福德女婿哈密尔顿公爵（Duck of Hamilton）的后人寻人对该瓷器进行了一次修复，同年将其以 27 英镑的价格卖给前都柏林博物馆。[5]之后甘尼尔凡提尔壶直到二十世纪 50 年代才重新出现在公众面前，现由都柏林的爱尔兰国家博物馆收藏。[6]

据说法国贝瑞公爵金恩还有另一件来自中国的玉壶春瓶[7]，白釉，瓶身上有浮雕花纹，其来源不详。说明当时的欧洲不止一件玉壶春瓶。

另一件著名的华瓷是卡岑埃尔恩博根瓷碗（The Katrenelnbogen Bowl），现在是德国黑森州立博物馆中的镇馆之宝。这件瓷器在 1453 年毫无疑问是属于卡岑埃尔恩博根伯爵菲利普（Count Philip of Katzenelnbogen）的。菲利普伯爵曾于 1433 至 1434 年在东方旅行，很有可能是在旅途中得到了这件华瓷。[8]据说这位伯爵前往圣地朝圣，在阿卡城购得带回。阿卡城是中国途径巴格达、大马士革与地中海地区进行商业贸易的一条通道的终点。证明了这一时期的华瓷主要是通过中东等地几经周转，通过交换和购买等形式传入德意志地区。

卡岑埃尔恩博根瓷碗是一青瓷碗。该瓷碗线条优美，上面覆有一层亮绿色的釉。是元朝或是明初于产于龙泉地区，款识为 1453 年（一说为 1435 年[9]）。该瓷碗瓷身宽阔，俯视为六边形。总高度 20.6 厘米，直径 16 厘米。碗缘由欧洲当地工匠镶上了金边和银边，据说某位王子曾使用过。[10]瓷碗附有镀金银座，此底座是由菲利普伯爵装上的，上有伯爵的纹章图案，其风格显示是 15 世纪莱茵河的作坊制作。

另外还有一件 15 世纪欧洲贵族收藏的华瓷流传了下来。是一件元代的龙泉瓷盘，现收藏在佛

---

[1] Stacey Pierson, Collectors, *Collections and Museums: The Field of Chinese Ceramics in Britain, 1560–1960*, Peter Lang, 2007, p. 17.

[2] 又译为路易大帝（Louis the Great）。

[3] 有学者认为这个底座是土耳其人加上去的。参见 Stacey Pierson, *Collectors, Collections and Museums: The Field of Chinese Ceramics in Britain, 1560–1960*, p. 18.

[4] 法国大革命后，法国王室的很多藏品流散到民间，英国的贵族和富商纷纷前往巴黎淘宝，甘尼尔凡提尔壶也是在这种情况下从法国到了英国。

[5] See Clive Wainwright, *The Romantic Interior: The British Collector at Home, 1750–1850*, London, 1989, pp. 135–136.

[6] Arthur Lane, "The Gaignières–Fonthill Vase; A Chinese Porcelain of about 1300", *The Burlington Magazine*, Vol. 103, No. 697, 1961, pp. 124–133.

[7] Lauren Arnold, *Princely gifts and papal treasures: the Franciscan mission to China and its influence on the art of the West, 1250–1350*, Hardcover, Desiderata Press, 1999, p. 133.

[8] David Whitehouse, "Chinese Porcelain in Medieval Europe", *Medieval Archaeology*, 1973, No. 16, p. 71.

[9] 参见伊瓦·斯托贝：《德雷斯顿的中国瓷器收藏》，吴鹏译，载《中国历史文物》，2005 年第 4 期，第 26 页。

[10] 朱培初：《明清陶瓷和世界文化的交流》，轻工业出版社 1984 年版，第 87 页。

罗伦萨银器博物馆。[①]该瓷盘是 1461 年埃及苏丹赠送给威尼斯总督帕斯夸莱·马利皮耶罗（Pasquale Malipiero）20 件瓷器礼物之一。[②]1487 年，埃及苏丹就曾赠给劳伦佐·德·美第奇（Lorenzo de Medici）一批中国产的美丽绝伦的青瓷花瓶。这批瓷器极具收藏价值，可惜在 1494 年劳伦佐死后被卖掉了，[③]除了这件龙泉瓷盘，其余的下落不明。

13—15 世纪西方收藏的华瓷中，还有一些是流入欧洲时间不能精确的华瓷。马可波罗瓷瓶（The Marco Polo Jar）就是其中的一例。

13 世纪时，中国专门出口给印度和波斯的瓷器渐渐流入意大利。[④]另有不少商人和旅行家也往来于波斯和意大利间，专门经营华瓷贸易。[⑤]现今收藏在威尼斯圣马可教堂的一件元代白瓷，据说是由马可·波罗带回意大利的，因此被称为马可·波罗瓷瓶，可以说是圣马可教堂的珍宝。大部分学者们确信这件瓷瓶是在 13 世纪的时候传到欧洲。确切的时间据说是在 1295 年，马可·波罗将一些中国瓷器带回威尼斯，[⑥]这个瓷瓶就是其中之一。但现在仍有一些学者对于是否是由马可·波罗带回的，持不同意见。有学者认为如果这件德化白瓷是马可·波罗带回的话，那它将是留存至今的最早一件流传至欧洲的中国瓷器。[⑦]

该瓷罐高 12 厘米，最大直径 8.1 厘米。瓶身俯视呈五边形，据判断应是个梅瓶[⑧]。瓶底有边，脖子短而细，底部比较厚。原有四个小环可以扣住瓶盖。瓷器是半透明的白瓷，除了瓶底外都上了浅绿色的釉。瓷器底部的釉有些开裂。瓶身饰有花瓣型的纹饰，下方有一条纹样作为花瓣的支撑。瓶口和瓶底有传统的花团状的装饰。这种装饰在中国东南部很常见。因此很多学者认为这件瓷器来自中国南方，应该是福建德化地区。

威尼斯圣马可教堂曾经藏有来自中国的另一件瓷器，是一个完整的八角形香炉。现属于法国卢浮宫博物馆，格朗迪迪埃（Grandidier）藏品系列。该香炉盖身齐全，来自中国福建。据说是在中世纪的时候传入威尼斯，一个掌管圣马可宝库的牧师送给了达维离耶（Davillier），达维离耶后来又卖给了格朗迪迪埃。也有学者认为该香炉是清代的产物，而格朗迪迪埃是被达维离耶蒙骗了。[⑨]

16 世纪前欧洲收藏的华瓷还有一件是青白瓷瓶，现在收藏在英国伦敦维多利亚和艾伯特博物馆，其编号为：acc. no. c68-1957。瓷器诞生的时间为 14 世纪左右，釉色呈淡蓝色，瓶身上绘有植物图案。瓶颈有损伤，这个缺陷在 1700 年后被德意志工匠以镀金所掩饰。有学者认为从材质上看不太像葡萄牙或是荷兰进口的，应该是在中世纪传入欧洲的，[⑩]但传入的具体时间不详。

达·伽马途径印度时，在当地购买了一些华瓷。回国之后将其中的一些精品献给了当时的葡萄牙国王曼努埃尔一世（Manuel I）。至此，葡萄牙王室开始了对华瓷的收藏。

---

① 也有学者认为瓷盘上后加的铭文说明了它是 1484 年由埃及苏丹赠与罗伦佐·美第奇的礼物。参见 H. Honour, *Chinoiserie: The Vision of Cathayl*, New York, 1973, p. 36; R. W. Lightbown, "Oriental Art and the Orient in Late Renaissance and Baroque Italy", *Journal of the Warburg and Courtauld Institutes*, 1969, No. 32, p. 229.

② P. Atterbury, *The History of porcelain*, London, Orbis, 1982, p. 80.

③ Ibid.

④ See W. Burton, *A General History of Porcelain*, vol. 1, New York, 1921, p. 111.

⑤ 参见朱培初：《明清陶瓷和世界文化的交流》，第 103 页。

⑥ Donald F. Lach, *Asia in the Making of Europe*, vol. II, Book one, p. 36.

⑦ Oliver Impey, *The Origins of Museums: The Cabinet of Curiosities in Sixteenth-and Seventeenth-Century*, London, 1998, p. 356.

⑧ 梅瓶是一种小口、短颈、丰肩、瘦底、圈足的瓶式，以口小只能插梅枝而得名。元代的梅瓶较多地继承宋制，但它的口部加高，口沿平坦，肩部较丰满，一般不带盖，元代的梅瓶在各地瓷窑中都有烧制。参见中国硅酸盐学会编：《中国陶瓷史》，第 346—347 页。

⑨ Oscar C. Raphael, "Chinese Porcelain Jar in the Treasury of San Marco, Venice", *Transactions of the Oriental Ceramic Society*, 1931–1932, pp. 13–15.

⑩ David Whitehouse, "Chinese Porcelain in Medieval Europe", p. 72.

二 考古出土的华瓷碎片

13—15 世纪传入欧洲的华瓷有一些在收藏和使用过程中被毁。通过考古出土的一些碎片成为了华瓷在欧洲收藏的一个佐证。

意大利卢切拉的一个古堡中发掘出一些瓷器碎片。其中一些是越窑瓷碗碎片，带碗沿，曾淡灰褐色，内含白色物质。碗内的釉厚于碗外，釉色中有呈乳状的白色物质。碗身饰有莲花花瓣图案，由底部放射性蔓延至瓷器下半部分，属于 11 世纪越窑的晚期作品。另外有两个青瓷碗碎片，带碗沿。釉色较厚，是比较明亮的浅灰色，混有一些天青色和深灰色的物质，部分青灰色的釉龟裂，专家认为属于 12 世纪的浙江青瓷。最后是一个小青白瓷碗的部分碎片。瓷碗属白瓷，碗内和碗外的底部上有暗青灰色的釉。碗身有一圈窄的植物花纹，釉下彩，是 12 至 13 世纪福建产品。①

英格兰威切斯特也出土了华瓷的碎片。在 14—15 世纪地层中出土了青花瓷碗或是青花瓷杯的碎片。下溪街（Lower Brook Street）同等地层中也出土了一些青瓷碎片。

匈牙利布达佩斯的一个 15 世纪灰坑中曾出土了橄榄绿的瓷盘和瓷壶。

欧洲还出土了中国专为中东生产的瓷器，说明这些华瓷在 16 世纪前也传入欧洲成为藏品。

在希腊的科林斯地区的一次考古发掘中，出土了一批拜占廷帝国晚期的堆积物，其中就有中国青花瓷器的碎片。②在塞浦路斯的尼科西亚（Nicosia in Cyprus）也出土了由中东地区进口的中国青花瓷碎片。③

西班牙的阿尔梅里亚（Almeria）一间当地博物馆收藏了该地出土的一些瓷器碎片。其中一个是直径 10.7 厘米的带碗边沿的碎片，硬质白瓷，釉色透明，瓷器底部外饰有莲花花瓣。内部有绿色的阿拉伯语铭文，是古兰经中的一句话："来自安拉的力量"，但是在拼写上有错误。另一个是直径 8 厘米的瓷碗底部残片。也是硬质白瓷，透明釉，内部釉下彩，同心圆类的装饰。还有一个是一片很小的白瓷碎片，很小。最后一个是 8.5 厘米的瓷碗碎片，相对前面几个碎片来说质量一般。器身不透明，也是无色釉。有专家认为这是专为中东生产的华瓷，也有可能是是中东仿制的。④

三 中世纪文献中的华瓷

中世纪文献中记载的华瓷是比较重要的研究来源。

1. 14 世纪欧洲文献中的华瓷

第一类是中世纪的遗嘱。

1323 年那不勒斯和西西里王后玛丽亚（Queen Maria of Naples and Sicily）的遗嘱中提到了华瓷。由于 13 世纪及其之前没有华瓷在欧洲的记录，因此这份文件可以说是中世纪欧洲保存下来的最早提到华瓷的文件。其原文如下：

Item Paulo Gerardi…Bocalettum unum cum coperculo qui ponitur in extimatione de sporchellano, et est de vitro, extimatum uncias duas pro uncia una. Item Baldo de Baldis scutellas duas de porchellana pro tarenis

---

① David Whitehouse, "Chinese Porcelain in Medieval Europe", pp. 66–67.
② Charles H. Morgan II, *The Byzantine Pottery*, Harvard University Press, 1942, p. 171.
③ A. H. S. Megaw, "Three medieval pit–groups from Nicosia", *Report Dep, Antiquities of Cyprus 1937–39*, pp. 145–168; cited from David Whitehouse, "Chinese Porcelain in Medieval Europe", p. 68.
④ David Whitehouse, "Chinese Porcelain in Medieval Europe", p. 69.

quindecim.[①]

学者克里兹金科维奇（Krisztinkovics）和科拉克（Korach）的研究指出王后在遗嘱中赠予巴尔杜斯·德·巴尔蒂斯（Baldus de Baldis）的是两个小瓷碗，只有 15 个塔里尼（tareni）[②]重。

在 14 世纪的那不勒斯，有记录可查的还有 4 件华瓷，其中之一的就是甘尼尔凡提尔壶，曾属于那不勒斯和西西里王室所有。

第二类是中世纪的私人财产目录。

1363 年诺曼底公爵的财产目录和 1372 年的简·戴福略（Jeanne d'Evreux）的财产目录显示，他们收藏了来自中国的瓷器[③]。学者普遍认为诺曼底公爵收藏的有碗和盘子，其中一件是青瓷。而戴福略所拥有的可能是一件白瓷。

1379—1380 年的安茹公爵路易斯一世（Louis I, duke of Anjou）的财产目录原文：

Une escuelle de pourcelaine à servir de fruit, garnie d'argent doré: et par le pié est à plusieurs savages; et dessus a vi esmaus, en chascun desquels a une teste d'apostre, et les bors sont esmailliés d'asur, et y a gens qui chacent et aucuns qui jouent à divers jeux. Et sur lesdis bors a trois escuons de nos armes pendants à avelez; et y aussi a trois fretelez dorez à perles et a petis grenas, et sur chascum fretez a une langue de serpent. Et poise en tout v mars vi onces.[④]

安茹公爵路易斯一世拥有的是一个水果盘，有银质镀金的底座和佩饰，盘内有人物嬉戏的纹饰图案。安茹公爵本在 1378 年被那不勒斯女王乔万娜一世（Joanna I）指定为继承人，但是都拉佐公爵查理三世（Charles III, duke of Durazzo）于 1378 年占领那不勒斯后他失去了继承权。学者普遍认为他是在去意大利之前得到并收藏了这些华瓷，因此很有可能是通过贸易或是外交礼物的形式而获得的。[⑤]

第三类是这一时期的公证文书。

意大利国家档案馆（Archivio di Stato）收藏了一份 1384 年的热那亚公证书。该文件公正了一批商品，其中就有华瓷。

2. 15 世纪中世纪文献中的华瓷

第一类也是当时欧洲的私人财产目录。

1416 年贝里公爵金恩（Jean, duke of Berry）的财产目录。

原文如下：

Une aiguière de porcelaine ouvrée, les pié, couvercle et biberon de laquelle sont d'argent doré et l'envoya nostre Sant Père le Pappe Jehan XXIIJe (sic), en don à Monsieur . . .

---

① 　Bela Krisztinkovics and Maurizio Korach, "Un antico documento sulla porcellana cinese in Europa", Faenza, LUI (lg67), pp. 27–30, citing Gustav Wenzel, *Monumenta Hungariae Historica: Diplomdciai emlekek az Anjou-Korbol* (Budapest, 1874), I, 239–40 and 244; cited from David Whitehouse, "Chinese Porcelain in Medieval Europe", p. 73.

② 　塔里尼（Tareni）又称 Tarì，是 913 年至 1859 年西西里、马耳他和意大利南部通用的、基督徒认可的一种伊斯兰金币。每枚金币含 1.05 克金。

③ 　"Deux plats, iiii écuelles et iiii saussières de porcelaine"；"Ung pot à eau de pierre de pourcelaine à ung couvercle d'argent; un pot à vin de pierre de pourcelaine plus blanche"；see H. Havard, *Dictionnaire de l'ameublement* (Paris, 1890), s.v. 'porcelaine'；David Whitehouse, "Chinese Porcelain in Medieval Europe", p. 73

④ 　H. Maranville, *Inventaire de l'orfeorerie et des joyaux de Louis I*, due d'Anjou, Paris, lg05, III, 518, item 3354, cited from David Whitehouse, "Chinese Porcelain in Medieval Europe", p. 74.

⑤ 　David Whitehouse, "Chinese Porcelain in Medieval Europe", p. 74.

Un plat fait de pourcelaine, sanz aucune garnison, estant dedans un estuy de cuir, non prisé pour ce qu'il a esté rompu en amenant de Bourges à Paris.

Un pot de pourcelaine à une ance d'argent et le demoirant, avec le couvercle, garny d'argent doré . . . . Un autre pot de porcelaine avec l'ance de mesme . . . .

Deux petites escuelles de pourcelaine, prisees i sol iij den.[①]

贝里公爵的这批瓷器来自教皇格利高里十二世（Gregorius XII）。而教皇又很可能是从罗马或者是佛罗伦萨在 1410 年至 1414 年间赠送的礼物中得到这批华瓷。里面有瓷壶，是一个执壶，上面有喜鹊纹，有疑为来欧洲后加上的银质镀金壶盖。此外还有一个瓷盘，两个瓷壶，其中一个有银质镀金的装饰。

1456 年那不勒斯和西西里国王、安茹公爵勒内一世（Rene I, duke of Anjou）的财产目录：

En la petite chambre dessus la Saulcerie, a plusieurs auriolles de verre, gardemangers de terre, plaz de pourcelaine et autres choses de verre, dont y plusieurs rompuiz et cassez.[②]

这一小段表明勒内一世在一个小房间中存放着华瓷、玻璃制品等，但是没有说明其收藏的数量。

1456 年佛罗伦萨统治者皮埃罗·德·美第奇（Piero de' Medici）的财产目录。原文如下：

Una choppa de porciellana leghata in oro....

Uno vaso di porciellana choi chopercio ....

Uno infreschatio di porciellana ....

Uno piatello di porciellana bigio (grey) ....

Uno orciuolo di porciellana ....

Uno vaso di porciellana leghato in horo col chopercio.[③]

以上记载的 6 件瓷器不是皮埃罗·德·美第奇藏品的全部，保守估计他拥有 11 件华瓷。目录没有详细描述这些华瓷的器型和种类，第一件和最后一件华瓷应该是装在一个金底座上，说明这一时期的华瓷在欧洲价值连城。第四件华瓷被描绘成灰色的瓷盘，很多学者对此比较疑惑，认为也许是是青瓷的一种。[④]

1464 年皮埃罗·德·美第奇的财产清单节选自：*Una coppa di porcellana legata in oro pie et coperchio punzonato*, fl. 200。[⑤]该清单显示，皮埃罗·德·美第奇拥有一个有贴金杯盖的瓷杯，价值 200 个佛罗林[⑥]。

1493 年，埃尔科莱·德·埃斯特（Ercole d'Este）的财产清单中也提到了华瓷。埃斯特家族对于华瓷的热爱不逊于美第奇家族。[⑦]

第二类是 15 世纪的信件，包括当时的外交信件和私人邮件。

1447 年一封写给查理七世的外交信件中表明了东方统治者将华瓷作为礼物送给法国查理七世，原文如下：

---

① Baron Davillier, *Les Origines de la porcelaine en Europe*, Paris and London, 1882, p. 9, cited from Arthur *Lane, Italian Porcelain*, London, 1954, p. 30.

② Baron Davillier, *Les Origines de la porcelaine en Europe*, Paris and London, 1882, p. 10, cited from cited from D. B. Whitehouse, "Chinese Porcelain from Lucera Castle", Faenza, LII, 1966, p. 93.

③ Eugene Muntz, *Les collections des Médicis au XVᵉ siècle: le musée, la bibliothèque, le mobilier*, Paris, 1888, pp. 16–33, cited from D. B. Whitehouse, "Chinese Porcelain from Lucera Castle", p. 93.

④ David Whitehouse, "Chinese Porcelain in Medieval Europe", p. 75.

⑤ David Whitehouse, "Chinese Porcelain from Lucera Castle", p. 93.

⑥ 1252 年在佛罗伦萨发行的一种金币，重量约 3.5 克左右。

⑦ Donald F. Lach, *Asia in the Making of Europe*, vol. II, Book one, p. 37.

. . . Si, te mande par ledit ambassadeur un present: c'est à sçavoir du baume fin de nostre saincte vigne; un bel liépart, trois escuelles de pourcelaine de Sinant (China), deux grandz platz ouvertz de pourcelaine, deux touques verdes de pourcelaine, deux bouquetz de pourcelaine, ung lavoir ès mains et un garde-manger de pourcelaine ouvré.[①]

达维利耶认为这份材料来自"埃及或巴比伦苏丹"写给查理七世的信。该苏丹很可能是埃及的马木路克苏丹马立克·阿尔－加西尔（Malik al-jahir）。这封信提到了法国商人给苏丹的建议：增加法国人在黎凡特的商业许可。信中明确表示送给法王的礼物中至少有三个是来自中国的瓷器，现代学者认为很有可能是三件青瓷碗。

1461 年的外交记录显示，埃及马木路克苏丹哈迈特（Abulfet Hamet）赠送了 20 件瓷器给威尼斯总督帕斯夸里·马利皮耶罗（Pasquale Malipiero）。

皮耶特罗·比别纳（Pietro Bibbiena）写给皮埃罗·德·美第奇的女儿克拉丽丝·德·美第奇的信中证实：1487 年，佛罗伦萨统治者洛伦佐·德·美第奇，得到了来自最后一位埃及马木路克苏丹的华瓷礼物。[②]

四　13—15 世纪欧洲华瓷收藏的特点

首先，是欧洲华瓷收藏在来源上的非单一性。

13—15 世纪以前欧洲的华瓷来源分为购买和获赠。购买这一途径又分为两类。第一类是旅行者从远东带回的华瓷。在这类华瓷中，有像马可·波罗直接从中国带回。也有像达·伽玛般，从印度购买华瓷带回欧洲。第二类是欧洲人前往近东或是中东旅行，从当地人手中购买流传到那里的华瓷。如卡岑埃尔恩博根伯爵菲利普带回的青花瓷碗。中东地区，埃及在 15 世纪华瓷传输中具有重要地位。法国国王、威尼斯总督和佛罗伦萨统治者都是从埃及接受的华瓷礼物。这与当时埃及的商贸及地理位置有关。由于当时很多华瓷由阿拉伯商人带至北非等地。因此欧洲权贵主要是从埃及得到华瓷藏品。

获赠这个途径，主要是以外交礼物的形式获得的。这也分为两类。如果甘尼尔凡提尔壶来源的传说是真实的话，第一种形式就是直接是来自中国的外交礼物。由中国使团在赴欧时赠送给当地的统治者。传说匈牙利拉约什一世就是从前去觐见教皇本笃十二世的中国使团那里获得了甘尼尔凡提尔壶。

第二种形式是获得华瓷的人转赠给别人。其一为教皇的赏赐。由于教皇经常获得各个阶层的献礼。而将瓷器作为贵重礼物献给教皇似乎已经成为传统，直到现在也经常有人将瓷器献给教皇。笔者在梵蒂冈博物馆中见到了历代教皇所得到的一小部分瓷器礼物，例如弗朗西斯·格雷维（Francese Grevy）献给教皇利奥十三世（Papa Leo XIII）一只高约 4 米的巨大的白底红花瓷瓶；德皇威廉一世（Wilhelm I）献给教皇庇护九世（Papa Pius IX）一只高约 3 米的双耳瓶，瓶柄是镀金兽头的形式，瓶身描绘了欧洲风光；美国纽约大主教区于 1976 年 6 月献给教皇保罗六世（Papa Paul VI）一组大型的瓷雕，名为《无声的和平天鹅》（Mute Swans of Peace）等等。教皇也经常将手中的瓷器赏赐给别人。如教皇约翰二十三世在 1410 至 1414 年间赐给贝里公爵的那件华瓷一样。其二是来自近东或中东统治者的礼物。近东或中东的统治者有条件有能力委托商人进口华瓷，因此他们获得华瓷要比当时的欧洲人容易一些。他们也常常将华瓷作为珍贵礼物送给欧洲的统治者们。例如 1447 年马木

---

① David Whitehouse, "Chinese porcelain from Lucera Castle", pp. 90-93

② A. Fabroni, *Laurentii Medicis Magnifici Vita*, Pisa, 1784, p. 337, cited from Arthur Lane, *Italian Porcelain*, London, 1954, p. 30.

路克苏丹马立克·阿尔－加西尔送给法国国王至少 3 件华瓷；另一个东方统治者埃及的马木路克苏丹哈迈特在 1461 年送给威尼斯总督 20 件华瓷，最后一位埃及马木路克苏丹在 1487 年增送给洛伦佐·美第奇一些华瓷作为礼物。

其次，是欧洲华瓷收藏在数量上的有限性。

华瓷数量的稀少跟其来源范围狭窄有很大关系。尽管这一时期华瓷来源具有非单一性。但是欧洲人没有得到直接同中国进行华瓷贸易这最为直接和便利的收藏途径，因此，华瓷在 16 世纪以期进入欧洲的渠道并不通畅，过程也极为曲折。由此导致了这一时期欧洲人获得的华瓷数量大多数是个位数，而数量最多的一次，不过是威尼斯总督一次性得到了 20 件华瓷。

最后，数量上的有限性导致了华瓷在欧洲收藏界的珍贵性。

数量的稀少导致华瓷成为一种珍贵的收藏品。尽管统治阶层也许可以通过购买或获赠的方式拥有华瓷，但是在葡萄牙人 16 世纪大量进口前，华瓷仍是相当珍贵的。没有证据显示当时社会大众拥有瓷器。在当时华瓷这种贵重的奢侈品主要是社会上层所拥有。从文献中我们得知华瓷被王室或贵族家庭所独占，从温切斯特和科林斯的考古发掘显示华瓷不光被社会最高阶层所垄断，富有的商人们也有可能占有瓷器。华瓷的珍贵性还表现在，收藏华瓷的欧洲精英连中东地区仿制华瓷的瓷器也一并收藏。另一方面，考古发掘表明，同伊斯兰瓷器碎片的分布相比，伊斯兰瓷器分布均匀，而华瓷碎片只在极少的地方出土，也说明了当时华瓷数量的稀少和珍贵。①此外，欧洲人在收藏华瓷时对进行的再加工，如镶金嵌银，或是加上豪华贵重的底座等，亦显示出华瓷在当时欧洲的珍贵性。

---

① 关于西欧出土的伊斯兰碎片参见 D. B. Harden, "Medieval glass in the west", *Proc. VIII*[th] *International Congress on Glass*, 1968 (Soc. Glass Technology, Sheffield, 1969), 102 f.; *id.*, "Ancient glass, III: post-Roman", *Archaeol. F.*, CXXVIII (1972), 106 f., cited from David Whitehouse, "Chinese Porcelain in Medieval Europe", p. 76.

西欧大学中的首位拜占廷教师
——拜占廷学者曼纽尔·克利索罗拉斯

张俊芳　天津医科大学

摘要：曼纽尔·克利索罗拉斯是文艺复兴时期第一位在西欧大学中任教的拜占廷学者，此后，众多拜占廷学者纷纷效仿他来到意大利担任各个大学的希腊语教师。他在佛罗伦萨大学的教学引发了意大利人学习希腊语言和文化的浓厚兴趣，为意大利培养了众多复兴希腊古典文化的健将，有力地推动了意大利文艺复兴运动的发展。然而，他到意大利不只是为了传播希腊文化，他更重要的目的是为陷入困境的拜占廷帝国寻求西方的军事援助。

关键词：文艺复兴； 拜占廷；首位；希腊语； 教师

Abstract：Manuel Chrysoloras was the first Byzantine scholar who had taught in a university of Western Europe during the Renaissance. Many Byzantine scholars had followed the example of him to come to Italy to be Greek Instructors in each university henceforward. His instruction in Florence University had aroused the Italian people's intense interest of studying Hellenic language and culture, trained many masters who had dedicated themselves to the revival of classic Hellenic culture for Italy, and had thus promoted the development of the Renaissance in Italy forcefully. However, he went to Italy not only for transmitting Hellenic culture, seeking military aid from the west for the Byzantine Empire which had fallen into difficult circumstances was his more important purpose.

Keywords：The Renaissance, Byzantium, The First, The Greek, Instructor

文艺复兴时期，南意大利的希腊人莱恩提乌斯·皮拉图（Leontius Pilatus）可以称得上是西欧最早出现的希腊语教师，但是，最先在大学中正式讲授希腊语并且影响深远的应当是拜占廷著名学者曼纽尔·克利索罗拉斯（Manuel Chrysoloras，1350 — 1415 年）。

一

曼纽尔·克利索罗拉斯出生于君士坦丁堡的贵族世家，他既是拜占廷帝国晚期帕列奥列格文艺复兴的杰出代表，也是著名的外交家，在拜占廷他被冠以修辞学家、哲学家等称号，他的研究范围涉及神学、修辞学、哲学等领域①。克利索罗拉斯为人谦和，举止得体，才思敏捷，学识渊博，法国文艺复兴史家蒙尼尔（Monnier）称他是"一位真正的希腊人……他了解最新的科学和哲学成就；他是通过在意大利教学恢复古典传统的第一位希腊教师"②。

早在 1391 年克利索罗拉斯作为外交官曾到过威尼斯，期间他教过罗伯特·罗西（Roberto Rossi）希腊语，后者把他介绍给当时的佛罗伦萨执政官克鲁乔·萨卢塔蒂（Coluccio Salutati）。萨卢塔蒂不仅是佛罗伦萨政府的执政官，还是意大利著名的人文主义者，在他的庇护下，佛罗伦萨的人文主义者经常集会讨论学术问题，他还慷慨地出借私人藏书，为人文主义者提供接触古典书籍的机会。在他的不懈努力下，14 世纪末佛罗伦萨终于成为意大利人文主义的中心。见到克利索罗拉斯之后，萨卢塔蒂立刻被他渊博的希腊学识所折服，内心已经萌发邀请他到佛罗伦萨之意。

但是，直接促使佛罗伦萨政府决定聘请拜占廷著名学者曼纽尔·克利索罗拉斯的是文化赞助人的支持。文艺复兴时期，意大利的文化赞助人大多是君主或者极有权势的富商。③新兴资产阶级凭借强大的经济实力成为社会上层阶级，他们雇佣、聘请大批诗人、学者和艺术家，并通过这些人的艺术创作展现自己的理想与价值观念。几乎每个佛罗伦萨显贵家族都有庇护文化的传统，譬如梅迪奇家族。拜占廷学者曼纽尔·克利索罗拉斯正是在佛罗伦萨金融实业家帕拉·斯特罗兹（Palla Strozzi）的赞助下，才有了佛罗伦萨之行。

1396 年，萨卢塔蒂写信邀请克利索罗拉斯，1397 年 2 月，克利索罗拉斯来到佛罗伦萨大学担任希腊语教师，这是意大利乃至整个西欧自中世纪以来第一次在大学中正式讲授希腊知识，对于文艺复兴时期意大利的古典文化复兴，具有举足轻重的意义。虽然文艺复兴先驱彼特拉克和薄伽丘激起了意大利人对希腊文化的兴趣，但这种热情仅限于佛罗伦萨的修道院和少数人文主义者之中。直到拜占廷学者曼纽尔·克利索罗拉斯来到佛罗伦萨以后，意大利的希腊研究才真正开始。对此，列奥纳多·布鲁尼（Leonardo Bruni）有一段话广为流传："在这一时期（即克利索罗拉斯应邀来佛罗伦萨讲学之际），文学在意大利强有力地发展着，希腊语在中断了 700 年之后又复活了。拜占廷的克利索罗拉斯，一位出身高贵和精通希腊语的学者，给我们带来了希腊语的知识……"④尽管这段话现在看起来并不准确，因为我们知道南意大利地区仍保留着希腊传统，并且早在 1380 — 81 年，拜占廷人西蒙·阿图曼诺（Simon Atumano）曾在意大利传授希腊语，但有一点是值得肯定的，那就是克利索罗拉斯在佛罗伦萨大学的讲授有力地推动了意大利的希腊文化复兴。

克利索罗拉斯是第一位在西欧大学中正式任教的拜占廷学者，而佛罗伦萨大学也是最先邀请拜占廷学者任教的西欧学校，此后，不断有拜占廷学者前往继任，佛罗伦萨大学由此形成了希腊语的教学传统，受其影响，意大利各个大学相继聘任拜占廷学者。事实上，文艺复兴时期，除了佛罗伦萨、罗马、帕多瓦这三个城市一直聘请拜占廷学者以外，维罗那、费拉拉、威尼斯、佩鲁贾、帕维亚和其他意大利城市也不时地出现来自拜占廷的希腊语教师⑤。

二

---

① Donald M. Nicol, *A Biographical Dictionary of the Byzantine Empire*, London: Seaby Ltd., 1991, p.24.
② A. A. Vasiliev, *History of the Byzantine Empire 324–1453*,Vol.II, Wisconsin: the University of Wisconsin Press, 1958, p.719.
③ C. G. Crump & E. F. Jacob, *The Legacy of the Middle Ages*, London: Oxford University Press, 1969, p.282.
④ 王挺之、徐波、刘耀春：《新世纪的曙光：文艺复兴》，北京：中国青年出版社 1999 年，第 151 页。
⑤ 雅各布·布克哈特著，何新译：《意大利文艺复兴时期的文化》，北京：商务印书馆 1996 年，第 192 页。

从 1397 年到达至 1400 年离开前往米兰，克利索罗拉斯在佛罗伦萨大学的实际任期仅仅 3 年，虽然任期较短，但是克利索罗拉斯的教学却是极其成功的，他超越了以前所有的希腊语教师，包括南意大利的皮拉图等人。

为了方便佛罗伦萨大学的初学者，克利索罗拉斯以问答形式编写了《语法》（*Erotemata*），与传统的语法教材相比，该书的突出特点是简洁易懂，譬如在拜占廷晚期学者曼纽尔·穆斯柯保罗斯（Manuel Moschopoulos）的《语法》中名词的种类有 56 种，而克利索罗拉斯的《语法》中仅有 10 种，并且这种简化不影响学生对希腊语法的理解 ①。克利索罗拉斯的语法教材很受初学者的欢迎，它的各种手抄本四处流传，在 1476 年康斯坦丁·拉丝凯里斯（Constantine Lascaris）的《语法》公开发行以前，克利索罗拉斯的《语法》是意大利唯一的一本通用的希腊语法教材，直到 16 世纪这本书仍被广泛使用 ②。关于克利索罗拉斯在佛罗伦萨大学的教学方法，没有留下文字记载，我们只能通过一些相关的史料，推测一下：这种教学方法强调准确的发音，要求学生有良好的记忆力，课前需要做大量准备工作，了解背景知识，课堂上还要不停地记录 ③。文艺复兴时期成千上万的西方学生之所以能够吸收大量的希腊语法、文化背景知识，正是得益于克利索罗拉斯的独特的教学方法的广为流传。

在希腊著作的翻译方法上，拜占廷学者曼纽尔·克利索罗拉斯也有独到的见解，他的学生森西奥·德·拉丝提锡（Cencio de Rustici）曾说过，克利索罗拉斯经常告诉他们，逐字逐句直译的方法很不准确，那样的翻译时常会曲解希腊原文。正确的翻译方法是根据原文的实质进行意译，同时还要避免过分地随意改动。④克利索罗拉斯采用这种方法翻译过一些希腊著作，他的译本不仅没有曲解希腊原文，还更加符合拉丁语的习惯用法，此前的翻译家们虽然对希腊原文理解地很透彻，但是却没有达到这一高度。在他的译著中有不少名篇，例如柏拉图的《理想国》（*Republic*）和托勒密的《地理学》（*Geographia*）。克利索罗拉斯的翻译方法深受意大利学生的推崇，效仿者众多。列奥纳多·布鲁尼是文艺复兴时期著名的人文主义者、翻译家，他最成功的译作是柏拉图的《政治学》，在该书的翻译过程中，布鲁尼使用的就是克利索罗拉斯的方法而非中世纪西方传统的莫贝克方法 ⑤。罗伯特·罗西也是克利索罗拉斯在佛罗伦萨教过的学生之一，他翻译过亚力士多德的部分著作，据说在意大利曾经盛行一时，同样，他也采纳了克利索罗拉斯的翻译方式。

拜占廷学者曼纽尔·克利索罗拉斯在佛罗伦萨大学任教期间的学生众多，其中不乏著名的意大利人文主义者，例如佛罗伦萨的列奥纳多·布鲁尼、尼克罗·尼科利、罗伯特·罗西、乌贝尔托·狄塞姆利奥、维罗那的瓜里诺（Guarino of Verona）和帕拉·斯特罗兹、帕多瓦的皮埃尔·保罗·维尔杰利奥（Pier Paolo Vergerio）等。

列奥纳多·布鲁尼是克利索罗拉斯最得意的学生之一，他精通拉丁文，曾在罗马教廷担任秘书，享有一定的声望，也是继萨卢塔蒂之后佛罗伦萨政治和文化生活的中心人物。在佛罗伦萨大学，布鲁尼跟随克利索罗拉斯学习过两年时间，这两年的学习为他打开了一扇通向古希腊文化宝库的大门，他由此接触到荷马、柏拉图、狄摩西尼等古希腊诗人、哲学家、演说家、历史学家的著作，并养成了对古典文学和历史学的喜好，后来他撰写了历史著作《佛罗伦萨人民史》（*History of the Florentine People*）。此外，布鲁尼还付出三十多年的心血，翻译了许多希腊著作，其中包括巴西里尔斯（Basilius）的《训诫》（*Homilia*）、柏拉图的《费多》（*Phaedon*）；还有古希腊埃斯琴斯（Aeschines）、普

---

①　Wilson, N. G., *From Byzantium to Italy*, London: Duckworth, 1992, p.9.

②　Thomson, Ian, "Manuel Chrysoloras and the Early Italian Renaissance", *Greek, Roman and Byzantine Studies*, 1996, (Vol.7), p.74.

③　Thomson, Ian, "Manuel Chrysoloras and the Early Italian Renaissance", p.67.

④　Wilson, N. G., *From Byzantium to Italy*, p.11.

⑤　Moerbeke：指中世纪神学家莫贝克逐字逐句直译古代文献的方法，也有现代学者认为他的方法更忠实于原文。

鲁塔克（Plutarch）、狄摩西尼（Demosthenes）、和亚力士多德（Aristotle）等人的作品。

克利索罗拉斯的声明远播和他的学生瓜里诺（1373—1460 年）有很大关系。瓜里诺是 15 世纪早期威尼斯文化界最重要的人物，他对于威尼斯的希腊文化复兴做出了重大的贡献。1414 年他创建了威尼斯第一所人文主义学校，希腊语言和文学是该校主要的教学内容，这所学校培养了众多优秀人才，例如著名的政治家兼人文主义者弗朗西斯科·巴巴罗（Francesco Barbaro）。在弗朗西斯科的学识形成过程中，来自东方的希腊文化起了决定性的作用，这自然是受益于瓜里诺的教学效果，而瓜里诺本人的希腊知识又来自于他的拜占廷老师克利索罗拉斯。

瓜里诺不只是在佛罗伦萨大学跟随克利索罗拉斯学习希腊知识，他甚至前往拜占廷继续向老师求教，在拜占廷学习期间，瓜里诺接受了全面的希腊教育，这为他后来的翻译工作奠定了坚实的基础。瓜里诺翻译过的著作有：希腊传记作家普鲁塔克(Plutarch)的《亚历山大》（Alexander）、希腊修辞学家鲁善(Lucian)的两篇文章、希腊戏剧家阿里斯托芬的三部戏剧，当然还有他的老师——曼纽尔·克利索罗拉斯的《语法》①。

瓜里诺把克利索罗拉斯比作"照亮意大利黑夜的一盏明灯"，在他看来，克利索罗拉斯对意大利最突出的贡献，就是帮助意大利恢复了古典文化研究的传统。瓜里诺认为不懂希腊语就不可能正确地理解拉丁语，而希腊语的传播必然带动拉丁语研究的兴起，因此克利索罗拉斯在意大利的教学活动不但复兴了希腊文化，而且唤醒了长期处于睡眠状态的意大利学术界。为此，他希望意大利为克利索罗拉斯建立一个凯旋门以示表彰。在克利索罗拉斯去世 40 年后，瓜里诺将所有纪念他的文章编辑成册，并命名为《克利索罗拉斯》（Chrysolorina）②。

对于克利索罗拉斯所提倡的希腊教育理想，他的学生、著名的人文主义者维尔杰利奥极为推崇。1404 年，维尔杰利奥撰写了论文《论文雅风范与青年的人文教养》（De ingenuis moribus et liberalibus studiis adolescentiae），在意大利学术界一举成名。该文中，他暗示中世纪西方的教育传统落后，建议恢复晚期希腊的教育传统。在晚期希腊教育中身体和智力同等重要，强调均衡、全面发展，通过加强体能的锻炼和良好品德的培养来实现教育的最高目标。按照这一理念，维尔杰利奥制订了新的课程计划，其中包括语法、逻辑学、修辞学、诗歌、音乐、数学、天文学、自然史、绘画、医学、法学、论理学和神学等内容，这显然比中世纪传统教育中的三、四门课程要丰富得多。维尔杰利奥的教育构想引发了意大利人文主义者的兴趣，他们先后开展了一系列的教育实践③。影响较大的有：1408—1420 年巴滋扎（Barzizza）在帕多瓦；1423—1446 年维陶里诺（Vittorino）在曼图亚（Mantua）；瓜里诺分别于 1414—1419 年在威尼斯、1420—1429 年在维罗那（Verona）、1430—1460 年在费拉拉进行试验。

拜占廷学者曼纽尔·克利索罗拉斯还引发了意大利人前往拜占廷学习希腊文化、收集古希腊手稿的热潮。1403 年当克利索罗拉斯返回拜占廷时，与其随行的还有几个他的意大利学生。例如，瓜里诺从 1403 到 1408 年间，一直在拜占廷首都君士坦丁堡学习希腊文化知识。从那时起直到拜占廷帝国末期甚至土耳其统治时期，前往君士坦丁堡和其它东部城市游学的意大利人文主义者仍络绎不绝，其中包括那个时代最杰出的希腊学专家，如意大利商人兼学者奥利斯帕（Aurispa）、陶泰利（Tortelli）、弗朗西斯科·费尔弗（Francesco Filelfo）等人。奥利斯帕先后于 1417 年和 1422 年两次从拜占廷托运古代手稿，其中仅第二次托运的手稿就有 238 卷，几乎涵盖了所有知名的古希腊著作。奥利斯帕曾说过"为了这些书，我的货物、现金甚至衣服都可以不要"。④费尔弗则在拜占廷成家立

① Wilson, N. G., *From Byzantium to Italy*, p.23.
② Sandys, John Edwin, *A History of Classical Scholarship*,Vol. II, Bristol: Thoemmes Press, 1998, p.21.
③ Thomson, Ian, "Manuel Chrysoloras and the Early Italian Renaissance", p.66.
④ Lindsay, Jack, *Byzantium into Europe*, London: The Bodley Head, 1952, p.449.

业，他是少数几个能用古希腊文写作的意大利人文主义者之一。①这些意大利学生在学成返乡时，不但带回了大量重要的古代希腊手稿，而且将拜占廷的学术传统也带回了意大利，譬如古典文本的翻译方法、学校教育中阅读教材的选定和教学课程的设置等，有力地推动了文艺复兴时期意大利人文主义者的希腊研究甚至拉丁研究。

三

作为意大利乃至西欧第一位具有深远影响的希腊语教师，拜占廷学者曼纽尔·克利索罗拉斯的重要地位毋庸置疑。克利索罗拉斯在佛罗伦萨大学的教学活动，激发了他的意大利学生对希腊古典文化研究的浓厚兴趣，他们不仅终身保持着对古典文化的持久热情，还致力于古典文化的推广和传播，这些人后来大多成为意大利文艺复兴时期复兴希腊文化的健将。不仅如此，克利索罗拉斯还起到了很好的示范效应，引发了大规模的拜占廷流亡学者西迁。由于他深受意大利学生的追捧，继他之后，更多的拜占廷流亡学者效仿他来到意大利寻求发展机会，其中比较突出的有：在费拉拉教学的塞奥多·加扎（Theodore Gaza）、在佛罗伦萨和罗马教学的约翰·阿基罗保罗斯（John Argyropoulos）、先后在帕多瓦、佛罗伦萨和米兰教学的德米特利尔斯·考坎迪利斯（Demetrios Chalcondylas）、在威尼斯和帕多瓦教学的马科斯·姆修拉斯（Marcus Musurus）。这些拜占廷流亡学者在意大利的教学活动，对于传播拜占廷文化和意大利的希腊古典文化复兴起到了至关重要的作用。

然而，克利索罗拉斯到意大利的目的并不只是为了担任希腊语教师，传播古典文化知识。克利索罗拉斯出身于贵族世家，在拜占廷拥有很高的社会地位，他既可以出入宫廷，又是学术圈里的首领，他不可能为了仅仅150金弗罗琳（gold florins，货币单位——笔者注）的年薪离开拜占廷前往佛罗伦萨。加之，克利索罗拉斯根本不懂意大利语，他的拉丁语水平也很有限，他可以想像得到远赴异乡生活的种种不便。假设克利索罗拉斯真的是为了经济利益前往佛罗伦萨，那么他就应该完成他的5年任期，事实上，在佛罗伦萨任教的3年内，他的薪水涨了2次，到1400年时总数已达到250金弗罗琳，尽管佛罗伦萨政府再三挽留，克利索罗拉斯还是决定离开。

其实，从他的繁忙的行程中，我们不难看出，曼纽尔·克利索罗拉斯在承担教学任务的同时，还肩负着特殊的外交使命。1400年，受拜占廷皇帝曼努埃尔的指派，克利索罗拉斯毅然地离开佛罗伦萨前往米兰；1402年他又接受维斯孔蒂的邀请到帕维亚任教；1403年克利索罗拉斯返回拜占廷。1407至1410年间，作为拜占廷皇帝的使节，克利索罗拉斯再次来到西方，先后访问过威尼斯、佛罗伦萨、巴黎、伦敦和罗马。1413年他和两位罗马的红衣主教一起到康斯坦斯筹备即将召开的宗教大会，1415年春，出席康斯坦斯宗教会议期间克利索罗拉斯去世，葬礼由他的两位意大利学生森西奥和波乔·布拉乔利尼操办。②

克利索罗拉斯如此频繁地在西欧各国间四处奔走，其目的只有一个，那就是为拜占廷帝国寻求西方的军事援助。因为此时日益强盛的奥斯曼土耳其帝国，不断蚕食拜占廷帝国的疆土，国力衰败的拜占廷需要来自外部的支援，而拜占廷与拉丁西方毕竟同属于基督教文化范畴，有着相同的古典文化背景，并且在中世纪期间双方或多或少地保持着一定的经济和文化交往。所以，面临异教徒入侵时，拜占廷人自然而然地转向拉丁西方寻求援助。事实上，很多拜占廷的宗教界和文化界上层人士都认为只有依靠教会联合，拜占廷才能摆脱土耳其的威胁，他们清楚地看到意大利人文主义者对

---

①　Kristeller, Paul Oskar, *Renaissance Thought and Its Sources*, New York: Columbia University Press, 1979, p.143.

②　Sandys, John Edwin. *A History of Classical Scholarship*, Vol. II, pp.20–21.

古希腊文化的大力追捧，他们希望以此为契机融合同源的两种基督教文明，促成东西方教会的联合。然后借此说服罗马教皇号召西欧各国组成十字军，阻止土耳其军队的入侵。很多晚期拜占廷学者都对教会合并抱有幻想，克利索罗拉斯就是其中的典型代表，他们认为抗击异教的奥斯曼土耳其人是所有基督徒的共同责任。遗憾的是，由于西方当权者缺乏远见，并未意识到拜占廷的安危在战略上对西方的重要性，因此，对于拜占廷的求助，他们表现的漠不关心，克利索罗拉斯所盼望的西方军事援助始终未曾到来。

　　总之，无论拜占廷学者曼纽尔·克利索罗拉斯出于何种目的前往佛罗伦萨大学任教，他对于文艺复兴时期意大利复兴古典文化的重大作用都是值得肯定的。克利索罗拉斯教给他的意大利学生的不仅仅是希腊知识，还有一种作为罗马共和国真正继承人的自信心和自豪感，这种自信心和自豪感在人文主义文化形成中的作用是难以估量的。正如文艺复兴史专家坚尼·布鲁克尔所说，14 世纪末"由曼纽尔·克利索罗拉斯提供的希腊语教学确实激励了对古典学术研究的兴趣，并促成了 15 世纪的人文学的热潮。"[1]

---

[1]　坚尼·布鲁克尔著，朱龙华译：《文艺复兴时期的佛罗伦萨》，北京：生活·读书·新知三联书店 1985 年，第 308 页。

简论 4 至 6 世纪拜占廷帝国基督教与古典文化 *

张日元 泰山学院

摘要： 在公元 4 至 6 世纪，随着拜占廷帝国基督教化的发展，如何处理与古典文化之间的关系成为基督教不可规避的一个问题。面对"根深蒂固"的古希腊、罗马文化，基督教采取了一种"接纳"和"为我所用"的态度。

关键词： 4 至 6 世纪；拜占廷帝国；基督教；古典文化

Abstracts： With the Christianizing of Byzantine Empire during the period from 4th to 6th century,

how to deal with the relationships with the Classical Culture was a question that Christianity had to face. Facing the 'popular' Classical Culture of Greek and Rome, Christianity took an attitude of 'adopting' and 'things-for-us'.

Keywords： from 4th to 6th century, Byzantine Empire, Christianity, the Classical Culture

按照传统观点，4世纪初《米兰敕令》颁布后，获得合法宗教地位的基督教在拜占廷帝国迅速传播，拜占廷帝国基督教化进程随之开始。而随着拜占廷帝国基督教化的发展，如何处理与古典文化之间的关系成为基督教不可规避的一个问题。本文拟在前贤研究的基础上，从历史的角度对上述问题作一简要论述。

一 古典文化渊源

拜占廷帝国初期，几乎每个有教养的基督徒都要受到希腊、罗马古典文化的熏陶，因为他们生活在一个古典文学和世俗教育体系占主导地位的社会中，不可能完全"超然"于这个世俗社会。特别是，如果一个人想要融入上流社会，或要在这个社会中"飞黄腾达"，无论他从事什么职业，他都必须要懂得异教著作；而对处于社会上层的基督徒父母来说，剥夺其子女的常规教育课程则是不可想象的。①

---

* 本文为山东省高校人文社科计划项目"罗马帝国晚期基督教兴起研究"（项目编号 J12WD58）阶段性成果之一。

① Jones, A.H.M., *Later Roman Empire 248-602: A Social, Economic, and Administrative Survey*, Oxford: Basil Blackwell, 1964, p.1006.

　　同时，在4至6世纪的拜占廷帝国，所有著名的中等学校都讲授希腊古典文学。学校一般设置的基础课程包括：讲授荷马（Homer）、欧里庇得斯（Euripides）、阿里斯托芬（Aristophanes）和德谟斯提尼（Demosthenes）的著述；更高年级的学生也阅读希罗多德（Herodotus）和修昔底德（Thucydides）、柏拉图（Plato）和亚里士多德（Aristotle）的著作。4世纪时，主要的古典高等教育学校集中于雅典和亚历山大里亚，这些著名的学校一直开办至6世纪。所有这些学校的创始者及其教师都是异教徒。而且，这个时期的拜占廷人所接受的启蒙教育通常是从《荷马史诗》开始，然后才是《圣经》。①甚至，当基督教成为国教时，如果基督徒的孩子们一定要学习"拼字法"（Orthography）和"语法"（Grammar）的话，他们必然要使用异教徒的课本，阅读异教徒的著作。②

　　因此，在拜占廷帝国初期如果一个基督徒想拥有良好教养，他就必须学习上述课程，并与异教徒一起在那些学校里学习。③早在3世纪，当时最重要的新柏拉图哲学家普罗提诺（Plotinus）和最渊博的基督教神学家奥立金就曾一起在亚历山大里亚求学并受教于同一位老师。④

　　在拜占廷帝国初期，基督教学者曾拜著名异教学者为师的现象也并不少见。例如，被称为4世纪"文学先生"的利班纽斯（Libanius，314–393年）是一位异教徒，并且是背教者朱利安的朋友和崇拜者，但基督徒圣约翰·克里索斯托、纳西昂的圣格里高利和叙利亚教会的重要神学家塞奥多利（Theodore of Mopsuestia）都曾投师于其门下。⑤5世纪时，基督教教会文学最早的代表，卡帕多西亚的圣瓦西里、纳西昂的圣格里高利、尼斯的圣格里高利、圣金口约翰、伊西多尔·贝鲁西奥特（死于436年）、亚历山大里亚的奚利尔（死于477年）、居鲁士的塞奥多利特（死于457年）等希腊教父都曾在雅典学园就读；卡帕多西亚的圣瓦西里和纳西昂的圣格里高利还与朱利安皇帝有同窗之谊。⑥

　　而且在拜占廷帝国初期，一些基督徒还以教授希腊、罗马古典文学为业。3世纪起，有许多杰出的教师是虔诚的基督徒。⑦例如，4世纪的基督教学者瓦西里（329–379年）在雅典大学教授语法、政治和历史，同时还在当地的职业学校担任算学和医学教师。⑧从背教者朱利安统治期间发生的一个"小插曲"中，我们也可以清楚地看到这一事实。该皇帝曾在一段时期内禁止基督徒教师讲述异教古典文学，但他的这一规定同时遭到了异教徒和基督徒的谴责。⑨当朱利安死后，基督徒教师们又开始教授异教古典文学。⑩

　　拜占廷帝国早期，基督教盛行的凯撒里亚和吉萨都拥有著名的修辞学学校。即使在基督教最早的学校，即教理问答学校中，"虽然这些学校以传授基督教教义为重点，但也教授如数学和医学等学科；当奥立金（'基督教学问之王'）在亚历山大里亚的学校接替克莱门特的职位时，他在课程中增加了语法科目"⑪。4世纪的圣瓦西里也曾以摩西和丹尼尔（Moses and Daniel）受益于异教学问

①　徐家玲：《拜占廷文明》，北京：人民出版社，2006年，第477页。

②　Baynes, N.H. and Moss, H.St.L.B.(eds.), *Byzantium: An Introduction to East Roman Civilization*, Oxford: The Clarendon Press, 1948, p.202.

③　Treadgold, W., *A History of the Byzantine State and Society*, Stanford: Stanford University Press, 1997, p.265. See also Baynes, N.H. and Moss, H.St.L.B.(eds.), *Byzantium: An Introduction to East Roman Civilization*, p.222.

④　Treadgold, W., *A History of the Byzantine State and Society*, p.127.

⑤　Mango, C. (ed.), *The Oxford History of Byzantium*, Oxford: Oxford University Press, 2002. p.102.

⑥　徐家玲：《拜占廷文明》，第458页。

⑦　Jones, A.H.M., *Later Roman Empire 248–602: A Social, Economic, and Administrative Survey*, pp.1005–1006.

⑧　陈志强：《拜占廷帝国史》，北京：商务印书馆，2006年，第482页。

⑨　Mango, C. (ed.), *The Oxford History of Byzantium*, p.103. See also: Jones, A.H.M., *Later Roman Empire 248–602: A Social, Economic, and Administrative Survey*, pp.1005–1006.

⑩　Scorates, *Scorates and Sozomenus Ecclesiastical Histories*, edit. By Schaff, P., New York: Christian Literature Publishing Co., 1886.3.16, p.165; 5.18, p.557.

⑪　阿尔文·施密特著、汪晓丹和赵巍译：《基督教对文明的影响》，北京：北京大学出版社，2004年，第153页。

为例，劝告年轻人要学习古典历史和文学。①从以弗所的约翰（John of Ephesus）口中，我们了解到圣者西蒙（Simeon）和瑟吉厄斯（Sergius）也传授过古典知识。这两位圣者在居住于阿米达（Amida）附近的一个村庄中时，曾创办了一所有 30 或 40 名学生的学校来维持生活，而他们在这所学校设置的课程包括阅读、写作和算术等。②

在 4—10 世纪的教区学校和主教制学校中，在主教的把持下，这些学校不仅教授基督教教义，也普遍地讲授七艺，即三科（语言、修辞和逻辑）以及四术（算术、音乐、几何和天文学）。

因此，拜占廷帝国接受基督教为国教虽对帝国文化产生了重大影响，但在 4 至 6 世纪期间并没有对古典文化造成太大冲击。自由的教育方式并没有发生根本的变化。③许多基督徒受到良好的希腊文化熏陶，他们中大多数人对希腊知识持尊重态度。在一些著名的希腊市镇上，主教已经成为当地知识分子中的一员。④

而且在 4 至 6 世纪时，教会主教大多由行省贵族或高级官员的子弟充任。如安布罗斯、诺拉的保林努斯（Paulinus of Nola）和许多其他世俗名门人士都成为了主教；同样，5 世纪与 6 世纪期间的高卢（Gaul）主教都出身于拥有较高文化素养和经济地位的名门望族。⑤自然，这些人都深受那个时代颇为普及的古典文化的熏陶，他们不但撰写了大量有关行政管理或宗教事务的书信，而且也写作了许多充分体现其古典文学和哲学素养的辩论文章和神学论文。例如，凯撒里亚的瓦西里因其在教会法方面的巨大贡献而成为拜占廷教会的重要人物；纳西昂的格里高利不但创作了具有高超修辞技巧的布道词，而且还写了大量可与古人相媲美的书信和诗篇，并且他在 380—381 年间曾出任君士坦丁堡大教长；而尼撒的格里高利则是基督教柏拉图哲学的诠释者。上述这些 4 世纪基督教学者的著作成为了以后拜占廷教会文学的典范⑥；它们标志着拜占廷"正统"文学的巅峰⑦。

甚至到 8、9 世纪时，一些著名的教会领袖也接受过传统的古典教育。例如，大教长塔拉修斯（Tarasius，去世于 806 年）、尼基弗鲁斯（Nicephorus，758–828 年）和斯图狄特的圣塞奥多利（St Theodore the Studite，759–826 年），他们在担任大主教之前都接受过传统修辞学的训练，并对古典哲学有一定的了解。⑧

而且在拜占廷帝国初期，帝国君主也对所有的文化知识都采取一种支持态度。例如，圣阿森尼乌斯（Arsenius，354–445 年）因其拥有渊博的希腊、罗马学问而享有盛誉，被塞奥多西一世从罗马请来教导他的两个儿子⑨；425 年，皇帝塞奥多西二世在君士坦丁堡设立了 30 个讲授语法、修辞学、哲学和法律的教授席位⑩。即使是一向以基督教的保护者自居的查士丁尼大帝，也没有完全使非基督教的古典传统在拜占廷灭绝。

---

① Baynes, N.H. and Moss,H.St.L.B.(eds.), *Byzantium:An Introduction to East Roman Civilization*, p.202.

② Jones, A.H.M., *Later Roman Empire 248–602: A Social, Economic, and Administrative Survey*, p.997.

③ Mango, C., *Byzantium: The Empire of New Rome*, New York: Charles Scribner's Sons, 1980,p.125.

④ Brown, P., *The World of Late Antiquity (AD150–750)*, London: Thames and Hudson Ltd, 1971,p.84.

⑤ Spieser, J.M., "The Christianisation of the City in Late Antiquity" ,p.8. In: Jean–Michel Spieser, *Urban and Religious Spaces in Late Antiquity and Early Byzantium*, Variorum Collected Studies: Aldershot, 2001.

⑥ 罗伯特·福西耶主编，陈志强、崔艳红等译：《剑桥插图中世纪史（350 年—950 年）》，济南：山东画报出版社，2006 年版，第 137 页。See also: Baynes, N.H. and Moss,H.St.L.B.(eds.), *Byzantium:An Introduction to East Roman Civilization*, p.226.

⑦ Baynes, N.H. and Moss,H.St.L.B.(eds.), *Byzantium:An Introduction to East Roman Civilization*, p.228.

⑧ Mango, C., *Byzantium: The Empire of New Rome*, p.137.

⑨ Baynes, N.H. and Moss,H.St.L.B.(eds.), *Byzantium:An Introduction to East Roman Civilization*, p.200.

⑩ Treadgold, W., *A History of the Byzantine State and Society*, p.91.

二 基督教的应对

面对上述现实，4 至 6 世纪的拜占廷帝国基督教对古典文化采取了一种"接纳"的态度。可以说，对古典文化的"接纳"一直是基督教发展的一个重要特征。正如教会史家沃尔克所言："基督教不可能建立在处女地上，而必须将已经存在的各种思想作为材料构筑自己的体系。"①早期教父也对此作出了自己的阐释，例如 3 世纪的著名教父奥立金认为：基督教是"自然"、"元初"宗教。耶稣基督已经将基督教教义的"种子"播撒到每个人心中，自从创世起，上帝就分别地照料着这些种子。基督"呵护"着希腊文化中最好的"种子"——特别是希腊哲学和伦理学。因而，一位基督徒不会拒绝接受希腊文化。②在实践中，奥立金也试图将流行的柏拉图学说融入到传统的基督教教义中。③

所以，"亚历山大里亚的基督教学者变成了希腊人的学生，这个说法并不是没有道理：虽然奥立金的观点可能被谴责为异端，但其对基督教思想的影响仍然是巨大的。"④

尽管在教会中也存在着一些不同之音，认为"《圣经》为人类提供了所需要的一切知识，其他知识来自于恶魔"⑤。例如教父德尔图良就对古典文化"深恶痛绝"。他把哲学视作与基督教格格不入的异教徒的智慧，认为哲学家比其他异教徒对基督教更危险。⑥但"在大多数场合，他的著作不乏说理充分、论辩严密、注重证据的哲学风格。即使在反驳一些希腊哲学家时，他也自觉或不自觉地利用另一些哲学家的观点，不可避免地运用他所鄙薄的辩证方法。"⑦

因此，尽管德尔图良的这种思想在一段时间内曾对早期教会产生了一定影响，但最终被教会所抛弃。"到 3 世纪末时，德尔图良完全排斥古典文化的思想对当时的基督徒几乎没有产生什么实际的影响。"⑧对古典文化的"接纳"成为 4 至 6 世纪拜占廷教会的一种主导思想。

于是我们看到，圣金口约翰曾呼吁家长们让自己的子女接受基督教早期教育，但他并不否定对青少年进行传统文化启蒙教育的必要性。⑨如现代学者琼斯所言，有教养的普通基督徒并不会对学习异教古典文学感到内疚，甚至连最严格的基要主义者也不得不承认，虽然对成年基督徒来说，为消遣而阅读古典文学是一种罪恶，但孩子们不得不在学校里学习这些古典文学。⑩

显然，在拜占廷帝国初期的基督徒心中，世俗的古典教育仍占有一席之地，教会领袖只是对此提出了一个"有益的告诫"：基督徒的孩子要远离那些邪恶的有关古老神灵的故事，而只学习那些虔诚、有益的古典知识。⑪拜占廷早期教会史家苏克拉底在 5 世纪 40 年代对此解释道，教会既不赞成也不拒绝 "希腊"（即异教的）教育，教会的这种态度有其合理的理由。因为基督教经典并没有向基督徒传授逻辑推理，因此，如果基督徒要驳斥真理的敌人，他们就应当使用异教徒自己的武器，以子之矛攻子之盾。⑫事实上，受益于修辞学教育的教会领袖们也确实将其在学校中学到的"希腊"

---

① 威利斯顿·沃尔克著、孙善玲等译、朱代强校：《基督教会史》，北京：中国社会科学出版社，1991 年，第 3 页。
② Brown, P., *The World of Late Antiquity (AD150–750)*, pp.82,84.
③ Frend, W. H. C., *Town and Country in the Early Christian Centuries*, London:Variorum Reprints, 1980.X, p.265.
④ Baynes, N.H. and Moss,H.St.L.B.(eds.), *Byzantium:An Introduction to East Roman Civilization*, p.222.
⑤ Frend, W. H. C., *Town and Country in the Early Christian Centuries*, VIII, p.72.
⑥ 赵敦华：《基督教哲学 1500 年》，北京：人民出版社，1994 年，第 105 页。
⑦ 赵敦华：《基督教哲学 1500 年》，第 107 页。
⑧ Frend, W. H. C., *The Rise of Christianity*, Philadelphia: Fortress Press, 1984.p.415.See also: Mango, C., *Byzantium: The Empire of New Rome*, p.132.
⑨ 徐家玲：《拜占廷文明》，第 458 页。
⑩ Jones, A.H.M., *Later Roman Empire 248–602: A Social, Economic, and Administrative Survey*, p.1005.
⑪ Mango,C. (ed.), *The Oxford History of Byzantium*, p.103.See also: Mango, C., *Byzantium: The Empire of New Rome*, p.133.
⑫ Mango,C. (ed.), *The Oxford History of Byzantium*, p.103.

知识运用到了他们的布道与写作中。

非常有趣的是，在背教者朱利安时期，有几个基督教学者试图向人们讲授《圣经》，但他们却留下了深刻的古典文学痕迹。如阿波利纳里（Apollinarii）父子，他们根据各种古希腊韵律将《旧约圣经》改编成了一部诗集，而将《新约圣经》变成了一部柏拉图式的对话集。①

甚至，一些异教哲学思想还被吸纳入基督教正统思想体系中，典型者如新柏拉图主义。该思想本身深刻地影响了卡帕多西亚教父（Cappadocian Fathers），像纳西昂的格里高利和尼撒的格里高利的神学思想；同时在其他地方，似乎是公元500年左右，一位在其著作上署名为使徒保罗的同时代人狄奥尼修斯（Dionysius the Areopagite）的无名作者也大量地借用了新柏拉图主义者普罗克洛斯（Proclus，410–485年）著作中的思想。当这些著作一旦被教会认可为是使徒时代的作品，新柏拉图思想便成为了拜占廷帝国教会正统神学的组成部分。②

伟大的希腊教父时代结束于5世纪中期，我们可以说这些希腊教父都曾经运用他们那渊博的世俗修辞学和哲学知识提出了新颖而有说服力的神学观点。③即使在6世纪中期以后，虽然再也没有出现著名的异教学者，且专业的世俗学者变得"稀少"，但基督教神学明显地开始吸收哲学知识。事实上可以说，基督教教义自始至终都"受惠"于希腊思想。④

因此，著名学者贝恩斯认为，"整个拜占廷文学史存在着一种连续性；这里同西部欧洲一样，并没有与古代世界断裂开来。"⑤学者罗德尼·斯塔克也表述了同样的观点："基督教不但与分散各地的犹太文化有高度的连续性，而且与希腊文化因素也有高度的一致性。"⑥彼得·布朗更深刻地阐述道，"4世纪，对于基督教的进一步发展更具有重要意义的是，教会领袖们，特别是在希腊世界，发现他们能够迎合每个富有的平民的文化、观念和信仰需要。"⑦

结　语

综上所述，我们可以看到在4至6世纪的拜占廷帝国，尽管基督教教会内部对古典文化的态度可能还存在着一些争议，但从总体上来说，教会消除了它早期对异教世界的文化所怀有的敌意，开始"务实"地对待古典希腊、罗马文化遗产，并尽力将其吸纳入自己的体系中。当然，基督教对于古典文化并不是完全不加选择地接受，而是采取了一种"为我所用"的态度。例如，对于讲述恶人或邪恶神灵的任何诗歌，他们像尤利西斯⑧对付塞壬⑨一样"塞住耳朵"。在所有古典文学中，他们如同飞舞于花丛中采粉酿蜜的蜜蜂一样，吸收对自身有益的营养。⑩

---

① Mango,C. (ed.), *The Oxford History of Byzantium*, p.103.
② Baynes, N.H. and Moss,H.St.L.B.(eds.), *Byzantium:An Introduction to East Roman Civilization*, p.223.
③ Treadgold, W., *A History of the Byzantine State and Society*,p.267.
④ Baynes, N.H. and Moss,H.St.L.B.(eds.), *Byzantium:An Introduction to East Roman Civilization*, p.222.
⑤ Baynes, N.H. and Moss,H.St.L.B.(eds.), *Byzantium:An Introduction to East Roman Civilization*, p.222.
⑥ 罗德尼·斯塔克著，黄剑波、高民贵译：《基督教的兴起：一个社会学家对历史的再思》，上海：上海古籍出版社，2005年，第167页。
⑦ Brown, P., *The World of Late Antiquity (AD150–750)*, p.82.
⑧ Ulysses，罗神，即希腊神话中的（Odysseus）奥德修斯。
⑨ Sirens，希神，半人半神的海妖，常以美妙歌声诱惑经过的海员而使航船触礁毁灭。
⑩ Baynes, N.H. and Moss,H.St.L.B.(eds.), *Byzantium:An Introduction to East Roman Civilization*, p.202.

【附录】

"古代文明的碰撞、交流与比较"
——"中国第四届世界古代史国际学术研讨会"综述

杨巨平、叶 民

2012 年 6 月 16–18 日，南开大学历史学院和中国世界古代中世纪史研究会在南开大学共同主办"中国第四届世界古代史国际学术研讨会"。本次会议的主题是："古代文明的碰撞、交流与比较——从地中海到黄河"，共分四个议题：（1）古代欧亚大陆文明的互动；（2）古代的中国与世界；（3）丝绸之路古国文明研究；（4）古代世界的历史、宗教与文化。与会中外学者约 200 位，其中国外代表 26 位。会议共收到正式的论文约 120 篇，内容广泛，视角新颖，涉及到丝绸之路、古代中外文化交流、中外古史比较、古希腊史、罗马史、古埃及史、古代西亚史、东亚史、中亚史以及欧洲中世纪史、拜占廷史等专门的研究领域。与会者就目前学界所关注的问题进行了深入的探讨。

一　古史比较的意义、方法和重点

美国斯坦福大学的沃尔特·塞德尔（Walter Scheidel）教授是国际著名的比较研究倡导者。他在"古代世界的比较研究：过去、现在和未来"一文中指出，古史比较的价值在于把历史发展的一般特征同文化发展的具体特征区分开来，使我们能够对特定历史发展结果起到关键作用的变量做出判定，对某种特定的制度在一种结构相似的体制背景下进行评估。他以自己主持的一系列中外对比项目为例指出，古代世界的研究成果在西方世界呈逐年上涨的趋势，中国古代史正在成为重要的比较对象，但是汉语（包括古汉语）一直是西方学者难以突破的障碍。然而这恰恰是中国古史研究者的长项，中国历史学者应当积极地参与到古史比较的研究中去。

国内刘家和教授多年来从事中外古史比较研究，他在给本次会议提交的《中西古代史学比较刍议》一文中，详细分析了古代中国史学与希腊罗马史学各自不同的特点。他认为，《荷马史诗》虽有史影，但还不能成为史书，《书》《诗》也未能成为史书，但其中却有殷鉴不远等对历史发展的某种规律性的认识。希罗多德的《历史》和修昔底德的《伯罗奔尼撒战争史》都是当时人写当时事的断代史，总体上为编年体，富有时代精神，但缺乏历史反省。在中国，形式相近的《左传》《国语》，虽为断代，却记载大量前言往行以为当时之事的历史渊源，表现了通史精神。此后，希腊罗马的史书大量出现，但都缺乏通史精神。但司马迁的《史记》和班固等的《汉书》却具有通史精神，因为西汉时期的文明史是中国古代文明史中的一个不可分离的部分。历代正史都是如此，政治上分段，文明却是连续的，这就是中国古代史学连续性存在的具体方式。古代中国在文明史层面上未曾发生断裂，在史学史层面上同样未曾发生断裂，原因就在于通史精神传统的确立。

德国德累斯顿大学穆启乐（F-H. Mutchler）教授的论文《古代中国与罗马历史写作中的行为与结果关系》通过对两地史家著述的一般性比较后指出，古代中国和罗马史家都非常重视分析"行为"与"结果"之间的联系，尤其是道德行为同政治结果之间的关系。他们一方面肯定历史自有"公论"，另一方面也看到了这种"行为"与"结果"完全相反的现实性。但他们始终要在历史现实的非正义和历史写作的公正性之间寻求平衡，他们力求公正地评价历史人物并将这种公正性传与后人。

罗马帝国与古代中国的比较研究是本次会议的一个热点。布鲁塞尔佛兰德大学保罗·埃德坎普（Paul Erdkamp）教授对古代中国和罗马帝国的生育率和人口增长模式进行了对比。认为古代中国为应对人口的增长，不仅调整生产技术，而且改变经济制度，刺激了经济的发展。丹麦哥本哈根大学的安娜·拉泽托（Anna Razeto）教授以汉代长安和罗马帝国时期的罗马城为例，对二者的建筑设施，尤其是城墙系统、城门建筑和道路网络做了对比分析，认为这些基础建设在政治象征意义上有很丰富的内涵。荷兰莱顿大学卢克·德·李特（Luuk De Ligt）教授也以罗马城和汉代长安城为例证，深入分析了汉帝国和罗马帝国的高度城市化现象。美国北卡罗来纳大学理查德·塔尔波特（Richard Talbert）教授以中华帝国和罗马帝国在古典时代（公元前 323 年至公元 316 年）之间道路系统为比较对象，将其视为帝国权威与文明的表现工具，并从文化、哲学和宗教方面分析了中外驿道系统的内涵。南京大学陈仲丹教授对中国史学大师陈寅恪先生早年对中国与罗马文明主体的比附与比较作了分析。

美国哥伦比亚大学威廉·哈里斯（William V. Harris）教授比较研究的视野更为开阔，他在《前现代世界的读写能力：地中海世界与东亚的相似性与不同点》一文中，分析了公元前 1000 年至公元 1900 年之间地中海范围内读写能力发展史的特征，指出，在前现代的中国社会，特别是战国和汉帝国时期，影响中国读写能力的因素同地中海世界大致相当。北京大学拱玉书教授的论文《六书与十二书》对汉字与楔形文字的形体和构成进行了比较分析，指出在汉字和楔形文字的发展和使用过程中都产生了《说文解字》。认为，《说文解字》是传承文字的有效手段，其中对文字结构的分析，在很大程度上反映了文字创造者在创造文字时所本的一些原则。北京大学黄洋教授对希罗多德《历史》和司马迁《史记》中对蛮族的记载做了对比研究，发现两者在构建"自我"与"他者"方面具有极大的相似性。原因在于在两位历史学家都处于本土文明与外部世界大规模冲突和碰撞的时代，都有了解外部世界的迫切必要。北师大蒋重跃教授和南开大学张晓芒教授则分别从中国学者的角度，对老子的"道论"与古希腊哲学中的本体论、墨家学派和亚里士多德的逻辑系统进行了比较。

二　文明互动的模式与研究

牛津大学奥斯温·默里（Oswyn Murray）教授在《古代历史的西方传统》一文中认为，在西欧"古代历史"的研究同古典传统和希腊罗马文化有直接的联系，但对古代以色列、埃及、近东、印度和远东国家古代文明的研究却处于边缘状态。他呼吁，21 世纪的古代史研究应该建立一种新的"古代历史"观念，这种观念不应当只把欧洲的传统看作是"古代历史"的基础，而应当将世界古代的重要文明如中国文明和近东文明包括其中。

南开大学王敦书教授在《中国学者论古代文明和文明的发展与交往》一文中对达尼列夫斯基、斯宾格勒、汤因比、麦克尼尔和亨廷顿等国外著名学者对文明的概念进行了深入的分析，并对照国内雷海宗等著名学人对古代文明和文明的发展与交往的看法，认为当今世界经济日益全球化和一体化，各地区文明之间更紧密频繁地展开多层面和全方位的交流，虽然存在文明冲突，但更多的是进行文明对话。人类是有理性和人性的高级生物，理性与人性也是文明所具有的根本特征。在21世纪，人类将根据理智和博爱的精神通过对话增进相互理解，和平公正地解决多种冲突，人类的文明、各地区民族的文明将空前繁荣昌盛。

美国布朗大学库尔特·拉夫劳布（Kurt Raaflaub）教授的《古代世界的政治思想起源：互动与比较》一文，以荷马和赫西俄德的作品为例证，证明古代近东的政治思想对公元前7世纪晚期到公元前6世纪早期的斯巴达和雅典的法律思想、公正思想、集体治理思想等都产生了一定的影响。

南开大学杨巨平教授在《希腊化文化信息在中国的回响（至公元七世纪）》一文中，利用中国的古代典籍以及传入中国的犍陀罗艺术、钱币等文化载体，分析了希腊化文化与古代中国之间的互动交流关系。他特别强调了亚历山大东征及希腊化世界的形成和张骞出使西域、丝绸之路开通在其中所发挥的先导和奠基作用。澳大利亚麦克夸利大学（悉尼）刘南强（Samuel N.C. Lieu）教授介绍了他主持（协调）的"中国与地中海世界——10世纪之前（中国唐代）的考古资源与文献资料"项目。该项目汇集了前伊斯兰时代的中亚地区的文献与铭文资料，文献涉及古拉丁语、古希腊语、古叙利亚语和古汉语等语言，目的在于促进中国学者对于关于希腊化、罗马和拜占廷历史的研究，其中部分资料已经用中文公布，便于中国学者查阅。南开大学王力平教授论述了敦煌文献中包含的外来文化因素，指出敦煌文书是进行中外文化交流研究的极其重要的史料，应该引起高度的重视。清华大学张绪山教授对中国史籍中频频出现的女人国的传说追根溯源，认为其属于希腊传说系统，是希腊渊源的"女人国"传说的翻版。中山大学林英教授则通过对近年在东魏和唐代墓中出土的具有动感的胡人形象和同时期静态的佛像的比较分析，指出这种胡人形象实际是犍陀罗艺术影响的结果，希腊罗马雕像与胡人俑之间有着密切的联系。暨南大学王银田教授通过对北魏平城历史遗迹的考察，论证了该城文化的多元性及其与丝绸之路的关系。

三　文明史、区域史与国别史的专题研究

古希腊史、罗马史是历次世界古代史会议关注度较高的研究领域。本次会议提供了中外古典学者平等对话的平台。上海师范大学裔昭印教授阐述了古希腊会饮的发展演变过程，并从社会性别的视角考察了古希腊会饮的性别关系与情爱特征。安徽师范大学解光云教授认为，在古希腊历史语境下，造船区、德莫和三一区具有相对的时空意义。三者是城邦公民的权力基础。中国人民大学王人庆副教授指出，奥林匹亚赛会是古希腊宗教仪式活动的派生物和外在表现形式之一，本身不仅具有"宗教性"和"神圣性"，也带有"世俗性"，并且经历了"世俗化"的过程。中国社会科学院世界史所邢颖博士则认为古代奥林匹亚赛会离不开希腊文明最本质性城邦特征，其产生方式、管理方式、建筑布局、竞争关系与荣誉授予方式都受到城邦制度的影响。华中师范大学徐晓旭教授在希腊族群认同问题上，提出了"希腊人的蛮族祖先与蛮族人的希腊祖先"这一相互关联的命题。认为神话里的希腊人和蛮族人在血缘上并无清晰的界限。当用血缘神话无力界定希腊人的时候，其他文化特征就成了区别希腊人和蛮族人的标准。东北师范大学张强教授考察了"philologia"一词的源流，指出西方古典文献学的名称与内容在不同历史时期、不同语境中均曾发生过变化，但总体上的沿革相类于中国古典文献学或传统文献学。南京师范大学祝宏俊教授对古代希腊派迪亚（paideia）和阿高盖（agōgē）两种教育模式的功能和作用做了比较，指出前者侧重于人文素养培养，后者侧重于专业技能培养，特别是体育、军事技能培养。徐松岩教授将雅典国家的发展道路归纳为"城邦——帝国——城邦"三段论，揭示了城邦内政变革与对外政策的互动关系。鲁东大学魏凤莲教授以内容与疯狂仪式相关的铭文为基础，分析了古希腊疯狂仪式的具体内容以及酒神狂女们在城邦中的身份和

地位。美国德堡大学刘津瑜博士通过对公元三世纪一块拉丁文颂碑的个案研究，分析了罗马骑士与地方元老贵族的关系。东北师范大学宫秀华教授探讨了罗马帝国统治下的高卢行省的罗马化进程及其表现。中国社会科学院胡玉娟研究员特别注意到了被保护人出身的平民家族在平民集团中的存在及其影响。

西亚北非古文明的研究近年来异军突起，进入了原始文献解读层面。东北师范大学郭丹彤教授对古代埃及文献中沙苏人的来源做了考证，指出古代埃及社会中的沙苏不是一个种族，而是一个带有军事色彩的阶层。中国社科院刘健研究员利用两河流域文献和考古资料，探讨了海湾及海湾地区的社会发展状态和政治联系特征。东北师范大学李晓东教授认为"玛阿特"是古埃及价值观念中的核心概念，为古埃及人判断一切的最高标准和终极的价值观。东北师范大学吴宇虹教授的论文释读了收藏于大不列颠博物馆编号为 CT3219 乌尔第三王朝时期的苏美尔楔形文字贡物名单。通过对贡物名单和进贡者身份的分析，还原了乌尔第三王朝末期同 Simurrrum 的战争背景和相互关系。北京大学李政教授从赫梯人的历史文化和目前国外赫梯学研究的客观现实状况两个方面对赫梯学研究的对象和范畴做了新的说明。

东亚史研究进入世界古代史学者的视野，是本次会议的特色之一。中国社科院世界史所徐建新研究员从对"古代东亚世界论"的评介入手，提出了"区域整体史"的概念，认为古代世界尚不存在真正意义上的世界史（"全球史"、"世界体系"），但古代世界存在着多个横向交往频繁、互动关系密切的区域。从实证的角度来讲，这样的区域大于某个古代民族生存的地区和某个国家存在的范围。南开大学杨栋梁教授对古代中日关系史做了系统的梳理，对各阶段二者关系的演变做了新的定性，李卓教授对关于日本文化深受中华文明影响的传统观点提出了质疑。郑州大学于向东教授重点分析了越南阮朝明命帝的海洋意识。南开大学李治安教授指出，中华文明由于受游牧民族南下的影响，在宋元之际出现了第二个南北子文明的分野和融汇，从而再次整合发展。美国明尼苏达大学的陈润成教授对十四世纪意大利圣方济各会修士奥多里克的《中国游记》中的传说与事实做了鉴别梳理，认为此书对于研究中世纪中西关系和西方在中国的传教活动很有价值。

从事中世纪史和拜占廷史研究的一些学者也参加了会议。东北师大徐家玲教授论述了十字军骑士与突厥人在近东的军事交往和互动，四川大学孙锦泉教授和邹薇博士分别撰文论述了华瓷在欧亚各地的传布与收藏。此外，南开大学郑玮副教授对古代晚期雅典的基督教化问题的关注，武鹏博士对《宋史》中有关拂菻记载的考辨，兰州大学姬庆红博士关于约翰长老传说的流布，以及涉及到拜占廷帝国的皇帝、教会、雇佣军、救灾等方面的一批论文都显示了国内中世纪史及拜占廷史研究的扩展和深入。

本次会议还有一个明显的特点，就是新一代的青年学人队伍壮大，成果斐然。他们在会上踊跃发言，敢于提出自己的观点。如田明关于古埃及白线陶的地域风格，蒋保关于荷马的怜悯情怀，冯金鹏关于伯利克里的泛希腊政策，李尚君关于对演说家的述职审查，王志超关于苏格拉底对雅典民主政治的认同，李永斌关于希腊的"东方化革命"，徐媛媛关于旅顺博物馆馆藏古代印度佛教造像等方面的论文都给人耳目一新之感，显示了我国世界古代史研究广阔的发展前景。

由于提交会议的论文数量众多且涉及领域非常广泛，受篇幅所限，本文不能一一列举，只能大体概括介绍。没有提及者，敬请见谅。我们将会出版会议论文集，所有参会者的研究成果都会得到全面的体现。会议承办者愿借此机会，对所有与会学者表示感谢。此次会议确实是一次国际学术盛会，它不仅体现了中国世界古代史研究的整体实力，也加强了各国学者之间的学术交流，拓宽了进一步合作研究的渠道，特别是使中国学者对本学科的发展趋势、特点有了更加深入的了解，这对于推动我国的世界古代史研究早日进入国际前沿应该具有十分重要的意义。

（原载《世界历史》2013 年第 2 期。发表时由于篇幅原因有所删节，此次全文刊出。）

后　记

　　2012 年是我国著名历史学家雷海宗先生诞辰 110 周年。值此之际，南开大学历史学院于 6 月 15 日隆重举行纪念大会，百余名雷先生昔日的学生、同事以及各地高校、科研机构的代表、本院师生济济一堂，深切缅怀这位为 20 世纪中国史学发展做出杰出贡献的学者。次日，南开大学历史学院和中国世界古代中世纪史研究会联合举办的"古代文明的碰撞、交流与比较"国际学术研讨会开幕，国内外专家学者、在读研究生约 200 人参加了大会。与会者提交论文近百篇，从不同的角度对古代世界东西方文明自身的发展与相互之间的交流、比较进行了深入的探讨。雷先生生前在南开大学专门讲授世界古代史，并著文论述古代世界游牧文明与农耕文明之关系，对中外古史比较研究亦有诸多独到见解，本次国际学术研讨会实际上就是对先生学术贡献的肯定和弘扬，是对先生百年诞辰的最好纪念。

　　两次会议的发言和论文，尤其对雷先生的回忆文章，弥足珍贵。为了让更多的学人能够了解雷先生的辉煌事业，能够分享这次国际学术盛宴，南开大学历史学院决定编辑出版两会文集。经过三年多的努力，本论文集终于正式出版。在此，编委会首先要代表南开大学历史学院和中国世界古代中世纪史研究会对本次会议的赞助者——著名国画家范曾先生表示感谢。范先生上个世纪五十年代在南开大学历史系就读期间，亲身聆听过雷先生教诲。为感谢师恩，他慷慨解囊，在南开大学历史学院设立了"雷海宗基金"。本次会议及文集的出版就得益于该项基金的资助。其次，要对所有的与会者再次表示感谢。雷先生的学生、亲炙弟子都过古稀或至耄耋之年，但他们有的亲临大会，有的撰文，让后人再次感受到了雷先生的大师风范。那些不远万里前来参会的国外学者，让我们近距离分享了他们最新的研究成果。最后对所有参与两会会务的领导、老师和学生也表示感谢。正是他们的辛勤工作、竭诚服务才使会议顺利进行，圆满成功。

　　文集的编辑历经两年，除了编委会的成员之外，南开大学历史学院世界古代史教研室的郑玮、武鹏二位老师也参与了文集的审稿工作。由于文集出版周期较长，有的作者的文章已经先期在正式学术刊物上发表，但由于本书是会议论文集，我们仍然按照当时参会者提交的文稿收入。编委会尊重作者个人的意愿，遵照"文责自负"的原则，只对文稿进行了技术性的编辑处理，其余全部保留。

编委会